Coincraft's
2000
Standard Catalogue
of English and UK Coins
1066 to Date

Richard Lobel
Publisher

Mark Davidson
Hammered Section

Allan Hailstone
Milled Section

Eleni Calligas
Editor

COINCRAFT

London 1999

First published in 1999
by Standard Catalogue Publishers Ltd for
Coincraft
44 & 45 Great Russell Street
London WC1B 3LU

British Library Cataloguing in Publication Data
A catalogue record for this book is available from the British Library

ISBN 0 9526228 82

Database typeset by Polestar Whitefriars Ltd
Printed and bound by Polestar Wheatons Ltd

This edition is dedicated to all the numismatists and dealers, past and present, who helped me through 44 years in coins. They had great patience and I hope that in some small way this book rewards their good deeds. My late Father, when asked once what he hoped I would be when I grew up, answered 'alive'!

Richard Lobel

About the Contributors

Richard Lobel

info@coincraft.com.uk

Richard was born in Cambridge Massachusetts in 1944 and moved to London in 1968. He is a member of the Professional Numismatic Guild since 1974 and of numerous numismatic societies world-wide. He holds a degree in International Business and Macro Economics from Boston University and was accepted to the Harvard Business School to study Finance but moved to England instead, mistakenly believing that he spoke the language.

His first mentor in the coin business was the late Maurice Gould, author of many numismatic research works. Over the years he has had the privilege of knowing many famous numismatists and learning from them. His serious interest in coins dates from his first paid subscription to a coin publication in June of 1955.

He founded Coincraft, which has become the second largest firm of coin dealers in the United Kingdom. Perhaps his proudest boast is that Coincraft sells more numismatic books retail than anyone else in the UK. They deal only with collectors and publish a monthly newspaper/catalogue called *The Phoenix* and a semi-annual magazine *The Coin Collector*.

He has been listed in the *Guinness Book of Records* many times, for the legendary Edward VIII Collection, the unique 1954 Penny and for heading the consortium that bought the largest, heaviest and most expensive lot of banknotes ever sold at auction.

This book was his brainchild, his way to repay something to the hobby which has supported him for so many years. Richard stated recently that if he knew how much effort and how much money this book was going to take, he would never have started it.

Mark Davidson

info@coincraft.com.uk

Born and raised in Surrey, Mark began collecting bun pennies by date at the age of six. Encouraged in his hobby by his parents and his uncle, he soon became a keen collector and purchased his first hammered coin from the then recently discovered Colchester hoard of Henry III and Edward I pennies. At sixteen he started working for Richard Lobel and received his 'apprenticeship in the coin trade'. He started his own business at the age of twenty, dealing in all types of coins, publishing catalogues and trading from the old Saturday Charing Cross market. When that market closed in 1987, Mark started a monthly London Coin fair with Linda Monk which still flourishes today and, on the death of John Hooper, he became a partner in Croydon Coin Auctions. Mark is very well known in the trade and attends most auctions and fairs, where he enjoys meeting collectors.

Allan Hailstone

aha@globalnet.co.uk

Allan was born in Coventry in 1938, and lived in various parts of England before moving to London in 1957 to read Chemical Engineering at Imperial College. Graduating in 1960, he entered industry but rapidly found that nobody appeared to know what a Chemical Engineer was. In 1962, he noticed a wants list of coins in a shop window in Canterbury, and decided on the spot to become a coin dealer.

With an amiable eccentric nature masking a deeply flawed personality, Allan met Richard Lobel many years ago, and recognised a kindred spirit; something akin to a friendship developed.

Allan can often be found perusing old books in the British Library or hiding behind a newspaper at any one of several London coffee shops. Caring more for accuracy, language and spelling than for his fellow man, he was a natural choice for producing the milled section of this book.

Dr Eleni Calligas

eleni@petasos.demon.co.uk

Born in Athens in 1960, Eleni is, by trade, a historian of nineteenth century Greece. She finds potted autobiographies misleading but can unequivocally state that after completing her BA degree in History at the American College of Greece, she continued her studies at the London School of Economics, receiving her MA in 1987 and her doctorate in 1994. She was among the founding editors of the Greek historical journal *Histor*, has published a book-length study on child welfare in 19th century Greece and contributed articles to historical journals in both Greek and English. As well as history and the written word, she likes cats, sunshine and Alice in Wonderland humour.

Acknowledgements

We would like to give special thanks to the following individuals and organisations for their assistance:

Airedale Coins

Lauri Andrews

Peter 'Maundy' Allen

Laurie Bamford

Joe Bispham

R. Blunt

James Brown

Garry Charman

Barry Clayden

Malcolm Coeshaw

Chris Comber

Colin Cooke

Anthony Dowle

Daniel Fearon

Patrick Finn

Michael Gouby

Eric Green

Anton Holt

Robert Ilsley

Peter Jackson

Ian Jull

Andrew Litherland

Claire Lobel

Dimitri Loulakakis

Nigel Mills

Peter Mitchell

Sylvia Mitchell

Graeme Monk

James Morton

Colin Narbeth

Paul Nicholson

William Paul

Mark Rasmussen

Alan Rayner

Roderick Richardson

M.R. 'Bob' Roberts

The Royal Mint

Douglas Saville

Michael Sharp

May Sinclair

Edward Smith

Alan Ward

Sydney J. Warner

Chris Webb

Colin Whitear

Barry Williams

E.J. Williams

We would also like to thank the following auction houses for their help:

Baldwins

Bonhams

Christies

Croydon Coin Auctions

Dix Noonan & Webb

Glendinings

Sothebys

Spink

We had a very warm response from readers who filled our 'error or omission' cards and would like to take this opportunity to thank them again for their interest.

Coincraft's Numbering System

The Coincraft numbering system is an intuitive system for listing British coins. In previous catalogues the numbers represented an arithmetic progression, 1, 2, 3 and so on. By combining an abbreviation of the monarch's name with an abbreviation of the denomination you have the first really useful numbering system. It won't tell you which date or variety a coin is, but it will tell you who struck it and what denomination it is.

There are many monarchs in this country's long history but they share a very small number of names. For Henry and Edward there were eight kings each. These are easy to abbreviate to just the letter 'H' or 'E' followed by their number from 1–8. Henry V is 'H5' and Henry VIII is 'H8'. It is simple but logical, a type of shorthand.

The denomination is also fairly easy to abbreviate as, over the centuries, there were not all that many different denominations struck. Here we have used an easy to understand and again logical usage of the actual denomination. Half crown becomes 'HC', crown 'CR', penny '1D' and so on. There is an easy to read and use chart which lists every denomination issued from 1066 and every monarch. By combining the monarch with the denomination we get H84D, which we know is a Henry VIII groat, an Edward VII shilling becomes E7SH and a George III guinea G3GN. This combination will tell you the monarch and the denomination, but not the exact variety which is listed as a number. This you will have to look up. G3GN-5 is a George III guinea dated 1761 and a G3GN-145 is one dated 1788, but both are 'G3GN' or George III Guineas.

Collectors using the New Numbering System: Please note that in most cases collectors will leave out the leading '0', thus '005' becomes '5' and '035' becomes '35'. The only time you will need the '0' is when you are putting your coins on a computer, then the zeros are required to sort the coins properly. Collectors will also want to use the full number, i.e. H84D-15. This will allow them to see the full description of the coin they own and will also facilitate the easy sorting of their collection by computer.

Dealers using the New Numbering System: Dealers will use the shortened version of the code. If I were listing George III guineas, I would have listed the 1761 guinea as SC-5 and the 1788 as SC-145. You know from the listing of the coin that it is a guinea and it is of George III, so why waste your time. 'SC', of course, stands for Standard Catalogue.

This numbering system is very easy to use, try it for a little while and I am sure you will wonder how you ever did without it. When I take notes of our collectors' wants, I do it in the Coincraft numbering shorthand. It is so much easier to write 'E3' than Edward III. Try it, I am sure that you will like it and it actually works!

A large number of auction houses world-wide are already using this numbering system. It won't be long before they are all using it! This new numbering system makes sense for both collectors and dealers. Collectors use the full numbering system and dealers use the shortened version and everyone is happy!

On the opposite page we list the various abbreviations used in the numbering system and on the following pages there are two easy to use **Quick-Index-Charts** which list the various denominations struck by each monarch from 1066 to date, with page references that correspond to this catalogue.

How to use the Quick-Index-Charts®

Perhaps one of the most useful features of this book are the *Quick-Index-Charts*. You can quickly and easily find the exact page you want for the exact coin that you are trying to look up. It is easy and quick to use.

The are two charts: one for Hammered Coins and one for Milled Coins.

Across the top of both charts are the abbreviations for the denominations: **CR** for Crown, **HG** for Half Guinea and so on (see 'How to use the Numbering System' above). Down the left hand side of the charts are the monarchs' names and down the right hand side the abbreviations: **Henry I** and **H1**, **William III** and **W3**, and so on. To use the charts, first find either the denomination or the monarch you want. Then go down the chart until you find the monarch or across the chart until you find the denomination. If you have ever used a chart to show the mileage between two destinations, then you already know how to use the *Quick-Index-Charts*.

Use these charts on a regular basis and you will find the coins you are looking for much quicker than by thumbing though the book. The number listed is the exact page number which refers to the coin you are looking for.

It is easy, it's fun and it's quick...

REF	Monarch	Reign
W1	William I	1066 – 1087
W2	William II	1087 – 1100
H1	Henry I	1100 – 1135
ST	Stephen	1135 – 1154
MT	Matilda	
H2	Henry II	1154 – 1189
R1	Richard I	1189 – 1199
JH	John	1199 – 1216
H3	Henry III	1216 – 1272
E1	Edward I	1272 – 1307
E2	Edward II	1307 – 1327
E3	Edward III	1327 – 1377
R2	Richard II	1377 – 1399
H4	Henry IV	1399 – 1413
H5	Henry V	1413 – 1422
H6	Henry VI (First reign)	1422 – 1461
E4	Edward IV (First reign)	1461 – 1470
H6	Henry VI (Restored)	1470 – 1471
E4	Edward IV (Second reign)	1471 – 1483
E5	Edward V	1483
R3	Richard III	1483 – 1485
H7	Henry VII	1485 – 1509
H8	Henry VIII	1509 – 1547
E6	Edward VI	1547 – 1553
MA	Mary	1553 – 1554
PM	Philip & Mary	1554 – 1558
EL	Elizabeth I	1558 – 1603
J1	James I	1603 – 1625
C1	Charles I	1625 – 1649
CW	Commonwealth	1649 – 1660
OC	Cromwell	
C2	Charles II	1660 – 1685
J2	James II	1685 – 1688
WM	William & Mary	1688 – 1694
W3	William III	1695 – 1701
AN	Anne	1702 – 1714
G1	George I	1714 – 1727
G2	George II	1727 – 1760
G3	George III	1760 – 1820
G4	George IV	1820 – 1830
W4	William IV	1830 – 1837
V	Victoria	1837 – 1901
E7	Edward VII	1902 – 1910
G5	George V	1910 – 1936
E8	Edward VIII	1936
G6	George VI	1937 – 1952
EZ	Elizabeth II	1952 –

REF	Decimal Coinage
D5P	Five Pounds
D2P	Two Pounds
D1P	Pound
D50	Fifty Pence
D25	Twenty Five Pence
D20	Twenty Pence
D10	Ten Pence
D05	Five Pence
D02	Two Pence
D01	Penny
DHP	Halfpence

REF	Denomination
AG	Angel
BR	Broad
CR	Crown
DC	Double Crown
DFL	Double Florin
18D	Eighteen Pence Token
FA	Farthing
50S	Fifty Shillings
5G	Five Guineas
5P	Five Pounds
FL	Florin
4M	Fourpence, Maundy
4D	Groat
GN	Guinea
HA	Half Angel
HC	Half Crown
HF	Half Farthing
HFL	Half Florin
2D	Halfgroat / Twopence, Copper
HG	Half Guinea
HL	Half Laurel
HN	Half Noble
HP	Half Pound
HS	Half Sovereign
HU	Half Unite
HD	Halfpenny
LA	Laurel
NB	Noble
1D	Penny
1M	Penny, Maundy
PD	Pound
QA	Quarter Angel
QF	Quarter Farthing
QFL	Quarter Florin
QG	Quarter Guinea
QL	Quarter Laurel
QN	Quarter Noble
RY	Ryal
SH	Shilling
6D	Sixpence
SV	Sovereign
TS	Testoon
TF	Third Farthing
TG	Third Guinea
3F	Three Farthings
3S	Three Shillings
3HD	Threehalfpence
3D	Threepence
3DB	Threepence, Brass
3M	Threepence, Silver
TU	Triple Unite
20D	Twenty Pence
2G	Two Guineas
2P	Two Pounds
2M	Twopence, Maundy
UN	Unite

Quick-Index-Charts®

Hammered Coins

	TU	SV	UN	LA	PD	RY	HS	DC	HL	HU	HP	NB	AG	FL	CR	CRR	HN	HA	
William I																			W1
William II																			W2
Henry I																			H1
Stephen																			ST
Matilda																			MT
Henry II																			H2
Richard I																			R1
John I																			JH
Henry III																			H3
Edward I																			E1
Edward II																			E2
Edward III												135		153			173		E3
Richard II												137					174		R2
Henry IV												138					175		H4
Henry V												139					176		H5
Henry VI (F)												140					176		H6
Edward IV (F)					142							142	145				177		E4
Henry VI (R)													145					179	H6
Edward IV (S)													145					179	E4
Edward V													146					180	E5
Richard III													146					180	R3
Henry VII		105				121							147					180	H7
Henry VIII		106						123				149	148		155	171		181	H8
Edward VI		108						124					149		157			181	E6
Mary I		108				121							149					182	MA
Philip & Mary													150					182	PM
Elizabeth I		108			109	121					125		150		158			182	EL
James I		109	110	110		121	127	127	127				151		159			183	J1
Charles I	103		111		116			128		130	130		151		162				C1
Commonwealth			119					132							168				CW
Charles II			119					132							169				C2

Milled Coins

	5G	5P	50S	2G	2P	BR	GN	SV	HG	HS	TG	QG	CR	DFL	3S	HC	FL	
Cromwell			433			443							477			499		OC
Charles II	421		435			445		461					477			499		C2
James II	422		435			446		461					479			501		J2
William & Mary	423			436			446	462					480			501		WM
William III	423			436			447	462					480			502		W3
Anne	424			437			448	462					481			504		AN
George I	425			437			448	463				475	482			505		G1
George II	425			437			449	463					483			506		G2
George III						451	453	464	467	473	475		484		497	507		G3
George IV		427			439			453	467				487			508		G4
William IV					439			454	467				487			509		W4
Victoria		427			440			454	468				488	495		509	517	V
Edward VII		428			440			457	470				490			511	519	E7
George V		429			440			458	470				490			512	520	G5
Edward VIII		429			441			459					491			513	521	E8
George VI		429			441			459	471				492			513	521	G6
Elizabeth II		430			441			459	471				492			514	522	EZ

	HFL	HC	20D	QN	QA	QFL	TS	SH	6D	4D	3D	2D	3HD	1D	3F	HD	FA	
William I														315				W1
William II														317				W2
Henry I														317		379		H1
Stephen														320				ST
Matilda														321				MT
Henry II														322				H2
Richard I														325				R1
John I														326				JH
Henry III			213											328		379	395	H3
Edward I										259				333		379	395	E1
Edward II														341		381	397	E2
Edward III	185			215		223				260		289		343		381	397	E3
Richard II				216						262		291		349		383	398	R2
Henry IV				217						262		291		350		384	398	H4
Henry V				217						263		292		351		384	399	H5
Henry VI (F)				218						264		293		353		385	399	H6
Edward IV (F)				219						267		295		356		387	400	E4
Henry VI (R)										270		297		359		388		H6
Edward IV (S)										270		298		359		388		E4
Edward V										271		298		362				E5
Richard III										272		298		362		389		R3
Henry VII							225			272		299		362		390	400	H7
Henry VIII		187			221	225				274		300		365		391	401	H8
Edward VI		188						226	247	277	283	304		368		393	401	E6
Mary										278		304		369				MA
Philip & Mary								228	247	278		305		369				PM
Elizabeth I		189			221			229	248	278	283	305	313	370	377	393		EL
James I		190						231	250			306		371		393	401	J1
Charles I		192						232	251	279	284	307		371		394	402	C1
Commonwealth		210						245	256			310		375		394		CW
Charles II		211						245	257	282	286	311		375				C2

	18D	SH	6D	4M	4D	3M	3DB	2M	2D	3HD	1M	1D	HD	FA	HF	TF	QF	MS	
Cromwell		525	541																OC
Charles II		525	541	553		561		571			579		593	605					C2
James II		526	541	553		561		571			579		593	605				*	J2
William & Mary		526	542	553		561		571			579		594	606				*	WM
William III		527	542	554		562		572			580		595	607				*	W3
Anne		528	544	554		562		572			580			607				*	AN
George I		530	544	554		562		572			580		596	608				*	G1
George II		531	545	555		563		572			581		597	609				*	G2
George III	523	532	545	555		563		573	575		581	583	597	609				*	G3
George IV		533	546	555		563		573			581	583	598	610	617	619		623	G4
William IV		534	547	556	559	564		573		577	582	584	599	611	617	619		623	W4
Victoria		534	547	556	559	564		573		577	582	584	599	611	617	619	621	624	V
Edward VII		536	549	556		565		574			582	588	601	613		620		625	E7
George V		536	549	556		566		574			582	588	602	613		620		625	G5
Edward VIII		537	550			567	569				589	602	614						E8
George VI		537	550	556		567	569	574			582	590	603	614				626	G6
Elizabeth II		538	551	556		567	570	574			582	591	603	615				626	EZ

* listed under individual coins

Contents

About the Contributors 4

Acknowledgements 5

How to use the Numbering System 6

Quick-Index-Charts 8

Preface to the Fifth Edition 17

An Introduction to Coin Collecting 53

Introduction 25

A coin per reign 31

Glossary 55

Questions & Answers 76

Hammered coins

Introduction to Hammered Coinage 81

Mintmarks 89

Triple Unite
Charles I (1625 – 49) 103

Sovereign Unite Laurel Pound
Henry VII (1485 – 1509) 105
Henry VIII (1509 – 47) 106
Edward VI (1547 – 53) 107
Mary (1553 – 54) 108
Elizabeth I (1558 – 1603) 108
James I (1603 – 25) 109
Charles I (1625 – 49) 111
Commonwealth (1649 – 60) 119
Charles II (1660 – 85) 119

Ryal
Henry VII (1485 – 1509) 121
Mary (1553 – 54) 121
Elizabeth I (1558 – 1603) 121
James I (1603 – 25) 121

Half Sovereign Double Crown Ten Shillings Halfpound Half Laurel
Henry VIII (1509 – 47) 123
Edward VI (1547 – 53) 124
Elizabeth I (1558 – 1603) 125
James I (1603 – 25) 126
Charles I (1625 – 49) 128
Commonwealth (1649 – 60) 132
Charles II (1660 – 85) 132

Noble
Edward III (1327 – 77) 135
Richard II (1377 – 99) 137
Henry IV (1399 – 1413) 138
Henry V (1413 – 22) 139
Henry VI First Reign (1422 – 61) 140

Edward IV First Reign (1461 – 70) 142

Angel
Edward IV First Reign (1461 – 70) 145
Henry VI Restored (Oct. 1470 – April 1471) ... 145
Edward IV Second Reign (1471 – 83) 145
Edward IV or V 146
Edward V (1483) 146
Richard III (1483 – 85) 146
Henry VII (1485 – 1509) 147
Henry VIII (1509 – 47) 148
Edward VI (1547 – 53) 149
Mary (1553 – 54) 149
Philip and Mary (1554 – 58) 150
Elizabeth I (1558 – 1603) 150
James I (1603 – 25) 151
Charles I (1625 – 49) 151

Florin or Double Leopard
Edward III (1327 – 77) 153

Crown
Henry VIII (1509 – 47) 155
Edward VI (1547 – 53) 157
Elizabeth I (1558 – 1603) 158
James I (1603 – 25) 159
Charles I (1625 – 49) 162
Commonwealth (1649 – 60) 168
Charles II (1660 – 85) ....

Crown of the Rose
Henry VIII (1509 – 47) 171

Half Noble
Edward III (1327 – 77) 173
Richard II (1377 – 99) 174
Henry IV (1399 – 1413) 175
Henry V (1413 – 22) 176
Henry VI First Reign (1422 – 61) 176
Edward IV First Reign (1461 – 70) 177

Half Angel
Henry VI Restored (Oct. 1470 – April 1471) ...179
Edward IV Second Reign (1471 – 83) 179
Edward IV or V 180
Edward V (1483) 180
Richard III (1483 – 85) 180
Henry VII (1485 – 1509) 180
Henry VIII (1509 – 47) 181
Edward VI (1547 – 53) 181
Mary (1553 – 54 182
Philip and Mary (1554 – 58) 182
Elizabeth I (1558 – 1603) 182
James I (1603 – 25) 183

Half Florin or Leopard
Edward III (1327 – 77) 185

Halfcrown
Henry VIII (1509 – 47).....................................187
Edward VI (1547 – 53).....................................188
Elizabeth I (1558 – 1603)...............................189
James I (1603 – 25)..190
Charles I (1625 – 49).....................................192
Commonwealth (1649 – 60) 210
Charles II (1660 – 85)....................................211

Twenty Pence
Henry III (1216 – 72).....................................213

Quarter Noble
Edward III (1327 – 77)...................................215
Richard II (1377 – 99)....................................216
Henry IV (1399 – 1413)..................................217
Henry V (1413 – 22).......................................217
Henry VI First Reign (1422 – 61) 218
Edward IV First Reign (1461 – 70) 219

Quarter Angel
Henry VIII (1509 – 47)...................................221
Elizabeth I (1558 – 1603)...............................221

Quarter Florin or Helm
Edward III (1327 – 77)...................................223

Shilling
Henry VII (1485 – 1509).................................225
Henry VIII (1509 – 47)...................................225
Edward VI (1547 – 53)...................................226
Philip and Mary (1554 – 58)..........................228
Elizabeth I (1558 – 1603)...............................229
James I (1603 – 25)..231
Charles I (1625 – 49).....................................232
Commonwealth (1649 – 60) 245
Charles II (1660 – 85)....................................245

Sixpence
Edward VI (1547 – 53)...................................247
Philip and Mary (1554 – 58)..........................247
Elizabeth I (1558 – 1603)...............................248
James I (1603 – 25)..250
Charles I (1625 – 49).....................................251
Commonwealth (1649 – 60) 256
Charles II (1660 – 85)....................................257

Groat
Edward I (1272 – 1307)..................................259
Edward III (1327 – 77)...................................260
Richard II (1377 – 99)....................................262
Henry IV (1399 – 1413)..................................262
Henry V (1413 – 22).......................................263
Henry VI First Reign (1422 – 61) 264
Edward IV First Reign (1461 – 70) 267
Henry VI Restored (Oct. 1470 – April 1471) ...270
Edward IV Second Reign (1471 – 83)..............270
Edward IV or V..271
Edward V (1483)..271
Richard III (1483 – 85)...................................272
Henry VII (1485 – 1509).................................272

Henry VIII (1509 – 47)...................................274
Edward VI (1547 – 53)...................................277
Mary (1553 – 54)...278
Philip and Mary (1554 – 58)..........................278
Elizabeth I (1558 – 1603)...............................278
Charles I (1625 – 49).....................................279
Charles II (1660 – 85)....................................282

Threepence
Edward VI (1547 – 53)...................................283
Elizabeth I (1558 – 1603)...............................283
Charles I (1625 – 49).....................................284
Charles II (1660 – 85)....................................286

Halfgroat
Edward III (1327 – 77)...................................289
Richard II (1377 – 99)....................................291
Henry IV (1399 – 1413)..................................291
Henry V (1413 – 22).......................................292
Henry VI First Reign (1422 – 61) 293
Edward IV First Reign (1461 – 70) 295
Henry VI Restored (Oct. 1470 – April 1471) ...297
Edward IV Second Reign (1471 – 83)..............298
Edward V (1483)..298
Richard III (1483 – 85)...................................298
Henry VII (1485 – 1509).................................299
Henry VIII (1509 – 47)...................................300
Edward VI (1547 – 53)...................................304
Mary (1553 – 54)...304
Philip and Mary (1554 – 58)..........................305
Elizabeth I (1558 – 1603)...............................305
James I (1603 – 25)..306
Charles I (1625 – 49).....................................307
Commonwealth (1649 – 60) 310
Charles II (1660 – 85)....................................311

Three Halfpence
Elizabeth I (1558 – 1603)...............................313

Penny
William I (1066 – 87)......................................315
William II (1087 – 1100) 317
Henry I (1100 – 35).......................................317
Stephen (1135 – 54).......................................320
Matilda...321
Henry II (1154 – 89).......................................322
Richard I (1189 – 99)......................................325
John (1199 – 1216)...326
Henry III (1216 – 72).....................................328
Cut Pennies 333
Edward I (1272 – 1307)..................................333
Distinguishing betweed E11D and E21D........334
Edward II (1307 – 27).....................................341
Edward III (1327 – 77)...................................343
Richard II (1377 – 99)....................................349
Henry IV (1399 – 1413)..................................350
Henry V (1413 – 22).......................................351
Henry VI First Reign (1422 – 61) 353

Edward IV First Reign (1461 – 70) 356
Henry VI Restored (Oct. 1470 – April 1471) ...359
Edward IV Second Reign (1471 – 83) 359
Edward IV or V...361
Edward V (1483)...362
Richard III (1483 – 85)................................362
Henry VII (1485 – 1509)..............................362
Henry VIII (1509 – 47).................................365
Edward VI (1547 – 53).................................368
Mary (1553 – 54)..369
Philip and Mary (1554 – 58).........................369
Elizabeth I (1558 – 1603)............................370
James I (1603 – 25).....................................371
Charles I (1625 – 49)...................................371
Commonwealth (1649 – 60).........................375
Charles II (1660 – 85).................................375

Three Farthings
Elizabeth I (1558 – 1603)............................377

Halfpenny
Henry I (1100 – 35).....................................379
Henry III (1216 – 72)...................................379
Edward I (1272 – 1307)...............................379
Edward II (1307 – 27)..................................381
Edward III (1327 – 77).................................381
Richard II (1377 – 99).................................383
Henry IV (1399 – 1413)...............................384
Henry V (1413 – 22)....................................384
Henry VI First Reign (1422 – 61) 385
Edward IV First Reign (1461 – 70) 387
Henry VI Restored (Oct. 1470 – April 1471) ...388
Edward IV Second Reign (1471 – 83) 388
Edward IV or V...389
Richard III (1483 – 85)................................389
Henry VII (1485 – 1509)..............................390
Henry VIII (1509 – 47).................................391
Edward VI (1547 – 53).................................393
Elizabeth I (1558 – 1603)............................393
James I (1603 – 25).....................................393
Charles I (1625 – 49)...................................394
Commonwealth (1649 – 60).........................394

Farthing
Henry III (1216 – 72)...................................395
Edward I (1272 – 1307)...............................395
Edward II (1307 – 27)..................................397
Edward III (1327 – 77).................................397
Richard II (1377 – 99).................................398
Henry IV (1399 – 1413)...............................398
Henry V (1413 – 22)....................................399
Henry VI First Reign (1422 – 61) 399
Edward IV First Reign (1461 – 70) 400
Henry VII (1485 – 1509)..............................400
Henry VIII (1509 – 47).................................401
Edward VI (1547 – 53).................................401
James I (1603 – 25).....................................401
Charles I (1625 – 49)...................................402

Forgeries of J1FA and C1FA 405
Elizabeth I Countermarked Coins 407
Elizabeth I Portcullis Coinage 408
Charles I Siege Issues.....................................
Unofficial Coins and Tokens.............................411
Jetons..411
Ecclesiastical Tokens 412
Trade Tokens 412
Coin Weights...412

Milled Coins

Introduction to the milled coinage section
A Guide to using the Tables...........................415
Translation of Foreign Legends......................416

Five Guineas
Charles II (1660 – 85) 421
James II (1685 – 88)....................................422
William and Mary (1688 – 94) 423
William III (1695 – 1701) 423
Anne (1702 – 14).......................................424
George I (1714 – 27) 425
George II (1727 – 60) 425

Five Pounds
George IV (1820 – 30)..................................427
William IV (1830 – 37).................................427
Victoria (1837 – 1901).................................427
Edward VII (1901 – 10)................................428
George V (1910 – 36)...................................429
Edward VIII (1936)......................................429
George VI (1937 – 52)..................................429
Elizabeth II (1952 –)..................................430

Fifty Shillings
Oliver Cromwell (Commonwealth
1649 – 60) 433

Two Guineas
Charles II (1660 – 85) 435
James II (1685 – 88)....................................435
William and Mary (1688 – 94) 436
William III (1695 – 1701) 436
Anne (1702 – 14).......................................437
George I (1714 – 27) 437
George II (1727 – 60) 437

Two Pounds
George IV (1820 – 30)..................................439
William IV (1830 – 37).................................439
Victoria (1837 – 1901).................................440
Edward VII (1901 – 10)................................440
George V (1910 – 36)...................................440
Edward VIII (1936)......................................441
George VI (1937 – 52)..................................441
Elizabeth II (1952 –)..................................441

Broad
Oliver Cromwell (Commonwealth
1649 – 60) 443

Guinea
Charles II (1660 – 85) 445
James II (1685 – 88) 446
William and Mary (1688 – 94) 446
William III (1695 – 1701) 447
Anne (1702 – 14) 448
George I (1714 – 27) 448
George II (1727 – 60) 449
George III (1760 – 1820) 451

Sovereign
George III (1760 – 1820) 453
George IV (1820 – 30) 453
William IV (1830 – 37) 454
Victoria (1837 – 1901) 454
Edward VII (1901 – 10) 457
George V (1910 – 36) 458
Edward VIII (1936) 459
George VI (1937 – 52) 459
Elizabeth II (1952 –) 459

Half Guinea
Charles II (1660 – 85) 461
James II (1685 – 88) 461
William and Mary (1688 – 94) 462
William III (1695 – 1701) 462
Anne (1702 – 14) 462
George I (1714 – 27) 463
George II (1727 – 60) 463
George III (1760 – 1820) 464

Half Sovereign
George III (1760 – 1820) 467
George IV (1820 – 30) 467
William IV (1830 – 37) 467
Victoria (1837 – 1901) 468
Edward VII (1901 – 10) 470
George V (1910 – 36) 470
George VI (1937 – 52) 471
Elizabeth II (1952 –) 471

Third Guinea
George III (1760 – 1820) 473

Quarter Guinea
George I (1714 – 27) 475
George III (1760 – 1820) 475

Crown
Oliver Cromwell (Commonwealth
(1649 – 60) 477
Charles II (1660 – 85) 477
James II (1685 – 88) 479
William and Mary (1688 – 94) 480
William III (1695 – 1701) 480
Anne (1702 – 14) 481
George I (1714 – 27) 482

George II (1727 – 60) 483
George III (1760 – 1820) 484
George IV (1820 – 30) 487
William IV (1830 – 37) 487
Victoria (1837 – 1901) 488
Edward VII (1901 – 10) 490
George V (1910 – 36) 490
Edward VIII (1936) 491
George VI (1937 – 52) 492
Elizabeth II (1952 –) 492

Double Florin
Victoria (1837 – 1901) 495

Three Shillings
George III (1760 – 1820) 497

Halfcrown
Oliver Cromwell (Commonwealth
1649 – 60) 499
Charles II (1660 – 85) 499
James II (1685 – 88) 501
William and Mary (1688 – 94) 501
William III (1695 – 1701) 502
Anne (1702 – 14) 504
George I (1714 – 27) 505
George II (1727 – 60) 506
George III (1760 – 1820) 507
George IV (1820 – 30) 508
William IV (1830 – 37) 509
Victoria (1837 – 1901) 509
Edward VII (1901 – 10) 511
George V (1910 – 36) 512
Edward VIII (1936) 513
George VI (1937 – 52) 513
Elizabeth II (1952 –) 514

Florin
Victoria (1837 – 1901) 517
Edward VII (1901 – 10) 519
George V (1910 – 36) 520
Edward VIII (1936) 521
George VI (1937 – 52) 521
Elizabeth II (1952 –) 522

Eighteen Pence Bank Token
George III (1760 – 1820) 523

Shilling
Oliver Cromwell (Commonwealth
1649 – 60) 525
Charles II (1660 – 85) 525
James II (1685 – 88) 526
William and Mary (1688 – 94) 526
William III (1695 – 1701) 527
Anne (1702 – 14) 528
George I (1714 – 27) 530
George II (1727 – 60) 531
George III (1760 – 1820) 532
George IV (1820 – 30) 533

William IV (1830 – 37)............534
Victoria (1837 – 1901)............534
Edward VII (1901 – 10)............536
George V (1910 – 36)............536
Edward VIII (1936)............537
George VI (1937 – 52)............537
Elizabeth II (1952 –)............538

Sixpence
Oliver Cromwell (Commonwealth
1649 – 60)............541
Charles II (1660 – 85)............541
James II (1685 – 88)............541
William and Mary (1688 – 94)............542
William III (1695 – 1701)............542
Anne (1702 – 14)............544
George I (1714 – 27)............544
George II (1727 – 60)............545
George III (1760 – 1820)............545
George IV (1820 – 30)............546
William IV (1830 – 37)............547
Victoria (1837 – 1901)............547
Edward VII (1901 – 10)............549
George V (1910 – 36)............549
Edward VIII (1936)............550
George VI (1937 – 52)............550
Elizabeth II (1952 –)............551

Maundy Fourpence
Charles II (1660 – 85)............553
James II (1685 – 88)............553
William and Mary (1688 – 94)............553
William III (1695 – 1701)............554
Anne (1702 – 14)............554
George I (1714 – 27)............554
George II (1727 – 60)............555
George III (1760 – 1820)............555
George IV (1820 – 30)............555
William IV (1830 – 37)............556
Victoria (1837 – 1901)............556
Edward VII (1901 – 10)............556
George V (1910 – 36)............556
George VI (1937 – 52)............556
Elizabeth II (1952 –)............556

Groat
William IV (1830 – 37)............559
Victoria (1837 – 1901)............559

Silver Threepence
Charles II (1660 – 85)............561
James II (1685 – 88)............561
William and Mary (1688 – 94)............561
William III (1695 – 1701)............562
Anne (1702 – 14)............562
George I (1714 – 27)............562
George II (1727 – 60)............563
George III (1760 – 1820)............563

George IV (1820 – 30)............563
William IV (1830 – 37)............564
Victoria (1837 – 1901)............564
Edward VII (1901 – 10)............565
George V (1910 – 36)............566
Edward VIII (1936)............567
George VI (1937 – 52)............567
Elizabeth II (1952 –)............567

Brass Threepence
Edward VIII (1936)............569
George VI (1937 – 52)............569
Elizabeth II (1952 –)............570

Silver Twopence
Charles II (1660 – 85)............571
James II (1685 – 88)............571
William and Mary (1688 – 94)............571
William III (1695 – 1701)............572
Anne (1702 – 14)............572
George I (1714 – 27)............572
George II (1727 – 60)............572
George III (1760 – 1820)............573
George IV (1820 – 30)............573
William IV (1830 – 37)............573
Victoria (1837 – 1901)............573
Edward VII (1901 – 10)............574
George V (1910 – 36)............574
George VI (1937 – 52)............574
Elizabeth II (1952 –)............574

Copper Twopence
George III (1760 – 1820)............575

Three Halfpence
William IV (1830 – 37)............577
Victoria (1837 – 1901)............577

Silver Penny
Charles II (1660 – 85)............579
James II (1685 – 88)............579
William and Mary (1688 – 94)............579
William III (1695 – 1701)............580
Anne (1702 – 14)............580
George I (1714 – 27)............580
George II (1727 – 60)............581
George III (1760 – 1820)............581
George IV (1820 – 30)............581
William IV (1830 – 37)............582
Victoria (1837 – 1901)............582
Edward VII (1901 – 10)............582
George V (1910 – 36)............582
George VI (1937 – 52)............582
Elizabeth II (1952 –)............582

Copper/Bronze Penny
George III (1760 – 1820)............583
George IV (1820 – 30)............583
William IV (1830 – 37)............584
Victoria (1837 – 1901)............584

Edward VII (1901 – 10).............................588
George V (1910 – 36)..............................588
Edward VIII (1936)................................589
George VI (1937 – 52).............................590
Elizabeth II (1952 –)............................591

Halfpenny
Charles II (1660 – 85)............................593
James II (1685 – 88)..............................593
William and Mary (1688 – 94)......................594
William III (1694 – 1701).........................595
George I (1714 – 27)..............................596
George II (1727 – 60).............................597
George III (1760 – 1820)..........................597
George IV (1820 – 30).............................598
William IV (1830 – 37)............................599
Victoria (1837 – 1901)............................599
Edward VII (1901 – 10)............................601
George V (1910 – 36)..............................602
Edward VIII (1936)................................602
George VI (1937 – 52).............................603
Elizabeth II (1952 –)............................603

Farthing
Charles II (1660 – 85)............................605
James II (1685 – 88)..............................605
William and Mary (1688 – 94)......................606
William III (1694 – 1701).........................607
Anne (1701 – 1714)................................607
George I (1714 – 27)..............................608
George II (1727 – 60).............................609
George III (1760 – 1820)..........................609
George IV (1820 – 30).............................610
William IV (1830 – 37)............................611
Victoria (1837 – 1901)............................611
Edward VII (1901 – 10)............................613
George V (1910 – 36)..............................613
Edward VIII (1936)................................614
George VI (1937 – 52).............................614
Elizabeth II (1952 –)............................615

Half Farthing
George IV (1820 – 30).............................617
William IV (1830 – 37)............................617
Victoria (1837 – 1901)............................617

Third Farthing
George IV (1820 – 30).............................619
William IV (1830 – 37)............................619
Victoria (1837 – 1901)............................619
Edward VII (1901 – 10)............................620
George V (1910 – 36)..............................620

Quarter Farthing
Victoria (1837 – 1901)............................621

Maundy Sets
George IV (1820 – 30).............................623
William IV (1830 – 37)............................623
Victoria (1837 – 1901)............................624

Edward VII (1901 – 10)............................625
George V (1910 – 36)..............................625
George VI (1937 – 52).............................626
Elizabeth II (1952 –)............................626

Touchpieces 629

Decimal Coinage
Base Metal Five Pounds 633
Base Metal Two Pounds 635
Base Metal One Pound 637
50 Pence 638
25 Pence 640
20 Pence 641
10 Pence 642
5 Pence 643
2 Pence 644
1 Penny 645
Half Penny..646

Britannia Coinage
100 Pounds 647
50 Pounds 647
25 Pounds 648
10 Pounds 458
2 Pounds 649
Pound 649
50 Pence 649
20 Pence 649

Proof Sets
George II (1727 – 60).............................651
George IV (1820 – 30).............................651
William IV (1830 – 37)............................651
Victoria (1837 – 1901)............................651
Edward VII (1901 – 10)............................652
George V (1910 – 36)..............................653
George VI (1937 – 52).............................653
Elizabeth II (1952 –)............................654

Specimen Sets 667

Mintage Figures.................................671

Mintage Figures, Decimal Coinage 685

Patterns

Hammered Patterns 691

Milled Patterns 705

Bibliography 739

Index of engravers and designers...........743

Index 751

Preface to the Fifth Edition

Another year, fewer coins and higher prices...!

As each new edition of *The Standard Catalogue* comes out, part of my job is to review what has happened in numismatics in the past year. It seems that I am always writing that there are fewer coins around and that prices are higher. So why should this year be any different? It isn't! There are fewer dealers with shops because the rents are so high, there are more auction houses chasing material that might be for sale and prices are in general higher! I have even heard of one auction house who, in order to secure a very important collection, worked on no commission at all! They had to pay all of their expenses out of the buyers premium. That shows just how much nice material is wanted.

There have been several very nice auctions this past year and the prices were very strong, if the auction house did a good catalogue and spent some money advertising the sale, it was a success. Two auctions that spring to mind are the collection of George III coins and the Stack's collection of hammered pennies et al. Before the sales there were worries that there wouldn't be enough money around to buy everything, how wrong they were. Nice material finds buyers — period. It is the same in banknotes and other collectables, at this time there is far more money around than there is material to be bought. Collectors are not fools, but they appear to be going that extra ten yards, sorry make that meters after all we are now Europeans, in order to get what they want...

That is not to say that prices have gone crazy as they did in the early 1980s, collectors are being sensible, but they are willing to pay that little bit extra. I have also seen a marked interest on the part of collectors to value quality higher than in the past. When I started in coins in 1955, a coin was either new or it was used and to be honest many of the coins called used were in fact new! With low prices you had less pressure to attract the collectors' attention with a flashy grade. You had far fewer collectors and there was more than enough material to go around. I remarked the other day that dealers and auction houses are now illustrating coins which in the past they wouldn't even have considered for inclusion in their sales. Less material makes what is available more attractive, Gresham's law is that bad money drives good money out of circulation. A dealer has to make a living and if Uncirculated coins are not available then he will sell Fine or Very Fine coins.

One must understand that not everyone can afford a Gothic crown in choice proof condition, but many collectors can afford the same coin in Very Fine or Extremely Fine. In the past when collectors could have their choice of twenty different choice Gothic crowns for the princely sum of £7.50, they could take their time and be choosy. Those who collected tended to be at the upper end of the socio-economic scale. They could afford to spend a week's wages for the average man on a single coin. Most of us were worrying about how we were going to pay the mortgage and feed the family. The idea of coins was to be used to pay bills and not to be collected! You collected enough coins until you had the required amount to settle your bill! Today that same Gothic crown would cost about £1,750.00 and there are still many collectors who can not afford it or refuse to pay that price! On the other hand they can afford and will buy a nice VF example at say £400. Tastes change and we are seeing that happen in today's market.

When we bought the 17,000,000 British Military banknotes at auction a number of years ago, most of the notes were Uncirculated, but some were used. We finally found some dealers in Indonesia that only wanted used notes and we were saved. The answer was that in Indonesia they only wanted used notes, because that meant that they were real because they had circulated. Perhaps today's collector feels the same way, used coins at a reasonable fraction of the Uncirculated price are real coins. I don't know the answer, in this case I am just posing the question, but I do know that circulated coins have increased in demand and in price.

We are seeing a new breed of collector and one that on a personal basis I strongly encourage. They are true collectors and want a nice example for their collection, on hammered coins that might be Fine and on milled it might be Very Fine. Nice coins which have seen reasonable circulation, but after all that is why coins were struck, to be used. This is also a change in collecting styles, that is more toward type collecting rather than trying to accumulate every date and mintmark of a particular series. While we still see a lot of date collectors in the more modern series, the earlier hammered coins have priced themselves out of that market. You just can not get or afford to buy one of each mint, moneyer and class of a monarch.

There have been some hoards which have come out on to the market recently, King Cnut pennies in particular spring to mind. The best pieces came out first and they have disappeared from the market. Then the Fines and Very Fines came out and they too are being absorbed into the market. Prices are much lower now, but as the supply is drying up, this might well be the time you add one to your collection. I bought a large part of the Reigate hoard of Henry VI groats a few years ago, now these coins have disappeared and prices have risen substantially. When a hoard comes out prices drop, a wise collector takes that opportunity to buy something that he always wanted but previously couldn't afford.

Certainly the high end coins are selling, but to be honest most are going through the auction houses. Sotheby managed to sell an 1819 Sovereign for some £55,000 including buyers premium, a world record price for a sovereign. There were two buyers who had to have it and they pushed each other up, I understand that the under bidder wishes he had bid even more...

Nice material is being collected and prices are going up. You have to understand that for too long the availability of British coins has been greater than the demand for them. An interesting example is the 1887 Queen Victoria jubilee head shilling. Always available in Uncirculated condition despite it being over 100 years old and very reasonably priced. Today it is harder to find an Uncirculated example and prices are higher, but are they over priced? Certainly not! Today you might pay say £25 for an nice Uncirculated example, a similar sized coin and of the same vintage from the United States, would cost £200 to £400. So the British shilling has gone up in value, yet it is still very reasonable in collector's terms.

So to summarise, material is getting tougher, prices have risen but there is no panic out there. Nice material for collectors will tend to go up in value, but at a reasonable rate. When a hoard comes out, I believe that it is the time to buy an example for your collection. It has been a good but sensible year in numismatics.

The Past

My friend David Rider was over from Australia the other week, he emigrated there a number of years ago. David, Michael Gouby, Claire and myself went out to dinner and reminisced, as usual. There are far fewer dealers in coins to today than there were twenty years ago. After all today a youngster can join a city firm or go into computers and make a lot more money than he can in coins. A dealer is someone who loves his coins, he would have to, when you consider all the time and effort that he puts into the business. The hours sorting and writing coins up, the weekends spent at coin shows, the lots of coins to be viewed at auctions and the many miles to be travelled every year. I believe that if the average dealer totalled up the number of hours that he worked and divided it by his take home pay, then he would be better off in a job! Of course the job wouldn't be as much fun and the people you meet might not be so interesting. You also have to remember that work is a four letter word!

Michael and I almost shared a flat some 31 years ago and David and I use to go out on the raze together when we were both single. So our relationships are first personal and then professional. They both love their coins and are of the old school, so to speak. Michael has written an important book on Victorian pennies and this is also one of David's loves. When I first came to London it was in David's back room that I stored by trunk and he was responsible for my 'taxi fetish'. Whenever I would ask him how to get somewhere, he would always say, 'take a taxi'.

We were talking about how cheap coins used to be and how much smaller the collector base is today. Yes, I know that some prices are higher today, but not all of them. In 1968 Coin Monthly had some 43,000 subscribers and a 1954 halfcrown Uncirculated wholesaled for £40.00! You must remember that at that time the average wage was only £15–20 a week. A 1953 plastic set sold for £12.50 and today... It was a time just before decimalization and everyone wanted to complete a date set of the coins of Elizabeth II. Prices were crazy in today's terms and in yesterday's terms they were insane!

It showed how rare and scarce some of the modern so called 'common coins' really were. Malcolm Coeshaw does quite a bit with decimal coins and he tells me that some dates are almost impossible to get. If too many people started to collect modern coins, many dealers would be surprised just how difficult some dates really are. Michael and David understood the pre-decimal market and some of the prices obtained were unbelievable. I think David sold a modified effigy penny to a collector in Bermuda for a gigantic price, he must have as he stood the drinks all night long. We were young, had money in our pockets and no responsibilities, it was a great life...

The dealers in those days were characters, unlike most of us today who are conservative businessmen. Well not exactly conservative businessmen, but we had a lot more fun in the old days and we were a lot freer of all the red tape and rules and regulations. There weren't so many catalogues and if you knew your stuff, you could make the occasional real buy. When your over heads are only £25–35 a week, a good buy could keep you going for some time.

There were three big firms in those days, two of which are still in existence, Seaby, Spink and Baldwin. There were a number of other important dealers who traded on their own account, Geoff and Bernard Hearn, Peter 'Maundy' Allen, Michael Millward just to name four. The numismatic world was very small and if someone went to another country on business, even in Europe, it was quite something. The auction houses were the preserve of dealers who sat around horseshoe shaped tables. Any collector who went to an auction might well have to bid against a dealer. That dealer might just bid the collector up just because the collector had the affront to be there! Business was done for the most part in cash and as the top tax rate was 94%, perhaps some of it fell through the cracks. I never saw a restaurant bill paid by cheque for example.

Sometimes dealers would play a little naughty themselves. I remember one dealer sitting next to me at the table at a Glendining's Auction and 'winning' a lot that I had been bidding on. I asked him what was in the lot and he said, 'lots of good things'. So I suspected that he was bidding on my bid, that is, he hadn't looked at the lot, but knew that I had and he was bidding on my knowledge. A couple of lots later he again outbid me on a lot and I believe that it cost him £1,250 at the time. I waited for about five lots before asking him the same question. You see after five lots it would be very hard to reopen the lot. He gave me the same reply and I nodded and said, 'I am glad of that, because I was bidding on the wrong lot and only had £250 on that one'. That dealer turned rather pale and never tried to bid on my bid again...!

Today the dealers are still friendly, but it is now business and they maybe your friend but they also want the coin you want. The dealers are getting older and there are far fewer of us than there were. I and Coincraft are now one of the senior dealers, it would have been hard to imagine all those years ago. Perhaps some day in the future someone will be sitting at a computer writing something about me. Until then, excuse me but you said that you wanted how much for that coin?

Selecting your Dealers

You should find dealers that you are comfortable with and feel you can trust. They may have a shop, they may have an office, they may have a market stall or they may just attend coin shows. Don't be put off by where the dealer operates from, it is the person you are dealing with, not the premises. I know rogues with elegant shops and very honourable people working out of their houses. Once you feel comfortable with a dealer, let him know your interests, what you want and what you can afford. Every dealer would love to have a Lottery winner come in and buy up the shop, but that hasn't happened yet! Let him know that a nice Very Fine coin is more than welcome, or if you only want Uncirculated coins, let him know that also. Any dealer worth his salt will try to supply you with nice coins which fit your budget; after all that's how he makes a living. Please, don't try and buy Uncirculated coins at Extremely Fine prices, it just can't be done! The coins may well look a bargain, but when you go to re-sell them you just might find out that they were only polished Very Fines in the first place. Get to know your dealer and work with him, he can give you the benefit of his experience.

Dealers offer collectors they like either first refusal on something special or perhaps a small discount, but never both! As a collector myself, I would rather have first refusal than a discount. I know that sounds strange, but think it over. If someone else gets first refusal then you may never get that special piece that you have always wanted. That first collector will surely have bought that coin. It is better to get a coin you need at a reasonable price, than **not** get the coin you wanted at a reduced price.

Dealers do not treat all their collectors equally! There are some collectors that you just like more than others. Believe it or not money doesn't really enter into it. Some collectors only have £10-£15 to spend and we enjoy dealing and spending time with them, because they are really interested in what they collect. You need your dealer and your dealer needs you! Try and work together and build a relationship.

You have to work with your dealer to establish a good relationship. I guess the most important thing is please, pay your bills promptly. We are in business to earn a living and we need to pay our bills too. If you would like something and can't afford it all in one go, talk to your dealer; in many cases you will find that something can be done to spread the payments over a period of time. Please don't tell a dealer that you can get something cheaper elsewhere. If it is that much cheaper then just go and get it, if it isn't that much cheaper, then let the dealer earn a little something from time to time. Please do not go and show your dealer what you bought elsewhere, they won't be all that pleased and they might even get upset. Would you go and show your dentist the nice bridge some other dentist just put in? Maintain a good relationship with your dealer. It will pay off in the long term with special offers, perhaps the occasional special price plus good feelings and friendship.

Prices

We have seen a tightening of the market for both high grade and lower grade coins. This is partly due to the shortage of material and I understand that this is also true in paintings, prints, ceramics and other collectable fields. Please note, too many dealers live in the past, which can be good for a collector especially if they don't realise the demand has increased...

There are more and more collectors coming into the market, many of them as interested in the history of the period as they are in the coins themselves. To them, to own a coin of Charles I or Edward I or Henry VIII seemed impossible outside a museum. The other point is that these new collectors are not burdened with knowledge about what prices used to be 10 or even 20 years ago. They look at a piece and if the price seems reasonable they will buy it. These new collectors are making today's and tomorrow's prices, they are dictating what coins are going to cost, not what they used to cost. Dealers when they get together, always talk about the coins they use to own. To many dealers the most pleasant times were the past, especially the distant past...

There has been a great shortage of top quality material around and collectors and dealers have had to settle for a little less. Nice solid middle grade coins, good Fine and Very Fine, are not only highly sought after, they are also much more difficult to get. When a nice coin becomes available, usually many collectors want to add it to their collection and you have to be quick off the mark.

Auction prices have been firm this year and the vast number of auction houses in London and the provinces all seem to be making a reasonable living. Richard Falkiner who writes the coin column for the Antiques Trade Gazette is always reporting record after record. This, despite the realisation that nothing of any really great consequence in English coins has been offered this past year. Should an outstanding collection come up for auction, I believe that prices will go through the roof. There is money available and a pent-up demand from collectors who want to add to their collections. There have been thousands of price changes in this edition of the Catalogue and the vast majority have been increases.

How do we arrive at the prices in this catalogue?

It is my contention that if you put every British coin for sale in this entire country on any given day into one room, you would have fewer than 1% of the coins listed in this book! That includes varieties of date, mint, mint mark and condition. How can anyone be expected to know what each and every coin is worth? They can't! What we have done is taken an educated 'guesstimate' at what we think a collector might have to pay when buying from an established dealer. You might get a bargain at a jumble sale or you might buy a pup, we have estimated what a coin dealer would charge you. On any given day, a coin may bring more or less than its catalogue value, depending on the market conditions on that day. A lot of people might be looking for say, a Maundy Set of 1948 to celebrate their 50th birthday or anniversary. The supply is finite, the actual price you will have to pay may well be more than the catalogue price. On the other hand, if at a coin fair there are three 1948 Maundy Sets on sale and you are the only buyer, you might well obtain a small discount. A lot of dealers price their coins according to what they have paid for them. If they made a good buy, you might well get a bargain and if they paid too much ...

Hammered coins are in general much more individual than milled coins, because they were struck by hand. You can put three Elizabeth I hammered sixpences on a table all grading Very Fine and I am willing to bet that the best Very Fine of the three will sell for 50% -100% more than the worst. It all has to do with centring, quality of strike and general overall eye appeal, yet, technically they are all Very Fine. A nice fully round hammered coin with a strong clear portrait will be worth substantially more than one weakly struck and on an irregular planchet. In many cases with hammered coins beauty is in the eyes of the owner. Pricing hammered coins is especially difficult and requires a good and well practised eye.

Milled or machine struck coins, do not have to have a milled edge. The early examples of milled coins were not all that well struck and it is my belief that the first coins to really get it right were the sixpences of Charles II and the William III coinage of 1700. Before that, the coins were not struck up and that in turn was due to incorrectly cut dies and not enough pressure being used. Again you can take three examples of say, the Gothic Florins of Queen Victoria all the same date and all in Uncirculated condition and lay them down next to each other. One will be weakly struck from a worn die, the second will be a sharply struck example from when the die was fresh and the third will have been struck when the die was new and has a Prooflike surface. All three coins are Uncirculated but all three will sell for widely differing prices.

The final price you pay is one that you will be happy with. If a coin seems too cheap it probably is! No one is going to give away nice coins, especially with the shortages on today's market. Remember, while we try to make all the prices correct, market forces will cause ups and downs, this Catalogue and any other can only be considered a guide to what the coins are worth today. A choice example of any coin Fine, Very Fine or Uncirculated will bring more than the catalogue price. That having been said, we got a lot of compliments on our last edition and hope that with the thousands of changes we have made this year's will be even better. Prices are changing constantly mostly up, but occasionally down, especially when a hoard is found. This Catalogue is a guide to prices and not an absolutely definitive price guide for every coin in every grade.

All prices in this catalogue are in British pounds sterling and at the time of going to press, July 26th 1999, one pound was worth:

Argentina Peso 1.5757	Luxembourg Lux FR 60.7508
Australia $2.4243	Macao Pataca 12.6371
Austria SCH 20.7226	Malaysia Ringgit 5.9900
Bahamas $1.5763	Malta Maltese Lira 0.6402
Bahrain Dinar 0.5943	Mexico Peso 14.7968
Belgium BFR 60.7058	Netherlands FLR 3.3187
Bermuda $1.5763	New Zealand NZ $2.9647
Brazil Real 2.8594	Norway NKR 12.4146
Brunei $2.6779	Oman Rial 0.6069
Canada $2.3735	Peru New Sol 5.2334
Cyprus £ 0.8707	Philippines Peso 60.4906
Denmark DKR 11.2089	Poland Zloty 6.0499
Egypt £5.3796	Portugal Escudo 301.920
Finland Markka 8.9541	Qatar Riyal 5.7385
France FF 9.8785	Russia Rouble 38.2805
Germany DM 2.9454	Saudi Arabia Riyal 5.9120
Greece Drachma 489.331	Singapore S$2.6779
Hong Kong HK $12.2338	South Africa Rand 9.6241
India Rps 68.2065	Spain Peseta 250.573
Indonesia Rup. 10939.5	Sweden SKR 13.2142
Irish Republic Punt £1.1861	Switzerland SFR 2.4176
Italy Lira 2915.97	Thailand Baht 58.9142
Japan Yen 183.458	Turkey Lira 678006.2
Korea South Won 1904.80	**United States $1.5763**
Kuwait Dinar 0.4820	**Euro 1.5060**

Where should I buy my coins?

If I were going to be totally honest to that question, I would have to say 'we would love you to buy all your coins from Coincraft'! But neither Coincraft nor any dealer in the world is going to have everything you want or be able to deal with every collector. Sometimes the material but not the chemistry is there and at other times geographical distances between dealer and collector are the problem.

You can buy from a dealer either in person or through the post. With more and more dealers putting out postal lists it is getting easier for a collector in Lands End to buy a coin from a dealer in John O'Groats. Almost every city or town has coin fairs, although the larger fairs tend to be in the larger cities. In London for instance, we have a monthly fair at the Commonwealth Institute and quarterly fairs at the Cumberland Hotel. Both are well attended, informal and a good way to see many dealers' stocks in one go. Check for local fairs, but again the larger cities will have the largest fairs with the largest number of dealers with tables in attendance.

There are two publications which deal with coins in this country and both offer you a listing of fairs and auctions. The information that you will gain about coins by reading the articles is well worth the cover prices alone. *Coin News* is devoted to numismatics while *Stamp & Coin Mart* is mainly stamps but has a coin section. For their addresses see the advertisement section of this book. An educated collector is the best collector.

Auctions

We dealers are in competition with the auction houses to get material from you, the collector. In many cases the right way to sell something is through an auction and in many cases you will get faster payment and more money from a dealer. The real secret is to know when to use an auction house and when to sell directly to a dealer. You have to study the auction houses and see which gets better prices for what type of material, which auction lots the coins to your advantage and which you feel comfortable with. Some of the auction houses lot each reasonably priced coin as a separate lot, others put a small collection into just one lot. Sometimes the first gets better prices and sometimes the second method will bring you more money, it depends on who is at the sale, the weather and how much publicity the auction house gets for your coins. If you are in a sale which gains enormous publicity, then you material will fare better then in a 'run of the mill sale'.

Many auction houses do not want an average collection and will discourage you in anyway they can. They may even say that it is of too little value, perhaps you would be better taking it to a dealer. There is also the sale's commission and the buyer's premium for you to consider. A number of auction houses charge 15% buyer's commission plus 17.5% VAT on that commission. They then charge you 10%-15% to sell your material. In many cases you will nett only 75% of the auction price. In some cases, that 75% may well be more than you would have netted from a dealer and in other cases it will not. You have to decide.

If you are selling material which falls into the generic coin category, such as gold sovereigns, Proofs Sets and modern material, then selling to a dealer will get you more money, more quickly than using an auction house. A dealer will pay you on the spot, an auction house will pay you 30–45 days after they have been paid themselves. As most dealers do, I sell through auctions from time to time. If I have something which is in an area where I do not have the expertise, then I consign it to auction. If I have material which for one reason or another I have been unable to sell, it may well be consigned to auction. Material which is from a collection and thus is considered 'fresh' to the market will do better than dealers' lots at auction. On the other hand, I have seen lots and even whole auctions which have died. No one was interested in bidding and I have personally bought lots at auction for less than their gold value. This does not happen often, but it can happen and if you have consigned coins to that sale and waited months and months, then you will be disappointed.

It is up to you to decide if you sell to a dealer or through auction, both have advantages and both have disadvantages. If you want money now, then unless the collection is worth tens of thousands you will probably be better selling directly to a dealer. If the collection is of outstanding quality and rarity then the choice is yours. Any collection of sufficient value sent for auction should allow the vendor to obtain an advance from the auction house. You will pay interest on this advance but it will cover your immediate needs. It is a tricky question and one that I have tried to answer honestly.

Grading

Grading is the biggest area of contention in coins. Because the price of a coin is in a great part dependent on its condition, this can be open to many interpretations, even leaving aside those dealers who deliberately overgrade their coins and then advertise them 'cheaply', to appear that they are giving you a bargain. The best advice I can give you is, *if it appears too cheap, there is a reason for it!*

To learn to grade properly takes years of experience and actually handling thousands of coins. You must also know how a coin was made; a hammered coin is vastly different from a milled coin. You have to know about the dies, how they were engraved, how long they lasted and what they looked like as they started to wear. You have to know what an Uncirculated example looks like before you can determine if a particular coin is worn, or if it was just struck that way. You have to learn to distinguish original lustre from something which may have been done in order to try and artificially replace that lustre. Grading correctly is even harder than it sounds.

In the old days a coin was either new or it was used, a used coin could be Fine or it could be Extremely Fine, it just was not new. Today, because of the difference in price between an almost new coin and a new coin, you have to be that much more careful. In the United States they have a crazy grading system in which there are no less than 10 different grades of Uncirculated. They grade an Uncirculated coin on a numerical basis, anywhere from 60 out of 70 to the ultimate which is 70 out of 70. The price difference between a 64/70 and a 65/70 can be anything up to ten times the price. I believe that there are three grades of Uncirculated: Uncirculated, meaning that there is no wear, Choice Uncirculated, a superior coin which might have a few light bag marks but is in the upper 10% in quality of all Uncirculated coins, and Gem Uncirculated which is in the upper 2% of coins.

Because grading is a subjective area it is best to be careful, especially if you do not know the person you are buying from. Again I suggest that you form a relationship with a coin dealer you feel comfortable with and trust. They will be happy to explain why they graded the coin as they have. Grading of coins can not be learnt overnight, but it is something that a collector has to learn.

Going from the lowest grade to the highest they are as follows. *Poor*: extremely worn and most of the detail will be missing but you will still be able to identify the coin as to type. *Fair*: there is much wear but more of the detail is visible and you will easily be able to identify the coin. *Good*: almost all of the lettering will still be there and the date will be easy to read in most cases. *Very Good*: all of the coin will be readable and some of the finer details will start to be discernible. *Fine*: the details are starting to take shape and the coin is becoming more collectable. *Very Fine*: the details are clear, there is wear on the high points but most of the fine detail shows clearly. *Extremely Fine*: there is wear on only the highest points and on copper and bronze there may even be lustre on the coin. *Uncirculated*: there is no wear on the high points but the design may not be fully struck up due to the engraving of the die or its wear. Copper and bronze may or may not have lustre, depending on where and how they were stored.

Be careful about grading and until you learn to grade yourself, deal with someone you can trust.

Below we list the grading system used in some other countries.

Britain	Proof	Unc	EF	VF	Fine	VG
Brazil	—	FDC	S	MBC	BC	BC/R
Denmark	M	0	01	1+	1	1−
Finland	00	0	01	1+	1	1?
France	FB	FDC	SUP	TTB	TB	B
Germany	PP	STG	VZ	SS	S	S.G.E
Italy	FS	FDC	SPL	BB	MB	B
Netherlands	—	FDC	Pr.	Z.f.	Fr.	Z.g.
Norway	M	0	01	1+	1	1−
Portugal	—	Soberba Bela	MBC	BC+	BC	
Spain	Prueba	SC	EBC	MBC	BC+	BC
Sweden	Polerad	0	01	1+	1	1?

Why are there no photographs on coin grading in the Catalogue?

This is a good question. The problem with grading is that sometimes it is the overall look and feel of a coin, as well as the actual strike and wear, that determine its grade. Especially in the higher grades, it is hard to show this with photographs. Perhaps one day, when we have three-dimensional pictures that you can actually turn over and view from all sides on a computer, it will be possible.

The other problem is that, if we illustrated an Elizabeth I sixpence, for example, in all the relevant grades, the results and comments would apply to that specific variety of sixpence only and little else. A more comprehensive approach would involve thousands of photographs and be impracticable; even then, there is no way to guarantee that it would be all that useful. There is no 'quick fix' on the grading side, it takes time and years of experience to grade properly. I feel that it is better to have no photographs of grading, rather than include illustrations which are likely to mislead.

Rarity

Rarity is a way of trying to describe how many examples of a coin exist. A coin may be common in circulated condition but in mint state it might be very scarce, even rare. On more modern coins where an accurate mintage figure is known, assigning a rarity value is relatively easy. Of course, you still have to take into account the amount struck, how many were minted and how many still exist.

The assignment of rarity is again a subjective process. One of my first mentors, Bill Ross, used to say 'it is hard to shut that press off after just one coin was struck'. He also said that 'when you go to value a coin, it is what you have not seen rather than what you have seen that matters'. By that he meant that, when you see a coin that you have never seen before, forget what it catalogues, it is rare! My colleague Alan Ward once spent seven years looking for a coin which catalogues only $1.50; when he saw it he bought it. Since then, he has seen only two other examples and he bought both of them. In this case the catalogue is wrong, this coin is rare and should catalogue much more.

All dealers have their own ideas about levels of rarity and how to list them. In the old days there was a listing from C2 (Very Common) to R7 (Unique), other areas were graded on a scale going up to R22. These are confusing and I do not feel that you can be that precise, especially on early coins. As a dealer, I use the following nomenclature: a coin which is *scarce* I will list as scarce, Scarce or SCARCE depending on just how scarce it is. A *rare* coin will be listed as rare, Rare, RARE, Extremely Rare or Unique. This method gives the flavour of the rarity without trying to put an exact definition excluding only Unique.

Comments & Suggestions

Errors and omissions are inevitable, especially in a work of this size and scope. We apologise in advance and ask for your help in correcting them. Bound in this catalogue is a card which you can fill in and send to us with any such comments you wish to make. Also please let us know if you have good quality photographs which we can use. We have had a very good response from readers and would like to express again our thanks for their time and interest, particularly as it is no longer possible for us to acknowledge letters personally. Every card is read carefully by the appropriate person, the information is researched and acted on when necessary.

Other Titles in the Series

Our new catalogue on the coinage of Scotland, Ireland, the Channel Islands and the Isle of Man is just out and the first responses have been great. It is the first new book on the subject in 15–20 years and our crew did a great job, as usual. It is well worth having a copy and the price is £34.50 plus postage (UK £4, Europe £7 and the rest of the world £13).

Our new *Checklist of British Coins 1656 to 1816* is out and you get a FREE copy with this catalogue, just fill in and send us the coupon.

Eleni is starting her editorial work on a new work on the medallions of the Crystal Palace by Leslie Allen which we hope to have out shortly. If you have a numismatic book that you have written and would like us to consider for publication contact Dr Eleni Calligas at Standard Catalogue Publishers Ltd, 44 & 45 Great Russell Street and I am sure she will be happy to hear from you.

We have many books in the works but we are still looking for more...

Richard Lobel

Introduction

For the best part of a thousand years the inhabitants of England made their presence felt and influenced events taking place in the world. The prosperity this prominence built up is reflected in the nation's coinage and its study gives an insight into English heritage.

Collectors of the series can confine themselves to a simple method of collecting, such as acquiring one coin of each monarch — or can delve more deeply into the types of coin, reasons for issue, the engravers and the multitude of factors involved in the process of putting a penny in your pocket. The importance of such study was first emphasised by the nineteenth century numismatist Alexander Del Mar, who wrote that 'the history of civilisation is the history of money'.

The collector certainly plays an important part in the study of coins in that he at least preserves coins for future students to examine. Remember, the collector does not really own his treasures, he is a custodian for future generations.

Just how important coins are to the study of our past can be gauged by the fact that the entire chronology of ancient art is based on a dating system by coins. Many of the long-lost masterpieces of bygone schools of art would be unknown but for coins. From early coins we can tell many things about a nation — its religions, its importance, who rules its wealth and so on. There exist coins of an ancient British ruler about whom nothing is known except for the coin inscription.

The problems of dating coins are not confined to ancient times and the British series has an area where experts are still not always in agreement! It all stems from the fact that we cannot necessarily believe what we see on a coin. In mediaeval times the majority of people could not read or write and the importance of the inscriptions was confined to the educated classes. Communications were sometimes poor, cost was a considerable factor, and all this combined to sometimes have the coinage retain the same inscription long after the death of the monarch it was intended for.

So we read the inscription HENRICUS on coins for Henry I that were also issued by Henry II, Richard I, John I and Henry III. Similarly, it is impossible to identify from the inscription the coins of Edward I, II and III. Many years of study have led numismatists to attribute these Edward pennies on a basis of stylistic differences. It gets worse! Some coins of Edward VI were issued with the name and portrait of Henry VIII. The testoon (forerunner of the shilling) of Edward VI has the distinction of being the first English coin to be dated. Although it does not apply to the English series, it is interesting to note that some coins actually give a wrong year date deliberately! The best example of this is the Maria Theresa dollar which is dated 1780. The inhabitants of the areas bordering the Red Sea came to trust this coin and, when trading, insisted on exchanging only for Maria Theresa dollars. The result is that such coins dated 1780 were minted well into the 20th century.

One of the principal methods of dating English coins is the 'privy' or mintmarks found on them. Die numbers found on many milled coins also provide useful information. The English series can absorb the attention of a collector for a lifetime. Some collectors specialise in certain areas, such as hammered coins, milled coins or even the coins of just one mint or monarch. The coinage of Charles I, for example, is full of varieties. Certainly, forming such collections is an interesting and exciting hobby which can give years of pleasure. It is often overlooked that collectors enjoy the advantage of meeting people of similar interests in coin clubs up and down the country. Club meetings are often as much social get-togethers as occasions to swap and study. The major museums of the nation are there to assist the student and are well worth visiting to examine the numismatic collections. The British Museum has the finest collection of coins in the world.

The new collector will soon come across the investment potential of coins. Investment is best left to experienced collectors as, without knowledge, it is a pure gamble. The best investment a collector can make is in enjoying the hobby itself which will keep his mind active, interested and healthy and may well lead to a long and happy life. Of course collecting coins can be a sound financial investment — but usually this is because of the passage of time. Few collectors who have spent more than 20 years at the hobby have ever lost out when they have decided to sell. Just look at a priced catalogue of 20 years ago and compare it with a current one!

The collector who puts together a selection of coins to illustrate an area of numismatics and who studies them and comes to understand them, is likely to unintentionally make a good investment. Of course the collector has to pay attention to the value of a coin. He wants to know that if he does decide to sell it later on, he will get at least some of his money back! There is no substitute quite as good as experience but beginners can at least follow the basic guidelines of all collecting areas: know your dealer! Has he been in business for a long time, has he got a shop where you can go back to? If he has, you will know that he has to be reasonably OK or he would not still be in business! And once you become a 'regular' customer, you will find most dealers pay attention to your specific interests and become very useful 'scouts' for locating material for your collection.

The singular most important effect on value is condition. This catalogue gives you detailed descriptions of the various numismatic grading terms. It is well worth taking time to study these. Never be afraid to ask a dealer about the condition of a coin. A good dealer will take time out to explain. It is a subjective matter and often one finds the condition of a coin goes up or down a grade depending on whether it is being sold or bought! The real problem comes when a coin has been cleaned. There is nothing basically wrong with a coin being cleaned. The world's museums have departments whose sole function is to restore, clean and preserve every type of artefact. Hammered coins found in the earth often need to be treated so that the inscriptions can be read. But there is a difference between cleaning to preserve and identify, and cleaning to make a coin look in better condition than it really is so as to get a higher price for it.

A beginner should never try to clean a coin. Leave it to the experts. Sound advice is to leave it altogether if it needs cleaning! Part of the skill of collecting coins is to select good examples. This means knowing when a bad-condition coin is worth having because it just does not turn up in better condition at an affordable price, and when a coin is easy to obtain in beautiful condition and therefore should be discarded in bad condition.

Collectors generally divide the English series into two halves. The first encompasses the hammered series, the second encompasses the milled series. Hammered coins get their name because they were literally hammered. The dies were similar to those used in ancient Greek and Roman times, but the lower die was now given a long spur, or tang, so that it would fit into a deep recess of the anvil. The upper die contained the reverse design and the lower die the obverse. Because the hammer blow directly impacted on the reverse die, it wore out more quickly than the lower, obverse die.

It follows that the quality of many of these coins was affected by the precision and strength of the hammer blow — and collectors pay more for a well struck and centred coin. In making the die itself, many different types of engraving instruments were used. Often two punches would be used to create one letter. Students can identify the use, on some coins, of the punch for the letter 'I' joined to a reversed 'C' to create the letter 'D'.

The 'milled' process has no connection with the milling round the edge of the coin. The name refers to the machinery which rolled silver to the right thickness and was driven by horse-power or water-power. It was Eloye Mestrelle of Paris who demonstrated to the Royal Mint the milled system and he was employed at the Mint to use his equipment which included a rolling-mill for making sheets of silver to an exact thickness, a cutter for the circular blanks and a press for even pressure when the die was stamped on to the coin blank.

As it happened, he did not last long because of opposition from the Mint authorities. The Warden of the Mint, Richard Martin, saw to it that he was sacked after holding a trial of skill between Mestrelle and the hammer-men. His lengthy report omitted all mention of the fact that Mestrelle was producing, for the first time, a coin of equal size, shape and with a perfect and uniform register of the die designs. Instead he reported that the hammer-men could work ten times faster and wrote: 'Wherefore neither the said engine nor any workmanship to be wrought thereby will be to the Queen's Majesty's profit.' Mestrelle went into business on his own account and was even less appreciated at Norwich where they hanged him and his three accomplices for making false money.

The hammered silver penny was the standard coin in England for around 500 years. The first recognisable portrayal of a king was that of King Offa. The inscription REX ANGLOR — King of the English, first appears on coins of King Alfred. But it was not until William the Conqueror that the English truly became one country and it is the last successful conquest of England, by William the Conqueror in 1066, that makes a good starting point for collectors of the English series. The Norman influence on design can be seen in the crosses.

When William I arrived he found that English coinage, which had once copied the French *denier* for its silver penny, was now superior to the continental coinage so he wisely left the system alone but introduced coins with his name. He inherited some 45 mints and by the close of his reign in 1087 England had about 70 mints working. Henry I re-introduced the halfpenny — last struck by Eadgar — but only a few have come to light. The dies for coins were made in London and sent to the provincial mints. There, the moneyers would place their own names on the reverses of the coins. This was not so much as an honour for them, as it was to ensure that the London authorities knew who made the actual coin. If it was not of the correct weight and fineness they knew who to see about it.

By the time Henry I came to the throne in 1100, forgers were operating very successfully. Merchants worried by the amount of forgery would cut into the coin to make sure it was silver. The general public then refused to take the coin because it was mutilated. To overcome this disastrous situation the government took the extraordinary step of requiring all coins to be cut.

Some of these official cuts extend a third of the way into a coin. While it may have overcome the problem of getting the public to use the coin, it did not stop forgery. Mint-masters were not above doing a bit of overtime on their own account and we learn from the Margam Annals that one Christmas Day on the King's orders, Bishop Roger of Sarum mutilated 94 moneyers at Winchester — about half the moneyers in England. It was not much of a Christmas for them as mutilation on that occasion involved the loss of their right hand and testicle. It did improve the coinage. Most people suspected of counterfeiting were found guilty because the initial examination involved placing their hands in fire. Innocent people were supposed to withstand the pain.

A foreign goldsmith, Philip Aimer of Tours, designed the short-cross coinage with the title HENRICUS REX which circulated from 1180 to 1247 — through the last eight years of Henry II, the reigns of Richard I and John and the first 30 years of Henry III. (Coins found named to King John were minted in Ireland). The short-cross was introduced to enable the coin to be divided into halves and quarters for small change. But clipping the edges to acquire the silver was so prevalent that a Council was held at Oxford to consider the matter in 1247. The result was the long-cross penny. The four ends of the cross were extended to the edge of the coin. Any coin which did not have the four ends of the cross clearly visible was an illegal coin. Despite the long cross, clipping continued and in 1290 the Jews were blamed for the practice and it was one of the reasons for their persecution and expulsion. Collectors who like the challenge of deep specialisation will find the short-cross or the long-cross coinages a real challenge with much research still needed, with the excitement of new hoard finds and possibly even new types.

Dating coins of the hammered period can be very difficult but one of the most important methods of attributing dates is the mintmark (also known as the 'privy mark' or the 'Initial'). These denote the place of issue and, by changing the mark, the period. These marks are usually found under the bust or by the legends. For most coins numismatists have been able to work out the date and place of issue to within a few years.

A new coinage was introduced by Edward I and he introduced the groat (a four-penny piece). The designs were improved to such an extent that they were copied on the Continent. He partly solved the problem of cutting pennies into halves and quarters by producing halfpennies and farthings.

Often coins tell us over which territories a king ruled. Edward III, for example, was shown as King of France on his coins from 1351–1361. Following the Treaty of Bretigny his coins show him as Lord of Aquitaine — and not King of France (1361–1369). Then, when the Treaty was broken, his coins show him as Lord of Aquitaine and King of France. Some of his coins name him as ruler of England, France, Ireland and Aquitaine. In the reign of Edward III an important numismatic event occurred with the introduction of the Trial of the Pyx. This was a random check on the quality of moneyers' coins and has been carried out ever since. The original law includes the passage '.. the Warden shall make a tryall of yt, and if yt shall not bee so good as yt is undertaken, yt shalbee retorned to the said Master to bee remolten at his owne proper costs.'

Although the silver penny was the standard coin for some 500 years, a gold currency was introduced in 1257 which included a pure gold penny, equal to 20 silver pennies. It was twice the weight of a silver penny but for various reasons soon disappeared from circulation.

Later the gold noble was issued. The design shows the king standing in a ship and there is a strong numismatic opinion that this represents the naval victory at Sluys in 1340. Angels and ryals were introduced in the succeeding years.

One of the great fascinations of coin collecting is that a collector can actually hold in his hand a coin minted, for instance, in the time of Henry V, victor of Agincourt, and it is surprising how inexpensive such items can be. The Wars of the Roses saw Henry VI removed from the throne in 1461 and captured at the Battle of St Albans in 1465. His place was taken by Edward IV but Henry VI was restored in 1470. His 'restored' coinage is scarce because the following year he was murdered and Edward IV began his second reign. There are many different varieties, mintmarks and mints in Henry VI's reign and the mintmarks enable us to date most of his coins to within a few years of issue.

For those who set out to obtain one specimen of each monarch there are problems with such historic figures as Richard III, who died in battle at Bosworth and had his crown picked up there and then and placed on the head of Henry VII. Coins of Richard III are scarce because of his short reign, from 1483 to 1485.

New denominations were brought in by Henry VII and the coinage saw the introduction of the famous gold sovereign in 1489. A wide range of coins were used including gold ryals, or nobles, angels, half-angels, silver testoons (shillings), groats, half-groats, pennies, halfpennies and farthings. Fortunately for collectors, the practice was resumed of giving the full title of the king. No longer was it just HENRICUS, it was now clearly HENRY VII. Another great improvement in the coinage was that the portrait ceased to be a stylistic impression of a king and became an actual likeness of the monarch.

These coins attract a lot of attention from collectors and such coins in superb condition command high prices. Yet very attractive examples can be bought quite inexpensively when one considers that the coin is a contemporary portrait produced by highly skilled engravers many centuries ago. Some collectors concentrate on portrait coins and the coinage of Henry VIII produces some very fine portraits.

Henry VIII soon debased the coinage that his father had kept at such a high standard. His subjects came to nickname him 'Old Coppernose' because the thin wash of silver on his coins soon wore off and the nose on the full-face portrait coins was the first to show the metal underneath. For some time certain people had been empowered to privately mint coins and one famous coin is Wolsey's groat, minted by Cardinal Thomas Wolsey while Archbishop of York. The coin depicts a cardinal's hat and the letters T and W. The Bill of Impeachment against Wolsey in 1530 included: 'of his pompous and presumptuous mind he hath enterprised to join and imprint the Cardinal's Hat under your Arms in your coin of groat made at your city of York, which like deed hath not yet been seen to have been done by any subject within your realm before this time.' Wolsey actually died before his trial and similar private ecclesiastical mints were curbed soon after.

Edward VI restored the fineness of the coinage and the famous silver crown was introduced in his reign. Crowns are very popular with collectors because the size allows greater freedom for the artist. The first crown shows the king on horseback. Shillings of this period are often found with the reverse worn completely smooth. This was because of the game, today known as shove-halfpenny. The shilling was in great demand for the game, so much so that the coin could on occasion fetch more than its face value.

Queen Mary came to the throne in 1553 and the following year a portrait of a Spanish king appears on English coins facing the portrait of Queen Mary, during the joint reign of Philip and Mary. The coin gave rise to the saying: 'Still amorous, cooing and billing, Like Philip and Mary on a Shilling.'

The regal portraits of Elizabeth I found on her coins are worthy additions to any collection. Some odd denominations were produced at this time, such as a three-halfpence and a three-farthings.

King James stopped the practice of private shopkeepers and traders issuing lead and pewter tokens and in its place he granted a licence to Lord Harrington to strike copper farthings. The licence was subsequently bought by the Duke of Lennox and later by Lord Maltrevers. The king, of course, shared in the profits.

A tremendous variety of coins exist for Charles I and many collectors concentrate their attention on this one reign. The milled process was re-introduced by the French die-engraver Nicholas Briot. But although the coins were superior, they could not be issued fast enough and hand-hammering had to continue. The Civil War has left a multitude of emergency issues and siege money often cut from plate. When the king raised his standard at Nottingham in 1642, he introduced propaganda to his coinage with the 'Declaration' coins. On these he declared war on Parliamentary rebels and promised to defend the Protestant religion, the liberties of Parliament and the laws of England. His belief in divine right was expressed on many of the coins with the legend: CHRISTO AUSPICE REGNO — I reign under the auspices of Christ.

At this time coins exhibited very high quality workmanship, like the beautiful pattern coin produced for Charles by Thomas Rawlins and known as the Oxford crown — showing a view of the city below the king's horse.

Cromwell besieged Pontefract himself and there the royalists struck coins which read 'While I live I hope'. After Charles was beheaded the castle gamely carried on with the legend: 'For the son after the death of the father.' Cromwell's coinage became known as 'Breeches' money because of the shape of the joined shields on the reverse. Lord Lucas is supposed to have remarked to Charles II 'A fit name for the coins of the Rump'. During the Civil War the Parliamentarians continued to strike coins in the name of the king. This could be taken to mean that there was no intention at first to depose the king, just to curb his powers — or to mean that while the king lived the public would not use another coin. Often considered the greatest of all English die-engravers, Thomas Simon, was working at the Royal Mint when it was finally seized by Parliament in 1642. He began to make his presence felt with a magnificent portrait of Cromwell. Milled experiments were gathering pace and the last hammered coinage was that hurriedly produced for the Restoration of Charles II in 1660. It is noteworthy that Charles II dated his coins with the regnal year on the edge, not from when he came to the throne but from the execution of his father.

It will be seen that a fascinating collection can be made to illustrate the great events of the Civil War. The importance of these coins as historical evidence cannot be underestimated, and often corroborates other source information.

Peter Blondeau whose machinery had been used during the Commonwealth, retired on a pension. But he was brought back by Charles II and made Provost of the Moneyers and Engravers of the Mint and agreed to divulge 'his secrets in rounding the pieces before they are seized, and in marking the edges of monies.' It was to mark the end of coin clipping. Edges of crowns and halfcrowns were inscribed DECUS ET TUTAMEN (ornament and safeguard). The quality of the coins has never been higher and was in part due to the competition between very competent engravers. John Roettier, a brilliant engraver, had the advantage that his family had helped Charles during his exile. Thomas Simon, chief engraver, had to face a trial of skill. Both patterns produced by the engravers were magnificent. The Dutchman won and his coins were accepted. Many felt that Thomas Simon's were better and Roettier's had only been accepted in recognition of his family's service to the king. Simon certainly felt so and produced the now famous Petition Crown — a truly beautiful piece. The petition, inscribed in two lines on the edge reads 'Thomas Simon most humbly prays your Majesty to compare this, his tryall piece, with the Dutch, and if more truly drawn and emboss'd, more gracefully ordered and more accurately engraven, to relieve him.' His petition was not granted but he was allowed to design some of the smaller denominations. He died a few years later of the plague.

For those collectors who wish to limit their collecting interest, the milled series makes a clean break from the hammered. As we have seen, there were mill and screw-press coins as early as Elizabeth by Mestrelle and some by Nicholas Briot under Charles I. Cromwell portrait coins were struck on Peter Blondeau's newly invented machine. But now all coins were produced by the milled process. For some time, when Welsh silver was used to make coins, a mark had been placed on the coin to denote this. In the reign of Charles II the practice was extended to include an elephant, or elephant and castle, to represent the African Guinea Co. and a rose for silver from the West of England mines. Collectors who wish to restrict their collecting of the milled series often choose a coin, most popular being the crown or shilling, and try and put together as complete a collection as possible of all the dates and marks.

Coins of James II (1685–1688) show a strong face and are of high quality, the dies being engraved by Roettier. Very attractive are the coins of William and Mary and later William III. There is some difficulty in attributing engravers to coins in this reign which still gives scope for research. John Roettier, through age and probably arthritis could no longer use his hands properly and had to get his sons to do most of the work. So we have coins engraved by James and Norbert Roettier as well as by John himself. To make matters more complicated, Norbert had to flee to France and James was dismissed in 1697 for smuggling coin dies to France. Henry Harris and John Croker replaced them and also engraved coins during the reign.

With the death of Mary the elegant conjoined busts of the monarchs cease and coins show only the head of William III (1694–1702). During his reign a complete recoinage was undertaken. A total prohibition was placed on all clipped coins, which effectively demonetised the hammered coinage still circulating as most of it was now badly worn or clipped. An entry in Evelyn's diary tells us: 'Many executed at London for clipping money, now done to that considerable extent, that there was hardly any money that was worth about halfe the nominal value'. New mints were opened at Bristol, Chester, Exeter, Norwich and York and a prodigious output of coins was undertaken — recognised by numismatists because the coins are relatively common. Old coins were accepted at face by the government and replaced with the new coinage. The cost of this was borne by the introduction of a 'Window Tax' which raised well over a million pounds for the purpose. To avoid the tax, many people bricked up windows which can still be seen in many old houses today. The tax proved to be very effective so the government levied it right up to 1851.

History is well reflected on coins and major events during the reign of Queen Anne, (1702–1714) are commemorated. The union with Scotland in 1707 saw a change in the royal arms which, after the Act of Union, show the arms of Scotland and England joined in one shield instead of using separate shields as previously. In 1702 coins were made from silver taken from captured Spanish galleons at Vigo Bay. The name VIGO was placed under the queen's bust to indicate this. Collectors look for other such marks which are found on British coins, WCC for Welsh Copper Company and SSC for South Sea Company.

George I had the distinction of using one of the longest titles. The Latin abbreviations on his coins translate 'By the grace of God, King of Great Britain, France and Ireland, Defender of the Faith, Duke of Brunswick and Luneburg, Archtreasurer and Elector of the Holy Roman Empire'.

Collectors who specialise in engravers' work find that George II portraits were first engraved by John Croker who had also produced the dies for Anne and George I. But the older portrait, produced in 1743, is the work of Tanner.

The early part of George III's reign saw very few coins minted but in 1787 an enormous issue of shillings and sixpences was put into circulation. Although many of these are still easy to obtain, there are some rarities like the Northumberland shilling. The Earl of Northumberland distributed £100 worth of these to mark his entry into Dublin as Lord Lieutenant.

The Spanish eight reales (the famous pirates' 'pieces of eight') was a universally used coin at this time and, as British supremacy at sea involved privateers relieving the Spanish of large quantities of coin, it was decided to make use of them. Silver coin was in short supply and in 1797 the Mint was instructed to countermark the pieces of eight with the head of George III in a small oval. Early examples were punchmarked with the 'duty paid' head used on silver hall marks.

Major changes came in the reign of Queen Victoria. Being a woman, she was not able to succeed to the Hanoverian throne so the Hanover shield had to be dropped from coins. A new piece, the florin, came into being as a result of campaigns for a decimal coinage. A motion before Parliament that silver coins of one-tenth and one-hundredth of a pound should be issued was withdrawn by agreement when the florin was produced. For some reason the normal lettering 'D.G.' for 'By the grace of God' was left out and the coin was quickly nicknamed 'the Godless florin'.

Numismatists interested in dies find Victoria's reign a treasure-trove. The die numbers were put on coins and after 1864 the die number can be seen at the base of the queen's portrait on florins, shillings and sixpences. This practice continued until 1879.

Edward VII had only one issue of coins and this was engraved by de Saulles. A very attractive coin is the florin which departs from the normal designs to show a standing Britannia.

George V's reign has many varieties but is perhaps most notable for the debasement of the coinage. In 1920 the price of silver rose so high that it was possible to melt silver coinage and make a profit. So coins were reduced to 50 per cent silver and 50 per cent alloy.

Although coin patterns exist for Edward VIII, his portrait coinage was never authorised for circulation and such pieces are very scarce. Coins of George V dated 1936 are generally regarded as posthumous issues of George V struck during the reign of Edward VIII.

The very attractive coins of George VI and Elizabeth II complete the series and give collectors much material for study. Coins of this period should be collected in mint condition where possible as they are comparatively easy to obtain. They are well worth studying and can lead to 'finds' of new varieties and errors. Modern coins have the advantage to collectors that they can examine large quantities. They may be common now but it is worth noting that all coins were 'new issues' once.

Colin Narbeth

A coin per reign

Many collectors enjoy having a coin from each reign so below we list the denominations which are most easily available. During the early reigns the penny was often the only denomination struck and, therefore, the most common issue. However, many coins were cut in half and quarters to produce halfpennies and farthings. These can be an ideal way of filling the gap for the budget collector.

For the later reigns we have often listed several denominations, many of which may have scarce varieties so collectors should refer to the Collecting Hints of each issue. Finally, the popularity of the denominations or the reign can reflect the value of the coin. In general, larger coins of famous monarchs are more popular than smaller denominations of less well known reigns.

Monarch	Denomination
William I	W11D
William II	W21D
Henry I	H11D
Stephen	ST1D
Matilda	MT1D
Henry II	H21D
Richard I	R11D
John I	JH1D
Henry III	H31D
Edward I	E11D
Edward II	E21D
Edward III	E34D –2D –1D –HD
Richard II	R21D –HD
Henry IV	H4HD
Henry V	H54D –1D –HD
Henry VI First Reign	H64D –2D –1D –HD
Edward IV First Reign	E44D –2D –1D
Henry VI Restored	H64D
Edward IV Second Reign	E44D –2D –1D
Edward V	all v. rare
Richard III	R34D –1D
Henry VII	H74D –2D –1D
Henry VIII	H84D –2D –1D
Edward VI	E6SH –6D
Mary I	MA4D
Philip & Mary	PMSH –4D
Elizabeth I	ELSH –6D –4D –3D –2D –1D
James I	J1SH –6D –2D –1D –FA
Charles I	C1HC –SH –6D –2D –1D –FA

Monarch	Denomination
Commonwealth/Cromwell	CW2D –1D
Charles II	C24DH –2DH –1DH
James II	J24M –3M
William & Mary	WM4M –3M
William III	W36D
Anne	ANSH –4M –3M
George I	G1SH
George II	G2SH –6D
George III	G3SH –6D
George IV	G4SH –6D
William IV	W4SH –6D –4D
Victoria	VOHC –OFL –OSH
Edward VII	E7HC –FL –SH
George V	G5HC –FL –SH –6D
Edward VIII	none
George VI	G6HC –FL –SH –6D –most others
Elizabeth II	EZ1D –HD –most others

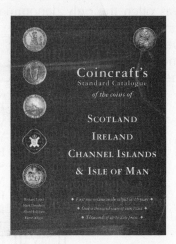
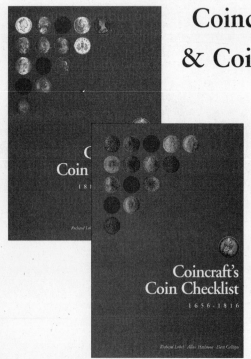

Comments & Suggestions

We welcome your comments and suggestions and would be glad to hear from you.

If you have spotted a mistake, or know of something that we have omitted, please fill in this card.

Although we are not always able to acknowledge individual letters, we do read all your comments and bear them in mind when producing future editions.

I would like to note the following:

....

....

....

....

....

....

Name ....

Address ....

....

Postcode ....Country.......................

CSC010900

Checklists & Standard Catalogues

➡ **USE THIS COUPON TO CLAIM YOUR FREE CHECKLIST**

STANDARD CATALOGUE PUBLICATIONS

Coincraft's 2000 Standard Catalogue of English & UK Coins 1066 to Date.   £19.95
plus **FREE** copy of *Coincraft's Coin Checklist 1656 to 1816*

Coincraft's Coin Checklist, 1816 to Date.   £6.95

Coincraft's Coin Checklist, 1656 to 1816.   £6.95
or **FREE** when you purchase *Coincraft's 2000 Standard Catalogue of English & UK Coins 1066 to Date*

Coincraft's Standard Catalogue of the Coins of Scotland, Ireland, Channel Islands & Isle of Man.   £34.50

For more information about any of these publications please contact Coincraft (Tel: 0207 636 1188 Fax: 0207 637 7635).

Please send me:

Publication	No of copies	Price
....	....	£ ......
....	....	£ ......
....	....	£ ......
COIN CHECKLIST 1656-1816	1	**FREE**

Please add postage (see reverse for details)   £ ....

TOTAL   £ ....

RETURN TO: COINCRAFT, FREEPOST,* 44 & 45 GREAT RUSSELL STREET, LONDON WC1B 3LU   TEL: 0207 636 1188
*UK only

CSC020900

Comments & Suggestions

By Air Mail
Par Avion

Please
place
stamp
here

Standard Catalogue Publishers

c/o Coincraft

44 & 45 Great Russell Street

London WC1B 3LU

UK

We welcome your comments and suggestions and would be glad to hear from you.

If you have spotted a mistake, or know of something that we have omitted, please fill in this card.

Although we are not always able to acknowledge individual letters, we do read all your comments and bear them in mind when producing future editions.

Checklists & Standard Catalogues

I enclose a cheque/PO for £..........made payable to Coincraft or please debit my:
Visa/Mastercard/Amex/Diners/Switch/Access/TrustCard/JCB

Card No ....

Expiry Date ....Issue No...............

Signature ....

Name ....

Address ....

....

Postcode....................................Country ....

RETURN TO: COINCRAFT, FREEPOST,* 44 & 45 GREAT RUSSELL STREET,
LONDON WC1B 3LU   TEL: 0207 636 1188
*UK only

PLEASE KEEP FOR FUTURE REFERENCE

POSTAGE COSTS

CHECKLISTS
Postage in the UK is FREE when ordering checklists with this coupon.
Postage for overseas orders will be subsidised when ordering with this coupon. Please phone or fax us for a quote.

STANDARD CATALOGUES
UK: £4.00
Europe: £7.00 airmail
Rest of the World: £13 airmail

If you are ordering books which have not yet been published your credit card will not be charged until they are available.

For more information please contact Coincraft
Tel: 0207 636 1188   Fax: 0207 637 7635

Overseas Distributors

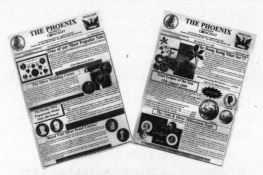

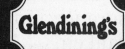

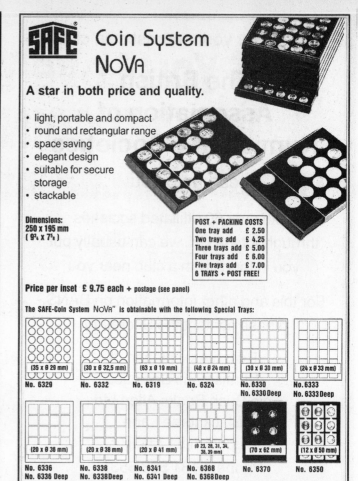

The Ecu Mint Set

This beautiful seven piece Mint Set contains the 1992 United Kingdom Ecus. Each collection comes in a full colour package, which gives you information about the pieces while keeping them safe.

Each Mint Set contains the 1/10th Ecu, 1/4 Ecu, 1/2 Ecu, 1, 2, 5 and 10 Ecus. The Crown sized 5 Ecu takes pride of place in the centre of the collection. With full colour packaging these make excellent gifts for collectors both in this country and overseas.

You get the whole seven piece collection in the full colour packaging for only £18.95 or order three for only £52.50. You will want one for yourself and your friends.

LEU9205	Ecu Mint Set in Full Colour Package	£18.95
LEU9290	3 Ecu Mint Sets in Full Colour Packages	£52.50

For the Ecu Mint Set, order by post or telephone quoting CSC040900 and the individual order codes above. Please add £1.95 per order for handling. Allow 14 days for delivery.

We accept Mastercard, Visa, Diners and American Express (quote card number and expiry date).

Send your order to Coincraft Customer Services at –

44 & 45 Great Russell Street, London WC1B 3LU
Tel: 0207-636 1188 Fax: 0207-637 7635
Email: info@ coincraft.com

Index of Advertisers

American Heritage Minting Inc	33	Anthony Halse	49
Bank of England Museum	44	Heritage Numismatic Auctions Inc	45
Bonhams	45	KB Coins	37
British Association of Numismatic		London Coin Auctions	42
Societies	49	Michael Coins	44
British Museum HSBC Money Gallery	48	Mynt & Seddel	42
Chelsea Coins	46	Peter Nichols	41
Classical Numismatic Group Inc	38	Numistory.Com	42
Coin News	35	Philip Phipps	39
Coinote Services Ltd	45	Pobjoy Mint Ltd	37
Coins on the Internet	46	Roderick Richardson	47
Collectors' Universe	51	William M. Rosenblum Rare Coins	46
Mark Davidson	47	Royal Gold Exchange	49
Davidson Monk Fairs	50	Royal Mint Coin Club	40
Davissons Ltd	48	Safe Albums (UK) Ltd	50
Den of Antiquity	50	The Searcher	34
Dix Noonan Webb	IBC	Simmons Gallery	48
Dorset Coin Co Ltd	50	Sotheby's	IFC
Edinburgh Coin Shop	38	Spink	43
Patrick Finn	46	States Treasury of Jersey	36
Format of Birmingham Ltd	42	J.J. Teaparty Inc	36
Giessener Munzhandlung	39	Treasure Hunting	38
Ronald J. Gillio Inc	44	Vera Trinder Ltd	34
Glendining's	48	Pam West	41
Phil Goodwin	41	Wynyard Coin Centre	36
Granta Coins, Stamps & Antiquities	38	York Coin Fair	49

An Introduction to Coin Collecting

I was a collector long before I became a dealer, I did not start dealing till 1956, by then I was already 12 years old. Coins have always fascinated me; the fact that the coin in my hand is so old has always excited me. Where has it been all these years, who owned it, who has handled it? The number one principle in collecting is: it must be something you do because you want to and because you enjoy it. Never believe that you are collecting for profit, you will be sadly disappointed. I do not sell coins for investments. Who can tell what is going to happen next? Not me, that's for sure. It is true that collectors who have stayed the course and have collected right along, when prices were high and when prices were low, have done very nicely when they sold their collections. But the reason they were collecting is that they enjoyed it and they learned about the coins in their collections. Someone who collects in a very narrow field will often know more than the dealers he buys from. After all, we dealers are a bit like General Practitioners, we know a little about a lot of things. You could well become the specialist in your chosen field, you just have to start somewhere.

The scarcer a coin is, the higher the price it will command, right? No! The price of a coin is determined in some unfathomable way by a combination of rarity, condition, desirability and collector interest. A common coin in choice condition will in many cases be more expensive than a rare coin in worn condition. In the old days collectors tried to obtain every variety that existed. Coin collecting tended to be an exclusive pastime which required disposable income and free time to study the coins. Today most collectors will try for a representative coin, a nice example of each major variety; we call this type collecting. What with the level of today's prices, it would be almost impossible to try and obtain one of everything. One nice coin is worth more than ten poor examples. A coin which is in choice Very Fine condition can have more 'eye appeal' than a coin that is in indifferent Extremely Fine quality.

Grading goes from the poorest to the finest as follows: Poor, Fair, About Good, Good, Very Good, Fine, Very Fine, Extremely Fine, Good Extremely Fine, About Uncirculated, Uncirculated, Choice Uncirculated and Gem Uncirculated. In this country Proof is a method of striking and not a condition, thus on the early proofs you can have an EF, Proof or even a Fine Proof. A Proof today is struck several times to get the best depth of design, on a polished planchet and with polished dies. The higher the grade, i.e. the less wear a coin has, the more expensive a coin will be. There are many coins in the hammered field which do not exist in grades higher than Very Fine; there are many milled coins which do not exist in Uncirculated condition. If you see a coin in a grade which is exceptional, then you can expect it to command an exceptional price. Novice collectors have to be aware that some dealers polish and/or over grade their coins to make them appear a better grade and thus sell for more money. If a coin looks too cheap there is something wrong, there is no Santa Claus! Polishing a coin, rather than increasing its value, in real terms decreases it and makes the coin harder to sell.

Coins with beautiful toning appeal to me because I know that they have lain undisturbed and no one has played with them for a long period of time. On the other hand, many collectors like their coins bright and shiny. Many new collectors regard a coin with toning as a 'dirty coin'. My sage advice to you is *do not clean your coins as you will hurt their value*! I have seen coins worth £500 which will bring only £50 after having been polished. Either learn to live with beautiful multi-coloured and hued toning or find untoned coins. Never clean your coins!

Coins cost much less today in terms of purchasing power than they did when they were originally issued. In the reign of Queen Anne a skilled craftsman working six days a week earned one shilling (5p) a week. Today a reasonable Queen Anne shilling sells for around £40 and a skilled craftsman earns £400 a week. The Queen Anne shilling is cheaper today, in terms of purchasing power, than it was when it was issued almost 300 years ago. In the time of Queen Anne one of her shillings would have been the equivalent of 60 hours' work today that same coin can be exchanged for only 3 hours' work. Coins today represent good value for money.

Getting back to how a coin is valued, the more people who collect a particular series, the more demand there will be for that series and the more people who will be willing to pay 'a price' for a particular coin from that series. There are some extremely rare hammered coins, but if there are only ten people who want an example and eleven coins on offer, prices will be low. On the other hand, if there were one hundred examples of an Edward VII coin and hundreds of collectors who wanted one, then prices would be high. Personally, I believe that when you know the history of hammered coins, then any coin which exists today is rare. There is no exact formula for determining what a coin will sell for, tastes change and with that prices also change. An educated collector is the best collector, so know your coins and get to know your dealer.

What should you collect? Rather than answer that, I would like to suggest a way that you might collect. Unless you have some specialist field which delights and consumes you, do not collect in too narrow a field to start. The mistake that many collectors make when first starting out is trying to decide immediately what they are going to collect. Buy whatever pleases and interests you, a little of this and a little of that. Over a period of time, nature will take its course and you will gradually narrow down your field of concentration. If you start collecting too narrowly in the beginning, you might well lose interest and stop collecting altogether. Let your imagination run wild. It is only after you have collected for a while and held and touched actual coins, that you will discover your true area of interest. I believe in the shotgun approach; a shotgun shell lets off many small pellets and one or more of them will usually find the target.

Some people collect by monarch, trying to get one coin from each reign, some by denomination such as shillings, halfcrowns or crowns. Others collect coins which are of historic significance to them, while yet others try to collect coins struck in and around their region. If you want to collect one coin of each monarch, then the penny is the only denomination which is listed continuously from the first to the last monarch in this book.

Why do people collect? I guess it is a disease and, as a sufferer myself, I know the symptoms. You want to own, to possess something, in this case a piece of history. It is not something to be ashamed of, rather something to be proud of. You are helping retain a part of our cultural history. It is a disease with no suffering and patients have the delusion that they are enjoying themselves. Welcome to the clinic!

Do not try to buy too many coins at the beginning; it is a temptation and as dealers we are here to tempt you — pass me that apple will you... The late J. William 'Bill' Ross told me, when I started in coins some 40 years ago, that 'there will always be more coins than there is money!'. By that he meant take your time, do not go in over your head when you start. There will come a time when you want a coin which costs more than you can afford. At that point you have three choices, one: selling something else in order to buy that new coin; two: talking to the dealer or auctioneer about perhaps spreading the purchase price over a few months; or three: forgetting it! Yes, you would like the coin, but there will be other coins around later, when you have the money available. There will always be more coins than there is money. Strange to hear a dealer say that, remember that I am a collector too; been there, done that...

Get to know a dealer and see what they have to offer, their best items will inevitably be offered to their favourite collectors and never go on display. We might have a nice coin and know that there are three collectors who need it. At that point your previous history comes into play; we will offer it to the collector who has been the least trouble or made himself most popular. If you haggle over the price, mess about over the arrangements or heaven forbid, bounce a cheque, it is to the back of the queue for you. Spend some time with your dealer, get to know them, let him get to know you. Remember that dealers make their living from coins, spend some money with them. There are few things that dealers hate more than collectors who take up their time asking about a coin, often one which they can't quite describe 'but it's old', only to reveal that they have used this free advice to buy that coin from another dealer. This may sound cold-hearted, but if you purchased a coin from another dealer, please do not show it to me. No dealer likes to see the 'bargains' that you bought from someone else. Would you make an appointment with your dentist to show him the work another dentist has done? I think not. Coin dealers are professionals who have put in long hours and many years studying our subject, treat us as professionals and we can make collecting fun for you.

The only way to get into coin collecting is to buy some coins. Many dealers have 'junk' boxes of low value coins, at Coincraft we even sell British and world coins by the kilo so the actual cost of coins can be in the pennies. Once you have seen and handled coins let your imagination run wild. Where has that coin been, who has handled it etc. Check with your local museum which may well have a coin collection, but it is no good studying coins if you have never actually handled them.

Collecting can be as inexpensive or as expensive as your budget will allow. The most important thing is to have fun! Do not let anyone tell you what to collect; buy a little of this and a little of that until you find what interests and excites you. Learn about the hobby and try and find a dealer or dealers that you are happy with and they are happy with you. Nothing gives a dealer a greater thrill than starting a new collector off and helping him build a nice collection. Take some time to look through this book, pick it up and open a page at random, let your eyes do the dancing. But most of all *enjoy yourself!*

Richard Lobel

Glossary

Aberystwyth Mint .... The first provincial mint to be established by Charles I. It was opened in Wales in 1638 by Sir Thomas Bushell, the lessee of the Welsh silver mines. His privy mark was an open book. Coins were struck at this mint from dies shipped in from London and their minting ceased before the Civil War started.

Adjustment Marks .... When a flan or planchet was too heavy for a particular denomination, an adjuster would scrape it by hand to bring it down to the correct weight.

AE .... Symbol for 'aes', an abbreviation for copper or bronze.

After Union .... Coins struck during the reign of Queen Anne after the Union of England and Scotland in 1707. Those struck at Edinburgh can be distinguished by an E or E* below the bust. Only silver coins are known with an E or E*.

Altered Date .... Where the date on a coin has been changed. Sometimes mints reuse dies and punch or re-engrave a new date over an old date. In some cases a coin will be altered unofficially to increase its collector value. An example is the 1933 penny, altered from 1935 into 1933.

Angel .... An English gold coin first issued in 1465 with a value of 6 shillings and 8 pence. St Michael spearing a dragon is on the obverse and a ship on the reverse. This denomination was struck under every monarch until the reign of Charles I.

Anglo-Hanoverian Coinage .... When Georg Ludwig became king of England in 1714, he retained his German dukedom of Brunswick-Luneberg in north central Germany -the name of which changed to Hannover in 1814 when it became a kingdom. Thus, George I, George II, George III, George IV and William IV were rulers of both Brunswick-Luneberg (Hanover) and the United Kingdom. As a result, coins of Brunswick-Luneberg issued between 1714 and 1837, though on a German standard and naturally showing German elements in the design, often portray the British monarchs, as well as their British regal titles and even, sometimes, the British coat of arms. On the accession of Victoria, due to Salic law which forbids the accession of a woman, the kingdom of Hanover passed to the Duke of Cumberland.

Annulet .... A ring, usually very small, in many cases used as a mintmark. Henry VI's coinage can be dated according to the placement of the annulet.

Ansell Sovereign .... Sovereigns struck in 1859 by the Royal Mint under G.F. Ansell to test the use of Australian gold. The gold proved too brittle for use in coinage. An Ansell sovereign can be distinguished by the line down the ribbon or tie in Victoria's hair; see p.454.

Anson, Admiral .... Admiral Anson circumnavigated the globe and brought back silver and gold which he had captured from the Spanish. But not off Lima Peru. The coins that were struck by George II with Lima below his bust might just indicate that the coins captured carried the Lima mintmark.

AR .... Denotes *Argentum*, i.e. silver.

Artificially Toned .... A coin which has been treated in some way to simulate a natural toning or give the appearance of age. It is sometimes done to disguise a badly cleaned coin. The colour is often very dark and somewhat lifeless. In some cases it can be rubbed away simply by touching the coin.

Assay .... A test to determine the actual metal content of an object or coin, i.e. the fineness of the precious metal as a percentage of the total content.

AU .... A grade which is designated as About Uncirculated.

Au .... Denotes *Aurum*, i.e. gold.

Bag Marks ....When coins are struck they are placed in bags and then moved to the place where they will be distributed to the public for everyday use. In that moving the coins rub up against each other and acquire small marks; these are called bag marks. The fewer the number and the less severity of the marks the higher the value of the coin.

Bank of England Dollar ....Struck from 1804 until about 1814 but still retaining the date 1804. It was issued by the Bank of England to help alleviate the shortage of change. They were overstruck on eight reales of the Spanish world to replace the countermarked coins. Previously a punch which had been used to hallmark silver with George III's portrait was used to countermark Spanish dollars and make them legal tender. A wit in those days said it was 'the head of an ass on the head of a fool'. Very wisely we do not know who said it.

Bank Token ....Issued by the Bank of England between 1811 and 1816, they were struck in silver with denominations of (a) one shilling and sixpence and (b) three shillings. The Bank's name does not appear on the coins, just the legend 'Bank Token'. There is also a pattern ninepence token known. From the condition of many of these Bank Tokens they saw considerable circulation.

Barton's Metal ....A very thin layer of gold which is laminated or bonded to a copper blank.

Base Metal ....A non-precious metal i.e. not silver, gold, platinum, or palladium. Usually copper or bronze but today it also includes aluminium, stainless steel and cupro-nickel.

Bath Metal ....A mixture of zinc (24.7%), copper (75%) and silver (0.3%), it is named after the city of Bath where it was invented. It was used in the 1720s to make coins for the American Colonies.

Beading ....The small dots sometimes found either around the rim of a coin or between the legend and a field.

Before Union ....Coin struck in the reign of Queen Anne before the union of England and Scotland in 1707.

Bell Metal ....Originally referred to coins struck from the melted church bells of France.

Bi-metallic ....A coin which is made up of two separate metals. In modern coins, they are usually in concentric circles. The James II tin coinage had a brass plug inserted in it to help stop counterfeiting.

Billon ....A mixture of silver and another metal where the silver makes up a maximum of 50% of the mixture. When first issued and still shiny from the mint, a billon coin will look like silver, but paler. After wear the other metal comes through and the coin will look coppery. The posthumous coinage of Henry VIII is a good example of what can happen and the reason he got the nickname 'Copper Nose'.

Blacksmith Half Crown ....A crude halfcrown struck in Kilkenny in Ireland during the Civil War. This is a very rare copy of the Tower Mint halfcrown.

Blank ....The metal disc, also called a planchet or flan, upon which the design of the coin is impressed. The blank is fed into a press where extreme pressure causes the metal of the blank to flow into the reversed design of the dies so the design comes out raised.

Blondeau, Pierre ....A French engraver who worked at the Tower Mint during the Commonwealth administration and Charles II's reign. He reintroduced the screw press for the making of milled or machine struck coins. It had not been used since Elizabeth I was on the throne. He also had the ability to put inscriptions or lettering on a coin's edge. This lettering was first used by Blondeau on pattern coins of 1651. It was not until 1658 that this process was regularly used on crowns and, after 1668, on five guineas. A lettered edge stopped the clipping of coins.

Blundered Inscription ....It will appear on a coin which has been struck several times and the slight shifting has made the legend unreadable.

Bob ....Slang term for shilling.

Bonnet Piece..............................A gold coin issued under James V of Scotland, it was valued at one ducat (3.5 grams). It was struck in 1539 from gold found at Crawford Muir. It is the first Scottish coin to bear a date.

Border..The outer part of a coin nearest to the edge and rim. Usually part of the design and used to ensure that the coin will wear better and longer.

Boulton, Matthew......................(1728-1809) A manufacturer of coinage machinery, from Birmingham. Most famous for his Soho Mint which issued many of the early copper coins of George III, including the famous Cartwheel twopence and penny, as well as the Bank of England dollar. Boulton was the first person to use steam power to strike coins.

Brass Threepence........................A denomination which was struck for circulation from 1937 until 1967 and then in the 1970 Proof Set. The twelve-sided coin was first designed for issue under Edward VIII and after he abdicated it bore the portrait of George VI.

Breeches Money........................A slang term for the coinage under the Commonwealth. The two shields looked like an inflated pair of men's breeches.

Brilliant Uncirculated................A condition of grading. On copper and bronze coins it means bright and shiny just as they came from the mint. On silver coins it means with little or no toning, perhaps the middle coins from a roll where the outer coins have toned.

Briot, Nicholas...........................(1580-1646) Arrived in England ca 1626 and believed in machine struck coinage. A superb engraver, perhaps the finest this country has ever known. His work was far superior to the crude coins that were being struck at that time. During the Civil War he was loyal to Charles I and worked at York and Oxford. His coinage is neat, precise and most attractive.

Britain Crown.............................A five shilling gold coin issued by James I in 1604. The legend reads HENRICUS ROSAS REGNA JACOBUS (Henry unites the roses, James the kingdoms)

Britannia Groat..........................William IV reintroduced the groat into general circulation. It had not been in regular use since Charles I. His new groat had the seated figure of Britannia on it; the final issue was the Jubilee issue of Victoria in 1888, which was struck exclusively for British Guinea.

Britannia....................................Her seated figure can first be seen on Roman coins under Hadrian and Antoninius Pius which were struck to commemorate their victories in the British dominions. Britannia is now depicted seated on a rock with a shield and trident in her hand.

Broad...A gold piece to the value of twenty shillings struck with the portrait of Oliver Cromwell, engraved by Thomas Simon and dated 1656.

Brockage....................................When a coin is stuck in a die and another planchet is introduced, that first coin makes an incused impression on the second coin. It acts like a miniature die. The second coin ends up with the same impression raised and incused.

Bronzed.....................................Copper coins which have been covered with a thin layer of bronze, usually on proof coins to make them more attractive.

Bull Head...................................The portrait depicting George III on the new halfcrown after the Currency Reform Act of 1816. It was only used in 1816 and 1817. While some collectors also use this term to describe the shilling and sixpence of this issue, I have my doubts. After all it was only the design of the halfcrown which was changed in 1817.

Bullion Coin...............................A coin which changes hands at or near its intrinsic value. In recent years usually struck and sold for the hoarding of precious metal. They are of no numismatic value except curiosity value. Some coins which sell at 'gold' or 'silver value' were legitimate issues: sovereigns, French 20 francs etc.

Bun Coinage..............................The bronze coinage of Queen Victoria with a youthful portrait and her hair tied up in a bun; it was issued from 1860-1894.

Bungtown Coppers ....Imitations of British copper coins struck mainly in the United Kingdom and also the American Colonies. There were many counterfeits of copper halfpennies, a number with most amusing legends. Also known as *Regal evasions*.

Bushell, Thomas ....The lessee of the North Wales silver mines. In 1637 Charles I gave him permission to strike coins at Aberystwyth. These coins have the Welsh plumes and a privy mark of an open book. The quality of the engraving is quite fine and the workmanship extremely neat. They are beautiful coins.

Cabinet Friction ....If coins are kept and displayed in wooden cabinets they tend to move about when the tray is taken out and rubbing or friction often occurs on the high points. These coins might not have seen circulation but unfortunately the cabinet friction does adversely affect their value.

Calais ....This French town came under English rule in 1363-1412 and again from 1424 to about 1440. English silver and gold coins were struck there and either have the legend VILLA CALESIE (many varieties exist) or a 'C' mintmark.

Carlisle, Siege Issues ....Carlisle, a town on the borders of England and Scotland, was besieged during the Civil War. From October 1644 to June 1645, octagonal shaped coins were struck there from dinner plates made of silver. The coins were valued at one and three shillings.

Cartouche ....A scroll-like ornamental design, usually containing some feature within it, e.g. the lion at the centre of the William III crown reverse.

Cartwheel ....A slang name for the copper coinage of 1797. The Soho Mint issued one and two penny coins which weighed one and two ounces respectively (28.35 and 56.7 grams). It was the only time a government tried to give value for money. As expected, the public hated the heavy two pence and the famous Cartwheel twopence was never issued again. The penny was actually struck for a number of years but all the coins bear the date 1797.

Cased Set ....A group of coins which is issued in some sort of casing or packaging. They are usually all of the same date and made other than for general circulation. They can be issued for a coronation, jubilee or the like.

Chevron Milling ....A 'V' shaped milling introduced to deter counterfeiting on the gold coinage of George II and George III.

Choice Uncirculated ....A grade. A coin is Uncirculated if it has never been in circulation and is without wear. But due to the vagaries of how coins are struck, how the dies were made and how the coins were treated after striking, there are different grades of Uncirculated. Choice Uncirculated is better than a normal Uncirculated coin with far fewer bag marks and is well struck with full and uninterrupted lustre.

Clash Marks ....The marks made on one die when it is struck by the other die without a flan or blank in between. When coins are struck from that die, they will have a minor impression from both dies.

Clipping ....The process by which a quantity of metal was unofficially removed from the edge of a coin, which would then be passed on for its original value. People would also take hammered coins, put them in a sack, then shake the sack vigorously for hours. The sack would then be melted down and any metal left would be the person's wages for the day. This was called 'sweating' the coins. It was illegal, but in the reign of Elizabeth I as long as the inner circle was not broken, the coin was still legal tender.

Coin Weight ....A piece of metal which exactly reproduces the weight of a known coin. This is used to check if a coin is of the proper weight and fineness. The coin goes in one side of a balance scale and the weight in the other; if the coin is of the correct weight then the scale will balance.

Coin ....A form of money, today the fractional part of a paper note. Usually round and struck in metal, but there have been square, triangular and other shapes also struck. In the 7th Century BC the first stamped piece of metal was issued in Lydia.

Collar ....The metal ring which retains the blank while a coin is being struck. A collar can also impart a lettering or design on the edge of a coin whilst it is being struck.

Commemorative ....A coin struck to honour or commemorate an event or person. In the past many commemoratives were issued at or near their face value. Today they are usually issued for collectors and to produce revenue for the issuing country or marketer. Many of the commemoratives issued today are not issued for general circulation and thus are *NCLT* (Non Circulating Legal Tender).

Condor Token ....Privately issued copper tokens to the value of a farthing, halfpenny or penny in the late 1700s. First issued by the Parys Mining Company in Wales. Due to the shortage of small change they were readily accepted as money and rapidly spread all over the country. The merchants made a small profit on the manufacture of the tokens and also advertised their wares for free on the tokens. The first widely used book on this subject was written by James Condor and thus they are often referred to as Condor Tokens.

Conjoined ....Two or more busts shown slightly overlapping and looking in the same direction. The only coins of this country to have conjoined busts were those of William and Mary.

Contemporary Forgery ....A copy of coin made during the time that the coin circulated.

Copper Nose ....A nickname given to Henry VIII whose posthumous coinage was so debased that, when it became worn, the copper showed through on Henry's nose. Thus he became known as 'Old Copper Nose'.

Copper-nickel ....See *Cupro-nickel*.

Copy ....A reproduction of something, in this case a coin. Museums make copies, some for their own collection and some for sale in their shops. Over the years some copies have become very collectable. For example the Renaissance copies of Roman coins known as Paduans are highly collected. Modern copies are often made to deceive collectors.

Corbet Farthing ....Andrew Corbet was granted a patent to strike farthings in 1693. This was almost immediately revoked, but a few pieces still exist.

Counterfeit ....A coin (or note) made outside the relevant issuing authority to cheat someone, although it may well have the same metal content as the original. Interestingly, when the sovereign was demonetised, Italian counterfeiters made sovereigns with slightly more gold than the originals. Because of this they could not be prosecuted and profited from the 44% premium over gold content that sovereigns sold for at the time.

Countermark ....A mark or design placed on a coin either by an issuing authority or by a private individual. During the reign of George III a small bust of the king was counterstamped on silver coins to make them legal tender in the United Kingdom. An individual can counterstamp a coin with his or her name or initials. In the 1800s many companies counterstamped advertising slogans on coins to get free advertising. It was later made illegal to deface coins by stamping anything on them.

Cracked Die ....When too much pressure is applied when striking coins or when the die is very worn it will start to crack. As the metal is pushed into the die it will also be pushed into the crack, so cracks will appear as raised lines on a coin. It is possible to estimate when during the life of a die the coin was made, by the state and length of the die crack on the coin. A famous example is the Cromwell Crown.

Crosier or crozier .... The hook shaped top part of a Bishop's staff, usually found as a mark in legends.

Crown Gold .... Henry VIII set the standard for gold to be .916 2/3 fine, known as 22 carat gold. The Mint still uses this standard today.

Crown .... The first English coin of this denomination was issued by Henry VIII in 1526. It was a gold coin with a face value of four shillings and sixpence. It is very rare because it was shortly replaced with the Crown of the Double Rose, which has a face value of five shillings. The first silver crown was issued in 1551 by Edward VI and the last crown to be issued was in 1981, for the wedding of Prince Charles and Lady Diana Spencer.

Cruciform Shields .... Shields in the form of a cross.

Cupro-nickel .... An alloy of copper and nickel. Today the usual ratio is 75% copper to 25% nickel.

Currency .... From the Latin *currentia*, a stream. Thus anything that flows from one hand to another: coins, banknotes, pigs, shells or any medium of exchange which is acceptable. Today we use the term to refer to paper money.

Cut Money .... In the early days when you wanted to pay someone a halfpenny and you only had a silver penny, you literally cut it in half. If you needed farthings then you cut the coin into quarters.

Debasement .... When a government uses less precious metal in the coining of money, while still retaining its original face or exchange value. The prime example is the posthumous coinage of Henry VIII which contained so much copper that the thin silver veneer wore off quickly.

Decimalization .... In 1971 the British monetary system was finally changed to one based on tens or decimals. The Pounds, Shillings and Pence or 'LSD' system (Libra, Solidus, Denarius) was withdrawn and a new system of 'New Pence' introduced. The pound was no longer divided into twenty shillings or 240d, but into 100p.

Declaration Type .... Coins of Charles I issued during the Civil War period, the reverse of which contained the official royalist declaration RELIGO PROTESTANTIUM LEGES ANGLIAE LIBERTAS PARLIAMENTI -The religion of the Protestants the laws of England the liberty of Parliament.

Demonetised .... A currency which is deemed to be no longer legal tender for debts both public and private. Under the Currency Reform Act of 1816 all coins issued before that date were demonetised, no longer legal tender. A period of grace was given during which the public could turn their old money in for the new coins. After that period of grace the coins were only worth their metal or intrinsic value.

Denomination .... The name given to value of the coin either real or implied. A florin is to the value of two shillings or ten pence.

Denticles .... Design objects used to create a border on a coin, usually round or wedge shaped. They go all around the edge of a coin next to the rim.

Device .... That part of the design which is not a portrait or lettering.

Die Axis .... There are two main types of die axis: coin alignment and medal alignment. In coin alignment if you are looking at the heads' side and turn the coin over through a vertical axis 180 degrees to the reverse, the reverse will be upside down. If on the other hand the reverse is right side up, then this is medal alignment.

Die Break .... A raised line which is caused by the metal of the flan being forced into a small crack or break in the die.

Die Numbering on Coins .... The Royal Mint used to number their dies between 1863 and 1880. It was for experimentation, the object of which has been lost. It has been mooted that the Mint was trying to see how long dies lasted.

Die Variety ....Because different pairs of dies are used to strike similar coins, there may be small differences on the coins. These small differences caused by different dies are called die varieties. As obverse and reverse dies wear out at different times, it is possible to link the dies used by comparing die combinations. Museums spend a lot of time in trying to follow the sequence of dies used and many scholarly papers have been written on the subject.

Die Wear ....Dies as they strike a vast number of coins start to show signs of wear; this causes the coins they strike to appear rather weakly struck. Coins can be as struck but appear to be only Very Fine.

Die ....The engraved metal piece which is used to strike coins and medallions. In the old days an engraver cut directly into and in reverse in the metal. Today a plaster is sculptured and a rubber is made which is then placed on a reduction machine. The end product is called a hub and is raised like coins. From this, dies are struck and then hardened before use.

Dorrien Magens Shilling ....A shilling issued in 1798 by the Royal Mint for the banking firm of Dorrien Magens. The government refused to allow this private enterprise to have its own coinage struck and so had all but about six examples melted down.

Double Florin............................A denomination of four shillings struck only three times in our history. The first was issued in 1887, the Jubilee year of Queen Victoria, and continued on in general circulation until 1890. It is also known as 'the barmaid's ruin'. When she had a few drinks she would often give change for a crown (5/-) instead of a double florin (4/-). This shortage would have to be made up out of her own wages. There were pattern issues in the reigns of George V, George VI and Elizabeth II. All these patterns are rare.

Drapery....................................Clothing or cloth in folds.

Dump Issue...............................A name used for the thick copper farthings and halfpennies of George I in 1717 and 1718.

Durham House ....This was the Palace of the Bishop of Durham in London, situated along what is now the Strand. It was in operation as a mint in the reign of Edward VI from 1548-1549.

Durham....................................A town where coins were issued over a very long period of time. Regal coinage was issued under William I onwards. Episcopal coinage started under Edward I and continued until the reign of Henry VIII.

E.I.C. ....The initials of the East India Company, which were used on some gold coins issued from 1729-1739.

Early Soho Striking ....A contemporary or near contemporary proof struck at the Soho mint, Birmingham, shortly after the dies were cut. See also *Late Soho Striking*.

Early Striking.............................When a new pair of dies is first used they are heavily polished and thus the first few coins struck will have a prooflike appearance. These coins tend to demand a premium price and in many cases are much rarer than proofs.

Edge Inscription ....Lettering on the edge of a coin which makes up a motto, first used on Cromwell coins. The inscription made it impossible to clip a coin.

Edge Nicks ....Because of the way coins are struck and then dumped into a bucket or some other receptacle, they fall on top of each other. The edge of the coins can sustain nicks some minute and some substantial. These nicks decrease the value of coins and some dealers will try to put the nick 'right'. Be careful.

Edge Ornament.........................A design on the edge of coin applied using a collar.

Edge Plain ....Indicates no milling or design on the edge of a coin. Often early proof coins will have a plain edge to differentiate proof coins from circulation strikes.

EF (Extremely Fine) ....A grade where there is little actual wear except on the high points. On copper and bronze original lustre might well still be in evidence. A most appealing and attractive grade, much undervalued by the market place in its inane seeking of the ultimate perfection.

Effigy...The bust or portrait on the coin or medallion.

Eighteen Pence Token................A silver token coinage issued by the Bank of England to help with a shortage of small change. Issued between 1811 and 1816.

Electrotype.............................A copy of a coin or medal which has been made by a process of electrolysis. These pieces are made in two parts and then glued or soldered together. They can be very deceptive but if lightly tapped on the rim, electrotypes will not give the characteristic ringing sound of a genuine coin.

Emergency Money....................Money which is issued outside the Mint during a time when the normal issuing authority cannot strike coins. It could be because of a siege (Civil War) or a shortage of small coins (Bank of England tokens).

En Medaille.............................If holding a coin between your fingers with the head side is upright, you flip it over 180° and the reverse side is upright, then this is struck en medaille. If the reverse is upside down then this is struck in coin rotation.

Enamelled Coins.....................In Victorian days fine engravers and jewellers made current and older coins into attractive jewellery by enamelling them. The surface was scraped off and the design re-engraved into the surface which was then filled with enamel. The workmanship ranged from poor to excellent. The latest coins that I have seen properly enamelled where those of Edward VII. The coins that are being sold today as enamelled are just piled high with acrylic paint and fired in a kitchen stove. Collectors will never collect these modern examples which prostitute the craftsmanship of Victorian and Edwardian times.

English Shilling.........................When George VI came to the throne a Scottish shilling was struck for the first time (1937). To balance this there was also a shilling with English representation. This continued until 1970 when the last shillings were struck.

Engrailing...............................The term for the type of lines on the edge of a coin.

Engraver's marks......................Sometimes die engravers are permitted to put their name or initials on a die, so every coin that is struck from it will bear their name or mark. Under William Wyon there were many varieties of his famous 'WW' engraver's mark on our coinage.

Engraver.................................The person who actually cuts the dies from which coins or medallions will be struck. He engraves into the metal.

Engraving...............................The action of cutting the dies from which coins are struck.

Error......................................Something which has gone wrong either in the striking of a coin or the printing of a banknote. Maybe the coin is struck off centre, double struck or struck on the wrong flan. Collectors will pay extra for a major error on a common coin; on a rare coin they will usually pay less.

Escutcheon.............................Shield bearing a coat of arms.

Essay.....................................A proposed design for a coin which may or may not be accepted.

Exergue..................................That part of a coin's design which is separated by a line below the base.

F (Fine)...................................A grade when the coin or note has seen considerable wear, but is still very collectable. Many collectors like a used coin because they feel that it has actually been somewhere. Collectors on a budget also like this grade.

Facing....................................When the portrait on a coin or medal is head on to the viewer.

Fair..A grade where the coin has seen much wear and it is only just discernible what the coin is. Collectors usually stay away from this grade unless the coin or note is especially rare or expensive.

Fantasy...................................A coin struck not to copy something else but rather to be something completely new out of someone's imagination. Over the years fantasy coins have the habit of becoming acceptable to collectors. Many have a very low mintage and can be far more attractive than regularly issued coins.

Farthing..................................The quarter part of a penny which is in turn the 240th part of a pound. The farthing was first introduced in the reign of Henry III and was last struck in 1956. The former was silver and the latter bronze.

FDC.......................................See *Fleur de Coin*

Fiat Money.................................A medium of exchange where we accept the value that a government or issuing body puts on something. Real money has an intrinsic or metal value, fiat money has the backing in principal of a government.

Field..That part of the coin where there are no portraits or devices.

Fifty Shillings.........................A rare gold coin of the Commonwealth period with Cromwell's portrait.

Filled Dies...............................From time to time a die will become filled with lint, grease or something else. When coins are struck from filled dies part of the design will not be struck up at all. A good example is the Gothic Florin whose design was so fine that occasionally parts of the coin would appear changed and this caused havoc in the roman numeral dates of this series.

Filler.......................................A coin in poor condition bought by a collector until a better example is found.

Fillet.......................................A head band; often used in describing Victoria's portraits which have either a plain or an ornamented fillet.

Find...The locating of a group of coins and or artefacts which have been buried or hidden. Two examples of famous finds are the two Colchester Hoards of Henry III pennies and the Reigate Hoard of Henry VI coins.

Fine Work................................William III's gold coinage of 1701 where the workmanship is of especially good quality.

Fishtail Lettering....................Style of lettering where the end of the letters resembles a fish tail, only used on the coinage of Richard II.

Flan...The piece of metal upon which the design of the coin will be struck, also called a planchet or blank.

Fleur de Coin..........................A French term which translates as 'flower of the die' and means Uncirculated. This term was used far more when coins were either mint or used. Today we use the term to represent a full mint state coin in impeccable condition (perfect Uncirculated of at least choice quality). Used far more on the Continent than in Great Britain today.

Florin......................................Originally a gold and a silver coin issued in Florence, Italy in 1252. First struck here in 1344 and then abandoned until 500 years later. Issued by Victoria as the first attempt at decimalization in 1849. Equivalent to two shillings or the tenth part of a pound, today it is ten pence.

Forgery...................................A copy of a coin or note made to deceive when exchanged for goods or services. In the old days you were hanged for just possessing a counterfeit, later convicted culprits were transported to Australia. See also *Contemporary Forgery*.

Fourpence...............................A denomination also called a groat, being one third of a shilling and one sixtieth of a pound. First issued under Edward I.

Frosting..................................Frosting can be the matting of the bust or lettering on a proof coin to show contrast with the brilliant field of the coin. Such a coin is the silver proof 1977 crown, which has almost a 'Wedgwood' effect. Frosting can also be part of the design of a coin such as the William and Mary halfcrown.

G (Good).................................A grade which denotes a considerable amount of wear. The coin is discernible but the lettering may not be clearly visible.

Gem Uncirculated...................A grade of a coin struck for circulation. I consider this to be the highest grade that a coin can achieve. There must be full and outstanding lustre, an exceptional strike, no nicks and only the smallest bag marks discernible under a strong glass. This quality is harder to achieve in larger sized coins than in smaller sized ones. Fewer than 2% of all Uncirculated coins can be called Gem.

George Noble..........................A rare denomination issued by Henry VIII, which had Saint George on it.

Ghosting.................................When dies come together without a flan in between, you may get a partial image of one die on the other. When coins are struck from this die the resulting coins will have one strong image and one weak image of the other die all on one side.

Gilt................................Gold plating on either silver or copper. In the reign of George III many of the proof issues were gold plated.

Godless............................The first florins issued during the reign of Victoria, in 1849. The legend omitted the phrase DEI GRATIA (-by the grace of God) and the issue became known as the Godless Florin. The coins were recalled and a new version was issued in 1851.

Gold................................A precious metal and, for most of history, the precious metal **par excellence**.

Gothic Crown..........................A crown issued in 1847 for circulation with a very ornate design, gothic in nature and thus became known as the Gothic Crown. Patterns were issued of this same design in 1846 and examples dated 1853 were included in the proof set of that year. Considered by many to be the most attractive British coin ever struck. The mintage of the 1847 issue is between 7 and 8,000 pieces.

Grade............................A verbal, or in the United States, a numerical way of trying to describe the quality of a coin. Because the price of a coin is in many ways dependent on the grade, some individuals will try to over state the grade of a coin.

Grain................................A weight where one grain equals 0.064799 grams.

Graining............................The milled edge design of a coin originally slanting rather than straight up and down.

Great Recoinage........................There have been a number of Great Recoinages over the years. There comes a point in time where coins have a problem circulating because they are of different weights and finenesses or have become very worn. Two recoinages which are very important are that of William III in 1696 and that of George III of 1816.

Groat................................A coin to the value of fourpence, first issued in the reign of Edward I and struck for use up until the time of Victoria. The coin is struck today for inclusion in the Maundy Set.

Guinea........................The denomination of a gold coin which had a face value of twenty-one shillings or £1.05 in new money. It got its name originally because much of the gold used in striking the coins came from Guinea in Africa. First issued under Charles II in 1663.

Half Crown..............................A denomination made up of two shillings and sixpence. The first silver issue was by Edward VI in 1551; before then it had been a gold coin.

Half Farthing............................A denomination used more in the colonies than in this country. Issued by George IV, William IV and Victoria.

Half Groat..........................Twopence or half of a fourpence groat.

Halfpenny..........................The half portion of a penny. The first halfpenny was issued by Henry I and the last predecimal coin was struck in 1970.

Hammered............................The striking of a coin by placing a flan or blank between two dies and then having someone swing a heavy hammer down on the dies to impress that piece of metal with the image on the dies. The other type of minting is called milled, which is a misnomer. The coins do not have to have milled edges, but rather be struck by machines.

Harp Strings............................In the reign of Charles II and some other reigns the number of harp strings on the reverse varied, possibly to indicate which dies were being used.

Harrington............................A licence was issued to Lord Harrington to strike farthings by James I. These coins were legal tender.

Hearts..........................Some George III shillings and sixpences dated 1787 have hearts in one section of the reverse shield and are known as the 'with hearts' variety, others omit them and are known as the 'no hearts' variety.

Heaton Mint..........................A private mint situated in Birmingham. Famous for the 'H' mintmark and has struck coins for many countries including British pennies in 1912, 1918 and 1919.

Hoard..A group of coins which have been buried or hidden by an someone in the past who anticipated coming back to dig them up. Usually, but not always, they are the same generic type of coin.

Holed..or **pierced**. The making of a hole in a coin after it has left the mint. Done to enable the coin to be worn or to demonetise it.

Hub...The positive pair of metal dies from which striking dies can be made. These reversed dies are then used to do the actual striking of the coins.

Imitation Money........................Copies of coins made usually as play money rather than to deceive anyone. The most famous of the manufacturers was Lauer of Nuremberg.

Imitation Spade Guinea.............A copy in brass of the George III gold guinea known as the spade guinea, because of the appearance of the shield on the reverse. There are many hundreds of different designs. The original pieces were struck by a company called Kettle. A Victorian actress was known to shower the audience with these at the end of her act. They are not valuable but make a wonderful area to attempt to collect.

Incuse ....A design which is sunk in rather than raised. Some initials on the coinage of William IV exist with both raised and incused lettering under the bust.

Initial Cross...............................The cross centred at the top of the coin. The legend will commence at this point.

Intrinsic.....................................The actual metal value of the coin. In the past the intrinsic or metal value was very close to the face value of the coin. It had to be that way otherwise no one would accept the coins in payment. Today we are told that the piece of metal has a face value of £5 and we accept it although the intrinsic value might well be only a few pence. See *fiat money*.

Jeton ....These are counters as used from the 12th to the 19th centuries, there are also later pieces which have advertising on them. Derived from the French, it is not a word that is used much in this country today. Jetons were used in mathematical calculations and later in games.

Joey..Slang name for a silver threepence, after Joseph Hume.

Jubilee Coinage.........................Queen Victoria finally allowed new coins to be issued with a portrait other than her young head. These young head coins were issued from 1838-1887. Her vanity was such that the coins carried her portrait as a 17 year old even when she was 67. On the Jubilee of her reign the new design was struck along with a new denomination (the double florin). The small crown placed on the back of the queen's head made her look a bit foolish and the jubilee head design was changed again in 1893 to the old or widow head coinage.

Key Date....................................The most difficult to obtain dates in a series. For example the 1952 sixpence and the 1950 and 1951 pennies. These are the dates which you would not find in your change no matter how hard you looked. You would need to go to a dealer and buy them to complete your collection.

Kings Norton Mint.....................A private mint situated in Birmingham. Known for the 'KN' mintmark. Issued many coins for overseas governments and struck pennies for this country in 1918 and 1919.

Late Soho Striking.....................Coins struck by the Soho mint some years after the dies were first cut. The coins will normally exhibit defects such as rust marks or die cracks, although usually these flaws are only noticeable on close inspection. In 1848 W.J. Taylor, a contemporary medallist, acquired many of the original dies from which he restruck many of the earlier Soho coins, including patterns, nearly always repolishing or re-engraving some elements of the original die before reusing them.

Laureate....................................A bust crowned with a wreath of laurel leaves.

Laurel...The James I gold twenty shilling piece first struck in 1619. It gets its 'name' from the laurel wreath on the king's head.

Legend ....The inscription found on a coin or medal. In many cases it will consist of a string of abbreviations of Latin words.

Lennox farthings ....Farthings struck under the licence that James I gave to Lord Lennox.

Leopard ....A rare gold coin issued by Edward III in 1344 with a value of three shillings. The figure shown is actually a lion and not a leopard.

Light Coinage ....Weights of coins reduced to make them more in line with the weight of European coins during the reigns of Henry IV and Edward IV.

Lima Coinage ....Coins issued in 1745 and 1746 by George II from silver captured by Anson from the Spanish. It is thought by some that the silver had originally come from Lima, Peru and it was George II's way of thumbing his nose at the Spanish by placing the name Lima below his bust on the coins.

Lion of Nassau ....The lion in the centre of the coins of William III.

Lombardic lettering ....Medieval lettering originating in Italy. More rounded and ornamental than the plainer styles that replaced it, it was used until about the time of Edward VI.

Long Cross Coinage ....The penny coinage first issued by Henry III where the cross on the reverse came to the outer edge of the coin. It is said that the cross came to the edge for either of two reasons, the first was to help with cutting the coin into halves or quarters and make change. The second was that it hindered the clipping of coins. As both halfpennies and farthings were introduced by Henry III (but are extremely rare), I am more convinced by the second reason!

Love Token ....A coin which is engraved with a sentiment, picture or both to show tenderness from one person to another. In Victorian times a young lady might be given any number of engraved threepences or sixpences in this way and it was customary to wear them on a charm bracelet.

Low Relief ....Dies which are cut with the design in relief which does not protrude from the surface a great deal.

Low Tide ....A variety on the 1902 penny and halfpenny coinage of Edward VII.

Lustre ....The brilliant rich colour that coins have when they have just been struck. It is impossible to replace this lustre once it has been lost, but some people will attempt to replace the colour, for profit. There is a certain swirl to the lustre. In copper and bronze coins, the more of the original orange brilliance a coin has, the more desirable it is.

Maltravers farthings ....Farthings struck by Lord Maltravers who had been licensed by Charles I.

Matt Proof ....A special finish which leaves a dull surface on the coin. This country issued matt proofs only in 1902 as an experiment; it was not repeated.

Maundy Money ....Associated with the royal ceremony celebrating Maundy Thursday which is believed to go back to the reign of Edward II. The first 'sets' can be made up from the hammered coins of Charles II but no real Maundy sets were made until the end of the reign of George III. A Maundy set consists of one of each of the denominations of fourpence, threepence, twopence and penny; mintages are low. Recipients of Maundy money get one penny for every year that the reigning monarch has been alive. So when Elizabeth II was 60, each person got 60 pence (six sets of four coins). When she was 61, they got six sets plus a 1 penny piece. When she was 62 they got six sets plus a 2 pence and so on.

Medal ....An award usually given for valour and intended to be worn. Given by the government or some official organisation.

Medalet ....A small sized medallion.

Medallion ....A commemorative piece struck to honour an individual, event, place, time or the like. May or may not be issued by a government. If the event is of importance, many different companies may issue many different pieces.

Mestrelle or Meystrell...............A French engraver who introduced the method of striking coins that we call today 'milled coinage'. Elizabeth I experimented with coins struck on a screw press between 1561 and 1571. Very neat workmanship and of a vastly superior quality than hammered coins. But the Mint employees feared that this new machinery would put them out of a job and Mestrelle was dismissed. In 1578 he was hung for counterfeiting!

Metal Transfer.........................During striking, metal flows from one side of the coin to the other to fill the die. A vague outline can be seen on the 'wrong' side of the coin. Not to be confused with clashed dies.

Military Guinea.........................The last gold guinea ever to be struck was dated 1813. It is called the Military Guinea not because of the design but because it was struck for paying troops rather than for general circulation.

Milled...A misnomer for machine struck coinage. Originally, one of the most important features of machine struck coins was that they could have their edge milled to prevent clipping. Milling was later replaced with lettering and then reintroduced. But the generic term milled indicates machine struck.

Milling..The actual lines or grooves around the edge of a coin which can be straight or slanting.

Mint abbreviation.....................On the early hammered coins the moneyer's name was spelled out in full but, due to lack of space on the reverse of a coin, the name of the mint might have to be abbreviated.

Mint Set....................................A set of uncirculated coins specially issued by a mint. The coins will usually have a special packaging and/or quality of the surfaces to distinguish them from regular circulation issues. The Royal Mint first issued Mint Sets in 1982 and have done so every year since.

Mint Sport.................................A coin struck illicitly but from genuine dies to produce an error or novelty of some kind.

Mint...As a grading term it is the same as Uncirculated, indicating a coin which has not seen circulation. Mint of course also refers to a place where coins are struck.

Mintage.....................................The number of coins of an issue that were struck.

Mintmark...................................Also known as 'privy mark'. A symbol or mark placed on a coin to differentiate it from other similar coins struck elsewhere and indicate where and by whom it had been struck. Used to control the quality of the coins being struck, these marks substituted the practice of including the moneyer's name in the legend. If something was wrong with the weight or the metal content of the coins, then the monarch knew who to 'speak to'. A mintmark was used for some hammered issues and on milled issues. It could help link dies to coins and sometimes undated coins can be dated accurately by their mintmark. See also separate 'Mintmark' chapter, p.89.

Mirror Finish............................When the surface of the planchet or flan has the appearance of brightness without flaws. This surface is found on proof coins where both the flan and the dies are polished to achieve perfection.

Misstrike...................................A coin which in any of a number of ways is not struck correctly. It might be off centre, it might be double struck or it might even be a brockage.

Model Coins..............................The model penny was struck by Joseph Moore of Birmingham ca 1844. It was a copper outer ring with a silvered inner part. It caused confusion with the public and the Mint had to tell the public that it was not legal tender. Other coins struck in much smaller size are usually by Lauer of Nuremberg; these were used as play money for children.

Modified Effigy........................Refers to a change in the design of the coinage of George V in 1926.

Moneyer....................................During the hammered coinage, a moneyer was the mint official responsible for the striking of the coins and ensuring they were of the legal weight and metal fineness. On late Anglo-Saxon and early post-Conquest coins, his name will appear on the reverse together with the name of the mint.

Mounting ....A coin can be mounted in either of two ways. The first is by attaching a loop to the coin with solder. The second is by constructing a ring or bezel to fit around the coin and placing a chain through a ring in the bezel. Both will decrease the value of a coin; one rapidly, the other slowly.

Mule..If you take one die from one coin and another die from a second coin and combine the two dies to make a third coin, this third coin is called a mule. When Taylor had the Soho Mint dies, he muled many different coins to come up with an equal number of new varieties.

NCLT...See *Non Circulating Legal Tender Coins*

'New' Coins ....An indication on the decimal coinage from 1968 to 1981 to show that these were New Pence, not old pence.

New Style Calendar..................In 1752 the calendar changed from Julian to Gregorian.

Newark ....A town in the Midlands which during the Civil War was surrounded and held to siege. Emergency coinage was 'struck' from cut up pieces of silver dinner plates. As some of the plates were gold plated silver so are the coins. They are dated 1645 and 1646 and the denominations are halfcrown, shilling, 9 pence and 6 pence.

No Hearts ....In the 1787 shillings and sixpences there are varieties with hearts in one of the quarters and another variety without hearts; this is known as the no hearts type.

Noble.......................................First struck in 1344 in the reign of Edward III, a gold coin to the value of six shillings and eight pence.

Non Circulating Legal Tender ...NCLT coins are the subject of much heated debate in the coin industry. Basically these are most of the commemorative and off metal strikes issued by the mints. They are made for collectors and to gain money for the issuing authority. But if you wanted to spend them in theory you could, thus they are legal tender.

Northumberland Shilling ....George III had struck £100 (2,000 pieces) of a special shilling in 1763. It was to be used by the Duke of Northumberland for largesse when he entered Dublin as the Lord Lieutenant of Ireland. It has a distinct bust.

Notaphily.................................The collecting of banknotes or financial instruments made of paper.

Numismatics ....The study of coins, medals, tokens, banknotes and other means of exchange. Such a broad field encompasses a very wide range of interests, from the historical developments associated with coins and banknotes or the technical aspects of production to the artistic aspect of the designs -to name but a few.

Obsidonal Currency..................From the Latin **obsedere**, to sit on, and indicating coins struck at a place that is besieged. In this country the term refers to the issues of the Civil War and encompasses Carlisle, Colchester, Newark, Pontefract and Scarborough. These issues are crude, being struck under extreme outside pressures and usually from cut up silverware.

Obverse ....The side of a coin which bears the monarch's portrait or the most important legend, which usually includes the name of the monarch or the country. This is considered the most important side of the coin and commonly known as 'heads'.

Off Metal Strike........................Sometimes a flan for one coin will accidentally be struck with the dies of another denomination. If these coins are issued in two different metals then the resulting coin will be known as an off metal striking. Today mints offer their coinage in both the original metal and in silver and gold strikings; there is confusion as to what to call these.

Off-centre ....A coin which is imperfectly struck so that part of the design is missing, as a result of careless minting procedures. In the case of hammered coins, such as those of Henry I and Stephen, they were met with very frequently. Off-centred coins are generally of less value than well-centred ones, even when the condition is otherwish excellent.

Old Head ....The last coinage of Queen Victoria which is also known as the widow head coins. She is portrayed wearing the veil of widowhood.

One Year Type ....A major variety which is only struck and issued for one year. Examples are the George IV 1821 shilling and 1849 florin of Victoria.

Ornamental Trident ....On the copper coins of Victoria, Britannia is holding a trident; this comes both plain and ornamented.

Overdate ....When dies have to be reused at a later date, rather than engrave new ones, a new date or part thereof is punched over the existing date. The overdate can only really be seen properly on high quality coins. In the Commonwealth there are some coins where the date has been repunched two or even three times. This saved the making of new dies, money and time.

Overseas Mints ....When English coins were struck at mints other than in Great Britain. Example Calais in the reign of Henry VI.

Overstrike ....When a coin is struck over an already existing coin. Examples are the Bank of England Dollar which was overstruck on Spanish eight reales.

Oxford Crown ....A now very rare silver crown issued for the City of Oxford during the Civil War. It is dated 1644, was designed by Thomas Rawlins and shows the City of Oxford below the king on horseback.

Parliament, Tower Mint under ..During the Civil War in the reign of Charles I, the Tower Mint fell under the control of Parliament and coins with the portrait of Charles I were struck.

Patina or Patination ....The toning that a coin has built up over a number of years. Many collectors, especially those just starting out, do not like what they call 'dirty' coins. I believe that nice patination not only enhances the appearance of coins but actually increases their value. Patina is something which comes naturally and cannot be reproduced artificially.

Pattern ....A proposed design for a new coin. When a new coin is going to be issued a number of engravers will be asked to submit their designs, before the final design is chosen. Once the actual design is chosen a number of examples will be struck before the date of issue for circulation. Even though these have the same appearance as the coin to be struck, because of the date they are considered to be patterns. An example is the 1848 florin of Victoria which is the same design as the issued 1849 coin. See p.691 for hammered patterns and p. for milled patterns.

Pax ....The word for Peace which appears on the pennies of William I and Henry I. It was a hope for peace in the country.

Peck, C. Wilson ....The author of the standard work on the copper and bronze coins of England.

Penny ....The denomination is from Denarius a Roman coin, which then became a denier in Europe and penny here which is abbreviated as 'd'.

Petition Crown ....Thomas Simon submitted the design for a crown to Charles II in 1663. The workmanship was excellent and Simon managed to get two lines of text on the edge of the coin. He petitioned the king to accept his designs but was turned down, reportedly because the king could not forgive him for the coins he had engraved in Cromwell's time.

Piedfort ....A French word for a coin which is thicker than the usual striking. There can be double, triple and six times thickness piedforts. In 1983 the Royal Mint started to issue special collectors examples of the new pound coin in silver proof piedfort and it proved to be very popular.

Pile ....The lower die in the pair of dies used to strike hammered coins. It usually had a sharp pointed end which could be stuck into the wood to hold it in place.

Pinches Family ....A family of medallists who became **the** engravers in the mid 1800s. Engraved coins and medallions and did some outstanding work.

Pingo, Lewis ....(1743-1830) Assistant engraver at the Royal Mint from 1776 and chief engraver from 1779-1815. Engraved many coins and patterns.

Pinhole .... On the edge of coins you will sometimes see two pin holes; these were made to hold the coin in a mount as jewellery.

Pistrucci, Benedetto .... (1784-1855) Engraver of gems as well as of the St George and the dragon reverse still used on coins today. The design was originally used on the 'new' sovereign of George III, struck in 1817.

Pitting .... Small holes in the surface of a coin or die caused by oxidation. If the die is pitted, then the coins it is used to strike will have small raised bumps on their surfaces. Many restrike coins can be told from the originals by the pitting or lack of it.

Plain Edge Proof .... Proofs of George III, William IV and Victoria often have plain edges to differentiate them from circulating coins.

Planchet .... The flan or blank that is used to strike coins.

Plaster .... A sculptor will use a round piece of plaster to engrave his design. From this plaster a rubber will be made. The rubber will be placed on a reduction machine to make hubs from which a die is made. The plaster will be much larger than the finished coin; this is to enable the fineness of the design to be engraved without the use of magnifying glass.

Plug .... Some coins have a plug in them to prevent counterfeiting such as the tin coins of James II. When a coin has been holed after striking, a plug may be placed in the hole to make the coin look more attractive.

Pontefract .... A Royalist stronghold in the Civil War, under siege from June 1648 until March 1649. Emergency moneys were issued struck from silver dinner plates.

Portcullis Coinage .... These were coins issued by Elizabeth I for use overseas by the East India Company in 1600-1601. They were trade coins and were struck with the denominations of 8, 4, 2 and 1 terstern and weighed the same as 8, 4, 2, and 1 reale respectively. They get their name by the depiction of a portcullis or drop gate on them.

Post-Union .... After the Union of England and Scotland in 1707.

Posthumous issue .... Coins of a monarch struck after his/her death.

Pre-Union .... Before the Union of England and Scotland in 1707.

Presentation Piece .... A coin specially struck to be given to a very important person. Sometimes the coin will be struck to a higher than normal quality, sometimes it will be struck in a more precious metal and sometimes it will be struck with a commemorative reverse. Presentation pieces were often made to show a monarch the new coinage or new designs.

Prince Elector Guinea .... The guinea of George I issued in 1714 where the legend reads PR EL in place of EL; it also has a very different head.

Privy mark .... See *Mintmark*.

Proof Set .... A set of coins issued in proof quality by a mint. The coins will, in modern times, come in a case or some sort of presentation packaging.

Proof .... In this country proof is a method of striking and not a condition. A proof coin is struck most carefully with polished dies and a polished flan. It will be struck more than once to get the high relief to show all the fine details. Sometimes you will get a lead piece with half of a coin, this is done to proof the die before striking.

Prooflike .... A condition when the coins are issued in a quality which is better than the normal circulation striking but not up to Proof quality. The surfaces will shimmer.

Provenance mark .... A symbol or mark on a coin to identify the origin of the metal it was struck on. Thus plumes, for example, indicate Welsh silver or silver from the Welsh Copper Co; roses, the mines in the West of England; VIGO, silver captured at the battle of Vigo in 1702.

Provincial Mints ....The Great Recoinage of 1696 caused so much work that provincial mints had to be opened again. They were Bristol, Chester, Exeter, Norwich and York.

Pseudo Coin ....A fantasy which purports to be a coin when it is usually a medallic piece.

Punch or Puncheon ....A design or lettering on a piece of metal which is then applied to make a portion of a die. The head of George III might be made as a punch so that every die made for that coin will have the same details. It could be for applying lettering or a mintmark.

Pyx, Trial of ....From the Greek *pyxis*, a box or vase. The Trial of the Pyx is the testing of the quality of the metal of coins by placing them in boxes at the Goldsmith's Hall, picking samples at random and assaying them to test the purity of the metal.

Quarter Farthing ....The smallest denomination ever struck in this country. There were 3,840 of these coins to the pound. They were issued by Victoria and struck in copper; they are scarce.

Quarter Guinea ....A gold coin with a face value of five shillings and three pence. Only issued by George I in 1718 and George III in 1762.

Quatrefoil ....Four pellets close together.

Raised Edge Proof ....On the 1935 George V crown the lettering on the edge of the coin was raised to differentiate it from the incuse lettering on the circulation strikes.

Rarity ....An attempt to describe how many examples of a coin still exist. When an exact number are not known then a scale of rarity is used. A scale might go from EC (Extremely Common) to S (Scarce), or from R for Rare to R5 for Extremely Rare. This 'guesstimate' of the number available is usually based on knowledge rather than mint reports of the number struck.

Rawlins, Thomas ....Charles I's chief coin and medal engraver during the Civil War. He worked at Oxford and did the beautiful Oxford Crown.

Re-issue ....When a mint strikes more coins than was originally planned. It should be in the same year or they then become restrikes. An example is the 1965 Canadian Mint Set. The Canadian Mint had so many orders that it reopened the ordering and struck as many sets as they had call for.

Recoinage ....When old coins are called in because they are no longer legal tender, melted down and then the metal is made into other coins. The last great recoinages were those of William III and George III.

Reddite Crown ....A pattern crown by Thomas Simon for Charles II.

Reducing Machine & Reduction Process ....Today when a coin is to be struck, an engraver carves his design in plaster. This plaster is used to make a metal or rubber master which is then placed on a reducing machine. This cuts an exact copy but in a size which is the same as the coin which is to be struck.

Reeding ....The milling on the edge of a coin.

Regnal Date ....The year on the edge of a coin which is taken from the date of the death of the proceeding monarch. As this may occur in the middle of the calendar year, a single year's coins will often carry two different regnal years during their striking. On the coinage of Charles II, this dates from the death of Charles I, 30 January 1649.

Relief ....The raised portion of the coin design.

Restrike ....When coins are struck from the original dies at a later time. Many of the coins from the Soho Mint were restruck when Taylor bought the old dies for scrap metal value. Until the 1960s the Indian government would strike coins going back to the period of Victoria for you if you gave them old rupees in their place. Collectors should be aware that restrikes exist and that they do not bring as much as the original strikes do. Restrikes also diminish the value of the original strikings.

Reverse ....The 'tails' side of the coin, the opposite of the obverse or 'heads' side.

Ribbon Stain ....In 1950 and 1951 proof sets the chemicals in the ribbon interact with the coins and often result in stains on the coins which cannot be removed.

Richmond Farthings ....The Duchess of Richmond was licensed to issue farthings by Charles I.

Rim ....The raised part of a coin, formed by the metal from the edge being extruded.

Rose Ryal ....A gold coin issued by James I. The king is sitting on his throne and the reverse has the Tudor Rose.

Rust Marks ....Unless carefully kept, dies will rust. Coins struck from rusted dies will show areas of pitting. It is more commonly found on hammered than milled coins, though some Soho Mint proof and pattern coins struck at a later date also show rust marks.

Ryal ....Edward IV first struck this gold coin in 1465; it had a value of ten shillings.

Scarborough ....A town which, when it was besieged during the Civil War, issued many different denominations, all cut from silver dinner plates. There are many known denominations and all are rare. Rather than try to have uniform denominations they cut the silver, weighed it and then stamped it with its value.

Scottish Shilling ....A variety of shilling issued from 1937 to 1970 (see also *English Shilling*).

Scratches ....Marks which are incused in the field of a coin. These may have been caused by any number of things. They detract from the appearance and value of a coin.

Seignorage ....The difference between the metal or intrinsic value of the planchet plus the cost of striking deducted from the face value of the coin. In the past this was a relatively small proportion of the value, today it is increasingly larger. It is interesting to note that some small denominations actually cost more to strike than their face value.

Shield Reverse ....This refers in particular to the first type of Victorian sovereign which had a shield or coat of arms on the reverse of the coin.

Shilling ....The first attempt at a shilling which was the twentieth part of a pound, was the Testoon of Henry VII introduced in 1504. The first actual shilling was issued by Edward VI. This is also the first dated English coin; the date was in Roman numerals.

Short Cross Coinage ....The penny coinage where the cross on the reverse fell well short of the edge of the coin, issued by Henry II, Richard I, John and Henry III. Henry III had both short and long cross coinage.

Shrewsbury ....The first Civil War mint to be opened to strike coinage for Charles I. Thomas Bushell was the mintmaster and took his privy mark of the Welsh plumes with him.

Siege Money ....Money issued by a locality under siege when the normal flow of money into and out of the location is impeded and inhabitants create their own form of exchange or money to service their economic transactions.

Silver Tokens ....Privately issued silver pieces struck around 1811 to alleviate the shortage of small change. Eventually the Bank of England also issued silver tokens, at which point the private issue ceased.

Sixpence ....A denomination of half a shilling containing the value of six one penny coins; there are Victorian patterns with the denomination of half a shilling. The sixpence was first struck in 1551 for the currency reform of Edward VI. It continued to be struck until 1970 and was legal tender till 1980.

Snick ....Small piece of metal, usually 'V' shaped, taken out of hammered coins to check their metal content.

Soho Mint ....Matthew Boulton's minting facilities in Birmingham, 1786-1809. Among the coins struck there, under contract for the British government, was the famous Cartwheel Twopence.

South Sea Company..................The South Sea Company had special coins struck for them in 1723 under George I. The coins were silver issues of sixpence, shilling, halfcrown and crown. They can be distinguished by the letters SSC in the angles between the arms on the reverse.

Sovereign....................................A gold coin first struck by Henry VII in 1489, to the value of twenty shillings. In 1816 under the Currency Reform Act the guinea was abolished and the sovereign made the unit of gold currency.

Spade Guinea...........................A gold coin to the value of 21 shillings issued by George III. The shield on the reverse looks like the metal part of a garden spade and thus it acquired the nickname Spade Guinea.

Specimen Set............................A set of coins struck for presentation purposes.

Specimen...................................A specially struck coin for presentation purposes. The surface is usually prooflike.

Spur Ryal...................................James I gold coin issued in 1604 with a face value of fifteen shillings. The sharp rays of the sun on the reverse look like a spur.

SSC...See *South Sea Company*.

Sterling......................................When it refers to the fineness of silver it is the British standard of 925 parts silver per 1,000 parts total. British coins were struck in Sterling Silver until 1919, at which point the metal content was changed to 500 fine silver.

Striation.....................................Marks on the coin usually from the scraping off of the excess metal of a coin. Sometimes from an improperly manufactured flan.

Tanner, John.............................Engraver of coins during the reign of George II and George III. A German who came to England in 1728 and died here in 1775, he was responsible for most of George II's coinage.

Tanner..Slang name for a sixpence.

Taylor, William Joseph.............(1802-1885) A medallist and die sinker who produced a number of coins and tokens, mainly for export. He is most famous for restriking of coins from the Soho Mint's dies.

Testoon......................................The forerunner of the shilling issued by Henry VII in 1504 and valued at twelve pence. It weighed 144 grains, twelve times the weight of a penny. A rare coin with his portrait and of artistic importance.

Third Farthing...........................A coin with the value of one third of a farthing, which in turn is a quarter of a penny which is again one 240th of a pound. Used in some of the colonies.

Third Guinea.............................A gold coin with the value of seven shillings (35p), three of which made up a guinea, only issued by George III.

Three Farthings........................A silver coin to the value of three quarters of a penny, struck only in the reign of Elizabeth I.

Three Halfpence.......................A coin to the value of one penny and a half issued by Elizabeth I and again by William IV and Victoria, when it was used in overseas colonies, Ceylon, Jamaica and British Guiana.

Three Shilling Token.................Bank token, struck in silver and issued by the Bank of England from 1811 until 1816. There are two busts of George III, the first in Roman armour and the second with a laurel wreath.

Threepence...............................A coin to the value of three pennies.

Tie..The bit on the bottom of the ribbon at the back of the head. Undergoes much change over the issues.

Token..A privately issued piece which stands in for a regal coin of a stated value. Many times the token will have an advertisement for the merchant who issued it. These pieces have less metal and cost less to strike than their purported face value. When there is a shortage of small change these pieces become more readily acceptable by the general populace. The vast influx of issues was in the 17th Century and then again in the late 18th Century. At the end, tokens were being issued for collectors rather than to fill a need in the community.

Toning...........................A coin over a period of time will react to its environment. The metal in a coin will change colour many times to a magnificent series of hues, and this is what we call toning. A toned coin is in fact more desirable than an untoned coin and in many cases will bring more money from a collector.

Tooling...........................The enhancement of a coin by burnishing the fields and getting the design to stand out more. It can also be to alter a coin's value by changing the date or some other part of the coin.

Touch Piece.....................When monarchs were held to rule by divine right, it was believed that the process of touching them with a coin and then wearing it constituted a cure for prevalent ailments. A 'Touching Ceremony' first took place in the reign of Edward the Confessor and last in the reign of Queen Anne, and special gold medalets were struck with which to 'touch' the monarch.

Tournai.............................French town were Henry VIII struck coins.

Tower Mint.....................The principal mint of England from Norman days, it was situated in and around the Tower of London. It was actually inside the Tower of London until the early 19th Century.

Triple Unite.....................Issued in the Civil War it is physically the largest gold coin ever struck and had a face value of sixty shillings. It was struck at Shrewsbury and Oxford from 1642 -1644.

Troy Weight.....................A measure of weight for precious metals. Where an ounce of feathers is weighed avoirdupois at 28 grams an ounce of gold is weighed in troy weight at 31.1 grams.

Truncation.......................The bottom part of a bust or neck on a coin, often where the engraver signs his name.

Type Coin.......................A coin which represents a major variety of a coinage rather than a specific date. Collectors often try and obtain one example of each major type rather than one of each date of coin issued.

Type Set...........................A collection of coins put together which shows the different major varieties of the coinage rather than all the dates.

Type...............................A major variety of a coinage such as Victorian crowns can be broken up into four different types: Young Head, Gothic, Jubilee Head and Old Head. A collector would attempt to gather one of each type of crown rather than to complete a date set of Victorian crowns.

Una & the Lion.................The design on the Victoria gold £5 issued in 1839.

Unc (Uncirculated)............A grade which indicates that a coin has never been released into circulation. Although a coin may be less than perfect when struck, with scratches and nicks, that does not mean that it is not Uncirculated. Over the years a coin may tone or a copper coin may change from bright to dark, again this does not mean that it is not Uncirculated. The term literally means a coin which has not seen circulation.

Uniface...........................Having a design on one side only.

Unite...............................A gold coin of James I, first issued in 1604 and with a face value of twenty shillings.

Unpublished Variety.........An example with a difference, i.e. lettering differential, metal content, overdate or unknown date which has never been listed in numismatic writings or in a journal.

V.I.P. Proof.....................A term sometimes used to describe proof coins struck in very small numbers for presentation.

VF (Very Fine).................A grade of coin where there has been obvious but relatively restricted wear on the highest portions of the coin.

VG (Very Good)................A grade where the coin has experienced a lot of wear and where the details are still discernible but worn.

Vigo Coinage...................The coinage of Queen Anne struck from silver and gold captured from the Spanish in the battle of Vigo.

WCC...............................See *Welsh Copper Company*

Weak Strike ....When not enough pressure is used to strike the coin, the design will appear to be weak and an Uncirculated coin will look like a used example.

Welsh Copper Company............Shillings were struck under George I with silver which came from the Welsh Copper Company. To distinguish these coins from the normal ones a small 'WCC' is under George's bust. These coins are all scarce and in higher grades are Rare.

Wire Money...............................Maundy money issued in 1792 by George III, where the shape of the numerals looked like a piece of wire. A one year type.

Wolsey ....Cardinal Wolsey had a mint at York from 1514-1526 and struck coins with his initials 'T. W.' on them. He struck a groat which caused problems and a trial. The king was incensed that he dared to strike groats and also that he had placed his initials on the coins.

Wreath Crown...........................A series of crowns issued from 1927 to 1936 excluding 1935, with a wreath on the reverse. This was the fourth coinage under George V; a proof set was issued in 1927 containing this coin. Mintages are low and it is also known as the Christmas Crown as it was given out as presents at that time of year.

Year Set ....A collection or set of coins containing all the coins that were issued in a specific year.

Yeo, Richard ....Engraver at the Royal Mint from about 1749. He produced the Northumberland Shilling and guineas of George III and died in 1779.

York..At this town there was an Episcopal mint from about 750 AD and it remained until Archbishop Wolsey struck groats bearing his own initials and the king closed him down. The city was also the location of a mint during the English Civil War and later during the Great Recoinage of 1696–97. The inscription on coins struck in York is EBOR.

Young Head...............................This has been used for the coinage of George II, George III and Victoria and helps to differentiate the first coins issued during a long reign.

Richard Lobel

Questions & Answers

Hammered Coins

How were hammered coins made?

A piece of metal was cut to shape, weighed and placed between two dies. The bottom die was fixed into a wooden table or stool, while the top die was held by the moneyer. The top die was hit, probably several times, and the coin was re-weighed to ensure the flan had not been damaged; the coin was then ready for circulation. It is probable that larger hammered coins such as Charles I silver pounds were struck with the silver flan heated so as to make the silver more supple.

What happened to people who counterfeited coins?

This offence was very serious and usually resulted in the culprit being hanged. Moneyers who were found guilty of producing underweight coins or of poor metal fineness could have had a hand cut off and even be castrated.

Why are hammered coins of a certain issue different sizes?

There are two answers to this question. Firstly, many hammered coins were clipped. Clipping was an illegal practice in which individuals cut small slithers of silver from the edge of the coin and then passed the under-weight coin on, so making a small illegal profit for themselves. The designs and styles of the coins were often changed to combat the problem but none was totally successful and it was not until milled coins were introduced that clipping ceased.

The second answer to the question is that the weight of the coins was more important than the size. Therefore, as long as the weight was correct, the coin would be readily acceptable.

Why were coins struck at many mints during the early reigns and at very few during the later ones?

During the reign of kings such as William I and II travelling in England was not only difficult but also hazardous. Most medieval people did not travel and many did not even leave the village they were born in. It was therefore easier and safer to bring the coin dies to the people rather than the coins themselves. Also, local minting helped enhance people's confidence in the coinage. As travelling improved and people became better educated, they were more willing to accept coins produced at the principal mints.

Why are so many hammered coins badly damaged or mutilated? On many coins it appears to be deliberate vandalism.

During the reign of William III many small denomination hammered coins were officially holed to reduce their face value, but the damage done unofficially by the public has a more varied and interesting explanation ranging from politics to love, leisure and business.

Some monarchs were unpopular, especially on religious grounds during the Tudor period, and it was considered preferable to vent one's anger on the portrait of a coin rather than risk imprisonment for attacking the monarch.

Coins such as sixpences were often buckled and given as tokens of affection to women when a man could not afford a ring. Others, particularly shillings, are often found with the obverse very badly worn. This was probably caused when they were used in a game similar to shove ha'penny and some of these coins actually bear the initials of the players on the reverse.

Finally many coins, in particular shillings, are found with a deliberate 'cross' scratched on the obverse. Although it is uncertain why this was done, it is possible that it constituted a form of accounting.

Which English hammered coin is most easily available?

The Edward I penny, see p.334.

What is the most valuable English hammered coin?

While the market is always changing and several issues can only be found in museums, the answer is probably the gold twenty pence of Henry III; a specimen sold in 1996 for £159,500, see p.213.

What was the largest hoard of hammered coins ever found?

In 1831 in Tutbury, 200,000 medieval pennies, mainly of Edward I, were found.

What was the largest hammered coin?

The Charles I silver pound struck during the Civil War at the Oxford and Shrewsbury mints, see p.116.

Which was the earliest dated hammered coin?

The first coin to be dated using Roman numerals was struck in 1548 and was a base shilling of Edward VI, see p.226. The first coin using Arabic numerals was a silver crown of Edward VI dated 1551, see p.157.

I	1d
II	halfgroat
III	threepence
IIII	groat
VI	sixpence
IX	ninepence
XII	shilling
XXX or II vi	halfcrown
V	crown
X	halfpound, double crown
XX	unite, pound

Did European coins circulate in England?

Yes, with coins worth their weight in gold or silver, many European coins circulated in England. Many of these coins had a fairly low silver content and some, in particular Venetian silver coins, could almost be classed as token coinage (see p.411). Scottish and Irish coins, in particular pennies, were also readily acceptable in England as they were the same weight and fineness as the English pennies.

When was the first milled coin introduced?

Milled coins were first struck in 1561 at the Tower Mint by the Frenchman Eloye Mestrelle. These coins were well struck and superior to the hammered issues but Mestrelle's presence at the mint was unpopular because he was French and because milled coins threatened moneyers' employment. Milled coins were not fully introduced until 1662, during the reign of Charles II.

Mark Davidson

Milled Coins

Why should I collect coins?

If you have no interest in history, or feel no sense of awe in handling items which have passed through countless hands for hundreds of years, then it may be that collecting coins is not for you. Even so, you may still wish to acquire a collection or accumulation of coins for investment purposes. There are few investment choices which are as easily marketable or transportable as are coins.

If you *are* one of those able to enjoy the myriad of experiences which coins offer, you are indeed lucky. How else could you acquire, at little cost, an item bearing a two thousand year old representation of a Roman Emperor? What other field could tantalise as one tries to fathom the minds of designers and engravers, such as those who encoded information into the minute die variations of the harp strings of the coinage of Charles II? Certainly, stamps do not offer anywhere near the same mystery; oil paintings, if one can afford them, possibly do, but they do not fit nearly so easily into registered envelopes.

What coins should I collect?

That depends on what sort of person you are. Primarily, it is best to collect what attracts you most. However, you should remember that there are alternatives to the obvious answer of collecting a particular denomination by date or by type. For example, you can collect thematically, buying examples of coins which depict particular items which interest you. Alternatively, you can take a totally original approach, for example collecting Victorian English silver coins by die number from 1 up to several hundreds.

What you collect will usually reflect something of your inner nature. An extrovert who wants to show off a collection will often collect crowns or five guinea pieces; an intellectual might collect, and study at length, Victorian farthings by date and die variety. The best rule is: do your own thing!

Should I buy coins as an investment?

There is no logical reason why items bought to bring pleasure should increase in value. If one's interests lie with computers or hi-fi equipment one does not expect to sell the used equipment for a profit at a later date. However, if one acquires collectable items for pleasure, it will often be the case that they increase in value at a rate higher than inflation over the years. Such appreciation in value should be regarded as a bonus on top of the enjoyment that one gets from their possession, and not as a right.

Which coins are likely to go up in value the most?

It is impossible to say. If you feel that you must buy with a view to profit, in general, it is usually wiser to concentrate on neglected areas rather than on popular ones, and to follow one's own hunches as to what seems to be good value. It is often a good ides to ignore 'hype' as to which fields are 'likely to go up in value'. Following emotion rather than intellect can surprisingly often guide one into anticipating trends.

How does age affect the value of coins?

The value of coins in a free market is determined by supply and demand. The supply of a coin is a function of its rarity. For example, Charles II milled coins in top condition are in general very rare, as they circulated widely, and few people thought to hoard them. They are also very popular, i.e. the demand is great. Consequently, the prices are high. Low grade Roman coins, much older, are in demand but the supply is very large, so they may be picked up relatively cheaply. Some modern coins, for example the 1934 crown, have both a low supply and a high demand. There is some correlation between age and value, but it is not clear-cut. It is a common fallacy amongst the unsophisticated public that the age of an item exclusively determines its price.

Which milled coins are the most attractive?

Attractiveness is too subjective to give a categorical answer, but it is generally accepted that the Gothic crown, the Victoria young head coinage by William Wyon and the early Charles II milled coins are amongst the most beautiful.

Which are the ugliest?

Again, a matter of opinion, but the Churchill crown and the first obverse of the George IV farthing might take some beating. The writer has been chided for daring to criticise adversely the reverse of the spade guinea, but some might agree.

Which are the largest and heaviest milled coins?

The cartwheel twopence of 1797, at 56.7 grams (2 ounces) far outweighs the gold five pound and five guinea pieces, and is also slightly larger (41 mm diameter).

Which is the smallest and lightest?

Not the quarter farthing, nor even the decimal halfpenny. Considerably smaller and lighter is the silver Maundy penny (0.5 grams; 11 mm in diameter).

Are there any unsolved mysteries about milled coins?

Many. For example, what is the significance of the word 'Lima' on some George II coins? What does the star mean on some Edinburgh mint Anne silver coins? What was the purpose of the 1847 Gothic crown — was it struck for the tenth anniversary of the accession? Who designed the early William and Mary heads on the half guinea?

Why are mis-strikes so inexpensive when errors on stamps fetch such high prices?

Because, as yet, there is little demand. Perhaps this is a good case for buying same (see earlier question).

Why have previous catalogues contained so many errors, or left out so much information?

You should ask their publishers.

Which common miscataloguings of milled coins has the Standard Catalogue clarified?

Many, including: the edge inscription on George I coins; the elephant symbol on William and Mary guineas; the William III guinea series; the order in which William III halfcrowns were struck; the supposedly rare variety of 1743 halfcrown reading GEORGIUS (all of them do!); the Gothic florin of 1887 with 33 arcs (does not exist); the entire Gothic florin series (with the aid of valuable work by Dickinson correcting hopelessly wrong research by others). In addition, the Standard Catalogue provides information not normally hitherto available in mainstream catalogues, e.g. edge inscriptions on five guinea pieces, weights, diameters and axis alignments on milled coins.

So, is the Standard Catalogue perfect?

By no means. It would be impossible to produce a work without errors. However, there should be fewer (in some cases, far fewer) than in other catalogues, and we are anxious to correct any that occur. If anything that you have pointed out to us is not in this edition, it is because verification has not yet been undertaken, or because a correction is not considered appropriate for some reason.

Where do we go from here?

You tell us.

Allan Hailstone

Hammered Coins
1066 to 1662

Introduction to Hammered Coinage

The pleasure and skill of discovering and collecting coins is greatly enhanced by an understanding of their underlying history, of the conflicts seen during various reigns and the inherent problems of producing hammered coinage. With this in mind, we will try to provoke your interest and understanding with the following brief historical summary.

Nearly all issues produced until 1662 were hammered. As the name suggests, they were made by placing the flan for the coin between two dies and striking the top die with a hammer so that the detail from the dies would be impressed on the flan of the coin. By law, the face value of the coin corresponded to its precious metal content and so, for example, a coin valued at twenty shillings would have to contain twenty shillings' worth of precious metal. If a coin was underweight or of low fineness it was in effect not worth its face value and, by issuing such inferior coins, a dishonest moneyer could make extra profit. This problem was addressed by having the name of the moneyer and mint included in the reverse legend so that any substandard coins could be attributed to their maker – a practice which continued up to the reign of Henry III and a few issues of Edward I. The details of all mints are to be found in the relevant chapters, but the collector might note that, as a general rule, the moneyer's name is found first on all issues and is usually followed by 'on' (meaning 'of') and the name of the mint. So, for example, the reverse legend might read 'Ricard on Lund', i.e. Richard (moneyer's name) of London (mint). It should also be stressed that in virtually all issues the mint names were not spelt as they are today and, to further complicate matters, the spelling often varied for each class or moneyer. Although we have listed all the mints and the known abbreviations and spellings with each issue, it is possible, particularly in the early issues, that some spellings and abbreviations have not been included. This is due primarily to the fact that many of these issues are rare and have not been recorded and, in such a case, a collector would need to use the process of elimination and possibly consult more specialist books.

In virtually all hammered issues the bust of the reigning monarch is to be found on the obverse with his or her name and, normally, title in the legend. The reverse usually bears some design and often the name of the town in which the coin was minted. We have enclosed the full obverse legend for all issues and accompanied it by a translation as, with the exception of the Commonwealth issues (1649 – 60), the legends are in Latin. Again however, a considerable number of dies were produced for a single issue and this often resulted in discrepancies and irregularities in spelling. Collectors should bear in mind that in such a case a coin with a different spelling may not necessarily be any more rare or valuable than the issues we have listed.

The other problem which plagued the hammered coinage was *clipping*, the fraudulent practice of cutting small parts off the edge of the coin. Individuals would then pass the coin on, having made a profit for themselves and a loss to the Crown. Clipped coins are worth less to collectors too. As each coin is different, it is difficult to value but a badly clipped coin might be worth up to 75% less than an unclipped one. The inexperienced collector should use the information in this book to ascertain the correct size of a coin to avoid unknowingly buying a clipped coin.

During most reigns, hammered coins from other European countries circulated freely in England as they were used in trade. Although such issues were only worth their weight in silver, English coins were, for most reigns, very highly prized in Europe because of their superior quality in both production and fineness. Since this often meant that large quantities of English coins ended up in Europe, during many reigns it was actually illegal to export English coins although it would appear that the law was difficult to enforce. As the value of silver rose over the years, speculators and merchants were often one step ahead of the moneyers and mints who produced coins with a metal content higher than their value, something which obviously cost many monarchs dearly. But since most monarchs were keen to produce coins of good metal content and a high value, this particular problem was never satisfactorily resolved.

The historical period covered in this book begins in 1066 with the ascendancy to the English throne of William the Conqueror. Born in 1027 and the illegitimate son of Duke Robert the Devil and a tanner's daughter, William based his claim to the throne on a promise made to him by the then king, Edward the Confessor, who was his second cousin. However, upon Edward's death in 1066, a Council of barons appointed to designate a successor elected Edward's brother-in-law, Harold Godwinson, instead. William launched an invasion from Normandy and, in the ensuing battle of Hastings, Harold was killed and his army defeated, whereupon the Council prudently decided to offer the throne to William. Crowned on Christmas Day 1066, he reigned for twenty-one years until his death in 1087 and had four sons and five daughters from his marriage to Matilda of Flanders.

William I's coinage saw very little change from previous issues, with the silver penny being the only coin produced. But, as the penny had a fairly high value, there was need for smaller denominations, a problem that merchants and traders solved by legally cutting coins in half and quarters and thus producing halfpennies and farthings. Coins constituted a political statement for a monarch and William I, wishing the entire country to be aware that he was king, had over fifty mints producing coins. A total of eight main types were issued, the most popular and common being the Pax, or Peace, issue which was struck during the end of his reign and reflected his feelings and hopes for the country. Yet, because the dies used by the provincial mints for most hammered issues were made in London and despatched to the mints, considerable control was exercised over the entire country's coinage and a degree of conformity in style and issues prevailed.

William the Conqueror left the English throne to his third and favourite son, William II nicknamed Rufus because of his flaming red hair. Born in 1056, Rufus ascended the throne in 1087 and reigned until 1100 when he was killed by a stray arrow in what might have been a hunting accident or an act of murder.

In terms of style, William II's coins were very much a continuation from his father's issues. They are, however, much scarcer since fewer mints were active probably because enough coins had been struck during William I's reign.

William II never married, nor did he leave any offspring so when he died in 1100, the throne went to his brother, Henry I (b. 1068) the fourth son of William the Conqueror. Henry I reigned for thirty-five years and was married twice; his first wife, Matilda of Scotland, bore him a daughter while his second wife, Adela of Louvain, a son.

Henry I's reign was a problematic time for England's coinage. The strict controls enforced during the reign of William I were, for the most part, disregarded, and this resulted in many moneyers producing quantities of coins that were underweight or of low metal fineness. The public, always wary of undervalued coins, often clipped the edges of a coin to inspect the silver inside it and thus exacerbated the situation, as people would not accept coins with clipped edges. In 1108 – 09 an extraordinary decision was taken, probably in desperation, to officially mutilate coins on the grounds that if they were clipped at the time of striking it would make them acceptable. But as this did not increase confidence in the coinage, in 1124 Henry I summoned all the moneyers to what became known as the 'Assize of the Moneyers' in Winchester.

They were required to explain their activities to him and many were severely punished for producing coins of inferior quality. During Henry I's reign a total of fifteen different issues were struck, the most common being the last two. This period also saw the re-introduction of the halfpenny which was produced at the Winchester mint and is extremely rare because very few coins were circulated.

After the death of his son and heir in 1120, Henry I nominated his daughter Matilda as his successor. But upon his death in 1135, the Council decided that a woman was unfit to rule and Stephen of Blois was offered the throne. Born in 1097, Stephen was Henry's nephew and William the Conqueror's grandson and reigned for nineteen years. It was a period of intense conflict as Henry I's daughter Matilda waged war on Stephen in a struggle for the throne. Meanwhile, Stephen married Matilda of Boulogne and had a son and two daughters. It was upon the death of this son in 1153 that an agreement was reached between Stephen and Matilda: Stephen would continue to reign until his death, where-upon Matilda's son would succeed him. He died in 1154.

The turbulence which marked Stephen's reign was reflected in the coinage, although some coins were produced, mainly from the South East mints which remained loyal to the king. These issues, which are all pennies, are very crude in style and design. At the same time Matilda, as well as some powerful barons, also produced coins. All issues are extremely rare and reflect the power struggle taking place at this time.

The death of Stephen saw the end of Norman rule as the throne passed to Henry of Anjou, the eldest son of Matilda and Geoffrey Plantagenet, Count of Anjou. Born in 1133 and ascending the throne in 1154 as Henry II, he became the first in a long line of fourteen Plantagenet kings whose name derives from 'planta genista', or yellow bloom, which Henry II's father wore in his helmet and was later incorporated in the family coat of arms. The Plantagenets consist of three related families: the Angevins (of Anjou), the Lancastrians (of Lancaster), and the Yorkists (of York).

Henry II, an Angevin, reigned for thirty-five years. Married to Eleanor of Aquitaine, he had five sons and three daughters. His reign saw the restoration of law and order amongst the population although the king lost his conflict with the Church in England. The church was determined to remain independent of royal power and the murder of Archbishop Thomas à Becket, with whom Henry had quarrelled bitterly over this issue, determined the outcome. Becket was murdered at Canterbury Cathedral in 1170 by men believing they were acting under Henry's instructions; the church gained a martyr and retained its independence.

Numismatically, Henry II's reign can be split into two main issues. Firstly there is the cross-and-crosslet coinage or Tealby issue – the name originating from a large hoard of these coins found at Tealby in Lincolnshire. There are six minor varieties of this issue. The obverse shows the king holding a sceptre and the reverse a large cross with a crosslet in each quarter. These coins were struck at some thirty mints but, being of very poor quality and strike, they were, as the issues from previous reigns, unacceptable. In an attempt to improve the quality, the short cross coinage was introduced in 1180. This issue lasted until 1247, being struck during the reigns of Richard I, John and part of Henry III's reign.

Upon Henry II's death in 1189 his second eldest son, Richard I (b. 1157), ascended the throne. Richard the Lionheart, 'Coeur-de-Lion', was a soldier, a crusader, and spent only ten months of his ten-year reign in England. He married Berengaria of Navarre but had no children. Control of England was left in the hands of Deputies who skilfully thwarted the intrigues of Richard's brother John. However, when Richard died in 1199, John, the fourth son of Henry II, ascended the throne and reigned for seventeen years. John's reign saw the loss of most of England's possessions in France, high taxation, misrule and finally a quarrel with the Church which led to the king's excommunication. The Church in Rome triumphed over John in its demand for rights for the people. In 1215, at Runnymede, the *Magna Carta*, stating these rights, was sealed by John. He broke his word. The nobility, with

aid from France organised an invasion. John died during the midst of this in 1216.

John's coinage showed the king's bust with a sceptre on the obverse and a small cross with four pellets in each quarter on the reverse and was very similar to the previous two reigns. For all four reigns the obverse legend reads HENRICUS — Henry. Possibly conformity had gone too far since as reigns changed the name of the king on the coin did not. Fewer mints were active during John's reign and it was the London and Canterbury mints which produced huge quantities of coins while provincial mints and dies for the coins were controlled from London. Constant improvement in transportation allowed for the easier distribution of coins around the country which meant that there was decreasing need for provincial mints. All short cross issues, because of the obverse legend and reverse cross, are fairly similar and the collector might find identifying the reign difficult. However, each reign had various issues, all of which are different. These minor varieties often consist of small differences in the lettering or style which was a form of quality control, allowing coins to be linked to specific dies should there be a problem with their weight or fineness. In the relevant chapters we have listed all the varieties, so the collector will be able to identify an issue.

King John was married twice and had two sons by his first wife, Isabelle of Gloucester, and three daughters by his second, Isabelle of Angouleme. John's son Henry III (b. 1207), ascended the throne in 1216 but, until he came of age in 1227, the government was controlled by deputies and it was they who succeeded in expelling the French invaders. Once again an unsatisfactory king ruled and from 1258 England saw the return of civil unrest. Henry III reigned for 56 years and married Eleanor of Provence with whom he had four sons and two daughters.

During the short cross coinage of Henry III the London mint produced silver halfpennies and farthings, which are now extremely rare. However, the need for smaller denominations was still met by cutting pennies into halves and quarters. The short cross coinage proved a tremendous success although its one flaw was that the cross on the reverse did not extend to the edge of the coin and so the public could not know how large the penny should be – which became especially confusing when the size was reduced during the reigns. This inconsistency allowed dishonest individuals to clip coins for profit with the inevitable result that underweight coins were in circulation, creating a dissatisfied public. In an effort to solve this problem, the long cross coinage was introduced in 1247. It was fairly similar to the short cross coinage, but had a long cross on the reverse that extended to the edge of the coin, breaking the legend, and this helped reduce clipping. This issue has many minor varieties. Also, for some time there had been a feeling in the country that a larger denomination was needed as, not only were several European states issuing gold coins during this period, but also gold Byzantine and Arabic coins, brought back from the Crusades, were in circulation. In response, Henry III instructed William of Gloucester to strike a gold twenty pence piece. The superb coin produced showed the king enthroned on the obverse and a long cross with a flower and pellets in each quarter on the reverse. Unfortunately, while beautifully designed, this issue was doomed because rising gold prices resulted in its gold content value outstripping its face value and so most of it was melted down on the Continent. The short and long cross coinages were popular and huge quantities of coins were produced. At last the population had coins they could trust and, when a coin was worn down, it could be exchanged at the mint for a new one and this further boosted public confidence in the coinage.

In 1272 Henry III died and his son Edward I (b. 1239) came to the throne. During his thirty-five year reign, Edward exhibited considerable abilities as a soldier, statesman and lawmaker, focusing particularly upon the workings of parliament and the judiciary. However, Edward's determination to rule an undivided nation was thwarted as both Wales and Scotland claimed independence. Wales was conquered but until his death in 1307 Edward waged an unsuccessful war against Scotland. Edward's first wife, Eleanor of Castile, gave him three sons and five daughters, while Margaret of France gave him two sons and one daughter.

Edward I's issues were a success, although clipping continued to be a major problem. For the first few years of Edward's reign, the long cross coinage was struck in Henry's name and, as well as being prone to clipping due to its crude strike, it was beginning to look old-fashioned. Various laws were again introduced to halt clipping but without much success so, in 1279, Edward I decided to introduce a totally new coinage, both in style and denomination. The penny was still the most important denomination, with millions of coins being produced at a total of twelve mints nationwide. At this time, the independent ecclesiastical privilege mints of York and Durham were established, coins being struck there under the control of the Archbishops who stood to make considerable profits out of such a rewarding enterprise as minting coins. Edward I's recoinage saw the introduction of the privy mark, a small detail or deformation of a detail that linked the coin to a particular die and moneyer as a form of quality control and replaced the moneyer's name, which is no longer found on the coins. With all the mints' dies except Berwick on Tweed being made in London, a conformity in style and design was achieved and there is a total of ten main types or classes, and several varieties within each class. The obverse of the coins carried the king's name and title, the reverse the mint's name – with the exception of some of the coins from Bury St Edmunds. The new denominations introduced by Edward's recoinage were the groat, halfpenny and farthing. The groat was an unpopular denomination because it was underweight; it had a value of fourpence, but four single pennies weighed more. As the public would not accept it in trade, the groat was discontinued and not reintroduced until the reign of Edward III, when it carried the correct weight and was finally a success. The farthing and halfpenny on the other hand were successful from the start, particularly as they facilitated trade and put an end to the inconvenience of having to cut coins in halves and quarters. The class system of these two denominations is slightly linked with that of the penny and both issues were struck mainly in London, although five provincial mints also produced them. Overall, Edward I's recoinage was superb in style and quality and determined the styling of coins until the reign of Henry VII. Also, the king's portrait for the first time attempted to be more of a true likeness. Yet the coinage became a victim of its own success due to its immense popularity abroad and the fact that several European countries, mainly the Low Countries, copied Edward's pennies using low grade silver. This resulted in the illegal trade of good English silver coins for inferior foreign imitations. Furthermore, clipping was rife once again in spite of various laws aimed at upholding the quality of the coins in circulation.

Edward I died in 1307 and was succeeded by his son Edward II (b. 1284) who, having inherited none of his father's qualities as a monarch, succeeded only in arousing opposition to his reign. His wife Isabella of France, who gave him two sons and two daughters, eventually deserted him; his opponents invaded England and finally, after a twenty-year reign, he abdicated in favour of his son Edward III (b. 1312). Edward II was imprisoned and, in 1327, murdered.

Edward II's coinage was very much a continuation from his father's reign. The class system of the recoinage was continued and all issues are very similar to those of Edward I. Edward III ascended the throne in 1327; married to Philippa of Hainault, they had six sons and five daughters. By 1337 he was at war with France, commencing a conflict that would span several reigns and become known as The Hundred Years War. Ostensibly the war was started in support of Edward III's claim to the French throne although controlling trade between the two countries was a decisive factor. Between 1348 – 50 the bubonic plague, or Black Death, decimated England. The war could not be maintained under such conditions and the Treaty of Brétigny was signed in 1360. After fifty years on the throne, Edward III died in 1377; only five fortified towns and accompanying lands in France remained in England's possession.

Edward III's first coinage was very much a continuation from the previous reign and all issues are rare, reflecting the shortage of bullion during this period. During the second silver coinage, however, the fineness of some issues was reduced from .925 to .833, an unpopular measure that provoked concern that English coinage would begin to imitate inferior European standards. Nevertheless, as several European states had successfully introduced gold coinage, Edward wished to do likewise and in 1343 engaged two Florentine engravers, George Kirkyn and Lotte Nicholyn, for this purpose. They produced three superb gold coins: the double leopard, the leopard and the helm. But it was necessary to ensure that the face value and metal content of the new coins accurately reflected the difference in bullion value between gold and silver; thus, for example, a gold coin with a face value of twenty pence would have to have a gold content equivalent to the value of twenty silver pennies. Unfortunately the new issue had been overvalued, so the coins were not worth their weight in gold and they were a failure. Although fairly large quantities of coins had been produced, most were melted down and it is hardly surprising that they are now extremely rare. Yet despite this setback, Edward III still wanted to introduce some gold denominations because England was beginning to fall behind in Europe and gold coins would greatly facilitate trade. In 1344 Percival of Lucca joined the royal mint and as a result the gold noble and quarter noble were introduced later that year, to be followed by the gold half noble in 1346. The gold noble had a value of 6s 8d (or eighty pence), the half noble forty pence. These superb issues showed the king in a ship on the obverse, while the reverse carried an ornate design. The quarter noble, with a value of twenty pence, was a small coin and only showed the royal shield on the obverse. But, as the first two issues were overweight, in 1351 the weight of all three denominations was reduced bringing them in line with their face value. This eliminated the profitability of overweight coins being melted down. The gold noble was a great success and happily accepted in Europe; it was in use until the reign of Edward IV. The groat and halfgroat were successfully introduced in 1351 with a value of fourpence and twopence respectively. The moneyers had accurately gauged weights and fineness, so the discerning public happily accepted these new denominations. The obverse for both denominations shows a crowned bust of the king and the reverse a long cross with three pellets in each quarter and two legends, the outer legend being a religious statement, the inner one the mint. Although Edward III's reign is very complicated numismatically because there are many varieties within the issues, it also saw the full introduction of the mintmark which is a symbol, or depiction of an object and found on the obverse and/or reverse, at the beginning of the legends. Mintmarks were a form of quality control, linking dies to coins and, with documentary and hoard evidence, many issues can be accurately dated. The mintmark was a popular idea and was used on nearly all hammered coins until the reign of Charles II. Several mints were active during Edward III's reign, the most notable ones being York and Calais in France, which was under English rule. There are many varieties in the obverse legends reflecting the changing fortunes occurring in the war with France. As with all varieties and issues, they are dealt with in great detail in the relevant chapters.

Edward III's eldest son Edward the Black Prince died a year before his father, so his son Richard (b. 1367) ascended the throne in 1377 and reigned for twenty-two years as Richard II. However, until he came of age, the country was ruled by the Royal Council which was led by Richard's uncle, Edward III's son, John of Gaunt. Neither Edward's first wife, Anne of Bohemia, nor his second, Isabella of France, gave him a child. Richard's succession to the throne saw the start of the Wars of the Roses, otherwise known as the Cousins' War, a fierce struggle for the crown undertaken by John of Gaunt and, after his death, by his son Henry of Bolingbroke, who finally succeeded in deposing Richard II in 1399. The latter was imprisoned and, in 1400, murdered. This was merely the beginning of the Cousins' War; it was to affect the reigns of several English kings up to Henry VII.

Richard II's coinage was very much a continuation in style and denominations to that of Edward III. All issues are fairly scarce, if not rare, and very few coins were produced in any quantity, probably due to there being sufficient coins in circulation from the reign of Edward III while the continuing war with France caused a bullion shortage.

Henry IV, Henry Bolingbroke of Lancaster (b. 1367), ascended the throne in 1399 and with his coronation comes the end of the Angevin line and the start of the Lancastrian. Henry's first wife was Mary de Bohun, his second Joan of Brittany; he had four sons and two daughters. The dispute over the rightful heir to the throne continued during his reign and England saw rebellions and Civil War.

By the time Henry IV came to the throne England's coinage was in a serious situation. There was a severe shortage of bullion because, compared with European issues, the coinage was undervalued and so English coins were constantly been drained away into other countries to be melted down for profit. In 1412 it was decided to reduce the weight of all coins; the gold issues were reduced by ten per cent, the silver by about sixteen per cent. The two coinages for this reign are, therefore, called the Heavy and Light coinage. All issues from this reign are very rare.

By the time Henry IV died, in 1413, the rebellions had been quelled allowing his son Henry V (b. 1387) to inherit the throne. Henry V renewed the war with France and the defeat of the French at Agincourt led to further successes, culminating in Henry V's marriage to Catherine of Valois, daughter of Charles VI, King of France, who also acknowledged Henry as his rightful heir and thus denying his son, the Dauphin, the right of succession. In 1422 Henry V died, leaving his son Henry VI to inherit the thrones.

During Henry V's reign the coinage improved, both in quality and quantity. This was due, in part, to the reduced weight introduced in Henry IV's reign. The success England was enjoying in its conflict with France was also a factor. The mintmark system, as well as other marks, continued. This resulted in the enforcing of good quality control.

In 1422 Henry VI inherited the English and, within a few months, the French throne. He had not yet celebrated his first birthday. A Council, led by his uncle Humphrey of Gloucester, ruled until Henry came of age. Inevitably there was war with France, which finally ended in 1453 by which time England had lost all of its French possessions with the exception of Calais. In 1445 Henry VI married Margaret of Anjou, who gave him a son. Unfortunately Henry VI had inherited the madness that ran in his mother's family. The illness overtook him in 1454, whereupon Richard, Duke of York and next in line to the throne after Henry's baby son, was appointed Regent. This appointment reopened the old conflict for the throne. Henry VI's recovery after a year saw him in control once again but open hostilities now broke out between the Houses of York and Lancaster. During this period of conflict Richard, Duke of York was killed. It was Richard's son Edward (b. 1442) who defeated the Lancastrians. In 1461 Edward, Duke of York, deposed Henry VI and became king as Edward IV. Henry VI was restored to the throne in 1470 but his second reign only lasted until 1471.

The first few years of Henry VI's first reign saw a plentiful supply of gold and silver. This resulted in large quantities of gold and silver coins being produced. The denominations were very much a continuation from the previous reign. The Calais mint, still under English rule, produced large quantities of gold and silver coins. Calais was used for two reasons; firstly as a political statement, confirming that England ruled this part of France and secondly to facilitate trade between England and Europe. As with the previous issue, mintmarks, as well as other marks, can be found. These will help the collector identify, date and class this issue correctly.

Having deposed Henry VI, Edward IV became the first Yorkist king. Edward reigned between 1461 – 70 and 1471 – 83. He married Elizabeth Woodville, who gave him two sons and seven daughters. Between 1461 – 70 Edward IV was occupied with various intrigues aimed at removing him from the throne and in

1470 his enemies prevailed, forcing him to flee the country. Henry VI returned to the throne.

Edward IV's first reign inherited the problem of a lack of bullion. So, in 1464, the weight of all silver coins was reduced by twenty per cent. The gold noble was replaced by a similar, but slightly heavier, coin called the rose noble or ryal. This coin had a lower metal content, and had a value of ten shillings. It was not to be a popular denomination. The gold angel, with a value of six shillings and eightpence, was introduced. The angel showed St Michael spearing a dragon on the obverse and a ship on the reverse. The reduction in the weights of the coins allowed the production of large quantities of coins. There was an urgent need for coinage, so several old mints were reopened.

Henry VI, imprisoned in the Tower of London from 1465, was restored to the throne in 1470. However, during this short reign, Henry was at war with Edward IV. This conflict resulted in the death of Henry VI's son, Prince Edward, and finally Henry's capture. Once again Henry VI was imprisoned in the Tower, where he was murdered in 1471.

The coinage of Henry VI's second reign was very much a continuation from Edward IV's. The unpopular rose noble, or ryal, had been discontinued. However, the angel, with the value of the old noble, was popular. Henry VI's second reign saw the introduction of the half angel. As one would expect, from such a short reign, very few coins were produced.

Edward IV's return to the throne, unsurprisingly, brought little change to the coinage. The angel and half angel were now important denominations and replaced the nobles and half nobles of previous reigns.

Upon Edward IV's death in 1483, his son, Edward V, inherited the throne. His was to be one of the shortest reigns. Edward V (b. 1470) was too young to rule so a Council, which included some of his uncles, took control. One of these uncles, Richard, Duke of Gloucester, seized the opportunity to usurp the Boy King. Richard crushed any opposition from the Queen-mother's family, imprisoned both Edward V and his only brother in the Tower of London and within a few months of Edward V's accession, had claimed the throne. Both Edward V and his brother were murdered in the Tower and Richard III was considered responsible for this infamous act.

Coins were issued during Edward V's brief reign. They are virtually identical to those of Edward IV. On the obverse of Edward V's coinage is the mintmark boar's head, while the reverse had the mintmark halved sun and rose. It is thought that issues with the mintmark halved sun and rose on the obverse and reverse were struck during Edward V's reign.

Richard III (b. 1452) reigned between 1483 – 85. He was married to Anne Neville, with whom he had one son. His usurpation of the throne alienated many nobles who had previously supported him and the murder of Richard's nephews in the Tower added to his unpopularity throughout the country. Henry, Earl of Richmond, to whom the Lancastrian claim to the throne had descended and who was exiled in Brittany, invaded. Richmond, and his supporters triumphed. This was to be the last important conflict in the War of the Roses. Richard III was killed in battle. Richmond became King Henry VII.

Richard III's coinage is very similar to previous reigns, but bears his own name.

Henry VII (b. 1457), the son of Edmund Tudor, ascended the throne in 1485. In 1486 Henry married Elizabeth of York, the eldest daughter of Edward IV. This marriage united the claims of Lancaster and York, the War of the Roses was over and the reign of Tudor kings began. Henry VII reigned for twenty-four years. From his marriage he had two sons and two daughters. Henry's aim was to bring peace and prosperity to England. Henry forged alliances with Spain and Scotland through the arranged marriages of his son and daughter. His son Arthur married the Spanish princess, Catherine of Aragon. His daughter Margaret married King James IV of Scotland. This reign was to see the end of medieval England and the beginning of the Renaissance.

During Henry VII's reign the gold sovereign, with a value of twenty shillings, was produced. This coin was the forerunner of the pound coin of today. The gold sovereign showed the king enthroned on the obverse. The reverse carried the royal arms over a rose. The gold Sovereign is rare. Gold angels and half angels were produced in large quantities. These denominations were the main gold coins circulating in England at this time. The first issues of Henry VII's silver coinage were very similar to previous reigns. This silver coinage included groats, halfgroats, pennies, halfpennies and farthings. Henry VII's early issues reflected the virtual uniformity seen since the reign of Edward III. On the Continent, however, the style of coinage was changing. It was decided that the English coinage should reflect this change in style. In 1494 Alexander of Brugsal, a German, was appointed as engraver to the mint in London. It was Alexander who developed the superb silver 'profile' issue. This issue showed a lifelike crowned portrait of the king on the obverse, while the reverse showed the royal arms over a cross. The testoon, with a value of twelve pence, was first produced during this reign. However, all specimens are very rare. The testoon was later to become known as the shilling. The groat and halfgroat were produced and in far larger quantities. All groats were struck at the Tower mint but the halfgroats were also struck at Canterbury and York. The style of the penny also changed as the obverse now showed the king enthroned and the reverse the royal shield. These pennies became known as sovereign pennies. In all issues the mintmark system continued, linking dies with a particular issue. This also means that the coins can be accurately dated, usually within a year or so.

The death of Henry VII in 1509 saw Henry VIII ascend the throne. Henry VII's eldest son Arthur had died in 1502. Henry VIII (b. 1491) was contracted to marry his brother's widow, Catherine of Aragon who thus became the first of Henry VIII's six wives. The fate of these wives reads as follows: divorced, beheaded, died, divorced, beheaded, survived (as the king died first), but only the first three marriages produced heirs, two daughters and a son in all. It was Henry VIII's first divorce which saw the beginning of the Reformation. The Pope refused to accept Henry's right to divorce. Henry broke ties with Rome. With the support of Parliament, Henry assumed the title of Protector and Supreme Head of the Church and Clergy of England. There followed the Dissolution of the Monasteries, which served two purposes, while further eradicating Roman jurisdiction, it stripped the monasteries of their wealth. Henry VIII reigned for thirty-eight years. The monarchy was technically constitutional, but Henry's power was practically absolute.

Henry VIII's first coinage, 1509 – 25, hardly changed in style from his father's. The only slight differences being the obverse legend, and the mintmarks. In 1526, however, the value of all gold coins was increased by about ten per cent. This was in response to the rising price of bullion. It would prevent gold coins vanishing into Europe. The sovereign now had a value of twenty-two shillings and sixpence, the gold angel a value of seven shillings and sixpence. Several new denominations were also introduced. Firstly there was the George noble with a value of six shillings and eightpence, then the half-George noble, followed by the gold crown of the rose, with a value of four shillings and sixpence. All three issues were very unpopular and were not continued. During the second coinage the gold crown and gold halfcrown were introduced with a value of five shillings and two shillings and sixpence respectively. Each issue showed a rose with a crown above on the obverse; the reverse showed a crown above the shield. The style of the silver coins was changed for the second coinage. The groat and halfgroat had a new, more mature bust of the king. Once Henry was in control of the Church he closed the Church's privilege mints. From this point on all mints were to be controlled by the king. Towards the end of Henry VIII's reign the third coinage was introduced. It was probably the most unpopular coinage ever to be produced by a monarch. Henry VIII's finances were in a shambles, due mainly to his extravagances. To increase revenue it was decided to drastically reduce the silver content of all silver coins. By the end of the third coinage, the 'silver' coins had a two-thirds copper content. For the first time in England's

history, the coins were not worth their metal content. It is not surprising, therefore, that this coinage was unpopular. This issue had a new style, older bust of the king. During this issue the testoon was successfully introduced. Gold issues were also struck, and the gold half sovereign was also successfully introduced. The weights, and gold content, of these issues varied. This was due to the devaluation of the gold content.

When Henry VIII died in 1547, his son, Edward VI, ascended the throne. Born in 1537, he was too young to rule and the Duke of Somerset, his uncle and 'Protector', virtually ruled the country. Edward reigned for six years, until his death in 1553 by which time, England was established as a Protestant state. This reign saw war with Scotland and general unrest.

Three main coinages were struck during Edward's reign. Firstly there was the posthumous coinage of his father Henry VIII which was very similar to Henry's third coinage, with base issue coins being produced. Secondly, there was the base issue coins bearing Edward VI's name, heraldic arms and portrait. Thirdly, there was the fine silver issue struck in 1551 – 53 which included the first silver crown, halfcrown, sixpence and threepence. With good quality silver used, this was a major step in the improvement of English coins. The crown and halfcrown, which are both dated, show the Boy King on horseback. The shilling, sixpence and threepence show a crowned bust of the king. Edward VI's base issue silver coins were unpopular. However, the base shillings were the first English coins to be dated. Roman numerals were used for the dates. Several gold denominations were struck during Edward's reign. Most of these were a continuation from previous reigns. By the end of Edward VI's reign, good quality coins were being produced. These coins had a high metal content and weight as well as being superbly designed.

The next in succession to Edward VI was his sister, Mary who was a devout Catholic. This was used to persuade Edward to exclude Mary's claim and name Lady Jane Grey as his heir. Lady Jane's father-in-law led this plot to alter the succession. The right to the throne would now pass from the Tudors to the Dudley family. Upon Edward's death Lady Jane Grey was proclaimed queen. However, the plot failed. Within ten days Mary and her supporters had reclaimed the Tudor throne and Lady Jane's father-in-law was executed. Having originally spared Lady Jane, Mary eventually had both Jane and her husband executed. Mary I (b. 1516) ascended the throne in 1553, becoming the first queen to reign. A devout Catholic, Mary was determined to re-introduce Catholicism. And she insisted on marrying her cousin, Philip of Spain who was a fanatical Roman Catholic. Although her choice led to three insurrections, Mary was victorious and the marriage took place in 1554. During the rest of her reign Mary tried to enforce the conversion of England by ruthlessly persecuting Protestants, some of whom were burnt at the stake, and earned herself the nickname Bloody Mary. Once again England went to war against France and lost Calais.

For the first two years of Mary's reign, only her own portrait is to be found on the coins. After her marriage to Philip of Spain, both their busts are to be found on the shilling and sixpence, although only Mary's bust appears on other silver issues. However, both their names are in the legend.

When Mary died in 1558, Henry VIII's daughter from his second marriage, Elizabeth, ascended the throne. Born in 1533, she was the last of the Tudors. With Elizabeth came a return to Protestantism and by the end of her forty-four year reign England had been transformed; religious conflicts had all but disappeared, the Spanish Armada was defeated, Sir Francis Drake circumnavigated the globe. This was a period of voyage and discovery, when internal conflicts were controlled.

Elizabeth I's reign is notable for the large quantities of coins, of various denominations, produced. Initially base issue coins, from previous reigns, still circulated. Elizabeth recognised the importance of having a sound coinage. This meant coins of good weight, metal content and a variety of denominations. As an act of urgency, Elizabeth immediately ordered the base issue shillings of Edward VI to be countermarked, and then devalued. Elizabeth also ordered base issue coins to be taken in and melted down. This was an expensive exercise. However, confidence in English coins was restored. All of Elizabeth's coinage was struck in London and silver from the newly discovered Americas was often used. The silver denominations were crowns, halfcrowns, shillings, sixpences, groats, threepences, halfgroats, three-halfpence, pennies, three farthings and halfpence. Several silver issues were dated and as all issues had mintmarks on the obverse and reverse, the collector will be able to date the issue. The gold issues were very much a continuation from previous reigns. Sovereigns, now with a value of thirty shillings, pounds (twenty shillings), ryals (fifteen shillings), halfpounds, angels, half-angels, quarter-angels, crowns and halfcrowns were produced. This was the most prolific reign for the number of denominations and with this comprehensive denomination structure, Elizabeth had considered the needs of both the rich and poor.

In 1561, milled coins were issued for the first time. These coins were introduced by a Frenchman, Eloye Mestrelle, employed by the mint in London. They were struck using a screw press powered by horses and were the forerunner to the coins of today. These milled issues were superior to the hammered ones but their manufacture was slow and, moreover, Mestrelle's presence in the mint was unpopular partly because he was French but more significantly because he was seen as threatening the moneyers' employment. Mestrelle was dismissed in 1572 and the production of milled coins ceased. Mestrelle turned to counterfeiting, for which he was hanged in 1578.

In 1600, at the Tower mint, trade coins, otherwise known as portcullis money, were produced. These were struck for the company of merchants in London trading into the East Indies. These issues, which are all rare, were struck with the equivalent weight in silver to Spanish silver coins. These coins were not for circulation in England. They were issues for trade in the East Indies.

Throughout her reign Elizabeth refused to marry and in 1603 died childless. This meant that James VI of Scotland ascended the English throne as James I; he was the first Stuart king. James had married Anne of Denmark in 1589 and they had three sons and four daughters. As King of Scotland, James had had a troubled reign and he brought these troubles to the English throne so once again there was conflict between Protestant and Catholic. In the Gunpowder Plot of 1605, Catholic sympathisers attempted to blow up the king and Parliament and, although the plot failed, it caused even greater prejudice against Catholics and religious intolerance prevailed. In 1611 the authorised version of the Bible was published and in 1620 the Pilgrim Fathers set sail for the Americas, to establish a community where their beliefs could flourish.

With both England and Scotland ruled by one monarch, the design of the coins changed slightly as the Scottish title was incorporated in the legend and the Scottish arms appeared as part of the royal shield. Large quantities of coins were struck during James I's reign. The price of gold rose steadily during this period resulting in new denominations and changing values of coins. The most important denomination was the gold unite which had a value of either twenty or twenty-two shillings, depending upon when it was circulating. The name unite represents the uniting of England and Scotland. At the end of James I's reign the unite was replaced by the laurel, depicting the bust of the king wearing a laurel wreath. Other gold denominations produced were the rose ryal (thirty shillings), sovereign (twenty shillings), spur ryal (fifteen shillings), angel, half laurel, double crown (each ten shillings), Britain crown, quarter laurel, crown, half angel (each five shillings), thistle crown (four shillings) and the halfcrown (two shillings and sixpence). It is important to note that the values and weights, of some of these issues, varied with the fluctuating gold price. James I's silver coinage was also produced in some quantity and was very similar to the previous reign although fewer denominations were struck. Those produced were the crown, halfcrown, shilling, sixpence, halfgroat, penny and halfpenny. For many years the public had been demanding lower denominations. In large towns such as London the poor used lead tokens as coinage.

However, in 1613, James granted a licence to Lord Harrington, allowing him to produce copper farthings. These coins were very popular and profitable to produce. The licence was later taken over by the Duke of Lennox.

James I died in 1625 and his second son, Charles I ascended the throne. Born in 1600, Charles married Henrietta Maria of France and had four sons and five daughters. His reign saw a power struggle between king and parliament, which was dissolved three times. After the third time, in 1629, Charles proceeded to rule without Parliament. England was divided into supporters of parliament and royalists and this state of affairs lasted eleven years until Civil War erupted in 1642 and Oliver Cromwell, parliamentarian, formed an army. In 1645, Cromwell's forces crushed the royalists and a year later Charles I surrendered to the Scots who handed him over to the English. Finally in 1648, after facing a tribunal, Charles was sentenced to death; he was beheaded in 1649. The Commonwealth period extends from 1649 to 1660; Cromwell becoming Lord Protector in 1653.

Initially Charles I's coinage was very much a continuation from the previous reign. The gold angel was produced for the last time, and is very rare. The Tower mint struck the gold denominations unite, double crown and crown. The other main denominations struck at the Tower mint were crowns, halfcrowns, shillings, sixpences, halfgroats, pennies and halfpennies, as well as copper farthings. Many varieties of most issues exist. Some of the issues, particularly the shilling, were fairly poorly made. For the first time since the reign of Elizabeth I, milled coins were produced and once again it was a Frenchman, Nicholas Briot, who introduced this coinage. The Briot issues were superb in both design and production; however, the machinery was too slow in the production of the coin and the presence of Nicholas Briot in the Tower mint was unpopular. This unpopularity once again stemmed from the fact that he was a Frenchman and also because the moneyers were worried about their own employment. Mintmarks continued to be used for all issues, and the denomination for the coin could be found, for most issues, indicated in Roman numerals behind the bust. Before the Civil War, which was caused by Charles I's poor political judgement, high spending and constant arguments with Parliament, virtually all coins were struck at the Tower mint in London. However, huge quantities of farthings were struck under licence of which various varieties exist. Coins were also struck under licence at the Aberystwyth mint in Wales where large quantities of silver were being mined.

The Civil War, as one would expect, caused considerable difficulties in the production and supply of coinage. The Tower mint in London remained open but under the control of Parliament although the coins it struck still bore the portrait and name of Charles I. This shows an interesting political statement revealing the real wish for Cromwell's supporters to restore Charles I as king but with parliamentary control. Most provincial mints, such as York, Exeter, Truro, Shrewsbury, Oxford, Worcester, Chester and Bristol among others, reopened and most were in the west of England and loyal to the king. The dies for these issues were hurriedly made while several mints often shared a particular die, because the urgency of production was so great. These coins, of varying denominations, were needed to pay the troops loyal to the king as well as to supply local trade should communications with the Tower mint be cut off. Most denominations were struck at the provincial mints and this was the first time that the triple unite, with a value of sixty shillings, as well as the silver pound and halfpound were produced outside London. Most of these provincial issues carry an abbreviation of what is known as the Declaration on the reverse: RELIG PROT LEG ANG LIBER PAR, (varieties exist) which in translation reads: 'the religion of the Protestants, the laws of England, the liberty of Parliament'. During the Civil War several towns, such as Newark and Pontefract, were besieged by Cromwell and their occupants produced emergency or siege money, which usually consisted of silver plates cut into shapes, weighed and then hammered with a fairly crude design and value. Numismatically, Charles I's reign is the most complicated and possibly the most interesting. The stages of the

Civil War can almost be traced by the mints and the production of coins as the king and his army moved around the country.

During the Commonwealth dated hammered coins with legends in English were produced. All issues had the heraldic arms of St George and Ireland in them; they were very plain in style, reflecting the Puritan aesthetic values. Unites, double crowns and crowns were the gold denominations which were produced while the silver denominations were crowns, halfcrowns, shillings, sixpences, halfgroats, pennies and halfpennies. During this period, due to the shortage of small change, towns and traders issued copper and brass pennies, halfpennies and farthings in enormous quantities, to facilitate trade. Milled coins were struck with the bust of Oliver Cromwell on the coin. All issues are considered patterns; they were however produced in some quantity and many coins saw circulation. The denominations struck were fifty shillings, broad (twenty shilling) crown, halfcrown, shilling, sixpence and farthing. Many varieties of the farthing were struck. They are sometimes considered as tokens as well as patterns.

Following the death of Cromwell, Charles II, who had been living in exile during the Commonwealth period, was asked by Parliament to return and in 1660 he was restored to the English throne. Hammered coins in gold and silver were again produced in some quantity. However, with the advancement of the machinery for making milled coins, hammered coins were becoming obsolete and in 1662 hammered coins were produced for the last time.

From a personal point of view, I find the hammered coinage fascinating because of the complexities of the issues and also because of the very real links the coins had with political events and history. At the onset of this book, people asked me to make the hammered coinage easily comprehensible. This is by no means easy because the hammered coinage is so difficult to understand and also because I wanted to introduce more information into this book than has been previously published in any general book on the subject. The book also seeks to address itself both to the total beginner as well as to the advanced collector. We hope we have succeeded in keeping all collectors happy. To the new collector the whole hammered section might at first seem rather daunting and I have been asked on numerous occasions for advice on how to understand and learn about the issues. My advice is to read up as much as you can on the issues, but remember that there is no substitute for handling and looking at the actual coins. Dealers often have 'lots' of very worn hammered coins that they might sell cheaply and it might be useful as an educational exercise to identify such coins. Many previously published books recommend that collectors start with either one denomination or one reign. Such an approach does simplify some aspects of collecting but, if you are like me and find the whole series interesting, it can seem far too restrictive.

Through my research for this book I have been amazed to see how the information on and knowledge of some numismatic periods has changed over the years. This is mainly due to new hoards being found and more documentary evidence coming to light, and it is particularly true of the provincial mints of Charles I. Even while writing this book, new important issues have been found. In many respects the history of hammered coins is still being written and I am sure that there are many more issues to be discovered.

The last twenty years have been a fascinating period for hammered coinage due mainly to the use of metal detectors. With these now sophisticated machines, tens of thousands of coins have been found including very small denominations. This has produced a wealth of new information, stimulated collectors' interest and put many more coins on the market. With the redevelopment of much of London in the 1980s, huge quantities of coins were found around or in the river Thames. This has often caused problems with archaeologists, when metal detectors were illegally used on listed sites, or when finds of coins were not properly declared as treasure troves.

Finally, it should be stated that the information in this book is by no means complete. We look forward to hearing from collectors who have varieties which we have not listed. For the first time in any book we have listed all obverse and reverse legends. We know many varieties exist in these legends and we have, where possible, listed the most common.

I hope you, the collector, will find this book useful and informative and that it will bring you many happy years of collecting.

Notes to the fifth edition
During the last year the demand for hammered coins has been considerable, with many collectors buying from auction houses as well as from dealers.

Collectors are becoming increasingly more quality conscious, chasing together with dealers a dwindling supply of high grade specimens. Coins with historic links are also becoming more popular, a good example being the siege issues of Charles I which have increased in value considerably. Coins of the more famous monarchs such as Richard I and Henry VIII are also gaining popularity, often being purchased by people interested in history rather than numismatics.

The last year has seen no significant hoards or major collections enter the market, resulting in growing demand and rising prices throughout the hammered series. This situation, I feel, will continue especially with more people becoming interested in history and realising how accessible and historically important the coinage of England is.

Mark Davidson

Mintmarks

The mintmark, or privy mark as it is sometimes known, evolved during the reign of Edward III. Since Anglo-Saxon times, the need to link coins to dies and therefore moneyers and mints was strongly felt by a population worried about underweight coins of low metal fineness. After Edward I's 1279 re-coinage, the moneyer's name was omitted from the coins but, instead, marks or variations in the lettering or the king's bust were deliberately included so a coin could be accurately linked to a die. The mintmark was very much a development of this idea and from the reign of Edward III a mark of a certain style was placed on virtually all hammered coins at the beginning of the obverse legend and usually at the beginning of the reverse legend. These marks are important as, not only do they help identify a coin, but also date it more accurately.

From the moneyers' point of view, dies could now be more easily checked for wear or damage and their production could be improved. Dies from various issues were sometimes swapped, especially if only half had been damaged, often resulting in the two sides of a coin having different mintmarks; we have listed most such cases when they occur. It was also not uncommon, particularly under James I and Elizabeth I, for one mintmark to be engraved over another, thus extending the life of a die.

Below we list the various mintmarks alphabetically, with an indication of the reign(s) in which they occur. This is followed by a chronological listing, giving the specific years within each reign that a mintmark was used. The last list of mintmarks is of James I and Charles I farthings, which do not always conform to the gold and silver issues. Finally, we have illustrated all mintmarks (in alphabetical order), to help collectors with identification.

Mintmarks by Reign

0	EL
1	EL
2	EL
6	E6
A	EL
acorn	H8, EL, C1
anchor	H7, EL, C1, CW
anchor & B	C1
annulet	E4
arrow	H8, E6
B	C1
bell	EL, J1, C1
billet	C1
blackamoor's head	C1
boar's head	R3, C1
book	J1, C1
book clasped	C1
bow	E6
BR	C1
bugle	C1
castle	H8, EL, J1, C1
castle with H	H8
Catherine Wheel	H8
cinquefoil	H7, J1
cinquefoil heraldic	E4
coronet	EL, J1
crescent	H8, EL, J1
cross & four pellets	E4
cross 1 broken	E3
cross 1 pommée	E3
cross 2	E3
cross 3	E3

cross calvary	C1
cross crosslet	H7, EL
cross fleurée	H6, E4
cross floriated	C1
cross in circle	E4
cross Latin	EL
cross long fitchée	E4, H7, H8
cross patonce	H6, H8
cross pattée	JH, H3, E1, E2, E3, R2, H4, H5, H6, E4, C1
cross pierced	H5, H6, E4
cross pierced & central pellet	H5, E4
cross pierced & pellet	E4
cross plain or Greek	E3, H6, E4, H7, H8, EL, J1
cross potent	E3
cross Restoration	H6
cross saltire	J1
cross short fitchée	H6, E4
cross voided	H6, H8
crown	C1, C2
crown	E3, E4
crozier	H7
dragon	H7
E	H8, E6
eglantine	EL
ermine	EL
escallop	H7, H8, E6, EL, J1
eye	C1
eye radiate	H7
flower	H8
flower & B	C1
gerb	C1
grapes	J1, C1
grapple	H8
greyhound's head	H7
halfrose	MA
halfrose & castle	PM
hand	EL
harp	C1
heart	C1
helmet	C1
K	H8
key	H8, EL, J1
leopard's head	E6, C1
leopard's head crowned	H7
lion	E6, EL, C1
lion rampant	C1
lis	H6, E4, R3, H7, H8, E6, PM, EL, J1, C1
lis issuant from rose	H7
lis rose dimidiated	H7
lis upon half rose	H7
lis upon sun & rose	H7
lozenge	C1
martlet	H7, H8, E6, EL, C1
mullet	J1, C1
mullet pierced	E6
ostrich's head	E6
P in brackets	C1
pall	E4
pansy	E4, H7, H8
pear	C1
pellet in annulet	E4, H8
pellet or pellets	C1
plume	C1

plume	C1
pomegranate	H8, MA
portcullis	EL, C1
portcullis crowned	H8
R in brackets	C1
rose	E4, H6, R3, H7, H8, E6, EL, J1, C1
rosette	C1
S.	H8
sceptre	C1
spur rowel	H8, J1
star	H8, EL, C1
star curved	H8
star radiant	H8
sun	C1, CW
sun	E4
sun halved & rose	E4, E5, R3, H7
sunburst	H8
swan	E6
sword	EL
T	H8, E6
TC	H8, E6
thistle	J1
trefoil	H6, E4, H8, J1
triangle	C1
triangle in circle	C1
tun	H7, E6, EL, J1, C1
two lions	C1
uncertain	H8
woolpack	EL
WS	H8
y or Y	E6

Mintmarks for gold & silver coins

Edward III

cross plain	uncertain
cross pattée (6)	1334 – 51
cross 1	1351 – 52
cross 1 broken	1352 – 53
cross 2	1354 – 55
crown	1356
cross 3	1356 – 61
cross potent	1361 – 69
cross pattée	1369 – 77

Richard II

cross pattée	1377 – 99

Henry IV

cross pattée	1399 – 1413

Henry V

cross pattée	uncertain
cross pierced	uncertain
cross pierced with pellet centre	uncertain

Henry VI 1st Reign

lis	uncertain
cross fleurée	uncertain
cross pierced	1422 – 27
cross pommée	1422 – 34
cross plain	1422 – 60
cross patonce	1427 – 34
cross voided	1434 – 35
lis	1460

Edward IV 1st Reign

lis	1461 – 64
cross fleury	1461 – 64
cross plain	1461 – 64
rose	1464 – 65
pall	1464 – 67
sun	1465 – 66
sun	1467 – 68
crown	1467 – 69
lis	1467 – 70
rose	1468 – 69
cross long fitchée	1469 – 70
sun	1469 – 70

Henry VI Restored

cross pattée	1470 – 71
cross Restoration	1470 – 71
cross short fitchée	1470 – 71
lis	1470 – 71
rose	1470 – 71
trefoil	1470 – 71

Edward IV 2nd Reign

sun halved & rose	uncertain
cross short fitchée	1471
annulet	1471 – 72
trefoil	1471 – 72
pansy	1471 – 73
lis	1471 – 83
rose	1471 – 83
annulet small	1472 – 73
sun	1472 – 73
cross & 4 pellets	1473 – 77
cross 1 pierced	1473 – 77
cross in circle	1473 – 77
cross pattée	1473 – 77
pellet in annulet	1473 – 77
cross 1 pierced & pellet	1477 – 80
cross 2 pierced	1477 – 80
cross pierced & central pellet	1477 – 80
cinquefoil heraldic	1480 – 83
cross long fitchée	1480 – 83

Edward IV or V

sun halved & rose	1483?

Edward V

boar's head	1483?
sun halved & rose	1483

Richard III

boar's head	1483 – 85
lis	1483 – 85
rose	1483 – 85
sun halved & rose	1483 – 85

Henry VII

lis rose dimidiated	1485 – 87
lis upon halfrose	1485 – 87
lis upon sun & rose	1485 – 87
rose	1485 – 87
sun halved & rose	1485 – 87
cross fitchée	1487

lis	1487
cross plain	1487 – 88
no marks	1488 – 89
cinquefoil	1489 – 93
crozier	1489 – 93
cross fitchée	1492
dragon	1493 – 95
escallop	1493 – 95
lis	1493 – 98
tun	1493 – 98
pansy	1495 – 98
leopard's head crowned	1498
lis issuant from rose	1498
tun	1498
anchor	1499 – 1502
greyhound's head	1502 – 04
lis	1502 – 04
martlet	1502 – 09
cross crosslet	1504 – 05
rose	1504 – 09
pheon	1505 – 09

Henry VIII

star radiant	1509 – 23
castle	1509 – 26
castle with H	1509 – 26
cross fitchée	1509 – 26
martlet	1509 – 26
pomegranate	1509 – 26
portcullis crowned	1509 – 26
lis	1509 – 44
pheon	1509 – 44
rose	1509 – 44
T crowned	1513 – 18
cross voided	1514 – 26
escallop	1514 – 26
pansy	1514 – 26
star	1514 – 26
spur rowel	1523 – 26
crescent	1526 – 29
flower 8 petals	1526 – 29
trefoil	1526 – 29
acorn	1526 – 30
cross	1526 – 30
cross patonce	1526 – 36
uncertain mark	1526 – 36
arrow	1526 – 44
star	1526 – 44
sunburst	1526 – 44
star radiant	1529 – 44
key	1530 – 44
Catherine Wheel	1533 – 44
E	1544 – 47
pellet in annulet	1544 – 47
S	1544 – 47
WS monogram	1546 – 49
annulet & pellet	1547
arrow	1547 – 49
E Roman	1547 – 49
K	1547 – 49
lis	1547 – 49
bow	1548 – 49
grapple	1549
rose	1549
TC monogram	1549
t	1549 – 50
martlet	1550 – 51

Edward VI

bow	1548 – 49
arrow	1549
grapple	1549
E Roman	1549
pheon	1549
t or T	1549
TC monogram	1549
swan	1549 – 50
Y	1549 – 50
6	1549 – 50
rose	1549 – 51
leopard's head	1550
martlet	1550
lion	1550 – 51
lis	1550 – 51
ostrich's head	1551
Y or y	1551
tun	1551 – 53
escallop	1551 – 53
mullet pierced	1552 – 53

Mary

halfrose	1553 – 54
pomegranate	1553 – 54

Philip & Mary

halfrose & castle	1554 – 58
lis	1554 – 58

Elizabeth I

lis	1558 – 60
cross crosslet	1560 – 61
martlet	1560 – 61
star	1560 – 66
pheon	1561 – 65
rose	1565
portcullis	1566
lion	1566 – 67
coronet	1567 – 70
lis	1567 – 70
castle	1569 – 71
ermine	1572 – 73
acorn	1573 – 74
eglantine	1573 – 77
cross Greek	1578 – 79
cross Latin	1580 – 81
sword	1582
bell	1582 – 83
A	1582 – 84
escallop	1584 – 86
crescent	1587 – 89
hand	1590 – 92
tun	1591 – 95
woolpack	1594 – 96
key	1595 – 98
anchor	1598 – 1600
0	1600
1	1601 – 02
2	1602

James I

thistle	1603 – 04
lis	1604 – 05
rose	1605 – 06
escallop	1606 – 07

grapes	1607
coronet	1607 – 09
key	1609 – 10
bell	1610 – 11
mullet	1611 – 12
tower	1612 – 13
trefoil	1613
cinquefoil	1613 – 15
tun	1615 – 16
book on lectern	1616 – 17
crescent	1617 – 18
cross plain	1618 – 19
cross saltire	1619
spur rowel	1619 – 20
rose	1620 – 21
thistle	1621 – 23
lis	1623 – 24
trefoil	1624

Charles I

lis	1625
cross calvary	1625 – 26
blackamoor's head	1626 – 27
castle	1627 – 28
anchor	1628 – 29
heart	1629 – 30
plume	1630 – 31
flower & B	1631 – 32
rose	1631 – 32
harp	1632 – 33
portcullis	1633 – 34
bell	1634 – 35
crown	1635 – 36
tun	1636 – 38
anchor	1638 – 39
anchor & B or mullet	1638 – 39
book	1638 – 42
triangle	1639 – 40
star	1640 – 41
triangle in circle	1641 – 43
bugle	1642 – 43
lion	1642 – 44
rose	1642 – 45
lis	1642 – 46
pellets or pellet	1642 – 46
plume	1642 – 46
acorn	1643
castle	1643
cross pattée	1643
helmet	1643
bird	1643 – 44
boar's head	1643 – 44
grapes bunch of	1643 – 44
leopard's head	1643 – 44
lion rampart	1643 – 44
lions two	1643 – 44
lis	1643 – 44
P in brackets	1643 – 44
rosette	1643 – 44
Br.	1643 – 45
pellets	1643 – 45
rosette	1643 – 45
cross floriated	1643 – 46
billet	1644
cross pattée	1644
lozenge	1644
mullet	1644
castle	1644 – 45
gerb	1644 – 45
pear	1644 – 45
R in brackets	1644 – 45

A	1645
eye	1645
sun	1645 – 46
B	1646
sceptre	1646 – 48
crown	1648 – 49

Commonwealth

sun	1649 – 57
anchor	1658 – 60

Cromwell

Charles II

crown	1660 – 62
none	1660 – 62

Mintmarks of James I & Charles I Farthings

As many of these mintmarks do not conform to the silver and gold issues, they have been listed separately. Accurate dating is uncertain and if the mintmarks are badly blundered or not listed here, the coin in question is probably a forgery.

James I Farthing
Harrington Type (1613 – 1614)

cinquefoil	martlet
crescent	millrind
cross saltire	mullet
ermine	pellet
lis	trefoil

Lennox Type (1614 – 1625 exact date uncertain)

A	lion passant
annulet	lion rampant
ball	lis
bell	mascle
coronet	quatrefoil
crescent	rose
cross fitchée	star
cross pattée	stirrup
dagger	thistle head
eagle's head	trefoil
flower	triangle
grapes	tun
	woolpack

Charles I Farthing
Royal & Maltravers Issues (1625 – 1642)

A	fusil two
annulet	gauntlet
annulet with pellet centre	halberd
bell	harp
book	heart
cinquefoil	horseshoe
crescent	leaf
cross calvary	lion passant
cross patonce	lion rampant
cross pattée	lis
cross pattée fitchée	martlet

cross saltire
cross with pellets in angles
dagger
ermine
estoile
estoile pierced
eye
fish hook
fleece
fusil

nautilus
quatrefoil
rose
shield
spearhead
three lis
tower
trefoil
woolpack
woolpack over annulet

Rose Farthing (1636 – 1644?)

crescent
cross pattée
lis

martlet
mullet

Illustrations of mintmarks

0

1

acorn

anchor

anchor

bell

coronet

crown

hand

harp

key

lis

P in brackets

portcullis

R in brackets

sun

swan

triangle

triangle in circle

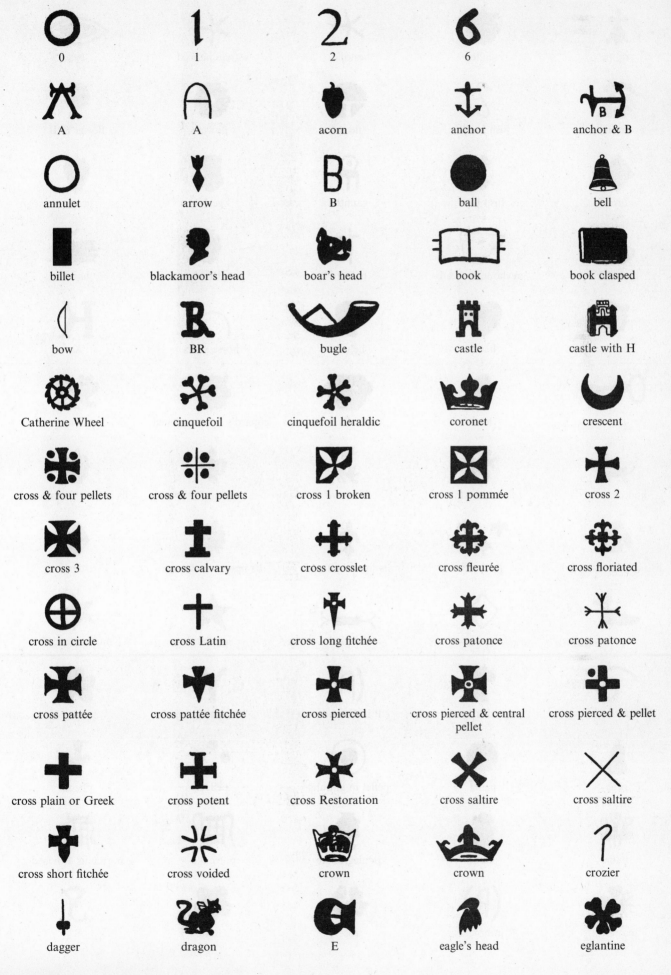

0	1	2	6	
A	A	acorn	anchor	anchor & B
annulet	arrow	B	ball	bell
billet	blackamoor's head	boar's head	book	book clasped
bow	BR	bugle	castle	castle with H
Catherine Wheel	cinquefoil	cinquefoil heraldic	coronet	crescent
cross & four pellets	cross & four pellets	cross 1 broken	cross 1 pommée	cross 2
cross 3	cross calvary	cross crosslet	cross fleurée	cross floriated
cross in circle	cross Latin	cross long fitchée	cross patonce	cross patonce
cross pattée	cross pattée fitchée	cross pierced	cross pierced & central pellet	cross pierced & pellet
cross plain or Greek	cross potent	cross Restoration	cross saltire	cross saltire
cross short fitchée	cross voided	crown	crown	crozier
dagger	dragon	E	eagle's head	eglantine

ermine	escallop	estoile	estoile pierced	eye
eye radiate	fish hook	fleece	flower	flower & B
fusil	fusil two	gauntlet	gerb	grapes
grapple	greyhound's head	halberd	halfrose	hand
harp	heart	helmet	horse shoe	K
key	leaf	leopard's head	leopard's head crowned	lion
lion passant	lion rampant	lions two	lis	lis issuant from rose
lis rose dimidiated	lis three	lis upon halfrose	lis upon sun & rose	lozenge
martlet	mascle	millrind	mullet	mullet pierced
nautilus	ostrich's head	P in brackets	pall	pansy
pear	pellet	pellet in annulet	pellets	pheon
plume	plume	pomegranate	portcullis	portcullis crowned
quatrefoil	R in brackets	rose	rosette	S

sceptre	shield	spear head	spur rowel	star
star radiant	stirrup	sun	sun	sun halved & rose
sunburst	swan	sword	T	TC
thistle	tower	trefoil	trefoil	triangle
triangle in circle	tun	uncertain	woolpack	woolpack over annulet
	WS	Y	y	

Issue marks, crowns and styles of lettering

annulet broken	crescent	crown bifoliate	crown trifoliate	crozier as on E21D Durham mint, classes 11A, 12, 13
leaf	lis	mascle	mullet	pellet
pinecone	plume Oxford	plume Shrewsbury	quatrefoil	quatrefoil
rosette	saltire	trefoil	trefoil slipped	trefoil, early style
open E	closed E	fishtail I	lombardic M	Roman M
fishtail N	Lombardic N	Roman N	reversed N	double barred N
wedge shaped R		reversed S		

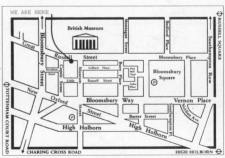

Location of mints

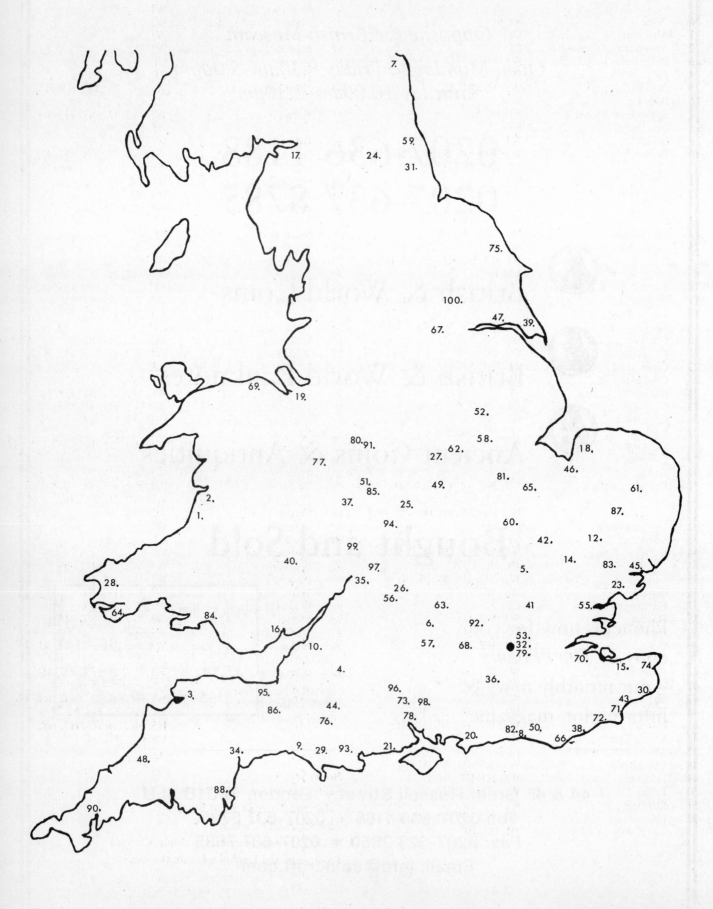

Below we list all the mints that were active from the reign of William I to the period of the Commonwealth in alphabetical order and note the monarchs who struck coins there. Each mint is numbered so it can be located on the map.

No — Mint	Reign
1 — Aberystwyth	C1
2 — Aberystwyth Furnace	C1
3 — Barnstaple	W1, H1
4 — Bath	W1, H1
5 — Bedford	W1, H1, ST, H2
6 — Bedwyn	W1
7 — Berwick on Tweed	E1, E2, E3
8 — Bramber	ST
9 — Bridport	W1
10 — Bristol	W1, W2, H1, ST, H2, H3, E1, E4, H6, H8, E6, C1
11 — Bur	W1
12 — Bury St Edmunds	W1, H1, ST, JH, H3, E1, E2, E3
13 — Calais	E3, R2, H4, H6
14 — Cambridge	W1, W2, H1, ST
15 — Canterbury	W1, W2, H1, ST, H2, R1, JH, H3, E1, E2, E3, E4, H7, H8, E6
16 — Cardiff	W1, H1, ST
17 — Carlisle	H1, ST, H2, R1, JH, H3, C1
18 — Castle Rising	ST
19 — Chester	W1, H1, ST, H2, E1, C1
20 — Chichester	W1, H1, ST, JH
21 — Christchurch	W1, H1
22 — Cipen	ST
23 — Colchester	W1, H1, ST, H2, C1
24 — Corbridge	ST
25 — Coventry	E4
26 — Cricklade	W1, W2
27 — Derby	W1, W2, H1, ST
28 — Devitum (St David's)	W1
29 — Dorchester	W1, W2, H1, ST
30 — Dover	W1, W2, H1, ST
31 — Durham	W1, H1, ST, H2, R1, JH, H3, E1, E2, E3, R2, H4, H5, H6, E4, R3, H7, H8
32 — Durham House	H8, E6
33 — Eden	ST
34 — Exeter	W1, W2, H1, ST, H2, R1, JH, H3, E1, C1
35 — Gloucester	W1, W2, H1, ST, H2, H3
36 — Guildford	W1, W2
37 — Hartlebury Castle	C1
38 — Hastings	W1, W2, H1, ST
39 — Hedon	ST
40 — Hereford	W1, W2, H1, ST, H2, H3, C1
41 — Hertford	W1, W2
42 — Huntington	W1, W2, H1, ST
43 — Hythe	W1, W2
44 — Ilchester	W1, W2, H1, H2, H3
45 — Ipswich	W1, W2, H1, ST, H2, JH
46 — King's Lynn	JH
47 — Kingston upon Hull	E1
48 — Launceston	W1, W2, H1, ST, H2
49 — Leicester	W1, H1, ST, H2
50 — Lewes	W1, H1, ST, H2
51 — Lichfield	R1
52 — Lincoln	W1, W2, H1, ST, H2, R1, JH, H3, E1
53 — London	W1, W2, H1, ST, H2, R1, JH, H3, E1, E2, E3, R2, H4, H5, H6, E4, E5, R3, H7, H8, E6, MA, PM, EL, J1, C1, CW, C2H
54 — Maint	W1
55 — Maldon (Essex)	W2
56 — Malmesbury	W1, W2
57 — Marlborough	W1, W2
58 — Newark	C1
59 — Newcastle	ST, H2, H3, E1
60 — Northampton	W1, H1, ST, H2, R1, JH, H3
61 — Norwich	W1, W2, H1, ST, H2, R1, JH, H3, E4
62 — Nottingham	W1, W2, H1, ST
63 — Oxford	W1, W2, H1, ST, H2, JH, H3, C1
64 — Pembroke	H1, ST, H2
65 — Peterborough	W1, ST?
66 — Pevensey	W1, W2, H1, ST
67 — Ponterfact	C1
68 — Reading	E1, E3
69 — Rhuddlan	W1, JH
70 — Rochester	W1, W2, H1, J
71 — Romney	W1, W2, H1
72 — Rye	ST
73 — Salisbury	W1, W2, H1, ST, H2
74 — Sandwich	W1, W2, H1, ST
75 — Scarborough	C1
76 — Shaftesbury	W1, W2, H1, ST
77 — Shrewsbury	W1, W2, H1, ST, H2, R1, H3, C1
78 — Southampton	H1, ST
79 — Southwark	W1, W2, H1, ST, H8, E6
80 — Stafford	W1, W2, H1, ST, H2
81 — Stamford	W1, W2, H1, ST
82 — Steyning	W1, W2, ST
83 — Sudbury	W1, W2, H1, ST
84 — Swansea	ST
85 — Tamworth	W1, W2, H1, ST
86 — Taunton	W1, W2, H1, ST
87 — Thetford	W1, W2, H1, ST, H2
88 — Totnes	W2, H1
89 — Tournais	H8
90 — Truro	C1
91 — Tutbury	ST
92 — Wallingford	W1, W2, H1, H2, H3
93 — Wareham	W1, W2, H1, ST
94 — Warwick	W1, W2, H1, ST
95 — Watchet	W1, W2, H1, ST
96 — Wilton	W1, W2, H1, ST, H2, H3
97 — Winchcombe	W1, H1
98 — Winchester	W1, W2, H1, ST, H2, R1, J, H3
99 — Worcester	W1, W2, H1, ST, H2, R1, C1
100 — York	W1, W2, H1, ST, H2, R1, JH, H3, E1, E3, R2, H4, H5, H6, E4, R3, H7, H8, E6, C1

Notes

BUR, uncertain, possibly Peterborough.

Calais and Tournais are in France.

EDEN, possibly Carlisle.

MARIT, location uncertain, possibly Thetford.

Tower mint and London mint are the same.

Triple Unite

The triple-unite, with a value of sixty shillings, was the highest denomination to be produced during the hammered coinage. Issued by Charles I at the Shrewsbury and Oxford mints during the Civil War, they are undoubtedly magnificent coins. All issues were made of gold and show the king holding a sword and an olive branch on the obverse and the Declaration with the date below on the reverse. The olive branch represented the king's desire for peace rather than war. The two mints are easily identified since Shrewsbury has the Declaration in two lines and Oxford in three.

Shrewsbury Mint (1642)

Collecting Hints

This issue is extremely rare.

Obverse Legend CAROLUS D.G. MAG BRIT FRAN ET HIBER REX — Charles by the grace of God King of Great Britain France and Ireland

Outer Reverse Legend EXURGAT DEUS DISSIPENTUR INIMICI — Let God arise and His enemies be scattered

Inner Reverse Legend RELIG PROT LEG ANG LIBER PAR — The religion of the Protestants the laws of England the liberty of Parliament

Obverse Crowned king holding sword, plume behind his head; no mintmark.

Reverse Three plumes and mark of value (III) above the two-line declaration, 1642 below.

C1TU-005 ex. rare

Oxford Mint (1642 – 1644)

Collecting Hints

These issues are rare, but usually obtainable. Specimens exist in all grades from Fine to EF but not below Fine; most are undamaged and well struck.

Obverse Legend CAROLUS D.G. MAG BRIT FR ET HIB REX — Charles by the grace of God King of Great Britain France and Ireland

Outer Reverse Legend EXURGAT DEUS DISSIPENTUR INIMICI — Let God arise and His enemies be scattered

Inner Reverse Legend RELIG PROT LEG ANG LIBER PAR — The religion of the Protestants the laws of England the liberty of Parliament

Obverse Half-length bust of king holding sword, plume behind; mintmark plume.

Reverse Declaration on three lines, above it value (III) with three plumes, below it 1642.

C1TU-010 F £4,000 VF £8,000

As previous, but the Declaration on the reverse in one continuous scroll; dated 1642 or 1643.

C1TU-015 F £4,000 VF £8,000

As previous, but a larger bust of fine style of king holding a short olive branch; mintmark small lis. Reverse as previous but dated 1643 only.

C1TU-020 ex. rare

As previous, but taller bust of king with scarf behind his shoulder; mintmark plume, dated 1643.

A slightly smaller coin with minor varieties in the bust; reverse as previous, but dated 1644.

| C1TU-025 | F £4,200 | VF £8,500 |

| C1TU-040 | F £4,000 | VF £8,000 |

As previous, but no scarf.

As previous, but OX instead of OXON below date.

| C1TU-030 | F £4,000 | VF £8,000 |

| C1TU-045 | F £4,200 | VF £8,500 |

As previous, but OXON below date.

| C1TU-035 | ex. rare |

Sovereign Unite Laurel Pound

The gold double-ryal, or sovereign as it became known, was introduced during the reign of Henry VII with a value of twenty shillings. It was the highest contemporary denomination and based on the *real d'or* of the Netherlands. While the coin's name reflected the sense of magnificence associated with it, its design and style complied with Renaissance rather than medieval aesthetic values.

During the second coinage of James I the gold unite was introduced, originally with a value of twenty shillings and a name that refered to James I's intentions regarding the union of the two kingdoms of England and Scotland. Then, during James' third coinage, the gold laurel was produced, again with a value of twenty shillings. This issue became known as the laurel because the king wears a laurel instead of a crown.

Under Charles I, superb silver pounds were struck at the Shrewsbury and Oxford mints. These issues, which depict the king on horseback, were mainly produced to pay royalist soldiers during the civil war.

The unite continued to be produced until 1662, when it was replaced by the guinea, a denomination of twenty-one shillings. However, the sovereign was reintroduced in 1817 and is still produced today although the coin was replaced by a banknote during World War I. In 1983 the pound note was discontinued and a pound coin with its old value of twenty shillings was introduced but, with this issue made of brass, it was a long way from the superb coins of Henry VII. The sovereign and pound coin might have an identical denomination value, but the sovereign is a bullion coin and valued at the price of its gold content. It remains popular in jewellery and with collectors.

Henry VII   (1485 – 1509)

Introduced in 1489, the sovereign had a value of twenty shillings. All issues were produced at the London mint and a mintmark can be found at the beginning of the obverse and reverse legends. Although varieties exist, the obverse always depicts the king enthroned and the reverse a Tudor rose with the royal shield in the centre. During this period, double and treble sovereigns were also produced using the sovereign dies (H7SV-025) but struck on flans two or three times thicker. These two issues are unique and were probably presentation pieces or patterns not intended for circulation; we have not, therefore, listed them as a separate denomination.

Collecting Hints

All issues are extremely rare as few specimens were struck. Coins are usually found in VF condition but other grades do exist.

Obverse Legend HENRICUS DEI GRATIA REX ANGLIE ET FRANCIE DNS IBAR (or HIB) (varieties exist) — Henry by the grace of God King of England and France Lord of Ireland

Reverse Legend IHESUS AUTEM TRANSIENS PER MEDIUM ILLORUM IBAT (varieties exist) — But Jesus passing through their midst went His way

Obverse Large figure of king sitting on a low-back throne, lis in background; mintmark none.

Reverse Large Tudor rose with small shield in centre; mintmark cross fitchée.

H7SV-005   ex. rare

Legends As previous.

Obverse As previous, but no lis in background; mintmark cinquefoil.

Reverse As previous, but crown over royal shield; mintmark cinquefoil.

H7SV-010   ex. rare

Legends As previous.

Obverse King on high-backed ornamental throne with a greyhound and dragon on side pillars; mintmark dragon.

Reverse Shield on Tudor rose; mintmark dragon.

H7SV-015   F £6,000   VF £16,000

Legends As previous.

Obverse As previous, but the throne has a high canopy which breaks the legend; mintmark lis.

Reverse As previous; mintmark dragon.

H7SV-020   F £5,800   VF £15,500

Legends As previous.

Obverse King on narrow throne with portcullis below his feet; mintmark lis.

Reverse As previous, but mintmark cross crosslet or pheon.

| H7SV-025 | F £5,800 | VF £15,500 |

Henry VIII (1509 – 1547)

Gold sovereigns were struck throughout Henry VIII's reign and there was also the posthumous issue struck under Edward VI. The first two issues (1509 – 44) are very similar to the last of Henry VII, the main difference being the mintmarks. During the third coinage, sovereigns were produced at the Southwark and Bristol mints as well as the Tower mint in London, with a new design of a lion and griffin holding the royal arms on the reverse; again, the mintmarks are most important for identification. The posthumous issue sovereigns, struck at the Bristol and Tower mints, are virtually identical to the third coinage apart from the use of Roman lettering instead of the more ornate Lombardic.

Collecting Hints

All issues of the first and second coinage are extremely rare. Coins, when available, are usually found undamaged in Fine to VF condition.

First Coinage (1509 – 1526)

Obverse Legend HENRICUS DEI GRATIA REX ANGLIE ET FRANC DNS HIB — Henry by the grace of God King of England and France Lord of Ireland

Reverse Legend IHESUS AUTEM TRANSIENS PER MEDIUM ILLORUM IBAT — But Jesus passing through their midst went His way

Obverse King enthroned, portcullis below; mintmark portcullis.

Reverse Royal shield over Tudor rose; mintmark portcullis.

| H8SV-005 | VG £1,500 | F £3,500 | VF £7,500 |

Second Coinage (1526 – 1544)

The value of the sovereign was raised to twenty-two shillings in 1526.

As previous, but mintmark sunburst or lis on the obverse and sunburst, lis or arrow on the reverse.

| H8SV-010 | VG £1,400 | F £3,200 | VF £7,000 |

Third Coinage (1544 – 1547)

The weight of the sovereign was reduced, as was its value, from twenty-two to twenty shillings. All third coinage sovereigns have Lombardic lettering in the legends.

Collecting Hints

There is little doubt that this issue saw more circulation than the previous ones. While still very rare, coins are usually found in Fine condition and are often slightly creased. VF and EF examples do exist and some issues, especially in the lower grades, look rather brassy in colour due to the fluctuating fineness of the gold. Also, the weights of some issues vary.

Tower Mint

Obverse Legend HENRIC 8 DI GRA ANGL FRANCIE ET HIBER REX (varieties exist) — Henry VIII by the grace of God King of England France and Ireland

Reverse Legend IHESUS AUTEM TRANSIENS PER MEDIUM ILLORUM IBAT (varieties exist) — But Jesus passing through their midst went His way

Obverse Large figure of king enthroned, candlesticks on throne pillars; mintmark lis.

Reverse Crowned royal arms, lion and dragon either side; mintmark lis.

| H8SV-015 | VG £2,000 | F £4,000 | VF £10,000 |

Legends As previous.

Obverse Smaller figure of king enthroned, birds on throne pillars; mintmark lis, pellet in annulet.

Reverse As previous; mintmark lis.

| H8SV-020 | VG £900 | F £2,500 | VF £6,500 |

Southwark Mint

This mint was located on the South Bank of the river Thames in London. This issue is only identifiable by the mintmark and an 'E' sometimes found below the shield on the reverse.

Legends As previous.

Obverse As previous, but mintmark 'S' or 'E', often muled.

Reverse As previous, but sometimes 'E' below the royal shield; mintmarks as obverse.

| H8SV-035 | VG £1,800 | F £4,800 | VF £9,500 |

| H8SV-025 | VG £900 | F £2,500 | VF £6,500 |

Bristol Mint

This issue is differentiated by the mintmark 'WS', usually found only on the obverse.

Legends As previous.

Obverse As previous; mintmark 'WS'.

Reverse As previous, but no 'E' below shield; mintmark none or, rarely, 'WS'.

| H8SV-030 | VG £1,500 | F £4,000 | VF £8,500 |

Posthumous Coinage (1547 – 1551)

These two rare issues were struck during the reign of Edward VI at the Tower and Bristol mints. They are virtually identical to the previous issues, with even the mintmarks remaining unchanged, but the legends are in Roman rather than Lombardic lettering.

Collecting Hints

These two issues are very rare. When available, coins are usually found in Fine condition and are sometimes creased although coins in the higher grades do exist.

Tower Mint

Legends As previous, but Roman lettering.

Obverse As previous, but mintmark lis.

Reverse As previous, but mintmark lis.

Bristol Mint

Legends As previous.

Obverse As previous, but mintmark 'WS'.

Reverse As previous, but mintmark 'WS'.

| H8SV-040 | VG £1,200 | F £2,800 | VF £5,500 |

Edward VI (1547 – 1553)

Edward VI issued four different gold sovereigns during his reign. After the posthumous issue in his father's name listed above, a similar style sovereign was produced at the London mint during Edward's second period (1549 – 50). Then, during the third period (1550 – 53) the fine sovereign was produced, with a value of thirty shillings. It is fairly similar in style to the issues of Henry VIII, with the king enthroned on the obverse and the royal arms over the Tudor rose on the reverse. Finally, the ordinary sovereign of twenty shillings was also produced during the third period bearing a half-length bust of the king facing right on the obverse and a crowned shield supported by a lion and dragon on the reverse. While the fine sovereign might well have commanded a separate denomination chapter, it was known as a sovereign and we feel that it should be listed here since the weight and gold content was the most important factor in valuing a coin at the time.

Second Period (Jan. 1549 – April 1550)

Collecting Hints

This issue is very rare and when available usually found in Fine condition; VF examples do exist but they are extremely rare.

Obverse Legend EDWARD VI DEI GRA AGL FRAN ET HIBER REX (varieties exist) — Edward VI by the grace of God King of England France and Ireland

Reverse Legend IHS AUTEM TRANSIENS PER MED ILLOR IBAT. — But Jesus passing through their midst went His way

Obverse King enthroned; mintmark arrow or 'Y'.

Reverse Crowned royal arms held by a lion and dragon, 'ER' below shield; mintmarks as obverse.

| E6SV-005 | VG £1,000 | F £2,800 | VF £6,000 |

| E6SV-015 | VG £700 | F £1,800 | VF £4,000 |

Third Period (1550 – 1553)

Fine Sovereign

This issue had a value of thirty shillings.

Collecting Hints

This issue is extremely rare.

Obverse Legend EDWARD VI D G ANGLIE FRANCIE Z HIBERNIE REX — Edward VI by the grace of God King of England France and Ireland

Reverse Legend IHESUS AUTEM TRANSIENS PER MEDIUM ILLORUM IBAT — But Jesus passing through their midst went His way

Obverse King enthroned, portcullis below him and decoration around the inner circle; mintmark tun or ostrich head.

Reverse Royal arms over Tudor rose; mintmarks as obverse.

| E6SV-010 | F £10,000 | VF £20,000 |

These dies were also used to strike the double sovereign. This coin, which was struck on a flan of double thickness, is probably unique and thought to be a presentation piece or pattern rather than a denomination for circulation.

Sovereign

This issue had a value of twenty shillings.

Collecting Hints

This coin is very rare and usually found in Fine condition, although specimens in VF and even EF exist.

Obverse Legend EDWARD VI D G AGL FRA Z HIBER REX — Edward VI by the grace of God King of England France and Ireland

Reverse Legend IHS AUTEM TRANSIE PER MEDI ILLORU IBAT — But Jesus passing through their midst went His way

Obverse Half-length bust of king facing right, holding orb and sword; mintmark 'Y' or tun.

Reverse Crowned royal arms with a lion and dragon on either side, 'E.R' below shield; mintmark as obverse.

Mary (1553 – 1554)

During Mary's reign the gold fine sovereign, with a value of thirty shillings, was produced. It shows the queen enthroned on the obverse and sometimes has the date in Roman numerals at the end of the legend. The reverse bears the royal arms over a Tudor rose. This issue shows much decoration and ornamentation, especially on the obverse.

Collecting Hints

This issue is very rare, with 1554 being much rarer than 1553. When available, it is usually found undamaged in Fine to VF condition. Modern forgeries of this issue exist.

Obverse Legend MARIA D G ANG FRA Z HIB REGINA (sometimes followed by MDLIII or MDLIIII; varieties exist) — Mary by the grace of God Queen of England France and Ireland (1553 or 1554)

Reverse Legend A. DNO FACTU EST ISTUD Z EST MIRA IN OCUL NRIS — This is the Lord's doing and it is marvellous in our eyes

Obverse Queen seated on ornamental throne, a portcullis below and decoration within the inner circle; mintmark pomegranate or halved rose.

Reverse Royal arms over Tudor rose; mintmarks as obverse.

| MASV-005 | VG £1,200 | F £3,500 | VF £7,000 |

No sovereigns were struck during the reign of Philip and Mary.

Elizabeth I (1558 – 1603)

During Elizabeth I's reign fine sovereigns with a value of thirty shillings were produced, as were gold pounds with a value of twenty shillings. The fine sovereign depicts the queen enthroned on the obverse and the royal arms over a Tudor rose on the reverse while the gold pound bears the bust of the queen on the obverse and a crowned shield on the reverse. All issues were struck at the Tower mint and have a mintmark on the obverse and reverse, at the beginning or end of the legend.

Fine Sovereign

Collecting Hints

All issues are very rare and are usually found undamaged in Fine or VF condition.

First – Third Issues (1559 – 1578)

Obverse Legend   ELIZABETH D G ANG FRA ET HIBE REGINA (minor varieties exist) — Elizabeth by the grace of God Queen of England France and Ireland

Reverse Legend   A DNO FACTU EST ISTUD ET EST MIRAB IN OCULIS NRIS — This is the Lord's doing and it is marvellous in our eyes

Obverse   Queen enthroned with a portcullis below; mintmark lis or cross crosslet.

Reverse   Royal arms over a Tudor rose; mintmarks as obverse.

| ELSV-005 | VG £1,200 | F £3,000 | VF £5,750 |

No sovereigns or pounds were struck for the fourth issue (1578 – 82).

Fifth Issue (1583 – 1600)

Legends   As previous.

Obverse   As previous, but the throne is lower; mintmark 'A', escallop, crescent, hand, tun.

Reverse   As previous; mintmarks as obverse.

| ELSV-010 | VG £1,200 | F £3,000 | VF £5,700 |

Gold Pound

Gold pounds were produced in some quantity during the fifth and sixth coinages (1592 – 1602). They had a value of twenty shillings.

Collecting Hints

These coins, while rare, are obtainable. They can be found in all grades from VG to EF but specimens are sometimes damaged. Collectors tend to pay particular attention to the obverse which bears a superb bust of the queen.

Obverse Legend   ELIZABETH D G ANG FRA ET HIB REGINA — Elizabeth by the grace of God Queen of England France and Ireland

Reverse Legend   SCUTUM FIDEI PROTEGET EAM — The shield of faith shall protect her

Obverse   Crowned bust of queen; mintmark tun, woolpack, key, anchor, O, 1, 2.

Reverse   Crown over royal arms and dividing 'E.R'; mintmarks as obverse.

| ELPD-015 | VG £600 | F £1,250 | VF £3,300 |

James I (1603 – 1625)

During the reign of James I three types of sovereign were produced. The regular sovereign was struck during the first coinage. It was largely a continuation from previous reigns in style and value (twenty shillings) and, like all gold issues from this coinage, is rare due to a contemporary shortage of gold. The second coinage saw the introduction of the gold unite, so called because the legends on the coin proclaimed James I's intentions regarding the union of the two kingdoms of England and Scotland. The value of the unite was twenty shillings until 1612, when it was raised to twenty-two due to the rise of the value of gold across Europe. Finally, the gold laurel with a value of twenty shillings was introduced during the third coinage. Named after the laurel that the king is portrayed wearing on his head, this issue was produced in some quantity but its quality in style and design was comparatively poor. All issues were struck at the Tower mint in London and have mintmarks at the beginning of the obverse and usually the reverse legend.

First Coinage (1603 – 1604)
Sovereign

Collecting Hints

This issue, which was only struck for two years, is very rare and usually found undamaged in Fine to VF condition. Specimens in the lower grades seem to be extremely rare.

Obverse Legend   IACOBUS D G ANG SCO FRAN ET HIB REX — James by the grace of God King of England Scotland France and Ireland

Reverse Legend   EXURGAT DEUS DISSIPENTUR INIMICI — Let God arise and His enemies be scattered

Obverse   Half-length crowned bust of king holding orb and sceptre; mintmark thistle.

Reverse   Royal arms with crown above dividing 'I.R.'; mintmark thistle.

| J1SV-005 | VG £450 | F £900 | VF £2,500 |

Legends   As previous.

Obverse   As previous, but the king is wearing decorated armour; mintmark thistle or lis.

Reverse   As previous, but mintmark thistle or lis.

| J1SV-010 | VG £450 | F £950 | VF £2,500 |

Second Coinage (1604 – 1619)
Unite

Collecting Hints

The gold unite is a superb, large, well designed coin and is usually available to collectors; it is an ideal coin to have from this period. It was produced in some quantity and collectors should have little difficulty obtaining an example. Unites can be found in all grades from poor to EF but many specimens are worn or damaged, reflecting considerable circulation. Also, many were made into jewellery or holed and then perhaps plugged at a later date. Collectors should beware of plugged or mounted coins when buying a specimen. Modern forgeries of coins with mintmark mullet exist.

Second Bust

Obverse Legend   IACOBUS D G MA BRI FRA ET HI REX (minor varieties exist) — James by the grace of God King of Great Britain France and Ireland

Reverse Legend   FACIAM EOS IN GENTEM UNAM — I will make them one nation

Obverse   Crowned king with pointed beard, holding orb and sceptre; mintmark lis or rose.

Reverse   Crown above royal arms dividing 'I.R'; mintmark lis or rose.

| J1UN-015 | VG £225 | F £450 | VF £750 |

Fourth Bust

Legends   As previous.

Obverse   Crowned king with long beard not tucked into his armour and holding an orb and sceptre; mintmarks rose, escallop, grapes, coronet, key, bell, mullet, tower, trefoil and cinquefoil.

Reverse   As previous; mintmarks as obverse.

| J1UN-020 | VG £225 | F £450 | VF £750 |

Fifth Bust

Legends   As previous.

Obverse   Crowned bust of king with short bushy beard and holding an orb and sceptre; mintmarks cinquefoil, tun, book, crescent, plain cross, saltire.

Reverse   As previous; mintmarks as obverse.

| J1UN-025 | VG £225 | F £450 | VF £750 |

Scotland also produced coins which are very similar to the unite but with a different style bust, different reverse shield and mintmark thistle.

Third Coinage (1619 – 1625)
Laurel

Collecting Hints

The gold laurel is scarcer than the gold unite and less popular with collectors as it is not as attractive. The laurel with the fifth bust is extremely rare, while the other two issues are usually found in Fine or VF condition. Like the unite, these issues are often found damaged in less than Fine condition and undoubtedly saw considerable circulation. Modern forgeries of this issue do exist.

First Bust

Obverse Legend   IACOBUS D G MAG BRI FRA ET HIB REX (minor varieties exist) — James by the grace of God King of Great Britain France and Ireland

Reverse Legend   FACIAM EOS IN GENTEM UNAM — I will make them one nation

Obverse   Large bust of king wearing a laurel, value (XX) behind his head; mintmark spur rowel.

Reverse   Long cross fleury over crowned square shield; mintmark spur rowel at end of legend.

J1LA-030   VG £240   F £450   VF £850

Second Bust

Legends   As previous.

Obverse   As previous, but slightly smaller bust; mintmark spur rowel or rose.

Reverse   As previous; mintmarks as obverse.

J1LA-035   VG £250   F £450   VF £850

Third Bust

Legends   As previous.

Obverse   Smaller, neater bust of king with his chin not protruding as much as the previous issue; mintmark rose or thistle.

Reverse   As previous; mintmarks as obverse.

J1LA-040   VG £250   F £450   VF £850

Fourth Bust

Legends   As previous.

Obverse   Laureate bust of king wearing new-style cloak; mintmarks lis or trefoil.

Reverse   As previous; mintmarks as obverse.

J1LA-045   VG £250   F £450   VF £850

Fifth Bust

Obverse Legend   As previous, but HI instead of HIB.

Reverse Legend   As previous.

Obverse   Smaller, crude bust of king of very poor style wearing laurel, with value behind; mintmark trefoil.

Reverse   As previous; mintmark trefoil.

J1LA-050   rare

Charles I   (1625 – 1649)

As mentioned earlier, the name of the denomination changed from 'sovereign' to 'unite' and 'laurel' although the values of the coins remained the same. During this period, the denomination was mainly referred to as twenty shillings, however, as today, coins of the same denomination had different names. During all of Charles I's reign gold unites were produced at the Tower mint. They depicted the crowned bust of the king on the obverse and a shield of varying styles, with a crown above, on the reverse. A mintmark can usually be found at the beginning of the obverse and reverse legends and issues struck while the mint was under the control of Parliament are easily identified by their mintmarks. Nicholas Briot also produced wonderful, machine-made unites in 1631 – 32. These issues, which are very rare, are superb in style and design and are greatly superior to the hammered issues of the Tower mint.

During the Civil War at the end of Charles I's reign provincial mints struck coins, often to pay troops loyal to the king, and gold unites and superb silver pounds were produced at several locations. Most provincial gold unites are extremely rare or even unique, although the Oxford mint did produce a small quantity of specimens. These issues, which are very crude in style, differ greatly from the regular Tower issue specimens in that the bust of the king is very different and the reverse does not bear a shield, but only the Declaration with the date below. The silver pounds, which were produced at the Shrewsbury and Oxford mints, can easily be recognised by the XX (20 shillings) above the Declaration on the reverse but, as the two issues are extremely similar in style, both should be studied when identifying a coin.

The issues of Charles I are numerous and we have included 'Collecting Hints' for each. It is important to remember that Charles II also issued unites and that in all cases the obverse legend of Charles I starts CAROLUS, whereas Charles II starts CAROLUS II.

Tower Mint

Tower Mint under King (1625 – 1642)

Collecting Hints

Most issues are fairly common and are usually available to the collector in VG to VF condition. Some issues are not fully round and although specimens may have been clipped, there is little doubt that moneyers sometimes paid little attention to the shape of a coin's flan. Furthermore, many issues are often damaged or worn, reflecting considerable circulation. Collectors should try to obtain an example with as good a portrait as possible.

The following line-drawings, from B.R. Osborne's archive on Charles I, depict the numerous styles of bust with the corresponding classes to which they relate. It is important to remember that, with the number of dies being used, varieties exist.

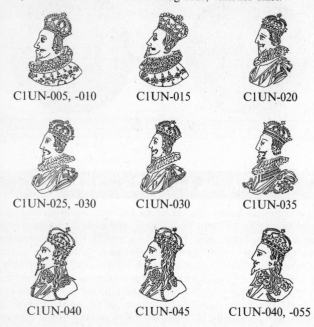

C1UN-005, -010   C1UN-015   C1UN-020

C1UN-025, -030   C1UN-030   C1UN-035

C1UN-040   C1UN-045   C1UN-040, -055

First Bust

Obverse Legend CAROLUS D G MAG BR FR ET HI REX — Charles by the grace of God Great King of Britain France and Ireland

Reverse Legend FLORENT CONCORDIA REGNA — Through concord kingdoms flourish

Obverse King wearing ruff and double-arched crown, value behind his head; mintmark lis or cross calvary.

Reverse Crown over square shield; mintmark as obverse.

C1UN-005   VG £220   F £425   VF £650

As previous, but extra garnishing to shield on reverse; mintmark lis.

C1UN-010   VG £220   F £425   VF £650

As C1UN-005 but king is wearing a flat-topped single-arched crown.

C1UN-015   VG £260   F £475   VF £850

As C1UN-010 but king is wearing a flat-topped crown.

C1UN-017   VG £220   F £425   VF £650

Second Bust

Obverse Legend As previous; minor varieties exist.

Reverse Legend As previous.

Obverse Smaller, thinner and neater bust of king with a smaller ruff; mintmark cross calvary, blackamoor's head, castle, anchor, heart.

Reverse Crown over square royal shield; mintmark as obverse.

C1UN-020   VG £260   F £475   VF £850

Obverse As previous, but larger bust with wider crown; mintmark heart or plume.

Reverse As previous; mintmarks as obverse.

C1UN-025   VG £220   F £450   VF £750

As previous, but with mintmark anchor below bust.

C1UN-030   VG £220   F £450   VF £750

Third Bust

Legends As previous.

Obverse King wears more visible armour; mintmark plume or rose.

Reverse Oval shield with crown above and dividing 'C.R'; mintmark as obverse.

| C1UN-035 | VG £210 | F £410 | VF £630 |

Fourth Bust

Legends   As previous.

Obverse   King with longer hair and smaller collar; mintmark harp, portcullis, bell, crown, tun.

Reverse   Oval shield with crown above, 'C.R' with small crowns above divided by shield; mintmark as obverse.

| C1UN-040 | VG £210 | F £475 | VF £775 |

No unites were struck with the fifth bust.

Sixth Bust

Legends   As previous.

Obverse   King with pointed beard (Briot-style bust) and large lace collar; mintmark anchor, triangle, star, triangle in circle.

Reverse   Crown over oval shield dividing crowned 'C R'; mintmark as obverse.

| C1UN-045 | VG £220 | F £450 | VF £750 |

Briot's Hammered Issue

Obverse   As previous; mintmark anchor. Briot's coinage.

Reverse   Crown over square-topped shield, dividing crowned 'C. R' (Briot-style reverse).

| C1UN-050 | v. rare |

Tower Mint under Parliament (1643 – 1648)

The mintmarks differentiate this issue from previous ones.

Collecting Hints

These issues are rarer than the previous ones. Specimens are usually found, often poorly struck, in Fine to VF condition.

The following line-drawings, from B.R. Osborne's archive on Charles I, depict the numerous styles of bust with the corresponding classes to which they relate. It is important to remember that, with the number of dies being used, varieties exist.

C1UN-040, -055   C1UN-060   C1UN-065

Fourth Bust

Legends   As previous.

Obverse & Reverse   As C1UN-040, but mintmark 'P'.

| C1UN-055 | VG £250 | F £475 | VF £900 |

Sixth Bust

Legends   As previous.

Obverse & Reverse   As C1UN-045, but mintmark '(P)', '(R)' or triangle in circle.

| C1UN-060 | VG £220 | F £500 | VF £1,000 |

Seventh Bust

Obverse   As previous, but bust of cruder style; mintmark eye, sun, sceptre.

Reverse   Crown over royal shield, dividing crowned 'C R'; mintmark as obverse.

| C1UN-065 | VG £200 | F £425 | VF £900 |

Briot's Coinage (1631 – 1632)

This issue is machine-made and easily identified by its mintmark and uniquely shaped reverse shield.

Collecting Hints

This is a superb issue and undoubtedly the finest unite struck under Charles I. It is also very rare, although specimens do exist in Fine to EF condition and are usually undamaged.

Obverse Legend   CAROLUS D. G. MAGN BRITANN FRAN ET HIBER REX — Charles by the grace of God King of Great Britain France and Ireland

Reverse Legend FLORENT CONCORDIA REGNA — Through concord kingdoms flourish

Obverse Crowned bust of king, value (XX) behind; mintmark flower and 'B'.

Reverse Crown over square-topped shield which divides crowned 'CR'.

| C1UN-070 | F £1,400 | VF £2,850 |

Provincial Issues

These rare unites were struck during the Civil War and were often used to pay royalist troops.

Chester Mint

This issue should not be confused with the Tower mint issues C1UN-035 and -040; not only is it poorer in style but also on the Tower issues the 'C R' on the reverse is uncrowned.

Collecting Hints

This issue is extremely rare.

Obverse Legend CAROLUS D.G. MA BR FR ET HI REX — Charles by the grace of God Great King of Britain France and Ireland

Reverse Legend FLORENT CONCORDIA REGNA — Through concord kingdoms flourish

Obverse Crowned bust with value behind; mintmark plume.

Reverse Crown over oval shield which divides crowned 'CR'; mintmark plume.

| C1UN-075 | ex. rare |

Oxford Mint

These issues are easily identified by the reverse design which has the Declaration with date below and plumes above; this is only shared by the extremely rare Bristol issue. Many varieties of the Oxford unite exist and we have listed them all.

Collecting Hints

All issues are very rare, but specimens for collectors do exist outside museums. The issues are extremely crude in style and often have weaknesses in the legends due to the poor strike. Specimens exist in VG to EF condition, but coins in EF are extremely rare.

Obverse Legend CAROLUS D. G. MAG BRIT FR ET HIB REX (many minor varieties exist) — Charles by the grace of God King of Great Britain France and Ireland

Outer Reverse Legend EXURGAT DEUS DISSIPENTUR INIMICI — Let God arise and His enemies be scattered

Inner Reverse Legend RELIG PROT LEG ANG LIBER PAR (many minor varieties exist) — The religion of the Protestants the laws of England the liberty of Parliament

Obverse Crowned bust of king holding olive branch, value (XX) behind; no mintmark.

Reverse The Declaration in two lines, three plumes above, date 1642 below.

| C1UN-080 | VG £600 | F £1,300 | VF £2,800 |

As previous, but the Declaration in three lines, dated 1642 or 1643 below.

| C1UN-085 | VG £600 | F £1,300 | VF £2,800 |

Obverse Larger bust of king holding sword.

Reverse As previous, but dated 1643 only.

| C1UN-090 | VG £600 | F £1,350 | VF £2,950 |

Obverse Shorter bust of king; mintmark plume.

Reverse As previous, but dated 1643 or 1645.

C1UN-095	VG £600	F £1,300	VF £2,800

C1UN-120	VG £600	F £1,350	VF £2,950

Bristol Mint

This issue is similar to C1UN-095 dated 1645, however, it has the mintmark 'BR' on the obverse.

As previous, but 'OX' below date 1644.

C1UN-100	VG £600	F £1,300	VF £2,800

Collecting Hints

This issue is extremely rare.

Obverse Tall new-style bust going to the edge of the coin, the legend starts near the bottom of the coin; no mintmark.

Reverse As previous, dated 1643.

Obverse Legend CAROLUS D.G. MAG BR FR ET HIB REX — Charles by the grace of God Great King of Britain France and Ireland

Outer Reverse Legend EXURGAT DEUS DISSIPENTUR INIMICI — Let God arise and His enemies be scattered

Inner Reverse Legend REL PROT LEG ANG LIB PAR — The religion of the Protestants the laws of England the liberty of Parliament

Obverse King holding sword, value (XX) behind; mintmark 'BR'.

Reverse Three plumelets over the Declaration, dated 1645 below.

C1UN-105	VG £600	F £1,300	VF £2,800

C1UN-125	ex. rare

Obverse Smaller bust of king as C1UN-095.

Reverse The Declaration on three straight lines, dated 1644 OX. Probably struck from a shilling die.

C1UN-110	ex. rare

Exeter Mint

This issue should not be confused with the more common Tower issue although both use the mintmark rose on the obverse and reverse. One Exeter issue has a different reverse legend, while the other has a crowned 'C' and 'R' on either side of the shield on the reverse; the Tower issues are uncrowned. This issue used to be classed under Truro.

Obverse Longer, narrow bust and not as small as previous.

Reverse As previous.

C1UN-115	VG £600	F £1,350	VF £2,950

Collecting Hints

The first issue is unique, the second extremely rare.

Obverse As previous.

Reverse A single plume above the Declaration instead of three; dated 1645 or 1646, OX.

Obverse Legend CAROLUS D.G. MAG BR FR ET HI REX — Charles by the grace of God Great King of Britain France and Ireland

Reverse Legend FLORENT CONCORDIA REGNA — Through concord kingdoms flourish

Obverse Crowned bust with value (XX) behind; mintmark rose.

Reverse Crowned oval garnished shield; mintmark rose.

C1UN-130   unique

As previous, but reverse legend reads CULTORES SUI DEUS PROTEGIT — God protects His worshippers.

C1UN-135   ex. rare

Worcester Mint (1643 – 1644)

This issue, which is extremely rare, can be identified by the lion paws on either side of the shield on the reverse.

Collecting Hints

This issue is extremely rare in any grade.

Obverse Legend   CAROLUS D G MAG BR FR ET HI RE[X] — Charles by the grace of God King of Great Britain France and Ireland

Reverse Legend   FLORENT CONCORDIA REGNA — Through concord kingdoms flourish

Obverse   Crowned bust with value (XX) behind; no mintmark.

Reverse   Crown over oval royal shield, a lion paw either side of the shield.

C1UN-140   ex. rare

Shrewsbury Mint (1644)

The mints of Shrewsbury and Worcester were very closely connected. The Shrewsbury issue is identical to the Worcester one, except for the mintmark lis which can only be found on the obverse, and the fact that on the reverse there are no lion paws either side of the shield.

Legend   As previous.

Obverse   As previous, but mintmark lis.

Reverse   As previous, but no lion paws and no mintmark.

C1UN-145   possibly unique

Shrewsbury and Oxford Silver Pounds

Silver pounds with a value of twenty shillings were produced at the Oxford and Shrewsbury mints between 1642 and 1644. Both these issues, which are very similar, show the king on horseback on the obverse with various designs below the horse and on the reverse the Declaration with plumes above and date below. The denomination, (XX) twenty shillings, can be found above the Declaration. These issues are very similar in style and design, and collectors will have to refer to both when identifying a coin. The main differences are as follows: the Shrewsbury mint has no mintmark at the beginning of the obverse legend, although most issues have a series of pellets; most Oxford issues use mintmark plume; all Shrewsbury issues are dated 1642, while Oxford issues are dated 1642 – 44. Also, Oxford plumes have a 'tie' at the bottom, whereas Shrewsbury plumes do not.

Collecting Hints

These large coins are very rare although specimens exist in VG to VF condition. They must have been difficult to strike and this is sometimes reflected in their condition.

Shrewsbury Mint (1642)

Obverse Legend   CAROLUS D G MAG BRIT FRA ET HIB REX — Charles by the grace of God King of Great Britain France and Ireland

Outer Reverse Legend   EXURGAT DEUS DISSIPENTUR INIMICI — Let God arise and His enemies be scattered

Inner Reverse Legend   RELIG PROT LEG ANGL LIBER PAR — The religion of the Protestants the laws of England the liberty of Parliament

Obverse   King on horseback with plume behind.

Reverse   Declaration in two lines, date 1642 below, value and three plumes above.

C1PD-150   VG £950   F £2,200   VF £4,000

As previous, but new-style, neater horseman walking over a pile of arms.

| C1PD-155 | VG £900 | F £2,200 | VF £4,000 |

| C1PD-165 | VG £1,100 | F £3,000 | VF £5,000 |

As previous, but a cannon below king's horse on the obverse and only one plume above Declaration on the reverse.

As previous, but the reverse is an Oxford die with Oxford plumes.

| C1PD-160 | VG £1,000 | F £2,500 | VF £4,250 |

Oxford Mint (1642 – 1644)

Obverse Legend CAROLUS D.G MAG BRIT FRA ET HIBER REX — Charles by the grace of God King of Great Britain France and Ireland

Outer Reverse Legend EXURGAT DEUS DISSIPENTUR INIMICI — Let God arise and His enemies be scattered

Inner Reverse Legend RELIG PROT LEG ANG LIBER PAR — The religion of the Protestants the laws of England the liberty of Parliament

Obverse Large horseman with king's sword breaking the inner circle, arms below horse; mintmark plume.

Reverse Declaration with date 1642 below, value (XX) and three Shrewsbury-style plumes above. This is a Shrewsbury die.

| C1PD-170 | VG £1,100 | F £3,000 | VF £5,000 |

As previous, but new-style horseman on the obverse with horse trampling on arms, exergual line below horse.

| C1PD-175 | VG £1,000 | F £2,400 | VF £4,200 |

117

As previous, but cannon amongst arms, dated 1642 or 1643.

| C1PD-180 | VG £1,000 | F £2,400 | VF £4,250 |

As previous, but the space below groundline on the obverse is chequered, dated 1642 only.

| C1PD-185 | VG £1,250 | F £3,250 | VF £6,000 |

As previous but Briot-style horseman, dated 1643.

| C1PD-190 | VG £1,250 | F £3,250 | VF £6,000 |

Legends   As previous.

Obverse   As C1PD-165 obverse.

Reverse   The Declaration in three lines in the form of a scroll, dated 1644 with OX below, value (XX) above and a single plume above value.

| C1PD-195   VG £2,000   F £4,000   VF £10,000 |
| EF Spink March '96 £17,000 |

Pontefract Siege Issue (1648 – 1649)

These issues were struck inside Pontefract Castle during the siege by Cromwell's army. After the death of Charles I, these were the first gold coins to be struck in the name of Charles II.

Collecting Hints

These issues are extremely rare.

Obverse Legend   DUM SPIRO SPERO — Whilst I live I hope

Reverse Legend   CAROLUS SECUNDUS 1648 — Charles II 1648

Obverse   Large crown over 'CR'.

Reverse   Castle gateway with flag.

| C1SV-200   ex. rare |

Obverse Outer Legend   CAROL II D.G. MAG B F ET H REX — Charles II by the grace of God King of Great Britain France and Ireland

Obverse Inner Legend   HANC DEUS DEDIT — God has given this

Reverse Legend   POST MORTEM PATRIS PRO FILIO — For the son after the death of his father

Obverse   Large crown, 1648.

Reverse   As previous.

| C1SV-205   ex. rare |

Commonwealth (1649 – 1660)

Gold unites with a value of twenty shillings were produced during most of the Commonwealth period. These issues are very plain in style when compared to previous ones, reflecting contemporary Puritan values. The obverse shows the arms of St George and bears a mintmark, the reverse has the date and, just below it, the value (XX). For the first time, the legends are in English rather than Latin echoing anti-Catholic feeling.

Collecting Hints

The first issue with the mintmark sun is rare but obtainable. Coins are found, sometimes damaged, in all grades from VG to EF. All issues with mintmark anchor are very rare and tend to be found in lower grades. Modern forgeries exist but are dated 1651 only.

The following are dates and rarity values for the Commonwealth unites:

Date	Rarity
1649	RR
1650	RR
1651	R
1652	RR
1653	R
1654	R
1655	R
1656	R
1657	R
1658	RRR
1660	RRR

Obverse Legend THE COMMONWEALTH OF ENGLAND

Reverse Legend GOD WITH US

Obverse St George's shield within wreath; mintmark sun.

Reverse St George's shield and Irish shield, value above, dated 1649 – 57.

CWUN-005 VG £450 F £900 VF £1,800

As previous, but mintmark anchor, dated 1658 or 1660.

CWUN-010 VG £800 F £1,750 VF v. rare

Charles II (1660 – 1685)

Hammered Coinage (1660 – 1662)

Gold unites with a value of twenty shillings were produced during Charles II's hammered coinage. These rare issues show the king's bust on the obverse and a crown above the royal arms on the

reverse. The gold unite was replaced by the milled gold guinea in 1663, with a value of twenty shillings subsequently rising to twenty-one shillings. It was not until 1817, at the end of George III's reign, that the sovereign was reintroduced with a value of twenty shillings.

Collecting Hints

Both issues are very rare. Examples are usually found undamaged in Fine or VF condition.

Obverse Legend CAROLUS II D G MAG BRIT FRAN ET HIB REX — Charles II by the grace of God King of Great Britain France and Ireland

Reverse Legend FLORENT CONCORDIA REGNA — Through concord kingdoms flourish

Obverse Bust of king wearing a laurel; mintmark crown.

Reverse Crown above oval royal shield which divides 'CR'.

C2UN-005 VG £600 F £1,300 VF £3,500

As previous, but value (XX) behind king's head.

C2UN-010 VG £600 F £1,300 VF £3,500

Ryal

With a value of ten shillings, the gold ryal was a replacement for the noble during the reign of Edward IV but, as it proved unpopular, it was later replaced by the angel. The Edward IV ryal is listed under the Noble Chapter as it is such a continuation in style. Although the ryal was reintroduced in 1487 under Henry VII, very few coins were issued and it continued to be unpopular, especially compared to the angel which was produced in some quantity. The ryal was not produced again until the reign of Mary, when its value was increased to fifteen shillings or half a fine sovereign.

Henry VII   (1485 – 1509)

Collecting Hints

This coin is extremely rare in any grade.

Obverse Legend   HENRIC D. GRA REX ANGL Z FRANC DNS IBAR — Henry by the grace of God King of England and France Lord of Ireland

Reverse Legend   IHC AUTEM TRANSIENS PER MEDIU ILLORU IBAT — But Jesus passing through their midst went His way

Obverse   King standing in a ship holding a sword and shield, two flags flying from ship.

Reverse   French shield over large Tudor rose; mintmark cross fitchée.

H7RY-005   F £8,000   VF £16,000

Mary   (1553 – 1554)

Collecting Hints

With a value of fifteen shillings, this issue is extremely rare; specimens are usually found in VF condition. In fact, in 1985, a VF specimen sold at auction for £13,000. Collectors should be aware that very good Victorian forgeries exist and can be detected by the lack of detail on the rose on the reverse of the coin.

Obverse Legend   MARIA DG. ANG FRA Z HIB REGINA MDLIII — Mary by the grace of God Queen of England France and Ireland 1553

Reverse Legend   A DNO FACTU EST ISTUD Z EST MIRA IN OCULNRIS — This is the Lord's doing and it is marvellous in our eyes

Obverse   Queen on a ship; mintmark pomegranate.

Reverse   Radiate rose in centre of design.

MARY-005   ex. rare

Elizabeth I   (1558 – 1603)

Collecting Hints

This is an extremely rare denomination, struck only between 1584 – 89. It is sought after as it is accepted as the last truly mediaeval English coin. Usually found in Fine to VF condition, it bears a mintmark only on the reverse.

Fifth Issue

Obverse Legend   ELIZAB D G ANG FR ET HIB REGINA — Elizabeth by the grace of God Queen of England France and Ireland

Reverse Legend   IHS AUT TRANSIENS PER MEIU ILLORUM IBAT — But Jesus passing through the midst of them went His way

Obverse   Queen standing in a contemporary sailing ship.

Reverse   Geometric design; mintmark 'A', escallop, crescent, hand.

ELRY-005   VG —   F £8,000   VF £12,000

James I   (1603 – 1625)

Rose Ryal

This rare issue was struck during the second and third coinage of James I. It was really a two-ryal piece and should not be classed as a sovereign which was valued at either twenty or twenty-two shillings. The obverse of these extremely decorative coins is fairly similar in style to the Elizabeth I fine sovereign which, of course, had the same value as the rose ryal. A mintmark can be found on the obverse and reverse and the value of the coin, (XXX) thirty shillings, appears above the royal shield on the reverse of the third coinage.

Second Coinage (1604 – 1619)

Obverse Legend IACOBUS DG MAG BRIT FRAN ET HIBER REX — James by the grace of God King of Great Britain France and Ireland

Reverse Legend A DNO FACTUM EST ISTUD ET EST MIRAB IN OCULIS NRIS — This is the Lord's doing and it is marvellous in our eyes

Obverse King enthroned, a portcullis below his feet; mintmark rose, escallop, grapes, coronet, key, mullet, tower, trefoil, cinquefoil, tun, closed book.

Reverse Royal arms over a rose; mintmarks as obverse.

| J1RY-005 | VG — | F £2,000 | VF £4,000 |

Third Coinage (1619 – 1625)

Obverse Legend IACOBUS DG MA BRI FR ET HI REX — James by the grace of God King of Great Britain France and Ireland

Reverse Legend As previous.

Obverse King enthroned, a portcullis below; mintmark spur rowel, rose, thistle, lis.

Reverse Royal shield, value (XXX) above circled by roses, lions and lis; mintmarks as obverse.

| J1RY-010 | VG — | F £2,000 | VF £4,200 |

As previous, but plain back to king's throne; mintmark trefoil.

| J1RY-015 | VG — | F £2,100 | VF £3,800 |

Spur Ryal

This issue, so called because the sun and rose on the reverse resemble a spur, was introduced during the second coinage. Originally its value was fifteen shillings but, in line with all gold coins, it was raised in 1612 to sixteen shillings and sixpence. During the third coinage a new-style spur ryal was introduced with its value and weight reduced to fifteen shillings. On the obverse it shows a crowned lion above the royal arms dividing the value (XV), while the reverse remains similar to previous issues.

Second Coinage (1604 – 1619)

Obverse Legend IACOBUS DG. MAG BRIT FRAN ET HIB REX — James by the grace of God King of Great Britain France and Ireland

Reverse Legend A. DNO FACTUM EST ISTUD ET EST MIRABILE — This is the Lord's doing and it is marvellous [in our eyes]

Obverse King in ship holding sword and shield; mintmark rose, escallop, coronet, mullet, tower, trefoil, cinquefoil, closed book.

Reverse Rose over radiant star, a lion and crown in each quarter; mintmarks as obverse.

| J1RY-020 | VG — | F £2,200 | VF £5,000 |

Third Coinage (1619 – 1625)

Obverse Legend IACOBUS DG MAG BRIT FRA ET HI REX — James by the grace of God King of Great Britain France and Ireland

Reverse Legend A DNO FACTUM EST ISTUD ET EST MIRABILE — This is the Lord's doing and it is marvellous [in our eyes]

Obverse Lion holding sceptre above the royal shield which divides 'XV'; mintmark spur rowel, rose, thistle, trefoil (at end of legend).

Reverse Rose over radiate star, a lion and crown in each quarter; mintmarks as obverse.

| J1RY-025 | VG — | F £2,200 | VF £5,000 |

Half Sovereign   Double Crown   Ten Shillings
Halfpound   Half Laurel

The gold half-sovereign with a value of ten shillings was introduced during the third coinage of Henry VIII. During the second coinage of James I it became known as the double crown and during the third coinage as the half-laurel after the laurel worn by the king instead of a crown. However, all gold issues from the reign of Charles I were known as double crowns. Also under Charles I, silver halfpounds were struck, mainly to pay troops loyal to the king during the civil war.

The half sovereign became a popular and much needed denomination and was produced for circulation as a gold coin until 1915 at the Royal Mint in London and then until 1926 at the Empire mint in South Africa. Thereafter, it was issued as a banknote until decimalization, when it was replaced by the fifty pence piece. Undoubtedly, the introduction of the half-sovereign, along with the gold crown, marked the start of the long haul towards decimalization and conformity.

Charles II's reign saw the introduction of the guinea and half-guinea which for a while replaced the sovereign and half-sovereign until the latter were re-introduced towards the end of George III's reign.

Gold ryals, also known as rose nobles, were produced during several reigns prior to Henry VIII and most, albeit not all, issues had a value of ten shillings. We have listed these issues in a separate chapter as they were not called half-sovereigns or fall into a wider scheme of creating a better denomination structure. Also listed separately are the gold angels which did sometimes have a value of ten shillings. Double crowns, ten-shillings, halfpounds and half-laurels can be found here.

Henry VIII   (1509 – 1547)

Half-sovereigns were produced during Henry VIII's third coinage (1544 – 47) at the Tower and Southwark mints in London and the Bristol mint. All issues are easily identified by the mintmarks found at the beginning of the legend, always on the obverse and sometimes on the reverse. After Henry VIII's death in 1547 and during the reign of his son Edward VI, half-sovereigns were produced in Henry's name at the Tower and Southwark mints. These issues are very similar to the third coinage and are included under Henry VIII. Collectors should refer to the third as well as the posthumous coinage when identifying an issue.

Collecting Hints

Both issues, while scarce, are obtainable. They are usually found in about Fine condition; VF and EF examples are very rare. Most coins are found unclipped and usually undamaged, but not well struck.

Third Coinage (1544 – 1547)

Tower Mint

Obverse Legend   HENRIC 8 DI GRA AGL FRANCI ET HIB REX (many varieties exist) — Henry VIII by the grace of God King of England France and Ireland

Reverse Legend   IHS AUTEM TRANSIENS PER MEDIV ILLORUM IBAT (many varieties exist) — But Jesus passing through their midst went His way

Obverse   King on throne holding orb and sceptre; mintmark lis or pellet in annulet.

Reverse   Crown over shield, lion and dragon either side.

| H8HS-005 | VG £240 | F £500 | VF £1,000 |

Southwark Mint

Legends   As previous.

Obverse   As previous, but mintmark 'S' or 'E'.

Reverse   As previous, but sometimes an 'E' below the shield; mintmarks as obverse, often muled.

| H8HS-010 | VG £240 | F £500 | VF £1,000 |

Bristol Mint

Legends   As previous.

Obverse   As previous, but mintmark 'WS'.

Reverse   As previous, but no 'E' below shield; sometimes no mintmark.

| H8HS-015 | VG £350 | F £750 | VF £1,700 |

Posthumous Coinage (1547 – 1551)

This issue closely resembles the previous one, but bears a youthful bust enthroned even though the obverse legend is the same.

Tower Mint

Legends   As previous.

Obverse   King with youthful bust sitting on the throne; mintmark arrow, annulet and pellet, lis, grapple, martlet.

Reverse   Crown over royal arms, lion and dragon either side; mintmark annulet and pellet, martlet.

| H8HS-020 | VG £250 | F £500 | VF £1,000 |

As previous, but a 'K' below the shield on the reverse, mintmark none, 'E' or 'K' as reverse mintmark only.

| H8HS-025 | VG £250 | F £500 | VF £1,000 |

As H8HS-020, but a grapple below the shield on the reverse; mintmark grapple or none.

| H8HS-030 | VG £250 | F £500 | VF £1,000 |

Southwark Mint

Legends As previous.

Obverse As H8HS-020; mintmark 'E' or none.

Reverse As H8HS-020, but sometimes 'E' below royal shield.

| H8HS-035 | VG £220 | F £450 | VF £950 |

Edward VI (1547 – 1553)

During Edward VI's reign a number of half-sovereigns of various styles were produced. The first issue was the posthumous Henry VIII, listed above. During the first period, half-sovereigns were produced very similar to the previous issue but with the obverse legend reading EDWARD 6 instead of HENRIC 8. During the second period, a variety of half-sovereigns were struck at the Tower mint as well as the Durham House mint, situated in London where the Strand is today. These issues show the bust of the Boy King, sometimes uncrowned, with a crown over the royal arms on the reverse. Finally, a half-sovereign was produced during the third period depicting a half-length figure of the king holding a sword and orb on the obverse and a crown over the royal arms on the reverse.

First Period (April 1547 – Jan. 1549)

Collecting Hints

These issues are quite rare and difficult to obtain. When available, they are usually in Fine condition.

Tower Mint

Obverse Legend EDWARD 6 DI GRA AGL FRANCI HIB REX — Edward VI by the grace of God King of England France and Ireland

Reverse Legend IHS AUTE TRANSIEN PER MEDIU ILLOR IBAT (minor varieties exist) — But Jesus passing through their midst went His way

Obverse King on throne holding orb and sceptre; mintmark arrow.

Reverse Crown over shield, lion and dragon either side.

| E6HS-005 | VG £300 | F £650 | VF £1,500 |

Southwark Mint

This issue is identical to the previous one except for the mintmark 'E' also, an 'E' of various styles can sometimes be found below the shield on the reverse.

| E6HS-010 | VG £350 | F £800 | VF £1,700 |

Second Period (Jan. 1549 – April 1550)

Collecting Hints

The issues from the Tower mint, while rare, are obtainable especially in Fine condition. However, all issues from Durham House are extremely rare and difficult to obtain in any grade. Collectors should pay particular attention to the obverse and reverse legend readings as this will help with identification.

Uncrowned Bust

Tower Mint

Obverse Legend TIMOR DOMINI FONS VITE MDXLIX — The fear of the Lord is the fountain of life 1549

Reverse Legend EDWARD VI D.G. AGL FRA Z HIB REX — Edward VI by the grace of God King of England France and Ireland

Obverse Uncrowned bust of king; mintmark arrow.

Reverse Crown over royal shield dividing 'E R' (EDWARD REX — Edward King).

E6HS-015   ex. rare

E6HS-035   VG £300   F £650   VF £1,500

Durham House Mint

Obverse Legend   As previous.

Reverse Legend   As obverse legend.

Obverse   Crowned bust of king; mintmark bow.

Reverse   As previous.

Varieties in the legends exist in this extremely rare issue as it sometimes muled with E6HS-030.

Obverse Legend   SCUTUM FIDEI PROTEGET EUM — The shield of faith shall protect him

Reverse Legend   As previous.

Obverse   As previous, but mintmark arrow or 'Y'. There is also an extremely rare variety with mintmark '6'.

Reverse   As previous.

E6HS-020   VG £325   F £750   VF £1,700

E6HS-040   ex. rare

Third Period (1550 – 1553)

Durham House Mint

Obverse Legend   As previous, but date MDXLVIII at end of legend.

Reverse Legend   As previous.

Obverse   As previous; mintmark bow.

Reverse   As previous.

E6HS-025   ex. rare

Collecting Hints

This most attractive issue is rare and difficult to obtain. When available, it is usually found in Fine or VF condition.

As previous, but undated.

E6HS-027   unique

Obverse Legend   EDWARD VI DG AGL FRA Z HIB REX — Edward VI by the grace of God King of England France and Ireland

Reverse Legend   IHS AUTEM TRANSIE PER MEDI ILLORU IBAT — But Jesus passing through their midst went His way

Obverse   Half-length figure of the king holding orb and sword; mintmark 'Y', tun.

Reverse   Crown over royal shield which divides 'E.R'.

Obverse Legend   LUCERNA PEDIBUS MEIS VERBUM TUUM — Thy word is a lamp unto my feet

Reverse Legend   As previous.

Obverse   As previous.

Reverse   As previous.

E6HS-030   ex. rare

E6HS-045   VG £450   F £1,250   VF £3,000

No half-sovereigns were produced during the reigns of Mary, and Philip and Mary.

Crowned Bust

Tower Mint

Obverse Legend   EDWARD VI DG AGL FRA Z HIBER REX — Edward VI by the grace of God King of England France and Ireland

Reverse Legend   SCUTUM FIDEI PROTEGET EUM — The shield of faith shall protect him

Obverse   Crowned bust of king; mintmark arrow, swan, grapple, 'Y', martlet.

Reverse   Crown over royal shield which divides 'E.R'.

Elizabeth I   (1558 – 1603)

During most of Elizabeth I's reign, hammered gold halfpounds with a value of ten shillings were produced. All issues show the bust of the queen on the obverse and a crown over the royal arms on the reverse while a mintmark can be found on the obverse and reverse at the beginning of the legends. During most of Elizabeth

125

I's reign gold angels with the same value as halfpounds were also produced; these issues can be found under the angels chapter. Gold halfpounds were also produced during the milled issue but in very small quantities.

Hammered Coinage Halfpound

Collecting Hints

These issues are attractive coins. They are usually found in Fine condition, however VF examples do exist. They are usually undamaged and unclipped but are sometimes creased; creasing occurs when a coin is folded or bent and then straightened, producing an area of flatness on its surface.

First – Third Issues (1559 – 1578)

The halfpounds for the first three issues hardly varied in style at all and were all struck at the Tower mint.

Obverse Legend   ELIZABETH DG ANG FR ET (or Z) HI REGINA — Elizabeth by the grace of God Queen of England France and Ireland

Reverse Legend   SCUTUM FIDEI PROTEGET EAM — The shield of faith shall protect her

Obverse   Youthful bust of queen crowned; wire-lined inner circles; mintmark lis.

Reverse   Crown over royal shield, 'E R.' (ELIZABETH REGINA) divided by crown.

| ELHP-005 | VG £350 | F £700 | VF £1,600 |

As previous, but beaded inner circles and mintmark cross crosslet, rose, portcullis, lion, coronet, castle.

| ELHP-010 | VG £300 | F £550 | VF £1,200 |

No halfpounds were struck for the fourth issue.

Fifth Issue (1583 – 1600)

Obverse Legend   ELIZAB(ETH) DG ANG FR ET HI REGINA — Elizabeth by the grace of God Queen of England France and Ireland

Reverse Legend   As previous.

Obverse   Older bust of queen with a more elaborate dress and a profusion of hair; mintmark tun, woolpack, key, anchor, 'O'.

Reverse   As previous.

| ELHP-015 | VG £350 | F £800 | VF £1,400 |

Sixth Issue (1601 – 1602)

As previous, but mintmark '1' or '2'.

| ELHP-020 | VG £400 | F £1,000 | VF £2,000 |

Milled Coinage Halfpound

This issue is easily differentiated from the hammered ones by style and the fact it has no inner circles. Minor varieties in the style and size of bust exist.

Collecting Hints

This issue which is usually found in Fine or VF condition is very rare and difficult to obtain.

Obverse Legend   ELIZABETH DG ANG FRA ET HIB REGINA — Elizabeth by the grace of God Queen of England France and Ireland

Reverse Legend   SCUTUM FIDEI PROTEGET EAM — The shield of faith shall protect her

Obverse   Crowned bust of queen; mintmark star or lis.

Reverse   Crown over royal shield which divides 'E.R'.

| ELHP-025 | VG £650 | F £1,600 | VF £3,800 |

James I   (1603 – 1625)

The erratic supply and fluctuating price of gold during the reign of James I was largely responsible for the lack of a comprehensive monetary policy regarding the denominations of gold coins. Half-sovereigns were produced during the first coinage but in very small numbers. Then, during the second coinage, double crowns were produced with a value of ten shillings until 1612 and eleven shillings after that. To avoid the ensuing confusion, the half-laurel was introduced during the third coinage; so called because the king was wearing a laurel wreath on his head instead of a crown. It bore its value of ten shillings behind the bust. Nevertheless, angels, which are listed in a separate chapter, were also produced at this time and usually had a value of ten shillings.

As previous, but fourth bust with the king's hair brushed forward and plainer armour; mintmark rose, escallop, grapes, coronet, key, bell.

| J1DC-015 | VG £180 | F £400 | VF £675 |

First Coinage (1603 – 1604)
Half Sovereign

Collecting Hints

This issue, easily identified by its unique legends, is extremely rare in any grade and collectors may encounter great difficulty in obtaining a specimen.

Obverse Legend   IACOBUS D G. ANGL SCO FRAN ET HIBER REX — James by the grace of God King of England Scotland France and Ireland

Reverse Legend   EXURGAT DEUS DISSIPENTUR INIMICI — Let God arise and His enemies be scattered

Obverse   Crowned bust of king; mintmark thistle.

Reverse   Crown above royal shield dividing 'I R' (IACOBUS REX).

As previous, but fifth bust with longer hair brushed back; several very minor varieties exist; mintmark mullet, tower, trefoil, cinquefoil, tun, book, crescent, plain cross, saltire, key.

| J1DC-020 | VG £180 | F £400 | VF £675 |

| J1HS-005 | VG — | F £2,000 | VF £4,500 |

Third Coinage (1619 – 1625)
Half Laurel

Collecting Hints

While scarce, this issue is obtainable especially in the lower grades. However, coins are sometimes found damaged and those in better than VF condition are extremely rare.

Obverse Legend   IACOBUS DG. MAG BRI FRA ET HIB REX — James by the grace of God King of Great Britain France and Ireland

Reverse Legend   HENRIC ROSAS REGNA IACOBUS — Henry united the roses, James the kingdoms

Obverse   Large bust of king wearing a laurel on his head; value (X) behind head; mintmark spur rowel.

Reverse   Cross over royal shield with crown above.

Second Coinage (1604 – 1619)
Double Crown

Collecting Hints

These issues, while scarce, are obtainable. There are minor varieties in the bust which we have listed. Coins, usually found unclipped and undamaged, are mostly available in Fine condition and although VF examples exist, they are rare.

Obverse Legend   IACOBUS DG. MAG BRIT FRAN ET HIB REX — James by the grace of God King of Great Britain France and Ireland

Reverse Legend   HENRICUS ROSAS. REGNA IACOBUS — Henry united the roses James the kingdoms

Obverse   Third bust of king with protruding, square-cut beard; mintmark lis, rose.

Reverse   Crown over royal shield dividing 'I R'.

| J1HL-025 | VG £225 | F £450 | VF £750 |

| J1DC-010 | VG £180 | F £400 | VF £675 |

As previous, but smaller, fourth bust; mintmark spur rowel, rose, thistle, lis, trefoil.

| J1HL-030 | VG £225 | F £450 | VF £750 |

Charles I   (1625 – 1649)

Both gold and silver coins with a value of ten shillings were issued under Charles I. The first issues struck at the Tower mint were gold and known as double crowns. Easily recognisable by the X for ten shillings found behind the king's bust, they were struck almost throughout Charles I's reign. The mintmarks and style of the bust and reverse shield differentiate the various issues. During 1631 – 32 Nicholas Briot introduced a superb milled ten-shillings. The quality and design of this issue is excellent and clearly differentiates it from other issues. During the Civil War the provincial mints of Oxford and Bristol produced gold half unites. Oxford and Shrewsbury produced a superb silver halfpound with a value of ten shillings.

Tower Mint Double Crown

Collecting Hints

Most issues, while scarce, are obtainable. The ones struck under the king tend to be more common than those struck under Parliament. Very large numbers of minor varieties exist and collectors should check all issues when identifying a coin. Most specimens are found in Fine condition, those in VF or better being very rare. These issues saw much circulation and are sometimes found damaged or clipped.

Tower Mint under King (1625 – 1643)

First Bust

Obverse Legend   CAROLUS DG MAG BRIT FRA ET HIB REX (many minor varieties exist) — Charles by the grace of God King of Great Britain France and Ireland

Reverse Legend   CULTORES SUI DEUS PROTEGIT — God protects His worshippers

Obverse   Bust of king wearing large ruff with value behind his head; mintmark lis, cross calvary.

Reverse   Crown above square-topped shield.

| C1DC-005 | VG £200 | F £400 | VF £800 |

Second Bust

Legends   As previous.

Obverse   Smaller bust of king wearing a ruff; mintmark cross calvary, blackamoor's head, castle, anchor, heart, plume.

Reverse   As previous.

| C1DC-010 | VG £200 | F £400 | VF £800 |

Third Bust

Legends   As previous.

Obverse   Shorter bust of king wearing heavier armour; mintmark plume or rose.

Reverse   Oval shield with crown above and dividing 'C.R.'.

| C1DC-015 | VG £200 | F £400 | VF £800 |

Fourth Bust

Legends   As previous.

Obverse   A slightly wider bust of king with a more pointed beard; several varieties of bust exist; mintmark harp, portcullis, tun, bell, crown, anchor.

Reverse   As previous, but a small crown over the 'C' and 'R'.

| C1DC-020 | VG £200 | F £400 | VF £800 |

Fifth Bust Aberystwyth Style

As previous, but large bust of good style; mintmark anchor, triangle.

| C1DC-025 | VG £200 | F £400 | VF £800 |

Sixth Bust Briot Style

As previous, but full, wide bust of king; mintmark triangle, star, triangle in circle.

| C1DC-030 | VG £225 | F £500 | VF £950 |

Briot's Hammered Issue

This issue is possibly a trial or pattern.

Legends   As previous.

Obverse   As previous; mintmark anchor.

Reverse   Rectangular shield with crown above, 'C.R' at sides.

| C1DC-035 | ex. rare |

Tower Mint under Parliament (1643 – 1648)

Legends   As previous.

Obverse   As C1DC-020, but mintmark eye.

Reverse   As C1DC-020.

| C1DC-040 | ex. rare |

Legends   As previous.

Obverse   As C1DC-025, but mintmark sun or sceptre.

Reverse   Oval shield.

| C1DC-045 | VG £350 | F £650 | VF £1,200 |

Legends   As previous.

Obverse   As C1DC-030, but mintmark '(P)'.

Reverse   As C1DC-030.

| C1DC-050 | VG £350 | F £650 | VF £1,200 |

Seventh Bust

As previous, but cruder bust of king with large nose; mintmark sun.

| C1DC-055 | VG £300 | F £600 | VF £1,300 |

As mentioned earlier, many varieties of most busts exist and it is important when identifying an issue to make sure the mintmark corresponds.

Briot's Milled Coinage (1631 – 1632)

Collecting Hints

This superb issue is rare. When available, it is usually found undamaged in Fine to EF condition.

Obverse Legend   CAROLUS DG MAG BRITAN FRAN ET HIB REX — Charles by the grace of God King of Great Britain France and Ireland

Reverse Legend   CULTORES SUI DEUS PROTEGIT — God protects His worshippers

Obverse   Detailed bust of king, value behind; mintmark 'B' and flower.

Reverse   Crown over square-topped shield, 'C.' and 'R' with small crowns above on either side of the shield; mintmark 'B' in legend.

| C1DC-060 | VG — | F £750 | VF £2,000 | EF £5,000 |

Provincial Mints

Bristol Half Unite

Obverse Legend   CAROLUS D.G. MAG BR FR ET H REX — Charles by the grace of God King of Great Britain France and Ireland

Outer Reverse Legend   EXURGAT DEUS DISSIPENTUR INIMICI — Let God arise and His enemies be scattered

Inner Reverse Legend   REL PRO LEG AN LIB PA — The religion of the Protestants the laws of England the liberty of Parliament

Obverse   Crowned left-facing bust holding sword and olive branch, 'X' behind bust; mintmark BR at start of legend.

Reverse   Declaration in a scroll, dated 1645, small plume with plumelet either side.

| C1HU-061 | ex. rare |

Oxford Mint

Oxford produced a gold half-unite, valued at ten shillings, and a silver halfpound. The gold half-unite bears the king's bust on the obverse and the Declaration in three lines on the reverse. The value of the coin can easily be distinguished by an X for ten shillings behind the king's bust. The only other gold half-unites were produced at the Tower mint and omit the Declaration on the reverse. The silver halfpound produced at Oxford is a superb, large coin. It shows the king on horseback on the obverse and, on the reverse, the Declaration in two lines with the date below it and the denomination X and three plumes above. This issue is very similar to the ones from Shrewsbury and collectors should refer to both mints for identification.

Gold Half Unite

Collecting Hints

This issue is very rare and usually found in Fine condition, sometimes damaged; it is very crude in style and production.

Obverse Legend   CAROLUS DG MAG BR FR ET HI REX — Charles by the grace of God King of Great Britain France and Ireland

Outer Obverse Legend   EXURGAT DEUS DISSIPERTUR INIMICI — Let God arise and His enemies be scattered

Inner Reverse Legend   RELIG PROT LEG ANG LIBER PAR — The religion of the Protestants the laws of England the liberty of Parliament

Obverse   Bust of king with value behind; no mintmark.

Reverse   Declaration in three straight lines, 1642.

| C1HU-065 | VG — | F £900 | VF £2,000 |

Obverse   As previous.
Reverse   Declaration in a scroll 1642 or 1643.

| C1HU-070 | VG £300 | F £700 | VF £1,400 |

Obverse   New-style bust to bottom of coin; legend begins at 7 o'clock.
Reverse   As previous, but dated 1643 only.

| C1HU-075 | VG £400 | F £1,000 | VF £2,000 |

As previous, but coin is dated 1644 with 'OX' below date.

| C1HU-080 | ex. rare |

Silver Halfpound

The Oxford halfpounds are very similar to the Shrewsbury issues but have minor differences, especially on the obverse. Collectors should pay particular attention to any mintmark and plume behind the king's head, as well as to whether the horse is on a groundline. All Oxford horses have a groundline while some Shrewsbury issues do not. Oxford issues are dated 1642 or 1643, Shrewsbury ones 1642 only. Oxford plumes have a 'tie' which is absent in Shrewsbury plumes. Collectors should refer to every issue from Oxford and Shrewsbury when identifying a coin and bear in mind that minor varieties exist in the legends.

Collecting Hints

While rare, these issues are available and usually found in Fine or VF condition, often with striking flaws or cracks in the flan.

Obverse Legend   CAROLUS DG MAG BRIT FRAN ET HIB REX — Charles by the grace of God King of Great Britain France and Ireland

Outer Reverse Legend   EXURGAT DEUS DISSIPENTUR INIMICI — Let God arise and His enemies be scattered

Inner Reverse Legend   RELIG PROT LEG ANG LIBER PAR — The religion of the Protestants the laws of England the liberty of Parliament

Obverse   King on horseback with plume behind; mintmark plume.

Reverse   Shrewsbury reverse die with three plumes without bands.

| C1HP-085 | VG £400 | F £800 | VF £2,500 |

As previous, but reverse has bands in the plumes; Oxford die.

| C1HP-090 | VG £400 | F £1,000 | VF £2,750 |

Shrewsbury Mint

These issues are very similar to the Oxford ones, where details on identification are given.

Collecting Hints

While rare, these issues are obtainable and usually found in Fine or VF condition, often with flaws or cracks in the flan due to striking.

Obverse Legend   CAROLUS D.G. MAG BRI FRA ET HIB REX —
Charles by the grace of God King of Great Britain France and Ireland

Outer Reverse Legend   EXURGAT DEUS DISSIPENTUR INIMICI —
Let God arise and His enemies be scattered

Inner Reverse Legend   RELIG PROT LEG ANGL LIBER PARL —
The religion of the Protestants the laws of England the liberty of
Parliament

Obverse   King on horseback with plume behind, no groundline;
mintmark nine pellets.

Reverse   Three plumes without bands and value X (ten shillings) above
Declaration, 1642 below.

C1HP-105   VG £450   F £1,000   VF £2,750

C1HP-095   VG £450   F £1,000   VF £2,750

As previous, but cannon and arms below horse; mintmark four pellets.

C1HP-110   VG £450   F £1,000   VF £2,750

As previous, but only two plumes on reverse above Declaration.

As previous, but just arms and no canon or plume on obverse.

C1HP-100   VG £450   F £1,000   VF £2,750

Obverse   King on horseback with groundline, plume behind.

Reverse   As C1HP-095.

C1HP-115   VG £450   F £1,000   VF £2,750

Exeter Mint

This issue is similar to the Exeter crown of Charles I. In fact it was struck from crown dies but is of double thickness, often known as a piedford, and therefore contains 10/-of silver.

Collecting Hints

This coin is extremely rare.

Obverse Legend   CAROLUS D.G. MAG BRI FRA ET HI REX — Charles by the grace of God King of Great Britain France and Ireland

Reverse Legend   CHRISTO AUSPICE REGNO — I reign under the auspices of Christ

Obverse   King on horseback; mintmark rose.

Reverse   Round garnished shield; mintmark rose.

C1HS-118   ex. rare

Colchester Siege Issue (1648)

Made of gold with a value of ten shillings, there is doubt as to whether this is a contemporary siege issue or a later, fantasy one. Although no documentary evidence exists to support its authenticity, we have decided to list it here.

Collecting Hints

This issue is of the highest rarity.

Obverse   Gateway to Colchester, 'C' and 'R' on either side, 'OBS COL 16SX48' in two lines; 'SX' stands for ten shillings.

Reverse   Plain.

C1HS-120   ex. rare

Commonwealth (1649 – 1660)

The Commonwealth double crown, struck in gold, is very similar to the other gold issues. The denomination is easily identifiable by an X for ten shillings above the two shields on the reverse. All issues are dated and have the mintmark sun or anchor on the obverse. Like all Commonwealth issues, the double crown is very plain in style and design, reflecting contemporary Puritan values.

Collecting Hints

The first issue is rare but obtainable, found in all grades from VG to EF. The issue with the mintmark anchor is extremely rare in all grades. Modern forgeries of this coin exist, dated 1651.

The following are dates and rarity values for the Commonwealth double crowns:

Date	Rarity
1649	R
1650	RR
1651	R
1652	RR
1653	R
1654	R
1655	R

1656	none were struck
1657	R
1660	RRR

Obverse Legend THE COMMONWEALTH OF ENGLAND

Reverse Legend GOD WITH US

Obverse St George's cross in shield within wreath; mintmark sun.

Reverse Shields of St George and Ireland; value X above, dated 1649 – 57.

CWDC-005 VG £280 F £550 VF £900

As previous, but mintmark anchor dated 1660.

CWDC-010 VG £750 F £1,800 VF £4,000

No double crowns were struck by Cromwell. The so-called half-broads of ten shillings are not contemporary.

Charles II   (1660 – 1685)

Hammered Coinage (1660 – 1662)

This rare gold issue bears a bust of the king on the obverse and a crown above the royal shield on the reverse. Should the bust be very different in style, it is probably an issue of Charles I.

Collecting Hints

Both issues are very rare and difficult to obtain. When available, they are usually in Fine or VF condition.

First Issue

Obverse Legend   CAROLUS II DG MAG BRIT FRAN ET HIB REX — Charles II by the grace of God King of Great Britain France and Ireland

Reverse Legend   FLORENT CONCORDIA REGNA — Through concord kingdoms flourish

Obverse   Bust of Charles II; mintmark crown.

Reverse   Crown over royal shield which divides 'C.R'.

C2DCH-005   VG £400   F £1,000   VF £2,400

Second Issue

As previous, but mark of value X behind king's bust.

C2DCH-010	VG £375	F £1,000	VF £2,400

Noble

During the reign of Edward III gold coins were produced in some quantity for the first time. The gold twenty-pence had been introduced in Henry III's reign and the gold leopard or florin at the beginning of Edward III's, but these issues are extremely rare and saw no circulation. However, this changed with the introduction of the gold noble. These issues, which were produced in some variety and quantity, show the king in a ship on the obverse and a cruciform design on the reverse. The value of the noble was six shillings and eightpence, i.e. eighty pence (80d). Smaller gold denominations, the half-noble and quarter-noble, complemented the monetary reform.

Edward III   (1327 – 1377)

Large quantities of gold nobles were produced with many varieties, all of which are minor. On Edward III's issues, the word EDWARD or EDWAR is found on the obverse legend and usually divided by the front of the ship. Although Edward IV also issued nobles, he used the mintmarks rose or lis, found on the obverse and/or reverse legends; and, should the coin have a rose on the king's ship, it is an Edward IV ryal. Many varieties of nobles exist, the main differences being the obverse legends which reflect the British monarch's claim to the sovereignty of all or part of France. During the second, third and fourth coinages Edward laid claim to the throne of France, so FRANC can be found in the obverse legend. Following the 1360 treaty (for details see p.343) FRANC was replaced by ACQ on the coins. After the treaty broke down in 1369, FRANC was reintroduced on the obverse legend of the nobles. Two mints were active producing nobles under Edward III, London, and Calais in France. Until 1361, all issues were struck in London but the town of Calais also produced nobles thereafter. Calais was chosen as a mint for two reasons: the fact that an English king struck English coins in France contained a very powerful political statement, also, with the growth of European commerce, it was useful for English merchants trading on the continent to have a supply of good quality coins. Issues from Calais can usually be identified by a C in the middle of the obverse cross and sometimes a flag on the stern of the ship. There are exceptions which are all listed in the various issues.

Collecting Hints

Most issues, while scarce, are obtainable and usually found unclipped in Fine to VF condition. Coins sometimes have solder marks where they have been made into jewellery (mounted), in which case they are worth considerably less than unmounted examples. Modern forgeries of the Treaty period are known to exist.

Second Coinage (1344 – 1346)

This issue weighs 138.5 grains (9.0 grams).

Obverse Legend EDWAR DGRA REX ANGL Z FRANC DNS HYB — Edward by the grace of God King of England and France Lord of Ireland

Reverse Legend IHC AUTEM TRANSIENS PER MEDIUM ILLORUM IBAT — But Jesus passing through their midst went His way

Obverse King holding sword and shield in ship, large lettering with Lombardic 'N'.

Reverse 'L' in centre of cross.

E3NB-005 ex. rare

Third Coinage (1346 – 1351)

This issue weighs 128.5 grains (8.3 grams).

As previous, but a large 'E' in centre of the reverse cross.

E3NB-010	VG —	F £1,200	VF £2,800

Fourth Coinage (1351 – 1377)

All issues weigh 120 grains (7.8 grams).

Pre-Treaty Period (1351 – 1361)

This issue was struck while Edward was laying claim to the French throne and FRANC can be found in the obverse legend. Many minor varieties exist and have been listed, however, no true gold nobles are known for series A as they are muled with series B.

Series B/A (1351)

Obverse Legend EDWARD DEI GRA REX ANGL Z FRANC D HYB(E) — Edward by the grace of God King of England and France Lord of the Irish

Reverse Legend IHE AUTEM TRANSIENS PER MEDIUM ILLORUM IBAT — But Jesus passing through their midst went His way

Obverse King holding sword and shield on ship, open 'C' and 'E', Roman 'M' and 'N' in legend; mintmark cross I.

Reverse Lombardic 'M' and 'N' in legends, 'E' in centre of reverse cross.

E3NB-015	VG £325	F £650	VF £1,000

Series C (1351 – 1352)

Similar to previous, but closed 'C' and 'E', Lombardic 'M', Roman 'N' and wedge-tailed 'R'; mintmark cross 1.

E3NB-020	VG £300	F £650	VF £1,000

Series D (1352 – 1353)

As above, but mintmark cross 1 or broken cross 2 on reverse only.

E3NB-025	VG £325	F £700	VF £1,150

Series E (1354 – 1355)

Mintmark cross 2 or cross 3 with broken letters in the legend, the 'V' often has a nick in the right limb.

E3NB-030	VG £325	F £600	VF £1,000

Series F (1356)

Mintmark crown only; the 'C's and 'E's are often broken at the top.

E3NB-035	VG £325	F £700	VF £1,150

Series G (1356 – 1361)

Mintmark cross 3 or cross 4; the 'E's in the legend are often broken and with an extra long middle bar.

E3NB-040	VG £300	F £550	VF £1,000

Many of the dies for these issues are muled. The following mules are very rare (the first letter refers to the obverse die, the second to the reverse):
B/A, C/D, E/F, G/F, F/G.

Transitional Period (1361)

This issue can be easily recognised by the obverse legend reading ACQ (many varieties exist) and omitting FRANC; mintmark cross potent.

Obverse Legend   EDWARD DEI GRA REX ANGL DNS HIB Z ACQ (many varieties exist) — Edward by the grace of God King of England Lord of Ireland and Aquitaine

Reverse Legend   IHC AUTE TRANSIES P MEDIUM ILLORR IBAT (many varieties exist and often entire words are missing) — But Jesus passing through their midst went His way

Obverse   King with sword and shield in ship; mintmark cross potent, abnormal size 'I', 'H', 'P', 'F' or 'N' sometimes in legends.

Reverse   'E' in centre of cross, annulet or pellet at corner of central cross.

E3NB-045	VG £250	F £500	VF £1,000

Treaty Period (1361 – 1369)

This issue is very similar to the previous one, with the mintmark cross potent and virtually identical obverse and reverse legends. However, in all cases a saltire or annulet can be found at the start of the obverse legend, just before EDWARD. During this period coins were also struck at Calais. Modern forgeries of the Treaty period are known to exist.

London Mint

Legends   As previous.

Obverse   As previous, but an annulet or saltire before EDWARD.

Reverse   As previous, but the 'A' in IBAT is unbarred.

E3NB-050	VG £280	F £550	VF £950

Calais Mint

Legends   As previous.

Obverse   As previous, with saltire, quatrefoil or nothing before EDWARD, all 'A's in the legend are unbarred, flag at stern of ship.

Reverse   'C' in centre of cross.

E3NB-055	VG £280	F £550	VF £950

As previous, but no flag at stern of ship.

E3NB-060	VG £280	F £550	VF £950

Post-Treaty Period (1369 – 1377)

During this period nobles were struck in London and Calais. Once again the obverse die has been changed and includes FRANC and also AQT (varieties). This legend is unique to the period and while many varieties exist, the words for France and Aquitaine always appear.

London Mint

Obverse Legend   EDWARD DEI G REX ANG Z FRA DNS HYB Z AQT — Edward by the grace of God King of England and France Lord of Ireland and Aquitaine

Reverse Legend   As previous.

E3NB-065	VG £280	F £550	VF £1,000

As previous, but a crescent on the forecastle of the king's ship.

E3NB-070	VG £280	F £550	VF £1,000

As ED3NB-065 with new-style thin, tall lettering, 'E' with a pellet in centre of reverse.

E3NB-075	VG £280	F £550	VF £1,000

As previous, but an 'E' with a saltire in the centre on the reverse.

E3NB-080	VG £280	F £550	VF £1,000

Calais Mint

Legends   As previous.
Obverse   Flag at stern of ship.
Reverse   'E' in centre of reverse.

E3NB-085	VG £280	F £550	VF £1,000

As previous, but an 'E' with pellet in centre of reverse.

E3NB-090	VG £280	F £550	VF £1,000

No flag on ship but a 'C' in centre of reverse.

E3NB-095	VG £280	F £600	VF £1,200

Richard II   (1377 – 1399)

During the reign of Richard II nobles were struck at the London and Calais mints. As with the previous reign, the obverse shows the king holding a sword and shield in a ship and the reverse an elaborate cross with decoration around it. The issues are fairly easy to identify as RICARD appears at the beginning of the obverse legend, broken by the bow of the ship. No other Richard issued gold coins so it can only be an issue of Richard II. The issues from the mint of Calais, which was under English rule at the time, are identified by the fact that the king's ship has a flag on it. The style of the letters in the legends of Richard II varies greatly and is important when identifying the issues.

Collecting Hints

All Richard II nobles are very rare and difficult to obtain. When available they are usually found in Fine to VF condition, unclipped and undamaged. These coins tend to have been found in hoards, hence the reasonable condition of the specimens.

London Mint

The first issue of Richard II's coinage used a reverse and/or an obverse die from an Edward III issue. On the obverse die Edward's name was altered to RICARD and an 'R' placed over the 'E' in the centre of the reverse. Various dies were used and the legends are the same as the issues of Edward III.

R2NB-005	VG £375	F £1,100	VF £2,000

Obverse Legend   RICARD DI G REX ANGL Z FR DNS HIBS Z AQT (minor varieties in abbreviation exist) — Richard by the grace of God King of England and France Lord of Ireland and Aquitaine

Reverse Legend   IHC AUTEM TRANSIENS PER MEDIUM ILLORR IBAT (many varieties exist) — But Jesus passing through their midst went His way

Obverse   King in the ship with a lis over the sail, lettering in the style of Edward III.

Reverse   Cross with 'R' in centre, decoration around cross.

R2NB-010	VG £375	F £1,000	VF £1,800

Obverse Legend   As previous, but sometimes omits FRA.
Reverse Legend   As previous.

Obverse   As previous, but no lis, annulet above the sail, straight-sided lettering in the legends.
Reverse   As previous.

| R2NB-015 | VG £340 | F £900 | VF £1,600 |

Obverse Legend   RICARD DI GR REX ANGL DNS HIBS Z AQT — Richard by the grace of God King of England Lord of Ireland and Aquitaine (NB: French title omitted)

Reverse Legend   As previous.

Obverse   Fishtail lettering in legends, sometimes with a lis or lion on the ship's rudder and/or a trefoil by the king's shield.

Reverse   As previous.

| R2NB-020 | VG £400 | F £1,000 | VF £2,000 |

Legends & Reverse   As previous.

Obverse   Dumpy style lettering with sometimes an escallop or crescent on the ship's rudder and/or a trefoil over the sail.

| R2NB-025 | VG £350 | F £950 | VF £1,700 |

Calais Mint

These issues can easily be identified by the flag on the stern.

Obverse Legend   As R2NB-005 (altered dies with France in the legend).

Reverse Legend   As previous.

Obverse   The king in a ship with a flag at stern.

Reverse   As previous.

| R2NB-030 | VG £400 | F £1,000 | VF £1,900 |

As R2NB-015 with straight-sided lettering and a quatrefoil over the sail.

| R2NB-035 | VG £400 | F £1,000 | VF £1,900 |

As R2NB-020, but with fishtailed lettering.

| R2NB-040 | VG £375 | F £975 | VF £1,850 |

As previous, but a lion on the ship's rudder.

| R2NB-045 | VG £425 | F £1,100 | VF £2,200 |

As R2NB-025 with small, dumpy-style lettering, sometimes a trefoil over sail or a crescent on the rudder.

| R2NB-050 | VG £375 | F £975 | VF £1,850 |

Henry IV   (1399 – 1413)

The gold nobles of Henry IV's reign can be divided into the heavy coinage (120 grains, 7.8 grams) and the light coinage (108 grains, 7.0 grams). The issue can be identified by several points; firstly HENRIC appears at the beginning of the obverse legend and is broken by the bow of the ship. But Henry IV was not the only Henry to produce nobles, Henry V and Henry VI (1st reign), also struck them. At a quick glance all issues look similar, but variations actually differentiate them from each other. It is important that collectors pay particular attention to the mintmark, which can sometimes be found clearly on the obverse and always on the reverse at the beginning of the legend. The only mintmark of Henry IV's issues was cross pattée. Minor marks and varieties are also found on all issues. If uncertain, collectors should check all issues from all reigns when identifying a noble. During the heavy coinage, London and Calais produced nobles. The Calais mint, like previous reigns, is identified by a flag at the stern of the king's ship.

Collecting Hints

All issues from the heavy coinage are extremely rare, and very difficult to obtain. The issues from the light coinage, while rare, sometimes appear on the market. They are usually found in the higher grades, with VF being the average condition; collectors will have great difficulty in obtaining an example. Modern forgeries of the heavy noble are known to exist.

Heavy Coinage (1399 – 1412)
London Mint

Obverse Legend   HENRIC DI GRA REX ANGL Z FRANC DNS HIB Z AQT (many varieties exist) — Henry by the grace of God King of England and France Lord of the Irish and Aquitaine

Reverse Legend   IHC AUTEM TRANSIENS PER MEDIUM ILLORR IBAT — But Jesus passing through their midst went His way

Obverse   The king standing in a ship, four lis on upper part of his shield, crescent on ship's rudder; mintmark cross pattée.

Reverse   H in cross, sometimes over 'R', obviously a Richard II reverse die.

| H4NB-005 | VG — | F — | VF £12,000 |

As previous, but three lis on shield, a crescent, pellet or lis on ship's rudder.

| H4NB-010 | VG — | F — | VF £12,000 |

Calais Mint

As H4NB-005 but a flag at the stern of the ship, a crown on or to the left of the ship's rudder.

| H4NB-015 | ex. rare |

As H4NB-010, but with a flag at the stern of the ship, a crown or saltire on the rudder.

| H4NB-020 | VG — | F — | VF £11,000 |

Light Coinage (1412 – 1413)

This issue was only struck at the London mint.

Legends As previous.

Obverse New-style shield with three lis, trefoil or trefoil and annulet on side of ship; mintmark cross pattée.

Reverse Trefoil on quarter.

| H4NB-025 | VG — | F £1,600 | VF £3,200 |

Henry V (1413 – 1422)

Henry V's issues closely resemble those of Henry IV and Henry VI. Collectors should refer to the general introduction to Henry IV to help identify the various issues and reigns. All of Henry V's issues were struck in London and the mintmarks used, which are unique to these issues, are cross pattée or pierced cross, both with central pellet. In all except class G, a quatrefoil can be found above the ship's sail and in one quarter of the reverse. These minor varieties are unique to these issues.

Class A

Obverse Legend HENRIC DI GRA REX ANGL Z FRANC DNS HYB (often abbreviated) — Henry by the grace of God King of England and France Lord of the Irish (NB: the omission of 'and Aquitaine' is another small difference between Henry IV and Henry V issues)

Reverse Legend IHC AUTEM TRAN(S)IENS PER MEDIUM ILLORR IBAT (varieties exist) — But Jesus passing through their midst went His way

Obverse King on a ship with a quatrefoil over the ship's sail, short broad lettering.

Reverse Cross with 'H' in centre, quatrefoil in second quarter of cross.

| H5NB-005 | ex. rare |

Class B

As previous, but ordinary lettering with barred 'H's, sometimes an annulet on the ship's rudder.

| H5NB-010 | VG £400 | F £750 | VF £1,500 |

Class C

New-style lettering, a mullet by the king's sword, sometimes an annulet on the ship's rudder or a broken annulet on the ship's side. Modern forgeries of this issue are known.

| H5NB-015 | VG £400 | F £750 | VF £1,500 |

Class D

Mullet and annulet by king's sword, a trefoil by the shield and a broken annulet on the ship's side.

| H5NB-020 | VG £350 | F £700 | VF £1,450 |

Class E

Pellet at king's sword point, annulet or trefoil on ship's side, trefoil by shield, unbroken annulet and sometimes a mullet by the king's sword-arm.

| H5NB-025 | VG £350 | F £700 | VF £1,450 |

Class F

Trefoil by king's shield, annulet or trefoil on ship's side, mullet and sometimes annulet by sword arm.

| H5NB-030 | VG £350 | F £700 | VF £1,450 |

Class G

No marks in field and no quatrefoil on obverse or reverse, annulet stops and mullet after HENRIC in obverse legend.

| H5NB-035 | VG £375 | F £850 | VF £1,650 |

Henry VI First Reign (1422 – 1461)

Nobles were struck throughout the reign of Henry VI, but the decline in the supply of gold was reflected in the quantity of coins struck. Thus, while fairly large numbers were produced in the first part of the reign, very few were issued towards the end of the period and then only at the London mint. As with all of Henry VI coins, the nobles can be divided into issues differentiated by various marks, usually in the legends. These marks were a form of quality control, so that the dies could be linked to various

issues. As was stated above, Henry VI issues are fairly similar to those of Henry IV and Henry V and collectors might have to refer to all three reigns when identifying a coin and pay particular attention to the different mintmarks and any unusual marks found on the coin or in the legend. No nobles were struck during Henry VI's second reign.

As with previous issues, the mintmark can be found on the reverse of the coin at the beginning of the legend. HENRIC can always be found on the obverse and is usually broken by the bow of the king's ship. Three mints, in London, Calais and York, were active during the first part of Henry VI's reign. The issues from Calais are easy to identify as they have a flag at the stern of the king's ship while those from York have no flag but a lis over the stern. The London issue have neither a flag nor a lis.

As England's European trade steadily increased from Edward I's reign onwards, large quantities of English coins, which were known for their quality, good weight and metal fineness, ended up in Europe despite various forms of currency control. Gold nobles in particular were so popular that they were imitated and produced in some quantity in the Low Countries. The style of these imitations however is different from the English issue.

Annulet Issue (1422 – 1427)

London Mint

Obverse Legend HENRIC DI GRA REX ANGL Z FRANC DNS HYB — Henry by the grace of God King of England and France Lord of the Irish

Reverse Legend IHC AUTEM TRANSIENS PER MEDIUM ILLORR IBAT — But Jesus passing through their midst went His way

Obverse King on ship holding sword and shield, annulet by his arm.

Reverse Annulets in legend and one annulet in the spandrel; mintmark lis.

| H6NB-005 | VG £250 | F £600 | VF £900 |

As previous, but the obverse die is from a Henry V issue and so bears no annulet. Forgeries of this issue are known.

| H6NB-010 | VG — | F £1,000 | VF £1,800 |

| H6NB-030 | VG £400 | F £900 | VF £1,850 |

Calais Mint

As H6NB-005 but a flag at the stern of the king's ship, 'H' in the centre of the reverse.

| H6NB-015 | VG £375 | F £750 | VF £1,200 |

As previous, but 'C' in the centre of the reverse.

| H6NB-020 | VG £250 | F £525 | VF £850 |

York Mint

As H6NB-005, but a lis over the stern of the ship.

| H6NB-025 | VG £400 | F £800 | VF £1,600 |

Rosette Mascle Issue (1427 – 1430)

London Mint

Legends As previous.

Obverse A lis by the sword arm, rosettes or rosettes and mascles in the legend.

Reverse Lis in second quarter, mintmark lis, rosettes or rosettes and mascles in the legend.

Calais Mint

Obverse As previous, but a flag on the stern of the ship.

Reverse Mintmark lis.

| H6NB-035 | VG £400 | F £900 | VF £1,850 |

Pinecone Mascle Issue (1430 – 1434)

Legends As previous.

Obverse Pinecone and mascle in legends.

Reverse A lis in one quarter, pinecones and mascles in the legend; mintmark lis.

| H6NB-040 | VG £400 | F £900 | VF £1,850 |

Leaf Mascle Issue (1434s – 1435)

Legends As previous.

Obverse A leaf in the sea, saltires and a mascle in the legend.

Reverse Saltires with one leaf and one mascle in the legend; mintmark lis.

| H6NB-045 | VG — | F £2,500 | VF ex. rare |

Leaf Trefoil Issue (1435 – 1438)

Legends As previous.

Obverse & Reverse Leaves and trefoils in legends.

| H6NB-050 | VG — | F £3,000 | VF £6,000 |

Trefoil Issue (1438 – 1443)

Legends As previous.

Obverse Trefoil to left of shield, saltires in legend.

Reverse Saltires, trefoils and a pellet in legend; mintmark lis.

| H6NB-055 | VG — | F £3,000 | VF ex. rare |

Leaf Pellet Issue (1445 – 1454)

Legends   As previous.

Obverse   An annulet, lis and leaf below the king's shield.

Reverse   A pellet before the 'H' in centre reverse, annulets and saltires in legend.

| H6NB-060 | VG — | F £2,500 | VF ex. rare |

Cross Pellet Issue (1454 – 1460)

Legends   As previous.

Obverse & Reverse   Details unknown.

| H6NB-065 | unique |

| E4NB-005 | VG — | F £5,000 | VF £10,000 |

As previous, but quatrefoil below the sword arm; mintmark rose on the obverse, lis on the reverse.

| E4NB-010 | ex. rare |

As previous, but rose in two spandrels on reverse; mintmark rose obverse and reverse.

| E4NB-015 | ex. rare |

Edward IV First Reign (1461 – 1470)

The gold noble, which had hardly changed in style, value or quality since the reign of Edward III, was produced for the last time during Edward IV's reign. The rise in the price of gold from the 1430s onwards meant that gold coins were worth more in Europe than in England and had resulted in a shortage in England, as gold coins were taken abroad for profit. The situation became particularly problematic during Edward IV's reign and only a small quantity of nobles was struck during the heavy coinage. Finally in 1464, to stop gold coins drifting to the Continent, the value of all gold nobles in circulation was raised from six shillings and eight pence to eight shillings and four pence and a new coin, the rose noble or ryal was introduced. With a value of ten shillings and weighing 120 grains (7.8 grams), the ryal is easily recognisable by the rose on the king's ship featured on the obverse and the different central design on the reverse. However, the new denomination proved unpopular and was discontinued after 1470. By contrast the angel, which was introduced in 1464 with a value of six shillings and eight pence as the original noble had been, soon became an important and popular denomination. Edward IV's heavy coinage nobles are fairly similar to those of Edward III except for the mintmarks which are unique to each issue; Edward III used various crosses, while Edward IV used mintmark rose or lis, sometimes muled.

Heavy Coinage (1461 – 1464)

London was the only mint that produced gold coins during the heavy coinage.

Collecting Hints

All three issues are extremely rare; when available, examples are usually found in Fine to VF condition.

Obverse Legend   EDWARD DI GRA REX ANGL Z FRANC DNS HYB — Edward by the grace of God King of England and France Lord of Ireland (legend starts at 11 o'clock)

Reverse Legend   IHC AUTEM TRANSIENS PER MEDIUM ILLOR IBAT — But Jesus passing through their midst went His way

Obverse   King with sword and shield in ship, a lis below the shield.

Reverse   Central cross; mintmark lis.

Light Coinage (1464 – 1470)
Rose Noble or Ryal

During this period, large quantities of gold coins needed to be produced and the provincial mints of Bristol, Coventry, Norwich and York as well as, of course, London took an active part. The various mints can easily be identified by their initials, found in the waves below the king's ship. These are none for London, 'B' for Bristol, 'C' for Coventry, 'N' for Norwich and 'E' for York.

In style as well as value, the rose noble was a popular coin on the Continent and various copies were struck throughout the 16th century, mainly in the Low Countries. They are all copies of the London mint and very crude in style with coarse features. Also, the flans of these copies are larger than the English issues.

Collecting Hints

All London issues, while scarce, are obtainable. They are usually found undamaged with full unclipped flans in Fine to VF condition. Coins from the provincial mints, in particular Coventry and Norwich, are much scarcer and more difficult to obtain.

London Mint

Obverse Legend   EDWARD D. GRA REX ANG Z FRANC DNS (H)IB — Edward by the grace of God King of England and France Lord of Ireland

Reverse Legend   IHC AUT TRANSIENS PER MEDIUM ILLOR IBAT — But Jesus passing through their midst went His way

Obverse   King holding sword and shield, large rose on side of ship, banner with E on stern; mintmark rose, sun or crown, sometimes only on reverse.

Reverse   Rose over radiate sun in centre, fleurs in spandrels.

| E4NB-020 | VG £300 | F £650 | VF £1,150 |

As previous, but small trefoils in spandrels on reverse; mintmark crown, sun over crown, long cross fitchée sometimes only on reverse.

| E4NB-025 | VG £300 | F £650 | VF £1,150 |

Bristol Mint

Legends As previous.
Obverse As E4NB-020, 'B' in waves below ship.
Reverse Large fleurs in spandrels; mintmark sun, crown.

| E4NB-030 | VG £375 | F £800 | VF £1,750 |

As previous, but small trefoils in spandrels; mintmark crown or sun only on reverse.

| E4NB-035 | VG £375 | F £750 | VF £1,450 |

Coventry Mint

Legends As previous.
Obverse As E4NB-020, but 'C' in waves below ship.
Reverse Mintmark sun.

| E4NB-040 | VG £500 | F £1,450 | VF £3,200 |

Norwich Mint

Modern forgeries of this issue are known.

Legends As previous.
Obverse As E4NB-020, but 'N' in waves below ship.
Reverse Mintmark rose? or sun.

| E4NB-045 | VG £500 | F £1,200 | VF £2,750 |

York Mint

Modern forgeries of this issue are known.

Legends As previous.
Obverse As E4NB-020, but 'E' in waves below ship; no mintmark.
Reverse Large fleurs in spandrels; mintmark sun, sun and lis, lis.

| E4NB-050 | VG £375 | F £800 | VF £1,600 |

As previous, but small fleurs in spandrels on reverse; mintmark lis or sun.

| E4NB-055 | VG £375 | F £800 | VF £1,600 |

Angel

During the reign of Edward IV the weights and values of coins had to be changed to bring them more in line with the fluctuating price of gold. The gold noble which had been a popular denomination, especially with merchants, with a value of six shillings and eight pence was replaced by the ryal or rose noble, with a value of ten shillings. Also, the value of all nobles from previous issues was raised to eight shillings and four pence, to prevent the export of coins from England. This, however, left an unwelcome gap in the denomination structure, so the gold angel was introduced with a value of six shillings and eight pence, the same as the earlier nobles. The design shows St Michael spearing a dragon on the obverse and a ship on the reverse. These issues were much more life-like in style when compared to earlier ones. The denomination was retained until the reign of Charles I and even though the value changed, the general design and style did not.

Edward IV First Reign (1461 – 1470)

The gold angel from the first reign of Edward IV is fairly easy to identify. The king's name is found at the beginning of the obverse legend and reads EDWARD and although angels were struck in Edward IV's second reign and under Edward V, each reign used different styles and mintmarks. The mintmark is found at the beginning of the legends, but not always on both sides of the coin.

Collecting Hints

All issues are extremely rare. The few examples we have traced are in VF to EF condition.

Obverse Legend EDWARD D GRA REX . ANGL FRANC DNS HB — Edward by the grace of God King of England France Lord of Ireland

Reverse Legend PER CRUCE TUA SALVA NOS XPC REDEMPTOR (minor varieties exist) — By Thy Cross save us O Christ our Redeemer

Obverse St Michael spearing a dragon.

Reverse Ship with cross and arms at centre, rays of sun at masthead, large rose and sun by mast; mintmark rose.

E4AG-005   ex rare

As previous, but small rose and sun at mast; mintmark crown.

E4AG-010   ex rare

Henry VI Restored (Oct. 1470 – April 1471)

During this very short period gold angels were struck at the London and Bristol mints which stylistically were very much a con-

tinuation from the reign of Edward IV. Henry VII and Henry VIII also produced angels, however, all issues of Henry VI have a lis beside the mast of the ship on the reverse, while the issues of Henry VII and Henry VIII have a rose. If uncertain, collectors should check the coin's mintmark, usually found on the obverse at the beginning of the legend. Moreover, the Bristol issue is easily identified by a 'B' in the waves on the reverse.

Collecting Hints

Considering that these issues were produced for such a short period, it is not surprising that they are both very rare. When available, they are usually found in Fine or VF condition.

London Mint

Obverse Legend HENRIC DI GRA REX ANGL Z FRANC (minor varieties exist) — Henry by the grace of God King of England and France

Reverse Legend PER CRUCE TUA SALVA NOS XPC REDEMPTOR — By Thy Cross save us O Christ our Redeemer

Obverse St Michael killing a dragon; mintmark Restoration cross or none.

Reverse Ship with arms and mast in the shape of a cross, an 'H' and a lis divided by the cross; mintmark cross pattée, lis or Restoration cross.

H6AG-005   VG £300   F £600   VF £1,200

Bristol Mint

Legends As previous.

Obverse As previous, but no mintmark.

Reverse As previous, but 'B' in the waves below the ship; mintmark Restoration cross or none.

H6AG-010   VG £400   F £1,000   VF £1,800

Edward IV Second Reign (1471 – 1483)

These two issues are very much a continuation from the reign of Henry VI. The style is not as detailed as that of Edward's first reign angel, but this issue is much more common. Mintmarks play an important part in identification and collectors should also refer

to the Edward V angel where the issues are discussed. As with the previous reign, the Bristol mint was also active and can easily be identified by a 'B' in the waves below the ship on the reverse.

London Mint

Obverse Legend   EDWARD DI GRA REX ANGL Z FRANC — Edward by the grace of God King of England and France

Reverse Legend   PER CRUCEM TUAM SALVA NOS XPC REDEMPTOR (varieties exist) — By Thy cross save us O Christ our Redeemer

Obverse   St Michael killing a dragon; mintmark short cross fitchée, annulet, pellet in annulet, cross and four pellets, heraldic cinquefoil, pierced cross, cross with pellet in one quarter.

Reverse   Ship with arms and mast in the shape of a cross, an 'E' and a rose divided by the mast.

| E4AG-015 | VG £230 | F £500 | VF £750 |

Bristol Mint

Legends   As previous.

Obverse   As previous, but mintmark annulet only.

Reverse   As previous, but a 'B' in waves below ship.

| E4AG-020 | VG — | F £1,000 | VF £2,000 |

Edward IV or V

Gold angels of the London mint with the mintmark of halved sun and rose are thought to have been struck under Edward V from dies made during the reign of Edward IV. These issues are identical to the Edward IV second reign angel except for the mintmark.

Obverse Legend   EDWARD DI GRA REX ANGL Z FRANC — Edward by the grace of God King of England and France

Reverse Legend   PER CRUCEM TUAM SALVA NOS CHRISTE REDEMPTOR — By Thy Cross save us O Christ our Redeemer

Obverse   St Michael killing a dragon; mintmark halved sun and rose.

Reverse   Ship with arms and mast in the shape of a cross, an 'E' and a rose divided by the mast.

| E4AG-025 | VG — | F £1,400 | VF £3,000 |

Edward V   (1483)

This issue is very much a continuation of the last one but again the mintmark is different. On the obverse there is the mintmark boar's head which was the personal emblem of Richard III who was Edward's 'Protector'; on the reverse the mintmark halved sun and rose is used again. This reverse die is from the previous issue, it is only the obverse die which is new.

As previous, but mintmark boar's head on the obverse.

| E5AG-005 | ex. rare |

Richard III   (1483 – 1485)

Very few coins were struck under Richard III and the gold angel was no exception. Several issues used altered dies from the previous reigns, all have an 'R' for Richard besides the ship's mast and in the two more common issues the king's name appears as RICARD or RICAD. All issues were struck at the London mint.

Obverse Legend   EDWARD DI GRA REX ANGL Z FRANC — Edward by the grace of God King of England and France

Reverse Legend   PER CRUCEM TUAM SALVA NOS CHRISTIE REDEMPTOR — By the Cross save us O Christ our Redeemer

Obverse   St Michael killing dragon; mintmark halved sun and rose.

Reverse   'R' over 'E' by ship's mast on reverse; mintmark sun and rose. This die was originally from Edward IV/V.

| R3AG-005 | probably unique |

As previous, but mintmark boar's head on obverse (Edward V die); reverse as previous.

R3AG-010	probably unique

Obverse Legend   RICARD DI GRA REX ANGL Z FRANC — Richard by the grace of God King of England and France

Reverse Legend   As previous.

Obverse   St Michael killing a dragon; mintmark sun and rose or boar's head.

Reverse   'R' by ship's mast, sometimes over 'E' (Edward IV/V die); mintmark sun and rose or boar's head, sometimes muled.

R3AG-015	VG £600	F £1,400	VF £2,200

Obverse Legend   RICA(R)D DI GRA REX ANGL Z FRANC — Richard by the grace of God King of England and France

Reverse Legend   As previous.

Obverse   As previous.

Reverse   'R' by mast, small cross on reverse; mintmark as previous.

R3AG-020	VG £600	F £1,400	VF £2,250

Henry VII   (1485 – 1509)

Throughout Henry VII's reign gold angels were produced at the London mint in some quantity. There are several varieties and we have listed them all. The main differences in type is that St Michael, instead of being a feathered figure, is wearing armour on the later issues and there are two different reverse legends which we have listed. Henry VIII also produced angels during the first part of his reign but these issues can be identified by the eight in either Roman (VIII) or Arabic (8) numerals after the king's name. Similarly, angels were produced in Henry VI's second reign but are distinguishable from their mintmarks, style and various marks on the coin.

Collecting Hints

All issues are rare but obtainable. Coins are usually found undamaged in Fine or VF condition. However, on some issues the legends are not all clear, due either to minor clip

ping or, more likely, the use of too small a flan when striking. It is important to also note that many of these issues are muled.

Class 1A

Obverse Legend   HENRIC DI GRA REX ANGL Z FRANC — Henry by the grace of God King of England and France

Reverse Legend   PER CRUCE TUA SALVA NOS XPC REDEMPTOR (many varieties) — By Thy Cross save us O Christ our Redeemer

Obverse   A feathered St Michael with one foot on a dragon; mintmark sun and rose, lis upon sun and rose, lis upon half rose.

Reverse   A ship with royal arms in centre and mast above, an 'H' and a rose divided by the mast.

H7AG-005	VG £225	F £450	VF £900

Class 1B

This is an altered die from the reign of Richard III. On the obverse RICARD has been altered to read HENRIC and on the reverse an Edward IV/V die has been altered with the 'H' over an 'E'. Mintmark rose on obverse only. It is possible other varieties exist.

H7AG-010	VG £300	F £700	VF £1,450

Class 2A

As Class 1A, but mintmark none, cinquefoil or escallop; often muled.

H7AG-015	VG £225	F £450	VF £900

Class 2B

Obverse Legend   As H7AG-005.

Reverse Legend   IHC AUTEM TRANSIENS PER MEDIUM ILLORUM IBAT — But Jesus passing through their midst went His way

Obverse   As previous; mintmark none or cinquefoil.

Reverse   As previous.

H7AG-020	VG £225	F £450	VF £900

Class 3A

Obverse Legend   As previous.

Reverse Legend   As Class 1A.

Obverse   New-style St Michael wearing armour with two feet on a dragon, large straight lettering in legends; mintmark escallop, pansy, lis issuant from rose, anchor, greyhound's head, sometimes muled.

Reverse   As previous.

H7AG-025	VG £225	F £450	VF £800

Class 3B

Obverse Legend As previous.

Reverse Legend IHC AUTEM TRANSIENS PER MEDIUM ILLORUM IBAT — But Jesus passing through their midst went His way

Obverse As previous; mintmark escallop.

Reverse As previous.

H7AG-030	VG £225	F £450	VF £800

Class 4A

Obverse Legend As previous.

Reverse Legend As Class 3A.

Obverse Small square lettering; mintmark greyhound's head.

Reverse As previous.

H7AG-035	VG £225	F £450	VF £800

Class 4B

Legends As previous, tall thin lettering.

Obverse As previous; mintmark cross crosslet or greyhound's head (mule from previous issue).

Reverse As previous; mintmark cross crosslet.

H7AG-040	VG £225	F £450	VF £800

Class 5

Legends As previous.

Obverse Large crook-shaped abbreviation after HENRIC; mintmark cross crosslet, pheon.

Reverse As previous, mintmark cross crosslet, pheon or none.

H7AG-045	VG £225	F £450	VF £750

Henry VIII   (1509 – 1547)

Gold angels were produced during Henry VIII's first, second and third coinages and are very much a continuation from the reign of Henry VII. The main difference is in the obverse legend, where Henry VII angels read HENRIC DEI GRA etc. while Henry VIII issues read HENRIC VIII (or 8) DI GRA or DG. The mintmarks are also different, with the exception of mintmark pheon which was used in both reigns.

During the second coinage Cardinal Wolsey introduced the George noble. This coin had a value of six shillings and eight pence which, of course, was the same as the angel. However, during the second coinage the value of the angel was increased to seven shillings and six pence, due partly to the rising price of gold, but also to Henry VIII's extravagant spending. The George noble, which is extremely rare, is included here and was intended to

continue as an important denomination but, with numerous other denominations being issued during this period, it was not really needed and the public preferred to use the more familiar angel.

Collecting Hints

All issues are rare but obtainable. Coins are usually found undamaged, but sometimes slightly clipped, in Fine or VF condition.

First Coinage (1509 – 1526)

Obverse Legend HENR(I)C VIII DI GRA REX AGL Z FRA — Henry by the grace of God King of England and France

Reverse Legend PER CRUCE TUA SALVA NOS XPE RED (varieties exist) — By Thy Cross save us O Christ our Redeemer

Obverse St Michael killing a dragon; mintmark pheon, castle, castle with 'H', crowned portcullis.

Reverse Ship with royal arms, an 'H' and rose divided by the ship's mast; mintmarks as obverse, sometimes muled.

H8AG-005	VG £225	F £425	VF £700

As previous, but no rose by the ship's mast; mintmark portcullis.

H8AG-010	VG £200	F £425	VF £800

Second Coinage (1526 – 1544)

The value of the angel was raised to seven shillings and sixpence.

Obverse Legend HENRIC VIII D G R AGL Z FRA — Henry VIII by the grace of God King of England and France

Reverse Legend As previous.

Obverse As previous; mintmark sunburst or lis.

Reverse As previous.

H8AG-015	VG £225	F £425	VF £700

George Noble

This coin, with a value of six shillings and eight pence, was produced to replace the angel denomination. Two varieties exist, one of which is unique. The obverse shows a ship with a rose in the centre and, for the first time, the reverse depicts St George killing a dragon.

Collecting Hints

The first type is extremely rare, while the second is unique. Coins are usually found undamaged in Fine to EF condition.

Obverse Legend   TALI DICA SIGNO MES FLUCTUARI NEQUIT — Consecrated by such a sign the mind cannot waver

Reverse Legend   HENRIC D G R AGL Z FRANC DNS HIBERNIE — Henry by the grace of God King of England and France Lord of Ireland

Obverse   St George on horseback killing a dragon.

Reverse   Ship with a rose on the mast,' H.K.' divided by the mast; mintmark rose.

H8AG-020   very rare

Obverse Legend   TALI DICATA SIGNO MEN FLUCTUARE NEQUIT — Consecrated by such a sign the mind cannot waver

Reverse Legend   HENRIC D G R AGL Z FRANC DNS HYB — Henry by the grace of God King of England and France Lord of Ireland

Obverse   St George on horseback brandishing a sword, a dragon below; mintmark rose.

Reverse   Ship with three masts, rose on centre mast.

H8AG-025   unique

Third Coinage (1544 – 1547)

This angel is very much a continuation from the second coinage, the main difference being that the Roman numeral VIII after the king's name is replaced by an Arabic 8. The 'Collecting Hints' are similar to those of the earlier issues. The value of the angel was eight shillings for this issue.

Obverse Legend   HENRIC 8 DG AGL FRA Z HIB REX — Henry VIII by the grace of God King of England France and Ireland

Reverse Legend   PER CRUCE TUA SALVA NOS XPE REDE — By Thy Cross save us O Christ our Redeemer

Obverse   St Michael killing a dragon, sometimes an annulet by St Michael's head; mintmark lis.

Reverse   Ship with royal arms, 'H' and rose divided by mast, sometimes an annulet on the ship; mintmark lis.

H8AG-030   VG £225   F £425   VF £750

No angels were struck during the posthumous coinage.

Edward VI   (1547 – 1553)

This issue, struck under Edward's name, is very much a continuation from his father's reign. Due to the shortage of metal, inflation and debasement in other denominations, the value of the angel was ten shillings. The obverse legend starts with the king's name EDWARD VI. It is important to remember that Edward IV and V both produced angels, but the styles, legends and mintmarks are very different.

Collecting Hints

This coin is extremely rare in any grade.

Obverse Legend   EDWARD VI D.G. AGL FRA Z HIB REX — Edward VI by the grace of God England France and Ireland King

Reverse Legend   PER CRUCE TUA SALVA NOS XPE REDE — By Thy Cross save us O Christ our Redeemer

Obverse   St Michael killing dragon; mintmark ostrich head or tun over ostrich head.

Reverse   Ship with royal arms in centre, a rose and an 'E' divided by the mast.

E6AG-005   VG —   F £5,000   VF £12,000

Mary   (1553 – 1554)

The gold angel was produced in some quantity during Mary's reign. Its value remained ten shillings and the design was very similar to previous issues. Angels were also struck under Philip and Mary, but are much rarer. The main differences between the issues lie in the obverse legends which start MARIA and PHILIP Z MARIA respectively; the mintmarks also vary for each issue.

Collecting Hints

This issue, while rare, is obtainable. Specimens are usually found undamaged in Fine or VF condition.

Obverse Legend   MARIA D G ANG FRA Z HIB REGINA — Mary by the grace of God Queen of England France and Ireland

Reverse Legend   A DNO FACTU EST ISTUD Z EST MIRABI — This is the Lord's doing and it is marvellous [in our eyes]

Obverse   St Michael killing a dragon; mintmark pomegranate or half rose and castle.

Reverse   Ship with royal arms in centre, an 'M' and a rose divided by the mast.

| MAAG-005 | VG £400 | F £1,150 | VF £3,000 |

Philip & Mary (1554 – 1558)

This issue, which is very rare, is differentiated from the previous one mainly by the obverse legend and the mintmarks.

Collecting Hints

These coins are extremely rare in any grade. When available they are usually found in Fine or VF condition.

Obverse Legend PHILIP Z MARIA DG. REX Z REGINA — Philip and Mary by the grace of God King and Queen

Reverse Legend A DNO FACTU EST ISTUD Z EST MIRABILE — This is the Lord's doing and it is marvellous [in our eyes]

Obverse St Michael killing a dragon, angel wings of varying size; mintmark lis.

Reverse Ship with royal arms in centre, 'P. M' divided by the mast; mintmark lis.

| PMAG-005 | VG — | F £2,000 | VF £4,500 |

Elizabeth I (1558 – 1603)

The gold angel, still with a value of ten shillings, was produced in some quantity throughout Elizabeth's long reign. All issues are hammered with no milled specimens existing for this denomination. The angel was popular even if it might have appeared old-fashioned in style when compared to some of the new denominations such as the sovereign. Moreover the halfpound was introduced at this time with an identical value of ten shillings. These issues circulated alongside the angel and, while popular, were not as popular as the old-style angel, which had changed very little in style from the reign of Edward IV. As with coinage today, Elizabethan England did not like change and the angel was to stay until the reign of Charles I.

Collecting Hints

Elizabeth I angels are rare but obtainable. They are usually found in Fine condition and are sometimes slightly buckled or bent. Angels in VF and EF condition exist, but it is obvious that these issues saw considerable circulation; after all, with inflation, ten shillings was no longer such a large denomination as it had been during the reign of Edward IV. Modern forgeries of some issues are known.

First – Third Issues (1559 – 1578)

There is nothing for the angel issues to differentiate the first three issues, so they have all been listed together. Many minor varieties exist in the legends.

Obverse Legend ELIZABETH D G ANG FRAN Z HIB REGI — Elizabeth by the grace of God Queen of England France and Ireland

Reverse Legend A. DNO. FACTUM EST ISTUD ET EST MIRABI — This is the Lord's doing and it is marvellous [in our eyes]

Obverse St Michael killing a dragon, wire lined or beaded inner circles; mintmark lis.

Reverse Ship with royal arms, an 'E' and rose divided by the ship's mast; mintmark as obverse.

| ELAG-005 | VG £275 | F £650 | VF £1,150 |

Legends As previous, except obverse legend reads FRA. ET. REGINA

Obverse As previous, but beaded inner circles; mintmark cross crosslet, lis, coronet, ermine, acorn and eglantine.

Reverse Ship facing right, royal arms and 'E' and rose divided by mast; mintmark as obverse.

| ELAG-010 | VG £275 | F £650 | VF £1,150 |

Legends As previous.

Obverse As previous, but mintmark ermine, acorn and eglantine.

Reverse Royal ship the bowsprit is at the stern, it has been incorrectly punched; mintmark as obverse.

| ELAG-015 | VG £275 | F £650 | VF £1,150 |

Fourth Issue (1578 – 1582)

This issue used gold of a slightly reduced fineness.

Legends As previous.

Obverse As previous; mintmark Greek cross, Latin cross or sword; beaded inner circles.

Reverse Ship facing right, royal arms and an 'E' and a rose divided by the mast; mintmark as obverse.

| ELAG-020 | VG £275 | F £650 | VF £1,150 |

Fifth Issue (1583 – 1600)

The fineness of gold was raised for this issue.

Legends   As previous.

Obverse   As previous, but mintmark bell, 'A', escallop, crescent, hand, tun, key, anchor or 0.

Reverse   As previous; mintmark as obverse.

| ELAG-025 | VG £250 | F £575 | VF £1,000 |

Sixth Issue (1601 – 1602)

The weight for this issue was very slightly reduced. The mint-marks denoted the year, thus 1 is for 1601 and 2 for 1602.

As previous, but mintmark 1 or 2.

| ELAG-030 | VG £300 | F £700 | VF £1,350 |

James I   (1603 – 1625)

Gold angels were introduced in 1605 during the second coinage with a value of ten shillings which in 1612, with the price of gold rising, was raised to eleven shillings. The second coinage angel is very similar in style to earlier reigns but a new style angel of lighter weight was introduced in the third coinage. The value of this coin was again ten shillings, which was obviously a more practical denomination. The obverse is fairly similar to previous issues while the reverse shows a more modern ship in full sail. Many angels from these issues have large holes, which was done officially to make them into 'touch' pieces. Touch pieces were used at 'touching' ceremonies, where people suffering from scrofula were brought to be cured. As under Elizabeth I, the gold angel circulated alongside denominations of similar value such as the double crown and half-laurel. The angel was a popular coin but now looked outdated in style when compared to issues such as the unite. It had lasted well since medieval times, but the coins were becoming much rarer and finally stopped being produced during the reign of Charles I.

Collecting Hints

All issues are very rare and coins are usually found in Fine condition. VF and EF examples exist but are very rare. As mentioned earlier, many angels were holed to make them into 'touchpieces' and, while interesting, such coins are worth considerably less than undamaged specimens. Prices are for unpierced specimens.

Second Coinage (1604 – 1619)

Obverse Legend   IACOBUS D G MAG BRIT ET F ET H REX — James by the grace of God King of Great Britain and France and Ireland

Reverse Legend   A DNO FACTUM EST ISTUD — This is the Lord's doing and it is marvellous in our eyes

Obverse   St Michael killing a dragon; mintmark rose, escallop, grapes, coronet, bell, mullet, tower, trefoil, cinquefoil, tun, book, crescent, plain cross or saltire.

Reverse   Ship with royal arms in centre, an 'I' and a rose divided by the ship's mast; mintmark as obverse.

| J1AG-005 | VG £300 | F £650 | VF £1,600 |

Third Coinage (1619 – 1625)

Obverse Legend   IACOBUS D G MAG BRI FRA ET HIB REX — James by the grace of God King of Great Britain France and Ireland

Reverse Legend   ADOMINO FACTUM EST ISTUD — This is the Lord's doing and is marvellous in our eyes

Obverse   St Michael killing a dragon; mintmark spur rowel, rose, thistle, lis or trefoil.

Reverse   A ship in full sail, mintmark as obverse.

| J1AG-010 | VG £350 | F £800 | VF £1,800 |

Charles I   (1625 – 1649)

Under Charles I, angels were struck at the Tower mint until 1643. Although they were produced most years, they are a very rare denomination. Stylistically, they are very much a continuation from James I's third coinage, with St Michael killing a dragon on the obverse and a ship in full sail on the reverse. The main differences in the two reigns are in the obverse legends and mintmarks. The value of the angel was ten shillings and on most coins a mark of value X (10 shillings) can be found in the obverse field. Again, many of these coins can be found officially holed so they could be used in 'touching' ceremonies, where those who suffered from scrofula were brought to be cured. Known as 'touch pieces', these coins are interesting but worth less than undamaged specimens. The gold angel finally stopped being produced when the king left London.

Collecting Hints

All issues are very rare and not usually found in better than Fine condition. VF examples exist but are extremely rare. Many coins, as mentioned earlier, are officially holed and some specimens are also damaged. Prices are for unpierced specimens.

Obverse Legend   CAROLUS D G MAG BRI FRA ET HIB REX (minor varieties exist) — Charles by the grace of God King of Great Britain France and Ireland

Reverse Legend   AMOR POPULI PRAESIDIUM REGIS — The love of the people is the King's protection

Obverse   St Michael killing a dragon; mintmark lis or cross calvary.

Reverse   Ship in full sail; mintmark as obverse.

C1AG-005	VG £350	F £900	VF £2,200

Legends   As previous.

Obverse   As previous, but mark of value to right of St Michael; mintmark blackamoor's head, castle, anchor or heart.

Reverse   As previous; mintmark as obverse.

C1AG-010	VG £300	F £800	VF £1,850

Legends   As previous.

Obverse   As previous, but mark of value to left of St Michael; mintmark blackamoor's head, heart, rose, harp, portcullis, bell, crown, tun, anchor, triangle star or triangle in circle.

Reverse   As previous; mintmark as obverse.

C1AG-015	VG £350	F £900	VF £2,200

Florin or Double Leopard

Edward III (1327 – 1377)

Instructed by Edward III to produce gold denominations for England in 1343, the two Florentines George Kirkyn and Lotte Nicholyn designed the florin or double leopard in 1344. The florin, based on the French gold issues and with a value of six shillings, was intended to be an issue for the whole of Europe, not just England. But as the gold used to strike the coins had been overvalued, the issue was unacceptable to merchants and had to be demonetised in August 1344. The coins were recalled, melted down and used to make the popular and acceptable gold noble. This issue is undoubtedly one of the most beautiful medieval English coins ever produced and it is a loss to collectors that virtually all specimens were destroyed.

Collecting Hints

This issue is extremely rare, however, most specimens exist in the higher grades.

Obverse Legend EDWR D GRA REX ANGL Z FRANC DNS HIB — Edward by the Grace of God King of England and France Lord of Ireland

Reverse Legend IHC TRANSIENS PER MEDIUM ILLORUM IBAT — But Jesus passing through their midst went His way

Obverse King enthroned beneath a canopy, two leopards' heads at sides.

Reverse Royal cross within a quatrefoil, a leopard in each spandrel.

E3FL-005 ex. rare

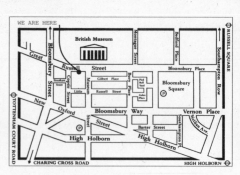

Crown

The crown, or the 'crown of the double rose' as it was known at the time, was introduced during Henry VIII's 1526 monetary reform. The first crowns were stuck in gold and it was not until Edward VI's reign that the silver crown was introduced. Many collectors believe that all crowns are silver but until the Commonwealth period gold crowns were produced in some quantity, except for the reign of Mary and Philip when no crowns were struck at all. However, silver as well as gold crowns were produced during the reigns of Elizabeth, James I and Charles I and during the period of the Commonwealth. With gold and silver in plentiful supply and the sizes of both coins being acceptable to the public, there was no reason why crowns could not be struck in silver as well as gold. Crowns were produced in all reigns from Elizabeth I to Elizabeth II and are still struck today but, despite being legal tender, they have become commemorative issues saved by collectors rather than being found in circulation. There has now been a move by the Royal Mint to produce five pound commemorative coins, which are the same size as the old crown and are referred to by many people as a 'crown'.

It should also be noted that the gold crown struck during James I's second coinage was known as the 'Britain crown' due to the fact that MAG BRIT appears for the first time on the legend, as James was king of both Scotland and England. At this time, the 'thistle crown' was also introduced, so called because of the thistle depicted on the reverse. Finally, James' third coinage, saw the introduction of quarter-laurels which portrayed the king wearing a laurel instead of a crown.

Henry VIII (1509 – 1547)

Gold crowns were produced during the second, third and posthumous issues of Henry VIII; they were all made of good quality 22 carat gold and unlike some of the silver issues were never debased. All issues have a crown over a rose on the obverse and a crown over a shield on the reverse; they also bear initials on the obverse and, sometimes, the reverse which, together with the mintmark, serve to identify issues. The Bristol mint struck crowns which bear the mintmark WS on the obverse and/or reverse during the second coinage while the Southwark mint, London's second mint located just south of the River Thames, struck crowns during the third and posthumous coinage. The posthumous issue can be identified easily as it omits the 8 after the king's name.

Collecting Hints

Most issues, while scarce, are obtainable; the Southwark posthumous issue in particular is extremely rare. Coins are usually available unclipped in Fine or VF condition.

Second Coinage (1526 – 1544)

All these issues were struck at the Tower mint. The various initials on the reverse refer to Henry VIII's various wives.

Obverse Legend HENRIC VIII RUTILANS ROSA SINE SPINA — Henry VIII a dazzling rose without a thorn

Reverse Legend DEI GR ANGLIE FRANC DNS HIBERNIE — By the grace of God King of England France Lord of Ireland

Obverse Rose with crown above, 'H.K' crowned initials; mintmark rose.

Reverse Crown above shield, no initials; mintmark rose.

H8CR-005	VG £225	F £400	VF £750

As previous, but 'HK' on obverse and reverse; mintmark rose (obverse) lis (reverse), lis or arrow.

H8CR-010	VG £225	F £400	VF £750

As previous, but 'HK' on obverse, 'HA' on reverse or vice versa; mintmark arrow.

H8CR-015	VG £250	F £425	VF £800

As previous, but 'HR' on obverse, 'HK' on reverse or vice versa; mintmark arrow.

H8CR-020	ex rare

As previous, but 'HA' on reverse; mintmark arrow.

H8CR-025	VG £250	F £425	VF £800

As previous, but 'HA' on obverse, 'HR' on reverse; mintmark arrow.

H8CR-030	ex. rare

As previous, but 'HI' on obverse and reverse; mintmark arrow. Some issues read HIBERIE.

H8CR-035	VG £250	F £425	VF £800

As previous, but 'HK' on obverse, 'HI' on reverse; mintmark arrow.

| H8CR-040 | VG £250 | F £425 | VF £850 |

As previous, but 'HR' on obverse, 'HI' on reverse; mintmark arrow.

| H8CR-045 | VG £250 | F £425 | VF £800 |

As previous, but 'HR' on reverse; mintmark arrow.

| H8CR-050 | VG £250 | F £450 | VF £850 |

As previous, but reverse legend reads DEI GR ANGLIE DNS HIBERIE REX; mintmark pheon.

| H8CR-055 | VG £250 | F £600 | VF rare |

Third Coinage (1544 – 1547)

This issue while similar to the previous one, has 8 instead of VIII in the obverse legend and different mintmarks.

Tower Mint

Obverse Legend   HENRIC 8 RUTILANS ROSA SINE SPINA — Henry VIII a dazzling rose without a thorn

Reverse Legend   DEI GRA ANGLIE FRANC HIBERNIE REX — By the grace of God King of England France and Ireland

Obverse   Rose with crown above initials H.R; mintmark pellet in annulet.

Reverse   Crown above shield initials 'HR'.

| H8CR-060 | VG £200 | F £375 | VF £700 |

As previous, but omits RUTILANS in obverse legend.

| H8CR-065 | VG £200 | F £375 | VF £700 |

As previous, but an annulet is found on the inner circle in the obverse legend.

| H8CR-070 | VG £200 | F £400 | VF £750 |

Southwark Mint

This issue can be identified by the mintmark only.

Legends   As H8CR-065.

Obverse   As H8CR-065; mintmark 'S', 'E', sometimes muled.

Reverse   As H8CR-065.

| H8CR-075 | VG £225 | F £400 | VF £800 |

Bristol Mint

The mintmark WS, which is unique for Bristol, can always be found on the obverse and/or reverse.

Obverse Legend   HENRIC VIII RUTILANS ROSA SINE SPINA — Henry VIII a dazzling rose without a thorn

Reverse Legend   DEI GRA ANGLIE FRANC HIBERNIE REX — By the grace of God King of England France Ireland

Obverse   As previous, but mintmark 'WS' or none.

Reverse   As previous, but mintmark 'WS' or none.

| H8CR-080 | VG £200 | F £400 | VF £800 |

As previous, but legend reads HENRIC 8 instead of HENRIC VIII.

| H8CR-085 | VG £200 | F £400 | VF £800 |

Posthumous Coinage (1547 – 1551)

This issue is very similar to the third coinage except for the legends and sometimes the mintmark. Produced during the reign of Edward VI, it should really be under Edward VI coinage but, as these issues are so similar to the issues of Henry VIII, they have been classed under Henry VIII for the convenience of the reader.

Tower Mint

Obverse Legend   HENRIC 8 RUTILANS ROSA SINE SPINA — Henry VIII a dazzling rose without a thorn

Reverse Legend   DEI GRA ANGLIE FRAN Z HIB REX — By the grace of God King of England France and Ireland

Obverse   Crown over rose, 'HR' initials; mintmark arrow, none (with 'K' on reverse), grapple, martlet.

Reverse   Crown over shield, 'HR' initials; mintmark as obverse.

| H8CR-090 | VG £225 | F £450 | VF £900 |

As previous, but the legend is in a different order with several varieties and omits the '8'.

| H8CR-095 | VG £275 | F £600 | VF £1,100 |

| E6CR-010 | VG £400 | F £1,000 | VF £2,200 |

Obverse Legend EDWARD VI DG AGL FR Z HIB REX — Edward VI by the grace of God King of England France and Ireland

Reverse Legend SCUTUM FIDEI PROTEGET EUM — The shield of faith shall protect him

Obverse Crowned bust of king; mintmark arrow, grapple, swan and 'Y'.

Reverse Crown over royal shield dividing 'ER'.

| E6CR-015 | VG £300 | F £700 | VF £1,500 |

Third Period (1550 – 1553)

Obverse Legend EDWARD VI DG ANGL FRA Z HIB REX — Edward VI by the grace of God King of England France and Ireland

Reverse Legend SCUTUM FIDEI PROTEGET EUM — The shield of faith shall protect him

Obverse Half length bust of king holding orb and sword; mintmark 'Y' or tun.

Reverse Crown over royal shield dividing 'ER.'.

| E6CR-020 | VG £450 | F £1000 | VF £2,200 |

Silver Issue (1551 – 1553)

This coin was struck during Edward VI's fine silver issue. Unlike some other earlier denominations, it was struck in good quality silver and was popular since it once again provided the public with silver coins which were worth their metal weight. Many of these crowns are overstruck dates. We have noted 1551/52 and 1553 over 1552 or 1551.

Collecting Hints

While these crowns are scarce they are obtainable in VG to VF condition; some however are found gilded and this detracts from their value. Being the first numerically dated English coin (Edward VI base shillings used Latin numbering) it is an historical issue and an important acquisition for any collection. There is no doubt that many different dies were used to strike these coins, producing a large number of varieties.

Obverse Legend EDWARD VI DG. AGL FRANC Z HIBER REX — Edward VI by the grace of God King of England France and Ireland

---

Southwark Mint

A variety of legend readings exists for this issue.

As H8CR-075 but mintmark 'E', with transposed legends; varieties exist.

| H8CR-100 | VG £275 | F £600 | VF £1,100 |

Edward VI (1547 – 1553)

During the reign of Edward VI there were three main issues of crowns. After the posthumous issue struck in Henry VIII's name and listed above, the second main issue consists of the gold crowns produced in Edward's name throughout all three periods of coinage; they are all very rare and the first issue is thought to be unique. The third main issue under Edward VI was the silver crown. Dated between 1551 and 1553, these coins are superb in style and production, with the obverse showing the Boy King on horseback and the reverse the royal arms over a cross.

Gold Issue

Collecting Hints

All issues are extremely rare and the first issue is presumed unique. When available, the second and third period coins are usually found in fine and VF condition, but collectors will have difficulty in obtaining a specimen.

First Period (April 1547 – Jan. 1549)

Obverse Legend RUTILANS ROSA SINE SPINA — A dazzling rose without a thorn

Reverse Legend EDWARD 6 DG AGL. FRA Z HIB REX — Edward VI by the grace of God King of England France and Ireland

Obverse Crown over rose dividing 'ER'.

Reverse Crown over shield dividing 'ER'; mintmark arrow.

| E6CR-005 | ex. rare, probably unique |

Second Period (Jan. 1549 – April 1550)

Obverse Legend SCUTUM FIDEI PROTEGET EUM — The shield of faith shall protect him

Reverse Legend EDWARD VI DG AGL FR Z HIB REX — Edward VI by the grace of God King of England France and Ireland

Obverse Uncrowned bust of king; mintmark arrow, '6', 'Y'.

Reverse Crown over royal shield dividing 'E.R.'.

Reverse Legend   POSUI DEUM ADIVITORE MEU (minor varieties) — I have made God my helper

Obverse   Boy King on horseback, date 1551 below horse; mintmark 'Y'.

Reverse   Royal arms over cross; mintmark 'Y' (Southwark mint).

E6CR-025	VG £300	F £550	VF £900

As previous, but mintmark tun.

E6CR-030	ex. rare

As previous, but '2' over '1' of date.

E6CR-035	v. rare

As previous, but dated 1552.

E6CR-040	VG £275	F £650	VF £1300

As previous, but dated 1553/2.

E6CR-045	rare

As previous, but dated 1553, flat-toppped '3' (altered die?).

E6CR-050	VG £230	F £550	VF £1,150

As previous, but a rounded '3' in date.

E6CR-055	rare

No crowns were struck during the reign of Mary or Philip and Mary.

Elizabeth I   (1558 – 1603)

Hammered gold crowns were struck during most of Elizabeth's reign. All issues had a bust of the queen on the obverse, a crowned shield dividing 'E R' (ELIZABETH REGINA) on the reverse and a mintmark at the beginning of both obverse and reverse legend. Issues are fairly easily identifiable by the various mintmarks and minor varieties in style. Milled gold crowns were also issued at the time and are very different in style from the gold hammered issues, mainly because they omit the inner circles. Finally, a silver crown, which is probably the best-known Elizabeth I crown, was struck during the last two years of her reign. Produced in some quantity, it is the most common issue, as well as the most popular with collectors. The obverse shows a superb bust of the queen and the reverse the royal shield over a cross, and a mintmark can be found at the beginning of the obverse and reverse legend.

Hammered Gold Issue

Collecting Hints

All issues are rare and the first is extremely rare. Coins are usually available in about Fine condition, often with minor flaws such as slight creasing where the coin has been bent and straightened, or cracks in the flan due to poor striking.

Obverse Legend   ELIZABETH DG ANG FR ET HI REGINA — Elizabeth by the grace of God Queen of England France and Ireland

Reverse Legend   SCUTUM FIDEI PROTEGET EAM — The shield of faith shall protect her

Obverse   Crowned bust of queen in plain dress, no inner circles; mintmark lis.

Reverse   Crown over royal shield dividing 'E.R.', wire lined inner circles.

ELCR-005	ex. rare, only two known

Obverse Legend   As previous, minor varieties exist.

Reverse Legend   As previous.

Obverse   As previous, but beaded inner circles; mintmark cross crosslet, rose, portcullis, lion, coronet or castle.

Reverse   As previous.

ELCR-010	VG £225	F £500	VF £1,000

Obverse Legend   ELIZAB DG ANG FRA ET HIB REGI — Elizabeth by the grace of God Queen of England France and Ireland

Reverse Legend   As previous.

Obverse   Crowned bust of queen with long hair and decorative dress; mintmark tun, woolpack, key, cypher, '1' or '2'. N.B. Sixth issue mintmark '1' and '2' are very rare.

Reverse   As previous.

ELCR-015	VG £225	F £500	VF £1,000

Milled Gold Issue

Collecting Hints

All milled gold crowns are extremely rare in any grade; when available, they are usually found in Fine or VF condition, sometimes damaged.

Obverse Legend   ELIZABETH DG ANG FRA ET HIB REGINA — Elizabeth by the grace of God Queen of England France and Ireland

Reverse Legend   SCUTUM FIDEI PROTEGET EAM — The shield of faith shall protect her

Obverse   Crowned bust of queen of various styles, no inner circle; mintmark star or lis.

Reverse   Crown over royal arms dividing 'E.R.'.

ELCR-020	VG £600	F £1,350	VF £2,750

Hammered Silver Issue

Collecting Hints

Even though this issue was struck for only two years, it is the most common and found in all grades from poor to EF. In many cases the obverse is more worn than the reverse

due to a weak strike. These issues whilst scarce are obtainable and very popular with collectors who should, however, be aware of tooled and plugged examples. The mintmarks 1 and 2 denote the dates in which the coins were issued, 1601 and 1602 respectively. Those bearing mintmark 2 are considerably scarcer than the 1601 issue.

Obverse Legend   ELIZABETH DG ANG FRA ET HIBER REGINA — Elizabeth by the grace of God Queen of England France and Ireland

Reverse Legend   POSUI DEUM ADIUTOREM MEUM — I have made God my helper

Obverse   Crowned bust of queen holding sceptre and orb; mintmark '1' or '2'.

Reverse   Royal arms in shield over long cross.

ELCR-025	VG £500	F £1,000	VF £2,000

James I   (1603 – 1625)

Gold as well as silver crowns were produced under James I, but fluctuations in the supply and price of gold meant that many denominations were devalued and this lack of consistency is reflected in the way coins have been listed. In the second coinage the value of a half angel was, for a period, five shillings but as it was not called a crown it is listed separately. Also during the second coinage, the thistle crown was introduced with a value of only four shillings, as was the Britain crown with a value of five shillings; they are both included here. The Britain crown derives its name from the MAG BRIT (Great Britain) in the obverse legend. During the third coinage, gold quarter-laurels were produced with the value of a crown and V for five shillings behind the bust of the king; they are included in this chapter. There is little doubt that the varieties of gold coins during this reign are confusing, but with erratic gold prices and the coins worth their weight in gold the government was compelled to vary the denominations and values.

Silver crowns were also produced during most of James's reign. They all have the king on horseback on the obverse, the royal shield, sometimes with a plume above, on the reverse and a mintmark at the beginning of the obverse and reverse legends. As the silver sixty-shillings produced in Scotland during this period is very similar in style and design to the English crown, collectors should carefully compare the two. First check the reverse legend; only the second and third coinages have the same legend readings as the Scottish issue. Then check the mintmark; on the Scottish issue it is thistle only, the second issue did not use mintmark thistle, the first one did but had a different reverse legend and the third coinage used the mintmark thistle but the style of the coin is different. In particular, the English issue has, in nearly all cases, a bird-headed harp in the royal shield as well as colon stops in the obverse legend while the Scottish issue has a very plain harp and single pellet stops in the legend. No issue from Scotland has a plume over the royal shield and, furthermore, on the obverse legend the English issue uses 'ET' and the Scottish issues '&'.

Gold Issue

First Coinage (1603 – 1604)

The first coinage can easily be distinguished from other issues by the reverse legend and mintmarks.

Obverse Legend   IACOBUS DG ANG SCO FRA ET HI REX — James by the grace of God King of England Scotland and Ireland

Reverse Legend   TUEATUR UNITA DEUS — May God guard these United [Kingdoms]

Obverse   Bust of king; mintmark thistle or lis.

Reverse   Crown above royal arms and dividing 'IR' (IACOBUS REX); mintmark thistle.

J1CR-005	VG —	F £1,000	VF £2,400

Second Coinage (1604 – 1619)

Large quantities of gold crowns were produced during this period. The first issue, known as the Britain crown, has a bust of the king of various styles on the obverse and a crown above the royal arms and dividing 'IR' (IACOBUS REX) on the reverse. The reverse legend is also different from the first coinage. The second issue, the thistle crown, had a denomination of only four shillings but is classed as a crown and easily identified as it omits the king's bust on the obverse and bears a thistle on the reverse.

Britain Crown

First Bust

Obverse Legend   IACOBUS D.G. MAG BRI FRA ET H. REX. — James by the grace of God King of Great Britain France and Ireland

Reverse Legend   HENRICUS ROSAS REGNA IACOBUS — Henry united the Roses, James the kingdoms

Obverse   Crowned bust of king with a rounded bust and a square beard; mintmark lis, rose, escallop, grapes and coronet.

Reverse   Crown over royal shields and dividing 'I.R.'.

J1CR-010	VG £135	F £240	VF £450

Third Bust

As previous, but crowned bust of king with square cut beard which projects; mintmark key, bell, mullet, tower, trefoil, cinquefoil.

J1CR-015	VG £135	F £240	VF £450

Fifth Bust

As previous, but crowned bust of king with longer hair brushed back and a beard that is not neat; mintmark cinquefoil, tun, book, crescent, plain cross, saltire.

J1CR-020	VG £135	F £240	VF £450

Thistle Crown

Obverse Legend   IA DG MAG BRIT ET H REX — James by the grace of God King of Great Britain and Ireland

Reverse Legend   TUEATUR UNITA DEUS — May God guard these United [Kingdoms]

Obverse   Crown above rose, 'I R' usually divided by rose; mintmark lis, rose, escallop, grapes, coronet, key, bell, mullet, tower, trefoil, cinquefoil, tun, book, crescent, plain cross.

Reverse   Crown above thistle usually dividing 'I.R.'.

J1CR-025	VG £145	F £260	VF £450

Third Coinage (1619 – 1625)

With gold prices and denomination values fluctuating, public faith in the coinage was severely shaken, so major monetary reforms were introduced with the third coinage in 1619. For the first time on gold crowns, the denomination V for five shillings can be found on the coin, behind the king's head. The bust is also very different, depicting the king uncrowned and wearing a laurel. This laurel actually gave the whole issue its name and the gold crown is known as the quarter-laurel.

Second Bust

Obverse Legend IACOBUS DG MAG BRI FR ET HIB REX — James by the grace of God King of Great Britain France and Ireland

Reverse Legend HENRICUS ROSAS REGNA IACOBUS — Henry united the Roses, James the kingdoms

Obverse Bust of king with large face wearing a laurel, value behind bust; mintmark spur rowel, rose, thistle, lis.

Reverse Crown over royal arms.

J1CR-030	VG £140	F £250	VF £400

Fourth Bust

There is no inner circle on the reverse of some issues.

As previous, but the king's bust is smaller and neater; mintmark lis, trefoil.

J1CR-035	VG £140	F £250	VF £400

Silver Issue

Collecting Hints

All silver crowns, while scarce, are obtainable, but the first coinage in particular is very scarce. Most issues are found unclipped and usually undamaged in Fine condition, those in VF or EF being very rare and desirable. Collectors should ensure that a coin is an English rather than a Scottish issue which, as we explained at the beginning of the chapter, are very similar.

First Coinage (1603 – 1604)

Obverse Legend IACOBUS DG ANG SCO FRAN ET HIBER REX — James by the grace of God King of England Scotland France and Ireland

Reverse Legend EXURGAT DEUS DISSIPENTUR INIMICI — Let God arise and His enemies be scattered

Obverse King on horseback; mintmark thistle, lis.

Reverse Royal arms in square garnished shield.

J1CR-040	VG £275	F £700	VF £1,700

Second Coinage (1604 – 1619)

Obverse Legend IACOBUS DG MAG BRIT FRAN ET HIB REX — James by the grace of God King of Great Britain France and Ireland

Reverse Legend QUAE DEUS CONIUNXIT NEMO SEPARET — What God hath joined let no man put asunder

Obverse As previous; mintmark lis, rose, escallop, grapes.

Reverse As previous.

J1CR-045	VG £275	F £600	VF £1,450

Third Coinage (1619 – 1625)

Legends As previous.

Obverse As previous, but colon dots in obverse legend as opposed to single stops; mintmark rose, thistle, lis, trefoil.

Reverse As previous, but no stops in reverse legend and the harp on the shield in most cases has a bird's head at the end.

J1CR-050	VG £275	F £500	VF £1,200

Legends As previous.

Obverse As previous; mintmark thistle, lis, trefoil.

Reverse As previous, but large plume (denoting silver mined in Wales) over the royal shield.

J1CR-055	VG £275	F £600	VF £1,350

Charles I (1625 – 1649)

During the reign of Charles I both gold and silver crowns were produced. With fairly plentiful supplies of gold and silver there was no reason why crowns could not be produced in both metals.

These issues gave the public a choice and also helped when trading on the Continent. All gold crowns were struck at the Tower mint in London and have a bust of the king with the value V (five shillings) behind the king's head on the obverse and the royal shield on the reverse. A mintmark can be found in nearly all cases at the beginning of the obverse and reverse legends. During the early part of the reign the silver issues were also stuck at the Tower mint and then at provincial mints during the Civil War.

Gold Issue (1625 – 1642)

Collecting Hints

Most issues are fairly common, however there are exceptions which we have listed. They are sometimes found damaged in Fine condition, but VF and EF examples do exist. These crowns tend to be slightly less popular with collectors who prefer the larger silver issues.

First Bust

Obverse Legend   CAROLUS DG MAG BR FR ET HI REX — Charles by the grace of God King of Great Britain France and Ireland

Reverse Legend   CULTORES SUI DEUS PROTEGIT — God protects His worshippers

Obverse   Crowned bust of king wearing a ruff, value behind; mintmark lis, cross calvary.

Reverse   Square-topped shield with crown above; minor varieties in the style of the shield exist.

C1CR-005	VG £150	F £250	VF £500

Second Bust

Legends   As previous.

Obverse   As previous, but a thinner bust of the king; mintmark cross calvary, blackamoor's head, castle, anchor, heart, plume.

Reverse   As previous, but sometimes no mintmark.

C1CR-010	VG £150	F £250	VF £500

Legends   As previous.

Obverse   As previous, but larger bust; mintmark plume, rose.

Reverse   As previous; mintmark plume over rose sometimes on reverse, crown above shield.

C1CR-015	VG £150	F £250	VF £500

Third Bust

Legends   As previous.

Obverse   Slightly wider bust of king wearing a larger crown; mintmark plume.

Reverse   Crowned oval shield; mintmark plume.

C1CR-020	VG £200	F £400	VF £700

Fourth Bust

Several very minor varieties of this issue exist. It was produced both under the king (1632–1641) and under Parliament (1643–1648) but, as only the mintmark differentiates the two, we have included them here together. Mintmarks (P), (R), eye, sun and sceptre were used under Parliament.

Legends   As previous.

Obverse   Larger bust of king not wearing a ruff; mintmark harp, portcullis, bell, crown, tun, anchor, triangle, star, triangle in circle, '(P)', '(R)' eye, sun, sceptre.

Reverse   Oval shield dividing crowned 'C.R'.

C1CR-025	VG £150	F £250	VF £400

Fifth Bust — Aberystwyth Style

This issue is known as the Aberystwyth bust because it is the style of bust used on the provincial issues of the Aberystwyth mint.

Legends   As previous.

Obverse   Smaller, neater bust of king without a ruff; mintmark anchor.

Reverse   As previous, but mintmark anchor.

C1CR-030	VG £200	F £300	VF £700

Sixth Bust — Briot Style

This issue, which is unique and possibly a pattern, was probably not by Briot but copied the bust of some of Briot's machine-made issues.

As previous, but new-style bust of king with more hair and wider crown; mintmark anchor.

C1CR-035	unique

Briot's Milled Coinage

This gold issue was machine made.

| C1CR-045 | VG £200 | F £450 | VF £900 |

Collecting Hints

This issue is excessively rare and very difficult to obtain.

Obverse Legend   CAROLUS D.G. MAG BRIT FR ET HIB REX — Charles by the grace of God King of Great Britain France Ireland

Reverse Legend   CULTORES SUI DEUS PROTEGIT — God protects His worshippers

Obverse   Bust of king with value behind; mintmark 'B'.

Reverse   Crown over royal shield which divides 'C.R'.

| C1CR-040   ex. rare |

Silver Issue

The following line-drawings, from B.R. Osborne's archive on Charles I, depict the numerous styles of horseman with the corresponding classes to which they relate. It is important to remember that, with the number of dies being used, varieties exist.

C1CR-045, -050   C1CR-055 to -065   C1CR-070, -075

C1CR-085   C1CR-090

Tower Mint under King (1625 – 1642)

These issues show the king on horseback on the obverse and the royal arms on the reverse. When identifying a coin collectors should also refer to the provincial mints and pay particular attention to the mintmark, which is found on the obverse and reverse at the beginning or the end of the legend, the shape of the reverse shield and the style of the horseman. Also note that all issues from the Tower Mint are undated.

Collecting Hints

Most issues, while scarce, are fairly easy to obtain in VG to Fine condition but rare and desirable in VF and EF. They tend not to be clipped or damaged, but some coins have areas on them that are particularly worn.

Class 1A

Obverse Legend   CAROLUS DG MAG BRIT FRA ET HIB REX — Charles by the grace of God King of Great Britain France and Ireland

Reverse Legend   CHRISTO AUSPICE REGNO — I reign under the auspices of Christ

Obverse   Horse with plume on head, king with sword raised; mintmark lis or cross calvary.

Reverse   Square-topped, garnished shield of royal arms.

Class 1B

As previous, but plume over shield on reverse; mintmarks lis, cross calvary, castle.

| C1CR-050 | VG £300 | F £650 | VF £1,400 |

Class 2A

Obverse Legend   As previous, minor varieties exist.

Reverse Legend   As previous.

Obverse   As previous, but smaller horseman, the king holds his sword on his shoulder; mintmark harp.

Reverse   Oval shield with 'C.R' above shield, no plume.

| C1CR-055 | VG £200 | F £400 | VF £900 |

Class 2B.1

As previous, but a plume dividing C.R; mintmark plume or rose.

| C1CR-060 | VG £210 | F £400 | VF £850 |

Class 2B.2

As previous, but the royal arms are over a cross fourchée; mintmark harp, plume.

| C1CR-065 | VG £225 | F £500 | VF £1,000 |

Class 3A

Obverse Legend   As previous, minor varieties exist.

Reverse Legend   As previous.

Obverse   King on horseback holding his sword in the air; mintmark bell, crown, tun, anchor, triangle, star.

Reverse   Oval shield with no plume or CR.

| C1CR-070 | VG £225 | F £425 | VF £800 |

Class 3B

As previous, but plume over shield on the reverse; mintmark portcullis, crown, tun.

| C1CR-075 | VG £225 | F £425 | VF £900 |

Briot Style Horseman

The obverse is fairly similar to contemporary Scottish issues. If a coin's reverse is different from the one described here, collectors should refer to issues of Scotland.

Obverse Legend   CAROLUS DG MAG BRIT FR ET HIB REX — Charles by the grace of God King of Great Britain France and Ireland

Reverse Legend   CHRISTO AUSPICE REGNO — I reign under the auspices of Christ

Obverse   King on horseback on small neater horse, there is a groundline below the horse and the king's sword is very long; mintmark triangle in circle.

Reverse   Royal arms in oval shield.

| C1CR-080 | ex. rare |

Tower Mint under Parliament (1642 – 1648)

This issue is very much a continuation of the Tower mint under the king although the style of the king's horse is slightly different and the issues can easily be identified by their unique mintmarks. The 'Collecting Hints' are similar to the previous issues except that these two classes are scarcer and tend to be found in the lower grades.

Class 4

Obverse Legend   CAROLUS D.G. MAG BRI FRA ET HIB REX — Charles by the grace of God King of Great Britain France and Ireland

Reverse Legend   CHRISTO AUSPICE REGNO — I reign under the auspices of Christ

Obverse   Foreshortened king on horseback; mintmark '(P)', '(R)', eye and sun.

Reverse   Royal arms in oval garnished shield.

| C1CR-085 | VG £200 | F £500 | VF £1,000 |

| C1CR-095 | VG £350 | F £850 | VF £2,000 |

Class 5

As previous, but larger, spirited horse and the king holding a long sword; mintmark sun. These coins are usually struck on larger flans than those of Class 4.

| C1CR-090 | VG £225 | F £525 | VF £1,100 |

Briot's Coinage (1631 – 1639)

Unlike Charles I's other issues which were all hammered, this superb, rare coin was milled and very different in style. The whole coin is very well proportioned and elegant and the issue can easily be identified by the mintmark flower on the obverse and a 'B' on both obverse and reverse. The 'B' stood for Briot and could be classed as an engraver's mark.

Collecting Hints

This issue is rare and usually found undamaged in Fine to VF condition; rarely found in the low grades due to the qualities of strike, it is also extremely rare in EF.

Obverse Legend CAROLUS D.G. MAGN BRITAN, FRAN ET HIBER REX — Charles by the grace of God King of Great Britain France and Ireland

Reverse Legend CHRISTO AUSPICE REGNO — I reign under the auspices of Christ

Obverse King on horseback with groundline; mintmark 'B' and flower.

Reverse Crown over royal arms which divide crowned 'C R'.

Provincial Issues

Crowns were struck during the Civil War at Shrewsbury, Oxford, Truro and Exeter. The Shrewsbury and Oxford issues are fairly similar and have the Declaration on the reverse. They can be distinguished by the dates, as Shrewsbury issues were only struck in 1642 while most Oxford issues were struck during 1643, and by the style of the horseman and the plumes. The Truro and Exeter issues are fairly similar to those of the Tower mint except that many are dated. Those that are undated also use the mintmark rose found on the Tower mint issue 2B, however the obverse and reverse are very different in style.

Shrewsbury Mint

Collecting Hints

The Shrewsbury-style horseman issue is rare and usually found undamaged in Fine or VF condition but the Aberystwyth-style horseman issue is extremely rare.

Shrewsbury Style Horseman

Obverse Legend CAROLUS D.G. MAG BRIT FRAN ET HIBER REX — Charles by the grace of God King of Great Britain France and Ireland

Outer Reverse Legend EXURGAT DEUS DISSIPENTUR INIMICI — Let God arise and His enemies be scattered

Inner Reverse Legend RELIG PROT. LEG ANG LIBER PAR — The religion of the Protestants the laws of England the liberty of Parliament

Obverse King on horseback with groundline, plume without band behind king's head. Many minor varieties of the Shrewsbury style horseman exist.

Reverse Three plumes and value V (five shillings) above Declaration, 1642 below.

| C1CR-100 | VG £300 | F £600 | VF £1,400 |

Aberystwyth Style Horseman

As previous, but Aberystwyth-style horseman with longer sword and king's scarf catching in the wind.

C1CR-105	ex. rare

Oxford Mint

Collecting Hints

All crowns from the Oxford mint are rare; nearly all are dated 1643 and there are very many minor varieties. Coins are usually found unclipped and undamaged in Fine condition although VF examples exist. One excessively rare issue shows the king on horseback with the City of Oxford in the distance on the obverse but collectors should be aware that many forgeries and electrotype copies (made by R. Ready) of this stunning and extremely rare coin exist.

Shrewsbury Obverse Die Issue

This issue used the obverse die from the Shrewsbury crown and the Oxford reverse, which has a different style in the three plumes above the Declaration.

Obverse Legend CAROLUS DG MAG BRIT FRAN ET HIBER REX — Charles by the grace of God King of Great Britain France and Ireland

Outer Reverse Legend EXURGAT DEUS DISSIPENTUR INIMICI — Let God arise and His enemies be scattered

Inner Reverse Legend RELIG PROT LEG ANG LIBER PAR — The religion of the Protestants the laws of England the liberty of Parliament

Obverse King on horseback with plume behind head.

Reverse Three Oxford-style plumes with denomination (V) above Declaration, dated below 1642 or 1643; N.B. Shrewsbury struck crowns are dated 1642 only.

C1CR-110	VG £300	F £650	VF £1,600

Oxford Style Horseman

This issue, dated 1643, is easily identified by the grass that is depicted on the groundline on the obverse. Minor varieties exist, particularly in the number and position of stops in the legend.

Legends As previous.

Obverse King on horseback with plume behind him; mintmark plume at beginning of obverse legend. The king's horse walks on groundline of grass.

Reverse Three plume and denomination above the Declaration, 1643 below.

C1CR-115	VG £300	F £700	VF £1,600

Rawlins Style Crown

The dies for this issue were made by Thomas Rawlins.

Legends As previous, but PARL instead of PAR in the Declaration.

Obverse King on horseback, view of Oxford behind.

Reverse Three plumes and denomination above floral scrolls, the Declaration in the centre with date 1644 below and OXON (Oxford) below date.

C1CR-120	ex. rare

Exeter Mint

Undated Issues (1642 – 1643)

All coins for this mint have the mintmark rose or castle. As mentioned earlier, mintmark rose was also used in the Tower mint class 2B. The two issues are easy to differentiate by the style of horseman and the reverse shield. The following three issues used to be classed under Truro mint.

Collecting Hints

Exeter crowns, while scarce, are obtainable and usually found undamaged and unclipped but fairly worn in VG to Fine condition; VF examples exist but are very rare.

Obverse Legend CAROLUS D.G. MAG BRI FRA ET HI REX — Charles by the grace of God King of Great Britain France and Ireland

Reverse Legend CHRISTO AUSPICE REGNO — I reign under the auspices of Christ

Obverse King on horseback with no groundline; mintmark rose.

Reverse Royal arms in garnished oval shield.

C1CR-125	VG £180	F £400	VF £700

As previous, but the royal shield is garnished with twelve scrolls.

C1CR-130	VG £220	F £450	VF £750

As C1CR-125, but with king looking sideways instead of forwards as on previous issues.

C1CR-135	VG £200	F £425	VF £725

Other very minor issues exist, mainly with different styles in horseman and the garniture of the royal shield.

Dated Issues (1644 – 1645)

Dated Exeter crowns are fairly easy to identify as they are all dated (1644 or 1645) at the end of the reverse legend and have the mintmark rose or castle. Many minor varieties of this issue exist, particularly in the style of the king's sash and the variety of mintmarks. The minor styles and varieties are all fairly common and make little difference to rarity or value.

Obverse Legend   CAROLUS D.G. MAG BRI FRA ET HI REX — Charles by the grace of God King of Great Britain France and Ireland

Reverse Legend   CHRISTO AUSPICE REGNO — I reign under the auspices of Christ

Obverse   King on horseback; mintmark castle or rose.

Reverse   Royal arms in oval garnished shield, dated 1644 or 1645 at end of legend; mintmark rose, castle, sometimes in legend, or EX.

C1CR-140	VG £200	F £425	VF £725

Truro Mint

This issue is very similar to the undated Exeter ones. In fact these Exeter issues used to be classed under Truro but recent research has re-classed them under Exeter. Truro crowns show the king's bust in profile rather than facing and also share the mintmark rose.

Collecting Hints

While scarce, these issues are obtainable and usually found undamaged and unclipped but fairly worn in VG to Fine condition; VF examples exist but are very rare.

Obverse Legend   CAROLUS DG MAG BRI FRA ET HI REX — Charles by the grace of God King of Great Britain France and Ireland

Reverse Legend   CHRISTO AUSPICE REGNO — I reign under the auspices of Christ

Obverse   King on horseback, king's head in profile, sash flies out in two ends; mintmark rose.

Reverse   Round garnished shield; mintmark rose.

C1CR-142	VG £180	F £360	VF £650

Scarborough Siege Issue

Scarborough was the only siege town to produce a crown. The denomination can be identified because below the castle on the obverse it is stamped 'S' then 'V' below followed by S.C.

Collecting Hints

This issue is extremely rare and collectors should be aware of forgeries.

Obverse   View of castle, counterstamped 'S.' with 'V' below SC.

Reverse   Plain.

C1CR-145   ex. rare

Commonwealth (1649 – 1660)

During the Commonwealth both gold and silver crowns were produced. They are very similar in style, having the date on the reverse and, for the first time, the legends in English. The coins are attractive but very plain in style with the obverse of both issues showing a St George cross within a wreath and the reverse the arms of Ireland with St George cross.

Gold Issue

Collecting Hints

All gold issues are rare, particularly that with the anchor mintmark dated 1658 or 1660. Coins tend to be available in the higher grades from Fine to EF and are usually undamaged, but collectors might have difficulty obtaining an example.

The following are dates and rarity values for the Commonwealth gold crowns:

Date	Rarity
1649	R
1650	RR
1651	RR
1652	R
1653	R
1654	R
1655	R
1656	R
1657	RR
1658/7	RRR
1658	RRR
1660	RRR

Obverse Legend THE COMMONWEALTH OF ENGLAND

Reverse Legend GOD WITH US

Obverse Shield of St George within wreath; mintmark sun.

Reverse Shield of St George and Ireland with date above (1649, 1650, 1651, 1652, 1653, 1654, 1655, 1656 or 1657).

CWCR-005 VG £250 F £500 VF £1,100

As previous, but mintmark anchor and date 1658 or 1660.

CWCR-010 VG £500 F £1,100 VF £2,200

Silver Issue

Collecting Hints

The silver crowns are much more common than the gold ones and tend to be found undamaged in VG to VF condition. The issue uses the mintmark sun only. Some dates are rarer than others and the prices given are for the common dates.

Obverse Legend   THE COMMONWEALTH OF ENGLAND

Reverse Legend   GOD WITH US

Obverse   Shield of St George within wreath; mintmark sun.

Reverse   Shield of St George and Ireland with value and date above. The following dates and varieties exist:

Date	Rarity
1649	RRR
1649 ....with wire line inner circles	RRR
1651	RRR
1652/1	RRR
1652	scarce
1652 ....date: large 2	RR
1653	scarce
1654	RRR
1656	RR
1656 ....date: small 6 over 4	scarce
1656 ....date: large 6 over small 6 over 4	R

CWCR-015 VG £325 F £650 VF £1,500

Charles II (1660 – 1685)

Hammered Issue (1660 – 1662)

During the hammered coinage of Charles II only gold crowns were struck. Two varieties were produced, both showing the bust of Charles II on the obverse and the royal shield with a crown above on the reverse. These issues were replaced in 1662 by the silver milled issue which is fairly common and listed in the milled section of this book.

Collecting Hints

These two issues are rare and difficult to obtain. When available, coins are usually found undamaged in Fine to VF condition.

Obverse Legend CAROLUS II D.G. MAG BRIT FR ET HIB REX — Charles II by the grace of God King of Great Britain France and Ireland

Reverse Legend FLORENT CONDORDIA REGNA — Through concord kingdoms flourish

Obverse Bust of king wearing laurel; mintmark crown.

Reverse Crown above oval shield dividing 'C.R'.

| C2CRH-005 | VG £275 | F £800 | VF £1,800 |

As previous, but value (V) behind king's bust.

| C2CRH-010 | VG £400 | F £850 | VF £1,900 |

Crown of the Rose

Henry VIII   (1509 – 1547)

The crown of the rose, with a value of four shillings and sixpence, was introduced for a short period during the second coinage of Henry VIII. It was made of 23 carat gold but was soon succeeded by a gold crown made of 22 carat gold and with a value of five shillings.

Collecting Hints

These issues are extremely rare.

Obverse Legend   HENRIC 8 DEI GRA REX ANGL Z FRAC — Henry VIII by the grace of God King of England France

Reverse Legend   HENRIC RUTILANS ROSA SINE SPINA — Henry a dazzling rose without a thorn

Obverse   Crown over royal shield; mintmark rose.

Reverse   Rose in centre of cross, two crowned 'H's and two lions in angles; mintmark rose.

H8CRR-005   ex. rare

As previous but reverse legend reads DNS HIB RUTILANS ROSA SINE SPINA — Lord of Ireland a dazzling rose without a thorn

H8CRR-010   ex. rare

Half Noble

The gold half-noble was introduced during the reign of Edward III as part of the 1346 monetary reform, and the extension of the denominations in circulation. It was exactly half the weight of the full noble and had a value of three shillings and fourpence. In virtually all issues, half-nobles are very similar in style, appearance and quality to nobles, depicting the king with a sword and a shield in a ship on the obverse and a cross surrounded by decoration on the reverse. A mintmark, which is important for identification, can be found in all cases on the obverse, either at the beginning or end of the legend.

Edward III   (1327 – 1377)

The half-noble was first introduced during the third coinage (1346–1351) and produced more widely during the fourth (1351–1377), becoming an important denomination both in England and with merchants in Europe. The obverse shows the king with a sword and shield in a ship; EDWARD is always broken by the ship's bow. Half-nobles are divided into several issues according to their obverse legends, which reflect Edward's territorial aspirations in France (for details, see p.343). Until 1361, half-nobles included FRANC on the legend; this was replaced by AQU until 1369 but FRANC returned in the final, post-treaty period. Two mints produced gold half-nobles during Edward III's reign, London and Calais. The issues from Calais can easily be identified by a flag at the ship's stern or a 'C' in the cross in the centre of the reverse. Calais, in Northern France, was under the control of Edward III and was used as a mint firstly to show English sovereignty in the area and secondly to supply English merchants trading in Europe.

Collecting Hints

Edward III's half-nobles are scarce but obtainable, however, although they are as scarce as the gold noble, this is not reflected in their value since collectors prefer to own a gold noble rather than a half-noble. With many half-nobles found in hoards, the condition of specimens is often very good and the average grade Fine to VF. Nevertheless, recent examples found by metal detectors indicate that many half-nobles saw considerable circulation and may be worn or clipped.

Third Coinage (1346 – 1351)

Obverse Legend   EDWAR D GRA REX ANGL Z FRA D — Edward by the grace of God King of England and France Lord (of the Irish)

Reverse Legend   DOMINE NE IN FURORE TUO ARGUAS ME — O Lord rebuke me not in Thine anger

Obverse   King on ship holding sword and shield, large lettering in legends with Lombardic 'N'.

Reverse   Mintmark cross pattée, closed 'E' in centre of reverse cross.

E3HN-005	VG —	F £1,500	VF £3,000

Fourth Coinage (1351 – 1377)

Pre Treaty Period (1351 – 1361)

We have listed the main varieties although, with muling, there is little doubt that other minor varieties do exist.

Obverse Legend   As previous; minor varieties.

Reverse Legend   As previous.

Obverse   King on ship holding sword and shield; Roman 'M' and 'N' ('N' sometimes reversely barred or unbarred), annulet stops in legend.

Reverse   As previous, actually with the last issue's reverse die, making this one a mule; Lombardic 'M' or 'N' in reverse legend.

E3HN-010	VG £200	F £400	VF £700

As previous, but a closed 'E' and 'C' and a Lombardic 'M' in legends.

E3HN-015	VG £200	F £400	VF £700

Broken letters in the legends with the 'V' often having a nick in the right arm.

E3HN-020	VG £300	F £600	VF £1,200

Transitional Period (1361)

Obverse Legend   EDWARDUS DEI G REX ANGL D or E D DEI GRA REX ANGL DNS HIB Z ACQ (several varieties exist) — Edward by the grace of God King of England Lord of Ireland and Aquitaine

Reverse Legend   DOMINE NE IN FURORE TUO ARGUAS ME — O Lord rebuke me not in Thine anger

Obverse   King on ship holding sword and shield, irregular sized lettering.

Reverse   'E' in centre of reverse, pellets or annulets in centre of cross; mintmark cross potent.

E3HN-025	VG £200	F £400	VF £700

Treaty Period (1361 – 1369)

These issues were struck at London and Calais. They had new-style letters of uniform size and a curule-shaped 'X' in the legends.

London Mint

Obverse Legend   EDWARD DEI G REX ANGL D HYB Z AQT — Edward by the grace of God King of England Lord of the Irish and Aquitaine

Reverse Legend   DOMINE NE IN FURORE TUO ARGUAS ME — O Lord rebuke me not in Thine anger

Obverse   King in ship holding sword and shield; a saltire before EDWARD.

Reverse   As previous; mintmark cross potent.

E3HN-030	VG £200	F £400	VF £700

As previous, but an annulet before EDWARD.

E3HN-035	VG £210	F £450	VF £750

Calais Mint

Legends As previous.

Obverse As previous, but a saltire before EDWARD, a flag at the ship's stern.

Reverse 'C' in centre on reverse.

E3HN-040	VG £210	F £450	VF £775

As previous, but no marks before EDWARD. Sometimes without a flag at the ship's stern.

E3HN-045	VG £225	F £500	VF £850

As previous, but a quatrefoil before EDWARD.

E3HN-050	VG £225	F £500	VF £850

Post Treaty Period (1369 – 1377)
London Mint

Obverse Legend EDWARD DI GRA REX ANGL Z FRANC D — Edward by the grace of God King of England and France Lord (of the Irish)

Reverse Legend As previous.

Obverse As previous, but annulet before EDWARD.

Reverse 'E' in centre with pellet; mintmark cross potent.

E3HN-055	F £900	VF £2,000

Calais Mint

Legends As previous.

Obverse King on ship with a flag at the stern.

Reverse 'E' in centre of reverse.

E3HN-060	VG £225	F £450	VF £900

As previous, but a 'C' on reverse. This issue is a mule using the reverse die from the Treaty issue (E3HN-040 to -050).

E3HN-065	VG £225	F £450	VF £900

Should your coin have a rose in the side of the king's ship it is a rose half-noble of Edward IV's first reign.

Richard II   (1377 – 1399)

During the reign of Richard II half-nobles were produced at the London and Calais mints. All issues have RICARD at the beginning of the obverse legend, broken by the ship's bow. Richard II was the only Richard to produce half-nobles. The issues are very similar in style to those of Edward III except for the obverse legend and an 'R' on the centre cross of the reverse, which however is sometimes omitted in the first issue. As mentioned earlier, Calais was an active mint producing gold coins during the reign of Richard II and its issues are easily identified by a flag at the ship's stern.

Collecting Hints

All issues are very rare but, when available, usually found in Fine to VF condition because most specimens in collections today have been found in hoards and are therefore usually neither damaged nor badly worn.

London Mint

Obverse Legend RICARD DI GRA REX ANGL Z FR D HIBS Z AQT (many varieties exist usually with abbreviations or FR omitted altogether) — Richard by the grace of God King of England and France Lord of the Irish and Aquitaine

Reverse Legend DOMINE NE IN FURORE TUO ARGUAS ME — O Lord rebuke me not in Thine anger

Obverse This issue is an altered die of Edward III and RICHARD is struck over EDWARD; king on ship holding sword and shield.

Reverse This again is sometimes an altered die of Edward III, an 'R' is struck over the 'E' in the central cross.

R2HN-005	VG £325	F £800	VF £1,600

In some cases only one die has been altered. These coins were struck right at the beginning of Richard II's reign while new dies were being prepared.

The following three issues for London are true issues of Richard II and the style of their lettering is different.

Legends   As previous.

Obverse   King in ship holding sword and shield, straight-sided lettering with an annulet over the sail.

Reverse   'R' in centre of cross; mintmark cross pattée. Straight-sided lettering in legends.

| R2HN-010 | VG £300 | F £750 | VF £1,650 |

Legends   As previous.

Obverse   Lion on rudder of ship, fishtailed lettering in legends.

Reverse   As previous, but fishtailed lettering in legends.

| R2HN-015 | VG £300 | F £750 | VF £1,650 |

Legends   As previous.

Obverse   Crescent on ship's rudder, small dumpy lettering in legends.

Reverse   As previous, but dumpy lettering.

| R2HN-020 | VG £325 | F £775 | VF £1,700 |

Calais Mint

All issues have a flag at the ship's stern to differentiate them from London issues.

Legends   As previous.

Obverse   As R2HN-005 (Edward III's die).

Reverse   As R2HN-005 (Edward III's die).

| R2HN-025 | VG £350 | F £850 | VF £1,800 |

Legends   As previous.

Obverse   Quatrefoil over sail, straight-sided lettering.

Reverse   'R' in centre of cross, straight-sided lettering; mintmark cross pattée.

| R2HN-030 | VG £300 | F £850 | VF £1,800 |

Legends   As previous.

Obverse   Lion on ship's rudder, fishtailed lettering in legend.

Reverse   As previous, but fishtailed lettering in legend.

| R2HN-035 | VG £325 | F £800 | VF £1,700 |

Legends   As previous.

Obverse   Crescent on ship's rudder, or trefoil over sail or saltire behind rudder; dumpy style lettering.

Reverse   As previous, but dumpy style lettering.

| R2HN-040 | VG £375 | F £950 | VF £2,000 |

Henry IV   (1399 – 1413)

All issues of Henry IV are rare and the half-noble is the rarest of them all. It is fairly similar to issues of Henry V and VI who also produced half-nobles. In Henry IV's case, HENRIC is found at the beginning of the obverse legend broken by the ship's bow and the mintmark cross pattée is found in all issues except Calais, at the start of the reverse legend. Of the three Henrys that produced half-nobles the cross pattée mintmark was used for Henry IV and Henry V. All issues of the three Henrys had various marks, such as annulets and mascles, on the coin that can differentiate the various issues and reigns. If uncertain, collectors should check all three reigns when trying to identify an issue, paying particular attention to mintmarks and other marks on the coins

With the value of gold and silver rising and the scarcity of bullion, the mints faced increasing difficulty producing coins, and those that were struck were often smuggled abroad for sale as their metal content was so high. So in 1412 the metal content of gold coins was reduced by 10% and the so-called light coinage replaced the heavy. A half-noble in particular, instead of weighing 60 grains (3.9 grams), now weighed 54 grains (3.5 grams).

London and Calais both produced half-nobles but the issues from Calais were only struck during the heavy coinage and are easily identified by a flag at the ship's stern.

Collecting Hints

All issues are extremely rare and collectors will have great difficulty in obtaining an example. The very few specimens we have seen have been in Fine to VF condition.

Heavy Coinage (1399 – 1412)

London Mint

Obverse Legend   HENRIC DI G REX ANGL Z FR DNS HIB AQT — Henry by the grace of God King of England and France Lord of the Irish and Aquitaine (often abbreviated)

Reverse Legend   DOMINE NE IN FURORE TUO ARGUAS ME — O Lord rebuke me not in Thine anger

Obverse   King in ship holding sword and shield with four lis in the two French quarters; this is known as the 'old arms' type.

Reverse   'H' in centre of cross; mintmark cross pattée.

| H4HN-005 | ex. rare |

As previous, but three lis in the two French quarters on the king's shield; known as the 'new arms' type.

| H4HN-010 | F £5,000 | VF — |

Calais Mint

As previous, but a flag on the ship's stern; mintmark crown.

| H4HN-015 | ex. rare |

Light Coinage (1412 – 1413)

This issue was only struck at the London mint. Should your coin have a quatrefoil above the ship's sail refer to Henry V.

Legends   As previous.

Obverse   King in ship holding sword and shield with new style arms, an annulet on the side of the ship.

Reverse   'H' in centre of reverse cross.

H4HN-020   VG £ —   F £4,000   VF —

Henry V   (1413 – 1422)

During the reign of Henry V half-nobles were produced at the London mint in some quantity. All issues used the mintmark cross pattée with pellet in centre or pierced cross, except for the first very rare issue which uses the Henry IV reverse die. Many coins can also be identified by a quatrefoil above the ship's sail on the obverse. Many issues are fairly similar to those of Henry VI and, if uncertain, collectors should refer to this chapter.

Collecting Hints

Most issues of Henry V are very rare and the first issue is extremely so. Coins when available are usually undamaged in Fine to VF condition as they have been found in hoards and rarely saw much circulation.

Obverse Legend   HENRIC DI GRA REX ANGL Z F — Henry by the grace of God King of England and France

Reverse Legend   DOMINE NE IN FURORE TUO ARGUAS ME — O Lord rebuke me not in Thine anger

Obverse   King on ship holding sword and shield, a quatrefoil above the sail.

Reverse   Mintmark cross pattée; this is a Henry IV die.

H5HN-005   ex. rare

Legends   As previous.
Obverse   As previous, but quatrefoil below sail, broken annulet on ship.
Reverse   'H' in centre of cross; mintmark cross pattée or pierced cross.

H5HN-010   VG £300   F £600   VF £1,200

Legends   As previous.
Obverse   Broken annulet on ship's side and a mullet above the shield.
Reverse   Broken annulet in upper right quarter of coin, the rest as previous.

H5HN-015   VG £300   F £600   VF £1,200

Legends   As previous.
Obverse   Mullet above shield, trefoil usually between shield and prow.
Reverse   As previous, usually using previous die.

H5HN-020   VG £325   F £700   VF £1,400

Legends   As previous.
Obverse   Quatrefoil over ship's sail, mullet sometimes after first word of legend.
Reverse   Mullet or annulet stops after first word of legend.

H5HN-025   VG £300   F £500   VF £1,000

Henry VI First Reign (1422 – 1461)

During the first few years of Henry VI's reign half-nobles were produced in some quantity. All issues bear HENRIC at the beginning of the obverse legend broken by the ship's bow while mintmarks and various other marks can class coins into issues. This form of quality control linked each coin to a particular die but it was particularly complex and as there is no easy way of identifying issues collectors might find it necessary to refer to all issues, even those of Henry IV and Henry V.

During Henry VI's reign three mints produced half-nobles: London, Calais and York. The Calais mint is identifiable by a flag at the stern of the ship and sometimes a 'C' instead of an 'H' in the centre of the reverse cross. The issues of York are identified by a lis over the ship's stern.

Collecting Hints

All issues are rare and the later issues extremely so. Coins are usually undamaged in Fine to VF condition as many have been found in hoards and so saw little circulation.

Annulet Issue (1422 – 1427)

London Mint

Obverse Legend   HENRIC DI GRA REX ANGL Z FRANC — Henry by the grace of God King of England and France

Reverse Legend   DOMINE NE IN FURORE TUO ARGUAS ME — O Lord rebuke me not in Thine anger

Obverse   King holding shield and sword on ship, annulet by sword, lis after HENRIC.

Reverse   Annulet in one spandrel on reverse, a mullet in legend, 'H' in centre cross.

H6HN-005   VG £220   F £400   VF £800

This issue is a mule and used the obverse die from issues of Henry V.

Obverse Legend   HENRIC DI GRA REX ANGL Z F (varieties exist) — Henry by the grace of God King of England and France

Reverse Legend   As previous.

Obverse   As (London) issues of Henry V, usually H5HN-025

Reverse   As previous.

H6HN-010   VG £275   F £525   VF £1,000

Calais Mint

Obverse Legend   As H6HN-005.

Reverse Legend   As previous.

Obverse   As H6HN-005 with a flag at the ship's stern.

Reverse   As H6HN-005, but sometimes 'C' instead of 'H' in centre of cross.

H6HN-015	VG £325	F £600	VF £1,200

York Mint

Legends   As previous.

Obverse   As previous, but a lis over ship's stern instead of a flag.

Reverse   As previous, but 'H' in centre of cross.

H6HN-020	VG £325	F £650	VF £1,300

Rosette Mascle Issue (1427 – 1430)
London Mint

Legends   As previous.

Obverse   King with sword and shield on ship, rosettes and mascle stops in legend.

Reverse   Lis in one quarter of reverse, rosette and mascle stops in legend; mintmark lis.

H6HN-025	VG —	F £1,000	VF £2,100

Calais Mint

Legends   As previous.

Obverse   King with sword and shield on ship, flag at stern, rosette stops in legend.

Reverse   Lis in one quarter of reverse, rosette stops in legend; mintmark lis.

H6HN-030	VG —	F £1,000	VF £2,100

Pinecone Mascle Issue (1430 – 1434)

This issue was struck in the London mint and is found only as a mule, using the obverse die from the previous issue.

Legends   As previous.

Obverse   King on ship holding sword and shield, rosettes and mascle stops.

Reverse   Mintmark lis; pinecones and mascle stops in legend.

H6HN-035	ex. rare

Leaf Mascle Issue (1434 – 1435)

Legends   As previous.

Obverse / Reverse   No details available.

H6HN-040	ex. rare

Leaf Trefoil Issue (1435 – 1438)

This issue is only found as a mule using the reverse die from the annulet issue.

Legends   As previous.

Obverse   King in ship with sword and shield, leaves and trefoils in legend.

Reverse   As H6HN-005.

H6HN-045	probably unique

No other half-nobles were produced during the later issues of Henry VI.

Edward IV First Reign (1461 – 1470)

The gold half-noble had hardly changed in style, value or quality since the previous century when it was first introduced. However, Henry VI's reign was the last period in which the true half-noble, with a value of three shillings and four pence, was to be issued. During the first period of Edward IV's reign (1461–1464), few nobles and no half-nobles were produced as the high gold price meant that the coins' metal value was higher than their intrinsic face value. In 1464, in response to this crisis the value of all half-nobles in circulation was increased to four shillings and twopence and a new coin of higher value and weight was introduced. Known as the rose half-noble or half-ryal, it had a value of five shillings. The half-ryal is fairly similar to the old-style half-nobles except for a rose on the ship on the obverse and a different central design on the reverse. However, the new denomination was unpopular and ceased at the end of Edward IV's first reign. Then, during Henry VI's second reign, the gold half-angel was introduced with a value of three shillings and fourpence which, of course, was the old value for the half-noble.

A total of five mints were actively producing the new half rose ryal during the reign of Edward IV and may be distinguished by a letter found in the waves below the ship. They were London (none), Bristol (B), York (E), Coventry (C) and Norwich (N).

Collecting Hints

While the London issue is rare, the provincial ones are very rare. Coins are usually found undamaged in Fine or VF condition.

London Mint

Obverse Legend   EDWARD DI GRA REX ANGL Z FRANC — Edward by the grace of God King of England and France

Reverse Legend   DOMINE NE IN FURORE TUO ARGUAS ME — O Lord rebuke me not in Thine anger

Obverse   King holding sword and shield on ship; mintmarks rose, crown, sun, long cross fitchée or none. Various combinations of mintmarks and muling exist.

Reverse   Rose upon a sun.

E4HN-005	VG £225	F £450	VF £900

Bristol Mint

Legends   As previous.

Obverse   As previous, but 'B' in waves below ship; no mintmark.

Reverse   As previous, but mintmark sun, crown, none, sun and crown.

E4HN-010	VG £240	F £600	VF £1,200

Coventry Mint

Legends   As previous.

Obverse   As previous, but 'C' below ship.

Reverse   As previous, but mintmark sun.

E4HN-015	ex. rare

Norwich Mint

Legends   As previous.

Obverse   As previous, but an 'N' below ship.

Reverse   As previous, but mintmark rose.

E4HN-020	VG £ —	F £2,000	VF —

York Mint

Legends   As previous.

Obverse   As previous, but 'E' (for EBORACI, Latin for York) below ship.

Reverse   As previous, but mintmark sun, lis, sun over crown, rose and lis.

E4HN-025	VG £225	F £450	VF £900

As previous, but a lis in the ship's side instead of 'E'.

E4HN-030	ex. rare

The three shillings Charles I Carlisle siege issue can be found in the chapter 'Charles I, Siege Issues' at the end of the hammered coinage section.

Half Angel

Even though the gold angel was introduced during the first reign of Edward IV the half-angel, or angelet as it was sometimes called later, was not introduced until the second reign of Henry VI. It had a value of three shillings and four-pence but was never produced in any quantity. The issues are virtually identical in style to the larger and more popular full angel, with St Michael killing the dragon on the obverse and a ship with arms in centre on the reverse. The mintmark, which is helpful in identification, is usually found at the beginning of the obverse and/or reverse legends.

Henry VI Restored (Oct. 1470 – April 1471)

These coins were struck at the London and Bristol mints and bear a mintmark only on the reverse. Henry VII and Henry VIII also struck half-angels, but in most cases the mintmark is different, the style and various marks which are found on the issues of Henry VIII can also help with identification. The king's name in all cases is found at the beginning of the obverse legend, and it should read HENRIC, HENRICU or HERIC — Henry.

The Bristol mint struck half-angels, however, it is thought only one specimen exists. This issue is identified by a 'B' in the waves below the ship.

Collecting Hints

Coins from the London mint are extremely rare, and when available are usually in Fine or VF condition. The issue from the Bristol mint, as mentioned earlier, is unique.

London Mint

Obverse Legend HE(N)RIC(U) DI GRA REX ANGL Z FRA (many varieties exist) — Henry by the grace of God King of England and France

Reverse Legend O CRUX AVE SPES UNICA (minor varieties exist) — Hail thou cross my only hope

Obverse St Michael killing a dragon; mintmarks none.

Reverse Ship with royal arms in centre, a mast in the shape of a cross above, an 'H' and lis either side of the royal arms; mintmark cross pattée, Restoration cross or lis.

H6HA-005   F £1,750   VF £3,500

Bristol Mint

Obverse Legend HENRIC DI GRA REX ANGL Z FRA — Henry by the grace of God King of England and France

Reverse Legend As previous.

Obverse As previous.

Reverse As previous, but mintmark Restoration cross only, 'B' in the waves below the ship.

H6HA-010   unique

Edward IV Second Reign (1471 – 1483)

These issues, which were all struck at the London mint, are very much a continuation from the previous reign. In all cases the mintmark can be found on the obverse and sometimes the reverse. The varieties of these three issues lie in the arrangement of the legends.

Edward V also produced half-angels which have the mintmark halved sun and rose on the obverse and reverse, or sometimes a boar's head on the obverse and a halved sun and rose on the reverse. When identifying an issue collectors should refer to these issues if necessary.

Collecting Hints

These issues are very rare and are usually found undamaged in Fine to VF condition.

Obverse Legend EDWARD DEI GRA REX ANG — Edward by the grace of God King of England

Reverse Legend O CRUX AVE SPES UNICA — Hail thou cross my only hope

Obverse St Michael killing the dragon; mintmark pierced cross and pellet, annulet, pierced cross central pellet, heraldic cinquefoil.

Reverse Ship with royal arms above, the mast in the shape of a cross, 'E' and rose either side of the mast; mintmarks as previous.

E4HA-005   VG £180   F £350   VF £750

Obverse Legend As E4HA-005 reverse.

Reverse Legend As E4HA-005 obverse.

Obverse As previous; mintmark short cross fitchée.

Reverse As previous; no mintmark.

E4HA-010   VG £225   F £500   VF £900

Obverse Legend As E4HA-005 obverse legend.

Reverse Legend As the obverse legend.

Obverse As previous; mintmark annulet.

Reverse As previous; no mintmark.

E4HA-015   VG £200   F £475   VF £800

Edward IV or V

There is uncertainty whether half-angels were struck during the reign of Edward V using the mintmark halved sun and rose. It is now thought that the dies were made during the reign of Edward IV, but were used to strike coins during the short reign of Edward V. Only the mintmark can differentiate these issues.

Collecting Hints

This issue is extremely rare.

Obverse Legend EDWARD DI GRA REX ANG — Edward by the grace of God King of England

Reverse Legend O CRUX AVE SPES UNICA — Hail thou cross my only hope

Obverse St Michael killing the dragon; mintmark halved sun and rose.

Reverse Ship with royal arms in centre, a mast in the shape of the cross above, 'E' and a rose either side of the cross; mintmark halved sun and rose.

E4HA-020 ex. rare

Edward V (1483)

This issue, which is unique, has the mintmark boar's head on the obverse and mintmark halved sun and rose on the reverse.

Collecting Hints

This coin is unique.

Obverse Legend EDWARD DI GRA REX ANG — Edward by the grace of God King of England

Reverse Legend O CRUX AVE SPES UNICA — Hail thou cross my only hope

Obverse St Michael killing the dragon; mintmark boar's head.

Reverse Ship with royal arms in centre, a mast in the shape of a cross with 'E' and a rose either side of the cross; mintmark halved sun and rose.

E5HA-005 unique

Richard III (1483 – 1485)

This issue is very much a continuation from the previous one. RICARD is found at the beginning of the obverse legend and the mintmark boar's head on the obverse and reverse. This issue was struck at London only.

Collecting Hints

This issue is extremely rare.

Obverse Legend RICARD DI GRA REX ANG — Richard by the grace of God King of England

Reverse Legend O CRUX AVE SPES UNICA — Hail thou cross my only hope

Obverse St Michael killing the dragon; mintmark boar's head.

Reverse Ship with royal arms in centre, a mast in the shape of a cross, 'R' and rose either side of mast; mintmark boar's head.

R3HA-005 ex. rare

Henry VII (1485 – 1509)

Half-angels were struck during most of Henry VII's reign; they were all struck at London and again are very much a continuation from the last reign. The first issue uses altered dies from Edward IV or V and the mintmark halved sun and rose; it is extremely rare. The next issues show a slightly more life-like St Michael with both feet, instead of just one, on the dragon.

Henry VIII also struck half-angels but used different mintmarks so coins can be easily identified. Should the mintmarks be unclear, we have listed minor varieties which will enable collectors to identify the issue. Henry VI's restored reign also produced half-angels but they show St Michael with just one foot on the dragon.

Collecting Hints

The first issue is extremely rare, the others rare. Coins are often found slightly damaged in Fine condition. However, VF and EF examples do exist but are very rare.

Obverse Legend HENRIC DI GRA REX ANG (altered dies) — Henry by the grace of God King of England

Reverse Legend O CRUX AVE SPES UNICA — Hail thou cross my only hope

Obverse St Michael with one foot on the dragon killing it; mintmark halved sun and rose or lis over halved sun and rose?

(altered die)

Reverse Ship with royal arms in centre, mast in shape of cross above, 'H' and rose either side.

H7HA-005 VG £200 F £425 VF £800

Obverse Legend HENRIC DI GRA REX ANGL — Henry by the grace of God King of England

Reverse Legend As previous.

Obverse St Michael with both feet on the dragon; mintmark pansy or anchor.

Reverse As previous; mintmark pansy or greyhound's head.

H7HA-010	VG £190	F £375	VF £700

As previous, but small square lettering; mintmark rose on obverse and reverse.

H7HA-015	VG £200	F £500	VF £900

As H7HA-010, but tall, thin lettering; mintmark rose (obverse), cross crosslet (reverse).

H7HA-020	VG £190	F £400	VF £800

As H7HA-010, but large crook-shaped abbreviation after HENRIC on the obverse; mintmark pheon.

H7HA-025	VG £185	F £375	VF £675

Henry VIII   (1509 – 1547)

Gold half-angels were struck during all three issues of Henry VIII's reign although not during the posthumous coinage. All issues are very much a continuation from the reign of Henry VII except for the mintmarks and, in some cases, the obverse legend; also the third issue often has annulets on the ship. We have listed all the varieties, but collectors should pay particular attention to the mintmark and, if uncertain, refer back to the reign of Henry VII.

During the first coinage the value of the half-angel remained three shillings and four pence. However, because English coins were being exported abroad where they had a higher value, the value of the half-angel was increased to three shillings and nine pence in 1526.

All half-angels were struck at the London mint.

Collecting Hints

Half-angels from the first coinage while rare are obtainable; from the second coinage they are very rare. Coins are usually found in Fine condition, while VF and even EF examples do exist. There is no doubt that many of these coins saw considerable circulation and this is reflected in their condition.

First Coinage (1509 – 1526)

Obverse Legend   HENRIC DI GRA REX AGL Z or HENRIC VIII DI GRA REX AL (many minor varieties exist) — Henry (VIII) by the grace of God King of England (and)

Reverse Legend   O CRUX AVE SPES UNICA — Hail thou cross my only hope

Obverse   St Michael killing the dragon; mintmark castle, castle with 'H' or portcullis crowned.

Reverse   Ship with royal arms in centre, a mast in the shape of a cross, 'H' and rose either side; mintmarks as obverse but also rose muled.

H8HA-005	VG £195	F £350	VF £650

Second Coinage (1526 – 1544)

Legends   As previous, but HENRIC VIII in obverse.

Obverse   As previous, but mintmark lis.

Reverse   As previous, but mintmark lis.

H8HA-010	VG £250	F £550	VF £1,100

Third Coinage (1544 – 1547)

Obverse Legend   HENRIC 8 D G AGL FR Z HIB REX — Henry VIII by the grace of God King of England France and Ireland

Reverse Legend   O CRUX AVE SPES UNICA — Hail thou cross my only hope

Obverse   As previous, but annulet on ship; mintmark lis.

Reverse   As previous.

H8HA-015	VG £195	F £350	VF £650

As previous, but no annulet on ship. This issue should not be confused with the second coinage; the only difference is the obverse legend.

H8HA-020	VG £195	F £350	VF £650

As previous, but three annulets on ship.

H8HA-025	VG £190	F £325	VF £625

Edward VI   (1547 – 1553)

Half-angels were produced during the third period of Edward VI's reign but only one specimen survives. The issue, which now had a value of five shillings, was produced at the Tower mint in London.

Collecting Hints

This issue is unique.

Obverse Legend   EDWARD VI D G AGL F Z HI REX — Edward VI by the grace of God King of England France and Ireland

Reverse Legend   PER CRU TUA SALVA NOS XPE — By Thy cross save us O Christ our Redeemer

Obverse   St Michael killing the dragon; mintmark ostrich's head.

Reverse   Ship with royal arms in centre, a mast in the shape of a cross, 'E' and a rose either side of mast.

E6HA-005   unique

Mary   (1553 – 1554)

Half-angels were struck during Mary's reign, however, they are rare. They were also struck during the reign of Philip and Mary, the main differences being the obverse legend. The style of the coin, with the exception of the legends, is very much a continuation of previous reigns.

Collecting Hints

This issue is extremely rare in any grade.

Obverse Legend   MARIA D G A FR Z HIB REGINA — Mary by the grace of God Queen of England France and Ireland

Reverse Legend   A DNO FACTU EST ISTVD Z — This is the Lord's doing and it is marvellous in our eyes (abbreviated)

Obverse   St Michael killing the dragon; mintmark pomegranate.

Reverse   Ship with royal arms in centre, a mast in the shape of a cross, 'M' and rose either side of the cross.

MAHA-005   F £2,500   VF £6,000

Philip & Mary   (1554 – 1558)

This issue, which is extremely rare, is very much a continuation from Mary's reign, the main difference being the obverse legend and the mintmark.

Collecting Hints

This issue is extremely rare.

Obverse Legend   PHILIP Z MARIA D G REX Z REGI — Philip and Mary by the grace of God King and Queen

Reverse Legend   A DNO FACTU EST ISTUD Z EST MIR — This is the Lord's doing and it is marvellous in our eyes

Obverse   St Michael killing the dragon; mintmark lis.

Reverse   Ship with royal arms in centre, a mast with PM either side.

PMHA-005   ex. rare

Elizabeth I   (1558 – 1603)

During the first five issues of Elizabeth I's reign half-angels were produced with a value of five shillings. They circulated alongside the crown of similar value, however, by now the half-angel's style, which had changed very little from the reign of Henry VI, was looking tired and old-fashioned, especially when compared to many of the other contemporary English gold coins.

Collecting Hints

All issues are rare and some extremely rare. Coins are usually found in Fine condition. However, VF and even EF specimens do exist. There is no doubt that these coins saw considerable circulation which is reflected in their grade.

First – Third Issues (1559 – 1578)

Obverse Legend   ELIZABETH D G A FR ET HI REGINA — Elizabeth by the grace of God Queen of England France and Ireland

Reverse Legend   A DNO FACTUM EST ISTUD ET EST MIRA — This is the Lord's doing and it is marvellous in our eyes

Obverse   St Michael killing the dragon; mintmark lis, wire lined inner circles.

Reverse   Ship with royal arms in centre, a mast in the shape of a cross above, 'E' and rose either side, wire lined inner circles; mintmark lis.

ELHA-005   ex. rare

Legends   As previous.

Obverse   As previous, but beaded inner circles; mintmark lis, cross crosslet, coronet, ermine, acorn, eglantine.

Reverse   As previous, but beaded inner circles, the ship now faces right.

ELHA-010   VG £200   F £350   VF £700

Fourth Issue (1578 – 1582)

The fineness of gold for this issue was slightly reduced.

Legends   As previous.

Obverse   As previous, but mintmark Greek cross or sword.

Reverse   As previous; mintmarks as obverse.

ELHA-015	VG £200	F £350	VF £700

As previous, but no 'E' or rose by mast of ship; mintmark Latin cross.

ELHA-020	VG £275	F £550	VF £1,100

Fifth Issue (1583 – 1600)

The fineness of gold for this issue was raised slightly.

Legends   As previous.

Obverse   As ELHA-015; mintmark bell, 'A', escallop, crescent, hand, key, anchor.

Reverse   As ELHA-015; mintmarks in obverse.

ELHA-025	VG £200	F £350	VF £700

James I   (1603 – 1625)

Gold half-angels were struck for a very short time during James I's second coinage. In 1612 the value of all half-angels was raised to five shillings and sixpence, and this included all coins from previous reigns and issues. However, the half-angel had become obsolete in denomination and style from medieval England, and production of the half-angel finally ceased in 1619.

Collecting Hints

All issues are extremely rare.

Obverse Legend   IACOBUS D G MA BRI FRA ET HI REX — James by the grace of God King of Great Britain France and Ireland

Reverse Legend   A DNO FACTUM EST ISTUD — This is the Lord's doing and it is marvellous in our eyes

Obverse   St Michael killing the dragon; mintmark tower, trefoil, cinquefoil, tun, closed book, plain cross, saltire cross.

Reverse   Ship with royal arms in centre, 'I' and rose either side of shortened mast; mintmarks as obverse.

J1HA-005	F £1,500	VF £3,500

Half Florin or Leopard

In 1344, a year after Edward III had instructed the Florentines George Kirkyn and Lotte Nicholyn to produce gold denominations for England, the half-florin or leopard was created. Largely based on the European gold issues, it was intended to be not just for England but for the whole of Europe. Its value was three shillings but as the gold used to strike the coins had been over-valued, the coins were unacceptable to the public. By August of that year the issue was demonetised and the coins recalled, melted down and used to make the popular and more acceptable noble issues. Nevertheless, this issue is undoubtedly one of the most beautiful medieval English coins ever produced and it is a loss to collectors that virtually all specimens were destroyed.

Collecting Hints

This issue is extremely rare; however, most specimens exist in the higher grades.

Obverse Legend   EDWAR D GRA REX ANGL Z FRANC DNS HIB — Edward by the grace of God King of England and France Lord of Ireland

Reverse Legend   DOMINE NE IN FURORE TUO ARGUAS ME — O Lord rebuke me not in Thy anger

Obverse   A leopard with a cloak of the royal arms.

Reverse   Royal cross in a quatrefoil, a leopard in each quarter.

E3HFL-005   ex. rare

Halfcrown

Henry VIII's monetary reform of 1526 introduced the halfcrown which, like most new denominations, was struck in some quantity. It was made of 22 carat gold and had the value of two shillings and sixpence. However, although the gold issue was important to the monetary reform it was really too small in size and could easily get lost. Furthermore, having a coin of such high value this small was unpopular so the silver halfcrown was introduced during Edward VI's fine silver issue. Made of good quality silver and beautifully designed, it was an important and acceptable denomination. Probably because there were enough numbers in circulation, halfcrowns were not struck again until the end of Elizabeth I's reign, except for some gold issues. However, during all future reigns and until 1967, large quantities of halfcrowns were produced for circulation.

Henry VIII (1509 – 1547)

Under Henry VIII gold halfcrowns were produced from 1526, during the second and third coinages as well as the posthumous coinage struck under Edward VI. All these issues are fairly similar. Halfcrowns were struck at the Tower mint during the second coinage, then also at Bristol and Southwark during the third coinage and finally at the two London mints, Tower and Southwark, during the posthumous coinage. To identify the mint and issue, collectors should pay particular attention to the mintmark at the beginning of the obverse and, in most cases, the reverse legend.

Collecting Hints

These issues are fairly scarce but tend to be unpopular with collectors as there is no bust of the king on the coin. Rarely found in better than Fine condition, they are sometimes damaged. Nevertheless, they are the first halfcrown struck and no serious collection of halfcrowns would be complete without an example.

Second Coinage (1526 – 1544)

Obverse Legend HENRIC 8 DI GRA REX AGL Z FRA — Henry VIII by the grace of God King of England and France

Reverse Legend RUTILANS ROSA SINE SPINA — A dazzling rose without a thorn

Obverse Crown above a rose; mintmark rose.

Reverse Crown over royal shield.

H8HC-005	VG £150	F £300	VF £600

As previous, but rose dividing 'HK' on both sides of the coin, uncrowned on obverse.

H8HC-010	VG £150	F £300	VF £600

As previous, but HK on the obverse only; mintmark rose on obverse and lis on reverse (the dies of this issue are muled), or lis, or arrow.

H8HC-015	VG £165	F £320	VF £650

As previous, but HI both sides of coin; mintmark arrow.

H8HC-020	VG £175	F £350	VF £700

As previous, except that the mintmark is a pheon, there is 'HR' on both sides of coin and the reverse legend reads HENRIC 8 D G AGL FR Z HIB REX (varieties exist) — Henry VIII by the grace of God King of England France and Ireland

H8HC-025	VG £200	F £450	VF £900

Third Coinage (1544 – 1547)

Unlike the silver issues of the third coinage, the gold issues were never debased.

Tower Mint

Obverse Legend HENRIC 8 DG AGL FR Z HIB REX — Henry VIII by the grace of God King of England France and Ireland

Reverse Legend RUTILANS ROSA SINE SPINA — A dazzling rose without a thorn

Obverse Crown above a rose; mintmark pellet in annulet, initials H.R.

Reverse Crown over shield, H.R.

H8HC-030	VG £160	F £300	VF £600

As previous, but an annulet on the inner circle.

H8HC-035	VG £160	F £300	VF £600

Southwark Mint

Southwark was London's second mint and operated just south of the river Thames. This issue used Roman and Lombardic lettering.

Legends As previous.

Obverse As H8HC-030, but mintmark 'S'.

Reverse As H8HC-030, but mintmark 'S'.

H8HC-040	VG £170	F £320	VF £600

Obverse Legend   HENRIC 8 ROSA SINE SPIN — Henry VIII a rose without a thorn

Reverse Legend   DEI GRA AGL FR Z HIB REX — By the grace of God King of England France and Ireland

Obverse   As previous, but mintmark 'E'.

Reverse   As previous, but mintmark 'E'.

H8HC-045	VG £175	F £400	VF £800

Bristol Mint

Obverse Legend   HENRIC 8 ROSA SINE SPINA — Henry VIII a rose without a thorn

Reverse Legend   DEI GRA AGL FRA Z HIB REX — By the grace of God King of England France and Ireland

Obverse   As previous, but mintmark 'WS' monogram.

Reverse   As previous, but no mintmark.

H8HC-050	VG £175	F £400	VF £800

Posthumous Coinage (1547 – 1551)

Tower Mint

On each issue a mintmark is found on the obverse and/or reverse.

Obverse Legend   RUTILANS ROSA SINE SPINA — A dazzling rose without a thorn

Reverse Legend   HENRIC 8 D GR AGL FRA HIB REX — Henry VIII by the grace of God King of England France and Ireland

Obverse   Crown over rose dividing 'H.R.'; mintmark arrow, none, 'K', grapple, or martlet.

Reverse   Crown over royal shield; mintmark arrow, none or martlet.

H8HC-055	VG £175	F £375	VF £750

Southwark Mint

As previous, but legends all in Roman lettering and mintmark 'E' or none.

H8HC-060	VG £175	F £375	VF £750

Edward VI   (1547 – 1553)

Three main types of halfcrown were produced during Edward VI's reign. Firstly there was Henry VIII's posthumous issue listed above. Then, gold halfcrowns were produced during the first, second and third periods (1547 – 53); the first being similar in style to that of Henry's except for bearing the king's own name and initials and the next two having the bust of the Boy King on the obverse and a crowned shield on the reverse. The third main issue of the reign is the fine silver issue and the halfcrown for this, struck in fine silver, is a superb coin depicting the Boy King on horseback with the date below on the obverse and the royal arms on the reverse. All of these issues were produced at the Tower mint.

Gold Issue

First Period (1547 – 1549)

Collecting Hints

This coin is extremely rare and collectors will have great difficulty in obtaining an example.

Obverse Legend   RUTILANS ROSA SINE SPINA — A dazzling rose without a thorn

Reverse Legend   EDWARD 6 D GR AGL FR Z HIB REX — Edward VI by the grace of God King of England France and Ireland

Obverse   Crowned rose dividing 'ER'.

Reverse   Crowned shield dividing 'ER'; mintmark arrow.

E6HC-005	ex. rare

Second Period (1549 – 1550)

Collecting Hints

All issues are very rare in any grade; when available they are usually in Fine to VF condition.

Obverse Legend   EDWARD VI DG AG FR Z HI REX — Edward VI by the grace of God King of England France and Ireland

Reverse Legend   SCUTUM FIDEI PROTEGET EUM — The shield of faith shall protect him

Obverse   Uncrowned bust of king; mintmark 'Y' or arrow.

Reverse   Crown over shield; mintmark 'Y' or none.

E6HC-010	VG £325	F £800	VF £1,600

As previous, but the king is crowned; mintmark arrow, swan, grapple or 'Y', sometimes a different mintmark on the obverse and reverse.

E6HC-015	VG £300	F £650	VF £1,300

As E6HC-010, but mintmark arrow or grapple and the obverse and reverse legends are transposed:

Obverse Legend   SCUTUM FIDEI PROTEGET EUM — The shield of faith shall protect him

Reverse Legend   EDWARD VI DG AG FR Z HI REX — Edward VI by the grace of God King of England France and Ireland

| E6HC-020 | VG £300 | F £675 | VF £1,400 |

Third Period (1550 – 1553)

Collecting Hints

This issue is very rare in any grade and when available is usually in Fine to VF condition.

Obverse Legend   EDWARD VI DG AG FR Z HI REX — Edward VI by the grace of God King of England France and Ireland

Reverse Legend   SCUTUM FIDEI PROTEGET EUM — The shield of faith shall protect him

Obverse   Crowned king holding orb and sceptre; mintmark 'Y' or tun.

Reverse   Crown over shield, dividing 'ER'.

| E6HC-025 | VG £400 | F £900 | VF £2,200 |

Fine Silver Issue (1551 – 1553)

Collecting Hints

This issue while scarce is obtainable usually undamaged in Fine condition; VF and even EF examples exist but are rare.

Obverse Legend   EDWARD VI DG AGL FRA Z HIB REX — Edward VI by the grace of God King of England France and Ireland

Reverse Legend   POSUI DEUM ADIVITORE MEUM — I have made God my helper

Obverse   Boy King on walking horse, a plume on the horse's head, the date 1551 below the horse; mintmark 'Y'.

| E6HC-030 | VG £200 | F £375 | VF £900 |

As previous, but the horse is galloping and there is no plume on its head; mintmark tun, dated 1551 – 52.

| E6HC-035 | VG £200 | F £400 | VF £950 |

As previous, but large walking horse; mintmark tun, dated 1553 only.

| E6HC-040 | VG £300 | F £600 | VF £2,000 |

No halfcrowns were struck during the reign of Mary or Philip and Mary.

Elizabeth I   (1558 – 1603)

Gold halfcrowns were produced during most of Elizabeth's reign; they were all hammered except for one very rare milled issue. Silver halfcrowns were only produced during the last two years of the reign, albeit in large quantities. The gold halfcrowns on the other hand were struck in fairly small numbers not only because many silver ones had been produced under Edward VI but also because the public disliked a small coin with such a high value. All halfcrowns were struck at the Tower Mint.

Hammered Gold Issue (1559 – 1602)

First – Third Issues (1559 – 1578)

Collecting Hints

Gold halfcrowns are rare. They are usually found in Fine condition, sometimes creased or holed; VF and even EF examples exist but are rare. However, the value of this issue does not reflect its rarity due to the fact that most collectors prefer to own either a silver halfcrown or a gold coin of larger value; a gold halfcrown may be rather difficult to obtain.

Obverse Legend   ELIZABETH DG ANG FRA ET HI REGINA (minor varieties exist) — Elizabeth by the grace of God Queen of England France and Ireland

Reverse Legend   SCUTUM FIDEI PROTEGET EAM — The shield of faith shall protect her

Obverse   Crowned bust of queen facing left, wire-line inner circles; mintmark lis.

Reverse   Crowned royal arms in shield which divides 'E.R.' (ELIZABETH REGINA).

ELHC-005   ex. rare only three known

As previous, but beaded inner circles; mintmark cross crosslet, rose, portcullis, lion, coronet, castle.

ELHC-010   VG £200   F £400   VF £825

No halfcrowns were struck for the fourth issue.

Fifth Issue (1583 – 1600)

As previous, but older bust of queen; mintmark tun, woolpack, key, anchor (which is unique) and 0.

ELHC-015   VG £200   F £400   VF £825

Sixth Issue (1601 – 1602)

As previous, but mintmark 1 or 2. This issue was struck alongside the silver halfcrown.

ELHC-020   ex. rare

Milled Gold Issue (1561 – 1570)

This extremely rare issue can easily be identified by the completely different style of the coin and the mintmark star and lis.

Collecting Hints

While all milled gold issues of Elizabeth I are rare, the milled halfcrown is by far the rarest. It will be extremely difficult for collectors to obtain this coin in any grade.

Obverse Legend   ELIZABETH D.G. ANG FRA (ET or Z) HIB REGINA — Elizabeth by the grace of God Queen of England France and Ireland

Reverse Legend   SCUTUM FIDEI PROTEGET EAM — The shield of faith shall protect her

Obverse   Crowned bust of queen facing left; mintmark star or lis.

Reverse   Crowned royal arms in shield which divides 'E.R.'.

ELHC-025   VG £700   F £1,600   VF £3,250

Hammered Silver Issue (1601 – 1602)

Even though the silver halfcrown was struck for only two years during the sixth coinage, it is more common than the gold issues due firstly to the fact that large quantities of silver were coming in to Europe mainly from the Americas and secondly to the popularity of the coin's size and quality. The obverse shows a superb bust of the queen holding a sceptre and the reverse the royal shield over a cross. The mintmark '1' or '2' denotes the year (1601 or 1602) and can be found at the beginning of the obverse and reverse legend.

Collecting Hints

Silver halfcrowns are available in most grades, the most common being about Fine. However, rare and desirable VF and EF examples exist. Similarly, worn specimens can be found, often with a very flat portrait and a much clearer shield on the reverse which is due to the quality of strike. These issues while rare are usually obtainable and are sought after by collectors. Coins of mintmark '2' (1602) are extremely rare, less than a dozen are known.

Obverse Legend   ELIZABETH D.G ANG FRA ET HIBER REGINA — Elizabeth by the grace of God Queen of England France and Ireland

Reverse Legend   POSUI DEUM ADIUTOREM MEUM — I have made God my helper

Obverse   Bust of queen holding sceptre; mintmark 1 or 2.

Reverse   Royal shield over cross.

ELHC-030   VG £275   F £550   VF £1,300

James I   (1603 – 1625)

Both gold and silver halfcrowns were produced during James I's reign; all have the king's bust on the obverse.

Gold Issue

Collecting Hints

The first coinage is very rare in any grade. The second coinage issues, while rare are usually available in Fine condition; VF examples also exist but are very rare. Many issues are pierced and there is speculation that this was officially done to devalue the coins in later reigns. However, the scarcity of these coins is not reflected in their value as collectors prefer the silver halfcrowns or a larger but more common gold denomination.

First Coinage (1603 – 1604)

Obverse Legend IACOBUS DG. AN SCO ET HI REX — James by the grace of God King of England Scotland and Ireland

Reverse Legend TUEATUR UNITA DEUS — May God guard these United [Kingdoms]

Obverse Crowned bust of king; mintmark thistle or lis.

Reverse Crown over royal shield, 'I R' divided by crown.

J1HC-005	VG £150	F £350	VF £750

Second Coinage (1604 – 1619)

The main differences between the first and second coinage are the obverse legend readings and the mintmarks. The busts of the king on the second and third type are also different.

Obverse Legend I DG ROSA SINE SPINA — James by the grace of God a rose without a thorn

Reverse Legend TUEATUR UNITA DEUS — May God guard these United [Kingdoms]

Obverse Crowned bust of king of similar style to the first coinage (first bust); mintmark lis, rose, escallop, grapes, coronet, key.

Reverse Crown over royal shield, 'I R' at sides of crown.

J1HC-010	VG £140	F £250	VF £400

As previous, but the king has a square beard that projects (third bust); mintmark key, bell, mullet, tower or trefoil.

J1HC-015	VG £140	F £250	VF £400

As previous, but the king has longer hair brushed back (fifth bust); mintmark cinquefoil, tun, book, crescent or plain cross.

J1HC-020	VG £140	F £250	VF £400

No gold halfcrowns were produced during the third coinage.

Silver Issue

Silver halfcrowns were produced during all three of James I's coinages. All issues show the king on horseback on the obverse and the royal arms on the reverse, and a mintmark can be found at the beginning of the obverse and reverse legend. These mintmarks are important for identification, particularly since Scotland struck coins that were very similar to the halfcrowns. All Scottish issues are mintmark thistle, while none of the second coinage English halfcrowns and only some of the first and third coinages used that mintmark. To distinguish these coins collectors need to look at the beginning of the reverse legend, which is QUAE DEUS for the Scottish coins and the second and third coinages, and EXURGAT for the first coinage, and then at the Irish harp on the reverse shield which in the English issue has a bird's head on the edge and on the Scottish one the end of the harp is turned in. The only English issue with a bird's head is the third coinage. It is important to check that the mintmarks correspond to the issue.

> ## Collecting Hints
>
> James I silver halfcrowns, while scarce, are obtainable in all grades. Many of these issues seem to have seen little circulation and are usually available undamaged in Fine condition. VF and even EF examples exist but are rare and desirable.

First Coinage (1603 – 1604)

Obverse Legend IACOBUS D.G. ANG SCO FRAN ET HIB REX — James by the grace of God King of England Scotland France and Ireland

Reverse Legend EXURGAT DEUS DISSIPENTUR INIMICI — Let God arise and His enemies be scattered

Obverse King on horseback; mintmark thistle or lis.

Reverse Royal shield.

J1HC-025	VG £225	F £450	VF £1,100

Second Coinage (1604 – 1619)

Obverse Legend IACOBUS DG MAG BRIT FRAN ET HIB REX — James by the grace of God King of Great Britain France and Ireland

Reverse Legend QUAE DEUS CONIUNXIT NEMO SEPARET — What God has joined together let no man put asunder

Obverse As previous, but mintmark lis, rose or escallop.

Reverse As previous.

J1HC-030	VG £200	F £400	VF £1,000

Third Coinage (1619 – 1625)

Legends As previous.

Obverse As previous, but mintmark rose, thistle, lis or trefoil.

Reverse Shield with bird-headed Irish harp.

| J1HC-035 | VG £120 | F £260 | VF £600 |

As previous, but there is no groundline on the obverse; mintmark rose.

| J1HC-040 | VG £150 | F £330 | VF £700 |

As J1HC-035, but plume over shield on reverse; mintmark thistle, lis or trefoil.

| J1HC-045 | VG £120 | F £300 | VF £600 |

Charles I (1625 – 1649)

During Charles I's reign large quantities of silver halfcrowns were produced, mainly at the Tower mint in London, although most provincial mints and several siege towns also struck them. Like many of Charles's other issues, the halfcrowns are very complex with many varieties and styles existing. In general the most common issues are those struck under the king at the Tower mint and if collectors are unsure of a coin they should refer to the Tower issues first and then the provincial ones. All except the siege pieces depict the king on horseback on the obverse and either the royal arms in a shield (Tower issues), or the royal arms or a legend in the centre (provincial issues) on the reverse. As stated earlier, many varieties exist. Unlike many of the provincial issues, all Tower halfcrowns are undated; also all except the siege issues have mintmarks, usually on the obverse and reverse legend. In identifying coins, collectors should always check that a mintmark ties in with a particular issue. They should also look carefully at the shapes and style of the royal arms on the reverse and at the king on horseback on the obverse as again many varieties exist, particularly regarding how the horse is walking, the position of the king's sword and the king's scarf. Unlike the smaller denominations, virtually all halfcrowns have no mark of value, however, all the smaller denominations did not have the king on horseback. The next higher denomination which used the king on horseback

was the crown which is much bigger, with a diameter of about 43 mm compared to the approximately 34 mm of the halfcrown.

Many forgeries of Charles I halfcrowns exist, most of them being good contemporary forgeries of the Tower mint issue, usually with a silvered layer over a copper or brass core. Although the style of these forgeries is usually good, the silver flakes off in most cases revealing the base metal underneath. The other main forgeries of halfcrowns that exist are nineteenth century 'museum' copies of the provincial mints. These were usually not produced as forgeries, however many have found their way into the market and can easily deceive an inexperienced collector. They are usually bright and untoned and often have very smooth edges whilst original coins tend to have rather ragged edges. Also some forgeries tend to be underweight and small in size. It is important, therefore, that collectors buy coins from these issues from a reputable dealer who has considerable knowledge.

The following line-drawings, from B.R. Osborne's archive on Charles I, depict the numerous styles of horseman with the corresponding classes to which they relate. It is important to remember that, with the number of dies being used, varieties exist.

C1HC-005   C1HC-010, -015   C1HC-020 to -030

C1HC-040 to -060   C1HC-065   C1HC-070

C1HC-075   C1HC-080   C1HC-085, -095

C1HC-090   C1HC-100

Tower Mint
Tower Mint under King (1625 – 1642)

Collecting Hints

Most Tower issues are fairly common, particularly the later ones. All issues are hammered, with the later ones often being poorly struck on flans of irregular size so perhaps not all of the legend will be clear. Collectors should try to obtain an example with a clear king on horseback, a clear mintmark and as much of the legend as possible. Many of these issues have been found in large hoards, often buried during the Civil War; they are usually available in VG to VF condition and, although EF examples exist, coins often left the mint in only VF condition. Moreover, many are found clipped, some so badly that they have no legend at all left. Also some coins are found with what look like deliberate nasty scratches and while the reason for this remains open to speculation, it could well have been the work of a contemporary ardent anti-royalist.

Obverse Legend CAROLUS·D.G. MAG BRI FRA ET HI REX — Charles by the grace of God King of Great Britain France and Ireland

Reverse Legend CHRISTO AUSPICE REGNO — I reign under the auspices of Christ

Obverse King riding decorated horse on a groundline, a rose on the horse's coat; mintmark lis.

Reverse Square-topped garnished shield over a cross.

C1HC-005	VG £75	F £150	VF £350

As previous, but a floriate spray instead of a rose on the horse's coat.

C1HC-010	ex. rare

As previous, but no groundline.

C1HC-015	VG £75	F £150	VF £350

Obverse Legend As previous; minor varieties exist.

Reverse Legend As previous.

Obverse As previous, but a rather clumsier-looking horse; mintmark cross calvary, blackamoor's head, castle.

Reverse Royal arms not over a cross.

C1HC-020	VG £60	F £120	VF £250

As C1HC-015, but the horse is on a groundline; mintmark lis.

C1HC-025	VG £250	F £500

As previous, but with a plume over the shield on the reverse; mintmark lis, cross calvary, blackamoor's head, castle or anchor.

C1HC-030	VG £300	F £500	VF £1,200

As previous, but a smaller horse with a rose on its coat on the obverse; mintmark heart or plume.

C1HC-035	ex. rare

Obverse Legend As previous; many minor varieties exist.

Reverse Legend As previous.

Obverse King on horseback with no groundline or rose on the horse's coat; mintmark lis over rose or lis or plume.

Reverse Royal arms in an oval garnished shield with 'CR' (CAROLUS REX) above it. Varieties of harp in shield exist.

C1HC-040	VG £50	F £90	VF £180

As previous, but a rose between 'CR' on the reverse.

C1HC-045	ex. rare

As previous, but a large plume dividing 'CR' on the reverse.

C1HC-050	VG £80	F £160	VF £320

As C1HC-040, but differently garnished oval shield which divides 'CR'; mintmark harp or portcullis.

| C1HC-055 | VG £45 | F £85 | VF £160 |

As previous, but the king's scarf flies from the shoulder; mintmark tun, anchor, triangle and star.

| C1HC-075 | VG £40 | F £75 | VF £150 |

As previous, but a plume over the shield on the reverse; mintmark harp.

| C1HC-060 | VG £200 | F £350 | VF £700 |

As previous, but rough ground under the horse; mintmark triangle and star.

| C1HC-080 | VG £40 | F £75 | VF £150 |

Obverse Legend   As previous, many varieties exist.

Reverse Legend   As previous.

Obverse   New-style king on horseback, the horse is undecorated, the king's sword is upright and his scarf flies out from the waist; mintmark anchor, bell, crown or tun.

Reverse   Round garnished shield.

| C1HC-065 | VG £40 | F £75 | VF £150 |

Obverse   This issue has a foreshortened horse with its mane in front of its chest and its tail between its rear legs; the king's scarf is flying from his shoulder; mintmark star and triangle in a circle.

Reverse   As previous.

| C1HC-085 | VG £40 | F £80 | VF £160 |

Tower Mint under Parliament (1642 – 1648)

With the Civil War dividing the country, this issue was struck under the orders of Parliament and it is interesting to note that the king still appeared on the coins. These issues are very much a continuation of the Tower mint under the king issues, but can easily be identified by their unique mintmarks.

As previous, but plume over the shield on the reverse; mintmark portcullis, bell, crown or tun.

| C1HC-070 | VG £70 | F £140 | VF £280 |

Collecting Hints

Two of these issues are fairly common while one is rare. They are all slightly scarcer than the Tower mint under the king issues and often found poor in style and production. Collectors should be able to obtain an example in VG or Fine condition, although VF is quite rare, due to the poor strikings. Remember to try to obtain an example with a clear mintmark. These issues do not tend to be so badly clipped as some of the later royal ones.

Obverse Legend   CAROLUS D.G. MAG BRI FRA ET HIB REX —
Charles by the grace of God King of Great Britain France and Ireland

Reverse Legend   CHRISTO AUSPICE REGNO — I reign under the
auspices of Christ

Obverse   King on horseback with sword pointing upwards and scarf
flying from his shoulder; mintmark '(P)', '(R)', eye, sun.

Reverse   Royal arms in a round shield.

C1HC-090	VG £40	F £90	VF £175

As previous, but the king is on a foreshortened horse with its mane in
front of its chest and its tail between its rear legs; mintmark '(P)'.

C1HC-095	VG £100	F £200	VF £400

The king is on a tall horse with a long bushy tail; mintmark sun, sceptre.

C1HC-100	VG £60	F £110	VF £220

Briot's Coinage
Milled Issues (1631 – 1639)

These milled or machine-made issues are superb in design and
quality and probably the finest halfcrowns produced under
Charles I. The obverse has the king on horseback while the
reverse has an oval shield below a crown; also a mintmark can
be found on the obverse of the first issue and on both sides of
the second issue. These mintmarks, which both incorporate the
letter B for Briot, are specific to these issues.

Collecting Hints

These issues are rare but when obtainable usually available
in Fine or VF condition. They are rarely found clipped and
are usually on full round flans.

First Milled Issue (1631 – 1639)

Obverse Legend   CAROLUS D.G. MAGN BRITAN FRAN ET HIB
REX — Charles by the grace of God King of Great Britain France and
Ireland

Reverse Legend   CHRISTO AUSPICE REGNO — I reign under the
auspices of Christ

Obverse   King on horseback holding sword; mintmark flower and 'B'.

Reverse   Crown over shield which divides 'CR'.

C1HC-105	VG £140	F £350	VF £750

Second Milled Issue (1638 – 1639)

Legends   As previous.

Obverse   As previous, except with mintmark anchor and 'B'.

Reverse   As previous, except with mintmark anchor and 'B' also on
reverse.

C1HC-110	VG £120	F £320	VF £650

Hammered Issue (1638 – 1639)

While there is no doubt that the dies for this very rare issue were
made by Briot, there is considerable evidence that the coins were
not struck by him. The obverse has a Briot-style horse and the
reverse a square-topped oval shield. In some cases, a reverse die
from a common Tower issue was used and in all cases mintmark
triangle has been used with a Briot obverse die.

Collecting Hints

All issues are extremely rare in any grade and rarely found
in better than Fine condition. Collectors should be careful
not to confuse this issue with the much more common
Tower mint hammered issues, previously listed.

Obverse Legend   CAROLUS DG MAG BRIT FR ET HIB REX —
Charles by the grace of God King of Great Britain France and Ireland

Reverse Legend   CHRISTO AUSPICE REGNO — I reign under the
auspices of Christ

Obverse   King on horseback holding sword; mintmark anchor.

Reverse   Square-topped shield; mintmark anchor.

C1HC-115	VG £300	F £750	VF £1,500

Obverse   As previous, but mintmark triangle over anchor.

Reverse   Round shield; mintmark triangle. This die is from a Tower mint issue.

C1HC-120   rare

Provincial Mints

York Mint (1643 – 1644)

These scarce but obtainable issues are easily recognisable by the mintmark lion which is specific to this issue and found at the beginning of the obverse and reverse legend. Also in many of the issues EBOR (short for EBORACUM, Latin for York) is found under the horse. Many issues appear to be very slightly oval in shape and are sometimes very slightly bent. This appears to be the way they were made and does not affect their value.

Collecting Hints

These coins are usually found unclipped and undamaged in various grades. Fine condition is probably the most common but VF and even EF examples exist.

Obverse Legend   CAROLUS DG MAG BRI FR ET HI REX — Charles by the grace of God King of Great Britain France and Ireland

Reverse Legend   CHRISTO AUSPICE REGNO — I reign under the auspices of Christ

Obverse   King on horseback holding sword, groundline below horse; mintmark lion.

Reverse   Square-topped shield dividing 'CR'; mintmark lion.

C1HC-125   VG £130   F £250   VF £650

As previous, but oval shield and no 'CR' on reverse.

C1HC-130   VG £100   F £220   VF £550

Obverse   As previous, but no groundline below the horse.

Reverse   A somewhat flattened shield.

C1HC-135   VG £90   F £220   VF £550

As previous, but EBOR below the horse on obverse. These coins were struck in fairly base metal. It is probable that they were contemporary forgeries which undoubtedly saw considerable circulation.

C1HC-140   VG £120   F £190   VF £400

Obverse Legend   CAROLUS DG MAG BRIT FRAN ET HIB REX — Charles by the grace of God King of Great Britain France and Ireland

Reverse Legend   CHRISTO AUSPICE REGNO — I reign under the auspices of Christ

Obverse   King on tall horse, EBOR below horse; mintmark lion.

Reverse   Square-topped shield with crown above, flowers in legend, 'CR' divided by shield.

C1HC-145   VG £100   F £170   VF £475

As previous, but oval shield on reverse.

C1HC-150   VG £100   F £170   VF £380

As previous, but the horse's tail is between its rear legs and on the reverse instead of 'CR' there are two lion's paws either side holding the shield.

| C1HC-155 | VG £100 | F £170 | VF £380 |

As previous, but a more spirited horse. Obverse legend reads FRAN ET HIB.

| C1HC-165 | VG £320 | F £525 | VF £1,600 |

Aberystwyth Mint (1638 – 1642)

This issue can easily be identified by the mintmark open book which can be found at the beginning of the obverse and reverse legends. The obverse die from this mint was used with reverse dies from other provincial mints to produce coins for other provincial mints. Therefore, check that the mintmark open book can be found on both obverse and reverse. If it is only found on the obverse, check the Shrewsbury mint issues.

As C1HC-160, but ground below horse.

| C1HC-170 | VG £350 | F £600 | VF £1,700 |

Aberystwyth Furnace Mint (1648 – 1649)

This issue, while fairly similar to the Aberystwyth ones, is differentiated by the mintmark crown found on the obverse and reverse. As it also has a plume behind the king, it can easily be distinguished from Tower mint issues which also used the mintmark crown.

Collecting Hints

This issue is very rare in any grade and usually available in Fine condition although VF examples do exist. Most specimens are usually unclipped and undamaged. Should collectors just want an example from the Aberystwyth mint, they should consider a groat or threepence as they are fairly common and easily obtainable in good condition.

Collecting Hints

This issue is very rare in any grade. Rarely found in better than Fine condition, it is much cruder in style than the Aberystwyth issues.

Obverse Legend CAROLUS DG MAG BRIT FRA ET HI REX — Charles by the grace of God King of Great Britain France and Ireland

Reverse Legend CHRISTO AUSPICE REGNO — I reign under the auspices of Christ

Obverse King on horseback holding sword, small plume behind king; mintmark open book.

Reverse Oval shield with large plume above; mintmark open book.

Obverse Legend CAROLUS DG MAG BRIT FRAN ET HI REX — Charles by the grace of God King of Great Britain France and Ireland

Reverse Legend CHRISTO AUSPICE REGNO — I reign under the auspices of Christ

Obverse King holding sword on horseback, plume behind king; mintmark crown.

Reverse Plume over oval shield.

| C1HC-160 | VG £300 | F £500 | VF £1,250 |

| C1HC-175 | VG £600 | F £1,200 | VF £3,000 |

Hereford Mint

While documentary evidence exists that silver for coins was brought to Hereford, there is no other conclusive source establishing that this extremely rare issue was actually produced in Hereford. It used to be attributed to the Combe Martin mint. So, although there is no doubt that it was made in the area, the site of the actual mint cannot be confirmed. After all, with the Civil War raging, the dies for this issue could have been moved from town to town.

Collecting Hints

All coins from this issue are very rare and always found very worn, usually in less than Fine condition; VF examples probably do not exist.

Obverse Legend   CAROLUS DG MAG BRI FRA ET HI REX — Charles by the grace of God King of Great Britain France and Ireland

Reverse Legend   CHRISTO AUSPICE REGNO — I reign under the auspices of Christ

Obverse   King holding sword on horseback; mintmark small lis.

Reverse   Royal arms with lion and unicorn either side, crown above dividing 'CR', dated 1645.

C1HC-180	VG £800	F £2,000

As previous, but undated.

C1HC-185	VG £1,200	F £3,000

Shrewsbury Mint (1642)

During the Civil War it was intended to open mints at the king's temporary capitals of York and Shrewsbury. The Aberystwyth mint which had been run under royal licence by Thomas Bushell before the conflict erupted was moved to Shrewsbury where it could be better protected by local royalists and produce money for royal troops. It was only active in 1642 and, due to a shortage of gold, virtually all coins were struck in silver which was mainly supplied by the universities and wealthy royalists. Various dies were used for the issues including odd ones from the Aberystwyth mint, others smuggled out of London and also locally-made dies. By the end of 1642 the king had established himself at Oxford so Bushell moved there to open a new mint and Shrewsbury was closed. Because dies from other provincial mints, notably Aberystwyth and Oxford, were often interchanged, these issues are fairly difficult to identify. Nevertheless, all Shrewsbury coins have the king on horseback on the obverse, the Declaration on the reverse and are dated 1642. This makes identification somewhat easier as most Oxford issues are dated 1643.

Collecting Hints

All Shrewsbury issues are scarce and the halfcrowns are no exception; they are usually available undamaged in Fine to VF condition.

Obverse Legend   CAROLUS DG MAG BRIT FRAN ET HIB REX — Charles by the grace of God King of Great Britain France and Ireland

Outer Reverse Legend   EXURGAT DEUS DISSIPENTUR INIMICI — Let God arise and His enemies be scattered

Reverse Centre Legend   RELIG PROT LEG ANGL LIBERT PAR — The religion of the Protestants the laws of England the liberty of Parliament

Obverse   King on horseback, plume behind and groundline below horseman; mintmark open book. This is the obverse Aberystwyth die.

Reverse   Single plume above Declaration dividing '2' and '6', 1642. This is a Shrewsbury die.

C1HC-190	ex. rare

Obverse   As previous, but fat plume behind king on horseback (Aberystwyth die).

Reverse   Three plumes above Declaration (Shrewsbury die).

C1HC-195	VG £200	F £500	VF £1,600

The following are all Shrewsbury dies except C1HC-215, but in certain cases the obverse or reverse die was used later to produce coins at Oxford.

Obverse Legend   CAROLUS DG MAG BR FR ET HIB REX — Charles by the grace of God King of Great Britain France and Ireland

Reverse Legends   As previous; minor varieties exist.

Obverse   New-style Shrewsbury horseman with plume behind.

Reverse   Single plume over Declaration and 1642 below.

C1HC-200	VG £180	F £500	VF £1,500

Obverse   As previous.

Reverse   The digits '2' and '6', for halfcrown, divided by a plume, over the Declaration.

C1HC-205	VG £300	F £600	VF £1,600

As previous, but groundline below horse.

C1HC-210   VG £250   F £550   VF £1,600

Obverse   As previous.

Reverse   Plume above shield; mintmark open book (Aberystwyth die).

C1HC-215   ex. rare

Obverse Legend   CAROLUS DG MAG BRIT FRAN ET HIB REX — Charles by the grace of God King of Great Britain France and Ireland

Outer Reverse Legend   EXURGAT DEUS DISSIPENTUR INIMICI — Let God arise and His enemies be scattered

Inner Reverse Legend   RELIG PROT LEG ANG LIBER PAR — The religion of the Protestants the laws of England the liberty of Parliament

Obverse   King on horseback, no plume behind king (Shrewsbury die); mintmark plume. All other Oxford halfcrowns have a plume behind the king.

Reverse   Three small plumes of different style above the Declaration, 1642.

Obverse   As previous.

Reverse   As C1HC-210, but three plumes above the Declaration and no denomination.

C1HC-220   VG £120   F £220   VF £500

C1HC-230   VG £100   F £300   VF £700

As previous, but no plume behind the king.

C1HC-225   VG £140   F £280   VF £600

Undoubtedly, other varieties exist due to the muling of dies and those issues would be much scarcer than the ones listed.

Obverse   Oxford die with Shrewsbury horseman.

Reverse   Shrewsbury die with three Shrewsbury plumes above the declaration.

C1HC-232   VG £100   F £300   VF £600

Oxford Mint (1642 – 1646)

As stated above, the Shrewsbury mint closed and moved to Oxford at the end of 1642. Thomas Bushell and William Parkhurst were in charge of the Oxford mint which produced large quantities of gold and silver coins with metal supplied mostly by the universities and wealthy royalists. Several of the old dies from the Aberystwyth and Shrewsbury mints were used alongside new dies made locally, some by the young talented engraver Thomas Rawlins. Coins were struck at Oxford until the city finally surrendered to Cromwell's army in June 1646. The Oxford issues are fairly complex; all have the king on horseback on the obverse and the Declaration with the date below on the reverse and a number of issues also have 'OX' for Oxford below the date. Although many of the Oxford issues are similar to those of Shrewsbury, an identification problem should only arise with coins dated 1642; Oxford coins bear the mintmark plume at the beginning of the obverse legend. For coins dated 1643, however, collectors should also bear in mind that the Bristol mint used Oxford dies.

Obverse   Oxford horse with plume behind; mintmark plume.

Reverse   Three plumes over Declaration, dated 1642.

C1HC-235   VG £95   F £180   VF £360

Obverse   Shrewsbury-style horse walking on groundline, plume behind king; mintmark plume.

Reverse   As C1HC-230.

C1HC-240   VG £95   F £160   VF £320

As previous, but no groundline.

C1HC-245   VG £95   F £180   VF £360

Oxford Style Horseman

Legends   As previous.

Obverse   New-style horse walking on groundline, plume behind king; mintmark plume.

Reverse   Three plumes above the Declaration, 1643.

C1HC-250   VG £95   F £180   VF £360

As previous, but without groundline, dated 1643.

C1HC-255   VG £95   F £180   VF £360

Briot Style Horseman

Legends   As previous, (minor varieties).

Obverse   New Briot-style horseman with grass under horse and plume behind king; mintmark plume.

Reverse   Three plumes above Declaration, dated 1643, 'OX' below date.

C1HC-260   VG £95   F £180   VF £400

Obverse   As previous; but lumpy ground below horseman.

Reverse   Three plumes, the central one being the largest; 1643 or 1644, 'OX' below date.

C1HC-265   VG £110   F £250   VF £550

Obverse   As previous, but grass below horseman.

Reverse   As C1HC-260 dated 1643, sometimes with 'OX'.

C1HC-270   VG £95   F £200   VF £400

Obverse   As previous.

Reverse   As C1HC-265, dated 1643 or 1644, 'OX' below date.

C1HC-275   VG £95   F £200   VF £400

Obverse   As previous, but plain ground under horse.

Reverse   As previous, dated 1644, 'OX' below date.

C1HC-280   VG £95   F £200   VF £400

Obverse   As previous.

Reverse   As C1HC-270, 1644 or 1645, 'OX' below date.

C1HC-285   VG £95   F £200   VF £400

Obverse   As previous.

Reverse   As C1HC-280, but large date.

C1HC-290   VG £110   F £250   VF £550

Obverse   As previous.

Reverse   As previous, but two small plumes either side of small date.

C1HC-295   VG £120   F £250   VF £550

Larger Briot Style Horseman

The horseman in this issue is large and clumsy and much poorer in style, but the legends and mintmarks remain the same.

Obverse   Larger Briot-style horseman on plain ground, plume behind king; mintmark plume.

Reverse   Three plumes over Declaration, 1644 or 1645 and 'OX' below.

| C1HC-300 | VG £95 | F £200 | VF £450 |

As previous, but lumpy ground under horse on obverse.

| C1HC-305 | VG £95 | F £200 | VF £450 |

Obverse   As previous.

Reverse   Large central plume between two small ones, dated 1644, 'OX' below.

| C1HC-310 | VG £95 | F £200 | VF £450 |

Obverse   As previous, but pebbly ground under horse.

Reverse   As C1HC-305, dated 1645 or 1646, 'OX' below.

| C1HC-315 | VG £95 | F £200 | VF £450 |

Obverse   As previous.

Reverse   Pellets or annulets by plumes and by date, 1645 – 46, 'OX' below.

| C1HC-320 | VG £95 | F £180 | VF £400 |

Obverse   As previous, but grass below horse.

Reverse   As C1HC-315, but pellets at date.

| C1HC-325 | VG £95 | F £250 | VF £550 |

Obverse   As previous.

Reverse   Rosettes by plumes and by date 1645, 'OX' below.

| C1HC-330 | VG £110 | F £225 | VF £550 |

Bristol Mint (1643 – 1645)

Most issues from the Bristol mint are fairly easy to identify as they have 'BR' either on the obverse below the horseman or on the reverse below the date or in the legend. Although some of the issues used the Oxford obverse die, they can easily be distinguished as they bear the mintmark 'BR' on the reverse. If an issue does not have a clear mintmark, the three plumes on the reverse are distinctive, especially on the 1643 issues, being very different in style to the plumes of the other mints. To identify a coin, collectors should also check it against the Shrewsbury and Oxford issues, paying particular attention to the date, the mintmark on the obverse and reverse, the number and size of the plumes on the reverse and the style of the horseman.

Collecting Hints

Most issues from the Bristol mint, while scarce, are obtainable. They are usually found in about Fine condition and VF examples are rare. Many issues tend to be slightly clipped, possibly due to an irregular flan, or have a small piercing in the centre, which appears to have been done officially, possibly to devalue the coin at the end of the seventeenth century. Also, hammered coins were holed through the centre at the time of the recoinage of 1697 – 98 to signify that they might circulate at face value for a limited time.

Obverse Legend   CAROLUS DG MAG BRIT FR ET HIB REX — Charles by the grace of God King of Great Britain France and Ireland

Outer Reverse Legend   EXURGAT DEUS DISSIPENTUR INIMICI — Let God arise and His enemies be scattered

Inner Reverse Legend   RELIG PROT LE AN LI PA — The religion of the Protestants the laws of England the liberty of Parliament

Obverse   King on horseback with plume behind; mintmark plume or pellet. This is an obverse Oxford die, several minor varieties exist.

Reverse   Three Bristol plumes above Declaration, 1643.

| C1HC-335 | VG £100 | F £190 | VF £350 |

As previous, but mintmark 'BR' on reverse and plume on obverse.

| C1HC-340 | VG £95 | F £180 | VF £340 |

Obverse As previous, but Shrewsbury plume behind king; mintmark plume.

Reverse 'BR' mintmark, 1643 or 1644.

| C1HC-345 | VG £95 | F £175 | VF £320 |

As previous, but 'BR' below date 1644 and below horseman; no mintmark on reverse.

| C1HC-350 | VG £95 | F £180 | VF £350 |

As previous, but 'BR' below horse and date 1644 or 1645, and horseman of slightly different style.

| C1HC-355 | VG £95 | F £180 | VF £350 |

As previous, but 'BR' mintmark on reverse 1644 or 1645.

| C1HC-360 | VG £100 | F £200 | VF £350 |

Late Declaration Issues (1645 – 1646)

These very rare issues can easily be recognised by the various markings found on the coins, however, many used altered dies from other provincial mints, particularly Bristol. They were previously ascribed to Lundy mint.

Collecting Hints

All issues are extremely rare and difficult to obtain in any grade.

Obverse Legend CAROLUS DG MAG BR FR ET HIB REX — Charles by the grace of God King of Great Britain France and Ireland

Outer Reverse Legend EXURGAT DEUS DISSSIPENTUR INIMICI — Let God arise and His enemies be scattered

Inner Reverse Legend REL PROT LE AN LI PA — The religion of the Protestants the laws of England the liberty of Parliament

Obverse King on horseback, plume behind king, letter 'A' below horse; mintmark plume.

Reverse Letter 'A' below date (sometimes over 'BR', Bristol die), 1645; mintmark 'A'.

| C1HC-365 | VG £500 | F £1,100 |

As previous, but no 'A' below date and no 'BR'. This is not a Bristol die.

| C1HC-370 | VG £400 | F £750 | VF £1,750 |

Obverse As previous.

Reverse Scroll above Declaration, 'B' below date 1646.

C1HC-375   ex. rare

C1HC-395   ex. rare two specimens known

Obverse   Plumelet below horse; mintmark plume.

Reverse   Scroll above Declaration; mintmark plume, 1646.

C1HC-380   VG £250   F £600   VF £1,400

As previous, but king is holding a sword.

C1HC-400   ex. rare

As previous, but plumelet below date.

C1HC-385   VG £270   F £650   VF £1,500

As previous, but 'CR' above the shield on the reverse.

C1HC-405   VG £450   F £1,000   VF £2,000

Truro Mint (1642 – 1643)

In November 1642 Sir Richard Vyvyan was commissioned to strike gold and silver coins at Truro and deliver them to Sir Ralph Hopton, the royalist Commander in Cornwall. Very few issues were dated but all used the mintmark rose and are fairly easy to distinguish. Although the Exeter mint also used the mintmark rose, Exeter coins are all dated after 1644; similarly, the Tower mint used the same mintmark, but the style of the coins is very different.

Obverse   The horse is trotting.

Reverse   'CR' at side of shield.

Collecting Hints

Most Truro halfcrowns are rare and in fact much rarer than crowns; they are usually found undamaged in about Fine condition.

Obverse Legend   CAROLUS D.G. MAG BRIT FRAN ET HIB REX — Charles by the grace of God King of Great Britain France and Ireland

Reverse Legend   CHRISTO AUSPICE REGNO — I reign under the auspices of Christ

Obverse   King on horseback galloping, holding a baton; mintmark rose.

Reverse   Oblong shield dividing 'CR', undated; mintmark rose.

C1HC-410   VG £250   F £600   VF £1,750

Obverse   The horse is walking, the king's head is in profile.

Reverse   As previous.

| C1HC-415 | VG £200 | F £650 | VF £1,750 |

As previous, but 'CR' above shield.

| C1HC-420 | VG £220 | F £650 | VF £1,750 |

Truro or Exeter Mint

The following issues, which are all undated and have a mintmark rose, are very much a continuation of the Truro mint's production but historical records indicate that they might also have been struck in nearby Exeter. In the constantly changing conditions of the war, moneyers might well have travelled with their dies from one town to another, supplying coins for the troops.

Obverse Legend As previous, (minor varieties exist).

Reverse Legend As previous.

Obverse King on horseback, sash tied in a bow behind him; mintmark rose.

Reverse Oblong shield dividing 'CR'.

| C1HC-425 | VG £125 | F £225 | VF £500 |

Obverse As previous.

Reverse Round shield with six or eight scrolls around it and no CR.

| C1HC-430 | VG £110 | F £200 | VF £400 |

Obverse King's sash flies out behind him.

Reverse Round shield.

| C1HC-435 | VG £120 | F £240 | VF £500 |

As previous, but reverse has an oblong shield.

| C1HC-440 | ex. rare |

Obverse Briot-style horseman on a groundline.

Reverse Round shield, sometimes with an inverted garnature.

| C1HC-445 | VG £120 | F £240 | VF £500 |

As previous, but with oblong shield.

| C1HC-450 | unique |

Exeter Mint (1643 – 1646)

The city of Exeter was captured by the royalist Prince Maurice in September 1643. The commission of Sir Richard Vyvyan, who had produced the previous Truro mint coinage, was renewed, he was placed in charge of the mint and commanded to hand the coinage produced over to Sir John Berkeley. After a dispute with Berkeley, Vyvyan was sent to prison for a time. Exeter finally surrendered to Cromwell in April 1646. Most Exeter issues use the mintmark rose, with only a few using mintmark castle or 'EX', and all are dated on the reverse either in the legend or below the Declaration. Thus, although the mintmark rose makes them very similar to the Truro issues, they can be distinguished since all Truro halfcrowns were undated except for a rare 1642 issue, and all Exeter ones were struck during 1644 or 1645. To identify an undated coin with mintmark castle or rose, collectors should refer to the Truro section as well as the Tower issues which also used these mintmarks but are very different in style.

Collecting Hints

Most Exeter issues are fairly scarce and those with the Declaration on the reverse are very rare. Most issues are usually obtainable undamaged in about Fine condition; better grade examples exist but are very rare. Also, the first three issues are extremely rare.

This issue used to be classed under Truro mint.

Obverse Legend CAROLUS DG MAG BR FR ET HI REX — Charles by the grace of God King of Great Britain France and Ireland

Reverse Legend CHRISTO AUSPICE REGNO — I reign under the auspices of Christ

Obverse King galloping over arms; mintmark rose.

Reverse Oval shield, dated 1642 below shield in cartouche.

C1HC-452	ex. rare

C1HC-470	VG £140	F £250	VF £500

Obverse Legend   CAROLUS DG MAG BR FR ET HI REX — Charles by the grace of God King of Great Britain France and Ireland

Reverse Legend   CHRISTO AUSPICE REGNO — I reign under the auspices of Christ

Obverse   King galloping over arms; mintmark rose. This appears to be the Truro obverse die.

Reverse   Oval shield, 1644 in legend.

Obverse   New-style horse with twisted tail; mintmark rose.

Reverse   Oval shield, dated 1644 or 1645 in legend.

C1HC-455	ex. rare

C1HC-475	VG £120	F £250	VF £500

Obverse   As previous.

Reverse   Mintmark castle, 1645 in legend.

As previous, but 1645; mintmark castle on reverse.

C1HC-460	probably unique

C1HC-480	VG £150	F £350	VF £750

Obverse   Short ill-proportioned horse; mintmark rose.

Reverse   Oval shield, dated 1644, sometimes intercepted by a rose.

As previous, but mintmark 'EX', 1645 in legend.

C1HC-465	VG £225	F £500	VF £1,750

C1HC-485	VG £150	F £350	VF £750

Declaration Type

Should the mintmarks of C1HC-490 and C1HC-495 not tie in, collectors should refer to other provincial mints, remembering that the obverse must have the mintmark rose.

Obverse Legend   As previous.

Outer Reverse Legend   EXURGAT DEUS DISSIPENTUR INIMICI — Let God arise and His enemies be scattered

Obverse   Briot-style horse on groundline; mintmark rose.

Reverse   Oval shield, 1644 in legend.

Inner Reverse Legend   REL PRO LE ANG LIB PAR (varieties) — The religion of the Protestants the laws of England the liberty of Parliament

Obverse   King on horseback; mintmark rose. .

Reverse   Mintmark 'EX' sometimes in legend, 1644 or 1645 below Declaration.

| C1HC-490 | VG £600 | F £1,200 |

As previous, but 'EX' below date 1644.

| C1HC-495 | VG £500 | F £1,100 |

Worcester Mint (1643 – 1644)

Very little is known about the Worcester mint. Numismatists even debate whether these rare and crude issues were struck at Worcester at all or, possibly, Weymouth as there is no hard evidence linking a mint with the Worcester area. All these issues are crude in style, design and production. While similar to other issues of Charles I they are all very different in the style of the reverse shield and legend. Collectors should pay particular attention to any marks under the horse.

Collecting Hints

All Worcester issues are rare; they are difficult to find in any grade and exceptionally rare in VF. Often the legends are poorly struck on irregular sized flans and so are partly illegible.

Obverse Legend   CAROLUS DG MAG BRIT FRAN ET HIB REX — Charles by the grace of God King of Great Britain France and Ireland

Outer Reverse Legend   EXURGAT DEUS DISSIPENTUR INIMICI — Let God arise and His enemies be scattered

Inner Reverse Legend   RELIG PROT LE AN LIB PA — The religion of the Protestants, the laws of England, the liberty of Parliament

Obverse   King on horseback; mintmark two lions, W below horse.

Reverse   Three plumes above Declaration, 1644 below.

| C1HC-500 | VG £325 | F £1,000 | VF £2,000 |

Obverse Legend   As previous.

Reverse Legend   CHRISTO AUSPICE REGNO — I reign under the auspices of Christ

Obverse   As previous, but mintmark castle or helmet, 'W' below horse.

Reverse   Square-topped shield with crown above.

| C1HC-505 | VG £250 | F £500 | VF £1,200 |

As previous, but oval shield with crown above on reverse; mintmark helmet.

| C1HC-510 | VG £300 | F £550 | VF £1,100 |

Obverse   Grass under horse, 'W' above grass; mintmark castle.

Reverse   Square-topped shield with crown above; mintmark helmet or none.

| C1HC-515 | VG £225 | F £650 | VF £1,500 |

As previous, but oval shield with crown above; lis or lions in legend.

| C1HC-520 | VG £250 | F £500 | VF £1,350 |

As previous, but oval shield dividing CR, roses in legend.

| C1HC-525 | VG £270 | F £525 | VF £1,350 |

Obverse Legend As previous.

Reverse Legend FLORENT CONCORDIA REGNA — Through concord kingdoms flourish

Obverse As previous.

Reverse Oval shield with a lion's paw either side and a crown above; no mintmark.

C1HC-530	VG £300	F £700	VF £1,600

Obverse Legend As previous.

Reverse Legend CHRISTO AUSPICE REGNO — I reign under the auspices of Christ

Obverse Tall horseman with no marks below bust; no mintmark.

Reverse Oval shield with crown above, lis, roses, lions or stars in legend.

C1HC-535	VG £250	F £550	VF £1,200

As previous, but square-topped shield with crown above; mintmark helmet.

C1HC-540	VG £300	F £700	VF £1,600

Obverse Legend As previous.

Reverse Legend FLORENT CONCORDIA REGNA — Through concord kingdoms flourish

Obverse As previous.

Reverse Oval shield with crown above; no mintmark.

C1HC-545	VG £250	F £500	VF £1,350

Obverse Legend As previous.

Reverse Legend CHRISTO AUSPICE REGNO — I reign under the auspices of Christ

Obverse Briot-style bust of king with sword slanting forwards, no or uncertain mintmark.

Reverse Oval shield with crown above roses in legends.

C1HC-550	VG £200	F £500	VF £1,450

As previous, but shield dividing 'CR' on the reverse.

C1HC-555	VG £250	F £500	VF £1,350

Legends As previous.

Obverse A fat, portly king on a crude horse; mintmark uncertain or none.

Reverse Oval shield with crown above, stars, lions, roses or lis in the legend.

C1HC-560	VG £200	F £475	VF £1,350

Obverse Thin king on rather scraggy horse; no or uncertain mintmark (leopard's head?).

Reverse Crown above oval royal shield; stars in the legend.

C1HC-565	VG £250	F £500	VF £1,400

Salopia or Shrewsbury Mint (1644)

Very little is known about these issues and there is even uncertainty about whether they were struck in Shrewsbury at all. Several issues bear 'SA' below the horse which would correspond to Salopia, the town's Latin name; on the other hand, the coins have little in common with the Shrewsbury 1642 issues which is unusual and puzzling considering that they were produced less than two years later. Stylistically, they are linked to the Worcester mint, and the geographic proximity of these two towns allows for a 'transit-mint' interpretation which was common at the time. However, in the absence of more concrete evidence, we have listed these rare issues separately and not under Shrewsbury.

> ## Collecting Hints
>
> All issues are very rare in any grade. They are usually found in about Fine condition, often on flans of irregular size and shape; coins in VF condition are extremely rare.

Obverse Legend CAROLUS DG MAG BR FRAN ET HI(B) REX — Charles by the grace of God King of Great Britain France and Ireland

Reverse Legend CHRISTO AUSPICE REGNO — I reign under the auspices of Christ

Obverse King on horseback, 'SA' below.

Reverse Crown over oval shield; mintmark helmet.

C1HC-570	ex. rare

Reverse Legend FLORENT CONCORDIA REGNA — Through concord kingdoms flourish

Obverse As previous.

Reverse As previous, but no mintmark.

C1HC-575	ex. rare

Obverse As previous, but 'SA' replaced by a large cannon ball.
Reverse As C1HC-570; mintmark lis in legend or helmet.

C1HC-580	VG £800	F £1,500	VF —

Obverse Tall horse with no marks below it; mintmark lis.
Reverse Crown above large round shield; mintmark helmet.

C1HC-585	VG £380	F £750	VF £1,600

Obverse As previous.
Reverse Small, uncrowned, square-topped shield with lion's paw above and at either side; mintmark helmet.

C1HC-590	VG £450	F £800	VF £1,700

Obverse As previous.
Reverse Small oval shield with crown above; mintmark lis, helmet or none.

C1HC-595	VG £380	F £700	VF £1,600

Reverse Legend FLORENT CONCORDIA REGNA — Through concord kingdoms flourish
Obverse As previous.
Reverse Oval shield with crown above; no mintmark.

C1HC-600	VG £450	F £800	VF £1,800

Obverse A much cruder horse, often with both eyes showing; mintmark lis.
Reverse Round shield with crown above; mintmark lis.

C1HC-605	VG £450	F £800	VF £1,850

Obverse As previous, but grass under horse; mintmark lis.
Reverse As previous; mintmark rose or lis.

C1HC-610	VG £475	F £900	VF £2,200

Reverse Legend FLORENT CONCORDIA REGNA — Through concord kingdoms flourish

Obverse As previous, but a line under horse and no grass; mintmark lis.
Reverse Oval shield with crown above; no mintmark.

C1HC-615	VG £450	F £800	VF £1,850

Hartlebury Castle Mint (1646)

Hartlebury Castle in Worcester was a royalist garrison from 1643 to 1646 and the only coin produced at its mint was the halfcrown. Virtually nothing is known about this issue although some numismatists believe it could have been a Chester issue. It is also known as the HC issue from the initials found at the base of the reverse shield.

Collecting Hints

This issue is extremely rare in any grade.

Obverse Legend CAROLUS DG MAG BRIT FRAN ET HIB REX — Charles by the grace of God King of Great Britain France and Ireland

Reverse Legend CHRISTO AUSPICE REGNO — I reign under the auspices of Christ

Obverse King on horseback; mintmark pear.

Reverse Oval shield, 'HC' in garniture below shield; mintmark three pears.

| C1HC-620 | VG £800 | F £1,700 | VF £4,000 |

Chester Mint (1644)

Records indicate that during 1644 the Chester mint was active producing mainly halfcrowns, but also some other denominations. These issues are easily distinguished by their mintmarks while in some cases CHST, the town name abbreviated, can be found below the horse. These issues are similar to the ones from Hartlebury Castle and, as mentioned previously, the two mints could have been linked.

Collecting Hints

All issues are very rare in any grade. They are usually found in Fine condition but VF examples do exist. Many issues were struck on flans of irregular size, which may lead to legends being unclear. While the style of some of the issues is good with many resembling those from York, the actual production of the coins was poor. Contemporary forgeries exist.

Obverse Legend CAROLUS DG MAG BRI FR ET HIB REX — Charles by the grace of God King of Great Britain France and Ireland

Reverse Legend CHRISTO AUSPICE REGNO — I reign under the auspices of Christ

Obverse King on horseback, plume behind; mintmark three gerbs and sword, CHST below horse.

Reverse Oval shield; mintmark as obverse.

| C1HC-625 | VG £300 | F £650 | VF £1,950 |

Obverse As previous; mintmark prostrate gerb, cinquefoil or none.

Reverse Crown over royal shield; mintmark triangle of pellets, cinquefoil.

| C1HC-630 | VG £300 | F £700 | VF £1,550 |

Obverse As previous; mintmark cinquefoil, three pellets or prostrate gerb. No plume behind king or CHST below horse.

Reverse As previous; mintmark as obverse.

| C1HC-635 | VG £320 | F £750 | VF £1,650 |

Obverse As previous; mintmark cinquefoil.

Reverse Square-topped shield with crown above, a rose in the legend.

| C1HC-640 | VG £350 | F £1,250 | VF £2,200 |

Obverse Legend As previous.

Outer Reverse Legend EXURGAT DEUS DISSIPENTUR INIMICI — Let God arise and His enemies be scattered.

Reverse Legend RELIG PRO ANG LIBER PAR — The religion of the Protestants the laws of England the liberty of Parliament

Obverse King on horseback, no plume behind or inscription below horse; mintmark three gerbs and a sword(?).

Reverse Three plumes over Declaration, dated 1644 below.

| C1HC-645 | VG £400 | F £950 | VF £2,000 |

Coventry or Corfe Castle

An incredibly rare issue with the mintmark interlinked 'C's was attributed to Coventry or Corfe Castle, near Swanage. Although listed in many reference books, it appears that this coin is a forgery.

Siege Issues

Newark (1645 – 1646)

This denomination may be distinguished by the XXX, for 30 pence or halfcrown, found below the crown on the obverse.

Collecting Hints

Newark siege halfcrowns, while scarce and popular, are obtainable. They are the scarcest of all Newark issues and found in all grades from Poor to VF. As they were made out of pieces of plate, they often show gilding from the original object which does not detract from their value.

Obverse   Crown dividing CR, denomination below.

Reverse   OBS NEWARK[E], 1645 or 1646 on three lines.

| C1HC-650 | VG £325 | F £700 | VF £1,650 |

Scarborough (1644 – 1645)

Collecting Hints

This issue is extremely rare in any grade and collectors should beware of forgeries.

Obverse   Castle with gateway to left, value punched below.

Reverse   None.

| C1HC-655 | VG — | F £6,000 | VF — |

Commonwealth   (1649 – 1660)

Halfcrowns were struck during most of the Commonwealth period. The denomination is easily identifiable by the markings II VI found above the two shields on the reverse. All issues are dated and have the value (II VI, two shillings and sixpence) on the reverse and bear a mintmark at the beginning of the obverse legend. In keeping with Puritan values, the legends are in English and the style of the coins, which were hammered, is very plain. Many varieties exist with misspellings in the legend and overdates which we list below.

Collecting Hints

Commonwealth halfcrowns, whilst scarce, are obtainable. They are usually found in less than Fine condition, often clipped; specimens in VF or better condition are rare. The most common issues have mintmark sun and are dated 1649, 1651 – 56; issues dated 1658 – 60 with mintmark an

chor are extremely rare. Collectors should be aware that forgeries are very common; most are contemporary forgeries made of base metal, which was often silvered. Remember, genuine coins were made of high quality silver and usually well struck.

Date	Rarity
1649	RRR
1651	RR
1651 ....proof	RRR
1652	R
1652/1	RR
1653	R
1653/1	R
1653/2	R
1653 over 1553 ...engraver's error	RRR
1654	R
1654/3	R
1655	RRR
1656	R
1656/5	R
1657 ....(Baldwin's, near VF £6,000)	2 known
1658 ....(Baldwin's, good F £1,300)	RRR
1658/7 ....(Baldwin's, good F £1,400)	RRR
1659	2 known
1660	RRR

Obverse Legend THE COMMONWEALTH OF ENGLAND

Reverse Legend GOD WITH US

Obverse Shield of St George within wreath; mintmark sun.

Reverse The arms of St George and Ireland, value and date above 1649, 1651 – 56. Coins dated 1651 are rare, while issues dated 1655 are very rare.

| CWHC-005 | VG £100 | F £225 | VF £450 |

As previous, but mintmark anchor. Dated 1658, 1659, 1660.

| CWHC-010 | VG £350 | F £1,000 | VF rare |

Charles II   (1660 – 1685)

Hammered Issue (1660 – 1662)

Three main types of hammered halfcrowns were struck under Charles II, from 1660 to 1662. All are undated and have a crowned bust of the king on the obverse, the king's arms on the reverse and mintmark crown on the obverse and, sometimes, the reverse. Unlike other denominations from this series, they cannot be confused with issues of Charles I which show the king on horseback.

C2HCH-015   VG £70   F £120   VF £400

Collecting Hints

The first and second issue are both very rare in any grade. The third issue, while scarce, is obtainable, especially in the lower grades. Undoubtedly, many of these coins saw considerable circulation and are often found very worn, sometimes also clipped. The portrait, while detailed, appears to have been weakly struck and the reverse of the coin is often in much better condition than the obverse. Issues with a good clear bust are of higher value.

Obverse Legend   CAROLUS II DG MAG BRIT FRAN ET HIB REX — Charles II by the grace of God King of Great Britain France and Ireland

Reverse Legend   CHRISTO AUSPICE REGNO — I reign under the auspices of Christ

Obverse   Crowned bust of king with no inner circles or mark of value; mintmark crown.

Reverse   Royal shield over cross; no mintmark or inner circles.

C2HCH-005   VG £300   F £500   VF £1,300

Obverse Legend   As previous, (minor varieties).

Reverse Legend   As previous.

Obverse   As previous, but mark of value XXX behind the bust.

Reverse   As previous.

C2HCH-010   VG £350   F £600   VF £1,650

Obverse Legend   As previous, (minor varieties).

Reverse Legend   As previous.

Obverse   As previous, but inner circles.

Reverse   As previous, but inner circles and mintmark crown.

Twenty Pence

Henry III (1216 – 1272)

Before Henry III's reign the need for higher denominations had been met, at least partly, by Byzantine and Arabic gold and silver issues that circulated among merchants and traders. But as commerce increased the monetary system also had to grow, so in 1257 the king instructed his goldsmith, William of Gloucester, to prepare a coinage of pure gold. The twenty-pence was one of the issues introduced, with an obverse depicting the king enthroned and a reverse bearing a long cross with a flower in each quarter and the moneyer's name in the legend. A total of four different dies were made, producing three minor varieties and indicating that the issue was not a pattern but a denomination intended for circulation. As, however, the issue had been undervalued and, by 1265, was worth twenty-four rather than twenty pennies in gold, it is thought that the majority of coins were melted down by unscrupulous individuals for profit. Consequently, the coinage was not a success and few specimens have survived. It was not until the reign of Edward III that gold coins would be minted again.

Collecting Hints

These coins are extremely rare. Modern forgeries are also known to exist.

Obverse Legend HENRICUS REX III — King Henry III

Reverse Legend WILLEM ON LUND — William of London

Obverse King holding sceptre and orb seated on a throne.

Reverse Long cross with rose in each quarter.

H320D-005 ex. rare (VF example sold for £159,500 in July 1996)

Quarter Noble

With a value of one shilling and eightpence, the gold quarter-noble was introduced under Edward III as part of the new denomination restructure. All issues have the king's arms in a shield on the obverse and a small cross surrounded by a design of arches, lis and lions and often a letter in the centre on the reverse. Many quarter-nobles have been found in hoards but, more recently, a great number have also been located with the help of metal detectors. This indicates that, unlike the nobles which were used primarily by wealthy merchants to trade with their European counterparts and are subsequently found in hoards, quarter-nobles were in general circulation at the time. Gold coins found with the help of metal detectors are usually dull in appearance with a matt surface and, under a magnifying glass, they show scratches and nicks due to movement in the soil where they lay. Coins with a dull, matt surface should not be cleaned or buffed up.

Edward III (1327 – 1377)

The gold quarter-noble was first introduced in 1344, during the second coinage. This issue weighed 34.5 grains (2.2 grams) but was subsequently reduced to 32 grains (2.1 grams) in the third coinage (1346 – 51). The second period issue, which is very rare, can be identified by an L for London in the centre of the reverse cross whereas most other issues bear an E for Edward instead. Most quarter-nobles were produced during the fourth coinage and can be identified by their obverse legends which reflect Edward III's claim to the throne of France (for details, see p.343). Being a popular and much needed denomination, the quarter-noble was produced during several reigns. The king's name can always be found at the beginning of the obverse legend and will read EDWARD, EDWARR or EDWAR; although Edward IV also struck quarter-nobles, only one example exists and can be distinguished by its mintmark at the beginning of the reverse legend, which was not used by Edward III. The obverse legend might also read RICARD or HENRIC, whereupon the coin is an issue of Richard II or Henry IV, V or VI. Two mints produced quarter-nobles under Edward III, London and Calais in France. The issues for Calais, which was used as a mint not only because coins were needed by English merchants in Europe but also as a political statement, were all struck during the treaty period of 1361 – 69 and bear various marks differentiating them from the more common London issues.

Collecting Hints

Most quarter-nobles, while scarce, are obtainable. Many varieties exist and collectors should not have too much difficulty in obtaining a more common variety. Quarter-nobles are found in all grades from VG to EF but are sometimes clipped, damaged or very worn, reflecting their considerable circulation.

Second Coinage (1344 – 1346)

Obverse Legend   EDWAR REX ANG Z FRANC D HYB — Edward King England and France Lord of the Irish

Reverse Legend   EXALTABITUR IN GLORIA — He shall be exalted in glory

Obverse   King's arms in arches of six arcs.

Reverse   'L' in centre of cross (this identifies the issue).

E3QN-005	F £1,500	VF £3,000

Third Coinage (1346 – 1351)

Obverse Legend   EDWAR R ANGL Z FRANC D HYB — Edward King of England and France Lord of the Irish

Reverse Legend   As previous.

Obverse   As previous, but large lettering and a Lombardic 'N' and 'M'.

Reverse   'E' in centre of reverse cross.

E3QN-010	VG £150	F £300	VF £600

Many varieties of this issue exist, often with muling but all issues have mintmark cross 3.

Obverse   Annulet stops in legend.

Reverse   Saltire stops in legend.

E3QN-015	VG £135	F £275	VF £450

As previous, but muled with E3QN-025.

E3QN-020	VG £135	F £275	VF £450

Saltire stops in legend, a pellet either side of one lis on the reverse.

E3QN-025	VG £135	F £275	VF £450

Large 'E' in centre of the reverse.

E3QN-030	VG £135	F £275	VF £450

Fourth Coinage (1351 – 1377)
Pre Treaty Period (1351 – 1361)

Many varieties exist for the three issues produced during this period but all include the French title in the legend and have eight arcs to the treasure on the obverse.

Class A

Obverse Legend   EDWAR D G REX ANGL Z FRAE or EDWARR ANGL Z FRANC D HYBER or EDWAR D G REX ANGL Z FRANC — Edward King of England and France

Reverse Legend   As previous.

Obverse   Royal shield in arcs of eight arches.

Reverse   'E' in centre cross.

E3QN-035	VG £135	F £225	VF £400

Class B

Legends   As previous.

Obverse   Royal shield with pellet below.

Reverse   Closed 'E' in centre of cross; mintmark cross I.

E3QN-040	VG £135	F £275	VF £450

Class C

Obverse   As previous.

Reverse   Wedge-tailed 'R' and annulet stops in the legend; mintmark cross I.

E3QN-045	VG £140	F £300	VF £475

Transitional Period (1361)

Obverse Legend   EDWAR DEI GRAC REX ANGL D — Edward by the grace of God King of England Lord [of Ireland]

Reverse Legend   As previous.

Obverse   Royal shield, often with trefoils or annulets at cusps.

Reverse   'E' in centre cross; mintmark cross potent.

E3QN-050	VG £135	F £300	VF £475

As previous, but cross in centre (no 'E').

E2QN-052	VG £135	F £300	VF £475

Treaty Period (1361 – 1369)
London Mint

Obverse Legend   EDWARD DEI GRA REX ANGL — Edward by the grace of God King of England

Reverse Legend   As previous.

Obverse   Royal arms.

Reverse   Lis in centre of reverse cross; mintmark cross potent.

E3QN-055	VG £135	F £300	VF £475

As previous, but an annulet before EDWARD.

E3QN-060	VG £135	F £300	VF £475

Calais Mint

As previous, but annulet in centre of cross on the reverse.

E3QN-065	VG £140	F £275	VF £450

As previous, but a cross in a circle above the royal shield on the obverse.

E3QN-070	VG £140	F £300	VF £475

As previous, but a quatrefoil in the centre cross on the reverse and just a cross over the shield on the obverse.

E3QN-075	VG £150	F £325	VF £500

As previous, but a crescent over the shield on the obverse.

E3QN-080	VG £160	F £350	VF £600

No quarter-nobles were produced during the post-treaty period.

Richard II   (1377 – 1399)

Fairly large quantities of quarter-nobles were produced under Richard II, all at the London mint. They were very similar in style and design to the previous, Edward III issues and one (R2QN-015) even used an altered die of that reign. They are, however, easy to distinguish as all bear RICARD at the beginning of the obverse legend and some also have an 'R' for Richard in the centre cross on the reverse. Moreover, no other Richard produced quarter-nobles.

Collecting Hints

All issues are rare but obtainable. Coins are usually found in Fine or VF condition.

Obverse Legend   RICARD DEI GRA REX ANGL (varieties exist) — Richard by the grace of God King of England

Reverse Legend   EXALTABITVR IN GLORIA — He shall be exalted in glory

Obverse   Royal arms.

Reverse   'R' in centre of reverse; mintmark cross pattée.

R2QN-005	VG £200	F £500	VF £900

As previous, but a lis or pellet in centre cross on reverse.

| R2QN-010 | VG £200 | F £500 | VF £900 |

Obverse die altered from an Edward III issue; reverse has pellet in centre of shield.

| R2QN-015 | VG £200 | F £500 | VF £900 |

As R2QN-010, but escallop over shield.

| R2QN-020 | VG £200 | F £550 | VF £950 |

As R2QN-010, but three annulets over shield.

| R2QN-025 | VG £200 | F £550 | VF £950 |

As R2QN-010, but quatrefoil, cross or trefoil over shield.

| R2QN-030 | VG £200 | F £550 | VF £950 |

Henry IV   (1399 – 1413)

Henry IV, V and VI all produced very similar gold quarter-nobles, with the royal shield on the obverse and a cross surrounded by decoration on the reverse. A differentiating mintmark can usually be found at the beginning of the obverse and reverse legends but, as it is not clear on some coins, collectors should also look for any unusual marks or designs and refer to all three monarchs. All Henry IV quarter-nobles have HENRIC at the beginning of the obverse legend.

Henry IV's issues are divided into the heavy and the light coinage. In 1412 following a shortage of coins in circulation, which was brought about when rising gold prices resulted in bullion coins being smuggled abroad to be melted down and sold for profit, it was decided to reduce the weight of gold coins by ten percent and align it with their value. Thus, towards the end of Henry's reign the light coinage was produced. It should also be noted that during the heavy coinage new royal arms were introduced which only lasted for this reign and are easily identified by an extra lis in the upper quarter of the shield. Finally, the two mints that produced quarter-nobles under Henry IV were London and Calais in France. The issue from Calais, which is very rare, has the mintmark crown to distinguish it from the London issues, which used the mintmark cross pattée.

Collecting Hints

Quarter-nobles are the most common gold issues of Henry IV; however, they are all very rare and difficult to obtain. Coins are usually found in Fine or VF condition.

Heavy Coinage (1399 – 1412)

London Mint

Obverse Legend   HENRIC DI GRA REX ANGL Z FRANC (varieties exist) — Henry by the grace of God King of England and France

Reverse Legend   EXALTABITUR IN GLORIA — He shall be exalted in glory

Obverse   Old-style royal arms with crescent above; mintmark cross pattée.

Reverse   Pellet in centre of reverse cross.

| H4QN-005 | VG £450 | F £1,400 | VF £2,800 |

As previous, but new-style royal arms on obverse with an extra lis in the top quarter.

| H4QN-010 | VG £400 | F £1,200 | VF £2,350 |

Calais Mint

Obverse   As previous.

Reverse   As previous, but mintmark crown.

| H4QN-015 | VG £425 | F £1,500 | VF £3,000 |

Light Coinage (1412 – 1413)

Legends   As previous.

Obverse   New-style royal arms with trefoils or trefoils and annulets at side.

Reverse   Lis in centre of reverse cross.

| H4QN-020 | VG £300 | F £800 | VF £1,500 |

Henry V   (1413 – 1422)

Under Henry V, quarter-nobles were only struck at the London mint. As mentioned earlier, they are very similar in style to the issues of Henry IV and Henry VI, but can be distinguished apart. Only Henry V used the mintmark cross pattée with pellet in centre or the mintmark pierced cross, moreover all his issues have a lis above the royal arms and in the centre cross on the reverse. Also in most issues, one or more mullets can be found somewhere on the coin and this is a mark that only Henry V used on quarter-nobles.

Collecting Hints

All quarter-nobles are rare but obtainable and usually found in Fine or VF condition.

Obverse Legend   HENRIC DI GRA REX ANGL — Henry by the grace of God King of England

Reverse Legend   EXALTABITVR IN GLORIA — He shall be exalted in glory

Obverse   Lis over royal shield, quatrefoil and annulet beside shield; the legend is in short, broad lettering.

Reverse   Lis in centre of reverse.

H5QN-005	VG £165	F £350	VF £600

Obverse   Royal shield and lis above, quatrefoil to the left and quatrefoil and mullet to the right; ordinary style lettering.

Reverse   As previous.

H5QN-010	VG £160	F £275	VF £500

Obverse   Royal shield and lis above, annulet to left and mullet to right of shield.

Reverse   As previous.

H5QN-015	VG £160	F £275	VF £500

Obverse   Royal shield and lis above, trefoil to left, mullet to right of shield.

Reverse   As previous.

H5QN-020	VG £160	F £285	VF £525

Obverse   Lis over royal arms, mullet after king's name, no other marks.
Reverse   As previous.

H5QN-025	VG £160	F £285	VF £525

Henry VI First Reign (1422 – 1461)

During the first part of Henry VI's reign, quarter-nobles were produced in some quantity. All are fairly similar to previous reigns, with the royal arms on the obverse and a lis in the centre of the reverse. The various Henry VI issues can be identified by the marks or stops, such as annulets, which are found in the legends and are specific to each issue. Again if collectors are uncertain when trying to identify a coin, they should refer to the issues of Henry IV and Henry V. Three mints produced quarter-nobles under Henry VI, London, Calais and York. They can be identified by the number of lis found over the royal shield on the obverse as London had one lis or none, York two and Calais either three or one and a small mintmark lis.

Collecting Hints

All issues, especially the provincial ones, are scarce, but collectors should be able to obtain a more common variety. Coins are usually found in Fine or VF condition.

Annulet Issue (1422 – 1427)
London Mint

Obverse Legend   HENRIC DI GRA REX ANGL — Henry by the grace of God King of England

Reverse Legend   EXALTABITUR IN GLORIA — He shall be exalted in glory

Obverse   Lis over royal arms; mintmark large lis.

Reverse   Lis in centre; annulets in reverse legend.

H6QN-005	VG £140	F £250	VF £450

As previous, but a trefoil below the shield.

H6QN-010	VG £140	F £250	VF £450

As previous, but a pellet below the shield. If the mintmark lis is very small refer to H6QN-030.

H6QN-015	ex. rare

Calais Mint

Legends   As previous.
Obverse   Three lis over royal shield, mintmark large lis.
Reverse   Lis in centre, annulets in legend.

H6QN-020	VG £160	F £300	VF £525

As previous, but the three lis on the obverse are around the royal shield.

H6QN-025	VG £160	F £300	VF £525

Only one lis above shield, but the mintmark lis is very small on the obverse and reverse; annulets in reverse legend.

| H6QN-030 | VG £160 | F £300 | VF £525 |

York Mint

As previous, but two lis over the royal shield; mintmark lis.

| H6QN-035 | VG £170 | F £350 | VF £650 |

Rosette Mascle Issue (1427 – 1430)
London Mint

Legends As previous.

Obverse A lis over the royal shield, rosette stops on legend; mintmark lis.

Reverse Lis in centre, rosette and mascle stops in legend.

| H6QN-040 | VG £185 | F £400 | VF £700 |

As previous, but no lis over royal shield.

| H6QN-045 | VG £175 | F £350 | VF £650 |

Calais Mint

Legends As previous.

Obverse Lis over royal shield, a rosette either side of shield; mintmark lis.

Reverse Lis in centre, rosette stops in legend.

| H6QN-050 | VG £200 | F £450 | VF £800 |

Pinecone Mascle Issue (1430 – 1434)

Legends As previous.

Obverse Lis over royal shield; mintmark lis.

Reverse Lis in centre, pinecone and mascle stops in legend.

| H6QN-055 | ex. rare |

Leaf Mascle Issue (1434 – 1435)

Legends As previous.

Obverse Lis above royal shield; mintmark lis.

Reverse A leaf below the 'R' in GLORI, saltire and mascle stops in legend.

| H6QN-060 | F £1,000 | VF £2,000 |

Leaf Trefoil Issue (1435 – 1438)

Legends As previous.

Obverse Lis over royal shield; mintmark lis.

Reverse Lis in centre, leaf and trefoil stops in legend.

| H6QN-065 | probably unique |

No quarter-nobles were struck for the rest of Henry VI's reign.

Edward IV First Reign (1461 – 1470)

During the early part of Edward IV's reign the rising price of gold created a shortage in the supply to the mint which in turn led to a decrease in the number of gold coins in circulation. The situation was exacerbated by merchants exporting English gold coins to the Continent to melt and sell at a profit. To counteract this practice, the value of every noble in circulation was raised from six shillings and eightpence to eight shillings and fourpence in 1464 and, the following year, the gold ryal or rose noble was introduced with a value of ten shillings. This 1465 issue, which included half-ryals and quarter-ryals, was a continuation of the noble series, so we have included the quarter-ryal here. The heavy coinage (1461 – 64) quarter-noble is unique; and although more would undoubtedly have been produced, they were probably melted down at the time. The new quarter-ryal was very close to the quarter-noble in style, bearing the royal shield on the obverse and a rose over a radiate sun over a centre cross on the reverse. Mintmarks can be found on obverse and reverse, and dies are often muled. All issues were struck at the London mint only, and the quarter-ryal had a value of two shillings and sixpence.

Quarter Noble
Heavy Coinage (1461 – 1464)

Collecting Hints

Only one coin survives.

Obverse Royal arms mintmark.

Reverse and Legends Details unknown.

| E4QN-005 | unique |

Quarter Ryal
Light Coinage (1464 – 1470)

Collecting Hints

The first issue listed is probably unique and is considered by some numismatists to be a Continental copy or forgery. The next two issues are rare and, when available, usually found undamaged in Fine to VF condition.

Obverse Legend EDWARD DI GRA REX ANG — Edward by the grace of God King of England (and France)

Reverse Legend   EXALTABITUR IN GLORIA — He shall be exalted in glory

Obverse   Royal arms with rose above; mintmark sun.

Reverse   A rose over a radiate sun over the centre reverse cross; mintmark rose.

E4QR-010   unique

Legends   As previous.

Obverse   E over royal shield, rose left of shield, sun to right; mintmark rose, sun, crown (often muled).

Reverse   As previous.

E4QR-015   VG £200   F £425   VF £850

As previous, but rose to right of shield and sun to left; mintmark crown, sun, rose, long cross fitchée, lis. Sometimes muled.

E4QR-020   VG £200   F £450   VF £900

Quarter Angel

The gold quarter-angel was introduced in Henry VIII's third coinage (1544 – 47), with a value of two shillings, as part of the new denomination structure. All issues show St Michael killing the dragon on the obverse and a ship with the royal arms in the centre on the reverse. Quarter-angels were only struck again under Elizabeth I but the two reigns are easily identified by the monarch's name at the beginning of the obverse legend. However, as the denomination proved unpopular, it was superseded by the popular shilling and halfcrown. This coin is also known as the angelet.

Henry VIII   (1509 – 1547)

This rare issue was struck at the London mint. Only one variety exists, always with the mintmark lis at the beginning of the obverse and reverse legend.

Collecting Hints

This issue is rare but obtainable. Coins are usually found in Fine condition, sometimes damaged or badly worn, reflecting considerable circulation. The style is not as good as the angel or half-angel as the die engraver would probably have found it difficult to put all the detail onto such a small die.

Obverse Legend   HENRICUS VIII D GRA AGL — Henry VIII by the grace of God [of] England

Reverse Legend   FRANCIE ET (or Z) HIBERNIE REX — France and Ireland King

Obverse   St Michael killing the dragon; mintmark lis.

Reverse   Ship with royal arms in centre, a mast in the shape of a cross above, 'H' and a rose either side.

H8QA-005	VG £150	F £325	VF £750

Elizabeth I   (1558 – 1603)

The gold quarter-angel was produced during most of Elizabeth's reign. As the angel had risen to ten shillings under Edward VI, the value of the quarter-angel was exactly two shillings and sixpence, the same as the gold halfcrown. These denominations circulated alongside each other; however, the quarter-angel was obsolete in design and value and stopped being produced in 1600 being replaced by the silver halfcrown, a denomination which was to be produced for circulation until 1967.

Collecting Hints

All Elizabeth's quarter-angels are rare. They are usually found in Fine condition, but VF examples do exist. The denomination is fairly unpopular with collectors as it is very small and poor in design when compared to large denomination gold coins.

First – Third Issues (1559 – 1578)

Obverse Legend   ELIZABETH DG ANG FRANCIE — Elizabeth by the grace of God [of] England France

Reverse Legend   ET HIBERNIE REGINA FIDEI — and Ireland Queen [defender] of the Faith

Obverse   St Michael killing the dragon; mintmark ermine, acorn and eglantine.

Reverse   Ship with royal arms in centre, a mast in the shape of a cross, 'E' and a rose either side; mintmark as obverse.

ELQA-005	VG £170	F £340	VF £675

Fourth Issue (1578 – 1582)

The gold used for this issue was of a slightly lower fineness.

Legends   As previous.

Obverse   As previous, but mintmark Greek cross, Latin cross or sword.

Reverse   As previous; mintmarks as obverse.

ELQA-010	VG £160	F £300	VF £600

Fifth Issue (1583 – 1600)

The coins for this issue had a slightly higher fineness of gold.

Legends   As previous.

Obverse   As previous, but mintmarks bell, 'A', escallop, crescent, hand, tun, woolpack, key or anchor.

Reverse   As previous; mintmarks as obverse.

ELQA-015	VG £160	F £300	VF £600

No quarter-angels were struck for the sixth issue.

Quarter Florin or Helm

Edward III   (1324 – 1377)

Acting on instructions that Edward III had issued in 1343 regarding the production of gold denominations for England, the Florentines George Kirkyn and Lotte Nicholyn designed the quarter-florin or helm in 1344. With a value of one shilling and sixpence and based largely on the European gold issues, it was intended to be not only for England but also for the whole of Europe. However, the gold used to make the coins had been over-valued so the issue was unacceptable to merchants and had to be demonetised in August 1344. The coins were recalled, melted down and used to make the popular and more acceptable nobles.

Collecting Hints

This issue is extremely rare and most specimens exist in the higher grades.

Obverse Legend   EDWR R ANGL Z FRANC D HIB — Edward King of England and France Lord of Ireland

Reverse Legend   EXALTABITUR IN GLORIA — He shall be exalted in glory

Obverse   Royal helmet surmounted by a lion and cap.

Reverse   Floriated cross with a quatrefoil in centre.

E3QFL-005   ex. rare

Shilling

The silver shilling or testoon was first introduced in the profile issue of Henry VII. Documentary evidence is scarce but it is thought that few issues were originally struck because, like so many new denominations, the shilling did not become popular for some time. It was reintroduced in Henry VIII's third coinage, when fairly large quantities were produced but the entire coinage was unpopular. Finally, the shilling was successfully introduced during the reign of Edward VI and was subsequently produced during every reign except Mary's. The combination of rising inflation and general prosperity in Europe, due mainly to large quantities of silver and gold coming from the Americas, meant that the shilling, together with other larger denominations, became more important in English everyday transactions.

Henry VII (1485 – 1509)

The shilling, known as the testoon, was introduced during Henry VII's profile issue but, with no documentary evidence surviving, little is known about it. It has been argued that the issues were trials or patterns but this seems unlikely since a total of three different dies were made. It is more probable that the shilling took some time to become popular as a denomination. It is important to remember that large quantities of European as well as English coins circulated in England at the time and merchants were in a position to choose which coins they would accept for their goods.

Profile Issue (1502 – 1504?)

Collecting Hints

All three issues are extremely rare. When available they are usually found in Fine or VF condition.

Obverse Legend HENRIC DI GRA REX ANGLIE Z FRAN — Henry by the grace of God King of England and France

Reverse Legend POSUI DEUM ADIVTOE MEU — I have made God my helper

Obverse Crowned bust of king to right; mintmark lis.

Reverse Royal shield over cross.

| H7TS-005 | F £5,000 | VF £12,000 |

As previous, but obverse legend reads HENRIC SEPTIM DI GRA REX ANGL Z FRA.

| H7TS-010 | F £6,000 | VF £12,500 |

As previous, but obverse legend reads HENRIC VII DI GRA REX ANGL Z FRA.

| H7TS-015 | F £6,500 | VF £13,500 |

Henry VIII (1509 – 1547)

The shilling, still known as the testoon, was reintroduced during Henry VIII's third coinage (1544 – 47) and continued to be produced in the posthumous coinage (1547 – 51) when coins bearing Henry's name and portrait were struck while his son Edward VI was on the throne and producing coins in his own name. As both Henry's issues were made of base silver (i.e. silver mixed with a metal of little value, usually copper, to produce a coin of low fineness), they were extremely unpopular because the public was accustomed to, and expected, bullion coins. The three mints producing testoons during the two coinages were London, now known as Tower mint, Southwark and Bristol. They can easily be distinguished by their reverse legends which read as follows: Tower — POSUI ADIVITOREM MEUM (minor varieties exist); Southwark — CIVITAS LONDON; Bristol — CIVITAS BRISTOLLIE.

Collecting Hints

All Henry VIII's testoons are fairly rare and usually available in less than Fine condition, often badly worn and scratched. The edges of the coin are often chipped, usually due to the poor striking and metal content rather than clipping. Coins in VF and EF condition are very rare.

Third Coinage (1544 – 1547)
Tower Mint

Obverse Legend HENRIC VIII DG AGL FR Z HIB REX — Henry VIII by the grace of God King of England France and Ireland

Reverse Legend POSUI DEUM ADIVTOREM MEUM (minor varieties) — I have made God my helper

Obverse Front-facing crowned bust of the king; mintmark lis, two lis or pellet in annulet.

Reverse Crown over rose with crowned 'H' and 'R' at sides.

| H8TS-005 | Poor £100 | VG £200 | F £500 | VF £1,500 |

As previous, but obverse legend starts HENRIC 8; mintmark lis or pellet in annulet.

| H8TS-010 | Poor £100 | VG £200 | F £550 | VF £1,600 |

Southwark Mint

This issue was also produced during the posthumous coinage using the same or identical dies.

Obverse Legend HENRIC 8 DG AGL FR Z HIB REX — Henry VIII by the grace of God King of England France and Ireland

Reverse Legend CIVITAS LONDON — City London

Obverse As previous, but mintmark 'S' or 'E'; varieties in muling.

Reverse As previous.

| H8TS-015 | Poor £100 | VG £200 | F £550 | VF £1,600 |

Bristol Mint

This issue was probably also struck during the posthumous coinage.

Obverse Legend As previous.

Reverse Legend CIVITAS BRISTOLLIE — City Bristol

Obverse As previous, but no mintmark.

Reverse As previous, but mintmark 'WS'.

| H8TS-020 | Poor £100 | VG £200 | F £550 | VF £1,600 |

Posthumous Coinage (1547 – 1551)
Tower Mint

Obverse Legend HENRIC 8. DG AGL FR Z HIB REX — Henry VIII by the grace of God King of England France and Ireland

Reverse Legend POSUI DEUM ADIVTOREM MEUM — I have made God my helper

Obverse Crowned bust of facing king; mintmark none or pellet in annulet.

Reverse Crown over rose with 'H' and 'R' at sides, sleeve or lozenge shaped stops usually either side of legend; mintmark pellet in annulet.

| H8TS-025 | Poor £120 | VG £225 | F £750 | VF £1,800 |

Edward VI (1547 – 1553)

From this period onwards, the shilling was no longer known as a testoon. The shillings struck under Edward VI fall into three categories, the posthumous coinage mentioned above, the base issue and finally the fine silver coinage. The base issue, struck in Edward's name, was very much a continuation from the previous reign and again made of low grade, base silver. The superb coins of the fine silver issue, on the other hand, were made of good quality silver and became extremely popular with the public who had coins worth their weight in silver once more. All of these silver issues were struck at the Tower mint in London.

Base Silver Issue

Many varieties in styles of bust and lettering exist but, due to the poor condition of most coins, they are very difficult to detect and we have only listed the main ones.

Collecting Hints

Most of these issues are fairly rare and very difficult to obtain in Fine or better condition. Often they are either clipped or have ragged edges due to striking and metal content; also they appear dull in colour and should never be cleaned. Collectors should pay particular attention to a clear portrait and, if seeking an example from the reign, might prefer a more attractive and easily obtainable fine silver issue. They should also note that contemporary forgeries struck in brass are quite common and appear to have seen some circulation, especially in Ireland and, finally, that the weights of some issues vary considerably although it would appear that the silver content remains the same.

First Period April (1547 – 1549)
Durham House Year MDXLVIII (1548)

This rare issue was struck in brass alloy at the Durham House mint. It has been considered a possible forgery or pattern and no records exist.

Obverse Legend EDWARD VI DG AGL. FR Z HIB REX — Edward VI by the grace of God King of England France and Ireland

Reverse Legend   TIMOR DOMINI FONS VITE MDXLVIII — The fear of the Lord is the fountain of life 1548

Obverse   Crowned bust of king right.

Reverse   Oval shield dividing 'ER'; mintmark bow.

E6SH-005   ex. rare

Second Period (Jan. 1549 – April 1550)

Three London mints (Tower, Southwark and Durham House) and two provincial ones (Bristol and Canterbury) were active in the second period. Although coins are fairly hard to identify correctly because of their poor condition, the various issues can be distinguished by the date which is found on the obverse and/or reverse. Should a coin be undated but with a reverse legend beginning INIMICOS, it is from Durham House mint. Coins with a clear date and mintmark are worth more than those without. For convenience, issues are listed here by date, with the mintmarks to distinguish the various mints.

Year MDXLIX (1549)

These coins, which were struck in January and February 1549, all bear bust 1.

Transposed Legends

Obverse Legend   TIMOR DOMINI FONS VITE MDXLIX (varieties in order) — The fear of the Lord is the fountain of life 1549

Reverse Legend   EDWARD VI DG AGL FRA Z HIB REX (varieties in order) — Edward VI by the grace of God King of England France and Ireland

Obverse   Crowned bust of king to right.

Reverse   Oval shield dividing 'ER'. The order of the legend might change in various issues.

Durham House Mintmark   Bow on reverse.

E6SH-010   VG £70   F £150   VF £450

Tower Mintmark   Arrow. There is also an extremely rare variety which bears bust 2 and mintmark arrow only on the reverse.

E6SH-015   VG £80   F £175   VF £450

Southwark Mintmark   Obverse 'Y' or 'EY'; reverse 'Y'.

E6SH-020   VG £150   F £300   VF £750

Canterbury Mintmark   Obverse none; reverse rose.

E6SH-025   ex. rare

Regular Legends

Obverse and reverse are as previous, but the legends are always in their correct order.

Obverse Legend   EDWARD VI DG AGL FRA Z HIB REX (varieties in order) — Edward VI by the grace of God King of England France and Ireland

Reverse Legend   TIMOR DOMINI FONS VITE (varieties in order) — The fear of the Lord is the fountain of life

Durham House Mintmark   Bow.

E6SH-030   VG £150   F £300   VF £750

Tower Mintmark   Obverse arrow, arrow over 6, grapple, grapple over '6', pheon, swan, swan over Y; reverse swan. One die omits the 'ER' beside the shield.

E6SH-035   VG £60   F £150   VF £400

Southwark Mintmark   Obverse 'Y', 'Y' over '6', 'Y'; reverse 'Y' over grapple.

E6SH-040   VG £80   F £180   VF £500

Bristol Mintmark   Obverse 'TC' over 'G'; reverse 'TC'. The initials TC are those of Thomas Chamberlain who put his initials over the 'G' which stood for George Gale who was treasurer at the York mint. This die, while prepared for the York mint, was subsequently sent to the Bristol mint and never used at York.

E6SH-045   VG £300   F £600   VF —

Canterbury Mintmark   't', 't' over 'G', 'T'.

E6SH-050   VG £80   F £180   VF £500

Year MDL (1550)

Obverse, reverse and legends are as previous.

Tower Mintmark   Obverse pheon and reverse swan, swan, martlet. There is also an extremely rare variety with mintmark crowned leopard's head.

E6SH-055   VG £60   F £150   VF £450

Southwark Mintmark 'Y'.

E6SH-060	VG £80	F £180	VF £500

Undated Issue

This issue, struck at the Durham House, has no date and a different reverse legend. Varieties exist, with the main difference being the order of the legends; the mintmark for all issues is bow.

Obverse Legend   As previous.

Reverse Legend   INIMICOS EIUS INDUAM CONFUSIONE — As for His enemies I shall clothe them with shame

Obverse & Reverse   As previous; mintmark bow.

E6SH-065	VG £100	F £200	VF £500

Third Period (1550 – 1551)
Year MDL (1550)

Obverse Legend   As previous.

Reverse Legend   As E6SH-015.

Obverse & Reverse   As previous.

Tower Mintmark   Lion over rose, or lis.

E6SH-070	VG £60	F £130	VF £300

Southwark Mintmark   Obverse lis; reverse 'Y'.

E6SH-075	VG £60	F £130	VF £350

Year MDLI (1551)

Legends   As previous.

Obverse & Reverse   As previous.

Tower Mintmark   Obverse rose, lion, lion; reverse rose over lion.

E6SH-080	VG £100	F £200	VF £450

Southwark Mintmark   Obverse 'Y'; reverse lis.

E6SH-085	VG £100	F £200	VF £450

Fine Silver Issue (1551 – 1553)

This high grade silver issue of good quality and style was extremely popular. Struck at the Tower mint, it has a superb portrait of the Boy King on the obverse and the royal arms on the reverse. However, it was struck alongside the base issue thus producing two standards of coins. This was mainly due to the fact that many of the members of the Council that governed the country until Edward became of age had an interest in keeping the base coinage in production because it was so profitable. The king himself was in fact instrumental in restoring the coinage.

Collecting Hints

Edward VI fine silver shillings are fairly common, usually available in about Fine condition but sometimes scratched or holed. Examples in VF and even EF condition exist and are very desirable. Compared to the contemporary base issues, these coins are superb with clear design and legible legends.

Obverse Legend   EDWARD VI DG AGL. FRA Z HIB REX — Edward VI by the grace of God King of England France and Ireland

Reverse Legend   POSUI DEU ADIUTORE MEUM — I have made God my helper

Obverse   Front-facing bust of crowned king, rose to left, value XII to right; mintmark 'Y' or tun.

Reverse   Royal shield over long cross, mintmark 'Y' or tun.

E6SH-090	Poor £30	VG £60	F £100	VF £275

Philip & Mary (1554 – 1558)

No shillings were struck during Mary's brief reign; however, large quantities were produced between 1554 and 1558 when, after an Act of Parliament pronouncing that a woman was unfit to rule alone, Mary reigned jointly with her husband Philip of Spain. To indicate duel sovereignty and boost Philip's popularity, both their busts are found on the coins. All issues were struck at the Tower mint and many were dated.

Collecting Hints

Philip and Mary shillings are fairly rare, especially in Fine or better condition. They are usually found, undamaged but worn, in less than Fine condition and although coins in VF and EF exist, they are very expensive and desirable. Forgeries, primarily modern ones, exist for most issues and include coins dated 1554 below the obverse busts and others dated 1557. Collectors should take care to buy from a reputable source.

Spanish Title

Obverse Legend   PHILIP ET MARIA DG R ANG FR NEAP PR HISP — Philip and Mary by the grace of God King and Queen of England France and Naples Prince [and Princess] of Spain

Reverse Legend   POSUIMUS DEUM ADIUTOREM NOSTRUM — We have made God our helper

Obverse   Busts of Philip and Mary facing each other with large crown above.

Reverse   Oval royal shield with crown above which divides the mark of value.

PMSH-005	VG £90	F £240	VF £650

As previous, with no mark of value.

PMSH-010	VG £120	F £280	VF £800

As PMSH-005, but dated 1554 on the obverse.

PMSH-015	VG £90	F £240	VF £650

English Title

Obverse Legend   PHILIP ET MARIA DG REX ET REGINA ANGL — Philip and Mary by the grace of God King and Queen of the English

Reverse Legend   As previous, but mark of value on the reverse.

Obverse   As previous, dated 1554 or 1555.

Reverse   As previous.

PMSH-020	VG £120	F £280	VF £800

As previous, but without mark of value on the reverse. The issue dated 1555 is extremely rare.

PMSH-025	VG £120	F £280	VF £800

As previous, but date below bust 1554 or 1555. This coin is rarely found in better than VG condition.

PMSH-030	VG £400	F —	VF —

As previous, but without ANG in obverse legend, dated 1555.

PMSH-035	VG £450	F —	VF —

Elizabeth I   (1558 – 1603)

Although a large quantity of shillings were produced under Elizabeth, there was a twenty year break in production between 1562 and 1582, probably because originally sufficient numbers were in circulation from Edward VI, Philip and Mary and the Great Recoinage of 1560 – 62. Nevertheless, several varieties of hammered shilling were struck during the early part of the reign while milled shillings were also produced in the 1560s. All issues show a bust of the queen on the obverse and the royal shield over a cross on the reverse; they are undated and have no mark of value. However, they cannot be confused with other issues, because no other denomination is at all like the shilling in style and, most importantly, size. All issues have a mintmark on the obverse and reverse, found at the top of the coin at the beginning of the legends. And, since mintmarks were a form of quality control linking coins with dies, all Elizabeth I shillings can be dated very accurately with the help of the mints' records and historical data. The mintmark and the date struck are here listed with each issue.

First Issue (1559 – 1560)

> ## Collecting Hints
>
> This issue is, for some reason, always found very worn and is fairly rare especially in better than VG condition. These coins are usually scratched or damaged.

Obverse Legend   ELIZABET(H) DG ANG FRA(N) Z HIB REGINA — Elizabeth by the grace of God Queen of England France and Ireland

Reverse Legend   POSUI DEUM ADIVTOREM MEUM — I have made God my helper

Obverse   Crowned bust to left; mintmark lis. Wire-line inner circles.

Reverse   Royal shield over cross.

ELSH-005	VG £80	F £200	VF £500

As previous, but wire-line and beaded inner circles.

ELSH-010	VG £50	F £100	VF £450

Second Issue (1560 – 1561)

The main differences from the previous issue are the mintmarks and that the 'Z' in the obverse legend has been replaced by 'ET'. Both issues have large thin flans.

Collecting Hints

This is more common than the first issue but is again nearly always found in the lower grades, rarely clipped or deliberately damaged but nearly always worn. Coins in VF and EF condition are rare and desirable.

Obverse Legend ELIZABETH DG ANG FRA ET HIB REGINA — Elizabeth by the grace of God Queen of England France and Ireland

Reverse Legend POSUI DEU ADIUTOREM MEU(M) — I have made God my helper

Obverse Bust of queen; mintmark cross crosslet or martlet (both 1560 – 61).

Reverse Royal shield over long cross.

ELSH-015	VG £30	F £100	VF £275

Milled Coinage (1560 – 1561)

During Elizabeth's reign the Frenchman Eloye Mestrelle was commissioned to produce machine-made coins using horsepower. First made in 1561 at the Tower mint, these milled issues are the predecessors of our modern coins and were of fine quality, well struck and fully round. The smaller denominations tend to be rare because of the difficulty in making small milled coins. However, although superior in quality, the milled issues took longer to produce than the hammered ones. Furthermore, Mestrelle was

unpopular at the mint firstly because he was French and secondly because the workers who produced hammered coins feared that the new technique would make them redundant. The disputes and animosity between Mestrelle and his fellow workers eventually resulted in his dismissal in 1572 and six years later he was hanged for counterfeiting. Under Elizabeth, milled issues were last struck in 1571; they were not introduced again until Nicholas Briot's issues of the 1630s.

Shillings were among the denominations that Mestrelle produced at the Tower mint using horsepower, but it is thought they were only made in 1560 – 61, alongside the hammered issue. All milled issues have the mintmark star on both sides and are very different in style to the hammered.

Collecting Hints

Most milled shillings appear to have been weakly struck, especially when compared to the sixpence. The obverse in particular is very weak and this is probably due to the striking techniques and the thickness of the silver. Coins are usually found in less than Fine condition and those in VF and EF are rare and desirable. Shillings, like sixpences, are often found gilded and it appears that they were popular as jewellery pieces. Milled shillings are rarely found clipped.

The diameter of the coin is over 31 mm.

Obverse Legend ELIZABETH D.G. ANG FRA ET HIB REGINA — Elizabeth by the grace of God Queen of England France and Ireland

Reverse Legend POSUI DEUM ADIVTOREM MEUM — I have made God my helper

Obverse Bust of queen with plain dress; mintmark star.

Reverse Royal arms over long cross.

ELSH-020	VG £175	F £350	VF £800

As previous, but the queen's dress is decorated.

ELSH-025	VG £100	F £200	VF £650

As previous, but the diameter of the coin is 30 – 31mm.

ELSH-030	VG £75	F £150	VF £400

As previous, but the diameter of the coin is under 30 mm.

ELSH-035	VG £75	F £150	VF £400

Fifth Issue (1582 – 1600)

The fifth and sixth issues are by far the most common of Elizabeth's shillings and, with a new portrait and different obverse legend, the whole style of the coin was changed. The two issues can be distinguished by the different mintmarks which are once more found on both sides of the coin. Varieties of bust exist.

Collecting Hints

The fifth issue is fairly easy to obtain, especially in VG to Fine condition; VF and EF examples exist but are quite rare. The coins are rarely found clipped or damaged and collectors should try to obtain one with a reasonable portrait and clear mintmark.

Obverse Legend ELIZAB DG ANG FR ET HIB REGI — Elizabeth by the grace of God Queen of England France and Ireland

Reverse Legend POSUI DEU ADIVTOREM MEU — I have made God my helper

Obverse Bust of queen. Minor varieties of bust exist.

Reverse Royal shield over long cross.

Mintmark Bell (1582 – 83), 'A' (1582 – 84), escallop (1584 – 86), crescent (1587 – 89), hand (1590 – 92), tun (1592 – 95), woolpack (1594 – 96), key (1595 – 98), anchor (1597 – 1600) or cypher (1600).

| ELSH-040 | VG £25 | F £55 | VF £150 |

Sixth Issue (1601 – 1602)

This issue is virtually identical to the previous one except for the mintmarks and a very small reduction in the weight of the coins.

Collecting Hints

The 'Collecting Hints' are the same as for the previous issue except that the sixth is slightly scarcer.

As previous, but mintmark '1' (1601) or '2' (1602).

| ELSH-045 | VG £30 | F £70 | VF £160 |

James I (1603 – 1625)

By the early seventeenth century, the shilling was established as an important denomination. All James I's issues are undated and have the bust of the king with the denomination behind on the obverse and the royal arms on the reverse. The various issues can be distinguished by the reverse legend, the mintmark at the beginning of the obverse and reverse legends, as well as by the style of the bust. However, should the bust be difficult to identify, some mintmarks are specific to particular issues and may be used to identify a coin. One scarce issue also has a large plume above the reverse shield. It should be noted that several Scottish issues, produced during the reigns of James VI and Charles I, are fairly similar to James I's English shillings, except for differences in the royal shield and, sometimes, the legends. However, should a coin have a large harp on the reverse only, it is an Irish issue.

Collecting Hints

Most James I shillings are fairly common and usually found in less than Fine condition, often with a very worn portrait. Although collectors should have little difficulty obtaining an example in Fine or VF, EF specimens are rare and desirable. Shillings are rarely clipped but often found with deliberate scratches on them for which there does not seem to be a plausible explanation. Because of the quality of the strike, the reverse of the coin is usually in better condition than the obverse.

First Coinage (1603 – 1604)

Obverse Legend IACOBUS DG. ANG SCO FRA ET HIB REX — James by the grace of God King of England Scotland France and Ireland

Reverse Legend EXURGAT DEUS DISSIPENTUR INIMICI — Let God arise and His enemies be scattered

Obverse Bust of the king with square-cut beard; mintmark thistle.

Reverse Royal arms.

| J1SH-005 | VG £30 | F £65 | VF £250 |

As previous, but the king's beard merges with his collar; mintmark thistle or lis.

| J1SH-010 | VG £28 | F £60 | VF £220 |

Second Coinage (1604 – 1619)

This issue can be easily differentiated from the first coinage by the reverse legend.

Obverse Legend IACOBUS MAG BRI(T) FRA ET HIB REX — James King of England France and Ireland

Reverse Legend QUAE DEUS CONIUNXIT NEMO SEPARET — What God hath joined together let no man put asunder

Obverse Bust of king with projecting, square-cut beard; mintmark lis (1604 – 05) or rose (1604 – 06).

Reverse As previous.

| J1SH-015 | VG £25 | F £55 | VF £180 |

Obverse As previous, but the king's hair is brushed forward and his armour is plainer; mintmark rose (1605 – 06), escallop (1606 – 07), grapes (1607), coronet (1607 – 09).

Reverse As previous.

| J1SH-020 | VG £25 | F £55 | VF £180 |

Obverse As previous, but slightly larger bust with longer hair brushed back; mintmarks coronet (1607 – 09), key (1609 – 10), mullet (1611 – 12), tower (1612 – 13), trefoil (1613), tun (1613 – 15), closed book (1615 – 16), plain cross (1617 – 18), cinquefoil (1613 – 15).

Reverse As previous.

| J1SH-025 | VG £25 | F £55 | VF £180 |

Third Coinage (1619 – 1625)

Legends As previous.

Obverse Bust of king with long, very curly hair; mintmarks spur rowel (1619 – 20), rose (1620 – 21), thistle (1621 – 23), lis (1623 – 24), trefoil (1624)

Reverse Royal arms in shield.

| J1SH-030 | VG £25 | F £55 | VF £180 |

As previous, but plume over shield on reverse; mintmark thistle (1621 – 23), lis (1623 – 24), trefoil (1624).

| J1SH-035 | VG £30 | F £80 | VF £300 |

Charles I (1625 – 1649)

Shillings were struck in large quantities and many varieties and styles during the reign of Charles I. The majority were produced at the Tower mint in London and have the king's portrait with the denomination (XII for twelve pence or shilling) behind on the obverse, the royal shield on the reverse and a mintmark at the beginning of the obverse and reverse legends. However, provincial mints were also active, especially during the Civil War when they produced money for the royal troops. Also, shillings were among the coins struck by royalists in besieged towns like Newark. These siege pieces are crude issues without a portrait and were produced, usually out of silver plate, to pay the troops defending the town from Cromwell's army. Although the denomination itself cannot be confused with any other because of the Roman numerals XII behind the king's bust, it is often only small marks and slightly different styles that differentiate the many issues of this reign. When identifying a coin, collectors should refer to the more common Tower mint issues first and bear in mind that mintmarks are in many cases specific to particular issues; also, collectors might also want to refer to the hammered issues of Charles II.

Tower Mint (1625 – 1648)

The issues of the Tower mint in London may be subdivided into the hammered issue struck under royal authority, the hammered issue struck under Parliament and Briot's distinctive milled issue. The Parliament issue is clearly distinguished by a different style bust and specific mintmarks while Briot's milled coins are superb in design and detail, and easily identified by their distinctive style.

Tower Mint under King (1625 – 1642)

Huge quantities of coins were produced at the Tower mint during this period and they have many styles and varieties, which we have listed. However many issues, due either to poor striking or clipping, have irregular sized flans and illegible or even non-existent legends.

Collecting Hints

Most issues are fairly common and usually found in about Fine condition; although VF and EF examples exist they are often on poor flans. Coins with full round flans and legible legends are much more desirable and collectors should also try to obtain a specimen with a good portrait and clear mintmark. Contemporary forgeries of some of the Tower mint issues exist, especially of the later classes. They can usually be identified by the coin's silver plating flaking off to reveal the copper or brass core underneath. These issues are also rather crude in style and judging by their condition were obviously in circulation for some time. The weights of the early issues varied, but all weights and issues were official.

The following line-drawings, from B.R. Osborne's archive on

Charles I, depict the numerous styles of bust with the corresponding classes to which they relate. It is important to remember that, with the number of dies being used, varieties exist.

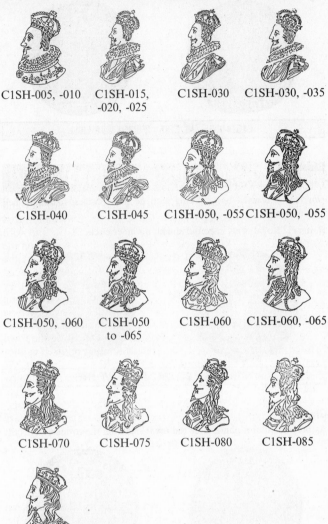

C1SH-005, -010	C1SH-015, -020, -025	C1SH-030	C1SH-030, -035
C1SH-040	C1SH-045	C1SH-050, -055	C1SH-050, -055
C1SH-050, -060	C1SH-050 to -065	C1SH-060	C1SH-060, -065
C1SH-070	C1SH-075	C1SH-080	C1SH-085

C1SH-090

Class 1

Obverse Legend CAROLUS DG. MAG BRIT FRA ET HIB REX — Charles by the grace of God King of Great Britain France and Ireland

Reverse Legend CHRISTO AUSPICE REGNO — I reign under the auspices of Christ

Obverse Crowned bust of king wearing ruff with value behind; mintmark lis or cross calvary.

Reverse Royal shield with square top over a cross.

C1SH-005	VG £30	F £60	VF £120

Class 1B

As previous, but of the lightweight issue at 81.5 grains (5.3 grams); mintmark cross calvary. All issues should weigh over 90 grains (5.8 grams).

C1SH-010	VG —	F £80	VF £200

Class 1C

As C1SH-005, but the ruff and the armour are concealed by a scarf; mintmark cross calvary, castle, blackmoor's head.

C1SH-015	VG £25	F £50	VF £100

Class 1D

As C1SH-005, but plume over shield on the reverse, no cross on the reverse; mintmark lis, cross calvary.

C1SH-020	VG £150	F £350	VF £750

Class 1E

As C1SH-015, but of the lightweight issue at 81.5 grains (5.3 grams); mintmark cross calvary. All issues should weigh over 90 grains (5.8 grams).

C1SH-025	VG —	F £120	VF £275

Class 1F

As C1SH-015, but plume over shield with no cross on the reverse; mintmark cross calvary, blackamoor's head, castle, anchor, heart, plume.

C1SH-030	VG £30	F £60	VF £100

Class 1G

As previous, but with cross over the shield on the reverse; mintmark blackamoor's head.

C1SH-035	VG £200	F £400

Class 2

Obverse Legend   CAROLUS D.G. MA(G) BRI(T) FR ET HIB REX (varieties exist) — Charles by the grace of God King of Great Britain France and Ireland

Reverse Legend   CHRISTO AUSPICE REGNO — I reign under the auspices of Christ

Obverse   Bust of king wearing ruff with more armour visible; mintmark plume or rose.

Reverse   Oval royal shield, with 'C.R.' (CAROLUS REX) above.

| C1SH-040 | VG £25 | F £45 | VF £90 |

Class 2A

As previous, but plume over shield on reverse dividing the 'C' and 'R'; mintmark plume or rose.

| C1SH-045 | VG £60 | F £120 | VF £250 |

Class 3

Obverse Legend   CAROLUS D.G. MA(G) BR(IT) FR(A) ET HIB REX (many varieties exist) — Charles by the grace of God King of Great Britain France and Ireland

Reverse Legend   CHRISTO AUSPICE REGNO — I reign under the auspices of Christ

Obverse   Crowned bust of king with lace collar; mintmark harp or portcullis.

Reverse   Royal arms in oval shield which divides 'C.R.'.

| C1SH-050 | VG £20 | F £40 | VF £90 |

Class 3A

As previous, but a plume over the shield on the reverse; mintmark harp.

| C1SH-055 | VG £175 | F £350 | VF £800 |

Class 3B

Legends   As previous.

Obverse   Crowned bust of king with no inner circles; mintmark bell, crown or tun.

Reverse   Royal arms in round shield, no inner circle.

| C1SH-060 | VG £20 | F £40 | VF £90 |

Class 3C

As previous, but a plume over the royal shield on the reverse.

| C1SH-065 | VG £30 | F £80 | VF £200 |

Class 4

This issue has a bust similar in style to that produced at the Aberystwyth mint but it has a different mintmark.

Obverse Legend   CAROLUS DG MA(G) BR(IT) FR(A) ET HI(B) REX (many varieties exist) — Charles by the grace of God King of Great Britain France and Ireland

Reverse Legend   CHRISTO AUSPICE REGNO — I reign under the auspices of Christ

Obverse   Large Aberystwyth-style bust of king with small value (XII) behind the bust; mintmark tun.

Reverse   Square-topped shield over cross.

| C1SH-070 | VG £30 | F £65 | VF £130 |

Class 4A

As previous, but the king has rounder shoulders and the denomination (XII) is larger than in the previous issue; mintmark anchor or triangle.

C1SH-075	VG £25	F £40	VF £80

Class 4B

As previous, but the bust is smaller, the king is wearing a double-arched crown, small denomination (XII) behind bust; mintmark tun.

C1SH-080	VG £25	F £45	VF £95

Class 4C

As previous, but single-arched crown and large denomination behind bust; mintmark tun, anchor or triangle.

C1SH-085	VG £25	F £45	VF £95

Class 4D

As previous, but an older-style bust with a very pointed beard; mintmark star, anchor, triangle or triangle in circle. This issue is often struck on flans of irregular size.

C1SH-090	VG £25	F £45	VF £100

Tower Mint under Parliament (1642 – 1648)

When London came under the control of Parliament during the Civil War, the shillings produced at the Tower mint were very similar in style to those previously struck under the king and it is interesting to note that the king's portrait, heraldic arms and royal inscription continued to be on the coins. Still, these issues can easily be identified by their unique mintmarks. It would, however, appear from the striking of many issues that little care was taken in producing these coins, which are often badly struck on irregular shaped pieces of metal. Because of the great similarity with the previous Tower mint issues, classes are numbered consecutively.

The following line-drawings, from B.R. Osborne's archive on Charles I, depict the numerous styles of bust with the corresponding classes to which they relate. It is important to remember that, with the number of dies being used, varieties exist.

C1SH-095	C1SH-100	C1SH-105	C1SH-105

Class 4E

Obverse Legend CAROLUS DG MAG BRI FRA ET HIB REX — Charles by the grace of God King of Great Britain France and Ireland

Reverse Legend CHRISTO AUSPICE REGNO — I reign under the auspices of Christ

Obverse Crowned bust of king with pointed beard and value behind; mintmark '(P)', '(R)', eye, sun.

Reverse Royal arms in square-topped shield over small cross.

C1SH-095	VG £30	F £60	VF £140

Class 4F

As previous, but long narrow bust; mintmark sun, sceptre.

C1SH-100	VG £32	F £60	VF £140

Class 4G

As previous, but short, broad older bust; mintmark sceptre. Varieties of king's crown exist.

C1SH-105	VG £32	F £65	VF £150

Briot's Coinage (1631 – 1639)

Milled Issues

These issues were milled producing a coin of better quality and are easily identifiable in both style and production. Furthermore the mintmark, which is similar to some issues, is nonetheless unique.

Collecting Hints

Without doubt, these issues are superb in quality, style and production. Usually available in Fine and VF condition, they were struck on full round flans with clear legible legends. Both issues are fairly scarce and, because of their style and production, very desirable.

First Milled Issue (1631 – 1632)

Obverse Legend CAROLUS DG. MAGN BRITANN FRAN ET HIB REX — Charles by the grace of God King of Great Britain France and Ireland

Reverse Legend CHRISTO AUSPICE REGNO — I reign under the auspices of Christ (the legend sometimes begins at the bottom of the coin)

Obverse Crowned bust of king with pointed beard and wearing a lace collar, value (XII) behind bust; mintmark flower and B/B.

Reverse Royal arms in square-topped shield over cross.

| C1SH-110 | VG £90 | F £175 | VF £450 |

Second Milled Issue (1638 – 1639)

Obverse As previous, with the king's bust and clothing of slightly different style and minor differences in legend; mintmark anchor and 'B' and anchor.

Reverse As previous, but the cross over the shield is smaller and does not extend across the flan.

| C1SH-115 | VG £60 | F £140 | VF £300 |

Hammered Issue (1635 – 1639)

This very rare hammered issue is virtually identical to the milled. There is uncertainty as to why it was made at all but evidence suggests that, while Briot's dies were used, the production was not actually under his control. Collectors should pay particular attention to the mintmark and obverse bust so as to avoid confusing this issue with the more common Tower mint ones that also use mintmark triangle.

Collecting Hints

This issue is very rare in any grade and collectors might have great difficulty obtaining an example.

Legends As previous.

Obverse As previous; mintmark anchor, triangle over anchor.

Reverse Several varieties exist. Square-topped shield over cross; sometimes mintmark triangle (Tower mint Class 4 die).

| C1SH-120 | VG £200 | F £500 |

Provincial Mints

York Mint (1643 – 1644)

Although there is considerable uncertainty regarding when the York mint was opened, it is thought that it became active in early 1642 and ceased production after the royalist defeat at Marston Moor in July 1644. The dies, which were probably styled or made by Nicholas Briot, were sent to York from London at the beginning of the Civil War but were captured by the Roundheads for a time. The York issues were not hammered but machine-struck on a rotary press and punched out by a mechanical cutter; this resulted in many coins being slightly bent. The issue is easily identified by the mintmark lion at the beginning of the obverse and reverse legend, while some issues also bear the word EBOR (for EBORACUM, York's Latin name) above or below the royal shield. It is important to note that several very minor varieties of the bust exist.

Collecting Hints

Struck for only two years, this issue is scarce but obtainable and usually available unclipped but creased in about Fine condition. Coins in VF condition exist due mainly to the good quality of strike, and while rare are available.

Obverse Legend CAROLUS D G. MAG BRI FRA ET HIB REX (minor varieties exist) — Charles by the grace of God King of Great Britain France and Ireland

Reverse Legend CHRISTO AUSPICE REGNO — I reign under the auspices of Christ

Obverse Crowned bust of king, value behind; mintmark lion.

Reverse EBOR over square-topped shield of the royal arms.

| C1SH-125 | VG £70 | F £150 | VF £350 |

As previous, but the bust is coarse in style and the armour plain.

C1SH-130	VG £75	F £160	VF £375

Obverse As C1SH-125.

Reverse EBOR below an oval shield of the royal arms.

Obverse Legend CAROLUS DG. MA(G) BR FR ET HI REX — Charles by the grace of God King of Great Britain France and Ireland

Reverse Legend CHRISTO AUSPICE REGNO — I reign under the auspices of Christ

Obverse Bust with large lace collar, plume before face and small XII behind bust, no inner circle; mintmark book.

Reverse Oval shield of royal arms with plume above, no inner circle.

C1SH-135	VG £75	F £160	VF £375

C1SH-150	VG £100	F £250	VF £550

As previous, but a crown over an oval shield.

As previous, but with inner circle on the reverse.

C1SH-140	VG £70	F £150	VF £350

C1SH-155	VG £80	F £200	VF £500

As previous, but the royal shield has lion-skin garniture around the edges.

C1SH-145	VG £70	F £150	VF £350

As C1SH-150, but large XII behind bust and inner circles on both sides of the coin.

Aberystwyth Mint (1638 – 1642)

The various varieties of this scarce issue can easily be identified by the mintmark book at the beginning of the obverse and reverse legend; also, a plume can be found both in front of the king's face and above the royal shield. When identifying a coin, collectors should refer to the Shrewsbury issues as well, because the obverse Aberystwyth die was sometimes used at Shrewsbury.

C1SH-160	VG £80	F £200	VF £500

As previous, but a smaller bust with a more rounded lace collar.

C1SH-165	VG £80	F £200	VF £500

Obverse   Briot's older bust similar to Tower mint class 4D, but single arched crown with a plume in front of the king's face. This obverse die was also used at the Shrewsbury mint but with a totally different reverse.

Reverse   Plume over oval shield.

C1SH-170	VG £100	F £250	VF £600

Aberystwyth Furnace Mint (1648 – 1649)

In 1648, at the end of the Civil War, Edmund Goore took control of the Welsh silver mines and, because Aberystwyth Castle had been badly damaged, the mint was moved to the silver mills. Although no accounts survive regarding the number of coins struck, it appears that very few were and the mint was closed in 1649. This extremely rare issue is similar to the Aberystwyth mint except for the mintmark crown, which is found on both sides of the coin, and the fact that the plume in front of the king's face is much smaller.

Collecting Hints

This issue is extremely rare in any grade and collectors may have great difficulty obtaining an example.

Obverse Legend   CAROLUS D G MAG BRI FRA ET HIB REX — Charles by the grace of God King of Great Britain France and Ireland

Reverse Legend   CHRISTO AUSPICE REGNO — I reign under the auspices of Christ

Obverse   Crowned bust of king with value behind and plume in front of face; mintmark crown.

Reverse   Plume over oval shield of royal arms.

C1SH-175	ex. rare

Shrewsbury Mint (1642)

This rare issue had two different obverse dies; one is from the Aberystwyth shilling with the mintmark book and the plume in front of the king's face and the other is Shrewsbury mint's own crude issue with the mintmark plume at the beginning of the obverse legend. In both cases the reverse has the Declaration on three lines, the date 1642 below and three plumes above the Declaration. Collectors should note that the second Shrewsbury die was also used for an Oxford issue.

Collecting Hints

Both these coins are rare and difficult to obtain in better than Fine condition. The Shrewsbury die issue in particular is usually found in less than Fine condition, due to rather inferior dies.

Obverse Legend   CAROLUS DG MAG BRIT FRA ET HI REX — Charles by the grace of God King of Great Britain France and Ireland

Outer Reverse Legend   EXURGAT DEUS DISSIPENTUR INIMICI — Let God arise and His enemies be scattered

Inner Reverse Legend   RELIG PROT LEG ANG LIB PAR — The religion of the Protestants the laws of England the liberty of Parliament

Obverse   Bust of king, value behind, plume in front of face; mintmark book (Aberystwyth die).

Reverse   Three plumes over the Declaration in three lines, date 1642 below.

C1SH-180	VG £250	F £600

Obverse Legend   CAROLUS D.G. MAG BR FR ET HIB REX — Charles by the grace of God King of Great Britain France and Ireland

Reverse Legends   As previous.

Obverse   Crude bust of king with denomination behind (XII); mintmark plume.

Reverse   As previous.

C1SH-185	VG £300	F £650

Oxford Mint (1642 – 1646)

There are many varieties of this scarce issue. The first variety used the second Shrewsbury obverse die (C1SH-185) but a less crudely styled, Oxford reverse die. In particular, note the differences in the three plumes on the reverse which easily differentiate the two mints. All the other issues were struck using Oxford dies. However, collectors should note that the obverse Oxford die was also used at the Bristol mint. Most Oxford issues may be easily identified by the abbreviation 'OX' found below the date on the reverse.

Collecting Hints

Even though this issue is scarce it is obtainable, especially in the lower grades; many specimens are weakly struck and bent. Coins in VF and EF condition are rare and desirable.

Shrewsbury Obverse Die

Obverse Legend   CAROLUS D.G. MAG BR FR ET HIB REX — Charles by the grace of God King of Great Britain France and Ireland

Outer Reverse Legend   EXURGAT DEUS DISSIPENTUR INIMICI — Let God arise and His enemies be scattered

Inner Reverse Legend   RELIG PROT LEG ANG LIBER PAR — The religion of the Protestants the laws of England the liberty of Parliament

Obverse   Crowned bust of king with value behind; mintmark plume.

Reverse   Three plumes over the Declaration, 1642 below.

C1SH-190	VG £60	F £140	VF £300

Oxford Dies

Obverse Legend   As previous, but varieties exist, especially in the spelling of the Irish title.

Reverse Legends   As previous.

Obverse   Small crowned bust of king with value behind; mintmark plume.

Reverse   As previous, dated 1642 or 1643.

C1SH-195	VG £80	F £170	VF £400

As previous, but coarser style of bust, dated 1643.

C1SH-200	VG £80	F £170	VF £400

As previous, but large bust of fine work, dated 1643.

C1SH-205	VG £80	F £170	VF £400

As previous, but 'OX' below the date on the reverse, dated 1644 or 1646.

C1SH-210	VG £85	F £180	VF £400

As previous, but bust with bent crown, no 'OX' on reverse and dated 1643.

C1SH-215	VG £85	F £180	VF £400

As previous, with 'OX' below date, 1644 which sometimes reads 1044 in error.

C1SH-220	VG £85	F £180	VF £400

Rawlins Issue

This issue used Rawlins' dies and can easily be identified by the 'R' on the truncation of the king's bust.

Obverse   As previous, but with an 'R' on the truncation.

Reverse   Dated 1644, no 'OX' below date.

C1SH-225	VG £125	F £275	VF £700

As previous, but 'OX' below date and Declaration framed in scrolls.

C1SH-230	VG £125	F £300	VF £650

Bristol Mint (1643 – 1645)

Bristol was an important seaport and soon after it became a royalist stronghold in July 1643, Thomas Bushell established a mint there using silver from the various Welsh mines. Cromwell's forces took the city in August 1645. The Bristol issues are quite similar to the Oxford ones except that many have a plume in front of the king's face and a 'BR' below the date on the reverse; moreover, the size of the date on the reverse is different, fairly large on Oxford issues and small and neat on Bristol ones. Most Bristol issues bear the mintmark plume at the beginning of the obverse legend and this, along with the reverse design, serves to distinguish them from the Aberystwyth issues that also have a plume in front of the face.

Collecting Hints

While all Bristol mint denominations are scarce, the shilling is probably the least so and coins are usually found in about Fine condition on full unclipped flans, sometimes creased. They are difficult to obtain in VF or EF condition, but collectors should not have too much difficulty finding the lower grades.

Obverse Legend   CAROLUS DG MAG BR FR ET HIB REX — Charles by the grace of God King of Great Britain France and Ireland

Outer Reverse Legend   EXURGAT DEUS DISSIPENTUR INIMICI — Let God arise and His enemies be scattered

Inner Reverse Legend   RELIG PRO LEG ANG LIB PAR — The religion of the Protestants the laws of England the liberty of Parliament

Obverse   Crowned bust of king with value behind; mintmark plume. This is an Oxford die.

Reverse   Three plumes of the same size and level over the Declaration, the date 1643 below. The only difference from the Oxford reverse is in the size and spacing of the plumes.

C1SH-235   VG £65   F £175   VF £400

Obverse   As previous, using the Oxford obverse die.

Reverse   New reverse with mintmark 'BR' in the legend; dated 1643 or 1644.

C1SH-240   VG £60   F £175   VF £400

Obverse   As C1SH-235, but Oxford(?) bust of crude style. There is uncertainty whether this is a Bristol or Oxford obverse die.

Reverse   As C1SH-235.

C1SH-245   VG £70   F £200   VF £450

Obverse   As previous.

Reverse   As C1SH-240, with 'BR' below date, dated 1644.

C1SH-250   VG £60   F £175   F £400

Legends   As previous.

Obverse   Crowned bust of king of good style, small plume in front of face; no mintmark in legend.

Reverse   The Declaration with three plumes above and dated 1644 or 1645; mintmark 'BR' in the legend.

C1SH-255   VG £65   F £190   VF £425

As previous, but with 'BR' below the date instead of in the reverse legend; dated 1644.

C1SH-260   VG £70   F £200   VF £425

As previous, but the king is wearing a round collar; 'BR' on its side below the date; dated 1644 – 45.

C1SH-265   F £70   F £200   VF £425

As previous, but the king is wearing a square collar; 'BR' in the reverse legend, dated 1645.

C1SH-270   VG £75   F £220   VF £450

Late Declaration Issues (1645 – 1646)

With documentary evidence scarce, very little is known about these issues which were thought to have been struck in Lundy Island, Appledore, Barnstaple or Bideford. However, recent research suggests that coins marked 'A' may have been struck in Ashby de la Zouch and those marked 'B' or with plumes in Bridgnorth-on-Severn. These mints were active in 1645 and 1646 and, with dies easy to transport, it is possible that the mint could have been moved either for safety or to produce urgently needed coinage in an area. These rare issues can easily be distinguished from those of Oxford or Bristol; they are the only ones to bear the date 1646 while the coins dated 1645 also bear the mintmark A in the reverse legend and an 'A' below the date.

Collecting Hints

These issues are all very rare, particularly those dated 1645. When available, they are usually in Fine condition and often of rather crude style and striking. Collectors may well have difficulty obtaining a specimen.

Obverse Legend CAROLUS DG MAG BR FR ET HIB REX — Charles by the grace of God King of Great Britain France and Ireland

Outer Reverse Legend EXURGAT DEUS DISSIPENTUR INIMICI — Let God arise and His enemies be scattered

Inner Reverse Legend REL PRO LEG ANG LIB PAR — The religion of the Protestants the laws of England the liberty of Parliament

Obverse Crowned bust of king, value behind and mintmark plume.

Reverse Mintmark 'A' in legend at the top of the coin; three plumes over the Declaration, dated 1645 with an 'A' below the date.

| C1SH-275 | VG £200 | F £400 | VF £1,100 |

As previous, but small plume before the king's face.

| C1SH-280 | VG £200 | F £400 | VF £1,100 |

As previous, but scroll above Declaration on reverse, dated 1646.

| C1SH-285 | VG £120 | F £300 | VF £700 |

As previous, but larger plume in front of face; the reverse has mintmark pellet and is dated 1646.

| C1SH-290 | VG £100 | F £250 | VF £600 |

Truro Mint

All issues from the Truro mint have mintmark rose and although some Exeter as well as some of the common Tower issues also use the same mintmark, they are different in style and design.

Collecting Hints

All Truro shillings are extremely rare. Several Exeter issues used to be classed under Truro.

Obverse Legend CAROLUS DG MAG BR FRA ET HI REX (varieties exist) — Charles by the grace of God King of Great Britain France and Ireland

Reverse Legend CHRISTO AUSPICE REGNO — I reign under the auspices of Christ

Obverse Small crowned bust of king with value behind; mintmark rose.

Reverse Royal arms in an oblong shield; mintmark rose.

| C1SH-295 | ex. rare |

Exeter Mint (1643 – 1646)

The third issue from the Exeter mint is quite similar to the ones from Truro and also uses the mintmark rose but is distinguished by the reverse. There is, however, another rarer Exeter issue with a reverse Declaration similar to that of Oxford and Bristol issues and it is probable that this reverse die actually came from the Oxford mint; but as the obverse has the rose mintmark, the issue can easily be differentiated. Several of these issues used to be classed under Truro.

Collecting Hints

Both issues are rare, in particular the Declaration type which is very rare. When available, coins are usually found in about Fine condition.

Obverse Legend CAROLUS D.G. MA BRI FRA ET HI REX — Charles by the grace of God King of Great Britain France and Ireland

Reverse Legend CHRISTO AUSPICE REGNO 1644 — I reign under the auspices of Christ 1644

Obverse Crowned bust of king with value behind; mintmark rose.

Reverse Round garnished shield, date in legend; mintmark rose.

| C1SH-300 | VG £275 | F £700 | VF rare |

As previous, but oval shield dividing 'C.R'.

| C1SH-305 | VG £275 | F £700 | VF rare |

Obverse   Larger bust of king with lank hair, value behind; mintmark rose.

Reverse   As previous.

| C1SH-310 | VG £250 | F £650 | VF rare |

Obverse   As previous.

Reverse   Royal arms in round shield surrounded by eight scrolls.

| C1SH-315 | VG £300 | F £700 | VF rare |

As previous, but only six scrolls around shield.

| C1SH-320 | VG £200 | F £500 | VF rare |

Obverse Legend   CAROLUS DG MA BR FRA ET HI REX — Charles by the grace of God King of Great Britain France and Ireland

Reverse Legend   CHRISTO AUSPICE REGNO — I reign under the auspices of Christ

Obverse   Bust of king with value behind; mintmark rose.

Reverse   Round shield with six scrolls, dated 1644 or 1645; mintmark rose, often splitting the date.

| C1SH-325 | VG £100 | F £250 | VF £550 |

Declaration Type

Obverse Legend   As previous.

Outer Reverse Legend   EXURGAT DEUS DISSIPENTUR INIMICI — Let God arise and His enemies be scattered

Inner Reverse Legend   RELIG PRO LEG ANG LIB PAR — The religion of the Protestants the laws of England the liberty of Parliament

Obverse   As previous.

Reverse   Three plumes above the Declaration, dated 1645; no mintmark.

| C1SH-330 | VG £250 | F £650 |

Worcester or Shrewsbury Mint

This issue is very easy to recognise by the very crude style of the design. It was probably made in a considerable hurry and little attention has been paid to the quality of dies or the striking. It should be noted that because the issues of this mint are so rare and in such poor condition, additional mintmarks might exist which we have not listed.

Collecting Hints

All issues are extremely rare and difficult to obtain in any grade.

Obverse Legend   CAROLUS DG MAG BRIT FR ET HI REX (varieties exist) — Charles by the grace of God King of Great Britain France and Ireland

Reverse Legend   CHRISTO AUSPICE REGNO — I reign under the auspices of Christ

Obverse   Bust of king to left; mintmark castle.

Reverse   Square-topped shield.

| C1SH-335 | VG £225 | F £600 | VF rare |

As previous, but 'C.R' above shield on reverse; mintmark helmet or pear.

| C1SH-340 | VG £225 | F £600 | VF rare |

As previous, but oval shield on reverse with no 'C.R'; mintmark lion, pear.

| C1SH-345 | VG £200 | F £550 | VF rare |

Legends   As previous.

Obverse   As C1SH-335, but an even cruder copy; mintmark boar's head, helmet.

Reverse   As C1SH-335, but cruder in style.

| C1SH-350 | VG £250 | F £650 | VF rare |

As previous, but 'CR' above the royal shield on the reverse.

| C1SH-355 | VG £250 | F £650 | VF rare |

As previous, but an oval shield on the reverse; mintmark lis.

| C1SH-360 | VG £225 | F £600 | VF rare |

As previous, but a round shield on the reverse; mintmark bird, lis.

| C1SH-365 | VG £250 | F £600 | VF rare |

Obverse   Bust to right, value behind king's head; mintmark pear.
Reverse   Oval shield dividing 'CR', rose and lis in legends.

| C1SH-370 | ex. rare |

Chester Mint (1644)

This extremely rare issue can be differentiated by its unique mint-mark three pellets, found on the obverse.

Collecting Hints

This issue is extremely rare in any grade, and collectors may have great difficulty obtaining an example in any condition.

Obverse Legend   CAROLUS DG. [uncertain] REX — Charles by the grace of God King [of Great Britain France and Ireland]. The only example that we have seen had an unclear legend.

Reverse Legend   CHRISTO AUSPICE REGNO — I reign under the auspices of Christ

Obverse   Crowned bust of king with value behind; mintmark triangle of pellets.

Reverse   Crowned oval shield.

| C1SH-375 | ex. rare |

As previous, but square shield over long cross on reverse.

| C1SH-380 | ex. rare |

As previous, but shield without cross.

| C1SH-385 | ex. rare |

Siege Issues
Carlisle (1644 – 1645)

These extremely rare issues are round in shape.

Collecting Hints

Rarely found in better than Fine condition, coins are some-times damaged and collectors may have great difficulty obtaining an example.

Obverse   Crown above 'C.R'; denomination XII below.
Reverse   OBS CARL 1645 — Siege Carlisle 1645; on three lines.

| C1SH-390 | VG £800 | F £2,200 | VF £5,000 |

As previous, but the reverse legend and date are on two lines.

| C1SH-395 | VG £800 | F £2,500 | VF £5,500 |

As C1SH-395, but struck on octagonal flan.

| C1SH-397 | ex. rare |

Newark (1645 – 1646)

Newark was besieged several times between 1645 and 1646 and finally surrendered to Cromwell's army in May 1646. The shillings are easily identified by the value XII below the crown on the obverse.

Collecting Hints

Shillings can be found in most grades with even VF spec-imens being obtainable. Many coins are found gilded, but this does not greatly detract from their value because the gilding comes from the original plate from which the coins were made.

Obverse   Flat-shaped crown dividing 'C.R' and denomination below.
Reverse   OBS NEWARKE 1645 on three lines.

| C1SH-400 | VG £300 | F £700 | VF £1,500 |

As previous, but high-arched crown.

| C1SH-405 | VG £270 | F £500 | VF £1,000 |

| C1SH-415 | VG £625 | F £1,000 | VF £2,500 |

As previous, but NEWARK omits last 'E'; dated 1645 or 1646.

| C1SH-410 | VG £260 | F £500 | VF £900 |

As previous, but no sword and 'P.C' on reverse divided by the value XII.

| C1SH-420 | VG £625 | F £1,000 | VF £2,500 |

As C1SH-415, but octagonal.

| C1SH-422 | VG £625 | F £1,200 | VF £3,000 |

As previous, but the 'R' on the obverse is reversed.

| C1SH-412 | VG £260 | F £500 | VF £900 |

As C1SH-420, but octagnal.

| C1SH-423 | VG £625 | F £1,200 | VF £3,000 |

Pontefract (1648 – 1649)

Pontefract, besieged from June 1648 to January 1649, was the last town to fall to Cromwell's troops. These rare issues can be found on flans of varying shapes but all have a crowned 'C.R' on the obverse and a castle gateway on the reverse. Most Pontefract issues do not bear a denomination, but as they weigh about the same as a shilling, it is presumed that this is what they were. Nevertheless, the weight of each coin varies, probably due to the haste in which they were produced. The last two issues were struck after the execution of Charles I and bear the name of his son, Charles II. Round issues are coins that have been cut down.

Obverse   As previous, but octagonal.

Reverse   CAROLUS SECUNDUS — Charles II and 1648 around castle gateway with flag flying.

| C1SH-425 | VG £600 | F £1,200 | VF £3,000 |

Collecting Hints

These issues are rare and difficult to obtain in any grade; collectors should be aware of forgeries in this series. These issues were made in a variety of shapes.

This issue is diamond shaped.

Obverse   DUM SPIRO SPERO — Whilst I live I hope (around 'C.R' crowned).

Reverse   Castle surrounded by OBS, 'P.C.', sword and 1648.

Obverse Outer Legend   CAROL II DG MAG BR H REX — Charles II by the grace of God King of Great Britain Ireland

Obverse Centre Legend   HANC DEUS DEDIT — God has given this (i.e. the crown)

Reverse Legend   POST MORTEM PATRIS PRO FILIO — For the son after the death of the father

Obverse   Crown above inscription, date 1648 below.

Reverse   Castle gate.

C1SH-430   VG £500   F £1,200   VF £2,800

Scarborough (1644 – 1645)

Like other siege issues, these coins were made from silver plate; the denomination is counterstamped on the coin.

Collecting Hints

Scarborough shillings are extremely rare in any condition and collectors should be aware that numerous forgeries exist.

Obverse   Castle gateway, value punched below.

Reverse   None.

C1SH-435   ex. rare

Obverse   Castle with two turrets, value punched below.

Reverse   None.

C1SH-440   ex. rare

The Newark siege ninepence of Charles I can be found in the chapter 'Charles I, Siege Issues' at the end of the hammered coinage section.

Commonwealth (1649 – 1660)

Shillings were struck in some quantity during the Commonwealth. They are very plain in style and design but for the first time the inscriptions are in English, rather than Latin. All coins are dated and have a mintmark above the single shield, while the denomination XII is clearly found above the two shields. Collectors should beware of contemporary forgeries which were usually made of silver plated brass or copper and although the silver plate usually flakes off, good forgeries also exist. Various minor varieties for both issues exist, often with misspelled words in the legends and overdates; they are all rare.

Collecting Hints

While scarce, Commonwealth shillings are obtainable, especially in the lower grades. They are often clipped but unlike other denominations rarely holed. Coins in Fine condition are obtainable but those in VF and EF are rare and desirable. Issues with mintmark anchor are all very rare.

Date	Rarity
1649	RR
1651	R
1651/49	RR
1652	R
1652/1	RR
1653	R
1653/2	RRR
1654	R
1654/3	RR
1655	RRR
1655/4	RRR
1656	R
1657	RRR
1658	RRR
1658/7	RRR
1659	unique?
1660	RRR

Obverse Legend THE COMMONWEALTH OF ENGLAND

Reverse Legend GOD WITH US

Obverse Shield of St George surrounded by palm and laurel; mintmark sun at start of legend.

Reverse Shield of St George and Ireland with denomination and date 1649, 1651 – 57 above. Issues dated 1655 and 1657 are extremely rare.

CWSH-005   VG £75   F £180   VF £350

As previous, but mintmark anchor, dated 1658 – 60. An issue dated 1659, possibly unique, exists.

CWSH-010   VG £200   F £600   VF rare

Charles II (1660 – 1685)

Hammered Issue (1660 – 1662)

During this short period three issues produced three different types of shilling. All are undated and have the king's bust on the obverse, the royal shield on the reverse and mintmark crown at the beginning of the obverse and sometimes the reverse legend. If a coin is hard to identify, collectors should check whether it is an issue of Charles I and bear in mind that all of Charles II's issues have mintmark crown and an obverse legend starting CAROLUS II DG.

Collecting Hints

The first two issues are rare, but usually found in Fine to VF condition, the third is fairly common in less than Fine condition and rare in VF or EF.

First Issue

Obverse Legend   CAROLUS II DG MAG BRIT FR ET HIB REX — Charles II by the grace of God King of Great Britain France and Ireland

Reverse Legend   CHRISTO AUSPICE REGNO — I reign under the auspices of Christ

Obverse   Bust of king; mintmark crown.

Reverse   Royal arms; no mintmark.

| C2SHH-005 | VG £90 | F £200 | VF £600 |

Second Issue

Obverse Legend   As previous, but with several minor varieties.

Reverse Legend   As previous.

Obverse   As previous, but mark of value (XII) behind the king's bust.

Reverse   As previous.

| C2SHH-010 | VG £150 | F £350 | VF £1,000 |

Third Issue

Legends   As previous.

Obverse   As previous, but with inner circles.

Reverse   As previous, but with inner circles and mintmark crown.

| C2SHH-015 | VG £50 | F £120 | VF £400 |

Sixpence

First introduced under Edward VI, the silver sixpence soon became one of the most popular denominations. During the reign of George II, it was also known as the tanner after Sigismund Tanner who designed some issues. Sixpences were struck during most reigns and last produced for circulation in 1967. Under Elizabeth I, sixpences were bent and given to ladies on their engagement if the gentleman could not afford a ring.

E66D-010	Poor £50	VG £100	F £185	VF £600

Edward VI   (1547 – 1553)

The sixpence was introduced into circulation during Edward VI's fine silver coinage and quickly established as a popular denomination. Usually it was some time before new denominations won the English public over but, with the sixpence being made of good quality silver of a high fineness, it was eagerly accepted and much more desirable than either Henry VIII's later issues or Edward's own base coinage. The coins were produced at the Tower and York mints; they can be distinguished by the reverse legend, which reads POSUI DEUM ADIVTOREM MEUM for the Tower and CIVITAS EBORACI for York.

Collecting Hints

Tower mint sixpences are fairly common, especially in the lower grades, and are usually available in about Fine condition. Coins are often badly cracked, probably due to the striking, sometimes holed or creased but rarely clipped; those in VF and EF are rare and desirable. The issue from the York mint is rare and difficult to obtain in any grade.

Tower Mint

Obverse Legend   EDWARD VI DG AGL FRA Z HIB REX — Edward VI by the grace of God King of England France and Ireland

Reverse Legend   POSUI DEUM ADIVTOREM MEUM — I have made God my helper

Obverse   Front-facing bust of king with rose to the left and denomination (VI) to the right; mintmark 'Y' or tun at start of legend.

Reverse   Long cross over royal shield; mintmark as obverse.

E66D-005	Poor £30	VG £50	F £100	VF £300

York Mint

Obverse Legend   As previous.

Reverse Legend   CITIVAS EBORACI — City of York

Obverse   As previous, but mintmark mullet.

Reverse   As previous; mintmark mullet.

Philip & Mary   (1554 – 1558)

Sixpences were not produced during the reign of Mary (1553 – 54) but reintroduced, with important new features, under Philip and Mary. The first novel feature of this issue was that the sixpences were dated, continuing a practice that was inaugurated with Edward VI's fine silver crown and halfcrown and of course still used today. As mentioned in previous chapters, undated coins can still be dated with considerable accuracy by the mintmark in conjunction with historical evidence. Some issues from the reign of Philip and Mary do not have mintmarks, but all later hammered issues have mintmarks with or without a date. The second novel feature of these sixpences was particular to the reign and shared by the other contemporary denominations; the coins had the busts of both Philip and Mary on the obverse. This had never been done before and was necessitated as much by the Act of Parliament that proclaimed Mary unfit to rule alone because she was a woman as by the hope that the popularity of her husband, Philip of Spain, might be boosted if his portrait was on the coins. Finally, sixpences were only struck at the Tower mint in London, a practice that would continue during the next two reigns.

Collecting Hints

Philip and Mary sixpences are fairly rare but obtainable, usually in about Fine condition although often damaged or creased; coins in VF and EF are very difficult to obtain and desirable. If collectors just want an example of this new-style coinage, they might consider obtaining a shilling instead, which is much more common. They should not however confuse the English sixpence with the more common Philip and Mary Irish groat, which has a large harp on the reverse.

Spanish Title

Obverse Legend   PHILIP ET MARIA D G R ANG FR NEAP PR HISP — Philip and Mary by the grace of God [King and Queen] of England France and Naples Prince [and Princess] of Spain

Reverse Legend   POSUIMUS DEUM ADIUTOREM NOSTRUM — We have made God our helper

Obverse   Facing busts of monarchs, crown above separating date 1554; no mintmark.

Reverse   Crown over royal shield and dividing mark of value VI.

PM6D-005	VG £70	F £150	VF £500

English Title

Obverse Legend   PHILIP ET MARIA DG REX ET REGINA AN — Philip and Mary by the grace of God King and Queen of England

Reverse Legend   As previous.

Obverse   As previous, but dated 1555; no mintmark.

Reverse   As previous.

PM6D-010	VG £75	F £200	VF £650

As previous, but dated 1557 with mintmark lis at start of obverse legend.

PM6D-015	VG £75	F £200	VF £650

As PM6D-010 but the obverse has a heavy-beaded inner circle between the legend and the busts. It is accepted that the obverse die from the Philip and Mary Irish groat was used to produce this coin. The reverse is as previous.

PM6D-020	ex. rare

This extremely rare issue is usually only obtainable in less than Fine condition.

Obverse Legend   As PM6D-010.

Reverse Legend   As PM6D-010.

Obverse   As PM6D-010 with no mintmark; the date (1554 or 1557) is below the busts.

Reverse   As PM6D-010.

PM6D-025	VG £250	F —	VF —

Elizabeth I   (1558 – 1603)

The sixpence became an important and well-established denomination under Elizabeth I and although none was produced in the short period of her first two issues, large quantities were struck in the third issue. The sixpence is easily identified as a denomination since, with one extremely rare exception, all issues are dated and, again with one extremely rare exception, all have a rose behind the queen's bust. Also, all sixpences have mintmarks at the beginning of the obverse and reverse legend which we have listed with the dates, as the poor condition of some coins results in unclear dates. Moreover, some dates, in particular 1568/1567, are overdates — i.e. a die has been altered from one year to another so as to avoid the expense of a new die. In rare cases the date is not complete on the coin, usually with the last number missing. With huge quantities of coins being produced from numerous dies, variations in style exist and there are particularly many styles of bust in the third coinage. Finally, milled sixpences were also produced under Elizabeth and are very different in style from the hammered issue.

Hammered Coinage

Collecting Hints

No collection should be without an Elizabeth I sixpence. They are fairly common, especially in VG to about Fine condition but VF and EF examples also exist and are desirable and obtainable. Sixpences are sometimes clipped, creased or holed. Collectors should try to obtain an example with a clear date, mintmark and portrait.

Third Issue (1561 – 1577)

Many slight varieties of bust exist; several issues have been found undated and were probably die trials, as it is known that the date was engraved last on the die. All undated sixpences are extremely rare.

Large Flan Issue

This issue was only struck in 1561 with a flan measuring 27mm or more in diameter as compared to the less than 26mm flan of regular issues.

Obverse Legend   ELIZABETH DG. ANG FRA ET HIB REGINA (varieties exist) — Elizabeth by the grace of God Queen of England France and Ireland

Reverse Legend   POSUI DEU ADIVTOREM MEU — I have made God my helper

Obverse   Large bust of queen with hair swept back, rose behind bust; mintmark pheon.

Reverse   Cross over royal shield, 1561 above shield.

EL6D-005	VG £80	F £180	VF £400

As previous, but smaller bust; mintmark pheon.

EL6D-010	Poor £15	VG £30	F £60	VF £180

Regular Issue

Legends As previous.

Obverse Bust of queen with rose behind; mintmark at beginning of legend.

Reverse Cross over royal shield, date above shield; mintmark at beginning of legend: *Mintmark* Pheon (1561 – 65), rose (1565), portcullis (1566), lion (1566 – 67, undated), coronet (undated, 1567 – 70), castle (1569 – 71), ermine (1572 – 73, undated), acorn (1573 – 74), eglantine (1573 – 77)

| EL6D-015 | Poor £10 | VG £22 | F £50 | VF £125 |

Another variety apparantly exists without a rose on the obverse, dated 1561; mintmark pheon. This issue is extremely rare and possibly a pattern or trial, or possibly the rose has been unofficially erased.

| EL6D-020 | ex. rare |

Fourth Issue (1578 – 1582)

Sixpences for this and the following issues tend to have slightly larger busts.

Legends As previous.

Obverse As previous, but with larger bust.

Reverse As previous.

Mintmark Plain cross (1578 – 79), long cross (1580 – 81), sword (1582), bell (1582).

| EL6D-025 | Poor £10 | VG £22 | F £50 | VF £150 |

Fifth Issue (1582 – 1600)

This issue is fairly similar to the previous one except for the obverse legend.

Obverse Legend ELIZAB D G ANG FR ET HIB REGI — Elizabeth by the grace of God Queen of England France and Ireland

Reverse Legend, Obverse & Reverse As previous.

Mintmark Bell (1582 – 83), A (1582 – 84), escallop (1584 – 86), crescent (1587 – 89), hand (1590 – 92), tun (1592 – 95), woolpack (1594 – 95), key (1595 – 98), anchor (1598 – 1600), cypher (1600).

| EL6D-030 | Poor £10 | VG £22 | F £50 | VF £150 |

Sixth Issue (1601 – 1602)

This issue is similar to the previous one and a continuation in style and design.

As previous, but mintmark '1' (1601 – 02), '2' (1602).

| EL6D-035 | Poor £12 | VG £22 | F £50 | VF £175 |

Milled Coinage

Elizabeth's milled sixpence, struck for eleven years at the Tower mint, can easily be distinguished from the hammered by its style and absence of inner circles. All issues are dated and have a rose behind the queen's bust, unlike the groat which has neither. For more details on Elizabeth's milled coinage, please refer to the Shilling Chapter.

Collecting Hints

Most types of milled sixpence are fairly common. They are usually available in about Fine condition, creased and often mounted or gilded as the coin was popular as jewellery. Coins in VF or EF, especially if uncreased, are obtainable and very desirable. This issue is never clipped and, because of the way the coins were produced, details are usually clear.

Obverse Legend ELIZABETH D G ANG FRA ET HIB REGINA — Elizabeth by the grace of God Queen of England France and Ireland

Reverse Legend POSUI DEUM ADIVITOREM MEUM — I have made God my helper

Obverse Small bust of queen, large rose behind; mintmark star.

Reverse Cross over royal shield, 1561 above shield.

| EL6D-040 | VG £40 | F £75 | VF £200 |

As previous, but tall narrow bust with plain dress; 1561 or 1562.

EL6D-045   VG £40   F £75   VF £200

As previous, but the dress is decorated; 1562.

EL6D-050   VG £40   F £75   VF £200

As previous, with large broad bust, small rose behind bust; 1562.

EL6D-055   VG £40   F £75   VF £200

As previous, but cross pattée on reverse over royal shield; 1562 – 64.

EL6D-060   VG £40   F £85   VF £225

As previous, but the queen has a low ruff, with a visible ear; the border of the coin is made up of pellets; dated 1564 or 1566.

EL6D-065   VG £45   F £110   VF £250

Smaller bust of queen; mintmark lis on obverse and reverse. Dated 1567 or 1568.

EL6D-070   VG £40   F £95   VF £235

Large crude bust of queen breaking the legend in lower half of coin. Dated 1570 with mintmark lis, or 1571/0 with mintmark castle.

EL6D-075   VG £100   F £300   VF rare

James I   (1603 – 1625)

The sixpences produced under James I were a continuation in style and quality from those of Elizabeth, except that the Scottish arms are to be found on the shield on the reverse. Struck at the Tower mint, all sixpences are dated on the reverse above the shield and have a mintmark at the beginning of the obverse and reverse legend. Issues are distinguished chiefly by the style of the king's bust. As James VI of Scotland, James I also produced a Scottish six-shilling piece which is similar to the English sixpence, but cruder in style. To ensure correct identification, collectors should always check that the mintmark corresponds to the date of a sixpence.

Collecting Hints

Most James I sixpences are fairly common and collectors will have little difficulty obtaining an example. They are usually found in less than Fine condition, often clipped and in some cases the coin appears weakly struck, with a rather faint portrait. Coins in Fine and VF condition are fairly common, but those in EF are very rare and desirable. As James I shillings tend to be found in better condition than sixpences, collectors who just want an example from this reign might consider a shilling.

First Coinage (1603 – 1604)

First Bust

Obverse Legend   IACOBUS D.G ANG SCO FRA ET HIB REX — James King of England Scotland France and Ireland

Reverse Legend   EXURGAT DEUS DISSIPENTUR INIMICI — Let God arise and His enemies be scattered

Obverse   Bust of king with small neat beard, value VI behind bust; mintmark thistle.

Reverse   Royal arms, 1603 above shield.

J16D-005   VG £30   F £55   VF £165

Second Bust

Legends   As previous.

Obverse   Bust of king with long pointed beard; mintmark thistle or lis.

Reverse   As previous, but dated 1603 or 1604.

J16D-010   VG £30   F £55   VF £165

Second Coinage (1604 – 1616)

Third Bust

Obverse Legend   IACOBUS D.G. MAG BRIT FRA ET HIB REX — James by the grace of God King of Great Britain France and Ireland

Reverse Legend   QUAE DEUS CONIUNXIT NEMO SEPARET — What God hath joined let no man put asunder

Obverse   Bust of king with square-cut beard; mintmark lis or rose.

Reverse   As previous, but dated 1604 – 05.

J16D-015   VG £30   F £50   VF £150

Fourth Bust

Legends   As previous.

Obverse   King's bust similar to previous one except that the beard is bushier and unkempt, and the armour is plainer in style.

Reverse   As previous, but dated 1605 – 18.

Mintmark   Rose (1605 – 06), escallop (1606 – 07), grapes (1607), coronet (1607 – 09), key (1609 – 10), bell (1610), mullet (1610 – 11), tower (1611 – 12), trefoil (1613), cinquefoil (1614 – 15), tun (1615), plain cross (1618).

J16D-020   VG £30   F £50   VF £150

Fifth Bust

The king's bust is larger than the previous one and the hair is brushed back; the mintmark is a plain cross and the date 1618. This issue should not be confused with the sixth bust.

J16D-025   unique

Third Coinage (1619 – 1625)

Sixth Bust

Legends   As previous.

Obverse   Bust of king with long curly hair.

Reverse   Royal arms, date above.

Mintmark   Rose (1621), thistle (1621 – 23), lis (1623 – 24), trefoil (1624).

J16D-030   VG £30   F £50   VF £150

Charles I   (1625 – 1649)

Charles I's reign was as complicated numismatically as it was turbulent politically. Large quantities of sixpences were produced mainly, but not exclusively, at the Tower mint; provincial mints also struck sixpences and there are a number of siege pieces. The early issues were dated and fairly similar in style to those of James I, but the later and more common Tower issues were undated. The denomination is easily identified as the mark of value (VI) can always be found behind the king's head.

Tower Mint

Most Tower mint issues are fairly common. The early ones, up to class 4B, were struck under the king and from 1642 onwards under Parliament. They can easily be identified by the mintmark, which is different in the earlier issues and found at the beginning of the obverse and reverse legend. In some, mostly later, issues mintmarks have been altered so that dies could be used for another year and this often results in the mintmark looking blundered.

Collecting Hints

Most of these issues should be fairly easy to obtain, especially in less than Fine or Fine condition but are fairly scarce in VF or EF. On many issues the coin's flan is irregular in shape and much of the legend is missing; this is due to poor striking rather than clipping. Collectors should try to obtain an example with a good portrait and clear mintmark, and not worry too much about the state of the legend.

Tower Mint under King (1625 – 1642)

Class 1

Obverse Legend   CAROLUS D.G. MAG BRI FRA ET HI REX — Charles by the grace of God King of Great Britain France and Ireland

Reverse Legend   CHRISTO AUSPICE REGNO — I reign under the auspices of Christ

Obverse   Bust of king wearing ruff, value behind; mintmark lis or cross calvary.

Reverse   Royal shield over a cross with date above, 1625 or 1626.

C16D-005	VG £40	F £60	VF £200

C16D-030	VG £22	F £45	VF £100

Class 1A

Legends   As previous.

Obverse   As previous, but the king's armour is concealed; mintmark cross calvary, blackamoor's head, castle, anchor, heart.

Reverse   As previous, dated 1625 – 29.

C16D-010	VG £40	F £60	VF £200

Class 1B

As previous, but no cross over the shield on the reverse, dated 1629 or 1630; mintmarks heart or plume.

C16D-015	VG £85	F £200	VF £450

Class 2A

Obverse Legend   As previous, but minor varieties exist.

Reverse Legend   As previous.

Obverse   Bust of king with more armour visible; mintmark plume or rose.

Reverse   Oval shield, no date, 'C.R.' above shield.

C16D-020	VG £30	F £50	VF £100

Class 2B

As previous, but a plume divides the 'C.R.' on the reverse.

C16D-025	VG £40	F £60	VF £120

Class 3

Legends   As previous.

Obverse   Bust of king with lace collar; mintmark harp or portcullis.

Reverse   Oval shield dividing 'C.R.'.

Class 3A

Legends   As previous.

Obverse   Bust of king without the inner circles usually found between the legend and the king's bust; mintmark bell, crown or tun.

Reverse   Oval shield, without either 'C.R' to sides or the inner circles usually found between the legend and shield.

C16D-035	VG £22	F £45	VF £100

Class 4

The size of the VI varies in this issue.

Legends   As previous.

Obverse   Bust of king within inner circles; mintmark tun or anchor.

Reverse   Square-topped shield with inner circle.

C16D-040	VG £22	F £45	VF £100

Class 4A

As previous, but a slightly different Aberystwyth bust, the king's crown sometimes has a single or double arch; mintmark anchor or triangle.

C16D-045	VG £22	F £45	VF £100

Class 4B

As previous, but older-looking bust of king; mintmark triangle or triangle in circle.

C16D-050	VG £22	F £45	VF £100

Tower Mint under Parliament (1642 – 1648)

This issue is easily identified by the unique mintmarks.

Class 4C

Legends   As previous.

Obverse   Bust of king similar to previous issue; mintmarks '(P)', '(R)', eye or sun.

Reverse   Square-topped shield over cross.

C16D-055	VG £25	F £60	VF £150

Class 4D

Similar to class 4A (C16D-045); mintmark '(R)', eye, sun or sceptre.

C16D-060	VG £25	F £60	VF £150

Class 4E

As previous, but large, squat bust of king; mintmark eye or sun.

C16D-065	VG £100	F £250	VF —

Briot's Milled Coinage (1631 – 1639)

Nicholas Briot joined the Tower mint in 1628 and was made sole designer for the bust of the royal coinage. In 1631 he introduced his milled, or machine-made, coinage which was high in quality, style and design and greatly superior to the hammered issues. Its main drawback appears to have been the length of time needed to produce the coins. Moreover, hammered coins were more popular with the moneyers at the mint, who were worried that machines would take over their jobs.

Collecting Hints

As with the other denominations, the quality of Briot's coins was much higher than that of contemporary hammered issues and this is reflected in the quality of the coins available today. Both issues are fairly scarce but obtainable, usually in Fine or VF condition. Due to the striking there is occasionally a weakness in parts of the legend, but the coins are usually round with complete legends unlike the Tower mint's hammered issues.

First Milled Issue (1631 – 1632)

Obverse Legend   CAROLUS D G MAGN BRITANN FR ET HIB REX — Charles King of Great Britain France and Ireland

Reverse   CHRISTO AUSPICE REGNO — I reign under the auspices of Christ

Obverse   Bust of king with value behind; mintmark flower and 'B'.

Reverse   Square-topped shield over cross, small 'B' sometimes at top of cross.

C16D-070	VG £50	F £100	VF £250	EF £500

Second Milled Issue (1638 – 1639)

Legends   As previous.

Obverse   Bust of slightly different style from last issue; mintmark anchor or mullet.

Reverse   Royal arms over smaller cross, the edges of which just go to the inner circle.

C16D-075	VG £35	F £90	VF £180	EF £450

Provincial Mints
York Mint (1643 – 1644)

This issue is fairly easy to distinguish by the mintmark lion.

Collecting Hints

York sixpences, unlike the other denominations, are fairly scarce especially in better than Fine condition.

Obverse Legend   CAROLUS D.G. MAG BRIT FRAN ET HIB REX — Charles by the grace of God King of Great Britain France and Ireland

Reverse Legend   CHRISTO AUSPICE REGNO — I reign under the auspices of Christ

Obverse   Bust of king with pointed beard, denomination behind the bust; mintmark lion.

Reverse   Oval shield with crown above.

C16D-080	VG £80	F £200	VF £450

As previous, but 'C.R' divided by shield on the reverse.

C16D-085	VG £70	F £180	VF £400

Aberystwyth Mint

This issue can easily be identified by the plume in front of the king's face and the mintmark book.

Collecting Hints

Sixpences from the Aberystwyth mint are fairly rare and difficult to obtain; when available, they are usually undamaged in Fine or VF condition.

Obverse Legend   CAROLUS D.G. MAG BR FR ET HI REX (minor varieties exist) — Charles by the grace of God King of Great Britain France and Ireland

Reverse Legend   CHRISTO AUSPICE REGNO — I reign under the auspices of Christ

Obverse   Bust of king with plume in front of face, value behind and no inner circle; mintmark book.

Reverse   Oval shield with plume above, no inner circle.

C16D-090	VG £80	F £180	VF £350

As previous, but inner circle on obverse.

C16D-095	VG £85	F £190	VF £375

As Tower bust 3 (C16D-030), but inner circle on obverse and reverse, a plume in front of the bust with value behind.

C16D-100	VG £100	F £250	VF £550

As previous, but on reverse the plume is square in shape.

C16D-105	VG £80	F £180	VF £350

As previous, but on obverse the king's crown breaks the inner circle.

C16D-110	VG £100	F £200	VF £400

Aberystwyth Furnace Mint (1648 – 1649)

This issue is fairly similar to the Aberystwyth one but has mintmark crown, and is a little cruder in style.

Collecting Hints

This issue is extremely rare in any grade.

Obverse Legend   CAROLUS D.G. MAG BRI FRA ET HIB REX — Charles by the grace of God King of Great Britain France and Ireland

Reverse Legend   CHRISTO AUSPICE REGNO — I reign under the auspices of Christ

Obverse   Bust of king, value behind and small plume in front of face; mintmark crown.

Reverse   Oval shield, plume above shield.

C16D-115	ex. rare

Oxford Mint (1642 – 1646)

This rare issue used the Aberystwyth obverse die, probably because coins needed to be struck urgently; the reverse has the Declaration in three lines with a date below.

Collecting Hints

All issues are fairly rare but, when available, usually found in Fine or VF condition.

Obverse Legend   CAROLUS D G. MAG BRIT FR ET HI REX — Charles by the grace of God King of Great Britain France and Ireland

Reverse Legend   EXURGAT DEUS DISSIPENTUR INIMICI — Let God arise and His enemies be scattered

Reverse Centre Legend   RELIG PROT LEG ANG LIBER PAR — The religion of the Protestants the laws of England the liberty of Parliament

Obverse   Aberystwyth bust of king with inner circle, value behind bust and plume in front of face; mintmark book.

Reverse   The Declaration in three lines, three plumes above and the date 1642 or 1643 below.

C16D-120	VG £75	F £175	VF £350

As previous, but smaller plumes of different style, known as Shrewsbury plumes, on the reverse; 1643.

| C16D-125 | VG £75 | F £175 | VF £350 |

As previous, but only one plume on reverse and a lis either side; dated 1644 with OX by date.

| C16D-130 | ex. rare |

Bristol Mint (1643 – 1645)

Collecting Hints

This rare issue is difficult to obtain in any grade.

Obverse Legend   CAROLUS D.G. MAG B F ET H REX — Charles by the grace of God King of Great Britain France and Ireland

Outer Reverse Legend   EXURGAT DEUS DISSIPENTUR INIMICI — Let God arise and His enemies be scattered

Inner Reverse Legend   RELIG PRO LEG ANG LIB PAR — The religion of the Protestants the laws of England the liberty of Parliament

Obverse   Coarse bust of king of poor style, value behind.

Reverse   Three small plumes over the Declaration, 1643 below.

| C16D-135 | VG £100 | F £275 | VF £600 |

As previous, but plumelet in front of face.

| C16D-140 | VG £70 | F £175 | VF £425 |

Late Declaration Issues (1645 – 1646)

These issues are different in style from the other provincial issues. The mintmarks 'B' and 'A' are specific to this issue. Although unconfirmed, it is thought that the mintmark might stand for the town that issued the coin, 'A' being for Appledore or Ashby de la Zouch and 'B' for Barnstaple, Bideford or Bridgnorth-on-Severn.

Collecting Hints

Both issues are fairly rare, especially the first which is usually available only in the lower grades. The second type is usually available in Fine or VF condition.

Obverse Legend   CAROLUS D G MAG BR FR ET HI REX — Charles by the grace of God King of Great Britain France and Ireland

Outer Reverse Legend   EXURGAT DEUS DISSIPENTUR INIMICI — Let God arise and His enemies be scattered

Inner Reverse Legend   REL PRO LEG ANG LIB PAR — The religion of the Protestants the laws of England the liberty of Parliament

Obverse   Bust of king with value behind, plumelet in front of face; mintmark sideways 'A'.

Reverse   Three plumelets above Declaration, 1645 below.

| C16D-145 | VG £100 | F £275 | VF £600 |

Obverse Legend   CAROLUS D.G. MAG B F ET H REX — Charles by the grace of God King of Great Britain France and Ireland

Outer Reverse Legend   As previous.

Inner Reverse Legend   As previous, but sometimes beginning TIN PRO instead of REL PRO which might be a die error.

Obverse   Bust of king with value behind, plume in front of face; mintmark 'B'.

Reverse   Scrolls and plumes above Declaration, 1646 below.

| C16D-150 | VG £80 | F £200 | VF £400 |

Exeter Mint

This rare issue has the date 1644 in the reverse legend and mintmark rose. The date in the legend is specific to this issue.

Collecting Hints

This issue, which is crude in style, is fairly rare. The coins are usually obtainable in about Fine condition, often damaged. Coins in better than Fine condition are rare.

Obverse Legend   CAROLUS DG. MA BR FR ET HI REX — Charles by the grace of God King of Great Britain France and Ireland

Reverse Legend   CHRISTO AUSPICE REGNO — I reign under the auspices of Christ

Obverse   Bust of king, value behind in varying sizes; mintmark rose.

Reverse   Oval garnished shield, dated 1644; mintmark rose. Two reverses exist, on one the rose divides the date, on the other it does not.

C16D-155	VG £90	F £225	VF £550

Worcester or Shrewsbury Mint

Very little is known about this very rare and crudely produced coin. Its style of production is unique and so are the mintmarks castle and boar's head, usually muled.

Collecting Hints

This coin is rare in any grade and probably does not exist in better than Fine condition.

Obverse Legend   CAROLUS DG MAG BR FR ET HI RX — Charles by the grace of God King of Great Britain France and Ireland

Reverse Legend   CHRISTO AUSPICE REGNO — I reign under the auspices of Christ

Obverse   Crude bust of king, value behind; mintmark castle.

Reverse   Square-topped shield; mintmark boar's head.

C16D-160	VG £300	F £600

Siege Issues

Newark (1646)

Newark was besieged several times between 1645 and 1646 and finally surrendered to Cromwell's army in May 1646. This issue can be easily identified from other denominations by the VI for sixpence below the crown on the obverse.

Collecting Hints

Only struck in 1646, the sixpence is one of the rarer denominations, usually obtainable in Fine condition and often holed. Some specimens are gilded, with the gilding coming from the article which was the original source of the coin. While interesting, gilded coins can be worth less because they are often unsightly where the gilding has worn.

Obverse   Crown dividing 'CR', denomination below.

Reverse   OBS NEWARK 1646 in three lines.

C16D-165	VG £200	F £500	VF £1,000

As previous, but a leopard's head countermark on reverse.

C16D-167	ex. rare

Scarborough (1644 – 1645)

Scarborough produced two differently styled sixpences. The value was stamped on the coins, which are roughly square in shape.

Collecting Hints

All issues are extremely rare in any grade and collectors should beware of forgeries.

Obverse   Castle with gateway to left, value (VI) punched below.

Reverse   Plain.

C16D-170	ex. rare

Obverse   Castle with two turrets, value (VI) punched below.

Reverse   Plain.

C16D-175	ex. rare

Commonwealth   (1649 – 1660)

Hammered sixpences, fairly plain in style, were struck during the Commonwealth. The issue is similar to the other denominations with the shield of St. George on the obverse and the shield of St George and Ireland with the denomination VI above on the reverse. All issues were dated.

Collecting Hints

The early issue (with mintmark sun) is fairly common, especially in the lower grades, but the later issue (mintmark anchor) is rare in all grades. Many coins are badly worn, bent or damaged and those in better than Fine condition are rare for both issues. Coins dated 1655 and 1657 are extremely rare.

Date	Rarity
1649	R
1651	R
1651/49	R
1652	R
1652/49	RR
1652/1	RR
1653	R
1654	RR
1654/3	RRR
1655	RRR
1656	R
1657	RRR
1658	RRR
1659	only 3? exist
1660	RRR

Obverse Legend THE COMMONWEALTH OF ENGLAND

Reverse Legend GOD WITH US

Obverse St George's arms in wreath; mintmark sun.

Reverse Arms of St George and Ireland, value above and date in legend, 1649, 1651 – 57.

CW6D-005 VG £60 F £120 VF £300

As previous, but mintmark anchor, dated 1658 – 60.

CW6D-010 VG £200 F £500 VF rare

Charles II (1660 – 1685)

Hammered Issue (1660 – 1662)

During this short period three different types of sixpence were produced, all of them undated with mintmark crown on the obverse.

Collecting Hints

The first issue is quite scarce, the second very rare but the third is fairly common; all three are usually obtainable in about Fine condition. VF and better examples exist but are rare and desirable. The average grade the coin is found in is less than Fine and specimens are often clipped, with weak portraits.

Obverse Legend CAROLUS II D.G. MAG BRIT FRAN ET HIB REX — Charles by the grace of God King of Great Britain France and Ireland

Reverse Legend CHRISTO AUSPICE REGNO — I reign under the auspices of Christ

Obverse Bust of king with no mark of value; mintmark crown.

Reverse Royal shield over cross.

C26DH-005 VG £75 F £150 VF £400

As previous, but mark of value behind the king's head.

C26DH-010 VG £300 F £600 VF —

As previous, but inner circles on obverse and reverse.

C26DH-015 VG £40 F £110 VF £300

257

Groat

The silver groat, with a value of fourpence, was first introduced during the recoinage of Edward I in 1279. Its name, which was derived from the French *gros* and the Italian *grosso*, roughly translated means great or thick. The groat constituted an important part of Edward's recoinage to introduce more denominations into circulation. In the 1260s the French had successfully introduced a large silver coin with a fairly similar value to the groat, the *gros tournois*. With England's European trade increasing, Edward I realised the importance of larger denominations. Although Edward's issues did not succeed, the groat was successfully introduced under Edward III and was produced by most monarchs for circulation until the reign of Queen Victoria. Even now, the groat is produced as a Maundy fourpence and distributed by the monarch every year.

The following linedrawings depict the basic common types of groat, although it should be noted that many varieties exist and these illustrations are mainly indicative of portrait style and legend rather than specific issues.

Edward III   Henry VI,   Edward IV   Henry VII
            1st Reign

Edward I   (1272 – 1307)

Until the reign of Edward I the only coins produced, except for a few rare exceptions, were pennies. Increased trade in a more prosperous England and Europe required a variety of both smaller and larger denominations and the need was met by Edward I's recoinage, when the groat or fourpence was also introduced. Many consider this rare issue to have been an experiment or pattern, but as a total of eight different varieties were issued, it would appear that it was intended for circulation. Its introduction, however, was not a success not only because the public was accustomed to the penny and wary of change, but also because the groat was underweight with four single pennies weighing more. Merchants, especially those trading on the Continent, preferred payment in pennies so the groat became unpopular and was not successfully introduced into circulation until Edward III's reign. All Edward I issues were struck at London; in total, eight slight varieties exist. The prices are the same for all, depending upon whether they are mounted or not.

mounted	VG £800	F £1,400	VF —

unmounted	VG £1,500	F £3,500	VF £5,500

Collecting Hints

Edward I groats are rare. Most specimens show traces of gilding and solder marks and appear to have been made into jewellery at some period. Undamaged coins are extremely rare and most of the damaged ones are in Fine condition.

Obverse Legend EDWARDUS DI GRA REX ANGL — Edward by the grace of God King of England

Reverse Legend DNS HIBNE DUX AQUT — Lord of Ireland Duke of Aquitaine

Reverse Inside Circle Legend LONDONIA CIVI — City of London

Obverse Front-facing bust of crowned king within a quatrefoil, a flower either side of his hair.

Reverse Long-cross with three pellets in each angle, reverse legend in two circles.

E14D-005

Obverse Triple pellet stops in legend, spearheads to king's crown; the king's drapery in two wedges and a trefoil below bust.

Reverse As previous.

E14D-010

As previous, but a pellet either side of the king's bust.

E14D-015

Double pellet stops in legend, pearls on crown and a trefoil below bust.

E14D-020

Double or triple pellet stops in legend, spearheads to crown, curved drapery on king, trefoil below bust.

E14D-025

Double pellet stops in legend, small pearls on crown, king's drapery in two wedges, small flower below bust.

E14D-030

Triple pellet stops in legend, pearls on crown and a small flower below bust.

E14D-035

Double pellet stops, spearheads on crown, the rest as previous.

E14D-040

Edward III   (1327 – 1377)

The groat was successfully introduced into circulation during Edward III's fourth coinage (1351 – 77). Like the groats of Edward I and Edward IV, which are all similar in style, Edward III issues bear the king's name at the beginning of the obverse legend but are distinguishable either by small particularities in the face, hair or legends or, in the case of Edward IV, by various marks in the legends and often in the field beside the king. However, collectors should note that there are many minor varieties of Edward III groats. The various issues based on the monarch's aspirations in France that are detailed in the relevant section of the Penny chapter also apply to the groat.

Collecting Hints

Edward III groats are fairly common; they can be found in VG to VF condition, EF specimens being rare. Many coins are clipped and some have weak areas where the legend is unclear. Collectors should try to obtain an example in Fine condition with good eye appeal and as round as possible.

Pre Treaty Period (1351 – 1361)

London Mint

Varieties exist in most classes, especially E34D-040. Letters are often missed out or words misspelt in the legends and London is sometimes spelt LONDOM. In most cases these varieties are not rare.

1351

Obverse Legend   EDWARD D G REX ANGL Z FRANC D HYB — Edward by the grace of God King of England and France Lord of Ireland. This is known as the French title.

Reverse Legend   POSVI DEUM ADIVTOREM MEUM — I have made God my helper

Reverse Inside Circle Legend   CIVITAS LONDON — City of London

Obverse   Front-facing bust of the king, with Roman 'M', open 'C' and 'E' in legend; mintmark cross '1'.

Reverse   Large cross with three pellets in each quarter.

E34D-005   VG £60   F £125   VF £300

As previous, but crown in each quarter of the reverse instead of pellets.

E34D-010   unique

1351 – 1352

Legends   As previous.

Obverse   Front-facing bust of king with French title; Lombardic 'M', closed 'C' and 'E', 'R' with wedge-shaped tail.

Reverse   Large cross with three pellets in each quarter.

E34D-015   VG £40   F £70   VF £150

1352 – 1353

As previous, but 'R' with normal tail; mintmark cross 1 or cross 1 broken.

E34D-020   VG £40   F £70   VF £150

1354 – 1355

As previous, but broken letters in legend, 'V' with nick in right limb; mintmark cross 2.

E34D-025   VG £40   F £70   VF £150

As previous, but a lis on the king's breast.

E34D-030   VG £45   F £80   VF £175

1356

As previous, but no lis on breast; mintmark crown.

E34D-035   VG £45   F £80   VF £175

1356 – 1361

Legends   As previous.

Obverse   Front-facing bust of the king, usually with annulet under it; mintmark cross 3.

Reverse   An annulet usually in one quarter.

E34D-040   VG £40   F £80   VF £150

York Mint

Obverse Legend   EDWARD D G REX ANGL Z FRANC D HYB — Edward by the grace of God King of England and France Lord of Ireland

Outer Reverse Legend   POSVI DEUM ADIVTOREM MEUM — I have made God my helper

Reverse Inner Circle Legend CIVITAS EBORACI — City of York

Obverse Front-facing bust of the king; mintmark cross 1 or cross 1 broken.

Reverse Large cross, three pellets in each quarter.

E34D-045 VG £45 F £90 VF £200

As previous, but broken letters in the legend and 'V' has a nick in the right limb.

E34D-050 VG £40 F £75 VF £180

Transitional Period (1361)

In this scarce issue the French title in the obverse legend is missing and the letters are of irregular size.

Obverse Legend EDWAR DEI GRAC REX ANGL — Edward by the grace of God King of England

Inner Reverse Legend POSVI DEUM ADIVTOREM MEU(M) — I have made God my helper

Outer Reverse Legend CIVITAS LONDON — City of London

Obverse Front-facing crowned bust of the king, annulet each side of crown, irregular size lettering; mintmark cross potent.

Reverse Large cross, three pellets in each quarter.

E34D-055 VG £60 F £150 VF £400

Treaty Period (1361 - 1369)

London Mint

This issue can be differentiated by the different obverse legend. Also the 'X' in REX is distinct, being a treaty cross similar to a cross pattée but used as a letter. As with previous issues, there are several varieties which include various stops and marks in the legend, also the A in ADIVTOREM is sometimes unbarred. None of these varieties are particularly rare.

Obverse Legend EDWARD D(EI) G REX ANGL D(NS) HYB Z AQT — Edward by the grace of God King of England Lord of Ireland and Aquitaine

Reverse Legend POSVI DEUM ADIVTOREM MEUM — I have made God my helper

Obverse Front-facing bust of king; mintmark cross potent.

Reverse Large cross with three pellets in each quarter.

E34D-060 VG £45 F £80 VF £150

As previous, but annulet before EDWARD in obverse legend.

E34D-065 VG £45 F £85 VF £175

As previous, but annulet on king's breast.

E34D-070 VG £45 F £85 VF £175

Calais Mint

Obverse Legend EDWARD D G REX ANGL D HYB Z AQT — Edward by the grace of God King of England Lord of Ireland and Aquitaine

Reverse Legend POSVI DEUM ADIVTOREM MEUM — I have made God my helper

Reverse Inside Circle Legend VILLA CALESIE — Town of Calais

Obverse Front-facing bust of king, annulet on breast; mintmark cross potent.

Reverse Large cross, three pellets in each quarter.

E34D-075 VG £70 F £150 VF £350

Post Treaty Period (1369 - 1377)

These issues were all struck at the London mint. The French title has been resumed in the obverse legend. Saltire stops are found in the legends. Also, the word or abbreviation for 'and' in the obverse legend is omitted, probably by mistake.

Obverse Legend EDWARD DI GRA REX ANGL FRANC — Edward by the grace of God King of England [and] France

Reverse Legend POSVI DEUM ADIVTOREM MEUM — I have made God my helper

Obverse Front-facing bust of king, 'F' in legend usually reversed with varieties in readings; mintmark cross pattée.

Reverse Large cross, three pellets in each quarter.

| E34D-080   VG £50   F £100   VF £350 |

Obverse Legend   EDWARD DI G REX ANGL F DNS HIB A (varieties exist) — Edward by the grace of God King of England [and] France Lord of Ireland [and] Aquitaine

Reverse Legend   POSVI DEUM ADIVTOREM MEUM — I have made God my helper

Obverse   Front-facing bust of king, row of annulets under bust that resembles chain mail; mintmark cross potent with four pellets around it.

Reverse   Cross with three pellets in each quarter.

| E34D-085   VG £100   F £225   VF rare |

Obverse Legend   EDWARD DI G REX ANGL FRANC D HIB — Edward by the grace of God King of England [and] France Lord of Ireland

Reverse Legend   As previous.

Obverse   Row of pellets across king's breast; mintmark as previous issue.

Reverse   As previous.

| E34D-090   VG £130   F £250   VF rare |

Richard II   (1377 – 1399)

Richard II's coinage continued in the style of Edward III's and all groats are rare. After checking that RICARD, rather than EDWARD or HENRI, is found at the top of the obverse legend and to distinguish it from a Richard III groat, collectors should pay particular attention to the face, hair and crown. Moreover, the two monarchs used different mintmarks; Richard II only used the cross pattée and Richard III used other mintmarks. Richard II issued four distinct types of groat and they were all struck at London.

Collecting Hints

Richard II groats are rare and usually found in about Fine condition, often clipped. Collectors should try to obtain the best possible example with a clear reading of RICARD.

Obverse Legend   RICARD DI GRA REX ANGL(IE) Z FR(ANC) — Richard by the grace of God King of England and France

Reverse Legend   POSVI DEUM ADIVTORE(M) MEU(M) — I have made God my helper

Obverse   Front-facing bust of king; mintmark cross pattée. Pay particular attention to the ET or 'Z' in the legend.

Reverse   Large cross with three pellets in each quarter.

| R24D-005   VG £200   F £400   VF £1,000 |

As previous, but new-style lettering, particularly the 'Z' before FRANC in the obverse legend.

| R24D-010   VG £150   F £300   VF £650 |

As previous, but a slightly different style of bust and fishtail serifs to lettering.

| R24D-015   VG £200   F £400   VF £1,000 |

As previous, but slightly different style to bust, a crescent on the king's breast.

| R24D-020   VG £750   F £1,200   VF rare |

Henry IV   (1399 – 1413)

All issues from the reign of Henry IV are rare and groats are no exception. No groats were struck in the heavy coinage (1399 – 1412) but three main varieties were issued during the light coinage of 1412 – 13. However, Henry IV's coins are fairly difficult to distinguish from the much more common issues of Henry V, VI and VII, all of which read HENRIC in the obverse legend — the first three Henrys (I-III) not having struck groats and those of Henry VIII being easily distinguishable. Henry VII's issues are also very different, particularly on the king's crown. Henry IV groats may be identified by the mintmark cross pattée (6) found above the crown in the legend (the only other Henry to use this mintmark is Henry VI Restored), the mint (London, found on the reverse inner circle legend) and the portraits, which have different style crown, hair and facial expressions. Having correctly identified the reign that a coin belongs to, collectors should look for any unusual marks on it such as annulets etc., to establish the issue.

Collecting Hints

Henry IV groats are extremely rare in any grade and the average condition they are found in is about Fine. Collectors will have difficulty obtaining any coin for their collection.

Obverse Legend   HENRIC DI GRA REX ANGL (Z FRANC) — Henry by the grace of God King of England (and France)

Reverse Legend   POSVI DEUM ADIVTOREM MEUM — I have made God my helper

Reverse Inside Circle Legend   CIVITAS LONDON — City of London

Obverse   Front-facing crowned bust of king, pellet to the left of crown, annulet to the right; the French title has been omitted on some issues; mintmark cross pattée (6). This is an altered Richard II die with HENRIC struck over RICARD and signs of the old lettering coming through.

Reverse   Large cross, three pellets in each quarter.

| H44D-005 | VG £800 | F £1,800 | VF £4,000 |

Obverse Legend   HENRIC DI GRA REX ANGL Z FRANC — Henry by the grace of God King of England and France

Reverse Legend   As previous.

Obverse   Front-facing bust of king, annulet to the left and pellet to the right of crown, eight or ten arches in tressure; mintmark cross pattée.

Reverse   As previous.

| H44D-010 | VG £700 | F £1,800 | VF £3,800 |

Obverse Legend   HENRIC DI GRA REX ANGL Z FRANC (IE) — Henry by the grace of God King of the English and France

Reverse Legend   As previous.

Obverse   As previous, but nine arches in tressure.

Reverse   As previous.

| H44D-015 | VG £700 | F £1,800 | VF £3,800 |

Henry V   (1413 – 1422)

As mentioned above, there are many similarities between the coinages of Henry IV, V and VI. However, Henry V used the mintmarks cross pattée or pierced cross, both with a central pellet. He also issued new marks, such as mullets or quatrefoils, which are usually found in the legends or the field of the coin; also the portrait, of which there are four main types, is different. Nevertheless, several of Henry V issues are muled using Henry IV dies. All Henry V groats were minted in London.

Collecting Hints

The first two varieties of Henry V groat are very rare, especially in better than Fine condition. The frowning bust type is fairly scarce and usually available in about Fine, although VF and even EF examples do exist; dedicated collectors should find little difficulty obtaining an example of a common issue.

Obverse Legend   HENRIC DI GRA REX ANGL Z FRANC — Henry by the grace of God King of England and France

Reverse Legend   POSVI DEUM ADIVITOREM MEUM — I have made God my helper.

Reverse Inner Circle Legend   CIVITAS LONDON — City of London

Obverse   Emaciated bust of king with no neck, short, broad letters in the legend, quatrefoil after HENRIC, fleurs over crown; mintmark cross pattée with central pellet.

Reverse   Long cross with three pellets in each quarter, quatrefoil after POSVI.

| H54D-005 | VG £700 | F £1,800 | VF £3,500 |

This issue is sometimes muled with a Henry IV reverse whereupon it does not have a quatrefoil nor is the lettering short and broad. However, it may also be muled with later issues of Henry V, whereupon the reverse lettering will again be different. All three varieties that make up this class are of equal rarity.

Legends   As previous.

Obverse   Scowling bust of king, ordinary lettering in legend, some issues have a quatrefoil after HENRIC; mintmark pierced cross with pellet in centre.

Reverse   Large cross with three pellets in each quarter, ordinary lettering.

| H54D-010 | VG £300 | F £800 | VF £1,500 |

A variety exists that has a mullet in the centre of breast.

| H54D-015 | VG £130 | F £260 | VF £500 |

As with the previous issue, the obverse was sometimes muled with either a Henry IV issue or a later Henry V issue.

As previous, but frowning bust of king, usually with a mullet on the right shoulder, sometimes a quatrefoil is found after HENRIC; mintmark pierced cross with pellet centre.

| H54D-020 | VG £70 | F £150 | VF £350 |

On one very rare variety, the obverse legend ends FRANIE instead of FRANC.

| H54D-025 | VG £70 | F £150 | VF £350 |

As previous, but the obverse legend ends FRANC and there are no marks such as mullet on the obverse.

H54D-030	VG £80	F £170	VF £400

Henry VI First Reign (1422 – 1461)

Henry VI's issues are fairly easy to distinguish by their style, mint-mark and various other marks even though the obverse legend reads, like on the issues of the other Henrys, HENRIC. To differentiate this reign from the groats of other Henrys, collectors should bear in mind that on Henry IV's issues the face and crown are different. Henry V's bust is distinct and a number of marks such as mullet on right shoulder differentiate these issues. Henry VI Restored is usually identified by the king's name on the obverse, which reads HENRICV instead of HENRIC. The style, particularly of the crown, of Henry VII's issues is different, while Henry VIII's coins have a totally different style.

As with all Henry VI's denominations, the groat can be classified into various issues depending on the marks, such as annulets or pinecones and mascles, found on it. Three mints were active producing groats under Henry VI, London, Calais and York (which is rare). The mint's name can be found on the reverse of the coin in the inner circle and reads CIVITAS LONDON for London, VILLA CALISIE for Calais or, for the annulet issue, CIVITAS EBORACI for York. However, as many of these issues have similar markings it is important that collectors check all markings when attributing a coin to a class.

Collecting Hints

Henry VI coins are common and the groat is probably the most abundant, especially the annulet issue which was struck in very large quantities in London and Calais, and is usually available in Fine and VF condition, although EF specimens are not uncommon. The other issues tend to be slightly rarer, but again are often available in Fine or VF condition. Henry VI groats tend to be unclipped but sometimes have weaknesses in the legend due to lack of silver in the flan during minting. Collectors just wanting an example should try to obtain an annulet issue.

Annulet Issue (1422 – 1427)

London Mint

Obverse Legend   HENRIC DI GRA REX ANGL Z FRANC — Henry by the grace of God King of England and France

Reverse Legend   POSVI DEUM ADIVTOREM MEUM — I have made God my helper

Reverse Inner Circle Legend   CIVITAS LONDON — City of London

Obverse   Front-facing bust of king.

Reverse   Annulet in two quarters.

H64D-005	VG £20	F £50	VF £90	EF £160

Calais Mint

Obverse & Reverse Legend   As previous.

Reverse Inner Circle Legend   VILLA CALISIE — Town of Calais

Obverse   Front-facing bust of king with an annulet either side of neck.

Reverse   An annulet in two quarters on reverse.

H64D-010	VG £20	F £50	VF £90	EF £160

As previous, but no annulets on reverse.

H64D-015	VG £30	F £60	VF £120	EF £250

York Mint

Obverse & Reverse Legend   As previous.

Reverse Inside Circle Legend   CIVITAS EBORACI — City of York

Obverse   Front-facing bust of king with lis either side of neck.

Reverse   Annulet in two quarters.

H64D-020	VG £350	F £700	VF £1,400	EF ex. rare

Annulet Trefoil Sub-Issue
London Mint

Obverse & Reverse Legend   As previous.

Reverse Inside Circle Legend   CIVITAS LONDON — City of London

Obverse   Front-facing bust of king with trefoil of pellets to left of crown.

Reverse   As previous.

H64D-025	VG £90	F £150	VF £300	EF rare

Calais Mint

Obverse & Reverse Legend   As previous.

Reverse Inside Circle Legend   VILLA CALISIE — Town of Calais

Obverse   As previous, with an annulet either side of neck.

Reverse   As previous.

H64D-030	VG £40	F £80	VF £180	EF £350

Rosette Mascle Issue (1427 – 1430)

This issue has rosettes or rosettes and mascles in the legends.

London Mint

Obverse & Reverse Legend   As previous.

Reverse Inside Circle Legend   CIVITAS LONDON — City of London

Obverse   Front-facing bust of king with no marks, but rosettes or rosettes and mascles in legend.

Reverse   Rosettes or rosettes and mascles in legends.

| H64D-035 | VG £35 | F £90 | VF £180 | EF £350 |

Calais Mint

Obverse & Reverse Legend   As previous.

Reverse Inside Circle Legend   VILLA CALISIE — Town of Calais

Obverse   As previous.

Reverse   As previous.

| H64D-040 | VG £30 | F £60 | VF £120 | EF £250 |

There is a variety where a mascle is found in the spandrels.

| H64D-045 | VG £35 | F £70 | VF £140 | EF £280 |

Pinecone Mascle Issue (1430 – 1434)

This issue has pinecones and mascles in the legend.

London Mint

Obverse & Reverse Legend   As previous.

Reverse Inside Circle Legend   CIVITAS LONDON — City of London

Obverse   Front-facing bust of king, no marks but pinecone and mascles in legend.

Reverse   Pinecones and mascles in legend.

| H64D-050 | VG £25 | F £60 | VF £125 |

Calais Mint

As previous, but reverse inside circle legend reads VILLA CALISIE — Town of Calais.

| H64D-055 | VG £25 | F £70 | VF £140 |

Leaf Mascle Issue (1434 – 1435)

This issue has a mascle in the legends and a leaf somewhere in the design.

London Mint

This issue is sometimes muled with other London issues, so the reverse often has different marks in the legend from its obverse class.

Obverse & Reverse Legend   As previous.

Reverse Inside Circle Legend   CIVITAS LONDON (or DONDON) — City of London

Obverse   Front-facing bust of king with leaf below bust and mascles in legend.

Reverse   Mascles in legend.

| H64D-060 | VG £50 | F £100 | VF £200 |

Calais Mint

Obverse & Reverse Legend   As previous.

Reverse Inside Circle Legend   VILLA CALISIE — Town of Calais

Obverse   Front-facing bust of king, leaf on breast and mascles in legend.

Reverse   Leaf usually below MEUM in legend.

| H64D-065 | VG £35 | F £70 | VF £150 |

Leaf Trefoil Issue (1435 – 1438)

This issue usually has leaves and trefoil of pellets in the legends.

London Mint

Obverse & Reverse Legend   As previous.

Reverse Inside Circle Legend   CIVITAS LONDON — City of London

Obverse   Front-facing bust of king, leaf on breast, leaves and trefoil of pellets in legend.

Reverse   Leaves and trefoil of pellets usually in legends.

| H64D-070 | VG £35 | F £70 | VF £150 |

As previous, but no leaf on breast.

| H64D-075 | VG £40 | F £80 | VF £160 |

Calais Mint

Obverse & Reverse Legend   As previous.

Reverse Inside Circle Legend   VILLA CALISIE — Town of Calais

Obverse   Front-facing bust of king, leaf on breast; leaves and trefoil usually in legend.

Reverse   As previous.

| H64D-080   ex. rare |

Trefoil Issue (1438 – 1443)

This issue usually has trefoil of pellets either side of neck and in the legends, as well as a leaf on the king's breast.

London Mint

Obverse & Reverse Legend   As previous.

Reverse Inside Circle Legend   CIVITAS LONDON — City of London

Obverse   Front-facing bust of king, leaf on breast and trefoils by neck; trefoil of pellets in legend.

Reverse   A leaf sometimes found before LON in legend.

| H64D-085 | VG £40 | F £80 | VF £160 |

Obverse & Reverse Legend   As previous.

Obverse   As previous, but fleurs in spandrels.

Reverse   There are sometimes extra pellets in the quarters.

| H64D-090 | VG £40 | F £80 | VF £160 |

As previous, but sometimes trefoils instead of fleurs.

| H64D-095 | VG £35 | F £75 | VF £150 |

Calais Mint

Obverse & Reverse Legend   As previous.

Reverse Inside Circle Legend   VILLA CALISIE — Town of Calais

Obverse   Front-facing bust of king, leaf on breast and trefoils by neck, trefoils in legend.

Reverse   Trefoils in legend.

| H64D-100 | VG £60 | F £150 | VF rare |

Trefoil Pellet Issue (1443 – 1445)

This issue was only struck at the London mint.

Obverse & Reverse Legend   As previous.

Reverse Inside Circle Legend   CIVITAS LONDON — City of London

Obverse   Front-facing bust of king, trefoils by neck, pellets by crown and small leaf on breast; trefoils in legend.

Reverse   Sometimes an extra pellet in two quarters.

| H64D-105 | VG £35 | F £70 | VF £200 |

Leaf Pellet Issue (1445 – 1454)

This issue usually has a leaf on breast and a pellet either side of the crown. It was only struck at the London mint.

Obverse & Reverse Legend   As previous.

Reverse Inside Circle Legend   CIVITAS LONDON — City of London

Obverse   Front-facing bust of king, leaf on breast and pellets by crown.

Reverse   An extra pellet in two quarters on reverse.

| H64D-110 | VG £30 | F £65 | VF £150 |

Similar to previous, but obverse legend reads ANGLI instead of ANGL and sometimes has a trefoil.

| H64D-115 | VG £30 | F £65 | VF £150 |

Obverse Legend   As H64D-110, usual reading of ANGL.

Reverse Legends   As previous.

Obverse   Front-facing bust of king, leaf on neck and pellets by crown.

Reverse   An extra pellet in two quarters.

| H64D-120 | VG £40 | F £80 | VF £180 |

As previous, but four pellets instead of two in the obverse field (two by the crown and two by the hair).

| H64D-125 | VG £45 | F £100 | VF £225 |

Unmarked Issue (1445 – 1454)

This issue was only struck at the London mint.

Obverse & Reverse Legend   As previous.

Reverse Inside Circle Legend   CIVITAS LONDON — City of London

Obverse   Front-facing bust of king, no marks.

Reverse   Two or four extra pellets.

H64D-130	VG £150	F £400	VF rare

Cross Pellet Issue (1454 – 1460)

This issue has a variety of markings and was struck at the London mint.

Obverse & Reverse Legend   As previous.

Reverse Inside Circle Legend   CIVITAS LONDON — City of London

Obverse   Saltire either side of neck, pellets by crown, leaf and fleur on breast.

Reverse   Two extra pellets in quarters.

H64D-135	VG £60	F £120	VF £250

Legends   As previous.

Obverse   Saltire on neck, pellets by crown, a mullet is usually found after HENRIC and FRANC.

Reverse   Usually two extra pellets in design, sometimes a mullet in legend.

H64D-140	VG £55	F £110	VF £230

As previous, but mascles instead of mullets in legend.

H64D-145	VG £60	F £120	VF £250

As previous, but the pellets are by the king's hair instead of the crown.

H64D-150	VG £80	F £140	VF £300

Lis Pellet Issue (1454 – 1460)

This issue was struck at the London mint.

Obverse & Reverse Legend   As previous.

Reverse Inside Circle Legend   CIVITAS LONDON — City of London

Obverse   Front-facing bust of king, lis on neck, pellets by crown; sometimes a mascle after HENRIC.

Reverse   Sometimes two extra pellets in quarters.

H64D-155	VG £100	F £250	VF £550

Edward IV First Reign (1461 – 1470)

As with all Edward IV issues, groats can be divided into the heavy and the light coinage, so called because of a 20% reduction in the weight of the coins in 1464 when groats changed from weighing 60 grains (3.9 grams) to 48 grains (3.1 grams). Edward IV groats are fairly distinctive and EDWARD is found at the top of the obverse legend. To distinguish these issues from those of other Edwards, collectors should bear in mind the following points: Edward I's portrait is quite distinct from any other issue. Edward III's portrait, hair, crown and style of lettering are different. Edward IV's heavy coinage is slightly larger and, of course, heavier than the light coinage and the style is slightly different. Edward IV's second reign coinage is fairly similar to that of Edward IV's light coinage but may be distinguished, either by various small differences or marks, or by the mintmarks which tend to be different. The coins classed as Edward IV or V have a mintmark of halved sun and rose and it is uncertain whether they were an issue of Edward IV or V.

Heavy coinage groats were all struck at London and all varieties are scarce. The light coinage issue is far more prolific and, as the demand for coins increased, Bristol, Coventry, Norwich and York as well as London became active mints; Coventry and Norwich however ceased by Edward IV's second reign. The mint's name is found on the reverse of the coin in the inner circle and reads CIVITAS LONDON for London; VILLA BRESTOLL, BRISTOLL, BRESTOW, BRISTOW for Bristol; CIVITAS COVETRE for Coventry; CIVITAS NORWIC, NORVIC for Norwich or CIVITAS EBORACI for York.

Collecting Hints

Edward IV's heavy coinage issue is fairly rare, but sometimes available in Fine or VF condition. Light coinage groats from the London mint are fairly common and usually found in about Fine condition, although VF and even EF examples are not uncommon. However, the issues of the provincial mints, with the exception of York, are fairly scarce and desirable, especially in better than Fine condition. Nevertheless, collectors should have little difficulty obtaining an Edward IV groat and many of the issues tend to be unclipped with few problems and readable legends.

Heavy Coinage (1461 – 1465)

These issues were all produced at the London mint.

Obverse Legend   EDWARD DI GRA REX ANGL Z FRANC — Edward by the grace of God King of England and France

Reverse Legend   POSVI DEUM ADIVTOREM MEUM — I have made God my helper

Reverse Inside Circle Legend   CIVITAS LONDON — City of London

Obverse   Front-facing bust of king with a lis on neck and pellets by crown; mintmark cross fleury, plain cross, lis. Sometimes muled.

Reverse   Long cross with three pellets in each quarter.

E44D-005	VG £50	F £100	VF £300

As previous, but no pellets either side of crown; mintmark plain cross or lis.

E44D-010	VG £60	F £100	VF £275

As previous, but front-facing bust of king, crescent on breast, quatrefoils by neck; mintmark rose.

| E44D-015 | VG £60 | F £120 | VF £325 |

As previous, but trefoil on king's breast; mintmark rose.

| E44D-020 | VG £50 | F £100 | VF £300 |

As previous, but an eye in the reverse inner circle legend.

| E44D-025 | VG £60 | F £120 | VF £300 |

As previous, but no quatrefoils by bust; mintmark rose.

| E44D-030 | VG £70 | F £120 | VF £325 |

As previous, but no trefoil on breast; mintmark rose.

| E44D-035 | VG £65 | F £120 | VF £300 |

Legends As previous.

Obverse Annulet at either side of king's neck; mintmark rose.

Reverse Eye in reverse legend after TAS.

| E44D-040 | VG £70 | F £140 | VF £350 |

Light Coinage (1464 – 1470)

London Mint

This coin was struck with dies from the last heavy coinage issue (E44D-040) and can only be differentiated by its weight, 48 grains (3.1 grams).

Obverse Legend EDWARD DI GRA REX ANGL Z FRANC — Edward by the grace of God King of England and France

Reverse Legend POSVI DEUM ADIVTOREM MEUM — I have made God my helper

Reverse Inside Circle Legend CIVITAS LONDON — City of London

Obverse Front-facing bust of king, annulets at neck; mintmark rose.

Reverse Eye after TAS.

| E44D-045 | VG £40 | F £75 | VF £150 |

As previous, but new dies with a slightly different style; eye on reverse after DON or TAS.

| E44D-050 | VG £45 | F £85 | VF £200 |

This issue, like E44D-045, was struck with heavy coinage dies of E44D-020 and may only be distinguished by its weight.

Legends As previous.

Obverse Front-facing bust of king with quatrefoils either side of neck; mintmark rose.

Reverse Eye after TAS in legend.

| E44D-055 | VG £40 | F £75 | VF £150 |

As previous, but new dies are used; mintmark rose.

| E44D-060 | VG £35 | F £65 | VF £140 |

As previous, but no marks by neck and an eye in reverse legend; mintmark rose.

| E44D-065 | VG £50 | F £100 | VF £250 |

Legends As previous.

Obverse Front-facing bust of king, quatrefoils at neck; mintmark rose, sun, crown and long-cross fitchée. The mintmarks of this issue are sometimes muled so there is a different mintmark on each side of the coin.

Reverse No marks (such as eyes in legend).

| E44D-070 | VG £35 | F £60 | VF £120 |

As previous, but a rose or quatrefoil on the king's breast; mintmark rose, crown and sun. Sometimes muled.

| E44D-075 | VG £35 | F £60 | VF £120 |

As previous, but no marks by neck; mintmark sun, crown and long-cross fitchée. Sometimes muled.

E44D-080	VG £35	F £60	VF £120

As previous, with trefoils or crosses at neck; mintmark long-cross fitchée, rose and sun. Sometimes muled.

E44D-085	VG £35	F £60	VF £120

Bristol Mint

Obverse Legend EDWARD DI GRA REX ANGL Z FRANC — Edward by the grace of God King of England and France

Reverse Legend POSVI DEUM ADIVTOREM MEUM — I have made God my helper

Reverse Inside Circle Legend VILLA BRESTOLL or BRISTOLL or BRESTOW or BRISTOW — Town of Bristol

Obverse Front-facing bust of king, 'B' on breast, quatrefoils at neck; mintmark sun, rose and crown. Usually muled.

Reverse Long-cross; no unusual marks in legends.

E44D-090	VG £40	F £90	VF £180

As previous, but without 'B' on king's breast; mintmark sun.

E44D-095	VG £40	F £90	VF £180

As E44D-090 with 'B' on breast but trefoils at neck; mintmark sun.

E44D-100	VG £35	F £85	VF £170

As previous, 'B' on king's breast but no marks by neck; mintmark sun.

E44D-105	VG £35	F £85	VF £170

Coventry Mint

Obverse & Reverse Legend As previous.

Reverse Inside Circle Legend CIVITAS COVETRE — City of Coventry

Obverse Front-facing bust of king with 'C' for Coventry on king's breast and quatrefoils at neck; mintmark sun or rose. Sometimes muled.

Reverse No marks on reverse.

E44D-110	VG £60	F £150	VF £250

There is a noticeable difference in style and engraving expertise between the previous issue (E44D-110) and the two subsequent ones.

As previous, but coins produced from local, crude, poor quality dies; mintmark rose.

E44D-115	VG £60	F £155	VF £270

As previous, but no 'C' or quatrefoils.

E44D-120	VG £65	F £160	VF £350

Norwich Mint

Obverse & Reverse Legend As previous.

Reverse Inside Circle Legend CIVITAS NORWIC or NORVIC — City of Norwich

Obverse Front-facing bust of king with N for Norwich on his breast and quatrefoils at neck; mintmark rose or sun. Sometimes muled.

Reverse No marks.

E44D-125	VG £50	F £100	VF £300

York Mint

Obverse & Reverse Legend As previous.

Reverse Inside Circle Legend CIVITAS EBORACI — City of York

Obverse Front-facing bust of king with 'E' for EBORACI on his breast and quatrefoils at neck; mintmark sun, lis or crown. Sometimes muled.

Reverse No marks.

E44D-130	VG £35	F £70	VF £150

As previous, but trefoils at neck; mintmark lis and sun. Sometimes muled.

E44D-135	VG £35	F £70	VF £150

As E44D-130, but no 'E' on the king's breast; mintmark lis.

E44D-140	VG £40	F £75	VF £165

Henry VI Restored (Oct. 1470 – April 1471)

This scarce issue is very similar to Henry VI's first reign groats, especially those from the London mint, but has no other marks except the mintmark which in some cases is actually unique to the Restored coinage. Although this fact alone distinguishes this issue from the majority of earlier ones, collectors should also bear in mind that on some of the obverse legends of the Restored coinage HENRIC reads HENRICV. Nevertheless, there is no easy way of identifying this issue and a process of elimination based on the marks, mintmarks and obverse legend readings of every Henry VI class may have to be employed to identify a coin accurately.

Collecting Hints

All groats from this reign are rare due to the fact that it only lasted a few months. Most coins are available in Fine condition, although VF examples are obtainable. Collectors should try to ensure that a specimen is of good enough condition to be safely attributed to this rare issue.

London Mint

Obverse Legend   HENRIC(V) DI GRA REX ANGL Z FRANC — Henry by the grace of God King of England and France

Reverse Legend   POSVI DEUM ADIVTOREM MEUM — I have made God my helper

Reverse Inside Circle Legend   CIVITAS LONDON — City of London

Obverse   Front-facing bust of king, no marks; mintmark cross pattée, Restoration cross, lis, short cross fitchée. Often muled.

Reverse   Long cross, three pellets in each quarter.

H64D-160	VG £100	F £200	VF £350

Bristol Mint

This issue is easily identified, being the only one to be struck by a Henry at the Bristol mint.

Obverse & Reverse Legend   As previous.

Reverse Inside Circle Legend   VILLA BRISTOW — Town of Bristol

Obverse   Front-facing bust of king, 'B' on his breast; mintmark Restoration cross, rose, trefoil, short cross fitchée. Sometimes muled.

Reverse   As previous.

H64D-165	VG £110	F £250	VF £450

York Mint

This issue is again easily identified as it is the only issue of a Henry struck at York that has an E for EBORACUM (York) on the king's breast.

Obverse & Reverse Legend   As previous.

Reverse Inside Circle Legend   CIVITAS EBORACI — City of York

Obverse   Front-facing bust of king, 'E' on king's breast; mintmark lis and sun. Sometimes muled.

Reverse   As previous.

H64D-170	VG £100	F £200	VF £400

Edward IV Second Reign (1471 – 1483)

The groats from Edward IV's second reign are very similar to the first reign light coinage issues, which is hardly surprising as the two periods were only seven months apart. In identifying a second reign groat, collectors should check firstly, that the mint on the reverse inner circle reads CIVITAS LONDON for London, VILLA BRISTOW (varieties) for Bristol or CIVITAS EBORACI for York. Secondly, that any marks, such as pellets or roses, correspond to those listed under the various classes, And thirdly, that the mintmark, found above the king's head on the obverse and at the beginning of the outer circle legend on the reverse, ties in with the appropriate class. However, in some cases dies were muled so a different mintmark appears on each side of the coin; this situation is not uncommon for coins from this period.

Collecting Hints

Most of these issues are fairly common and coins are usually found in Fine condition although VF and EF examples are not uncommon. Most coins tend to be unclipped with full, readable legends.

London Mint

Obverse Legend   EDWARD DI GRA REX ANGL Z FRANC — Edward by the grace of God King of England and France

Reverse Legend   POSVI DEUM ADIVTOREM MEUM — I have made God my helper

Reverse Inside Circle Legend   CIVITAS LONDON — City of London

Obverse   Front-facing bust of king, no marks by bust, trefoils on cusps; mintmark short cross fitchée, annulet, trefoil, sun, pellet in annulet, cross and four pellets, cross in circle.

Reverse   Long cross, three pellets in each quarter.

E44D-145	VG £30	F £55	VF £125

As previous, but a rose either side of the bust; mintmark pellet in annulet.

E44D-150	VG £30	F £60	VF £125

Legends As previous.

Obverse Front-facing bust of king, no marks by bust, fleurs on cusps; mintmark pierced cross, pierced cross and pellet, pierced cross with central pellet.

Reverse As previous.

E44D-155	VG £30	F £60	VF £125

As previous, but a pellet either side of the bust; mintmark pierced cross.

E44D-160	VG £40	F £90	VF £225

As E44D-155, but rose on breast; mintmark heraldic cinquefoil.

E44D-165	VG £30	F £60	VF £125

Bristol Mint

This issue is very similar to the one from Edward IV's first reign. Check mintmarks on both sides of the coin for accurate identification.

Obverse & Reverse Legend As previous.

Reverse Inside Circle Legend VILLA BRISTOW (possible varieties) — Town of Bristol

Obverse Front-facing bust of king, 'B' for Bristol on his breast; mintmark rose, annulet, sun, or none on reverse. Sometimes muled.

Reverse As previous.

E44D-170	VG £40	F £90	VF £200

York Mint

Both Edward IV reigns use mintmark lis but the earlier issues from the first reign have marks by the king's neck or no 'E' on the king's breast.

Obverse & Reverse Legend As previous.

Reverse Inside Circle Legend CIVITAS EBORACI — City of York

Obverse Front-facing bust of king, 'E' for EBORACI on his breast; mintmark lis.

Reverse As previous.

E44D-175	VG £40	F £90	VF £200

Edward IV or V

It is uncertain whether this issue was struck for Edward IV or Edward V but most numismatists consider that the dies were made for Edward IV and used for the production of coins under Edward V. This issue can only be differentiated from the more common issues of Edward IV by the mintmark halved sun and rose which is found on both sides of the coin.

Collecting Hints

This issue is very rare in any grade but Fine and VF examples do exist. It is most important that collectors obtain an example with a clear mintmark which could not be confused with mintmark rose or heraldic cinquefoil of the more common earlier issues of Edward IV.

Obverse Legend EDWARD DI GRA REX ANGL Z FRANC — Edward by the grace of God King of England and France

Reverse Legend POSVI DEUM ADIVTOREM MEUM — I have made God my helper

Reverse Inside Circle Legend CIVITAS LONDON — City of London

Obverse Front-facing bust of king, no marks, fleurs on cusps; mintmark halved sun and rose.

Reverse Long cross, three pellets in each quarter; mintmark halved sun and rose.

E44D-180	VG £200	F £600	VF £1,450

Edward V (1483)

This extremely rare issue can be distinguished from the previous, more common ones of Edward IV only by the mintmark boar's head. The boar's head was the personal emblem of Richard III who was the young king's 'protector', even though he was later considered responsible for the boy's murder. On this rare issue, the boar's head mintmark is found on the obverse, and the halved sun and rose mintmark from the previous issue is found on the reverse.

Collecting Hints

This issue is extremely rare in any grade; Fine and VF examples exist, but rarely appear on the market. Collectors should ensure a specimen has clear mintmarks to avoid confusion with coins from the reign of Edward IV.

Obverse Legend EDWARD DI GRA REX ANGL Z FRANC — Edward by the grace of God King of England and France

Reverse Legend POSVI DEUM ADIVTOREM MEUM — I have made God my helper

Reverse Inside Circle Legend CIVITAS LONDON — City of London

Obverse Front-facing bust of king, fleurs on cusps, no marks by king; mintmark boar's head.

Reverse Long cross, three pellets in each quarter; mintmark halved sun and rose.

E54D-005	ex. rare

Richard III (1483 – 1485)

Richard III's coinage is easily identified by the obverse legend which starts RICARD; the only other Richard to issue groats was Richard II but they are very different in style and mintmarks.

Collecting Hints

Richard III groats are rare but obtainable and usually found in Fine condition, mostly unclipped with clear legends. VF and even EF examples exist, but are very rare.

London Mint

Obverse Legend RICARD DI GRA REX ANGL Z FRANC — Richard by the grace of God King of England and France

Reverse Legend POSVI DEUM ADIVTOREM MEUM — I have made God my helper

Reverse Inside Circle Legend CIVITAS LONDON — City of London

Obverse Front-facing bust of king; mintmark halved sun and rose, or boar's head, or none. Often muled, with varieties in style of mintmark.

Reverse Long cross, three pellets in each quarter; mintmark as obverse.

R34D-005	VG £250	F £550	VF £1,200

As previous, but pellet below bust.

R34D-010	VG £250	F £550	VF £1,200

York Mint

Obverse & Reverse Legend As previous.

Reverse Inside Circle Legend CIVITAS EBORACI — City of York

Obverse Front-facing bust of king without pellet; mintmark halved sun and rose.

Reverse No mintmark.

R34D-015	VG £300	F £700	VF £1,400

Henry VII (1485 – 1509)

Numismatically, Henry VII's reign can be divided into two sections, the front-facing bust issue and the profile issue. The first is in many respects similar to that of previous reigns, but the superb profile issue depicts a lifelike portrait of the king and is wonderful in detail and manufacture. The dies were engraved by Alexander of Brugsal and the coins of this period reflect Renaissance aesthetic values and the change that was sweeping through Europe. The only mint that produced groats during Henry VII's reign was London and CIVITAS LONDON is found on the reverse inner circle legend of the front-facing bust issues.

Front-facing Bust Issue (1485 – 1505)

As stated above, Henry VII's front-facing bust issue is similar to other reigns and the obverse legend begins HENRIC. However, not only is the crown quite distinct, being taller with arches and often jewelled, but also the king's portrait is different in style, and so is his hair. Finally, although the mintmarks used for this issue are also found on coins of other kings, such as Edward IV, they were not often used for any other Henry.

Collecting Hints

Front-facing bust groats, except for the first two classes, are fairly common and usually available unclipped in Fine or VF condition. Coins of lower grades are often damaged; EF examples are rare, but occasionally obtainable. The mintmarks on some of the issues, such as the greyhound's head, are often very bold and this makes the coin more desirable.

Obverse Legend HENRIC DI GRA REX ANGL Z FRANC — Henry by the grace of God King of England and France

Reverse Legend POSVI DEUM ADIVTOREM MEUM — I have made God my helper

Reverse Inside Circle Legend CIVITAS LONDON — City of London

Obverse Front-facing bust of king, old-style open crown; mintmarks halved sun and rose, lis upon halved sun, lis upon sun and rose, lis-rose dimidiated. Sometimes muled.

Reverse Long cross, three pellets in each quarter.

H74D-005	VG £40	F £150	VF £350

As previous, but crosses or saltires by neck; mintmark rose, cross fitchée or lis.

N.B. This issue shares the same mintmarks as Henry VI both reigns.

| H74D-010 | VG £45 | F £150 | VF £350 |

New Crown Type

Obverse & Reverse Legend   As previous.

Obverse   Front-facing bust of king, the crown has two plain arches either side; mintmark none or cinquefoil.

Reverse   As previous.

| H74D-015 | VG £35 | F £70 | VF £140 |

As previous, but crosses either side of neck; mintmark lis or none.

| H74D-020 | VG £38 | F £75 | VF £150 |

An extremely rare variety has a portcullis in the centre of the reverse; mintmark none on the obverse, lis on the reverse.

| H74D-025 | ex. rare |

Obverse Legend   HENRIC DI GRA REX ANGL Z FRA (varieties in abbreviation) — Henry by the grace of God King of England and France

Reverse Legends   As previous.

Obverse   Front-facing bust of king, crown has two jewelled arches; mintmark cinquefoil.

Reverse   As H74D-020.

| H74D-030 | VG £38 | F £75 | VF £150 |

Similar but with more realistic hair; mintmark escallop, pansy.

| H74D-035 | VG £32 | F £65 | VF £130 |

As previous, but crown has one plain and one jewelled arch; mintmark pansy, crowned leopard's head, lis issuant from rose, anchor, greyhound's head. Sometimes muled.

| H74D-040 | VG £38 | F £75 | VF £150 |

As previous, but the crown is arched with a single bar rather than four separate arches; mintmark greyhound's head, rose, cross-crosslet. Sometimes muled.

| H74D-045 | VG £38 | F £75 | VF £150 |

As previous, but the single arch is now a double bar made up of two lines; mintmark greyhound's head, cross-crosslet. Sometimes muled.

| H74D-050 | VG £38 | F £75 | VF £150 |

Profile Issue (1502 – 1509)

With this issue Tudor England left its medieval past and entered the Renaissance, an exciting time of learning and discovery. The profile issue caused considerable interest at the time not least because the general style of coins had not changed much during the last two centuries. Notably, the practice of life-like portraits still continues today. This issue is unlike any previous ones apart from Henry VIII's first issue, but can easily be distinguished by the obverse legend which reads HENRIC VII (or variations) for Henry VII, and HENRIC VIII for Henry VIII. Although there is no mention on the design of where the coin was struck, the only mint used for the profile issue was London. The dies for this issue were made by a German engraver, Alexander of Brugsal.

Tentative Issue (1502 – 1505)

These issues were trials using various dies and styles but, as most were issued into circulation, they cannot really be considered patterns. With such a new style and design and a fairly uneducated public, it took time to introduce new coins into circulation and, like today, there was a general dislike of change and hesitation in accepting new coins.

Obverse Legend HENRIC VII DI GRA REX ANGL Z F — Henry VII by the grace of God King of England and France

Reverse Legend POSVI DEUM ADIVTOE MEU — I have made God my helper

Obverse Crowned bust right; mintmark none, lis, crosslet, greyhound's head. Sometimes muled.

Reverse Royal shield over cross fourchée which divides the legend.

| H74D-055 | VG £70 | F £150 | VF £325 |

Obverse Legend HENRIC DEI GRA REX ANGLI Z FRA — Henry by the grace of God King of England and France

Reverse Legend As previous.

Obverse As previous; mintmark lis, none, greyhound's head. Sometimes muled.

Reverse As previous.

| H74D-060 | VG £120 | F £250 | VF £600 |

Obverse Legend HENRIC SEPTIM DI GRA REX ANGL Z FR — Henry Seventh by the grace of God King of England and France

Reverse Legend As previous.

Obverse As previous; no mintmark.

Reverse As previous; mintmark lis.

| H74D-065 | ex. rare |

Obverse Legend HENRIC VII DI GRA REX ANGL Z F — Henry VII by the grace of God King of England and France

Reverse Legend As previous.

Obverse As previous, but the bust within tressure of arches; mintmark crosslet.

Reverse As previous; mintmark crosslet.

| H74D-070 | ex. rare |

Regular Issue

This issue is by far the most common; it was in no way a trial or pattern.

Legends & Reverse As previous.

Obverse Crowned bust facing right, triple band to king's crown; mintmark crosslet, pheon/crosslet, pheon. Slightly different in style from previous issues and sometimes muled.

| H74D-075 | VG £60 | F £120 | VF £275 |

Henry VIII (1509 – 1547)

Henry VIII groats may be classed in four main types, the first, second, third and posthumous issues. The first coinage (1509 – 26) was virtually identical to Henry VII's profile issue except for different mintmarks and the obverse legend reading HENRIC VIII instead of HENRIC VII, but still with the previous king's portrait. The portrait changed to that of Henry VIII in the second coinage (1526 – 44), which has several varieties and was minted in London and York. The third coinage (1544 – 47) was made of very base metal; it was struck with three slightly different styles of bust at the Tower mint, Southwark, Bristol, Canterbury and York. Finally, the posthumous issue of 1547 – 51 was produced during the first few years of Edward VI's reign but with Henry VIII's portrait and titles in the legends; three different busts were used for this issue with coins struck at the Tower mint, Southwark, Durham House, Bristol, Canterbury and York.

From the third coinage onwards two new London mints became active, Southwark and Durham House, and to avoid confusion, what was previously known as the London mint is henceforth referred to as Tower mint, from its location in the Tower of London. Coins may be linked to specific mints because they bear either the name of a mint or a legend exclusively attributed to one. They are the following: CIVITAS LONDON (City of London) for Southwark; POSVI DEUM ADIVTORE MEU(M) (I have made God my helper) for the Tower mint; REDDE CVIQUE QVOD SVVM EST (Render to each that which is his own) for Durham House; CIVITAS CANTOR for Canterbury; CIVITAS EBORACI for York and CIVITAS BRISTOLI for Bristol.

Collecting Hints

Most Henry VIII groats are fairly common. The first and second coinages, being made of good quality silver, are more attractive and usually obtainable unclipped with full legible legends on round flans in Fine condition, although VF examples are not uncommon; EF examples also exist and are extremely desirable. By comparison, the third and posthumous issues are, in most cases, extremely ugly coins. Not only is the old bust of the king less attractive, but also the low quality of the metal often produced a poor striking with weak legends and features and made the coins look dull, often with more mixed colours in the surface. Collectors should never attempt to clean coins of these issues, not even with a light duster, because they will appear copper in colour. Nevertheless, the groat is one of the most desirable coins of this reign and no collection should be without several examples.

First Coinage (1509 – 1526)

London Mint

Obverse Legend HENRIC VIII DI GRA REX AGL Z FRA — Henry VIII by the grace of God King of England and France

Reverse Legend POSVI DEU ADIVTORE MEU — I have made God my helper

Obverse Crowned bust of Henry VII facing right; mintmark pheon, castle, portcullis crowned.

Reverse Royal shield over cross fourchée which divides legend.

| H84D-005 | VG £60 | F £120 | VF £250 |

As previous, but the king's hair touches his collar, the lettering is mainly Lombardic; mintmark rose.

| H84D-025 | VG £50 | F £110 | VF £200 |

Tournai Mint

This mint was in France but under English control.

Obverse Legend As previous.

Reverse Legend CIVITAS TORNACEN — City of Tournai

Obverse As previous, but mintmark crowned 'T'.

Reverse As previous.

| H84D-010 | VG £150 | F £400 | VF £1,200 |

As previous, but the king's hair is over his collar, mostly Lombardic lettering; mintmark rose.

| H84D-030 | VG £50 | F £100 | VF £180 |

Second Coinage (1526 – 1544)

London Mint

Obverse Legend HENRIC VIII DI GRA REX AGL Z FR — Henry VIII by the grace of God King of England and France

Reverse Legend POSVI DEU ADIVTORE MEU — I have made God my helper

Obverse Youthful bust of king facing right with hair not touching the collar, Roman lettering except for the Lombardic 'H' in HENRIC; mintmark rose.

Reverse Long-cross fourchée over royal shield.

| H84D-015 | VG £80 | F £150 | VF £320 |

As previous, but all Lombardic lettering; mintmark lis, sunburst, arrow, pheon. Sometimes muled.

| H84D-035 | VG £50 | F £100 | VF £180 |

As previous, but the king's bust has slightly different features, with the hair above the collar and all the letters in the legend are Lombardic; mintmark lis, arrow, pheon, sunburst.

| H84D-040 | VG £50 | F £100 | VF £180 |

Irish Title

Obverse Legend HENRIC 8 DI GRA HIB REX AGL Z F (varieties exist) — Henry VIII by the grace of God King of Ireland England and France

Reverse Legend As previous.

Obverse As previous; mintmark pheon, lis; often muled.

Reverse As previous.

As previous, but Lombardic lettering; mintmark rose.

| H84D-020 | VG £50 | F £110 | VF £220 |

| H84D-045 | VG £100 | F £300 | VF £700 |

York Mint

The ecclesiastical mint of York was under Archbishop Thomas Wolsey.

Obverse Legend HENRIC VIII DI GRA AGL Z FRA — Henry VIII by the grace of God King of English and France

Reverse Legend CIVITAS EBORACI — City of York

Obverse Youthful bust of king facing right; mintmark voided cross, acorn, sometimes muled.

Reverse Long-cross fourchée over royal shield dividing 'T.W.' (Thomas Wolsey) and cardinal's hat below the shield.

H84D-050	VG £60	F £150	VF £300

As previous, but omits 'T.W.'; mintmark voided cross, acorn.

H84D-055	VG £200	F £450	VF £900

Third Coinage (1544 – 1547)

Made of base silver, these coins are usually dull in colour. The different styles of bust all depict an ageing king and were used for most of the provincial mints. Third coinage issues are often difficult to distinguish from posthumous coinage ones, especially if the portrait or mintmark are unclear. However, the style of lettering of most issues can help identify them. Illustrations of these styles may be found in the Mintmark Chapter and details of the lettering are given with each coin.

Tower Mint

Obverse Legend HENRIC 8 D G AGL FRA Z HIB REX — Henry VIII by the grace of God King of England France and Ireland

Reverse Legend POSVI DEUM ADIVTORE MEU — I have made God my helper

Obverse Crowned bust of king; mintmark lis. Lombardic lettering.

Reverse Royal shield over long-cross.

H84D-060	VG £35	F £70	VF £160

As previous, but with an annulet in the cross ends. Lombardic lettering.

H84D-065	VG £45	F £90	VF £200

Southwark Mint

Obverse Legend As previous.

Reverse Legend CIVITAS LONDON — City of London

Obverse Crowned bust of varying styles; mintmark none, lis, 'S' or 'S' and 'E'. Lombardic or Roman lettering.

Reverse As previous.

H84D-070	VG £40	F £80	VF £180

Bristol Mint

Obverse Legend As previous.

Reverse Legend CIVITAS BRISTOLI — City of Bristol

Obverse As previous; no mintmark. Lombardic lettering.

Reverse As previous, but mintmark 'W S'.

H84D-075	VG £45	F £90	VF £200

Canterbury Mint

Obverse Legend As previous.

Reverse Legend CIVITAS CANTOR — City of Canterbury

Obverse As previous; no mintmark. Usually Roman lettering.

Reverse As previous, but no mintmark.

H84D-080	VG £45	F £90	VF £200

York Mint

Obverse Legend As previous.

Reverse Legend CIVITAS EBORACI — City of York

Obverse As previous; no mintmark. Lombardic or Roman lettering.

Reverse As previous.

| H84D-085 | VG £45 | F £90 | VF £200 |

Posthumous Coinage (1547 – 1551)

These issues were again of base silver. Three new busts were used, although busts from the third coinage were also employed, albeit rarely, in the Tower and Bristol mints; these issues may be distinguished by the mintmarks.

Tower Mint

Obverse Legend HENRIC 8 DG AGL FRA Z HIB REX — Henry VIII by the grace of God King of England France and Ireland

Reverse Legend POSVI DEUM ADIVTORE MEU — I have made God my helper

Obverse Crowned busts of king of varying styles; mintmark lis, arrow, 'K', grapple, martlet or none. Often muled. Roman lettering.

Reverse Royal shield over cross.

| H84D-090 | VG £35 | F £75 | VF £160 |

Southwark Mint

Obverse Legend As previous.

Reverse Legend CIVITAS LONDON — City of London

Obverse As previous; mintmarks lis, 'E' or none. Roman lettering.

Reverse As previous.

| H84D-095 | VG £40 | F £80 | VF £180 |

Durham House Mint

Obverse Legend As previous.

Reverse Legend REDDE CVIQUE QVOD SVVM EST — Render to each that which is his own

Obverse Crowned bust of king; mintmark bow. Roman lettering.

Reverse As previous.

| H84D-100 | VG £75 | F £150 | VF £350 |

Bristol Mint

Obverse Legend As previous.

Reverse Legend CIVITAS BRISTOLI — City of Bristol

Obverse As H84D-075; no mintmark. Bristol lettering.

Reverse As previous, but mintmark 'WS' or 'TC'.

| H84D-105 | VG £40 | F £120 | VF £250 |

Canterbury Mint

Obverse Legend As previous.

Reverse Legend CIVITAS CANTOR — City of Canterbury

Obverse Crowned bust of king; mintmark none or rose. Roman lettering.

Reverse Royal shield over cross.

| H84D-110 | VG £40 | F £90 | VF £200 |

York Mint

Obverse Legend As previous.

Reverse Legend CIVITAS EBORACI — City of York

Obverse As previous; mintmark lis or none. Roman lettering.

Reverse As previous.

| H84D-115 | VG £45 | F £90 | VF £200 |

Edward VI (1547 – 1553)

The groat was only produced during Edward's first coinage (1547 – 49) at the same time as Henry VIII's posthumous issue. In fact the posthumous issue groat seems to have been more acceptable to the public, probably because Edward was just a boy with virtually no power in the country. Moreover, very few Edward VI groats were struck, at first because large quantities had been produced under Henry and in the posthumous coinage, and then because the production of the sixpence and threepence in the later part of the reign made this denomination appear redundant. All Edward VI groats were struck in base silver; they look dull in colour and often have a porous surface.

277

Tower Mint

Obverse Legend EDWARD D.G.

Reverse Legend POSVI

Obverse Crowned bust right; mintmark arrow.

Reverse Royal shield over cross.

| E64D-005 | VG £100 | F £300 | VF rare |

As previous, but obverse legend reads EDOARD 6.

| E64D-010 | ex. rare |

Southwark Mint

Obverse Legend As E64D-005.

Reverse Legend CIVITAS LONDON — City of London

Obverse As previous; mintmark 'E' or none.

Reverse As previous.

| E64D-015 | VG £120 | F £325 | VF rare |

Mary (1553 – 1554)

The coinage of Mary falls into two distinct categories. Firstly there is her own issue, which can be easily identified by the obverse legend which starts MARIA. The second category is for the period when Mary shared the throne with her husband Philip, and the obverse reads PHILIP Z MARIA. The groat was reintroduced as a denomination during Mary's reign. Although Edward VI and his council seem to have favoured the shilling, sixpence and threepence, the increased volume of groats struck under Mary indicate a desire to return to it as a principal silver denomination. Very large quantities of groats were produced throughout her reign and all bear a superb detailed portrait of

the queen: Philip's portrait was only included on the shilling and sixpence.

Obverse Legend MARIA D G ANG FRA Z HIB REGI — Mary by the grace of God Queen of England France and Ireland

Reverse Legend VERITAS TEMPORIS FILIA — Truth is the daughter of time

Obverse Crowned left-facing bust of queen; mintmark pomegranate after queen's name.

Reverse Royal shield over cross; mintmark as obverse after VERITAS.

| MA4D-005 | Poor £20 | VG £40 | F £85 | VF £250 |

Philip & Mary (1554 – 1558)

Obverse Legend PHILIP Z MARIA D G REX Z REGINA — Philip and Mary by the grace of God King and Queen

Reverse Legend POSUIMUS DEUM ADIVTO NOS — We have made God our helper

Obverse As previous, but mintmark lis at start of legend.

Reverse As previous; mintmark lis at start of legend.

| PM4D-005 | Poor £20 | VG £45 | F £95 | VF £280 |

Elizabeth I (1558 – 1603)

Groats continued to be struck in quite large numbers during the first few years of Elizabeth's reign but a desire to return to the predominance of the threepence, sixpence and shilling as the main silver denominations meant there was no further need for the groat. All groats, including the rare milled issue, were produced at the Tower mint. Due to their similar size and weight, groats might easily be confused with sixpences, but whereas none of the groats are dated, all sixpences are (except for some extremely rare examples); also all sixpences, except again for a few very rare issues, bear a large rose behind the queen's head.

Hammered Coinage

Collecting Hints

Groats are fairly common and usually available in about Fine condition; VF and EF examples are rare, but obtainable. Most coins are unclipped with clear legends.

First Issue (1559 – 1560)

Obverse Legend   ELIZABETH D G ANG FRA Z HIB REGI — Elizabeth by the grace of God Queen of England France and Ireland

Reverse Legend   POSUI DEU ADIUTOREM MEU(M) — I have made God my helper

Obverse   Crowned left-facing bust, wire-line inner circles; mintmark lis.

Reverse   Royal shield over cross.

| EL4D-005 | VG £60 | F £150 | VF £400 |

As previous, but wire-line and beaded inner circles.

| EL4D-010 | VG £25 | F £70 | VF £140 |

There is a rare variety with a very small bust. This issue uses the half-groat bust punch.

| EL4D-015 | rare |

Second Issue (1560 – 1561)

Obverse Legend   ELIZABETH D G ANG FRA ET HIB REGINA — Elizabeth by the grace of God Queen of England France and Ireland

Reverse Legend   POSUI DEU ADIUTOREM MEU — I have made God my helper

Obverse   Crowned left-facing bust, beaded circles; mintmarks cross crosslet or martlet.

Reverse   Royal shield over cross.

| EL4D-020 | VG £20 | F £50 | VF £100 |

Milled Coinage

This rare issue was struck in 1561; it is distinguishable from the sixpence by being undated and omitting the rose behind the queen's head. Milled coins are different in style from hammered, with the detail and striking usually clearer.

Collecting Hints

This issue is usually found in the lower grades, sometimes damaged. Elizabeth milled groats are considerably scarcer than the milled sixpences.

Obverse Legend   ELIZABETH D G ANG FRA ET HIB REGINA — Elizabeth by the grace of God Queen of the English France and Ireland

Reverse Legend   POSVI DEUM ADIVTOREM MEUM — I have made God my helper

Obverse   Crowned left-facing bust, no inner circles; mintmark star.

Reverse   Queen's shield over cross.

| EL4D-025 | VG £60 | F £140 | VF £350 |

Charles I   (1625 – 1649)

No groats were issued under James I, being replaced by the two-pence, sixpence and shilling. The denomination was reintroduced under Charles I and, although no groats were produced at the Tower mint, several provincial mints were active. They can all be easily distinguished from other denominations by the Roman numerals IIII by the king's bust.

Aberystwyth Mint

The mint in the royal castle of Aberystwyth was created in 1637 by indenture between the king and the moneyer Thomas Bushell so as to utilise the locally-mined silver. All Aberystwyth issues use the mintmark open book which symbolised Bushell's accountability to the king. The dies for these issues were made in London and the mint closed in 1642.

Collecting Hints

This issue can be found in all grades from VG to EF. They are well struck and the quality of coins found is higher than other issues.

Obverse Legend   CAROLUS D G M B F ET H REX — Charles by the grace of God Great King of Britain France and Ireland

Reverse Legend   CHRISTO AVSPICE REGNO — I reign under the auspices of Christ

Obverse   Large left-facing bust with lace collar, no armour on shoulder and a plume in front of the king's face, value behind; mintmark book.

Reverse   Plume over oval shield with royal arms.

C14D-005	VG £30	F £45	VF £90	EF £200

As previous, but smaller bust.

C14D-010	VG £30	F £45	VF £90	EF £250

Larger bust and the king has armour on shoulder.

C14D-015	VG £30	F £50	VF £100	EF £275

Aberystwyth Furnace Mint

Collecting Hints

This issue is rare in any grade. Coins are often found holed, which was probably done officially at a later date. Most coins appear to have seen considerable circulation.

Obverse Legend   CAROLUS D G MAG BR FRA ET HIB REX — Charles by the grace of God King of Great Britain France and Ireland

Reverse Legend   CHRISTO AVSPICE REGNO — I reign under the auspices of Christ

Obverse   Left-facing bust of king with IIII behind the head and small plume in front of the face; mintmark crown.

Reverse   Oval shield with plume above it.

C14D-020	VG £90	F £200	VF £450

Oxford Mint

Collecting Hints

While scarce, these issues are obtainable, especially in the lower grades. Coins are sometimes found bent, damaged or holed.

Obverse Legend   CAROLUS D G M B F ET H REX — Charles by the grace of God King of Great Britain France and Ireland

Outer Reverse Legend   EXURGAT DEUS DISSIPENTUR INIMICI — Let God arise and His enemies be scattered

Reverse Centre Legend   RELIG PRO LEG ANG LIBER PA(R) — The religion of the Protestants the laws of England the liberty of Parliament

Obverse   Bust of king with IIII behind head and plume in front of face; mintmark book. This die was from the Aberystwyth mint.

Reverse   Declaration in centre, plume above, dated 1644, 'OX' below date; the outer legend starts three-quarters of the way around the coin.

C14D-025	VG £55	F £90	VF £275

As previous, but three plumes above Declaration.

C14D-030	VG £55	F £100	VF £300

As previous, but lion's head on shoulder.

C14D-035	VG £50	F £90	VF £275

As previous, but large bust with the king's crown reaching to the top of the coin.

C14D-040	VG £60	F £110	VF £300

Large bust to the bottom of the coin and obverse legend starting two-thirds of the way around coin instead of at the top.

C14D-045	VG £60	F £100	VF £300

Similar to previous, but no inner circles. This issue uses a Rawlins die and there is an 'R' on the king's shoulder.

C14D-050	VG £60	F £125	VF £350

As C14D-035, but dated 1645.

C14D-055	VG £60	F £125	VF £350

As C14D-045, but dated 1645.

C14D-060	VG £60	F £110	VF £325

Similar to C14D-050 with large single plume over Declaration which is in cartouche; dated 1645 or 1646.

C14D-065	VG £55	F £125	VF £325

Bristol Mint

These issues are very similar to the Oxford ones except that they sometimes have 'BR' instead of 'OX' below the date and the Declaration is between two straight lines with three plumes above. Because groats are often in poor condition, collectors might have to check through all Charles I issues to find the correct type.

Collecting Hints

While scarce, these issues are obtainable, especially in the lower grades. Coins are sometimes found bent, damaged or holed.

Obverse Legend   CAROLUS D G MAG BR FR ET HI REX — Charles by the grace of God King of Great Britain France and Ireland

Reverse Legend   EXURGAT DEUS DISSIPENTUR INIMICI — Let God arise and His enemies be scattered

Reverse Centre Legend   REL PROT LEG ANG LIB PAR — The religion of the Protestants the laws of England the liberty of Parliament

Obverse   Crowned left-facing bust, value behind, nothing in front of face; mintmark pellet.

Reverse   Three plumes above Declaration; 1644 below.

C14D-070	VG £85	F £190	VF £400

As previous, but plumelet before face.

C14D-075	VG £85	F £190	VF £400

As previous, but 'BR' for Bristol below date.

C14D-080	VG £80	F £180	VF £360

Late Declaration Issue (1645 – 1646)

There is considerable debate regarding where these coins were struck. Previously attributed to Lundy Island or Barnstaple, it is now thought that they may have been struck at Bridgnorth or Ashby de la Zouch. The main difference from previous issues is the date.

Collecting Hints

The first issue is of the highest rarity; the second is rare but obtainable, usually in the lower grades.

Obverse Legend   CAROLUS D G MAG BR FR ET HIB REX — Charles by the grace of God King of Great Britain France and Ireland

Outer Reverse Legend   EXURGAT DEUS DISSIPENTUR INIMICI — Let God arise and His enemies be scattered

Inner Reverse Legend   REL PRO LEG ANG LIB PAR — The religion of the Protestants the laws of England the liberty of Parliament

Obverse   Bust of king, value behind the head and plumelet in front.

Reverse   Three plumelets above Declaration, dated 1645.

C14D-085	ex. rare

As previous, but upper Declaration line is in two scrolls, dated 1646; mintmark plumelet on the obverse and plume or pellet on the reverse .

C14D-090	VG £70	F £150	VF £350

Exeter Mint

Collecting Hints

While scarce, this issue is obtainable and usually found un-damaged in VG to Fine condition.

Obverse Legend 1644 CAROLUS D G M B F ET H REX — 1644 (date) Charles by the grace of God King of Great Britain France and Ireland

Reverse Legend CHRISTO AUSPICE REGNO — I reign under the auspices of Christ

Obverse Bust of king, value behind; mintmark rose.

Reverse Oval shield.

C14D-095	VG £50	F £140	VF £400

Worcester, Salopia (Shrewsbury) or possibly Hereford Mint

There is great uncertainty regarding which mint struck this issue, especially as dies could have been transported to all three mints.

Collecting Hints

This issue is very rare and the coins were struck with extremely crude dies.

Obverse Legend CAROLUS D G M B F ET H REX — Charles by the grace of God King of Great Britain France and Ireland

Reverse Legend CHRISTO AUSPICE REGNO — I reign under the auspices of Christ

Obverse Crowned left-facing bust in very crude style, value behind; mintmark rose or lis over rose.

Reverse Oval shield; mintmark helmet.

C14D-100	VG £220	F £500	VF rare

No groats were issued during the Commonwealth.

Charles II (1660 – 1685)

Hammered Issue (1660 – 1662)

The hammered groat was only struck once during Charles II's reign, in the third issue.

Collecting Hints

This issue is fairly common especially in Fine or less condition; VF and even EF examples are not uncommon. Many of the coins lack some of the legends due either to a small flan or clipping.

Obverse Legend CAROLUS D G MAG BRIT FR ET HIB REX — Charles by the grace of God King of Great Britain France and Ireland

Reverse Legend CHRISTO AVSPICE REGNO — I reign under the auspices of Christ

Obverse Left-facing bust of king, mark of value behind, inner circles; mintmark crown.

Reverse Shield over cross; mintmark crown.

C24DH-005	VG £20	F £50	VF £100

Threepence

First introduced in Edward VI's fine silver coinage, the threepence was of good quality silver and formed part of a new set of denominations. But as with most newly introduced denominations it was not very popular and the next two reigns reverted back to the groat. Although it was an easier denomination to work with in the context of pounds and shillings, the public preferred the groat which had, of course, been in circulation since the reign of Edward I.

Edward VI   (1547 – 1553)

The threepence, introduced during the fine silver issue and made of good quality silver, is easily distinguished from the other denominations by the Roman numeral III for threepence found to the side of the king's head. Threepences were struck at London and York.

Collecting Hints

Edward VI threepences are fairly rare, especially in a good grade, and many are very badly cracked. This cracking does not appear to have been a fault of striking but, for some reason, deliberate vandalism. Coins are usually available in about Fine condition and VF and EF examples are extremely rare.

London Mint
Obverse Legend   EDWARD VI D G ANG FRA Z HIB REX — Edward VI by the grace of God King of England France and Ireland

Reverse Legend   POSUI DEUM ADIUTOREM MEUM — I have made God my helper

Obverse   Front-facing bust of king with rose to the left and III to the right; mintmark tun.

Reverse   Long cross over royal shield.

E63D-005	VG £70	F £250	VF £550

York Mint
Obverse Legend   As previous.

Reverse Legend   CIVITAS EBORACI — City of York

Obverse   As previous, but mintmark mullet.

Reverse   As previous.

E63D-010	VG £100	F £300	VF £650

No threepences were struck during the reigns of Mary or Philip and Mary.

Elizabeth I   (1558 – 1603)

The threepence was reintroduced under Elizabeth I, who realised the importance of smaller denominations, and it played an important part in a varied structure of denominations. With a 21 mm diameter for most 1561 issues and 19 mm for all other, the threepence is fairly similar in size to the groat and halfgroat but may easily be distinguished as, unlike them, it is dated and has a rose behind the queen's bust. The coins also have mintmarks on both sides which facilitates dating when the date itself is weak. Milled threepences were also produced and although they too are dated and have a rose behind the queen's bust, they differ from the hammered issue in style, being more ornate and lacking inner circles to divide the legend from the bust or shield. Three-halfpences were also introduced under Elizabeth but, although they are fairly similar in style to the threepence, they are much smaller with a maximum diameter of 17 mm on some 1561 issues and 16 mm on all others.

Hammered Coinage

No threepences were struck during the first or second issues.

Collecting Hints

Hammered threepences are fairly common in Fine condition, while even VF or EF examples are desirable but not very rare. Issues are usually unclipped, but sometimes slightly bent. Collectors should try to obtain an example in at least Fine condition, with a clear date and reasonable portrait.

Third Issue (1561 – 1577)

Large Flan Issue (21 mm)
Obverse Legend   ELIZABETH D G. ANG FR ET HIB REGINA — Elizabeth by the grace of God Queen of England France and Ireland

Reverse Legend   POSUI DEU ADIUTOREM MEU — I have made God my helper

Obverse   Crowned bust of queen, rose behind head; mintmark pheon.

Reverse   Shield over long cross, dated 1561.

EL3D-005	VG £30	F £60	VF £120

Regular Flan Issue (19 mm)
Legends   As previous.

Obverse   Crowned bust of queen, rose behind; mintmark as listed below.

Reverse   Shield over long cross, date (listed below) over shield.

Mintmark & Date   Pheon (1561 – 65), rose (1565), portcullis (1566), lion (1566 – 67), coronet (1567 – 70), castle (1570 – 71), ermine (1572 – 73), acorn (1573 – 74) eglantine (1573 – 77).

| EL3D-010 | VG £20 | F £40 | VF £80 |

As previous, but tall narrow bust with large rose, dated 1562; mintmark star.

| EL3D-030 | VG £60 | F £140 | VF £280 |

As previous, but omitting rose behind the queen's head on the obverse, dated 1568; mintmark coronet.

| EL3D-015 | four known |

As previous, but short bust with small rose.

| EL3D-035 | VG £70 | F £160 | VF £300 |

Fourth Issue (1578 – 1582)

This issue is identical to the third issue except that its silver content is fractionally lower.

As previous, but mintmark and date as listed below.
Mintmark & Date   Plain cross (1578 – 79), long cross (1580 – 82), sword (1582).

| EL3D-020 | VG £20 | F £40 | VF £80 |

No threepences were issued during the fifth or sixth issues.

As previous, but the long cross on the reverse is a cross pattée; dated 1563 or 1564.

| EL3D-040 | VG £80 | F £250 |

No threepences were struck during the reign of James I.

Charles I (1625 – 1649)

Under Charles I, no threepences were struck at the Tower mint but most provincial mints were active producing them, sometimes in considerable quantities. The denomination is identified by the Roman numeral III behind the king's bust.

York Mint (1638 – 1649)

Milled Coinage (1561 – 1564)

Collecting Hints

The milled issue is fairly rare, especially in Fine or better condition and many coins are creased. Issues are often pierced or gilded as this coin was obviously later popular as a jewellery piece.

Obverse Legend   ELIZABETH D G. ANG FRA ET HIB REGINA — Elizabeth by the grace of God Queen of England France and Ireland

Reverse Legend   POSUI DEUM ADIUTOREM MEUM — I have made God my helper

Obverse   Small bust of queen with plain dress, rose behind bust; mintmark star.

Reverse   Shield over long cross, dated 1561.

| EL3D-025 | VG £60 | F £140 | VF £280 |

Collecting Hints

These machine made coins are the most common of the York issues. They are available in all grades from VG to VF and, while rare, EF examples do exist. Many issues have a central piercing, undoubtedly done officially, probably towards the end of the 17th century to devalue the coins.

Obverse Legend   CAROLUS D.G. MAG BR FR ET HI REX — Charles by the grace of God King of Great Britain France and Ireland

Reverse Legend   CHRISTO AUSPICE REGNO — I reign under the auspices of Christ

Obverse   Crowned bust of king facing left; mintmark lion.

Reverse   Royal shield over cross, EBOR (York) over shield.

| C13D-003 | VG £30 | F £65 | VF £150 |

Aberystwyth Mint (1638 – 1642)

Bristol and Oxford often used obverse or reverse dies from the Aberystwyth threepence, so collectors should also refer to those issues when identifying a coin which may be from Aberystwyth.

Collecting Hints

Aberystwyth threepences are by far the most common and usually available in Fine or VF condition; EF examples are rare but obtainable.

Obverse Legend   CAROLUS DG M(A)B. F(R) ET H(I)(B) REX — Charles by the grace of God King of Great Britain France and Ireland

Reverse Legend   CHRISTO AUSPICE REGNO — I reign under the auspices of Christ

Obverse   Bust of king with plumes in front of face and the denomination behind his head; mintmark book.

Reverse   Large oval shield with plumes above.

| C13D-005 | VG £25 | F £55 | VF £110 | EF £200 |

As previous, but the king's crown cuts the inner circles.

| C13D-010 | VG £25 | F £55 | VF £110 | EF £200 |

Aberystwyth Furnace Mint (1648/1649)

Collecting Hints

This issue is rare in any grade and very difficult to obtain.

Obverse Legend   CAROLUS D.G. MAG BR FR ET HI REX — Charles by the grace of God King of Great Britain France and Ireland

Reverse Legend   CHRISTO AUSPICE REGNO — I reign under the auspices of Christ

Obverse   Crowned bust, plumelet in front of face, value behind; mintmark crown.

Reverse   Small oval shield with large plumes above.

| C13D-015 | VG £100 | F £250 | VF £450 |

Oxford Mint

Collecting Hints

Oxford threepences are fairly common, especially in the lower grades, but the urgency to strike coins was such that many issues used an Aberystwyth die. Coins in better than Fine condition are rare. Many coins from this issue are often damaged and holed.

Obverse Legend   CAROLUS D G MAG BR FR ET H. REX — Charles by the grace of God King of Great Britain France and Ireland

Outer Reverse Legend   EXURGAT DEUS DISSIPENTUR INIMICI — Let God arise and His enemies be scattered

Inner Reverse Legend   RELI PRO LEG ANG LIB PAR. 1644 OX — The religion of the Protestants the laws of England the liberty of Parliament. 1644 Oxford

Obverse   Aberystwyth die; plume in front of king's face with value behind.

Reverse   The Declaration in three lines.

| C13D-020 | VG £50 | F £100 | VF £225 |

Obverse Legend   CAROLUS D.G. M BR F ET H REX — Charles by the grace of God King of Great Britain France and Ireland

Reverse Legend   CHRISTO AUSPICE REGNO — I reign under the auspices of Christ

Obverse   Bust of king with denomination behind bust and 'R' (for Rawlins, the die maker of the obverse) below the king's shoulder.

Reverse   Aberystwyth die with large oval shield and plumes above; mintmark book.

| C13D-025 | VG £50 | F £100 | VF £225 |

Obverse Legend   As previous.

Reverse Legend   As C13D-020 but sometimes omits 'OX'.

Obverse   As previous, but without 'R' on the king's shoulder.

Reverse   As C13D-020, dated 1644 or 1646.

| C13D-030 | VG £50 | F £100 | VF £225 |

Bristol Mint

Collecting Hints

This issue is rare in any grade and particularly difficult to obtain in better than Fine, while coins are often damaged or holed.

Obverse Legend   CAROLUS D G. MAG B F ET H REX — Charles by the grace of God King of Great Britain France and Ireland

Outer Reverse Legend   EXURGAT DEUS DISSIPENTUR INIMICI — Let God arise and His enemies be scattered

Inner Reverse Legend   REL PRO LEG AN LIB PA 1644 — The religion of the Protestants the laws of England the liberty of Parliament. 1644

Obverse This is an Aberystwyth die, with a plume in front of the king's face and denomination behind; mintmark book.

Reverse Three small plumes above the Declaration, date below.

C13D-035	VG £70	F £175	VF £350

As previous, but plume with bands before face, denomination behind king's head; mintmark pellet (local die).

C13D-040	VG £70	F £175	VF £350

Legends As previous.

Obverse As previous, but plumelet before king's face.

Reverse Only one plumelet above the declaration, 1645.

C13D-045	ex. rare

Exeter Mint

Collecting Hints

This issue is obtainable but fairly scarce, particularly in better than Fine condition and is often holed or damaged.

Obverse Legend CAROLUS D.G. MA BR F ET H RE — Charles by the grace of God King of Great Britain France and Ireland

Reverse Legend CHRISTO AUSPICE REGNO — I reign under the auspices of Christ

Obverse Bust of king with denomination behind the head; mintmark rose.

Reverse Royal shield with date 1644 above.

C13D-050	VG £60	F £150	VF £325

Worcester or Shrewsbury Mint

Collecting Hints

This issue is very crude in style but extremely rare and difficult to obtain in any grade.

Obverse Legend CAROLUS DG. MB F ET H REX — Charles by the grace of God King of Great Britain France and Ireland

Reverse Legend CHRISTO AUSPICE REGNO — I reign under the auspices of Christ

Obverse Crude bust of king with denomination behind; mintmark lis.

Reverse Oval shield.

C13D-055	VG £150	F £350	VF —

Chester Mint

It is not certain that this issue is from the Chester mint at all and until a hoard or documentary evidence appears, it will not be possible to class it correctly.

Collecting Hints

This issue is extremely rare in any grade and collectors may have great difficulty obtaining an example.

Obverse Legend CAROLUS. D.G. MAG. BRIT. FRAN. ET HIB REX. — Charles by the grace of God King of Great Britain France and Ireland

Reverse Legend CHRISTO AUSPICE REGNO — I reign under the auspices of Christ

Obverse Bust of king with denomination behind; no mintmark.

Reverse Square shield undated; mintmark prostrate gerb.

C13D-060	ex. rare

Late Declaration

Collecting Hints

These issues are rare and when available are found, sometimes damaged, in VG to Fine condition.

Obverse Legend CAROLUS D G M B F ET HI REX — Charles by the grace of God King of Great Britain France and Ireland

Outer Reverse Legend EXURGAT DEUS DISSIPENTUR INIMICI — Let God arise and His enemies be scattered

Inner Reverse Legend REL PRO LEG AN LIB PA 1646 — The religion of the Protestants the laws of England the liberty of Parliament

Obverse Crowned bust, plumelet before bust, value behind; mintmark plume.

Reverse Declaration, one plume above and a scroll either side.

C13D-065	VG £100	F £225	VF £400

As previous, but no scroll, 1645.

C13D-070	VG £100	F £250	VF rare

No threepences were struck under the Commonwealth or Cromwell.

Charles II (1660 – 1685)

Hammered Coinage (1660 – 1662)

Threepences were only struck during the third issue of the hammered coinage (1660 – 62).

Collecting Hints

This issue is fairly common and usually easily obtainable in Fine condition; VF examples are not uncommon.

Obverse Legend   CAROLUS II D G. MAG BRI F ET H REX — Charles by the grace of God King of Great Britain France and Ireland

Reverse Legend   CHRISTO AUSPICE REGNO — I reign under the auspices of Christ

Obverse   Bust of king within an inner circle, mark of value behind bust; mintmark crown.

Reverse   Royal shield over cross.

C23DH-005	VG £20	F £40	VF £80	EF £150

Halfgroat

Introduced under Edward III in 1351, the silver halfgroat or two-pence was stylistically very similar to the groat with only its size and weight reduced. It was a popular denomination and issued by all monarchs until George III, when it was continued as a Maundy coin. The halfgroat was also issued as legal tender in several British colonies during the 19th century.

Edward III (1327 – 1377)

Edward III realised the importance of having varied denominations in circulation to facilitate trade and the halfgroat, introduced in 1351 during the fourth coinage, became one of the most important. Although Edward's halfgroat closely resembles the contemporary groat, its design and style are fairly different from later issues of Edward IV, Richard II or the Henrys (IV, V, VI and VII). The halfgroat bears the king's name, EDWARDUS, at the top of the obverse legend and although Edward III was not the only Edward to issue halfgroats, the ones from Edward IV's two reigns are very different in style, slightly smaller and lighter. Three mints produced halfgroats during Edward III's reign, London, York and Calais, which was under English rule at the time and was used for political as well as monetary reasons. The mint name can be found on the inner reverse legend and reads CIVITAS LONDON for London, CIVITAS EBORACI for York and VILLA CALESIE for Calais. The various issues based on Edward's aspirations in France that are detailed in the relevant section of the Penny chapter also apply to the halfgroat.

Collecting Hints

Edward III halfgroats are fairly common and usually obtainable in about Fine condition, often clipped; VF examples are rare, but exist. Coins tend to be found in lower grades than the groat, where large hoards are available in slightly better condition. However, all Edward III coins from the Calais mint are rare.

Pre Treaty Period (1351 – 1361)

These issues have the French title in the obverse legend.

London Mint
1351

Obverse Legend EDWARDUS REX ANGL (Z or reversed F) FRAN — Edward King of England and France

Outer Reverse Legend POSVI DEUM ADIVTOREM MEU(M) — I have made God my helper

Inner Reverse Legend CIVITAS LONDON — City of London

Obverse Front-facing crowned bust of king, Roman 'M', open 'C' and 'E' in legend; mintmark cross 1.

Reverse Long cross, three pellets in each quarter.

| E32D-005 | VG £40 | F £70 | VF £150 |

1351 – 1352

As previous, but a Lombardic 'M', closed 'C' and 'E', and the 'R' has a wedge-shaped tail.

| E32D-010 | VG £20 | F £40 | VF £80 |

1351 – 1353

As previous, but 'R' with normal tail; mintmarks cross 1 or cross 1 broken.

| E32D-015 | VG £20 | F £40 | VF £80 |

As previous, but the letters in the legends are broken, often with parts missing, the 'V' usually has a nick in the right arm; mintmark cross 2.

| E32D-020 | VG £20 | F £40 | VF £80 |

As previous, but mintmark crown.

| E32D-025 | VG £22 | F £45 | VF £85 |

As previous, but mintmark cross 3.

| E32D-030 | VG £22 | F £45 | VF £85 |

As previous, but an annulet in one quarter and sometimes under the king's bust; mintmark cross 3.

| E32D-035 | VG £25 | F £50 | VF £100 |

York Mint

Obverse & Outer Reverse Legend As previous.

Inner Reverse Legend CIVITAS EBORACI — City of York.

Obverse Front-facing crowned bust of king, similar to E32D-015.

Reverse Large cross, three pellets in each quarter.

| E32D-040 | VG £30 | F £60 | VF £125 |

As E32D-020 with inner reverse legend as previous.

| E32D-045 | VG £30 | F £60 | VF £125 |

As previous, but with a lis on the king's breast.

| E32D-050 | VG £35 | F £65 | VF £130 |

Transitional Period (1361)

This issue, which omits the king's French title, was only struck at the London mint.

Obverse Legend   EDWARD REX ANGLIE DNS HIB — Edward King of England Lord of Ireland

Outer Reverse Legend   POSVI DEUM ADIVTOREM MEU(M) — I have made God my helper

Inner Reverse Legend   CIVITAS LONDON — City of London

Obverse   Front-facing crowned bust of king with an annulet either side of crown, the letters of the legend are irregular in size and there are only seven arches in the tressure; mintmark cross potent.

Reverse   Large cross, three pellets in each quarter.

| E32D-055 | VG £60 | F £130 | VF £250 |

Treaty Period (1361 – 1369)

London Mint

Obverse Legend   EDWARDUS REX ANGL DNS HYB — Edward King of the English Lord of Ireland

Outer Reverse Legend   POSVI DEUM ADIVTOREM MEU(M) — I have made God my helper

Inner Reverse Legend   CIVITAS LONDON — City of London

Obverse   Front-facing bust of king, new-style 'X' in REX similar to a cross pattée; mintmark cross potent.

Reverse   Large cross, three pellets in each quarter.

| E32D-060 | VG £25 | F £50 | VF £100 |

As previous, but annulet before EDWARDUS in the obverse legend and an unbarred 'A' in ADIVTOREM in the reverse legend.

| E32D-065 | VG £25 | F £50 | VF £100 |

As previous, but annulet on the king's breast and barred 'A' in ADIVTOREM.

| E32D-070 | VG £35 | F £70 | VF £140 |

Calais Mint

Obverse & Outer Reverse Legend   As previous.

Inner Reverse Legend   VILLA CALESIE — Town of Calais

Obverse   Front-facing bust of king, annulet on his breast; mintmark cross potent.

Reverse   Large cross, three pellets in each quarter.

| E32D-075 | VG £60 | F £130 | VF £250 |

Post Treaty Period (1369 – 1377)

This issue has the French title in the obverse legends once more; also the 'X' in REX resembles a St Andrew's cross while the abbreviation for ET (and) is a reversed 'F'.

Obverse Legend   EDWARD DI GRA REX ANGL F (reversed) FR — Edward by the grace of God King of England and France

Outer Reverse Legend   POSVI DEUM ADIVTOREM MEU(M) — I have made God my helper

Inner Reverse Legend   CIVITAS LONDON — City of London

Obverse   Front-facing bust of king, row of pellets across one side of his breast (this is called chain mail); mintmark cross pattée.

Reverse   Large cross, three pellets in each quarter.

| E32D-080 | VG £100 | F £200 | VF — |

Obverse Legend   EDWARDUS REX ANGL F (reversed) FRANC — Edward King of England and France

Reverse Legends   As previous.

Obverse   Front-facing bust of king, a pellet either side of crown's central lis.

Reverse   As previous.

| E32D-085   VG £60   F £120   VF £250 |

| R22D-005   VG £175   F £300   VF £650 |

Obverse Legend   EDWARD REX ANGL F (reversed) FRANC(IE) — Edward King of England and France

Reverse Legends   As previous.

Obverse   Front-facing bust of king; the size of the bust sometimes varies.

Reverse   As previous.

Legends   As previous.

Obverse   Front-facing bust of king with bushy hair, fishtail lettering in legends; mintmark cross pattée.

Reverse   As previous, but fishtail lettering.

| E32D-090   VG £60   F £120   VF £250 |

This issue was probably struck at the time of Edward III's death.

Obverse Legend   EDWARDUS REX ANGL F(reversed) FRAC — Edward King of England and France

Reverse Legends   As previous.

Obverse   Front-facing bust of king, possibly Richard II, with small head and long neck; mintmark cross potent.

Reverse   As previous.

| E32D-095   ex. rare |

| R22D-010   VG £185   F £330   VF £675 |

Several of Richard II's issues were muled with those of Edward III. The obverse die was changed to read RICARD instead of EDWARD, and often the original name can be seen underneath.

There are several varieties due to the muling of dies in this very rare issue.

Obverse Legend   RICARD DI GRA REX ANGL Z FRANC (varieties) — Richard by the grace of God King of England and France

Reverse Legends   As previous.

Obverse   Front-facing bust of king, which is often Edward III depending on which die has been muled.

Reverse   Long cross, three pellets in each quarter. This is often a Edward III die.

| R22D-015   VG £250   F £500   VF £900 |

Richard II   (1377 – 1399)

All of Richard II's halfgroats are rare. They were only struck in London, often using altered Edward III dies so that the king's name reads RICARD instead of EDWARD, thus facilitating identification. However, as Richard III also issued halfgroats, it is important to check the mintmarks which constitute the main difference between the two reigns although there are also differences in the style of the halfgroats too. Richard II only used mintmark cross pattée, while Richard III used either a halved sun and rose, or boar's head.

Obverse Legend   RICARD DI GRA REX ANGLI — Richard by the grace of God King of England

Reverse Legends   As previous

Obverse   New-style bust and crown of king.

Reverse   Long cross with three pellets in each quarter.

| R22D-020   VG £350   F £600   VF — |

Henry IV   (1399 – 1413)

All Henry IV issues are very rare and the halfgroat is no exception. Numismatically the reign can be divided into the heavy and the light coinage; the latter being introduced in 1412, when the weight of the halfgroat dropped from 36 grains 2.3 grams to 30 grains 1.9 grams. London was the only mint to produce halfgroats during this reign.

Like Henry IV's other denominations, the halfgroat is fairly difficult to identify because, although it bears the king's name HENRIC at the start of the obverse legend, a number of Henrys issued halfgroats. Nevertheless, those struck under Henry VI and Henry VII are very different in style from Henry IV's. Furthermore, despite the existence of numerous varieties for the issues of these two reigns, most of Henry V's coins have mullets somewhere in their design while none of Henry IV's halfgroats bear this mark.

Collecting Hints

All of Richard II's halfgroats are rare. In fact, they are much scarcer than the groat and usually found in Fine condition, although they are sometimes damaged and clipped. VF or better examples exist but are extremely rare.

Obverse Legend   RICARD DI GRA REX ANGLI — Richard by the grace of God King of England (varieties exist)

Outer Reverse Legend   POSVI DEUM ADIVTOREM MEU(M) — I have made God my helper

Inner Reverse Legend   CIVITAS LONDON — City of London

Obverse   Front-facing bust of king, new-style lettering in legend; mintmark cross pattée.

Reverse   Long cross, three pellets in each quarter.

Collecting Hints

Henry IV halfgroats are extremely rare in any grade and collectors may have difficulty obtaining an example regardless of its condition. They should, moreover, take particular care to ensure that a coin of this series has been identified correctly.

Heavy Coinage (1399 – 1412)

Obverse Legend   HENRIC DI GRA REX ANGL Z FRANC — Henry by the grace of God King of England and France

Outer Reverse Legend   POSVI DEUM ADIVTOREM MEU(M) — I have made God my helper

Inner Reverse Legend   CIVITAS LONDON — City of London

Obverse   Front-facing bust of king with star on his breast; mintmark cross pattée.

Reverse   Long cross with three pellets in each corner, unbarred 'N's in LONDON.

| H42D-005 | VG £600 | F £1,400 | VF £3,000 |

Light Coinage (1412 – 1413)

Obverse Legend   As previous, but omitting FRANC.

Reverse Legends   As previous.

Obverse   Altered Richard II dies with front-facing bust of king, pellet to left and annulet to right of crown; mintmark cross pattée.

Reverse   Long cross with three pellets in each quarter.

| H42D-010 | VG £500 | F £1,250 | VF £2,500 |

Obverse Legend   As H42D-005 with full French title.

Reverse Legends   As previous.

Obverse   Henry IV's own dies with front-facing bust of king, annulet to left and pellet to right of crown; mintmark cross pattée.

Reverse   As previous.

| H42D-015 | VG £450 | F £1,250 | VF £2,000 |

Henry V   (1413 – 1422)

Henry V halfgroats, which were only minted in London, are rare particularly compared to the groat or penny. They are also fairly difficult to identify as they closely resemble Henry IV's issues. Apart from the details listed under Henry IV on how to distinguish the various reigns apart, we should add that Henry V's issues have various marks which are specific to their particular class. Also, a close study of the bust reveals that the neck is often much slimmer than that of other monarchs and many of the facial expressions are specific to this reign. Collectors should ensure that every detail on a coin is meant to be there and, if something is missing or added, check through both reigns to identify the specimen correctly.

Collecting Hints

Henry V halfgroats are rare and usually obtainable in about Fine condition, although VF examples exist. The lower grade coins are often damaged, making it difficult to identify the issue and collectors should try to obtain a coin in Fine condition, which is easily identifiable. If collectors merely want a coin from Henry V's reign, it would perhaps be wiser to consider a groat or penny.

Obverse Legend   HENRIC DI GRA REX ANGL (or ANGLIE) Z F — Henry by the grace of God King of England and France

Outer Reverse Legend   POSVI DEUM ADIVTOREM MEU(M) — I have made God my helper

Inner Reverse Legend   CIVITAS LONDON — City of London

Obverse   Front-facing bust of king with no neck, annulet or pellet sometimes by crown, short broad lettering in legend; mintmark cross pattée.

Reverse   Long cross, three pellets in each corner.

| H52D-005 | VG £250 | F £600 | VF rare |

As previous, but ordinary lettering, no marks by crown; this issue is sometimes muled with a Henry IV reverse.

| H52D-010 | VG £120 | F £300 | VF £700 |

As previous, but front-facing bust with neck which has an oval swelling, there is a broken annulet to left of crown and sometimes a mullet on the right shoulder or in the centre of the king's breast. One variety has a broken annulet either side of crown. Also a mule with a Richard II reverse is known.

| H52D-015 | VG £50 | F £100 | VF £200 |

As previous, but front-facing bust of king with trefoil to right and annulet to left of crown and mullet on breast.

| H52D-020 | VG £50 | F £100 | VF £200 |

Legends   As previous.

Obverse Front-facing bust of king, neat in style with a hollow neck, no marks by neck or crown; mintmark pierced cross or pierced cross pellet centre.

Reverse As previous, but sometimes muled with a Henry VI reverse.

| H52D-025 | VG £60 | F £120 | VF £240 |

| H62D-010 | VG £20 | F £50 | VF £85 | EF £150 |

As previous, but only one annulet on reverse.

| H62D-015 | VG £35 | F £55 | VF £120 | EF £200 |

As previous, but no annulets on reverse.

| H62D-020 | VG £20 | F £40 | VF £65 | EF £125 |

York Mint

Obverse & Outer Reverse Legend As previous.

Inner Reverse Legend CIVITAS EBORACI — City of York

Obverse Front-facing bust of king, a lis either side of neck.

Reverse Long cross with three pellets in each quarter, an annulet in two quarters.

| H62D-025 | VG £400 | F £800 | VF £1,800 | EF rare |

Annulet Trefoil Sub Issue

This issue was only struck at the Calais mint.

Obverse & Outer Reverse Legend As previous.

Inner Reverse Legend VILLA CALISIE — Town of Calais

Obverse Front-facing bust of king, annulets either side of neck, trefoil to left of crown.

Reverse Long cross with three pellets in each quarter, an annulet in two quarters.

| H62D-030 | VG £40 | F £80 | VF £160 |

Rosette Mascle Issue (1427 – 1430)

This issue has rosettes and mascles in the legends.

London Mint

Obverse & Outer Reverse Legend As previous.

Inner Reverse Legend CIVITAS LONDON — City of London

Obverse Front-facing bust of king, rosettes and mascles somewhere in the legend.

Reverse Rosettes and mascles in legends.

| H62D-035 | VG £25 | F £50 | VF £110 |

Calais Mint

As previous, but inner reverse legend reads VILLA CALISIE — Town of Calais.

| H62D-040 | VG £20 | F £40 | VF £90 |

Henry VI First Reign (1422 – 1461)

Like all silver Henry VI denominations, halfgroats may be categorised into issues according to the marks on the coin which may be by the king's head or in the legends. All halfgroats bear the king's name, HENRIC, in the obverse legend and have a different, more lifelike bust than the issues of the two previous Henrys. Collectors should also pay particular attention to the mintmark, found above the king's head at the beginning of the obverse legend; Henry IV and Henry V used only three mintmarks between them but Henry VI used a total of seven different mintmarks. A total of three mints were active during Henry VI's reign; London and Calais were by far the most prolific but the York mint did produce some very rare issues during the early part of the reign. The mint's name can be found in the inner legend on the reverse and reads CIVITAS LONDON for London, CIVITAS EBORACI for York and VILLA CALISIE for Calais.

Collecting Hints

Henry VI's halfgroats are fairly common, but not as common as groats. They are usually obtainable unclipped and undamaged in Fine condition, VF examples are not uncommon while those in EF are rare.

Annulet Issue (1422 – 1427)

London Mint

Obverse Legend HENRIC DI GRA REX ANGL Z FR — Henry by the grace of God King of England and France

Outer Reverse Legend POSVI DEUM ADIVTOREM MEU(M) — I have made God my helper

Inner Reverse Legend CIVITAS LONDON — City of London

Obverse Front-facing bust of king; mintmark pierced cross.

Reverse Long cross, three pellets in each quarter and with an annulet in two quarters.

| H62D-005 | VG £20 | F £45 | VF £90 | EF £175 |

Calais Mint

Obverse & Outer Reverse Legend As previous.

Inner Reverse Legend VILLA CALISIE — Town of Calais

Obverse Front-facing bust of king, an annulet either side of his neck.

Reverse Long cross with three pellets in each quarter, two annulets in quarters.

A mascle is sometimes found between the inner curves and the beaded circle.

| H62D-045 | VG £30 | F £60 | VF £120 |

Pinecone Mascle Issue (1430 – 1434)

This issue has pinecones and mascles in the legend.

London Mint

Obverse & Outer Reverse Legend   As previous.

Inner Reverse Legend   CIVITAS LONDON — City of London

Obverse   Front-facing bust of king, pinecones and mascles in legend.

Reverse   Pinecones and mascles in legend.

| H62D-050 | VG £25 | F £50 | VF £100 |

Calais Mint

As previous, but inner reverse legend reads VILLA CALISIE — Town of Calais.

| H62D-055 | VG £25 | F £50 | VF £100 |

Leaf Mascle Issue (1434 – 1435)

This issue has a mascle in the legend and a leaf below the bust.

London Mint

Obverse & Outer Reverse Legend   As previous.

Inner Reverse Legend   CIVITAS LONDON — City of London

Obverse   Front-facing bust of king, leaf under bust.

Reverse   Mascle in legend; pellet under TAS and DON in reverse legend.

| H62D-060 | VG £30 | F £70 | VF £150 |

Calais Mint

Obverse & Outer Reverse Legend   As previous.

Inner Reverse Legend   VILLA CALISIE — Town of Calais

Obverse   Leaf below front-facing bust of king.

Reverse   Leaf sometimes on reverse, mascle in legend.

| H62D-065 | VG £75 | F £150 | VF £350 |

Leaf Trefoil Issue (1435 – 1438)

Mostly with leaves and trefoils in the legends, this issue was only struck at the London mint.

Obverse & Outer Reverse Legend   As previous.

Inner Reverse Legend   CIVITAS LONDON — City of London

Obverse   Front-facing bust of king, leaf on breast, leaves in obverse legend.

Reverse   Long cross, three pellets in each quarter, no leaves or trefoil.

| H62D-070 | VG £25 | F £50 | VF £120 |

As previous, but trefoils in legends on obverse and reverse.

| H62D-075 | VG £35 | F £70 | VF £140 |

As previous, but no leaf on breast but leaves and/or trefoils in legends.

| H62D-080 | VG £50 | F £100 | VF £200 |

Trefoil Issue (1438 – 1443)

London Mint

Legends   As previous.

Obverse   As H62D-070.

Reverse   As H62D-070, but trefoils in legend.

| H62D-082 | VG £80 | F £200 | VF £400 |

Leaf Pellet Issue (1445 – 1454)

Calais Mint

Obverse Legend   As previous.

Outer Reverse Legend   As previous.

Inner Reverse Legend   VILLA CALISIE — Town of Calais

Obverse   As previous.

Reverse   As H62D-065.

| H62D-083 | v. rare |

Leaf Pellet Issue (1445 – 1454)

This issue was only struck at the London mint and usually has a leaf on the king's breast and a pellet on either side of the crown.

Obverse & Outer Reverse Legend   As previous.

Inner Reverse Legend   CIVITAS LONDON — City of London

Obverse   Front-facing bust of king, pellets either side of crown and leaf on his breast.

Reverse   Long cross with an extra pellet in two quarters, making a total of fourteen.

| H62D-085 | VG £25 | F £55 | VF £120 |

As previous, but sometimes no leaf on the king's breast and no stops or marks in the reverse legend.

H62D-090	VG £25	F £55	VF £120

Unmarked Issue (1453 – 1454)

This issue, which was only struck at the London mint, has no marks in the field or in the legends except for one saltire stop on the reverse. It also has two extra pellets on the reverse, making a total of fourteen.

Obverse & Outer Reverse Legend As previous.

Inner Reverse Legend CIVITAS LONDON — City of London

Obverse Front-facing bust of king.

Reverse An extra pellet in two quarters.

H62D-095	VG £150	F £250	VF £500

Cross Pellet Issue (1454 – 1460)

This issue was only struck at the London mint and has a saltire (small cross) on neck and a pellet either side of crown.

Legends As previous

Obverse Front-facing bust of king, saltire on neck, a pellet either side of crown.

Reverse An extra pellet in two quarters, making a total of fourteen, mullets in legends.

H62D-100	VG £150	F £250	VF £500

No halfgroats were struck for the rare lis pellet issue of 1456 – 60.

Edward IV First Reign (1461 – 1470)

This reign can be divided into the heavy and the light coinages. Heavy coinage halfgroats were struck between 1461 and 1464; the light coinage was issued from 1464 to 1470. Halfgroats from the heavy coinage weigh 30 grains (1.9 grams), which at the time was heavier than their actual value. This was due to the increasing price of silver which in turn was caused by a shortage and high demand in Europe. To address this problem, the weight of the coins was reduced by 20% in 1464. Many heavy coinage halfgroats were melted down, either officially or unofficially, producing a 20% profit.

Heavy Coinage

All these issues were struck at the London mint.

Collecting Hints

All heavy coinage halfgroats are rare and difficult to obtain in any condition. They were all struck at London and can be easily confused with the light coinage issues which are far more common. Collectors should pay particular attention to the various marks, especially the mintmarks.

Obverse Legend EDWARD DI GRA REX ANGL Z FRAN — Edward by the grace of God King of England and France

Outer Reverse Legend POSUI DEUM ADIUTOREM MEUM — I have made God my helper

Inner Reverse Legend CIVITAS LONDON — City of London

Obverse Front-facing crowned bust of king, lis on his breast, a pellet either side of crown; mintmark cross fleury or plain cross.

Reverse Long cross, four pellets in two quarters.

E42D-005	VG £170	F £450	VF £1,000

Legends As previous.

Obverse Front-facing bust of king, crescent on his breast, quatrefoil either side of neck; mintmark rose.

Reverse Long cross, three pellets in each quarter.

E42D-010	VG £120	F £300	VF £650

Legends As previous.

Obverse Crowned bust of king, trefoil on breast, quatrefoils either side of neck; mintmark rose.

Reverse As previous, but an eye in the inner legend.

E42D-015	VG £120	F £300	VF £650

As previous, but no marks on king's breast.

E42D-020	VG £120	F £300	VF £650

Legends As previous.

Obverse Crowned bust of king, an annulet either side of neck; mintmark rose.

Reverse As previous, but sometimes omits eye in legend.

E42D-025	VG £110	F £280	VF £550

Light Coinage

Collecting Hints

The light coinage issues were struck at six mints and in enormous quantities, especially at the London and Canterbury mints. This reflects the urgent need for coinage be cause so many coins from previous coinages had been melted down for profit. Coins are available in most grades from VG to VF and are sometimes damaged. There is no doubt that these issues circulated for a considerable time. Many varieties exist and collectors should also refer to the second reign of Edward IV when identifying an issue.

London Mint

This issue uses the same dies as the previous one; the only difference in the coins is the weight.

As previous, but no eye in the reverse legend.

E42D-030	unique

Legends As previous.

Obverse Crowned bust of king, quatrefoils at neck; mintmark rose, sun, crown, none, sometimes muled.

Reverse Long cross, three pellets in each quarter.

E42D-035	VG £40	F £80	VF £160

As previous, but saltires at neck; mintmark sun, crown, sometimes muled.

E42D-040	VG £40	F £80	VF £160

As previous, but trefoils at neck; mintmark sun, crown, long cross fitchée, sometimes muled.

E42D-045	VG £35	F £70	VF £150

As previous, but no marks by neck; mintmark sun and long cross fitchée always muled.

E42D-050	VG £60	F £150	VF £300

Bristol Mint

Obverse Legend As previous.

Outer Reverse Legend As previous.

Inner Reverse Legend VILLA BRISTOW (or BRESTOW or BRISTOLL) — Town of Bristol

Obverse Crowned bust of king, crosses or saltires either side of neck; mintmark rose, sun or crown, often muled.

Reverse Long cross, three pellets in each quarter.

E42D-055	VG £60	F £140	VF £300

As previous, but quatrefoils by neck.

E42D-060	VG £60	F £140	VF £300

As previous, but trefoils by neck; mintmark crown.

E42D-065	VG £70	F £160	VF £350

As previous, but no marks at neck; mintmark crown obverse, sun reverse.

E42D-070	VG £70	F £160	VF £350

Canterbury Mint
Ecclesiastical Mint under Archbishop Bourchier

Obverse Legend As previous.

Outer Reverse Legend As previous.

Inner Reverse Legend CIVITAS CANTOR — City of Canterbury

Obverse Crowned bust of king, a knot below the bust, quatrefoils either side of neck; mintmark pall.

Reverse Long cross, three pellets in each quarter, mintmark none, rose, sun.

E42D-075	VG £18	F £35	VF £80

As previous, but no quatrefoil at neck; mintmark pall.

E42D-080	VG £18	F £35	VF £80

As previous, but saltires by neck; mintmark pall, sometimes sun on reverse.

E42D-085	VG £20	F £40	VF £85

As previous, but trefoils by neck; mintmark pall.

E42D-090	VG £40	F £90	VF £180

As previous, but wedges by hair or neck; mintmark pall, sometimes rose or sun on reverse.

| E42D-095 | VG £20 | F £40 | VF £85 |

As E42D-075 or E42D-080 but no knot below king's bust.

| E42D-100 | VG £25 | F £50 | VF £120 |

Royal Mint

Legends As previous.

Obverse Crowned bust of king, quatrefoils at neck; mintmark crown.

Reverse As previous; mintmark crown or none.

| E42D-105 | VG £20 | F £40 | VF £90 |

As previous, but saltires by neck; mintmark as previous.

| E42D-110 | VG £20 | F £40 | VF £90 |

As previous, but trefoils by neck; mintmark crown, rose, sometimes sun on reverse.

| E42D-115 | VG £22 | F £45 | VF £100 |

As previous, but no marks at neck; mintmark sun.

| E42D-120 | VG £40 | F £90 | VF £200 |

Coventry Mint

Obverse Legend As previous.

Outer Reverse Legend As previous.

Inner Reverse Legend CIVITAS COVETRE — City of Coventry

Obverse Crowned bust of king, crosses either side of neck; mintmark sun.

Reverse Long cross, three pellets in each quarter.

| E42D-125 | ex. rare |

Norwich Mint

As previous, but inner reverse legend reads CIVITAS NORVIC — City of Norwich; and there are saltires instead of crosses by king's neck on the obverse.

| E42D-130 | ex. rare |

York Mint

Obverse Legend As previous.

Outer Reverse Legend As previous.

Inner Reverse Legend CIVITAS EBORACI — City of York

Obverse Crowned bust of king, quatrefoils by neck; mintmark sun or lis.

Reverse Long cross, three pellets in each quarter, mintmark sun, lis or none.

| E42D-135 | VG £40 | F £90 | VF £180 |

As previous, but saltires by neck; mintmark lis.

| E42D-140 | VG £40 | F £90 | VF £180 |

As previous, but trefoils by neck; mintmark lis or none (reverse).

| E42D-145 | VG £40 | F £90 | VF £180 |

As E42D-135 but an E on the king's breast; mintmark lis, none on reverse.

| E42D-150 | VG £35 | F £85 | VF £170 |

Henry VI Restored (Oct. 1470 – April 1471)

During this very short period, London and York produced halfgroats. The London issue is very similar to the first reign ones except that it is lighter in weight, it has no marks such as annulets or mascles, and uses the mintmark Restoration cross which was not used at all during the first reign. The extremely rare York issue is easily identified by the 'E' (for EBORACI) on the king's breast as no other Henry used this mark on halfgroats.

Collecting Hints

Coins from this period are all rare and the halfgroat is no exception. The coins from the London mint are difficult to obtain in any condition but Fine and VF examples exist. The issues from York are extremely rare in any grade.

London Mint

Obverse Legend HENRIC (V) DI GRA REX ANGL Z FR(A)(NC) — Henry by the grace of God King of England and France

Outer Reverse Legend POSVI DEUM ADIVTOREM MEU(M) — I have made God my helper

Inner Reverse Legend CIVITAS LONDON — City of London

Obverse Front-facing bust of king; mintmarks Restoration cross, Restoration cross and none.

Reverse Long cross, three pellets in each quarter.

| H62D-105 | VG £150 | F £350 | VF £700 |

York Mint

Obverse & Outer Reverse Legend As previous.

Inner Reverse Legend CIVITAS EBORACI — City of York

Obverse Front-facing bust of king, 'E' on breast; mintmark lis.

Reverse As previous, but mintmark lis or sun.

| H62D-110 | ex. rare |

Edward IV Second Reign (1471 – 1483)

Numismatically, Edward IV's second reign is a continuation from his first, which is hardly surprising given there is only a seven month gap between them. There are however minor distinguishing differences mainly in the mintmarks and other marks.

Collecting Hints

Coins from the second reign tend to be slightly scarcer than those of the first although the most common mints (London and Canterbury) are usually obtainable in Fine condition, sometimes clipped; VF and EF examples exist but are not common. Collectors should try to obtain an unclipped example with a clear mintmark.

London Mint

Obverse Legend   EDWARD DI GRA REX ANGL Z FRA — Edward by the grace of God King of England and France

Outer Reverse Legend   POSVI DEUM ADIVTOREM MEUM — I have made God my helper

Inner Reverse Legend   CIVITAS LONDON — City of London

Obverse   Front-facing bust of king, trefoils on cusps; mintmark short cross fitchée, annulet, trefoil, pellet in annulet, cross and four pellets, cross in circle, cross pattée, pierced cross (varieties), rose or heraldic cinquefoil.

Reverse   Long cross, three pellets in each quarter.

| E42D-155 | VG £20 | F £50 | VF £100 |

Bristol Mint

Obverse & Outer Reverse Legend   As previous.

Inner Reverse Legend   VILLA BRISTOW — Town of Bristol

Obverse   Front-facing bust of king, 'B' on breast; mintmark rose, short cross fitchée.

Reverse   As previous.

| E42D-160 | ex. rare |

Canterbury Royal Mint

Obverse & Outer Reverse Legend   As previous.

Inner Reverse Legend   CIVITAS CANTOR — City of Canterbury

Obverse   Front-facing bust of king, trefoils on cusps; mintmark rose, long cross fitchée, long cross fitchée and heraldic cinquefoil, or heraldic cinquefoil.

Reverse   As previous.

| E42D-165 | VG £20 | F £50 | VF £100 |

As previous, but a 'C' on king's breast; mintmark rose.

| E42D-170 | VG £18 | F £50 | VF £100 |

As previous, but 'C' also in centre of reverse; mintmark rose.

| E42D-175 | VG £18 | F £50 | VF £100 |

As previous, but 'C' on the king's breast and a rose in the centre of the reverse; mintmark rose.

| E42D-180 | VG £18 | F £50 | VF £100 |

York Mint

Obverse & Outer Reverse Legend   As previous.

Inner Reverse Legend   CIVITAS EBORACI — City of York

Obverse   Front-facing bust; mintmark lis.

Reverse   As previous.

| E42D-185 | VG £70 | F £140 | VF £280 |

Edward V   (1483)

While it is believed that halfgroats were produced for this reign, it appears that none have survived. This issue would, however, be easily identified by the mintmark halved sun and rose, or boar's head. The obverse legend would be similar to that of Edward IV and the coin would only have been struck at London.

Richard III   (1483 – 1485)

During this short reign, halfgroats were only produced at the London mint. They bear the king's name, RICARD, on the obverse and may be distinguished from Richard II's issues by differences in style and weight, as well as by the mintmark which is cross pattée for Richard II and either halved sun and rose or boar's head for Richard III.

Collecting Hints

Richard III halfgroats are very rare in any condition; Fine and VF examples exist but are extremely rare. The groat from this reign, while rare, is much more common than the halfgroat.

Obverse Legend   RICARD DI GRA REX ANGL Z FRA — Richard by the grace of God King of England and France

Outer Reverse Legend   POSVI DEUM ADIVTOREM MEUM — I have made God my helper

Inner Reverse Legend   CIVITAS LONDON — City of London

Obverse   Front-facing bust of king; mintmark halved sun and rose.

Reverse   Long cross, three pellets in each quarter.

| R32D-005 | VG £500 | F £1,200 | VF £2,500 |

As previous, but pellet below bust; mintmarks halved sun and rose on obverse and boar's head on reverse.

| R32D-010 | VG £600 | F £1,350 | VF £2,700 |

As previous, but pellet below bust; mintmark sun and rose.

R32D-015 unique

Henry VII (1485 – 1509)

The so-called profile issue divides Henry VII's reign in two distinct numismatic styles. Until its introduction in 1502, the king's bust was in the standard medieval style with a rather unrealistic portrait; but the new design, by the German Alexander of Brugsal, was a product of the Renaissance and showed a lifelike profile portrait in incredible detail.

Henry's first issue is fairly easy to distinguish from earlier examples by the crown which, except for a few cases, has arches going over the top, and by the bust, especially the neck and rather unkempt hair. Although a few halfgroat issues have the early crown and might easily be confused with earlier issues of Henry VI, they also have specific mintmarks. The king's name, HENRIC, is found at the beginning of the obverse legend on all issues. Three mints were active during this period, London, Canterbury (ecclesiastical) and York (ecclesiastical and royal) and their name is found in the inner reverse legend: CIVITAS LONDON for London, CIVITAS CANTOR for Canterbury and CIVITAS EBORACI for York.

Collecting Hints

In the front-facing bust issues, most classes and all mints are fairly common and easy to obtain, usually in Fine condition. VF examples are not rare but EF ones are both rare and desirable. Many issues tend to be clipped or struck on rather small flans. Unclipped coins with full legible legends are more desirable.

London Mint

Obverse Legend HENRIC D(E)I GRA REX ANGL Z FR — Henry by the grace of God King of England and France

Outer Reverse Legend POSVI DEUM ADIVTOREM MEU(M) — I have made God my helper

Inner Reverse Legend CIVITAS LONDON — City of London

Obverse Front-facing bust of king, open crown similar to previous issues; mintmark lis on rose.

Reverse Long cross, three pellets in each quarter.

H72D-005 VG £200 F £400 VF £800

As previous, but front-facing bust of king with double-arched crown, rosettes on tressures; mintmark escallop.

H72D-010 ex. rare

As previous, but no rosettes on tressure, lozenge panel in centre of reverse; mintmark lis.

H72D-015 VG £25 F £50 VF £100

As previous, with a lis on the king's breast; mintmark lis.

H72D-020 VG £25 F £50 VF £100

Legends As previous.

Obverse Front-facing bust of king, unarched crown; mintmark lis.

Reverse Lozenge panel in centre of reverse.

H72D-025 VG £20 F £40 VF £80

As previous, but struck on a smaller die with smaller lettering.

H72D-030 VG £20 F £40 VF £80

Canterbury Mint
Ecclesiastical Mint under Archbishop Morton
(1486 – 1490)

Obverse & Outer Reverse Legend As previous.

Inner Reverse Legend CIVITAS CANTOR — City of Canterbury

Obverse Front-facing bust of king wearing an open crown, crosses either side of neck; mintmark tun.

Reverse 'M' in centre of cross.

H72D-035 VG £20 F £40 VF £80

As previous, with a double-arched crown; no mintmark.

H72D-040 VG £20 F £40 VF £80

Under King and Archbishop Jointly (1490 – 1500)

As previous, but without 'M' on the reverse; mintmarks lis, tun, pansy. Several minor varieties exist with different style lettering and various marks and stops in the legend.

H72D-045 VG £18 F £35 VF £70

York Mint
Royal Mint

Obverse & Outer Reverse Legend As previous.

Inner Reverse Legend CIVITAS EBORACI — City of York

Obverse Front-facing bust of king wearing a double-arched crown, lis on his breast; mintmark lis.

Reverse Lozenge panel in centre.

| H72D-050 | VG £20 | F £40 | VF £80 |

As previous, but no lis on king's breast; mintmark lis.

| H72D-055 | VG £20 | F £40 | VF £80 |

As H72D-050, but unarched crown.

| H72D-060 | VG £18 | F £38 | VF £75 |

Ecclesiastical Mint under Archbishop Savage

Several varieties of this coin exist, with different style lettering.

Legends As previous.

Obverse Front-facing bust of king wearing double arched crown, keys either side of neck; mintmark martlet.

Reverse Long cross with three pellets in each quarter.

| H72D-065 | VG £18 | F £38 | VF £75 |

Sede Vacante Issue (1507 – 1508)

As previous, but with no keys by bust; mintmark martlet.

| H72D-070 | VG £22 | F £45 | VF £90 |

Profile Issue

The stunning profile issue shows superb craftsmanship in design and production. It is easily recognisable but, because Henry VIII used the same portrait in his first coinage, it is important to ensure that the obverse legend reads HENRIC VII or HENRIC for Henry VII rather than HENRIC VIII. There are also several differences in the mintmarks and reverse legends. Unlike previous issues, Henry VII's mints are not marked by names but by symbols, such as keys below the reverse shield for York, and collectors should check all classes when identifying a coin.

London Mint

Obverse Legend HENRIC VII DI GRA REX AGL Z — Henry by the grace of God King of England and [France]

Reverse Legend POSVI DEUM ADIVTOREM MEU(M) — I have made God my helper

Obverse Profile bust of king; mintmark lis and pheon, sometimes muled.

Reverse Cross over royal shield.

| H72D-075 | VG £35 | F £70 | VF £170 |

As previous, but the obverse legend reads HENRIC omitting the VII.

| H72D-080 | ex. rare |

Canterbury Mint

As H72D-075, but mintmark martlet or rose.

| H72D-085 | VG £30 | F £60 | VF £140 |

York Mint under Archbishop Bainbridge

As H72D-075, but two keys below shield on reverse; mintmark martlet or rose.

| H72D-090 | VG £30 | F £60 | VF £140 |

As previous, but 'X.B.' either side of reverse shield and no keys below; mintmark rose obverse and martlet reverse.

| H72D-095 | VG £35 | F £65 | VF £145 |

Henry VIII   (1509 – 1547)

There were three main coinages during Henry VIII's reign and the posthumous coinage which bears Henry's portrait but was struck under his son. Henry's own first coinage bears the portrait of his father, Henry VII, but has HENRIC VIII in the obverse legend as well as different mintmarks and reverse legends; the second coinage shows the young portrait of the king. The third and posthumous coinages, which are very similar in style, were both struck in base silver and proved very unpopular. Base silver is produced when copper is added to silver, resulting in poor quality coins of a low fineness and Henry VIII introduced this coinage in an effort to relieve the financial troubles caused by overspending.

First Coinage (1509 – 1526)

Four mints produced halfgroats during the first coinage, London, Canterbury, York and Tournai in France. Some issues are just marked with symbols, such as keys, to differentiate the mint but others bear its name in full.

London Mint

Obverse Legend HENRIC VIII DI GRA REX AGL Z — Henry VIII by the grace of God King of England and [France]

Reverse Legend POSVI DEV ADIVTOE MEV — I have made God my helper

Obverse Profile bust of Henry VII; mintmark portcullis crowned.

Reverse Royal shield over cross.

| H82D-005 | VG £60 | F £130 | VF £220 |

Canterbury Mint under Archbishop Warham

As previous, but mintmark rose on the obverse. The only difference between this and the previous issue is the mintmark.

| H82D-010 | VG £50 | F £100 | VF £200 |

As previous, but 'WA' above shield on reverse; mintmark martlet.

| H82D-015 | VG £45 | F £90 | VF £170 |

As previous, but 'W.A.' divided by shield; mintmark cross fitchée.

| H82D-020 | VG £35 | F £70 | VF £160 |

Obverse Legend As previous.

Reverse Legend CIVITAS CANTOR — City of Canterbury

Obverse As previous; mintmarks pomegranate, lis, cross fitchée and lis.

Reverse 'W.A.' divided by shield.

| H82D-025 | VG £35 | F £70 | VF £160 |

York Mint
Ecclesiastical Mint under Archbishop Bainbridge (1508 – 1514)

Obverse Legend As previous.

Reverse Legend POSVI DEV ADIVTOE MEU — I have made God my helper

Obverse Profile bust of Henry VII; mintmark martlet.

Reverse Cross over royal shield, keys below shield.

| H82D-030 | VG £35 | F £70 | VF £160 |

As previous, but 'X.B' divided by shield; mintmark martlet.

| H82D-035 | VG £40 | F £80 | VF £180 |

Ecclesiastical Mint under Archbishop Wolsey (1514 – 1530)

As previous, with keys, but no 'X.B' by shield, Cardinal's hat below shield; mintmarks martlet or radiant star.

| H82D-040 | VG £60 | F £120 | VF £250 |

Royal Mint

Obverse Legend As previous.

Reverse Legend CIVITAS EBORACI — City of York

Obverse Profile bust of king; mintmark radiant star, star, pansy, escallop or voided cross.

Reverse Cross over royal shield, keys either side and Cardinal's hat below shield.

| H82D-045 | VG £40 | F £80 | VF £175 |

As previous, with 'T.W' divided by shield; mintmark voided cross.

| H82D-050 | VG £45 | F £90 | VF £200 |

Tournai Mint

Only groats and halfgroats were produced at this mint, which was located in France.

Obverse Legend As previous.

Reverse Legend CIVITAS TORNACEN — City of Tournai

Obverse As previous; mintmark crowned 'T'.

Reverse Cross over royal shield.

| H82D-055 | probably unique |

Second Coinage (1526 – 1544)

The second coinage (1526 – 44) bears a youthful portrait of Henry VIII and was struck at London, Canterbury and York. Either the mint's name or an identifying legend on the reverse distinguishes the three mints. For London it is POSVI DEV ADIVTOE MEU

(I have made God my helper), for Canterbury CIVITAS CANTOR, and for York CIVITAS EBORACI.

Collecting Hints

Halfgroats from the second coinage are fairly common. They are usually obtainable in Fine condition; VF examples are not uncommon but EF ones are rare and desirable. Most coins are unclipped but the legends can sometimes be slightly weak in places due to poor striking.

London Mint

Obverse Legend HENRIC VIII D.GR AGL Z FR — Henry VIII by the grace of God of England and France

Reverse Legend POSVI DEV ADIVTOE MEU — I have made God my helper

Obverse Youthful bust of king; mintmarks, rose, lis, sunburst, arrow.

Reverse Cross over royal shield.

| H82D-060 | VG £30 | F £60 | VF £120 |

Obverse Legend HENRIC D.G. AGL Z HIB REX — Henry by the grace of God King of England and Ireland

Reverse Legend As previous.

Obverse As previous, but mintmark pheon.

Reverse As previous.

| H82D-065 | VG £200 | F £400 | VF — |

Canterbury Mint
Royal Mint

Obverse Legend HENRIC VIII D GR AGL Z FR — Henry VIII by the grace of God of England and France

Reverse Legend CIVITAS CANTOR — City of Canterbury

Obverse Youthful bust of king; mintmark uncertain, rose, cross patonce, or 'T', sometimes muled.

Reverse 'W.A' divided by shield.

| H82D-070 | VG £20 | F £60 | VF £120 |

As previous, but nothing beside the shield; mintmark uncertain.

| H82D-075 | VG £30 | F £65 | VF £150 |

Ecclesiastical Mint under Archbishop Cranmer

As previous, but 'T.C' beside shield; mintmark Catherine Wheel.

| H82D-080 | VG £25 | F £60 | VF £120 |

York Mint
Ecclesiastical Mint under Archbishop Wolsey

Obverse Legend As previous.

Reverse Legend CIVITAS EBORACI — City of York

Obverse Youthful bust of king; mintmark voided cross.

Reverse Cross over shield, 'T.W' divided by shield with Cardinal's hat below.

| H82D-085 | VG £20 | F £60 | VF £120 |

Sede Vacante Issue (1530 – 1531)

As previous, but no marks such as letters or Cardinal's hat on the reverse; mintmark key.

| H82D-090 | VG £30 | F £60 | VF £120 |

Ecclesiastical Mint under Archbishop Lee

As previous, but 'E.L' or 'L.E' divided by the reverse shield; mintmark key.

| H82D-095 | VG £20 | F £60 | VF £120 |

Third Coinage (1544 – 1547)

As mentioned earlier, the third coinage was made from base silver and coins from this issue are usually dull in appearance but should not be cleaned, because they will then look as if they have been made of copper. A total of five mints produced halfgroats during this period: Bristol, Canterbury and York and two London-based mints. The second London mint was Southwark mint, just south of the River Thames and, to avoid confusion, what was previously referred to as London mint is henceforth the Tower mint. The mint can be found by referring to the reverse legends which read POSUI DEVM ADIVTOE MEU (I have made God my helper) for the Tower Mint, CIVITAS LONDON for Southwark, CIVITAS CANTOR for Canterbury, CIVITAS EBORACI for York and CIVITAS BRISTOLI for Bristol.

Halfgroat issues of the third coinage are often difficult to distinguish from those of the posthumous coinage, particularly if the portrait or mintmark are unclear. Differences in the style of lettering can, however, help identify most issues. Illustrations of these styles may be found in the Mintmark Chapter and details of the lettering are given below with each coin.

Collecting Hints

Even though the third coinage was only struck for three years it is fairly common, especially in the lower grades. It is usually dull in appearance and often clipped or with a flaking surface due to the metal content. Fine examples are fairly common but VF and EF examples are quite rare.

Tower Mint

Obverse Legend   HENRIC 8 D.G. AGL F Z HIB REX (many varieties) — Henry VIII by the grace of God King of England France and Ireland

Reverse Legend   POSVI DEUM ADIVTOE MEU — I have made God my helper

Obverse   Bust of ageing king; mintmark lis or none. Lombardic lettering.

Reverse   Cross over royal shield.

| H82D-100 | VG £40 | F £80 | VF £180 |

Southwark Mint

Obverse Legend   As previous.

Reverse Legend   CIVITAS LONDON — City of London

Obverse   Bust of ageing king, Roman and Lombardic lettering; mintmark 'S' or 'E' in forks or none. Mixed Lombardic and Roman lettering.

Reverse   As previous.

| H82D-105 | ex. rare |

Bristol Mint

Obverse Legend   As previous.

Reverse Legend   CIVITAS BRISTOLI — City of Bristol

Obverse   As previous, but mintmark on reverse only. Lombardic or Bristol lettering.

Reverse   As previous; mintmark 'WS'.

| H82D-110 | VG £35 | F £70 | VF £180 |

Canterbury Mint

Obverse Legend   As previous.

Reverse Legend   CIVITAS CANTOR — City of Canterbury

Obverse & Reverse   As previous, no mintmark. Lombardic or mixed Lombardic and Roman lettering.

| H82D-115 | VG £35 | F £65 | VF £180 |

York Mint

Obverse Legend   As previous.

Reverse Legend   CIVITAS EBORACI — City of York

Obverse & Reverse   As previous, no mintmark. Lombardic or mixed Lombardic and Roman lettering.

| H82D-120 | VG £40 | F £80 | VF £180 |

Posthumous Coinage (1547 – 1551)

After Henry VIII's death in 1547, his son Edward ascended the throne but until 1551 continued to issue coins with Henry VIII's portrait and name. This is known as the posthumous coinage. Although very similar to Henry's third coinage, these issues have different mintmarks, and some of the York mint have a different style bust. Moreover, a third mint opened in London during this coinage at Durham House, a former palace on the Strand owned by the Bishop of Durham. The reverse reading for this mint is REDD CUIQ QD SUUM EST (Render to each that which is his own); the other mints remain as in the previous issue.

Collecting Hints

Most coins are usually dull in appearance due to their low silver content. Coins are usually found in VG or F condition while coins in VF and EF do exist from the common mints.

Tower Mint

Obverse Legend   HENRIC 8 D G AGL FR Z HI REX (many varieties) — Henry VIII by the grace of God King of England France and Ireland

Reverse Legend   POSVI DEUM ADIVTOE MEU — I have made God my helper

Obverse   Ageing bust of king, Roman lettering; mintmarks arrow, 'K', grapple, lis, martlet, none, often muled. Roman lettering.

Reverse   Cross over royal shield.

| H82D-125 | VG £35 | F £65 | VF £180 |

Southwark Mint

Obverse Legend   As previous.

Reverse Legend   CIVITAS LONDON — City of London

Obverse   As previous; mintmark 'E', pheon, 'K' and none, often muled. Roman lettering.

Reverse   As previous.

| H82D-130 | VG £35 | F £65 | VF £180 |

Durham House Mint

Obverse Legend   As previous.

Reverse Legend   REDD CUIQ QD SUUM EST — Render to each that which is his own

Obverse   As previous, but mintmark bow, often just on reverse. Roman lettering.

Reverse   As previous.

H82D-135	VG £200	F £400	VF rare

Bristol Mint

This issue can be identical to H82D-110.

Obverse Legend   As previous.

Reverse Legend   CIVITAS BRISTOLI — City of Bristol

Obverse   As previous, no mintmark. Bristol lettering.

Reverse   As previous; mintmark 'T.C' or 'WS'.

H82D-140	VG £35	F £70	VF £180

Canterbury Mint

Obverse Legend   As previous.

Reverse Legend   CIVITAS CANTOR — City of Canterbury

Obverse   As previous, lozenge stops in legend; mintmark none, or 'T'. Lombardic or mixed Lombardic and Roman lettering.

Reverse   As previous; mintmark none, or 'T'.

H82D-145	VG £35	F £65	VF £150

York Mint

Obverse Legend   As previous.

Reverse Legend   CIVITAS EBORACI — City of York

Obverse   As previous, but two styles of bust; no mintmark. Roman lettering.

Reverse   As previous.

H82D-150	VG £35	F £65	VF £180

Edward VI (1547 – 1553)

Halfgroats were produced in considerable quantities during Edward VI's reign but all the common issues were in the name of his father, Henry VIII (the posthumous coinage listed above), and those struck in his own name are rare. The latter were produced for only a short period (April 1547 to January 1549) and in very base silver; no halfgroats were struck during Edward's fine silver issues. The three mints that produced halfgroats, the Tower and Southwark in London and the Canterbury mint, are distinguished by the reverse legends which read POSUI etc. (I have made God my helper) for the Tower, CIVITAS LONDON for Southwark and CIVITAS CANTOR for Canterbury.

Collecting Hints

Edward VI halfgroats are rare in any condition; Fine and VF examples exist but are often dull in appearance and the metal tends to flake due to the poor metal mixture.

Tower Mint

Obverse Legend   EDOARD [uncertain]

Reverse Legend   POSUI [uncertain]

Obverse   Crowned bust to right; mintmark arrow.

Reverse   Royal shield over cross.

E62D-005	VG £175	F £350	VF £750

Southwark Mint

Obverse Legend   As previous.

Reverse Legend   CIVITAS LONDON — City of London

Obverse   Crowned bust to right; mintmark arrow or 'E'.

Reverse   As previous.

E62D-010	VG £175	F £350	VF £750

Canterbury Mint

Obverse Legend   EDOARD [uncertain]

Reverse Legend   CIVITAS CANTOR — City of Canterbury

Obverse   Crowned bust to right; no mintmark.

Reverse   As previous.

E62D-015	VG £125	F £225	VF £500

Mary (1553 – 1554)

Although large quantities of groats were produced during Mary's reign, very few halfgroats were struck, probably due to there being sufficient numbers in circulation from previous reigns. Also, because of inflation and the falling value of silver, there was a need at this time for larger denominations. Unlike several of the previous issues, Mary's halfgroats were struck in good quality silver; they were only produced at the Tower mint and can easily be distinguished from Philip and Mary's 1554 – 58 issue by the legends.

Collecting Hints

This issue is extremely rare in any grade but usually found in about Fine, often holed. VF examples exist but are very rare and collectors should note that good quality forgeries of this issue also exist.

Obverse Legend   MARIA D.G. ANG FRA Z HIB REGI — Mary by the grace of God Queen of England France and Ireland

Reverse Legend   VERITAS TEMPORIS FILIA — Truth is the daughter of time

Obverse   Crowned bust of queen facing left; mintmark pomegranate.

Reverse   Royal shield over long cross.

MA2D-005   ex. rare

Philip & Mary   (1554 – 1558)

Philip and Mary halfgroats are not as rare as Mary's issue and were again only struck at the Tower mint. They can easily be differentiated from the previous issue as both the obverse and reverse legends are different.

Collecting Hints

This issue is very rare in any grade and usually found in about Fine, often holed. VF examples exist, but are very rare and collectors should note that good quality forgeries of this issue exist.

Obverse Legend   PHILIP ET MARIA D.G. REX ET REGINA — Philip and Mary by the grace of God King and Queen

Reverse Legend   POSUIM DEUM ADIVTO NOS — We have made God our helper

Obverse   Crowned bust of Mary facing left; mintmark lis.

Reverse   Royal shield over cross.

PM2D-005   VG £200   F £450   VF £1,400

Elizabeth I   (1558 – 1603)

Elizabeth I and her government recognised the importance of having a large number of small denominations in the coinage and the halfgroat was produced during most of her reign, circulating together with other denominations which were very close in value, such as the threepence. Each denomination was produced in quantity and helped to facilitate trade. Under Elizabeth, halfgroats were only struck at the Tower mint in London.

Identifying Elizabeth's coinage is not in itself difficult as in virtually all silver issues, including the halfgroats, the queen's distinctive bust appears on the obverse with her name in the legend. But distinguishing the various denominations is sometimes more complicated and collectors should bear in mind that none of the halfgroats but all threepences and three-halfpence from this reign are dated and that threepences and three-halfpence, with one exception, have a rose behind the queen's bust which is omitted in the halfgroat. Moreover, in the fifth and sixth issue halfgroats, two pellets denoting two pence can be found behind the queen's bust. Finally, accurately to identify a particular issue, collectors should locate the mintmark, which is specific to each issue. Collectors will also find that the earlier issues tend to be slightly larger than the later ones.

Collecting Hints

Elizabeth's halfgroat is fairly common with the exception of the first issue and the milled coinage. Fine and VF examples are not uncommon while EF examples also exist and are desirable. The portrait on the coin is usually reasonable but the legends are sometimes a little weak.

First Issue (1559 – 1560)

Obverse Legend   ELIZABETH D.G. ANG FRA Z HIB REG — Elizabeth by the grace of God Queen of England France and Ireland

Reverse Legend   POSUI DEU ADIVTOREM MEU — I have made God my helper

Obverse   Crowned bust of queen facing left, a wire-line inner circle; mintmark lis.

Reverse   Shield over long cross.

EL2D-005   VG £100   F £200   VF £400

Second Issue (1560 – 1561)

Apart from the mintmark, there is a slight difference between the first and second issue obverse legend where Z, denoting 'and', is replaced by ET.

Obverse Legend   ELIZABETH D.G. ANG FRA ET HIB REGINA — Elizabeth by the grace of God Queen of England France and Ireland

Reverse Legend   As previous.

Obverse   As previous, but beaded inner circle, mintmark cross-crosslet or martlet.

Reverse   As previous, beaded inner circle.

EL2D-010   VG £20   F £40   VF £80

Third Issue (1561 – 1572)

As previous, but a slightly different style in bust; mintmarks portcullis, lion, coronet or castle.

EL2D-015   VG £25   F £50   VF £100

No halfgroats were struck for the fourth issue.

Fifth Issue (1582 – 1600)

Obverse Legend   E.D.G. ROSA SINE SPINA — Elizabeth by the grace of God a rose without a thorn

Reverse Legend   CIVITAS LONDON — City of London

Obverse   Crowned bust of queen facing left, two pellets behind the bust; mintmark bell, 'A', escallop, crescent, hand, tun, woolpack, key, anchor or cypher. Some very early issues of mintmark bell omit the pellets or have the pellets struck over II.

Reverse As previous.

| EL2D-020 | VG £18 | F £35 | VF £70 |

Sixth Issue (1601 – 1602)

Legends As previous

Obverse Bust of queen with two pellets behind; mintmark '1' or '2'.

Reverse As previous.

| EL2D-025 | VG £25 | F £50 | VF £100 |

Milled Coinage

Although milled halfgroats were produced during Elizabeth's reign, it is thought that they were not a success due to the difficulties in producing such a small coin. Like the hammered issue, they can be differentiated from the threepence by the absence of a date and of the rose behind the queen's bust.

Collecting Hints

They are rare and are usually found in VG or F condition often damaged.

Obverse Legend ELIZABETH D.G. ANG FRA ET HIB REGINA — Elizabeth by the grace of God Queen of England France and Ireland

Reverse Legend POSUI DEUM ADIUTOREM MEUM — I have made God my helper

Obverse Crowned bust of queen left; mintmark star.

Reverse Square shield over cross, no inner circles.

| EL2D-030 | VG £80 | F £200 | VF £500 |

James I (1603 – 1625)

Although James I issued fewer denominations than Elizabeth, the halfgroat continued to be struck throughout his reign and falls in two main types according to design. In the first coinage, the halfgroat bore the king's bust on the obverse and the royal shield with no legend on the reverse. But in the second and third coinages it omitted the bust and depicted a crowned rose on the obverse and a crowned thistle on the reverse. This was the first halfgroat to omit the monarch's portrait since the denomination was introduced under Edward III and was probably intended as a political statement, stressing, in combination with the reverse legend, the link that England had achieved with Scotland.

Collecting Hints

James I's first issue is fairly scarce, especially in the better grades; the average condition in which it is found is less than Fine, although Fine and VF examples exist and are obtainable. The later issues are fairly common; Fine and VF examples are fairly easy to obtain while EF examples also exist but are rare and desirable.

First Coinage (1603 – 1604)

Obverse Legend I.D.G ROSA SINE SPINA — James by the grace of God a rose without a thorn

Reverse Legend None.

Obverse Crowned bust of king right with II behind; mintmarks thistle or lis.

Reverse Royal shield with mintmark above.

| J12D-005 | VG £20 | F £40 | VF £100 |

Second Coinage (1604 – 1619)

Obverse Legend I.D.G ROSA SINE SPINA — James by the grace of God a rose without a thorn

Reverse Legend TUEATUR UNITA DEUS — May God guard these united (kingdoms)

Obverse Rose with large crown above; mintmark lis, rose, escallop, grapes or coronet.

Reverse Thistle with large crown above and stops or dots in legend.

| J12D-010 | VG £15 | F £30 | VF £50 | EF £100 |

Legends As previous.

Obverse Rose with small crown above; mintmark coronet, key, bell, mullet, tower, trefoil, cinquefoil, tun, book or plain cross.

Reverse Thistle with small crown above.

| J12D-015 | VG £18 | F £35 | VF £60 | EF £120 |

Third Coinage (1619 – 1625)

Legends As previous.

Obverse Rose with small crown above; mintmark spur rowel, none, rose, thistle, lis, trefoil or trefoil and lis.

Reverse Thistle with small crown above, no stops in legend.

| J12D-020 | VG £15 | F £30 | VF £50 | EF £100 |

Charles I (1625 1649)

Halfgroats were struck in great quantities and numerous varieties during Charles I's reign. Most were produced at the Tower mint in London, either from hand-hammered dies or under Nicholas Briot's supervision from milled dies; the two issues being struck alongside each other. Many provincial mints also opened, especially during the Civil War when the Roundheads gained control of the capital and the Tower mint. Most of Charles' halfgroats have the Roman numeral II by the king's bust, denoting the denomination. Finally, many halfgroats are found holed and this was probably done officially at the end of the 17th century, to devalue the coin.

Tower Mint

Tower Mint under King (1625 – 1642)

There are two main types but many varieties of this issue; the first has a crowned rose on either side of the coin. This design only occurs in Charles I's reign and should not be confused with James I's second and third coinages, which have a crowned rose on the obverse and a crowned thistle on the reverse.

Collecting Hints

All the varieties from this issue are fairly common, the average grade being less than Fine although VF or even EF examples exist. The legends are often weak, usually due to poor striking and considerable circulation.

Crowned Rose Issue

Obverse Legend   C D G ROSA SINE SPINA — Charles by the grace of God a rose without a thorn

Reverse Legend   IUS THRONUM FIRMAT — Justice strengthens the throne

Obverse   Crowned rose with inner circles; mintmarks lis, cross calvary, blackamoor's head.

Reverse   Crowned rose with inner circles.

| C12D-005 | VG £20 | F £40 | VF £100 |

Legends   As previous.

Obverse   Crowned rose with no inner circles; mintmark blackamoor's head, castle, anchor, heart or plume.

Reverse   Crowned rose with no inner circles.

| C12D-010 | VG £15 | F £30 | VF £60 |

Bust Issue

Many varieties in the obverse legend exist but all issues will read one of the following:

CAROLUS D G MAG B F ET H REX
CAROLUS D G MA B F ET H REX
CAROLUS D G MB F ET H REX
CAROLUS D G M B FRA ET HIB REX
CAROLUS D G M A B F ET H REX.

Due to the muling of the various issues and the many varieties, the obverse legend is only listed once.

Obverse Legend   CAROLUS D G M(A)(G) B F(RA) ET H(IB) REX — Charles by the grace of God King of Great Britain France and Ireland

Reverse Legend   IUSTITIA THRONUM FIRMAT — Justice strengthens the throne

Obverse   Bust of king wearing ruff and mantle; mintmark plume or rose.

Reverse   Oval shield.

| C12D-015 | VG £15 | F £28 | VF £50 |

As previous, but plume over reverse shield.

| C12D-020 | VG £20 | F £35 | VF £60 |

Obverse   Bust of king wearing lace collar; mintmark harp, crown or portcullis.

Reverse   'C.R' divided by oval shield, no inner circles.

| C12D-025 | VG £15 | F £28 | VF £50 |

As previous, with inner circles on obverse and reverse; mintmark harp or portcullis.

| C12D-030 | VG £20 | F £35 | VF £60 |

As previous, but inner circle on reverse only.

| C12D-035 | VG £15 | F £35 | VF £60 |

As previous, but inner circle on obverse only.

| C12D-040 | VG £15 | F £28 | VF £50 |

Bust and shield as previous, but no 'C.R' divided by shield, inner circles on both sides; mintmark portcullis.

C12D-045   VG £15   F £28   VF £50

As previous, but inner circle only on obverse.

C12D-050   VG £15   F £28   VF £50

Obverse   New style bust of king, no inner circles; mintmark bell, crown, tun, anchor, triangle, star or triangle in circle.

Reverse   Rounder shield, no inner circle.

C12D-055   VG £15   F £28   VF £50

As previous, but inner circle on obverse; mintmark triangle.

C12D-060   VG £15   F £28   VF £50

As previous, but inner circles on both sides; mintmark triangle, star or triangle in circle.

C12D-065   VG £15   F £28   VF £50

Obverse   New-style bust similar to the Aberystwyth mint issues, no inner circles; mintmark anchor.

Reverse   Rounder shield, no inner circles.

C12D-070   VG £20   F £35   VF £60

As previous, but inner circles on reverse; mintmark anchor.

C12D-075   VG £20   F £35   VF £60

Obverse   Very small bust of king, no inner circles; mintmark anchor.

Reverse   Rounder shield, no inner circles.

C12D-080   VG £20   F £35   VF £60

Tower Mint under Parliament (1642 – 1648)

London and the Tower mint came under the control of Parliament in 1642. The halfgroats produced during this period are fairly similar to the previous issues except for the mintmark and it is interesting to note that the Roundheads retained the king's portrait and emblems on the coins.

Collecting Hints

Both varieties from this period are slightly scarcer than the previous issues. They are usually obtainable in about Fine condition but better grade coins do exist. It is important that a coin bears a clear mintmark for accurate identification.

Obverse Legend   CAROLUS D G M B F ET HIB REX — Charles by the grace of God King of Great Britain France and Ireland

Reverse Legend   IUSTITIA THRONUM FIRMAT — Justice strengthens the throne

Obverse   Bust of king, inner circles on obverse and reverse; mintmarks '(P)', '(R)', eye, sun, sceptre.

Reverse   Rounder shield of royal arms.

C12D-085   VG £25   F £50   VF £100

Obverse Legend   CAROLUS D G M B F ET H REX — Charles by the grace of God King of Great Britain France and Ireland

Reverse Legend   IUSTITIA THRONUM FIRMAT — Justice strengthens the throne

Obverse   Older, shorter bust of king with pointed beard; mintmarks eye, sun, sceptre. Inner circles both sides.

Reverse   Rounder shield.

C12D-090   VG £25   F £50   VF £100

Briot's Milled Issue (1631 – 1632)

Collecting Hints

The halfgroat from this issue is fairly scarce but, due to the good quality of production, is often found in better grades than the hammered. Specimens are usually obtainable in Fine to VF condition and even EF examples are not rare.

Obverse Legend   CAROLUS D.G MAG BRIT FR ET HIB R — Charles by the grace of God [King of] Great Britain France and Ireland

Reverse Legend   IUSTITIA THRONUM FIRMAT — Justice strengthens the throne

Obverse   Bust of king, II behind and 'B' below bust; no mintmark.

Reverse   Square topped shield of royal arms over cross; no mintmark.

C12D-095   VG £30   F £50   VF £120   EF £250

Provincial Mints

Halfgroats were produced at several provincial mints and many issues look fairly similar. When identifying a coin, collectors should check through all the provincial mints, ensuring that the mintmark corresponds to the issue. Also, in every issue the halfgroat as a denomination can be identified by the Roman numeral II behind the bust of the king.

Aberystwyth Mint

This issue, which had four varieties, can be identified by the large plume on the reverse and mintmark open book.

> ## Collecting Hints
>
> This issue is fairly scarce but usually obtainable undamaged in VG or Fine condition.

Obverse Legend CAROLUS D.G. M B F ET H REX — Charles by the grace of God King of Great Britain France and Ireland

Reverse Legend IUSTITIA THRONUM FIRMAT — Justice strengthens the throne

Obverse Bust of king with lace collar, no inner circles, value behind.

Reverse Large plume, no inner circles.

| C12D-100 | VG £40 | F £70 | VF £140 | EF £250 |

Similar to last, but the king's lace collar is square.

| C12D-105 | VG £35 | F £65 | VF £130 | EF £230 |

As C12D-100, but inner circles on both sides of the coin.

| C12D-110 | VG £30 | F £60 | VF £120 | EF £220 |

Briot-style bust, similar to that of the Tower mint's first coinage, inner circles on both sides of the coin. This issue was hammered.

| C12D-115 | VG £35 | F £65 | VF £130 | EF £230 |

Aberystwyth Furnace Mint (1648 – 1649)

This issue is very similar to the Aberystwyth one except for the mintmark crown and the slightly different design of the plume on the reverse.

> ## Collecting Hints
>
> The coin is very rare in any grade.

Obverse Legend CAROLUS D G MA BR FR ET HIB REX — Charles by the grace of God King of Great Britain France and Ireland

Reverse Legend IUSTITIA THRONUM FIRMAT — Justice strengthens the throne

Obverse Bust of king and inner circles; mintmark crown.

Reverse Large plume with band inscribed ICH DIEN — I serve, inner circles.

| C12D-120 | VG £100 | F £220 | VF £450 |

Oxford Mint

Two very different issues were produced at the Oxford mint. The first resembles the Aberystwyth issue with a large plume on the reverse which, however, is of a different style; it also has mintmark lis or cross. The second issue has a very distinct reverse, with the Declaration in three lines, the date 1644 and OX (for Oxford) below the date.

> ## Collecting Hints
>
> Both Oxford issues are rare; often found holed or damaged, they are rarely available in VF condition.

Obverse Legend CAROLUS D G M B F ET H(IB) REX — Charles by the grace of God King of Great Britain France and Ireland

Reverse Legend IUSTITIA THRONUM FIRMAT — Justice strengthens the throne

Obverse Bust of king; mintmark lis or cross, value behind head.

Reverse Large plume in centre.

| C12D-125 | VG £60 | F £120 | VF £250 |

Obverse Legend As previous.

Outer Reverse Legend EXURGAT DEUS DISSIPENTUR INIMICI — Let God arise and His enemies be scattered

Inner Reverse Legend RELIG PROT LEG ANG LIBER — The religion of the Protestants the laws of England the liberty of Parliament

Obverse Bust of king.

Reverse Declaration on three lines, three fleur-de-lis above, date 1644 below and OX below that; the outer legend does not start at the top of the coin.

| C12D-130 | VG £80 | F £150 | VF £300 |

Bristol Mint

Only one issue was produced at the Bristol mint and has a very different style reverse.

> ## Collecting Hints
>
> This issue is rare in any grade and is often damaged.

Obverse Legend CAROLUS D G M B F ET H REX — Charles by the grace of God King of Great Britain France and Ireland

Outer Reverse Legend EXURGAT DEUS DISSIP INIMICI — Let God arise and His enemies be scattered (abbreviated)

Reverse Centre Legend RE PR LE AN LI PA — The religion of the Protestants the laws of England the liberty of Parliament

Obverse Bust of king; no mintmark.

Reverse Declaration on three lines, undated, BR for Bristol below declaration.

C12D-135	VG £150	F £300	VF —

Late Declaration Silver

Very little is known about this issue which is often known as the Plumes mint and easily identifiable, being the only halfgroat issued with the date 1646.

Collecting Hints

Coins from this issue are very rare in any grade and are often damaged.

Obverse Legend CAROLUS D G M B F ET H REX — Charles by the grace of God King of Great Britain France and Ireland

Reverse Legend IUSTITIA THRONUM FIRMAT — Justice strengthens the throne

Obverse Bust of king; no mintmark.

Reverse Large plume dividing date 1646.

C12D-140	VG £150	F £300	VF rare

Exeter Mint

Two issues were struck at Exeter. The first resembles the common Tower mint issues except that that it is dated (1644) and has mintmark rose. The second issue is easily identifiable; it is also dated 1644 and has a large rose in the centre of the reverse.

Collecting Hints

Both issues are rare in any grade. Coins are often damaged or badly struck, those in VF or better condition being very rare.

Obverse Legend CAROLUS D G M B F ET HI REX — Charles by the grace of God King of Great Britain France and Ireland

Reverse Legend THRO IUSTI FIRMAT 1644 — Justice strengthens the throne 1644

Obverse Bust of king; mintmark rose.

Reverse Royal shield.

C12D-145	VG £60	F £100	VF £300

As previous, but large rose in the centre of the reverse.

C12D-150	VG £80	F £140	VF £350

Worcester or Salopia (Shropshire)

This issue is very crude in style with a tall bust of little detail. It is easily identified by its design, the mintmark lis and the reverse legend.

Collecting Hints

This issue is extremely rare in any grade.

Obverse Legend CAROLUS D G M B F ET H REX — Charles by the grace of God King of Great Britain France and Ireland

Reverse Legend CHRISTO AUSPICE REGNO — I reign under the auspices of Christ

Obverse Crude bust of king; mintmark lis.

Reverse Crude round shield.

C12D-155	VG £200	F £400	VF —

During Charles I's reign Briot struck pattern twopences, with the king's bust on the obverse and two 'C's joined with a crown on the reverse. While classed as patterns, these issues are fairly common and obviously saw circulation. As collectors may come across them, we have noted them; several varieties exist.

Commonwealth (1649 – 1660)

Halfgroats were struck throughout the Commonwealth period; all bearing no legends, date or mintmark. The halfgroat is virtually identical to the penny except for the Roman numeral II above the reverse shields denoting the denomination.

Collecting Hints

Halfgroats are fairly common. Many are found clipped and/or holed, which was done officially during later reigns to devalue the coin. Coins in Fine or VF condition are not uncommon and EF examples also exist. A fully round coin is of considerably more value than a clipped specimen.

Obverse Legend None.

Reverse Legend None.

Obverse Shield of St George within wreath.

Reverse Shield of St George and Ireland with II above.

| CW2D-005 | VG £25 | F £50 | VF £100 | EF £200 |

Charles II (1660 – 1685)

Hammered Issue (1660 – 1662)

Charles II's hammered and machine-made issues are fairly common. While they were only struck for a few years, large quantities and several varieties were produced. All issues have the denomination in Roman numerals (II) behind the king's bust but are easily distinguished from Charles I's issues by the distinct portrait of Charles II and the obverse legend reading CAROLUS II instead of just CAROLUS. They were all struck at the Tower mint.

Collecting Hints

All issues are fairly common and usually obtainable in Fine condition although VF or even EF examples are not uncommon. Many coins have parts of their legends missing but this is usually due to poor striking rather than clipping.

First Issue

Obverse Legend CAROLUS II DG MAG BRIT FR ET H REX — Charles II by the grace of God King of Great Britain France and Ireland

Reverse Legend CHRISTO AUSPICE REGNO — I reign under the auspices of Christ

Obverse Bust of king with no mark of value and no inner circles; mintmark crown.

Reverse Royal shield over cross; no mintmark.

| C22DH-005 | VG £15 | F £30 | VF £60 | EF £120 |

Second Issue

As previous, but with mark of value behind the king's bust and mintmark crown on obverse, none on reverse.

| C22DH-010 | VG £80 | F £200 | VF £400 | EF rare |

As previous, but mintmark also on reverse. This issue was machine-made and is usually much rounder than others.

| C22DH-015 | VG £14 | F £30 | VF £60 | EF £120 |

This issue was also machine-made.

Legends As previous.

Obverse Bust of king to edge of coin, the crown has a single arch and the legend starts at bottom left of coin.

Reverse As previous.

| C22DH-020 | VG £16 | F £35 | VF £70 | EF £140 |

Third Issue

This issue was hammered and coins were often fairly badly struck.

Legends As previous.

Obverse Bust of king in an inner circle, value behind the head and the legend starts at the top of the coin; mintmark crown.

Reverse As previous.

| C22DH-025 | VG £15 | F £30 | VF £60 | EF £120 |

Three Halfpence

Elizabeth I (1558 – 1603)

The silver penny-halfpenny, or three-halfpence, was introduced in Elizabeth I's third and fourth issues as part of a plan to produce large quantities of coins of varying denominations and high metal content. It depicts the bust of the queen with a rose behind on the obverse and the royal shield with the date above on the reverse; a mintmark can be found at the beginning of the obverse and reverse legend. All three halfpence issues were struck at the Tower mint. Although this denomination may easily be confused with the threepence or three-farthings which were both produced at the time, the diameters of the coins vary and, for unclipped specimens, are as follows:

threepence: 1561 large flan 21 mm, all others 19 mm

three-halfpence: 1561 large flan 17 mm, all others 16 mm

three-farthings: 14 mm flan

However, halfgroats and pennies were also struck under Elizabeth. To distinguish the three-halfpence from these, collectors should bear in mind that the halfgroat and penny omit the rose behind the queen's bust and the date except for an extremely rare 1558 penny which is dated but can easily be identified since no three-halfpences were issued that year.

Collecting Hints

This issue is scarce but obtainable. Coins are usually found in VG to Fine condition and undoubtedly saw considerable circulation. Specimens in VF or EF are rare.

Obverse Legend   E. D. G. ROSA SINE SPINA — Elizabeth by the grace of God a rose without a thorn

Reverse Legend   CIVITAS LONDON — City of London

Obverse   Crowned bust of queen with rose behind; mintmark as listed below.

Reverse   Royal arms with date above; mintmark at start of legend.

Mintmark   Pheon (1561 – 62, 1564), rose (1565), portcullis (1566), lion (1567), coronet (1567 – 69), castle (1570), ermine (1572 – 73), acorn (1572 – 74), eglantine (1573 – 77), plain cross (1578 – 79), long cross (1581) or sword (1582).

EL3HD-005	VG £25	F £50	VF £100

No three-halfpences were struck after 1582 and the denomination was discontinued because both James I and Charles I produced large quantities of halfpennies and farthings.

Penny

The silver penny probably was first introduced in England during the reign of Offa in 757 AD. The origin of the word is uncertain but possibly comes from the German *pfennig* which was a German denomination. The issues were similar in size and weight to the continental *deniers* of this period. The abbreviation 'd' came from the Roman denomination *denarius* and was used up until the 1970s. The penny up until the reign of Edward III was the most important denomination and from then on was produced during every reign and is in circulation today.

William I (1066 – 1087)

William I continued the previous Anglo-Saxon system of coinage, with the silver penny being the only denomination struck. As it was a fairly large denomination at the time, when smaller monetary units were needed, pennies were cut in half or even quarters. Most pennies have a front-facing bust of the king on the obverse, which was a departure from the sideways bust of most earlier Anglo-Saxon coins, and a design surrounded by the legend with the moneyer's name and the mint on the reverse. Of the eight major types of pennies, the most famous and popular is the Pax (Peace) penny, produced at most mints in 1086 – 87 and thought to reflect the peace that prevailed after the conquest, as powerful notables pledged their allegiance to the king.

To satisfy the demand for coinage, some 70 mints were active during William's reign, but it was the moneyers who were personally responsible for maintaining the weight (20 to 22 grains, 1.3 to 1.4 grams for pennies) and the silver fineness of the coins they produced. So although there was only a small amount of space on the reverse for the 'identification details', the moneyer's name was considered more important than the mint and rarely abbreviated, albeit often 'misspelt'. The moneyer's name begins the legend after a small cross and is usually followed by ON and then the town's name; for example '+ GODRIC ON LEMRE' i.e. 'Godric of Leicester'. One should note that letters are sometimes unintelligible due to the poor cutting of dies while certain letters, such as 'N', are often reversed and 'U' is written as a 'V'. In cases where the legend is particularly bad, a coin might be traced through the moneyer's name, specialist books and an elimination process. Below we list the various mints and the abbreviations of their name that are most commonly found on the coins, although it should be stressed that more varieties could very possibly exist — and we have listed the coins of William I and William II together as the two reigns are so similar in this respect.

Collecting Hints

William I pennies can usually be found in Fine to VF condition and, as most have come from hoards, they will have an attractive appearance. However, all coins are fairly fragile and should be handled with care as it is not uncommon for them to break when mistreated; bent coins should never be straightened. In some cases the legends may be blundered or damaged but collectors should ensure that the moneyer's name and mint are legible. Many of the provincial mints are reasonably plentiful and some collectors collect by mint, others try to obtain representative examples of all eight major types.

Profile, Cross Fleury Issue (1066 – 1068)

Obverse Legend   PILLEMUS REX (I or A) — King William

Reverse Legend   Moneyer's name and mint.

Obverse   Left profile of king crowned, with sceptre.

Reverse   Cross fleury with annulet at centre.

W11D-005	VG £140	F £350	VF £700

Bonnet Issue (1068 – 1071)

Obverse Legend   PILLEMUS REX (I or A) — King William

Reverse Legend   Moneyer's name and mint.

Obverse   Crowned front-facing bust of king with two fillets falling from crown each side of head, looking like a bonnet.

Reverse   Cross voided with annulet in centre, pellet (or dot) between two crescents at end of each limb.

W11D-010	VG £135	F £300	VF £600

Canopy Issue (1071 – 1074)

Obverse Legend   PILLEMUS REX (I) — King William

Reverse Legend   Moneyer's name and mint.

Obverse   Crowned front-facing bust within canopy supported by two columns.

Reverse   Double quadrilateral with incurved sides, fleur at the angles, annulet in centre.

W11D-015	VG £150	F £350	VF £650

Two Sceptres Issue (1074 – 1077)

Obverse Legend   PILLEM REX ANGLOR — William King of the English

Reverse Legend   Moneyer's name and mint.

Obverse   Crowned front-facing bust of king with sceptre either side of bust.

Reverse   Cross fleury with annulet in centre over saltire botonnée.

W11D-020	VG £150	F £350	VF £600

Two Stars Issue (1077 – 1080)

Obverse Legend PILLEM REX AN. — William King of the English

Reverse Legend Moneyer's name and mint.

Obverse Crowned front-facing bust of king with a star at either side.

Reverse Cross botonnée over quadrilateral with incurved sides, annulet in centre.

W11D-025	VG £150	F £350	VF £600

Sword Issue (1080 – 1083)

Obverse Legend PILLELM REX I. — King William

Reverse Legend Moneyer's name and mint.

Obverse Crowned front-facing bust of king holding sword in his right hand.

Reverse Cross pattée over quadrilateral with incurved sides, fleury at angles.

W11D-030	VG £175	F £400	VF £700

Right Profile, Cross and Trefoils Issue (1083 – 1086)

This issue, which was only produced at the London mint, has recently been found struck in lead. The original dies were used and it is uncertain whether this issue is a trial striking or, more likely, a forgery.

Obverse Legend PILLELM REX — King William

Reverse Legend Moneyer's name and mint.

Obverse Crowned bust to right-facing sceptre.

Reverse Cross pattée with annulet in centre with a voided trefoil in each angle.

W11D-035	VG £175	F £400	VF £700

Pax Issue (1086 – 1087)

Obverse Legend PILLELM REX — King William

Reverse Legend Moneyer's name and mint.

Obverse Crowned front-facing bust of king holding sceptre; there are three different styles of crown in this issue.

Reverse Cross pattée, in each angle an annulet containing one letter of PAXS (peace).

W11D-040	VG £100	F £240	VF £375

William I & William II Mints

Rarity of Mints

We have listed all main issues of William I and II. The prices given refer to common mints. All mints with a single 'R' would fall under this pricing. As a rule mints with 'RR' would be worth approximately 50% more. Mints with 'RRR' are extremely rare and could be worth twice as much as the prices given. This rarity system however is only a guide because with the use of metal detectors more coins are being found and the rarity of a mint can quickly change. Also demand for various mints can change with collectors' interest.

Mint	Abbreviation	Rarity
Barnstaple	BARD(I)	RR
Bath	BADN	RR
Bedford	B(E)D, BEDEFO	RR
Bedwyn	BEDEWIND	RRR
Bridport	BRDPHT, BRIPUT, BRID	RRR
Bristol	BRI(GCTSO), BRICSI, BRICA	RR
Bury St Edmunds	EDM DM	RR
Cambridge	GRINNT, GRANT	RR
Canterbury	CATPAI, C(NT), CANTO, EANT, CNTLI	R
Cardiff	CAIRDI, CARITI	RRR
Chester	LECI, CESTR(E), LEGECE	RR
Chichester	CISSAN, CICEST	RR
Christchurch	TWIN, TPIN	RRR
Colchester	CO(LE), CO(L)EC, COLI	RR
Cricklade	CRIC	RRR
Derby	D(E)RBI	RR
Devitum (probably St Davids, Wales)	DEVITUM	RRR
Dorchester	DORECES	RR
Dover	DOF R, DOI, DOVOR	R
Durham	DUN(E)	RR
Exeter	IEXE(C), EXEC(S)I, EXCI	RR
Gloucester	GLPEC, GEP, GLE(PI)	RR
Guildford	GILDEF, GLDF	RRR
Hastings	AESTI, HIEST	RR
Hereford	HEREFORI, HRF	RR
Hertford	HRTFR, RETEF	RR
Huntingdon	HVNTEN, HVT(D), H(V)	RR
Hythe	HIDEN	RRR
Ilchester	GIVELCSTI, GIF	RR
Ipswich	GIP(E), GIPSP	R
Launceston	STEFNI	RRR
Leicester	LEMRE, LEGRI	RR
Lewes	LIEWIE, LAEPES	RR
Lincoln	LINCOLN(E), LINC, LINI	R
London	LVNDN(E), LVNDENI, LVN(I), L(V)I, LOUN	R
Maint	MAINT	RRR
Maldon (Essex)	MIEL, MLD	RR
Malmesbury	MALME	RRR
Marlborough	MIERLEBH	RRR
Northampton	HMTVI, HATVI	RR
Norwich	N(ORI), NORDPI(C), NODP, NORD(I)	RR
Nottingham	SNOTI(NGI)	RR
Oxford	OXSN, OXNE(F), OX(S)I	R
Peterborough	BURI	RRR
Pevensey	PEFNESE	RRR
Rhuddlan	RUDILI	RRR
Rochester	ROF ECS	RRR
Romney	RV(ME), RUMN	RRR
Salisbury	SIER(BI), SEBR	RR
Sandwich	SANDP	RRR
Shaftesbury	S, SC(IE)F	RRR
Shrewsbury	SCRUB	RRR
Southwark	SDEP, SVDE(P)	RR

Stafford	STEFFOR, STAEF	RRR
Stamford	STN, STI	R
Steyning	STNI(G)	RRR
Sudbury	SVBR, SVD(I)	RRR
Tamworth	TAMP	RRR
Taunton	TV, T(A)NT	RRR
Thetford	DEOTF(ORI), DTF(RD)I	RR
Totnes	TOTN	RRR
Wallingford	PALL(IG), P(A), PAL(I)	RR
Wareham	PERE	RRR
Warwick	PERI, VERI, PERP	RRR
Watchet	PICEDI	RRR
Wilton	PILTV, PILTUNAP	RR
Winchcombe	WINCL, PNCL	RRR
Winchester	PINC(E), PICES, PNCE	RR
Worcester	PIH(R)	RRR
York	EOF (I), EOF E, ERP, EOI, IIIFERP, EFR(PI), EFRP(ICI)	RR

William II (1087 – 1100)

William II was the second son of William I and succeeded him in 1087. He continued to strike pennies but standards of production progressively deteriorated, with badly produced dies being used and the resultant coins often having blundered legends and weak flat parts. This can make it difficult to decipher the mint and moneyer's name. There are five main designs of William II's coins which, like those of his father, were struck throughout the country despite the fact that many mints closed during his reign so that only 34 remained active at his death, as opposed to over fifty during the earlier part of his reign.

Collecting Hints

All William II coins are rare and usually of poor quality. Collectors should try to obtain a Fine example, with lettering clear enough to make out the mint name.

Profile Issue (1087 – 1090)

Obverse Legend PILLEM R. — King William

Reverse Legend Moneyer's name and mint.

Obverse Crowned bust right, holding a sword.

Reverse Cross pattée with annulet at centre over cross fleury.

W21D-005	VG £200	F £500	VF £1,100

Cross in Quatrefoil Issue (1090 – 1093)

Obverse Legend PILLELM RE (X or sometimes I) — King William

Reverse Legend Moneyer's name and mint.

Obverse Crowned bust front-facing, holding sword.

Reverse Quatrefoil with pellet at each angle enclosing a cross pattée with annulet at centre.

W21D-010	VG £200	F £500	VF £1,100

Cross Voided Issue (1093 – 1096)

Obverse Legend PILLELM R(I, A, EX or sometimes EI) — King William

Reverse Legend Moneyer's name and mint.

Obverse Front-facing crowned bust between two stars; except for the Dover, Hastings, Northampton and Norwich mints which omit the stars.

Reverse Voided cross pattée with annulet in centre over a cross annulettée.

W21D-015	VG £200	F £500	VF £1,100

Cross Pattée and Fleury Issue (1096 – 1099)

Obverse Legend PILLELM RE(X or sometimes I) — King William

Reverse Legend Moneyer's name and mint.

Obverse Front-facing crowned bust of king holding sword.

Reverse Cross pattée over a cross fleury.

W21D-020	VG £200	F £550	VF £1,200

Cross Fleury and Piles Issue (1099 – 1100)

The coins of this issue are very blundered.

Obverse Legend PILLELM (I) RI — King William

Reverse Legend Moneyer's name and mint.

Obverse Crowned front-facing bust holding a sceptre in right hand and a star to right of bust.

Reverse Cross fleury with a pile surmounted by a pellet in each angle.

W21D-025	VG £200	F £550	VF £1,200

Henry I (1100 – 1135)

The penny continued to be the main denomination during Henry's relatively long reign because although the halfpenny was introduced, it proved very unpopular and only three or four specimens are known today. Fifteen major types of pennies were issued yet the quality of production continued to be poor. Coins were struck at various mints countrywide and it is obvious from the early issues that little central control could be imposed on the activities of the moneyers who made a very large seniorage or profit by producing coins that were underweight and below fineness. In 1124, Henry finally summoned the moneyers to Winchester and called them to account for their activities; a number of them were even mutilated for issuing coins of inferior quality. As a result, the coinage did improve in fineness and weight, although not always in production.

Around 54 mints were intermittently active during this period and, as previously, the mint and moneyer's name were included in the coin's reverse legend which usually starts with a small cross followed by the moneyer's name, the word ON and the mint. Again, the moneyer's name was written in full even if long but the town name might well be abbreviated, often to a few letters. Thus for example, a coin may read '+ AHGEMVND:ION:C', i.e. + moneyer's name of C (Canterbury, abbreviated due to a long name), or '+ RODBERT:ON:CAN', i.e. + moneyer's name of CAN (Canterbury, not abbreviated as much due to the moneyer's shorter name). Words are usually separated by two pellets (:) and it should be noted that letters were often left out or legends were blundered because of bad dies. Owing to the originally poor quality of the coin, it is often impossible to identify the mint. The mints are listed below, with some of the abbreviation often found on the coin.

Collecting Hints

As previously noted, most of Henry I's coinage is of fairly poor quality. Collectors wishing to obtain an example of this reign might well choose a class XIV or XV penny as, being struck after 1124, they tend to be of better quality and have clearer mints. Many Henry I pennies have a small cut in the edge, produced by contemporaries checking the fineness of the coin, which sometimes makes them unsightly and a bad cut reduces the coin's value. Furthermore, a fair number of coins turn up cracked, often because of the small clip in the edge, and those with bad cracks should be avoided as they can break easily. Dealers have been known to send out a cracked coin in one piece, only to have it arrive in two or more.

Annulet Issue (1101 – 1102)
Obverse Legend HENRI (CUS) REX N — King Henry

Reverse Legend Moneyer's name and mint.

Obverse Crowned front-facing bust with an annulet either side of neck.

Reverse Cross fleury with annulet in centre and in each angle three pellets on a pile which rests on the inner circle.

H11D-005 VG £200 F £450 VF £900

Profile Issue (1102 – 1103)
Obverse Legend HENRI REX — King Henry

Reverse Legend Moneyer's name and mint.

Obverse Crowned bust facing left holding sceptre.

Reverse Cross fleury with annulet at centre.

H11D-010 VG £200 F £450 VF £900

Pax Issue (1103 – 1104)
The PAX (peace) issue is thought to refer to the Alton treaty which marked Henry's success in negotiating peace with his brother Robert and quelling a rebellion amongst Robert's supporters.

Obverse Legend HENRY REX (EI) — King Henry

Reverse Legend Moneyer's name and mint.

Obverse Front-facing crowned bust of king with an annulet on right shoulder and a trefoil on the left.

Reverse PAX between two beaded lines, two annulets above and below.

H11D-015 VG £250 F £500 VF £900

Annulets and Piles Issue (1104 – 1105)
Obverse Legend HENRIC RE — King Henry

Reverse Legend Moneyer's name and mint.

Obverse Front-facing crowned bust with sceptre over right shoulder.

Reverse Four annulets between four piles.

H11D-020 VG £250 F £500 VF £900

Voided Cross and Fleurs Issue (1105 – 1106)
Obverse Legend HENRIC REX. — King Henry

Reverse Legend Moneyer's name and mint.

Obverse Front-facing crowned bust with sceptre over right shoulder and star in field.

Reverse Voided cross with fleur in each angle.

H11D-025 VG £325 F £700 VF £1,400

Pointing Bust and Stars Issue (1106 – 1107)
Obverse Legend HENRI REX. — King Henry

Reverse Legend Moneyer's name and mint.

Obverse Crowned bust three quarters right holding sceptre in right hand and pointing with left; three stars in the right part of the field.

Reverse Cross pattée over saltire with a star in each angle.

H11D-030 VG £400 F £1,000 VF £2,000

Quatrefoil and Stars Issue (1108 – 1109)
Obverse Legend HENRI RE (X) — King Henry

Reverse Legend Moneyer's name and mint.

Obverse Crowned front-facing bust.

Reverse Quatrefoil with piles, annulet with pellet in centre.

H11D-035 VG £200 F £450 VF £800

Larger Profile, Cross and Annulets Issue (1109 – 1110)

Obverse Legend HENRI REX. — King Henry

Reverse Legend Moneyer's name and mint.

Obverse Crowned bust facing left, facing sceptre.

Reverse Cross with annulet in each angle.

| H11D-040 | VG £400 | F £800 | VF £1,600 |

Cross in Quatrefoil Issue (1107 – 1108)

Obverse Legend HENRI REX. — King Henry

Reverse Legend Moneyer's name and mint.

Obverse Crowned front-facing bust with a sceptre in right hand and a star and a quatrefoil of annulets to the right of bust. A quatrefoil of annulets is four annulets next to each other touching in a diamond shape.

Reverse Cross in quatrefoil, quatrefoil of annulets in the four angles of the quatrefoil.

| H11D-045 | VG £300 | F £650 | VF £1,300 |

Full Face, Cross Fleury Issue (1114 – 1119)

Obverse Legend HENRICUS REX A (N) — Henry King of England

Reverse Legend Moneyer's name and mint.

Obverse Crowned front-facing bust.

Reverse Cross fleury with annulet in centre.

| H11D-050 | VG £175 | F £375 | VF £650 |

Double Inscription Issue (1110 – 1114)

Obverse Legend HENR (IR). — King Henry

Reverse Legend In most cases the outer circle has the name of the moneyer and the inner circle the mint from which the coin was issued.

Obverse Crowned bust facing left, holding sceptre.

Reverse Double inscription between three beaded circles, the outer one divided by four quatrefoils, small cross in centre.

| H11D-055 | VG £400 | F £800 | VF £1,600 |

Smaller Profile, Cross and Annulet Issue (1119 – 1120)

Obverse Legend HENRICUS — Henry

Reverse Legend Moneyer's name and mint.

Obverse Small crowned bust facing left, a rosette in the field.

Reverse Cross pattée with an annulet enclosing a pellet in each angle.

| H11D-060 | VG £250 | F £450 | VF £900 |

Star in Lozenge Fleury Issue (1120 – 1122)

Obverse Legend HENRICUS — Henry

Reverse Legend Moneyer's name and mint.

Obverse Crowned bust left holding sceptre.

Reverse Quadrilateral with incurved sides, fleur at each angle, trefoil of annulets between each pair of fleurs, star in centre.

| H11D-065 | VG £250 | F £450 | VF £900 |

Pellets in Quatrefoil Issue (1122 – 1124)

Obverse Legend HENRICUS R(EX) — King Henry

Reverse Legend Moneyer's name and mint.

Obverse Crowned front-facing bust holding sceptre, a star to the right of bust and in a few cases an annulet on the king's shoulder.

Reverse Quatrefoil with star in centre and pellets on limbs, a lis in each angle.

| H11D-070 | VG £130 | F £260 | VF £450 |

Quadrilateral on Cross Fleury Issue (1125 – 1136)

Obverse Legend HENRICUS — Henry

Reverse Legend Moneyer's name and mint.

Obverse Crowned bust three quarters facing left, holding sceptre.

Reverse Quadrilateral with incurved sides over cross fleury.

| H11D-075 | VG £100 | F £225 | VF £400 |

Mints

Rarity of Mints

The most common mints are 'R' while the rarest are 'RRR'. We have listed prices for each issue and these refer to the most common mints (R). It is often difficult to identify mints due to the poor condition of the coins. As a general rule, issues with 'RR' are worth approximately 50% more and those with 'RRR' 100% more of the prices given. The rarities of issues will change as more coins come on to the market with the help of metal detectors, and the varying demands of collectors.

Mint	Abbreviation	Rarity
Barnstaple	BARD	RR
Bath	BA(DA)	RRR
Bedford		RRR
Bristol	BRIS(TO)	RR

Bury St		
Edmunds	SAN EDMN, SEDM	RR
Cambridge		RRR
Canterbury	C, CA(T)N, CANTLEI	R
Cardiff		RRR
Carlisle	CARLI, CARD	RRR
Chester	CESTRE, LEGL	RR
Chichester	CIC(ES)	RR
Christchurch		
(Twynham)	TVEHAM, TPN	RRR
Colchester	COL(E)	RR
Derby	DERBIP, DERBEREI	RRR
Dorchester	DOREC	RR
Dover	DOI, DOF	RR
Durham	DVRHAM	RRR
Exeter	EX	RRR
Gloucester	GLOWA, GLE	RRR
Hastings	HIEST, HAS	RRR
Hereford	HEREF	RRR
Huntingdon	HUN	RRR
Ilchester	IVELCE	RRR
Ipswich	GIPE	RRR
Launceston	LANTSA	RRR
Leicester	LE(I), LECE	RRR
Lewes	LIEIP, LEP	RRR
Lincoln	LINC	RR
London	LVN, LVND(EN)	R
Northampton	NORH(AM)	RR
Norwich	NORPI(C), NOR(DE)	RR
Nottingham	NO(T), SNOT(I)	RRR
Oxford	OX(ENN)	RR
Pembroke	PEI	RRR
Pevensey		RRR
Rochester	ROFI	RRR
Romney	RUME	RR
Salisbury	SEBR, SERR	RR
Sandwich	SAN	RR
Shaftesbury	S(EFTE)	RRR
Shrewsbury		RRR
Southampton		RRR
Southwark	SVDPE, SVTP	RR
Stafford		RRR
Stamford		RR
Sudbury	SVD, SUTB	RRR
Tamworth		RRR
Taunton	TANTV	RRR
Thetford	TET(F), DTF	RR
Totnes		RRR
Wallingford	WALL	RRR
Wareham	PERA, WARE	RRR
Warwick	WAR, PARPIC	RRR
Watchet		RRR
Wilton	PIL(TV)	RRR
Winchcombe		RRR
Winchester	PIN(CE)	RR
Worcester	PIRE(CES)	RRR
York	EVER, EBO	RR

Stephen   (1135 – 1154)

Stephen's reign was a period of almost dual monarchy, as well as civil war and anarchy. Henry I had wanted his daughter Matilda to succeed him but both she and his nephew Stephen claimed the throne when he died. The cousins arrived in England from France almost simultaneously and set up rival courts, in Bristol and London respectively. The location of their courts was reflected in the minting of their coins, with Stephen's coins being struck mostly in the east and south of the country while Matilda's were in the west. However, with the prevalent uncertainty a number of powerful Earls, especially those in the Northern Border region, started to strike coins in their own names. All the coins produced at this time were pennies and although the quality was very poor,

numerous designs and styles were used since there were so many issuers, die makers and mints. We have listed the five main types of Stephen pennies and although there are many variants of each type, particularly the 'Watford' one, the variants themselves are rare, often unique, albeit in appalling condition. As with Henry I's coins, the moneyer's name and the mint, often abbreviated, are found on the reverse, but as the legends are very blundered it is often impossible to decipher the mint even on a Fine condition coin. Listed below are the mint names with their usual abbreviation but it is important to remember that letters were often omitted or joined together by their vertical stem to save space, especially if the moneyer's name was long. In fact, many of the mints for Stephen pennies can not be worked out.

Collecting Hints

Stephen's pennies are always popular and not as rare as one might expect, especially the Watford type. By contrast, coins of Matilda or the Earls are very rare and infrequently appear on the market although the advent of metal detectors may alter the situation dramatically at any time. Should collectors require just one example from the reign, they should look for a Watford type as, with patience, these coins can be found in Fine even though their average condition is only fair. Collectors should also try to obtain a coin with a clear mint, keeping in mind that the mint's name is often obliterated in coins of even Fine condition, because like Henry I's pennies, those of Stephen are crude, frequently struck on irregular shaped flans and often off-centre. Specimens with a round flan and a centred strike are more desirable and rare. Collectors interested in coins of Matilda and the Earls should be prepared for a long wait and plenty of searching. These coins are all very rare, very desirable and rarely come on to the market.

Watford Issue

The issue derives its name from a hoard found in Watford and contains several minor varieties including no inner circle on the obverse, annulets in the crown or crescents before the nose.

Obverse Legend   STIEFNE (R, RE or REX) — King Stephen

Reverse Legend   Moneyer's name and mint.

Obverse   Crowned bust facing right holding sceptre.

Reverse   Cross moline with a fleur in each angle.

ST1D-005	VG £100	F £220	VF £450

Watford Issue with different Obverse Legend

The obverse legend of this issue, PERERIC(M), cannot actually be translated and is thought to have been constructed to look like HENRICUS, the name of the previous monarch. Wishing to extricate themselves from the conflict over the throne and realising the importance of supplying adequate quantities of coinage during this turbulent period, the moneyers seem to have adopted this novel solution which, in part, was acceptable because the vast majority of the population were illiterate.

Obverse Legend   PERERIC(M)

Reverse Legend   Moneyer's name and mint.

Obverse   Crowned bust facing right holding sceptre

Reverse   Cross moline with a fleur in each angle.

ST1D-010   VG £200   F £450   VF —

Voided Cross Issue

Obverse Legend   STIEFNE — Stephen

Reverse Legend   Moneyer's name and mint.

Obverse   Crowned bust, three-quarters left holding sceptre.

Reverse   Plain cross voided with a mullet in each angle.

ST1D-015   VG £150   F £300   VF £600

Profile, Cross and Piles Issue

There is also a variety where the bust faces right rather than left.

Obverse Legend   STIEFNE — Stephen

Reverse Legend   Moneyer's name and mint

Obverse   Crowned bust facing left holding sceptre.

Reverse   Cross fleury with a pile and a trefoil of annulets in each angle.

ST1D-020   VG £200   F £450   VF £1,100

Awbridge or Cross Pommée Issue

So named because many coins of this type were found in a hoard in Awbridge.

Obverse Legend   STIEFNE — Stephen

Reverse Legend   Moneyer's name and mint.

Obverse   Bearded crowned bust facing three quarters left and holding sceptre in right hand.

Reverse   Voided cross pommée with a lis in angles.

ST1D-025   VG £150   F £350   VF £800

Mints

Rarity of Mints

As with previous reigns, we have listed rarities of mints. As mentioned however, it is impossible to identify most coins' mints. A clear, identifiable mint adds value to a coin and mints with 'RR' are very rare while those with 'RRR' are extremely rare. An issue with 'RRR' could be worth twice as much as the price given while an issue with 'RR' could be worth up to 50% more. Rarity of these issues is always changing due to more coins being found.

Mint	Abbreviation	Rarity
Bedford	BED	RRR
Bramber	BRAN	RRR
Bristol	BRIST	RRR
Bury St Edmunds	EDM	RR
Cambridge		RRR
Canterbury	CANT	R
Cardiff	CARDI	RRR
Carlisle	CARDI	RRR
Castle Rising	RIS	RR
Chester	CES	RR
Chichester	CICES	RRR
Cipen (possibly Ipswich)	CIPEN	RRR
Colchester	COLE	RRR
Corbridge		RRR
Derby	DURBI	RRR
Dorchester		RRR
Dover	DOFVER	RRR
Durham	DVNHO	RRR
Eden (possibly Carlisle)	EDEN	RRR
Exeter	EXE	RRR
Gloucester	GLO	RRR
Hastings	HAS	RR
Hendon (near Hull)	HEDON	RRR
Hereford	HEREFO	RRR
Huntingdon	HUN	RRR
Ipswich	GIP	RRR
Launceston	LANSA	RRR
Leicester	LEREC	RRR
Lewes	LEP(E), LEV, LIEIP	RRR
Lincoln	LINCOL, NIC	R
London	LUND	R
Newcastle	NE(VCAS), NI(VCA)	RRR
Northampton	NORHAN	RRR
Norwich	NORPT	RRR
Nottingham	SNOT	RRR
Oxford	OXEN	RR
Pembroke	PAN	RRR
Peterborough?	BUR	RRR
Pevensey	PEVEN	RRR
Rye	RIE	RRR
Salisbury	SAL	RRR
Sandwich	SAN	RRR
Shaftesbury	SCIEFT	RRR
Shrewsbury	SALOPES	RRR
Southampton		RRR
Southwark	SUTHGEW	RRR
Stafford	STAFO	RRR
Stamford	STANF	RR
Steyning	(S)TEN	RRR
Sudbury	SUD	RRR
Swansea	SWENSI, SVENSHI	RRR
Tamworth		RRR
Taunton	TANTVN	RRR
Thetford	FORT, TETFOR	R
Tutbury		RRR
Wareham	PARHAM	RRR
Warwick	PAR	RRR
Watchet	WACET	RRR
Wilton	PILT	RR
Winchester	PINCE	RR
Worcester	PIREC	RRR
York	EVER	RRR

Matilda

The style of Matilda's issues tended to be cruder than that of the regular issues of Stephen, reflecting the production of dies and coins in the provincial mints.

The design of this style is quite similar to Stephen's Watford type penny, but there is also a variety of the reverse with cross pattée over cross fleury.

Obverse Legend MATILDI IMP. — Empress Matilda

Reverse Legend Moneyer's name and mint.

Obverse Crowned bust facing right holding a sceptre.

Reverse Cross moline with a fleur in each angle.

MT1D-005	VG £1,000	F £2,500	VF £6,000

Mints

Mint	Abbreviation
Bristol	BRIS
Calne?	CA
Canterbury?	CA
Cardiff	CAIERDI
Gloucester	GLO
Oxford	OX
Wareham	WARHA

Henry II (1154 – 1189)

Peace was restored in England under Henry II, who ascended the throne in 1154 as the first Plantagenet king, but at first Stephen's coinage continued to be minted and retained its poor quality, with many coins being underweight and of low silver fineness. To restore public confidence in the currency a new standard and type of coin, the cross and crosslets penny, was introduced in 1158 and is often referred to as the Tealby penny, after the hoard in which many of these coins were found. A total of thirty-one mints was employed in the recoinage but, once the new issue was complete, only twelve mints were allowed to remain active and this reduction began the gradual decline in the number of mints used to strike English coins.

The Tealby coinage was acceptable in terms of weight and silver fineness but the overall quality of production was appalling so in 1180, Henry II introduced a new style of coinage, the short cross penny, with better made dies. Despite being fairly ugly, the style remained more or less unaltered until 1247 which was quite a departure from the past practice of changing it every few years. However, retaining a single style gave a sense of greater stability both to the currency and the country itself. Greater uniformity was also achieved by the further reduction in the number of mints. As with previous coinages, the moneyer's name and mint, often abbreviated, were on the reverse which also bore a small cross in the centre with four pellets in each quarter. This enabled merchants to make halfpennies and farthings out of the pennies by simply cutting along the lines of the cross, thus producing an abundance of change since the penny was still the only denomination produced throughout Henry's reign.

Tealby Issue

Although six different designs were used on the obverse of the Tealby penny, the layout of the reverse remained unchanged. The legend consists of a small cross preceding the moneyer's name

which is given in full and followed by ON (for 'of') and the mint name, often abbreviated. For example, a coin might read 'ROBERD ON GIPE', Roberd of Ipswich or 'RICARD ON LERE', Ricard of Leicester. In identifying the mints it is important to bear in mind that, apart from being misspelt on occasion, town names were often different from their modern equivalents and were sometimes shortened or even lengthened, often by an additional E at the end, so as to accommodate the size of the die; in general, the longer a moneyer's name, the shorter the mint abbreviation. Collectors should also remember that varieties of some mints exist. Owing to the poor quality of striking, the mint is often unclear but if the moneyer's name is legible it is possible to identify the mint with reference to specialist books and a process of elimination aided by the fact that in some cases there was only one moneyer of that name working in the country.

A (1158 – 1161)

Obverse Legend HENRI REX ANG — Henry King of England

Obverse Crowned front-facing bust with no hair, wearing armour with sceptre in right hand.

Reverse Cross potent with small cross potent in each angle.

H21D-005	VG £50	F £90	VF £180

B (1161 – 1165)

Obverse Legend HENRY REX AN — Henry King of England

Obverse Crowned front-facing bust with no hair, wearing armour with sceptre in right hand. Mantle design slightly different from previous issue.

Reverse As previous.

H21D-010	VG £50	F £90	VF £180

C (1161 – 1165)

Obverse Legend HENRI R ANG — Henry King of England

Obverse Crowned front-facing bust with single curl of hair. Wearing armour designed of sweeping lines. Sceptre in right hand and collar decorated.

Reverse As previous.

H21D-015	VG £50	F £90	VF £180

D (1165 – 1168)

Obverse Legend HENRI REX — King Henry

Obverse Crowned front-facing bust, sceptre in right hand. Similar to H21D-015 with decorated collar and H21D-020 has a decorated shoulder.

Reverse As previous.

H21D-020	VG £50	F £90	VF £180

E (1168 – 1170)

Obverse Legend HENRI REX A — Henry King of England

Obverse Crowned front-facing bust, sceptre in right hand. Mantle sweeps from left shoulder across body with shoulder not decorated.

Reverse As previous.

H21D-025	VG £50	F £100	VF £200

F (1170 – 1180)

Obverse Legend HENRI REX — King Henry

Obverse Crowned front-facing bust, holding sceptre in right hand, with the king's hair in a bunch of curls to the right of his head.

Reverse As previous.

H21D-030	VG £50	F £100	VF £200

Tealby Issue Mints

Rarity of Mints

We have given rarities of all the mints. 'R' is rare, 'RR' very rare and 'RRR' extremely rare. As mentioned, many coins even in Fine condition will not show the mint name due to poor striking. Prices for 'RR' coins are approx. 50% above those listed while those with 'RRR' are up to twice the value.

Mint	Abbreviation	Rarity
Bedford	BED	RRR
Bristol	BRIS	RRR
Bury St Edmunds	S.EDM	R
Canterbury	CANTO	R
Carlisle	CARDU	R
Chester	CESTE	RR
Colchester	COLE	RRR
Durham	DVNHOL	RRR
Exeter	EXC	RRR
Gloucester	GLOECE	RRR
Hereford	HEREFOR	RRR
Ilchester	IVELCE	RRR
Ipswich	GIPES	R
Launceston	LANST	RRR
Leicester	LERE	RR
Lewes	LEVAS	RRR
Lincoln	LINC	R
London	LUND	R
Newcastle	NIV	RR
Northampton	NORHA	RR
Norwich	NORED	R
Oxford	OXENE	RR

Pembroke	PAIN	RRR
Salisbury	SALEB	RRR
Shrewsbury	SALOPES	RRR
Stafford	STA	RRR
Thetford	TED	R
Wallingford	WELL	RRR
Wilton	PIL	RRR
Winchester	WINC	RR
York	EVERWI	RR

Short Cross Coinage

As stated above, the short cross coinage was introduced in 1180 and continued to be struck, virtually unchanged, for nearly 70 years, thus covering not only Henry II's reign but also those of Richard I, John I and the early part of Henry III. Furthermore, all the coins look fairly similar with identical obverse legends of HENRICUS REX. It was therefore necessary to break the short cross coinage into classes based on small differences in, for example, the hair, lettering or facial features, so that a coin can be attributed to a particular reign by identifying its class. Collectors should bear in mind that Henry II pennies tend to be larger than those of the other three monarchs while Richard I's issues tend to be more blundered. It is also important to pay particular attention to the 'X' on the obverse legend of John and Henry III pennies as a number of classes depend mainly on this one letter.

Short Cross Coinage Classes by Reign

Henry II 1A, 1B, 1C
Richard I 2, 3A, 3B, 4A, 4B
John I 4C, 5A, 5B, 5C, 6A.1, 6A.2, 6A. 2A
Henry III 6B, 6C, 7, 8A, 8B.1, 8B.2, 8B.3

Collecting Hints

Short cross pennies are fairly easy to obtain and collectors should aim for an example in at least Fine condition, with a clear mint and moneyer's name.

Classes

Class 1A	Class 1B	Class 1C

Class 1A

Obverse Legend HENRICUS REX — King Henry

Obverse Front-facing crowned bust of king holding sceptre, the face is narrow and there is a square 'E' and sometimes a square 'C' in the legend, as well as pellets.

Reverse Small cross, four pellets in each quarter.

H21D-035	VG £100	F £225	VF £450

Class 1B

Obverse Legend As previous.

Obverse Front-facing crowned bust of king holding sceptre, his hair has two curls to left and five curls to right; pellets in the legend and the 'E' and 'C' are more rounded.

Reverse As previous.

H21D-040	VG £40	F £80	VF £160

Class 1C

Obverse Legend As previous.

Obverse Front-facing crowned bust of king holding sceptre. The style is becoming a little blundered now, with no stops or pellets in the legend.

Reverse As previous.

H21D-045	VG £40	F £80	VF £160

Mints

Below we have listed all the mints which struck coins for Henry II, the mint name or abbreviation, as it is found on the coins, the moneyer and finally the class and subsection in which the moneyer struck coins. Often however a moneyer was active through several reigns and this has to be taken into account when identifying a coin's class. And once again, the mint's and moneyer's names were often misspelt and abbreviated while letters were sometimes pushed together to share the same vertical stem.

Mint Abbreviation	Moneyer	Class
Carlisle		
CARDI	ALAIN	1B, 1C
Exeter		
EXERI	ASKETIL	1A, 1B
	IORDAN	1A, 1B
	OSBER	1A, 1B
	RAUL	1B
	RICARD	1B, 1C
	ROGER	1B
Lincoln		
NICOLE	EDMUND	1B, 1C
	GIRARD	1B
	HUGO	1B
	LEFWINE	1B, 1C
	RODBERT	1B
	WALTER	1B
	WILL.D.F.	1B
	WILLELM	1B, 1C
London		
LUND	AIMER	1
	ALAIN	1
	ALAINV	1A, 1B
	ALWARD	1B
	DAVI	1B, 1C
	FIL AIMER	1A, 1B
	GILEBERT	1C
	GODARD	1B
	HENRI	1A, 1B
	HENRI PI	1A, 1B
	IEFREI	1A, 1B C
	IOHAN	1A, 1B
	OSBER	1B
	PIERES	1A, 1B, 1C
	PIERES M	1A, 1B
	RANDUL	1A, 1B
	RAUL	1B, 1C

Mint	Moneyer	Class
	REINALD	1B
	WILLELM	1A, 1B, 1C
Northampton		
NOR	FILIPE	1A, 1B
	HUGO	1A, 1B
	RAUL	1A, 1B, 1C
	REINALD	1A, 1B
	SIMUND	1B
	WALTER	1
	WILLELM	1A, 1B
Norwich	**(possibly Northampton)**	
NOR	REINALD	1B, 1C
	WILLELM	1B
Oxford		
OXEN	ASKETIL	1B
	IEFREI	1B
	OWEIN	1B
	RICARD	1B, 1C
	RODBERT	1B
	RODBT.F.B.	1B
	SAGAR	1B
Wilton		
WILT	OSBER	1A, 1B
	RODBERT	1A, 1B
Winchester		
WINCE	ADAM	1B, 1C
	CLEMENT	1A, 1B
	GOCELM	1
	HENRI	1A
	OSBER	1A, 1B
	REINIER	1B
	RICARD	1B
	RODBERT	1A, 1B
Worcester		
WIREC	EDRICH	1B
	GODWINE	1B, 1C
	OSBER	1B
York		
EVERWIC	ALAIN	1A, 1B
	EFRARD	1
	GERARD	1B
	HUGO	1B, 1C
	HUNFREI	1A, 1B
	ISAC	1A, 1B
	TURKIL	1
	WILLELM	1A, 1B

Pricing

We have priced all the coins in their classes in VG, Fine and VF condition; these prices are for the most common mints, usually London and Canterbury. We have also priced coins by mint and these prices are for the most common class of each mint; coins of a rare class would be valued at higher prices.

Mint	VG	F	VF
Carlisle	70	140	280
Exeter	65	130	260
Lincoln	60	120	220
London	40	80	160
Northampton	60	120	220
Norwich	60	120	220
Oxford	75	150	300
Wilton	70	140	280
Winchester	40	80	160
Worcester	75	150	300
York	40	80	160

Richard I (1189 – 1199)

The pennies of the short cross coinage continued throughout Richard I's reign and, although the quality of production became cruder, the style remained fairly similar. The obverse legend of all Richard's pennies reads HENRICUS REX (King Henry) and the reverse continued to have a small cross with four pellets in each quarter and a legend with the moneyer's name and mint; what changed from one class to another was the bust of the king. All of Richard I's issues are very much a continuation from the short cross coinage of Henry II but the classes, while similar in style, are different to those of John and Henry II. Collectors might need to refer to all reigns when identifying a coin. The reverse legend on the coin gives the moneyer's name and the mint. The legend starts with the moneyer's name, followed by ON (of) and then the mint, which is usually abbreviated. We have listed the mint, mint abbreviation and moneyer's name and the classes which each struck to help identification.

Collecting Hints

These coins while scarce are obtainable and always popular with collectors. They tend to be slightly crude in style and when available are usually found in VG to Fine condition. Several of the mints are rare and difficult to obtain. Collectors should remember when identifying a mint that the letters are sometimes blundered or missing.

Classes

Class 2

Class 3A

Class 4A

Class 4B

Class 2

Obverse Round front-facing face, curls both sides of head, large pellets for eyes and a bushy beard, sceptre in hand and five or more pearls in crown.

Reverse Short cross, four pellets in each quarter.

R11D-005	VG £60	F £125	VF £250

Class 3A

Obverse Long thin face with pellet eyes, seven pearls in crown with a beard of small curls, sceptre in hand.

Reverse As previous.

R11D-010	VG £60	F £125	VF £250

Class 3B

Obverse Similar to above but annulet instead of pellet eyes.

Reverse As previous.

R11D-015	VG £50	F £100	VF £200

Class 4A

This class includes a variety that has colon stops instead of a single stop on the reverse of the coin.

Obverse Similar to previous, but beard of pellets rather than curls.

Reverse As previous, but colon stop in legend.

R11D-020	VG £50	F £100	VF £200

Class 4B

Obverse Very crude front-facing bust, the hair represented by a couple of crude curves and the beard by just a few pellets; sceptre in hand.

Reverse As R11D-015.

R11D-025	VG £50	F £100	VF £200

Mints

Mint Abbreviation	Moneyer	Class
Canterbury		
CANT	GOLDWINE	2, 3, 4A, 4B
	HERNAUD	4B
	IO(H)AN	4B
	MEINIR	2, 3, 4A, 4B
	REINALD	2, 3, 4A, 4B
	REINAUD	2, 3, 4A
	ROBERD	2, 3, 4A, 4B
	SAMUEL	4B
	ULARD	2, 3, 4A, 4B
Carlisle		
CARDI	ALEIN	3, 4A, 4B
Durham		
DURE, DUNO	ADAM	4A
	ALEIN	4A, 4B
Exeter		
EXEN	RICARD	3B
Lichfield		
LIHEFL	IOAN	2
Lincoln		
NICOLE	EDMUND	2
	LEFWINE	2
	WILLELM	2
London		
LUND	AIMER	2, 3, 4A, 4B

	FULKE	4A, 4B
	GOLDWINE	4A
	HENRI	4A, 4B
	RAUL	2
	RICARD	2, 3, 4A, 4B
	STIVENE	2, 3, 4A, 4B
	WILLELM	2, 3, 4A, 4B

Northampton
NOR	GEFERI	4A
	ROBERD	3
	WALTIR	3

Norwich
NOR	RANDUL	4A, 4B
	WILLELM	4A, 4B

Shrewsbury
SALOP	IVE	4B
	REINALD	4A, 4B
	WILLELM	4A

Winchester
WINCE	ADAM	3A
	GOCELM	2, 3
	OSBERN	3, 4A
	PIRES	4A
	WILLELM	2, 3, 4A, 4B

Worcester
WIREC	OSBERN	2

York
EVERIC	DAVI	4B
	EVERARD	2, 3, 4A, 4B
	HUE	2, 3, 4A
	NICOLE	4B
	TURKIL	2, 3, 4A, 4B

Pricing

Prices are for the most common types.

Mint	VG	F	VF
Canterbury	45	90	180
Carlisle	100	220	400
Durham	110	250	450
Exeter	90	200	380
Lichfield	RRR		
Lincoln	80	150	300
London	45	90	180
Northampton	90	200	380
Norwich	90	200	380
Shrewsbury	130	250	450
Winchester	50	100	200
Worcester	RRR		
York	50	100	200

John (1199 – 1216)

The short cross coinage continued through John's reign, with the obverse legend still reading HENRICUS REX (King Henry) and the reverse having the moneyer's name and mint around a small cross with four pellets in each quarter. The first class is fairly similar to Richard's coinage but the rest of John's pennies are of a higher standard, with neater work and a slightly more lifelike portrait. The later issues are very similar to those of Henry III. The mints and moneyers are very much a continuation from the previous reign where they have been discussed in greater detail.

Collecting Hints

The coins while scarce are obtainable in all grades. They are sometimes clipped or damaged and there is no doubt that many of them saw considerable circulation. Many of these issues are very similar to those of Richard I and Henry III. Collectors might need to refer to both reigns when identifying a coin.

Classes

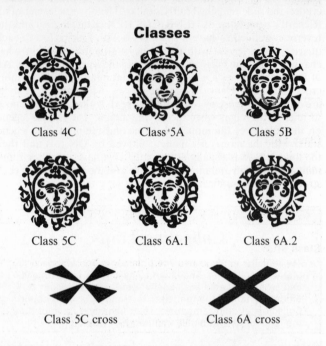

Class 4C — Class 5A — Class 5B

Class 5C — Class 6A.1 — Class 6A.2

Class 5C cross — Class 6A cross

Class 4C

Obverse Crude front-facing bust, sceptre in hand. Similar to previous issues of Richard I except that the letter 'S' in the legend is reversed.

Reverse As previous.

JH1D-005	VG £45	F £90	F £180

Class 5A

Front-facing bust holding sceptre; new neater style, 'S' is reversed, cross pommée in reverse legend. Some coins of this class have ornamented letters, with extra and often more exaggerated curves, which gives the impression that the whole legend is more ornate.

JH1D-010	VG £40	F £75	VF £150

Class 5B

Obverse Similar to above except that the 'S' is not reversed and the cross pommée has been replaced by a cross pattée.

Reverse As previous.

JH1D-015	VG £40	F £75	VF £150

Class 5C

Obverse Similar to above but 'X' in obverse legend composed of four strokes in the form of a St Andrew's cross.

Reverse As previous.

| JH1D-020 | VG £45 | F £90 | VF £180 |

Class 6A.1

Obverse Slightly coarser style with slightly taller face, 'X' in legend is composed of two strokes in the form of a St Andrew's cross.

Reverse As previous.

| JH1D-025 | VG £40 | F £75 | VF £150 |

Class 6A.2

Obverse Similar to above but a very slightly rounder face and the 'X' in the obverse legend has arms at right angles with rounded ends.

Reverse As previous.

| JH1D-030 | VG £40 | F £75 | VF £150 |

Class 6A.2A

Obverse Similar to above but the 'X' has arms at right angles and more rounded edges looking almost as if it is made up of four pellets.

Reverse As previous.

| JH1D-035 | VG £35 | F £70 | VF £145 |

Muling of obverses and reverses of different classes was not uncommon during this period, particularly in Class 5.

Mints

Mint Abbreviation	Moneyer	Class
Bury St Edmunds		
S.EDM, SANTEA	FULKE	5B, 5C
Canterbury		
CANT	ARNAUD	5
	COLDWINE	4C, 5
	(H)ERNAUD	4C, 5
	HUE	4C, 5
	IO(H)AN	4C, 5
	IOHAN B	5B, 5C
	IOHAN M	5B, 5C
	RAUF	5C
	ROBERD	4C, 5
	SAMUEL	4C, 5
	SIMON	5A or 5C
	SIMUN	4C, 5A, 5B
Carlisle		
CARDI	TOMAS	5B
Chichester		
CICST	PIERES	5B
	RAUF	5A, 5B
	SIMON	5A, 5B
	WILLELM	5B
Durham		
DURO, DUNO	PIERES	4C, 5, 6A
Exeter		
EX	GILEBERT	5A, 5B
	IOHAN	5A, 5B
	RICARD	5A, 5B
Ipswich		
GIPE	ALISANDRE	5B, 5C
	IOHAN	5B, 5C
King's Lynn		
LE(N), LENE, LENN	IOHAN	5B
	NICOLE	5B
	WILLELM	5B
Lincoln		
NICOLE	ALAIN	5A
	ANDREU	5
	HUE	5B, 5C
	IOHAN	5A
	RAUF	5A, 5B
	RICARD	5A
	TOMAS	5A, 5B
London		
LUND	ABEL	5C, 6A
	ADAM	5B, 5C
	ARNAUD	5B
	BENEIT	5B, 5C
	FULKE	4C, 5A
	HENRI	4C, 5A, 5B
	ILGER	5B, 5C, 6A
	IOHAN	5B
	RAUF	5C, 6A
	RENER	5B, 5C
	RICARD	4C, 5A, 5B
	RICARD B	5B, 5C
	RICARD T	5B
	WALTER	5C, 6A
	WILLELM	4C, 5
	WILLELM B	5B, 5C
	WILLELM L	5B, 5C
	WILLELM T	5B, 5C
Northampton		
NORHT	ADAM	5B, 5C
	RANDUL	4C
	ROBERD	5B
	ROBERD T	5B
Norwich		
NOR	GIFREI	5
	IOHAN	5
	RENALD	5A
	RENAUD	5
Oxford		
OXEN	AILWINE	5B
	HENRI	5B
	MILES	5B
Rhuddlan		
RULA(N), RUTL(A)N, RUTN	HALLI	
	HENRICUS	
	TOMAS	
	SIMOND	
Rochester		
ROFE	ALISANDRE	5B
	HURFREI	5B
Winchester		
WIN	ADAM	5
	ANDREU	5
	BARTELME	5B, 5C
	HENRI	5A
	IOHAN	5
	LUKAS	5B, 5C
	MILES	5
	RAUF	5B, 5C

	RICARD	5A, 5B
York		
EVERIC	DAVI	4C, 5A, 5B
	NICOLE	4C, 5
	RENAUD	5B
	TOMAS	5B

1. The Rhuddlan mint, which is believed to have been active during John's reign, does not conform to the normal classes in this series. The dies are of local manufacture and so the coins are crude in style.

Rhuddlan Mint

Pricing

The prices below are for the most common types.

Mint	VG	F	VF
Bury St			
Edmunds	50	100	200
Canterbury	40	70	145
Carlisle	85	170	320
Chichester	60	120	240
Durham	70	140	280
Exeter	50	100	200
Ipswich	50	100	200
King's Lynn	100	200	400
Lincoln	50	100	200
London	40	70	145
Northampton	50	100	200
Norwich	50	100	200
Oxford	50	100	200
Rhuddlan	80	160	300
Rochester	90	180	360
Winchester	45	80	150
York	50	90	160

Henry III (1216 – 1272)

The short cross coinage continued under Henry III until 1247 and, although the mints issuing coins were reduced to six, London and Canterbury were extremely prolific. Having lasted for 67 years, the short cross coinage was undoubtedly a success. Being of reasonable quality, acceptable design and good fineness, it was popular with the public and brought a much needed stability to the country. The only problem was that many of the coins in circulation were underweight through no fault of the moneyers, because of the illegal practice of clipping. This was facilitated by the cross on the reverse not extending to the edge of the coin, which meant that the public often could not know exactly how large the coin should be. So, in 1247, the short cross was replaced by a longer one that reached to the very edge of the coin, the rest of the design remaining mainly unaltered. Because of the introduction of the new coinage, many of the old mints were reopened to supply sufficient quantities of coins. As with the short cross penny, the long cross one could be cut along the lines of the cross to produce halfpennies and even farthings.

Short Cross Coinage

Henry's short cross coinage is similar in style to that of previous reigns, especially John's, and the system of classification is continued. The obverse legend of all classes still reads HENRICUS REX and the reverse bears the moneyer's name and mint in the legend, with a small cross in the centre and four pellets in each angle.

Classes

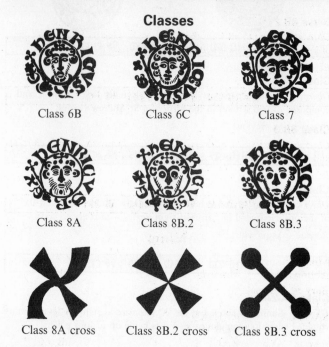

Class 6B	Class 6C	Class 7
Class 8A	Class 8B.2	Class 8B.3
Class 8A cross	Class 8B.2 cross	Class 8B.3 cross

Class 6B

Obverse Very tall lettering in legends with the king's face often thin.

Reverse Cross with four pellets in each quarter.

H31D-005	VG £18	F £35	VF £65

Class 6C

Obverse The king has a very pointed face with larger staring eyes. There is also a fairly scarce variety of this type with ornamental lettering in the legend, see line drawing.

Reverse As previous.

H31D-010	VG £18	F £35	VF £65

Class 7

Obverse The bust of the king has no neck. There are various styles of hair and eyes in this class.

Reverse As previous, but without stops between the words in the legend.

H31D-015	VG £18	F £35	VF £65

Class 8A

Obverse New style with large bust, 'X' in REX curule shaped.

Reverse As previous, mintmark cross pattée.

H31D-020   ex. rare

Class 8B.1

Obverse Similar to Class 8A.

Reverse As previous, but mintmark cross pommée.

H31D-025   VG £20   F £40   VF £75

Class 8B.2

Obverse Similar to 8B.1 but the bust is cruder with the beard being made of just a few sharp lines; wedge shaped 'X' in legend.

Reverse As previous.

H31D-030   VG £20   F £40   VF £75

Class 8B.3

Obverse As previous, but very crude bust with two large pellets for eyes and four large curls for hair, 'X' in legend is a cross pommée.

Reverse As previous.

H31D-035   VG £20   F £40   VF £75

Mints

Mint Abbreviation	Moneyer	Class
Bury St Edmunds		
S.EDM, SANTEA	IO(H)AN	7, 8
	NORMAN	7
	RAUF	6B, 6C, 7
	SIMUND	7
	WILLELM	7
Canterbury		
CANT	ARNOLD	6C
	HENRI	6B, 6C, 7
	HIUN	6B, 6C, 7
	IUN	7
	IO(H)AN	6B, 6C, 7, 8
	IOAN CHIC	7
	IOAN F.R.	7
	NICOLE	7, 8
	NORMAN	7
	OSMUND	7
	ROBERD	6B
	ROBERT	7
	ROBERT VI	7
	ROGER	6B, 6C, 7
	ROGER OF R	7
	SALEMUN	6C, 7
	SAMUEL	6B, 6C, 7
	SIMON	7
	SIMUN	6B, 6C, 7
	TOMAS	6C, 7
	WALTER	6B, 6C, 7
	WILLELM	7, 8
	WILLEM TA	7
Durham		
DURO, DUNO	PIERES	7
London		
LUND	ABEL	6B, 6C, 7
	ADAM	7
	(H)ELIS	7
	GIFFREI	7
	ILGER	6B, 6C, 7
	LEDULF	7
	NICHOLE	7, 8
	RAU(L)F	6B, 6C, 7

	RICARD	7
	TERRI	7
	WALTER	6B, 6C
Winchester		
WIN	HENRI	6C
York		
EVERIC	IOHAN	6C
	PERES	6C
	TOMAS	6C
	WILAM	6C

Pricing

The prices below are for the most common types.

Mint	VG	F	VF
Bury St Edmunds	25	50	100
Canterbury	18	35	65
Durham	100	200	350
London	18	35	65
Winchester	25	50	100
York	100	200	350

Long Cross Coinage (1247 – 1272)

There are two main varieties of long cross pennies, depending on whether a sceptre is found on the obverse or not; but within these varieties, the long cross coinage is again broken up into classes according to slight differences of style. The reverse legend is similar to that of the short cross coinage, bearing the moneyer's name and mint, often abbreviated, except for Class 1A which omits both moneyer and mint, and Class 1B which only omits the moneyer. This however was highly unpopular because it reduced the moneyers' accountability and it was precisely this absence of control that had allowed the production of underweight, low fineness coins in previous reigns. When the moneyer's name and mint were reintroduced, the same considerations regarding abbreviation applied and the legend again started with the moneyer's name, followed by ON (of) and the mint name. We have listed the mint names, their abbreviations, the moneyer's names and the class in which each moneyer was active.

Collecting Hints

Henry III's long cross coinage is plentiful due to the discovery of hoards, the most notable of which was found in Colchester. It is relatively easy to find coins in Fine or VF condition and even EF coins appear occasionally. Collectors should aim for a coin in the best possible condition, with a fully readable legend. Examples from many of the regional mints, however, are fairly scarce and may take some time and effort to obtain, They also tend to come in slightly lesser grades than, for instance, the London issue. Finally, the last two classes of the long cross coinage tend to be crude and are usually found in the lower grades.

Classes

Class 1A

Class 1B

Class 2A

Class 2B   Class 3A   Class 3B

Class 3C   Class 4A   Class 4B

Class 5A   Class 5B   Class 5C

Class 5D   Class 5E   Class 5H

Class 5G   Class 5G cross

Obverse without Sceptre

Class 1A

This issue omits both the moneyer's name and the mint but is considered to have been struck in London and Canterbury.

Obverse Legend   HENRICUS REX — King Henry

Reverse Legend   ANGLIE TERCI — Third of England

Obverse   King's bust.

Reverse   Long cross with three pellets in each quarter.

| H31D-040 | VG £125 | F £250 | VF £500 |

Class 1B

Due to lack of space the obverse legend is broken halfway through the word ANGLIE and continued on the reverse which then bears the mint name abbreviated to LON, CAN or AED.

Obverse Legend   HENRICUS REX ANG — Henry King of England

Reverse Legend   LIE TERCI LON (or CAN or AED) — the Third London (Canterbury or Bury St Edmunds)

Obverse   Front-facing bust of king.

Reverse   As previous.

| H31D-045 | VG £45 | F £90 | VF £180 |

Class 2A

The new reverse legend with the moneyer's name and mint is continued through all the rest of Henry III's classes.

Obverse Legend   HENRICUS REX TERCI — King Henry the Third

Reverse Legend   Moneyer's name and mint.

Obverse   Bust of king.

Reverse   As previous.

| H31D-050 | VG £22 | F £45 | VF £90 |

Class 2B

As previous, but the letter 'X' is formed of two straight limbs.

| H31D-052 | VG £22 | F £45 | VF £90 |

Class 3A

Obverse Legend   HENRICUS REX III — King Henry III

Obverse   The king has a thinner face.

| H31D-055 | VG £20 | F £38 | VF £70 |

Class 3B

Obverse Legend   HENRICUS REX III — King Henry III

Obverse   The king has a smaller, rounder face.

| H31D-060 | VG £20 | F £38 | VF £70 |

Class 3C

Obverse Legend   As Class 3B.

Obverse   More pointed chin on bust with the neck indicated by two lines and the eyes by pellets in annulets.

| H31D-065 | VG £20 | F £38 | VF £70 |

Obverse with Sceptre

The design of the reverse remained unaltered.

Class 4A

Obverse Legend   HENRICUS REX III — King Henry III

Obverse   Similar to Class 3C but king is holding a sceptre.

| H31D-070 | VG £50 | F £100 | VF £200 |

Class 4B

Obverse Legend As Class 4A.

Obverse The king has a slightly larger face and a crown of a slightly different design.

| H31D-075 | VG £55 | F £110 | VF £220 |

Class 5A

The obverse legend does not start at the top of the coin, but just after the sceptre and this position is retained on all the rest of Henry III's classes.

Obverse Legend HENRICUS REX III — King Henry III

Obverse The bust is similar to Class 4B except that the king has rounder eyes.

| H31D-080 | VG £20 | F £40 | VF £80 |

Class 5B

As Class 5A, but the king has a narrower face, round eyes and the tails of the 'R's in the legends are wedge shaped.

| H31D-085 | VG £20 | VF £38 | VF £75 |

Class 5C

As Class 5B, but the king has oval eyes.

| H31D-090 | VG £20 | F £38 | VF £75 |

Class 5D

New-style portrait with a different crown with correctly-shaped fleur, and the tails of the 'R's in the legend are not wedge shaped.

| H31D-095 | VG £35 | F £70 | VF £140 |

Class 5E

As Class 5D, but the crown is decorated by beads.

| H31D-100 | VG £90 | F £180 | VF £350 |

Class 5F

The king has a slightly larger face and the crown is of a different style, with a double band along it.

| H31D-105 | VG £20 | F £40 | VF £80 |

Class 5G

As Class 5F, but the crown has a flatter base and a single band. Curule 'support to a chair' shaped 'X' in obverse legend.

| H31D-110 | VG £20 | F £40 | VF £80 |

Class 5H

As Class 5G, but much cruder in style and with pellets instead of fleur in crown.

| H31D-115 | VG £20 | F £40 | VF £80 |

Class 5I

Even cruder than Class 5H and the king has a triple line of pellets for a beard.

| H31D-120 | ex. rare |

Mints

Mint Abbreviation	Moneyer	Class
Bristol		
BRUSTOV	ELIS	3
	HENRI	3B
	IACOB	3
	ROGER	3
	WALTER	3B, 3C
Bury St Edmunds		
SANTED		2, 3, 4, 5A, 5G, 5H, 5I
	ION, IOHS	5 except 5G,
	RANDULF	5H, 5I
	RENAND	5G
	STEPHANE	5G
Canterbury		

331

CANT	ALEIN	5G, 5H
	GILBERT	2, 3, 4, 5 except 5E, 5H, 5I
	ION, IOH, IOHANES	3C, 4, 5 except 5E, 5H, 5I
	NIC(H)OLE	1B, 2, 3, 4, 5 except 5I
	RICARD	5G, 5H
	ROBERT	5C, 5D, 5E, 5F, 5G, 5H
	WALTER	5C, 5D, 5E, 5F, 5G, 5H
	WILLEM(E)	1B, 2, 3, 4, 5 except 5E, 5H, 5I
Carlisle CARLEL	ADAM	3A, 3B
	ION	3A, 3B
	ROBERT	3A, 3B
	WILLEM	3A, 3B
Durham DVRH	PHILIP	3B
	RICARD	5B, 5C
	ROGER	5G
	WILLEM	5G
Exeter ECCETRE	ION	2, 3
	PHILIP	2, 3
	ROBERT	2, 3
	WALTER	2, 3A, 3B
Gloucester GLOECES	ION	2, 3
	LUCAS	2, 3
	RICARD	2, 3
	ROGER	2, 3
Hereford HERE	HENRI	3A, 3B
	RICARD	3
	ROGER	3
	WALTER	3
Ilchester IVELCE	HUGE	3
	IERVEIS	3
	RANDULF	3
	STEPHE	3
Lincoln NICOLE	ION	2, 3
	RICARD	2, 3
	WALTER	2, 3
	WILLEM	2, 3
London LUND	DAVI(D)	3C, 5F
	HENRI	3, 4, 5 except 5E, 5H, 5I
	ION, IOH(S), IOHAN	5C, 5D, 5G
	NICOLE	1B/2mule, 2, 3, 4, 5A, 5B, 5C
	RENAUD	5G, 5H, 5I
	RICARD	3C, 4, 5 except 5H, 5I
	ROBERT	5G
	THOMAS	5G
	WALTER	5C, 5D, 5E, 5F, 5G
	WILLEM	5C, 5D, 5E, 5F, 5G

Newcastle NEVECA	ADAM	3A, 3B
	HENRI	3
	ION	3
	ROGER	3
Northampton NORHA	LUCAS	2, 3A, 3B
	PHILIP	2, 3
	TOMAS	2, 3
	WILLEM	2, 3
Norwich NORWIC	HUGE	2, 3
	JACOB	2, 3
	ION	2, 3
	WILLEM	2, 3
Oxford OXON	ADAM	2, 3
	GEFREI	2, 3
	HENRI	2, 3
	WILLEM	2, 3
Shrewsbury SROSEB	LORENS	3
	NICOLE	3
	PERIS	3
	RICARD	3
Wallingford VALI, WALI	ALISANDRE	3A, 3B
	CLEMERT	3A, 3B
	RICARD	3A, 3B
	ROBERT	3A, 3B
Wilton WILT	HUGE	3B, 3C
	ION	3
	WILLEM	3
Winchester WINT	HUGE	2, 3
	IORDAN	2, 3
	NICOLE	2, 3
	WILLEM	2, 3
York EVERWIC	ALAIN	2, 3A, 3B
	IEREMIRE	2, 3A, 3B
	ION	2, 3
	RENER	2, 3
	TOMAS	3B, 3C

Bury St Edmunds Mint

Canterbury Mint

Durham Mint

Exeter Mint

Gloucester Mint

Ilchister Mint

Lincon Mint

London Mint

Newcastle Mint

Northampton Mint

Norwich Mint

York Mint

Pricing

The prices below are for the most common types.

Mint	VG	F	VF
Bristol	25	50	100
Bury St Edmunds	25	50	100
Canterbury	20	38	75
Carlisle	50	100	225
Durham	60	120	250
Exeter	40	80	150
Gloucester	30	60	120
Hereford	40	80	150
Ilchester	70	140	280
Lincoln	30	60	120
London	20	38	75
Newcastle	30	60	120
Northampton	30	60	120
Norwich	30	55	110
Oxford	35	70	140
Shrewsbury	45	90	180
Wallingford	45	90	180
Wilton	45	90	180
Winchester	25	50	100
York	25	50	100

Cut Pennies from William I to Henry III

As mentioned earlier, for over 200 years the penny was the sole denomination to be struck, except for a couple of very rare issues of Henry I and Henry III. As it was such a large denomination, traders met the need for small change by cutting coins in half or quarters. Cut pennies of the earlier reigns are fairly scarce because many coins come from large hoards which were probably set aside as savings rather than exchanged for goods. However, with the advent of metal detecting more cut coinage has been found, especially from the short and long cross series. Every collection should have a few of these fractional pennies and for collectors on a limited budget they can provide an inexpensive example of an early coin.

Edward I (1272 – 1307)

Edward I succeeded his father, Henry III, in 1272 although he was absent on a crusade at the time of Henry's death. Obviously, coin production could not be arrested until Edward's return, so the long cross coinage was continued in a similar style. Two types were produced during these seven years; the first is very crude but the second is of better quality. Most of the examples from these classes that are on the market today come from the Colchester Hoard, found in 1969.

As Edward crossed Europe on his return from the crusades in 1279, he was able to conclude an important wool trade treaty with the Low Countries, an indication of the steady increase in Anglo-European commerce. The king acknowledged the need to improve the style and fineness of English coinage and avoid the inferior quality coins that had occasionally been produced under previous reigns and shaken public confidence in the economy. There was also a need for both larger and smaller denominations than the penny, which had not changed much for about five hundred years, and so the groat (fourpence), halfpenny and farthing were introduced. Finally, there was the problem of clipping for which the Jews were unfairly blamed, often being either killed or forced to flee abroad. Their unpopularity stemmed from the fact that many were money-lenders and even Edward owed them money; by persecuting them for clipping, powerful individuals avoided paying their debts.

In response to these pressures, a new coinage was introduced in 1279 with a different design. Millions of coins were struck, mostly in London and Canterbury, and the public could take their old, underweight long or short cross pennies to the mints and exchange them for new coins of correct weight and fineness. These new-style pennies soon became the envy of Europe and were copied extensively, although often in low fineness silver. But as this only made Edward's coins even more popular and severely drained the local supply, exporting English coins abroad became illegal in 1299. The strong, good quality currency helped strengthen the economy and England enjoyed considerable prosperity. Moreover, although clipping still occurred and the relevant penalties continued to be enforced during Edward's reign, the new design made it much easier to detect if a coin had been clipped.

Edward I's coinage was prolific in both numbers and varieties, with many of these issues looking very similar, especially to a new collector. After checking that the reverse bears the long cross, collectors should look at the portrait paying attention to the size (earlier issues tend to be larger than later ones), as well as the design of the crown, eyes, hair style and garments, and ensure that a specimen is not from Edward II or Edward III. If a coin looks very crude in style it could be an issue from the Berwick mint and if it has a major discrepancy, such as no crown or a different legend, it could be a Continental imitation. When reading the reverse legend for the mint, it is important to remember that not only did die-makers often make mistakes but also the script was slightly different to today's, letters such as N might be reversed and, to save space, a comma might replace a letter or two letters might share the same stem.

Long Cross Coinage

The class numbering is continued from Henry III's reign as Edward's coins are so similar. The obverse legend still reads HENRICUS REX III and the reverse bears a long cross and the moneyer's name and mint in the legend; we have listed the relevant details below. It should be noted that only three mints were active at the time.

Collecting Hints

As mentioned earlier, Edward's Class 6 long cross penny is very crude and even VF coins often look very ugly. The second type is of better quality but examples are rare. Of the three mints London and Durham are rare, Bury St Edmunds is common especially in Class 6. Collectors who simply want an example of this interesting type might well opt for a Bury St Edmunds Class 6 in the best grade possible.

Below we list the two classes, followed by the mints and prices.

Classes

Class 6   Class 7

Class 6

Obverse   Crude bust of king holding sceptre. The king has large eyes and long realistic curly hair.

Reverse   Long cross, three pellets in each quarter.

Class 7

Similar to the previous design, but of much better quality with smaller eyes and sharper features. Lombardic 'U' in obverse legend.

Mints

Bury St Edmunds

| SANTED | IOCE | 7 |
| | ION or IOH | 6, 7 |

Durham

| DURH | ROBERD | 6 |
| | ROBERT | 7 |

London

| LUND | PHELIP | 7 |
| | RENAUD | 7 |

Pricing

No.	Mint	Class	VG	F	VF
E11D-005	Bury St Edmunds	6	25	45	100
E11D-010		7	50	100	200
E11D-015	Durham	6	150	300	—
E11D-020		7	150	300	—
E11D-025	London	7	50	100	200

The 1279 Recoinage

The 1279 coinage differed from previous issues in many ways. There is a more realistic, lifelike front-facing bust of the crowned king on the obverse and the legend is longer, usually reading EDW REX ANGL DNS HYB (Edward King of England Lord of Ireland). The reverse has a large cross, going from the middle to the edge of the coin with three pellets in each quarter; the moneyer's name is omitted from the legend (except in one issue from Bury St Edmunds), but the mint name is usually given in full, e.g. CIVITAS LONDON (City of London) or VILLA NOVI CASTRI (Town of Newcastle). The new coinage also contained a privy mark, a slight difference such as a rose on the king's breast, or an alteration in the size of the king's eyes or the style of a letter, that distinguished each issue. These differences were not due to lack of care in producing dies but done deliberately, replacing the moneyer's name as a form of quality control; any coin appearing underweight or of low fineness could be returned to the moneyer and compared to the original die. Excluding a few provincial issues, there are about 34 different styles of Edward I penny which look fairly similar to an untrained eye since, after all, they only needed to be distinguishable to moneyers and mint officials. The various types are categorised into classes and to identify a coin correctly, collectors should pay particular attention to the hair style, any marks on the king's breast and the shape of the king's eyes as well as to the general style of lettering. The later classes tend to be slightly smaller than the earlier issues.

Distinguishing between E11D and E21D

Collectors often find it very difficult to distinguish between the pennies of Edward I and those of Edward II as the two reigns are so similar. This was no coincidence, since Edward II wanted his issues to be a continuation of Edward I's, which had been so popular in England and heavily imitated on the continent. Nevertheless, it was still imperative that each issue was slightly different so that moneyers responsible for substandard coins could held to account. Admittedly, the minor varieties that can be found on all issues were of more help to the mint officials of the day than to the modern collector who often has to identify a worn coin, but they remain an important key of classification.

Thus, the first step in identifying a coin is finding which mint struck it. The name of the mint can be found in the reverse legend and below we give details of the various spellings and the reign in which they can be attributed to.

It is however important to remember that minor varieties exist.

Mint	Reverse Legend	Reign
Berwick on Tweed [1]	VILLA BERREWYCI	E1 & E2
Bristol	VILL BRISTOLIE	E1
	VILLA BRISTOLLIE	E1
Bury St Edmunds	ROBERT DE HADELEIE	E1
	ROBERTUS DE HADL	E1
	VILA SCI EDMVDI	E1
	VILA SCI EDMVNDI	E1
	VILL SCI EDMVNDI	E2
	VILLA S EDMVDI	E1
	VILLA S EDMVNDI	E1
	VILLA SCI EDMVDI	E1
	VILLA SCI EDMVNDI	E1
Canterbury	CIVITAS CANTOR	E1 & E2
	CIVITAS CANTVR	E1
Chester	CIVITAS CESTRIE	E1
Durham	CIVITAS DVNELM	E2
	CIVITAS DVREME	E1 & E2
	CIVTAS DVREME	E1
Exeter	CIVTAS EXONIE	E1
Kingston upon Hull	VIL' KYNCESTON	E1
	VILL KYNCESTON	E1
Lincoln	CIVITAS LINCOL'	E1
London	CIVITAS LONDON	E1 & E2
Newcastle	VIL' NOV' CASTRI	E1
	VILA NOVI CASTRI	E1
	VILL NOV' CASTRI	E1
	VILL NOVI CASTRI	E1
Reading	CIVITAS LONDON [2]	E1
York	CIVITAS EBORACI	E1

1. Berwick on Tweed mint struck coins outside this class system and they have been classed separately in this catalogue.
2. Annulet on king's breast; mule.

As Edward I struck coins at a total of 13 mints and Edward II only at five, many Edward I issues may be identified correctly with this information alone. However the two most common mints, London and Canterbury, were active during both reigns, so the collector will have to refer to minor marks and varieties of design to identify a coin from these mints.

Although all the issues of both reigns depict a crowned, front-facing bust of the king on the obverse and a long cross on the reverse, they are divided into fifteen classes according to minor differences. Classes 1 to 10 were struck under Edward I and classes 11 to 15 under Edward II.

To identify an issue a collector should pay close attention to the obverse legend and in particular to the way the king's name is spelt. Below we list the varieties of the obverse legend according to class. And although various classes have the same spelling, the process will have narrowed down the number of possible issues.

Class	Obverse Legend
1A	EDW REX ANGL DNS HYB
1B	ED REX ANGLIE DNS HYBN
1C	EDW REX ANGL DNS HYB
1D	EDW R ANGL DNS HYB
2	EDW R ANGL DNS HYB
3	EDW R ANGL DNS HYB
4	EDW R ANGL DNS HYB
5	EDW R ANGL DNS HYB
6A	EDW R ANGL DNS HYB
6B	EDWR (or EDWA) ANGL DNS HYB
7	EDW R ANGL DNS HYB
8A	EDWR (or EDWA) ANGL DNS HYB
8B	EDWR (or EW or EDW) ANGL DNS HYB
9	EDWR (or EW or EDW) ANGL DNS HYB
10A	EDWARD R ANGL DNS HYB
10B	EDWARR ANGL DNS HYB
10C	EDWA R ANGL DNS HYB
10D	EDWAR ANGL DNS HYB
10E	EDWAR ANGL DNS HYB
10F	EDWAR ANGL DNS HYB
11	EDWAR ANGL DNS HYB
12	EDWAR ANGL DNS HYB
13	EDWAR ANGLIE DNS HYB
14	EDWAR ANGL DNS HYB
15	EDWAR ANGL DNS HYB

The second main difference is to be found in the style of the coin and stylistically the crowns of Edward I and Edward II can be divided into two: the trifoliate and the bifoliate crown. The trifoliate crown has three prongs at each end, while the bifoliate has two prongs at each end, as illustrated below.

trifoliate crown   bifoliate crown

This distinction helps with identification considerably because all Class 1 to 10A pennies have trifoliate crowns while Classes 10B to 15C have the bifoliate. Thus, if the issue has a trifoliate crown it is one of Edward I. If however a coin has a bifoliate crown it could be a late issue of Edward I (Class 10B — 10F) or one of Edward II. Again however, there are certain differences and below we illustrate the four main types of bifoliate crown.

Class 10C   Class 11A-B

Class 12 (fleur of crown)   Class 13 (central cross of crown as Greek double axe)

Class 15 (flat crown, spears at end usually bent leftwards)

These crowns are unique to each class or classes so a coin can be narrowed down to just a few issues. Then, in conjunction with the descriptions of each class (see under Edward II), a coin can be correctly classed and identified. We have also listed, for both reigns, the various classes that were issued by each mint. It is therefore sensible, as an added check, to check that the mint produced the corresponding class.

Collecting Hints

Edward's post-1279 pennies are common and fairly easily obtainable even though comparatively few of the millions that were produced have survived, because when coins became worn they would have been exchanged at the mint. Nevertheless, large hoards of Edward I pennies have been found, often in nice condition, and collectors can easily obtain an example in Fine or VF, even EF sometimes. It is important to seek a well struck and fully round coin. Although some people collect by the various mints and others by class, all would agree that an Edward I penny is a specimen from an important issue as well as the product of fine medieval craftsmanship.

Classes

All issues have a crowned bust of the king. The reverse bears a long cross with three pellets in each quarter. The reverse legend shows the mint name.

Class 1A   Class 1B   Class 1C

Class 1D   Class 2A   Class 2B

Class 3A   Class 3B   Class 3C

Class 3D   Class 3E   Class 3F

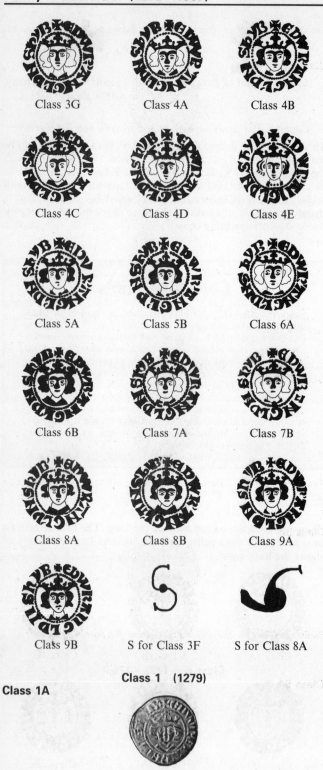

Class 3G   Class 4A   Class 4B

Class 4C   Class 4D   Class 4E

Class 5A   Class 5B   Class 6A

Class 6B   Class 7A   Class 7B

Class 8A   Class 8B   Class 9A

Class 9B   S for Class 3F   S for Class 8A

Class 1 (1279)

Class 1A

This coin was only struck at the London mint.

Obverse Legend EDW REX ANGL DNS HYB — Edward King of England Lord of Ireland

Reverse Legend The mint's name.

Obverse Crowned bust of king with plain band to crown, Lombardic 'N' in legend.

Reverse Long cross with three pellets in each quarter.

Class 1B

Obverse Legend ED REX ANGLIE DNS HYBN — As above

Similar to Class 1A, but no drapery on bust and Roman 'N' reversed on obverse and reverse legends.

Class 1C

Obverse Legend EDW REX ANGL DNS HYB — As above

Similar to Class 1A, but the lettering is smaller and there is a Roman 'N', often reversed, in the obverse legend.

Class 1D

Obverse Legend EDW R ANGL DNS HYB — As above

The face and lettering are larger than Class 1C although the same in terms of style.

Class 2 (1280)

With very few exceptions, which we have listed, the obverse legend for the rest of Edward's pennies reads EDW R ANGL DNS HYB.

Class 2A

Obverse Legend EDW R ANGL DNS HYB — As above

Large face and short neck similar to Class 1D but the crown is slightly different in style with the right hand side of the central lis normally broken.

Class 2B

Similar to Class 2A, but the king has a high neck and narrower face; 'N' in legend reversed.

Class 3 (1280 – 1281)

Class 3A

This issue was only struck in London. Crescent shape to base of neck; there are more facial features, and pearls (or dots) in the crown.

Class 3B

Similar to Class 3A, but the king's neck and drapery on bust looks like a segment of a circle.

Class 3C

Similar to Class 3A, but no pearls on crown; the king's drapery is in one piece and hollowed in centre.

Class 3D

Normal crown and bust, but the drapery is in two pieces and the king's face is broad.

Class 3E

Long narrow face. This issue was only struck in Durham, Newcastle and both of the York mints; the York ecclesiastical issue often has a quatrefoil in the centre on the reverse and, sometimes, on the breast.

Class 3F

Broad bust with a large nose. This issue tends to be poorer in style and some of the lettering is made up to look like wedges; on the reverse the 'S' is different in style.

Class 3G

Smaller, neater bust with a narrow face, the fleurs on the edge the of crown have a slightly different design.

Class 4 (1282 – 1289)

Class 4A

Fairly similar to Class 3G, but the drapery is in the shape of two wedges; the 'C' and 'E' in the lettering are open.

Class 4B

Similar to Class 4A, but shorter face and hair.

Class 4C

Similar to Class 4A, but larger face and more hair; unbarred 'A' in legend.

Class 4D

Similar to Class 4C, but pellet or dot at the beginning of obverse and/or reverse legend.

Class 4E

Similar to Class 4D, but three pellets on king's breast and a pellet in reverse legend.

Class 5 (1290 – 1291)

Class 5A

Similar to Class 4, but the coin is well spread out and there is a pellet on the king's breast.

Class 5B

Similar to Class 5A, but with taller lettering and narrower face.

Class 6 (1292 – 1296)

Class 6A

This issue was only minted at London and is somewhat smaller in size. The cross above the king's crown is almost plain in style and the crown is slightly different in style.

Class 6B

Obverse Legend EDWR (or EDWA) ANGL DNS HYB — As above

Similar but slightly better style; cross pattée above king's crown, closed 'E' in legend and the 'N' on the reverse is usually double barred.

Class 7   (1294 – 1296)

Class 7A

Obverse Legend   As Class 2A.

Similar to Class 6B, but with a rose on breast and almond shaped eyes; double barred 'N' in legend.

Class 7B

Very similar to 7A, but king has longer hair and a slightly different crown.

Class 8   (1294 – 1300)

Class 8A

Obverse legend as Class 6B; smaller crown, no rose on bust with an unusual shaped 'S'; the king also has a longer neck.

Class 8B

Similar to Class 9A but still has unusual shaped 'S' in legend and nothing on breast.

Class 9   (1300 – 1302)

Class 9A

Obverse Legend   EDWR (or EW or EDW) ANGL DNS HYB — As above

Similar to Class 8B, but the drapery is in two wedges and the king has a narrow face; there usually is a star on the breast and the crown is flatter.

Class 9B

These coins tend to be slightly smaller in size. The 'N' in the legend is of various styles, barred, unbarred or pothook; often there is also a star or pellet on the breast.

Class 10   (1302 – 1310)

Class 10A

Obverse Legend   EDWARD R ANGL DNS HYB — As above

Very narrow lettering with concave sides and narrow face.

Class 10B

All classes onwards have a bifoliate crown, with two leaves at each end instead of three.

Obverse Legend   EDWARR ANGL DNS HYB — As above

Similar to Class 10A, but some issues have an earlier style crown.

Class 10C

Obverse Legend   EDWA R — King Edward

Identical to 10B except for the obverse legend; new-style crown as standard.

Class 10D

Obverse Legend   EDWAR ANGL DNS HYB — As above

Similar to Class 10C, but with a slightly wider face and more ornate letters in legend.

Class 10E

Obverse Legend   EDWAR ANGL DNS HYB — As above

Similar to 10D, but the king's face is squarer and has a shorter neck.

Class 10F

Obverse Legend   EDWAR ANGL DNS HYB — As above

Similar to Class 10E, but the cross above the king's crown is dumpier in shape.

Mints

Although most of Edward I's coins were struck at London and Canterbury, dies were also made for various provincial mints. The coins from provincial mints conform in almost every detail to the 10 major classes laid out previously but there are a few exceptions where small marks or a slightly different design were added to the coin to distinguish them. The mint is found on the reverse, usually preceded by CIVITAS (city) or VILLA (town). Below we have listed all the mints that issued coins and the inscriptions found on the reverse legend, with slashes marking where the long cross breaks the legend. We have also given the class in which the coins were issued and any unusual marks found on them.

Bristol Mint

VILL/ABR/ISTO/LLIE	2B, 3B, 3D, 3F, 3G
VILL/BRI/STO/LIE	9B

Bury St Edmunds Mint

This mint is the one exception that had a moneyer's name, Robert de Hadelie, rather than the mint name on some issues.

Robert de Hadelie issue   mint name issue

ROBE/RTU/SDEH/ADL	3C
ROBE/RTUS/DEH/ADL	4A
ROBE/RTDE/HADE/LEIE	3C, 3D, 3G, 4A, 4B, 4C
VIL/LAS/EDM/VDI	4E, 5B
VIL/LAS/EDM/VNDI	5B
VILA/SCI/EDM/VDI	6B
VILL/ASCI/EDM/VNDI	7A, 8A
VILL/ASCI/EDM/VDI	7A
VILA/SCIE/DMV/NDI	8, 9A
VILL/SCIE/DMV/NDI	9B
VILL/SCIE/DMV/NDI	10A, 10B

Canterbury Mint

CIVI/TAS/CAN/TOR	2, 3B, 3C, 3D, 3F, 3G, 4A, 4B, 4C, 4E, 5, 6, 7, 9, 10A, 10B
CIVI/TAS/CAN/TVR	2A, sometimes 2B

Chester Mint

CIVI/TAS/CES/TRIE	3G, 9B
CIVI/TAS/CEST/RIE	3G sometimes

Durham Mint

Durham was an ecclesiastical privilege mint, having a 'favour' from the king that allowed coins to be struck there under the watchful eye of the powerful Bishops — an important source of revenue for the Church. Several Bishops introduced small marks on their coin using their family crests.

CIV/TAS/DVR/ EME		9B, 10A, 10B, 10E,
	Regular Issue [1]	10F
CIVI/TAS/DVR/ EME	Regular Issue [1]	10A
CIV/TAS/DVR/ EME	Bishop de Insula [2]	2B, 3B, 3C, 3E, 3G, 4A
CIV/ITAS/DVR/ EME	Bishop Bec [3]	4B, 4E, 5B, 6B, 7B
CIV/ITAS/DVR/ ENE	Bishop Bec	9A
CIV/ITA/SDVR/ ENE	Bishop Bec [4]	9A
CIV/ITAS/DVR/ EME	Bishop Bec	4B

1. King's receiver, no distinguishing marks
2. No distinguishing marks
3. Cross moline as initial mark on both sides of coin.
4. There is also a variety where a cross moline is found in one quarter on the reverse

Exeter Mint

CIV/TAS/EXO/NIE	9B

Kingston upon Hull Mint

VILL/KYN/CES/TON	9B
VIL'/KYN/CES/TON	9B

London Mint

CIVI/TAS/LON/DON	all classes except 3E

Lincoln Mint

CIVI/TAS/LIN/COL'	3C, 3D, 3F, 3G

Newcastle Mint

VIL/ANO/VICA/STRI	3E
VILL/NOVI/CAS/TRI	10A, 10B
VILL/NOV'/CAS/TRI	9B, 10A, 10B
VIL'/NOV'/CAS/TRI	9B, 9C

Reading Mint

CIVI/TAS/LON/ DON	annulet on king's breast; mark of Abbot of Reading	1D

York Mint

As well as a royal mint, York had an ecclesiastical privilege mint like Durham. The two types of coins had to look different so, although the legends remained the same, a quatrefoil was placed in the centre of the reverse cross of those struck at the ecclesiastical mint.

| CIVI/TAS/EBO/ RACI | royal mint | 2, 3B, 3C, 3E, 3F, 9B |
| CIVI/TAS/EBO/ RACI | ecclesiastical mint | 3E, 3G, 9B |

Pricing

No.	Mint	Class	VG	F	VF
E11D-030	Bristol	2B	30	50	100
E11D-035		3B	35	60	120
E11D-040		3D	25	45	90
E11D-045		3F	35	60	120
E11D-050		3G	25	50	100
E11D-055		9B	25	50	100
E11D-060	Bury St Edmunds. Robert de Hadelie rev.	3C	40	80	160
E11D-065		3D	40	80	160
E11D-070		3G	40	80	160
E11D-075		4A	40	90	180
E11D-080		4B	40	80	160
E11D-085		4C	40	80	160
E11D-090	Bury St Edmunds. Mint name rev.	4E	25	50	100
E11D-095		5B	40	100	—
E11D-100		6B	40	100	—
E11D-105		7A	40	100	—
E11D-110		8A	25	50	100
E11D-115		8B	30	60	120
E11D-120		9A	25	50	100
E11D-125		9B	25	50	100
E11D-130		10A	25	55	110
E11D-135		10B	25	50	100
E11D-140	Canterbury	2A	22	40	80
E11D-145		2B	20	35	70
E11D-150		3B	25	55	100
E11D-155		3C	20	30	60
E11D-160		3D	20	30	60
E11D-165		3F	30	70	120
E11D-170		3G	30	30	60
E11D-175		4A	22	35	70
E11D-180		4B	20	30	60
E11D-185		4C	20	30	60
E11D-190		4D	20	40	75
E11D-195		4E	20	40	75
E11D-200		5A	30	75	150
E11D-205		5B	30	75	150
E11D-210		6A	60	140	300
E11D-215		6B	40	100	200
E11D-220		7A	40	100	200
E11D-225		7B	40	100	200
E11D-230		9A	22	35	75
E11D-235		9B	20	30	60
E11D-240		10A	20	30	60
E11D-245		10B	60	30	60
E11D-250	Chester	3G	40	80	150
E11D-255		9B	35	70	140
E11D-260	Durham	2B	25	50	100
E11D-265		3B	30	60	120
E11D-270		3C	25	50	100
E11D-275		3E	25	50	100
E11D-280		3G	25	50	100
E11D-285		4A	25	50	100
E11D-290		4B	25	50	100
E11D-295		4E	25	50	100
E11D-300		5B	30	70	125
E11D-305		6B	40	100	200
E11D-310		7B	40	100	200
E11D-315		9A	25	50	100
E11D-320		9B	25	50	100
E11D-325		10A	25	50	100

No.	Mint	Class	VG	F	VF
E11D-330		10B	25	50	100
E11D-335		10E	25	50	100
E11D-340		10F	25	50	100
E11D-345	Exeter	9B	35	70	140
E11D-350	Kingston upon Hull	9B	40	80	150
E11D-355	London	1A	200	450	—
E11D-360		1B	200	500	—
E11D-365		1C	25	45	125
E11D-370		1D	25	45	90
E11D-375		2A	20	30	60
E11D-380		2B	20	30	60
E11D-385		3A	30	70	120
E11D-390		3B	30	60	100
E11D-395		3C	20	30	60
E11D-400		3D	20	30	60
E11D-405		3F	22	50	100
E11D-410		3G	20	30	60
E11D-415		4A	20	35	65
E11D-420		4B	20	30	60
E11D-425		4C	20	30	60
E11D-430		4D	20	30	60
E11D-435		4E	20	35	65
E11D-440		5A	30	70	120
E11D-445		5B	30	70	120
E11D-450		6A	60	140	220
E11D-455		6B	40	100	200
E11D-460		7A	40	100	200
E11D-465		7B	40	100	200
E11D-470		8A	25	50	100
E11D-475		8B	25	50	100
E11D-480		9A	20	30	60
E11D-485		9B	20	30	60
E11D-490		10A	20	30	60
E11D-495		10B	20	30	60
E11D-500		10C	20	30	60
E11D-505		10D	20	30	60
E11D-510		10E	20	30	60
E11D-515		10F	20	35	80
E11D-520	Lincoln	3C	25	45	90
E11D-525		3D	25	45	90
E11D-530		3F	30	60	110
E11D-535		3G	25	45	90
E11D-540	Reading	1D	120	250	—
E11D-545	Newcastle	3E	25	45	90
E11D-550		9B	25	45	90
E11D-555		9C	25	45	90
E11D-560		10A	25	45	90
E11D-565		10B	25	45	90
E11D-570	York	2A	25	50	100
E11D-575		2B	25	50	100
E11D-578		3B	25	55	100
E11D-580		3C	20	40	90
E11D-585		3E	25	50	100
E11D-590		3F	30	60	120
E11D-595		3G	20	40	80
E11D-600		9B	20	40	80

Berwick on Tweed Mint

The coins of Berwick on Tweed have not been included in the previous listing because they do not conform to the classes of Edward I. As mentioned earlier, dies were usually made in London and sent out to the provincial mints, thus ensuring conformity both in production and style. But the dies used at Berwick were of local manufacture, because, due to its proximity to Scotland, the town was a constant battle-ground between Scots and English and often changed hands as battles progressed. So, although Berwick was hardly the safest location for a royal mint, there was a need for coinage not least for the payment of the English troops and local dies were made to strike it. The coins produced were all pennies and can be divided into four classes.

Collecting Hints

Berwick coins tend to be crude in style and a portrait with large staring eyes. Many seem to have a lower silver content than the regular issues. Berwick pennies are common, but nice VF examples are hard to find. Collectors should try to obtain an example in at least Fine condition and visually attractive.

Class 1

Obverse Legend   EDW R ANGL DNS HYB — Edward King of England and Lord of Ireland

Reverse Legend   VILLA BEREVVICI — Town of Berwick

Obverse   Front-facing bust of king wearing crown.

Reverse   Similar to all reverses on Edward I pennies.

E11D-605   VG £20   F £50   VF £120

Class 2

Obverse Legend   EDW(A), R ANGL DNS HYB — As above

Reverse Legend   VILLA BERREWYCI (or BERREVICI) — Town of Berwick

Obverse   As previous, but very crude in style; the king's crown is also ornamented with large pellets

Reverse   As previous.

E11D-610   VG £20   F £50   VF £120

Class 3

This is identical to Class 1, except that the obverse legend reads EDWA instead of EDWR.

E11D-615   VG £20   F £50   VF £120

Class 4

Obverse Legend   EDWA R ANGL DNS HYB — As above

Reverse Legend   VILLA BEREVVICI — Town of Berwick

Obverse   Neater bust with large eyes and a pellet on the breast.

Reverse   As previous.

E11D-620   VG £22   F £60   VF £60   EF £130

Edward II   (1307 – 1327)

Edward II succeeded Edward I in 1307 and although his reign was neither as prosperous nor as peaceful as his father's, there is very little difference in their coinage. The penny continued as the main denomination, and the halfpennies and farthings that were also struck are now scarce. Stylistically, the two reigns are also similar, with virtually identical reverses and only minor differences on the obverse. The obverse legend reads EDWA(R) R ANGL DNS HYB, which is different from most of Edward I's pennies except for some of the later classes. The crown on Edward II's pennies is bifoliate, having two prongs on each end, while most Edward I issues have a crown with three prongs — except for Class 10, which also has a bifoliate crown. However, the most common Edward II pennies are those of Class 11, which have a broken pearl to the left of the crown; the later classes (12 to 15) omit the broken pearl but all have a bifoliate crown and the same legend. Most of these later classes differ from the previous ones in the style of the crown. Finally, many of Edward II's pennies tend to be a little smaller than those of Edward I.

A more detailed description of the differences between the two reigns is given above, p.334.

Collecting Hints

Edward II pennies are relatively easy to obtain and although most have come from hoards, their quality and condition is slightly inferior to that of Edward I's and some may be clipped. Collectors should try to obtain a coin in at least Fine condition and with as large a flan as possible.

Classes

Classes are numbered consecutively from the previous reign because the coins are so similar.

Class 11A   Class 11C   Class 12

Class 13   Class 14

Class 15A   Class 15B   Class 15C

Class 11   (1310 – 1314)

Class 11A

Obverse Legend   EDWAR ANGL DNS HYB — Edward King of England and Lord of Ireland

Obverse   Front-facing crowned bust of king; crown with broken pearl to left of centre, straight-sided 'N' in legend.

Reverse   Similar to all Edward I reverses.

Class 11B

Similar to Class 11A, but face slightly smaller, large serifs to 'N's in legend, 'E' with an angular back.

Class 11C

Similar to Class 11B, but 'A' of legend is double-barred at vertical side and flat topped.

Class 12   (1314)

The crown has its central fleur formed of three wedges, rather than a curved lis style as previous classes.

Class 13   (1315 – 1318)

Very similar to previous issues, but the central fleur of crown is in the form of a Greek double-axe.

Class 14   (1318 – 1320)

Very similar to Class 13 but the central fleur is taller and the king has a slightly larger face with leering eyes.

Class 15   (1320 – 1335)

Class 15A

The bust is similar to Class 14, but the crown is smaller and flatter and its spearheads or points are often bent to the left.

Class 15B

Similar to Class 15A, but a slightly smaller face.

Class 15C

Similar to previous issues, but the king has a larger face and the 'E' in the legend is large.

Mints

Only five mints were active under Edward II, probably because large quantities of coins had been produced in the previous reign and the need for new coinage was not acute. We have listed the mints below, along with their inscriptions with slashes marking where the long cross breaks the legend, the classes in which the issues were struck and, where appropriate, any distinguishing marks. These reverses are very similar to those of Edward I. If necessary, collectors should refer back to that section for identification.

Bury St Edmunds Mint

VILL/SCIE/DMV/NDI   all Edward II classes

Canterbury Mint

CIVI/TAS/CAN/TOR   all Edward II classes

London Mint

CIVI/TAS/LON/DON   all Edward II classes

Durham Mint

Durham continued as an ecclesiastical privilege mint, producing coins under the control of the Bishops. However, the first issue is known as the King's Receiver Issue because it was struck by a Receiver under strict instructions from Edward II who had been displeased with Bishop Bec for putting his own small marks on the coins.

CIVI/TAS/DVN/ ELM CIVI/TAS/ DVR/EME	King's Receiver, plain cross mm	11A, 14
CIVI/TAS/DVR/ EME	Bishop Bec, cross moline mm (obv.)	11A
CIVI/TAS/DVN/ ELM	Bishop Kellawe, crozier end to long cross (rev.)	11A, 12, 13
CIVI/TAS/DVN/ ELM	Bishop Beaumont, lion and lis mm (obv.)	13, 14, 15
CIVI/TAS/DVN/ ELM	Sede Vacante, plain cross (obv.)[1]	15C

1. There is confusion as to when and why this issue was produced. The coins were struck under the authority of the king rather than the Bishop and some experts consider them to be London-Durham mules. There are several varieties.

Pricing

No.	Mint	Class	VG	F	VF
E21D-005	Bury St Edmunds	11A	22	45	90
E21D-010		11B	22	45	90
E21D-015		11C	25	50	100
E21D-020		12	22	45	90
E21D-025		13	22	45	90
E21D-030		14	22	45	90
E21D-035		15A	22	45	90
E21D-040		15B	22	45	90
E21D-045		15C	25	50	100
E21D-050	Canterbury	11A	22	45	90
E21D-055		11B	22	45	90
E21D-060		11C	25	50	100
E21D-065		12	22	45	90

No.	Mint	Class	VG	F	VF
E21D-070		13	22	45	90
E21D-075		14	22	45	90
E21D-080		15A	22	45	90
E21D-085		15B	22	45	90
E21D-090		15C	25	50	100
E21D-095	London	11A	22	35	70
E21D-100		11B	22	35	70
E21D-105		11C	25	30	100
E21D-110		12	22	40	80
E21D-115		13	20	35	70
E21D-120		14	20	30	60
E21D-125		15A	20	32	65
E21D-130		15B	20	32	65
E21D-135		15C	20	32	65
E21D-140	Durham	11A	25	50	100
E21D-145		11B	25	50	100
E21D-150		11C	25	50	100
E21D-155		12	25	50	100
E21D-160		13	25	50	100
E21D-165		14	25	50	100
E21D-170		15A	25	55	110
E21D-175		15B	25	55	110
E21D-180		15C	40	90	180

Berwick on Tweed Mint

The Berwick pennies of Edward II continue from the previous reign and again form a separate category (please see above for details). Like the previous issues, coins tend to be crude, often made of rather base metal and found in fairly poor condition. In all of the classes the obverse legend translates as 'Edward King of England and Lord of Ireland' and the reverse as 'Town of Berwick', while the reverse design is a long cross with three pellets in each quarter.

Class 5   (1310)
Obverse Legend   EDWA(R) ANGL DNS HYB — Edward King of England and Lord of Ireland

Reverse Legend   VIL/LAB/ERE/WICI (or /WYCI) — Town of Berwick

Obverse   Front-facing bust of king with bifoliate crown with a broken spearhead.

E21D-185   VG £30   F £80   VF £180

Class 6
Obverse Legend   EDWAR ANGL DNS HYB

Reverse Legend   VIL/LAB/ERE/WICI (or /WYCI or /WYC')

Obverse   As previous, but the king has a trifoliate (three pronged) crown.

E21D-190   VG £35   F £90   VF £200

Class 7
Obverse Legend   EDWAR ANGL DNS HYB

Reverse Legend   VILL/ABE/REV/VICI (or /ICI)

Obverse   As previous, the face often has squinting eyes and the whole coin is very crude.

E21D-195   VG £40   F £100   VF £220

There is also a very rare variety which has a bear's head in one quarter of the reverse.

E21D-200   very rare

Edward III   (1327 – 1377)

Edward III succeeded his father at the age of fourteen and reigned for fifty years, although during the early period the country was in fact ruled by his mother, Queen Isabella. Edward's reign was a period of conflict, not only with the Scots but also with France as he laid claim to the French throne and the vicissitudes of that enterprise are reflected in the legends of his coins. Moreover, when the town of Calais became English after a treaty with France, coins were also struck there partly for convenience and partly as a political statement.

During the first part of Edward's reign only a small quantity of pennies was produced, similar in style to those of his father. However, a new series of coins was introduced when increasing trade with Flanders necessitated the production of good quality gold currency and a variety of denominations. The gold noble, half-noble, and quarter-noble were introduced to be followed later by the groat, or fourpence, which became very popular and eventually superseded the penny in importance, and the halfgroat, which again proved popular. The penny itself changed in style, with a bust that was very different from that on the issues of the two preceding monarchs, while halfpennies and farthings were also produced. There was, at last, an adequate supply of varying denominations, which benefited both the internal market and trade with Europe, where English coins of all denominations were readily acceptable.

Edward's long reign resulted in numerous varieties in the coinage but identifying an Edward III penny is fairly easy, except for the first coinage of 1327 – 35. As with the other four Edwards who struck pennies, the obverse legend begins with EDWARDUS or some abbreviation which in this case will read at least EDWA; the portrait is quite distinct however as, in contrast to the other four, Edward III, who is depicted with long hair, kept his youthful looks on all his coins.

A total of five mints were active from 1344 to 1377 and their legends, found on the reverse of the coin, read as follows:

CIVITAS LONDON	City of London
CIVITAS DUREME (varieties)	City of Durham
VILLA CALESIE	Town of Calais
VILLA RADINGY	Town of Reading
CIVITAS EBORACI	City of York

Once the above details have been identified, the obverse legend will help indicate the particular issue and it often helps to write a coin's legend out in full before attempting to match it. Finally, look for any unusual marks such as annulets or saltires, which are often in the legend or on or below the king's breast and constituted a form of quality control by being individual to a particular die. In this way, if there was a problem with a coin, it could have been traced back to the original die and moneyer.

The main varieties of marks are:
an annulet, usually in the legend or king's breast and sometimes in the four quarters on the reverse;
an escallop in one quarter on coins from the Reading mint;
a quatrefoil usually in the centre of the reverse on coins from York;
a crown found at 12 o'clock on the obverse legend;
a crozier on the reverse of coins from Durham;
a trefoil of pellets sometimes on the king's breast;
a quatrefoil enclosing a pellet in the centre of the reverse from some coins of York;
a double annulet sometimes found in the legends;
a pellet sometimes found in the legend, or an extra one in the quarters on the reverse;
a voided quatrefoil sometimes on the king's breast;

a lis sometimes on the king's breast.

Collecting Hints

Except for the first coinage and certain varieties and mints, Edward III pennies are available but usually found in a lower grade than those of the first two Edwards. Although coins in EF condition tend to be rare, it should not be difficult to find an example in Fine or even VF. Many of the lower grade coins tend to be clipped and, due to poor striking, parts of the legend are often flat. Collectors should try to obtain an unclipped example with as much detail showing as possible.

First Coinage (1327 – 1335)

Because of the extensive similarities in style, the class numbering system continues from the previous reign. This small and scarce issue is very similar to Class 15 of Edward II but has Lombardic 'N's in the legend. The reverse of the coin is determined by the mint and the various details are listed below.

Class 15D

Obverse Legend   EDWAR ANGL DNS HYB — Edward King of England and Lord of Ireland

Obverse   Front-facing bust of king as Class 15 but Lombardic 'N's in legend.

Mints

As well as London, five provincial mints were active during the first coinage, four of which have the Class 15D obverse. The provincial issues are all scarce or rare and have Lombardic 'N's in legend; the points where the long cross breaks the legend are represented below by slashes. Collectors should also cross reference with the provincial mints of Edward I and Edward II to ensure that they have the correct issue.

London Mint

Reverse Legend   CIVITAS LONDON — City of London

Reverse   Long cross, three pellets in each quarter.

E31D-005	VG £200	F £400	VF £800

Bury St Edmunds Mint

Reverse Legend   VILL/SCIE/DMV/NDI — Town of Bury St Edmunds

E31D-010	ex. rare

Canterbury Mint

Obverse   Mintmark cross pattée with pellet centre or pellet by mintmark, Roman or Lombardic 'N' in D.N.S.

Reverse   Long cross, three pelltes in each quarter, sometimes extra pellets in one quarter.

E31D-015	VG £175	F £350	VF £750

Durham Mint

Reverse Legend   CIVI/TAS/DVN/ELM — City of Durham

Reverse   A small crown can be found on the reverse.

E31D-020	VG £300	F £600	VF v. rare

York Mint

Reverse Legend   CIVI/TAS/EBO/RACI — City of York

Reverse   Four varieties exist:
1. a quatrefoil in the centre of the reverse cross;
2. a small pellet in each quarter of the obverse mintmark;
3. three extra pellets in one quarter;
4. sometimes a Roman 'N' only on the obverse legend.

E31D-025	VG £150	F £275	VF £550

Berwick on Tweed Mint

As with the previous two reigns, the Berwick issues do not conform to the regular classes. This type was issued around 1344.

Obverse Legend   EDWARDUS ANGL HIB

Reverse Legend   VIL/LAB/ERW/ICI

Obverse   Crowned bust of king.

Reverse   A bear's head in one quarter.

E31D-030	VG £200	F £400	VF £800

No pennies were produced during the second coinage (1335 – 43). This was probably because there were adequate reserves in circulation from the previous two reigns since, by contrast, large quantities of halfpennies were struck to satisfy demand.

Third or Florin Coinage (1344 – 1351)

The third, or florin coinage, spans the period from 1344 to 1351 and derived its name from the fact that the dies were made by two Florentine craftsmen. Because the new style for the penny is so different, the class numbering system is discontinued after the first coinage. The obverse still bears a front-facing bust of the king but the main difference is in the style of hair, Edward III's being long and unkempt while Edward I's is much neater; also, the neck and shoulders differ in style, as does the lettering. As with previous issues, the mint can be found on the reverse and, of the five mints that were active at the time, London was the most prolific.

London Mint

Obverse Legend   EDW R ANGL DNS HYB — Edward King of England and Lord of Ireland

Reverse Legend   CIVITAS LONDON — City of London

Obverse   Front-facing bust with bushy hair and broad neck and shoulders; Lombardic 'N's in the legend, as well as annulets; mintmark cross pattée.

E31D-035	VG £18	F £38	VF £80

As previous, but the obverse legend reads EDWAR ANGL DNS HYB.

E31D-040	VG £16	F £35	VF £80

Similar to E31D-040, but a Roman 'N', sometimes reversed, is found on the obverse legend.

E31D-045	VG £16	F £35	VF £80

As previous, but there are no annulet stops in the legend and a variety of 'N's are used.

E31D-050	VG £16	F £35	VF £80

Canterbury Mint

Obverse Legend   As E31D-040.

Reverse Legend   CIVI/TAS/CAN/TOR — City of Canterbury

Obverse   As previous.

E31D-055	VG £35	F £75	VF £150

Obverse Legend   EDWR ANGL DNS HYB. Reversed Roman 'N' in legend.

E31D-060	VG £35	F £75	VF £150

Durham Mint

All the coins from the Durham mint are rare. Many varieties of the reverse legend exist and we have listed the major ones below.

Obverse Legend   EDWARDUS REX AIN — Edward King of England

Reverse Legend   CIV/ITAS/DUN/ELM or DUN/OLME — City of Durham. Crozier in reverse.

E31D-065	VG £75	F £175	VF £350

Obverse Legend   EDWR ANGL DNS HYB — Edward of England Lord of Ireland

Reverse Legend   CIVITAS DUN/ELM or DUN/OLM — City of Durham

E31D-070	VG £35	F £75	VF £150

Obverse Legend   EDWR ANGL DNS YB — Edward of England Lord of Ireland. Usually one Lombardic and one Roman 'N'.

Reverse Legend   As previous.

E31D-075	VG £35	F £75	VF £150

Obverse Legend   EDWAR R ANG DNS HYB. — Edward of England Lord of Ireland. Lombardic Ns.

Reverse Legend   CIVI/TAS DUN/ELM, CIVI/TAS DUN/OLM, CIVI/TAS DUN/OLME, VIL/ADU/NOL/MIE, VIL/LAD/UR/REM — City or Town of Durham

E31D-080	VG £75	F £175	VF £350

Obverse Legend   EDWARDUS REX ANGLIE — Edward King of England

Reverse Legend   VILA DUNO LMIE — Town of Durham

E31D-085	VG £75	F £175	VF £350

Reading Mint

Obverse Legend   EDWR ANGL DNS HYB

Reverse Legend   VIL/LA R/ADI/NGY — Town of Reading

An escallop can be found in one quarter of the reverse instead of the usual three pellets.

E31D-090	VG £175	F £400	VF £850

York Mint

Obverse Legend   EDWR ANGL DNS HYB

Reverse Legend   CIVI/TAS/EBO/RACI — City of York

Obverse   Variety of 'N's in legends.

Reverse   Long cross, quatrefoil in centre, three pellets in each quarter.

E31D-095	VG £25	F £50	VF £100

Fourth Coinage (1351 – 1377)

Edward III's fourth coinage is an important turning point in English numismatic history, involving the successful introduction of the groat and halfgroat as well as the gold noble, half-noble and quarter-noble. It constitutes the beginning of the modern varied denomination system. However, as well as being a historical landmark, the fourth coinage was itself influenced by contemporary events and is classified according to the obverse legend which charts the progress of Edward's claim to the French throne. Based on the 1360 Treaty of Brétigny that granted Edward land in France, the coinage is subdivided into the pre-treaty, transitional, treaty and post-treaty periods. During the pre-treaty and post-treaty periods, when Edward's claims were not recognised, FRANC (France) appeared in the legends of most of his coins.

It was omitted for the six years that the treaty was upheld. In some cases, but not on the penny, FRANC was replaced by AQT for Aquitaine, the French territory granted to Edward. After the treaty was repudiated by the French in 1369, the two countries went to war again and England lost most of its French possessions except Calais and Bordeaux. However, the one feature of the coinage that remained constant was the king's portrait with the result that even at the age of sixty, Edward retain his youthful looks on the coins.

Pre Treaty Period (1351 – 1361)

Many of the coins produced between 1351 and 1361 bear the word FRANC, but the penny does not. Three mints were active in the production of coins during this decade.

London Mint

Minor varieties of this issue exist.

Class B

Obverse Legend   EDWARDUS REX ANGLI — Edward King of England

Reverse Legend   CIVI/TAS/LON/DON — City of London

Obverse   Front-facing bust with round eyes.

Reverse   Lombardic 'M' and 'N' in legend with an annulet in each quarter; mintmark cross pattée.

E31D-100	VG £40	F £100	VF £200

Class C

As previous, but closed 'C' and 'E', and 'R' with wedge-shaped tail in legend; an annulet in each quarter of the reverse.

E31D-105	VG £18	F £35	VF £75

Class D

As previous, but 'R' with normal tail.

E31D-110	VG £18	F £35	VF £75

Class E

The legend has broken letters and an annulet can not always be found in each quarter.

E31D-115	VG £18	F £35	VF £75

Class F

The mintmark crown can be found on the obverse of the coin.

E31D-120	VG £20	F £38	VF £75

Class G

Annulet in one quarter on reverse.

E31D-125	VG £18	F £35	VF £75

An annulet can be found below the bust.

E31D-130	VG £22	F £45	VF £90

A saltire can be found in one quarter on the reverse.

E31D-135	VG £30	F £60	VF £120

Durham Mint

This issue was struck under Bishop Hatfield.

Obverse Legend   EDWARDUS REX ANGLI — Edward King of England

Reverse Legend   VILLA DURREM — Town of Durham

There is an extra pellet in each quarter and a crozier in the reverse legend.

E31D-140	VG £100	F £200	VF £400

Obverse Legend   As previous.

Reverse Legend   CIVITAS DUNELMIE — City of Durham

Obverse   As E31D-105.

E31D-145	VG £30	F £60	VF £120

Legends   As previous.

Obverse   As E31D-110.

E31D-150	VG £30	F £60	VF £120

Legends   As previous.

Obverse   As E31D-115.

E31D-155	VG £25	F £50	VF £100

Obverse Legend   As previous.

Reverse Legend   CIVITAS DVREME — City of Durham

Obverse   As E31D-120.

E31D-160	VG £30	F £60	VF £120

Legends As previous.
Obverse As E31D-125.

E31D-165 VG £22 F £45 VF £90

Legends As previous.
Obverse As E31D-130.

E31D-170 VG £20 F £40 VF £80

Legends As previous.
Obverse As E31D-135.

E31D-175 VG £20 F £40 VF £80

Legends As previous.
Obverse An annulet can be found on each of the king's shoulders.

E31D-180 VG £20 F £40 VF £80

Legends As previous.
Obverse A trefoil of pellets can be found on the king's shoulders.

E31D-185 VG £22 F £45 VF £90

Obverse Legend As previous.
Reverse Legend CIVITAS DVRELMIE — City of Durham
Obverse Plain bust of king.
Reverse Crozier in legend.

E31D-190 VG £22 F £45 VF £90

York Mint
Royal Mint
Obverse Legend EDWARDUS REX ANGLI — Edward King of England
Reverse Legend CIVITAS EBORACI — City of York
Obverse As E31D-110.
Reverse Plain cross to centre.

E31D-195 VG £30 F £60 VF £120

As previous, but some letters in legend are broken.

E31D-200 VG £20 F £38 VF £75

Episcopal Mint under Archbishop Thorsby
Obverse Legend EDWARDUS REX ANGLI — Edward King of England
Reverse Legend CIVITAS EBORACI — City of York
Obverse Similar to E31D-110.
Reverse Cross with quatrefoil in centre.

E31D-205 VG £25 F £50 VF £100

Similar to previous but sometimes annulet in one quarter on the reverse and sometimes under bust of king.

E31D-210 VG £20 F £38 VF £80

As previous, but an annulet or saltire on breast.

E31D-215 VG £22 F £45 VF £90

Transitional Period (1361 – 1363)

This small and scarce issue can be easily identified as it omits REX (king) from the obverse legend. Most of the lettering in this issue is of irregular size. The same three mints were active during this period.

London Mint
Obverse Legend EDWAR(D)ANGLIE DNS HIB — Edward of England and Lord of Ireland
Reverse Legend CIVITAS LONDON — City of London
Obverse Front-facing bust of king; annulet in two upper quarters of mintmark cross.

E31D-220 VG £60 F £120 VF £240

York Mint
At the time, York was an ecclesiastical mint under the control of Archbishop Thorsby.
Obverse Legend As previous.
Reverse Legend CIVITAS EBORACI — City of York
Reverse Quatrefoil enclosing pellet in centre of reverse.

E31D-225 VG £45 F £90 VF £180

Durham Mint
At the time, Durham was an ecclesiastical mint under the control of Bishop Hatfield.
Obverse Legend As previous.
Reverse Legend CIVITAS DORELME or DURENE — City of Durham
Reverse The reverse legend is preceded by a crozier.

E31D-230 VG £55 F £110 VF £220

Treaty Period (1361 – 1369)

During this short period of peace, coins were also struck at Calais which became an important mint and continued to be active intermittently until Henry VI's reign.

London Mint
Obverse Legend EDWARD ANGL R DNS HYB — Edward of England and Lord of Ireland
Reverse Legend CIVITAS LONDON — City of London
Obverse Double annulet stops in legend and unbarred 'A' in CIVITAS.

E31D-235	VG £20	F £40	VF £85

There is also a variety similar to the above. It has a barred 'A' on the reverse legend, and a pellet before EDWARD.

Calais Mint

Obverse Legend   As previous.

Reverse Legend   VILLA CALISIE — Town of Calais

Obverse   Double annulet stops in legend.

Reverse   Pellet after LA in legend.

E31D-240	VG £60	F £125	VF £250

York Mint

Obverse Legend   EDWARDUS REX ANGLI — Edward King of England (varieties exist)

Reverse Legend   CIVITAS EBORACI — City of York

Obverse   Pellet stops in legend.

Reverse   Long cross, quarterfoil in centre.

E31D-245	VG £60	F £125	VF £250

Similar to above, but the king has a voided quatrefoil on his breast. Most of this issue appears to have been made with locally produced, poor quality dies.

E31D-250	VG £70	F £150	VF £300

Similar to E31D-245, but with an annulet before EDWARDUS.

E31D-255	VG £60	F £125	VF £250

Obverse Legend   EDWARD ANGL R DNS HYB — Edward King of England Lord of Ireland

Reverse Legend   As previous.

Obverse & Reverse   Similar to the London issue, but sometimes with a pellet before EDWARD.

E31D-260	VG £60	F £125	VF £250

Many varieties of the obverse legend exist.

Obverse Legend   EDWARDUS DEI G REX AN — Edward by the grace of God King of England (abbreviated)

Reverse Legend   CIVITAS EBORACI — City of York

Obverse   Single annulet stops in legend.

Reverse   Quatrefoil in centre of reverse.

E31D-265	VG £30	F £60	VF £120

Durham Mint

Obverse Legend   EDWARDUS REX ANGLI — Edward King of England

Reverse Legend   CIVITAS DUREME — City of Durham

Obverse   Single annulet stops in legend.

Reverse   Crozier at the beginning of legend.

E31D-270	VG £40	F £80	VF £160

Obverse Legend   As previous.

Reverse Legend   CIVITAS DUNELMIS — City of Durham

This issue has no crozier in the legend.

E31D-275	VG £45	VG £90	VF £180

Post Treaty Period (1369 – 1377)

Three mints were active during this period and, for the first time, FRANC (France) can be found in some of the legends. In many cases the 'F' of FRANC is reversed, probably due to an error in the die production.

London Mint

Obverse Legend   EDWARD R ANGL FRANC or EDWARDUS REX ANGLIE FR — Edward King of England and France

Reverse Legend   CIVITAS LONDON — City of London

Obverse   The king sometimes has a pellet on his breast.

Reverse   Roman 'N' in reverse legend is sometimes reversed.

E31D-280	VG £40	F £80	VF £160

Obverse Legend   EDWARDUS REX ANGLIE — Edward King of England

Reverse Legend   CIVITAS LONDON — City of London

Obverse   A cross, annulet or quatrefoil or nothing on the king's breast.

Reverse   Usually extra pellets on the reverse.

E31D-285	VG £45	F £90	VF £180

York Mint

York was an ecclesiastical mint under the control of Archbishops Thorsby or Neville.

Obverse Legend   EDWARD REX ANGL FR (ANC sometimes) — Edward King of England and France

Reverse Legend   CIVITAS EBORACI — City of York

Obverse   A double annulet, large pellet or saltire stops in legend. Some coins have a cross or annulet on breast; mintmark plain cross.

Reverse   Quatrefoil in centre of reverse. Sometimes a plain cross at the start of the legend.

E31D-290   VG £25   F £50   VF £100

Obverse Legend   EDWARD DI GRA REX ANG — Edward by the grace of God King of England

Reverse Legend   As previous.

Obverse   Saltire stops in the legend.

Reverse   As previous.

E31D-295   VG £30   F £60   VF £120

Obverse Legend   EDWARDUS REX ANGLIE (ET) — Edward King of England (and)

Reverse Legend   As previous; crozier in legend.

Obverse   There is usually an annulet, lis or cross on the king's breast. This issue usually has saltire stops in the legend.

Reverse   As previous.

E31D-300   VG £25   F £50   VF £100

Durham Mint

Durham was an ecclesiastical mint under the control of Bishop Hatfield.

Obverse Legend   EDWARDUS REX ANGL FR — Edward King of England [and] France

Reverse Legend   CIVITAS DUNOLM — City of Durham

Obverse   Double annulets and saltires in legend; mintmark plain cross.

Reverse   Long cross, three pellets in each quarter, crozier in legend.

E31D-305   VG £45   F £90   VF £180

Obverse Legend   EDWARDUS REX ANGLIE — Edward King of England

Reverse Legend   As previous.

Obverse   Annulet, lis or nothing on king's breast.

Reverse   As previous.

E31D-310   VG £50   F £100   VF £200

Richard II   (1377 – 1399)

The last quarter of the fourteenth century was a time of problems and difficulties for England and this was reflected in the quantity and quality of the coins produced. Because Edward III's son the Black Prince died in 1376, when the king himself died a year later the throne went to his eleven year old grandson, Richard II. During Richard's reign, England continued to lay claim to the French throne and was at war with France until 1396. High taxation was imposed to meet the costs of the war and this caused several peasant uprisings.

Moreover during this period, large quantities of poor quality European coins, inferior in both weight and fineness, circulated alongside England's high quality coinage. Large profits could be made by smuggling English coins to the Continent where they would be melted down and, after other valueless metals had been added to the alloy, the coinage would be produced and returned to England. To an uneducated eye, the baser coins looked just the same. This not only made small change scarce, but caused a problem for the mints which were also having difficulties obtaining sufficient quantities of silver for the production of more coins. The situation was in fact a good illustration of Gresham's law that bad money drives good money out of circulation.

The 'new' denominations of Edward III continued into Richard II's reign. Pennies were produced at London, York and Durham.

Collecting Hints

Richard II's pennies are fairly easy to obtain in the lower grades and the average condition in which they are found is Poor to Fair. Often clipped or damaged, they tend not to be attractive coins. York pennies are much more common than those of London and Durham, but many of the York coins were struck from poor quality, locally produced dies and often look very blurred and crude. Collectors should try to obtain an example in at least VG, if not Fine condition but may find it very difficult to obtain specimens in VF or better condition.

London Mint

Obverse Legend   RICARDUS REX ANGLIE — Richard King of England

Reverse Legend   CIVITAS LONDON — City of London

Obverse   Front-facing bust of king; mintmark cross pattée.

Reverse   Reversed 'N's in legend.

R21D-005   VG £150   F £300   VF £600

Obverse Legend   RICARDUS REX ANGLE Z FRANC — Richard King of England and France

Reverse Legend   As previous.

Obverse   As previous, but the king has a lis on his breast.

R21D-010   VG £150   F £300   VF £600

Obverse Legend   RICARD REX ANGLIE — Richard King of England

Reverse Legend   As previous.

Obverse   Front-facing bust with bushy hair; the legend's lettering is fishtailed in shape at the ends.

R21D-015   VG £200   F £400   VF £750

York Mint

A quatrefoil can be found on the reverse in all cases.

Obverse Legend   RICARDUS REX ANGLIE — Richard King of England

Reverse Legend   CIVITAS EBORACI — City of York

Obverse   Lis, cross or nothing on breast.

Reverse   Quatrefoil in centre of reverse.

| R21D-020 | VG £50 | F £100 | F £200 |

| R21D-055 | VG £200 | F £350 | VF — |

Obverse Legend   RICARDUS REX ANGLIE Z — As previous.

Reverse Legend   As previous.

Obverse   Pellets by shoulders, cross on breast.

| R21D-025 | VG £50 | F £100 | F £200 |

Obverse Legend   RICARDUS REX ANGLIE — As previous.

Reverse Legend   As previous.

Obverse   No marks on bust or in the field; a breastline is indicated.

| R21D-030 | VG £45 | F £85 | VF £170 |

Similar to previous, but without breastline.

| R21D-035 | VG £55 | F £110 | VF £220 |

As previous, but two extra pellets in reverse quarters.

| R21D-038 | rare |

Obverse Legend   RICARD REX ANGL Z FRANC — Richard King of England and France

Reverse Legend   As previous.

Obverse   Coarse, rather crude bust.

Reverse   As previous, but scallop after 'TAS'.

| R21D-040 | VG £55 | F £110 | VF £220 |

Similar to previous, but the bust is of fine work.

| R21D-045 | VG £60 | F £120 | VF £240 |

Obverse Legend   RICARD REX ANGLIE or RICARDUS REX ANGL Z F — Richard King of England (and France)

Reverse Legend   As previous, no marks.

Obverse   The king has bushy hair.

Reverse   'R' in centre of quatrefoil.

| R21D-050 | VG £200 | F £400 | VF — |

Durham Mint

Obverse Legend   RICARDUS REX ANGLIE — Richard King of England

Reverse Legend   CIVITAS DUNOLM — City of Durham

Obverse   Front-facing bust of king with a lis or cross on breast.

Reverse   Long cross, three pellets in each quarter.

Henry IV   (1399 – 1413)

Henry Duke of Lancaster, who also was a grandson of Edward III, usurped Richard II in 1399 and ruled as Henry IV. He encountered serious opposition, however, and it was a time of problems and conflict in the country with various attempts being made against the king's life. Also, England was at war with both Scotland and Wales. Henry IV inherited the coinage problems of Richard II. As noted earlier, the price of silver and gold was low in England compared with Europe and, although it was illegal, coins were smuggled out of England to be melted down on the Continent and sold at a profit. This caused major problems for England as not only were there insufficient coins in circulation, but also, the mints could not obtain enough bullion to issue more.

Henry IV's pennies are divided into the heavy and the light coinages. The heavy coinage is so called because the weight of the coins had not been changed in line with the Continental silver price. These coins tend to be somewhat similar to Richard II's issues and cruder in style. The light coinage was issued in 1412 when the weight was reduced to correspond with Continental silver pieces and so put an end to the illegal export of English coinage. This issue was a great success even though it lasted less than two years. The style of the coins was much better, with a more lifelike portrait.

Collecting Hints

All of Henry IV's coins are rare and the penny is no exception. The average condition is VG to about Fine; coins in Fine or better are rare. Many coins tend to be clipped, have flattened legends or creases in the flan. All these features make it difficult to differentiate Henry IV's coins from other more common issues of earlier or later reigns. Using the information listed, collectors should check that a coin is correctly identified. When buying a Henry IV penny from a dealer, collectors should also ensure that the dealer guarantees not only the authenticity of the coin, but also the description. To identify these coins it is necessary to pay particular attention to the obverse legend and to the various marks found on the obverse and reverse of the coin. The mintmark is found at the start of the obverse legend and all issues only used the mintmark cross pattée.

Heavy Coinage (1399 – 1412)

London Mint

Obverse Legend   HENRIC DI GRA REX ANGL — Henry by the grace of God King of England

Reverse Legend   CIVITAS LONDON — City of London

Obverse   Front-facing bust of king with long hair and a long neck. This die was originally used for a Richard II penny as HENRIC appears to have been struck over RICARDUS. A cross pattée can be found at 12 o'clock in the legend.

Reverse   Large cross in centre breaking legends, four pellets in two quarters and three pellets in the two remaining quarters. The reverse die was for Henry IV issues only.

| H41D-005 | VG £325 | F £750 | VF £1,500 |

Similar to the previous issue, but a star can be found on the breast and there are two pellets above the central fleur on the crown. On the reverse some varieties have either 12 or 14 pellets in the quarters.

| H41D-010 | VG £325 | F £750 | VF £1,500 |

Obverse As H41D-005, but the king has a short neck.

Reverse As previous, but Lombardic 'N'.

| H41D-015 | VG £325 | F £750 | VF £1,500 |

York Mint

Reverse Legend CIVITAS EBORACI — City of York

Obverse Similar to H41D-005 with the king having a long neck.

Reverse Quatrefoil in centre of reverse cross.

| H41D-020 | VG £200 | F £400 | VF £900 |

As previous, but the king has a broader face and rounder chin.

| H41D-025 | VG £200 | F £400 | VF £900 |

Light Coinage (1412 – 1413)

London Mint

Obverse Legend HENRIC REX ANGLIE — Henry King of England

Reverse Legend CIVITAS LONDON — City of London

Obverse Front-facing bust of king, pellet to left and annulet to right of crown and a trefoil on breast.

Reverse As previous issues, with three pellets in each quarter, trefoil at beginning of legend and Lombardic 'N's in LONDON.

| H41D-030 | VG £300 | F £600 | VF £1,200 |

As previous, but with annulet to left and pellet to right of crown.

| H41D-035 unique |

Similar, but the obverse legend reads HENRIC DI GRA REX ANGL — Henry by the grace of God King of England.

| H41D-040 | VG £300 | F £600 | VF £1,200 |

Similar to H41D-035, but the king has a small bust with short hair.

| H41D-045 ex. rare |

York Mint

Obverse Legend HENRIC REX ANGLIE — Henry King of England

Reverse Legend CIVITAS EBORACI — City of York

Obverse Front-facing bust of king with an annulet on breast and after HENRIC.

Reverse Quatrefoil in centre and annulet stops in legend.

| H41D-050 | VG £200 | F £400 | VF £800 |

Durham Mint

Obverse Legend As previous.

Reverse Legend CIVITAS DVNOLM — City of Durham

Obverse Front-facing bust of king, trefoil on breast.

Reverse Plain cross.

| H41D-055 | VG £180 | F £375 | VF £750 |

Collectors may wonder why we have given no weights to help to differentiate the two coinages. This is because most specimens tend to be clipped, damaged or worn, making it difficult to give an accurate weight.

Henry V (1413 – 1422)

Henry V, Henry IV's eldest son, ascended the throne at the age of 25, upon the death of his father. It was to be a fairly short reign and once again a time of war with France. Henry V claimed the throne of France and the famous battle of Agincourt took place during his reign. In both style and weight, Henry V's coinage was a continuation of his father's successful light coinage but can be differentiated from Henry IV's coinage in several ways.

Firstly, a cross pattée can be found in the obverse legend of all Henry IV's pennies, at 12 o'clock. By contrast Henry V's coins bear a cross pattée with a pellet in the centre or a pierced cross instead.

Secondly, it is a matter of elimination; most issues tend to have marks such as annulets and trefoils on the coin, so collectors should check all the varieties to see which type a specimen falls into. It is also important to check the reverse legend to ensure that you have the correct mint. It will either be London, York, Durham, Calais (Henry VI) or Canterbury (Henry VII).

And thirdly, compare the portraits which are slightly different, particularly in the hair.

Collecting Hints

Henry V's pennies are fairly easy to obtain but tend to be found in less than Fine condition and are often slightly crude in style and manufacture. Collectors should try to obtain an example in at least Fine condition; coins in VF or better condition are rare. Heavily clipped coins in base metal, similar in style to the pennies of this era, are often found and are contemporary forgeries which may easily be distinguished by their low silver content.

London Mint

Obverse Legend (usually found) HENRIC REX ANGL — Henry King of England

Reverse Legend CIVITAS LONDON — City of London

Obverse 'Emaciated' front-facing bust of king, short and broad lettering in legend, with annulet and pellet usually by crown.

Reverse Large plain cross, three pellets·in each quarter, annulet after LON in legend.

| H51D-005 | VG £175 | F £350 | VF — |

Legends As previous.

Obverse die of a Henry IV penny, but a mullet has been punched over pellet to right of crown. The reverse has ordinary lettering. This variety sometimes has a broken annulet added by crown.

| H51D-010 | VG £150 | F £300 | VF — |

As previous, but the king has a tall neck with a mullet to left and broken annulet to right of the crown.

| H51D-015 | VG £25 | F £50 | VF £100 |

As previous, but with a whole instead of a broken annulet.

| H51D-020 | VG £25 | F £50 | VF £100 |

As previous, but with a trefoil to the right of the crown; mullet still to left.

| H51D-025 | VG £30 | F £55 | VF £110 |

Obverse Legend HENRIC DI GRA REX ANGL — Henry by the grace of God King of England

Reverse Legend As previous.

Obverse New neat bust with no marks on coin

The obverse die for this type is sometimes used for coins of Henry VI.

| H51D-030 | VG £30 | F £55 | VF £110 |

Durham Mint

Obverse Legend Similar to H51D-005.

Reverse Legend CIVITAS DUNOLM — City of Durham

Obverse Front-facing bust of king with tall neck. Mullet to left and broken annulet to right of crown.

| H51D-035 | VG £45 | F £90 | VF £180 |

Similar, but complete annulet instead of broken annulet to side of crown.

| H51D-040 | VG £40 | F £80 | VF £160 |

New neat bust with mullet to left and annulet to right of crown; also with an annulet in one quarter of the reverse.

| H51D-045 | VG £40 | F £80 | VF £160 |

York Mint

Obverse Legend Similar to H51D-015.

Reverse Legend CIVITAS EBORACI — City of York

Obverse Front-facing bust of king with tall neck; mullet to left and broken annulet to right of crown.

Reverse Quatrefoil in centre of reverse cross.

| H51D-050 | VG £25 | F £45 | VF £90 |

As previous, but a whole instead of a broken annulet beside the king.

| H51D-055 | VG £25 | F £50 | VF £100 |

As previous, but with a pellet above the mullet.

| H51D-060 | VG £40 | F £80 | VF £160 |

Sometimes with a trefoil above the mullet or with mullet to left and trefoil to right of crown.

| H51D-065 | VG £25 | F £45 | VF £90 |

New neat bust with mullet to left and trefoil to right of crown.

| H51D-070 | VG £30 | F £60 | VF £120 |

As previous, but made with local dies which make the lettering slightly crude in style. Mullet to left and lis to right of crown and an annulet in one quarter of the reverse.

| H51D-075 | VG £25 | F £55 | VF £110 |

Henry VI First Reign (1422 – 1461)

Henry VI, Henry V's son, became king while still an infant and until he came of age the controlling power in the country rested with the King's Council. Henry VI favoured peace with France but Richard Duke of York, a descendant from the second son of Edward III and heir apparent to the English throne, favoured war. In 1455 this difference precipitated the War of the Roses, the conflict between the Lancastrians (Henry VI) and the Yorkists (Edward IV). The nobility attached itself to either faction but changed allegiance as the balance of power shifted. Eventually in 1461, Henry VI was defeated by Richard's son Edward, who became Edward IV.

Henry VI's long reign is interesting from a numismatic point of view. Despite the immense upheaval and even a civil war, an adequate supply of coinage was maintained throughout the period. Several mints were active, in particular Calais. Henry's coinage may be divided into various classes, distinguished by minor varieties on the coins such as annulets or trefoils. These marks, each specific to a particular moneyer and die, were used as a form of quality control so that if there was a problem with a coin, the person responsible could be identified. There are eleven different issues in total, and all can be dated accurately. Stylistically, Henry VI's coins tend to be very different from previous issues. When identifying pay particular attention to the legend, the mint (if it is Calais it is almost definitely Henry VI), and any marks in the field or legends, such as annulets. The Henry V penny is very crude, compared to the Henry VI one which is neat. It must also be remembered that some of Henry VI's issues were muled with the last issues of Henry V. For coins from the Durham mint, if the reverse legend reads CIVITAS DUNOLIN collectors should refer to Edward IV's First Reign.

Collecting Hints

Henry VI's pennies are fairly common. Collectors simply wanting one or two examples should have no trouble; some varieties are rare, but, Fine or better examples may be found. Even VF examples are fairly common, but EF are rare. Collectors should try to obtain a fully round coin, with a good portrait and a clear legend.

Annulet Issue (1422 – 1427)

London Mint

Obverse Legend   HENRICUS REX ANGLIE — Henry King of England

Reverse Legend   CIVITAS LONDON — City of London

Obverse   Front-facing bust of king.

Reverse   Large cross with three pellets in each quarter, annulet in two quarters.

| H61D-005 | VG £25 | F £50 | VF £100 |

Calais Mint

Obverse Legend   As previous.

Reverse Legend   VILLA CALISIE — Town of Calais

Obverse   Front-facing bust of king with an annulet either side of neck.

Reverse   As previous.

| H61D-010 | VG £22 | F £45 | VF £90 |

As previous, but only one annulet in quarter on the reverse.

| H61D-015 | VG £25 | F £50 | VF £100 |

York Mint

Obverse Legend   As previous.

Reverse Legend   CIVITAS EBORACI — City of York

Obverse   Front-facing bust of king, a lis either side of neck.

Reverse   Annulets in two quarters on reverse.

| H61D-020 | VG £300 | F £650 | VF — |

Annulet Trefoil Sub-Issue
Calais Mint

Similar to H61D-010, but a trefoil of pellets to left of crown; two annulets on the reverse.

| H61D-025 | VG £50 | F £100 | VF £200 |

Similar to above, but only one annulet on the reverse.

| H61D-030 | VG £60 | F £120 | VF £240 |

Rosette Mascle Issue (1427 – 1430)

All these issues have rosettes and mascles somewhere in the legends.

London Mint

Obverse Legend HENRICUS REX ANGLIE — Henry King of England

Reverse Legend CIVITAS LONDON — City of London

Obverse Front-facing bust of king, no marks by crown or neck.

Reverse Cross with three pellets in each quarter.

| H61D-035 | VG £40 | F £80 | VF £160 |

Calais Mint

As previous, but the reverse legend reads VILLA CALISIE — Town of Calais.

| H61D-040 | VG £30 | F £60 | VF £120 |

York Mint

York was an ecclesiastical mint under the control of Archbishop Kemp. Many of these issues appear to be clipped.

Obverse Legend As previous.

Reverse Legend CIVITAS EBORACI (sometimes misspelt) — City of York

Obverse Front-facing bust of king, crosses by hair, no rosette in legend.

Reverse Cross with quatrefoil in centre.

| H61D-045 | VG £25 | F £50 | VF £100 |

As previous, but saltires by hair.

| H61D-050 | VG £25 | F £50 | VF £100 |

As previous, but no saltires by hair, with a mullet either side of crown.

| H61D-055 | VG £25 | F £50 | VF £100 |

Durham Mint

At the time, Durham was an ecclesiastical mint under the control of Bishop Langley.

Obverse Legend As previous.

Reverse Legend CIVITAS DVNOLMI — City of Durham

Obverse Star to left of crown, no rosettes in legend.

Reverse Plain cross in centre, three pellets in each quarter.

| H61D-060 | VG £50 | F £100 | VF £200 |

Pinecone Mascle Issue (1430 – 1434)

All the coins from this issue have a pinecone and a mascle in the legend.

London Mint

Obverse Legend HENRICUS REX ANGLIE — Henry King of England

Reverse Legend CIVITAS LONDON — City of London

Obverse Front-facing bust of king, no marks in field.

Reverse Plain cross, three pellets in each quarter.

| H61D-065 | VG £50 | F £100 | VF £200 |

Calais Mint

As previous, but the reverse legend reads VILLA CALISIE — Town of Calais.

| H61D-070 | VG £25 | F £50 | VF £100 |

York Ecclesiastical Mint under Archbishop Kemp

Obverse Legend As previous.

Reverse Legend CIVITAS EBORACI — City of York

Obverse Mullet by crown.

Reverse Quatrefoil in centre of cross.

| H61D-075 | VG £25 | F £50 | VF £100 |

Legends As previous.

Obverse Rosette on breast.

Reverse No quatrefoil in centre of the reverse cross.

| H61D-080 | VG £25 | F £50 | VF £100 |

As previous, but a mullet on breast instead of a rosette.

| H61D-085 | VG £25 | F £50 | VF £100 |

Durham Mint

Durham was an ecclesiastical mint under the control of Bishop Langley.

Obverse Legend As previous.

Reverse Legend CIVITAS DVNOLMI — City of Durham

Obverse Front-facing bust of king, no marks.

Reverse Cross with three pellets in each quarter.

| H61D-090 | VG £50 | F £100 | VF £200 |

Leaf Mascle Issue (1434 – 1435)

London Mint

Obverse Legend HENRICUS REX ANGLIE — Henry King of England

Reverse Legend CIVITAS LONDON — City of London

Obverse Front-facing bust of king, leaf on breast, mascle and saltires in legend.

Reverse Plain cross with three pellets in each quarter.

H61D-095 VG £40 F £80 VF £160

Calais Mint

Obverse Legend   As previous.

Reverse Legend   VILLA CALISIE — Town of Calais

Obverse   Front-facing bust of king, leaf on breast.

Reverse   As previous, but mascle and saltires in legend and a leaf below SIE.

H61D-100   VG £40   F £80   VF £160

Leaf Trefoil Issue (1435 – 1438)
London Mint

Obverse Legend   HENRICUS REX ANGLIE — Henry King of England

Reverse Legend   CIVITAS LONDON — City of London

Obverse   Front-facing bust of king, leaf on breast, saltires and trefoil in legend.

Reverse   Plain cross with three pellets in each quarter, leaf and trefoil in legend.

H61D-105   VG £50   F £100   VF £200

Calais Mint

As previous, except that the reverse legend reads VILLA CALISIE — Town of Calais.

H61D-110   ex. rare

Durham Mint

Obverse Legend   HENRICUS REX ANGLIE — Henry King of England

Reverse Legend   CIVITAS DUNOLM — City of Durham

Obverse   Front-facing bust of king, leaf on breast, saltires and leaf in legend.

Reverse   Cross on reverse with two rings in centre, no marks in legend.

H61D-115   VG £75   F £150   VF £300

No pennies were struck for the trefoil issue (1438 – 1454).

Leaf Pellet Issue (1445 – 1454)
London Mint

Obverse Legend   HENRICUS REX ANGLIE — Henry King of England

Reverse Legend   CIVITAS LONDON — City of London

Obverse   Front-facing bust of king with leaf on breast, a pellet either side of crown, saltires in legend.

Reverse   Plain cross sometimes with an extra pellet in two quarters.

H61D-120   VG £35   F £70   VF £140

As previous, but no pellets by crown.

H61D-125   VG £35   F £70   VF £140

Similar to H61D-120, but a trefoil in obverse legend.

H61D-130   VG £40   F £80   VF £160

York Mint

York was an ecclesiastical mint under the control of Archbishop Booth.

Obverse Legend   HENRICUS REX ANGLIE — Henry King of England

Reverse Legend   CIVITAS EBORACI — City of York

Obverse   Front-facing bust of king sometimes with leaf on breast; a pellet either side of crown.

Reverse   Quatrefoil and pellet in centre of reverse, sometimes an extra pellet in two quarters.

H61D-135   VG £25   F £50   VF £100

There is also a variety, slightly crude in style, which was struck with local dies. It is identical to the previous issue, but there is another pellet either side of the king's hair.

H61D-140   VG £25   F £50   VF £100

Durham Mint

Durham was an ecclesiastical mint under the control of Bishop Neville.

Obverse Legend   As previous.

Reverse Legend   CIVITAS DUNOLM — City of Durham

Obverse   Front-facing bust of king with leaf on breast, sometimes trefoil in legend.

Reverse   Cross with two rings in centre.

H61D-145   VG £75   F £150   VF £300

No pennies were struck during the unmarked issue (1453 – 54).

Cross Pellet Issue (1454 – 1460)
London Mint

Obverse Legend   HENRICUS REX ANGLIE — Henry King of England

Reverse Legend   CIVITAS LONDON — City of London

Obverse   Front-facing bust of king, a saltire on neck and a pellet either side of crown.

Reverse   Plain cross, three pellets in each quarter, mascle(s) or mullet and mascle in legend.

H61D-150   VG £80   F £160   VF £320

York Mint

York was an ecclesiastical mint under the control of Archbishop William Booth.

Obverse Legend   As previous.

Reverse Legend   CIVITAS EBORACI — City of York

Obverse   Front-facing bust of king, leaf sometimes on breast, saltires beside neck.

Reverse   Quatrefoil in centre of cross.

H61D-155   VG £50   F £100   VF £200

Durham Mint

Durham was an ecclesiastical mint under the control of Bishop Laurence Booth.

Obverse Legend   HENRICUS REX ANGLIE — Henry King of England

Reverse Legend   CIVITAS DUNOLM — City of Durham

Obverse   Saltire and 'B' either side of neck, a pellet either side of crown.

Reverse   Two rings in centre of cross, the three pellets in each quarter are sometimes linked by lines.

| H61D-160 | VG £100 | F £200 | VF £400 |

No pennies were struck for the lis-pellet issue (1456 – 60).

Edward IV First Reign (1461 – 1470)

In 1461, Edward Duke of York deposed Henry VI and proclaimed himself King Edward IV of England. With the Lancastrians defeated, Henry fled and was finally captured and imprisoned in the Tower of London. He was released and restored to the throne in 1470, but only for a few months. Throughout this period virtual civil war raged in England but the continuing conflict did not affect the output of coinage, not least because issuing coins in the name of a new king was a means of manifesting his authority.

Under Edward IV, the heavy and the light coinages were produced. With the rising value of silver in Europe, coins from England were again being smuggled abroad, melted down and sold at a profit. As a result, in 1464, the weight of all coins was reduced by about 20%, producing the light coinage. Heavy coinage pennies weigh about 15 grains (1.0 gram) and those from the light coinage weigh 12 grains (0.8 grams). Edward's coins are quite easy to distinguish. Above, in the section devoted to Edward III, we have listed how these coins differ from the previous issues of Edward I to Edward III. In order to identify an Edward IV penny, collectors should first check that the obverse legend bears the king's name EDWARD. Secondly look at the face, which in Edward IV's case will be fairly youthful. Compare it to Edward I, II, III, and also Edward IV's second reign, paying particular attention to the crown and hair style. The coins from Edward IV's second reign tend to be very crude in style. It is also important to remember that the coinage became progressively smaller in size.

Having identified the monarch, it is important to find the mint, which is on the reverse, preceded by the word VILLA (town) or CIVITAS (city). For Edward IV they are the following:

CIVITAS LONDON	City of London
CIVITAS DVNOLIN	City of Durham
CIVITAS BRISTOLI or BRISTOW	City of Bristol
CIVITAS CANTOR	City of Canterbury
CIVITAS EBORACI	City of York

If a coin is not from one of the above mints, it is not Edward IV's first reign.

After finding the correct mint, look for marks of interest on the coin, usually found on the obverse near the king's head. When you have found some marks, go through the following pages until you find the exact variety. If it is not there, check Edward IV's second reign carefully.

Heavy Coinage (1461 – 1464)

Weighing 15 grains (1.0 gram), these coins are, in some cases, very similar to the light coinage. Collectors should check every detail carefully and, if necessary, weigh the coin; also note that several dies from this issue omitted DI GRA in the obverse legend.

London Mint

Obverse Legend   EDWARD DI GRA REX ANGL — Edward by the grace of God King of England

Reverse Legend   CIVITAS LONDON — City of London

Obverse   Front-facing bust of king, lis on breast, pellet either side of crown and mascle after REX; mintmark plain cross.

Reverse   Extra pellet in two quarters of the reverse cross.

| E41D-005 | VG £125 | F £250 | VF £500 |

Legends   As previous.

Obverse   Front-facing bust of king, quatrefoils by neck; mintmark rose.

Reverse   Cross with three pellets in each quarter.

| E41D-010 | ex. rare |

As previous, but an eye after 'TAS' in reverse legend.

| E41D-015 | VG £150 | F £300 | VF £600 |

Legends   As previous.

Obverse   Front-facing bust of king, annulets by neck; mintmark rose.

Reverse   Cross with three pellets in each quarter.

| E41D-020 | VG £160 | F £350 | VF £650 |

York Mint

York was an ecclesiastical mint under the control of Archbishop Booth.

Obverse Legend   EDWARD DI GRA REX ANG — Edward by the grace of God King of England

Reverse Legend   CIVITAS EBORACI — City of York

Obverse   Front-facing bust of king, quatrefoils by bust, mintmark rose.

Reverse   Voided quatrefoil in centre of reverse cross.

E41D-025	VG £125	F £250	VF £500

Durham Mint

There is uncertainty as to where to class this type. It would appear that the obverse is from a Henry VI penny. The reverse, with the spelling of Durham DUNOLIN, appears to be that of Edward IV. Both have mintmarks of plain cross and this was used during the reigns of both Henry VI and Edward IV. Sometimes this issue has one or more pellets beside the crown and, on the reverse, a rose in the centre and an extra pellet in the quarters.

Obverse Legend   HENRICUS REX ANGLIE (or altered die) — Henry King of England

Reverse Legend   CIVITAS DUNOLIN — City of Durham

Obverse   Front-facing crowned bust of Henry VI.

Reverse   As previous.

E41D-030	VG £125	F £250	VF £500

Light Coinage (1464 – 1470)

These pennies weigh 12 grains (0.8 grams); sometimes DI GRA is omitted from the obverse legend. Also, some words miss out odd letters.

London Mint

Obverse Legend   EDWARD DI GRA REX ANGL — Edward by the grace of God King of England

Reverse Legend   CIVITAS LONDON — City of London

Obverse   Front-facing bust of king, annulets by neck; mintmark rose.

Reverse   Plain cross, three pellets in each quarter.

This coin was struck using the heavy coinage die; the weight should, therefore, be checked.

E41D-035	VG —	F £150	VF £300

As previous, but quatrefoils at neck, mintmark sun or crown.

E41D-040	VG £30	F £60	VF £120

As previous, but trefoil and quatrefoil by neck; mintmark crown.

E41D-045	VG £32	F £65	VF £130

As previous, but saltires by neck; mintmark crown.

E41D-050	VG £32	F £65	VF £130

As previous, but trefoils by neck; mintmark crown or long cross fitchée.

E41D-055	VG £30	F £60	VF £120

As previous, but front-facing bust of king without marks; mintmark long cross fitchée.

E41D-060	ex. rare

Bristol Mint

Obverse Legend   EDWARD DI GRA REX ANGL — Edward by the grace of God King of England

Reverse Legend   VILLA BRISTOW — Town of Bristol

Obverse   Front-facing bust of king, quatrefoils or saltires by neck; mintmark crown.

Reverse   Plain cross, three pellets in each quarter.

E41D-065	VG £90	F £180	VF £360

Obverse Legend   As previous.

Reverse Legend   VILLA BRI (trefoil) STOLL — Town of Bristol

Obverse   As previous, with quatrefoils by neck.

Reverse   As previous, but trefoil in legend.

E41D-070	VG £100	F £200	VF £400

Obverse Legend   As previous.

Reverse Legend   VILLA BRISTOLL — Town of Bristol

Obverse   Trefoil to right of neck.

Reverse   As previous.

E41D-075	VG £110	F £225	VF £450

Canterbury Mint

Two mints were active in Canterbury during this period. The ecclesiastical mint under Archbishop Bourchier, and the royal mint under the control of the king.

Canterbury Ecclesiastical Mint

Obverse Legend   EDWARD DI GRA REX ANGL — Edward by the grace of God King of England

Reverse Legend   CIVITAS CANTOR — City of Canterbury

Obverse   Front-facing bust of king, quatrefoils or saltires by neck, knot on breast; mintmark pall.

Reverse   Plain cross, three pellets in each quarter.

E41D-080	VG £75	F £150	VF £300

As previous, but no marks by neck.

E41D-085	VG £75	F £150	VF £300

As E41D-080, but no knot on king's breast.

E41D-090	VG £80	F £160	VF £320

As previous, but crosses by neck.

E41D-095	VG £75	F £150	VF £300

Canterbury Royal Mint

As previous, but quatrefoils by neck; mintmark crown.

E41D-100	VG £125	F £250	VF £500

Durham Mint
King's Receiver

Varieties of this type exist. The legends are often blundered for Durham and York, especially with the locally made dies issue.

Obverse Legend   EDWARD REX ANGLIE — Edward by the grace of God King of England (varieties exist)

Reverse Legend   CIVITAS DUNOLM, DVNOLI, DER(H)AM — City of Durham (varieties)

Obverse   Front-facing bust of king; mintmark plain cross or rose.

Reverse   Rose usually in centre.

E41D-105	VG £20	F £40	VF £80

Bishop Booth

Legends   As previous.

Obverse   'B' and 'D' either side of neck; mintmark rose.

Reverse   'B' in centre.

E41D-110	VG £30	F £60	VF £120

As previous, but quatrefoil and 'B' by neck; mintmark sun.

E41D-115	VG £30	F £60	VF £120

Legends   As previous.

Obverse   'D' and quatrefoil by neck; mintmark sun.

Reverse   Plain cross.

E41D-120	VG £30	F £60	VF £120

Legends   As previous.

Obverse   Quatrefoils by neck, mintmark crown.

Reverse   Plain cross.

E41D-125	VG £30	F £60	VF £120

As previous, but trefoils by neck; mintmark crown.

E41D-130	VG £30	F £60	VF £120

As previous, but lis by neck; mintmark crown.

E41D-135	VG £32	F £65	VF £130

York Mint
Sede Vacante Issue (1464 – 1465)

Obverse Legend   EDWARD DI GRA REX ANGL — Edward by the grace of God King of England

Reverse Legend   CIVITAS EBORACI — City of York

Obverse   Front-facing bust of king; quatrefoils either side of neck; mintmark sun or rose.

Reverse   Plain cross.

E41D-140	VG £45	F £90	VF £180

Ecclesiastical Mint under Archbishop Neville (1465 – 1470)
This issue was rather crude in style, being struck from locally made dies.

Legends   As previous.

Obverse   Front-facing bust of king, a 'G' and key by neck; mintmark plain cross or rose.

Reverse   Quatrefoil in centre.

E41D-145	VG £32	F £65	VF £130

As previous, but struck from better quality London-made dies and bearing different mintmarks: sun, lis, or long cross fitchée.

E41D-150	VG £22	F £45	VF £90

As previous, but no marks by neck; mintmark large lis.

E41D-155	ex. rare

As previous, but quatrefoils by neck.

E41D-160	VG £32	F £65	VF £130

As previous, but trefoils by neck.

E41D-165	VG £40	F £80	VF £160

Henry VI Restored
(Oct. 1470 – April 1471)

During Edward IV's reign England was being torn apart by the War of the Roses and in October 1470 the king was forced to flee to the Continent, and Henry VI was released from the Tower and restored to the throne. This second reign of his however only lasted a few months as Edward, having mustered support for his own restoration, returned to England in 1471, defeated his enemies and regained the throne. Henry VI was once again imprisoned in the Tower, where he was murdered the same night.

Despite the brevity of Henry VI's second reign, three mints were active and, in the case of the London mint, three different dies were used. The coins of Henry VI's restored reign are fairly similar to those of his first reign but with a few minor differences. Firstly, the mintmark, found in the legend above the king's head, which for London is a cross pattée, Restoration Cross or a short cross fitchée; Henry's first reign coinage did not use these mintmarks. However, Henry V did use a cross pattée, but this had a pellet in the centre. If the mintmark is not clearly visible, collectors will have to compare the styles of Henry V and Henry VI; they are very different, with the Henry V issues being very crude in style.

The minor differences between the reigns are as follows :
1. A cross pattée with a pellet in the centre is found on issues of Henry V.
2. There is a slight difference in the obverse legend, which for Henry VI Restored is HENRIC (or HENRICU, HERICU) DI GRA REX ANGL (or ANG). The legend of Henry VI's first reign usually reads HENRICUS REX ANGLIE. Pay particular attention to the king's name and the spelling, as in all cases it is different from the previous issue.

Collecting Hints

The short period of Henry VI's second reign explains why all issues are rare, in every grade. Collectors should try to obtain an example in at least Fine condition, so that it can be easily differentiated from previous issues.

London Mint

Obverse Legend   HENRIC DI GRA REX ANGL — Henry by the grace of God King of England

Reverse Legend   CIVITAS LONDON — City of London

Obverse   Front-facing bust of king; mintmarks cross pattée, Restoration cross, short cross fitchée.

Reverse   Cross with three pellets in each quarter.

H61D-165	VG £225	F £500	VF £1,000

Bristol Mint

This coin is of the highest rarity.

Obverse Legend   As previous.

Reverse Legend   CIVITAS BRISTOW — City of Bristol

Obverse   As previous, with mintmark cross fitchée only.

Reverse   As previous.

H61D-170   ex. rare

York Mint

Obverse Legend   As previous.

Reverse Legend   CIVITAS EBORACI — City of York

Obverse   Front-facing bust of king, 'G' and a key either side of neck; mintmark lis.

Reverse   A quatrefoil in centre of the reverse cross.

H61D-175	VG £150	F £400	VF £800

Edward IV Second Reign
(1471 – 1483)

Edward IV landed in England in 1471 to recover the throne from Henry VI and, after two victories at Barnet and Tewkesbury, succeeded.

The coinage of Edward's second reign continued from the first reign. All the denominations and styles remained the same.

The 'initial mark', or mintmark, was becoming increasingly more important as a form of quality control, linking coins to specific dies without the coins having to look different to the general public which in England, as elsewhere, wanted conformity in the coinage. It is important to bear in mind that a coin had to be actually worth its weight in silver or gold, it was not a token or a promissory issue but a penny's worth of silver. Before accepting it in payment, traders would inspect a coin carefully, particularly as forgeries were produced in large quantities and clipped coins and inferior European issues were in circulation. But the mintmark also served another purpose, which is especially useful to the collector, as coins can be accurately dated using the mintmark. In previous issues, such as Henry VI's and Edward IV's first reigns, many issues can be dated to within a few years. However, during Edward IV's second reign, the use of the mintmark to denote the date was firmly established.

As mentioned earlier, the issues of the second reign are very similar to those of the first and in that section we have given full details on how to differentiate Edward IV's reign from others. Then, an elimination process has to be used to differentiate between Edward IV's own two reigns. Firstly, find the mint where the coin was issued. This can be found on the reverse of the coin and should read as follows:

CIVITAS LONDON	City of London
CIVITAS BRISTOW or BRISTOLL	City of Bristol
CIVITAS CANTOR	City of Canterbury
CIVITAS DERAM or DUNOLMIE	City of Durham
CIVITAS EBORACI	City of York

Now that you know where the coin was issued, look for the mintmark in the obverse legend above the king's head. Finally, look for any unusual marks on the coin. These can often be found on either side of the king's neck. Then, using an elimination process, go through the various types until you find one which corresponds to your coin.

Should you have difficulty in classifying your coin, re-check the obverse legend making sure it is a coin of Edward. Then re-check, using the information on Edward IV's first reign, to make sure that you have the correct Edward. Do not be too concerned if your coin is not exactly like the coin in the illustration. Many different dies were used, and no two dies are exactly the same.

Also bear in mind that letters, during this period, were not always written as they are today.

The mintmarks found on coins from Edward IV's second reign are as follows:

Mint	Mintmark	Date
York or Durham	rose	1471-83
	short cross fitchée	1471
	large annulet, trefoil	1471-72
Bristol	rose	1471-72
Durham	pansy	1471-73
	small annulet	1472-73
Bristol	sun	1472-73
	pellet in annulet	1473-77
	cross and four pellets	
	cross in circle	
	cross pattée	1473-77
	pierced cross	
	pierced cross and pellet	1477-80
	pierced cross	
	pierced cross and central pellet	
Canterbury	rose	
	heraldic cinquefoil	1480-83
Canterbury	long cross fitchée	
	halved sun and rose?[1]	

1. It is uncertain whether this mintmark is for Edward IV or for Edward V.

Collecting Hints

As already mentioned Edward IV second reign is very much a continuation of his first reign and this is found in the quality of coins, which are usually obtainable in VG to Fine condition and are often clipped and damaged.

London Mint

Obverse Legend EDWARD DI GRA REX ANGL — Edward by the grace of God King of England

Reverse Legend CIVITAS LONDON — City of London

Obverse No marks by bust; mintmarks from 1471 short cross fitchée to 1480 – 83 heraldic cinquefoil (refer to table).

Reverse Plain cross, three pellets in each quarter.

E41D-170	VG £30	F £60	VF £120

Bristol Mint

This issue is of the highest rarity.

Obverse Legend As previous.

Reverse Legend CIVITAS BRISTOW — City of Bristol

Obverse As previous; mintmark rose.

Reverse As previous.

E41D-175	ex. rare

Canterbury Mint

Obverse Legend As previous.

Reverse Legend CIVITAS CANTOR — City of Canterbury

Obverse As previous; mintmark rose or long cross fitchée.

Reverse As previous.

E41D-180	VG £60	F £120	VF £240

As previous, but a 'C' on the king's breast and mintmark rose only.

E41D-185	VG £65	F £130	VF £250

Durham Mint

This was an ecclesiastical mint under the control of Bishop Booth.

Obverse Legend As previous.

Reverse Legend CIVITAS DERAM or DUNOLMIE — City of Durham

Obverse No marks on coin; mintmark short cross fitchée or trefoil.

Reverse No marks in centre of cross.

E41D-190	VG £22	F £45	VF £90

Legends As previous.

Obverse 'B' and trefoil by neck; mintmark trefoil, rose or pellet in annulet.

Reverse 'D' in centre of reverse cross.

E41D-195	VG £25	F £50	VF £100

Legends As previous.

Obverse A lis either side of the neck; mintmark rose.

Reverse 'D' in centre of reverse cross.

E41D-200	VG £22	F £45	VF £90

The following issues (E41D-205 – 235) were struck from locally made dies.

Legends As previous.

Obverse Crosses over crown and on breast; mintmark rose.

Reverse 'D' in centre of reverse cross, extra pellet in one or four quarters.

E41D-205	VG £22	F £45	VF £90

Legends As previous.

Obverse Crosses over crown; mintmark rose or pansy.

Reverse 'D' in centre of cross, a 'V' under CIVI in legend.

E41D-210	VG £25	F £50	VF £100

As previous, but 'B' to left of crown, 'V' on breast; mintmark pansy.

E41D-215	VG £20	F £40	VF £80

As previous, but crosses by shoulders.

E41D-220	VG £20	F £40	VF £80

Sede Vacante Issue (1476)

Legends As previous.
Obverse Plain bust, no marks; mintmark rose.
Reverse 'D' in centre of reverse.

| E41D-225 | VG £35 | F £70 | VF £140 |

Bishop Dudley Issue

Legends As previous.
Obverse 'V' to right of neck; mintmark rose.
Reverse 'D' in centre of reverse cross.

| E41D-230 | VG £25 | F £50 | VF £100 |

Legends As previous.
Obverse 'D' and 'V' either side of neck; mintmark heraldic cinquefoil.
Reverse In most cases a 'D' in the centre of reverse cross.

| E41D-235 | VG £20 | F £40 | VF £80 |

York Ecclesiastical Mint

Archbishop Neville Issue (1471 – 1472)

Obverse Legend As previous.
Reverse Legend CIVITAS EBORACI — City of York
Obverse Front-facing bust of king, quatrefoils by neck; mintmark short cross fitchée over lis.
Reverse Quatrefoil in centre of reverse cross.

| E41D-240 | VG £100 | F £200 | VF £400 |

As previous, but 'G' and key either side of neck on obverse; mintmark short cross fitchée over lis.

| E41D-245 | VG £20 | F £40 | VF £80 |

Sede Vacante Issue (1472 – 1475) (Archbishop Neville suspended)

As previous, but plain cross in centre of reverse, no quatrefoil.

| E41D-250 | VG £20 | F £40 | VF £80 |

Legends As previous.
Obverse No marks by neck; mintmark small annulet, cross in circle or rose. A few issues have a rose on the breast
Reverse Quatrefoil in the reverse cross in most cases.

| E41D-255 | VG £100 | F £200 | VF £400 |

Legends As previous.
Obverse 'E' and rose either side of neck; mintmark rose.
Reverse Quatrefoil in centre.

| E41D-260 | VG £22 | F £45 | VF £90 |

Archbishop Neville restored (1475 – 1476)

As previous, but 'G' and rose either side of king's neck; mintmark rose.

| E41D-265 | VG £22 | F £45 | VF £90 |

As previous, but 'G' and key either side of neck; mintmark rose over annulet.

| E41D-270 | VG £25 | F £50 | VF £100 |

As previous, but mintmark rose.

| E41D-275 | VG £22 | F £45 | VF £90 |

Sede Vacante Issue (1476)

As previous, but no marks by neck; mintmark rose. Rose on king's breast. Quatrefoil on reverse.

| E41D-280 | VG £25 | F £50 | VF £100 |

Archbishop Lawrence Booth Issue (1476 – 1480)

As previous, but 'B' and key either side of neck; mintmark rose and cinquefoil.

| E41D-285 | VG £22 | F £45 | VF £90 |

Sede Vacante Issue (1480)

Legends As previous.
Obverse 'B' and key either side of neck; mintmark rose.
Reverse Plain cross, no quatrefoil.

| E41D-290 | VG £25 | F £50 | VF £100 |

Archbishop Rotherham Issue (1480 – 1483)

Legends As previous.
Obverse 'T' and key either side of neck; mintmark rose.
Reverse Quatrefoil in centre.

| E41D-295 | VG £25 | F £50 | VF £100 |

As previous, but a star on the king's breast.

| E41D-300 | VG £100 | F £250 | VF — |

As previous, but a star on the king's breast and to the right of the king's crown.

| E41D-305 | VG £65 | F £150 | VF £300 |

Edward IV or V

As mentioned earlier, there is uncertainty regarding which reign this issue should be classed in, but most numismatists are of the opinion that, while the dies were made for Edward IV's second reign, they were used to produce coinage under Edward V. Despite the uncertainty, the issue is extremely rare. It was struck at the London mint and the only way to differentiate it is through the mintmark which is halved sun and rose.

Obverse Legend   EDWARD DI GRA REX ANGL — Edward by the grace of God King of England

Reverse Legend   CIVITAS LONDON — City of London

Obverse   Plain bust of king, no marks, but mintmark halved sun and rose.

Reverse   Plain cross, three pellets in each quarter.

E41D-310	VG —	F £1,000	VF £2,200

Edward V   (1483)

Edward V was only 12 years old when, upon his fathers death, he inherited the throne. As the country could obviously not be governed by a child, rival factions tried to obtain control and Richard Duke of Gloucester, who was the younger brother of Edward IV, proclaimed himself Protector of the Realm. To consolidate power he executed his rivals and placed Edward V and his younger brother Richard in the Tower of London where they were murdered a few months later.

While evidence exists that pennies were struck, it is uncertain that any have survived. From records we believe that the London mint produced coins for this period with a boar's head as mintmark. From what we can ascertain from contemporary evidence, this issue is as follows:

Obverse Legend   EDWARD DI GRA REX ANGL — Edward by the grace of God King of England

Reverse Legend   CIVITAS LONDON — City of London

Obverse   Front-facing bust of king, no marks; mintmark boar's head.

Reverse   Cross, three pellets in each quarter.

E51D-005	ex. rare

Richard III   (1483 – 1485)

Richard Duke of Gloucester usurped his nephew Edward V in 1483 and reigned as Richard III. He was, however, blamed for the murder of the young king and his ruthlessness alienated many of the nobility who had previously supported him. Having survived one rebellion, Richard was killed during the Battle of Bosworth.

This short reign produced few changes in the coinage but all of Richard III's coins are rare, and fairly easy to differentiate. Firstly, the obverse legend begins with the king's name, RICARD, and only one other issue is similar, that of Richard II. Richard I's coins read HENRICUS. To distinguish between the coins of Richard II and Richard III look at the different style of hair, eyes and the size. Then look at the mintmark, in the legend above the king; Richard II only used mintmark cross pattée while Richard III's coinage did not use this but the mintmarks boar's head, sun and rose, or rose and lis instead.

Collecting Hints

All of Richard III's coins are rare. Pennies tend to be found in about Fine condition, often on small flans with weaknesses in the legend. It is fairly difficult to find a coin in Fine or better condition. Collectors who simply want a coin from this reign might well consider a groat, which is a more attractive and more readily available coin, but please note that any Richard III coin is expensive.

London Mint

Obverse Legend   RICARD DEI GRA REX ANG(L) — Richard by the grace of God King of England

Reverse Legend   CIVITAS LONDON — City of London

Obverse   Front-facing bust of king; mintmark boar's head.

Reverse   Plain cross, three pellets in each quarter.

R31D-005	unique

York Mint

This was an ecclesiastical mint under the control of Archbishop Rotherham.

Obverse Legend   As previous.

Reverse Legend   CIVITAS EBORACI — City of York

Obverse   Bust of king with no marks; mintmark sun and rose.

Reverse   Quatrefoil in centre.

R31D-010	VG £250	F £500	VF £1,000

As previous, but 'T' and key either side of neck; mintmark rose or boar's head.

R31D-015	VG £150	F £300	VF £600

Durham Mint

This was an ecclesiastical mint under the control of the Bishop of Sherwood.

Obverse Legend   As previous.

Reverse Legend   CIVITAS DURRAM — City of Durham

Obverse   'S' on king's breast; mintmark lis.

Reverse   'D' in centre of reverse cross.

R31D-020	VG £125	F £250	VF £600

Henry VII   (1485 – 1509)

In 1485, Henry Tudor sailed with his army from France and landed at Milford Haven in Wales. He confronted Richard III at the Battle of Bosworth, defeating his army and killing him, whereupon he assumed the English throne as Henry VII. Although Henry was a Tudor, he descended from Lancastrians and by his marriage to Elizabeth of York finally succeeded in ending the Wars of the Roses.

Henry VII's reign was important for the production of coinage and new denominations were introduced, such as the sovereign (20 shillings) and the testoon (one shilling). Moreover the whole style of the coinage, which had remained more or less unaltered for over two hundred years, changed; this is particularly noticeable with denominations such as the groat and though somewhat less noticeable with the penny. The king's bust became much more lifelike and the reverse shields far more detailed. Undoubtedly influenced by the European Renaissance, the quality of coins was improved. Henry VII's pennies can be divided into two main types: the old type which, at a rough glance, is similar to that of previous kings, such as Henry VI, and the so-called 'sovereign' type which depicts the king seated on the throne on the obverse and the royal shield over a cross dividing the legend on the reverse.

First Coinage

This fairly scarce issue is similar to that of Henry VI and Henry V. However, there are some important differences. Having established that a penny is a Henry by checking that the obverse legend begins with HENRIC, compare the styles using the illustrations below; Henry VII's hair and crown are very different in style. Also look at the reverse where the centre cross on Henry VII's coinage is usually thinner and the three pellets in each quarter smaller. Finally pay attention to the mintmark, found above and slightly to the right of the king's head; Henry VII used mintmarks that are not found on the previous issues.

Collecting Hints

Pennies from this issue are surprisingly difficult to obtain, especially when compared to the groats and halfgroats which tend to be readily available. Collectors should try to obtain an example in at least Fine condition. When this issue is available it tends to be in reasonable condition, unclipped and usually on full flans.

London Mint

Obverse Legend   HENRIC DI GRA REX ANG (varieties) — Henry by the grace of God King of England

Reverse Legend   CIVITAS LONDON — City of London

Obverse   Front-facing bust of king; mintmark lis upon sun and rose.

Reverse   Cross with three pellets in each quarter.

| H71D-005 | VG £225 | F £450 | VF £900 |

A very rare variety exists with crosses either side of bust.

| H71D-010 | ex. rare |

Canterbury Mint

While the crown looks similar to that of Henry VI, this issue is the only one with the letter M in the centre of the reverse cross.

Obverse Legend   As previous.

Reverse Legend   CIVITAS CANTOR — City of Canterbury

Obverse   The king has an open instead of an arched crown; mintmark tun.

Reverse   'M', for Archbishop Morton, in centre of cross.

| H71D-015 | ex. rare |

Legends   As previous.

Obverse   The king has an arched crown; mintmark tun.

Reverse   Plain cross in centre.

| H71D-020 | VG £40 | F £80 | VF £160 |

Durham Mint

Obverse Legend   As previous.

Reverse Legend   CIVITAS DERAM — City of Durham

Obverse   'S', for Bishop Sherwood, on king's breast; mintmark cross.

Reverse   'D' in centre of reverse cross.

| H71D-025 | VG £70 | F £140 | VF £280 |

York Mint

Obverse Legend   As previous.

Reverse Legend   CIVITAS EBORACI — City of York

Obverse   'T' and cross either side of king's bust. This issue sometimes has a cross on the king's breast; mintmark lis upon sun and rose.

Reverse   'H' in centre of reverse cross.

| H71D-030 | VG £35 | F £70 | VF £140 |

Legends   As previous.

Obverse   'T' and trefoil either side of king's bust; mintmark lis over sun and rose.

Reverse   Quatrefoil in centre of cross, and an extra pellet in two quarters.

| H71D-035 | VG £40 | F £80 | VF £160 |

Sovereign Coinage

The sovereign coinage is so called because the new style, showing the sovereign on the throne, was first used in the production of Henry VII sovereigns. That coin dramatically put an end to the two hundred year old style which had changed little since the reign of Edward I, signalling the close of medieval England and the dawn of the Renaissance period.

The weight of the coins remained the same as in the previous issues but, as you can see, the new issue was far more detailed. The mintmark system remained and the mintmark, which as mentioned earlier was a form of quality control and can also be used to date various issues, can be found just to the right of the king's crown. The mint's name can also be found on the coin and, as with earlier issues, it makes up the reverse legend. The first word is always CIVITAS (City of) followed by LONDON, EBORACI (York), DERAM or DIRHAM (Durham).

As with previous issues, many varieties exist. We have listed them all. Should a coin not fall into any of these classes, remember that Henry VIII also issued sovereign pennies and refer to that section for details on how to differentiate the two reigns.

Collecting Hints

Henry VII sovereign pennies are available, usually in VG to about Fine condition. They are often slightly clipped with legends difficult to read. Collectors should try to obtain an example in at least Fine condition. VF and EF coins sometimes become available. However, as with previous issues, these are very popular with collectors and tend to sell quickly.

London Mint

Obverse Legend   HENRICUS DI GRA REX ANG (varieties) — Henry by the grace of God King of England

Reverse Legend   CIVITAS LONDON — City of London

Obverse   King seated on throne, no pillars to side of throne, no stops in legend; no mintmark.

Reverse   The king's shield over a cross.

H71D-040	ex. rare

As previous, but single pillar to throne on king's right side; mintmark lis, cinquefoil or nothing.

H71D-045	VG £20	F £45	VF £100

As previous, but ornate lettering in obverse legend with rosette stops; mintmark lis.

H71D-050	VG £25	F £50	VF £110

As previous, but two pillars either side of king; mintmark pansy or nothing, saltire stops in obverse legend.

H71D-055	VG £20	F £45	VF £100

As previous, but small square lettering in obverse legend; no mintmark.

H71D-060	VG £20	F £45	VF £100

As previous, but two double pillars either side of king; mintmark, nothing, crosslet or pheon. The legends are slightly neater in style.

H71D-065	VG £25	F £50	VF £110

Durham Ecclesiastical Mint
Bishop Sherwood

Obverse Legend   As previous.

Reverse Legend   CIVITAS DERAM or DIRHAM — City of Durham

Obverse   King seated on throne that has one pillar, crozier to right of king; no mintmark.

Reverse   'D' and 'S' either side of shield.

H71D-070	VG £25	F £55	VF £120

As previous, but the king's throne now has two pillars, no crozier.

H71D-075	VG £30	F £60	VF £130

Bishop Fox

Legends   As previous.

Obverse   King's throne with one pillar.

Reverse   Bishop's mitre above shield, 'RD' or 'DR' divided by shield.

H71D-080	VG £25	F £55	VF £120

As previous, but the king's throne has two pillars.

H71D-085	VG £25	F £55	VF £120

York Ecclesiastical Mint
under Archbishop Rotherham

Obverse Legend   As previous.

Reverse Legend   CIVITAS EBORACI — City of York

Obverse   King seated on throne with no pillars; trefoil stops in legend.

Reverse   A key either side of shield.

H71D-090	VG £25	F £55	VF £110

As previous, with a single pillar to throne.

H71D-095	VG £25	F £55	VF £110

As previous, but single pillar to throne, rosette or no marks in the legend; also the lettering is more ornate.

H71D-100	VG £25	F £55	VF £110

As previous, but a pillar either side of king, sometimes with crosses between legs of throne.

H71D-105	VG £25	F £50	VF £110

Henry VIII   (1509 – 1547)

Henry VIII's reign was not only historically important, but also saw several important numismatic changes. Henry VIII, who came to the throne at the age of only nineteen and has become notorious for his numerous wives, first married Katherine of Aragon and remained married to her for twenty-four years. During the first sixteen years of Henry's reign, the first coinage was issued; it was fairly similar to the last issue of his father, Henry VII. However, the second coinage of 1526 – 44 changed in many respects. Not only were new gold denominations introduced but, with higher bullion prices on the Continent, the weight of the silver coins was reduced to bring their value more in line with their European equivalents. Finally the style of the coins changed, except for the penny and halfpenny. Henry VIII's first coinage bore his father's portrait but his second had his own.

When Henry decided to marry Anne Boleyn, the Pope refused to dissolve his marriage with Katherine of Aragon whereupon the king broke all ties with Rome and the Catholic Church. Proclaiming himself head of the English Church, Henry precipitated a major crisis in the country as monasteries and church property were destroyed and people executed for not recognising Henry VIII as head of the Church. During this period of uncertainty the only change numismatically was the closure of the ecclesiastical privilege mints of Canterbury, York and Durham which had been an added source of revenue for the Church of Rome. From this period onwards, all mints were royal mints under the control of the crown which received all the revenue.

Although Henry profited considerably from taking over the Church, by 1544 he was running short of money not least because of his extravagant personal lifestyle and expenditure. He decided therefore to debase the silver coinage as this would provide him with huge profits. The third coinage of 1544 – 47 was duly debased and only about one third of the coins' content was actually silver, the rest being copper. This was the first time in English history since the Roman period when the intrinsic silver value of the coins did not correspond to the denominational value and the debased coinage was, understandably, extremely unpopular. The third coinage also bore a new portrait of a much older Henry while the sovereign penny was discontinued and replaced by an issue with a front-facing bust of the king. New gold denominations were introduced, due mainly to the fluctuating gold price on the Continent. Also, the testoon, the forerunner of the shilling, was successfully introduced into circulation in some quantity. Upon Henry's death in 1547, England was on the verge of a crisis; the coinage was in a poor state, the English Church was almost non existent and the legacy of Henry's tumultuous marital life were two daughters, Mary and Elizabeth, and a frail, sickly son Edward, who would succeed him.

On the face of it, Henry VIII sovereign pennies are fairly similar to those of Henry VII. When trying to identify them, collectors might be hampered by the fact that many of the coins only turn up in VG condition and are sometimes clipped, thus losing vital clues as to which issue they belong. Collectors should bear these few points in mind when identifying an issue:

– The obverse legends of Henry VII and the first issue of Henry VIII are the same, but Henry VIII's second issue bears a different legend.
– The coin's mint is found in the reverse legend.
– Having identified the mint, collectors will notice on most issues various letters beside the shield, or symbols such as keys. By going through the various issues of that mint it is possible to place the coin in its correct issue.

– If it is clear, check the mintmark which in all cases is found just to the right of the king's crown, at the beginning of the legend. Then check that the mintmark falls into the correct issue.
– Refer to the illustrations for each issue, as in some issues there are varieties, such as different styles of throne.

First Coinage (1509 – 1526)

Collecting Hints

Henry VIII's sovereign pennies are not rare and usually found in VG to about Fine condition. They are often clipped and with difficult to read legends; collectors should try to obtain an example in Fine condition. VF and EF examples sometimes become available but are usually difficult to obtain and can be expensive.

London Mint

Obverse Legend   HENRIC DI GRA REX ANGL — Henry by the grace of God King of England

Reverse Legend   CIVITAS LONDON — City of London

Obverse   Seated king on throne; mintmark castle or portcullis.

Reverse   The king's shield over a cross.

H81D-005	VG £35	F £75	VF £150

Canterbury Ecclesiastical Mint under Archbishop William Warham

Obverse Legend   As previous.

Reverse Legend   CIVITAS CANTOR — City of Canterbury

Obverse   As previous; mintmark martlet.

Reverse   'WA' above shield.

H81D-010	ex. rare

Legends   As previous.

Obverse   As previous; mintmark pomegranate.

Reverse   Shield dividing 'WA'.

H81D-015	VG £35	F £75	VF £150

Durham Ecclesiastical Mint
Bishop Thomas Ruthall (1509 – 1523)

Obverse Legend   As previous.

Reverse Legend   CIVITAS DVRRAM — City of Durham

Obverse   As previous; mintmark lis.

Reverse   'TD' above shield.

H81D-020	VG £30	F £60	VF £130

Legends   As previous.

Obverse   As previous; mintmark lis or radiant star.

Reverse   Shield dividing 'TD'.

H81D-025	VG £30	F £60	VF £130

Bishop Thomas Wolsey (1523 – 1529)

Even though this issue continued into the second coinage by some three years, the obverse legend remained the same as for all the first issues.

Legends   As previous.

Obverse   As previous; mintmark spur rowel.

Reverse   Shield dividing 'TW', Cardinal's hat below.

H81D-030	VG £60	F £150	VF £300

Second Coinage (1526 – 1544)

Collecting Hints

As for the first coinage.

London Mint

Obverse Legend   H.D.G. ROSA SIE SPIA — Henry by the grace of God a rose without a thorn (abbreviated)

Reverse Legend   CIVITAS LONDON — City of London

Obverse   Sovereign type, king on throne; mintmark rose, lis, arrow or sunburst.

Reverse   King's shield over cross.

H81D-035	VG £30	F £60	VF £120

Canterbury Ecclesiastical Mint
Archbishop William Warham

Obverse Legend   As previous.

Reverse Legend   CIVITAS CANTOR — City of Canterbury

Obverse   As previous; mintmark 'T', cross patonce, uncertain.

Reverse   Shield dividing 'WA'.

H81D-040	VG £60	F £125	VF £250

Archbishop Thomas Cranmer

Legends   As previous.

Obverse   As previous; mintmark Catherine Wheel.

Reverse   Shield dividing 'TC'.

H81D-045	VG £50	F £100	VF £200

Durham Ecclesiastical Mint
Bishop Wolsey (1529)

Obverse Legend   As previous.

Reverse Legend   CIVITAS DVRRAM — City of Durham

Obverse   As previous; mintmark trefoil, crescent, star, cross with pellet in one angle.

Reverse   Shield dividing 'TW', Cardinal's hat below shield.

H81D-050	VG £20	F £45	VF £80

Sede Vacante Issue (1529 – 1530)

Legends   As previous.

Obverse   As previous; mintmark star or radiant star.

Reverse   Plain shield and cross; no marks on reverse.

H81D-055	VG £40	F £80	VF £160

Bishop Cuthbert Tunstall (1530)

Legends & Obverse   As previous.

Reverse   Shield dividing 'CD'.

H81D-060	VG £20	F £45	VF £80

York Ecclesiastical Mint
under Archbishop Edward Lee

Obverse Legend   As previous.

Reverse Legend   CIVITAS EBORACI — City of York

Obverse   As previous; mintmark key.

Reverse   Shield dividing 'EL'.

H81D-065	VG £60	F £120	VF £240

Third Coinage or Debased Issue (1544 – 1547)

As mentioned earlier, by 1544 Henry VIII was running short of money and decided to drastically lower the fineness of his silver coins to about one third silver and two thirds copper. He also changed his portrait on the coinage; he now looked much older and had a beard. With Henry VIII head of the Church, there were no more ecclesiastical mints and mints such as York and Canterbury were controlled by the king. During this period two mints were active in London, the Tower mint and Southwark, which was situated just south of the River Thames. Southwark became an important mint so, instead of referring to a London mint, a differentiation is made henceforth between the Tower and the Southwark mints. In the third coinage there are three slightly different styles of bust which however are often difficult to recognise on small denominations such as the penny. As a result, a coin may not look exactly like the one that is photographed. Finally, collectors should bear in mind that the third coinage is fairly similar to the posthumous issue of 1547 – 51.

It should also be mentioned that, as with the groats and half-groats, pennies struck during the posthumous coinage of Henry VIII are often difficult to distinguish from issues of the third coinage, particularly if the portrait or mintmark are unclear. However, an important aid to identification for most issues is the style of lettering used in the legends. Illustrations of the various styles appear in the Mintmark chapter and below we list the style used under each coin.

Collecting Hints

Due to the poor metal content, these coins tend to be unattractive. They often look like zinc or, if they have been cleaned, the copper shines through. They also tend to be fairly small and often have parts of their legends missing. The average grade in which they are found is VG. Nevertheless, as this issue is one of historical importance and interest, collectors should try to obtain the best possible example for their collection.

Tower Mint

Obverse Legend   H.D.G. ROSA SINE SPINA — Henry by the grace of God a rose without a thorn (abbreviated)

Reverse Legend   CIVITAS LONDON — City of London

Obverse   Front-facing bust of king; mintmark lis (Lombardic lettering) or none (Lombradic or mixed Roman and Lombardic lettering, with Roman on reverse).

Reverse   King's shield over cross.

H81D-070	VG £35	F £70	VF £150

Southwark Mint

Legends   As previous.

Obverse   Front-facing bust of king; mintmark none.

Reverse   In forks of cross mintmark 'S' (Roman lettering) or 'SE' (Lombardic or mixed Roman and Lombardic lettering).

H81D-075	ex. rare

Bristol Mint

Obverse Legend   As previous.

Reverse Legend   CIVITAS BRISTOLI — City of Bristol

Obverse   Front-facing bust of king; no mintmark. Lombardic lettering.

Reverse   King's shield over cross.

H81D-080	VG £40	F £80	VF £160

Canterbury Mint

Obverse Legend   As previous.

Reverse Legend   CIVITAS CANTOR — City of Canterbury

Obverse   Front-facing bust of king; no mintmark, sometimes saltires or trefoil in legend. Lombardic lettering.

Reverse   As previous, but sometimes has a spur.

H81D-085	VG £40	F £85	VF £170

York Mint

Obverse Legend   As previous.

Reverse Legend   CIVITAS EBORACI — City of York

Obverse   Front-facing bust of king; no mintmark. Roman and Lombardic lettering.

Reverse   As H81D-070.

H81D-090	VG £40	F £85	VF £170

Posthumous Coinage

Edward VI, Henry's son from his marriage to Jane Seymour, was only nine when his father died and he inherited the throne. As he was too young to govern, the affairs of England were assumed by a Council. From 1547 to 1551 the posthumous coinage of Henry VIII was produced, still bearing Henry's name and bust. This was a period of economic unrest, generated by the inflation which was caused by the circulation of low quality coins of poor silver content. Moreover, the huge influx of South and Central American gold and silver into Spain and from there into the rest of Europe destabilised the price of bullion metals and aggravated the situation.

The posthumous issue varied little from the previous one, with the silver coins being heavily debased. The only difference with the penny was a slightly altered bust and the mintmark, which often appeared only on the reverse. The third and posthumous issues can be differentiated by the busts, as the posthumous issue has a three-quarters bust; it is also important to pay particular attention to the mintmark and ensure it matches the issue. The reverse remained the same as the third issue. During this period a new mint opened in London, the Durham House mint. Located in the Strand in what was formerly a palace of the Bishops of Durham, it became for a short period London's third mint.

Collecting Hints

The same as for the third issue.

Tower Mint

Obverse Legend   H.D.G. ROSA SINE SPINA — Henry by the grace of God a rose without a thorn (abbreviated)

Reverse Legend   CIVITAS LONDON — City of London

Obverse   Front-facing or three-quarters bust of king; mintmark arrow, 'K', grapple or none. Roman lettering.

Reverse   King's shield over cross; mintmarks as obverse.

H81D-095	VG £30	F £65	VF £130

Southwark Mint

As previous, but mintmark 'E' only. Roman lettering.

H81D-100	VG £60	F £125	VF —

Durham House Mint

Obverse Legend   As previous.

Reverse Legend   RED CUIQ Q S EST — Render to each that which is his own

Obverse   As previous, but mintmark bow. Roman lettering.

Reverse   As previous.

H81D-105   VG £100   F £200   VF—

Bristol Mint

Obverse Legend   As previous.

Reverse Legend   CIVITAS BRISTOLI — City of Bristol

Obverse   Front-facing bust of king with more body; no mintmark. Roman lettering.

Reverse   As previous.

H81D-110   VG £35   F £75   VF £150

Canterbury Mint

Obverse Legend   As previous.

Reverse Legend   CIVITAS CANTOR — City of Canterbury

Obverse   Bust of king with more body; no mintmark. Lozenge stops in legend and Lombardic lettering.

Reverse   As previous.

H81D-115   VG £30   F £70   VF £150

York Mint

Obverse Legend   As previous.

Reverse Legend   CIVITAS EBORACI — City of York

Obverse   Bust of king; no mintmark. Roman lettering.

Reverse   As previous.

H81D-120   VG £30   F £70   VF £150

Edward VI   (1547 – 1553)

Edward VI assumed the throne in 1547 at the age of nine and died in 1553, having been sickly throughout his short life and leaving no male heir. Although his reign was short, it was an important time of change for the coinage. With the English economy in a poor state, due mainly to the debasement of silver coinage, a change was necessary. Although Edward's first three issues (1547 – 53) all produced base silver coinage, the fine silver issue was introduced during the third coinage. This issue was one of new denominations, the silver crown, halfcrown, shilling, sixpence and threepence, which would last until decimalization in 1971. The coins were of good silver and high quality design. The aim was to revitalise the economy with a well produced quality coinage, which would be readily acceptable both in England and in Europe. As inflation had been rising over the previous thirty years, the penny was becoming much less important. In fact, during the next few reigns, the most common coins were the shilling, sixpence and groat. Although the main reason for the growth in larger denomination coins was the huge influx of silver

from South America coupled with inflation, England was also becoming wealthier.

First Period (1547 – 1549)

Tower Mint

Obverse Legend   E.D.G. ROSA SINE SPINA — Edward by the grace of God a rose without a thorn (abbreviated)

Reverse Legend   CIVITAS LONDON — City of London

Obverse   Side bust of crowned king; mintmark arrow.

Reverse   King's shield over cross.

E61D-005   VG £150   F £300   VF £800

Southwark Mint

As previous, but mintmark 'E' on reverse.

E61D-010   VG £150   F £300   VF £800

Bristol Mint

Obverse Legend   As previous.

Reverse Legend   CIVITAS BRISTOLI — City of Bristol

Obverse   As previous, but no mintmark.

Reverse   As previous.

E61D-015   VG £150   F £300   VF £800

No pennies were struck during the second coinage from 1549 – 50.

Third Coinage (1550 – 1553)

London Issue

It is uncertain at which London mint this issue was struck.

Obverse Legend   E.D.G. ROSA SINE SPINA — Edward by the grace of God a rose without a thorn (abbreviated)

Reverse Legend   CIVITAS LONDON — City of London

Obverse   Large rose in centre; mintmark escallop.

Reverse   Long cross over king's shield.

E61D-020   VG £50   F £100   VF £200

York Mint

This issue was struck in York but circulated mainly in Ireland.

Obverse Legend   As previous.

Reverse Legend   CIVITAS EBORACI — City of York

Obverse   As previous, but mintmark mullet.

Reverse   As previous.

E61D-025	VG £45	F £90	VF £200

Fine Silver Issue

This coin is of the highest rarity and possibly unique.

Obverse Legend   E.D.G. ROSA SINE SPI — Edward by the grace of God a rose without a thorn (abbreviated)

Reverse Legend   CIVITAS LONDON — City of London

Obverse   Sovereign-type king enthroned holding orb and sceptre.

Reverse   As previous.

E61D-030	ex. rare

Mary   (1553 – 1554)

Mary was Henry VIII's eldest child, by his first wife Katherine of Aragon and the throne would have passed to her upon Edward VI's death. Just before the young king died, however, he was persuaded by the Duke of Northumberland to exclude her from the succession because she was a staunch Catholic and Lady Jane Grey, Northumberland's daughter-in-law, was named in her stead. But, due to the Duke of Northumberland's unpopularity, the plan miscarried and Mary assumed the throne. Lady Jane Grey and her husband were put to death and Elizabeth, Mary's younger sister, imprisoned in the Tower of London. Mary proceeded with the restoration of the Roman Catholic faith to England and the punishment of those who had supported the Protestant Reformation.

Only four gold and three silver denominations were issued during Mary's reign. The groat is by far the most common, the other issues tending to be rare.

Collecting Hints

The fine silver issue is rare in any condition and very difficult to obtain, while collectors should be aware that Victorian copies exist. As an example from Mary's reign, collectors might well consider a groat instead, as these coins have an attractive portrait and are easier to find.

Obverse Legend   M.D.G. ROSA SINE SPINA — Mary by the grace of God a rose without a thorn (abbreviated)

Reverse Legend   VERITAS TEMP FILIA — Truth is the daughter of time

Obverse   Crowned bust left of queen; mintmark pomegranate.

Reverse   Long cross over royal shield.

MA1D-005	VG £200	F £600	VF £1,400

As previous, but reverse legend reads CIVITAS LONDON — City of London (Tower mint); no mintmark.

MA1D-010	VG £200	F £600	VF £1,400

Base Issue

Despite existing controversy, we believe that this issue is genuine and not a forgery.

Obverse Legend   M.D.G. ROSA SINE SPINA — Mary by the grace of God a rose without a thorn

Reverse Legend   CIVITAS LONDON — City of London

Obverse   A rose; mintmark rose.

Reverse   As previous.

MA1D-015	VG £50	F £100	VF —

Philip & Mary   (1554 – 1558)

Although it was hoped in England that Mary would marry an Englishman, she had set her heart on her cousin Philip, the Prince of Spain, who was a devout Catholic and they married in 1554, whereupon Philip became the King Consort. In an attempt to boost his popularity, Mary had Philip's portrait placed on the coins as well as her own. This was the first time that the portrait of a joint ruler can be found on any English coin. Owing to inflation and the abundance of silver in Europe, the penny continued to be superseded in importance by the shilling and sixpence, which were re-introduced after a brief absence, and the groat. Philip and Mary pennies are classed in two distinct types, the fine silver and the base issue.

Collecting Hints

Fine silver issue pennies are rare in any condition and Victorian copies exist. The average grade of the base issue is about Fine and due to their low silver content coins often appear to have been made from lead or zinc. For an example from this reign, collectors might opt for a shilling, sixpence or groat, which are relatively common and far more attractive.

Fine Silver Issue

Obverse Legend   P Z M D G ROSA SINE SPINE — Philip and Mary by the grace of God a rose without a thorn (abbreviated)

Reverse Legend   CIVITAS LONDON — City of London (Tower mint)

Obverse   Crowned bust of queen left; mintmark lis.

Reverse   Long cross over royal shield.

PM1D-005	VG £200	F £400	VF £800

Base Issue

Obverse Legend   As previous.

Reverse Legend   CIVITAS LONDON — City of London (Tower mint)

Obverse   Rose; mintmark halved rose and 'H' (or castle).

Reverse   Long cross over royal shield.

PM1D-010	VG £50	F £100	VF £225

Elizabeth I   (1558 – 1603)

Before her death in 1558, Mary had secured the right of succession for Elizabeth, Henry VIII's second daughter. By the middle of the sixteenth century, England was impoverished and in religious turmoil; but Elizabeth's reign was a creative, adventurous and eventually very prosperous period marked by the multifarious contributions of such figures as Shakespeare, Francis Drake and Walter Raleigh. The Queen was an able monarch, strong willed but inspiring. Guided as much by political considerations and a desire to distance the country and her court from the Catholic centres of power as by religious faith, Elizabeth reestablished Protestantism in England. The country prospered under Elizabeth, not least by engaging in piratical attacks on the Spanish ships returning from their colonies in South America loaded with silver and gold. The breakdown of relations with Spain culminated in the defeat of the Spanish Armada in 1588 which further enhanced England's international position. The confidence and prosperity of the country, as in previous times, was reflected in its coinage with bold, good quality coins being produced.

Henry VIII had left the coinage of England in a poor state and little had been done subsequently to improve either the quantity or the quality of the coins in circulation. The coinage system as a whole required reform, with high quality coins of good weight and high silver content, and this was a task Elizabeth boldly set about to accomplish. Throughout her reign large quantities of both gold and silver coins of many different denominations were produced thus meeting a need in England, but also on the Continent where they facilitated commerce. Much of the silver used to strike coins was captured from the Spanish, and a wide range of silver denominations was introduced, the shilling and sixpence being the most important. At the end of the period, a silver crown and halfcrown were introduced and replaced the gold denominations of these coins. Small denomination coins were also struck and were very popular with the small traders and merchants. The groat (fourpence), threepence, halfgroat (twopence), three-halfpence, penny, three-farthings and halfpenny were all introduced but no farthings were produced because they would have been too small to handle and easily lost. For the first time a milled or machine-made coinage was struck, produced by an ex-employee of the Paris mint, Eloye Mestrell. This issue was fairly successful but there was animosity in the Tower mint towards Mestrell, which ultimately led to his dismissal, as it was felt by the mint employees that his machinery would cause unemployment. Some of Elizabeth's denominations were dated and those that were not carry a mintmark, usually found on both sides of the coin, which can be used to accurately date a coin. As before, mintmarks were used as a form of quality control, so that each coin could be linked to a particular die and thus moneyer.

Unlike some rulers, Elizabeth recognised the need for small denomination coinage and the penny was produced throughout her reign although it was not one of the denominations made during the milled coinage trials. This was probably due to the difficulty in making such a small sized coin. Elizabeth's hammered coinage can be divided into six issues, distinguishable by slight differences in the features but all bearing the same legends, which read

E.D.G. ROSA SINE SPINA on the obverse and CIVITAS LONDON on the reverse. All of Elizabeth's issues were struck at the Tower mint.

Collecting Hints

Most of Elizabeth I's coins are readily available and the penny is no exception; it can usually be found in VG to VF condition but is sometimes creased or bent. One problem with this denomination is that it is very small in size and collectors may want a larger coin, such as a shilling or sixpence, in order to fully appreciate the fine work and detail of these issues.

First Issue (1559 – 1560)

There is an excessively rare variety of this coin that is dated 1558 in the obverse legend.

Obverse Legend   E.D.G. ROSA SINE SPINA — Elizabeth by the grace of God a rose without a thorn

Reverse Legend   CIVITAS LONDON — City of London (Tower mint)

Obverse   Bust of Elizabeth facing left; mintmark lis, wire-line inner circle.

Reverse   Royal shield over long cross.

EL1D-005	VG £150	F £300	VF £700

Second Issue (1560 – 1561)

Obverse   Bust of Elizabeth facing left; mintmark cross crosslet or martlet; beaded inner circles.

Reverse   Royal shield in centre over long cross.

EL1D-010	VG £20	F £45	VF £90

Third Issue (1561 – 1577)

As previous, but mintmark rose, portcullis, lion, coronet, castle, acorn, eglantine; beaded inner circles.

EL1D-015	VG £18	F £35	VF £70

Fourth Issue (1578 – 1582)

As previous, but mintmark Greek cross, Latin cross, sword; beaded inner circles.

EL1D-020	VG £18	F £35	VF £70

Fifth Issue (1582 – 1600)

As previous, but mintmark bell, 'A', escallop, crescent, hand, tun, woolpack, key, anchor, '0'.

N.B. Pennies of mintmarks key, anchor and '0' bear the mintmark on the obverse only.

EL1D-025	VG £16	F £30	VF £60

Sixth Issue (1601 – 1602)
As previous, but mintmark '1' (for 1601) or '2' (for 1602).

EL1D-030	VG £22	F £45	VF £90

While many of the previous issues hardly vary in style, we have listed them by their six classes to correspond with the other denominations produced, where there is considerable differences in some of the issues.

James I (1603 – 1625)

When Elizabeth died unmarried and childless in 1603, the English throne went to James VI of Scotland who was the son of Mary Queen of Scots and the great-grandson of Margaret Tudor, daughter of Henry VII. Unlike many previous kings, James I was used to royal duties as he had ruled Scotland since infancy and was 37 years old when he assumed the English crown. England continued to prosper due mainly to the initiative of merchants who traded goods from the newly found colonies, but this was also a time of political intrigue and there was the well known attempt on James I's life and that of the entire Parliament in 1605, the Gunpowder Plot.

James I's coinage changed little from that of Elizabeth I, except for the gold denominations, in production and in style. The most notable feature was the introduction of the copper farthing, which was issued to help with the problem of small change. Continuing a trend caused by inflation and the large quantities of silver and gold being imported into Europe, mainly by the Spanish, the penny became increasingly less important as a denomination. Two main types of penny were produced, the first bearing the king's bust on the obverse, the second just a rose. The only coin to be dated during James's reign was the sixpence but, as the mintmark system continued during this period, coins can be accurately dated accordingly. The mintmark is found on the obverse and/or reverse of the coin. Finally, another significant change to the coins was in the design of the reverse shield, which is found on most denominations. Since James was king of both England and Scotland, his heraldic emblem included the Scottish coat of arms.

Collecting Hints

James I's first coinage penny is fairly difficult to obtain, especially in better than Fine condition, probably because it was only issued in 1603 – 04. Collectors should try to obtain a full round example, in at least Fine condition. The second and third coinage issues are fairly common and easy to obtain in Fine to VF condition and even EF examples can be found and appear to have come from the same source, probably an unrecorded hoard.

First Coinage (1603 – 1604)
Obverse Legend   I.D.G. ROSA SINE SPINA — James by the grace of God a rose without a thorn

Obverse   Bust of king facing right, letter I behind head to denote denomination (1 penny).

Reverse   Square shield with mintmark above; mintmark thistle or lis. No legend.

J11D-005	VG £30	F £60	VF £120

Second Coinage (1604 – 1619)
The mintmark does not always appear on both sides. There is also a very rare variety which has the same obverse and reverse legend. This variety is found with the mullet mintmark and plain cross over book.

Obverse Legend   I.D.G. ROSA SINE SPINA — James by the grace of God a rose without a thorn

Reverse Legend   TUETUR UNITA DEUS — May God guard these (kingdoms) united

Obverse   Rose in centre of coin; mintmark lis, rose, escallop, grapes, coronet, key, bell, mullet, tower, trefoil, cinquefoil, plain cross or none.

Reverse   Thistle in centre of coin.

J11D-010	VG £12	F £25	VF £50

Third Coinage
Legends   As previous.

Obverse   As previous, but mintmarks spur rowel, none, lis or trefoil.

Reverse   As previous, but no stops in the legend.

J11D-015	VG £14	F £28	VF £55

Charles I (1625 – 1649)

Upon the death of James I in 1625 his twenty-five year old son Charles inherited the throne. Charles I was James's second son, his elder brother Henry having died while James was still reigning. Charles later married Henrietta Maria, daughter of Henry IV of France. Unfortunately, Charles's political judgement was appalling and he soon made enemies at a period when the whole of Europe was questioning the moral basis of absolute monarchy. Charles refused to accept direction from Parliament and for eleven years ruled without convening it. England was divided between the royalists and those who supported Parliament and when Civil War eventually broke out, Charles and his supporters were defeated.

Numismatically, Charles I's reign is unarguably the most interesting and complicated reign of any English monarch. This is not only because of the many varieties produced by the Tower mint, but also due to the re-opening of a number of provincial mints during the Civil War. The quantities, style and denominations are very diverse, thus giving the collector a rich field to collect. During the early part of Charles' reign, the Tower mint in London produced huge quantities of coins to satisfy demand; the penny was no exception: the number of varieties and variations in both style and design is immense. During the 1630s Nicholas Briot, a Frenchman who had worked at the Paris mint, struck machine-made milled coins at the Tower mint. These were far superior to the hammered issues, both in quality and design; Briot's coinage is always neat and well designed. A new mint at Aberystwyth, Wales was opened during Charles reign, located so as to strike silver coinage from the newly mined silver from the Welsh mines.

During the turmoil of the Civil War there was, once again, a need for provincial mints to become active as the transportation of coins was difficult and hazardous. These mints were royalist controlled and needed to produce coinage quickly, often to pay the troops' wages. For this reason, most of the denominations produced by these provincial mints were large, usually from the shilling upwards, as it was not possible in the strained circumstances of the Civil War to provide the country with a balanced coinage. Another interesting feature of the period are the siege pieces produced in towns such as Newark and Pontefract when they were besieged by Parliamentarian forces. These emergency issues were often made by cutting up silver plates and striking them with home-made dies. All of these siege pieces are interesting and under-appreciated. In 1642, the Tower mint in London fell under control of Parliament, but coins with the bust of Charles I were still produced there until 1648. The quantity and diversity of Charles I's coinage is immense. In each denomination section we have tried to provide information linking the coins to this turbulent period of English history.

Collecting Hints

Charles I pennies are fairly common and may be considered an almost insignificant denomination in contemporary terms as the penny had little buying power and, with growing prosperity, was becoming of little importance. Pennies were also becoming very small and this hinders the collector, as often the legends and mintmarks are unclear and difficult to read. The coins are usually found in about Fine condition, but VF examples can be obtained. They are often found holed and in poor condition and it is thought that this was done officially to make the coins invalid or to lower the denomination during the later part of the 17th century, when the production of milled coins was the norm. Most pennies were issued at the Tower mint, between 1625 and 1642. However, several provincial mints also produced pennies, most of which are rare and difficult to obtain.

Tower Mint

Tower Mint under King (1625 – 1642)

Obverse Legend   C.D.G. ROSA SINE SPINA — Charles by the grace of God a rose without a thorn

Reverse Legend   IUS THRONUM FIRMAT — Justice strengthens the throne

Obverse   Rose in centre.

Reverse   Rose in centre; mintmark lis, blackamoor's head, two pellets.

| C11D-005 | VG £12 | F £25 | VF £50 |

As previous, but no inner circles.

| C11D-010 | VG £12 | F £25 | VF £50 |

As previous, but inner circle on reverse only.

| C11D-015 | VG £10 | F £22 | VF £45 |

Obverse Legend   CAROLUS D.G.MA.B.F.ET HI REX. — Charles by the grace of God King of Great Britain France and Ireland

Reverse Legend   IUSTITIA THRONUM FIRMAT — Justice strengthens the throne

Obverse   Bust of king facing left wearing a ruff and mantle, figure 'I' behind head to denote denomination; mintmark plume or rose.

Reverse   Oval shield.

| C11D-020 | VG £10 | F £22 | VF £45 |

As previous, but no inner circles; mintmark plume or rose.

| C11D-025 | VG £10 | F £22 | VF £45 |

More armour visible, no inner circles; mintmark plume, rose.

| C11D-030 | VG £12 | F £25 | VF £50 |

As previous, but inner circle on obverse; mintmark plume, rose.

| C11D-035 | VG £12 | F £25 | VF £50 |

As previous, but inner circle both sides; mintmark plume over rose.

| C11D-040 | VG £12 | F £25 | VF £50 |

As previous, but inner circle on reverse; mintmark rose on obverse and plume on reverse.

| C11D-045 | VG £12 | F £25 | VF £50 |

Legends   As previous.

Obverse   Bust of king facing left wearing a lace collar, figure 'I' behind king's head to denote denomination, no inner circles; mintmark harp, one or two pellets.

Reverse   Oval shield dividing 'C.R.' (CAROLUS REX).

| C11D-050 | VG £20 | F £45 | VF £90 |

As previous, but no 'C.R.' on reverse.

| C11D-055 | VG £10 | F £22 | VF £45 |

As previous, inner circle on obverse; mintmark harp.

| C11D-060 | VG £10 | F £22 | VF £45 |

As previous, inner circle on reverse; mintmark harp.

C11D-065	VG £12	F £25	VF £50

As previous, but shield round in shape on reverse, no inner circles; mintmark bell, triangle, one or two pellets.

C11D-070	VG £12	F £25	VF £50

As previous, but inner circle on obverse; mintmark triangle or two pellets.

C11D-075	VG £12	F £25	VF £50

Aberystwyth Bust Type

Legends As previous.

Obverse Bust of king facing left, wearing pointed lace collar, small flat single arched crown, inner circle sometimes on obverse; mintmark one or two pellets, or none.

Reverse Shield.

C11D-080	VG £14	F £28	VF £55

Tower Mint under Parliament (1642 – 1648)

As previous, but the king looks considerably older; mintmark pellets, inner circle on obverse only.

C11D-085	VG £22	F £45	VF £90

Briot's Coinage (1631 – 1639)

These coins were milled, i.e. struck by machine, at the Tower mint by Nicholas Briot and the quality of production was superb. Coins can be found in Fine or even VF condition. They are usually well struck, and with all the details clearly visible. I have often wondered why Briot did not produce more coins, and why the entire output of coins from the Tower mint was not converted to milled coinage. It was probably due to the animosity felt against the Frenchman coupled with professional jealousy. The workers used to making hammered issues were afraid of losing their jobs if the new process was accepted.

Obverse Legend CARO MAG. BRIT FR ET HI R(EX.) — Charles King of Great Britain France and Ireland

Reverse Legend IUSTITIA THRONUM FIRMAT — Justice strengthens the throne

Obverse Crowned bust of king with value behind. Legend starts at the bottom of the coin.

Reverse Square-topped shield over cross.

C11D-090	VG —	F £70	VF £150

No pennies were issued during the second coinage of 1638 – 39.

Provincial Mints

The penny in most of the provincial issues, apart from Aberystwyth, appears to have been more of an afterthought since the main purpose of these mints was to produce coinage for the payment and armament of the royalist troops. Moreover, money was important as a vehicle of propaganda, informing the population which areas were controlled by the king and, with messages such as the Declaration on the coins, reinforcing the royalist cause.

Aberystwyth Mint (1638 – 1642)

The Aberystwyth mint, opened in 1638, used locally mined silver to produce reasonable quality hammered coins; the dies for this issue were made in London. The mint concentrated on the production of smaller denomination coins, i.e. from the halfcrown to the penny. Plumes can be found on coins from this mint, and the penny is no exception having plumes in the centre of the obverse, where a shield is usually found on the other issues. N.B. Should the reverse mintmark be different from those listed, check the coin in the Oxford listings (C11D-120 & -125).

Obverse Legend CARO D.G. M B F ET H REX — Charles by the grace of God King of Great Britain France and Ireland

Reverse Legend IUSTITIA THRONUM FIRMAT — Justice strengthens the throne

Obverse Bust of king, figure 'I' behind king's head, no inner circles; mintmark book

Reverse Plumes.

C11D-095	VG £60	F £120	VF £240

As previous, but with inner circles.

C11D-100	VG £60	F £120	VF £240

As previous, but obverse legend reads CAROLUS instead of CARO.

C11D-105	VG £60	F £120	VF £240

Briot Bust

Similar, but Briot-style bust on the obverse. The king's crown touches the inner circle.

C11D-110	VG £65	F £130	VF £260

Aberystwyth Furnace Mint (1648 – 1649)

This mint, actually situated at the silver mine itself, opened for a very short time. The castle at Aberystwyth had been damaged and there was need in the area for coinage. However, no records survive from the mint. The mintmark will easily differentiate this issue from the earlier issues, which had an open book as a mintmark. This issue uses the mintmark crown.

Collecting Hints

All issues are scarce, especially the penny, which is very rare in any condition.

Legends   As previous.

Obverse   As previous, but mintmark crown, with inner circles.

Reverse   As previous; the plumes are of different design to the regular issue of Aberystwyth mintmark crown on reverse, inner circles.

C11D-115	VG £300	F £550	VF —

Oxford Mint (1642 – 1646)

By 1642 Civil War was imminent, Parliament had taken control of the Tower mint in London and, towards the end of the year, Charles established his permanent headquarters in Oxford and made preparations to set up a mint there. He summoned Thomas Bushell, who had set up the mint in Aberystwyth, and for metal the king borrowed gold and silver plates from the University colleges, which he promised to repay. The Oxford mint produced some spectacular coins including the triple unite and a silver pound, as well as more mundane coins such as the penny. The Oxford pennies sometimes used the obverse die from the Aberystwyth mint and collectors should compare an example with the other provincial mints in order to identify it correctly, paying particular attention to the mintmark on both sides of the coin and the style of plumes. The use of the obverse Aberystwyth die was probably due to the great urgency for coins; as a result the usual formalities of mintmarks had to be discarded.

Collecting Hints

The pennies of Oxford are all fairly rare, often turning up in poor condition with the legends difficult to read. Collectors should try to obtain an example in Fine condition but, if simply wanting an example from the mint, they should try to obtain a more common denomination such as the halfcrown or shilling, as these can be found in better grades.

Obverse Legend   CARO D G M B F ET H REX — Charles by the grace of God King of Great Britain France and Ireland

Reverse Legend . As previous.

Obverse   Bust of king with large lace collar; mintmark book. This is an Aberystwyth die.

Reverse   Small plume; mintmark pellet.

C11D-120	VG £75	F £150	VF £350

Legends   As previous.

Obverse   As previous, but narrower bust; mintmark book.

Reverse   Large plume; mintmark four pellets.

C11D-125	VG £75	F £150	VF £350

Legends   As previous.

Obverse   Fine bust of king, not from Aberystwyth dies; mintmark lis.

Reverse   Small plume; mintmark mullet or pellet.

C11D-130	VG £75	F £150	VF £350

Legends   As previous.

Obverse   Wider bust of king; mintmark lis.

Reverse   Small plumes, mintmark lis.

C11D-135	VG £90	F £180	VF £400

Declaration Type

The obverse of this issue is very similar to all the issues from the Oxford mint. However, it is very rare in any grade.

Obverse Legend   As previous, but CAROL instead of CARO

Reverse Legend   As previous.

Obverse   Bust of king, no mark behind his head; mintmark lis.

Reverse   The declaration in centre of coin: RELIG PRO LEG ANG LIBER PAR. 1644 — The religion of the Protestants the laws of England the liberty of Parliament

C11D-140	VG £300	F £500	VF —

Bristol Mint (1643 – 1645)

Bristol was captured by the Royalists in July 1643 and Charles I immediately asked Thomas Bushell to set up a mint there. It was an important mint producing reasonable quality silver coins and a few extremely rare gold issues but in 1645 Bristol fell to the Parliamentarians and the mint was closed. Collectors should pay particular attention to the mintmark and the style of plumes when ascertaining which mint a coin is from.

Collecting Hints

Pennies from Bristol mint are rare in any grade; large denominations, however, tend to be more available.

Obverse Legend   CARO D G M BF ET H REX — Charles by the grace of God King of Great Britain France and Ireland

Reverse Legend   IUSTITIA THRONUM FIRMAT — Justice strengthens the throne

Obverse   Crowned bust facing left, with 'I' behind the king's head; mintmark pellet.

Reverse   Large plumes.

C11D-145	VG £180	F £400	VF £800

Exeter Mint (1643 – 1646)

Exeter was captured by Royalists in 1643. It became a fairly important mint producing mainly crowns and halfcrowns but also some pennies. The town finally surrendered to the Parliamentarians in April 1646.

Collecting Hints

Exeter pennies are rare in any grade. Many are found clipped and/or holed, which was done officially during later reigns to devalue the coins.

Obverse Legend CARO M B F E H R — Charles by the grace of God King of Great Britain France and Ireland

Reverse Legend THRO IUS FIRMAT 1644 — Justice strengthens the throne 1644

Obverse Crowned bust of king facing left, 'I' behind king's head; mintmark rose.

Reverse Large rose in centre; mintmark rose.

| C11D-150 | VG £125 | F £250 | VF £550 |

Commonwealth (1649 – 1660)

This issue, which has no legends and was purposefully simple in design, was struck for the full Commonwealth period.

Collecting Hints

This issue is fairly common, especially in the lower grades. Many specimens are found clipped and sometimes holed. This was done officially during later reigns to devalue the coins.

Obverse St George's shield within wreath.

Reverse St George's shield and Irish shield, value (I) above.

| CW1D-005 | VG £25 | F £50 | VF £120 |

Charles II (1660 – 1685)

Charles II, nicknamed the Merry Monarch, returned to England from exile in 1660. Oliver Cromwell had died and his younger brother had no intention of continuing to rule. With the restoration of the monarchy there was also a move away from the strict Puritanism of the Commonwealth which had banned games, fairs and sports.

From 1660 to 1662 hammered and machine-made coins were struck in three separate issues. The penny, which was a fairly common denomination by this time, was produced in all three issues. Thomas Simon produced the dies for the three issues, so all show superb detail.

Hammered and Machine-Made Issue (1660 – 1662)

Collecting Hints

This undated issue is fairly common and easily available in Fine condition. VF and EF examples do exist but tend to be scarce and under-appreciated. Often, due to the coin's small size, much of the legend is missing, and some coins have ragged edges. Collectors should try to obtain a coin in at least Fine condition with as round a planchet and as much legend showing as possible.

First Issue

Obverse Legend CAROLUS II D G MAG BRI F ET H REX — Charles II by the grace of God King of Great Britain France and Ireland

Reverse Legend CHRISTO AUSPICE REGNO — I reign under the auspices of Christ

Obverse Bust facing left; mintmark crown, no mark of value behind king's head and no inner circles.

Reverse The king's shield over a cross.

| C21DH-005 | VG £18 | F £40 | VF £80 |

As previous, but omitting mintmark.

| C21DH-010 | VG £18 | F £40 | VF £80 |

Machine-made Issue

There is also a variety with a single arched crown, and the obverse legend starting at 8 o'clock.

As previous, but with mark of value (I) behind king's head; mintmark on both sides. The obverse legend starts at the bottom or top of the coin.

| C21DH-015 | VG £16 | F £35 | VF £70 |

As previous, but legend starts at the top of the coin, no inner circles.

| C21DH-017 | VG £40 | F £80 | VF £150 |

Third Issue

Legends As previous.

Obverse Bust of king facing left, legend starts at top of coin; mintmark crown, mark of value (I) behind king's head, inner circles.

Reverse As previous, but inner circles.

| C21DH-020 | VG £20 | F £40 | VF £80 |

Three Farthings

Elizabeth I   (1558 – 1603)

The silver three-farthings was introduced in Elizabeth I's third and fourth issues as part of a plan to produce large quantities of coins of varying denominations and high metal content. It bears a bust of the queen with a rose behind on the obverse and the royal shield with the date above on the reverse, while a mintmark can be found at the beginning of the obverse and reverse legend. The three-farthings closely resembles the three-halfpence, differing only in the diameter which for unclipped specimens is 14 mm for the three-farthings and 16 mm for the three-halfpence. Halfgroats and pennies were also produced at the time but are all undated, except for the extremely rare 1558 penny, and they also omit the rose behind the queen's head. No three-farthings were issued in 1558, so the penny can be easily identified.

Collecting Hints

This issue used to be very rare, but significant quantities have been found in the last twenty years, either with metal detectors or by beach-combers in the river Thames, mostly in Poor to VG condition. Many coins are clipped and fragmented and often holed, due to their thinness or the acidic mud in which they have been found. Moreover, the dates are often crudely engraved. Coins in VF or EF condition are very rare.

Obverse Legend   E. D. G. ROSA SINE SPINA — Elizabeth by the grace of God a rose without a thorn

Reverse Legend   CIVITAS LONDON — City of London

Obverse   Bust of queen with rose behind; mintmark at beginning of legend.

Reverse   Royal arms with date above; mintmark at beginning of legend.

Mintmark   Pheon (1561 – 62), coronet (1567 – 68), ermine (1572 – 73), acorn (1573), eglantine (1573 – 77), plain cross (1578 – 79), long cross (1581) or sword (1582).

EL3F-005	VG £45	F £100	VF £300

Milled Issue

Only three examples of this issue are known to exist.

Obverse Legend   E. D. G. ROSA SINE SPINA — Elizabeth by the grace of God a rose without a thorn

Reverse Legend   CIVITAS LONDON — City of London

Obverse   Bust of queen with rose behind; mintmark star.

Reverse   Square shield over cross, 1563 above; mintmark star.

EL3F-010	ex. rare

Halfpenny

The halfpenny was successfully introduced under Edward I. During previous reigns, silver pennies had been cut in half and sometimes quarters to produce halfpennies and farthings. Some examples are illustrated below.

Thanks to metal detectors, Henry I and Henry III halfpennies have been found in recent years but they are all extremely rare and very little is known about them. They circulated alongside the more common cut coinage and although it is possible that they were patterns or trials, these specimens did see circulation. No documentary evidence exists, and it is possible that there are coins and issues which are still to be discovered.

Henry I   (1100 – 1135)

During the last few years, Henry I silver halfpennies have been found in the London area. This issue was possibly a pattern or trial but it is obvious that several specimens entered circulation. However, it was not until Edward I's reign that the halfpenny was successfully introduced.

Collecting Hints

Both issues are extremely rare; however, owing to metal detectors, they are becoming more common.

Obverse Legend   HENRIC REX — King Henry
Reverse Legend   GODWIN A ON WI — Godwin of Winchester
Obverse   Uncrowned front-facing bust.
Reverse   Cross potent with cross of pellets in each angle.

H1HD-005   ex. rare

As previous, but crowned bust.

H1HD-010   ex. rare

Henry III   (1216 – 1272)

These two issues, which were both struck at the London mint, have been discovered recently. They are of the short-cross coinage 1216 – 47 and similar in style to the pennies, but only half the size. They circulated alongside the much more common cut pennies, which served as halfpennies.

Collecting Hints

All issues are extremely rare.

Obverse Legend   HENRICUS REX — King Henry
Reverse Legend   TERRI (or ELIS) ON LUND — Terry (or Elis) of London
Obverse   Crowned bust of king holding sceptre.
Reverse   Short cross, four pellets in each quarter.

H3HD-005   ex. rare

Edward I   (1272 – 1307)

Edward I successfully introduced the halfpenny as part of the new coinage. It was an important and much needed denomination. Before the issue was introduced traders produced halfpennies by cutting pennies in half, which was obviously impractical in some cases and often inconvenient. The new denominations issued under Edward I allowed trade to increase and facilitated the country's prosperity.

Halfpennies from all hammered reigns tend to be difficult to identify. Most coins are small, often clipped or in poor condition. Moreover, many appear to have blundered legends due to the difficulty in making dies small enough for the denomination. The fact that Edward II, III and IV also issued halfpennies can hamper the collector when trying to identify an issue. All Edward I issues are linked to the classification system used for the penny. In general, Edward I's issues are larger than those of later kings. Throughout this chapter we will be show how to identify different reigns but many coins are often impossible to identify due to their poor condition.

As with other denominations, although London is by far the most common mint it was not the only mint to strike halfpennies, and five other mints were active during Edward I's reign. The entire legend on the reverse of the coin is the mint's name and read CIVITAS LONDON or LONDONIENSIS for London, VILLA BRISTOLLIE for Bristol, CIVITAS LINCOL for Lincoln, NOVI CASTRI for Newcastle-upon-Tyne, CIVITAS EBORACI for York, or VILLA BEREVVICI (varieties) for Berwick. Varieties exist in most cases and legends are often blundered or illegible in parts.

As with the other coins of this period, the denomination is not written on the coin, which was worth its weight in silver. Thus, a halfpenny would be half the size and weight of the penny. In all issues the king's name is found on the obverse of the coin. It is the first word in the obverse legend. It will read EDWA or EDWR (minor varieties). If it reads RICARD or HENRI it is an issue of Richard or Henry.

Collecting Hints

Edward I halfpennies are fairly common and usually available in about Fine condition. However, better examples exist and are not rare. All the provincial mints are rare and difficult to obtain. Collectors should try to obtain unclipped, undamaged examples in at least Fine condition so that they may be fairly easy to identify.

London Mint

As mentioned earlier, the class numbering system relates to the penny issue, as the two denominations are fairly similar.

Class 3B

Obverse Legend   EDW R ANGL DNS HYB — Edward King of England Lord of Ireland

Reverse Legend   LONDONIENSIS or CIVITAS LONDON — London or City of London

Obverse   Front-facing bust of king, his drapery as a segment of a circle.

Reverse   Long cross, three pellets in each quarter.

E1HD-005	VG £25	F £45	VF £90

As previous, but reversed 'N's in reverse legend.

E1HD-010	VG £30	F £50	VF £100

Class 3C

As previous, but front-facing bust of king, drapery as two wedges.

E1HD-015	VG £25	F £45	VF £90

Class 3G

As previous, but larger letters and wider crown.

E1HD-020	VG £25	F £45	VF £90

Class 4C

As previous, but larger face with much more hair, comma abbreviation marks and thick-waisted 'S' in obverse legend.

E1HD-025	VG £25	F £50	VF £100

Class 4E

As previous, but three pellets on king's breast on obverse and a pellet in reverse legend.

E1HD-030	VG £30	F £60	VF £120

Class 6

Legends   As previous.

Obverse   Front-facing bust of king, small lettering and double-barred 'N' in legend.

Reverse   Long cross, three pellets in each quarter.

E1HD-035	VG £30	F £60	VF £120

Class 7

As previous, but larger lettering.

E1HD-040	VG £30	F £60	VF £120

Class 9

As previous, but pot-hook 'N' in obverse legend, sometimes star on the king's breast with the crown band curved at the edges.

E1HD-045	VG £25	F £45	VF £90

Class 10

A piedford striking of this issue exists.

Obverse Legend   EDWAR R ANGL DNS HYB (varieties exist) — Edward King of England Lord of Ireland

Reverse Legend   As previous.

Obverse   Narrow letters in legend, the king has a long face.

Reverse   As previous.

E1HD-050	VG £25	F £45	VF £90

Bristol Mint

Obverse Legend   As Class 3C.

Reverse Legend   VIL(L)A BRISTOLLIE — Town of Bristol. There is one die reading IIISTOLLIE, this is a die-maker's error.

Obverse   Similar to Class 3C.

Reverse   As previous.

E1HD-055	VG £45	F £90	VF £200

As previous, but similar to Class 3G.

E1HD-060	VG £45	F £90	VF £200

Lincoln Mint

Obverse Legend   As Class 3C.

Reverse Legend   CIVITAS LINCOL or LINCOC — City of Lincoln

Obverse   Similar to Class 3C.

Reverse   As previous.

E1HD-065	VG £50	F £100	VF £200

Newcastle Mint

Obverse Legend   As previous.

Reverse Legend   NOVI CASTRI — Newcastle-upon-Tyne

Obverse   As Class 3C but king has a long narrow face.

Reverse   Long cross with single pellet in each angle.

E1HD-070	VG £100	F £200

York Mint

Obverse Legend   As previous.

Reverse Legend   CIVITAS EBORACI — City of York

Obverse   As Class 3B.

Reverse   Long cross, three pellets in each quarter.

E1HD-075	VG £40	F £75	VF £150

Berwick Mint

The rare halfpenny issue, like the pennies, does not fall into the usual classes of Edward I's coinage. This is because the dies for this issue were not made in London but produced locally.

Collecting Hints

All issues are rare in any grade. Many issues are very crude in design.

Obverse Legend   EDW R ANGL DNS HYB — Edward King of England Lord of Ireland

Reverse Legend   VILLA BEREVVICI — Town of Berwick

Obverse   Front-facing bust of king wearing trifoliate crown, Lombardic 'E' in legend.

Reverse   Long cross, three pellets in each quarter, Roman 'E' in legend.

E1HD-080	ex. rare

Obverse Legend   As previous

Reverse Legend   VILLA BERREWYCI (or BERREVICI) — Town of Berwick

Obverse   King wearing bifoliate crown, sometimes pellets in legend.

Reverse   As previous, but Lombardic 'E'.

E1HD-085	ex. rare

As previous, but EDWA instead of EDWR and Lombardic 'N' in obverse legend.

E1HD-090	VG £60	F £140	VF £250

As previous, but Roman 'N' in obverse legend.

E1HD-095	VG £60	F £140	VF £250

The later Berwick issues are listed under Edward II and Edward III respectively.

Edward II (1307 – 1327)

Only two mints produced halfpennies during the reign of Edward II, London and Berwick, probably because there were sufficient halfpennies circulating from Edward I's new coinage. The main difference between Edward II's halfpennies and Edward I's is the obverse legend which, on Edward II's London issue reads EDWARDUS REX A(NG). Also, on some issues, the central fleur of the king's crown looks like a battle axe.

London Mint

Collecting Hints

This issue is rare. It is often difficult to identify in low grade. The collector should try to obtain an example with a clear legend. This will allow the coin to be easily identified.

Obverse Legend   EDWARDUS REX A(NG) — Edward King of England

Reverse Legend   CIVITAS LONDON — City of London

Obverse   Front-facing bust of king, usually with the central fleur of the crown in the shape of a battle axe.

Reverse   Long cross, three pellets in each quarter.

E2HD-005	VG £40	F £80	VF £150

Many very minor varieties of this issue exist. Some numismatists consider some of the issue could be varieties of Edward I Class 10. However, we feel coins with this obverse legend should be included in Edward II, in particular, those with the new style crown, as this corresponds with Edward II's penny issues.

Berwick Mint

As with Edward I's Berwick halfpenny issue, those of Edward II do not fall into the usual issues. This is because the dies for this issue were not made in London, but produced locally.

Collecting Hints

All issues are rare in any grade. They are often crude in style.

Obverse Legend   EDWARDUS REX AN — Edward King of England

Reverse Legend   VILLA BEREWICI (varieties) — Town of Berwick

Obverse   Front-facing bust of king. Lombardic 'E' in legend

Reverse   As previous issues, colon before VIL in legend.

E2HD-010	VG £60	F £140	VF £250

Edward III (1327 – 1377)

Many different varieties of halfpennies were issued during the reign of Edward III. We will point out why a particular issue is unique. Halfpennies are difficult to identify, mainly because of their size. It is often difficult to see marks on the coins, especially those in the lower grades. It is important, when identifying your halfpenny, to check the obverse legends. Most reigns are slightly different. Look at the bust of the king. Does it look like the coin in our illustration? Also, look for any unusual marks on the coin. Many of Edward III's issues had a star in the legends. To identify an Edward halfpenny it may be necessary to refer to the chapters of Edward I, II and III. Edward IV's halfpennies are very different in style from those of the first three Edwards, and they are much smaller. It is also important to bear in mind that a coin of

Edward will have his name on the obverse at the top and will read EDWARD, EDWA and the other varieties. If a coin reads RICARD or HENRI, it is an issue of Richard or Henry.

Three mints were active during the reign of Edward III. They were London, Reading and Berwick. The Reading and Berwick mints are both very rare. The mint's name can be found on the reverse of the coin. The three mints read CIVITAS LONDON for London, VILLA BERV(V)ICI for Berwick and VILLA RADINGY (the N often reversed or unbarred) for Reading.

During this period, the English coinage was the envy of much of Europe as it could be relied upon for good weight and good metal content. It is not surprising, therefore, that the English coinage was copied on the Continent where many coins look very similar to the English issues; however, there are differences. During Edward III's reign copies of halfpennies were produced on the Continent; they are very similar in style to those of Edward III, except that the obverse legend reads, in most cases, EDWARDIENSIS. These coins are an interesting addition to any collection.

Collecting Hints

Most of Edward III's London issues are fairly common. This is due to the fact that several hoards have been found. Coins are usually found in about Fine condition. However, VF examples are not uncommon. Often coins are damaged, or poorly struck. This makes it difficult to identify the issues. The collector should try to obtain a coin in, at least, Fine condition. It should have clear legends, portrait and any marks. All issues from the two provincial mints are rare in any grade, and difficult to obtain.

First Coinage (1327 – 1335)

Struck only at the Berwick mint, this issue is very easy to recognise as in all cases there is either one or two bear's heads in the reverse quarters.

Obverse Legend EDWARDUS ANGLIE D OR EDWARDUS DEI GRA R (varieties) — Edward by the grace of God King of England

Reverse Legend VILLA BERV(V)ICI — Town of Berwick

Obverse Front-facing bust of king.

Reverse Bear's head in one or two quarters.

E3HD-005	VG £40	F £80	VF £160

Second Coinage (1335 – 1343)

Coins from this issue were struck in silver of slightly less fineness; in fact the silver content was reduced from .925 to .833. This unpopular change was reversed with the introduction of the third coinage. The London issue is again easily identifiable by a star at the end of the obverse legend.

London Mint

This issue is very similar to the previous issue of Edward II. However, the obverse legend is slightly different; also, there is a star at the end of the legend. Halfpennies were also struck for the first coinage issue using Edward II dies. This issue is indistinguishable.

Obverse Legend EDWARDUS REX A(NG) — Edward King of England

Reverse Legend CIVITAS LONDON — City of London

Obverse Front-facing bust of king, star at end of legend, very neat bust with a flat crown.

Reverse Long cross, three pellets in each quarter.

E3HD-010	VG £18	F £35	VF £70

Reading Mint

Obverse Legend As previous.

Reverse Legend VILLA RADINGY — Town of Reading

Obverse Front-facing bust of king, star at end of legend.

Reverse Escallop in one quarter of reverse.

E3HD-015	VG £225	F £450	VF —

Third or Florin Coinage (1344 – 1351)

Two mints were active during this issue, London and Reading. This issue has a fairly distinct type of bust. The king has much more bushy hair, and has a broad neck and shoulders, there is no star at the end of the legends. However, other marks can be found on the coin.

London Mint

Obverse Legend EDWARDUS REX (AN) — Edward King of England

Reverse Legend CIVITAS LONDON — City of London

Obverse Front-facing bust of king, sometimes two pellets by REX, sometimes pellet or small saltire either side of crown.

Reverse Long cross, three pellets in each quarter.

E3HD-020	VG £18	F £35	VF £70

As previous, but an extra pellet or saltire in one quarter of the reverse.

E3HD-025	VG £22	F £40	VF £75

Obverse Legend EDWARDUS REX — King Edward

Reverse Legend As previous.

Obverse Two pellets, two saltires or nothing before REX in legend, sometimes a pellet either side of crown.

Reverse Long cross, three pellets in each quarter.

E3HD-030	VG £22	F £40	VF £75

Reading Mint

Obverse Legend EDWARDUS REX (AN) — Edward King of England

Reverse Legend VILLA RADINGY — Town of Reading

Obverse Front-facing bust of king.

Reverse Long cross, escallop in one quarter, three pellets in the other three quarters.

E3HD-035	VG £200	F £425

As previous, but a saltire in the obverse legend.

Fourth Coinage (1351 – 1377)

Pre Treaty Period (1351 – 1361)

This very rare issue is extremely difficult to identify. The main difference is in the lettering. Many of the letters are broken or have parts missing. The mintmark, which is found on the obverse above the king's head, is cross 2(3), however, the mintmark in many issues is not clear.

Obverse Legend   EDWARDUS REX AN — Edward King of England

Reverse Legend   CIVITAS LONDON — City of London

Obverse   Front-facing bust of king, broken letters in legend; mintmark cross 2(3).

Reverse   Long cross, three pellets in each quarter.

E3HD-045   VG £80   F £150   VF £300

Another extremely rare variety exists which was struck in 1356

Obverse Legend   EDWARDUS REX — King Edward

Reverse Legend   CIVITAS LONDON — City of London

Obverse   Front-facing bust of king; mintmark crown.

Reverse   As previous, but an annulet in one quarter.

E3HD-050   ex. rare

Transitional Treaty Period

The only point which distinguishes this issue is that there are two pellets above the mintmark cross potent (5). This issue is rare.

Obverse Legend   EDWARDUS REX AN — Edward King of the English

Reverse Legend   CIVITAS LONDON — City of London

Obverse   Front-facing bust of king, two pellets over mintmark cross potent (5). The lettering of both obverse and reverse legends sometimes varies in size.

Reverse   Long cross, three pellets in each quarter.

E3HD-055   VG £70   F £150   VF £300

Treaty Period (1361 – 1369)

This issue is differentiated by several minor marks, which are specific to this issue.

Obverse Legend   EDWARDUS REX AN — Edward King of England

Reverse Legend   CIVITAS LONDON — City of London

Obverse   Front-facing bust of king; mintmark cross potent.

Reverse   Double or single pellet stops after DON, unbarred 'A' in TAS.

E3HD-060   VG £20   F £40   VF £75

Legends   As previous.

Obverse   As previous, but pellet before EDWARDUS.

Reverse   Two or one annulet after DON, barred 'A' in TAS.

E3HD-065   VG £20   F £40   VF £75

No halfpennies were produced during the post-treaty period (1369 – 77).

Richard II   (1377 – 1399)

Richard II produced three main types of halfpennies during his reign. All were produced at the London mint and are fairly easy to identify. All obverse legends start with the king's name RICARD; should the coin read HENRI or EDWARD it is an issue of either Henry or Edward. Richard III also produced halfpennies, which are very rare. To differentiate between the two Richards' halfpennies refer to the mintmark, found above the king's head, just before the start of the obverse legend. In Richard II's coinage, in all cases, the mintmark is cross pattée whereas in Richard III's issues the mintmark is sun and rose or boar's head. Should the mintmark not be clear, refer to the various marks found on the coin. For example, the early style of Richard II had marks on the king's breast, the later style had fishtail lettering. Fishtail lettering is when the ends of most letters in the legends are broken and curved outwards, so looking like a fishtail.

Collecting Hints

Richard II halfpennies, while scarce, are obtainable. The average grade is about Fine. VF examples do exist. For the budget collector looking for a reasonable grade coin from this reign, the halfpenny is probably the best choice. The issue is rarely clipped and, in most cases, the king's name is clear. The other issues from this reign are rare, except for the penny issues of the York mint. These, however, are usually found in poor to fair grade.

First Issue

Obverse Legend   RICHARD REX ANGL — Richard King of England

Reverse Legend   CIVITAS LONDON — City of London

Obverse   Front-facing bust of king, annulet or saltire on breast, reversed Roman 'N's in legend.

Reverse   Long cross, three pellets in each quarter.

R2HD-005   VG £40   F £80   VF £180

Intermediate Issue

Legends   As previous.

Obverse   No marks on king's breast, Lombardic 'N's in legend.

Reverse   Usually Lombardic 'N's in legend.

R2HD-010   VG £30   F £55   VF £100

Late Bust Issue

Fishtail Lettering

Obverse Legend   RICARD REX ANGL (F or I sometimes) — Richard King of England

Reverse Legend   CIVITAS LONDON — City of London

Obverse   Front-facing bust of king but no marks on bust; the legend has fishtail lettering making all the letters look very fancy.

Reverse   Fishtail lettering in the legend.

R2HD-015	VG £30	F £55	VF £100

As previous, but short stubby lettering.

R2HD-020	VG £35	F £70	VF £140

Henry IV   (1399 – 1413)

Henry IV's halfpennies are very difficult to identify. This is mainly due to the fact that they are usually clipped or in poor condition, making it very difficult to see marks which would differentiate them from more common reigns. To identify a coin, firstly check that the obverse legend reads HENRIC; if it reads EDWARD or RICARD it is an issue from the reign of Edward or Richard. Secondly, the mint, found in the reverse legend, should read CIV-ITAS LONDON, as London was the only mint that produced halfpennies under Henry IV. Thirdly, try to distinguish the mint-mark, which in all cases is cross pattée, with nothing in the centre. This mintmark is specific to Henry IV but might not be clear on a coin. Then pay attention to the king's bust, as Henry IV's busts are different from those of other reigns. In particular, pay close attention to the reign of Henry V. Finally, look for any marks, such as annulets, on the coin. Then see if any issue has these markings in it. When trying to identify a Henry IV halfpenny, also check the issues of Henry V, VI and VII.

Collecting Hints

All of Henry IV's coins are very rare and usually difficult to identify, and the halfpenny is no exception. Halfpennies are often found in about Fine condition, clipped and with weak legends. Collectors should try to obtain an example with as many clear distinguishing marks as possible. Also, when obtaining this coin from a dealer, ensure that the coin is guaranteed to be an issue of Henry IV.

Heavy Coinage (1399 – 1412)

Coins from the heavy coinage weigh some 20% more than the light coinage. The weight difference is not a simple way to identify this issue due to the fact that most issues were clipped and are worn. Accurate weighing of the two issues would be most misleading.

Obverse Legend   HENRIC REX ANGL — Henry King of England

Reverse Legend   CIVITAS LONDON — City of London

Obverse   Front-facing small bust of king; mintmark cross pattée.

Reverse   Long cross, three pellets in each quarter.

H4HD-005	VG £100	F £250	VF £500

As previous, but larger bust with rounded shoulders.

H4HD-010	VG £100	F £200	VF £425

Light Coinage (1412 – 1423)

This issue used the same dies as the heavy coinage. An unclipped example from the heavy coinage should weigh 0.70 grams and from the light coinage 0.35 grams. However, due to clipping and wear most coins from these issues can not be classed.

Legends   As previous.

Obverse and Reverse   As previous.

H4HD-015	VG £110	F £250	VF £500

This issue used a new set of dies which were very different from the previous one.

As previous, but whole or broken annulets usually either side of crown or neck.

H4HD-020	VG £110	F £275	VF £550

As previous, but with two pellets to right of neck.

H4HD-025	rare

Henry V   (1413 – 1422)

Henry V's coins are somewhat easier to identify than those of the previous reigns, because they bear a number of distinguishing marks. Firstly, check that the coin has the king's name at the start of the obverse legend and reads HENRIC; should it read RICARD or EDWARD the coin is an issue of Richard or Edward. Now check that the mint, on the reverse legend, reads CIV-ITAS LONDON, because during this reign halfpennies were only produced at the London Mint. The mintmarks on all issues are either cross pattée with pellet in centre, or pierced cross. The only certain way for collectors to identify an issue is to check through each class, paying particular attention to the various marks and the king's bust. If a coin is not found, collectors should refer to Henry IV, VI and VII.

Collecting Hints

Henry V's halfpennies are fairly common and usually obtainable in Fine condition. They are mostly unclipped with clear legends and marks. Collectors should try to obtain an example in at least Fine condition with clear legends.

Obverse Legend   HENRIC REX ANGL — Henry King of England
Reverse Legend   CIVITAS LONDON — City of London
Obverse   Very thin emaciated bust of king, annulet either side of crown.
Reverse   Long cross, three pellets in each quarter.

H5HD-005   VG £20   F £40   VF £90

As previous, but the obverse is an altered die of Henry IV's last issue (H4HD-020); a mullet over the annulet to right of crown differentiates this issue.

H5HD-010   VG £60   F £125   VF £225

As previous, but new-style bust of king of usual style, a broken annulet either side of crown.

H5HD-015   VG £20   F £40   VF £90

As previous, but broken annulet by hair.

H5HD-020   VG £20   F £40   VF £90

As previous, but one annulet broken by crown and another annulet unbroken by crown.

H5HD-025   VG £30   F £60   VF £110

As previous, but annulet to one side and trefoil to the other side of crown.

H5HD-030   VG £20   F £40   VF £90

This issue was probably struck during the reign of Henry VI. The obverse die is obviously that of Henry V, while the reverse die is that of Henry VI.
Legends   As previous.
Obverse   New, neat bust with hollow neck; no marks on coin.
Reverse   Widely separated pellets on reverse.

H5HD-035   VG £50   F £100   VF £180

Henry VI First Reign (1422 – 1461)

As with all other denominations, many issues of halfpenny were produced during the reign of Henry VI. Each issue is easily identifiable by specific markings which were put on the coins as a form of quality control so that, if a problem arose, a coin could be returned to the appropriate mint and checked for weight and metal fineness. Firstly, to find that you have a coin of Henry, check that the obverse legend reads HENRIC. Then check the mint, on the reverse legend. Three mints were active under Henry VI, London, York and Calais in France, which was under English rule during this period, and their reverse legends read CIVITAS LONDON, CIVITAS EBORACI, VILLA CALIS (minor varieties are known) respectively. Finally, collectors should look for any unusual marks, such as annulets, rosettes or mascles, and go through each issue to see if the coin ties in with a particular class. If unsuccessful, also check the reigns of Henry IV, V and VI second reign, as well as Henry VII.

Annulet Issue (1422 – 1427)

This issue has annulets somewhere on the coin.

London Mint
Obverse Legend   HENRIC REX ANGL — Henry King of England
Reverse Legend   CIVITAS LONDON — City of London
Obverse   Front-facing bust of king.
Reverse   Annulets in two quarters.

H6HD-005   VG £15   F £30   VF £60

Calais Mint
Obverse Legend   As previous.
Reverse Legend   VILLA CALIS(IE) — Town of Calais
Obverse   Front-facing bust of king, annulet by neck.
Reverse   As previous.

H6HD-010   VG £15   F £30   VF £60

York Mint
Obverse Legend   As previous.
Reverse Legend   CIVITAS EBORACI
Obverse   Front-facing bust of king, a lis either side of neck.
Reverse   As previous.

H6HD-015   VG £200   F £400   VF £750

Rosette Mascle Issue (1427 – 1430)

This issue has a rosette and mascles somewhere in the legend.

London Mint

Obverse Legend   As previous.

Reverse Legend   CIVITAS LONDON — City of London

Obverse   Front-facing bust of king, rosettes and mascles in legend.

Reverse   Long cross, three pellets in each quarter.

H6HD-020	VG £20	F £40	VF £75

Calais Mint

As previous, but reverse legend reads VILLA CALIS(IE) — Town of Calais.

H6HD-025	VG £20	F £40	VF £75

Pinecone Mascle Issue (1430 – 1434)

This issue has pinecones and mascles in the legends.

London Mint

Obverse Legend   As previous.

Reverse Legend   CIVITAS LONDON — City of London

Obverse   Front-facing bust of king, pinecones and mascles in legend.

Reverse   As previous.

H6HD-030	VG £22	F £45	VF £80

Calais Mint

As previous, but reverse legend reads VILLA CALIS(IE) — Town of Calais.

H6HD-035	VG £22	F £45	VF £80

Leaf Mascle Issue (1434 – 1435)

This issue has a leaf somewhere on the coin and a mascle usually in the obverse or reverse legend.

London Mint

Obverse Legend   As previous.

Reverse Legend   CIVITAS LONDON — City of London

Obverse   Leaf on king's breast.

Reverse   Leaf below 'N' of LON or 'S' of TAS.

H6HD-040	VG £20	F £40	VF £80

Calais Mint

Obverse Legend   As previous.

Reverse Legend   VILLA CALIS(IE) — Town of Calais

Obverse   Front-facing bust of king with leaf on breast.

Reverse   Leaf under SIE of legend.

H6HD-045	VG £30	F £60	VF £120

Leaf Trefoil Issue (1435 – 1448)

This issue sometimes has a leaf on the king's breast, and has a trefoil of pellets in the legend.

London Mint

Obverse Legend   As previous.

Reverse Legend   CIVITAS LONDON — City of London

Obverse   Front-facing bust of king, leaf on breast, trefoil in legend.

Reverse   Long cross, three pellets in each quarter.

H6HD-050	VG £20	F £40	VF £75

As previous, but no leaf on breast.

H6HD-055	VG £25	F £50	VF £85

Calais Mint

The Calais mint also produced a piedfort, or double thickness, coin for this issue, which, however, is considered a pattern and is extremely rare.

As H6HD-050 except for reverse legend, which reads VILLA CALIS(IE).

H6HD-060	ex. rare

Trefoil Issue (1438 – 1443)

This issue, struck at the London mint, has trefoils either side of neck and a leaf on the breast.

Obverse Legend   As previous.

Reverse Legend   CIVITAS LONDON — City of London

Obverse   Front-facing bust of neck and a leaf on the king's breast, sometimes trefoils in legend.

Reverse   Long cross, three pellets in each quarter. One die has an extra pellet in two quarters.

H6HD-065	VG £25	F £50	VF £90

No halfpence were struck for the trefoil pellet issue.

Leaf Pellet Issue (1445 – 1454)

This issue, struck at the London mint, has a leaf on the king's breast and pellet either side of crown.

Obverse Legend   HENRIC REX ANGLI — Henry King of the English

Reverse Legend   CIVITAS LONDON — City of London

Obverse   Front-facing bust of king, leaf on king's breast and pellet either side of crown.

Reverse   As previous.

H6HD-070	VG £20	F £40	VF £80

No halfpennies were issued for the unmarked issue of 1453 – 54.

Cross Pellet Issue (1454 – 1460)

This issue, struck at the London mint, has a saltire or cross on the obverse.

As previous, but a saltire either side of king's neck.

H6HD-075	VG £40	F £80	VF £150

As previous, but a single saltire on the king's neck, a mullet can also be found after HENRIC in the obverse legend. The reverse is the same as the previous issue.

H6HD-080	VG £30	F £60	VF £120

Edward IV First Reign (1461 – 1470)

During Edward IV's first reign halfpennies were produced at four mints, London, Bristol, Canterbury and York. The provincial mints are all rare but the London mint produced a considerable number of coins. Edward IV's first reign coinage can be divided into the heavy and the light. The heavy coinage was only produced at the London mint and, with one rare exception, can be easily identified by the mintmark rose. The light coinage, so called because of the reduced weight of the coins, is very similar to Edward IV's second reign coinage, which is not surprising, as the two reigns were only divided by a few months. Collectors should check both reigns when identifying an issue. Edward IV's halfpennies are fairly easy to identify; firstly check that the obverse legend, starting at the top, reads EDWARD. If it reads RICARD or HENRIC it is an issue of Richard or Henry. Although Edward I, II and III also produced halfpennies, the issues are very different in style and size and the coins from the earlier reigns are larger. Edward IV's coins have a varied selection of mintmarks which are not found on the earlier issues, also the busts are different in style and size.

As mentioned earlier, four mints were active during Edward IV's reign. The mint's name can be found on the reverse legend and read CIVITAS LONDON for London, CIVITAS CANTOR for Canterbury, CIVITAS EBORACI for York and VILLA BRIS-TOW for Bristol. It is important to remember that Edward IV had two reigns; should collectors not find a coin in the first reign, they should refer to the second reign.

Collecting Hints

Most Edward IV halfpenny issues are fairly rare, especially the provincial mints. However, some issues from the London mint are quite common. These are usually available in about Fine condition. VF examples, while rare, are available. Many issues tend to be slightly clipped. They often look oval in shape, probably due to the tall bust of the king. In most cases there is a clear mintmark.

Heavy Coinage (1461 – 1464)

Collectors should check the mintmark, as well as all the other marks on the coin, when identifying this series. During this issue only the London mint was active.

Obverse Legend   EDWARD DI GRA REX — Edward by the grace of God King

Reverse Legend   CIVITAS LONDON — City of London

Obverse   Front-facing bust of king, lis on breast and a pellet either side of crown; mintmark plain cross.

Reverse   Long cross, three pellets in each quarter, but in some cases four pellets in two quarters.

E4HD-005	VG £60	F £120	VF £250

Legends   As previous.

Obverse   Front-facing bust of king, quatrefoils either side of bust; mintmark rose.

Reverse   Long cross, three pellets in each quarter.

E4HD-010	VG £40	F £80	VF £160

As previous, but saltires by bust; mintmark rose.

E4HD-015	VG £50	F £100	VF £180

As previous, but no marks by bust; mintmark rose.

E4HD-020	VG £35	F £75	VF £140

As previous, but annulet by bust; mintmark rose.

E4HD-025	VG £35	F £75	VF £140

Light Coinage (1464 – 1470)

London Mint

Obverse Legend   EDWARD DI GRA REX (A) — Edward by the grace of God King

Reverse Legend   CIVITAS LONDON — City of London

Obverse   Front-facing bust of king, saltires by neck; mintmark sun, crown or rose.

Reverse   Long cross, three pellets in each quarter.

E4HD-030	VG £35	F £65	VF £120

As previous, but trefoils at neck; mintmark sun, crown or long cross fitchée.

E4HD-035	VG £20	F £40	VF £80

As previous, but no marks at neck; mintmark long cross fitchée.

E4HD-040	ex. rare

Bristol Mint

Obverse Legend As previous.

Reverse Legend VILLA BRISTOW — Town of Bristol

Obverse Front-facing bust of king, crosses by neck; mintmark crown.

Reverse Long cross, three pellets in each quarter.

E4HD-045	VG £70	F £150	VF £300

As previous, but trefoils by neck; mintmark crown.

E4HD-050	VG £55	F £100	VF £200

Canterbury Mint

Ecclesiastical Mint under Archbishop Bourchier

Obverse Legend As previous.

Reverse Legend CIVITAS CANTOR — City of Canterbury

Obverse Front-facing bust of king, trefoils by neck; mintmark pall.

Reverse Long cross, three pellets in each quarter.

E4HD-055	VG £60	F £120	VF £240

As previous, but no marks by king's neck; mintmark pall.

E4HD-060	VG £60	F £120	VF £240

Royal Mint

Legends As previous.

Obverse Front-facing bust of king, saltires by neck; mintmark crown.

Reverse Long cross, three pellets in each quarter.

E4HD-065	VG £40	F £80	VF £160

As previous, but trefoils at neck; mintmark crown.

E4HD-070	VG £40	F £80	VF £160

Norwich Mint

Obverse Legend As previous.

Reverse Legend CIVITAS NORWIC — City of Norwich

Obverse Crowned bust of king, a quatrefoil on either side of his neck.

Reverse Long cross, three pellets in each quarter.

E4HD-072	ex. rare

York Royal Mint

Obverse Legend As previous.

Reverse Legend CIVITAS EBORACI — City of York

Obverse Front-facing bust of king, saltires by neck; mintmark lis or sun.

Reverse As previous.

E4HD-075	VG £40	F £80	VF £160

As previous, but trefoils at neck; mintmark lis.

E4HD-080	VG £40	F £80	VF £160

Henry VI Restored (Oct. 1470 – April 1471)

During this very short period two mints produced halfpennies, London and Bristol. The London issue is fairly similar to the first reign of Henry VI although there are several differences. Firstly the obverse legend reads HENRIC DI GRA REX, also the mintmark short cross fitchée, which can be found on this issue, was not used on a halfpenny by any other Henry. The Bristol halfpenny, which is extremely rare, is easily identifiable being the only halfpenny produced at this mint by a Henry.

Collecting Hints

The London issue is very rare in any grade. Collectors should make sure that the coin they are buying has a clear legend and mintmark. In this way it can be easily differentiated from other more common issues. As mentioned earlier, the Bristol issue is extremely rare in any grade.

London Mint

Obverse Legend HENRIC DI GRA REX — Henry by the grace of God King

Reverse Legend CIVITAS LONDON — City of London

Obverse Front-facing bust of king, no marks; mintmark short cross fitchée.

Reverse Long cross, three pellets in each quarter.

H6HD-085	VG £120	F £250	VF £500

Bristol Mint

Obverse Legend As previous.

Reverse Legend VILLA BRISTOW — Town of Bristol

Obverse Front-facing bust of king; mintmark cross

Reverse As previous.

H6HD-090	ex. rare

Edward IV Second Reign (1471 – 1483)

The halfpennies for the second reign of Edward IV are very much a continuation from the first reign, which is hardly surprising as the two periods were only separated by a few months. During Edward's second reign the London and Royal Canterbury mint continued production; also, the Durham mint produced halfpennies for this reign only. We have given details in Edwards IV's first reign of how to identify the various issues; the only new detail is, of course, the Durham mint. The production of halfpennies at this mint is unique to this reign. The mint's name, as with other issues, is found on the reverse of the coin and reads CIVITAS DERAM. It is important that, should collectors not find a coin under the second coinage, they should refer to the first coinage which is in many cases very similar.

Collecting Hints

The London mint of the second coinage is, like the first coinage, fairly common. It is usually obtainable in about Fine condition. VF examples, while rare, are obtainable. Both the Canterbury and Durham mint issues are rare in any grade.

London Mint

Obverse Legend   EDWARD DI GRA REX — Edward by the grace of God King

Reverse Legend   CIVITAS LONDON — City of London

Obverse   Front-facing bust of king, no marks by neck; mintmark short cross fitchée, annulet, pellet in annulet, cross and four pellets, cross in circle, pierced cross, cross and one pellet, cinquefoil.

Reverse   Long cross, three pellets in each quarter.

E4HD-085	VG £60	F £100	VF £200

As previous, but pellet either side of neck; mintmark pierced cross.

E4HD-090	VG £20	F £40	VF £80

Canterbury Royal Mint

Obverse Legend   As previous.

Reverse Legend   CIVITAS CANTAR — City of Canterbury

Obverse   Front-facing bust of king, 'C' on king's breast; mintmark rose.

Reverse   Long cross, three pellets in each quarter, large 'C' in centre of cross.

E4HD-095	VG £40	F £80	VF £150

As previous, but no 'C' on reverse; mintmark rose.

E4HD-100	VG £35	F £70	VF £140

As previous, without 'C'; mintmark long cross fitchée.

E4HD-105	VG £40	F £80	VF £150

Durham Ecclesiastical Mint
under Bishop Booth

Obverse Legend   As previous.

Reverse Legend   CIVITAS DERAM — City of Durham

Obverse   Front-facing bust of king; mintmark rose.

Reverse   Long cross, three pellets in each quarter with large 'D' in centre of cross.

E4HD-110	VG £60	F £130	VF £250

As previous, but 'V' to left of neck.

E4HD-115	VG £60	F £130	VF £250

Edward IV or V

As with other denominations, there is uncertainty over which reign this issue should be classed in, but most numismatists are of the opinion that, while the dies were made for Edward IV's second reign, they were used to produce coins under Edward V.

Collecting Hints

This very rare coin is very difficult to obtain in any grade. As the only mark that differentiates it from the more common issues is the mintmark, collectors purchasing one of these rare specimens should ensure that the mintmark is clear.

Obverse Legend   EDWARD DI GRA REX — Edward by the grace of God King

Reverse Legend   CIVITAS LONDON — City of London

Obverse   Front-facing bust of king, no mark in field; mintmark halved sun and rose.

Reverse   Long cross, three pellets in each quarter.

E4HD-120	VG £200	F £400	VF £800

No halfpennies were issued using dies from the reign of Edward V.

Richard III   (1483 – 1485)

During Richard III's short reign only the London mint produced halfpennies. The issues are fairly easy to identify as RICARD can be found on the obverse, at the beginning of the legend. The only other Richard to produce halfpennies was Richard II, but his issues are very different in style. Also different mintmarks were used by the two monarchs; Richard II used cross pattée and Richard III used mintmark sun and rose and boar's head.

Collecting Hints

Richard III halfpennies are extremely rare in any grade.

Obverse Legend   RICARD DI GRA REX — Richard by the grace of God King

Reverse Legend   CIVITAS LONDON — City of London

Obverse   Front-facing bust of king; mintmark sun and rose.

Reverse   Long cross, three pellets in each quarter.

R3HD-005	VG £200	F £500	VF £1,000

As previous, but mintmark boar's head.

R3HD-010	VG £225	F £550	VF £1,100

Henry VII   (1485 – 1509)

During Henry VII's reign quantities of halfpennies were produced at the London, Canterbury and York mints. All issues are of the front-facing bust variety because the coins were becoming too small for the profile style. This is unfortunate, as the quality of workmanship, in both design and style, was much better in the profile issue.

Henry VII's halfpennies are fairly easy to identify. The obverse legend, starting at the top, reads HENRIC. If it reads RICARD or EDWARD it is an issue of Richard or Edward. Henry IV, V and VI (both reigns) all issued halfpennies, but Henry VII's issues are different in many ways. The portraits are different in style, the king's crown has an arch in the more common issues and Henry VII used different mintmarks. Another feature, on the reverse of the coin, is the centre cross which is ornate at the edges in most issues whereas previously it had been a plain cross.

It is important to remember that many issues from the same reign are slightly different. Collectors might have to check through several reigns when identifying a coin, especially if it is in poor condition. Remember to check the mintmark, also look for any unusual marks on the coins.

Three mints were active producing Henry VII halfpennies. The mint name can be found on the reverse of the coin and reads CIVITAS LONDON for London, CIVITAS CANTOR for Canterbury and CIVITAS EBORACI for York.

Collecting Hints

The London issue halfpennies are fairly common; they are usually available in about Fine condition, VF examples are scarce but obtainable. Both the Canterbury and York mints are fairly scarce. Many issues are very small, sometimes missing parts of their legend. Usually this is due not to clipping, but to the way the coins were struck. With the price of silver rising over the last few centuries, coins were getting smaller. The halfpenny would, during this period, be considered a small denomination with fairly little buying power.

London Mint

Open Crown Issue

Obverse Legend   HENRIC D (E) I GRA REX — Henry by the grace of God King

Reverse Legend   CIVITAS LONDON — City of London

Obverse   Front-facing bust of king with open crown; mintmark lis upon sun and rose or lis-rose dimidiated.

Reverse   Long cross, three pellets in each quarter.

H7HD-005	VG £40	F £100	VF £180

As previous, but trefoil at king's neck; mintmark rose.

H7HD-010	VG £40	F £100	VF £180

As previous, but crosses by king's neck; mintmark rose or cross fitchée.

H7HD-015	VG £35	F £80	VF £160

Arched Crown Issue

As previous, but front-facing bust of king wearing an arched crown; mintmark none or cinquefoil.

H7HD-020	VG £18	F £35	VF £70

As previous, but saltires by neck; no mintmark.

H7HD-025	VG £18	F £35	VF £70

As H7HD-020, but crown has a lower arch, the lettering in the legends is also more ornate; no mintmark.

H7HD-030	VG £20	F £38	VF £75

As previous, but much smaller portrait; mintmark pheon or lis.

H7HD-035	VG £25	F £45	VF £85

Canterbury Mint

Ecclesiastical Issue under Archbishop Morton

Obverse Legend   As previous.

Reverse Legend   CIVITAS CANTOR — City of Canterbury

Obverse   Front-facing bust of king wearing open early style crown; no mintmark.

Reverse   As previous, but 'M' in centre of reverse.

H7HD-040	ex. rare

Obverse Legend   As previous, except for horizontal lines before king's name.

Reverse Legend   As previous.

Obverse Front-facing bust of king wearing double-arched crown, the four lines in the legend are probably an uncertain mintmark.

Reverse As previous.

H7HD-045 ex. rare

This issue was issued by the king and Bishop jointly.

Obverse Legend As H7HD-040.

Reverse Legend As previous.

Obverse Front-facing bust of king wearing arched crown; mintmark none or lis.

Reverse No 'M' in centre.

H7HD-050 VG £50 F £50 F £100 VF £200

York Mint

York was an ecclesiastical mint under the control of Archbishop Savage.

Obverse Legend As previous.

Reverse Legend CIVITAS EBORACI — City of York

Obverse Front-facing bust of king wearing single-arched crown, key below king's bust; mintmark uncertain.

Reverse Long cross, three pellets in each quarter.

H7HD-055 VG £50 F £100 VF £200

Henry VIII   (1509 – 1547)

Henry VIII produced a variety of halfpennies. During the first and second coinage the issues are fairly similar to those of his father, Henry VII. However, the issues, which all have an arched crown, tend to be slightly crude in style and the mintmarks used are different. The provincial mints had various marks or letters in the field specific to their class, moreover, during the second coinage the obverse legend changed radically to H.DG ROSA SIE SPIA — Henry by the grace of God a rose without a thorn.

During the third and the posthumous coinages, the king has a more life-like bust similar to the one used on larger denominations such as the groat; the reverse, however, remains the same. The third and posthumous issues were struck in base silver. A total of four mints struck halfpennies during Henry VIII's reign: London, Canterbury, York and Bristol. The London mint is henceforth referred to as Tower mint to avoid confusion with the other two mints which operated in London around this period. The mint's name can be found on the reverse of the coin in the legends and read as follows for the various issues:

London — CIVITAS LONDON (1st and 2nd coinage)
Bristol — CIVITAS BRISTOLI (3rd coinage)
Canterbury — CIVITAS CANTOR (1st, 2nd and 3rd coinage)
York — CIVITAS EBORACI (2nd and 3rd coinage)
Tower — CIVITAS LONDON (3rd coinage)

Collecting Hints

The halfpenny was becoming a less important denomination and this is clearly illustrated by the rather poor production of these issues. Many of the issues are unclear, often with legends that are difficult to read. The average condition in which all issues are available is less than Fine. Collectors should try to obtain a coin in the best possible grade, preferably with a legible mint-name and portrait.

First Coinage (1509 – 1526)

London Mint

Obverse Legend HENRIC DI GRA REX AGL — Henry by the grace of God King of England

Reverse Legend CIVITAS LONDON — City of London

Obverse Front-facing bust of king; mintmark castle or portcullis crowned.

Reverse Long cross, three pellets in each quarter.

H8HD-005 VG £20 F £45 VF £80

Canterbury Mint

Obverse Legend As previous.

Reverse Legend CIVITAS CANTOR — City of Canterbury

Obverse Front-facing bust of king dividing 'W.A.' (for Archbishop Warham); mintmark pomegranate or cross fitchée.

Reverse As previous.

H8HD-010 VG £60 F £120 VF £220

Second Coinage (1526 – 1544)

This issue can be easily differentiated from the first coinage by the new obverse legend, and different mintmark.

London Mint

Obverse Legend H DG ROSA SIE SPIA — Henry by the grace of God a rose without a thorn

Reverse Legend CIVITAS LONDON — City of London

Obverse Front-facing bust of king; mintmark rose, lis, arrow or sunburst

Reverse Long cross, three pellets in each quarter.

H8HD-015 VG £20 F £45 VF £80

Canterbury Mint

Obverse Legend As previous.

Reverse Legend CIVITAS CANTOR — City of Canterbury

Obverse Front-facing bust of king dividing 'W.A' (for Archbishop Warham); mintmark 'T' or cross patonce. Mainly Lombardic lettering in the legend.

Reverse As previous.

H8HD-020 VG £35 F £60 VF £120

As previous, but 'T.C.' (for Thomas Cranmer) divided by bust; mintmark Catherine Wheel.

H8HD-025 VG £30 F £55 VF £110

York Mint

Obverse Legend   As previous.

Reverse Legend   CIVITAS EBORACI — City of York

Obverse   Front-facing bust of king dividing 'T.W.' (for Thomas Wolsey); mintmark voided cross or acorn.

Reverse   As previous.

| H8HD-030 | VG £30 | F £55 | VF £110 |

Sede Vacante Issue

Legends   As previous.

Obverse   Front-facing bust of king, key below bust; mintmark cross voided.

Reverse   As previous.

| H8HD-035 | VG £40 | F £75 | VF £150 |

As previous, but front-facing bust of king dividing 'E.L' or 'LE' (Archbishop Lee) on the obverse; mintmark key on the obverse only.

| H8HD-040 | VG £30 | F £55 | VF £110 |

Third Coinage (1544 – 1547)

This issue is very different from the first and second coinages as the obverse has a more life-like bust of the ageing king; it is, however, very similar to the posthumous issue. In most cases, due to the poor condition of the coins, the issues are impossible to distinguish and class. Tiny differences have been listed in all cases but unfortunately it is often impossible to see these small marks and differences on the coins. The reverse of the coin, in all cases, remained very similar to the first and second coinages.

Tower Mint

Obverse Legend   H.D.G ROSA SINE SPINA — Henry by the grace of God a rose without a thorn

Reverse Legend   CIVITAS LONDON — City of London

Obverse   Front-facing, ageing bust of king; mintmark lis or none. Lombardic lettering in the legend.

Reverse   Long cross, three pellets in each quarter, pellet in annulet in centre.

| H8HD-045 | VG £30 | F £50 | VF £90 |

Bristol Mint

Obverse Legend   As previous.

Reverse Legend   CIVITAS BRISTOLI — City of Bristol

Obverse   As previous, but no mintmark.

Reverse   As previous, but no pellet in annulet.

| H8HD-050 | VG £40 | F £80 | VF £90 |

Canterbury Mint

Obverse Legend   As previous, but some read H8 D.G instead of H.D.G.

Reverse Legend   CIVITAS CANTOR — City of Canterbury

Obverse   As previous, trefoil stops in legend; no mintmark. Lombardic or mixed lettering

Reverse   As previous, trefoil stops in legend.

| H8HD-055 | VG £30 | F £50 | VF £90 |

York Mint

Obverse Legend   As H8HD-045.

Reverse Legend   CIVITAS EBORACI — City of York

Obverse   As previous; no mintmark. Mixed lettering and trefoil stops in the legend.

Reverse   As previous.

| H8HD-060 | VG £30 | F £50 | VF £90 |

Posthumous Coinage (1547 – 1551)

As mentioned earlier, the halfpennies for the posthumous issue are virtually identical to those of the third issue. The main differences are as follows: the third coinage issues of the Tower and Canterbury mints have Lombardic lettering while the posthumous issue has Roman lettering which looks more like the lettering of today. However, the third coinage sometimes does have some Roman lettering in the legends. The main difference with the York mint is the stops which are found on the coin; in the third coinage they are trefoils and the posthumous issue has either single pellets or lozenges.

Tower Mint

Obverse Legend   H. DG ROSA SINA SPINA — Henry by the grace of God a rose without a thorn

Reverse Legend   CIVITAS LONDON — City of London

Obverse   Front-facing bust of ageing king; no mintmark. Roman lettering in the legend.

Reverse   Long cross, three pellets in each quarter.

| H8HD-065 | VG £30 | F £50 | VF £100 |

Canterbury Mint

Obverse Legend   As previous, but sometimes reads H8.

Reverse Legend   CIVITAS CANTOR — City of Canterbury

Obverse   As previous. Roman lettering

Reverse   As previous.

| H8HD-070 | VG £35 | F £60 | VF £120 |

York Mint

Obverse Legend   As H8HD-065.

Reverse Legend   CIVITAS EBORACI — City of York

Obverse   As previous; no mintmark. Lozenge or pellet stops in the legend, mixed style of lettering.

Reverse   As previous.

| H8HD-075 | VG £30 | F £50 | VF £100 |

| E6HD-015 | VG £150 | F £300 | VF £600 |

No halfpennies were struck during the reigns of Mary or Philip and Mary.

Edward VI (1547 – 1553)

During this short reign, several issues of halfpenny were produced in Edward VI's name. The first issue, produced during the first period from April 1547 to January 1549, was struck at the Tower and Bristol mints. These two issues are both extremely rare and had the crowned bust of the king on the obverse, while the reverse still had the long cross with three pellets in each quarter. During the third period (1550 – 53), a halfpenny was produced which omitted the king's head on the obverse and replaced it with a rose; the royal shield is found on the reverse. This issue is very rare, but not as rare as the issues from the first period. All these coins were struck in base silver and no halfpennies were produced during Edward VI's fine silver issue.

Collecting Hints

These issues are rare in any grade. Collectors will have great difficulty obtaining a specimen.

First Period April (1547 – Jan 1549)

Tower Mint

Obverse Legend EDG ROSA SIN SPIN — Edward by the grace of God a rose without a thorn

Reverse Legend CIVITAS LONDON — City of London

Obverse Crowned bust of king; mintmark uncertain.

Reverse Long cross with three pellets in each angle.

| E6HD-005 | VG £200 | F £400 | VF £800 |

Bristol Mint

Obverse Legend As previous, or ED6 DG instead of EDG.

Reverse Legend CIVITAS BRISTOLI — City of Bristol

Obverse As previous, but no mintmark.

Reverse As previous.

| E6HD-010 | VG £180 | F £350 | VF £700 |

Third Period (1550 – 1553)

This issue was only struck at the Tower mint and often used as a farthing because of its base silver content.

Obverse Legend EDG ROSA SINE SPINA — Edward by the grace of God a rose without a thorn

Reverse Legend CIVITAS LONDON — City of London

Obverse Rose in centre; mintmark escallop.

Reverse Royal shield over cross.

Elizabeth I (1558 – 1603)

Although no halfpennies were struck during the first twenty years of Elizabeth's reign, they were produced in some quantity during the fifth and sixth issues (1582 – 1602). These halfpennies, due to their very small size, did not have either the queen's portrait or legends; there was, however, a portcullis on the obverse and the reverse had a cross with three pellets in each quarter. Most issues had mintmarks which are found on the obverse above the portcullis.

Collecting Hints

Elizabeth's halfpennies are fairly scarce but obtainable. They are usually available in the higher grades. Fine and VF examples are not uncommon. They are rarely found damaged or clipped.

Fifth Issue (1582 – 1600)

Obverse Portcullis; mintmarks none, 'A', escallop, crescent, hand, tun, woolpack, key, anchor or '0'.

Reverse Cross with three pellets in each quarter.

| ELHD-005 | VG £20 | F £40 | VF £90 |

Sixth Issue (1601 – 1602)

The mintmark denoted the date the coin was made, '1' for 1601 and '2' for 1602.

Obverse As previous, but mintmark '1' or '2'.

Reverse As previous.

| ELHD-010 | VG £22 | F £45 | VF £90 |

James I (1603 – 1625)

Halfpennies were produced during all three coinages of James I. The first coinage issue is very similar to the issues of Elizabeth I; the only difference is the mintmark. James I used mintmark thistle and lis. During the second and third coinages the style was completely changed; on the obverse is a simple rose and a thistle on the reverse. The second coinage coins have a mintmark above the thistle but the third coinage coins have no mintmark.

Collecting Hints

Halfpennies from the first coinage are fairly scarce, due to the fact that they were only produced for two years; however, they are usually obtainable in Fine condition, VF examples are not rare. Halfpennies from the second and third coinages are fairly common and usually obtainable in Fine to EF condition.

First Coinage (1603 – 1604)

Obverse   Portcullis; mintmark thistle or lis.

Reverse   Long cross, three pellets in each quarter.

J1HD-005	VG £20	F £30	VF £50

Second Coinage (1604 – 1619)

Obverse   Rose.

Reverse   Thistle with mintmark lis, rose, escallop, grapes, coronet, key, bell, mullet and cinquefoil.

J1HD-010	VG £18	F £28	VF £50	EF £80

Third Coinage (1619 – 1625)

Obverse   Rose.

Reverse   Thistle; no mintmark.

J1HD-015	VG £18	F £28	VF £50	EF £80

Charles I   (1625 – 1649)

Hardly any halfpennies were produced during Charles I's reign. This is surprising considering the diversity, and quantity, of denominations that Charles I produced. The first, and most common, issue was struck at the Tower mint. This issue is easily recognisable, simply having a rose either side of the coin; there is no legend or mintmark. The only other Charles I halfpenny was produced at the Aberystwyth mint. This issue has a rose on the obverse, plumes on the reverse. As with the Tower mint issue, it has no legend or mintmark.

Collecting Hints

The Tower mint issue is fairly common, usually obtainable in about Fine condition. VF examples exist and are obtainable. The Aberystwyth issue is rare and difficult to obtain in any grade.

Tower Mint

Obverse   Rose, no mintmark.

Reverse   Rose.

C1HD-005	VG £18	F £30	VF £50

Aberystwyth Mint (1638 – 1642)

Obverse   Rose, no mintmark.

Reverse   Plumes.

C1HD-010	VG £80	F £150	VF £250

Commonwealth   (1649 – 1660)

The Commonwealth period was the last to produce the silver halfpenny which was replaced by a milled copper coin during Charles II's reign. The halfpennies of the Commonwealth are very plain, with no mintmark. There is the St George's cross on the obverse and the Irish harp on the reverse. Forgeries of this issue are quite common, they are usually very thick and the style is slightly different.

Collecting Hints

This issue is fairly scarce; coins are usually available in Fine or VF condition. Sometimes the coins are clipped or officially holed to devalue them.

Obverse   St George's cross.

Reverse   Arms of Ireland.

CWHD-005	VG £25	F £60	VF £125

No halfpennies were produced during the hammered coinage of Charles II (1660 – 62).

Farthing

Silver farthings, with one exception, were first produced in England during the reign of Edward I. The exception is an extremely rare specimen which was produced for Henry III. Farthings were part of Edward I's recoinage plan and were one of several new denominations introduced. Previously, the need for smaller denominations had been met by cutting pennies in half or quarters.

Any problem encountered by collectors is likely to be due to the farthing's size and value. Being the smallest denomination, it was seldom hoarded and in fact farthings, unlike pennies, have not been found in large hoards. Most issues are also extremely small, which has made it difficult to locate them with metal detectors as few can pick up a signal the size of a farthing. For these reasons, farthings tend to be rare.

Another difficulty could be identification. If the farthing is unclipped and in at least Fine condition, this problem should not arise. However, most issues are often weakly struck and sometimes clipped, making them difficult to identify. Also, halfpennies were often clipped and so resemble farthings.

Farthings were not produced in such a variety as denominations such as the penny were, but they were produced in most reigns. It is important to remember that all farthings were issued with full legends. If unsure, collectors should also refer to the halfpenny chapter when identifying an issue they think is a farthing.

Henry III (1216 – 1272)

This issue has only recently been discovered and is extremely rare. It was struck at the London mint during the short-cross coinage. It is similar to the penny in style, but very small. It is uncertain whether this issue can be considered a pattern as no documentary evidence exists. At the time of writing, with only two specimens known, this issue cannot be considered important as a denomination, but rather a trial issue.

Obverse Legend HENRICUS REX — King Henry

Reverse Legend TERRI (or ELIS or RALPH) ON LUND — Terry (or Elis or Ralph) of London

Obverse Bust of king holding sceptre.

Reverse Short cross, three pellets in each quarter.

H3FA-005	ex. rare

Edward I (1272 – 1307)

Edward I farthings were produced in very large quantities; London was by far the most prolific mint although Berwick, Bristol, Lincoln, Newcastle and York all issued farthings. These mints, in most cases, are very rare. The farthing, in all cases, is fairly similar to Edward's penny issues. The obverse has a crowned front-facing bust of the king, the legend starts EDWARDUS or ER for Edward. The reverse has the mint's name in the legend, a long cross dividing the coin and three pellets in each quarter.

The weight and fineness of Edward's farthing issues, unlike the other denominations, varies. The first three issues from the London mint weigh 6.85 grains (0.44 grams), the rest of the issues weigh 5.5 grains (0.36 grams); the value of the coins, however, remained the same. This was because the heavier issues had a lower fineness, or silver content, than the lighter issues. It is thought that the coins were made larger in order to make them easier to strike and handle. Coins of low fineness have never been popular in England and the public preferred the inconvenience of a smaller coin with a high metal content.

As mentioned earlier, six mints were active during Edward I's reign. The mint's name can be found on the reverse of the coin. They read LONDONIENSIS or CIVITAS LONDON for London, VILLA BEREVVICI for Berwick, VILLA BRISTOLLIE for Bristol, CIVITAS LINCOL for Lincoln, NOVICASTRI for Newcastle, and CIVITAS EBORACI for York.

When identifying farthings, use the same procedure as with pennies or groats. Firstly check the obverse legend; there are varieties, which are important. These varieties are one of the main, and easiest, ways of identifying farthings from the first three reigns of Edward. However, the farthing may not fall into a class, as many issues share the same obverse legend. Collectors should then check through each issue, looking for the various marks or differences, as they will differentiate the issue.

London Mint

Heavy Weight 6.65 grains (0.44 grams)

Class 1A

Obverse Legend EDWARDUS REX — King Edward

Reverse Legend LONDONIENSIS — London

Obverse Front-facing bust of king wearing bifoliate crown.

Reverse Long cross, three pellets in each quarter.

E1FA-005	VG £20	F £50	VF £125

Class 1C

As previous, but the king is wearing a trifoliate crown.

E1FA-010	VG £25	F £60	VF £140

Class 2

As previous, but reversed 'N's in reverse legend.

E1FA-015	VG £20	F £45	VF £125

Class 3C

As E1FA-010, but the king has a larger face and bushier hair.

| E1FA-020 | VG £20 | F £45 | VF £125 |

Reduced Weight 5.5 grains (0.36 grams)

Class 3D/3E

Obverse Legend   ER ANGLIE — Edward King of England

Reverse Legend   LONDONIENSIS — London

Obverse   Front-facing bust of king, no inner circle.

Reverse   As previous.

| E1FA-025 | VG £20 | F £45 | VF £125 |

Class 4

Obverse Legend   As previous

Reverse Legend   CIVITAS LONDON — City of London

Obverse   As previous, but king wears a tall narrow crown.

Reverse   As previous.

| E1FA-030 | VG £35 | F £60 | VF £140 |

Class 5

As previous, but the king has a wider crown; large irregular lettering in the legends.

| E1FA-035 | VG £35 | F £60 | VF £140 |

Class 6/7

As previous, but king has almond shaped eyes; double-barred 'N' in legend.

| E1FA-040 | VG £70 | F £140 | VF £220 |

Class 8

Obverse Legend   ER ANGL DN — Edward King of England Lord (of Ireland)

Reverse Legend   As previous.

Obverse   Closed 'E' in legend.

Reverse   As previous.

| E1FA-045 | VG £35 | F £60 | VF £140 |

Class 9

Similar to previous but pot-hook, unbarred 'N's in legend. This issue is probably a variety of Class 6/7 (E1FA-040), since no independent records exist for it at the mint.

| E1FA-050 | VG £35 | F £60 | VF £140 |

Class 10 (& 11)

This issue is often struck on an oval flan, and was possibly also struck during Edward II's reign.

Obverse Legend   EDWARDUS REX A(N) — Edward King of England

Reverse Legend   CIVITAS LONDON — City of London

Obverse   Inner circle, the king has a narrow face and narrow lettering in the legend.

Reverse   As previous.

| E1FA-055 | VG £20 | F £50 | VF £90 |

Berwick Mint

Obverse Legend   EDWARDUS REX — King Edward

Reverse Legend   VIIIA BERVVICI — Town of Berwick

Obverse   Front-facing bust of king.

Reverse   Long cross, three pellets in each quarter.

| E1FA-060 | ex. rare |

Bristol Mint

Class 3C

Obverse Legend   EDWARDUS REX — King Edward

Reverse Legend   VILLA BRISTOLLIE — Town of Bristol

Obverse   Large face with bushy hair.

Reverse   As previous.

| E1FA-065 | VG £50 | F £100 | F £200 |

Class 3G

Obverse Legend   E R ANGLIE — Edward King of England

Reverse Legend   As previous.

Obverse   No inner circle.

Reverse   As previous.

| E1FA-070 | VG £60 | F £120 | VF £220 |

Lincoln Mint

Class 3G

Obverse Legend   E R ANGLIE — Edward King of England

Reverse Legend   CIVITAS LINCOL — City of Lincoln

Obverse   No inner circle.

Reverse   As previous.

| E1FA-075 | VG £80 | F £150 | VF £300 |

Newcastle Mint

Class 3E

Obverse Legend   E R ANGLIE — Edward King of England

Reverse Legend   NOVI CASTRI — Newcastle

Obverse   Front-facing bust with no inner circle.

Reverse   As previous, but pellet-barred 'N's on reverse.

| E1FA-080 | VG £150 | F £300 |

As previous, but only one pellet in each quarter on reverse.

E1FA-085 ex. rare

York Mint

Class 3C

Obverse Legend EDWARDUS REX — King Edward

Reverse Legend CIVITAS EBORACI — City of York

Obverse Inner circles, and the king has a large face with bushier hair.

Reverse Long cross, three pellets in each quarter.

E1FA-090 VG £125 F £200 VF £350

Class 3E

Obverse Legend E R ANGLIE — Edward King of England

Reverse Legend As previous.

Obverse No inner circle.

Reverse As previous.

E1FA-095 VG £125 F £200 VF £350

Edward II (1307 – 1327)

Of the two mints which produced farthings during Edward II's reign, Berwick is extremely rare and London is rare. The London issue is very similar to Edward I's last London farthing, although there are a few differences. The combination of rarity and poor condition has resulted in little research being done towards classing these issues. In fact, in most cases, it appears probable that Edward I's last issue was in production during Edward II's reign. Although the obverse legend of Edward II farthings is often unclear, and varieties seem to exist, one of the main difference between the two reigns is in the lettering. In most of Edward II's issues the 'N's are unbarred and the 'E' is slightly different in style. Also, in many of Edward II's issues, the king has a more pointed face; in Edward I's issues the king has a rounder face.

Collecting Hints

As mentioned earlier, Edward II farthings are difficult to obtain and identify. They are usually found in less than Fine condition. Coins with clear legends and marks, such as unbarred Ns, are desirable.

London Mint

Obverse Legend EDWARDUS REX (AN) — Edward King of England

Reverse Legend CIVITAS LONDON — City of London

Obverse Front-facing bust of king with inner circle, crown with wedge-shaped or uneven petals to central lis, usually with unbarred 'N's in legend; mintmark plain Initial cross or Initial cross pattée.

Reverse Long cross, three pellets in each quarter.

E2FA-005 VG £40 F £80 VF £180

Berwick Mint

Obverse Legend EDWARDUS REX — King Edward

Reverse Legend VILLA BERVICCI — Town of Berwick

Obverse This issue is virtually identical to that of Edward I, except that on Edward II issues one of the spears in the crown is broken.

Reverse Long cross, three pellets in each quarter.

E2FA-010 VG £100 F £200

Edward III (1327 – 1377)

Edward III's issues, while fairly similar to those of the two previous reigns, are fairly easy to identify, having various markings or different obverse legends. Three mints produced Edward III's farthings; London was the most prolific, while Berwick is rare and the farthing from the Reading mint is unique. In all issues the king's name appears on the obverse of the coin, starting at the top. If instead of EDWARDUS it reads RICARD or HENRI, it is an issue of Richard or Henry.

Collecting Hints

All Edward III issues are rare and usually obtainable unclipped in Fine condition. VF examples exist but are rare.

First Coinage (1327 – 1335)

London Mint

Obverse Legend EDWARDUS REX (A) — King Edward

Reverse Legend CIVITAS LONDON — City of London

Obverse Front-facing bust of king, the crown is flat.

Reverse Long cross, three pellets in each quarter.

E3FA-005 VG £60 F £150 VF £300

Berwick Mint

Obverse Legend EDWARDUS REX — King Edward

Reverse Legend VILLA BERVICCI — Town of Berwick

Obverse Front-facing bust of king.

Reverse Bear's head in two quarters of reverse.

E3FA-010 VG £100 F £250 VF —

Second Coinage (1335 – 1343)

This issue was struck at the London mint in .833 silver although the usual silver content for coins of this period was .925.

Obverse Legend EDWARDUS REX A — Edward King of England

Reverse Legend CIVITAS LONDON — City of London

Obverse Similar to E3FA-005, except that this issue is rougher in style, the king's crown is taller and there is a star at the end of the legend.

Reverse Long cross, three pellets in each quarter.

E3FA-015 VG £40 F £80 VF £150

Third or Florin Coinage (1344 – 1351)

This issue was struck in .925 silver.

London Mint

Obverse Legend EDWARDUS REX — King Edward

Reverse Legend CIVITAS LONDON — City of London

Obverse Front-facing bust of king with bushy hair, broad neck and shoulders; the crown has neat broad fleurs or prongs.

Reverse As previous.

| E3FA-020 | VG £40 | F £65 | VF £120 |

Reading Mint

As previous, but escallop in one quarter of reverse and reverse legend reads VILLA RADINGY — Town of Reading.

| E3FA-025 | unique |

Fourth Coinage

These issues were struck in London.

Series E (1354 – 1355)

Obverse Legend EDWARDUS REX (AN) — King Edward

Reverse Legend CIVITAS LONDON — City of London

Obverse Front-facing crowned bust of king, broken letters in legend; mintmark cross 2.

Reverse Long cross, three pellets in each quarter.

| E3FA-030 | VF £100 | F £200 | VF — |

As previous, but annulet in one quarter of reverse.

| E3FA-035 | ex. rare |

Treaty Period (1361 – 1369)

Obverse Legend EDWARDUS REX — King Edward

Reverse Legend CIVITAS LONDON — City of London

Obverse Front-facing bust of king, pellet stop in legend.

Reverse As previous.

| E3FA-040 | VG £80 | F £180 | VF £300 |

Post Treaty Period (1369 – 1377)

Obverse Legend EDWARD REX ANGL — Edward King of England

Reverse Legend CIVITAS LONDON — City of London

Obverse The king has a large head and no neck.

Reverse As previous.

| E3FA-045 | VG £100 | F £200 | VF £325 |

Richard II   (1377 – 1399)

Richard II was the only Richard to produce farthings and this makes identifying an issue fairly easy as the coins bear the king's name, RICARD, on the obverse. All farthings issued by Richard are rare and were only struck at the London mint.

Collecting Hints

All issues of Richard II are rare in any grade. They are usually available in about Fine condition but VF examples exist. Collectors may have great difficulty in obtaining an example.

Obverse Legend RICARD REX ANGL — Richard King of England

Reverse Legend CIVITAS LONDON — City of London

Obverse Front-facing small bust of king.

Reverse Long cross, three pellets in each quarter.

| R2FA-005 | VG £125 | F £275 | VF £500 |

As previous, but a small rose after REX.

| R2FA-010 | VG £140 | F £300 | VF £550 |

As R2FA-005, bust but larger bust.

| R2FA-015 | ex. rare |

As previous, but on reverse a rose in each quarter instead of pellets.

| R2FA-020 | VG £250 | F £550 | VF £1,100 |

Henry IV   (1399 – 1413)

Farthings were issued during both the heavy and the light coinages of Henry IV. The heavy coinage is approximately 20% heavier than the light coinage but both issues are very rare. The two issues have variations which differentiate them from other reigns; not only is HENRIC found on the obverse, starting at the top but also the coins show a face of the king without a neck, whereas all other reigns have a proper bust. On the light coinage there is a slipped trefoil after REX in the obverse legend. Also, LONDON on the obverse legend appears to be spelled LOIDOI.

Collecting Hints

All coins from Henry IV's reign are very rare and the farthing is no exception. Collectors may have great difficulty in obtaining an example in any grade.

Heavy Coinage (1399 – 1412)

Obverse Legend HENRIC REX ANGL — Henry King of England

Reverse Legend CIVITAS LONDON — City of London

Obverse Face of king with no neck.

Reverse Long cross, three pellets in each quarter.

| H4FA-005 | VG £300 | F £600 | VF £1,200 |

Light Coinage (1412 – 1413)

Obverse Legend As previous.

Reverse Legend CIVITAS LONDON (appears LOIDOI) — City of London

Obverse Small face without neck, slipped trefoil after REX.

Reverse As previous.

| H4FA-010 | VG £325 | F £700 | VF £1,250 |

Henry V   (1413 – 1422)

Only one issue of farthing was produced during the reign of Henry V and it is very different from that of Henry IV as the king has a neck. However, this issue is fairly similar to those of Henry VI and the main difference is that Henry VI's issues have various marks, such as annulets, on the coin. Collectors should check both reigns when identifying farthings from this period as both reigns have the obverse legend starting with the king's name, HENRIC. During Henry V's reign the farthing was only produced at the London mint.

Collecting Hints

This issue is very rare. It is usually obtainable in about Fine condition but VF examples exist.

Obverse Legend HENRIC REX ANGL — Henry King of England

Reverse Legend CIVITAS LONDON — City of London

Obverse Front-facing bust of king with small face but with a neck; no marks elsewhere on coin.

Reverse Long cross, three pellets in each quarter

| H5FA-005 | VG £100 | F £250 | VF £425 |

Henry VI First Reign (1422 – 1461)

Farthings were produced for most of Henry VI's issues and struck at the London and Calais mints. Each issue is easily identifiable by various marks which are found on the coin. To the untrained eye, a Henry V issue is fairly similar to Henry VI's issues and both reigns should be referred to when identifying a coin from this period. In all cases the king's name is found in the obverse legend, at the top of the coin, and should read HENRIC; if it reads RICARD or EDWARD, it is an issue of Richard or Edward. The mint's name can be found on the reverse of the coin and for the issues of Henry VI reads CIVITAS LONDON for London or VILLA CALIS for Calais (possible varieties exist).

Collecting Hints

All Henry VI farthings are fairly rare and usually obtainable in at least Fine condition, VF and EF examples exist. The issues from Calais are rarer than the London ones.

Annulet Issue (1422 – 1427)

London Mint

Obverse Legend HENRIC REX ANGL — Henry King of England

Reverse Legend CIVITAS LONDON — City of London

Obverse Front-facing bust of king; mintmark cross pommée.

Reverse Long cross, three pellets in each quarter and two annulets in two quarters.

| H6FA-005 | VG £100 | F £225 | VF £400 |

Calais Mint

Obverse Legend As previous.

Reverse Legend VILLA CALIS — Town of Calais

Obverse Front-facing bust of king, annulet either side of neck.

Reverse As previous, but no annulets.

| H6FA-010 | VG £150 | F £375 | VF £700 |

Rosette Mascle Issue (1427 – 1430)

This issue has rosettes and mascles somewhere in the legends.

London Mint

Obverse Legend As previous.

Reverse Legend CIVITAS LONDON — City of London

Obverse Front-facing bust of king, rosettes and mascles in legend.

Reverse Long cross, three pellets in each quarter.

| H6FA-015 | VG £80 | F £150 | VF £300 |

Calais Mint

Obverse Legend As previous.

Reverse Legend VILLA CALIS — Town of Calais

Obverse As previous; mintmark cross pommée.

Reverse As previous.

| H6FA-020 | VG £85 | F £160 | VF £325 |

Pinecone Mascle Issue (1430 – 1434)

This issue has pinecones and mascles in the legend.

London Mint

Obverse Legend As previous.

Reverse Legend CIVITAS LONDON — City of London

Obverse Front-facing bust of king, pinecones and mascles in the legend.

Reverse Long cross, three pellets in each quarter.

| H6FA-025 | VG £80 | F £150 | VF £300 |

Calais Mint

As previous, but reverse legend reads VILLA CALIS — Town of Calais.

H6FA-030	VG £100	F £225	VF £400

Leaf Trefoil Issue (1435 – 1438)

This issue was only struck at the London mint.

Obverse Legend   As previous.

Reverse Legend   CIVITAS LONDON — City of London

Obverse   Front-facing bust of king, leaf on breast, trefoil and saltire stops in legend.

Reverse   Long cross, three pellets in each quarter.

H6FA-035	VG £80	F £150	VF £300

Leaf Pellet Issue (1443 – 1445)

This issue was only struck at the London mint.

Legends   As previous.

Obverse   Front-facing bust of king with leaf on breast, with a pellet either side of crown.

Reverse   As previous, but usually extra pellet in two quarters.

H6FA-040	VG £100	F £225	VF £375

Cross Pellet Issue (1454 – 1460)

This issue was only struck at the London mint.

As previous, but a saltire either side of the neck and a pellet either side of the crown.

H6FA-045	VG £100	F £225	VF £375

Edward IV First Reign (1461 – 1470)

Edward IV had two issues, the light and the heavy coinage, so called because of the difference in weight but in the case of farthings weight cannot be used to help identify various issues. Farthings were struck during both coinages of Edward IV but only at the London mint. The king's name is always found on the obverse of the coin at the top and should read EDWARD.

Collecting Hints

These issues are extremely rare and difficult to obtain in any grade.

Heavy Coinage (1461 – 1464)

Obverse Legend   EDWARD REX ANGLI — Edward King of England

Reverse Legend   CIVITAS LONDON — City of London

Obverse   Front-facing bust of king; mintmark plain cross.

Reverse   Long cross, three pellets in each quarter.

E4FA-005	VG £400	F £650	VF £1,400

Light Coinage (1464 – 1470)

Obverse Legend   EDWARD DI GRA REX — Edward King by the grace of God

Reverse Legend   As previous.

Obverse   Front-facing bust of king; mintmark rose.

Reverse   As previous.

E4FA-010	VG £300	F £500	VF £1,100

As previous, but trefoil either side of neck; mintmark crown.

E4FA-015	VG £500	F £700	VF £1,500

No farthings were struck for Henry VI Restored, Edward IV's second reign, Edward IV/V, Edward V or Richard III.

Henry VII   (1485 – 1509)

Only one type of farthing was issued during the reign of Henry VII. It is a very rare issue and was struck at the London mint. It is easily identifiable by its unique obverse legend, while the style of bust is also very different to any other issues. Collectors should not confuse the farthing with the halfpenny issue of the same reign; pay particular attention to the size of the coins. Remember, issues of later kings tend to be smaller than the issue of earlier kings because the weights of the coins were being reduced.

Collecting Hints

This issue is very rare in any grade and difficult to obtain; the usual grade in which they are found is Fine.

Obverse Legend   HENRIC DI GRA REX — Henry King by the grace of God

Reverse Legend   CIVITAS LONDON — City of London

Obverse   Front-facing crowned bust of King with arched crown; mintmark uncertain.

Reverse   Long cross, three pellets in each quarter.

H7FA-005	VG £125	F £200	VF £350

Henry VIII   (1509 – 1547)

Collecting Hints

All issues of Henry VIII farthings are extremely rare and collectors will have great difficulty in obtaining an example.

First Coinage (1509 – 1526)

Obverse Legend   HENRIC DI GRA REX — Henry King by the grace of God

Reverse Legend   CIVITAS LONDON — City of London

Obverse   Portcullis; mintmark portcullis in legend.

Reverse   Rose on long cross.

| H8FA-005 | VG £350 | F £650 | VF £1,100 |

Second Coinage (1526 – 1544)

Obverse Legend   RUTILANS ROSA — A dazzling rose

Reverse Legend   DEO GRACIA — By the grace of God

Obverse   Portcullis; mintmark probably lis in legend, or rose or sunburst.

Reverse   Long cross with one pellet in each quarter; no mintmark.

| H8FA-010 | VG £350 | F £650 | VF £1,100 |

Obverse Legend   As previous

Reverse Legend   DEO GRACIS — By the grace of God

Obverse   Portcullis; mintmark arrow in legend.

Reverse   Rose on long cross.

| H8FA-015   ex. rare |

An issue exists as H8FA-015, but with mintmark Catherine wheel. This is probably from the Canterbury mint, which used this mintmark under Archbishop Thomas Cranmer.

| H8FA-020   ex. rare |

Third Coinage (1544 – 1547)

Collecting Hints

This issue is extremely rare.

Obverse Legend   RUTILANS ROSA — A dazzling rose

Reverse Legend   DEO GRACIA — By the grace of God

Obverse   A rose; mintmark ?none.

Reverse   Cross and pellets.

| H8FA-025 ex. rare |

Edward VI (1547 – 1553)

Edward VI's farthing was issued in base silver during the third period of coinage (1550 – 53). The issue is fairly similar to that of Henry VIII, with a portcullis on the obverse, but the obverse legend is different. The reverse differs by not having a rose in the centre of the long cross.

Collecting Hints

This issue is extremely rare in any grade; collectors may have great difficulty in obtaining an example.

Obverse Legend   E. D.G. ROSA SINE SPI — Edward by the grace of God a rose without a thorn

Reverse Legend   CIVITAS LONDON — City of London

Obverse   Portcullis; mintmark uncertain.

Reverse   Long cross, three pellets in each quarter.

| E6FA-005   ex. rare |

No farthings were struck during the reign of Mary, Philip and Mary or   Elizabeth I due mainly to the fact that a silver farthing was just too small to be struck and was also easily lost. And although the farthing was a useful denomination for the less affluent, the rich and powerful citizens of the land did not need it, so none were produced. During this period lead tokens were produced by small businessmen, especially in London. It is thought that these tokens represented the value of a farthing. These issues often had a simple design or the issuer's initials but very little is known about them and no law was passed making them legal tender. However, they became an acceptable part of life, particularly in London.

James I (1603 – 1625)

During James I's reign the first copper farthings were introduced. James, who was also King of Scotland, realised that small denomination coins of base metal would be acceptable to the English especially as copper coins had been circulating successfully in Scotland and Europe for some considerable time. However, the English seemed to have had an obsession with gold and silver, trusting the real market value these precious metals had. This is illustrated in the havoc caused by Henry VIII's large denomination base silver coins. James I decided not to issue the farthings himself; instead, the production was put into the hands of John Harrington, Lord of Exton. Lord Harrington was heavily charged for this privilege but also made a large profit. Unlike larger denominations, they did not contain their value in metal. The issues produced by Lord Harrington are known as Harringtons. Lord Harrington died in 1614 and the right to produce farthings passed to his son, who died a few months later, and then back to Harrington's wife, Lady Anne Harrington. It appears that Lady Harrington either sold, or gave, the farthing patent to Lodewicke, Duke of Lennox. The issues of the Duke of Lennox were larger than Harrington's. Several varieties of each issue exist but in all cases the obverse has a crown with sceptres behind and a crowned harp is found on the reverse. These issues, especially the Lennox, are fairly similar to those of Charles I. However, they can be very easily identified by referring to the obverse legend. All coins of James I bear the king's name, IACO, while those of Charles I read CARO, CARA or CAROLUS.

Collecting Hints

James I farthings are fairly common, usually obtainable in Fine and VF condition; EF examples are not uncommon. In the last 20 years many coins have been found in the River Thames. Examples are often bent but can be easily straightened and, unlike silver coins, leave little damage. Forgeries of this reign exist. Collectors should refer to the information given about forgeries after Charles I.

Harrington Issues

Tin Surface Issue

These issues originally had a surface of tin which served two purposes. Firstly, to make counterfeiting more difficult; secondly, to make the coins look like silver and, therefore, more acceptable. Issues with original tin showing are more valuable than issues without and coins in VF or better condition must have a full tin surface to command the values stated here. These small Harringtons are on a 12.25 mm flan.

Obverse Legend   IACO DG MAG BRIT — James by the grace of God King of Great Britain

Reverse Legend (continued from the obverse legend) FRA ET HIB REX — France and Ireland

Obverse Two sceptres through a crown.

Reverse Crowned harp.

| J1FA-005 | VG £15 | F £35 | VF £70 | EF £110 |

As previous, but central jewel on circlet of crown.

| J1FA-010 | VG £20 | F £40 | VF £70 | EF £110 |

Larger Size Issue

This issue is larger (15 mm flan) and the coin surface was not tin washed. From now on no other issues were washed in tin.

As previous, but crowned harp is reversed.

| J1FA-015 | VG £8 | F £20 | VF £35 | EF £65 |

Lennox Issue

This issue can be easily differentiated by referring to the obverse legends. The Lennox obverse legend starts at the top, or bottom of the coin while the Harrington issue has the legend starting before the top of the coin. All Lennox issues are of the new larger size (15 mm flan).

Legends As previous.

Obverse Crown with sceptres in centre; no mintmark. The legend starts at the top of the coin.

Reverse Crowned harp; mintmark at start of legend.

| J1FA-020 | VG £6 | F £18 | VF £35 | EF £60 |

As previous, but mintmark both sides.

| J1FA-025 | VG £6 | F £18 | VF £35 | EF £60 |

As previous, but mintmark on obverse only.

| J1FA-030 | VG £6 | F £18 | VF £35 | EF £60 |

As previous, but larger crowns on obverse and reverse.

| J1FA-035 | VG £6 | F £18 | VF £35 | EF £60 |

This issue is oval, the legends start at the bottom of the coin and there is a mintmark on both sides.

Obverse Legend As previous.

Reverse Legend As previous.

Obverse As previous, with long sceptres.

Reverse As previous.

| J1FA-040 | VG £20 | F £45 | VF £80 |

Charles I (1625 – 1649)

All of Charles I's farthings were made under the king's licence, as with the previous issues of James I; neither the Tower nor any provincial mints produced farthings. In 1623, during James I's reign, the Duke of Lennox had also become Duke of Richmond but died a few months later. The farthing patent passed jointly to his widow Frances, Duchess of Richmond, and Sir Francis Crane. The first issues of Charles I are known as Richmond issues, after the patent holder. In 1634 another farthing patent was issued, to Lord Maltravers, Henry Howard and Sir Francis Crane; these issues are known as Maltravers. During this period huge quantities of forged farthings were in circulation and the situation became unacceptable as the poor felt conned and unfairly treated by the authorities. As a result Lord Maltravers was asked to introduce a new style denomination. This was called the Rose farthing, it was much smaller and also thicker. However, the main difference was the metal and the way in which it was made. Most of the coin was made of copper, but a small brass 'plug' was inserted into part of the coin. This made the issue almost impossible to forge and the production of forgeries swiftly ended.

Collecting Hints

Most Charles I farthings are fairly common, usually obtainable in Fine and VF condition; EF examples also exist. Most issues are undamaged and bent examples can be easily straightened. There are, however, forgeries of most issues. Please refer to the listings of forgeries at the end of this chapter. The majority of Charles I's farthings have been found in the River Thames. They are often fairly bright in colour.

Richmond or Royal Issues

This issue is an altered die from James I's Lennox issue (J1FA-030).

Obverse Legend   CARO (over IACO) D.G. MAG BRI — Charles by the grace of God King of Great Britain

Reverse Legend   FRA ET HIB REX — France and Ireland

Obverse   Crown with two sceptres; mintmark above crown.

Reverse   Crown over harp; no mintmark.

| C1FA-005 | VG £5 | F £18 | VF £30 | EF £50 |

As previous, but new die with king's name spelt CARA; mintmark on obverse.

| C1FA-010 | VG £40 | F £90 | VF £180 | EF ex. rare |

As previous, with new die with king's name spelt CARO.

| C1FA-015 | VG £5 | F £18 | VF £30 | EF £50 |

The next four issues, instead of having single stops in the legend, have apostrophe stops.

Obverse Legend   As previous.

Reverse Legend   As previous.

Obverse   As previous.

Reverse   As previous, but the harp has an eagle's head.

| C1FA-020 | VG £5 | F £18 | VF £30 | EF £50 |

As previous, but the harp is beaded.

| C1FA-025 | VG £5 | F £18 | VF £30 | EF £50 |

As previous, but the harp is scroll fronted with five jewels.

| C1FA-030 | VG £10 | F £25 | VF £40 | EF £60 |

As previous, but with seven jewels.

| C1FA-035 | VG £5 | F £18 | VF £30 | EF £50 |

Transitional Issue

This issue is fairly similar to the previous one, however, it has a double arched crown on both sides as used for the Maltravers issue.

| C1FA-040 | VG £25 | F £30 | VF £60 | EF £100 |

Maltravers Issues

This issue is easily identified because it has inner circles on the obverse and reverse.

Obverse Legend   CAROLUS D.G. MAG BR — Charles by the grace of God King of Great Britain

Reverse Legend   FRAN ET HIB REX — France and Ireland

Obverse   Crown with two sceptres in inner circles; mintmark at start of legend.

Reverse   Harp with crown above; no mintmark.

| C1FA-045 | VG £8 | F £25 | VF £40 | EF £60 |

As previous, but mintmark both sides.

| C1FA-050 | VG £5 | F £18 | VF £30 | EF £50 |

As previous, but different mintmark either side (i.e. muled).

| C1FA-055 | VG £5 | F £18 | VF £30 | EF £50 |

Oval Issues

These reasonably scarce issues are fairly similar to the last issues of James I. In fact Charles I's first issue actually uses the James I die. However, the king's name has been altered to CARO from

IACO. These issues are oval and, in all cases, the legend starts at the bottom of the coin.

Obverse Legend CARO (over IACO) DG MAG BRI — Charles by the grace of God King of Great Britain

Reverse Legend FRA ET HIB REX — France and Ireland

Obverse Crown with two long sceptres; mintmark on both sides. The king's name is over that of James I, this is just an altered die from the previous reign.

Reverse Crown and harp.

| C1FA-060 | VG £15 | F £30 | VF £50 | EF £100 |

As previous, but mintmark on obverse only.

| C1FA-065 | VG £12 | F £25 | VF £45 | EF £90 |

Maltravers Issue

Maltravers oval type, with king's full name but no inner circles. Note the double-arched crown which makes this a Maltravers issue.

Obverse Legend CAROLUS DG MAG BRIT — Charles by the grace of God King of Great Britain

Reverse Legend FRAN ET HIB REX — France and Ireland

Obverse Crown and sceptre; mintmark both sides.

Reverse Harp and crown.

| C1FA-070 | VG £15 | F £30 | VF £60 | EF £100 |

It is important to note that, for all the previous issues, varieties exist in the legends. When identifying an issue it is most important that collectors should refer to the number of arches on the crown, to the point where the legend starts and to any inner circles and stops in the legend.

Rose Farthing

These issues are smaller and thicker than the previous ones. They are made of copper, with a brass plug in the coin to deter forgers. On many coins of poorer condition the plug has fallen out and this leaves a rather unsightly gap. The obverse of the coin has a crown with two sceptres. The reverse a crowned rose, hence the name Rose farthing.

Obverse Legend CAROLUS D G MAG BRIT — Charles by the grace of God King [of] Great Britain

Reverse Legend FRAN ET HIB REX — France and Ireland

Obverse Double-arched crown with small sceptres in inner circle.

Reverse Double rose within inner circle.

| C1FA-075 | VG £10 | F £20 | VF £30 | EF £40 |

As previous, but sceptres on obverse just break inner circle.

| C1FA-080 | VG £8 | F £16 | VF £24 | EF £34 |

As previous, but sceptres almost reach outer circle.

| C1FA-085 | VG £6 | F £14 | VF £22 | EF £32 |

As previous, but obverse legend reads CAROLUS DG. MAG BRI.

| C1FA-090 | VG £15 | F £30 | VF £42 | EF £55 |

As previous, but muled with the next issue: the obverse has a double-arched crown, the reverse a single-arched crown.

| C1FA-095 | VG £8 | F £16 | VF £24 | EF £34 |

Obverse Legend CAROLUS D G. MAG BRI — Charles by the grace of God King of Great Britain

Reverse Legend FRA ET HIB REX — France and Ireland

Obverse Single-arched crown over two sceptres.

Reverse Single plain rose with crown above.

| C1FA-100 | VG £6 | F £14 | VF £22 | EF £32 |

As previous, but sceptres below crown and the king's name in the obverse legend shortened to CAROLU.

| C1FA-105 | VG £20 | F £50 | VF £100 | EF — |

Forgeries (J1FA & C1FA)

There are large numbers of forged James I, and particularly, Charles I farthings and although no small Harrington farthings appear to have been forged, many Lennox, Richmond and Maltravers have been. The following information will explain the differences between the genuine coins and the forgeries:

Forgeries tend to have erratic lettering and spelling; the whole layout of the coin can look a mess.

Many forgeries are irregular in shape, often with excess metal outside the legends.

The harp and the crown often lack detail and are erratic in style.

Many forgeries tend to be thin and bent although some forgeries are too thick; a genuine coin should feel very springy with a flat, even surface.

Genuine coins tend to be of correct shape and are usually not clipped.

Commonwealth and Cromwell
(1649 – 1660)

No farthings were issued for circulation during this period. However, a fairly large number of patterns were struck. There is no doubt that these issues circulated, many as tokens or patterns. This reflected the need for small change. During the period from 1648 to 1670 huge quantities of tokens were issued. These were mainly farthings and halfpennies. The tokens were issued by small traders or the towns themselves. The government seemed unable, or unwilling, to produce small denomination coins. There was, undoubtedly, an enormous need for small denomination coins and it was finally met by Charles II who, in 1672, introduced huge quantities of halfpennies and farthings into circulation.

Elizabeth I   (1558 – 1603)

Countermarked Coins

During the beginning of Elizabeth I's long reign there was a considerable number of base issue coins in circulation from the reigns of Henry VIII and Edward VI. But, recognising the importance of having good quality coins of high fineness in circulation, Elizabeth I decided to withdraw the base issues in 1559 and replace them with good quality silver coins of high fineness. Among the many denominations thus returned to the mint were base issue shillings from Edward VI's second and third period coinages. Probably due to the urgent need for low denomination coins, it was decided to counterstamp some of these shillings; the second period shillings were counterstamped with a portcullis, the third period issues with a greyhound. They were then returned to circulation with a value of fourpence-halfpenny and twopence-farthing respectively, in accordance with their true silver content. Nevertheless, this short-term solution was unpopular and the large quantities of good quality silver coins being produced in the 1560s also made it unnecessary. The replacement of the base coinage was a considerable expense to Elizabeth I. It shows Elizabeth's determination to bring good quality coins of high fineness into circulation. No records exist of how many coins were counterstamped, however, very few examples exist. Although other coins exist with these countermarks on, they are not considered to be contemporary.

Collecting Hints

All issues are extremely rare. The condition of the host coin varies from Poor to Fine. Forged false countermarks exist.

Fourpence Halfpenny

Obverse   Edward VI second period base shilling counterstamped with a portcullis.

Reverse   Edward VI base shilling.

ELCTM-005   ex. rare

Twopence Farthing

Obverse   Edward VI third period base shilling counterstamped with a seated greyhound.

Reverse   Edward VI base shilling.

ELCTM-010   ex. rare

Portcullis Coinage

These coins, which were struck by the Tower mint for the Company of Merchants, were bullion coins for world-wide trading. They were struck for trading in the East Indies and were produced from 1600 – 01. They were struck to weigh the same as the Spanish silver 8, 4, 2, 1 *reale* respectively.

N.B. Varieties in the legends exist.

Collecting Hints

All issues are rare and are usually found in Fine to VF condition, and rarely in low grades.

Eight Testern

Obverse Legend ELIZABETH D.G. ANG FR ET HIB REGINA — Elizabeth by the grace of God Queen of England, France and Ireland

Reverse Legend POSUI DEUM ADIVTOREM MEUM — I have made God my helper

Obverse Crown over royal shield, crowned E.R. either side of shield; mintmark '0'.

Reverse Crowned portcullis, chain either side; mintmark '0'.

| ELPOR-005 | F £1,400 | VF £3,450 |

Four Testern

As previous, but FRA ET HIBER instead of FR ET HIB in obverse legend.

| ELPOR-010 | F £1,000 | VF £2,000 |

Two Testern

As previous, but FR ET HIBER REGIN in obverse legend.

| ELPOR-015 | F £1,000 | VF £2,000 |

One Testern

As previous, but FR ET HI REGINA in obverse legend.

| ELPOR-020 | F £800 | VF £1,300 |

Charles I (1625 – 1649)

Siege Issues

Unusual and irregular denominations were struck in besieged towns, due to the urgency and lack of facilities. Regular siege issue denominations such as shillings and halfcrowns are listed under their relative denominations but unusual denominations are listed in this chapter. In some cases, the reverse legends bear the name of the town and OBS for OBSESSA, siege.

Carlisle Three Shillings

Collecting Hints

These issues are extremely rare and when available usually found in Fine to VF condition.

Obverse Crowned CR with rosette on each side and IIIS (3 shillings) below.

Reverse OBS CARL 1645 in three or two lines.

C1SG-005	VG £1,500	F £3,500	VF £8,500

Newark Ninepence

Collecting Hints

This is one of the most common siege issues. Specimens are available in most grades and often show original gilding from the host plates from which they were made.

Obverse Large crown between CR, IX below.

Reverse OBS NEWARKE or NEWARK 1645 or 1646 in three lines.

C1SG-010	VG £250	F £500	VF £1,000

Pontefract Two Shillings

Collecting Hints

This issue is extremely rare.

This coin is diamond shaped.

Obverse Legend DUM SPIRO SPERO — Whilst I live I hope

Reverse Legend None.

Obverse Large crown over CR.

Reverse Castle gateway with P.C at sides and vertically to the left of the tower.

C1SG-015	ex. rare

Scarborough Besieged

Because of the way the coins were produced, a very large number of denominations exist for this siege town. Silver plates were literally cut into squares, weighed and the value was then punched below. A castle, either with a gateway or two turrets, was then struck above the denomination. The following denominations exist:

Five shillings and eightpence; crown; three shillings and fourpence; three shillings; two shillings and tenpence; halfcrown; two shillings and fourpence; two shillings and twopence; two shillings (varieties exist); one shilling and ninepence; one shilling and sixpence; one shilling and fourpence; one shilling and threepence; one shilling and twopence; one shilling and a penny; one shilling; eleven pence; tenpence; ninepence; seven pence; sixpence; fourpence.

Collecting Hints

All these denominations are extremely rare. Nineteenth century forgeries exist for many issues. These forgeries can be very good and collectors should exercise extreme caution when purchasing an example.

Several fantasy issues also exist for other towns. They were struck in the nineteenth century, when there was a revival of interest in the history of this period.

Unofficial Coins and Tokens circulating in England

This book is solely devoted to English coins. However, during the hammered coinage, coins from other countries, as well as tokens and jetons, circulated alongside English coins. As these issues are often found by metal detectors we have decided to list the most common. These coins circulated because many of them were silver and had a similar value to the English coins. After all, all coins during this period were simply worth their weight in gold or silver. As a result of there often being a shortage of small denominations, these foreign issues became a useful source of small change.

Richard I Denier of Poitou
This province of France was controlled by England during this period.

French Denier

Irish Henry III Penny

Irish Penny

Low Countries' Sterlings
These coins were copies of Edward I's pennies. All legends are different from the Edward issues. Most of continental issues have an uncrowned bust of the king.

Venetian Silver Coins
These coins from the 13th and 14th centuries have been found in large quantities in the river Thames.

Venetian Coins

Irish Philip and Mary Groat
The obverse is similar to the English sixpence; however, the reverses show a large harp.

Jetons

English Jetons
Jetons were used from Edward I's reign to the early part of the 20th century. They were first used as reckoning counters in mathematics and finance, in a similar way as an abacus is used. The later issues were used as gaming counters. The early English issues, which were made of brass, are nearly always holed. These usually show the bust of the king on the obverse.

English Jeton

Foreign Jetons
Most jetons were produced in France and Germany. Many of these were exported to England. The most common were the Nuremberg jetons produced by the Krauvinkle family. These jetons were produced in huge quantities and are very common.

Foreign Jetons

Ecclesiastical Tokens

Boy Bishop Tokens

Boy Bishop tokens are ecclesiastical issues or tokens; they were only used in Medieval times in the Suffolk area. It is thought that they were given to the poor on religious holidays and could perhaps have been redeemed for food. These issues usually show a Bishop's head on the obverse while the reverse bears a long cross with three pellets in each quarter. There are many varieties of these issues.

Boy Bishop Token

Ecclesiastical Issues (?)

Very little is known about the following tokens. They were used over a considerable period of time and are often found in farmland.

Ecclesiastical issues (?)

Trade Tokens

The other main lead issue was thought to have been produced by local traders, mainly in large towns. Most have been found in London and often have a variety of designs. There are virtually no records relating to these tokens and this, combined with the fact that the issuer's name or town rarely appears on these issues, explains why very little has been discovered about them.

The lead tokens are often known as 'wine tavern' tokens, and probably had a value of a fraction of a penny. These tokens were the forerunners to the popular brass and copper 17th century issues, which were produced in large quantities by most traders, in most towns.

Tokens were produced to compensate for the lack of small denominations. They illustrate the failure of certain monarchs to be aware of the needs of the poor by providing adequate small denominations. However, Charles II recognised the problem and in the 1670s introduced large quantities of copper farthings and half-pennies. As a result, the tokens in circulation became unnecessary and obsolete; their production was finally forbidden by law in the late 1670s.

Lead tokens

Brass and copper tokens

Coin Weights

Merchants and traders needed to confirm that the coinage they received in payment for goods was of the full correct weight. As a result, it became necessary to introduce coin weights for most large gold and silver denominations. These weights were made of brass. They often had a portrait of the reigning monarch on the obverse, the weight on the reverse. Most European gold coins of this period had coin weights produced for them and many merchants carried weights for both English and foreign issues. The Low Countries produced large quantities of coin weights, often for export. These issues can usually be identified by a 'hand' counterstamped on the weight.

James I gold unite (after 1612)

James I half unite (after 1612)

Charles I gold crown

Milled Coins
1658 to date

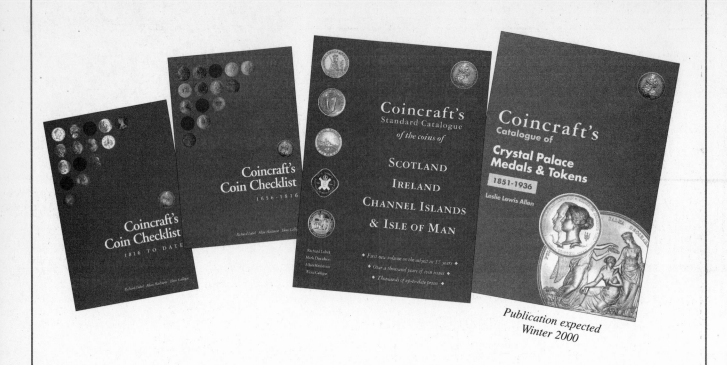

Publication expected
Winter 2000

Would you like to see your book on the shelf?

Have you ever thought of writing a book on some area of numismatics? Have you written a book but not yet had it published? Have you always wanted to see your work in print? Well here may be your chance to make your wish a reality…

Standard Catalogue Publishers Ltd, a division of Coincraft, are interested in publishing books on coins, medals, tokens or paper money. Having already gained world-wide recognition as the publishers of Coincraft Standard Catalogues, we are now looking to publish other similar works that have a broad numismatic appeal.

If you would like to see your work published, please submit a brief outline or synopsis of your proposal to: *Dr Eleni Calligas, editor at Standard Catalogue Publishers Ltd.*

Standard Catalogue Publishers Ltd

c/o Coincraft

44 & 45 Great Russell Street

London WC1B 3LU

Tel: (0207) 636 1188 : (0207) 637 8785

Fax: (0207) 637 7635 : (0207) 323 2860

Email: info@coincraft.com

Get your *free* copy of The Phoenix

The Phoenix, the only monthly coin, bank-note and antiquities newspaper in the UK!

- 24 tabloid-sized pages
- Hundreds of items on offer
- British and World Coins
- British and World Banknotes
- Greek & Roman Coins
- Greek, Roman and Egyptian antiquities
- Special offers and discounts
- Hundreds of photographs in every issue

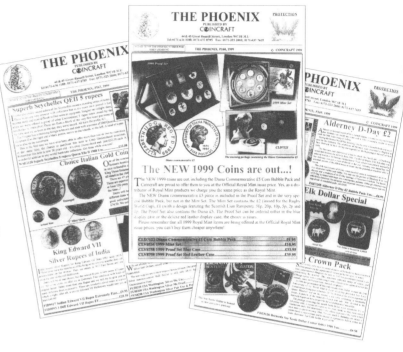

Coincraft is a family firm which has dealt in coins for over 40 years. At Coincraft we believe in old fashioned values; such as the collector is always right, even when occasionally he or she is wrong!

ORDER WITH CONFIDENCE!

Our guarantee to you

All items listed in *The Phoenix* are guaranteed authentic. If for any reason you are dissatisfied with anything ordered from *The Phoenix*, simply return it to us in undamaged condition within 30 days for a full no-questions-asked refund.

We have total confidence in the goods we sell. We want YOU to have total confidence in us!

Please send me a complimentary copy of *The Phoenix* – your monthly catalogue of British and World Coins, British and World Banknotes, ancient coins, medals, tokens and antiquities.

NAME..

ADDRESS...

....

....

....

POSTCODE..................... COUNTRY.................

CSC030900

Get your *free* copy of The Phoenix

The Phoenix,

the only monthly

coin, banknote

and antiquities

newspaper in

the UK!

- 24 tabloid-sized pages
- Hundreds of items on offer
- British and World Coins
- British and World Banknotes
- Greek and Roman Coins
- Greek, Roman and Egyptian antiquities
- Special offers and discounts
- Hundreds of photographs in every issue

Coincraft is a family firm which has dealt in coins for over 40 years. At Coincraft we believe in old fashioned values; such as the collector is always right, even when occasionally he or she is wrong!

Introduction to the milled coinage section

A Guide to using the Tables

Following the descriptive information, history and collecting hints relating to the denomination, the tables for each reign generally comprise three sections. Certain conventions have been used in the layout, and these are detailed below.

SECTION 1: The Broad Definition (5 columns)

Column 1: The name of the denomination.

Column 2: The metal from which the coin is made. If described as 'gold' the coin is, unless otherwise stated, of 22 carat gold, i.e. 22/24 (0.917) pure. If 'silver' it is of sterling silver (0.925 fine) unless another fineness is given.

Column 3: The weight of the coin in grams. If found specimens vary markedly from the official weight, a weight range of most commonly found specimens is given.

Column 4: The diameter, usually to the nearest millimetre (mm).

Column 5: The reverse alignment. This means the alignment of the reverse seen if the coin is firstly held at the rim between two fingers, top and bottom, with the obverse facing and upright, and then rotated 180 degrees between the fingers.

Further information relating to the points above may be given as a footnote to the 5-column broad definition table.

SECTION 2: The Description

Each different obverse used during the reign is listed in sequence as Obverse 1, 2, etc. and briefly described. The different portrayals of the monarch are listed as Head 1, 2, etc. and the placement of the head facing left or right is stated. The legend on the obverse then follows in block capitals, without punctuation. There are often so many different variations of punctuation within a given reign that it is more appropriate to refer to the relevant photograph and correlate it with punctuation varieties given in Section 3.

Any bracketed wording in italics following the legend description does not form part of the legend on the coin but is intended to provide information on the relevant issue, usually in the case of the commemorative issues. If this information is obvious from the legend then this bracketed information is omitted.

The reverses are similarly listed as Reverse 1, 2, etc. following the obverse list. Provenance marks (e.g. roses and plumes) or their absence are not considered to constitute a different obverse or reverse but are listed in Section 3 as variations within a single obverse or reverse.

The edge is then described (e.g. 'milled') or in the case of a lettered edge, the edge legend is given. The term 'milled' denotes straight-across milling or graining. If diagonal, chevron or other pattern milling exists, then it is described as such.

With all legends, bracketed information not italicized indicates information not as written but a variable which is listed in Section 3, e.g. (date). The terms 'regnal date' and 'edge date' are interchangeable.

SECTION 3: The Main Table

The table columns usually (but not invariably) are in the following sequence for each variety:

1. The reference number of the variety.

2. The date as depicted on the coin.

3. (optional) The mintmark as it appears on the coin. The name of the mint and the position of the mintmark will usually appear immediately above Section 3.

4. Features of the coin. These are the characteristics which qualify the coin as a distinct variety of the series, e.g. 'proof' or 'edge plain'. If no entry appears, it is usually the date which forms the characteristic feature. An entry reading, e.g., '9 over 8' refers to an overdate, where '9' occurs in the corrected date. Where the corrected date contains two or more identical digits, the entry will read, e.g. 'first 3 over 2', 'latter 7 over 6'.

5. (optional) The edge date or regnal date which forms part of the legend in Section 2.

6. The obverse number as in Section 2.

7. The reverse number as in Section 2.

8. The retail price in the various grades in which the coin is usually found. Prior to 1816 the highest grade given is usually EF, and the price for an FDC specimen of a proof coin is given in this column. The prices are in Pounds Sterling and are those which one would expect to pay from a reputable dealer, including handling fees, tax, etc. For very low priced items these ancillary charges form a disproportionate, and therefore substantial, fraction of the price quoted.

Many price boxes are left blank. This is because a price is considered inappropriate; for example, the coin may not exist in the grade stated, or it may be impossible to distinguish it (e.g. a proof in fine condition). Alternatively, it may be of negligible value in the grade stipulated.

The term 'BV' in the prices column denotes that the price one should expect to pay will bear a relationship to the bullion value of the metal in the piece. It must be stressed that this does not mean that the coin can be acquired for simply its bullion value. To this figure must be added any applicable local taxes (e.g. value added tax, sales tax), together with any handling fees and a reasonable profit margin to be charged by the dealer. Demand may also render the market value above the bullion value even though the one value may bear a relationship to the other.

Footnotes to the table are cross-referenced to notes in the table itself, usually in the Features column.

Translation of Foreign Legends

Below are listed most of the foreign legends on the milled coinage, together with English translations. Abbreviations are translated directly rather than the reader being referred to the unabbreviated word. Some duplication has been used to allow for easy location of the translation; if any difficulty is encountered it may help to break the foreign legend into sections and to look these up separately. Latin regnal years (after the term 'Anno Regni') should be split into separate words and the resulting translated numbers added together. Error legends are included and translated directly; the corrected foreign legend is given after the English version.

All legends are in Latin unless stated otherwise before the English version.

Legend	English translation
ANG	England
ANNA	(Queen) Anne
ANNA DEI GRATIA	(Queen) Anne, by the Grace of God
ANNO	Year (In the year of)
ANNO EGNI	In the year of the reign..... *(error: should be ANNO REGNI)*
ANNO REGNI	In the year of the reign....
BBITANNIAR	Of the British territories *(error: should be BRITANNIAR)*
BRIIT	Of the British territories *(error: should be BRITT)*
BRITANNIA REX FID DEF	King of Britain, Defender of the Faith
BRITANNIAB	Of the British territories *(error: should be BRITANNIAR)*
BRITANNIAE EEGINA	Queen of the British territories *(error: should be BRITANNIAR REGINA)*
BRITANNIAR	Of the British territories
BRITANNIAR REG FID DEF	Queen of the British territories, Defender of the Faith
BRITANNIAR REGINA	Queen of the British territories
BRITANNIAR REX FID DEF	King of the British territories, Defender of the Faith
BRITANNIARUM REGINA FID DEF	Queen of the British territories, Defender of the Faith
BRITANNIARUM REX FID DEF	King of the British territories, Defender of the Faith
BRITANNIARUM REX FIDEI DEFENSOR	King of the British territories, Defender of the Faith
BRITT	Of the British territories
BRITT OMN REGINA	Queen of all the British territories,
BRITT REGINA	Queen of the British territories
BRIVANNIA	Britain (or Britannia) *(error: should be BRITANNIA)*
BRVN ET L DVX S R I A TH ET EL	Duke of Brunswick and Lueneburg, Arch-Treasurer and Elector of the Holy Roman Empire
BRVN ET L DVX S R I A TH ET PR EL	Duke of Brunswick and Lueneburg, Arch-Treasurer and Prince Elector of the Holy Roman Empire
BRVN ET LVN DVX S R I A TH ET PR EL	Duke of Brunswick and Lueneburg, Arch-Treasurer and Prince Elector of the Holy Roman Empire
CAROLVS	Charles
CAROLVS A CAROLO	Charles, son of Charles
CAROLVS II	Charles II
CAROLVS II D G M B F H REX	Charles II, by the Grace of God, King of Great Britain, France and Ireland
CHRISTO AVSPICE REGNO	I reign under the auspice of Christ
CRAOLVS	Charles *(error: should be CAROLVS)*
D G	By the Grace of God
D G BR OMN REX F D IND IMP	By the Grace of God, King of all the British territories, Defender of the Faith, Emperor of India
DECIMO	Ten
DECUS ET TUTAMEN ANNO REGNI	An ornament and a safeguard; in the year of the reign
DECUS ET TUTAMEN	An ornament and a safeguard
DECVS ANNO REGNI ET TVTAMEN	An ornament and a safeguard; in the year of the reign. *(error: transposed word order)*
DECVS ET TVTAMEN AN REG	An ornament and a safeguard; in the year of the reign.....
DECVS ET TVTAMEN ANNO REGNI	An ornament and a safeguard; in the year of the reign.....
DECVS ET TVTAMEN	An ornament and a safeguard
DEI GARTIA	By the Grace of God. *(error: should be DEI GRATIA)*
DEI GRA BRITT OMN REGINA F D	By the Grace of God, Queen of all the British territories, Defender of the Faith
DEI GRA BRITT OMN REX FID DEF IND IMP	By the Grace of God, King of all the British territories, Defender of the Faith, Emperor of India
DEI GRATIA REGINA F D	By the Grace of God, Queen, Defender of the Faith
DEI GRATIA	By the Grace of God
DIEU ET MON DROIT (French)	God and my right
DIRIGE DEUS GRESSUS MEOS	May the Lord direct my steps
DIRIGIT DEUS GRESSUS MEOS	The Lord directs my steps
DRITANNIAR	Of the British territories. *(error: should be BRITANNIAR)*
DVODECIMO	Twelve
EDWARDVS VII	Edward VII
EDWARDVS VIII D G BR OMN REX F D IND IMP	Edward VIII, by the Grace of God, King of all the British territories, Defender of the Faith, Emperor of India
EDWARDVS VIII	Edward VIII
ELIZABETH II DEI GRA BRITT OMN REGINA F D	Elizabeth II, by the Grace of God, Queen of all the British territories, Defender of the Faith

ELIZABETH II DEI GRA REG F D ... Elizabeth II, by the Grace of God, Queen, Defender of the Faith

ELIZABETH II DEI GRATIA BRITT OMN REGINA FIDEI DEFENSOR ... Elizabeth II, by the Grace of God, Queen of all the British territories, Defender of the Faith

ELIZABETH II DEI GRATIA BRITT OMN REGINA ... Elizabeth II, by the Grace of God, Queen of all the British territories

ELIZABETH II DEI GRATIA REGINA F D ... Elizabeth II, by the Grace of God, Queen, Defender of the Faith

ELIZABETH II DEI GRATIA REGINA ... Elizabeth II, Queen by the Grace of God

ERA ... France *(error: should be FRA)*

F D ... Defender of the Faith

FID DEF BRITT REG ... Queen of the British territories, Defender of the Faith

FID DEF ... Defender of the Faith

FIDEI DEFENSOR BRITANNIARUM REX ... King of the British territories, Defender of the Faith

FOEDUS INVIOLABILE ... An unbreakable treaty

FRA ... France

GEI GRA ... By the Grace of God. *(error: should be DEI GRA)*

GEOE III ... George III *(error: should be GEOR III)*

GEOGIVS ... George *(error: should be GEORGIVS)*

GEOR III D G BRITT REX F D ... George III, by the Grace of God, King of the British territories, Defender of the Faith

GEORGIUS II REX ... King George II

GEORGIUS III ... George III

GEORGIUS III D G BRITANNIARUM REX F D .... George III, by the Grace of God, King of the British territories, Defender of the Faith

GEORGIUS III DEI GRATIA REX ... George III, King, by the Grace of God

GEORGIUS IIII ... George IV

GEORGIUS IIII D G BRITANNIAR REX F D ... George IV, by the Grace of God, King of the British territories, Defender of the Faith

GEORGIUS IV ... George IV

GEORGIVS ... George I (or George)

GEORGIVS D G M BR ET HIB REX F D ... George I, by the Grace of God, King of Great Britain and Ireland, Defender of the Faith

GEORGIVS D G M BR FR ET HIB REX F D ... George I, by the Grace of God, King of Great Britain, France and Ireland, Defender of the Faith

GEORGIVS DEI GRA ... George I, by the Grace of God

GEORGIVS II ... George II

GEORGIVS II REX ... King George II

GEORGIVS III ... George III

GEORGIVS III DEI GRATIA .. George III, by the Grace of God

GEORGIVS REX ... King George I

GEORGIVS V ... George V

GEORGIVS V D G BRITT OMN REX F D IND IMP ... George V, by the Grace of God, King of all the British territories, Defender of the Faith, Emperor of India

GEORGIVS V DEI GRA BRITT OMN REX FID DEF IND IMP ... George V, by the Grace of God, King of all the British territories, Defender of the Faith, Emperor of India

GEORGIVS VI ... George VI

GEORGIVS VI D G BR OMN REX F D IND IMP ... George VI, by the Grace of God, King of all the British territories, Defender of the Faith, Emperor of India

GEORGIVS VI D G BR OMN REX FIDEI DEF ... George VI, by the Grace of God, King of all the British territories, Defender of the Faith

GEORIVS ... George *(error: should be GEORGIVS)*

GRACIA ... By the Grace *(error: should be GRATIA)*

GRI ... George (VI), King and Emperor

GULIELMUS IIII ... William IV

GULIELMUS IIII D G BRITANNIAR REX F D ... William IV, by the Grace of God, King of all the British territories, Defender of the Faith

GULIELMUS IIII DEI GRATIA ... William IV, by the Grace of God

GVIELMVS ... William *(error: should be GVLIELMVS)*

GVILELMVS ... William *(error: should be GVLIELMVS)*

GVIR ... King George VI

GVLEELMVS ... William *(error: should be GVLIELMVS)*

GVLELMVS ... William *(error: should be GVLIELMVS)*

GVLIEEMVS ... William *(error: should be GVLIELMVS)*

GVLIEIMVS ... William *(error: should be GVLIELMVS)*

GVLIELMS ... William *(error: should be GVLIELMVS)*

GVLIELMVS ET MARIA ... William and Mary

GVLIELMVS ET MARIA D G ... William and Mary, by the Grace of God

GVLIELMVS III ... William III

GVLIELMVS TERTIVS ... William III

GVLIEMVS ... William *(error: should be GVLIELMVS)*

GVLILMVS ... William *(error: should be GVLIELMVS)*

HAS NISI PERITVRVS MIHI ADIMAT NEMO ... Let nobody remove these (letters) from me on pain of death

HI ... Ireland

HIB ... Ireland

HIB REX ET REGINA ... King and Queen of Ireland

HIPEX ... King of Ireland *(error: should be HIB REX)*

HIPREX ... King of Ireland *(error: should be HIB REX)*

HONI SOIT QUI MAL Y PENSE (French) ... Evil to him who evil thinks

IACOBVS II ... James II

IACOBVS II DEI GRATIA ... James II, by the Grace of God

IACOBVS SECVNDVS ... James II

ICH DIEN (German) ... I serve

IIIB... Ireland *(error: should be HIB)*

INCORRUPTA FIDES VERITASQUE........................ Uncorrupted faith and truth

IND IMP............................. Emperor (or Empress) of India

M B F ET H REX F D B ET L D S R I A T ET E................. King of Great Britain, France and Ireland, Defender of the Faith, Duke of Brunswick and Lueneburg, Arch-Treasurer and Elector of the Holy Roman Empire

MAB BR............................ Great Britain. *(error: should be MAG BR)*

MAG BR(I) FR(A) ET HI(B) REX ET REGINA.................. King and Queen of Great Britain, France and Ireland

MAG BR(I) FR(A) ET HIB REG...................................... Queen of Great Britain, France and Ireland

MARIA................................ Mary

MDCCCLI CIVIUM INDUSTRIA FLORET CIVITAS MCMLI.................... 1851 By the Industry of its people the State flourishes 1951

MRG BR............................. Great Britain. *(error: should be MAG BR)*

MVRIA................................ Mary *(error: should be MARIA)*

NEMO ME IMPUNE LACESSIT............................. Nobody provokes me with impunity

NONO.................................. Nine

NVMMORVM FAMVLVS....... The servant of the coinage (i.e. a minor coinage)

OCTAVO.............................. Eight

OLIVAR D G R P ANG SCO HIB &c PRO.......................... Oliver, by the Grace of God, Protector of the Republic of England, Scotland, Ireland, etc

PAX QVAERITVR BELLO...... Peace is sought through war

PLEIDIOL WYF I'M GWLAD (Welsh)................................. I am true to my country

PRIMO................................. One

PROTECTOR LITERIS LITERAE NVMMIS CORONA ET SALVS............................ A protector of the letters, the letters are a garland and a safeguard to the coinage

QVARTO.............................. Four

QVATTVOR MARIA VINDICO............................. I conquer the four seas

QVINTO.............................. Five

REGINA............................... Queen

REX..................................... King

RRITANNIAR...................... Of the British territories *(error: should be BRITANNIAR)*

SECVNDO............................ Two

SEPTIMO............................. Seven

SEXTO................................. Six

SIC VOC NON VOBIS............ We labour thus, but not for ourselves

SOLI DEO GLORIA................ Glory to God alone

TERTIO................................ Three

TERTIVS.............................. Third

TIRTIO................................ Three *(error: should be TERTIO)*

TRICESIMO.......................... Thirty

TUEATUR UNITA DEUS....... May God protect the Union

UNDECIMO......................... Eleven

VICESIMO........................... Twenty

VICTORIA D G BRIT REG F D.. Victoria, by the Grace of God, Queen of Britain (or British Territories), Defender of the Faith

VICTORIA D G BRITANNIAR REGINA F D... Victoria, by the Grace of God, Queen of the British territories, Defender of the Faith

VICTORIA D G BRITANNIARUM REGINA F D.. Victoria, by the Grace of God, Queen of the British territories, Defender of the Faith

VICTORIA D G BRITT REG F D.. Victoria, by the Grace of God, Queen of the British territories, Defender of the Faith

VICTORIA DEI GRA BRITT REGINA FID DEF IND IMP... Victoria, by the Grace of God, Queen of the British territories, Defender of the Faith, Empress of India

VICTORIA DEI GRATIA BRITANNIAR REG F D........ Victoria, by the Grace of God, Queen of the British territories, Defender of the Faith

VICTORIA DEI GRATIA BRITT REGINA F D.............. Victoria, by the Grace of God, Queen of the British territories, Defender of the Faith

VICTORIA REGINA.............. Queen Victoria

VIS VNITATE FORTIOR........ Strength is stronger through unity

First use of mark of denomination on milled coins

Denomination	Date
Gold two pounds	1986
Sovereign	1989
Crown	1927
Five shillings	1951
Three shillings token	1811
Halfcrown	1893
Florin	1849
One shilling and sixpence token	1811
Shilling	1831
Sixpence	1831
Small silver ('Maundy')	undated Charles II
Groat	1836
Silver threepence (in words)	1927
Brass threepence	1937
Three-halfpence	1834
Bronze penny	1860
Bronze halfpenny	1860
Farthing	1799 [1]
Half farthing	1839
Third farthing	1866
Quarter farthing	1839
Decimal coins	Normally all carry mark of denomination.

1. First use in words of denomination on any English coin.

Can you help?

We need information on the following coins, and would appreciate hearing from anyone who owns or has access to them:

No. & Date		Features
WMGN-040	(1692)	elephant only below bust not closely placed against truncation
WMGN-055	(1693)	elephant only below bust not closely placed against truncation
WMHG-035	(1692)	elephant only below bust not closely placed against truncation
C2CRM-055	(1663)	no regnal edge date
VGCR-105	(1853)	plain edge proof
VYCR-110	(1879)	proof
G5CR-090	(1935)	section of edge lettering missing
G1HC-015	(1715)	edge lettering transposed
VGFL-002	(1848)	milled edge
VGFL-175	(1867)	42 arcs obverse
W3SH-120	(1697)	rotated shields
Shilling	(1879)	proof with 1839 obverse
G6SH-330	(1952)	nickel proof
W36D-025	(1696)	shield of Scotland at date
W36D-030	(1696)	shield of France at date
W36D-190	(1697-C)	shield of Ireland at date
W36D-235	(1697-y)	shield of Ireland at date
AN6D-040	(1707)	After Union reverse with legend ...BR FRA...

Victorian sovereigns and half sovereigns with unusually high die numbers

Five Guineas

Charles II (1660 – 1685)

The British five guinea piece is one of the most spectacular and impressive series of machine struck currency ever produced. The Charles II coin, minted each year from 1668 until the last of the king's reign in 1684, comprises a formidable series.

The coin, although now invariably referred to as the five guinea piece, was in the 17th and 18th centuries also known as the five pound piece. It must be remembered that the guinea was not always valued at twenty-one shillings as it was in later times. During the reign of Charles II it had a value of twenty shillings, and thereafter until fixed by Proclamation in 1717 it fluctuated, rather like the value of bullion gold does today.

The obverse and reverse of the Charles II five guinea piece were designed by John Roettier (1631–c.1700). Evelyn's diary says that the drawing for the King's portrait was made by Cooper on 6 January 1662 (1661 old style calendar). The coin is similar in size to the crown, and is the only gold coin to bear an inscription on the edge. Like that on the crown and halfcrown, the inscription includes a regnal year, that is, a date counting from the inception of the king's reign. However, in the case of Charles II, the regnal year counts from the death of Charles I (by execution) rather than from 1660. The obverse and reverse of the five guinea piece are somewhat similar to those of the crown, but the portrait is different, especially at the truncation. The angles between the reverse shields are bisected by sceptres instead of interlinked 'C's. The latter do appear, however, as a group of four in the centre of the reverse.

The edge inscription was not, as is commonly thought, applied to the finished struck coinage. However, in later years the striking of the two sides and the edge may have been effected simultaneously. In the earlier years the blanks were first cut out from metal which had been rolled into strips using horse power. These blanks were then sent to have the edges impressed by a secret process devised by one Pierre Blondeau, an ex-engineer from the Paris mint, who jealously guarded his methods. The blanks were then returned to the mint to have their obverses and reverses struck in a hand-operated press. A long and detailed description of rolling, cutting and striking of blanks is contained in Pepys's Diary for 19 May 1663.

The wording of the edge inscription DECUS ET TUTAMEN was said by Leake, writing in 1726, to have been suggested by Mr Evelyn, based on a vignette of Cardinal de Richelieu's Greek Testament, printed at the Louvre in Paris.

The elephant (with or without castle) occurs more frequently on the five guinea piece than on the crown. This symbol indicates that the gold has been imported from the Africa Company.

value provides some sort of base price for valuation, even if the coin is badly worn or damaged. Generally speaking, one does not come across specimens below fine condition, although sometimes the coins are mounted on the edge, and this area of the coin must always be carefully examined.

Denomination	Metal	Weight (grams)	Diameter (mm)	Rev. alignment
Five Guineas 1668–69	Gold	41.0–42.0	37	↓
Five Guineas 1670–84	Gold	41.0–41.8	37	↓

Obverse 1 Head 1, right; pointed truncation; lock of hair to right of truncation; CAROLVS II DEI GRATIA

Obverse 2 Head 2, right; larger, rounded truncation, without lock of hair to right; same legend

Reverse 1 Four crowned cruciform shields between which are four sceptres, with four interlinked 'C's at the centre; MAG BR FRA ET HIB REX (date)

Edge DECVS ET TVTAMEN ANNO REGNI (regnal date)

Obv. 1

Obv. 2

Rev. 1

No.	Date	Features	Edge date	Obv.	Rev.	F	VF	EF
C25GM-005	1668		VICESIMO	1	1	1100	2200	5500
C25GM-010	1668	elephant below head	VICESIMO	1	1	1100	2200	5500
C25GM-015	1669		VICESIMO PRIMO	1	1	1100	2200	5500
C25GM-020	1669	elephant below head	VICESIMO PRIMO	1	1	1200	2500	5500
C25GM-025	1670		VICESIMO SECVNDO	1	1	1100	2200	5500
C25GM-030	1671		VICESIMO TERTIO	1	1	1200	2500	6000
C25GM-035	1672		VICESIMO QVARTO	1	1	1100	2200	5500
C25GM-040	1673		VICESIMO QVINTO	1	1	1100	2200	5500
C25GM-045	1674	1	VICESIMO SEXTO	1	1	1200	2500	6000

No.	Date	Features	Edge date	Obv.	Rev.	F	VF	EF
C25GM-050	1675	2	VICESIMO SEPTIMO	1	1	1100	2200	5500
C25GM-055	1675	elephant below head 2	VICESIMO SEPTIMO	1	1	1200	2500	6000
C25GM-060	1675	elephant and castle below head 2	VICESIMO SEPTIMO	1	1	2500		
C25GM-065	1676	3	VICESIMO SEPTIMO	1	1	1100	2200	5500
C25GM-070	1676		VICESIMO OCTAVO	1	1	1200	2500	6000
C25GM-075	1676	elephant and castle below head	VICESIMO OCTAVO	1	1	1100	2200	5500
C25GM-080	1677		VICESIMO NONO	1	1	1100	2200	5500
C25GM-085	1677	elephant and castle below head	VICESIMO NONO	1	1	1200	2500	6000
C25GM-090	1678		TRICESIMO	1	1	1100	2200	5000
C25GM-095	1678	8 over 7	TRICESIMO	1	1	1100	2200	5000
C25GM-100	1678	elephant and castle below head; 8 over 7	TRICESIMO	1	1	1200	2500	6000
C25GM-105	1678	8 over 7	TRICESIMO	2	1	1200	2500	6000
C25GM-110	1679		TRICESIMO PRIMO	2	1	1100	2200	5000
C25GM-115	1680		TRICESIMO SECVNDO	2	1	1100	2200	5000
C25GM-120	1680	elephant and castle below head	TRICESIMO SECVNDO	2	1	2500		
C25GM-125	1681		TRICESIMO TERTIO	2	1	1100	2200	5000
C25GM-130	1681	elephant and castle below head	TRICESIMO TERTIO	2	1	1200	2500	6000
C25GM-135	1682		TRICESIMO QVARTO	2	1	1100	2200	5000
C25GM-140	1682	elephant and castle below head	TRICESIMO QVARTO	2	1	1100	2200	5000
C25GM-145	1683		TRICESIMO QVINTO	2	1	1100	2200	5000
C25GM-150	1683	elephant and castle below head	TRICESIMO QVINTO	2	1	1200	2500	6000
C25GM-155	1684		TRICESIMO SEXTO	2	1	1100	2200	5000
C25GM-160	1684	elephant and castle below head	TRICESIMO SEXTO	2	1	1100	2200	5000

1. Minor alterations to head from 1674.
2. Edge date shared with 1676.
3. Edge date shared with 1675.

James II   (1685 – 1688)

John Roettier continued to design the dies for the five guinea piece. Although the facial features are very similar to the portrait he produced for the silver coins, there are marked differences in the area of the truncation.

The 1686 five guinea piece is frequently described as having misplaced or transposed sceptres, although very few catalogues explain what this means. On a correctly oriented coin, if the date is placed at 'North', the sceptre ending in a harp is pointing in a 'North-West' direction, while the one ending in a lis is pointing 'South-West'. On the 1686 coin, these two sceptres have changed places. A similar variety exists on the 1700 guinea, which it is believed appears in this book for the first time in any catalogue.

Collecting Hints

Although there are two slightly different types, collectors will usually be satisfied with one specimen for this reign. A good fine or very fine piece should prove acceptable.

Denomination	Metal	Weight (grams)	Diameter (mm)	Rev. alignment
Five Guineas	Gold	41.5–42.0	37	↓

Obverse 1   Head 1, left; IACOBVS II DEI GRATIA

Obverse 2   Head 2, left, hair arrangement slightly different and further forward; same legend

Reverse 1   Four crowned cruciform shields between which are four sceptres wrongly arranged (see above); MAG BR FRA ET HIB REX (date)

Reverse 2   Similar but sceptres are correctly arranged; the four crowns are slightly larger; same legend

Edge   DECVS ET TVTAMEN ANNO REGNI (regnal date)

Obv. 1   Obv. 2

Rev. 1

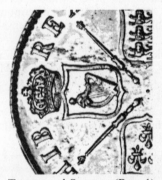 

Transposed Sceptres (Rev. 1)   Normal Sceptres (Rev. 2)

No.	Date	Features	Edge date	Obv.	Rev.	F	VF	EF
J25G-005	1686	1	SECVNDO	1	1	1500	2700	6500
J25G-010	1687		TERTIO	1	2	1200	2200	5500
J25G-015	1687	elephant and castle below head	TERTIO	1	2	1300	2500	6000
J25G-020	1687		TERTIO	2	2	1200	2200	5500
J25G-025	1687		QVARTO	1	2	1200	2200	5500
J25G-030	1688	elephant and castle below head	QVARTO	1	2	1300	2500	6000
J25G-035	1688		QVARTO	2	2	1200	2200	5500

1. So-called 'sceptres misplaced' variety.

Rev. 1

Rev. 2

William & Mary   (1688 – 1694)

Following the removal of James II, his daughter Mary and her husband Prince William of Orange ruled jointly by agreement. Their heads were placed in conjoined fashion on the coinage, with William's head uppermost. This classical style owed much to Greek and Roman coinage, as coins of later periods with joint rulers were normally designed showing them face to face.

The reign of William and Mary saw a departure from previous designs for the reverse of the five guinea piece. Although the cruciform shields design was retained on the crown piece, the shilling and the sixpence, the five guinea piece and other gold coins followed the halfcrown in introducing a crowned shield on the reverse. Curiously, however, by the time the first five guinea pieces were struck in 1691, the halfcrown had reverted to the cruciform shield design.

There is some doubt about the attribution of William and Mary coinage, but the five guinea piece was probably the work of James and/or Norbert Roettier.

The elephant and castle symbol continued to be placed on some of the coins to indicate gold from the Africa Company. Such coins were struck in each of the four years of minting, and are slightly scarcer than those struck without the symbol.

No.	Date	Features	Edge date	Obv.	Rev.	F	VF	EF
WM5G-005	1691		TERTIO	1	1	1000	2200	4800
WM5G-010	1691	elephant and castle below head	TERTIO	1	1	1100	2200	5000
WM5G-015	1692		QVARTO	1	2	1000	2000	4800
WM5G-020	1692	elephant and castle below head	QVARTO	1	2	1100	2200	5000
WM5G-025	1693		QVINTO	1	2	1000	2000	4800
WM5G-030	1693	elephant and castle below head	QVINTO	1	2	1100	2200	5000
WM5G-035	1694		SEXTO	1	2	1200	2200	5500
WM5G-040	1694	4 over indeterminate figure	SEXTO	1	2	1300	2300	5800
WM5G-045	1694	elephant and castle below head	SEXTO	1	2	1100	2200	5000
WM5G-050	1694	elephant and castle below head; 4 over indeterminate figure	SEXTO	1	2	1400	2500	5800

Collecting Hints

A very fine or better specimen is needed to appreciate the design of this somewhat flatly struck denomination.

Denomination	Metal	Weight (grams)	Diameter (mm)	Rev. alignment
Five Guineas	Gold	41.5–41.8	36	↓

Obverse 1   Heads 1, right; GVLIELMVS ET MARIA DEI GRATIA

Reverse 1   Crowned shield; MAG BR FR ET HIB REX ET REGINA (date)

Reverse 2   Similar but central lion on shield is smaller

Edge   DECVS ET TVTAMEN ANNO REGNI (regnal date)

Obv. 1

Rev. 1

Rev. 2

William III   (1695 – 1701)

The William III five guinea piece was minted only in the final three years of the reign of the king. There are thus no specimens corresponding to the early head seen on the silver coinage, and no gold was struck at the five provincial mints.

The design of this series was probably Johann Crocker (aka John Croker), James Roettier having died in 1698 and his brother Norbert having moved to France in 1695 under a cloud. The series is probably best known for the so-called 'fine work' piece of 1701, an engraving of intricate detail, especially in the hair, and sharply struck, almost to proof standard. The reverse of the series reverted to the cruciform shields of Charles II and James II. The shield reverse of William and Mary had not proved successful.

Collecting Hints

A coin in fine to very fine condition will usually prove acceptable, although a better specimen may be required to appreciate the intricacy of design of the 1701 coin.

Denomination	Metal	Weight (grams)	Diameter (mm)	Rev. alignment
Five Guineas	Gold	41.6–41.7	37	↓

Obverse 1   Head 1, right; GVLIELMVS III DEI GRA

Obverse 2   Head 2, right, larger, more detailed and sharply struck; same legend

Reverse 1   Four crowned cruciform shields between which are four sceptres, with central lion of Nassau; MAG BR FRA ET HIB REX (date)

Reverse 2   Similar but details slightly redesigned. The harp is much larger, the crowns slightly smaller;

Reverse 3   Similar but sceptres are more ornamented

Edge   DECVS ET TVTAMEN ANNO REGNI (regnal date)

Obv. 1   Obv. 2

Rev. 1   Rev. 2

Plain Sceptre (Rev. 2)   Ornamental Sceptre (Rev. 3)

No.	Date	Features	Edge date	Obv.	Rev.	F	VF	EF
W35G-005	1699		UNDECIMO	1	1	1000	2000	4500
W35G-010	1699	elephant and castle below head	UNDECIMO	1	1	1400	2800	6500
W35G-015	1700		DVODECIMO	1	1	1100	2100	4800
W35G-020	1701	1	DECIMO TERTIO	2	2	1100	2200	5000
W35G-025	1701	1	DECIMO TERTIO	2	3	1100	2200	5000

1. 'Fine work' type; each '1' in date now resembles a 'J'.

Anne (1702 – 1714)

The series began with one of the most exotic and valuable of all British coins, the Vigo piece of 1703. Only a very few remain in existence. The provenance mark VIGO indicates that the gold from which the coins were struck was captured from Spanish galleons at the battle at Vigo Bay in October 1702. The Warrant of 10 February 1703 (1702 old style calendar) authorized the VIGO mark to be placed 'under our effigies, which inscription we intend as a mark of distinction from the rest of our gold and silver moneys to continue to posterity the rememberence of that glorious action'.

The Glendining's catalogue for the sale of the 'Vigo Bay' Collection in October 1992 states that three different obverse dies were used for the striking of the Vigo five guinea piece, and that 'certainly less (*sic*) than twenty pieces survive'. If one compares the illustration in this catalogue with that in *The Milled Coinage of England* (Spink), it is clear that there is a marked difference in the positioning of the VIGO mark; moreover, the MCE specimen appears to have no stops on the obverse, whereas on the Glendining pieces they are clearly evident.

After the Vigo coin, the five guinea piece was struck again in 1705 and 1706 before the Union of England and Scotland necessitated a redesign in the reverse shields to indicate the Union. It is worthy of note that the five guinea piece is the only British coin to be struck with a post-Union reverse dated 1706, even though the Union occurred on 1 May 1707 (just over a month after the calendar year changeover from 1706 to 1707, which in those days occurred in England in March). The Bill for the Act of Union received Royal assent on 6 March 1707 (1706 old style calendar in England; 1707 in Scotland).

A further apparent date anomaly has a simple explanation. If one compares the regnal edge year on five guinea pieces with those on crowns and halfcrowns, in some cases they are the same, and in others the regnal year is one year earlier on the five guinea piece, e.g. QVARTO (4th year) on the 1705 five guinea piece, but QVINTO (5th year) on the silver. The explanation is that the five guinea pieces were being struck early enough in the year to take the monarch's preceding regnal year. The edge date was changed on the anniversary of the accession, not at the beginning of the calendar year.

Post-Union type five guinea pieces were struck in five years up to 1714, the year of Anne's death.

The first head of Anne was engraved by John Croker from a portrait by Sir Godfrey Kneller. The later head, introduced in 1711, was engraved either by Croker or his assistant Samuel Bull. The reverses were probably by Croker and/or Bull. The first reverse is considered to be by Croker.

Collecting Hints

One specimen of any type in fine to very fine condition will be acceptable to most collectors.

Denomination	Metal	Weight (grams)	Diameter (mm)	Rev. alignment
Five Guineas	Gold	41.6–41.8	37–38	↓

Obverse 1   Head 1, left; ANNA DEI GRATIA

Obverse 2   Head 2, left, older portrait, hair arrangement different; same legend

Reverse 1   Four crowned cruciform shields (of England, Scotland, France, Ireland) between which are four sceptres; central rose; MAG BR FRA ET HIB REG (date)

Reverse 2   Similar but two shields separately show conjoined English/Scottish arms; central Star of the Order of the Garter instead of rose; shields are broader; crowns redesigned; MAG BRI FR ET HIB REG (date). Lettering and date are smaller.

Reverse 3   Similar but shields are narrower and taller; lettering and date as large as on Reverse 1 harp is different; other minor modifications; same legend

Reverse 4   Similar to Reverse 2 but lettering as large as on Reverse 1

Edge   DECVS ET TVTAMEN ANNO REGNI (regnal date)

Obv. 1   Obv. 2

Rev. 1   Rev. 2

Rev. 3   Rev. 4

No.	Date	Features	Edge date	Obv.	Rev.	F	VF	EF
AN5G-005	1703	VIGO below head; stops on obverse [1]	SECVNDO	1	1	20000	30000	50000
AN5G-010	1703	VIGO below head; no stops on obverse	SECVNDO	1	1	20000	30000	50000
AN5G-015	1705		QVARTO	1	1	1100	2500	7000
AN5G-020	1706		QVINTO	1	1	1100	2500	7000
AN5G-025	1706		QVINTO	1	2	1100	2500	7000
AN5G-030	1709		OCTAVO	1	3	1100	2500	7000
AN5G-035	1711		DECIMO	2	4	1100	2500	7000
AN5G-040	1713		DVODECIMO	2	4	1100	2500	7000
AN5G-045	1714		DECIMO TERTIO	2	4	1100	2500	7000
AN5G-050	1714	4 over 1 or 3	DECIMO TERTIO	2	4	1100	2500	7000

1. Three slightly different obverses; position of VIGO differs markedly.

George I (1714 – 1727)

The series is a standard type, using an obverse by Croker and a reverse by J.R. Ochs, senior. The general overall design of the previous reign is followed, but both sides of the coin bear the long abbreviated Hanoverian titles of the king. The portrait is similar to that on the crown but the neck is bare.

The value of the guinea had fluctuated over the years from twenty shillings to about thirty shillings and back to a level of twenty-one shillings and sixpence at the beginning of the reign. A Proclamation in December 1717 reduced the value to twenty-one shillings.

Collecting Hints

The series is scarce, especially in the higher grades, only four dates being struck. A fine condition coin should be adequate.

Denomination	Metal	Weight (grams)	Diameter (mm)	Rev. alignment
Five Guineas	Gold	41.7–41.8	37	↓

Obverse 1   Head 1, right; GEORGIVS D G M BR FR ET HIB REX F D

Reverse 1   Four crowned cruciform shields between which are four sceptres; central Star of the Order of the Garter; BRVN ET L DVX S R I A TH ET EL (date)

Edge   DECVS ET TVTAMEN ANNO REGNI (regnal date) (but note 1720 footnote 2 below)

Obv. 1   Rev. 1

No.	Date	Features	Edge date	Obv.	Rev.	F	VF	EF
G15G-005	1716	[1]	SECVNDO	1	1	1500	3500	7500
G15G-010	1717	[1]	TERTIO	1	1	1500	3500	7500
G15G-015	1717	D of DECVS inverted (edge) [1]	TERTIO	1	1	1500	3500	7500
G15G-020	1720	[2]	SEXTO	1	1	1500	3500	7500
G15G-025	1726		DECIMO TERTIO	1	1	1500	3500	7500
G15G-030	1726	each N on edge inverted (top left of N has no serif) [3]	DECIMO TERTIO	1	1	1800	4000	8500

1. Cross before DECVS and after TVTAMEN (edge) on 1716 and 1717 only.
2. Edge reads DECUS ET TUTAMEN not DECVS ET TVTAMEN.
3. A similar variety occurs on the 1726 crown.

George II (1727 – 1760)

The five guinea pieces of George II were the last of this denomination struck as regular coinage. The series began in 1729, the obverse again the work of John Croker, who by this time was approaching retirement. Some of the coins of 1729 bear the provenance mark 'E.I.C' below the head, denoting gold obtained from the East India Company. At least some of the work on the reverses was done by Tanner, who was Croker's apprentice from January 1729 (1728 old style calendar).

Tanner was the subject of a report of 30 January 1729 (1728 o.s.) from the Master of the Mint to the Treasury: 'I beg leave to recommend John Sigismund Tanner, who is a protestant, has the character of being very honest, sober and industrious, is but 24 years of age and has shown by several specimens made properly by him for a trial that he is further advanced in the art of taking a likeness and embossing in steel than any who have offered themselves for His Majesty's service.'

A change to an older head was made in 1746. The 1741 coin bearing the young head was the last gold coin struck before the changeover. A warrant of 11 December 1745 authorized the placing of the mark LIMA below the head on the 1746 five guinea piece, denoting that the gold had been obtained during Admiral Anson's circumnavigation of the world. The use of the word LIMA is something of a mystery, as there appears to be no direct connection with the Peruvian port of that name.

The older portrait was the work of John Croker and Tanner. The last five guinea piece for general circulation was issued in 1753.

Collecting Hints

The young head coinage was struck in relatively high relief, and coins need to be in about very fine condition to retain most of the detail. One specimen of each reign is all that most collectors will aim for, and it is probably advisable to select the somewhat more flatly struck old head type, where a fine condition specimen is still an attractive coin. Edges of five guinea pieces of George II should always be carefully examined for mount marks and pinholes.

Denomination	Metal	Weight (grams)	Diameter (mm)	Rev. alignment
Five Guineas	Gold	41.8–42.0	37	↓

Obverse 1   Head 1, left; GEORGIVS II DEI GRATIA

Obverse 2   Head 2, left, older portrait; same legend

Reverse 1   Crowned shield; M B F ET H REX F D B ET L D S R I A T ET E (date)

Reverse 2   Similar but shield slightly redesigned

Edge   DECVS ET TVTAMEN ANNO REGNI (regnal date)

Obv. 1   Obv. 2

Rev. 1   Rev. 2

No.	Date	Features	Edge date	Obv.	Rev.	F	VF	EF
G25G-005	1729		TERTIO	1	1	1000	2000	4200
G25G-010	1729	PROOF; edge plain [1]		1	1			25000
G25G-015	1729	EIC below head	TERTIO	1	1	1000	1900	4000
G25G-020	1731		QVARTO	1	2	1000	1800	4000
G25G-025	1731	PROOF [2]	QVARTO	1	2			30000
G25G-030	1735		OCTAVO	1	2	1000	1800	4000
G25G-035	1738	[3]	DVODECIMO	1	2	1000	1800	4000
G25G-040	1741		DECIMO QVARTO	1	2	1000	1800	4000
G25G-045	1741	41 over 35	DECIMO QVARTO	1	2	1000	1800	4000
G25G-050	1746	LIMA below head	DECIMO NONO	2	2	1000	2000	4500
G25G-055	1748		VICESIMO SECVNDO	2	2	1000	2000	4200
G25G-060	1753		VICESIMO SEXTO	2	2	1000	2000	4200

1. May weigh below 40 grams.
2. The portrait is very slightly different from the regular piece (hair slightly forward); minor reverse differences also exist.
3. Obverse lettering is smaller than on previous dates.

Minor reverse variations occur, especially to the harp and shield border.

Five Pounds

George IV (1820 – 1830)

The so-called five guinea piece was known at its inception as a five pound piece. The guinea had a variable value, usually between about twenty or thirty shillings, and only later was its value fixed at the 21 shilling level recognised and used until comparatively recent times. There is thus some case for viewing the modern five pound piece as a continuation of the five guinea piece. However, the series is separate from its predecessor, and it will be treated thus in this catalogue. The value of the pieces struck from 1826 onwards was fixed at five pounds rather than five pounds five shillings. Moreover, coins struck after the 'Great Recoinage' of 1816 have a more modern 'feel' than those struck earlier.

The only five pound pieces struck for George IV were those of 1826 issued in the cased proof set of that year, and the unique 1829 coin. The obverse was by William Wyon from a bust of the monarch by Sir Francis Chantrey and the bust was depicted unlaureate at the express command of the king. The reverses were by Johann Baptiste Merlen.

Collecting Hints

This coin will normally be found in the cased proof set, although isolated examples sometimes come up for sale. Occasionally, specimens exhibit signs of repair in the obverse field.

Denomination	Metal	Weight (grams)	Diameter (mm)	Rev. alignment
Five Pounds	Gold	39.8–40.0	38	↓

Obverse 1 Head 1, left; GEORGIUS IV DEI GRATIA 1826

Obverse 2 Head 2, left; same legend but date 1829

Reverse 1 Shield within mantle, crown above; BRITANNIARUM REX FID DEF

Edge DECUS ET TUTAMEN ANNO REGNI SEPTIMO

Obv. 1   Rev. 1

No.	Date	Features	Obv.	Rev.	EF	FDC
G45P-005	1826	PROOF [1]	1	1	7000	10000
G45P-010	1826	PROOF; edge plain [2]	1	1	15000	20000
G45P-015	1826	PROOF on thick flan; edge plain [3]	1	1	18000	
G45P-020	1829	PROOF or pattern; edge plain [4]	2	1		90000

1. Issued in cased proof sets.
2. Possibly a pattern.
3. Possibly a pattern; weight 46.5 grams; probably unique.
4. Unique; weight 38.7 grams.

William IV (1830 – 1837)

Unusually, no five pound pieces were struck for this reign, even though a proof set was issued in 1831 containing a two pound piece. Note, however, the existence of the crown piece of 1831 struck in gold. This weighs about 40 grams, possibly intentionally corresponding to the usual weight of a five pound piece.

Victoria (1837 – 1901)

The first five pound piece issued for this reign is one of the most famous and attractive of all British coins. Known colloquially as the 'Una and the Lion' piece, it was issued in 1839 in the cased proof sets of that year. The coin was designed by William Wyon, and it depicts on the reverse Queen Victoria, representing Una, leading the British Lion.

The Una and the Lion five pound piece has acquired a cult status in numismatics, similar to that of the Gothic crown. The coin comes up for sale only rarely, and probably most remain within the cased proof sets. There are a number of varieties, as well as pieces of a similar nature struck in various metals. These are properly regarded as patterns. Indeed, some might be equally regarded as pattern crowns, since the coin bears no mark of value and is medallic in appearance. A few even bear an obverse similar to the 1839 proof crown.

The next five pound piece to be struck has come to be regarded almost as the definitive example of this coin. This was the piece struck for the 1887 Golden Jubilee. At first sight, this coin resembles a crown piece struck in gold, but there are distinct differences. The principal designs on both the obverse (by Boehm) and the reverse (by Pistrucci) are smaller than on the crown. Although not rare, the 1887 five pound piece is universally popular. Proofs were struck for inclusion in the proof sets of that year.

In 1893 a similar issue of proof and non-proof five pound pieces marked the introduction of the new veiled head obverse on the gold and silver coinage. This obverse was by Thomas Brock. The issue retained the Pistrucci reverse.

Collecting Hints

Although the 'Una' coin needs to be in mint condition for the quality of this piece to be fully appreciated, this coin would probably take pride of place in a collection whatever its condition.
Care needs to be taken with the 1887 and 1893 five pound pieces because of the widespread existence of forgeries, known euphemistically as restrikes or as being 'wrong'. Many of these are of high quality and of correct weight, and they often mislead experienced dealers. For the aver

age collector or investor, the 1887 and 1893 five pound pieces are amongst the few coins where it is probably advisable to aim for a specimen in no higher than about very fine condition. A genuine coin will often have an 'old' look, frequently with numerous minor surface marks while a forgery often has a 'clean' look and a somewhat weak strike. Many coins of the 1887 issue are early strikings, and these are easily confused with proofs. Familiarisation with genuine proofs will enable one to distinguish them with relative ease. The proofs have wide, clearly defined rims, and the milling on the edge has a cutting feel to the fingers.

Denomination	Metal	Weight (grams)	Diameter (mm)	Rev. alignment
Five Pounds 1839	Gold	38.7–39.3	38	↑
Five Pounds 1887–93	Gold	40.0	37	↑

Obverse 1   Head 1, left; VICTORIA D G BRITANNIARUM REGINA F D

Obverse 2   Head 2, left; VICTORIA D G BRITT REG F D

Obverse 3   Head 3, left; VICTORIA DEI GRA BRITT REGINA FID DEF IND IMP

Reverse 1   Victoria as Una, standing, leading a lion left; DIRIGE DEUS GRESSUS MEOS; MDCCCXXXIX (= 1839) in exergue

Reverse 2   Similar but DIRIGIT instead of DIRIGE, and Garter Star missing from robes

Reverse 3   St George and Dragon; (date) and initials B.P. in exergue

Edge 1   (in relief) DECUS ET TUTAMEN ANNO REGNI TERTIO in large letters

Edge 2   Similar but small lettering

Edge 3   plain

Edge 4   milled

Obv. 1   Obv. 2

Obv. 3   Rev. 1

Rev. 2   Rev. 3

Young Head

No.	Date	Features	Edge	Obv.	Rev.	VF	EF	UNC
VY5P-005	1839	1	2	1	1	6000	12000	20000
VY5P-010	1839		3	1	1			25000
VY5P-015	1839	1	1	1	2			25000
VY5P-020	1839		3	1	2			30000

1. Fillet decorations vary (obv.).

Jubilee Head

No.	Date	Features	Edge	Obv.	Rev.	VF	EF	UNC
VJ5P-025	1887		4	2	3	450	600	850
VJ5P-030	1887	PROOF	4	2	3			2500
VJ5P-035	1887	PROOF; no initials B.P. in exergue	4	2	3			4000

Old Head

No.	Date	Features	Edge	Obv.	Rev.	VF	EF	UNC
VO5P-040	1893		4	3	3	500	900	1200
VO5P-045	1893	PROOF	4	3	3			3000

Patterns exist of the 1839 issue in several metals, some of which are identical in design to the above.

Commonwealth Mint

Mintmark: S: Sydney, Australia

Position of mintmark: On ground line above centre of date (reverse)

No.	Date	Features	mm	Obv.	Rev.	FDC
VJ5P-050	1887	PROOF	S	1	1	75000

Edward VII   (1901 – 1910)

A five pound piece was struck in 1902 to mark the coronation of Edward VII. Matt proof specimens were included in the cased proof set, and a very small number of proof pieces bearing an 'S' (Sydney) mintmark exist. This mark is at the centre of the ground line above the date.

The issue used the portrait of Edward VII by George William de Saulles (1862–1903), while the reverse retained the Pistrucci depiction of St George and the dragon.

Collecting Hints

Very competent forgeries exist. Matt proofs usually exhibit faint hairlines which may be a product of mint finishing.

Denomination	Metal	Weight (grams)	Diameter (mm)	Rev. alignment
Five Pounds	Gold	39.9–40.0	37	↑

Obverse 1 Head 1, right; EDWARDVS VII DEI GRA BRITT OMN REX FID DEF IND IMP

Reverse 1 St George and dragon, 1902 in exergue

Edge milled

Obv. 1   Rev. 1

No.	Date	Features	Obv.	Rev.	VF	EF	UNC
E75P-005	1902		1	1	500	650	850
E75P-010	1902	matt PROOF [1]	1	1			800

1. Issued in cased proof sets.

Commonwealth Mint

Mintmark: S: Sydney, Australia

Position of Mintmark: On ground line above centre of date (reverse)

No.	Date	Features	mm	Obv.	Rev.	FDC
E75P-015	1902	matt PROOF	S	1	1	75000

George V (1910 – 1936)

As with the previous reign, a five pound piece was struck in 1911 to mark the coronation. However, for some reason no ordinary (non-proof) specimens were struck, and only proof examples from the sets exist.

The portrait of the king was designed by Sir Bertram Mackennal (1863–1931), while the Pistrucci reverse was again retained.

Collecting Hints

Despite the fact that this is a proof-only issue, forgeries exist. One also frequently comes across specimens which have been extensively scuffed, and some doubt has been cast on the genuineness of some of these. If a coin appears weakly struck it should be avoided.
The 1911 coin is difficult to find as a single coin. This is because there is no non-proof issue, and most of the proofs are still in the sets.
The apparent 'dig' on the king's head above the ear is part of the design.

Denomination	Metal	Weight (grams)	Diameter (mm)	Rev. alignment
Five Pounds	Gold	39.9–40.0	37	↑

Obverse 1 Head 1, left; GEORGIVS V DEI GRA BRITT OMN REX FID DEF IND IMP

Reverse 1 St George and dragon; 1911 in exergue

Edge milled

Obv. 1   Rev. 1

No.	Date	Features	Obv.	Rev.	EF	FDC
G55P-005	1911	PROOF [1]	1	1	900	1400

1. Issued in cased proof sets.

Edward VIII (1936)

The Edward VIII five pounds is strictly speaking a pattern, as probable royal approval was about to be granted at the time of the abdication. However, because its official status rests only on this technicality, and to provide continuity, it is included here.

The portrait of Edward VIII is by Thomas Humphrey Paget, and faces left at the insistence of the king, who considered this placement more flattering and wished to discontinue the tradition of opposite facings for successive monarchs. The reverse is the St George and dragon design of Pistrucci.

Denomination	Metal	Weight (grams)	Diameter (mm)	Rev. alignment
Five Pounds	Gold	40.0	37	↑

Obverse 1 Head 1, left; EDWARDVS VIII D G BR OMN REX F D IND IMP

Reverse 1 St George and dragon; 1937 in exergue

Edge milled

Obv. 1   Rev. 1

No.	Date	Obv.	Rev.	FDC
E85P-005	1937	1	1	175000

George VI (1937 – 1952)

Coronation issue five pound pieces of 1937 were again issued only in cased proof sets. These sets contained four coins, each of which comprised the only British coin of that denomination for the reign.

The obverse portrait was by Thomas Humphrey Paget, the reverse again being the Pistrucci St George and dragon.

<table>
<tr><td>

Collecting Hints

Gold coins of 1937 must always be examined carefully for edge damage. The tight fitting inserts in the case often meant that the coins were prised out, and the plain edge was very susceptible to marks.

</td></tr>
</table>

Denomination	Metal	Weight (grams)	Diameter (mm)	Rev. alignment
Five Pounds	Gold	39.9–40.0	37	↑

Obverse 1   Head 1, left; GEORGIVS VI D G BR OMN REX F D IND IMP

Reverse 1   St George and dragon, 1937 in exergue

Edge   plain

Obv. 1

Rev. 1

No.	Date	Features	Obv.	Rev.	EF	FDC
G65P-005	1937	PROOF [1]	1	1	600	750

1. Issued in cased proof sets.

Elizabeth II   (1952 –)

With the accession of Elizabeth II there was a departure from normal practice in the issuing of gold coinage. No gold coins were included in the proof sets of 1953 issued for the coronation, and the only British gold coins struck in that year were a small number struck in order to provide continuity of the series. These were not released, nor were similar coins dated 1957. The coins bore the obverse portrait of Elizabeth II by Mary Gillick, and the Pistrucci St George and dragon reverse.

No further five pound pieces were struck until 1980, nine years after decimalization. They then continued to be issued in a somewhat irregular fashion, both as individual cased coins and in cased sets. The coins from 1980 to 1984 bore a portrait of the queen by Arnold Machin, and those from 1985 used later portraits by Raphael David Maklouf. The 1989 issue commemorating the 500th anniversary of the gold sovereign differed markedly from the regular issue.

Denomination	Metal	Weight (grams)	Diameter (mm)	Rev. alignment
Five Pounds	Gold	40.0	36	↑

Obverse 1   Head 1, right; ELIZABETH II DEI GRA BRITT OMN REGINA F D

Obverse 2   Head 1, right; ELIZABETH II DEI GRATIA REGINA F D

Obverse 3   Head 2, right; same legend

Obverse 4   Head 3, right; ELIZABETH II DEI GRA REG F D

Obverse 5   Head 4, right; same legend

Obverse 6   Queen facing on throne, holding orb and sceptre; ELIZABETH II DEI GRA REG FID DEF (*for the 500th anniversary of the gold sovereign*)

Obverse 7   Similar but 'U' in circle below throne

Obverse 8   Head 5, right; ELIZABETH II DEI GRA REGINA FID DEF

Reverse 1   St George and dragon, (date) in exergue

Reverse 2   Similar but 'U' in circle to left of date

Reverse 3   Crowned shield within double rose; ANNIVERSARY OF THE GOLD SOVEREIGN 1489–1989

Edge   milled

Obv. 1

Obv. 3

Obv. 4

Obv. 6

Rev. 1

Rev. 2

Rev. 3

No.	Date	Features	Obv.	Rev.	Unc
EZ5P-005	1953	PROOF or pattern	1	1	200000
EZ5P-010	1957	PROOF	2	1	150000
EZ5P-015	1980	PROOF [1]	3	1	550
EZ5P-020	1981	PROOF [1]	3	1	550
EZ5P-025	1982	PROOF [1]	3	1	550
EZ5P-030	1984	[2]	3	2	450
EZ5P-035	1984	PROOF [1]	3	1	550
EZ5P-040	1985	[2]	4	2	450
EZ5P-045	1985	PROOF [3]	4	1	550
EZ5P-050	1986	[2]	4	2	450
EZ5P-055	1987	[2]	5	2	450
EZ5P-060	1988	[2]	5	2	450

No.	Date	Features	Obv.	Rev.	Unc
EZ5P-065	1989	2	7	3	550
EZ5P-070	1989	PROOF [1]	6	3	650
EZ5P-075	1990	2	4	2	500
EZ5P-080	1990	PROOF [1]	4	1	550
EZ5P-085	1991	2	4	2	500
EZ5P-090	1991	PROOF [1]	4	1	600
EZ5P-095	1992	2	4	2	500
EZ5P-100	1992	PROOF [1]	4	1	600
EZ5P-105	1993	2	4	2	550
EZ5P-110	1993	PROOF [1]	4	1	600
EZ5P-115	1994	2	4	2	550
EZ5P-120	1994	PROOF [3]	4	1	600
EZ5P-125	1995	2	4	2	550
EZ5P-130	1995	PROOF [1]	4	1	600
EZ5P-135	1996	2	4	2	550
EZ5P-140	1996	PROOF [1]	4	1	600
EZ5P-145	1997	2	4	2	550
EZ5P-150	1997	PROOF [1]	4	1	600
EZ5P-155	1998	2	8	2	550
EZ5P-160	1998	PROOF [3]	8	1	600

1. Issued cased and in cased proof sets.
2. Issued cased.
3. Issued in cased proof sets.

The gold strikings of the 1990 and later cupronickel five pounds are listed in the decimal section and do not appear in the table above.

Fifty Shillings

The gold 50 shillings of Oliver Cromwell was, together with the broad, the first gold coin styled similarly to modern coinage. It was designed by Thomas Simon (also called Symonds) and depicts Cromwell as a Roman Emperor.

This coin seldom comes up for sale, and only eleven specimens are thought to exist. Snelling considered the fifty shillings to be no more than the proof version of the broad.

Denomination	Metal	Weight (grams)	Diameter (mm)	Rev. alignment
Fifty Shillings	Gold	22.7	30	↓

Obverse 1 Head 1, left; OLIVAR D G R P ANG SCO HIB &c PRO

Reverse 1 Crowned shield; PAX QVAERITVR BELLO 1656

Edge (in relief): PROTECTOR LITERIS LITERAE NVMMIS CORONA ET SALVS

Obv. 1

Rev. 1

No.	Date	Obv.	Rev.	VF	EF
OC50S-005	1656	1	1	15000	20000

London, The Royal Mint

Two Guineas

Obv. 1

Obv. 2

Rev. 1

Charles II (1660 – 1685)

The coin nowadays known as the two guinea piece was first minted in 1664. The nominal value of the piece was forty shillings, and it was known initially as a forty-shilling piece, then later as a double-guinea or a two guinea piece. The term 'guinea' was a colloquial name referring to the place of origin of much of the gold used to produce the coins. However, although the two guinea piece began at a value of forty shillings, its value fluctuated over the years until set at forty-two shillings by Proclamation early in the 18th century.

The obverse and reverse of the new coin were designed by John Roettier (1631–c.1700). The designs are similar to those used on the five guinea piece, with significant modifications compared with the halfcrown design being made. These modifications were made to prevent gilding and passing off halfcrowns as the gold coin. The two guinea piece was considered too thin to allow an edge inscription to be used, as on the five guinea piece. This was a further distinguishing mark from the halfcrown, which bore a lettered edge. From 1664 to 1669 a perpendicular graining was used on the two guinea piece to deter filing or clipping. It was then decided that diagonal graining would afford greater security, and this was used from 1671 onwards.

The elephant (with or without castle) denotes gold obtained from the African Company in Guinea. The charter granted to the company included a clause allowing the insertion of this symbol on the coins.

No.	Date	Features	Obv.	Rev.	F	VF	EF
C22GM-005	1664		1	1	550	1200	4000
C22GM-010	1664	elephant below head	1	1	450	1000	3500
C22GM-015	1665	1	1	1			
C22GM-020	1669	2	1	1	3000		
C22GM-025	1671	3	1	1	550	1200	4000
C22GM-030	1675		2	1	550	1200	4000
C22GM-035	1676		2	1	450	1000	3000
C22GM-040	1676	elephant and castle below head	2	1	450	1000	3000
C22GM-045	1677		2	1	450	1000	3000
C22GM-050	1678	usually or always 8 over 7	2	1	450	1000	3000
C22GM-055	1678	elephant below head	2	1	4000		
C22GM-060	1678	elephant and castle below head	2	1	450	1000	3000
C22GM-065	1679		2	1	450	1000	3000
C22GM-070	1680		2	1	450	1000	3000
C22GM-075	1681	4	2	1	450	1000	3000
C22GM-080	1682		2	1	450	1000	3000
C22GM-085	1682	elephant and castle below head	2	1	450	1000	3000
C22GM-090	1683		2	1	450	1000	3000
C22GM-095	1683	elephant and castle below head	2	1	450	1000	3000
C22GM-100	1684		2	1	450	1000	3000
C22GM-105	1684	elephant and castle below head	2	1	450	1000	3000

1. Possibly unique.
2. Extremely rare.
3. Last 1 of date is reversed from usual orientation.
4. Lettering slightly larger.

Collecting Hints

As with all Charles II coins, the two guinea piece is rare in top condition. Luckily, however, the coin retains considerable attractiveness in fine condition. Coins are sometimes found which have toned to a superb rose red hue, and such a specimen in fine or better will enhance any collection. Usually a coin with an elephant below the head is significantly scarcer than one without, but care must be taken with the 1664 two guinea piece. This date with the elephant is possibly the most prevalent of the entire series. Some of the later dates occur somewhat weakly struck.

Denomination	Metal	Weight (grams)	Diameter (mm)	Rev. alignment
Two Guineas 1664–69	Gold	16.6–16.8	30–32	↓
Two Guineas 1671–84	Gold	16.5–16.7	30–32	↓

Obverse 1 Head 1, right; pointed truncation; lock of hair to right of truncation; CAROLVS II DEI GRATIA

Obverse 2 Head 2, right; larger, rounded truncation, without lock of hair to right; same legend

Reverse 1 Four crowned cruciform shields between which are four sceptres, with four interlinked 'C's at the centre; MAG BR FRA ET HIB REX (date)

Edge (1664–69) milled (vertically); (1671–84) milled (diagonally)

James II (1685 – 1688)

This series consists of only two dates, 1687 and 1688, and is a one-type issue. The design is by John Roettier. There are again marked differences between the obverse and reverse of this coin and those of the silver halfcrown, to prevent unscrupulous conversions from being attempted.

There are no elephant or elephant and castle provenance marks on this series. However, it should be mentioned that Ruding reported a 1686 coin with elephant and castle below the head. This coin appears to be unknown today.

Denomination	Metal	Weight (grams)	Diameter (mm)	Rev. alignment
Two Guineas	Gold	16.7	31–32	↓

Obverse 1   Head 1, left; IACOBVS II DEI GRATIA

Reverse 1   Four crowned cruciform shields between which are four sceptres; MAG BR FRA ET HIB REX (date)

Edge   milled (diagonally)

Obv. 1	Rev. 1

No.	Date	Features	Obv.	Rev.	F	VF	EF
J22G-005	1687		1	1	750	1700	4200
J22G-010	1688	usually or always 8 over 7	1	1	800	1800	4500

William & Mary   (1688 – 1694)

Apart from a very rare 1691 piece, the first two guinea piece of this reign struck for regular use was minted in 1693. This was well after the other gold coinage had entered circulation. By this time, the value of the guinea had risen to almost 30 shillings, from the 20 shillings which had been its value at the beginning of the reign of Charles II.

The reverse of the two guinea piece of William and Mary was radically redesigned from that of previous reigns. At first sight, this seems a curious decision. Deliberate design alterations had always been incorporated to differentiate it from the halfcrown, which was of a similar size. The new shield reverse was, however, very similar to the redesigned reverse of the William and Mary halfcrown of 1689–90. However, it must be remembered that by 1693 the halfcrown had again reverted to the cruciform shield reverse.

Although there is doubt about the exact attribution of much of the William and Mary coinage, it appears likely that the two guinea piece was the work of James and Norbert Roettier. The reverse is not the happiest of designs. It is a confusion of intricate detail, and is usually encountered weakly or flatly struck.

The elephant and castle symbol was reintroduced on all dates to denote gold obtained from the African Company.

Denomination	Metal	Weight (grams)	Diameter (mm)	Rev. alignment
Two Guineas	Gold	16.7–16.8	31–32	↓

Obverse 1   Heads 1, right; GVLIELMVS ET MARIA DEI GRATIA

Reverse 1   Crowned shield; MAG BR FR ET HIB REX ET REGINA (date)

Edge   milled (diagonally)

Obv. 1	Rev. 1

No.	Date	Features	Obv.	Rev.	F	VF	EF
WM2G-005	1691	elephant and castle below head	1	1	2000		
WM2G-010	1693		1	1	700	1200	3500
WM2G-015	1693	elephant and castle below head	1	1	800	1500	4000
WM2G-020	1694	usually or always 4 over 3	1	1	700	1200	3500
WM2G-025	1694	elephant and castle below head; usually or always 4 over 3	1	1	800	1500	4000

William III   (1695 – 1701)

There were no two guinea pieces minted depicting the early head of William III as on the other gold coins, and the only date minted was the 1701 'fine work' specimen corresponding to the five guinea piece with an almost identical portrait.

The reverse again depicted the cruciform shields of the Charles II and James II era, as the shield reverse of the William and Mary series had proved unsuccessful. Although the reverse appears at first glance to be identical to that of the five guinea piece, there are marked differences. The crowns and the harp are in particular very different.

The 1701 two guinea piece was probably designed by Johann Crocker, aka John Croker. James Roettier died in 1698 and his brother Norbert had moved to France in 1695.

Denomination	Metal	Weight (grams)	Diameter (mm)	Rev. alignment
Two Guineas	Gold	16.7	31–32	↓

Obverse 1   Head 1, right; GVLIELMVS III DEI GRA

Reverse 1   Four crowned cruciform shields between which are four sceptres, with central lion of Nassau; MAG BR FRA ET HIB REX (date)

Edge   milled (diagonally)

Obv. 1

Rev. 1

No.	Date		Obv.	Rev.	F	VF	EF
W32G-005	1701		1	1	1000	2000	4500

Anne (1702 – 1714)

The only two guinea pieces of Anne were struck as a one-type issue after the Union of England and Scotland. There is no transition to a slightly more mature head, as with the five guinea piece.

The portrait of Anne was engraved by Croker from a design by Sir Godfrey Kneller. The reverse is considered to be by either Croker or Bull, or possibly both.

The 1714 coin is usually catalogued as being with the 4 of the date over a 3. However, careful examination reveals that the faint overdate may be a 4 over a 1 instead of a 3. It must be remembered that the 'J-type' 1 has several of the characteristics of a 3.

Collecting Hints

A specimen in fine to Very fine condition will be adequate. This series frequently occurs mounted and gilt.

Denomination	Metal	Weight (grams)	Diameter (mm)	Rev. alignment
Two Guineas	Gold	16.7–16.8	31–32	↓

Obverse 1   Head 1, left; ANNA DEI GRATIA

Reverse 1   Four crowned cruciform shields between which are four sceptres; central Star of the Order of the Garter; MAG BRI FR ET HIB REG (date)

Edge   milled (diagonally)

Obv. 1

Rev. 1

No.	Date	Features	Obv.	Rev.	F	VF	EF
AN2G-005	1709		1	1	650	1100	3000
AN2G-010	1711		1	1	650	1100	3000
AN2G-015	1713		1	1	700	1200	3500
AN2G-020	1714		1	1	650	1100	3000
AN2G-025	1714	4 over 1 or 3 [1]	1	1	700	1100	3000

1. See comments above.

George I (1714 – 1727)

The series is a one-type issue, struck only in 1717, 1720 and 1726. The obverse was by Croker and the reverse by J. R. Ochs, senior.

The general design is a scaled-down version of the five guinea piece.

The value of the guinea had fluctuated over the years from twenty shillings to about thirty shillings and back to a level of twenty-one shillings and sixpence at the beginning of the reign. A Proclamation in December 1717 reduced the value to twenty-one shillings.

Collecting Hints

A fine condition coin should be acceptable to most collectors.

Denomination	Metal	Weight (grams)	Diameter (mm)	Rev. alignment
Two Guineas	Gold	16.8	31–32	↓

Obverse 1   Head 1, right; GEORGIVS D G M BR FR ET HIB REX F D

Reverse 1   Four crowned cruciform shields between which are four sceptres; central Star of the Order of the Garter; BRVN ET L DVX S R I A TH ET EL (date)

Edge   milled (diagonally)

Obv. 1

Rev. 1

No.	Date	Features	Obv.	Rev.	F	VF	EF
G12G-005	1717		1	1	750	1500	3500
G12G-010	1720		1	1	700	1400	3000
G12G-012	1720	0 over 1	1	1	750	1600	3500
G12G-015	1726	[1]	1	1	650	1400	3000

1. Date numerals larger and formed differently from previous dates.

George II (1727 – 1760)

Although in previous reigns the two guinea piece has in general mirrored the issue of five guinea pieces, during the reign of George II there were marked differences. No coins bearing the provenance marks E.I.C. or LIMA were issued. The main difference between the two issues was that three different portraits were used on the two guinea piece instead of two. The second head, used in 1739 and 1740, has become known as the 'intermediate head', as the other two are in common parlance termed the 'young' and 'old' heads. However, these terms derive mainly from the silver coinage. Since the heads on the gold are in any case different in many ways from those on the silver, the terms 'young', 'intermediate' and 'old' are something of a misnomer when applied to the gold, but nevertheless they persist. The intermediate and old heads are in fact very similar to each other. The chief difference on the obverses is the reversion of the 'U' in the king's name back to a 'V'.

The first two guinea piece was issued relatively late into the reign, in 1734 (following a 1733 pattern). This was some years after the silver denominations had begun. The series seems to have been widely circulated, and is often found in only fine condition. Hammered gold had been demonetized in 1732 and 1733. The last two guinea piece was struck in 1753, and the denomination terminated, although later dates may be found in the section on patterns (p.708).

A change was made to the graining (milling) during the reign of George II. Leake, writing in the 18th century, noted that 'in 1739 ... the graining which had hitherto been diagonal strokes was now made angular, upon occasion of a gang of guinea filers, who had taken more liberty than usual with the guineas, and for the discovery of whom a reward was publicly advertised. This alteration in the graining is certainly an improvement.' The 'angular' graining referred to is the shape of a chevron, or arrow-head.

The first head of George II was by Croker. The second and third heads were generally by Tanner, with some assistance from Croker on the earlier type. The reverses may have been by Tanner and/or Ochs, junior.

Obv. 1   Obv. 2

Obv. 3

Collecting Hints

A fine condition coin will normally be acceptable to most collectors.
Modern forgeries exist for some dates, notably 1738, 1739 and 1748. A genuine 1739 'intermediate head' (Head 2) coin will normally have a very tiny raised flaw in the field behind the king's head. A genuine 1738 coin frequently has a scratch-like flaw resembling an arc of a circle under the head.

Rev. 1   Rev. 2

Denomination	Metal	Weight (grams)	Diameter (mm)	Rev. alignment
Two Guineas	Gold	16.8	31–32	↓

Obverse 1 Head 1, left; GEORGIVS II DEI GRATIA

Obverse 2 Head 2, left, older portrait; GEORGIUS II DEI GRATIA

Obverse 3 Head 3, left, very similar but hair slightly more profuse; GEORGIVS II DEI GRATIA

(note the difference in spelling on Obverse 2)

Reverse 1 Crowned shield; M B F ET H REX F D B ET L D S R I A T ET E 1734

Reverse 2 Similar but crown and shield are somewhat different; same legend (date)

Edge (1734–38) milled (diagonally); (1739–53) milled (with chevrons)

No.	Date	Features	Obv.	Rev.	F	VF	EF
G22G-005	1734	4 over 3	1	1	1300	3000	
G22G-010	1735		1	2	500	800	1500
G22G-015	1738	[1]	1	2	400	650	1100
G22G-020	1739	[2]	1	2	400	650	1100
G22G-025	1739	[2]	2	2	400	650	1100
G22G-030	1740		2	2	420	700	1200
G22G-032	1740	4 over 3 or 40 over 39	2	2	450	900	1600
G22G-035	1748	[2]	3	2	450	900	1600
G22G-040	1753	[3]	3	2	600	1050	2200

1. DEI can occur widely spaced (obv.).
2. Lettering size varies.
3. Reverse has small lettering; graining is coarse.

Two Pounds

George IV   (1820 – 1830)

As the five pound piece replaced the five guinea piece, so after the Great Recoinage the two guinea piece gave way to the gold two pound coin. However, unlike its larger counterpart, the first two pounds struck was a currency piece, the well known and much admired 1823 coin, known at the time as the 'double sovereign'.

The obverse portrait of the king was designed by Johann Baptiste Merlen. This designer was known primarily for his reverses, and the portrait for the 1823 two pound piece was the only obverse he engraved, using as a basis a model by Sir Francis Chantrey. The elegance of this portrait compared with Pistrucci's portrait for the sovereign reveals that the choice of designer and engraver was a wise one. Apparently, Pistrucci was unwilling to work from the model of another artist. The quality of the strike was exceptional, producing what some consider to be the most beautiful two pound piece ever produced. The reverse of this coin (by Pistrucci) has been the basis for the design of this denomination up to the present day.

In 1826, a proof two pounds was struck for inclusion in the proof set. The obverse was by William Wyon from a bust of the monarch by Chantrey, and the reverse was by Johann Baptiste Merlen. This coin was very similar to the proof five pound piece struck for the same set.

Rev. 1   Rev. 2

No.	Date	Features	Edge date	Obv.	Rev.	F	VF	EF	UNC
G42P-005	1823		IV	1	1	300	450	850	1400
G42P-010	1823	PROOF	IV	1	1				4000
G42P-012	1824	PROOF or Pattern	QUINTO	2	2				12000
G42P-015	1825	PROOF or pattern; edge plain		2	2				5000
G42P-020	1826	PROOF [1]	SEPTIMO	2	2		800	2000	3500
G42P-025	1826	PROOF on thick flan; edge plain [2]		2	2				15000

1. Issued in cased proof sets.
2. Possibly a pattern; weight 21.5 grams; probably unique.

William IV   (1830 – 1837)

A proof two pound piece designed by William Wyon was struck in 1831 for inclusion in the cased proof set. This was the largest gold coin struck during this reign. The obverse was engraved by William Wyon after a bust designed by Sir Francis Chantrey. The reverse was designed and engraved by Johann Baptiste Merlen.

Collecting Hints

The 1823 two pound piece can occur so well struck that it appears to be a proof. The edge should always be examined for pinholes. Any isolated examples of the 1826 coin should be similarly examined. Many of these coins have also been privately gilded; some of the gilt 1823 coins are very attractive and can appear in better grade than they actually are. Particular attention should be paid to the highest points of both sides, such as the king's hair and the sword, head and breast of St George.

Collecting Hints

This coin is rarely found outside the proof set. The broad edge is somewhat susceptible to edge knocks.

Denomination	Metal	Weight (grams)	Diameter (mm)	Rev. alignment
Two Pounds	Gold	16.0	28	↓

Obverse 1   Head 1, left; GEORGIUS IIII D G BRITANNIAR REX F D

Obverse 2   Head 2, left; GEORGIUS IV DEI GRATIA 1826

Reverse 1   St George and dragon; 1823 in exergue

Reverse 2   Shield within mantle, crown above; BRITANNIARUM REX FID DEF

Edge   DECUS ET TUTAMEN ANNO REGNI (regnal date)

Denomination	Metal	Weight (grams)	Diameter (mm)	Rev. alignment
Two Pounds	Gold	15.9	28	↓

Obverse 1   Head 1, right; GULIELMUS IIII D G BRITANNIAR REX F D. WW on truncation of head

Reverse 1   Crowned shield on mantle; ANNO 1831

Edge   plain

Obv. 1   Obv. 2

Obv. 1   Rev. 1

No.	Date	Features	Obv.	Rev.	EF	FDC
W42P-005	1831	PROOF [1]	1	1	3000	5000

1. Issued in cased proof sets.

Victoria   (1837 – 1901)

The omission of a two pound piece from the proof set of 1839 was curious when one considers the coverage of this set from the five pounds to the farthing. The 1853 set also did not include this denomination, and it was not struck during this reign until 1887. This piece, minted for the Golden Jubilee, resembles a smaller version of the five pounds, with an obverse by Boehm and using the Pistrucci St George and dragon reverse. This is probably the best known and most popular example of this denomination, and proofs were struck for inclusion in the proof sets.

In 1893 a two pound piece was struck in both ordinary and proof versions to mark the introduction of the new veiled head obverse by Thomas Brock. The Pistrucci reverse was retained.

Collecting Hints

A large number of forgeries exist, especially of the 1887 coin. Many of these are of poor quality and 'wear' differently from genuine coins, especially around the head and breast of St George. However, many of the fakes are very difficult to detect. Because of the prevalence of these 'restrikes', as some dealers like to call them, it is probably advisable to look for coins in about very fine condition with a genuinely old appearance.

As with five pound pieces, care must be taken not to confuse proofs with early strikings. The rims and milling of genuine proofs should be examined whenever so that one becomes familiar with their appearance.

Denomination	Metal	Weight (grams)	Diameter (mm)	Rev. alignment
Two Pounds	Gold	16.0	28	↑

Obverse 1   Head 1, left; VICTORIA D G BRITT REG F D

Obverse 2   Head 2, left; VICTORIA DEI GRA BRITT REGINA FID DEF IND IMP

Reverse 1   St George and dragon; (date) and initials B.P. in exergue

Edge   milled

Obv. 1

Obv. 2

Rev. 1

Jubilee Head

No.	Date	Features	Obv.	Rev.	VF	EF	UNC
VJ2P-005	1887		1	1	220	350	500
VJ2P-010	1887	PROOF	1	1		500	1000
VJ2P-015	1887	PROOF no initials B.P. in exergue	1	1		600	1200

Old Head

No.	Date	Features		Obv.	Rev.	VF	EF	UNC
VO2P-020	1893			2	1	280	400	600
VO2P-025	1893	PROOF		2	1		550	1200

Commonwealth Mint

Mintmark: S: Sydney, Australia

Position of mintmark: On ground line above centre of date (reverse)

No.	Date	Features	mm	Obv.	Rev.	EF	UNC
VJ2P-030	1887	PROOF	S	1	1		30000

Edward VII   (1901 – 1910)

A two pound piece was struck in 1902 to mark the coronation of Edward VII. Matt proof specimens were included in the cased proof set, and a very small number of proof pieces bearing an 'S' (Sydney) mintmark exist. This mark is at the centre of the ground line above the date.

The issue used the portrait of Edward VII by George William de Saulles (1862–1903), while the reverse retained the Pistrucci depiction of St George and the dragon.

Collecting Hints

Very competent forgeries exist.

Denomination	Metal	Weight (grams)	Diameter (mm)	Rev. alignment
Two Pounds	Gold	16.0	28	↑

Obverse 1   Head 1, right; EDWARDVS VII DEI GRA BRITT OMN REX FID DEF IND IMP

Reverse 1   St George and dragon; 1902 in exergue

Edge   milled

Obv. 1

Rev. 1

No.	Date	Features	Obv.	Rev.	VF	EF	UNC
E72P-005	1902		1	1	240	320	450
E72P-010	1902	matt PROOF [1]	1	1		320	450

1. Issued in cased proof sets.

Commonwealth Mint

Mintmark: S: Sydney, Australia

Position of mintmark: On ground line above centre of date (reverse)

No.	Date	Features	mm	Obv.	Rev.	UNC
E72P-015	1902	matt PROOF	S	1	1	30000

George V   (1910 – 1936)

As with the previous reign, a two pound piece was struck in 1911 to mark the coronation. However, for some reason no ordinary (non-proof) specimens were struck, and only proof examples from the sets exist.

The portrait of the king was designed by Sir Bertram Mackennal (1863–1931), while the Pistrucci reverse was again retained.

Collecting Hints

Despite the fact that this is a proof-only issue, forgeries exist. One also frequently comes across specimens which have been extensively scuffed, and some doubt has been cast on the genuineness of some of these. Genuine single pieces are somewhat difficult to find, as most of the proofs are still in the sets.
The apparent 'dig' on the king's head above the ear is part of the design.

Denomination	Metal	Weight (grams)	Diameter (mm)	Rev. alignment
Two Pounds	Gold	16.0	28	↑

Obverse 1   Head 1, left; GEORGIVS V DEI GRA BRITT OMN REX FID DEF IND IMP

Reverse 1   St George and dragon, 1911 in exergue

Edge   milled

Obv. 1   Rev. 1

No.	Date	Features	Obv.	Rev.	EF	FDC
G52P-005	1911	PROOF [1]	1	1	450	800
G52P-010	1911	matt PROOF	1	1		3000

1. Issued in cased proof sets.

Edward VIII   (1936)

The Edward VIII two pounds is strictly speaking a pattern, as probable royal approval was about to be granted at the time of the abdication. However, because its official status rests only on this technicality, and to provide continuity, it is included here.

The portrait of Edward VIII is by Thomas Humphrey Paget, and faces left at the insistence of the king, who considered this placement more flattering and wished to discontinue the tradition of opposite facings for successive monarchs. The reverse is the St George and dragon design by Pistrucci.

Denomination	Metal	Weight (grams)	Diameter (mm)	Rev. alignment
Two Pounds	Gold	16.0	28	↑

Obverse 1   Head 1, left; EDWARDVS VIII D G BR OMN REX F D IND IMP

Reverse 1   St George and dragon, 1937 in exergue

Edge   milled

Obv. 1   Rev. 1

No.	Date		Obv.	Rev.		FDC
E82P-005	1937		1	1		70000

George VI   (1937 – 1952)

Coronation issue two pound pieces of 1937 were again issued only in cased proof sets. These sets contained four coins, each of which comprised the only British coin of that denomination for the reign.

The obverse portrait was by Thomas Humphrey Paget, the reverse again being the Pistrucci St George and dragon.

Collecting Hints

Gold coins of 1937 must always be examined carefully for edge damage. The tight fitting inserts in the case often meant that the coins were prised out, and the plain edge was very susceptible to marks.

Denomination	Metal	Weight (grams)	Diameter (mm)	Rev. alignment
Two Pounds	Gold	16.0	28	↑

Obverse 1   Head 1, left; GEORGIVS VI D G BR OMN REX F D IND IMP

Reverse 1   St George and dragon, 1937 in exergue

Edge   plain

Obv. 1   Rev. 1

No.	Date	Features	Obv.	Rev.	EF	FDC
G62P-005	1937	PROOF [1]	1	1	320	480

1. Issued in cased proof sets.

Elizabeth II   (1952 –)

With the accession of Elizabeth II there was a departure from normal practice in the issuing of gold coinage. No gold coins were included in the proof sets of 1953 issued for the coronation, and the only British gold coins struck in that year were a small number struck in order to provide continuity of the series. These were not released. The coins bore the obverse portrait of Elizabeth II by Mary Gillick, and the Pistrucci St George and dragon reverse.

No further two pound pieces were struck until 1980, nine years after decimalization. They then continued to be issued in a somewhat irregular fashion, both as individual cased coins and in cased sets. The coins from 1980 to 1983 bear a portrait of the queen by

Arnold Machin, and those from 1985 use later portraits by Raphael David Maklouf.

The proof gold two pounds of 1986, 1994, 1995 and 1997 are unusual in that they may be regarded either as gold versions of the base metal two pounds or as true gold issues. Gold versions of base metal coins are not unusual (e.g. the 1990 and 1993 five pounds) but the incorporation of the coins into proof sets of gold coinage is a somewhat unusual step. The gold versions are, therefore, listed in this catalogue primarily as true gold issues, with entries in the base metal section bearing the same reference number as in the gold section.

Denomination	Metal	Weight (grams)	Diameter (mm)	Rev. alignment
Two Pounds	Gold	16.0	28.4	↑

Obverse 1   Head 1, right; ELIZABETH II DEI GRA BRITT OMN REGINA F D

Obverse 2   Head 2, right; ELIZABETH II DEI GRATIA REGINA F D

Obverse 3   Head 3, right; ELIZABETH II DEI GRA REG F D

Obverse 4   Head 3, right; ELIZABETH II DEI GRATIA REGINA F D TWO POUNDS

Obverse 5   Queen facing on throne, holding orb and sceptre; ELIZABETH II DEI GRA REG FID DEF *(for the 500th anniversary of the gold sovereign)*

Obverse 6   Head 3, right within beaded circle; ELIZABETH II DEI GRATIA REGINA F D

Obverse 7   Head 4, right; ELIZABETH II DEI GRA REGINA FID DEF

Obverse 8   Head 4, right within beaded circle; ELIZABETH II DEI GRA REG FID DEF

Reverse 1   St George and dragon, (date) in exergue

Reverse 2   Thistle on St Andrew's Cross; 1986 *(for the Commonwealth Games)*

Reverse 3   Crowned shield within double rose; ANNIVERSARY OF THE GOLD SOVEREIGN 1489–1989

Reverse 4   Bank of England's Corporate Seal with Crown and Cyphers of William and Mary; BANK OF ENGLAND 1694 1994

Reverse 5   Dove carrying olive branch *(for 50th anniversary of end of World War II)*

Reverse 6   Array of flags rising from UN 50 logo; NATIONS UNITED FOR PEACE 1945–1995 *(for 50th anniversary of United Nations)*

Reverse 7   Four concentric circles depicting Man's technological advancement from Iron Age to the Internet; TWO POUNDS 1997

Reverse 8   Rugby ball and posts; 1999 TWO POUNDS

Edge   (except EZ2P-080) milled;
(EZ2P-080) (incuse): 1945 IN PEACE GOODWILL 1995

	Obv. 4	Obv. 5	Obv. 6
	Obv. 8	Rev. 1	Rev. 2
	Rev. 3	Rev. 4	Rev. 5
	Rev. 6	Rev. 7	Rev. 8

No.	Date	Features	Obv.	Rev.	FDC
EZ2P-005	1953	PROOF or pattern	1	1	75000
EZ2P-010	1980	PROOF [1]	2	1	250
EZ2P-015	1982	PROOF [1]	2	1	250
EZ2P-020	1983	PROOF [1]	2	1	250
EZ2P-025	1985	PROOF [2]	3	1	250
EZ2P-030	1986	PROOF [1]	4	2	250
EZ2P-035	1987	PROOF [1]	3	1	250
EZ2P-040	1988	PROOF [1]	3	1	250
EZ2P-045	1989	PROOF [1]	5	3	320
EZ2P-050	1990	PROOF [1]	3	1	250
EZ2P-055	1991	PROOF [1]	3	1	280
EZ2P-060	1992	PROOF [1]	3	1	280
EZ2P-065	1993	PROOF [1]	3	1	280
EZ2P-070	1994	PROOF [1]	4	4	350
EZ2P-075	1994	PROOF [3]	3	4	450
EZ2P-080	.1995	PROOF [4]	4	5	350
EZ2P-085	1995	PROOF [4]	4	6	350
EZ2P-090	1996	PROOF [4]	3	1	350
EZ2P-095	1997	PROOF [4]	6	7	350
EZ2P-100	1998	PROOF [1]	7	1	350
EZ2P-105	1999	PROOF [1]	8	8	350

1. Issued cased and in cased proof sets.
2. Issued in cased proof sets.
3. Error obverse; Royal Mint will exchange for correct obverse coin; issued cased.
4. Issued cased.

The 1997 issue has an inner disc of Gold 91.67%, Silver 4.17%, Copper 4.17% (yellow gold) and an outer ring of Gold 91.67%, Copper 8.33% (red gold).

| Obv. 1 | Obv. 2 | Obv. 3 |

Broad

Oliver Cromwell
(Commonwealth 1649 – 1660)

The Cromwell broad of twenty shillings was the forerunner of the guinea and the sovereign. Designed by Thomas Simon (also called Symonds), it was struck by Blondeau prior to his return to France in 1656. It is of similar size to the 50 shilling piece.

Although the broad is now usually encountered in the higher grades, a Mr Pinkerton, writing at the time, observed that many of the pieces in circulation were so worn as to be almost flat.

Denomination	Metal	Weight (grams)	Diameter (mm)	Rev. alignment
Broad	Gold	9.0–9.1	29–30	↓

Obverse 1   Head 1, left; OLIVAR D G R P ANG SCO HIB &c PRO

Reverse 1   Crowned shield; PAX QVAERITVR BELLO 1656

Edge   milled

Obv. 1   Rev. 1

No.	Date	Obv.	Rev.	VF	EF
OCBR-005	1656	1	1	3500	6000

Guinea

Charles II (1660 – 1685)

The guinea of 1663 was the first machine-struck gold coin to be struck. The coin was first struck on 6 February 1663 (1662 old style), and made current by a Proclamation of 27 March 1663. Relatively few of this date were issued, and the king's portrait was redesigned twice during the following year. The denomination was originally equivalent to one pound, or twenty shillings, but during the reign the rise in the price of gold led to its changing hands at a premium. In 1670 the weight of the coin was reduced, but the price of gold continued to rise, and the guinea traded at 22 shillings in the 1680s.

The term 'guinea' was not an official name. Much of the gold used to produce the early coins came from Guinea in Africa. The African Company was granted a Charter which allowed them to place their symbol (an elephant, or later an elephant and castle) on the coins, and the colloquial term 'guinea' originated thus. The placement of this symbol may have been responsible for the re-design of the early guineas. It is noticeable that the first head had an almost straight truncation, and the elephant symbol appeared uncomfortably squashed beneath it. The head was hastily redesigned in 1664, one of the new features being an incuse indentation cut into the centre of the truncation. The elephant symbol was now larger, and fitted neatly into the indentation. The symbol fell into disuse in 1668, but was revived in 1674, redesigned as an elephant and castle. Curiously, however, there are two very rare pieces of 1677 and 1678 bearing the elephant only symbol.

In 1672 the head was again redesigned to accommodate the older features of the king, and the truncation was rounded as on the larger gold.

The guinea coinage was designed by John Roettier. With its various revisions in design, it is a more complex series than either the two guinea piece or the five guinea piece. Like the larger gold coins, deliberate design differences vis-à-vis the silver designs were introduced. This was intended to prevent fraud and confusion with a silver coin, in this case the shilling, although occasionally one comes across a gilded shilling which has had sceptres engraved on the reverse.

Collecting Hints

The series is an interesting and rewarding one to collect, if one has the resources. The Charles II guinea is priced below the larger gold coins of the reign, but collecting guineas by date is rare enough for there to be very little in the way of catalogue documentation. For this reason, opportunities exist to explore uncharted waters. No doubt several varieties exist which are unrecorded, a situation which is less likely in, say, the Charles II shilling series.

The existence of four distinct heads in this series makes the guinea more interesting than the larger gold coins. Some of the dates are no doubt rarer than usually given credit for.

While a collector by date will usually be satisfied with a specimen in any condition, a collector by type should aim for a coin in fine to very fine condition. As with all Charles II coins, the price increases steeply as the grade increases. Coins in extremely fine condition are extremely rare.

Denomination	Metal	Weight (grams)	Diameter (mm)	Rev. alignment
Guinea 1663–69	Gold	8.4–8.5	25	↓
Guinea 1670–84	Gold	8.3–8.4	25	↓

Average gold content 0.9100 (from assays carried out in 1773, figures corrected).

Obverse 1 Head 1, right; truncation almost straight and is pointed at the front; lock of hair to right of truncation; CAROLVS II DEI GRATIA

Obverse 2 Head 2, right, truncation indented, otherwise slightly redesigned; same legend

Obverse 3 Head 3, right; tie higher; hair slightly different; same legend

Obverse 4 Head 4, right; older portrait, rounded truncation, without lock of hair to right; same legend

Reverse 1 Four crowned cruciform shields between which are four sceptres, with four interlinked 'C's at the centre; MAG BR FRA ET HIB REX (date)

Reverse 2 Similar but sceptres are longer

Edge (1663–69) milled (vertically); (1670–84) milled (diagonally)

Obv. 1   Obv. 2

Obv. 3   Obv. 4

Rev. 1   Rev. 2

No.	Date	Features	Obv.	Rev.	F	VF	EF
C2GNM-005	1663		1	1	500	1700	4000
C2GNM-010	1663	elephant below head	1	1	450	1500	3500
C2GNM-015	1664		2	2	400	1100	2500
C2GNM-020	1664	elephant below head	2	2	1000		
C2GNM-025	1664		3	2	260	750	2000
C2GNM-030	1664	elephant below head	3	2	270	900	2400
C2GNM-035	1665		3	2	270	850	2400
C2GNM-040	1665	elephant below head	3	2	270	900	2400
C2GNM-045	1666		3	2	260	750	2000
C2GNM-050	1667		3	2	260	750	2000
C2GNM-055	1668		3	2	260	750	2000
C2GNM-060	1668	elephant below head	3	2	900	2500	
C2GNM-065	1669		3	2	260	750	2000
C2GNM-070	1670		3	2	260	750	2000
C2GNM-075	1671		3	2	260	750	2000
C2GNM-080	1672		3	2	260	750	2000
C2GNM-085	1672		4	2	220	650	1600
C2GNM-090	1673		3	2	260	750	2000
C2GNM-095	1673		4	2	220	650	1600
C2GNM-100	1673	CRAOLVS instead of CAROLVS (obv.)	4	2	320	1200	4000
C2GNM-105	1674		4	2	300	850	2200

No.	Date	Features	Obv.	Rev.	F	VF	EF
C2GNM-110	1674	elephant and castle below head	4	2	700	1800	6000
C2GNM-115	1675		4	2	240	700	1800
C2GNM-120	1675	CRAOLVS instead of CAROLVS (obv.)	4	2	320	1200	4000
C2GNM-125	1675	elephant and castle below head	4	2	240	700	2000
C2GNM-130	1676		4	2	220	650	1600
C2GNM-135	1676	elephant and castle below head	4	2	240	700	2000
C2GNM-140	1677		4	2	220	650	1600
C2GNM-145	1677	elephant below head latter 7 over 5	4	2	700	1800	
C2GNM-150	1677	elephant and castle below head	4	2	240	700	2000
C2GNM-155	1678		4	2	220	650	1600
C2GNM-160	1678	elephant below head	4	2	700	1800	
C2GNM-165	1678	elephant and castle below head	4	2	320	800	2500
C2GNM-170	1679		4	2	220	650	1600
C2GNM-175	1679	elephant and castle below head	4	2	240	700	2000
C2GNM-180	1680		4	2	220	650	1600
C2GNM-185	1680	elephant and castle below head	4	2	320	800	2500
C2GNM-190	1681		4	2	220	650	1600
C2GNM-195	1681	elephant and castle below head	4	2	240	700	2000
C2GNM-200	1682		4	2	220	650	1600
C2GNM-205	1682	rev. → [1]	4	2	240	700	2000
C2GNM-210	1682	elephant and castle below head	4	2	270	800	2200
C2GNM-215	1683		4	2	220	650	1600
C2GNM-220	1683	elephant and castle below head	4	2	320	800	2500
C2GNM-225	1684		4	2	220	650	1600
C2GNM-230	1684	elephant and castle below head	4	2	270	800	2200

1. Cf. halfcrown 1682 variety.

James II (1685 – 1688)

The guinea was struck in each of the four years of this reign, and exists both with and without the elephant and castle mark for each year. There are two very similar portraits, with a changeover during 1686. The difference between the two heads is not as significant as on the halfcrown, the only other denomination to undergo a portrait change. Writing in 1742, Peter Vallavine observed that the legends on the second obverse were closer to the rim, and that at first he thought that this was the result of the coins having been filed down. However, when he weighed the coins, he found that this was not the case.

The James II coinage was the work of John Roettier.

Collecting Hints

Although a fine to very fine specimen will normally be acceptable, the higher grades are often exceptionally well struck and have much detail. Unfortunately, these command high prices.

Denomination	Metal	Weight (grams)	Diameter (mm)	Rev. alignment
Guinea	Gold	8.5	25–26	↓

Average gold content 0.9094 (from assays carried out in 1773, figures corrected)

Obverse 1 Head 1, left; IACOBVS II DEI GRATIA

Obverse 2 Head 2, left, slightly redesigned, nostrils more prominent; same legend

Reverse 1 Four crowned cruciform shields between which are four sceptres; MAG BR FRA ET HIB REX (date)

Edge milled (diagonally)

Obv. 1	Obv. 2	Rev. 1

No.	Date	Features	Obv.	Rev.	F	VF	EF
J2GN-005	1685	[1]	1	1	270	750	2200
J2GN-010	1685	elephant and castle below head	1	1	320	850	2800
J2GN-015	1686		1	1	270	750	2200
J2GN-020	1686	elephant and castle below head	1	1	500	1500	
J2GN-025	1686		2	1	270	750	2200
J2GN-030	1686	elephant and castle below head	2	1	350	1100	3500
J2GN-035	1687		2	1	270	750	2200
J2GN-040	1687	7 over 6	2	1	300	750	2400
J2GN-045	1687	elephant and castle below head	2	1	320	850	2800
J2GN-050	1688		2	1	270	750	2200
J2GN-055	1688	elephant and castle below head	2	1	320	850	2800

1. Some struck on broad flan.

The harp varies somewhat in shape through this series.

William & Mary (1688 – 1694)

By the end of the reign of William and Mary the guinea had risen in value to nearly 30 shillings. The exchanges between gold and silver were accompanied by much haggling, the cause of which was invariably the prevalence of clipped silver coinage and the extent of the clipping. The exchange rate for full weight silver coins was nearer the original 20 shillings rate.

In common with the other gold coinage, the reverse of the William and Mary guinea broke with tradition. The depiction of a shield was similar to the new reverses on the larger gold coins, but it was of irregular shape rather than being straight sided with ornamentations.

The guinea was the work of James and Norbert Roettier. Unlike the half guinea, there was only one basic obverse design, although the elephant and castle symbol can be found on all of the dates struck. The reappearance of the elephant only symbol on some coins of 1692 and 1693, both rare, is curious after so many years. However, these coins usually (always?) occur with the symbol placed so tightly against the truncation that there is room for doubt as to whether it is really an elephant and castle after all, with the castle obliterated by the busts. Kenyon (*Gold Coins of England*, 1884) lists no William and Mary coinage exhibiting the elephant alone. This is a field requiring further research.

Collecting Hints

This series should be acquired in at least fine to very fine condition.

Denomination	Metal	Weight (grams)	Diameter (mm)	Rev. alignment
Guinea	Gold	8.5	25	↓

Obverse 1 Heads 1, right; GVLIELMVS ET MARIA DEI GRATIA

Reverse 1 Crowned shield; MAG BR FR ET HIB REX ET REGINA (date)

Edge milled (diagonally)

Obv. 1   Rev. 1

No.	Date	Features	Obv.	Rev.	F	VF	EF
WMGN-005	1689		1	1	240	600	1800
WMGN-010	1689	elephant and castle below head	1	1	270	800	2000
WMGN-015	1690		1	1	240	600	1800
WMGN-020	1690	elephant and castle below head	1	1	270	800	2000
WMGN-025	1691		1	1	240	600	1800
WMGN-030	1691	elephant and castle below head	1	1	270	800	2000
WMGN-035	1692		1	1	240	600	1800
WMGN-040	1692	elephant below head [1]	1	1	320	900	2400
WMGN-045	1692	elephant and castle below head	1	1	270	800	2000
WMGN-050	1693		1	1	240	600	1800
WMGN-055	1693	elephant below head [1]	1	1		800	
WMGN-060	1693	elephant and castle below head	1	1		800	
WMGN-065	1694		1	1	240	600	1800
WMGN-070	1694	4 over 3	1	1	240	600	1800
WMGN-075	1694	elephant and castle below head	1	1	270	800	2000
WMGN-080	1694	elephant and castle below head 4 over 3	1	1	270	800	2000

1. See under main heading above.

The harp on the reverse shield varies considerably in shape and orientation.

William III   (1695 – 1701)

The shield reverse of the William and Mary gold coinage was apparently considered unsatisfactory, and the William III guinea reverted to the cruciform shields reverse of Charles II and James II. At the centre was depicted the lion of Orange-Nassau.

The series was probably designed by John Croker. In common with the half guinea, the first guinea was issued in 1695, some years before the two guinea and five guinea pieces were issued.

The situation with regard to the exchange of gold and silver coins was becoming chaotic at the beginning of the reign. Exchanges between the guinea and clipped and unclipped hammered and milled silver coins produced a variety of rates of exchange. A decision was taken in Parliament to limit the exchange rate of the guinea to 25 shillings, and to prohibit the minting or import of guineas from 2nd March 1695 to 1st January 1696. Later, the rate was reduced to 22 shillings and the importation rule cancelled.

The William III guinea is not a well documented series. Catalogues exist in which the descriptions are confusing or wanting, with the die allocations incorrect. There are probably a number of varieties which are unrecorded. The 1700 misplaced sceptres guinea listed below appears to be hitherto unknown. The silver coinage of William III is notorious for errors and varieties, and it is probably only because the gold is not so widely collected and available that similar varieties have not been documented. However, the use of provincial mints was no doubt responsible for many of the errors encountered in the silver series. No gold was struck at provincial mints.

Collecting Hints

The William III guinea is attractive in fine to very fine condition. This series is an excellent one for collectors interested in researching new varieties.

Denomination	Metal	Weight (grams)	Diameter (mm)	Rev. alignment
Guinea 1695–1700	Gold	8.4	25–26	↓
Guinea 1701	Gold	8.4	26–27	↓

Average gold content 0.9123 (from assays carried out in 1773, figures corrected).

Obverse 1   Head 1, right; GVLIELMVS III DEI GRA

Obverse 2   Head 2, slightly different, right; same legend

Obverse 3   Head 3, very different, more detailed and sharply struck, right; same legend

Reverse 1   Four crowned cruciform shields between which are four sceptres, with central lion of Nassau; MAG BR FRA ET HIB REX (date)

Reverse 2   Similar but slightly redesigned; a different harp

Reverse 3   Slightly redesigned; another harp; the English lions are much narrower; the 7 in 1700 is much thinner

Reverse 4   As Reverse 3 but two of the sceptres are misplaced as on the 1686 Five Guineas

Reverse 5   Redesigned; the English lions are as wide as on Reverses 1 and 2; the crowns are narrower compared with the shields

Reverse 6   As Reverse 5 but the sceptres are slightly more ornamented

Reverse 7   As Reverse 6 but the sceptres are less ornamented than on Reverse 5

Edge   milled (diagonally)

Obv. 1   Obv. 2   Obv. 3

Rev. 1   Rev. 2   Rev. 4

Rev. 5   Rev. 6   Rev. 7

No.	Date	Features	Obv.	Rev.	F	VF	EF
W3GN-005	1695		1	1	200	500	1200
W3GN-010	1695	5 over indeterminate digit	1	1	250	600	1400
W3GN-015	1695	elephant and castle below head	1	1	250	700	1500
W3GN-020	1696		1	1	200	500	1200
W3GN-025	1696	elephant and castle below head	1	1	800		
W3GN-030	1697		1	2	200	500	1200
W3GN-035	1697		2	2	200	500	1200
W3GN-040	1697	elephant and castle below head	2	2	400	1200	3000
W3GN-045	1698	[1]	2	2	200	400	1000
W3GN-050	1698	large date and lettering (rev.)	2	2	200	400	1000
W3GN-055	1698	elephant and castle below head	2	2	250	600	1600

No.	Date	Features	Obv.	Rev.	F	VF	EF
W3GN-060	1699		2	2	200	500	1200
W3GN-065	1699	elephant and castle below head	2	2	800		
W3GN-070	1700		2	2	200	450	1000
W3GN-075	1700	elephant and castle below head	2	2	300	750	1500
W3GN-080	1700		2	3	250	500	1200
W3GN-085	1700	[2]	2	4	450	900	2000
W3GN-090	1701		2	5	200	450	1000
W3GN-095	1701	elephant and castle below head	2	5	1000		
W3GN-100	1701		2	6	200	450	1000
W3GN-105	1701		2	7	300	800	2500
W3GN-110	1701	[3]	3	5	500	1400	4500

1. Size of lions varies.
2. See p.422 for description of misplaced sceptres.
3. 'Fine work' type.

1695–1700: '1' in date is reversed-Z type

1701: '1' in date is J-type

Almost all of the 1701 issue was coined from withdrawn foreign gold coinage in circulation.

Anne   (1702 – 1714)

The guinea was minted from the first year of Anne's accession with the basic design virtually unchanged. The portrait of Anne differed very little from that used on the shilling; the customary 'undraped bust' for gold was considered unsuitable. In a warrant dated 30 June 1702, Anne directed that a dress should be added below the neck to a pattern guinea that had been sent to her. The reverse continued the cruciform shields theme, but the lion of Nassau was replaced by a rose, and subsequently by a Star of the Order of the Garter following the Union of Scotland and England.

Some guineas were struck in 1703 bearing the VIGO provenance mark, but all VIGO gold is rare. Phillips's 'State of the Nation', 1726, records that only 34 lb. weight of gold was struck in 1703, compared with 3642 lb. in 1702. No pre-Union guineas were struck with the elephant and castle mark, but post-Union specimens exist dated 1707, 1708, 1709. These are significantly scarcer than the 'plain' type.

The series was probably engraved by John Croker, assisted by Samuel Bull. The first head of Anne was designed by Sir Godfrey Kneller.

Collecting Hints

While a fine to very fine condition specimen will be satisfactory for most purposes, coins in very fine to extremely fine are most attractive and are often sharply struck with a prooflike appearance. The series is under-documented and careful study may well yield new varieties. The elephant and castle specimens are possibly scarcer than sometimes thought.

Denomination	Metal	Weight (grams)	Diameter (mm)	Rev. alignment
Guinea	Gold	8.3	25	↓

Average gold content 0.9134 (from assays carried out in 1773, figures corrected)

Obverse 1   Head 1, left; ANNA DEI GRATIA

Obverse 2   Head 2, left; hair arrangement at top different; same legend

Obverse 3   Head 3, slightly different, left; same legend

Reverse 1   Four crowned cruciform shields between which are four sceptres; central rose; MAG BR FRA ET HIB REG (date)

Reverse 2   Similar but two shields separately show conjoined English/Scottish Arms; central Star of the Order of the Garter instead of rose; shields are broader; MAG BRI FR ET HIB REG (date).

Edge milled (diagonally)

Obv. 1   Obv. 2   Obv. 3

Rev. 1   Rev. 2

Before Union of England and Scotland

No.	Date	Features	Obv.	Rev.	F	VF	EF
ANGN-005	1702	[1]	1	1	220	600	1800
ANGN-010	1702	PROOF; edge plain	1	1		2500	5000
ANGN-015	1703	VIGO below head	1	1	3000	6000	12000
ANGN-020	1705		1	1	250	700	2000
ANGN-025	1706		1	1	250	700	2000
ANGN-030	1707		1	1	250	700	2000

1. Almost all coined from withdrawn foreign gold in circulation.

After Union of England and Scotland

No.	Date	Features	Obv.	Rev.	F	VF	EF
ANGN-035	1707		1	2	220	600	1800
ANGN-040	1707	elephant and castle below head	1	2	500	1000	3000
ANGN-045	1707		2	2	500	1000	3500
ANGN-050	1708		1	2	500	1000	3500
ANGN-055	1708		2	2	220	500	1500
ANGN-060	1708	elephant and castle below head	2	2	450	1000	3000
ANGN-065	1709		2	2	220	500	1500
ANGN-070	1709	elephant and castle below head	2	2	450	1000	3000
ANGN-075	1710		3	2	220	400	900
ANGN-080	1711		3	2	220	400	900
ANGN-085	1712	[1]	3	2	220	400	900
ANGN-090	1713		3	2	220	400	900
ANGN-095	1713	3 over 1	3	2	220	400	900
ANGN-100	1714		3	2	220	400	900
ANGN-105	1714	both 'A's in GRATIA unbarred (obv.)	3	2	220	400	900

1. Occurs with lettering very close to rim.

Minor reverse variations occur.

George I   (1714 – 1727)

The guinea series of George I is notable for the five different obverse portraits of the king. The first of these was on the guinea of 1714, itself a remarkable piece for a number of reasons. It was the only denomination in any metal struck in 1714, the first year of the reign, and a date shared with many coins of Anne. In addition, the reverse legend is unlike any other of this reign, as it includes the term PR (princeps), using smaller lettering overall to allow its inclusion. The head of George I on the obverse is also unique to this date. This coin has become known as the 'Prince Elector' guinea, and is much sought after. The piece was authorized by a warrant of 5 January 1715 (1714 old style calendar).

The second head of George I was introduced in 1715, but with very large numbers struck was changed during that year to one with less profusion of hair. Further changes in design were introduced in 1716 and 1723. Curiously, Leake, writing in the 18th century, noted that 'the Guinea of 1722 is supposed to have His Majesty's face the most resembling him of any'. Leake further notes the 1724 guinea being 'remarkable for a very broad margin between the legend and the edge of the coin'.

The obverse dies were largely the work of John Croker, but the low relief third type has been attributed to Croker and/or Samuel Bull. The reverses were by Croker and/or J. R. Ochs, senior.

Kenyon, writing in *Gold Coins of England* refers to a 1727 guinea with a somewhat different head, which 'cannot have been engraved by Croker'. It is probable that this coin is a pattern.

The elephant and castle provenance mark made its last appearance during this reign, bowing out on the 1726 coin.

The value of the guinea had fluctuated over the years from twenty shillings to about thirty shillings and back to a level of twenty-one shillings and sixpence at the beginning of the reign. A Proclamation of 22 December 1717 reduced the value to twenty-one shillings.

Collecting Hints

Unless one is aiming to collect one of each type, a single specimen of this reign in fine to very fine condition should be acceptable. The last head on a somewhat broader flan than usual is arguably the most attractive, and the date 1726 is the best value for money.

Denomination	Metal	Weight (grams)	Diameter (mm)	Rev. alignment
Guinea	Gold	8.3–8.4	25–26	↓

Average gold content 0.9135 (from assays carried out in 1773, figures corrected).

Obverse 1 Head 1, right; GEORGIVS D G MAG BR FR ET HIB REX F D

Obverse 2 Head 2, right, less profuse hair; GEORGIVS D G M BR FR ET HIB REX F D

Obverse 3 Head 3, right, lower relief, still less hair; same legend

Obverse 4 Head 4, right, different tie and hair; same legend

Obverse 5 Head 5, right, smaller and older; same legend

Reverse 1 Four crowned cruciform shields between which are four sceptres; central Star of the Order of the Garter; BRVN ET LVN DVX S R I A TH ET PR EL 1714

Reverse 2 Similar but larger lettering reading BRVN ET L DVX S R I A TH ET EL (date)

Edge milled (diagonally)

Obv. 1 Prince Elector

Obv. 3

Obv. 4

Obv. 5

Rev. 1 Prince Elector

Rev. 2

No.	Date	Features	Obv.	Rev.	F	VF	EF
G1GN-005	1714	[1]	1	1	350	800	2500
G1GN-010	1715		2	2	240	550	1400
G1GN-015	1715		3	2	200	450	1200
G1GN-020	1716		3	2	200	450	1200
G1GN-025	1716		4	2	200	450	1200
G1GN-030	1717		4	2	200	450	1200
G1GN-035	1718		4	2	800		
G1GN-040	1718	8 over 7	4	2	1000		
G1GN-045	1719		4	2	200	450	1200
G1GN-050	1720		4	2	200	450	1200
G1GN-055	1721		4	2	200	450	1200
G1GN-060	1721	elephant and castle below head	4	2	1400		
G1GN-065	1722		4	2	200	450	1200
G1GN-068	1722	latter 2 over 0 [2]	4	2	250	600	1500
G1GN-070	1722	elephant and castle below head	4	2	1400		
G1GN-075	1723		4	2	200	450	1200
G1GN-080	1723		5	2	200	450	1200
G1GN-085	1724		5	2	200	450	1200
G1GN-090	1725		5	2	200	450	1200
G1GN-095	1726		5	2	200	450	1200
G1GN-100	1726	elephant and castle below head [3]	5	2	500		
G1GN-105	1727		5	2	200	450	1200

1. 'Prince Elector' type.
2. Overdate often remarkably clear.
3. Tie slightly different from above coin (obv.).

George II (1727 – 1760)

The guinea series of George II is a complex one. The coin was struck for almost every year of this relatively long reign, and the designs underwent a number of subtle changes, especially with regard to lettering size. The so-called 'intermediate head' also makes an appearance. Provenance marks E.I.C. (East India Company) and LIMA (gold obtained during Anson's voyage around the world) also occur. In 1732 the old hammered gold pieces were demonetized, and some of the gold from these may have been recoined into the current issues.

The reverse of the guinea reverted to the shield design last seen under William and Mary. This seems at first a curious decision, as this reverse had not been a success. However, it was considered unwise to retain a design so near that of the shilling reverse. A proclamation of 1741 stated that gilt shillings of Anne had been particularly susceptible to being passed off as guineas, as the heads on the two coins were virtually identical. It was decreed that 'if any person colours or alters any shilling or sixpence, either lawful or counterfeit, to make them respectively resemble a guinea or halfguinea, or any halfpenny or farthing, to make them respectively resemble a shilling or sixpence, this is also high treason'.

Gilding of shillings was not the only problem. In 1739, the diagonal milling had to be changed to a more sophisticated chevron design 'upon occasion of a gang of Guinea-filers, who had taken more liberty than usual with the Guineas' (Martin-Leake, writing

449

at the time). These filers had found it easy to restore diagonal milling to clipped coins. A vicar from the Isle of Thanet, Kent, came to the rescue.

The Rev. Peter Vallavine was an unusual man of the cloth. He spent a great deal of his time minutely observing gold and silver coins, both weighing and measuring them accurately. When, in July 1738 a reward was offered for the apprehension of persons who had illegally clipped gold, he formulated his ideas, and in December of that year presented his proposals, in particular directing his attention to the false milling placed on clipped coins after gold had been removed: 'The milled money hath been found liable to be diminished by filing the edges, and the crannelling work thereon is so nearly imitated by some of these artists, that the difference is hardly to be discovered but by a curious observation'. His main proposals were for 'the King's name, stile and titles to be placed as near as possible to the edge of the piece' and 'a new method or form of edging the coin'. This was to take the form of a chevron-shaped milling, considered to be much more difficult to counterfeit. Vallavine pointed out that some types of guinea had been found to be much more clipped than others; William and Mary pieces were hardly clipped at all, but, for example, the 1733 coin was often 10 to 12 grains light. There seemed to be a definite correlation between the tendency of a guinea to be clipped and the distance of the legend from the edge.

Vallavine pointed out that a reward had been offered for the capture of guinea-filers, and that some monetary appreciation might be shown to someone who prevented future clipping. Accordingly, a payment of one hundred pounds was made for his work, and the new dies and milling were used from 1739 onwards. Vallavine returned to his church work, and died in January 1767.

The guinea and the shilling were the only coins struck in 1727, the first year of the reign. J.R. Ochs, senior was responsible for the reverses of both of these early coins, and they were the only coins of George II designed by him. The obverses 1 to 4 were by Croker, with obverses 5 to 7 by Tanner. Reverses 2 to 4 were probably by Tanner, with reverse 5 being by Ochs, junior.

Collecting Hints

A fine to very fine condition coin will normally be acceptable for this series. The early head by Ochs is best appreciated in very fine or better condition.

Denomination	Metal	Weight (grams)	Diameter (mm)	Rev. alignment
Guinea 1727 Obv. 2: Rev. 2	Gold	8.3–8.4	24–25	↓
Guinea all others 1727–60	Gold	8.3–8.4	25–26	↓

Average gold content 0.9140 (from assays carried out in 1773, figures corrected).

Obverse 1 Head 1, left; GEORGIVS II DEI GRATIA in small lettering

Obverse 2 Head 1, left; same legend but larger

Obverse 3 Head 2, narrower, left; same legend

Obverse 4 Head 2, left; same legend, even larger

Obverse 5 Head 3, left; same legend but GEORGIUS (lettering slightly smaller)

Obverse 6 Head 3, left; same legend but larger

Obverse 7 Head 4, older, left; same legend but GEORGIVS

Obverse 8 Head 4, left; same legend but even larger

Reverse 1 Crowned shield; M B F ET H REX F D B ET L D S R I A T ET E (date) in small lettering and numerals

Reverse 2 Similar but shield smaller; lettering and numerals slightly larger

Reverse 3 Similar but shield squarer

Reverse 4 Similar but lettering and numerals slightly larger and the shield is slightly different

Reverse 5 Similar but lettering and numerals larger

Edge (1727–38) milled (diagonally); (1739–60) milled (with chevrons)

Obv. 1   Obv. 2   Obv. 3

Obv. 4   Obv. 5   Obv. 6

Obv. 7   Obv. 8

Rev. 1   Rev. 2   Rev. 3

Rev. 4   Rev. 5

No.	Date	Features	Obv.	Rev.	F	VF	EF
G2GN-005	1727		1	1	400	1000	2000
G2GN-008	1727	PROOF; edge plain	1	1			4000
G2GN-010	1727	[1]	2	2	250	700	1400
G2GN-015	1728		2	2	250	700	1400
G2GN-020	1729	PROOF; edge plain [2]	3	3			4000
G2GN-025	1729	PROOF; edge plain; rev. ↑ [2]	3	3			4500
G2GN-030	1729	E.I.C. below head	3	3	300	800	1600
G2GN-035	1730		3	3	250	700	1400
G2GN-040	1731		3	3	250	700	1400
G2GN-045	1731	E.I.C. below head	3	3	300	800	1600
G2GN-050	1732		3	3	250	700	1400
G2GN-055	1732	E.I.C. below head	3	3	300	800	1600
G2GN-060	1732		4	3	200	500	1200
G2GN-065	1732	E.I.C. below head	4	3	350	900	1800
G2GN-070	1733		4	3	200	500	1200
G2GN-075	1734		4	3	200	500	1200
G2GN-080	1735		4	3	200	500	1200
G2GN-085	1736		4	3	200	500	1200
G2GN-090	1737		4	3	200	500	1200
G2GN-095	1738		4	3	200	500	1200
G2GN-100	1739	[3]	5	4	200	450	1000

No.	Date	Features	Obv.	Rev.	F	VF	EF
G2GN-105	1739	E.I.C. below head	5	4	350	900	1800
G2GN-110	1740		5	4	200	450	1000
G2GN-115	1741	41 over 39	5	4	1000		
G2GN-120	1743		5	4	2000	4500	
G2GN-125	1745		6	4	250	600	1400
G2GN-130	1745	LIMA below head	6	4	500	1200	2200
G2GN-135	1746		7	4	220	500	1100
G2GN-140	1747		8	5	170	350	750
G2GN-145	1748		8	5	170	350	750
G2GN-150	1749		8	5	170	350	750
G2GN-155	1750		8	5	170	350	750
G2GN-160	1751		7	5	160	320	700
G2GN-165	1752		7	5	160	320	700
G2GN-170	1753		7	5	160	320	700
G2GN-175	1755		7	5	160	320	700
G2GN-180	1756		7	5	160	320	700
G2GN-185	1758		7	5	160	320	700
G2GN-190	1759		7	5	160	320	700
G2GN-195	1760		7	5	160	320	700

1. Flan slightly smaller than usual.
2. Weight can be c.8.0 grams.
3. 'Intermediate head'.

George III (1760 – 1820)

When one considers the extensive gaps between issues of silver coinage during this long reign, the regularity with which the guinea was struck appears remarkable. The coin was issued almost every year for the first forty years of the reign. However, the relatively high price of silver compared with face value of silver coins prevented the use of this metal for coinage until later in the reign.

George III reigned for sixty years, and during this time the guinea underwent a number of changes. No fewer than six different portraits of the monarch were used. In 1774 almost 20 million worn guineas of William III and Anne were melted and recoined as guineas and half guineas.

The issue of guineas from 1787 to 1799 has become known in common parlance as the 'spade guinea' because of the spade-shaped shield on the reverse. In Victorian times the coin was popular as a fob piece attached to gold watch chains. The overall popularity of the coin has arguably been undeserved; the coin has a somewhat mechanical design, and the shield looks as if it is drawn with a ruler and a pair of compasses. The bust is flat and lacking in detail. The coin does not even have rarity to commend it; it is the most frequently encountered type of guinea.

Towards the end of the century, gold began to become scarce and to rise in value. Revolution and war in Europe had drained resources, and many people were hoarding the metal. Parliament passed a Bill making banknotes legal tender to any amount, and by 1799 the issue of spade guineas was at an end. Half-and third-guineas continued to be struck, however. In 1800, Great Britain and Ireland were united, and the King's titles were altered. An Order in Council of 5 November 1800 directed the Master of the Mint to prepare new coinage, but although designs were prepared, no guineas were authorized. The shortage of guineas continued, and at the beginning of 1812, Sir Edward Thomason, writing in his memoirs, observes: 'In this year an English guinea was worth 27 shillings, according to the Mint price of gold; and so scarce was the coin, and the panic so great, that every maiden lady hoarded up all the gold she received'.

In 1813, a one-year type guinea was struck to pay Wellington's army on the Pyrenees, as the local populace would accept only gold for purchases. The issue was 80,000 pieces, and the gold for the issue was imported from India in the form of gold mohur and pagoda coins. The coin has become known as the 'military guinea'. Gold was still scarce, and the guinea was trading on the fee market at about 27 shillings in paper money. The coining of this piece for the special requirement of supplying the army was therefore a poor deal for the British government, and the 1813 guinea was the last guinea to be struck.

The guineas from 1761 to 1773 were engraved by Richard Yeo. The reverses were from a design by Tanner. The guinea of 1774–86 was the work of Thomas Pingo. His son Lewis was appointed Chief Engraver in December 1779 on the death of Richard Yeo, and designed the spade guinea and the military guinea. The head for the latter was based on a design by Nathaniel Marchant.

Collecting Hints

Specimens in very fine condition will usually be adequate. The spade guinea of 1787–99 is one of the few coins which possibly are more attractive in very fine than in extremely fine condition. In higher grades there is very little more detail visible, and a very fine coin seems to have more character.

Care must be taken with guineas dated 1798, as modern forgeries exist, another reason why fine to very fine condition coins may be considered preferable. In particular, beware any coin on which the central vertical line on the shield continues above the top of the shield to touch the base of the crown. It does seem, however, that a few genuine pieces have this characteristic.

Denomination	Metal	Weight (grams)	Diameter (mm)	Rev. alignment
Guinea 1761–86	Gold	8.4	24	↓
Guinea 1787–1813	Gold	8.4	24	↑

Average gold content 0.9146 at beginning of reign (from assays carried out in 1773, figures corrected).

Obverse 1 Head 1, right; GEORGIVS III DEI GRATIA

Obverse 2 Head 2, right, hair more profuse; same legend

Obverse 3 Head 3, right, slightly different; same legend

Obverse 4 Head 4, larger, right; hair extends below truncation; same legend

Obverse 5 Head 5, smaller, right; truncation more pointed; same legend

Obverse 6 Head 6, smaller, very different, right; same legend

Obverse 7 Head 7, right; the truncation is more rounded than on Obverse 6

Reverse 1 Crowned shield; M B F ET H REX F D B ET L D S R I A T ET E ; (date) divided by crown

Reverse 2 Crowned spade-shaped shield; same legend but in opposite position around rim; (date) at bottom

Reverse 3 Crowned shield in Garter; BRITANNIARUM REX FIDEI DEFENSOR; HONI SOIT QUI MAL Y PENSE on Garter; Date 1813 between Garter and edge legend

Edge milled (with chevrons)

Obv. 1   Obv. 2   Obv. 3

Obv. 4   Obv. 5   Obv. 6 Military Type

451

Rev. 1	Rev. 2	Rev. 3 Military Type

No.	Date	Features	Obv.	Rev.	F	VF	EF
G3GN-005	1761		1	1	500	1000	2500
G3GN-010	1761	PROOF; edge plain	1	1			3500
G3GN-012	1761	PROOF; edge plain; rev ↑	1	1			4500
G3GN-015	1763		2	1	300	600	1500
G3GN-020	1764		2	1	300	600	1500
G3GN-025	1765		3	1	140	250	500
G3GN-028	1765	PROOF; edge plain	3	1			3500
G3GN-030	1766		3	1	130	220	450
G3GN-035	1767		3	1	140	250	500
G3GN-040	1768		3	1	140	250	500
G3GN-045	1769		3	1	140	250	500
G3GN-050	1770		3	1	140	250	500
G3GN-055	1771		3	1	140	250	500
G3GN-060	1772		3	1	140	250	500
G3GN-065	1773	[1]	3	1	140	250	500
G3GN-068	1773	3 over 2	3	1	160	350	700
G3GN-070	1774	[2]	4	1	130	200	400
G3GN-075	1774	PROOF; edge plain; rev. ↑ [3]	4	1			1800
G3GN-080	1775		4	1	130	200	400
G3GN-085	1776		4	1	130	200	400
G3GN-090	1777		4	1	130	200	400
G3GN-095	1778		4	1	130	200	400
G3GN-100	1779		4	1	130	200	400
G3GN-105	1781	[4]	4	1	130	200	400
G3GN-110	1782		4	1	130	200	400
G3GN-115	1783		4	1	140	240	500
G3GN-120	1784		4	1	130	200	400
G3GN-125	1785		4	1	130	180	350
G3GN-130	1786		4	1	130	180	350
G3GN-135	1787		5	2	120	170	320
G3GN-140	1787	PROOF; edge plain [5]	5	2			2000
G3GN-145	1788		5	2	120	170	320
G3GN-150	1789		5	2	120	170	320
G3GN-155	1790		5	2	120	170	320
G3GN-160	1791		5	2	120	170	320
G3GN-165	1792		5	2	120	170	320
G3GN-170	1793		5	2	120	170	320
G3GN-175	1794		5	2	120	170	320
G3GN-180	1795		5	2	130	210	400
G3GN-185	1796		5	2	130	210	400
G3GN-190	1797		5	2	120	170	320
G3GN-195	1798	[6]	5	2	115	160	280
G3GN-200	1798	8 over 7	5	2	150	210	400
G3GN-205	1799		5	2	140	210	400
G3GN-210	1813	[7]	6	3	250	450	750
G3GN-215	1813	PROOF [7]	7	3			2500

1. Differences in laurel berries occur (obv.).
2. Many struck from reclaimed gold from William III and Anne guineas.
3. Usually has die flaw in reverse field.
4. Date change; see comment below.
5. Can occur with weight as low as 7 grams.
6. Several counterfeits exist.
7. 'Military' guinea.

Reverse 1: from 1761 to 1779 the '1' in the date is a 'J' type; from 1781 to 1786 it is a Roman I.

Sovereign

George III (1760 – 1820)

The proclamation of 1 July 1817 giving legal tender to the sovereign introduced a coin which was to become of major importance. The guinea of twenty-one shillings had last been minted in 1813, and the sovereign, valued at twenty shillings, took its place in the new order after the Great Recoinage. It was obviously not realised at the time how important the sovereign would become as a unit in transactions of gold bullion.

As with the other new coinage, the quality of striking of the sovereign was very high. In practice, it was not invariably so, and extremely fine or better specimens can vary slightly in the sharpness of strike. Nevertheless, the workmanship and strike are consistently better than on the sovereigns produced today.

The public did not immediately take to the sovereign, preferring paper money. In addition, many of the coins were hoarded as curiosities. This explains why the 1817 coin often turns up in higher grades. Because of lack of demand, fewer coins were minted in subsequent years.

The obverse and reverse were designed by Benedetto Pistrucci. The reverse of the 1817 sovereign was the first use of the St George and dragon design.

Thomas Wyon died on 22 September 1817, and his office of Chief Engraver needed to be filled. Pistrucci, although not actually appointed, came to fulfil all of the duties of the post on a *de facto* basis.

Collecting Hints

The George III sovereign is a popular coin in all grades from fine upwards. If looking for specimens in extremely fine condition, one should try to obtain one with a sharp strike and prooflike fields.

Denomination	Metal	Weight (grams)	Diameter (mm)	Rev. alignment
Sovereign	Gold	8.0	22	↓

Obverse 1 Head 1, right; GEORGIUS III D G BRITANNIAR REX F D (date)

Reverse 1 St George and dragon; HONI SOIT QUI MAL Y PENSE on Garter

Edge milled

Obv. 1   Rev. 1

No.	Date	Features	Obv.	Rev.	F	VF	EF	UNC
G3SV-005	1817		1	1	120	190	400	800
G3SV-010	1817	PROOF	1	1				5000
G3SV-015	1818	[1]	1	1	130	240	800	1200
G3SV-020	1818	PROOF	1	1				6500
G3SV-025	1819	[2]	1	1	10000	20000		
G3SV-030	1820	[3]	1	1	120	190	400	800

1. Minor alterations in lettering occur.
2. Unknown in higher grades.

Notes continued
3. Date numerals vary in size.

George IV (1820 – 1830)

Pistrucci continued as the designer, and sovereigns were struck for each year of the reign. The reverse was modified, discarding the Garter with its legend, but retaining the St George and dragon theme. This design is very similar to that used in modern times. The early obverse portrait of the king by Pistrucci compared unfavourably with those on the five and two pound pieces by William Wyon and Johann Baptiste Merlen respectively. It was disliked by the king and replaced in 1825 with a bare head design by William Wyon. The reverse was altered to a crowned shield design by Merlen.

Proofs were struck in 1826 for inclusion in the cased proof sets.

Collecting Hints

This series should be collected in very fine or better condition. Counterfeits exist for a number of dates, and coins with a pitted surface or poor definition should be avoided.

Denomination	Metal	Weight (grams)	Diameter (mm)	Rev. alignment
Sovereign	Gold	8.0	22	↓

Obverse 1 Head 1, left; GEORGIUS IIII D G BRITANNIAR REX F D

Obverse 2 Head 2, left; GEORGIUS IV DEI GRATIA (date)

Reverse 1 St George and dragon; (date) in exergue

Reverse 2 Crowned shield; BRITANNIARUM REX FID DEF

Edge milled

Obv. 1   Obv. 2

Rev. 1   Rev. 2

No.	Date	Features	Obv.	Rev.	F	VF	EF	UNC
G4SV-005	1821		1	1	110	170	350	600
G4SV-010	1821	PROOF	1	1				3500
G4SV-015	1822		1	1	110	170	350	600
G4SV-020	1823		1	1	200	500	1000	1750
G4SV-025	1824		1	1	110	170	350	600
G4SV-030	1825		1	1	140	280	750	1100
G4SV-035	1825		2	2	110	170	350	600
G4SV-038	1825	struck in platinum [1]	2	2				
G4SV-040	1825	PROOF; edge plain	2	2				4000
G4SV-045	1826		2	2	110	170	350	600

No.	Date	Features	Obv.	Rev.	F	VF	EF	UNC
G4SV-050	1826	PROOF [2]	2	2				2500
G4SV-055	1827	[3]	2	2	110	170	350	600
G4SV-060	1828	[4]	2	2	1500	3000	4500	
G4SV-065	1829		2	2	110	170	350	600
G4SV-070	1830		2	2	110	170	350	600

1. This piece, weight 9.4 grams and cut into two pieces, is in the British Museum.
2. Issued in cased proof sets.
3. Struck until end November 1828.
4. Struck in December 1828.

William IV   (1830 – 1837)

The general overall design continued during this reign. The obverse portrait was by William Wyon from a bust by Sir Francis Chantrey, and the reverse was a slightly modified shield design by Johann Baptiste Merlen. Proofs were struck in 1831 for inclusion in the cased proof sets, and these differ from the ordinary coin in having a plain edge.

Collecting Hints

Fine to very fine condition specimens should be adequate. There is little increase in visible detail in the higher grades, especially on the reverse.

Denomination	Metal	Weight (grams)	Diameter (mm)	Rev. alignment
Sovereign	Gold	8.0	22	↓

Obverse 1   Head 1; GULIELMUS IIII D G BRITANNIAR REX F D W.W. (with stops) on truncation of head

Reverse 1   Crowned shield on mantle; below: ANNO (date)

Edge   milled

Obv. 1   Rev. 1

No.	Date	Features	Obv.	Rev.	F	VF	EF	UNC
W4SV-005	1831		1	1	120	200	500	750
W4SV-010	1831	PROOF edge plain [1]	1	1				2700
W4SV-015	1831	WW without stops (obv.)	1	1	120	200	500	750
W4SV-020	1832	[2]	1	1	110	180	450	700
W4SV-025	1832	PROOF	1	1				5500
W4SV-030	1832	WW without stops (obv.) [2]	1	1	110	180	450	700
W4SV-035	1833		1	1	110	180	450	700
W4SV-040	1835		1	1	110	180	450	750
W4SV-045	1836		1	1	110	180	450	700
W4SV-048	1836	raised 'N' on shield above ANNO (rev.)	1	1	500	1200		
W4SV-050	1837		1	1	110	180	450	750

1. Issued in cased proof sets.
2. Slightly different head introduced during this year.

Victoria   (1837 – 1901)

The Victorian sovereign is one of the most important and popular series in the world, and yet it is curiously under-researched. Because few people collect the sovereign by date, the varieties within the series are largely unknown to the average collector. Others have no doubt yet to be discovered.

Sovereigns were minted for almost every year of the queen's reign, and the series is further complicated on two counts: firstly, the production of the coins at three mints in Australia, and secondly, the adoption of the St George and dragon reverse from 1871 while the shield reverse continued to be in use until 1874 in London and until 1887 in Australia, many of the latter being exported to India. The result, coupled with the longevity of Victoria, was one of the longest and complex series of a denomination within one reign. No London sovereigns were struck from 1881 to 1883 because of extensive renovations at the Royal Mint.

The sovereign is nowadays one of the main coins used in trading of gold bullion throughout the world. Although sovereigns of the earlier reigns are occasionally dealt with in bulk quantities between dealers, the Victorian and later sovereigns are given daily buy-sell quotations on bullion markets around the world.

It is not generally realised that the dies for the sovereigns up to 1859 were the same as those used for the copper farthings. From comparison of the two series, it appears that a given die was used firstly to strike sovereigns, and then, when it became a little worn, it was transferred to strike farthings, which were not considered so important. The use of die numbers may have been to help in providing information on how many coins could be struck from one die. Normally, a die could be relied upon to produce about 100,000 pieces.

The 1859 sovereign listed below with obverse 4 is usually known as the 'Ansell' sovereign. Mr. G. F. Ansell of the Royal Mint experimented with a sample of Australian gold containing antimony, arsenic and lead, from which these sovereigns were produced in June and July 1859. Before treatment of the metal by Ansell it had proved too brittle for use in coinage.

The young head of Victoria was designed by William Wyon. This continued to be used until 1887, even though Wyon had died in 1851. The jubilee head was engraved by Leonard Charles Wyon from a design by Sir Joseph Edgar Boehm. The veiled head was designed by Sir Thomas Brock. The reverses are in some doubt, but the shield reverse was possibly the work of Johann Baptiste Merlen, while the St George and dragon reverse was originally by Pistrucci but engraved by other hands. In 1887, a plume was added to the helmet of St George on the reverse, restoring a feature which had appeared on Pistrucci's original design for the five and two pound pieces. The plume was subsequently redesigned for the 1893 issue.

Collecting Hints

One example of each type in extremely fine or better condition will be adequate for most collectors. Specimens of the veiled head type in top grades are surprisingly scarce. Many forgeries exist of Victorian sovereigns. These are not too difficult to spot when one has handled genuine specimens on a regular basis, but to a novice they can be deceptive. Often the date numerals appear not quite 'right'; the lettering may be unevenly spaced or the surface may be somewhat rough. A forgery's 'ring' when dropped on to a hard surface is often duller than that of a genuine coin. Another characteristic, which needs to be learnt by experience, is that the coin does not reflect light in the same way as a genuine coin, and the way in which the coin has worn appears strange. Some forgeries have the edge milling at a slight diagonal instead of 'straight across'. Poorly made Italian forgeries may be too large and some even have 'impossible' obverse/reverse matches. Some counterfeits dated before 1887 have a plume on St George's helmet.

Denomination	Metal	Weight (grams)	Diameter (mm)	Rev. alignment
Sovereign 1838–87 obv.7	Gold	8.0	22	↓
Sovereign 1887 obv.8–1901	Gold	8.0	22	↑

Obverse 1   Head 1, left; WW in relief on truncation; VICTORIA DEI GRATIA (date)

Obverse 2 Head 2, left, slightly larger, WW in relief, neck and hair slightly different, rim slightly thicker; same legend (date)

Obverse 3 Head 2, left; WW incuse; same legend (date)

Obverse 4 Head 3, left; WW incuse, raised line along lower edge of rear ribbon; same legend (date) (= 1859)

Obverse 5 Head 4, left; WW in relief, truncation more rounded; same legend (date)

Obverse 6 Head 5, left; WW in relief, only partially visible; VICTORIA D G BRITANNIAR REG F D (no date)

Obverse 7 Head 6, left; WW in relief bolder and fully visible, hair at neck slightly different; same legend

Obverse 8 Head 7, 'Jubilee' type, left; VICTORIA D G BRITT REG F D

Obverse 9 Head 8, veiled, left; VICTORIA DEI GRA BRITT REGINA FID DEF IND IMP

Reverse 1 Crowned shield within wreath; BRITANNIARUM REGINA FID DEF

Reverse 2 Similar but shield narrower; harp, crown, orb and ornamentation below shield slightly different; same legend

Reverse 3 Similar but legend orientation slightly different; rim slightly thicker. Some coins have die number below wreath (see listings)

Reverse 4 St George and Dragon; horse's tail is short; large BP and (date) in exergue; no plume on St George's helmet

Reverse 5 Similar but plume added to St George's helmet

Reverse 6 Similar but plume redesigned

Edge milled

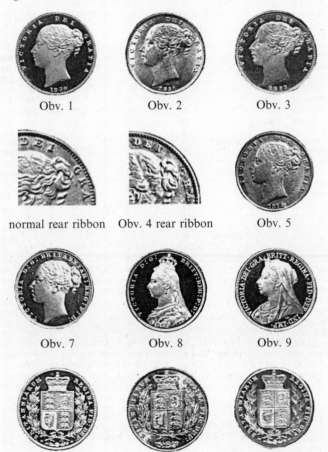

Obv. 1   Obv. 2   Obv. 3

normal rear ribbon   Obv. 4 rear ribbon   Obv. 5

Obv. 7   Obv. 8   Obv. 9

Rev. 1   Rev. 2   Rev. 3

Rev. 4

Young Head

No.	Date	Features	Obv.	Rev.	F	VF	EF	UNC
VYSV-005	1838	[1]	1	1	100	120	250	600
VYSV-008	1838		1	2	1000	1500		
VYSV-010	1838	PROOF; edge plain [2]	1	1				3500
VYSV-015	1838	PROOF; edge plain; rev. ↑	1	1				3500
VYSV-020	1839		1	1	150	250	800	1200
VYSV-025	1839	PROOF	1	1				4500
VYSV-030	1839	PROOF; edge plain [3]	1	1				2500
VYSV-035	1839	PROOF; edge plain; rev. ↑	1	1				3500
VYSV-040	1839	PROOF [4]	1	3				5000
VYSV-045	1841		1	1	450	850	2000	4000
VYSV-050	1842		1	1	70	80	180	240
VYSV-055	1843		1	1	70	80	180	240
VYSV-060	1843	3 over 2	1	1	120	160	240	300
VYSV-065	1843	[5]	1	2	1500	2500	3500	5000
VYSV-070	1844		1	1	70	80	180	300
VYSV-075	1844	first 4 over inverted 4	1	1	120	160	250	320
VYSV-080	1845		1	1	70	80	180	300
VYSV-085	1846		1	1	70	80	180	300
VYSV-090	1847		1	1	70	80	180	300
VYSV-095	1848		1	1	200	280	400	600
VYSV-100	1848		2	3	70	80	180	300
VYSV-105	1849		2	3	70	80	180	300
VYSV-110	1850		2	3	70	80	180	300
VYSV-115	1851		2	3	70	80	180	300
VYSV-118	1851	latter 1 over 0	2	3	110	120	240	400
VYSV-120	1852		2	3	70	80	180	300
VYSV-125	1853		2	3	70	80	180	300
VYSV-130	1853		3	3	70	80	180	300
VYSV-135	1853	PROOF [3]	3	3				5500
VYSV-140	1853	PROOF; rev. ↑	3	3				5500
VYSV-145	1854		2	3	70	80	180	300
VYSV-150	1854		3	3	70	80	180	300
VYSV-155	1855		2	3	70	80	180	300
VYSV-160	1855		3	3	70	80	180	300
VYSV-165	1856		3	3	70	80	180	300
VYSV-170	1857		3	3	70	80	180	300
VYSV-175	1858		3	3	70	80	250	600
VYSV-180	1859		3	3	70	80	180	300
VYSV-185	1859	[6]	4	3	180	400	1000	
VYSV-190	1860		3	3	70	80	160	300
VYSV-195	1861		3	3	70	80	160	300
VYSV-200	1862		3	3	70	80	160	300
VYSV-205	1863	no die number below wreath (rev.)	3	3	70	80	160	300
VYSV-210	1863	no die number below wreath (rev.) '827' in raised numerals on truncation instead of 'WW' (obv.) [7]	3	3	1500	2500		
VYSV-215	1863	die number below wreath (rev.)	3	3	70	80	160	300
VYSV-220	1863	die number 22 below wreath (rev.) '827' in raised numerals on truncation instead of 'WW' (obv.) [7]	3	3	1200	2000		
VYSV-225	1864	die number below wreath (rev.)	3	3	70	80	160	300
VYSV-230	1864	PROOF raised 'I' to left of incuse 'WW' (obv.) [8]	3	3				5000
VYSV-235	1865	die number below wreath (rev.)	3	3	70	80	160	240
VYSV-240	1866	die number below wreath (rev.)	3	3	70	80	160	240
VYSV-245	1868	die number below wreath (rev.)	3	3	70	80	160	240

No.	Date	Features	Obv.	Rev.	F	VF	EF	UNC
VYSV-250	1869	die number below wreath (rev.)	3	3	70	80	160	240
VYSV-255	1870	die number below wreath (rev.)	3	3	70	80	160	240
VYSV-260	1870	die number below wreath (rev.)	5	3	70	80	150	230
VYSV-265	1871	die number below wreath (rev.)	5	3	70	80	150	230
VYSV-270	1871		6	4	BV	70	120	160
VYSV-275	1871	PROOF	6	4				3000
VYSV-280	1871	PROOF; rev. ↑	6	4				3000
VYSV-285	1871	PROOF; edge plain; rev. ↑ [9]	6	4				2000
VYSV-290	1872	no die number below wreath (rev.)	2	3	70	80	150	230
VYSV-295	1872	die number below wreath (rev.)	5	3	70	80	150	230
VYSV-300	1872		6	4	BV	70	120	160
VYSV-305	1873	die number below wreath (rev.)	5	3	70	80	150	230
VYSV-310	1873		6	4	BV	70	120	160
VYSV-315	1874	die number below wreath (rev.)	5	3	400	1000	1800	
VYSV-320	1874		6	4	70	80	130	160
VYSV-325	1876		6	4	70	80	130	160
VYSV-330	1878		6	4	70	80	130	160
VYSV-335	1879		6	4	100	200	700	1200
VYSV-338	1879	PROOF	5	3				10000
VYSV-340	1880	PROOF; edge plain	5	3				6000
VYSV-345	1880		6	4	70	80	130	160
VYSV-350	1880	[10]	7	4	80	90	150	180
VYSV-355	1880	PROOF	7	4				4500
VYSV-360	1884		6	4	70	80	130	160
VYSV-365	1884		7	4	70	80	130	160
VYSV-370	1885		6	4	75	85	140	170
VYSV-375	1885		7	4	75	85	140	170
VYSV-380	1887	PROOF	5	3				5000
VYSV-385	1887	PROOF; edge plain	5	3				6000

1. Variety exists with minor reverse differences.
2. Minor design differences from usual; possibly a pattern.
3. Issued in cased proof sets.
4. With this reverse, presumably struck in 1848 or later.
5. Possibly a pattern.
6. The 'Ansell' sovereign; see above.
7. Possibly a trial piece to test new position for die number.
8. Possibly a trial piece to test new position for die number; a similar farthing exists (q.v.).
9. Varieties exist: small or large BP in exergue (rev.).
10. No BP in exergue (rev.).

Jubilee Head

No.	Date	Features	Obv.	Rev.	F	VF	EF	UNC
VJSV-390	1887		8	5	BV	70	110	140
VJSV-395	1887	PROOF [1]	8	5				700
VJSV-400	1888		8	5	BV	BV	90	120
VJSV-405	1889		8	5	BV	BV	90	120
VJSV-410	1890		8	5	BV	BV	90	120
VJSV-415	1891		8	5	BV	BV	90	120
VJSV-420	1891	PROOF in lead [2]	8	5		1000		
VJSV-425	1892		8	5	BV	BV	90	120

1. Position of JEB on truncation varies (obv.).
2. Edge plain; weight c.5.4 grams; probably unique.

Old Head

No.	Date	Features	Obv.	Rev.	F	VF	EF	UNC
VOSV-430	1893		9	6	BV	BV	90	120
VOSV-435	1893	PROOF [1]	9	6				900
VOSV-440	1894		9	6	BV	BV	90	110
VOSV-445	1895		9	6	BV	BV	90	110
VOSV-450	1896		9	6	BV	BV	90	110
VOSV-455	1898		9	6	BV	BV	90	110
VOSV-460	1899		9	6	BV	BV	90	110
VOSV-465	1900		9	6	BV	BV	90	110
VOSV-470	1901		9	6	BV	BV	90	110

1. Issued in cased proof sets.

Minor design variations occur to Reverse 4, especially to the horse's tail and initials BP.

Commonwealth Mints

Mintmarks

M: Melbourne, Australia (opened June 1872)
P: Perth, Australia (opened June 1899)
S: Sydney, Australia (opened May 1855)

Position of Mintmarks

Obverses 6 and 7   Below head
Reverse 3   Below shield
Reverse 4   On ground line above centre of date

Young Head

No.	Date	Features	mm	Obv.	Rev.	F	VF	EF	UNC
VYSV-475	1871		S	3	3	100	130	220	300
VYSV-480	1871		S	5	3	85	100	160	220
VYSV-485	1871	PROOF	S	3/5?	3				7000
VYSV-490	1871		S	6	4	80	90	130	180
VYSV-495	1871	PROOF	S	6	4				6000
VYSV-500	1872		M	5	3	85	100	160	220
VYSV-505	1872	rev. ↑	M	5	3	400	600	1000	1500
VYSV-510	1872	2 over 1 [1]	M	5	3	300	500	800	1200
VYSV-515	1872		M	6	4	100	140	300	420
VYSV-520	1872		S	5	3	85	100	160	220
VYSV-525	1872		S	6	4	80	90	130	180
VYSV-530	1873		M	6	4	80	90	130	180
VYSV-535	1873		S	5	3	85	100	160	220
VYSV-540	1873		S	6	4	80	90	130	180
VYSV-545	1874		M	5	3	90	110	240	
VYSV-550	1874		M	6	4	80	90	130	180
VYSV-555	1874		S	6	4	80	90	130	180
VYSV-560	1875		M	6	4	80	90	130	180
VYSV-565	1875		S	5	3	85	95	150	220
VYSV-570	1875	PROOF	S	5	3				7000
VYSV-575	1875		S	6	4	80	90	130	180
VYSV-580	1876		M	6	4	80	90	130	180
VYSV-585	1876		S	6	4	80	90	130	180
VYSV-590	1877		M	6	4	80	90	130	180
VYSV-595	1877		S	5	3	85	95	150	220
VYSV-600	1878		M	6	4	80	90	130	180
VYSV-605	1878		S	5	3	85	95	150	220
VYSV-610	1879		M	6	4	80	90	130	180
VYSV-615	1879		S	5	3	85	95	150	220
VYSV-620	1879		S	6	4	80	90	130	180
VYSV-625	1880	[2]	M	5	3	400	800	1500	
VYSV-630	1880		M	6	4	80	90	130	180
VYSV-635	1880		S	5	3	85	95	150	220
VYSV-640	1880	PROOF	S	5	3				7000
VYSV-645	1880		S	6	4	80	90	130	180
VYSV-650	1880		S	7	4	80	90	130	180
VYSV-655	1880	PROOF	S	6/7?	4				6000
VYSV-660	1881		M	5	3	100	150	350	600
VYSV-665	1881		M	6	4	80	90	130	180
VYSV-670	1881		S	5	3	85	95	150	220
VYSV-675	1881		S	6	4	80	90	130	180
VYSV-680	1881		S	7	4	80	90	130	180
VYSV-685	1881	PROOF	S	6/7?	4				6000
VYSV-690	1882		M	5	3	85	100	180	250
VYSV-695	1882	PROOF	M	5	3				7000
VYSV-700	1882		M	6	4	80	90	130	180
VYSV-705	1882		M	7	4	80	90	130	180
VYSV-710	1882	[3]	S	5	3	85	95	150	220
VYSV-715	1882		S	7	4	80	90	130	180
VYSV-720	1883		M	5	3	150	300	900	2000
VYSV-725	1883		M	6	4	80	90	130	180
VYSV-730	1883		M	7	4	80	90	130	180
VYSV-735	1883		S	5	3	85	95	150	220
VYSV-740	1883	PROOF	S	5	3				7000
VYSV-745	1883		S	7	4	80	90	130	180
VYSV-750	1884		M	5	3	85	100	180	240
VYSV-755	1884		M	6	4	80	90	130	180
VYSV-760	1884		M	7	4	80	90	130	180
VYSV-765	1884	PROOF	M	6/7?	4				6000
VYSV-770	1884		S	5	3	85	95	150	220
VYSV-775	1884		S	7	4	80	90	130	180
VYSV-780	1885		M	5	3	85	100	180	240
VYSV-785	1885	PROOF	M	5	3				7000
VYSV-790	1885		M	7	4	80	90	130	180
VYSV-795	1885	PROOF	M	7	4				6000
VYSV-800	1885		S	5	3	85	95	150	220
VYSV-805	1885		S	7	4	80	90	130	180
VYSV-810	1886		M	5	3	1200	2000	3000	
VYSV-815	1886	PROOF	M	5	3				10000
VYSV-820	1886		M	7	4	80	90	130	180
VYSV-825	1886		S	5	3	85	95	150	220
VYSV-830	1886	PROOF	S	5	3				7000
VYSV-835	1886		S	7	4	80	90	130	180

No.	Date	Features	mm	Obv.	Rev.	F	VF	EF	UNC
VYSV-840	1887		M	5	3	500	1000	2200	
VYSV-845	1887		M	7	4	80	90	130	180
VYSV-850	1887	PROOF	M	7	4				6000
VYSV-855	1887		S	5	3	85	95	150	220
VYSV-860	1887	PROOF	S	5	3				7000
VYSV-865	1887		S	7	4	80	90	130	170

1. Opening of Melbourne mint delayed from 1871.
2. Obverse slightly modified during 1880.
3. Two slightly different obverses exist.

Jubilee Head

No.	Date	Features	mm	Obv.	Rev.	F	VF	EF	UNC
VJSV-870	1887		M	8	5	BV	BV	100	130
VJSV-875	1887	PROOF	M	8	5				6000
VJSV-880	1887		S	8	5	100	150	300	600
VJSV-885	1887	PROOF	S	8	5				6000
VJSV-890	1888		M	8	5	BV	BV	90	120
VJSV-895	1888	PROOF	M	8	5				6000
VJSV-900	1888		S	8	5	80	100	140	180
VJSV-905	1889		M	8	5	BV	BV	90	120
VJSV-910	1889	PROOF	M	8	5				6000
VJSV-915	1889		S	8	5	BV	BV	90	120
VJSV-920	1890		M	8	5	BV	BV	90	120
VJSV-925	1890	PROOF	M	8	5				6000
VJSV-930	1890		S	8	5	BV	BV	90	120
VJSV-935	1891		M	8	5	BV	BV	90	120
VJSV-940	1891		S	8	5	BV	BV	90	120
VJSV-945	1892		M	8	5	BV	BV	90	120
VJSV-950	1892		S	8	5	BV	BV	90	120
VJSV-955	1893		M	8	5	BV	BV	90	120
VJSV-960	1893	PROOF	M	8	5				6000
VJSV-975	1893		S	8	5	BV	BV	90	120
VJSV-980	1893	PROOF	S	8	5				6000

Old Head

No.	Date	Features	mm	Obv.	Rev.	F	VF	EF	UNC
VOSV-965	1893		M	9	5	BV	BV	90	110
VOSV-970	1893	PROOF	M	9	5				6000
VOSV-985	1893		S	9	6	BV	BV	90	110
VOSV-990	1893	PROOF	S	9	6				6000
VOSV-995	1894		M	9	6	BV	BV	90	110
VOSV-1000	1894	PROOF	M	9	6				6000
VOSV-1005	1894		S	9	6	BV	BV	90	110
VOSV-1010	1894	PROOF	S	9	6				6000
VOSV-1015	1895		M	9	6	BV	BV	90	110
VOSV-1020	1895	PROOF	M	9	6				6000
VOSV-1025	1895		S	9	6	BV	BV	90	110
VOSV-1030	1896		M	9	6	BV	BV	90	110
VOSV-1035	1896	PROOF	M	9	6				6000
VOSV-1040	1896		S	9	6	BV	BV	90	110
VOSV-1045	1897		M	9	6	BV	BV	90	110
VOSV-1050	1897	PROOF	M	9	6				6000
VOSV-1055	1897		S	9	6	BV	BV	90	110
VOSV-1060	1898		M	9	6	BV	BV	90	110
VOSV-1065	1898	PROOF	M	9	6				6000
VOSV-1070	1898		S	9	6	BV	BV	90	110
VOSV-1075	1899		M	9	6	BV	BV	90	110
VOSV-1080	1899	PROOF	M	9	6				6000
VOSV-1085	1899		P	9	6	100	140	250	350
VOSV-1090	1899	PROOF	P	9	6				6000
VOSV-1095	1899		S	9	6	BV	BV	90	110
VOSV-1100	1900		M	9	6	BV	BV	90	110
VOSV-1105	1900	PROOF	M	9	6				6000
VOSV-1110	1900		P	9	6	BV	BV	100	150
VOSV-1115	1900		S	9	6	BV	BV	90	110
VOSV-1120	1901		M	9	6	BV	BV	90	110
VOSV-1125	1901	PROOF	M	9	6				6000
VOSV-1130	1901		P	9	6	BV	BV	90	150
VOSV-1135	1901	PROOF	P	9	6				6000
VOSV-1140	1901		S	9	6	BV	BV	90	110

Edward VII   (1901 – 1910)

Matt proof sovereigns were struck in 1902 for the cased matt proof set of that year, and ordinary specimens were minted for each year of the reign at the London, Melbourne, Perth and Sydney mints. Coins were struck for the first time at the Ottawa mint during 1908, 1909, and 1910. These bear the mintmark 'C', unusual in denoting the name of the country instead of the city.

The sovereign uses the portrait of Edward VII by George William de Saulles (1862–1903) and the reverse St George and dragon by Pistrucci.

Denomination	Metal	Weight (grams)	Diameter (mm)	Rev. alignment
Sovereign	Gold	8.0	22	↑

Obverse 1   Head 1, right; EDWARDVS VII D G BRITT OMN REX F D IND IMP

Reverse 1   St George and dragon, (date) in exergue

Edge   milled

Obv. 1   Rev. 1

No.	Date	Features	Obv.	Rev.	F	VF	EF	UNC
E7SV-005	1902		1	1	BV	BV	BV	85
E7SV-010	1902	matt PROOF [1]	1	1	BV	BV	85	120
E7SV-015	1903		1	1	BV	BV	BV	85
E7SV-020	1904		1	1	BV	BV	BV	85
E7SV-025	1905		1	1	BV	BV	BV	85
E7SV-030	1906		1	1	BV	BV	BV	85
E7SV-035	1906	matt PROOF	1	1				10000
E7SV-040	1907		1	1	BV	BV	BV	85
E7SV-045	1908		1	1	BV	BV	BV	85
E7SV-050	1909		1	1	BV	BV	BV	85
E7SV-055	1910		1	1	BV	BV	BV	85

1. Issued in cased proof sets.

Commonwealth Mints
Mintmarks
C: Ottawa, Canada (opened January 1908)
M: Melbourne, Australia
P: Perth, Australia
S: Sydney, Australia

No.	Date	Features	mm	Obv.	Rev.	F	VF	EF	UNC
E7SV-060	1902		M	1	1	BV	BV	BV	90
E7SV-065	1902		P	1	1	BV	BV	BV	90
E7SV-070	1902	matt PROOF [1]	P	1	1				
E7SV-075	1902		S	1	1	BV	BV	BV	90
E7SV-080	1902	matt PROOF	S	1	1				3500
E7SV-085	1903		M	1	1	BV	BV	BV	90
E7SV-090	1903		P	1	1	BV	BV	BV	90
E7SV-095	1903		S	1	1	BV	BV	BV	90
E7SV-100	1904		M	1	1	BV	BV	BV	90
E7SV-105	1904	PROOF	M	1	1				2500
E7SV-110	1904		P	1	1	BV	BV	BV	90
E7SV-115	1904		S	1	1	BV	BV	BV	90
E7SV-120	1905		M	1	1	BV	BV	BV	90
E7SV-125	1905		P	1	1	BV	BV	BV	90
E7SV-130	1905		S	1	1	BV	BV	BV	90
E7SV-135	1906		M	1	1	BV	BV	BV	90
E7SV-140	1906		P	1	1	BV	BV	BV	90
E7SV-145	1906		S	1	1	BV	BV	BV	90
E7SV-150	1907		M	1	1	BV	BV	BV	90
E7SV-155	1907		P	1	1	BV	BV	BV	90
E7SV-160	1907		S	1	1	BV	BV	BV	90
E7SV-165	1908	satin PROOF	C	1	1	1500	3000	4500	
E7SV-170	1908		M	1	1	BV	BV	BV	90
E7SV-175	1908		P	1	1	BV	BV	BV	90
E7SV-180	1908		S	1	1	BV	BV	BV	90

No.	Date	Features	mm	Obv.	Rev.	F	VF	EF	UNC
E7SV-185	1909		C	1	1		180	250	400
E7SV-190	1909		M	1	1	BV	BV	BV	90
E7SV-195	1909		P	1	1	BV	BV	BV	90
E7SV-200	1909		S	1	1	BV	BV	BV	90
E7SV-205	1910		C	1	1		180	250	400
E7SV-210	1910		M	1	1	BV	BV	BV	90
E7SV-215	1910	PROOF	M	1	1				2500
E7SV-220	1910		P	1	1	BV	BV	BV	90
E7SV-225	1910		S	1	1	BV	BV	BV	90

1. Exists?

George V (1910 – 1936)

Proof sovereigns were struck at the London mint for inclusion in some of the proof sets of 1911. These coins are of high quality and, unlike those struck for the 1902 sets, have a polished field. Sovereigns were struck for every year from 1911 to 1932 at one or more of the British or Commonwealth mints, but notable gaps occur at some of the mints, and some of the date/mintmark combinations are very rare. With the outbreak of war in August, 1914, the Treasury opted to replace the sovereign with the one pound note. These were issued the same month, and the sovereign soon ceased to be a circulation coin. Large quantities of London mint sovereigns dated 1925 were struck to replace lightweight coins in the Bank of England, and these continued to be issued with the same date as late as 1952.

Sovereigns were struck for the first and only time at the Bombay mint, in 1918. These coins have an 'I' (India) mintmark. Coins were also struck at Pretoria, South Africa, from 1923 to 1928 ('SA' mintmark), including the 1923 proof, which was included in a cased set of proof coins of South Africa.

In 1935, the State of Victoria in Australia sought to strike a sovereign to commemorate the centenary of the foundation of Melbourne in 1835. Permission from London was not forthcoming, and a commemorative florin was issued instead.

Many sovereigns were exported to the United States for redemption of debts. The holding of gold in the form of foreign coins became illegal in that country after the passing of the Gold Reserve Act of 1934 and the coins were melted down into ingots. Consequently, some dates such as 1917 (London mint) are now virtually unobtainable.

The series divides into two main types. Sir Bertram Mackennal (1863–1931) designed the two portraits of George V, while the reverse continued the Pistrucci St George and dragon design. The latter also appears in two different designs, which can be distinguished at a glance by an experienced eye, but which on close examination appear surprisingly similar. The sword and broken lance have slight differences, but the chief distinction lies in the different way in which the two designs strike into the metal. All of the London mint coins are of the first type.

Collecting Hints

The series is an interesting one because of the degrees of rarity of some of the date/mintmark combinations. Some of these have proved to be considerably rarer, and some less rare, than at one time thought.
Forgeries exist, some of which are crude and even grotesque. See under Victoria.

Denomination	Metal	Weight (grams)	Diameter (mm)	Rev. alignment
Sovereign	Gold	8.0	22	↑

Obverse 1 Head 1, left; GEORGIVS V D G BRITT OMN REX F D IND IMP

Obverse 2 Head 2, left, smaller; same legend

Reverse 1 St George and dragon, (date) in exergue

Reverse 2 Similar but slightly redesigned

Edge milled

Obv. 1   Obv. 2

Rev. 1   Rev. 2

No.	Date	Features	Obv.	Rev.	VF	EF	UNC
G5SV-005	1911		1	1	BV	BV	BV
G5SV-010	1911	PROOF [1]	1	1	BV	100	300
G5SV-015	1912		1	1	BV	BV	BV
G5SV-020	1913		1	1	BV	BV	BV
G5SV-025	1914		1	1	BV	BV	BV
G5SV-030	1915		1	1	BV	BV	BV
G5SV-035	1916	2	1	1	70	80	100
G5SV-040	1917	3	1	1	2000	3000	4000
G5SV-045	1925	4	1	1	BV	BV	BV

1. Issued in cased proof sets.
2. Many were melted down.
3. Almost all were melted down; crude forgeries exist.
4. Many were struck as late as 1952.

Commonwealth Mints

Mintmarks
I: Bombay, India (opened August 1918)
M: Melbourne, Australia
P: Perth, Australia
S: Sydney, Australia
SA: Pretoria, South Africa (opened December 1922)

No.	Date	Features	mm	Obv.	Rev.	VF	EF	UNC
G5SV-050	1911		C	1	1	75	100	130
G5SV-055	1911		M	1	1	BV	BV	BV
G5SV-060	1911	PROOF	M	1	1			3000
G5SV-065	1911		P	1	1	BV	BV	BV
G5SV-070	1911		S	1	1	BV	BV	BV
G5SV-075	1912		M	1	1	BV	BV	BV
G5SV-080	1912		P	1	1	BV	BV	BV
G5SV-085	1912		S	1	1	BV	BV	BV
G5SV-090	1913		C	1	1	400	550	750
G5SV-095	1913		M	1	1	BV	BV	BV
G5SV-100	1913		P	1	1	BV	BV	BV
G5SV-105	1913		S	1	1	BV	BV	BV
G5SV-110	1914		C	1	1	250	400	550
G5SV-115	1914		M	1	1	BV	BV	BV
G5SV-120	1914		P	1	1	BV	BV	BV
G5SV-125	1914		S	1	1	BV	BV	BV
G5SV-130	1914	PROOF	S	1	1			2500
G5SV-135	1915		M	1	1	BV	BV	BV
G5SV-140	1915		P	1	1	BV	BV	BV
G5SV-145	1915		S	1	1	BV	BV	BV
G5SV-150	1916		C	1	1	6000	8000	15000
G5SV-155	1916		M	1	1	BV	BV	BV
G5SV-160	1916		P	1	1	BV	BV	BV
G5SV-165	1916		S	1	1	BV	BV	BV
G5SV-170	1917		C	1	1	75	100	130
G5SV-175	1917		M	1	1	BV	BV	BV
G5SV-180	1917		P	1	1	BV	BV	BV
G5SV-185	1917		S	1	1	BV	BV	BV
G5SV-190	1918		C	1	1	75	100	130
G5SV-195	1918		I	1	1	BV	BV	BV
G5SV-200	1918		M	1	1	BV	BV	BV
G5SV-205	1918		P	1	1	BV	BV	BV
G5SV-210	1918		S	1	1	BV	BV	BV
G5SV-215	1919		C	1	1	75	100	130

No.	Date	Features	mm	Obv.	Rev.	VF	EF	UNC
G5SV-220	1919		M	1	1	BV	75	100
G5SV-225	1919		P	1	1	BV	BV	BV
G5SV-230	1919		S	1	1	BV	BV	BV
G5SV-235	1920		M	1	1	1500	2500	4000
G5SV-240	1920		P	1	1	BV	BV	BV
G5SV-245	1920		S	1	1	30000	60000	80000
G5SV-250	1921		M	1	1	3000	5000	7000
G5SV-255	1921		P	1	1	BV	75	90
G5SV-260	1921		S	1	1	800	1200	1600
G5SV-265	1922		M	1	1	2000	5000	8000
G5SV-270	1922		P	1	1	BV	75	90
G5SV-275	1922		S	1	1	4000	8000	12000
G5SV-280	1923		M	1	1	BV	80	100
G5SV-285	1923		P	1	1	BV	75	85
G5SV-290	1923		S	1	1	2500	5000	8000
G5SV-295	1923	[1]	SA	1	1	700	1500	4000
G5SV-300	1923	PROOF [2]	SA	1	1			500
G5SV-305	1924		M	1	1	BV	90	110
G5SV-310	1924		P	1	1	BV	100	120
G5SV-315	1924		S	1	1	400	600	900
G5SV-320	1924		SA	1	1	1500	2500	4000
G5SV-325	1925		M	1	1	BV	BV	BV
G5SV-330	1925		P	1	1	BV	100	120
G5SV-335	1925		S	1	1	BV	BV	80
G5SV-340	1925		SA	1	1	BV	BV	BV
G5SV-345	1926	[3]	M	1	1	BV	BV	90
G5SV-350	1926		P	1	1	150	250	500
G5SV-355	1926		S	1	1	8000	12000	18000
G5SV-360	1926	PROOF	S	1	1			25000
G5SV-365	1926		SA	1	1	BV	BV	BV
G5SV-370	1927		P	1	1	BV	100	120
G5SV-375	1927		SA	1	1	BV	BV	BV
G5SV-380	1928		M	1	1	1200	1800	2500
G5SV-385	1928		P	1	1	BV	100	120
G5SV-390	1928		SA	1	1	BV	BV	BV
G5SV-392	1929	[4]	M	1	1			40000
G5SV-395	1929		M	2	2	2000	3000	4500
G5SV-400	1929		P	2	2	BV	BV	80
G5SV-405	1929		SA	2	2	BV	BV	BV
G5SV-410	1930		M	2	2	120	220	300
G5SV-415	1930		P	2	2	BV	BV	80
G5SV-420	1930		SA	2	2	BV	BV	BV
G5SV-425	1931		M	2	2	180	300	450
G5SV-430	1931		P	2	2	BV	BV	80
G5SV-435	1931		SA	2	2	BV	BV	BV
G5SV-440	1932		SA	2	2	BV	BV	80

1. VF specimens may be worn proofs.
2. Issued in cased proof sets of South Africa.
3. Edge milling varies in fineness.
4. One known (in Dixson Library, Sydney).

Edward VIII   (1936)

The Edward VIII sovereign is strictly speaking a pattern, as probable royal approval was about to be granted at the time of the abdication. However, because its official status rests only on this technicality, and to provide continuity, it is included here.

The portrait of Edward VIII is by Thomas Humphrey Paget, and faces left at the insistence of the king, who considered this placement more flattering and wished to discontinue the tradition of opposite facings for successive monarchs. The reverse is the St George and dragon design originally by Pistrucci. The edge is milled, unlike that of the George VI proof.

Denomination	Metal	Weight (grams)	Diameter (mm)	Rev. alignment
Sovereign	Gold	8.0	22	↑

Obverse 1   Head 1, left; EDWARDVS VIII D G BR OMN REX F D IND IMP

Reverse 1   St George and dragon, 1937 in exergue

Edge   milled

Obv. 1   Rev. 1

No.	Date		Obv.	Rev.		UNC
E8SV-005	1937		1	1		50000

George VI   (1937 – 1952)

The only George VI sovereigns struck were the proofs included in the cased proof sets of 1937. These sets contained four coins, each of which comprised the only British coin of that denomination for the reign. Curiously, through an oversight, the sovereign was not legal tender because the Proclamation of March 1937 happened to specify that legal tender sovereigns have a milled edge.

The obverse portrait was by Thomas Humphrey Paget, the reverse again being the Pistrucci St George and dragon.

Collecting Hints

Gold coins of 1937 must always be examined carefully for edge damage. The tight fitting inserts in the case often meant that the coins were prised out, and the plain edge was very susceptible to marks.

Denomination	Metal	Weight (grams)	Diameter (mm)	Rev. alignment
Sovereign	Gold	8.0	22	↑

Obverse 1   Head 1, left; GEORGIVS VI D G BR OMN REX F D IND IMP

Reverse 1   St George and dragon, 1937 in exergue

Edge   plain

Obv. 1   Rev. 1

No.	Date	Features	Obv.	Rev.	EF	FDC
G6SV-005	1937	PROOF [1]	1	1	350	480

1. Issued in cased proof sets.

Elizabeth II   (1952 –)

No gold coins were included in the proof sets of 1953 issued for the coronation, and the only British sovereigns struck in that year were a small number struck in order to provide continuity of the series. These were not released. The coins bore the obverse portrait of Elizabeth II by Mary Gillick, and the Pistrucci St George and dragon reverse.

The production of sovereigns was resumed in 1957. The portrait was similar to the 1953 piece but the obverse legend was revised. The coin was struck for most of the years up to 1968, then resumed in 1974 (post-decimalization) using an older portrait by Arnold Machin. From 1979 many proofs were struck for inclusion in proof sets and as individually cased proofs. In 1985 a new portrait by Raphael David Maklouf was introduced.

The reverse uses the Pistrucci St George and dragon design throughout, except for 1989 when a proof sovereign was struck for the 500th anniversary of the sovereign. This had a completely new obverse and reverse.

Collecting Hints

This series normally occurs in extremely fine or mint state. Forgeries exist of the non-proof coins.

Denomination	Metal	Weight (grams)	Diameter (mm)	Rev. alignment
Sovereign	Gold	8.0	22	↑

Obverse 1 Head 1, right; ELIZABETH II DEI GRA BRITT OMN REGINA F D

Obverse 2 Head 1, right; ELIZABETH II DEI GRATIA REGINA F D

Obverse 3 Head 2, right; same legend

Obverse 4 Head 3, right; ELIZABETH II DEI GRA REG F D

Obverse 5 Queen facing on throne, holding orb and sceptre; ELIZABETH II DEI GRA REG FID DEF *(for the 500th anniversary of the gold sovereign)*

Obverse 6 Head 4, right; ELIZABETH II DEI GRA REGINA FID DEF

Reverse 1 St George and dragon, (date) in exergue

Reverse 2 Crowned shield within double rose; ANNIVERSARY OF THE GOLD SOVEREIGN 1489–1989

Edge milled

Obv. 1   Obv. 2   Obv. 3

Obv. 4   Obv. 5   Obv. 6

Rev. 1   Rev. 2

No.	Date	Features	Obv.	Rev.	UNC
EZSV-005	1953	PROOF or pattern [1]	1	1	30000
EZSV-010	1957	[2]	2	1	BV
EZSV-015	1957	PROOF	2	1	3000
EZSV-020	1958		2	1	BV
EZSV-025	1958	PROOF	2	1	3000
EZSV-030	1959		2	1	BV
EZSV-032	1959	PROOF	2	1	6000
EZSV-035	1962		2	1	BV
EZSV-038	1962	PROOF	2	1	6000
EZSV-040	1963		2	1	BV
EZSV-042	1963	PROOF	2	1	6000
EZSV-045	1964		2	1	BV
EZSV-050	1965		2	1	BV
EZSV-055	1966		2	1	BV
EZSV-060	1967		2	1	BV
EZSV-065	1968		2	1	BV
EZSV-070	1974		3	1	BV
EZSV-075	1976		3	1	BV
EZSV-080	1978		3	1	BV
EZSV-085	1979		3	1	BV
EZSV-090	1979	PROOF [3]	3	1	100
EZSV-095	1980		3	1	BV
EZSV-100	1980	PROOF [4]	3	1	100
EZSV-105	1981		3	1	BV
EZSV-110	1981	PROOF [4]	3	1	100
EZSV-115	1982		3	1	BV
EZSV-120	1982	PROOF [4]	3	1	100
EZSV-125	1983	PROOF [4]	3	1	100
EZSV-130	1984	PROOF [4]	3	1	100
EZSV-135	1985	PROOF [4]	4	1	100
EZSV-140	1986	PROOF [4]	4	1	100
EZSV-145	1987	PROOF [4]	4	1	110
EZSV-150	1988	PROOF [4]	4	1	115
EZSV-155	1989	PROOF [4]	5	2	170
EZSV-160	1990	PROOF [4]	4	1	140
EZSV-165	1991	PROOF [4]	4	1	140
EZSV-170	1992	PROOF [4]	4	1	140
EZSV-175	1993	PROOF [4]	4	1	140
EZSV-180	1994	PROOF [4]	4	1	140
EZSV-185	1995	PROOF [4]	4	1	140
EZSV-190	1996	PROOF [4]	4	1	140
EZSV-195	1997	PROOF [4]	4	1	140
EZSV-200	1998	PROOF [4]	6	1	140
EZSV-205	1999	PROOF [4]	6	1	140

1. Possibly about 10 exist.
2. Milling finer than on subsequent years.
3. Issued cased.
4. Issued cased and in cased proof sets.

Half Guinea

<table>
<tr><th>No.</th><th>Date</th><th>Features</th><th>Obv.</th><th>Rev.</th><th>F</th><th>VF</th><th>EF</th></tr>
<tr><td>C2HGM-085</td><td>1678</td><td>8 over 7 elephant and castle below head</td><td>2</td><td>1</td><td>300</td><td>700</td><td>2500</td></tr>
<tr><td>C2HGM-090</td><td>1679</td><td></td><td>2</td><td>1</td><td>180</td><td>450</td><td>1500</td></tr>
<tr><td>C2HGM-095</td><td>1680</td><td></td><td>2</td><td>1</td><td>220</td><td>550</td><td>2200</td></tr>
<tr><td>C2HGM-100</td><td>1680</td><td>elephant and castle below head</td><td>2</td><td>1</td><td>500</td><td>1000</td><td></td></tr>
<tr><td>C2HGM-105</td><td>1681</td><td></td><td>2</td><td>1</td><td>220</td><td>550</td><td>2200</td></tr>
<tr><td>C2HGM-108</td><td>1681</td><td>elephant and castle below head</td><td>2</td><td>1</td><td>800</td><td>1500</td><td></td></tr>
<tr><td>C2HGM-110</td><td>1682</td><td></td><td>2</td><td>1</td><td>220</td><td>550</td><td>2200</td></tr>
<tr><td>C2HGM-115</td><td>1682</td><td>elephant and castle below head</td><td>2</td><td>1</td><td>300</td><td>700</td><td>2500</td></tr>
<tr><td>C2HGM-120</td><td>1683</td><td></td><td>2</td><td>1</td><td>220</td><td>550</td><td>2200</td></tr>
<tr><td>C2HGM-125</td><td>1683</td><td>elephant and castle below head</td><td>2</td><td>1</td><td>500</td><td>1000</td><td></td></tr>
<tr><td>C2HGM-130</td><td>1684</td><td></td><td>2</td><td>1</td><td>200</td><td>500</td><td>1800</td></tr>
<tr><td>C2HGM-135</td><td>1684</td><td>elephant and castle below head</td><td>2</td><td>1</td><td>240</td><td>550</td><td>2000</td></tr>
</table>

Charles II (1660 – 1685)

The first milled half guinea was struck in 1669. This was some years after the guinea had entered circulation, and the various alterations made to the portrait to accommodate the elephant and castle symbol had already occurred by 1669. The result was that the half guinea series has only two main obverse types instead of four. Although the portrait with the indentation to accommodate the symbol was used until 1672, no coins with the elephant and castle are known before the 1676 coin, by which time the larger head was in use. Unlike the guinea, no half guineas display the elephant only symbol.

The half guinea was designed by John Roettier.

Collecting Hints

This is a scarce series, and Charles II half guineas in high grades command high prices. In general, prices are higher than for guineas in similar grades. Because the half guinea is an expensive series to collect, and because pieces are seen so seldom, documentation of varieties has not been as thorough as on silver coinage, and no doubt a number of unrecorded varieties exist.

<table>
<tr><th>Denomination</th><th>Metal</th><th>Weight (grams)</th><th>Diameter (mm)</th><th>Rev. alignment</th></tr>
<tr><td>Half guinea</td><td>Gold</td><td>4.2</td><td>20</td><td>↓</td></tr>
</table>

Obverse 1 Head 1, right; pointed truncation with lock of hair to right of truncation; CAROLVS II DEI GRATIA

Obverse 2 Head 2, right; older portrait, rounded truncation, without lock of hair to right; same legend

Reverse 1 Four crowned cruciform shields between which are four sceptres, with four interlinked 'C's at the centre; MAG BR FRA ET HIB REX (date)

Edge (1669) milled (vertically); (1670–84) milled (diagonally)

Obv. 1

Obv. 2

Rev. 1

<table>
<tr><th>No.</th><th>Date</th><th>Features</th><th>Obv.</th><th>Rev.</th><th>F</th><th>VF</th><th>EF</th></tr>
<tr><td>C2HGM-005</td><td>1669</td><td></td><td>1</td><td>1</td><td>250</td><td>700</td><td>2500</td></tr>
<tr><td>C2HGM-010</td><td>1670</td><td></td><td>1</td><td>1</td><td>220</td><td>500</td><td>2000</td></tr>
<tr><td>C2HGM-015</td><td>1671</td><td></td><td>1</td><td>1</td><td>250</td><td>700</td><td>2500</td></tr>
<tr><td>C2HGM-020</td><td>1672</td><td></td><td>1</td><td>1</td><td>250</td><td>700</td><td>2500</td></tr>
<tr><td>C2HGM-025</td><td>1672</td><td></td><td>2</td><td>1</td><td>220</td><td>500</td><td>2000</td></tr>
<tr><td>C2HGM-030</td><td>1673</td><td></td><td>2</td><td>1</td><td>250</td><td>700</td><td>2500</td></tr>
<tr><td>C2HGM-035</td><td>1674</td><td></td><td>2</td><td>1</td><td>250</td><td>700</td><td>2500</td></tr>
<tr><td>C2HGM-040</td><td>1675</td><td></td><td>2</td><td>1</td><td>500</td><td>1800</td><td></td></tr>
<tr><td>C2HGM-045</td><td>1676</td><td></td><td>2</td><td>1</td><td>220</td><td>500</td><td>2000</td></tr>
<tr><td>C2HGM-050</td><td>1676</td><td>latter 6 over 4 or 5</td><td>2</td><td>1</td><td>240</td><td>550</td><td>2200</td></tr>
<tr><td>C2HGM-055</td><td>1676</td><td>elephant and castle below head</td><td>2</td><td>1</td><td>350</td><td>1000</td><td>5000</td></tr>
<tr><td>C2HGM-060</td><td>1677</td><td></td><td>2</td><td>1</td><td>220</td><td>500</td><td>2000</td></tr>
<tr><td>C2HGM-065</td><td>1677</td><td>elephant and castle below head</td><td>2</td><td>1</td><td>350</td><td>1000</td><td>3500</td></tr>
<tr><td>C2HGM-070</td><td>1678</td><td></td><td>2</td><td>1</td><td>220</td><td>500</td><td>2000</td></tr>
<tr><td>C2HGM-075</td><td>1678</td><td>8 over 7</td><td>2</td><td>1</td><td>240</td><td>550</td><td>2200</td></tr>
<tr><td>C2HGM-080</td><td>1678</td><td>elephant and castle below head</td><td>2</td><td>1</td><td>300</td><td>700</td><td>2500</td></tr>
</table>

James II (1685 – 1688)

John Roettier designed the head of James II for this series, which uses the basic design layout of the previous reign. There is, however, no motif of interlinked initials at the centre of the reverse. Unlike the guinea, there is only one obverse type. The elephant and castle symbol was used only during 1686, and this variety is particularly scarce. All James II half guineas are rare in extremely fine condition.

Collecting Hints

This is an attractive coin, but for most collectors a specimen in fine condition will be acceptable. However, much more obverse detail is visible on a very fine coin.

<table>
<tr><th>Denomination</th><th>Metal</th><th>Weight (grams)</th><th>Diameter (mm)</th><th>Rev. alignment</th></tr>
<tr><td>Half guinea</td><td>Gold</td><td>4.2</td><td>20</td><td>↓</td></tr>
</table>

Obverse 1 Head 1, left; IACOBVS II DEI GRATIA

Reverse 1 Four crowned cruciform shields between which are four sceptres; MAG BR FRA ET HIB REX (date)

Edge milled (diagonally)

Obv. 1

Rev. 1

<table>
<tr><th>No.</th><th>Date</th><th>Features</th><th>Obv.</th><th>Rev.</th><th>F</th><th>VF</th><th>EF</th></tr>
<tr><td>J2HG-005</td><td>1686</td><td></td><td>1</td><td>1</td><td>240</td><td>600</td><td>2000</td></tr>
<tr><td>J2HG-008</td><td>1686</td><td>IACOBVS over IACBVS (rev.)</td><td>1</td><td>1</td><td>300</td><td>750</td><td>2400</td></tr>
<tr><td>J2HG-010</td><td>1686</td><td>elephant and castle below head</td><td>1</td><td>1</td><td>600</td><td>1700</td><td>4500</td></tr>
<tr><td>J2HG-015</td><td>1687</td><td></td><td>1</td><td>1</td><td>240</td><td>600</td><td>2000</td></tr>
<tr><td>J2HG-020</td><td>1688</td><td></td><td>1</td><td>1</td><td>240</td><td>600</td><td>2000</td></tr>
</table>

William & Mary (1688 – 1694)

The credit for the design of the heads of William and Mary for the gold coinage is generally given to James and Norbert Roettier. However, the first type of half guinea in 1689 deserves careful study. The somewhat caricatured heads appear to be very much in the style of George Bower (?–1689/90), an artist who had been appointed an 'engraver in ordinary' in 1664 and who designed the first type of halfpenny and farthing in 1689, having also produced a number of medals with somewhat grotesque and cartoon-like busts. Records show that Bower was ordered in July 1689 'to make a puncheon for the Halfe Guinneys ande to worke it in the Mint'. The heads of the king and queen on the halfpenny, farthing and the first type of half guinea do not possess the mutual harmony and statesmanlike appearance of the later Roettier work.

The half guinea was minted each year of the reign until Mary's death in 1694. The elephant and castle symbol appeared on some coins of 1691 and 1692, and there is a rare variety of 1692 apparently bearing the elephant only symbol. However, see p. 446 for comments on the status of similar guineas of William and Mary.

Collecting Hints

The detail on this series is best appreciated in very fine or better condition. The reverses are of inferior execution and this should be taken into account when grading the coins.

Denomination	Metal	Weight (grams)	Diameter (mm)	Rev. alignment
Half guinea	Gold	4.2	20	↓

Obverse 1 Heads 1, right; GVLIELMVS ET MARIA DEI GRATIA

Obverse 2 Heads 2, right; same legend

Reverse 1 Crowned shield; MAG BR FR ET HIB REX ET REGINA (date)

Reverse 2 Similar but shield is differently shaped; crown and harp are very different

Edge milled (diagonally)

Obv. 1   Obv. 2

Rev. 1   Rev. 2

No.	Date	Features	Obv.	Rev.	F	VF	EF
WMHG-005	1689		1	1	300	700	2000
WMHG-010	1690		2	2	220	600	1800
WMHG-015	1691		2	2	220	600	1800
WMHG-020	1691	elephant and castle below head	2	2	220	600	1800
WMHG-025	1692		2	2	220	600	1800
WMHG-030	1692	elephant and castle below head	2	2	220	600	1800
WMHG-035	1692	elephant below head [1]	2	2	400		
WMHG-040	1693		2	2	700	1800	
WMHG-045	1693	3 over 2	2	2	800	2000	
WMHG-050	1694		2	2	220	600	1800

No.	Date	Features	Obv.	Rev.	F	VF	EF
WMHG-055	1694	4 over 3	2	2	250	650	2000

1. See comments under Guinea, p. 446.

William III (1695 – 1701)

On the death of Mary from smallpox in 1694, the obverse of the half guinea was redesigned to depict the undraped bust of William alone. The shield reverse of William and Mary had not been a success. It was a poorly proportioned effort, and the intricate design on the shield within such a small area had only led to a confusion of detail. The reverse was therefore recut using the cruciform shields design of earlier reigns, but with the lion of Orange-Nassau at the centre.

One detail which the reverses share with the silver coinage but not with the other gold denominations is the variation in the shape of the harp usually known as 'early harp' and 'late harp' on the silver. As far as is known, there are no harp variations within any particular date, the 'late harp' being introduced in 1697.

The elephant and castle symbol appears on three dates, 1695, 1696 and 1698. The 1696 coin is unusual in that no half guineas were struck in this year without the symbol.

The half guinea was probably the work of James Roettier and/or John Croker. The reverse of the 'late harp' type is considered to be by Croker alone.

Collecting Hints

A good fine specimen will be acceptable to most collectors of this series.

Denomination	Metal	Weight (grams)	Diameter (mm)	Rev. alignment
Half guinea	Gold	4.2	20	↓

Obverse 1 Head 1, right; GVLIELMVS III DEI GRA

Reverse 1 Four crowned cruciform shields between which are four sceptres, with central lion of Nassau; MAG BR FRA ET HIB REX (date)

Reverse 2 Similar but harp larger and of different design

Edge milled (diagonally)

Obv. 1   Rev. 1   Rev. 2

No.	Date	Features	Obv.	Rev.	F	VF	EF
W3HG-005	1695		1	1	130	350	750
W3HG-010	1695	elephant and castle below head	1	1	180	500	1300
W3HG-015	1696	elephant and castle below head	1	1	150	400	950
W3HG-020	1697		1	2	150	400	950
W3HG-025	1698		1	2	130	350	750
W3HG-030	1698	elephant and castle below head	1	2	180	500	1300
W3HG-035	1700		1	2	130	350	750
W3HG-040	1701		1	2	130	350	750

Anne (1702 – 1714)

Pre-Union half guineas were struck in 1702, 1703 and 1705. The coin of 1703 includes the provenance mark VIGO below the head and is very rare. Gold to produce this coin was captured from Spanish galleons at the battle at Vigo Bay in October 1702. Half guineas with the post-Union reverse were minted in 1707 and each year thereafter until Anne's death in 1714. Pre-Union coins depict a rose in the centre of the reverse, and post-Union coins a Star of the Order of the Garter.

Gold of previous reigns had used an undraped bust of the monarch to prevent fraudulent conversion of silver coins, which had depicted an undraped bust. However, the use of an undraped bust was not considered appropriate for Anne, with the result that many sixpences were gilded, engraved with sceptres, and passed off as half guineas. Subsequent coins of the Georges again used differing types of busts.

Unlike the guinea, the half guinea has only one type of obverse. This runs across the change from pre-Union to post-Union and is a characteristic shared with the sixpence. The obverse was the work of John Croker, from an original design by Sir Godfrey Kneller. The first reverse was by Croker and the second by Croker and/or Bull.

Collecting Hints

Coins in fine condition will probably be adequate for most collectors, but very fine specimens are considerably more attractive.

Denomination	Metal	Weight (grams)	Diameter (mm)	Rev. alignment
Half guinea	Gold	4.2	20	↓

Obverse 1 Head 1, left; ANNA DEI GRATIA

Reverse 1 Four crowned cruciform shields between which are four sceptres; central rose; MAG BR FRA ET HIB REG (date)

Reverse 2 Similar but two shields separately show conjoined English/Scottish arms; central Star of the Order of the Garter instead of rose; shields are broader; MAG BRI FR ET HIB REG (date).

Edge milled (diagonally)

Obv. 1   Rev. 1 Before Union Rev. 2 After Union

No.	Date	Features	Obv.	Rev.	F	VF	EF
ANHG-005	1702		1	1	1500	3500	
ANHG-010	1703	VIGO below head	1	1	3000	7000	
ANHG-015	1705		1	1	1500	3500	
ANHG-020	1707		1	2	180	450	1200
ANHG-025	1708		1	2	180	450	1200
ANHG-030	1709		1	2	180	450	1200
ANHG-035	1710		1	2	180	450	1200
ANHG-040	1711		1	2	180	450	1200
ANHG-045	1712		1	2	180	450	1200
ANHG-050	1713		1	2	180	450	1200
ANHG-055	1714		1	2	180	450	1200

George I (1714 – 1727)

Although at first sight the half guinea appears to continue the design used during the reign of Anne, there are important differences. The long and greatly abbreviated German titles of the king were incorporated into the legends, and the arms of Brunswick, Lüneburg, Saxony and the crown of Charlemagne were all crammed into one of the reverse shields. Clearly, the half guinea was too small a coin to depict such minutiae, but the overall impression is not unpleasing. The convention of the undraped bust on the gold to distinguish it from the silver was resumed.

There was no half guinea equivalent to the 'Prince Elector' guinea of 1714. The denomination ran from 1715 to 1727, with two different obverses rather than the five known on the guinea. The elephant and castle symbol made its last appearance on a half guinea in 1721. This piece is very rare.

The half guinea was the work of John Croker and/or J. R. Ochs, senior. The work of Ochs was probably restricted to the reverses.

The value of the guinea had fluctuated over the years from twenty shillings to about thirty shillings and back to a level of twenty-one shillings and sixpence at the beginning of the reign. A Proclamation in December 1717 reduced the value to twenty-one shillings.

Collecting Hints

Fine condition coins are often considerably lacking in detail on the obverse. A very fine coin should be looked for if possible. The elephant and castle coin of 1721 is greatly valued in any condition.

Denomination	Metal	Weight (grams)	Diameter (mm)	Rev. alignment
Half guinea	Gold	4.2	20	↓

Obverse 1 Head 1, right; GEORGIVS D G M BR FR ET HIB REX F D

Obverse 2 Head 2, right, smaller and older; same legend

Reverse 1 Four crowned cruciform shields between which are four sceptres; central Star of the Order of the Garter; BRVN ET L DVX S R I A TH ET EL (date)

Edge milled (diagonally)

Obv. 1   Obv. 2   Rev. 1

No.	Date	Features	Obv.	Rev.	F	VF	EF
G1HG-005	1715		1	1	160	320	800
G1HG-010	1717		1	1	160	320	800
G1HG-015	1718		1	1	150	300	700
G1HG-020	1718	8 over 7	1	1	160	320	800
G1HG-022	1718	second 1 over indeterminate digit (8?)	1	1	180	360	950
G1HG-025	1719	[1]	1	1	150	300	700
G1HG-030	1720		1	1	160	320	800
G1HG-035	1721		1	1	350	800	
G1HG-040	1721	elephant and castle below head	1	1	1500		
G1HG-045	1722		1	1	160	320	800
G1HG-050	1722	latter 2 over 0 [2]	1	1	170	350	850
G1HG-055	1723		1	1	220	450	1200
G1HG-060	1724		1	1	160	320	800
G1HG-065	1725		2	1	140	280	700
G1HG-070	1726		2	1	140	280	700
G1HG-075	1727	[3]	2	1	140	280	700

1. Occurs with lettering very close to rim.
2. Overdate often remarkably clear.
3. Date resembles 1721.

Some specimens of 1725 and 1726 have a line running down the king's forehead parallel to the profile line (cf. quarter guinea 1718, obverse 2).

George II (1727 – 1760)

The half guinea series of George II approximately parallels the guinea, with several differences. There was no issue corresponding to the first two types of guinea of 1727, bearing the obverse by J. R. Ochs, and no half guineas were struck at all that year. The variations in size of lettering are also less prevalent on the half guinea.

Fraudulent conversion of sixpences by gilding and passing them off as half guineas had become an epidemic. Because of this, with this issue the reverse was given a crowned shield design. This was a more pleasing effort than that used on the William and Mary coinage, and it proved successful in stopping the counterfeiters. While the milling on the guinea was in 1739 changed to a chevron design to thwart 'guinea-filers', the half guinea was too thin to permit this conversion.

John Croker initially prepared the dies for the George II half guinea. Subsequent work was by Tanner (who succeeded as Chief Engraver in 1791) and Ochs, junior.

Collecting Hints

A fine to very fine condition specimen will be adequate for most purposes.

Denomination	Metal	Weight (grams)	Diameter (mm)	Rev. alignment
Half guinea	Gold	4.2	20	↓

Obverse 1 Head 1, left; GEORGIVS II DEI GRATIA

Obverse 2 Head 2, left; same legend but GEORGIUS

Obverse 3 Head 2, left; same legend but GEORGIVS

Obverse 4 Head 3, left, older; same legend but larger lettering

Reverse 1 Crowned shield; M B F ET H REX F D B ET L D S R I A T ET E (date) in small lettering and numerals

Reverse 2 Similar but shield slightly different

Edge milled (diagonally)

Obv. 1   Obv. 2   Obv. 4   Rev. 1

No.	Date	Features	Obv.	Rev.	F	VF	EF
G2HG-005	1728		1	1	200	500	1400
G2HG-010	1728	PROOF; edge plain [1]	1	1			4000
G2HG-015	1728	PROOF; edge plain; rev. ↑	1	1			4500
G2HG-020	1729		1	1	200	500	1400
G2HG-025	1729	E.I.C. below head	1	1	350	800	2000
G2HG-030	1730		1	1	700	1500	
G2HG-035	1730	E.I.C. below head	1	1	350	900	2500
G2HG-040	1731		1	1	240	700	1700
G2HG-045	1731	E.I.C. below head	1	1	900	2000	
G2HG-050	1732		1	1	200	500	1400
G2HG-055	1732	E.I.C. below head	1	1	900	2000	
G2HG-060	1734		1	1	180	450	1100
G2HG-065	1736		1	1	200	500	1400
G2HG-070	1737		1	1	800	2000	
G2HG-075	1738		1	1	170	420	1000
G2HG-080	1739		1	1	170	420	1000
G2HG-085	1739	E.I.C. below head	1	1	900	2000	
G2HG-090	1740	[2]	2	1	240	700	1700
G2HG-095	1743	[3]	2	1	2000		
G2HG-100	1745		2	1	240	700	1700
G2HG-105	1745	LIMA below head	2	1	650	1800	3500
G2HG-110	1746		3	1	180	450	1100
G2HG-115	1747		4	2	200	550	1500
G2HG-120	1748		4	2	180	450	1000
G2HG-125	1749		4	2	500	1400	
G2HG-130	1750		4	2	170	400	850
G2HG-135	1751		4	2	170	420	900
G2HG-140	1751	latter 1 over 0	4	2	200	480	1000
G2HG-145	1752		4	2	170	420	900
G2HG-150	1753	[4]	4	2	160	380	750

No.	Date	Features	Obv.	Rev.	F	VF	EF
G2HG-155	1755		4	2	160	380	750
G2HG-160	1756		4	2	140	320	650
G2HG-165	1758		4	2	140	320	650
G2HG-170	1759		4	2	130	280	550
G2HG-175	1759	9 over 8	4	2	200	400	800
G2HG-180	1760		4	2	130	280	550

1. Reverse ↓ as ordinary issue.
2. 'Intermediate head'.
3. Possibly only one exists.
4. 3 in date has a straight top.

George III   (1760 – 1820)

The half guinea was minted for almost every year of this long reign. Seven different heads of the monarch by four different designers span the series. Beginning in 1762, the first two heads were by Richard Yeo, the last of this type being struck in 1775. In 1774 and 1775 there also appeared a new type bearing a head designed by Thomas Pingo. This was of inferior workmanship and struck up so poorly that it is surprising that any were issued. This type is rarely encountered, and it was replaced during 1775 by a coin having a much improved portrait by the same designer. Thus, in 1775 there were issued three completely different versions of the half guinea. Many of these would have been from recalled gold coins of William III and Anne, 20 million of which were remelted at this time.

Thomas Pingo's son Lewis was appointed Chief Engraver in January 1780. Lewis Pingo produced a very different head for the 'spade' half guinea of 1787–1800. This was slightly modified for the issue of 1801–03, on which the 'spade' shield was replaced by a shield in garter design. From 1800 to 1811 only half guineas and third guineas were issued. In 1801, the king relinquished his claim to the French throne, and the reverse legend was altered to reflect this. The Hanoverian quartering was also moved from the royal arms on the reverse on to an escutcheon at the centre of the shield. This reverse then continued until 1813 using another very different head (1804–13) engraved by Lewis Pingo from a design by Nathaniel Marchant.

The reverses initially carried over the Tanner design from the previous reign. However, Tanner's eyesight was now failing, and the engraving was possibly done by Richard Yeo.

Collecting Hints

Generally speaking, the half guinea is attractive enough in fine condition for most purposes. Certainly the somewhat flatly struck 'spade' type does not exhibit much greater detail in higher grades. Thus, one of each main type in fine condition should be adequate.
One does not have to be so vigilant about forgeries as in the guinea series, but possibly one should be cautious of 'hype' regarding the 1813 coin. The guinea of this date, a one-year type, commands a good premium. The half guinea of 1813 is somewhat scarce, but that is all. The fact that most collectors of half guinea do not collect by date is also a factor to be taken into account when pricing this coin.

Denomination	Metal	Weight (grams)	Diameter (mm)	Rev. alignment
Half guinea 1762–86	Gold	4.2	20	↓
Half guinea 1787–1813	Gold	4.2	20–21	↑

Obverse 1 Head 1, right; GEORGIVS III DEI GRATIA

Obverse 2 Head 2, right, slightly different; same legend

Obverse 3 Head 3, right, poorly executed and struck; same legend

Obverse 4 Head 4, right, similar but better crafted; same legend

Obverse 5 Head 5, right, somewhat similar; same legend

No.	Date	Features	Obv.	Rev.	F	VF	EF
G3HG-205	1800		5	2	150	300	550
G3HG-210	1801		6	3	80	120	200
G3HG-215	1802		6	3	80	120	240
G3HG-220	1803		6	3	80	120	240
G3HG-225	1804		7	3	80	120	240
G3HG-228	1804	PROOF; edge plain [3]	7	3			4000
G3HG-230	1805		7	3	500		
G3HG-235	1806		7	3	80	120	240
G3HG-240	1808		7	3	80	120	240
G3HG-245	1809		7	3	80	120	240
G3HG-250	1810		7	3	80	120	240
G3HG-255	1811		7	3	110	180	320
G3HG-260	1813		7	3	100	170	290

1. Weight c.5.3 grams; usually has die flaws on reverse.
2. Date change; Rev. 1: from 1762 to 1779 the '1' in the date is a 'J' type; from 1781 to 1786 it is a Roman I.
3. Weight 4.8 grams.

Obverse 6   Head 6, right, similar but slightly broader; same legend

Obverse 7   Head 7, very different, right; same legend

Reverse 1   Crowned shield; M B F ET H REX F D B ET L D S R I A T ET E; (date) divided by crown

Reverse 2   Crowned spade-shaped shield; same legend but in opposite position around rim; (date) at bottom

Reverse 3   Crowned shield in Garter; BRITANNIARUM REX FIDEI DEFENSOR; HONI SOIT QUI MAL Y PENSE on Garter; (date) between Garter and edge legend

Edge   milled (diagonally)

Obv. 1   Obv. 2   Obv. 3

Obv. 4   Obv. 5   Obv. 7

Rev. 1   Rev. 2   Rev. 3

No.	Date	Features	Obv.	Rev.	F	VF	EF
G3HG-005	1762		1	1	250	800	1800
G3HG-010	1763		1	1	280	820	1900
G3HG-015	1764		2	1	140	380	900
G3HG-020	1765		2	1	220	650	1800
G3HG-025	1765	5 over 4	2	1	220	650	1800
G3HG-030	1766		2	1	140	380	900
G3HG-035	1768		2	1	140	380	900
G3HG-040	1769		2	1	140	380	900
G3HG-045	1772		2	1	400	1200	3000
G3HG-050	1773		2	1	140	380	900
G3HG-055	1774		2	1	200	550	1500
G3HG-060	1774		3	1	700	1900	
G3HG-065	1775		2	1	200	550	1500
G3HG-070	1775		3	1	250	700	1800
G3HG-075	1775	PROOF; edge plain [1]	3	1			5000
G3HG-080	1775		4	1	110	200	420
G3HG-085	1776		4	1	110	200	420
G3HG-090	1777		4	1	110	200	420
G3HG-095	1778		4	1	110	200	420
G3HG-100	1779		4	1	120	230	480
G3HG-105	1781	[2]	4	1	110	200	420
G3HG-110	1783		4	1	250	700	
G3HG-115	1784		4	1	110	200	400
G3HG-120	1785		4	1	110	200	400
G3HG-125	1786		4	1	110	200	400
G3HG-130	1787		5	2	100	170	350
G3HG-135	1787	PROOF; edge plain	5	2			1000
G3HG-140	1787	PROOF in silver; edge plain	5	2			750
G3HG-145	1788		5	2	100	170	350
G3HG-150	1789		5	2	100	170	350
G3HG-155	1790		5	2	100	170	350
G3HG-160	1791		5	2	100	170	350
G3HG-165	1792		5	2	500	1500	
G3HG-170	1793		5	2	100	170	350
G3HG-175	1794		5	2	100	170	350
G3HG-180	1795		5	2	110	190	400
G3HG-185	1796		5	2	100	170	350
G3HG-190	1797		5	2	100	170	350
G3HG-195	1798		5	2	95	160	320
G3HG-200	1798	8 over 7	5	2	140	220	450

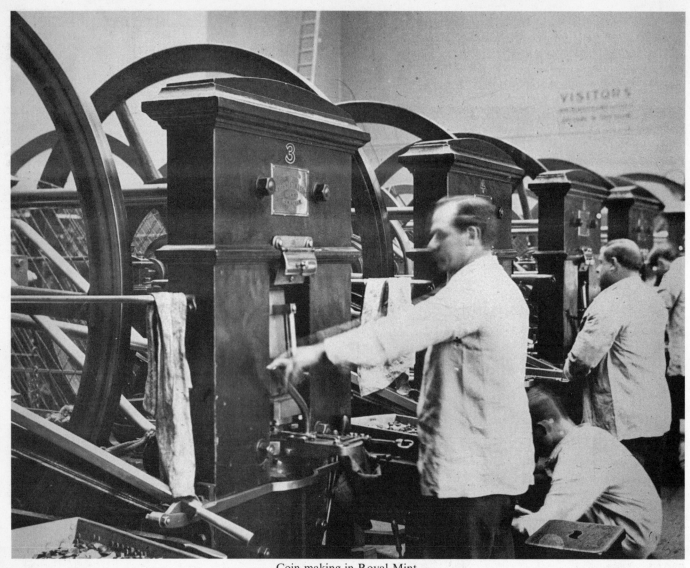

Coin making in Royal Mint

Half Sovereign

George III (1760 – 1820)

With the Great Recoinage, the half sovereign was struck as the companion piece to the sovereign, and became the smallest gold coin in regular use. The workmanship and striking of the half sovereign was not quite up to the standard of the sovereign. However, the coin received more extensive use and turns up in worn condition more often than the sovereign.

The obverse was designed by Benedetto Pistrucci, and the reverse was engraved by William Wyon, possibly from a design by Pistrucci.

Denomination	Metal	Weight (grams)	Diameter (mm)	Rev. alignment
Half Sovereign	Gold	4.0	19	↓

Obverse 1 Head 1, right; GEORGIUS III DEI GRATIA (date)
Reverse 1 Crowned shield; BRITANNIARUM REX FID DEF
Edge milled

Obv. 1   Rev. 1

No.	Date	Features	Obv.	Rev.	F	VF	EF	UNC
G3HS-005	1817		1	1	75	120	200	420
G3HS-010	1817	PROOF	1	1				2000
G3HS-015	1818		1	1	80	130	220	500
G3HS-020	1818	latter 8 over 7	1	1	120	200	300	600
G3HS-025	1818	PROOF	1	1				5000
G3HS-030	1820		1	1	75	120	200	420

George IV (1820 – 1830)

The George IV half sovereign occurs with two different obverse portraits and three different reverses. The first reverse was struck only in 1821, and depicts an ornate garnished shield. This coin is seldom found in any condition, and was withdrawn because of its similarity to the sixpence. The laureate head on the obverse of this coin was retained when the new reverse was introduced in 1823. In 1826 both the obverse and reverse were redesigned following the king's displeasure with his portrait, and proof specimens of the new type of half sovereign were included in the 1826 proof sets.

The first obverse was designed by Pistrucci and the second by William Wyon. The reverses were by Johann Baptiste Merlen. The reverse of the 1821 coin includes the initials WWP (for William Wellesley Pole, the Master of the Mint) hidden in the centres of the three shamrock leaves. Both obverses use the same dies as used for the sixpence.

Denomination	Metal	Weight (grams)	Diameter (mm)	Rev. alignment
Half Sovereign	Gold	4.0	19	↓

Obverse 1 Head 1, left; GEORGIUS IIII D G BRITANNIAR REX F D
Obverse 2 Head 2, left; GEORGIUS IV DEI GRATIA (date)
Reverse 1 Crowned shield garnished with rose, shamrock, thistle; ANNO 1821
Reverse 2 A square topped shield, ungarnished except at foot; ANNO (date)
Reverse 3 Somewhat different shield, lightly garnished; BRITANNIARUM REX FID DEF
Edge milled

Obv. 1   Obv. 2

Rev. 1   Rev. 2   Rev. 3

No.	Date	Features	Obv.	Rev.	F	VF	EF	UNC
G4HS-005	1821		1	1	200	450	1200	1700
G4HS-010	1821	PROOF	1	1				2500
G4HS-015	1823		1	2	100	250	500	750
G4HS-020	1823	PROOF	1	2				3500
G4HS-025	1824		1	2	100	250	500	700
G4HS-030	1825		1	2	90	220	450	650
G4HS-035	1825	PROOF [1]	1	2				2000
G4HS-040	1825	PROOF; edge plain	1	2				2000
G4HS-045	1826		2	3	100	240	480	650
G4HS-050	1826	PROOF [2]	2	3				1100
G4HS-055	1827		2	3	110	200	350	550
G4HS-060	1828	[3]	2	3	110	200	350	550

1. Head very slightly different; possibly a pattern.
2. Issued in cased proof sets.
3. Some possibly struck in 1829.

William IV (1830 – 1837)

The half sovereign is arguably the most interesting of the denominations of this short reign. It begins with a plain edge proof issue of 1831 on a flan somewhat smaller than used hitherto. It was intended to distinguish the piece from the sixpence and it is possible that the diameter of 18mm was chosen so that the obverse dies could be prepared from the same master tools used for the Maundy fourpence. After a regular issue in 1834 on a similar flan, the diameter of the flan was increased from 1835 onwards to the 19mm used in previous reigns. The smaller coin was not well received and some of the 1834 issue was recoined in 1835 into pieces of normal size. Varieties of the last two dates, 1836 and 1837, are known which have different obverses, apparently taken from the dies for the sixpence. This may have been the result of an error.

The obverse of the series was engraved by William Wyon from a design by Sir Francis Chantrey. The reverses were designed and engraved by Johann Baptiste Merlen.

Collecting Hints

Isolated examples of the 1831 proof issue are difficult to obtain, although they occasionally turn up, sometimes heavily scuffed. The ordinary issue coins should be sought in at least fine to very fine condition. The reverse is very slightly convex and tends to wear in the centre even when the obverse is still fine or better.

Denomination	Metal	Weight (grams)	Diameter (mm)	Rev. alignment
Half Sovereign 1831–34	Gold	4.0	18	↓
Half Sovereign 1835–37	Gold	4.0	19	↓

Obverse 1   Head 1; GULIELMUS IIII D G BRITANNIAR REX F D

Obverse 2   Similar but struck on larger flan. The Head is the same size as on Obverse 1

Obverse 3   Similar but head slightly larger and lettering orientation slightly different (from a sixpence die)

Reverse 1   Crowned and garnished shield; below: ANNO (date)

Reverse 2   Similar but struck on larger flan. Very slightly different design from Reverse 1

Edge   milled

Obv. 1   Obv. 3   Rev. 1

No.	Date	Features	Obv.	Rev.	F	VF	EF	UNC
W4HS-005	1831	PROOF; edge plain [1]	1	1				1400
W4HS-008	1831	PROOF; edge milled [2]	1	1				3000
W4HS-010	1834		1	1	100	150	450	650
W4HS-015	1835		2	1	90	150	450	650
W4HS-020	1836		2	2	100	200	500	750
W4HS-025	1836		3	2	700	1400	2500	4000
W4HS-030	1837		2	2	100	175	450	700
W4HS-035	1837		3	2	700	1400	2500	4000

1. Issued in cased proof sets.
2. Probably unique.

Victoria   (1837 – 1901)

The Victorian half sovereign was a much-used coin, and in general received even more circulation wear than the sovereign. It was minted almost every year of the reign, but specimens in extremely fine condition are difficult to find. This applies especially in the case of the young head coins bearing the Australian mintmarks. As with the sovereign, the series is not extensively collected by date, and no doubt unrecorded varieties occur.

The young head of Victoria was designed by William Wyon, the jubilee head by Sir Joseph Edgar Boehm and the old head by Sir Thomas Brock. The shield reverse was slightly modified from the

design for William IV by Johann Baptiste Merlen. The later St George and dragon reverses were based on the old Pistrucci design, but the initials BP do not appear. How the egotistical Italian, who spelt his name in full on the 1818 crown, would have hated that!

Collecting Hints

A specimen of each type in very fine or extremely fine condition will be acceptable to most collectors. Forgeries are not so much of a problem as they are with sovereigns.

Denomination	Metal	Weight (grams)	Diameter (mm)	Rev. alignment
Half Sovereign Obv.1–3	Gold	4.0	19	↓
Half Sovereign Obv.4–6	Gold	4.0	19	↑

Obverse 1   Head 1, left;. VICTORIA DEI GRATIA (date)

Obverse 2   Head 2, left, left-hand fillet is narrower; same legend (date)

Obverse 3   Head 3, left in slightly lower relief; truncation slightly different; same legend (date)

Obverse 4   Head 4, left, 'Jubilee' type; VICTORIA DEI GRATIA; initials JEB on truncation

Obverse 5   Similar but no JEB on truncation

Obverse 6   Head 5, left, veiled; VICTORIA DEI GRA BRITT REGINA FID DEF IND IMP

Reverse 1   Crowned and garnished shield; BRITANNIARUM REGINA FID DEF. Some coins have die number below wreath (see listings)

Reverse 2   Similar but redesigned; the crown is very different (Imperial); same legend (date)

Reverse 3   St George and dragon; (date) in exergue

Edge   milled

Obv. 1   Obv. 4   Obv. 6

Rev. 1   Rev. 2   Rev. 3

Young Head

No.	Date	Features	Obv.	Rev.	F	VF	EF	UNC
VYHS-005	1838		1	1	80	120	250	450
VYHS-010	1839	PROOF; edge plain [1]	1	1				1400
VYHS-015	1839	PROOF; edge plain; rev.↑	1	1				1400
VYHS-020	1839	PROOF in silver; edge plain	1	1				1500
VYHS-025	1841		1	1	85	130	270	420
VYHS-030	1842		1	1	70	90	180	300
VYHS-035	1843		1	1	85	130	270	420
VYHS-040	1844		1	1	75	100	200	350
VYHS-045	1845		1	1	120	200	600	1200
VYHS-050	1846		1	1	75	100	200	350
VYHS-055	1847		1	1	80	120	250	400
VYHS-060	1848		1	1	75	100	200	400
VYHS-065	1848	latter 8 over 7	1	1	100	140	270	450
VYHS-070	1849		1	1	70	90	170	300
VYHS-075	1850		1	1	85	125	450	800
VYHS-080	1851		1	1	65	80	140	240
VYHS-085	1852		1	1	75	100	200	320

No.	Date	Features	Obv.	Rev.	F	VF	EF	UNC
VYHS-090	1853		1	1	75	100	200	320
VYHS-095	1853	PROOF [1]	1	1				2500
VYHS-100	1854		1	1	1200			
VYHS-105	1855		1	1	70	90	170	240
VYHS-110	1856		1	1	70	90	170	240
VYHS-115	1857		1	1	75	95	180	260
VYHS-120	1858	[2]	1	1	70	90	170	240
VYHS-125	1859	[3]	1	1	70	90	170	240
VYHS-130	1860		1	1	70	90	170	240
VYHS-135	1861		1	1	70	90	170	240
VYHS-140	1862		1	1	200	500	1750	3500
VYHS-145	1863	no die number below wreath (rev.)	1	1	70	90	170	240
VYHS-150	1863	die number below wreath (rev.)	1	1	80	110	190	280
VYHS-155	1864	die number below wreath (rev.)	1	1	65	85	150	200
VYHS-160	1865	die number below wreath (rev.)	1	1	65	85	150	200
VYHS-165	1866	die number below wreath (rev.)	1	1	65	85	150	200
VYHS-170	1867	die number below wreath (rev.)	1	1	65	85	150	200
VYHS-175	1869	die number below wreath (rev.)	1	1	65	85	150	200
VYHS-180	1870	die number below wreath (rev.)	1	1	65	85	150	200
VYHS-185	1871	die number below wreath (rev.) [4]	1	1	65	85	150	200
VYHS-188	1871	die number below wreath (rev.); both sides have coarse border teeth [8]	1	1	200	400	600	1000
VYHS-190	1871	PROOF; die number below wreath (rev.) [5]	1	1				3000
VYHS-195	1871	PROOF; edge plain die number below wreath (rev.) [5]	1	1				3500
VYHS-200	1872	die number below wreath (rev.) [6]	1	1	65	80	140	180
VYHS-205	1873	die number below wreath (rev.)	1	1	65	80	140	180
VYHS-210	1874	die number below wreath (rev.)	1	1	65	80	140	180
VYHS-215	1875	die number below wreath (rev.)	1	1	65	80	140	180
VYHS-220	1876	die number below wreath (rev.)	1	1	65	80	140	180
VYHS-225	1876	die number below wreath (rev.)	2	1	65	80	140	180
VYHS-230	1877	die number below wreath (rev.)	1	1	65	80	130	170
VYHS-232	1877	PROOF; die number below wreath (rev.)	1	1				3500
VYHS-235	1877	die number below wreath (rev.)	2	1	65	80	130	170
VYHS-240	1878	die number below wreath (rev.)	2	1	65	80	130	170
VYHS-245	1878	PROOF; die number below wreath (rev.)	2	1				4500
VYHS-250	1879	die number below wreath (rev.)	2	1	65	80	150	200
VYHS-255	1880	die number below wreath (rev.)	2	1	65	80	130	170
VYHS-260	1880	die number below wreath (rev.)	3	1	65	80	130	170
VYHS-265	1880	no die number below wreath (rev.) [7]	3	1	65	80	130	170
VYHS-270	1880	PROOF; no die number below wreath (rev.)	3	1				2500
VYHS-275	1883		3	1	65	75	120	160
VYHS-280	1884		3	1	65	75	120	160
VYHS-285	1885		3	1	65	75	120	160
VYHS-290	1886	PROOF	3	1				2500
VYHS-292	1887	PROOF	3	1				4000

1. Issued in cased proof sets.
2. Minor obverse lettering orientation differences introduced during this year.
3. Date slightly larger than previous years.
4. Minor obverse orientation differences occur.
5. Usually die number 1?
6. Minor obverse and reverse differences introduced.
7. Minor reverse differences introduced.

No.	Date	Features	Obv.	Rev.	F	VF	EF	UNC
8. Usually or always die number 10.								

Jubilee Head

No.	Date	Features	Obv.	Rev.	F	VF	EF	UNC
VJHS-295	1887	[1]	4	2	50	60	75	90
VJHS-300	1887	PROOF [2]	4	2				400
VJHS-305	1887		5	2	120	300	800	
VJHS-315	1890		4	2	250			
VJHS-320	1890		5	2	50	60	80	100
VJHS-325	1891		5	2	50	60	85	110
VJHS-330	1892		5	2	50	60	85	110
VJHS-335	1893		5	2	60	80	110	150

1. Size of JEB on truncation varies (obv.).
2. Issued in cased proof sets.

Old Head

No.	Date	Features	Obv.	Rev.	F	VF	EF	UNC
VOHS-340	1893		6	3	50	60	80	100
VOHS-345	1893	PROOF [1]	6	3				450
VOHS-350	1894		6	3	50	60	80	100
VOHS-355	1895		6	3	50	60	80	100
VOHS-360	1896		6	3	50	60	80	100
VOHS-365	1897		6	3	50	60	80	100
VOHS-370	1898		6	3	50	60	80	100
VOHS-375	1899		6	3	50	60	80	100
VOHS-380	1900		6	3	50	60	80	100
VOHS-385	1901		6	3	50	60	80	100

1. Issued in cased proof sets.

Commonwealth Mints
Mintmarks
M: Melbourne, Australia (opened June 1872)
P: Perth, Australia (opened June 1899)
S: Sydney, Australia (opened May 1855)

Position of Mintmarks
Reverse 1   Below shield
Reverse 2   Below shield
Reverse 3   On ground line above centre of date

Young Head

No.	Date	Features	mm	Obv.	Rev.	F	VF	EF	UNC
VYHS-390	1871		S	1	1	75	150	700	1400
VYHS-395	1871	PROOF	S	1	1				3000
VYHS-400	1872	[1]	S	1	1	85	180	750	1500
VYHS-405	1873		M	1	1	85	180	800	1700
VYHS-410	1875		S	1	1	85	170	750	1500
VYHS-415	1877		M	2	1	85	170	800	1700
VYHS-420	1879		S	2	1	85	180	750	1500
VYHS-425	1880		S	3	1	85	180	900	2000
VYHS-430	1880	PROOF	S	3	1				6000
VYHS-435	1881		M	3	1	120	280	1300	2500
VYHS-440	1881	PROOF	M	3	1				4000
VYHS-445	1881		S	3	1	120	250	1300	2500
VYHS-450	1882		M	2	1	85	170	800	1700
VYHS-455	1882		M	3	1	85	170	600	900
VYHS-460	1882		S	3	1	120	400	2000	4000
VYHS-465	1883		S	3	1	85	170	750	1500
VYHS-470	1883	PROOF	S	3	1				3000
VYHS-475	1884		M	3	1	120	320	1200	2500
VYHS-480	1884	PROOF	M	3	1				4000
VYHS-485	1885		M	3	1	140	500	2500	5000
VYHS-490	1886		M	3	1	80	250	1200	3000
VYHS-495	1886	PROOF	M	3	1				3000
VYHS-500	1886		S	3	1	85	170	800	1700
VYHS-505	1887		M	3	1	130	500	2500	5000
VYHS-510	1887		S	3	1	80	200	800	2000

No.	Date	Features	mm	Obv.	Rev.	F	VF	EF	UNC
VYHS-515	1887	PROOF	S	3	1				2500

1. Minor differences on obverse and reverse.

Jubilee Head

No.	Date	Features	mm	Obv.	Rev.	F	VF	EF	UNC
VJHS-520	1887		M	4	2	100	140	250	700
VJHS-525	1887	PROOF	M	4	2				3000
VJHS-530	1887		S	4	2	90	160	400	700
VJHS-535	1887	PROOF	S	4	2				3000
VJHS-540	1889		S	5	2	90	150	250	1000
VJHS-545	1891		S	5	2	100	180	400	700
VJHS-550	1891	PROOF	S	5	2				3000
VJHS-555	1893		M	5	2	110	200	550	800
VJHS-560	1893	PROOF	M	5	2				3000

Old Head

No.	Date	Features	mm	Obv.	Rev.	F	VF	EF	UNC
VOHS-565	1893		M	6	3	800			
VOHS-570	1893	PROOF	M	6	3				5000
VOHS-575	1893		S	6	3	60	90	180	250
VOHS-580	1893	PROOF	S	6	3				2500
VOHS-585	1896		M	6	3	65	100	300	700
VOHS-590	1896	PROOF	M	6	3				2500
VOHS-595	1897		S	6	3	60	90	180	250
VOHS-600	1899		M	6	3	60	90	250	800
VOHS-605	1899	PROOF	M	6	3				2500
VOHS-610	1899	PROOF [1]	P	6	3				
VOHS-615	1900		M	6	3	60	90	180	250
VOHS-620	1900	PROOF	M	6	3				5000
VOHS-625	1900		P	6	3	100	300	600	1800
VOHS-630	1900		S	6	3	70	95	200	500
VOHS-635	1901	PROOF	P	6	3				5000

1. Authenticity in question.

Edward VII   (1901 – 1910)

Half sovereigns were struck at the London mint for each year of the reign, and at the three Australian mints for some of the years. Unlike the sovereign, the half sovereign was not struck at the Ottawa mint. Matt proof half sovereigns were struck in 1902 at the London mint for inclusion in the proof sets.

The portrait of Edward VII was by George William de Saulles (1862–1903); the reverse retains the Pistrucci St George and dragon.

Collecting Hints

Choice extremely fine or better specimens are scarce.

Denomination	Metal	Weight (grams)	Diameter (mm)	Rev. alignment
Half Sovereign	Gold	4.0	19	↑

Obverse 1   Head 1, right; EDWARDVS VII D G BRITT OMN REX F D IND IMP

Reverse 1   St George and dragon; (date) in exergue; no BP in exergue

Reverse 2   Similar but with BP (initials of designer) in exergue and other minor differences

Edge   milled

Obv. 1

Rev. 1

No.	Date	Features		Obv.	Rev.	VF	EF	UNC
E7HS-005	1902			1	1	50	65	80
E7HS-010	1902	matt PROOF [1]		1	1			95
E7HS-015	1903			1	1	50	65	80
E7HS-020	1904			1	1	50	65	80
E7HS-025	1904			1	2	50	65	80
E7HS-030	1905			1	2	50	65	80
E7HS-035	1906			1	2	50	65	80
E7HS-040	1906	matt PROOF		1	2			2500
E7HS-045	1907			1	2	50	65	80
E7HS-050	1908			1	2	50	65	80
E7HS-055	1909			1	2	50	65	80
E7HS-060	1910			1	2	50	65	80

1. Issued in cased proof sets.

Commonwealth Mints

Mintmarks
M: Melbourne, Australia
P: Perth, Australia
S: Sydney, Australia

Position of Mintmarks
On ground line above centre of date

No.	Date	Features	mm	Obv.	Rev.	VF	EF	UNC
E7HS-065	1902		S	1	1	70	150	250
E7HS-070	1902	matt PROOF	S	1	1			2500
E7HS-075	1903		S	1	1	70	140	230
E7HS-080	1904		P	1	1	250	600	1200
E7HS-085	1904		P	1	2	250	600	1200
E7HS-090	1906		M	1	2	70	150	240
E7HS-095	1906		S	1	2	70	140	220
E7HS-100	1907		M	1	2	70	150	250
E7HS-105	1908		M	1	2	70	150	250
E7HS-110	1908		P	1	2	250	600	1200
E7HS-115	1908		S	1	2	70	140	220
E7HS-120	1909		M	1	2	70	150	240
E7HS-125	1909		P	1	2	200	500	900
E7HS-130	1910		S	1	2	70	130	200

George V   (1910 – 1936)

The half sovereign series of George V is not as extensive as the sovereign series. Proofs were struck in 1911 for the cased set, and ordinary coins for each year up to 1915, but no further London mint half sovereigns were minted during this reign.

Commonwealth mint sovereigns were struck during a number of years. These included the 1923 Pretoria mint proof pieces which formed part of the cased proof set of that year.

The obverse portrait of George V was designed by Sir Bertram Mackennal (1863–1931). The reverse continued to use the Pistrucci St George and dragon design.

Collecting Hints

The George V half sovereign is easier to find in extremely fine or better condition than those of previous reigns. In particular the Australian mint coins occur in quantities in top condition.

Denomination	Metal	Weight (grams)	Diameter (mm)	Rev. alignment
Half Sovereign	Gold	4.0	19	↑

Obverse 1   Head 1, left; GEORGIVS V D G BRITT OMN REX F D IND IMP

Reverse 1   St George and dragon, (date) in exergue

Edge   milled

Obv. 1　　　　　　　　Rev. 1

Obv. 1　　　　　　　　Rev. 1

No.	Date	Features		Obv.	Rev.	VF	EF	UNC
G5HS-005	1911			1	1	50	55	65
G5HS-010	1911	PROOF [1]		1	1			180
G5HS-015	1912			1	1	50	55	65
G5HS-020	1913			1	1	50	55	65
G5HS-025	1914			1	1	50	55	65
G5HS-030	1915			1	1	50	55	65

1. Issued in cased proof sets.

No.	Date	Features		Obv.	Rev.	VF	EF	FDC
G6HS-005	1937	PROOF [1]		1	1	100	150	200

1. Issued in cased proof sets.

Commonwealth Mints

Mintmarks

M: Melbourne, Australia
P: Perth, Australia
S: Sydney, Australia
SA: Pretoria, South Africa

Position of Mintmarks

On ground line above centre of date

No.	Date	Features	mm	Obv.	Rev.	VF	EF	UNC
G5HS-035	1911		P	1	1	55	70	80
G5HS-040	1911		S	1	1	55	70	80
G5HS-045	1911	PROOF	S	1	1			2500
G5HS-050	1912		S	1	1	55	70	80
G5HS-055	1914		S	1	1	55	70	80
G5HS-060	1915		M	1	1	55	75	90
G5HS-065	1915		P	1	1	55	70	80
G5HS-070	1915		S	1	1	50	55	65
G5HS-075	1916		S	1	1	50	55	65
G5HS-080	1918		P	1	1	200	300	500
G5HS-085	1919	[1]	P	1	1			
G5HS-090	1920	[1]	P	1	1			
G5HS-095	1923	PROOF [2]	SA	1	1			250
G5HS-100	1925		SA	1	1	50	60	70
G5HS-105	1926		SA	1	1	50	60	70

1. Struck but not circulated.
2. Issued in cased proof sets of South Africa.

George VI (1937 – 1952)

The only George VI half sovereigns struck were the proofs included in the cased proof sets of 1937. These sets contained four coins, each of which comprised the only British coin of that denomination for the reign.

The obverse portrait was by Thomas Humphrey Paget, the reverse again being the Pistrucci St George and dragon.

Denomination	Metal	Weight (grams)	Diameter (mm)	Rev. alignment
Half Sovereign	Gold	4.0	19	↑

Obverse 1　Head 1, left; GEORGIVS VI D G BR OMN REX F D IND IMP

Reverse 1　St George and dragon, 1937 in exergue

Edge　plain

Elizabeth II (1952 –)

No gold coins were included in the proof sets of 1953 issued for the coronation, and the only British half sovereigns struck in that year were a small number struck in order to provide continuity of the series. These were not released. The coins bore the obverse portrait of Elizabeth II by Mary Gillick, and the Pistrucci St George and dragon reverse.

There was no issue of half sovereigns corresponding to the pre-decimal sovereign issue of 1957–68. After decimalization, the denomination was struck for most years from 1980 onwards as a cased proof, and in 1982 as a non-proof coin.

The first head of the monarch was designed by Arnold Machin and the second head by Raphael David Maklouf. The reverse continues the Pistrucci St George and dragon design.

Denomination	Metal	Weight (grams)	Diameter (mm)	Rev. alignment
Half Sovereign	Gold	4.0	19	↑

Obverse 1　Head 1, right; ELIZABETH II DEI GRA BRITT OMN REGINA F D

Obverse 2　Head 2, right; ELIZABETH II DEI GRATIA REGINA F D

Obverse 3　Head 3, right; ELIZABETH II DEI GRA REG F D

Obverse 4　Queen facing on throne, holding orb and sceptre; ELIZABETH II DEI GRA REG FID DEF *(for the 500th anniversary of the gold sovereign)*

Obverse 5　Head 4, right; ELIZABETH II DEI GRA REGINA FID DEF

Reverse 1　St George and dragon, (date) in exergue

Reverse 2　Crowned shield within double rose; ANNIVERSARY OF THE GOLD SOVEREIGN 1489–1989

Edge　milled

Obv. 1　　　　Obv. 2　　　　Obv. 3

Obv. 4

Obv. 5

Rev. 1

Rev. 2

No.	Date	Features	Obv.	Rev.	UNC
EZHS-005	1953	PROOF or pattern	1	1	20000
EZHS-010	1980	PROOF [1]	2	1	55
EZHS-015	1982		2	1	BV
EZHS-020	1982	PROOF [1]	2	1	55
EZHS-025	1983	PROOF [1]	2	1	55
EZHS-030	1984	PROOF [1]	2	1	55
EZHS-035	1985	PROOF [1]	3	1	65
EZHS-040	1986	PROOF [1]	3	1	65
EZHS-045	1987	PROOF [1]	3	1	65
EZHS-050	1988	PROOF [1]	3	1	65
EZHS-055	1989	PROOF [1]	4	2	95
EZHS-060	1990	PROOF [1]	3	1	70
EZHS-065	1991	PROOF [1]	3	1	70
EZHS-070	1992	PROOF [1]	3	1	70
EZHS-075	1993	PROOF [1]	3	1	70
EZHS-080	1994	PROOF [1]	3	1	75
EZHS-085	1995	PROOF [1]	3	1	75
EZHS-090	1996	PROOF [1]	3	1	75
EZHS-095	1997	PROOF [1]	3	1	75
EZHS-100	1998	PROOF [1]	5	1	75
EZHS-105	1999	PROOF [1]	5	1	75

1. Issued cased and in cased proof sets.

Third Guinea

George III (1760 – 1820)

The third guinea is unique amongst the gold coinage in being the only denomination struck entirely within a single reign. At its inception in 1797, the financial situation at the Bank of England was precarious. The stocks of gold were very low, and banknotes were given legal tender status. In order to help pay its dividends, an issue of what were at that time known as 'seven shilling pieces' was made, with the odd amounts of each dividend being made up in silver. The issue was authorised in October, 1797, with an initial order of £315,000 face value.

The denomination was struck almost every year until 1813. From 1800 to 1811 only half guineas and third guineas were issued. In 1801, the king relinquished his claim to the French throne, and the reverse legend was altered to reflect this.

The first type of third guinea was designed and engraved by Lewis Pingo. The portrait of the king is somewhat curious and is by no means the designer's best work. In 1804, Lewis Pingo engraved a very different bust after a design by Nathaniel Marchant. This is similar to that seen on the Military Guinea of 1813, and is Nathaniel Marchant's first work on the coinage. Both reverses were the work of Lewis Pingo.

Collecting Hints

Specimens in very fine to extremely fine condition are needed to show this coin to its full advantage. Always check for mount marks on the edge.

Denomination	Metal	Weight (grams)	Diameter (mm)	Rev. alignment
Third Guinea	Gold	2.8	17	↑

Obverse 1 Head 1, right; GEORGIVS III DEI GRATIA

Obverse 2 Head 2, right; same legend

Reverse 1 Crown; MAG BRI FR ET HIB REX (date)

Reverse 2 Crown (slightly different), with date immediately below; FIDEI DEFENSOR BRITANNIARUM REX with cross at top of legend

Reverse 3 Similar but a mullet at top of legend

Edge milled

Obv. 1	Obv. 2	Rev. 1	Rev. 3

No.	Date	Features	Obv.	Rev.	F	VF	EF
G3TG-005	1797		1	1	65	95	150
G3TG-010	1798		1	1	65	95	150
G3TG-015	1799		1	1	75	110	200
G3TG-020	1800		1	1	65	95	150
G3TG-025	1801		1	2	65	95	150
G3TG-030	1802		1	2	65	95	150
G3TG-035	1803		1	2	65	95	150
G3TG-038	1803	broken 0 in date and in DEFENSOR (rev)	1	2	65	95	150
G3TG-040	1804		2	3	65	95	150
G3TG-042	1804	PROOF; edge plain [1]	2	3			3000
G3TG-045	1806		2	3	65	95	150
G3TG-050	1808		2	3	65	95	150
G3TG-055	1809		2	3	65	95	150
G3TG-060	1810		2	3	65	95	150
G3TG-065	1811		2	3	150	350	800
G3TG-070	1813		2	3	100	200	400
G3TG-075	1813	PROOF	2	3			1500

1. Weight 3.1. grams.

Quarter Guinea

George I (1714 – 1727)

At the beginning of the reign of George I the price of silver had risen considerably, resulting in much of the silver coinage being melted down. Consequently, relatively few silver coins were struck. Sir Isaac Newton, in a minute dated 21 September 1717, blamed an overvaluation of the guinea at 21 shillings and sixpence, and a Proclamation of 20 December of that year lowered its value to 21 shillings. In 1718 it was thought appropriate to strike a new gold denomination equal to a quarter of a guinea to provide a useful coin approximating in value to the crown piece. The coin had to be proportionate in weight to the other gold coins. What was not realised at the time was that a coin of such small size would prove unpopular and impractical in use. 37,380 pieces were struck, but many were put aside as keepsakes, and of those which entered circulation a considerable number were lost. Leake, writing at the time, complained that the coins were 'too diminutive for use'. The coin was discontinued after the 1718 issue, and in the following few years there was a slightly increased output of guineas and half guineas.

Despite the small size of the quarter guinea, the coin took the form of a scaled-down version of the guinea and half guinea, with all of the intricate detail on the shields and with the long German titles of the king being retained. The coin is an attractive piece nevertheless, even though some magnification is needed to examine it properly. It was the work of Croker and/or J. R. Ochs, senior.

Collecting Hints

Because many of the coins were kept as keepsakes when first issued, the quarter guinea is not difficult to find in the higher grades. A specimen in very fine to extremely fine condition is adequate for most purposes.

It is not generally known that there are two slightly different busts on this series. On one, there is a line running down the forehead of the king, and this coin is often catalogued as having a scratch on the bust. Consequently, it may be possible to pick up such a piece at auction or elsewhere at a reduced price. Specimens in fine condition or thereabouts must be examined carefully for mount marks on the edge. Crimped specimens are not uncommon.

Denomination	Metal	Weight (grams)	Diameter (mm)	Rev. alignment
Quarter guinea	Gold	2.1	16	↓

Obverse 1 Head 1, right; GEORGIVS D G M BR FR ET HIB REX F D

Obverse 2 Head 2, right, similar but with line running down forehead parallel to profile line

Reverse 1 Four crowned cruciform shields between which are four sceptres; central Star of the Order of the Garter; BRVN ET L DVX S R I A TH ET PR EL 1718

Edge milled diagonally

Obv. 1

Rev. 1

Obv. 1   Obv. 2

No.	Date	Obv.	Rev.	F	VF	EF
G1QG-005	1718	1	1	65	120	200
G1QG-010	1718	2	1	65	120	200

George III (1760 – 1820)

When George III came to the throne, the price of silver had again risen dramatically. No silver coins were minted for several years, with the exception of the few 'Northumberland' shillings struck, and crown pieces had become very scarce. Despite the unpopularity of the gold quarter guinea during the reign of George I, it was again considered necessary to produce this denomination to fill the gap between the low denomination silver and the larger gold coins. Unfortunately, the coin met the same fate as its predecessor, and was struck for only one year, 1762.

The quarter guinea was mainly the work of Richard Yeo, who designed and engraved the obverse. The reverse was engraved by him based on the Tanner designs for the George II gold coinage.

Collecting Hints

As with the George I coin, this piece is not difficult to find in high grade. Low grade specimens often have mount marks, and creased specimens are even more prevalent than with the George I coin.

Denomination	Metal	Weight (grams)	Diameter (mm)	Rev. alignment
Quarter Guinea	Gold	2.1	16	↓

Obverse 1 Head 1, right; GEORGIVS III DEI GRATIA

Reverse 1 Crowned shield; M B F ET H REX F D B ET L D S R I A T ET E; 1762 divided by crown

Edge milled diagonally

Obv. 1

Rev. 1

No.	Date	Obv.	Rev.	F	VF	EF
G3QG-005	1762	1	1	65	120	200

Re-melting old silver coins returned from Bank of England

Crown

Oliver Cromwell (Commonwealth 1649 – 1660)

The 1658 crown of Oliver Cromwell was the first of the struck portrait crowns. Although sometimes considered to be technically a pattern, it deserves a place in any catalogue of regular coinage as the coins obviously entered circulation. It must be remembered that this was at a time when it was estimated that the united weekly earnings of a man, his wife and two children was ten shillings (two crowns).

The crown was designed by Thomas Simon (also called Symonds) with technical assistance from Peter Blondeau, and portrays Cromwell as a Roman Emperor, draped and laureate.

Collecting Hints

The most noticeable feature of the Cromwell crown is often the die flaw across the lower half of the obverse. The flaw is always present to some degree, but coins with only a trace of flaw command somewhat higher prices. Some collectors like to acquire an example with the flaw markedly formed.

The 'Tanner's Copy' was struck in the 18th century, and is outside the scope of this book.

Denomination	Metal	Weight (grams)	Diameter (mm)	Rev. alignment
Crown	Silver	30.0	40–41	↓

Obverse 1   Head 1, left; OLIVAR D G R P ANG SCO HIB &c PRO
Reverse 1   Crowned shield; PAX QVAERITVR BELLO 1658
Edge   (in relief): HAS NISI PERITVRVS MIHI ADIMAT NEMO

Obv. 1   Rev. 1

No.	Date	Features	Obv.	Rev.	F	VF	EF
OCCR-005	1658	8 over 7	1	1	850	1600	2700
OCCR-010	1658	struck in gold; 8 over 7 [1]	1	1			75000

1. Die flaw prominent; weight 46 or 50 grams; 2 known.

Charles II   (1660 – 1685)

An issue of Charles II hammered crowns was authorised, but never produced. The crowns of 1662 thus became the first coins struck for circulation of the new milled, or machine struck, coinage. This took its place alongside the earlier hammered coinage still in circulation, although a Proclamation in September 1661 had demonetised the Commonwealth coinage from November

1661, later postponed to March 1662 (1661 old style Calendar). The contract for Chief Engraver was won by John (aka Jan) Roettier (1631–c.1703), a native of Antwerp, in a hard-fought contest against Thomas Simon (1618–65).

Crowns of Charles II are relatively plentiful in very good and even in fine condition, but considerably scarcer in very fine or better. The earlier dates are particularly attractive in the higher grades. It is possible that the reason why so many crowns were struck was the payment by Louis XIV to the British in 1662 to purchase the town of Dunkirk. This payment was in the form of 1.5 million silver ecus, which may have been recoined into crowns.

The crowns of 1662 and 1663 are slightly larger in diameter than those of 1664 and later. The weight, however, remained constant, and the post–1663 coins must, therefore, have been struck on a slightly thicker flan. The rose below the head on many of the 1662 coins indicates silver from the West of England mines. 1662 crowns were struck from 6 February and in March 1663 (new style Calendar), which under the old style was still 1662. They were made current by a Proclamation of 27 March 1663.

The scarcity of the issues of 1665 and, to a lesser extent, 1666 is due probably to the ravages of the Great Plague and the Fire of London. The elephant occasionally encountered below the head of the 1666 coin (and the elephant and castle below some issues of 1680 and 1681) denote silver from the Africa Company in Guinea. The most commonly found Charles II crown is the third head type, with its somewhat unattractive flat appearance, giving the illusion that the coin is more worn than it actually is.

With the advent of the milled coinage, the practice arose of marking the edge of the larger denominations with an inscription in raised lettering which included the year of the reign, referred to in this catalogue as the 'regnal date'. Thus, for example, the first year of the reign is regnal date 1, the second is regnal date 2, and so on. It is interesting to note that the monarch's regnal date in the case of Charles II is calculated from the death of Charles I in 1649 rather than from the beginning of the reign of Charles II.

The reason for and the method of application of the edge inscription is of interest. Filing and clipping of coinage to acquire silver had become endemic in the years of hammered coins. It was considered that an edge inscription (or milling on the smaller coins) would render these activities more detectable and also serve as a deterrent. The wording of the edge inscription 'Decus et Tutamen' was said by Leake, writing in 1726, to have been suggested by Mr. Evelyn, based on a vignette of Cardinal de Richelieu's Greek Testament, printed at the Louvre, Paris. The French began to mark their ecus with edge lettering shortly after the first British issue of lettered crowns.

The edge inscription was not, as is commonly thought, applied to the finished struck coinage. However, in later years the striking of the two sides and the edge may have been effected simultaneously. In the earlier years the blanks were first cut out from metal which had been rolled into strips using horse power. These blanks were then sent to have the edges impressed by a secret process devised by one Pierre Blondeau, an ex-engineer from the Paris mint, who jealously guarded his methods. The blanks were then returned to the Mint to have their obverses and reverses struck in a hand-operated press.

A long and detailed description of rolling, cutting and striking of blanks is contained in Pepys's Diary for 19 May 1663.

Very large numbers of Charles II crowns were minted, and collectors will recognise the relative scarcity of other denominations in comparison. It seems strange that such a large quantity of high denomination coins should be minted until one remembers that much low denomination hammered coinage was still in circulation. In addition, the gold crown was now discontinued, and the crown had to bridge the gap between the halfcrown and the guinea until the first half guineas were minted in 1669.

Obv. 3   Obv. 3 elephant below

Obv. 4   Obv. 5

Rev. 1   Rev. 2

Collecting Hints

A collection of one specimen of each date in fine condition will produce an attractive set of this underpriced series.
For the more sophisticated collector, an upgrading to very fine and/or inclusion of several varieties will give an outstanding and enviable collection.
For the truly serious numismatist, a collection in extremely fine or of a grade as close as possible to extremely fine as possible (one for each major type) is probably all that can be hoped for; lack of buying opportunity and funds will normally prohibit the inclusion of many different dates or minor varieties from a collection in these grades. As with almost all Charles II coinage, the price of specimens rises steeply with each increase in grade.

Denomination	Metal	Weight (grams)	Diameter (mm)	Rev. alignment
Crown 1662–63	Silver	29.8–30.1	40	↓
Crown 1664–69	Silver	29.8–30.1	38	↓
Crown 1670–84	Silver	29.8–30.1	39	↓

But note exceptions below.

Obverse 1   Head 1, right, rose below; CAROLVS II DEI GRA.

Obverse 2   Head 1 with minor alterations, right, no rose; CAROLVS II DEI GRATIA

Obverse 3   Head 2, smaller than Head 1, right; same legend

Obverse 4   Head 3, right; larger, with flat appearance in higher grades; same legend

Obverse 5   Head 4, right; largest head with longer tie; same legend

Reverse 1   Four cruciform shields, top and bottom two quartered (England/France), interlinked pairs of 'C's in angles. MAG BR FRA ET HIB REX (date)

Reverse 2   Similar but shields of England and France separated and not quartered; crowns and harp slightly different

Edge   (in relief): Usually DECVS ET TVTAMEN ANNO REGNI (regnal date) but may vary as in tables below. From 1663 to 1666 the regnal date is in Roman numerals; from 1667 onwards it is in words, except for the rare 1667 numeral edge variety C2CRM-120

Obv. 1   Obv. 2

No.	Date	Features	Edge date	Obv.	Rev.	F	VF	EF
C2CRM-005	1662	[1]		1	1	70	400	1800
C2CRM-010	1662	PROOF [2]		1	1			6000
C2CRM-015	1662	rev. ↑ [2]		1	1	75	500	2000
C2CRM-020	1662	[3]	1662	1	1	80	600	2200
C2CRM-025	1662	[1]		2	1	80	600	2200
C2CRM-030	1662	rev. ↑ [2]		2	1	85	650	2300
C2CRM-035	1662	PROOF; edge plain		2	1			8000
C2CRM-037	1662	PROOF [2]		2	1			10000
C2CRM-038	1662	PROOF [4]		2	1			10000
C2CRM-040	1662	[3]	1662	2	1	85	650	2300
C2CRM-045	1663	[5]	XV	2	2	70	400	1800
C2CRM-050	1663	no stops rev.	XV	2	2	80	400	2000
C2CRM-055	1663	[6]		2	2	500		
C2CRM-060	1663	PROOF [7]	XV	2	2			7000
C2CRM-065	1663	PROOF in gold [8]	XV	2	2			40000
C2CRM-070	1664	[9]	XVI	3	2	70	250	1300
C2CRM-075	1664	PROOF	XVI	3	2			7000
C2CRM-080	1665		XVI	3	2	500		
C2CRM-085	1665		XVII	3	2	250	1500	
C2CRM-090	1665	5 over 4	XVII	3	2	250	1500	
C2CRM-095	1666		XVIII	3	2	120	900	
C2CRM-100	1666	ANN instead of ANNO (edge)	XVIII	3	2	150	1200	
C2CRM-105	1666	RE.X instead of REX (rev.)	XVIII	3	2	200	1500	
C2CRM-110	1666	elephant below head	XVIII	3	2	300	1500	
C2CRM-115	1666	elephant below head reads RE.X on rev.	XVIII	3	2	400	1200	
C2CRM-120	1667		XVIII	3	2	1500		
C2CRM-125	1667	[10]	DECIMO NONO	3	2	85	350	1700
C2CRM-130	1668		VICESIMO	3	2	75	300	1500

No.	Date	Features	Edge date	Obv.	Rev.	F	VF	EF
C2CRM-135	1668	DECVS ET TVTAMEN inverted relative to rest of inscription (edge)	VICESIMO	3	2	350	1500	
C2CRM-138	1668	8 over 5	VICESIMO	3	2	120	600	
C2CRM-140	1668	8 over 7	VICESIMO	3	2	85	450	1700
C2CRM-145	1669		VICESIMO PRIMO	3	2	300	1700	
C2CRM-150	1669	9 over 8	VICESIMO PRIMO	3	2	300	1700	
C2CRM-152	1669	REGN instead of REGNI; ICESIMO instead of VICESIMO (edge)	VICESIMO PRIMO	3	2	600		
C2CRM-155	1670		VICESIMO SECVNDO	3	2	85	350	1700
C2CRM-160	1670	70 over 69	VICESIMO SECVNDO	3	2	100	600	
C2CRM-165	1671	11	VICESIMO TERTIO	3	2	75	250	1500
C2CRM-170	1671	T of ET over R (rev.)	VICESIMO TERTIO	3	2	100	500	
C2CRM-175	1671	ET over FR or BR (rev.)	VICESIMO TERTIO	3	2	140	700	
C2CRM-180	1671		VICESIMO TERTIO	4	2	75	250	1500
C2CRM-185	1671	21	VICESIMO QVARTO	4	2	700	2000	
C2CRM-190	1672	9	VICESIMO QVARTO	4	2	75	250	1500
C2CRM-195	1673		VICESIMO QVARTO	4	2	700	2000	
C2CRM-200	1673	12	VICESIMO QVINTO	4	2	75	250	1500
C2CRM-205	1673	3 over 2 12	VICESIMO QVINTO	4	2	85	350	1700
C2CRM-210	1674	13	VICESIMO SEXTO	4	2	8000		
C2CRM-215	1675		VICESIMO SEPTIMO	4	2	400		
C2CRM-220	1675	EGNI instead of REGNI (edge)	VICESIMO SEPTIMO	4	2	500		
C2CRM-225	1675	5 over 3 14	VICESIMO SEPTIMO	4	2	300		
C2CRM-230	1676		VICESIMO OCTAVO	4	2	75	220	1300
C2CRM-235	1676	EGNI instead of REGNI (edge)	VICESIMO OCTAVO	4	2	85	300	1600
C2CRM-240	1677	15	VICESIMO NONO	4	2	75	250	1500
C2CRM-245	1677	7 over 6 16	VICESIMO NONO	4	2	95	350	1800
C2CRM-250	1678	8 over 7 17	TRICESIMO	4	2	160	900	
C2CRM-255	1679		TRICESIMO PRIMO	4	2	75	220	1300
C2CRM-260	1679		TRICESIMO PRIMO	5	2	85	350	1700
C2CRM-265	1679	reads HIBR.EX (rev.)	TRICESIMO PRIMO	5	2	85	400	1800
C2CRM-270	1680		TRICESIMO SECVNDO	4	2	85	350	1700
C2CRM-275	1680	80 over 79	TRICESIMO SECVNDO	4	2	80	300	1500
C2CRM-280	1680		TRICESIMO SECVNDO	5	2	65	250	1500
C2CRM-285	1680	80 over 79	TRICESIMO SECVNDO	5	2	85	300	1600
C2CRM-290	1681		TRICESIMO TERTIO	5	2	85	300	1600
C2CRM-295	1681	elephant and castle below head	TRICESIMO TERTIO	5	2	1200	5000	
C2CRM-300	1682	18	TRICESIMO QVARTO	5	2	120	600	2200
C2CRM-305	1682	2 over 1	TRICESIMO QVARTO	5	2	85	400	1800
C2CRM-310	1682	QVARTO appears to read QVRRTO (edge) 19	TRICESIMO QVRRTO	5	2	95	500	2000

No.	Date	Features	Edge date	Obv.	Rev.	F	VF	EF
C2CRM-315	1682	2 over 1; QVARTO appears to read QVRRTO (edge) 19	TRICESIMO QVRRTO	5	2	100	600	2400
C2CRM-320	1683	20	TRICESIMO QVINTO	5	2	140	1000	
C2CRM-325	1684		TRICESIMO SEXTO	5	2	95	500	

1. Edge reads DECVS ET TVTAMEN; minor varieties exist.
2. Edge reads DECVS ET TVTAMEN.
3. Edge reads DECVS ET TVTAMEN 1662; minor stop and other varieties exist.
4. Edge reads DECVS ET TVTAMEN 1662.
5. Some have the crowns and harp of Rev. 1.
6. No edge date.
7. Some or all have the crowns and harp of Rev. 1.
8. Has the crowns and harp of Rev. 1; weight c.60 grams.
9. Minor obverse varieties exist.
10. Edge stop varieties exist.
11. Occurs with and without stop after HIB (rev.).
12. Minor stop varieties exist.
13. Possibly only one or two exist.
14. Harp alignment varies (rev.).
15. Alignment of latter 7 in date varies.
16. Some have die flaw above head resembling a boar's head.
17. 8 probably always over 7.
18. Coin without overdate rarer.
19. Edge probably QVARTO over TERTIO.
20. Rarer than denoted in some catalogues.
21. Wyndham Boundy has suggested that this may be the result of a trial for a new edge on an edgeless 1671 crown.

The number of harp strings varies through this series. It is possible that the variation constituted a form of internal code denoting the die number.

James II   (1685 – 1688)

John Roettier continued as chief engraver during the reign of James II. The short and eventful reign of James II was marked by a brief series of coinage spanning just three dates, with no rare varieties and no proofs or patterns.

Collecting Hints

Assembling a set of James II crowns in fine condition, either by date and variety or by type, should present only moderate difficulty; however, some of the varieties are quite rare in very fine or better. Many of the crowns of this series are weakly struck, especially at the top of the wreath on the obverse and at the date. Consequently, very fine specimens may appear to be in a lower grade than they actually are. Adjustment marks are often seen on James II crowns. These marks appear similar to scratches, and were caused by filing the coins before issue to ensure that the weight was correct.

Denomination	Metal	Weight (grams)	Diameter (mm)	Rev. alignment
Crown	Silver	29.8–30.2	38–39	↓

Obverse 1 Head 1, left; IACOBVS II DEI GRATIA

Obverse 2 Head 2, left; smaller, with shorter tie; same legend

Reverse 1 Four cruciform shields; MAG BR FRA ET HIB REX (date)

Edge (in relief): DECVS ET TVTAMEN ANNO REGNI (regnal date)

Obv. 1

Obv. 2

Rev. 1

Denomination	Metal	Weight (grams)	Diameter (mm)	Rev. alignment
Crown	Silver	29.6–30.0	38–39	↓

Obverse 1   Heads 1, right; GVLIELMVS ET MARIA DEI GRATIA

Reverse 1   Four cruciform shields around lion of Orange-Nassau. MAG BR FR ET HI REX ET REGINA. Monogrammed 'WM' and one digit of date in each angle.

Edge   (in relief): DECVS ET TVTAMEN ANNO REGNI (regnal date)

Obv. 1

Rev. 1

No.	Date	Features	Edge date	Obv.	Rev.	F	VF	EF
J2CR-005	1686		SECVNDO	1	1	90	400	2000
J2CR-010	1686	no stops on obv. [1]	SECVNDO	1	1	110	700	5000
J2CR-015	1687	[2]	TERTIO	2	1	80	300	800
J2CR-020	1687	struck on 41mm diameter flan	TERTIO	2	1	110	450	1100
J2CR-025	1688		QVARTO	2	1	90	400	1000
J2CR-030	1688	A in IACOBVS and latter A in GRATIA unbarred	QVARTO	2	1	100	500	1200
J2CR-035	1688	8 over 7	QVARTO	2	1	100	500	1200

1. Rare in very fine or better.
2. Edge lettering size varieties exist.

No.	Date	Features	Edge date	Obv.	Rev.	F	VF	EF
WMCR-005	1691		TERTIO	1	1	250	600	2000
WMCR-010	1691	TERTTIO instead of TERTIO (edge)	TERTTIO	1	1	300	700	2400
WMCR-015	1692		QVARTO	1	1	250	600	2000
WMCR-020	1692	2 over inverted 2 [1]	QVARTO	1	1	400	1000	3000
WMCR-025	1692	2 over inverted 2	QVINTO	1	1	300	700	2200

1. Rarer than denoted in most catalogues.

The number of harp strings varies through this series. It is possible that the variation constituted a form of internal code denoting the die number.

The number of harp strings varies through this series. It is possible that the variation constituted a form of internal code denoting the die number.

William & Mary   (1688 – 1694)

Following the removal of James II, his daughter Mary and her husband Prince William of Orange ruled jointly by agreement. Their heads were placed in conjoined fashion on the coinage, with William's head uppermost. This classical style owed much to Greek and Roman coinage, as previous hammered coinage depicting joint rulers was normally designed showing them face to face.

Crowns were not struck until the latter part of the brief reign of William and Mary. Only one type of crown was issued, with no patterns or proofs. The design was unusual in a number of respects: the conjoined heads of a dual monarchy; the central lion of Orange-Nassau on the reverse, and the placement of the date around its four quarters. The happy coincidence of 'W' and 'M' resembling each other when inverted gave rise to the attractive lattice design in the angles of the reverse, and the letters fit so neatly that it is quite possible to collect the coins for years without realising the significance of the lattices.

The William and Mary crown was probably designed by James Roettier aided by his brother Norbert.

William III   (1695 – 1701)

The short reign of William III, following Mary's death from smallpox in 1694, produced one of the most interesting series of crowns to be minted. The early dies were engraved by James Roettier and, following Roettier's dismissal for smuggling, by John Croker (1670–1740 old style). They include probably the most frequently encountered 17th century crown and also some of the rarest dates and varieties.

Unlike the minor silver coinage, the crowns of William III were not minted at the provincial mints, and thus did not suffer the many spelling and orientation errors which were prolific on the provincial mint coins. The only major spelling error encountered on the crown is the 1696 issue with GEI instead of DEI on the obverse.

Collecting Hints

Whether collecting by date or by type, this series presents a formidable challenge. The stumbling block is the 1697, which is needed whether collecting by date or by type, and which is notoriously difficult to obtain in nice condition. There are a number of minor edge errors which are worth looking out for, and the obverse of any 1696 crown should always be checked for the GEI error.

An attempt should be made to acquire all of the major varieties in fine or better condition. One of the scarcer dates, 1700, is possibly more plentiful in very fine or better condition than in fine, as a hoard was found several years ago. Anyone able to assemble a set including all of the major dates and varieties in very fine grade can be justifiably proud of such an achievement.

Denomination	Metal	Weight (grams)	Diameter (mm)	Rev. alignment
Crown	Silver	29.4–30.0	38–39	↓

Obverse 1 Head 1, curved breastplate, right; GVLIELMVS III DEI GRA

Obverse 2 Head 2, right; straight breastplate, hair at top more profuse. Same legend.

Obverse 3 Head 3, right; very similar but die re-engraved, tie of finer design.

Reverse 1 Four cruciform shields, the top of each of which is convex, i.e. points outwards in the centre. Harp with top of left side higher than right. MAG BR FRA ET HIB REX (date)

Reverse 2 Similar but redesigned harp with left and right sides of similar height; shields larger, with centre of top concave, i.e. pointing inwards; central cartouche and lion smaller

Reverse 3 Similar but a different harp

Edge (in relief): DECVS ET TVTAMEN ANNO REGNI (regnal date)

Obv. 1   Obv. 2

Obv. 3   Rev. 1

Rev. 2   Rev. 3

No.	Date	Features	Edge date	Obv.	Rev.	F	VF	EF
W3CR-005	1695		SEPTIMO	1	1	60	180	700
W3CR-010	1695		OCTAVO	1	1	50	150	600
W3CR-015	1695	[1]	OCAVO	1	1	70	250	1000
W3CR-020	1695	PROOF; edge plain [2]		1	1			3500
W3CR-025	1696		OCTAVO	1	1	60	170	600
W3CR-030	1696	NNO instead of ANNO (edge)	OCTAVO	1	1	80	250	950
W3CR-035	1696	[1]	OCAVO	1	1	80	250	950
W3CR-040	1696	PROOF; edge plain [3]		1	1			6000
W3CR-045	1696	PROOF; edge plain; rev. ↑ [3]		1	1			6000
W3CR-050	1696	6 over 5	OCTAVO	1	1	100	300	1200
W3CR-055	1696	6 over 9 or inverted 6	OCTAVO	1	1	100	300	1200
W3CR-060	1696	no stops in obv. legend	OCTAVO	1	1	90	250	1000
W3CR-065	1696	G of GRA over D (obv.)	OCTAVO	1	1	80	250	950
W3CR-070	1696	GEI instead of DEI (obv.) [4]	OCTAVO	1	1	120	2000	
W3CR-072	1696	GEI instead of DEI (obv.); G of GRA over F (obv.) [4]	OCTAVO	1	1	160	2500	
W3CR-075	1696	[5]	OCTAVO	2	1	90	300	1000
W3CR-080	1696	no stops in rev. legend	OCTAVO	2	1	120	350	1400
W3CR-085	1696	edge lettering blundered	OCTOCTAVO OCTAVTAVO or similar	2	1	120	500	2000
W3CR-090	1696		TRICESIMO	2	1	1000		
W3CR-095	1697	[6]	NONO	2	2	400	2000	
W3CR-100	1700	[7]	DVODECIMO	3	3	100	150	500
W3CR-105	1700		DECIMO TERTIO	3	3	150	250	1000
W3CR-110	1700	D over inverted D in DECIMO (edge)	DECIMO TERTIO	3	3	180	300	1200

1. Edge date misspelt.
2. Border teeth wider; reverse ↓ as ordinary issue; may have die flaws.
3. Reverse differs slightly from usual Rev. 1.
4. Extremely rare above fine condition.
5. Reverse stops vary.
6. May not exist in EF+.
7. Possibly most plentiful date in VF+ grade.

The number of harp strings varies through this series. It is possible that the variation constituted a form of internal code denoting the die number.

Anne (1702 – 1714)

For the coinage of Anne, John Croker, together with his assistant Samuel Bull (d. 1726), produced a portrait of the queen based on a painting by Sir Godfrey Kneller.

This series includes a number of notable 'firsts'. Provenance marks (marks showing the origin of the metal) used for the first time are: VIGO for silver obtained by Sir George Rooke from Spanish galleons at Vigo Bay in 1702; plumes (in the angles on the reverse) for silver from Wales and also from Derbyshire; roses and plumes (also in the reverse angles) for silver from the 'Company for smelting down lead with Pitcoale and Seacoale'. Stephen

Martin Leake, writing at the time, comments that roses and plumes coins were referred to as 'Quaker's Money', because Quakers were considered prominent amongst the owners of the mines. E below the head of Anne indicates that the coins were struck at Edinburgh.

After the Union of England and Scotland in 1707, the top and bottom shields on the reverse were each divided into the arms of England and Scotland. Before the Union the arms of England and Scotland had been allocated separate shields.

Obv. 3

Rev. 1   Rev. 2

Collecting Hints

With the possible exception of 1705, a serious collector will attempt to obtain a specimen of each main date or type in very fine or better condition. The 1703 and 1713 are actually easier to find in very fine than are the otherwise more plentiful dates such as 1707 and 1708. However, the overall date scarcity of 1703 and 1713 still makes them more expensive than 1707 and 1708. All dates are rare in UNC condition.

Adjustment marks continue to be a problem with crowns of this period. Further care must also be taken because Anne crowns are sometimes found with traces of brooch mounting on the reverse. The marks often coincide with the position of the crowns above the shields, and can be easily missed if one is not careful. Care must also be taken that hairlines have not been re-engraved.

Before Union of England and Scotland

No.	Date	Features	Edge date	Obv.	Rev.	F	VF	EF
ANCR-005	1703	VIGO below head [1]	TERTIO	1	1	150	400	1200
ANCR-010	1705	plumes on rev.	QVINTO	1	1	220	600	2000
ANCR-015	1706	roses and plumes on rev. [2]	QVINTO	1	1	140	450	1400
ANCR-020	1707	roses and plumes on rev.	SEXTO	1	1	110	350	1000

1. Reverse is struck in lower relief than later pieces; flan sometimes slightly larger than most other dates.
2. Flan often slightly larger than most other dates.

Denomination	Metal	Weight (grams)	Diameter (mm)	Rev. alignment
Crown	Silver	29.9–30.3	38–40	↓

Obverse 1   Head 1, left; ANNA DEI GRATIA

Obverse 2   Head 2, slightly larger, left; same legend

Obverse 3   Head 3, older, left; hair re-engraved and more detailed; same legend

Reverse 1   Four undivided cruciform shields around central lion of the Garter; MAG BR FRA ET HIB REG (date). Usually known as the 'Before Union' reverse

Reverse 2   Similar but shields are wider and the top and bottom are each divided into the arms of England and Scotland. BR FRA of legend now becomes BRI FR. Known as 'After Union' reverse.

Edge   (in relief): DECVS ET TVTAMEN ANNO REGNI (regnal date)

After Union of England and Scotland

No.	Date	Features	Edge date	Obv.	Rev.	F	VF	EF
ANCR-025	1707	E below head	SEXTO	2	2	90	300	900
ANCR-030	1707	E below head	SEPTIMO	2	2	1500		
ANCR-035	1707		SEPTIMO	2	2	100	350	1000
ANCR-040	1708		SEPTIMO	2	2	150	500	1300
ANCR-045	1708	plumes on rev.	SEPTIMO	2	2	110	400	1100
ANCR-055	1708	E below head	SEPTIMO	2	2	100	350	950
ANCR-060	1708	8 over 7 E below head	SEPTIMO	2	2	110	400	1100
ANCR-065	1713	roses and plumes on rev.	DVODECIMO	3	2	110	300	900
ANCR-070	1713	roses and plumes on rev.	DVODECIM (error)	3	2	120	400	1000

The number of harp strings varies through this series. It is possible that the variation constituted a form of internal code denoting the die number.

George I (1714 – 1727)

John Croker and a Swiss engraver, Johann Rudolf Ochs (b. 1673), appear to have been responsible for engraving the dies for this series, which continues the general overall design of earlier series, with some modifications.

With the accession of George Louis, Elector of Hanover, as King George I, the crown was redesigned to include the Hanoverian

Obv. 1   Obv. 2

line. The German titles of the king appear in the reverse legend, while one of the reverse shields now contain the arms of Brunswick-Lüneburg.

The title of FIDEI DEFENSOR (Defender of the Faith), often shortened to FID DEF, or in this case F.D., appears for the first time.

Provenance marks of this series are: roses and plumes (in the angles on the reverse) for silver from the 'Company for smelting down lead with Pitcoale and Seacoale', and SSC in the reverse angles, denoting silver from the South Sea Company.

There are no pattern or proof crowns of George I.

No.	Date	Features	Edge date	Obv.	Rev.	F	VF	EF
G1CR-040	1726	roses and plumes on rev.; each N on edge inverted (top left of N has no serif) [3]	DECIMO TERTIO	1	1	320	700	1700

1. Edge reads QUINTO, not QVINTO as in some catalogues.
2. Roses and plumes are slightly smaller than on previous dates.
3. A similar variety occurs on the 1726 five guineas.

The number of harp strings varies through this series. It is possible that the variation constituted a form of internal code denoting the die number.

George II (1727 – 1760)

The crowns of George II are of two distinct types, those bearing the young head designed by Croker and those depicting the old head designed by Tanner (d. 1775), who had come to England from Germany in 1728, and who succeeded Croker as Chief Engraver after the latter's death in 1740. Although there are ten different dates, all crowns of George II are scarce, and particularly so in the high grades.

Provenance marks seen for the first time are: roses (without plumes), denoting silver from mines in the West of England; and LIMA below the head, for coins struck from silver captured by Admiral Anson during his voyages around the world. The use of the term LIMA has not been satisfactorily explained, and the Proclamation of 11 December 1745 authorizing the mark does nothing to clarify the matter. Presumably it is possible that the mark was meant to duplicate the mintmark on some of the captured silver coinage. It may, therefore, be wrong to call it a provenance mark.

It was noted towards the end of the 18th century that George II crowns 'disappeared as soon as coined, and, indeed, are too burdensome for common use, two halfcrowns better answering the purpose'. Snelling too, in 1766 noted that 'it is but very seldom a crown piece is to be seen'.

Collecting Hints

George I crowns are scarce in any grade, but one should attempt to obtain a minimum standard of good fine. Choice very fine to extremely fine specimens with original toning are highly desirable and much sought after.
As with crowns of Anne, George I crowns should always be examined for traces of mounting before buying any coin. The reverse should be particularly examined closely.

Denomination	Metal	Weight (grams)	Diameter (mm)	Rev. alignment
Crown	Silver	30.0	38–39	↓

Obverse 1 Head 1, GEORGIVS D G M BR FR ET HIB REX F D

Reverse 1 Four cruciform shields. BRVN ET L DVX S R I A TH ET EL (date)

Edge (in relief): (1716 & 1726) DECVS ET TVTAMEN ANNO REGNI (regnal date)

(1718–23) DECUS ET TUTAMEN ANNO REGNI (regnal date)

Obv. 1   Rev. 1

No.	Date	Features	Edge date	Obv.	Rev.	F	VF	EF
G1CR-005	1716	roses and plumes on rev.	SECVNDO	1	1	220	450	1200
G1CR-010	1718	roses and plumes on rev. [1]	QUINTO	1	1	300	750	2000
G1CR-015	1718	8 over 6 roses and plumes on rev. [1]	QUINTO	1	1	270	600	1600
G1CR-020	1720	roses and plumes on rev.	SEXTO	1	1	300	750	2000
G1CR-025	1720	20 over 18 roses and plumes on rev.	SEXTO	1	1	270	600	1600
G1CR-030	1723	SSC on rev.	DECIMO	1	1	240	600	1500
G1CR-035	1726	roses and plumes on rev. [2]	DECIMO TERTIO	1	1	260	700	1600

Collecting Hints

The young head crowns (1732 to 1741) are struck in unusually high relief, with the result that strictly fine condition specimens have a great deal of detail missing, especially on the monarch's hair and on the eye; for this reason specimens in very fine or better grade should be acquired. Fine condition old head crowns have more of the original detail, but for standardisation of the set very fine specimens will usually be looked for.
The 1746 proof should be sought whenever one of these rarities becomes available; it differs from the 1746 currency crown in the important characteristic of having no LIMA mark below the head, as well as being the only piece bearing the edge year VICESIMO. It also has wider beading than the currency crowns.

Denomination	Metal	Weight (grams)	Diameter (mm)	Rev. alignment
Crown	Silver	29.5–30.0	38–39	↓

Obverse 1 Head 1, GEORGIVS II DEI GRATIA

Obverse 2 Head 2, older; same legend but GEORGIUS instead of GEORGIVS

Obverse 3 Head 2; same legend but GEORGIVS

Reverse 1 Four crowned cruciform shields. M B F ET H REX F D B ET L D S R I A T ET E (date)

Reverse 2 Similar but a different harp

Edge (in relief): DECVS ET TVTAMEN ANNO REGNI (regnal date)

Obv. 1   Obv. 3

Rev. 1   Rev. 2

Rev. 1   Rev. 2

No.	Date	Features	Edge date	Obv.	Rev.	F	VF	EF
G2CR-075	1750		VICESIMO QVARTO	3	2	350	550	1100
G2CR-080	1751	[4]	VICESIMO QVARTO	3	2	380	600	1300

1. Plain in reverse angles; reported by Folkes in 1763 to weigh 30.0 grams; possibly a pattern; existence unknown today.
2. Often struck on slightly ovoid flan.
3. No LIMA below head; wider beading and smaller edge lettering than on currency crowns.
4. Same regnal edge year as 1750 coin.

The number of harp strings varies through this series. It is possible that the variation constituted a form of internal code denoting the die number.

The reverse legend and date on the 1750 and 1751 coins are more finely formed than on previous dates.

George III (1760 – 1820)

The crown series of George III, using the term in its broadest sense, is extraordinary! For many years, hardly any silver coinage was produced, owing to an acute shortage of the metal. Although a profusion of shillings and sixpences was issued in 1787, it became apparent towards the end of the century that a new issue of crowns and halfcrowns was needed. A large number of captured Spanish American silver dollars (8 reales) was available, and, in fact, were being unofficially used as currency. It was therefore decided to countermark the obverse of each Spanish 8 reales with an oval stamp bearing the head of George III. The punch was the official one used at Goldsmith's Hall for marking silver, but the counterstamping itself was done at the mint. These countermarked dollars were issued in 1797 with a nominal value of 4 shillings and 9 pence. A few silver ecus of France and American dollars also appear to have been counterstamped at that time. A good deal of satirical comment was passed about the counterstamping of the Spanish coins, including the saying that the product depicted 'the head of a fool on the head of an ass', and 'two Kings' heads are not worth a crown', this last being a comment on the nominal value of 4 shillings and 9 pence. Records show that a total of 3,744,583 foreign silver dollars were countermarked.

It soon became apparent that a large quantity of coins bearing forged countermarks were in circulation. An alteration was therefore made to the shape and size of the counterstamp. This was changed to an octagonal form with a larger head of the king. Taken from a Maundy penny die, this too proved a target for forgers, and often the striking was too shallow. In 1804 it was decided that the Spanish dollars should be completely overstruck with new dies. These were made by Küchler at Matthew Boulton's Soho mint in Birmingham. It was to create a new issue, to be called 'Bank of England Dollars'. This issue includes a large number of die varieties and proofs, and carried the first depiction of Britannia on a silver coin. A further issue was made in 1810 and 1811, all of the coins still bearing the date 1804.

Curiously, the only issue of true crowns was struck during just the last three years of the long reign of George III, beginning in October 1818. This marked the beginning of the 'Great Recoinage of 1816' using new equipment in new premises at Tower Hill, London. The striking is of unusually fine quality. Although struck in fairly low relief, it is not uncommon for high grade specimens to be mistaken for proofs because of their mirror fields. The design by Benedetto Pistrucci (1784–1855) includes the first representation of St George and the dragon on a silver coin, a tradition that has continued on coinage to the present day. At the time, Pistrucci was living at Brunet's Hotel, Leicester Square, London, and St George is said to have been modelled on a waiter at the hotel.

Benedetto Pistrucci was a temperamental Italian gem-engraver who had found favour with William Wellesley Pole, the Master of the Mint. Some measure of his egotism can be determined by the placement of his name in full on both obverse and reverse of

No.	Date	Features	Edge date	Obv.	Rev.	F	VF	EF
G2CR-005	1731	[1]	(unknown)	1	1			
G2CR-010	1732	roses and plumes on rev. [2]	SEXTO	1	1	280	500	1100
G2CR-015	1732	roses and plumes on rev. PROOF; edge plain		1	1			3000
G2CR-020	1734	roses and plumes on rev. [2]	SEPTIMO	1	2	350	550	1200
G2CR-025	1734	roses and plumes on rev.; edge reads DEC...AME ...NNO REGNI [2]	SEPTIMO	1	2	450	800	
G2CR-030	1735	roses and plumes on rev. [2]	OCTAVO	1	2	300	500	1100
G2CR-035	1735	roses and plumes on rev.; each 'E' on edge is over a 'B' [2]	OCTAVO	1	2	400	650	1400
G2CR-040	1735	T of OCTAVO over V (edge) [2]	OCTAVO	1	2	400	650	1400
G2CR-045	1736	roses and plumes on rev.	NONO	1	2	280	500	1100
G2CR-050	1739	roses on rev.	DVO-DECIMO	1	2	270	480	1000
G2CR-055	1741	roses on rev.	DECIMO QVARTO	1	2	270	500	1100
G2CR-060	1743	roses on rev.	DECIMO SEPTIMO	2	2	270	480	1000
G2CR-065	1746	LIMA below head	DECIMO NONO	3	2	300	500	1100
G2CR-070	1746	PROOF [3]	VICESIMO	3	2			2000

the crown. Although he was considered by many to be a slow worker, he was very defensive about this reputation.

Collecting Hints

Almost all collectors of countermarked Spanish American dollars will collect one of each type of counterstamp combined with one of each mintmark of the original coin, i.e. Mexico City, Lima, etc. However, there is no reason at all why one should not collect also by date of the original coin, although it would be a formidable, yet fascinating task, not least because of its educational value.

It should be remembered that the grade of a countermarked coin is normally taken as the grade of the countermark, but obviously if the original coin is in superior condition the piece will be that much more desirable. Since the octagonal counterstamp was taken from the Maundy penny die, comparison with the penny provides a useful way of detecting the many coins bearing false octagonal counterstamps.

The most interesting characteristics of the series of Bank Dollars are the diverse die varieties of both obverse and reverse. The various combination of these produce a wide array of collectable material. The copper proofs are an integral part of the series and should not be ignored. This series was overstruck on Spanish American dollars, and sometimes one comes across a piece on which the original date on the underlying coin is visible. Even more interestingly, one can also occasionally encounter specimens on which the date on the underlying coin is after 1804. This clearly shows that the dollars were overstruck with the 1804 date for some years after that date.

Only in extremely fine or better condition can the quality of the excellent striking of the series of crowns of 1818 to 1820 be appreciated. The novice collector may understandably sometimes believe he has acquired a proof, owing to the high quality of the finish, but the true proofs are sharper, often with a steely blue hue around the main design.

Countermarked Dollar

Denomination	Metal	Weight (grams)	Diameter (mm)	Rev. alignment
Counterstamped Spanish/Sp American dollar	Silver	c.27	38–40	↑

Denomination	Metal	Weight (grams)	Diameter (mm)	Rev. alignment
Counterstamped French ecu or US dollar	Silver	27–30	c.40	as host coin

Oval Counterstamp

Obverse 1   George III head, right, in oval counterstamped on Mexico 8 reales obverse

Obverse 2   Similar but on Peru 8 reales

Obverse 3   Similar but on Bolivia 8 reales

Obverse 4   Similar but on Guatemala 8 reales

Obverse 5   Similar but on Chile 8 reales

Obverse 6   Similar but on Spain 8 reales

Obverse 7   Similar but on France ecu

Obverse 8   Similar but on American dollar

Octagonal Counterstamp

Obverse 9   George III head in octagon counterstamped on Mexico 8 reales obverse

Obverse 10   Similar but on Peru 8 reales

Obverse 11   Similar but on Bolivia 8 reales

Obverse 12   Similar but on Guatemala 8 reales

Obverse 13   Similar but on Spain 8 reales

Obverse 14   Similar but on France ecu

Obverse 15   Similar but on American dollar

Obverse 16   Similar but on Chile 8 reales

Reverse   As of the appropriate host coin, partially flattened where stamped

Edge   As of the appropriate host coin

Obv. oval counterstamp

Obv. octagonal counterstamp

Rev. 1

No.	Date	Obv.	Rev.	F	VF	EF
G3CR-005	none	1	1	90	160	300
G3CR-010	none	2	2	120	210	400
G3CR-015	none	3	3	150	250	550
G3CR-020	none	4	4	200	400	700
G3CR-025	none	5	5	300	600	1000
G3CR-030	none	6	6	300	600	1000
G3CR-035	none	7	7	500		
G3CR-040	none	8	8	3000		
G3CR-045	none	9	9	140	260	450
G3CR-050	none	10	10	350	700	
G3CR-055	none	11	11	200	400	700
G3CR-060	none	12	12	600	1200	
G3CR-065	none	13	13	600	1000	
G3CR-070	none	14	14	2500		
G3CR-075	none	15	15	2000		
G3CR-078	none	16	16	2000	3000	

Bank of England Dollar

Denomination	Metal	Weight (grams)	Diameter (mm)	Rev. alignment
Bank of England Dollar	Silver	25–28	41	↑

485

Obverse 1 Head 1, right; C.H.K.(with stops) on truncation. GEORGIUS III DEI GRATIA REX (stop after REX); top leaf points to left hand side of 'E'

Obverse 2 As obverse 1 but C.H.K reads CHK (no stops)

Obverse 3 As obverse 1 but leaf points to centre of 'E'

Obverse 4 As obverse 3 but no stop after REX

Obverse 5 As obverse 1 but leaf points to right hand side of 'E'

Reverse 1 Britannia seated, with shield, in oval garter, this inscribed FIVE SHILLINGS DOLLAR; BANK OF ENGLAND 1804 around rim. Small 'K' in relief below shield

Reverse 2 As Reverse 1 but 'K' is inverted (in relief)

Reverse 3 As Reverse 1 but 'K' is inverted and incuse

Edge plain or with faint patterning of squares

Obv. 1

Obv. 1 details

Obv. 3   Obv. 4   Obv. 5

Rev. 1

No.	Date	Features	Obv.	Rev.	F	VF	EF
G3CR-080	1804		1	1	75	130	300
G3CR-085	1804	PROOF	1	1			800
G3CR-090	1804	PROOF in copper	1	1			600
G3CR-100	1804		2	1	100	200	500
G3CR-105	1804	PROOF	2	1			950
G3CR-110	1804		3	1	100	200	500
G3CR-115	1804	PROOF	3	1			700
G3CR-120	1804	PROOF in silver gilt	3	1			1800
G3CR-125	1804	PROOF in copper	3	1			700

No.	Date	Features	Obv.	Rev.	F	VF	EF
G3CR-128	1804	PROOF in copper; reverse ↓	3	1			900
G3CR-130	1804		3	2	100	200	500
G3CR-135	1804	PROOF	3	2			800
G3CR-140	1804	PROOF in copper	3	2			700
G3CR-145	1804		3	3	100	200	500
G3CR-150	1804	PROOF in copper	3	3			900
G3CR-155	1804		4	1	85	150	350
G3CR-160	1804	PROOF	4	1			800
G3CR-162	1804	PROOF on thick flan; reverse ↓ [1]	4	1			1700
G3CR-165	1804	PROOF in copper; reverse ↓ [2]	4	1			700
G3CR-170	1804		5	1	150	300	700
G3CR-175	1804		5	2	120	240	600
G3CR-180	1804	PROOF	5	2			800
G3CR-182	1804	PROOF in gilt silver	5	2			1800
G3CR-185	1804	PROOF in copper	5	2			800
G3CR-190	1804		5	3	120	240	600
G3CR-195	1804	PROOF in copper	5	3			800

1. Weight 31.8 grams.
2. Flan thickness varies; weight can be up to 36 grams.

Crown

Denomination	Metal	Weight (grams)	Diameter (mm)	Rev. alignment
Crown	Silver	28.3	39	↓

Obverse 1 Head 1, right; GEORGIUS III D G BRITANNIARUM REX F D (date)

Reverse 1 St George and dragon within Garter. HONI SOIT QUI MAL Y PENSE

Edge (in relief): DECUS ET TUTAMEN ANNO REGNI (regnal date)

Obv. 1   Rev. 1

No.	Date	Features	Edge date	Obv.	Rev.	F	VF	EF	UNC
G3CR-200	1818		LVIII	1	1	20	60	250	450
G3CR-205	1818	PROOF	LVIII	1	1				1200
G3CR-210	1818	edge DECVS ANNO REGNI ET TVTAMEN [1]	LVIII	1	1	800	2000	4500	
G3CR-215	1818		LIX	1	1	20	60	250	450
G3CR-220	1819	[2]	LIX	1	1	20	60	250	450
G3CR-225	1819	9 over 8	LIX	1	1	25	90	400	700
G3CR-230	1819	no edge stops [2]	LIX	1	1	25	90	400	700
G3CR-235	1819	[3]	LX	1	1	20	70	280	500
G3CR-240	1819	PROOF	LX	1	1				1200
G3CR-245	1819	PROOF; edge plain; reverse ↑		1	1				5000
G3CR-250	1820	[4]	LX	1	1	20	60	250	450
G3CR-255	1820	20 over 19	LX	1	1	25	90	400	700
G3CR-260	1820	S of SOIT over T (rev.)	LX	1	1	25	80	300	500
G3CR-265	1820	PROOF	LX	1	1				1200

1. Error edge; wording transposed.
2. Variety occurs with garter slightly wider.
3. Occurs with and without stop after TVTAMEN (edge).
4. Occurs with and without stop after TVTAMEN (edge); this date continued to be minted after death of George III.

Currency coins of this series were struck almost to proof standard.

George IV (1820 – 1830)

Benedetto Pistrucci, the designer of the George III head, executed a laureate head of George IV for the crown, while on the reverse the St George and dragon were enlarged and the surrounding Garter and legend omitted. Although now considered by many a handsome piece, the king considered the portrait unflattering, and the 1826 proof coinage exhibited a new and younger portrait by William Wyon (1795–1851), based on a bust by Sir Francis Legatt Chantrey (1781–1842). The practice of depicting a king as a laureated Roman emperor was now coming to an end. The St George and dragon reverse was also discontinued in favour of an elaborate crowned shield design, although the use of Pistrucci's St George and dragon design was far from over.

The initials W.W.P. appear in tiny letters in the ground line to the left of the dragon on the reverse, and are those of William Wellesley Pole, Master of the Mint.

Collecting Hints

As with the crowns of George III, fine condition specimens do not allow one to appreciate the characteristic high quality of production of this series; an 'as struck' specimen of an 1821 or 1822 crown is a delight to the eye, especially if with an original tone. Look for signs of wear on St George reverses in the form of a whiteness on St George's head and breast, on the dragon's body, and down the central line of the sword. Beware of buying 1821 and 1822 crowns unseen from abroad, as fine condition specimens are often graded as VF by dealers who do not handle them frequently.

Proof 1826 crowns will normally be in high grade, and most collectors will require only perfect or near-perfect specimens.

Denomination	Metal	Weight (grams)	Diameter (mm)	Rev. alignment
Crown	Silver	28.3	39	↓

Obverse 1 Head 1, laureate, left; GEORGIUS IIII D G BRITANNIAR REX F D

Obverse 2 Head 2, so-called 'bare head', left; GEORGIUS IV DEI GRATIA 1826

Reverse 1 St George and dragon, date in exergue below. WWP (see above) in groundline

Reverse 2 Crowned garnished shield; BRITANNIARUM REX FID DEF; scroll below inscribed DIEU ET MON DROIT

Edge (in relief): DECUS ET TUTAMEN ANNO REGNI (regnal date). The edge lettering is smaller on the 1826 issue

Obv. 1   Obv. 2

Rev. 1   Rev. 2

No.	Date	Features	Edge date	Obv.	Rev.	F	VF	EF	UNC
G4CR-005	1821		SECUNDO	1	1	25	80	450	900
G4CR-010	1821	WWP initials inverted (rev.)	SECUNDO	1	1	50	150	750	1300
G4CR-015	1821	PROOF	SECUNDO	1	1				2000
G4CR-020	1821	PROOF in copper	SECUNDO	1	1				900
G4CR-025	1821	PROOF in copper; edge plain		1	1				900
G4CR-030	1821	PROOF [1]	TERTIO	1	1				4000
G4CR-035	1822		SECUNDO [2]	1	1	30	120	700	1200
G4CR-040	1822	PROOF	SECUNDO [2]	1	1				3500
G4CR-045	1822		TERTIO	1	1	28	100	600	1100
G4CR-050	1822	PROOF	TERTIO	1	1				2500
G4CR-055	1823	PROOF; edge plain; rev. ↑		1	1				30000
G4CR-060	1823	PROOF in white metal; edge plain		1	1				15000
G4CR-065	1825	PROOF or pattern; edge plain		2	2				5000
G4CR-070	1825	PROOF or pattern in Barton's metal; edge plain		2	2				3500
G4CR-075	1826	PROOF [3]	SEPTIMO	2	2		750	1800	3500
G4CR-080	1826	PROOF; edge plain [4]		2	2				5000
G4CR-085	1826	PROOF (?) [5]	LVIII	2	2				7000

1. Error edge; see comment below.
2. This edge issued only until 29 January.
3. Issued in cased proof sets.
4. Some may weigh below 28 grams.
5. Incuse edge lettering; possibly unique; see comment below.

The fact that the 1821 error edge crowns are all proofs possibly indicates that this coin is more in the nature of a pattern than a genuine error coin.

Barton's metal is a laminated product consisting of thin sheets of gold bonded to a copper base.

James Morton has pointed out that, although the 1826 proof crown with regnal year LVIII is usually described as having an error date of the previous reign, the edge closely resembles in style that of the young head Victorian crown. He suggests that the coin may have been struck as a trial piece for the Victorian edge collar (around 1840?) and that the use of George IV dies may have been fortuitous.

William IV (1830 – 1837)

One of the rarest issues, the series has an obverse by William Wyon and a reverse by Jean Baptiste Merlen and is highly prized by collectors. The crowns can perhaps be properly described either as patterns or proofs. Certainly the inclusion of the 1831 in the proof set of that year merits its inclusion in this section of the catalogue. In 1830, Wyon had received a letter from a potential benefactor: 'I should like to see a new crown in circulation, with the King's Arms in full, and elegantly done, instead of St George fighting naked! If you would engrave and exhibit next year ... I would put you down in my will for 500 pounds with the greatest pleasure.'

Denomination	Metal	Weight (grams)	Diameter (mm)	Rev. alignment
Crown	Silver	27.0–28.0	39	↓

Obverse 1 Head 1, right; GULIELMUS IIII D G BRITANNIAR REX F D; W W incuse on truncation of head

Obverse 2 Head 1, right; same legend; W WYON in relief on truncation

Reverse 1 Crowned shield on mantle; below: ANNO (date)

Edge (on 1832 only) DECUS ET TUTAMEN ANNO REGNI TERTIO (in raised lettering) divided by rose, shamrock, thistle, lion, all between two ornate raised borders

Obv. 1   Rev. 1

Obv. 1   Obv. 2

No.	Date	Features	Edge date	Obv.	Rev.	EF	FDC
W4CR-005	1831	PROOF; edge plain [1]		1	1	2500	4000
W4CR-010	1831	PROOF in gold; edge plain [2]		1	1		60000
W4CR-015	1831	PROOF; edge plain [3]		2	1	3800	5200
W4CR-020	1831	PROOF; edge plain; rev. ↑		2	1		7000
W4CR-022	1831	PROOF [4]	LVIII	2	1		
W4CR-025	1832	PROOF in lead [5]	TERTIO	1	1	4000	
W4CR-030	1834	PROOF; edge plain		1	1	9000	11000

1. Issued in cased proof sets.
2. Weight 39 to 41 grams, possibly made to correspond to 5 pound piece weight.
3. Reverse ↓ as stated above; see also W4CR-020.
4. Incuse edge lettering DECUS ET TUTAMEN ANNO REGNI LVIII; possibly unique; cf G4CR-085.
5. Weight 28.3 grams; minor reverse differences from usual Rev. 1; possibly only two exist.

Victoria (1837 – 1901)

The first crowns of Victoria were the plain edge proofs struck in 1839 for incorporation in the cased proof sets of that year. No currency crowns were struck at that time, but a slightly modified design was used to strike currency pieces in 1844, 1845 and 1847.

In 1847 there was issued one of the most famous and elegant coins ever struck, the Victorian 'Gothic' crown. Its design was a bold and daring departure from previous issues, and Victoria is reported to have been delighted with it. The reason for its issue remains a mystery, but possibly it was connected with the tenth anniversary of the accession. The lettering on both sides and on the edge is in superbly crafted Gothic script, with the date in Roman numerals. The queen is wearing a crown, not nowadays considered unusual on a coin, but at that time not seen on a British coin since the 17th century.

The Gothic crown was reissued in 1853 for inclusion in the cased proof set, and, apart from patterns, occurs only with these two dates. There is, however, something of a mystery resulting from Victorian numismatic literature. Many books refer to a crown dated 1851, usually of the young head type, whereas no such coin appears to exist. It seems that plagiarism without checking facts was rife in Victorian numismatic circles. Possibly the story emanated from a source who was unable to read Gothic numerals correctly! Another mystery is that several books of 1850–70 fail to mention the Gothic crown in the listings. Possibly the Gothic crown was considered a pseudo-medal? It certainly resembles a medal in some ways, although it must be remembered that it appears in the 1853 proof sets, presumably as a crown piece.

The 1879 crown is a curious piece. According to the Royal Mint, it appears to have been struck for exhibition and presentation purposes, with some being supplied to 'certain well-placed individuals'. Note also the existence of proofs of other denominations dated 1879.

The crowns of 1887 to 1892 were the first to be issued with a milled edge, and circulated widely. However, they were disliked because of the portrait of the Queen wearing a ridiculously small crown. The 1893 to 1900 issue was better received.

H. W. Henfrey wrote, puzzlingly, of the denomination in 1885: 'They were driven out of circulation by the bankers, who sent to the Mint for silver, and the employers who sent to their banks for silver, both of whom so constantly stipulated against taking five-shilling pieces that they remained in the hands of the Mint. Yet about £2000 worth of these coins are made every year to go to the Falkland Islands. There, the whalers, English, German, Swedes and Americans assemble to pass the winter in harbour, and amongst them the only accepted currency is the English five-shilling piece; for them, therefore, it is manufactured, and to the Falkland Islands it is sent. This noble coin, by far the handsomest in our country, is now no longer issued in this country, and will soon become as much a thing of the past as guineas'.

The young head and Gothic crown obverses were designed by William Wyon. The young head reverse was probably by Johann Baptiste Merlen, and the Gothic reverse was by William Dyce. With regard to the 1887 to 1900 issue, the reverses used the old Pistrucci St George and dragon design from the crowns of 1821 and 1822. The jubilee head obverse was by Sir Joseph Edgar Boehm and the veiled head by Sir Thomas Brock.

beautiful crown minted. It is not a rare coin but high international demand maintains its high price and ensures that it will in turn always be resaleable. Many forgeries exist; a genuine 1847 lettered edge coin will usually 'look' old and have sharp edge lettering in the higher grades. The 'V' of 'Victoria' will align approximately with 'et' on the edge and with 'tur' of 'tueatur' on the reverse. However, note that the alignment of the plain edge type is exactly opposite to this, i.e. at 180 degrees. In this case, of course, the 'et' on the edge will not be evident. This alignment check is also useful in determining whether a lettered edge type has had its edge lettering removed. Always carefully check the date and the edge in case the dealer or auction house has been careless – you may pick up a bargain, even an 1846 pattern! The Jubilee and Old Head series should be collected in at least extremely fine condition, preferably with each regnal date variety. When grading, attention should be paid to the sharpness of the edge lettering as well as that of the design.

Care must be taken in distinguishing the 1887 proof crown from the many early strikings of the ordinary coin. On the proof, the 'knife edge' of the milling is of the same width straight across, and is so sharp that it almost cuts the fingers; on an ordinary coin the indentations forming the milling have a slightly convex appearance.

Obv. 3 / Obv. 4 / Obv. 5 / Rev. 1 / Rev. 2 / Rev. 3

Denomination	Metal	Weight (grams)	Diameter (mm)	Rev. alignment
Crown 1839	Silver	28.1–28.3	39	↑
Crown 1844–53	Silver	28.3	39	↓
Crown 1887–1900	Silver	28.3	39	↑

Obverse 1 Head 1, left; VICTORIA DEI GRATIA with 'T' of Victoria level with tip of nose. Date below head

Obverse 2 Head 1, left; VICTORIA DEI GRATIA in larger lettering with 'O' of VICTORIA level with tip of nose. Date below head

Obverse 3 Head 2, 'Gothic' type, left; VICTORIA DEI GRATIA BRITANNIAR REG F D in Gothic script

Obverse 4 Head 3, 'Jubilee' type with small crown on head, left; VICTORIA D G BRITT REG F D

Obverse 5 Head 4, 'Old Head' type, left; VICTORIA DEI GRA BRITT REGINA FID DEF IND IMP

Reverse 1 Crowned shield within branches. BRITANNIARUM REGINA FID DEF

Reverse 2 'Gothic' type. Cruciform shields, TUEATUR UNITA DEUS ANNO DOM (date in numerals) in Gothic script

Reverse 3 St George and dragon, date in exergue below

Edge 1844–47, head 1: (incuse) DECUS ET TUTAMEN ANNO REGNI (regnal date).
1847–53, head 2, Gothic issue: (in relief): DECUS ET TUTAMEN ANNO REGNI (regnal date).
1887–92: milled.
1893–1900: (in relief): DECUS ET TUTAMEN ANNO REGNI (regnal date)

Obv. 1

Obv. 2

Young Head

No.	Date	Features	Edge date	Obv.	Rev.	F	VF	EF	UNC
VYCR-005	1839	PROOF; edge plain [1]		1	1			2000	3500
VYCR-010	1844	[2]	VIII	2	1	25	65	650	2200
VYCR-015	1844	edge inscription struck twice in different positions	VIII	2	1	100	400		
VYCR-020	1844	PROOF	VIII	2	1				8000
VYCR-025	1845	[2]	VIII	2	1	25	65	650	2200
VYCR-028	1845	4 in date has large upper serif	VIII	2	1	50	120	1000	
VYCR-030	1845	AANNO instead of ANNO (edge)	VIII	2	1	40	120		
VYCR-035	1845	PROOF	VIII	2	1				8000
VYCR-040	1845	PROOF; edge plain		2	1				10000
VYCR-045	1845	PROOF; edge plain; rev. ↑		2	1				10000
VYCR-050	1847		XI	2	1	28	100	1000	2500
VYCR-055	1847	edge milled [3]		2	1				15000

1. Issued in cased proof sets.
2. Type of edge stops vary; date numeral size varies on 1845.
3. Possibly struck around 1887.

'Gothic' issue

No.	Date	Features	Edge date	Obv.	Rev.	F	VF	EF	UNC
VGCR-060	1847	PROOF	UNDECIMO	3	2	270	400	800	1400
VGCR-065	1847	PROOF in fine silver; heavily frosted; rev. ↑ [1]	UNDECIMO	3	2				2000
VGCR-070	1847	PROOF; edge plain; rev. ↑ [2]		3	2	350	500	900	1700
VGCR-075	1847	PROOF, frosted [3]	UNDECIMO	3	2				2200
VGCR-080	1847	PROOF; edges chamfered; lettering weak; rev. ↑	UNDECIMO	3	2				2200
VGCR-085	1847	PROOF in gold; edge plain		3	2				100000
VGCR-090	1847	PROOF in white metal; edge plain		3	2				2800
VGCR-095	1847	PROOF; rev. ↑ [4]	DECIMO SEPTIMO	3	2				8000
VGCR-100	1853	PROOF [5]	DECIMO SEPTIMO	3	2			2500	4000
VGCR-105	1853	PROOF; edge plain		3	2				8000

1. Struck at a much later date as Mint visit presentation pieces.
2. May weigh below 28 grams; some or all may be struck in fine silver.
3. Sealed in glass for 1851 Exhibition; inscription is on outer silver surround.
4. Minted in 1853 or later with error date; weight 27.6 grams; probably unique; see comment below.
5. Issued in cased proof sets.

Young Head

No.	Date	Features	Edge date	Obv.	Rev.	F	VF	EF	UNC
VYCR-110	1879	PROOF; edge plain [1]		2	1				50000

1. Reverse ↑ as other 1879 proofs

Jubilee Head

No.	Date	Features	Edge date	Obv.	Rev.	F	VF	EF	UNC
VJCR-115	1887			4	3	14	20	40	80
VJCR-120	1887	PROOF [1]		4	3				500
VJCR-125	1888			4	3	26	50	120	200
VJCR-130	1888	narrow date [2]		4	3	18	35	80	140
VJCR-135	1889			4	3	12	20	50	110
VJCR-140	1890			4	3	14	25	60	150
VJCR-145	1891			4	3	14	30	70	180
VJCR-150	1892			4	3	14	40	90	200

1. Issued in proof sets.
2. Minor reverse differences from previous coin; streamer thicker.

Old Head

No.	Date	Features	Edge date	Obv.	Rev.	F	VF	EF	UNC
VOCR-155	1893		LVI	5	3	14	30	110	200
VOCR-160	1893	PROOF [1]	LVI	5	3				550
VOCR-165	1893		LVII	5	3	16	45	160	320
VOCR-170	1894	[2]	LVII	5	3	16	45	140	260
VOCR-175	1894	[2]	LVIII	5	3	16	45	140	260
VOCR-180	1895		LVIII	5	3	16	45	140	240
VOCR-185	1895		LIX	5	3	16	45	140	240
VOCR-190	1896		LIX	5	3	16	50	160	300
VOCR-195	1896		LX	5	3	16	45	140	240
VOCR-200	1897		LX	5	3	16	45	140	240
VOCR-205	1897		LXI	5	3	16	45	140	220
VOCR-210	1898	[3]	LXI	5	3	17	55	180	300
VOCR-215	1898	[3]	LXII	5	3	16	45	140	240
VOCR-220	1899		LXII	5	3	16	45	140	240
VOCR-225	1899		LXIII	5	3	16	45	140	240
VOCR-230	1900		LXIII	5	3	16	45	140	240
VOCR-235	1900		LXIV	5	3	16	45	140	240

1. Issued in cased proof sets.
2. A reverse slightly different from other dates.
3. Minor reverse differences exist.

The 1847 Gothic crown bearing the regnal edge date DECIMO

SEPTIMO (not SEPTIMO as sometimes recorded) is usually referred to as an error edge coin, This is a misdescription, barring the unlikely event that it was known in 1847 that the next issue was to be minted in 1853, the date corresponding to DECIMO SEPTIMO. It is thus listed as an error date, and was presumably struck in 1853, or possibly later. It might be more correctly termed an error reverse coin than an error edge.

Edward VII   (1901 – 1910)

The king's portrait on the one-year type crowns of Edward VII was designed by George William de Saulles (1862–1903), while the reverse retained the Pistrucci St George and dragon. An interesting comment on the engraver appears in *The Times* of 26 January 1902: 'Contrary to some unauthorised rumours, Mr. de Saulles is not a foreigner. He is an Englishman, born of English parents in Birmingham.'

Unlike on previous crowns, only one regnal date was used on the whole of the issue for the calendar year.

Collecting Hints

Mint state or near for the ordinary issue, and FDC for the matt proof are the minimum criteria to aim for. Condition is critical in the case of the proof, as the original matt surface is impaired with even a trace of wear. To the untrained eye, a slightly impaired coin can appear perfect, and a beginner should take any opportunity of inspecting a set of FDC matt proofs, if the occasion arises.

Denomination	Metal	Weight (grams)	Diameter (mm)	Rev. alignment
Crown	Silver	28.3	39	↑

Obverse 1   Head 1, right; EDWARDVS VII DEI GRA BRITT OMN REX FID DEF IND IMP

Reverse 1   St George and dragon, date in exergue below

Edge   (in relief): DECUS ET TUTAMEN ANNO REGNI II

Obv. 1   Rev. 1

No.	Date	Features	Obv.	Rev.	F	VF	EF	UNC
E7CR-005	1902		1	1	35	45	90	130
E7CR-010	1902	matt PROOF [1]	1	1			90	120

1. Issued in cased proof sets.

George V   (1910 – 1936)

Although George V reigned for over a quarter of a century, the issue of crowns spans only ten years. The absence of a crown in 1911 was a major omission in the numismatic scene, especially as three different types of official proof sets were struck. The Deputy Master of the Royal Mint announced at the time that the crown piece 'may now be considered to be definitely abandoned'. Ironically, the series of George V crowns later came to be dominated by one of the most famous and sought after types, the 'wreath' crown, which can be regarded as the last series of circulating crowns as a true denomination, bearing the same design in consecutive years. Today we have a succession of isolated commemorative issues. Next to the rarest date, the 1934, stands the ubiquitous 1935, without which crowns of George V would have been scarce as a single type. Although the 1935 crown is plentiful, the so-called 'raised edge' proof variety, issued in a red box, is scarce and much sought after. The unusual 'specimen' issue with incuse edge, also issued in a red box, is equally popular, though not as scarce. It is worthy of note that the raised edge type is not legal tender, as the proclamation conferring legality on 1935 crowns specified that the edge was to be incusely marked.

The issue of the wreath crown in 1927 coincided with a redesign of the whole series (apart from Maundy), and a cased proof set was issued to commemorate this. For the first time, the mark of denomination 'CROWN' appeared, and each of the other five pieces in the new set now bore a mark of denomination in words.

The obverse of both types of crown was designed by Sir Bertram Mackennal (1863–1931). The reverse of the wreath crown was by George Kruger Gray (1880–1943), and that of the 1935 crown by Percy Metcalfe.

Collecting Hints

The wreath crown is a scarce series and is collectable in any grade, but it will generally be encountered in about very fine condition. Extremely fine specimens can be found without great difficulty, although the 1934 can present a real problem.

The 1935 crown, at first sight a common and somewhat bland coin, is in fact probably the most interesting coin of all. There are a number of varieties, and fascinatingly some of these are at times overlooked by one or more parties to a transaction; certainly a number of error edge raised lettering issues have passed through major London salerooms without being spotted by the cataloguers, and the order of words on the edge must always be checked (not too obviously!) when one is offered a 'raised edge' crown. Similarly, raised lettering crowns in about fine condition occasionally appear in bulk dealer lots of standard 1935 crowns.

Denomination	Metal	Weight (grams)	Diameter (mm)	Rev. alignment
Crown	0.500 Silver	28.3	39	↑

Obverse 1   Head 1, left; GEORGIVS V DEI GRA BRITT OMN REX

Obverse 2   Head 2, left; GEORGIVS V DG BRITT OMN REX FD IND IMP *(for the Silver Jubilee)*

Reverse 1   Crown, date above, these within wreath; FID DEF IND IMP CROWN

Reverse 2   St George and dragon in 'art deco' style; CROWN 1935 *(for the Silver Jubilee)*

Edge, Obv. 1/Rev. 1: milled.
Obv. 2/Rev. 2 (incuse): DECUS ET TUTAMEN ANNO REGNI XXV

Obv. 1

Obv. 2

Rev. 1

Rev. 2

'Wreath' Issue

No.	Date	Features	Obv.	Rev.	F	VF	EF	UNC
G5CR-005	1927	PROOF [1]	1	1	70	90	110	150
G5CR-010	1927	PROOF from sandblasted dies [2]	1	1				1000
G5CR-015	1928		1	1	75	95	130	160
G5CR-020	1928	PROOF	1	1				900
G5CR-025	1929		1	1	75	100	140	170
G5CR-030	1929	PROOF	1	1				900
G5CR-035	1930		1	1	75	100	140	170
G5CR-040	1930	PROOF	1	1				1000
G5CR-045	1931		1	1	75	110	150	200
G5CR-050	1931	PROOF	1	1				1000
G5CR-055	1932		1	1	90	125	170	240
G5CR-060	1932	PROOF	1	1				1500
G5CR-065	1933		1	1	75	95	130	150
G5CR-070	1933	PROOF	1	1				1000
G5CR-075	1934		1	1	400	600	900	1300
G5CR-080	1934	PROOF	1	1				4000

1. Issued in cased proof sets.
2. Struck to facilitate photography of coin.

Jubilee Issue

No.	Date	Features	Obv.	Rev.	F	VF	EF	UNC
G5CR-085	1935		2	2	6	8	16	25
G5CR-090	1935	edge error [1]	2	2	100	150	250	350
G5CR-095	1935	SPECIMEN [2]	2	2			30	55
G5CR-100	1935	PROOF in sterling silver	2	2				2000
G5CR-105	1935	PROOF; raised edge lettering [3]	2	2			160	250
G5CR-110	1935	PROOF; raised error edge lettering reads DECUS ANNO REGNI ET TVTAMEN. XXV [3]	2	2			700	900
G5CR-115	1935	PROOF or pattern with edge inscription in finer lettering	2	2				2000
G5CR-120	1935	PROOF in gold; raised edge lettering [4]	2	2				10000

1. DECUS ET TVTA section of edge legend missing.
2. Prooflike field; issued in red box.
3. Issued in red box.
4. Issued in red box; 25 to 30 issued to recipients chosen by ballot; weight c.48 grams.

'Wreath' Issue

No.	Date	Features	Obv.	Rev.	F	VF	EF	UNC
G5CR-125	1936		1	1	90	130	200	300
G5CR-130	1936	PROOF	1	1				1500

Edward VIII (1936)

The Edward VIII crown is strictly speaking a pattern, as probable royal approval was about to be granted at the time of the abdication. However, because its official status rests only on this technicality, and to provide continuity, it is included here.

The portrait of Edward VIII is by Thomas Humphrey Paget (1893–1974), and faces left at the insistence of the king, who considered this placement more flattering and wished to discontinue the tradition of opposite facings for successive monarchs. The reverse is by George Kruger Gray.

Denomination	Metal	Weight (grams)	Diameter (mm)	Rev. alignment
Crown	Silver	28.2	39	↑

Obverse 1   Head 1, left; EDWARDVS VIII D G BR OMN REX

Reverse 1   Royal arms supported and crowned; FID DEF IND IMP CROWN 1937

Edge   milled

Obv. 1   Rev. 1

No.	Date		Obv.	Rev.		Unc
E8CR-005	1937		1	1		100000

George VI (1937 – 1952)

The only two crowns of George VI were issued for the Coronation in 1937 and for the Festival of Britain in 1951. Both used obverses by Paget, with reverses by Kruger Gray in 1937 and of the Pistrucci St George and dragon in 1951. The latter was the first British crown struck in cupronickel, 400 years after the first was struck in silver, and it was struck only as a proof. Besides marking the Festival of 1951, it also commemorates the 100 years anniversary of the Great Exhibition held in London's Hyde Park in 1851. It was said that the reverse of this crown was made from a punch originally manufactured for an 1899 crown. The 1951 crown was issued to the public at a price of 5 shillings and 6 pence, and some were struck at the Festival site on London's South Bank. Unfortunately, no special mintmark was incorporated into the design. The forward-looking mood of the nation was reflected in the change of the denomination legend from 'crown' to 'five shillings'.

Collecting Hints

None of the George VI crowns is difficult to obtain, unless one is seeking the more exotic frosted varieties. Indeed, perhaps the most difficult items are original 1951 cardboard boxes (maroon and green) in pristine state with official leaflet. The boxes occur both with slide-off and pull-off lids, the latter being scarcer. Contrary to what one is sometimes told, the 1951 proof crowns in boxes and those in proof sets are identical.

Denomination	Metal	Weight (grams)	Diameter (mm)	Rev. alignment
Crown 1937	0.500 Silver	28.3	39	↑
Crown 1951	Cupronickel	28.3	39	↑

Obverse 1   Head 1, left; GEORGIVS VI D G BR OMN REX *(for the Coronation)*

Obverse 2   Head 2, left; GEORGIVS VI D G BR OMN REX F D FIVE SHILLINGS *(for the Festival of Britain)*

Reverse 1   Royal arms supported and crowned; FID DEF IND IMP CROWN 1937 *(for the Coronation)*

Reverse 2   St George and dragon, 1951 in exergue below *(for the Festival of Britain)*

Edge   (1937) milled;
(1951) incusely inscribed MDCCCLI CIVIUM INDUSTRIA FLORET CIVITAS MCMLI

Obv. 1   Obv. 2

Rev. 1   Rev. 2

No.	Date	Features	Obv.	Rev.	F	VF	EF	UNC
G6CR-005	1937	[1]	1	1	6	9	14	25
G6CR-010	1937	PROOF [2]	1	1			20	50
G6CR-015	1937	PROOF heavily frosted [3]	1	1				120
G6CR-020	1937	PROOF from sandblasted dies [4]	1	1				800
G6CR-025	1951	PROOF [5]	2	2			6	8
G6CR-028	1951	PROOF; edge lettering blundered [5]	2	2				150
G6CR-030	1951	PROOF, heavily frosted with brilliant field [6]	2	2				450
G6CR-035	1951	PROOF from sandblasted dies [4]	2	2				800
G6CR-040	1951	PROOF; edge plain	2	2				200

1. Issued for several years.
2. Issued in cased proof sets.
3. Possibly in sterling silver.
4. Struck to facilitate photography of coin.
5. Issued in card box and in cased proof sets.
6. Edge lettering finer than on previous coin.

Elizabeth II (1952 –)

Crowns of Elizabeth II are characterised by high mintage issues struck not for circulation but to commemorate events or anniversaries. They are generally collected for the sake of completeness rather than for their artistic merit, although the proofs in original cases are attractive.

The unusual obverse of the 1953 crown was designed by G. Ledward and was inspired by press photographs of the Queen riding 'Winston' at the Trooping of the Colour ceremony in London. The reverse, also carried forward to the 1960 coin, was by Fuller and Thomas.

Collecting Hints

Elizabeth II crowns are encountered in extremely fine or mint state more frequently than in any other grade, and the perverse collector may wish to acquire a specimen of each in the worst possible grade. It is surprising how many of these crowns exist in fair to fine condition. There are no doubt many who would say that the beauty of the Churchill crown increases in direct proportion to the amount of wear it has sustained.

No.	Date	Features	Obv.	Rev.	VF	EF	UNC
EZCR-005	1953	1	1	1	4	6	8
EZCR-010	1953	YO instead of YOU (edge)	1	1	40	60	80
EZCR-015	1953	PROOF 2	1	1		10	25
EZCR-020	1953	PROOF from sandblasted dies 3	1	1			800
EZCR-025	1960		2	1	3	6	8
EZCR-030	1960	polished die specimen	2	1		7	14
EZCR-035	1960	PROOF frosted bust	2	1			400
EZCR-040	1965	4	3	2		1	2
EZCR-045	1965	satin finish	3	2			450

1. Minor obverse varieties occur.
2. Issued in cased proof sets.
3. Struck to facilitate photography of coin.
4. 'R' in CHURCHILL varies (rev.).

For later crown-sized pieces, see the decimal section, p.633.

Denomination	Metal	Weight (grams)	Diameter (mm)	Rev. alignment
Crown	Cupronickel	28.3	39	↑

Obverse 1   Queen on horseback; ELIZABETH II DEI GRATIA BRITT OMN REGINA FIDEI DEFENSOR FIVE SHILLINGS

Obverse 2   Head 1, right; ELIZABETH II DEI GRATIA REGINA F D; below head: FIVE SHILLINGS *(for the British Trade Fair in New York)*

Obverse 3   Head 1, right; ELIZABETH II DEI GRATIA REGINA F D with wider spacing than above; below head: 1965

Reverse 1   Cruciform shields and emblems around crown, date below

Reverse 2   Head of Churchill; CHURCHILL

Edges   (1953) FAITH AND TRUTH I WILL BEAR UNTO YOU (incuse); (1960–65) milled

Obv. 1

Obv. 2

Obv. 3

Rev. 1

Rev. 2

Double Florin

Victoria (1837 – 1901)

The double florin is one of the shortest denominations on record, yet it includes a number of interesting varieties. Like the florin of 1887 it uses a reverse design based on that originally used by John Roettier on the gold of Charles II. This comprised four cruciform shields with sceptres laid out in the angles between them. The obverse of the double florin used the controversial Boehm portrait of the queen, engraved by Leonard Charles Wyon.

The 1887 coin with Arabic style '1' in the date was included in the proof sets of 1887, and proofs also exist of the type with Roman 'I' in the date. This denomination, unpopular at the time of issue, lasted until 1890, when it had outlived its usefulness. The use of the Boehm portrait no doubt accelerated its demise.

Collecting Hints

This is a popular series amongst collectors, and it is challenging to attempt to collect a complete set, including all varieties. Acquiring both types of proofs can, in particular, prove difficult.

Although many double florins received extensive circulation wear, this coin is not too difficult to find in Extremely Fine condition. The 1888 and 1889 varieties with 'inverted 1' in VICTORIA are the result of a broken punch. Although they are well-known coins much in demand, they might not have attracted so much attention if the series had been a longer one (it is interesting to note that the similar 1888 penny with broken serifs is not nearly so well known).

Denomination	Metal	Weight (grams)	Diameter (mm)	Rev. alignment
Double Florin	Silver	22.6	36	↑

Obverse 1 Head 1, left; VICTORIA DEI GRATIA. The field is flat.

Obverse 2 Similar but many minor differences. The field is slightly concave.

Reverse 1 Four crowned cruciform shields with sceptres in angles; FID DEF BRITT REG (date). Roman I instead of 1 in 1887

Reverse 2 Similar but many minor differences. Arabic 1 in date. The field is very slightly concave

Edge milled

Obv. 1   Rev. 1

No.	Date	Features	Obv.	Rev.	F	VF	EF	UNC
VJDFL-005	1887	Roman I in date	1	1	12	20	30	55
VJDFL-010	1887	PROOF Roman I in date	1	1				400
VJDFL-015	1887	Arabic 1 in date	1	2	12	18	26	50
VJDFL-020	1887	Arabic 1 in date	2	2	12	18	26	50
VJDFL-025	1887	PROOF Arabic 1 in date [1]	2	2				150
VJDFL-030	1888		2	2	13	24	35	70
VJDFL-035	1888	second I in VICTORIA is inverted '1'	2	2	18	35	90	150
VJDFL-040	1889		2	2	12	22	35	65
VJDFL-045	1889	second I in VICTORIA is inverted '1'	2	2	20	45	120	200
VJDFL-050	1890	[2]	2	2	13	25	40	90

1. Issued in cased proof sets.
2. Reverse design is very slightly larger than on previous years.

Three Shillings

George III   (1760 – 1820)

In 1811 there was a shortage of silver coinage for circulation. Although the countermarked dollars and five shilling bank tokens had been useful in this respect, no halfcrowns had been minted since 1751, and the last issue of shillings and sixpences for general use had been in 1787. In many parts of the country tradesmen issued private silver tokens during 1811, but these were not accepted outside the immediate area where they were issued.

To alleviate the situation, the Bank of England issued its own tokens for three shillings and for eighteen pence. Silver was at a high price, and the weights of these denominations were proportionately lower than normal. The fact that these issues were tokens rather than true coins rendered this shortfall acceptable.

The silver tokens of three shillings and eighteen pence were to some extent unofficially melted to produce private tokens. A proclamation of 20 July 1812 decreed that after 25 March 1813 no silver tokens except those produced by the Banks of England and Ireland should be current. This date was later extended, with an Act of Parliament finally outlawing the private tokens after the end of 1815.

The issue of three shilling tokens was a short one, from 1811 to 1816, and comprises two distinct types. The 1811 issue includes a number of minor varieties on both obverse and reverse. The tokens were withdrawn from issue in March 1820, thereafter being accepted only as bullion by weight.

The first type of three shillings token (1811–12) was probably designed by Lewis Pingo. The second type (1812–16) used the Marchant design employed on the gold coinage. This was engraved by Thomas Wyon, who designed and engraved the reverse.

Obv. 1   Obv. 2

Rev. 1   Rev. 2

No.	Date	Features	Obv.	Rev.	F	VF	EF	UNC
G33S-005	1811	[1]	1	1	14	30	70	110
G33S-010	1811	PROOF [1]	1	1				600
G33S-015	1812		1	1	14	32	75	120
G33S-020	1812	[2]	2	2	14	32	75	120
G33S-025	1812	PROOF	2	2				600
G33S-030	1812	PROOF in gold [3]	2	2				10000
G33S-035	1812	PROOF in platinum [4]	2	2				7000
G33S-040	1813		2	2	14	32	75	120
G33S-045	1814		2	2	14	32	75	120
G33S-050	1815		2	2	14	32	75	120
G33S-055	1816		2	2	150	300		

1. Wreath and lettering orientation varies (obv.); number of acorns varies (rev.).
2. Lettering orientation varies (obv.).
3. Weight 28.8 grams.
4. Weight 33.1 grams.

Denomination	Metal	Weight (grams)	Diameter (mm)	Rev. alignment
Three Shillings	Silver	15.0	35	↑

Obverse 1   Head 1, right; GEORGIUS III DEI GRATIA REX

Obverse 2   Head 2, right; same legend

Reverse 1   BANK TOKEN 3 SHILL (date) within wreath of oak leaves

Reverse 2   Similar but less profuse wreath of oak and olive

Edge   plain

Stirring pot of silver

Halfcrown

Oliver Cromwell (Commonwealth 1649 – 1660)

The halfcrown is unique in the short Cromwell series in that it occurs not only with two dates but as two types. The 1656 halfcrown is therefore the earliest milled coin having what became for the milled coinage a conventional layout, with an obverse bust and a heraldic reverse, both with lettering around the rim of each face. The coinage was struck under a patent dated 9 July 1656, but there appears to be no evidence that it was decreed to be legal tender currency.

The coin was designed by Thomas Simon (also called Symonds) with technical assistance from Peter Blondeau, and portrays Cromwell as a Roman Emperor, draped and laureate.

The 'Tanner's Copy' was struck in the 18th century, and is outside the scope of this book.

Collecting Hints

Unlike on the crown, there is no die flaw on the halfcrown. The coin is collectable in fine condition or above.

Denomination	Metal	Weight (grams)	Diameter (mm)	Rev. alignment
Halfcrown	Silver	14.6–15.1	32–34	↓

Obverse 1 Head 1, left; OLIVAR D G R P ANG SCO HI &c PRO

Obverse 2 Similar but HIB instead of HI

Reverse 1 Crowned shield; PAX QVAERITVR BELLO (date)

Edge (in relief) HAS NISI PERITVRVS MIHI ADIMAT NEMO

Obv. 2   Rev. 1

No.	Date	Features	Obv.	Rev.	F	VF	EF
OCHC-005	1656		1	1	800	1500	4000
OCHC-010	1658		2	1	450	750	1400
OCHC-015	1658	PROOF in gold [1]	2	1			30000

1. Weight c.27 grams; about 6 known.

Charles II   (1660 – 1685)

The first machine-struck halfcrown was issued in 1663, the year after the issue of the first crown, on whose design by Roettier it is based. The new minor silver coinage was not universally popular. Pepys records in his diary for 23 November 1663 that the financier Blackwell found it 'deadly inconvenient for telling, it is so thick and the edges are made to turn up'. The issue of halfcrowns continued for over twenty years, broken only in 1665 during the Great Plague, and used a design which continued throughout the reign with only minor modifications. It is believed that the ravages of the plague were also responsible for the low issue of halfcrowns up to 1669, almost all of which used over-strikings of 1664 and possibly other dates.

Provenance marks used in this series are: elephant and castle (or elephant) denoting silver from the Africa Company; plume for silver from Welsh mines.

Collecting Hints

Although a prolific issue spanning almost a quarter of a century, the halfcrowns were well circulated and few survive in near-perfect condition. A good fine condition specimen is, however, still an attractive coin, and many collectors will content themselves with such a piece to represent each date or type.

There are a number of interesting varieties, and it is prudent to examine all aspects of a coin, including the edge, when contemplating a purchase. Specimens of 1670 should always be checked for the MRG reverse, as this coin does turn up occasionally.

Very fine or better specimens of this series required by serious collectors are comparatively expensive owing to their scarcity and the high demand for them.

Denomination	Metal	Weight (grams)	Diameter (mm)	Rev. alignment
Halfcrown 1663	Silver	15.0–15.5	33–34	↓
Halfcrown 1664–84	Silver	14.8–15.3	32–34	↓

Obverse 1 Head 1, right; CAROLVS II DEI GRATIA

Obverse 2 Head 2, right; same legend

Obverse 3 Head 3, smaller, right; same legend

Obverse 4 Head 4, very similar to 3, right; same legend

Obverse 5 Head 5, much larger, right; same legend

Reverse 1 Four cruciform shields with pair of interlinked 'C's in angles. MAG BR FRA ET HIB REX. Date at top

Edge (in relief) (all dates except 1667) DECVS ET TVTAMEN ANNO REGNI (regnal date); (1667 only) DECVS ET TVTAMEN AN REG (regnal date). From 1662 to 1666 the regnal year is in Roman numerals; from 1667 onwards it is in words.

Obv. 1   Obv. 2

Obv. 3

Obv. 4

Obv. 5

Rev. 1

No.	Date	Features	Edge date	Obv.	Rev.	VG	F	VF	EF
C2HCM-005	1663		XV	1	1	30	50	250	1200
C2HCM-010	1663	rev. ↑	XV	1	1	35	60	350	1500
C2HCM-015	1663	rev. 90 degrees anticlockwise	XV	1	1	35	60	350	1500
C2HCM-020	1663	no stops on obv.	XV	1	1	35	60	350	1500
C2HCM-030	1663	V of CAROLVS over S (obv.)	XV	1	1	35	60	350	1500
C2HCM-035	1663	no stops on obv. and V of CAROLVS over S (obv.)	XV	1	1	40	70	400	1700
C2HCM-040	1663	PROOF	XV	1	1				8000
C2HCM-045	1664		XVI	2	1	50	80	450	2000
C2HCM-050	1666	last 6 over indeterminate digit [1]	XVIII	3	1	500	800	4000	
C2HCM-055	1666	last 6 over 4 elephant below head [1]	XVIII	3	1	250	350	1200	6000
C2HCM-060	1666	last 6 over indeterminate digit elephant below head [1]	XVIII	3	1	250	350	1200	6000
C2HCM-065	1667	7 over 4 [1]	DECIMO NONO	3	1	1200	2000		
C2HCM-070	1668	8 over 4 [1]	VICESIMO	3	1	60	100	600	2500
C2HCM-072	1668	8 over 4: CAROL∀S instead of CAROLVS (obv.) [1]	VICESIMO	3	1	70	120	750	3000
C2HCM-075	1669		VICESIMO PRIMO	3	1	140	250	1200	
C2HCM-080	1669	R of PRIMO over I (edge)	VICESIMO PRIMO	3	1	140	250	1200	
C2HCM-085	1669	9 over 4	VICESIMO PRIMO	3	1	70	130	700	
C2HCM-090	1670		VICESIMO SECVNDO	3	1	25	45	170	1000
C2HCM-092	1670	V of CAROLVS over S (obv.)	VICESIMO SECVNDO	3	1	35	60	250	
C2HCM-095	1670	MRG instead of MAG (rev.)	VICESIMO SECVNDO	3	1	50	90	600	
C2HCM-100	1670	A of MAG over R (rev.)	VICESIMO SECVNDO	3	1	35	60	250	
C2HCM-102	1670	E of ET over R (rev.) [2]	VICESIMO SECVNDO	3	1	35	60	250	
C2HCM-105	1671		VICESIMO TERTIO	4	1	25	45	140	900
C2HCM-110	1671	A of MAG over R (rev.)	VICESIMO TERTIO	4	1	40	60	220	
C2HCM-115	1671	1 over 0	VICESIMO TERTIO	4	1	30	50	160	950
C2HCM-120	1672		VICESIMO TERTIO	4	1	150	300		
C2HCM-125	1672		VICESIMO QVARTO	4	1	25	45	140	900
C2HCM-130	1672		VICESIMO QVARTO	5	1	50	80	250	1500
C2HCM-135	1673		VICESIMO QVINTO	5	1	25	45	130	900
C2HCM-140	1673	B of BR over R (rev.)	VICESIMO QVINTO	5	1	30	50	150	1000
C2HCM-145	1673	A of FRA over R (rev.)	VICESIMO QVINTO	5	1	30	50	150	1000
C2HCM-150	1673	EGNI instead of REGNI (edge)	VICESIMO QVINTO	5	1	40	60	160	1000
C2HCM-155	1673	plume below head [3]	VICESIMO QVINTO	5	1	1000	1500		
C2HCM-160	1673	plume below head and in centre of rev.	VICESIMO QVINTO	5	1	2000	3000		
C2HCM-165	1674		VICESIMO SEXTO	5	1	60	100	400	1500
C2HCM-170	1674	4 over 3	VICESIMO SEXTO	5	1	70	120	500	2000
C2HCM-175	1675		VICESIMO SEPTIMO	5	1	40	70	300	1200
C2HCM-180	1675	EGNI instead of REGNI (edge)	VICESIMO SEPTIMO	5	1	50	80	400	1300
C2HCM-185	1675	reversed 1 in date	VICESIMO SEPTIMO	5	1	70	120	500	
C2HCM-190	1676		VICESIMO OCTAVO	5	1	25	45	110	750
C2HCM-195	1676	EGNI instead of REGNI (edge)	VICESIMO OCTAVO	5	1	35	60	130	950
C2HCM-198	1676	R of BR over I (rev.)	VICESIMO OCTAVO	5	1	30	50	120	850
C2HCM-200	1676	reversed 1 in date [4]	VICESIMO OCTAVO	5	1	30	45	120	800
C2HCM-202	1676	reversed 1 in date; F of FRA over H; R of BR over T [4]	VICESIMO OCTAVO	5	1				
C2HCM-205	1677 [5]		VICESIMO NONO	5	1	25	45	120	800
C2HCM-210	1678		TRICESIMO	5	1	60	100	500	
C2HCM-212	1678	RRGNI or RBGNI instead of REGNI (edge)	TRICESIMO	5	1	90	150	800	
C2HCM-215	1679		TRICESIMO PRIMO	5	1	25	45	90	600
C2HCM-218	1679	REG instead of REGNI (edge)	TRICESIMO PRIMO	5	1	40	70	150	
C2HCM-220	1679	GRATTA instead of GRATIA (obv.)	TRICESIMO PRIMO	5	1	30	50	110	700
C2HCM-225	1679	DECNS instead of DECVS (edge)	TRICESIMO PRIMO	5	1	30	50	110	700
C2HCM-230	1679	DNCVS instead of DECVS (edge)	TRICESIMO PRIMO	5	1	30	50	110	700
C2HCM-235	1679	both 'V's on edge are inverted 'A's	TRICESIMO PRIMO	5	1	25	45	110	700
C2HCM-240	1679	N in REGNI is inverted R (edge)	TRICESIMO PRIMO	5	1	40	60	120	750
C2HCM-245	1679	PRICESIMO instead of TRICESIMO (edge)	PRICESIMO PRIMO	5	1	30	50	110	650
C2HCM-250	1680		TRICESIMO SECVNDO	5	1	60	100	500	
C2HCM-252	1680	H of HIB unbarred (rev.)	TRICESIMO SECVNDO	5	1	70	120	700	
C2HCM-255	1680	RGNI instead of REGNI (edge)	TRICESIMO SECVNDO	5	1	70	120	700	
C2HCM-258	1680	DECV instead of DECVS (edge)	TRICESIMO SECVNDO	5	1	70	120	700	
C2HCM-260	1680	D in SECVNDO inverted (edge)	TRICESIMO SECVN(D)O	5	1	60	110	600	
C2HCM-265	1681		TRICESIMO TERTIO	5	1	30	50	160	800

No.	Date	Features	Edge date	Obv.	Rev.	VG	F	VF	EF
C2HCM-270	1681	1 over 0	TRICESIMO TERTIO	5	1	35	60	180	1000
C2HCM-275	1681	elephant and castle below head	TRICESIMO TERTIO	5	1	800	1200		
C2HCM-280	1682		TRICESIMO QVARTO	5	1	40	70	250	1200
C2HCM-285	1682	PROOF (?) rev. ↑ 6	TRICESIMO QVARTO	5	1	50	80	350	1500
C2HCM-290	1682	2 over 1	TRICESIMO QVARTO	5	1	50	80	350	1500
C2HCM-295	1682	82 over 79	TRICESIMO QVARTO	5	1	50	80	350	1500
C2HCM-300	1683		TRICESIMO QVINTO	5	1	25	45	140	800
C2HCM-305	1683	plume below head 7	TRICESIMO QVINTO	5	1				
C2HCM-310	1684	4 over 3 1	TRICESIMO SEXTO	5	1	40	70	400	

1. This date always overstruck.
2. Some struck on 34–35 mm flans.
3. Broken 3 in date exists.
4. See comments below.
5. A variety is reported with the bust slightly modified.
6. See comments below; cf. 1682 guinea variety.
7. Only recorded specimen in poor to fair condition realised £3200 at auction (Spink June 1980).

The 1676 variety sometimes known as 'inverted 1' is the same as that recorded here as 'reversed 1'; the digit is not inverted, nor is the coin rare as some reference books imply.

The 1682 with reverse ↑ has been noted in VF condition with an unusually sharp strike, and may have been struck as a proof. See also the 1682 guinea with unusual die axis.

The number of harp strings varies through this series. It is possible that the variation constituted a form of internal code denoting the die number.

James II (1685 – 1688)

John Roettier, continuing as Chief Engraver, produced this short series of only four dates, which nevertheless includes a number of varieties of interest.

Collecting Hints

Some of the varieties of this series are difficult to find in the higher grades, and the characteristic slightly weak strike can sometimes make extremely fine specimens look as if they have some degree of wear. Haymarking and flecking are prevalent on many coins, and the individual collector must decide for himself whether these characteristics constitute blemishes or not.
The 1687 halfcrown with the later head is not as rare as some catalogues suggest.

Denomination	Metal	Weight (grams)	Diameter (mm)	Rev. alignment
Halfcrown	Silver	14.9–15.1	33	↓

Obverse 1 Head 1, left; tie turns down at end; IACOBVS II DEI GRATIA

Obverse 2 Head 2, slightly larger, left; tie turns up at end; same legend

Reverse 1 Four cruciform shields with surmounting crowns; MAG BR FRA ET HIB REX (date)

Edge (in relief) DECVS ET TVTAMEN ANNO REGNI (regnal date)

Obv. 1

Obv. 2

Rev. 1

No.	Date	Features	Edge date	Obv.	Rev.	F	VF	EF
J2HC-005	1685		PRIMO	1	1	75	190	900
J2HC-010	1686		SECVNDO	1	1	75	190	900
J2HC-015	1686	6 over 5	SECVNDO	1	1	90	300	1200
J2HC-020	1686		TERTIO	1	1	80	220	1000
J2HC-025	1686	V of IACOBVS over B (obv.)	TERTIO	1	1	85	240	1100
J2HC-030	1686	V of IACOBVS is a ∀ over S (obv.)	TERTIO	1	1	85	240	1100
J2HC-032	1686	IACOB∀S instead of IACOBVS (obv.)	TERTIO	1	1	90	270	1200
J2HC-035	1687		TERTIO	1	1	75	190	900
J2HC-040	1687	7 over 6	TERTIO	1	1	80	220	1100
J2HC-045	1687	6 over 8	TERTIO	1	1	110	300	1200
J2HC-050	1687		TERTIO	2	1	80	220	1100
J2HC-055	1687	PROOF	TERTIO	2	1			6000
J2HC-060	1688		QVARTO	2	1	80	220	1100

The number of harp strings varies through this series. It is possible that the variation constituted a form of internal code denoting the die number.

William & Mary (1688 – 1694)

The halfcrowns were, apart from the so-called 'Maundy Money', the first silver coins issued in the reign of William and Mary. The depiction of a single crowned shield on the reverse was a radical departure from the design used during the previous two reigns. During 1689 the first and fourth quarters of the shield were themselves quartered, displaying the arms of France and England. In 1691 this design reverted to the old four-shield motif, while at the same time a very different design of busts was introduced on the obverse.

It is interesting to note that, while on the crowns and the 1691 and 1693 halfcrowns the date is placed to be read from one position, on the 1692 halfcrown it rotates around the central lion. This anomaly may have been responsible for the (later recut) error inverting of some of the last date digits on a few of the halfcrowns and crowns.

The attribution of William and Mary coinage is not always clear. John Roettier was ill, and probably delegated work to his sons James and Norbert. The two main types of halfcrown are so different, not only in the concept of the reverse but also in the style of the busts, that it is difficult to believe that they are by the same designer. The first resembles the work of Norbert Roettier, and the second that of James. It is known that James Roettier preferred to work in lower relief than his brother. However, Rayner considers that the second obverse may possibly be the work of Henry Harris.

Henry Harris was a designer to whom little of the coinage can be attributed with any degree of confidence. He succeeded George Bower as Chief Engraver on the latter's death in 1690. He had worked on seals and signets since 1670, but on his appointment had not had much coinage experience. Consequently, immediately on his appointment he agreed with James and Norbert Roettier that they would act as advisory assistants, and for this Harris paid them £175 out of his annual salary of £325.

No provenance marks or proofs exist in this series.

Rev. 3

No.	Date	Features	Edge date	Obv.	Rev.	F	VF	EF
WMHC-005	1689	[1]	PRIMO	1	1	40	120	450
WMHC-010	1689	FRA instead of FR (rev.)	PRIMO	1	1	55	150	550
WMHC-015	1689	second L of GVLIELMVS over M (obv.)	PRIMO	1	1	50	130	500
WMHC-020	1689	first V of GVLIELMVS over A (obv.)	PRIMO	1	1	50	130	500
WMHC-022	1689	DECV instead of DECVS (edge)	PRIMO	1	1	60	150	600
WMHC-025	1689	no stops on obv.	PRIMO	1	1	50	150	550
WMHC-030	1689	[1]	PRIMO	1	2	50	150	550
WMHC-035	1690		SECVNDO	1	2	85	210	800
WMHC-040	1690	GRETIA instead of GRATIA; second V of GVLIELMVS over S (obv.)	SECVNDO	1	2	100	240	1000
WMHC-045	1690		TERTIO	1	2	95	240	900
WMHC-050	1691		TERTIO	2	3	55	150	550
WMHC-055	1692		QVARTO	2	3	55	150	550
WMHC-060	1692		QVINTO	2	3	100	250	1200
WMHC-065	1693		QVINTO	2	3	55	150	550
WMHC-070	1693	3 over inverted 3	QVINTO	2	3	65	170	600
WMHC-075	1693	3 of date inverted	QVINTO	2	3	150	400	1500

1. Design variations on reverse crown exist.

Reverse 3: variations occur in the monogrammed 'WM'.

The 1691 to 1693 dates are read in two lines, left to right, with the English shield at the top of the coin.

Collecting Hints

Only the most avid collector of varieties will attempt to assemble a set of the minor variations of the crown on the reverse of the 1689 halfcrown, but this coin should always be checked for the very striking L over M type and for the 'FRA' reverse, both scarce. Similarly, the 1690, in itself a particularly scarce date, must always be examined for the major 'GRETIA' variety.

The later type of 1691–93 is struck in very low relief and a very fine or extremely fine specimen may appear as fine or very fine to the untrained eye. In addition, these pieces are frequently found with haymarking.

Interesting contemporary forgeries exist which command unusually high prices. Some exhibit non-existent die/date/edge combinations.

Denomination	Metal	Weight (grams)	Diameter (mm)	Rev. alignment
Halfcrown	Silver	14.7–15.0	33–34	↓

Obverse 1 Heads 1, right; GVLIELMVS ET MARIA DEI GRATIA

Obverse 2 Heads 2, closer together and in low relief, right; same legend

Reverse 1 Crown above quartered shield, each quarter undivided; MAG BR FR ET HIB REX ET REGINA. Date divided by crown.

Reverse 2 Similar but first and fourth quarters themselves divided into arms of England and France.

Reverse 3 Four crowned cruciform shields around lion of Orange-Nassau, with monogrammed 'WM' and one digit of date in each angle; MAG BR FR ET HI REX ET REGINA

Edge (in relief) DECVS ET TVTAMEN ANNO REGNI (regnal date)

Obv. 1   Obv. 2

Rev. 1   Rev. 2

William III   (1695 – 1701)

Because of the large quantity of halfcrowns minted during the reign of William and Mary, the halfcrown was the only major silver denomination not to be issued in 1695. When it resumed in 1696, there began a series of halfcrowns which was to become unrivalled in the complexity of its varieties, oddities and errors. With the withdrawal of hammered coinage, it was necessary to use provincial mints at Bristol, Chester, Exeter, Norwich and York using local labour which was responsible for a plethora of mistakes, all of which render the series of absorbing interest. A proposed mint at Hereford never opened. There are so many minor variations in the design and size of, for example, the shields, the harp and the central lion that the noted scholar and numismatist Jackson Kent proffered the opinion that it would be 'an impossible task' to produce a complete list. For this reason we have selected those varieties which can be regarded as noteworthy, while making annotations on the minor ones. It should be mentioned that, for the sake of expediency, some varieties (such as the harp variations of 1699–1701) are referred to only in annotated form when they would probably have been noted as separate varieties if they had occurred, say, in the reign of James II. For these reasons, there is an inconsistency for which we offer no apology; otherwise the listing, after permutating each variety with each other and with the mintmark, could have covered scores of pages and been of very little interest to the majority of collectors, and even then would be incomplete.

In view of the above, it is remarkable that the obverse head of the monarch remained virtually identical throughout the series. The oddly designed head of one excessively rare 1696 coin is almost certainly a pattern.

In several reference works the 1696 halfcrown with large shields and so-called 'early harp' is referred to as type 1, while the small shield coinage is called type 3. Mr Jackson Kent disputed this notation, and the cataloguer, on examining the evidence, is inclined to agree. For this reason, the usual notation of types 1, 2 and 3 become in this catalogue reverses 2, 3 and 1 respectively. The reasoning is as follows:

1. The small shields with convex tops closely resemble those of the last issue of William and Mary, and the central lion and escutcheon are also very similar. It would be unusual for a radical change of design to be made which then reverts almost exactly to that of the previous reign.

2. The large shields with concave tops continue into 1697 and through to 1701. We are thus asked to believe not only that the design reverts during 1696 to that of William and Mary but that at the beginning of 1697 it switches back to the design used in the first half of 1696.

3. The reason for the notation used in E.S.C. and other works appears to be due solely to the fact that the so-called 'early harp' resembles that used on the 1695 crowns. However, there is no other factor in support of the usual notation; even the 1695 shields are convex, as are those on the reverse denoted in this catalogue as 'Reverse 1'.

Provenance marks (on 1701 halfcrowns only) are: plumes (silver from Welsh mines); elephant and castle below head (silver from the Africa Company).

Obv. 1   Rev. 1

Rev. 2   Rev. 3

No.	Date	Features	Edge date — mm	Obv.	Rev.	F	VF	EF
W3HC-005	1696		OCTAVO	1	1	45	100	350
W3HC-010	1696	[1]	OCTAVO — B	1	1	50	130	500
W3HC-015	1696	PROOF	OCTAVO — B	1	1			8000
W3HC-020	1696		OCTAVO — C	1	1	65	190	700
W3HC-025	1696		OCTAVO — E	1	1	85	280	950
W3HC-030	1696	DECVS AMEN AMEN instead of DECVS ET TVTAMEN (edge)	OCTAVO — E	1	1	100	350	1200
W3HC-035	1696	[1]	OCTAVO — N	1	1	50	140	500
W3HC-040	1696		OCTAVO — y	1	1	65	190	700
W3HC-045	1696		OCTAVO	1	2	50	110	400
W3HC-050	1696	PROOF on thick flan; edge plain [2]		1	2			3500
W3HC-055	1696		OCTAVO — B	1	2	55	130	450
W3HC-060	1696	struck on thick flan [3]	OCTAVO — B	1	2	1200		
W3HC-065	1696		OCTAVO — C	1	2	60	150	550
W3HC-070	1696		OCTAVO — E	1	2	70	180	650
W3HC-075	1696	E over B (mintmark)	OCTAVO — E	1	2	80	210	700
W3HC-080	1696		OCTAVO — N	1	2	100	300	1100
W3HC-085	1696		OCTAVO — y	1	2	60	150	500
W3HC-090	1696	y over E (mintmark)	OCTAVO — y	1	2	70	170	600
W3HC-095	1696	arms of Scotland at date	OCTAVO — y	1	2	800		
W3HC-100	1696		OCTAVO	1	3	80	250	1000
W3HC-105	1696		OCTAVO — C	1	3	80	250	1000
W3HC-110	1696		OCTAVO — E	1	3	80	250	1000
W3HC-115	1696		NONO — E	1	3	200	800	3000
W3HC-120	1696		OCTAVO — N	1	3	100	400	1500
W3HC-125	1697		NONO	1	3	45	100	350
W3HC-130	1697	7 over 6	NONO	1	3	60	140	550
W3HC-135	1697	GRR instead of GRA (obv.)	NONO	1	3	120	400	1000
W3HC-138	1697	GRA instead of GRA (obv.)	NONO	1	3	70	180	600
W3HC-140	1697	GVLIEIMVS instead of GVLIELMVS (obv.)	NONO	1	3	70	180	600
W3HC-142	1697	DECVS ET TVTAMEN instead of DECVS ET TVTAMEN (edge)	NONO	1	3	70	180	600
W3HC-145	1697	PROOF; edge plain		1	3			8000
W3HC-150	1697		NONO — B	1	3	50	130	500
W3HC-155	1697	no stops on rev.	NONO — B	1	3	60	160	650

Collecting Hints

If, as Jackson Kent said, it is an impossible task to list all of the varieties of the William III halfcrown, the difficulty of assembling a collection of varieties can be imagined. A comprehensive collection by date and variety would be a life's work and a source of endless fascination, and it would probably yield several new discoveries. In more practicable terms, one should attempt to acquire any piece which differs from anything in one's collection to any marked degree. Certainly most collectors will require specimens of each provincial mintmark; such pieces are particularly difficult to find in very fine or better.

Denomination	Metal	Weight (grams)	Diameter (mm)	Rev. alignment
Halfcrown	Silver	14.6–15.1	33	↓

Obverse 1   Head 1, right; GVLIELMVS III DEI GRA

Reverse 1   Four cruciform shields, each convex at the top and similar in width to each surmounting crown, all around central lion of Nassau; the harp with Irish shield has top left and top right roughly level; MAG BR FRA ET HIB REX (date) (with or without stops)

Reverse 2   Similar but the shields are wider than the crowns and are concave at the top; the lion is smaller; the harp has top left well above top right; same legend

Reverse 3   Similar but the harp is somewhat similar to that on Reverse 1, with both tops of sides level; the harp and the lion can vary in shape and size

Edge   (in relief) DECVS ET TVTAMEN ANNO REGNI (regnal date)

No.	Date	Features	Edge date — mm	Obv.	Rev.	F	VF	EF
W3HC-160	1697	no harp strings	NONO — B	1	3	60	160	650
W3HC-165	1697	PROOF on thick flan [4]	NONO — B	1	3			10000
W3HC-170	1697		NONO — C	1	3	55	140	550
W3HC-175	1697	no harp strings	NONO — C	1	3	65	170	700
W3HC-180	1697		NONO — E	1	3	50	130	500
W3HC-185	1697	T∇TAMEN instead of TVTAMEN (edge)	NONO — E	1	3	70	160	650
W3HC-190	1697	E over C (mintmark) [5]	NONO — E	1	3	80	180	800
W3HC-195	1697	E over B (mintmark) [5]	NONO — E	1	3	80	180	800
W3HC-200	1697	[6]	OCTAVO — E	1	3	400	1500	
W3HC-205	1697		NONO — N	1	3	50	130	500
W3HC-210	1697	arms of Scotland at date	NONO — N	1	3	600	2500	
W3HC-215	1697	[6]	OCTAVO — N	1	3	200	800	3000
W3HC-220	1697	[7]	NONO — y	1	3	50	120	450
W3HC-225	1697	no harp strings	NONO — y	1	3	60	140	550
W3HC-230	1697	[6]	OCTAVO — y	1	3	200	800	3000
W3HC-235	1698		DECIMO	1	3	40	85	300
W3HC-240	1698	8 over 7	DECIMO	1	3	90	200	800
W3HC-245	1698	GRA instead of GRA (obv.)	DECIMO	1	3	50	100	400
W3HC-250	1698	GVLIEIMVS instead of GVLIELMVS (obv.)	DECIMO	1	3	80	170	650
W3HC-255	1698	[8]	UNDECIMO	1	3	250	850	
W3HC-260	1698	[6]	OCTAVO	1	3	1000		
W3HC-265	1699	[9]	UNDECIMO	1	3	60	130	500
W3HC-268	1699	GRA instead of GRA (obv); each N in REGNI UNDECIMO is inverted (edge)	UNDECIMO	1	3	100	200	800
W3HC-270	1699	T∇TAMEN instead of TVTAMEN (edge)	UNDECIMO	1	3	70	150	650
W3HC-275	1699	DEC∇S ET T∇TAMEN instead of DECVS ET TVTAMEN	UNDECIMO	1	3	90	190	850
W3HC-280	1699	arms of Scotland at date [8]	UNDECIMO	1	3	700		
W3HC-285	1699	central lion inverted (rev.)	UNDECIMO	1	3	100	250	1000
W3HC-290	1700		DVODECIMO	1	3	50	100	350
W3HC-295	1700	[10]	DECIMO TERTIO	1	3	50	100	350
W3HC-300	1700	DEC∇S instead of DECVS (edge)	DECIMO TERTIO	1	3	60	120	450
W3HC-305	1701	[11]	DECIMO TERTIO	1	3	60	120	400
W3HC-310	1701	no stops on rev. [12]	DECIMO TERTIO	1	3	70	140	500
W3HC-315	1701	elephant and castle below head [13]	DECIMO TERTIO	1	3	1200		
W3HC-320	1701	plumes on rev. [14]	DECIMO TERTIO	1	3	70	180	650

1. Shield width varies.
2. Weight 23.3 grams; some are reverse ↑.
3. Weight 21.3 grams.
4. Weight c.21 grams; mintmark partially removed from coin (not die); edge lettering larger than regular issue.
5. May read T∇TAMEN (edge).
6. Error edge. Examples of the 1697 variety are known with 6 and with 7 harp strings.
7. Variety exists with badly cut 'y'.
8. Variety reads GRA (obv.).
9. Harp varies.
10. Lettering and harp vary.
11. Lettering and harp vary; see comment below.
12. See comment below.
13. Has large reverse lettering; see comment below.
14. Has small reverse lettering; see comment below.

The number of harp strings varies through this series. It is possible that the variation constituted a form of internal code denoting the die number.

Halfcrowns of 1701 have each L in GVLIELMVS with a much more prominent lower serif than those of other dates

Marks and Operating Periods of Provincial Mints

B: BRISTOL: September 1696 to September 1698
C: CHESTER: October 1696 to June 1698
E: EXETER: August 1696 to July 1698
N: NORWICH: September 1696 to April 1698
y: YORK: September 1696 to April 1698

Anne   (1702 – 1714)

John Croker continued as Chief Engraver, assisted by Samuel Bull. Croker produced a portrait based on a painting of Anne by Sir Godfrey Kneller. After the complexities of the William III coinage, the Anne series appears at first sight fairly simple, but collectors will find that it is not without challenge; it also straddles the union of England and Scotland, and thus has interesting historical significance. Provenance marks used are: VIGO for silver gleaned from Spanish galleons at Vigo Bay in 1702; plumes (in the reverse angles) for silver from Wales; roses and plumes (alternately in the angles of the reverse) for silver from the 'Company for smelting down lead with Pitcoale and Seacoale'. The mintmark E below the head of Anne represents coins struck at Edinburgh.

After the Union in 1707, the top and bottom shields on the reverse were each divided into the arms of England and Scotland.

Collecting Hints

Fine condition specimens are relatively plentiful and most collectors will require very fine or extremely fine coins. Some of the rarities are, however, difficult to find in the higher grades. This is particularly true of the 1709E, a piece which exhibits inferior workmanship and which is rarely encountered in above fine condition. Curiously, the 1703 VIGO is probably more easily found in very fine condition than in fine, probably the result of hoarding of the first date struck. Any coin offered as 1703 without VIGO must be examined closely for signs of artificial removal of the provenance mark.

Some dates, notably 1709 (plain), often occur with a slightly concave reverse. These coins suffer less wear on the reverse than on the obverse.

Denomination	Metal	Weight (grams)	Diameter (mm)	Rev. alignment
Halfcrown	Silver	14.8–15.0	33–34	↓

Obverse 1   Head 1, left; ANNA DEI GRATIA

Reverse 1   Four undivided cruciform shields with surmounting crowns; MAG BR FRA ET HIB REG (date); usually known as 'Before Union' reverse.

Reverse 2   Similar but top and bottom shields are each divided into the arms of England and Scotland; crowns are thinner; MAG BRI FR ET HIB REG (date); known as 'After Union' reverse.

Edge   (in relief) DECVS ET TVTAMEN ANNO REGNI (regnal date)

Obv. 1

Rev. 1

Rev. 2

Before Union of England and Scotland

No.	Date	Features	Edge date	Obv.	Rev.	F	VF	EF
ANHC-005	1703	VIGO below head	TERTIO	1	1	40	110	400
ANHC-010	1703		TERTIO	1	1	400	1200	
ANHC-015	1704	plumes on rev.	TERTIO	1	1	70	220	800
ANHC-020	1705	plumes on rev.	QVINTO	1	1	50	140	450
ANHC-025	1706	roses and plumes on rev.	QVINTO	1	1	40	120	350
ANHC-028	1706	T of QVINTO over V (edge)	QVINTO	1	1	60	180	500
ANHC-030	1707	roses and plumes on rev.	SEXTO	1	1	30	85	250

After Union of England and Scotland

No.	Date	Features	Edge date	Obv.	Rev.	F	VF	EF
ANHC-035	1707	E below head	SEXTO	1	2	26	65	170
ANHC-040	1707	E below head; ET*T*TAMEN instead of ET TVTAMEN	SEXTO	1	2	70	170	400
ANHC-045	1707	E below head [1]	SEPTIMO	1	2	800	2000	5000
ANHC-050	1707		SEPTIMO	1	2	30	75	200
ANHC-055	1707	E-T.T.TVTAMEN instead of ET TVTAMEN (edge)	SEPTIMO	1	2	70	170	400
ANHC-060	1707	struck on thick flan [2]	SEPTIMO	1	2	1000		
ANHC-065	1708	E below head [3]	SEPTIMO	1	2	30	75	200
ANHC-070	1708		SEPTIMO	1	2	30	65	180
ANHC-075	1708	plumes on rev.	SEPTIMO	1	2	35	90	240
ANHC-080	1709		OCTAVO	1	2	30	75	200
ANHC-085	1709	E below head; rev. ↑ [4]	OCTAVO	1	2	75	400	2000
ANHC-090	1710	roses and plumes on rev.	NONO	1	2	35	110	350
ANHC-095	1712	roses and plumes on rev.	UNDECIMO	1	2	35	100	280
ANHC-098	1712	roses and plumes on rev.; DECⱯS instead of DECVS (edge)	UNDECIMO	1	2	50	130	350
ANHC-100	1713		DVODECIMO	1	2	35	80	220

No.	Date	Features	Edge date	Obv.	Rev.	F	VF	EF
ANHC-105	1713	roses and plumes on rev.	DVODECIMO	1	2	35	90	280
ANHC-108	1713	roses and plumes on rev.; DECⱯS ET TⱯTAMEN instead of DECVS ET TVTAMEN (edge)	DVODECIMO	1	2	50	130	400
ANHC-110	1714	roses and plumes on rev.	DECIMO TERTIO	1	2	35	90	270
ANHC-115	1714	roses and plumes on rev.; ANN instead of ANNO (edge)	DECIMO TERTIO	1	2	70	200	500
ANHC-120	1714	4 over 3 roses and plumes on rev.	DECIMO TERTIO	1	2	35	90	280

1. At least one specimen exists in EF condition.
2. Weight 20–21 grams.
3. 1 in date varies.
4. Inferior workmanship; numerals different from those on London 1709 coin. The '1' is a reversed-Z instead of the J-type.

Minor obverse varieties occur. The number of harp strings varies through this series. It is possible that the variation constituted a form of internal code denoting the die number.

George I (1714 – 1727)

The halfcrown series was redesigned to accommodate the Hanoverian accession and the reverse legend includes a greatly abbreviated form of the German titles of the new king. The reverse translates from the Latin as: 'Duke of Brunswick and Lüneburg, Arch-Treasurer of the Holy Roman Empire, and Elector'. The Brunswick-Lüneburg arms are incorporated in one of the reverse shields.

The design was the work of John Croker, aided by J. R. Ochs, senior.

Provenance marks are: roses and plumes (see Anne); SSC (silver from The South Sea Company).

Collecting Hints

The George I halfcrown is a handsome coin even in fine condition, and its scarcity renders it perfectly acceptable in this grade to many collectors, although very fine or better specimens are much more desirable. The short series has a number of interesting varieties and rarities. In top grades, the most plentiful date is probably 1723.

Denomination	Metal	Weight (grams)	Diameter (mm)	Rev. alignment
Halfcrown	Silver	15.0–15.1	33–34	↓

Obverse 1 Head 1, right; GEORGIVS D G M BR FR ET HIB REX F D

Reverse 1 Four crowned cruciform shields; BRVN ET L DVX S R I A TH ET EL (date)

Edge (in relief) DECVS ET TVTAMEN ANNO REGNI (regnal date) (but see G1HC-040, note 5)

Obv. 1   Rev. 1

No.	Date	Features	Edge date	Obv.	Rev.	F	VF	EF
G1HC-005	1715	PROOF or PATTERN; edge plain [1]		1	1			6000
G1HC-010	1715	roses and plumes on rev.	SECVNDO	1	1	90	250	800
G1HC-012	1715	roses and plumes on rev.; NNO instead of ANNO (edge)	SECVNDO	1	1	130	350	1200
G1HC-015	1715	roses and plumes on rev.; edge lettering blundered	SECVNDO	1	1	300		
G1HC-020	1715	roses and plumes on rev.; edge plain		1	1	500	1800	
G1HC-025	1717	roses and plumes on rev. [2]	TIRTIO [3]	1	1	90	250	800
G1HC-030	1720	roses and plumes on rev. [4]	SEXTO	1	1	120	320	1000
G1HC-035	1720	20 over 17 roses and plumes on rev.	SEXTO	1	1	90	250	800
G1HC-040	1723	SSC on rev. [5]	DECIMO	1	1	90	250	800
G1HC-045	1726	roses and plumes on rev. [6]	DECIMO TERTIO	1	1	900	2000	

1. Plain in angles; usually has die flaw by GEORGIVS (obv.).
2. Regnal edge date always misspelt.
3. Marshall considers that this edge may be TLRTIO.
4. Unaltered date.
5. Edge reads DECUS ET TUTAMEN not DECVS ET TVTAMEN.
6. Roses and plumes smaller than on earlier dates.

Each '1' in the date on the 1715 coin is a 'J' type. Subsequent dates have a 'Z' type '1'.

George II (1727 – 1760)

As with the crowns, the early head of the king by Croker contrasts with the later head by Tanner, as do the relative scarcities of the two types. The first type is struck in relatively high relief and consequently can be difficult to find in top grades, and commands high prices thus. In 1742, Peter Vallavine observed that half-crowns 'are rarely to be met with'. The later LIMA halfcrown with the older head is one of the most popular and frequently encountered coins of this denomination.

Provenance marks are: roses (or roses and plumes) as on earlier issues; LIMA below the head for coins struck in silver captured by Admiral Anson. The reason for the use of the word LIMA has never been satisfactorily established, and it may therefore be wrong to call it a provenance mark.

Compared with the George I coinage, some of the German titles of the king are transferred from the obverse to the reverse. The reverse translation now reads: 'King of Great Britain, France and Ireland, Defender of the Faith, Duke of Brunswick and Lüneburg, Arch-Treasurer of the Holy Roman Empire and Elector'.

Collecting Hints

The young head halfcrowns (1731–41) are moderately scarce and a minimum grade of fine should be sought. The older head type is fairly easily found and most collectors will look for a very fine or better coin. The last two dates minted (1750 and 1751) are both scarce but a higher proportion of them have survived in very fine or extremely fine condition, possibly as a result of their being collected after the death of the king.

The 1745 and 1746 halfcrowns frequently occur with edge pinholes, no doubt the result of a short-lived fashion for mounting the pieces for personal adornment; consequently, the edges of coins from this period must always be carefully examined.

English Silver Coinage lists a 'very rare' variety of 1743 halfcrown which has U instead of V in GEORGIUS. In fact, all halfcrowns of this date are of this type.

Denomination	Metal	Weight (grams)	Diameter (mm)	Rev. alignment
Halfcrown	Silver	14.8–15.1	34	↓

Obverse 1   Head 1, left; GEORGIVS II (Head) DEI GRATIA

Obverse 2   Head 2, left; GEORGIUS II (Head) DEI GRATIA

Obverse 3   Head 2, left; same legend but GEORGIVS instead of GEORGIUS

Reverse 1   Four crowned cruciform shields; M B F ET H REX F D B ET L D S R I A T ET E (date)

Edge   (in relief) DECVS ET TVTAMEN ANNO REGNI (regnal date)

Obv. 1   Obv. 3

Rev. 1

No.	Date	Features	Edge date	Obv.	Rev.	F	VF	EF
G2HC-005	1731	PROOF or PATTERN; edge plain		1	1			2500
G2HC-010	1731	roses and plumes on rev. [1]	QVINTO	1	1	60	180	900
G2HC-015	1732	roses and plumes on rev.	SEXTO	1	1	50	150	750
G2HC-020	1734	roses and plumes on rev.	SEPTIMO	1	1	50	150	750
G2HC-025	1735	roses and plumes on rev.	OCTAVO	1	1	50	150	750

No.	Date	Features	Edge date	Obv.	Rev.	F	VF	EF
G2HC-030	1736	roses and plumes on rev.	NONO	1	1	55	170	850
G2HC-035	1739	roses on rev.	DVODECIMO	1	1	40	110	350
G2HC-038	1739	roses on rev.; TVTAME instead of TVTAMEN (edge)	DVODECIMO	1	1	65	200	600
G2HC-040	1741	roses on rev. [2]	DECIMO QVARTO	1	1	45	130	400
G2HC-045	1741	41 over 39 roses on rev.	DECIMO QVARTO	1	1	40	110	350
G2HC-050	1743	roses on rev.	DECIMO SEPTIMO	2	1	40	100	280
G2HC-055	1745	roses on rev.	DECIMO NONO	2	1	40	100	280
G2HC-060	1745	5 over 3 roses on rev.	DECIMO NONO	2	1	45	120	350
G2HC-065	1745	LIMA below head [3]	DECIMO NONO	2	1	35	60	180
G2HC-070	1746	LIMA below head [3]	DECIMO NONO	3	1	30	55	160
G2HC-075	1746	6 over 5 LIMA below head	DECIMO NONO	3	1	45	75	240
G2HC-080	1746	PROOF [4]	VICESIMO	3	1			900
G2HC-082	1746	PROOF; E of DECVS over A [4]	VICESIMO	3	1			900
G2HC-085	1750		VICESIMO QVARTO	3	1	70	200	750
G2HC-090	1751		VICESIMO QVARTO	3	1	80	200	700

1. Q of QVINTO appears to be on its side on some or all specimens (edge).
2. A variety has slightly larger obverse lettering.
3. Scottish arms vary.
4. The head is very slightly different from that on the ordinary issue; the edge lettering is also smaller.

The number of harp strings varies through this series. It is possible that the variation constituted a form of internal code denoting the die number.

George III   (1760 – 1820)

The scarce countermarked Spanish or Spanish-American 4 reales was a by-product of the much larger issue of countermarked 8 reales, the result of the silver shortage of the period. Around 1804, many complaints were voiced about the lack of silver coinage below the value of 5 shillings. Although the government promised that the matter would receive attention and that a supply of coins was being prepared, the first true halfcrown of the reign was issued only during its last five years, using the new equipment at Tower Hill, and yet it yielded two quite different designs for the portrait.

Thomas Wyon engraved the portrait of the king for the first halfcrown, from a design by Benedetto Pistrucci. Wyon designed and engraved the reverse. The first type of halfcrown has become known as the 'Bull Head' type, and it was replaced during 1817. The replacement bore a smaller and more attractive head, also by Wyon after Pistrucci, with a reverse by Pistrucci himself. Thomas Wyon died of consumption in September 1817, and it fell to Pistrucci to engrave the dies subsequently.

The new designs for the halfcrown after the 'Great Recoinage' incorporated a number of innovations. Indeed, the designs owed more to those of the Spanish coinage which had been counterstamped and used as currency. The date was placed under the head as on the 4 reales rather than, as previously, on the reverse. The reverse design of the halfcrown is similar to that of the 4 reales, and for the first time the reverse is not inverted relative to the obverse. This, too, is characteristic of the Spanish coinage.

Denomination	Metal	Weight (grams)	Diameter (mm)	Rev. alignment
Counterstamped Spanish 4 reales or Spanish-American 4 reales	Silver	13–14	32–34	↑
Counterstamped other foreign coins (halfcrown size)	Silver	as host coin	as host coin	as host coin

Oval Counterstamp

Obverse 1   George III head, right, in oval counterstamped on Spanish 4 reales obverse

Obverse 2   Similar but on Spanish-American 4 reales obverse

Obverse 3   Similar but on other foreign coins (halfcrown size)

Octagonal Counterstamp

Obverse 4   George III head in octagon counterstamped on Spanish 4 reales obverse

Obverse 5   Similar but on Spanish-American 4 reales obverse

Obverse 6   Similar but on other foreign coins (halfcrown size)

Reverse   As of the appropriate host coin, partially flattened where stamped

Edge   As of the appropriate host coin

Obv. oval counterstamp   Obv. octagonal counterstamp

Rev.

No.	Date		Obv.	Rev.	F	VF	EF
G3HC-005	none		1	1	100	200	400
G3HC-010	none		2	2	150	300	700
G3HC-015	none		3	3	300	500	900

No.	Date		Obv.	Rev.	F	VF	EF
G3HC-020	none		4	4	150	300	600
G3HC-025	none		5	5	200	400	750
G3HC-030	none		6	6	400	650	1100

Occasionally one meets a piece with the reverse counterstamped, or with the counterstamp inverted.

Denomination	Metal	Weight (grams)	Diameter (mm)	Rev. alignment
Halfcrown	Silver	14.1	32	↑

Obverse 1   Head 1, right; GEORGIUS III (Head) DEI GRATIA (date)

Obverse 2   Head 2, smaller, right; GEORGIUS III DEI GRATIA (date)

Reverse 1   Shield with Garter, crown above; BRITANNIARUM REX FID DEF; on Garter HONI SOIT QUI MAL Y PENSE

Reverse 2   Similar but differently designed; same legends

Edge   milled

Obv. 1   Obv. 2

Rev. 1   Rev. 2

No.	Date	Features	Obv.	Rev.	F	VF	EF	UNC
G3HC-035	1816	[1]	1	1	14	35	120	220
G3HC-040	1816	PROOF	1	1				1100
G3HC-045	1816	PROOF; edge plain	1	1				1300
G3HC-050	1817		1	1	12	30	110	170
G3HC-055	1817	D of DEI over T (obv.)	1	1	18	55	200	300
G3HC-057	1817	E of DEF over R (rev.)	1	1				500
G3HC-058	1817	S of PENSE over I (rev.)	1	1	24	65	250	400
G3HC-060	1817	PROOF	1	1				1200
G3HC-065	1817	PROOF; edge plain	1	1				1700
G3HC-070	1817	PROOF in copper	1	1				1000
G3HC-075	1817		2	2	12	30	110	170
G3HC-080	1817	each 'S' in Garter motto reversed (rev.)	2	2	30	70	200	300
G3HC-085	1817	PROOF	2	2				1200
G3HC-090	1817	PROOF; edge plain	2	2				1000
G3HC-095	1818		2	2	16	40	130	200
G3HC-098	1818	'S' in garter motto reversed (rev.)	2	2	50	120	350	600
G3HC-100	1818	PROOF	2	2				2000
G3HC-105	1819		2	2	12	30	110	170
G3HC-110	1819	9 over 8	2	2	50	100	400	600
G3HC-115	1819	PROOF	2	2				1700
G3HC-120	1820	[2]	2	2	14	35	120	180
G3HC-125	1820	PROOF	2	2				2200
G3HC-130	1820	PROOF; edge plain	2	2				2000

1. Issued in 1817.
2. Reverse orientation slightly different from previous dates.

George IV   (1820 – 1830)

The first issue of halfcrowns used the laureate head of the monarch by Benedetto Pistrucci as on the crowns, which was changed in 1824/25 to the Wyon portrait owing to the king's disapproval of his portrayal. The reverse underwent two major changes of design, resulting in 1825 in an obverse and reverse both very similar to those on the 1826 proof crown. The axis alignment reverted to that used on pre-George III coinage. It is not generally appreciated that the reverses include the carefully hidden initials both of William Wellesley Pole, Master of the Mint, in the centres of the shamrocks, and those of Johann Baptiste Merlen, designer of the reverse, in the beading around the rim.

Collecting Hints

Most of the dates are not too difficult to find in extremely fine or near, but the 1823 with the early reverse is a real rarity, seldom offered in the major salerooms, and even then usually only in fair or fine condition.

Denomination	Metal	Weight (grams)	Diameter (mm)	Rev. alignment
Halfcrown	Silver	14.1	32	↓

Obverse 1   Head 1, laureate, left; GEORGIUS IIII D G BRITANNIAR REX F D

Obverse 2   Head 2, so-called 'bare head', left; GEORGIUS IV DEI GRATIA (date)

Reverse 1   Garnished shield with surmounting large crown; ANNO (date)

Reverse 2   Similar but many minor differences (thistle leaves, harp strings, shamrock stalks, crown, etc.)

Reverse 3   Crowned shield within Garter and collar; ANNO (date); on Garter HONI SOIT QUI MAL Y PENSE

Reverse 4   Garnished flat-top shield with surmounting helmet and small crown; BRITANNIARUM REX FID DEF; on scroll DIEU ET MON DROIT

Edge   milled

Obv. 1   Obv. 2

Rev. 1   Rev. 2

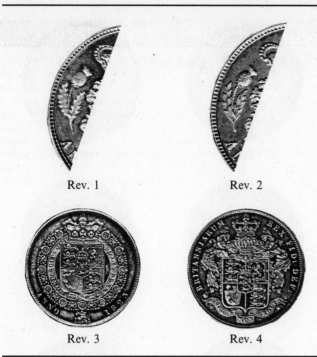

Rev. 1   Rev. 2

Rev. 3   Rev. 4

Obverse 1   Head 1, right; W.W. incuse on truncation in small block capitals; GULIELMUS IIII D G (Head) BRITANNIAR REX F D

Obverse 2   Similar but W.W. incuse in script, somewhat larger; hair slightly differently arranged

Reverse 1   Crowned shield on mantle; below ANNO (date)

Edge   milled

Obv. 1   Rev. 1

No.	Date	Features	Obv.	Rev.	F	VF	EF	UNC
G4HC-005	1820		1	1	12	35	120	200
G4HC-010	1820	PROOF	1	1				800
G4HC-015	1820	PROOF; edge plain	1	1				1400
G4HC-020	1820	PROOF	1	2				1000
G4HC-025	1821		1	1	12	35	120	200
G4HC-030	1821		1	2	25	60	300	450
G4HC-035	1821	PROOF	1	2				1200
G4HC-040	1823	[1]	1	2	250	800		
G4HC-045	1823		1	3	15	50	150	240
G4HC-050	1823	PROOF	1	3				1500
G4HC-055	1824		1	3	18	60	180	280
G4HC-060	1824	PROOF	1	3				1800
G4HC-065	1824	PROOF in copper; edge plain [1]	1	3				800
G4HC-070	1824		2	4	500			
G4HC-075	1825		2	4	15	40	130	220
G4HC-080	1825	PROOF	2	4				650
G4HC-085	1825	PROOF; edge plain	2	4				700
G4HC-090	1825	PROOF in Barton's metal; edge plain [2]	2	4				1700
G4HC-095	1826		2	4	12	35	120	200
G4HC-100	1826	PROOF [3]	2	4				750
G4HC-105	1828		2	4	18	65	240	350
G4HC-110	1829		2	4	15	50	180	280

1. See pattern section.
2. Barton's metal is a laminated product consisting of thin sheets of gold bonded to a copper base.
3. Issued in cased proof sets.

No.	Date	Features	Obv.	Rev.	F	VF	EF	UNC
W4HC-005	1831		1	1	600			
W4HC-010	1831	PROOF; edge plain [1]	1	1				600
W4HC-015	1831	PROOF	2	1				3000
W4HC-020	1831	PROOF; edge plain [2]	2	1				800
W4HC-025	1831	PROOF; edge plain; rev. ↑ [3]	2	1				1200
W4HC-030	1834		1	1	20	90	300	500
W4HC-035	1834	PROOF	1	1				1800
W4HC-040	1834		2	1	12	40	140	240
W4HC-045	1834	PROOF	2	1				1200
W4HC-050	1834	PROOF; edge plain	2	1				3000
W4HC-055	1835		2	1	15	70	300	500
W4HC-060	1836		2	1	12	40	140	240
W4HC-065	1836	6 over 5	2	1	15	60	200	300
W4HC-070	1836	PROOF; edge plain	2	1				3000
W4HC-075	1837		2	1	15	70	300	500

1. Issued in cased proof sets; hair arrangement slightly different from that on usual obverse 1; obverse border teeth finer.
2. A few were issued in cased proof sets; may weigh only c.13 grams.
3. Rim may be shallower than on other plain edge proofs of this date; possibly struck at a later date.

William IV   (1830 – 1837)

The design of the halfcrown by William Wyon (obv.) and Johann Baptiste Merlen (rev.) was very similar to that of the proof crown, and remained identical throughout the reign except for the variation of Wyon's initials on the obverse.

Victoria   (1837 – 1901)

Although the halfcrown series of Victoria began with an interesting and complex set of varieties for the first date, 1839, it continued in a lower key with only the change of date, and occasionally of type, providing interest. After 1850, a long gap in the series was occasioned by an attempt to promote the florin as a precursor of decimal currency, but in 1874 the halfcrown was reintroduced, and the elegant high relief portrait of the first decade gave way to a low relief and less attractive example. It had unfortunately been found that the high relief coinage wore too quickly for practical purposes. The unpopular Boehm portrait of 1887 and the Brock 1893 design were similar to those on the other silver denominations. The 1893 coin is the first bearing the denomination mark 'HALF CROWN'.

Collecting Hints

The coins should be collected in extremely fine or better condition. This is not a scarce series, with the possible exception of the 1835; however, very fine pieces do retain most of the detail of the design, especially on the reverse, and may be satisfactory to collectors wishing to concentrate on acquiring better pieces of more interesting series.

Collecting Hints

The serious collector will look only for extremely fine or better specimens throughout this series. The quality of the early high relief pieces up to 1850 can only be appreciated properly in these grades, and the later halfcrowns are so prolific in fine or very fine that their appeal will be mainly directed towards making up date sets rather than serious study of the workmanship.
The note in the crown section on distinguishing the 1887 proof crown applies equally to the 1887 and 1893 halfcrowns.
Occasionally one comes across halfcrowns dated 1866,

Denomination	Metal	Weight (grams)	Diameter (mm)	Rev. alignment
Halfcrown	Silver	14.1	32	↓

1868 and 1871, always in fair or fine condition. These exhibit marked differences from the regular coins, and are forgeries, even though at least one is reported to have been authenticated by the Royal Mint.

In particular, the lettering is irregular and poorly formed, and the background lines are not parallel to the axis of the shield. The view has been expressed that they may have been copies made in about 1870, but the portrait resembles the later 1874 type, indicating that they were fabricated after that date, possibly around 1910. The forgeries are sought by collectors, and change hands for up to £100.

Obv. 5

Obv. 6

Obv. 7

Obv. 8

Denomination	Metal	Weight (grams)	Diameter (mm)	Rev. alignment
Halfcrown 1839–87 rev. 1	Silver	14.1	32	↓
Halfcrown 1887–1901 revs 2, 3	Silver	14.1	32	↑

Obverse 1   Head 1, left; one plain and one ornate fillet in the hair, W.W. in relief on the truncation. VICTORIA DEI GRATIA (date)

Obverse 2   Head 2, left; similar but both fillets are ornate. W.W. in relief; same legend

Obverse 3   Head 3, left; similar but both fillets are plain. W.W. in relief; same legend

Obverse 4   Head 4, left; both fillets are plain. W.W. incuse; same legend

Obverse 5   Head 5, left; both fillets are plain. No initials on truncation; same legend

Obverse 6   Head 6, in lower relief, left; both fillets plain. No initials on truncation; same legend but slight spacing variations

Obverse 7   Head 7, 'Jubilee' type with small crown on head, left. VICTORIA (Head) DEI GRATIA

Obverse 8   Head 8, 'Old Head' type, left. VICTORIA DEI (Head) GRA BRITT REG

Reverse 1   Crowned shield within branches. BRITANNIARUM REGINA FID DEF. Slight variations from 1879

Reverse 2   Crowned shield within Garter and collar. BRITANNIARUM REGINA FID DEF (date)

Reverse 3   Crowned 'spade' shield in collar of the Garter. FID DEF IND IMP HALF (date) CROWN

Edge   milled

Rev. 1

Rev. 2

Rev. 3

large date

small date (double struck)

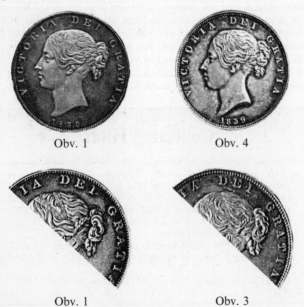

Obv. 1

Obv. 4

Obv. 1

Obv. 3

Young Head

No.	Date	Features	Obv.	Rev.	F	VF	EF	UNC
VYHC-005	1839		1	1	500	1100	4000	7500
VYHC-010	1839	PROOF	1	1				3000
VYHC-015	1839	PROOF; edge plain; rev. ↑ [1]	1	1				600
VYHC-020	1839	PROOF; edge plain [1]	1	1				600
VYHC-025	1839	PROOF; edge plain	2	1				2000
VYHC-030	1839	PROOF; edge plain; rev. ↑	3	1				5000
VYHC-035	1839		4	1	500	1100	4000	
VYHC-040	1839	PROOF	4	1				3500
VYHC-045	1839	PROOF; edge plain	4	1				3000
VYHC-050	1840		4	1	18	70	200	350
VYHC-055	1841		5	1	100	300	700	1800
VYHC-060	1842		5	1	14	50	160	250

No.	Date	Features	Obv.	Rev.	F	VF	EF	UNC
VYHC-065	1843		5	1	25	80	250	400
VYHC-068	1844	plain 4 in date	5	1	18	65	200	350
VYHC-070	1844	crosslet 4 in date	5	1	12	45	140	220
VYHC-075	1844	struck on large flan; edge plain	5	1	100	400		
VYHC-080	1845		5	1	12	45	140	220
VYHC-085	1846		5	1	15	55	170	270
VYHC-088	1846	8 over 1	5	1	22	75	240	400
VYHC-089	1846	8 over 6	5	1	50	150	500	
VYHC-090	1848	²	5	1	50	160	700	1000
VYHC-095	1848	latter 8 over 6	5	1	40	140	600	900
VYHC-100	1848	latter 8 over 7	5	1	120	350	1100	1800
VYHC-105	1849	large date	5	1	20	70	200	350
VYHC-108	1849	large date; 9 over 7	5	1	500			
VYHC-110	1849	small date	5	1	50	160	500	1000
VYHC-115	1850		5	1	20	75	250	450
VYHC-120	1850	PROOF	5	1				2500
VYHC-125	1853	PROOF ¹	5	1				1500
VYHC-130	1862	PROOF	1	1				1500
VYHC-135	1862	PROOF; edge plain; rev. ↑	1	1				3000
VYHC-140	1864	PROOF; rev. ↑ ³	1	1				2500
VYHC-145	1864	PROOF; edge plain; rev. ↑ ³	1	1				2500
VYHC-150	1874		6	1	10	30	100	140
VYHC-155	1874	PROOF	6	1				800
VYHC-160	1874	PROOF; edge plain	6	1				1500
VYHC-162	1874	PROOF; edge plain; rev ↑	6	1				2500
VYHC-165	1874	PROOF in gold; edge plain	6	1				15000
VYHC-170	1875		6	1	10	35	110	150
VYHC-175	1875	PROOF	6	1				1200
VYHC-180	1875	PROOF; edge plain	6	1				5000
VYHC-185	1876		6	1	12	35	120	160
VYHC-190	1876	6 over 5	6	1	18	50	150	200
VYHC-195	1877		6	1	12	35	120	160
VYHC-200	1878		6	1	12	35	120	160
VYHC-205	1878	PROOF	6	1				1500
VYHC-210	1879	⁴	6	1	12	35	120	160
VYHC-215	1879	PROOF; rev. ↑	6	1				1000
VYHC-220	1879	PROOF; edge plain; rev. ↑	6	1				1500
VYHC-225	1880	⁵	6	1	12	35	120	160
VYHC-230	1880	PROOF	6	1				1500
VYHC-235	1881	⁶	6	1	10	30	100	140
VYHC-240	1881	PROOF	6	1				1200
VYHC-245	1881	PROOF; edge plain	6	1				4000
VYHC-250	1882		6	1	12	35	120	160
VYHC-255	1883		6	1	10	30	100	140
VYHC-260	1884		6	1	10	30	100	140
VYHC-265	1885		6	1	10	30	100	140
VYHC-270	1885	PROOF	6	1				1500
VYHC-275	1886	⁷	6	1	10	30	100	140
VYHC-280	1886	PROOF	6	1				3000
VYHC-285	1887		6	1	10	28	90	120
VYHC-290	1887	PROOF	6	1				3000

1. Issued in cased proof sets.
2. Obverse lettering irregularly spaced.
3. Struck for Albert Memorial opening.
4. Minor obverse differences occur.
5. Number of border teeth vary on reverse.
6. Minor obverse orientation differences occur.
7. This date often occurs with unsightly streaking.

Jubilee Head

No.	Date	Features	Obv.	Rev.	F	VF	EF	UNC
VJHC-295	1887	¹	7	2	6	9	18	30
VJHC-300	1887	PROOF ²	7	2				130
VJHC-305	1888		7	2	7	12	45	85
VJHC-310	1889	³	7	2	7	11	40	60
VJHC-315	1890		7	2	7	16	60	120
VJHC-320	1891		7	2	7	16	60	120
VJHC-325	1892		7	2	7	16	60	130

1. Minor differences occur in crown (obv.).
2. Issued in cased proof sets.
3. Reverse border teeth vary in size; other minor differences occur.

Old Head

No.	Date	Features	Obv.	Rev.	F	VF	EF	UNC
VOHC-330	1893	¹	8	3	7	14	45	75
VOHC-335	1893	PROOF ²	8	3				160
VOHC-340	1894		8	3	8	20	80	130
VOHC-345	1895		8	3	8	18	70	110
VOHC-350	1896		8	3	8	17	65	100
VOHC-355	1897		8	3	7	14	50	75
VOHC-360	1898		8	3	7	17	65	95
VOHC-365	1899		8	3	7	16	60	90
VOHC-370	1900		8	3	7	14	50	75
VOHC-375	1901		8	3	7	14	45	70

1. Reverse border teeth vary in size; other minor differences occur.
2. Issued in cased proof sets.

Edward VII   (1901 – 1910)

The obverse portrait of Edward by George William de Saulles (1862–1903) was produced by a mechanical reduction process from the original master. The series was a one-type issue. It was the first which included a dated coin for every year of a monarch's reign.

Collecting Hints

Although, with the exception of the 1905, Edward VII half-crowns are easily found in fine condition, in top grades they can be surprisingly elusive. Moreover, the nature of the striking, and the manner in which they wear, can deceive the inexperienced eye as to how much wear a coin has sustained. Careful comparison with both the obverse and reverse of, say, a 1902 matt proof halfcrown will often show that one's optimism has not been justified. In the lower grades the 'P' of 'PENSE' is usually the first letter of the reverse to become worn off.
Clever forgeries of the 1905 halfcrown exist, and any coins with concave or 'blistered' fields should be suspect.

Denomination	Metal	Weight (grams)	Diameter (mm)	Rev. alignment
Halfcrown	Silver	14.1	32	↑

Obverse 1   Head 1, right; EDWARDVS VII DEI GRA BRITT OMN REX

Reverse 1   Crowned shield within Garter; FID DEF IND IMP HALF (date) CROWN

On Garter HONI SOIT QUI MAL Y PENSE

Edge   milled

Obv. 1   Rev. 1

No.	Date	Features	Obv.	Rev.	F	VF	EF	UNC
E7HC-005	1902		1	1	7	14	40	60
E7HC-010	1902	matt PROOF ¹	1	1			35	50
E7HC-015	1903		1	1	30	100	350	600
E7HC-020	1904		1	1	12	50	300	500
E7HC-025	1905		1	1	120	400	1000	1800
E7HC-030	1906		1	1	7	18	80	180
E7HC-035	1907		1	1	7	18	80	180
E7HC-040	1908		1	1	8	20	100	250
E7HC-045	1909		1	1	7	18	80	200

No.	Date	Features	Obv.	Rev.	F	VF	EF	UNC
E7HC-050	1910		1	1	7	18	70	130

1. Issued in cased proof sets.

George V   (1910 – 1936)

As with Edward VII, the halfcrown was struck for each year of the reign, and used the well-known portrait of the monarch by Sir Bertram Mackennal, whose initials B.M. appear on the truncation. The first reverse, although similar to that of the Edward VII coinage, is struck and wears so differently from its predecessor that many collectors would be forgiven for believing it to be a different reverse, and most would be baffled if asked to differentiate between the two. In fact, apart from minor differences in lettering, the main alteration is the omission of the beaded circle around the shield. The George V coins also have a slightly concave or 'dished' appearance contrasting with the rather 'flat' look of the Edward VII halfcrowns.

On 11 February 1920, silver was trading at 7s 5½d per ounce on the London market, and the intrinsic value of a sterling silver halfcrown was 3s 2d. It was clearly ridiculous that a coin should circulate for less than it would cost to produce, and furthermore such coins would soon disappear from circulation to be melted down. Consequently, the alloy was changed to include 50% of silver instead of 92.5%. Coins up to 1922 tarnished very unattractively, and a change in the base metal (non-silver) constituents after then rendered the alloy more acceptable in this respect.

In the first two editions of this catalogue, the writer tendered his opinion that the pre-1920 halfcrowns differed in appearance from the later type solely because of the relative difference in hardness between the two alloys used. He is now prepared to fall on his sword following valuable research by Chris Rigby, who has pointed out design differences between the obverses of the two types. The portrait on the later halfcrown is 1 mm larger from the top to the truncation, and the top and bottom of each 'E' in the legend has a tiny serif on the earlier type, with none on the later one. Consequently, the obverses have now been renumbered.

The reverse of the halfcrown was altered in 1927 as part of a radical redesigning of the silver currency by George Kruger Gray (1880–1943). The 1927 halfcrown bearing the new design was issued only as a proof as part of the cased proof set of that year, the first currency issue being in 1928. The reverse again sported a shield, but of a very different design. One of its more unusual features was a large slot at the top left corner, intended to represent the hole through which the lance was meant to pass.

From 1928 onwards small quantities of proofs were struck each year for record purposes. These were sent to museums, other mints, and occasionally presented to important visitors.

The new design of halfcrown was minted until a few months after the death of the king in 1936.

Collecting Hints

This series should be collected in extremely fine or better condition. Those looking for a sequence of dates in fine or very fine should not find the task of assembling them too difficult. A few of the dates are surprisingly difficult to find in top condition.
Care should be taken in grading; it is, for example, easy to overestimate the grade of the reverses of the halfcrowns of 1928–36 and particular attention should be paid to the amount of detail present in the hair of the obverse portrait. Conversely, many collectors undergrade extremely fine coins between 1920 and 1927.
What sometimes appears as a 'dig' on the portrait of the early dates, especially the 1911 proof, is in fact part of the design, as can be seen clearly if one inspects a 1911 proof set. Single 1911 proof coins are occasionally catalogued as

being 'with nick on the portrait' in auctions. It may be worth bidding on these!
The use of 'silver dip' is not normally recommended, but there is no doubt that chemical removal of the ugly yellow tarnish often seen on very fine to extremely fine pieces in the period 1920–22 does enhance their appearance.

Denomination	Metal	Weight (grams)	Diameter (mm)	Rev. alignment
Halfcrown 1911–19	0.925 Silver	14.1	32	↑
Halfcrown 1920–22	Silver 50%; copper 40%; nickel 10%	14.1	32	↑
Halfcrown 1922–27	Silver 50%; copper 50%	14.1	32	↑
Halfcrown 1927–36	Silver 50%; copper 40%; nickel 5%; zinc 5%	14.1	32	↑

Obverse 1   Head 1, 24 mm from top of head to tip of truncation; B.M. on truncation, left; GEORGIVS DEI GRA BRITT OMN REX

Obverse 2   Head 2, similar but 25 mm from 'top to tip'; same legend

Obverse 3   Head 3, so-called 'modified effigy', left; BM (no stops) further to right; same legend. beading recut; beads are wider than previously, and fewer in number

Reverse 1   Crowned shield within Garter; FID DEF IND IMP HALF (date) CROWN

On Garter HONI SOIT QUI MAL Y PENSE

Reverse 2   Shield with flanking interlinked and crowned 'G's. FID DEF IND IMP HALF CROWN (date)

Edge   milled

Obv. 1   Obv. 3

Rev. 1   Rev. 2

Sterling Silver Issue

No.	Date	Features	Obv.	Rev.	F	VF	EF	UNC
G5HC-005	1911		1	1	4	10	35	80
G5HC-010	1911	PROOF [1]	1	1			35	75
G5HC-015	1912		1	1	5	12	40	85
G5HC-020	1913		1	1	5	14	50	110
G5HC-025	1914		1	1	4	8	16	30
G5HC-030	1915		1	1	4	8	14	25
G5HC-035	1916		1	1	4	8	14	25
G5HC-040	1917		1	1	4	8	16	30
G5HC-045	1918		1	1	4	8	14	25

No.	Date	Features	Obv.	Rev.	F	VF	EF	UNC
G5HC-050	1919		1	1	4	10	20	40

1. Issued in cased proof sets.

50% Silver Issue

No.	Date	Features	Obv.	Rev.	F	VF	EF	UNC
G5HC-055	1920	1	1	1	4	10	25	55
G5HC-058	1920		2	1	4	10	25	55
G5HC-060	1921		2	1	4	10	12	30	55
G5HC-065	1922	2	2	1	4	10	25	55
G5HC-070	1923		2	1	4	8	16	22
G5HC-075	1924		2	1	4	14	35	65
G5HC-080	1925		2	1	5	20	140	300
G5HC-085	1926	3	2	1	4	10	35	90
G5HC-090	1926	4	3	1	4	10	35	100
G5HC-095	1927	4	3	1	3	7	25	40
G5HC-098	1927	struck in a gold alloy 5	3	1				7000
G5HC-100	1927	PROOF in nickel	3	1				2000
G5HC-105	1927	PROOF 6	3	2	10	15	25	35
G5HC-110	1927	PROOF from sandblasted dies 7	3	2				500
G5HC-115	1928	8	3	2	3	6	10	15
G5HC-120	1928	PROOF	3	2				500
G5HC-125	1929	8	3	2	3	6	10	15
G5HC-130	1929	PROOF	3	2				500
G5HC-135	1930		3	2	5	15	90	200
G5HC-140	1930	PROOF	3	2				1000
G5HC-145	1931		3	2	3	6	10	20
G5HC-150	1931	PROOF	3	2				550
G5HC-155	1932		3	2	3	7	20	45
G5HC-160	1932	PROOF	3	2				600
G5HC-165	1933		3	2	3	6	10	20
G5HC-170	1933	PROOF	3	2				500
G5HC-175	1934		3	2	3	8	35	65
G5HC-180	1934	PROOF	3	2				500
G5HC-185	1935		3	2	3	6	10	15
G5HC-190	1935	PROOF	3	2				500
G5HC-195	1936		3	2	3	6	8	12
G5HC-200	1936	PROOF	3	2				600

1. A few may exist in sterling silver.
2. Minor reverse differences occur; metal composition changes during year; see table above.
3. Defective obverse legend stops exist.
4. Reverse beading recut.
5. About four pieces exist, the result of trials by the Royal Mint at the request of overseas governments to test alloys of gold with silver and copper in various proportions. Weights 17.4 to 19.9 grams.
6. Issued in cased proof sets.
7. Struck to facilitate photography of coin.
8. Minor reverse varieties occur.

Edward VIII (1936)

The Edward VIII halfcrown is strictly speaking a pattern, as probable Royal approval was about to be granted at the time of the abdication. However, because its official status rests only on this technicality, and to provide continuity, it is included here.

The portrait of Edward VIII is by Thomas Humphrey Paget, and faces left at the insistence of the king, who considered this placement more flattering and wished to discontinue the tradition of opposite facings for successive monarchs. The reverse is by George Kruger Gray (1880–1943)

Denomination	Metal	Weight (grams)	Diameter (mm)	Rev. alignment
Halfcrown	Silver	14.1	32	↑

Obverse 1 Head 1, left; EDWARDVS VIII D G BR OMN REX

Reverse 1 Standard Flag bearing Royal arms flanked by interlinked 'E's on each side forming an internal figure '8'; FID DEF IND IMP HALF CROWN 1937

Edge milled

Obv. 1   Rev. 1

No.	Date	Obv.	Rev.	UNC
E8HC-005	1937	1	1	20000

George VI (1937 – 1952)

Thomas Humphrey Paget designed the portrait of George VI facing left, as on the George V coinage. The reverse was by George Kruger Gray, and was a redesigned version of the George V reverse. However, curiously, the shield hangs from a nail; a touch of humour, or surrealism, perhaps?

Proofs were struck in 1937 for the proof set, and in small quantities each year, possibly for testing purposes. The next official release of proofs was for the proof sets of 1950 and 1951. By this time, the coins were being struck in cupronickel.

Collecting Hints

Collect only in mint state, unless one is investing in silver, or enjoying the fun of assembling a date set. Always examine the edges of 1950 and 1951 proofs for corrosion. The 1950 is particularly susceptible, being in the corner of the cardboard box and liable to attack from a damp atmosphere. Resist the temptation to silver dip streaky cupronickel proofs, or indeed any coins in this metal. The marks will disappear, but will come back within days.

Denomination	Metal	Weight (grams)	Diameter (mm)	Rev. alignment
Halfcrown 1937–46	0.500 Silver	14.1	32	↑
Halfcrown 1947–52	Cupronickel	14.1	32	↑

Obverse 1 Head 1, left; GEORGIVS VI D G BR OMN REX

Reverse 1 Shield, flanked by crowned interlinked 'G's. FID DEF IND IMP HALF CROWN (date)

Reverse 2 Similar but IND IMP missing

Edge milled. The milling is finer from 1947–52

Obv. 1

Rev. 1   Rev. 2

50% Silver Issue

No.	Date	Features	Obv.	Rev.	F	VF	EF	UNC
G6HC-005	1937		1	1	2	3	4	7
G6HC-010	1937	PROOF [1]	1	1				20
G6HC-015	1937	PROOF from sandblasted dies [2]	1	1				300
G6HC-020	1938		1	1	2	3	8	20
G6HC-025	1938	PROOF	1	1				500
G6HC-030	1939		1	1	2	3	5	9
G6HC-035	1939	PROOF	1	1				500
G6HC-040	1940		1	1	2	3	5	9
G6HC-045	1940	PROOF	1	1				500
G6HC-050	1941		1	1	2	3	5	9
G6HC-055	1941	PROOF	1	1				500
G6HC-060	1942		1	1	2	3	5	8
G6HC-065	1943		1	1	2	3	5	8
G6HC-070	1943	PROOF	1	1				500
G6HC-075	1944		1	1	2	3	5	8
G6HC-080	1945		1	1	2	3	5	8
G6HC-085	1945	PROOF	1	1				500
G6HC-090	1946		1	1	2	3	5	8
G6HC-095	1946	PROOF	1	1				500

1. Issued in cased proof sets.
2. Struck to facilitate photography of coin.

Cupronickel Issue

No.	Date	Features	Obv.	Rev.	F	VF	EF	UNC
G6HC-100	1946	PROOF in cupronickel	1	1				1500
G6HC-105	1947		1	1	2	2	3	5
G6HC-110	1947	PROOF	1	1				500
G6HC-115	1948		1	1	2	2	3	5
G6HC-120	1948	PROOF	1	1				500
G6HC-125	1949		1	2	2	2	3	6
G6HC-130	1949	PROOF	1	2				500
G6HC-135	1950		1	2	2	2	3	6
G6HC-140	1950	PROOF [1]	1	2				8
G6HC-142	1950	PROOF reverse; ordinary obverse	1	2				50
G6HC-145	1950	PROOF from sandblasted dies [2]	1	2				300
G6HC-150	1951		1	2	2	2	3	6
G6HC-155	1951	PROOF [1]	1	2				8
G6HC-160	1951	PROOF from sandblasted dies [2]	1	2				300
G6HC-165	1952	[3]	1	2	12000			
G6HC-170	1952	PROOF [3]	1	2				20000

1. Issued in cased proof sets.
2. Struck to facilitate photography of coin.
3. Possibly unique.

Elizabeth II (1952 –)

The original design by Mary Gillick for the Queen's portrait resulted in a weak striking lacking in detail, and the dies were soon
recut to provide a sharper image. The first year (1953) is the only
coin bearing the obverse 'BRITT OMN' (transl: of all the British
possessions). The reverse was designed by Fuller and Thomas.

The beginning of the modern practice of collecting by date in the
early sixties came too late to preserve in mint state many of the
otherwise common pieces of the fifties, with the consequence that
some of the dates are difficult to find thus.

Denomination	Metal	Weight (grams)	Diameter (mm)	Rev. alignment
Halfcrown	Cupronickel	14.1	32	↑

Obverse 1 Head 1, right; ELIZABETH II DEI GRATIA BRITT OMN
REGINA

Obverse 2 Head 1 (recut), right; ELIZABETH II DEI GRATIA
REGINA

Reverse 1 Crowned shield flanked by E and R; FID DEF HALF
CROWN (date)

Edge milled

Obv. 1   Obv. 2

Rev. 1

No.	Date	Features	Obv.	Rev.	EF	UNC
EZHC-005	1953	[1]	1	1	2	5
EZHC-010	1953	PROOF [2]	1	1		8
EZHC-015	1953	PROOF from sandblasted dies [3]	1	1		300
EZHC-020	1954	[4]	2	1	4	20
EZHC-025	1954	PROOF	2	1		450
EZHC-030	1955		2	1	2	5
EZHC-035	1955	PROOF	2	1		400
EZHC-040	1956		2	1	2	5
EZHC-045	1956	PROOF	2	1		400
EZHC-050	1957		2	1	2	4
EZHC-055	1957	PROOF	2	1		400
EZHC-060	1958		2	1	4	16
EZHC-065	1958	PROOF	2	1		400
EZHC-070	1959		2	1	4	18
EZHC-075	1959	PROOF	2	1		400
EZHC-080	1960		2	1	2	4
EZHC-085	1960	PROOF	2	1		400
EZHC-090	1961	[5]	2	1	2	4
EZHC-095	1961	struck from polished blanks [6]	2	1	2	6
EZHC-100	1961	PROOF	2	1		400
EZHC-105	1962	[7]	2	1	2	3
EZHC-110	1962	PROOF	2	1		400
EZHC-115	1963		2	1	2	3
EZHC-120	1963	PROOF	2	1		400
EZHC-125	1964		2	1	2	3
EZHC-130	1964	PROOF	2	1		400
EZHC-135	1965		2	1	2	3
EZHC-140	1965	PROOF	2	1		300
EZHC-145	1966		2	1	2	3
EZHC-150	1966	PROOF	2	1		300
EZHC-155	1967	[8]	2	1	2	3
EZHC-160	1967	PROOF	2	1		300

No.	Date	Features	Obv.	Rev.		EF	UNC
EZHC-165	1970	PROOF [9]	2	1		2	3

1. Some have recut head; other obverse varieties occur.
2. Issued in cased proof sets.
3. Struck to facilitate photography of coin.
4. Reverse border teeth slightly larger than on other years.
5. May have no 'E.F.' initials below shield (filled die).
6. Often wrongly termed 'polished die' variety; see below.
7. Minor obverse varieties occur.
8. Issued for some years.
9. Issued in sealed cased proof sets; no ordinary issue coins of this date.

It has been surmised that the 1961 halfcrowns struck on polished blanks may have used blanks remaining from the issue of 1953 proof halfcrowns.

The halfcrown ceased to be legal tender after 31 December 1969.

Weighing finished coins. £200-worth weighed at a time

Florin

Victoria (1837 – 1901)

In 1847 Sir John Bowring proposed a motion in the House of Commons for the introduction of a decimal currency, and the striking of coins to the value of one-tenth and one-hundredth of a pound. The motion was subsequently withdrawn on the understanding that a one-tenth pound coin would be struck to test public opinion. Much discussion ensued as to the name of the proposed coin. Pattern coins of 1848 exist with the names Centum, Decade and Dime, but eventually the term 'florin' was adopted. This was an old English coinage term, but the name probably found favour because coins of similar size and value in some European countries had become known as florins.

The first adopted design for the florin was rather unusual. We are now used to seeing a crowned monarch on coinage, but the portrait of Victoria wearing a crown must have been a shock to the public when one considers that such a device had not been seen on coinage for nearly 200 years. Even more of a shock, including allegedly to the queen herself, was the omission of the term D.G. (=DEI GRATIA = by the grace of God). This omission caused the coin to be known popularly as the 'Godless Florin'.

The Godless florin was minted for one year only, 1849, although it may have been issued also during 1850 and 1851, but bearing the 1849 date. In 1851 a more elegant design was introduced which was similar in many respects to the Gothic crown of 1847. By now, the halfcrown had been discontinued as a further step to establishing the florin as a decimal coin. The Gothic florin was struck until 1887, when it was superseded by the jubilee and later the veiled head issues with obverses similar to the other silver coinage of the period.

One particular issue of Gothic florin deserves special mention. Salzman has suggested that the 1867 coin with the 42 arcs obverse may have been an error date, but examination of the details establishes this fact beyond all reasonable doubt. The minting of a 42–arc florin as the only piece in a 48–arc series is highly unlikely ten years before the 42–arc design was introduced. The highest die number recorded in ESC for 1867 is 9, with the exception of the 42–arc 1867 coin, which is die 32! Furthermore, the variety has no WW on the obverse, unlike all others of 1851 to 1876. The coin was undoubtedly struck in 1877 with the date wrongly 'spelt', that is, if it exists at all, about which there are doubts!

The alteration of the term BRIT to BRITT in 1867 may have been to denote a Latin abbreviation plural, representing 'Britains', i.e. Britain and its Colonies.

The Godless and Gothic florins had obverses designed by William Wyon and reverses by William Dyce. The jubilee florin had an obverse designed by Sir Joseph Edgar Boehm and engraved by Leonard Charles Wyon. Wyon is credited with designing the reverse, but this is obviously heavily influenced by the John Roettier design of the Charles II gold coinage. The veiled head florin had its obverse designed by Brock and the reverse by Sir Edward Poynter.

Denomination	Metal	Weight (grams)	Diameter (mm)	Rev. alignment
Florin 1849	Silver	11.3	28	↓
Florin 1851–87 (Gothic type)	Silver	11.3	30	↓
Florin 1887–92 (Jubilee type)	Silver	11.3	29.5	↑
Florin 1893–1901	Silver	11.3	28.5	↑

Obverse 1   Head 1, left; VICTORIA REGINA 1849

Obverse 2   Head 2, left; VICTORIA D G BRIT REG F D (date); WW below head; 48 ornamental arcs between legend and rim

Obverse 3   Head 3, left, slightly older; legend and date as Obverse 2 but BRITT instead of BRIT; WW; 48 arcs

Obverse 4   Similar but no WW; 48 arcs

Obverse 5   Similar but 42 arcs

Obverse 6   Head 4, left, slightly older; legend and date as Obverse 3 no WW; 39 arcs

Obverse 7   Head 3, no WW, left; 34 arcs

Obverse 8   Head 4, no WW, left; 34 arcs

Obverse 9   Head 3, no WW, left; 46 arcs

Obverse 10   Head 5, left; VICTORIA DEI GRATIA

Obverse 11   Head 6, left, slightly redesigned; same legend

Obverse 12   Head 7, left; VICTORIA DEI GRA BRITT REGINA FID DEF IND IMP

Note that on obverses 2 to 9 the date is in Roman numerals. The legend and date are in Gothic script.

The 34 arc obverses are also known as 33 arc obverses in some catalogues.

Reverse 1   Four crowned cruciform shields with rose at centre; rose, thistle, rose and shamrock in angles; ONE FLORIN ONE TENTH OF A POUND

Reverse 2   Similar but redesigned; cross in centre; same legend but in Gothic script

Reverse 3   Four crowned cruciform shields with Star of Garter in centre and sceptres in angles; FID DEF BRITT REG (date)

Reverse 4   Three shields separated by rose, shamrock and thistle; Garter; crown above; ONE FLORIN TWO SHILLINGS (date)

Edge   milled

Obv. 1   Obv. 2

Obv. 3 Obv. 5

Obv. 6 Obv. 8

Obv. 9 Obv. 10

Obv. 12

Rev. 1 Rev. 2

Rev. 3 Rev. 4

'Godless' Issue

No.	Date	Features	Obv.	Rev.	F	VF	EF	UNC
VGFL-002	1848		1	1	250	400	800	
VGFL-003	1848	PROOF	1	1				1500
VGFL-004	1848	PROOF; rev. ↑	1	1				1500
VGFL-005	1849	WW next to date	1	1	10	30	80	140

No.	Date	Features		Obv.	Rev.	F	VF	EF	UNC
VGFL-010	1849	WW next to date partially erased		1	1	10	30	85	150

For 1848 plain edge pieces, see the Pattern section, p.723.

'Gothic' Issue

No.	Date	Features	Date on coin*	Obv.	Rev.	F	VF	EF	UNC
VGFL-015	1851	[1]	mdcccli.	2	2	2000			
VGFL-020	1851	PROOF; edge plain	mdcccli.	2	2				6000
VGFL-022	1851	PROOF; edge plain; rev. ↑	mdcccli.	2	2				8000
VGFL-025	1851	PROOF	mdcccli.	2	2				5000
VGFL-030	1852		mdccclii.	2	2	12	40	110	140
VGFL-035	1852	2 over 1 [2]	mdccclii.	2	2	20	70	180	260
VGFL-040	1852	PROOF	mdccclii.	2	2				1000
VGFL-045	1853		mdcccliii	2	2	12	40	110	150
VGFL-050	1853	PROOF	mdcccliii	2	2				1200
VGFL-055	1854		mdcccliv	2	2	250	700	1500	
VGFL-058	1854	ONC TENTH instead of ONE TENTH (rev.)	mdcccliv	2	2	300	800		
VGFL-060	1855		mdccclv	2	2	12	45	120	160
VGFL-065	1856		mdccclvi	2	2	12	45	130	180
VGFL-070	1857		mdccclvii	2	2	12	45	130	180
VGFL-075	1858		mdccclviii	2	2	16	60	170	250
VGFL-080	1859		mdccclix	2	2	24	90	250	400
VGFL-085	1859		mdccclix.	2	2	16	60	170	250
VGFL-090	1859	m in date is double struck inverted m [3]	mdccclix.	2	2	50	180	600	1000
VGFL-095	1860		mdccclx.	2	2	12	45	130	180
VGFL-100	1862	[4]	mdccclxii	2	2	40	100	300	500
VGFL-105	1862	PROOF; edge plain [4]	mdccclxii	2	2				3000
VGFL-110	1863		mdccclxiii	2	2	100	200	600	1300
VGFL-115	1863	PROOF; edge plain	mdccclxiii	2	2				3000
VGFL-120	1864	with die number	mdccclxiv	2	2	12	45	120	160
VGFL-125	1864	struck on thick flan; with die number [5]	mdccclxiv	2	2	400	550	700	900
VGFL-130	1864	PROOF; struck on thick flan; with die number	mdccclxiv	2	2				2500
VGFL-135	1865	with die number	mdccclxv	2	2	12	50	130	170
VGFL-140	1865	with die number [6]	mdccclxv:	2	2	15	70	180	240
VGFL-145	1865	with die number; rev. →	mdccclxv:	2	2	18	85	220	300
VGFL-150	1866	with die number	mdccclxvi	2	2	16	80	200	270
VGFL-155	1866	with die number	mdccclxvi:	2	2	28	140	350	500
VGFL-160	1867	with die number [7]	mdccclxvii	2	2	40	120	320	450
VGFL-165	1867	PROOF	mdccclxvii	3	2				2500
VGFL-170	1867	PROOF; edge plain; rev. ↑	mdccclxvii	3	2				2500
VGFL-175	1867 (1877)	with die number [8]	mdccclxvii	5	2	1200			
VGFL-180	1868	with die number	mdccclxviii	3	2	12	45	130	180
VGFL-185	1869	with die number	mdccclxix	3	2	12	40	120	160
VGFL-190	1869	PROOF; with die number	mdccclxix	3	2				2000
VGFL-195	1870	with die number	mdccclxx	3	2	12	40	120	160
VGFL-200	1870	PROOF; with die number [9]	mdccclxx	3	2				3000
VGFL-205	1871	with die number	mdccclxxi	3	2	12	40	120	160
VGFL-210	1871	PROOF; with die number; rev. ↑	mdccclxxi	3	2				2500
VGFL-215	1871	PROOF; with die number; edge plain; rev. ↑ [10]	mdccclxxi	3	2				2500

No.	Date	Features	Date on coin*	Obv.	Rev.	F	VF	EF	UNC
VGFL-220	1872	with die number	mdccclxxii	3	2	10	35	110	150
VGFL-225	1873	with die number	mdccclxxiii	3	2	10	35	100	150
VGFL-230	1873	PROOF; with die number	mdccclxxiii	3	2				2500
VGFL-235	1874	with die number	mdccclxxiv	3	2	12	40	120	180
VGFL-240	1874	4 over 3; with die number [11]	mdccclxxiv	3	2	25	80	200	350
VGFL-245	1875	with die number	mdccclxxv	3	2	12	40	120	180
VGFL-250	1876	with die number	mdccclxxvi	3	2	12	45	130	190
VGFL-255	1877	with die number [12]	mdccclxxvii	3	2	12	45	130	190
VGFL-260	1877	with die number	mdccclxxvii.	4	2	12	45	130	190
VGFL-265	1877	with die number [12]	mdccclxxvii.	5	2	12	45	130	190
VGFL-270	1877		mdccclxxvii.	5	2	100	400		
VGFL-175 duplicated entry	1877 (1867)	with die number [13]	mdccclxvii (.)	5	2	1200			
VGFL-275	1878	with die number	mdccclxxviii	5	2	12	40	120	160
VGFL-280	1878	PROOF; with die number	mdccclxxviii	5	2				2500
VGFL-285	1879	with die number	mdccclxxix	3	2	50	200		
VGFL-290	1879		mdccclxxix	3	2	50	200		
VGFL-292	1879	briit over britt (obv.)	mdccclxxix	3	2	100	400		
VGFL-295	1879		mdccclxxix	5	2	12	40	120	180
VGFL-300	1879		mdccclxxix	6	2	12	40	120	180
VGFL-305	1879	PROOF	mdccclxxix	6	2				1500
VGFL-308	1879	PROOF; rev. ↑	mdccclxxix	6	2				1500
VGFL-310	1879	PROOF; edge plain; rev. ↑	mdccclxxix	6	2				1500
VGFL-315	1880		mdccclxxx	7	2	14	45	130	190
VGFL-320	1880		mdccclxxx	8	2	12	40	120	180
VGFL-325	1880	PROOF	mdccclxxx	8	2				2500
VGFL-330	1881		mdccclxxxi	8	2	8	30	85	120
VGFL-335	1881	[14]	mdccclxxri	8	2	12	45	120	160
VGFL-340	1881	PROOF	mdccclxxxi	8	2				2500
VGFL-345	1881	PROOF; edge plain; rev. ↑	mdccclxxxi	8	2				3000
VGFL-350	1883		mdccclxxxiii	8	2	8	30	85	120
VGFL-355	1884		mdccclxxxiv	8	2	8	30	85	120
VGFL-360	1885		mdccclxxxv	8	2	8	30	85	120
VGFL-365	1885	PROOF	mdccclxxxv	8	2				3000
VGFL-370	1886		mdccclxxxvi	8	2	8	30	85	120
VGFL-375	1886	PROOF	mdccclxxxvi	8	2				3000
VGFL-380	1887		m-dccclxxxvii	9	2	10	35	100	130
VGFL-385	1887	PROOF	m-dccclxxxvii	9	2				3000

* Including following punctuation.
1. Any extant are possibly all worn proofs; florin not legal tender until March 1852.
2. Last i of date is over stop.
3. Most have larger pellet shaped stops on obverse.
4. Stop after 'brit' (see below).
5. Specimens recorded with die nos. 32, 40, 47; weight 14.5–14.8 grams.
6. Usually die numbers 44 to 51.
7. Frequently die number 1.
8. Error date possibly struck in 1877. Catalogued also under date 1877; not known whether with stop after date; may not exist.
9. Recorded by Dickinson.
10. Some or all have die number 43.
11. Overdate: last v of date appears over ii; usually die nos. 29 and 30.
12. Die number position varies (see below).
13. Error date reads 1867. Catalogued also under date 1867; not known whether with stop after date; may not exist.
14. Last x of date appears as r (broken punch).

Jubilee Head

No.	Date	Features	Obv.	Rev.	F	VF	EF	UNC
VJFL-390	1887	[1]	10	3	5	8	14	18
VJFL-395	1887	PROOF [2]	10	3				120
VJFL-400	1888	[3]	11	3	6	10	30	40
VJFL-405	1889	[4]	11	3	6	10	30	40
VJFL-410	1890		11	3	8	20	60	80
VJFL-415	1891		11	3	12	50	120	160
VJFL-420	1892		11	3	12	50	130	180

No.	Date	Features	Obv.	Rev.	F	VF	EF	UNC
VJFL-425	1892	PROOF [5]	11	3				2500

1. Initials JEB on truncation vary in size and position (obv.).
2. Issued in cased proof sets.
3. Minor obverse differences exist.
4. Minor reverse differences exist.
5. Possibly 5 struck.

Old Head

No.	Date	Features	Obv.	Rev.	F	VF	EF	UNC
VOFL-430	1893	[1]	12	4	5	10	40	65
VOFL-435	1893	PROOF [2]	12	4				150
VOFL-440	1894	[3]	12	4	6	14	50	110
VOFL-445	1895	[3]	12	4	6	14	50	80
VOFL-450	1896	[3]	12	4	6	15	60	90
VOFL-455	1897		12	4	6	12	40	75
VOFL-460	1898		12	4	6	15	60	90
VOFL-465	1899		12	4	6	15	60	90
VOFL-470	1900		12	4	6	12	40	75
VOFL-475	1901		12	4	6	12	40	70

1. Minor obverse differences exist.
2. Issued in cased proof sets.
3. Minor obverse and reverse differences exist.

Florins of 1862 appear to have stops after 'brit' instead of a colon. However, examples exist with a colon having its upper stop faintly visible, so the stop is probably a colon resulting from using a deficient punch.

Florins have no die numbers except for coins of 1864 to 1879 when stated. Die numbers are on obverse under Victoria's bust to the right of her brooch. Some examples of 1877 have the die number to the left of the brooch.

Edward VII   (1901 – 1910)

The florin of Edward VII, designed by George William de Saulles (1862–1903), displayed a most unusual and original reverse. The low-relief finely detailed standing Britannia design was a complete departure from anything seen previously. Coin design is generally highly derivative from previous reigns, and it was a bold move to introduce such a variation of the Britannia theme.

Matt proofs were struck in 1902 for inclusion in the cased sets, and the florin was subsequently struck for each year of the reign.

Collecting Hints

The last numeral of the date frequently wears off before any of the legends, and this can lead to confusion as to the date on coins bordering on fine condition. '3' and '5' are particularly liable to be confused. However, it should be remembered that the 1905 florin is not as scarce as the halfcrown of that date.

The obverse of the Edward VII florin is often weakly struck.

Denomination	Metal	Weight (grams)	Diameter (mm)	Rev. alignment
Florin	Silver	11.3	28.5	↑

Obverse 1   Head 1, right; EDWARDVS VII DEI GRA BRITT OMN REX FD IND IMP

Reverse 1   Britannia standing with shield and spear; ONE FLORIN TWO SHILLINGS (date)

Edge   milled

Obv. 1

Rev. 1

No.	Date	Features	Obv.	Rev.	F	VF	EF	UNC
E7FL-005	1902		1	1	6	12	35	55
E7FL-010	1902	matt PROOF [1]	1	1			35	50
E7FL-015	1903		1	1	8	16	80	120
E7FL-020	1904		1	1	10	20	90	160
E7FL-025	1905		1	1	20	60	350	600
E7FL-030	1906		1	1	6	15	60	90
E7FL-035	1907		1	1	7	18	90	180
E7FL-040	1908		1	1	8	18	100	240
E7FL-045	1909		1	1	8	22	100	160
E7FL-050	1910		1	1	6	15	55	80

1. Issued in cased proof sets.

Minor differences of orientation and lettering size in word 'FLORIN' (rev.) occur from 1902 to 1904.

George V   (1910 – 1936)

The florin was minted for every year of this reign except 1934. Throughout the series the reverse used the cruciform shields and sceptres motif last seen on the Victoria jubilee head florin. From 1911 to 1926 the design of this was very similar to the jubilee design, but from 1927 the motif was radically redesigned with much larger sceptres in the angles.

The obverse portrait of George V was from a design by Sir Bertram Mackennal (1863–1931). Curiously, the (re-)designer of the 1911–26 reverse was not recorded, but the 1927–36 reverse was by George Kruger Gray (1880–1943). It is interesting to note the evolution of the cruciform shields and sceptres design from the John Roettier guinea of 1663 to the florin of 1936.

Because of the increase in the price of silver, in 1920 the alloy was changed to include 50% of silver instead of 92.5%. Coins up to 1922 tarnished very unattractively, and a change in the base metal (non-silver) constituents after then rendered the alloy more acceptable in this respect. The striking of the 50% silver coinage appears in lower relief relative to that of the 1911–19 coinage due possibly either to the different metal resistance to pressure or to a change in the method of striking to accommodate the new alloy.

From 1928 onwards small quantities of proofs were struck each year for record purposes. These were sent to museums, other mints, and occasionally presented to important visitors.

Collecting Hints

This series should be collected in extremely fine or better condition. Those looking for a sequence of dates in fine or very fine should not find the task of assembling them too difficult. A few of the dates are surprisingly difficult to find in top condition.
Care should be taken in grading; it is, for example, easy to overestimate the grade of the reverses of the florins of 1928–36 and particular attention should be paid to the amount of detail present in the hair of the obverse portrait. What sometimes appears as a 'dig' on the portrait of the early dates, especially the 1911 proof, is in fact part of the design, as can be seen clearly if one inspects a 1911 proof set. Single 1911 proof coins are sometimes knocked down

cheaply in salerooms because they have been catalogued as 'with nick on the portrait'.
The use of 'silver dip' is not normally recommended, but there is no doubt that chemical removal of the ugly yellow tarnish often seen on very fine to extremely fine pieces in the period 1920–22 does enhance their appearance.

Denomination	Metal	Weight (grams)	Diameter (mm)	Rev. alignment
Florin 1911–19	0.925 Silver	11.3	28.5	↑
Florin 1920–22	Silver 50%; copper 40%; nickel 10%	11.3	28.5	↑
Florin 1922–26	Silver 50%; copper 50%	11.3	28.5	↑
Florin 1927–36	Silver 50%; copper 40%; nickel 5%; zinc 5%	11.3	28.5	↑

Obverse 1 Head 1, left; B.M. on truncation; depression on neck above BM; GEORGIVS V D G BRITT OMN REX F D IND IMP

Obverse 2 Head 2, left, no depression

Obverse 3 Head 3, so-called 'modified effigy', left; BM (no stops) further to right; beading recut; beads are wider than previously, and fewer in number; GEORGIVS V DEI GRA BRITT OMN REX

Reverse 1 Four crowned cruciform shields with sceptres in angles; ONE FLORIN (date)

Reverse 2 Similar but redesigned; FID DEF IND IMP (date) ONE FLORIN

Edge milled

Obv. 1   Obv. 3

Rev. 1   Rev. 2

Sterling Silver Issue

No.	Date	Features	Obv.	Rev.	F	VF	EF	UNC
G5FL-005	1911		1	1	4	10	32	50
G5FL-010	1911	PROOF [1]	1	1			45	75
G5FL-015	1911		2	1	4	10	32	50
G5FL-020	1912		2	1	4	12	40	80
G5FL-025	1913	[2]	2	1	5	15	55	100
G5FL-030	1914	[3]	2	1	4	8	14	20
G5FL-035	1915		2	1	4	8	16	35
G5FL-040	1916		2	1	4	8	14	25
G5FL-045	1917		2	1	4	8	18	35
G5FL-050	1918		2	1	4	8	16	24
G5FL-055	1919		2	1	4	8	18	30

1. Issued in cased proof sets.
2. Date spacing varies.
3. Rim teeth size vary.

50% Silver Issue

No.	Date	Features	Obv.	Rev.	F	VF	EF	UNC
G5FL-060	1920	[1]	2	1	3	10	25	45
G5FL-065	1921		2	1	3	10	25	35
G5FL-070	1922	[2]	2	1	3	10	25	35
G5FL-075	1922	PROOF in pure gold on thick flan [3]	2	1				8000
G5FL-078	1922	PROOF in gold alloy [4]	2	1				6000
G5FL-080	1923		2	1	3	8	18	25
G5FL-085	1924		2	1	3	12	35	50
G5FL-090	1925		2	1	4	15	90	160
G5FL-095	1926		2	1	3	12	35	50
G5FL-100	1927	PROOF [5]	3	2	25	30	35	50
G5FL-105	1927	PROOF from sandblasted dies [6]	3	2				350
G5FL-110	1928		3	2	3	6	9	15
G5FL-115	1928	PROOF	3	2				500
G5FL-120	1929		3	2	3	6	10	18
G5FL-125	1929	PROOF	3	2				500
G5FL-130	1930		3	2	3	7	12	30
G5FL-135	1930	PROOF	3	2				500
G5FL-140	1931		3	2	3	6	10	20
G5FL-145	1931	PROOF	3	2				500
G5FL-150	1932		3	2	5	10	75	180
G5FL-155	1932	PROOF	3	2				1000
G5FL-160	1933		3	2	3	6	10	18
G5FL-165	1933	PROOF	3	2				500
G5FL-170	1935		3	2	3	6	9	12
G5FL-175	1935	PROOF	3	2				500
G5FL-180	1936		3	2	3	5	7	10
G5FL-185	1936	PROOF	3	2				500

1. Metal composition change; see first table; minor obverse differences exist.
2. Metal composition changes during year; see first table.
3. Weight 25.4 grams. See note for similar 1927 halfcrown.
4. Weight 17.4 grams. See note for similar 1927 halfcrown.
5. Issued in cased proof sets.
6. Struck to facilitate photography of coin.

Coins struck in 0.925 silver appear to be struck in higher relief than those on 0.500 silver. This may be due to the purer metal being softer and thereby having a lower resistance to pressure.

Edward VIII (1936)

The Edward VIII florin is strictly speaking a pattern, as probable royal approval was about to be granted at the time of the abdication. However, because its official status rests only on this technicality, and to provide continuity, it is included here.

The portrait of Edward VIII is by Thomas Humphrey Paget, and faces left at the insistence of the king, who considered this placement more flattering and wished to discontinue the tradition of opposite facings for successive monarchs. The reverse is by George Kruger Gray (1880–1943).

Denomination	Metal	Weight (grams)	Diameter (mm)	Rev. alignment
Florin	0.500 Silver	11.3	28.5	↑

Obverse 1 Head 1, left; EDWARDVS VIII D G BR OMN REX

Reverse 1 Crowned rose flanked by thistle and shamrock, E and R below last two; FID DEF IND IMP TWO SHILLINGS 1937

Edge milled

Obv. 1   Rev. 1

No.	Date	Obv.	Rev.	Unc
E8FL-005	1937	1	1	15000

George VI (1937 – 1952)

Thomas Humphrey Paget designed the portrait of George VI facing left, as on the George V coinage. The reverse was by George Kruger Gray, and depicted a crowned rose between a thistle and a shamrock. The denomination 'ONE FLORIN' was now discontinued in favour of 'TWO SHILLINGS'.

Proofs were struck in 1937 for the proof set, and in small quantities each year, possibly for testing purposes. The next official release of proofs was for the proof sets of 1950 and 1951. By this time, the coins were being struck in cupronickel.

Collecting Hints

Collect only in mint state, unless one is investing in silver, or enjoying the fun of assembling a date set. Always examine the edges of 1950 and 1951 proofs for corrosion. Resist the temptation to silver dip streaky cupronickel proofs, or indeed any coins in this metal. The marks will disappear, but will come back within days.

Denomination	Metal	Weight (grams)	Diameter (mm)	Rev. alignment
Florin 1937–46	0.500 Silver	11.3	28.5	↑
Florin 1947–51	Copper 75%; nickel 25%	11.3	28.5	↑

Obverse 1 Head 1, left; GEORGIVS VI D G BR OMN REX

Reverse 1 Crowned rose flanked by thistle and shamrock, G and R below last two; FID DEF IND IMP TWO SHILLINGS (date)

Reverse 2 Similar but IND IMP missing

Edge milled. The milling is finer from 1947–51

Obv. 1   Rev. 1   Rev. 2

50% Silver Issue

No.	Date	Features	Obv.	Rev.	F	VF	EF	UNC
G6FL-005	1937		1	1	1	3	5	7
G6FL-010	1937	PROOF [1]	1	1			8	12
G6FL-015	1937	PROOF from sandblasted dies [2]	1	1				250
G6FL-020	1938		1	1	1	3	8	15
G6FL-025	1938	PROOF	1	1				400
G6FL-030	1939		1	1	1	3	5	9
G6FL-035	1939	PROOF	1	1				400
G6FL-040	1940		1	1	1	3	5	9
G6FL-045	1940	PROOF	1	1				400
G6FL-050	1941		1	1	1	3	5	8
G6FL-055	1941	PROOF	1	1				400
G6FL-060	1942		1	1	1	3	5	7
G6FL-065	1942	PROOF	1	1				400
G6FL-070	1943		1	1	1	3	5	7
G6FL-075	1944		1	1	1	2	3	5
G6FL-080	1944	PROOF	1	1				400
G6FL-085	1945		1	1	1	2	3	5
G6FL-090	1945	PROOF	1	1				400
G6FL-095	1946		1	1	1	2	3	5
G6FL-100	1946	PROOF	1	1				400

1. Issued in cased proof sets.
2. Struck to facilitate photography of coin.

Cupronickel Issue

No.	Date	Features	Obv.	Rev.	F	VF	EF	UNC
G6FL-105	1946	PROOF in cupronickel [1]	1	1				1200
G6FL-110	1947		1	1			2	5
G6FL-115	1947	PROOF	1	1				380
G6FL-120	1948		1	1			2	5
G6FL-125	1948	PROOF	1	1				380
G6FL-130	1949		1	2			3	10
G6FL-135	1949	PROOF	1	2				380
G6FL-140	1950		1	2			2	8
G6FL-145	1950	PROOF [2]	1	2				7
G6FL-150	1950	PROOF from sandblasted dies [3]	1	2				250
G6FL-155	1951		1	2			2	10
G6FL-160	1951	PROOF [2]	1	2				7
G6FL-165	1951	PROOF from sandblasted dies [3]	1	2				250

1. Trial piece for cupronickel coinage.
2. Issued in cased proof sets.
3. Struck to facilitate photography of coin.

Elizabeth II (1952 –)

The original design by Mary Gillick for the queen's portrait resulted in a weak striking lacking in detail, and the dies were soon recut to provide a sharper image. The first year (1953) is the only coin bearing the obverse 'BRITT OMN' (transl: of all the British possessions).

The beginning of the modern practice of collecting by date in the early sixties came too late to preserve in mint state many of the otherwise common pieces of the fifties, with the consequence that some of the dates are difficult to find thus.

Collecting Hints

Collect in mint state. Acquiring examples of the unofficially struck proofs is an interesting challenge.

Denomination	Metal	Weight (grams)	Diameter (mm)	Rev. alignment
Florin 1953–70	Copper 75%; nickel 25%	11.3	28.5	↑

Obverse 1 Head 1, right; ELIZABETH II DEI GRATIA BRITT OMN REGINA

Obverse 2 Head 1 (recut), right; ELIZABETH II DEI GRATIA REGINA

Reverse 1 Concentric roses in centre surrounded by thistles, shamrocks, leeks; FID DEF TWO SHILLINGS (date)

Edge milled

Obv. 1   Obv. 2   Rev. 1

No.	Date	Features	Obv.	Rev.	EF	UNC
EZFL-005	1953	[1]	1	1	3	5
EZFL-010	1953	PROOF [2]	1	1		9
EZFL-015	1953	PROOF from sandblasted dies [3]	1	1		300
EZFL-020	1954		2	1	6	32
EZFL-025	1954	PROOF	2	1		300
EZFL-030	1955		2	1	3	5
EZFL-035	1955	PROOF	2	1		300

No.	Date	Features	Obv.	Rev.	EF	UNC
EZFL-040	1956		2	1	3	5
EZFL-045	1956	PROOF	2	1		300
EZFL-050	1957		2	1	5	24
EZFL-055	1957	PROOF	2	1		300
EZFL-060	1958		2	1	4	16
EZFL-065	1958	PROOF	2	1		300
EZFL-070	1959		2	1	5	30
EZFL-075	1959	PROOF	2	1		300
EZFL-080	1960		2	1	2	4
EZFL-085	1960	PROOF	2	1		300
EZFL-090	1961		2	1	2	4
EZFL-095	1961	PROOF	2	1		300
EZFL-100	1962	[4]	2	1	1	3
EZFL-105	1962	PROOF	2	1		300
EZFL-110	1963		2	1	1	3
EZFL-115	1963	PROOF	2	1		300
EZFL-120	1964		2	1	1	2
EZFL-125	1964	PROOF	2	1		300
EZFL-130	1965		2	1	1	2
EZFL-135	1965	struck in brass or nickel-brass [5]	2	1		300
EZFL-140	1965	PROOF	2	1		300
EZFL-145	1966		2	1	1	2
EZFL-150	1966	PROOF	2	1		300
EZFL-155	1967	[6]	2	1	1	2
EZFL-160	1967	struck on both sides with rev. design	rev. 1	1	90	120
EZFL-165	1967	PROOF	2	1		300
EZFL-170	1970	PROOF [7]	2	1	2	4

1. Some have recut head; other minor obverse differences exist.
2. Issued in cased proof sets.
3. Struck to facilitate photography of coin.
4. Several very minor varieties exist.
5. Weight 9.5 grams.
6. Issued for some years.
7. Issued in sealed cased proof sets; no ordinary issue coins of this date; minor obverse differences exist, e.g. size and number of border beads.

The florin continued as legal tender for several years after decimalization as an equivalent to the 10 pence coin.

Eighteen Pence Bank Token

In 1811 there was a shortage of silver coinage for circulation. Although the countermarked dollars and five shilling bank tokens had been useful in this respect, no halfcrowns had been minted since 1751, and the last issue of shillings and sixpences for general use had been in 1787. In many parts of the country tradesmen issued private silver tokens during 1811, but these were not accepted outside the immediate area where they were issued.

To alleviate the situation, the Bank of England issued its own tokens for three shillings and for eighteen pence. Silver was trading on the free market at a high price, and the weights of these denominations were proportionally lower than normal. The fact that these issues were tokens rather than true coins rendered this shortfall acceptable.

As with the three shilling tokens, the issue of eighteen pence tokens was a short one, from 1811 to 1816, and comprised two distinct types. They were withdrawn from issue in March 1820, and were accepted after this date only as bullion by weight.

The first type (1811–12) was probably designed by Lewis Pingo. The second type (1812–16) used the Marchant design employed on the gold coinage. The actual engraving of the die is usually attributed to Thomas Wyon, who designed and engraved the reverse, but some doubt exists as to whether he engraved the obverse.

An unusual feature of the reverse is the use of the abbreviations 's' and 'd' for shilling and pence.

Denomination	Metal	Weight (grams)	Diameter (mm)	Rev. alignment
Eighteen Pence	Silver	7.4	27	↑

Obverse 1   Head 1, right; GEORGIUS III DEI GRATIA REX

Obverse 2   Head 2, right; same legend

Reverse 1   BANK TOKEN 1s 6d (date) within wreath of oak leaves

Reverse 2   Similar but lettering different and less profuse wreath of oak and olive

Edge: plain

Obv. 1   Obv. 2

Rev. 1   Rev. 2

No.	Date	Features	Obv.	Rev.	F	VF	EF	UNC
G318D-005	1811		1	1	10	20	45	85
G318D-010	1811	PROOF	1	1				450
G318D-015	1812		1	1	10	20	45	85
G318D-020	1812		2	2	10	18	40	80
G318D-025	1812	PROOF	2	2				450
G318D-030	1812	PROOF; small lettering on rev.	2	2				1500
G318D-035	1812	PROOF in platinum [1]	2	2				3000
G318D-040	1813		2	2	10	18	40	80
G318D-045	1813	PROOF in platinum	2	2				3000
G318D-050	1814		2	2	10	18	40	80
G318D-055	1815		2	2	10	18	40	80
G318D-060	1816		2	2	10	18	40	80

1. Two specimens weigh 15.7 and 16.6 grams.

Cutting shilling silver coins from silver strips

Shilling

Oliver Cromwell (Commonwealth 1649 – 1660)

Unlike the halfcrown, the Cromwell shilling occurs only with the date 1658. It was designed by Thomas Simon (also called Symonds) with technical assistance from Peter Blondeau, and portrays Cromwell as a Roman Emperor, draped and laureate. The 'Tanner's Copy', struck in the 18th Century, is outside the scope of this book. The 1656 shilling reported by Snelling appears not to exist.

Collecting Hints

Forgeries exist. On genuine specimens there is usually a die flaw near the top laurel wreath. The coin should be collected in fine condition or better.

Denomination	Metal	Weight (grams)	Diameter (mm)	Rev. alignment
Shilling	Silver	6.0	25–26	↓

Obverse 1 Head 1, left; OLIVAR D G R P ANG SCO HIB &c PRO

Reverse 1 Crowned shield; PAX QVAERITVR BELLO 1658

Edge milled

Obv. 1

Rev. 1

No.	Date	Features	Obv.	Rev.	F	VF	EF
OCSH-005	1658	1	1	1	300	500	900

1. Usually a die flaw near top laurel leaf (obv.).

Charles II (1660 – 1685)

The new machine-struck shilling was designed by John Roettier (1631–c.1703). It was first struck in 1663, but, without any struck the following year, the ravages of the Plague and Great Fire had taken their toll before the issue resumed in 1666. It is possible that at least one original die was lost in the fire, and certainly the curious use of the guinea dies during 1666 lends credence to the theory that an emergency issue was necessary.

The subsequent issues up to 1684 are of much interest, the various combinations of date, head and provenance marks producing many pieces of considerable rarity.

Provenance marks are: plumes (below head and/or in centre of reverse) for silver from Welsh mines; elephant and castle or elephant alone (below head) for silver from the Africa Company. The Welsh mines had been taken over in 1670 by a company which included Prince Rupert, whose influence led to the privilege of the use of the plume on coinage struck from Welsh silver.

Collecting Hints

The series is a very difficult one to collect exhaustively, many of the date/head/silver-provenance combinations being very rare in any condition; in addition, the rarity of even common pieces of Charles II coinage in very fine or better condition renders the acquisition of a comprehensive collection a very difficult task. One should be perhaps thankful that the edges were milled rather than bearing regnal years with their attendant errors and varieties.

For a series of such complexity, one should attempt to acquire varieties in any condition; rejection of a rare piece purely on grounds of condition may result in a gap in one's collection which proves permanent. Indeed, there is a mystique about a very worn coin of such age, bearing a smudge clearly identifiable as, say, a plume, and acquired after much searching.

Denomination	Metal	Weight (grams)	Diameter (mm)	Rev. alignment
Shilling 1663	Silver	6.0	25–26	↓
Shilling 1666–84	Silver	5.7–5.9	25–26	↓

Obverse 1 Head 1, right; CAROLVS II DEI GRATIA

Obverse 2 Head 2, right; minor differences in hair arrangement; same legend

Obverse 3 Head 3, right; very different and without drapery, identical to head on guinea (always with elephant below); same legend

Obverse 4 Head 4, right; similar to Heads 1 and 2 but laurel wreath and tie slightly different; same legend

Obverse 5 Head 5, much larger, right; ties point slightly downwards; same legend

Obverse 6 Head 6, slightly redesigned, right; ties almost straight; same legend

Reverse 1 Central star enclosed by four cruciform shields with surmounting crowns; MAG BR FRA ET HIB REX (date). On examples with plume on reverse, the plume *replaces* the star.

Edge 1663–68: milled (vertically); 1669–84: milled (diagonally). Some coins of 1663 have a fine line through the centre of the milling and encircling the coin.

Obv. 1   Obv. 2   Obv. 3

Obv. 4   Obv. 5   Obv. 6

Rev. 1   Rev. 1 shields transposed

No.	Date	Features	Obv.	Rev.	F	VF	EF
C2SHM-005	1663		1	1	50	160	600
C2SHM-010	1663	rev. ↑	1	1	80	320	1000
C2SHM-015	1663	GARTIA instead of GRATIA (obv.)	1	1	120	800	
C2SHM-020	1663	Scotland/Ireland shields transposed	1	1	100	600	
C2SHM-025	1663	A of FRA over G (rev.)	1	1	80	300	950
C2SHM-030	1663	PROOF in copper; edge plain	1	1			1500
C2SHM-035	1663		2	1	50	200	750
C2SHM-040	1666	[1]	2	1	400	1200	2500
C2SHM-045	1666	elephant below head	2	1	240	900	2500
C2SHM-050	1666	elephant below head	3	1	850	2200	
C2SHM-055	1666		4	1	500	1500	
C2SHM-060	1668		2	1	240	800	2200
C2SHM-065	1668		4	1	40	180	650
C2SHM-070	1668	8 over 3 (?)	4	1	60	240	750
C2SHM-075	1669	9 over 6 (?) [2]	2	1	400	1200	
C2SHM-080	1669		4	1	1000		
W3SH-035	1669	head of William III [3]			750		
C2SHM-085	1670		4	1	70	300	1100
C2SHM-090	1671		4	1	80	450	1300
C2SHM-095	1671	plume both sides	4	1	150	600	1500
C2SHM-100	1672		4	1	50	240	900
C2SHM-105	1672	2 over 1	4	1	60	260	950
C2SHM-110	1673		4	1	70	300	1100
C2SHM-115	1673	3 over 2	4	1	80	350	1300
C2SHM-118	1673	E of ET over R (rev.)	4	1	80	350	1300
C2SHM-120	1673	plume both sides	4	1	150	600	
C2SHM-125	1674		4	1	70	300	1100
C2SHM-130	1674	4 over 3	4	1	70	320	1200
C2SHM-135	1674	plume both sides	4	1	200	700	1400
C2SHM-140	1674	plume on rev.	4	1	250	1000	
C2SHM-145	1674		5	1	200	800	
C2SHM-150	1675		5	1	100	450	1300
C2SHM-155	1675	5 over 3	5	1	100	450	1400
C2SHM-160	1675		4	1	120	550	2000
C2SHM-165	1675	5 over 4	4	1	120	550	2000
C2SHM-170	1675	plume both sides	4	1	150	600	3000
C2SHM-172	1675	plume both sides; 5 over 3	4	1	250	1000	
C2SHM-175	1676		4	1	50	180	650
C2SHM-180	1676	6 over 5	4	1	70	220	750
C2SHM-185	1676	plume both sides	4	1	200	750	
C2SHM-190	1677		4	1	70	220	750
C2SHM-195	1677	plume below head	4	1	250	1200	
C2SHM-200	1678		4	1	120	300	1100
C2SHM-205	1678	8 over 7	4	1	120	300	1100
C2SHM-210	1679		4	1	60	170	600
C2SHM-215	1679	9 over 7	4	1	70	200	700
C2SHM-220	1679	plume both sides	4	1	150	600	
C2SHM-225	1679	plume below head	4	1	150	800	
C2SHM-230	1680		4	1	500	1200	2500
C2SHM-235	1680	80 over 79	4	1	400	1000	2200
C2SHM-240	1680	plume both sides	4	1	500	1400	3000
C2SHM-245	1681		4	1	100	400	1000
C2SHM-250	1681	1 over 0	4	1	100	400	1000
C2SHM-255	1681	1 over 0 elephant and castle	4	1	3000		
C2SHM-260	1682	2 over 1	4	1	400	1000	2500
C2SHM-265	1683		4	1	700	2000	
C2SHM-270	1683		6	1	100	350	950
C2SHM-275	1684	[4]	6	1	130	450	1200

1. At least one exists in EF condition.
2. A few with straight milling.
3. Error date (1696); see William III; reference number cross-indexed.
4. Rarer than indicated in some catalogues.

James II (1685 – 1688)

The cruciform shields design of John Roettier was continued during the reign of James II. The brief series includes a number of interesting varieties, but no patterns or proofs. The only provenance mark noted is the plume on the reverse of the very rare

variety of 1685. There is doubt whether the intention was to denote Welsh silver, and it is thought probable that confusion occurred with a punch from a Charles II coin. Unusually, here a provenance mark replaces part of the design, i.e. the central star.

Denomination	Metal	Weight (grams)	Diameter (mm)	Rev. alignment
Shilling	Silver	5.7–6.0	25–26	↓

Obverse 1   Head 1, left; IACOBVS II (head) DEI GRATIA

Reverse 1   Central star enclosed by four cruciform shields with surmounting crowns; MAG BR FRA ET HIB REX (date). On the 1685 plume variety, the plume *replaces* the star

Edge   milled (diagonally)

Obv. 1   Rev. 1

No.	Date	Features	Obv.	Rev.	F	VF	EF
J2SH-005	1685	[1]	1	1	70	220	650
J2SH-010	1685	no stops on rev.	1	1	100	320	900
J2SH-015	1685	plume on rev. [2]	1	1	7500		
J2SH-020	1686	[1]	1	1	70	220	650
J2SH-025	1686	latter 6 over 5	1	1	120	400	1000
J2SH-030	1686	V of IACOBVS over S (obv.) [1]	1	1	75	280	700
J2SH-035	1686	G of MAG over A (rev.)	1	1	90	350	950
J2SH-040	1687	[3]	1	1	80	270	800
J2SH-045	1687	7 over 6	1	1	70	220	650
J2SH-050	1687	7 over 6 G of MAG over A (rev.) [4]	1	1	75	240	700
J2SH-055	1688	[5]	1	1	80	270	750
J2SH-060	1688	latter 8 over 7 [6]	1	1	90	340	900

1. Minor varieties of reverse stops exist.
2. Plume replaces central star.
3. 7 not over 6.
4. G over A variety possibly occurs without overdate.
5. Latter 8 not over 7.
6. Most or all have no stop after HIB (rev.).

The number of harp strings varies through this series. It is possible that the variation constituted a form of internal code denoting the die number.

William & Mary (1688 – 1694)

John Roettier, the Chief Engraver, developed an affliction of the hands at the beginning of this reign, and he delegated work to his two sons, James (1663–98) and Norbert (1665–?). The low relief style suggests the work of James Roettier, but Rayner states that this may be the work of Henry Harris. A design of shilling very similar to those of preceding reigns was continued. The practice of placing a motif of interlinked initials in the angles, discontinued during the reign of James II, was revived, with a clever lattice design formed of a linked 'W' and 'M'. The series comprises two dates, with no patterns, proofs or provenance marks.

Collecting Hints

Fine condition specimens, although attractive, should be improved upon whenever possible because much delicate portrait detail is lost in this grade. The coinage is quite difficult to find in top condition.

Denomination	Metal	Weight (grams)	Diameter (mm)	Rev. alignment
Shilling	Silver	5.9–6.0	25–26	↓

Obverse 1 Heads 1, right; GVLIELMVS ET MARIA DEI GRATIA

Reverse 1 Four cruciform shields around lion of Orange-Nassau, with monogrammed 'WM' and one digit of date in each angle; MAG BR FR ET HI REX ET REGINA

Edge milled (diagonally)

Obv. 1

Rev. 1

No.	Date	Features	Obv.	Rev.	F	VF	EF
WMSH-005	1692	[1]	1	1	60	250	850
WMSH-010	1692	inverted 1 in date [1]	1	1	70	300	950
WMSH-015	1693	[2]	1	1	50	200	600
WMSH-020	1693	9 over 0 or 6 or inverted 9	1	1	80	350	1000
WMSH-025	1693	3 over inverted 2	1	1	80	350	1000

1. Minor stop varieties exist.
2. Minor stop varieties exist; orientation of head against legend differs.

William III   (1695 – 1701)

As with the sixpence, the first issue of the shilling coinage in 1695 was of a single type without varieties, but in 1696, with the withdrawal of the hammered coinage, the London and five provincial mints embarked upon a series of considerable complexity and interest. Included were a large number of errors, several of which are remarkable in nature. These were no doubt due to the use of new and inexperienced workers in the local mints.

The early coinage was probably engraved by James Roettier before his conviction at a mint enquiry in 1697 for smuggling dies to France; later work was by John Croker, but some doubt remains about the exact attribution of several pieces of 1696–97.

As with the halfcrowns, the variegation of the series, especially with reference to such details as harp design, is so complex that expediency requires some abbreviation. Therefore, some minor varieties are omitted or referred to only in note form.

Jackson Kent has pointed out that the conventionally accepted title of 'Third Bust Variety' is unfortunate, since the so-called 'First' and 'Third' busts resemble each other more closely than do the 'Third' and 'Third Variety' busts. Moreover, the so-called 'Second Bust' is almost certainly a pattern.

Provenance marks are: plumes (either in angles on reverse or singly below head) for silver from Welsh mines; roses (in angles) for silver from West of England mines.

Collecting Hints

Because of the number of varieties and errors in this series, many of which are quite rare, collectors will find that if they insist on a minimum grade, say fine, they will end up with many gaps in their collection. Consequently, one should acquire any example offered of the rarer varieties, provided that it bears sufficient detail to identify the piece. The fact that there is only one reverse for this series makes the task of completing the set somewhat easier.

Although the 1696 and 1697 are probably overall the commonest dates, the 1700 is arguably the most frequently encountered in extremely fine or better condition. This is because a large quantity in mint state was discovered in a bank vault towards the end of the 19th century.

All of the shield positional varieties involve the Irish shield, directly or indirectly, and one should therefore always examine all reverses with the date at the top, and check that the harp is on the left. This is advisable also for other denominations of this period, but particularly so with this series.

Shillings of William III are frequently marked by the twin curses of weak striking and adjustment marks, and it is up to the individual collector to decide whether these afflictions detract from the coin or simply form part of its mintage history. A very weakly struck extremely fine coin of this series can sometimes appear to the uninitiated as about fine to very fine, while a heavily adjusted piece will seem to be badly scratched. In fact, the filing adjustment was carried out before issue to correct the weight to that officially authorised.

The first head shilling lacking the tie at the back of the head is not a true variety, nor is that reading GVLIEIMVS; these apparent varieties are caused by die wear in various degrees.

Denomination	Metal	Weight (grams)	Diameter (mm)	Rev. alignment
Shilling	Silver	5.8–6.2	25–26	↓

Obverse 1 Head 1, right; GVLIELMVS (head) III DEI GRA

Obverse 2 Head 2, right; same legend

Obverse 3 Head 3, right; same legend

Obverse 4 Head 4, right; same legend

Obverse 5 Head 5, very different, right; known as 'flaming hair' type; same legend but different lettering style

Obverse 6 Head 6, right; known as 'high hair' type; same legend

Heads 1, 3, 4 are all very similar; note especially the arrangement of the hair at the back of the head, and the tie

Reverse 1 Four cruciform shields around lion of Nassau; MAG BR FRA ET HIB REX (date)

Edge milled (diagonally)

Obv. 1   Obv. 2

Obv. 3

| Obv. 5 | Obv. 6 | Rev. 1 |

No.	Date	Features	mm	Obv.	Rev.	F	VF	EF
W3SH-005	1695			1	1	30	100	300
W3SH-010	1696	1		1	1	20	60	130
W3SH-015	1696	no rev. stops		1	1	25	75	160
W3SH-020	1696	MAB instead of MAG (rev.)		1	1	150	500	
W3SH-025	1696	GVLIEMVS instead of GVLIELMVS (obv.)		1	1	60	180	
W3SH-030	1696	GVLIELM∀S instead of GVLIELMVS (obv.)		1	1	40	120	400
W3SH-035	1669	1669 instead of 1696 2		1	1	750		
W3SH-040	1696	PROOF on thick flan		1	1		1000	3500
W3SH-045	1696		B	1	1	30	110	350
W3SH-050	1696	struck over hammered shilling	B	1	1	50	150	500
W3SH-055	1696		C	1	1	30	110	350
W3SH-060	1696	PROOF on thick flan	C	1	1		1200	4000
W3SH-065	1696		E	1	1	30	110	350
W3SH-070	1696	3	N	1	1	30	130	600
W3SH-075	1696		y	1	1	30	100	300
W3SH-080	1696		Y	1	1	35	110	350
W3SH-085	1696	Y over inverted Y (mintmark)	Y	1	1	45	140	500
W3SH-090	1696	4		2	1			
W3SH-095	1696		C	3	1	60	200	800
W3SH-100	1696		E	3	1	800		
W3SH-105	1696		y	3	1	600		
W3SH-110	1697	5		1	1	20	60	150
W3SH-115	1697	Scotland/ Ireland shields transposed (rev.)		1	1	250	1000	
W3SH-120	1697	shields rotated clockwise 90 degrees (rev.)		1	1	250	1000	
W3SH-125	1697	no rev. stops		1	1	25	70	180
W3SH-130	1697	GVLELMVS instead of GVLIELMVS (obv.)		1	1	70	200	500
W3SH-135	1697	GRI instead of GRA (obv.)		1	1	90	300	800
W3SH-140	1697	DE(over A)I instead of DEI (obv.)		1	1	50	140	500
W3SH-145	1697		B	1	1	30	110	350
W3SH-150	1697		C	1	1	30	110	350
W3SH-155	1697	Scotland/ Ireland shields transposed (rev.)	C	1	1	250	1000	
W3SH-160	1697		E	1	1	30	110	400
W3SH-165	1697		N	1	1	30	120	450
W3SH-170	1697		y	1	1	30	100	300
W3SH-175	1697	France/ Ireland shields transposed (rev.)	y	1	1	600		
W3SH-180	1697	Scotland/ Ireland shields transposed (rev.)	y	1	1	600		
W3SH-185	1697		Y	1	1	35	110	350
W3SH-190	1697	6		3	1	20	65	170

No.	Date	Features	mm	Obv.	Rev.	F	VF	EF
W3SH-195	1697	6	B	3	1	35	110	350
W3SH-200	1697	7	C	3	1	35	110	350
W3SH-205	1697	no rev. stops	C	3	1	40	120	380
W3SH-210	1697	Scotland shield at date	C	3	1	250	1000	
W3SH-215	1697		E	3	1	35	110	350
W3SH-220	1697	6	N	3	1	35	110	350
W3SH-225	1697		y	3	1	35	110	350
W3SH-230	1697			4	1	20	65	170
W3SH-235	1697	GVLIELM∀S instead of GVLIELMVS (obv.)		4	1	40	120	400
W3SH-240	1697		B	4	1	35	110	350
W3SH-245	1697		C	4	1	70	200	650
W3SH-250	1697	struck on thick flan 8	C	4	1	200	600	
W3SH-255	1698			4	1	30	90	250
W3SH-260	1698	PROOF; edge plain		4	1			1500
W3SH-265	1698	plumes on rev.		4	1	80	250	800
W3SH-270	1698	9		5	1	50	140	450
W3SH-275	1698	PROOF; edge plain		5	1			2000
W3SH-280	1699			5	1	35	100	300
W3SH-285	1699	struck on thick flan 10		5	1	300		
W3SH-290	1699			6	1	35	100	300
W3SH-295	1699	PROOF; edge plain		6	1			1600
W3SH-300	1699	plumes on rev.		6	1	70	200	500
W3SH-305	1699	roses on rev.		6	1	80	280	700
W3SH-310	1700	11		6	1	30	60	140
W3SH-315	1700	plume below head 12		6	1	1400		
W3SH-320	1701	9		6	1	35	100	300
W3SH-325	1701	plumes on rev.		6	1	70	200	500

1. Flan diameter varies.
2. Error date.
3. Very rare in EF plus.
4. Probably unique (VF); sold at Spink auction no.3, February 1979 for £13000.
5. Lions, harps, stops vary.
6. Lettering size varies.
7. Sometimes reads FR.A instead of FRA (rev.).
8. Weight c.9.0–10.2 grams.
9. Lions vary (rev.).
10. Weight 8.3 grams.
11. 'O's in date vary; reverse stops vary.
12. About 5 known.

The number of harp strings varies through this series. It is possible that the variation constituted a form of internal code denoting the die number. Other minor reverse variations occur, notably to the harp.

Marks and Operating Periods of Provincial Mints
B: BRISTOL: September 1696 to September 1698
C: CHESTER: October 1696 to June 1698
E: EXETER: August 1696 to July 1698
N: NORWICH: September 1696 to April 1698
y or Y: YORK: September 1696 to April 1698

Anne   (1702 – 1714)

The shilling series is the most complex denomination of Anne in its diversity of varieties. Straddling the Union of England and Scotland, it also exhibits a number of new provenance marks and mintmarks.

At the beginning of the reign, the Chief Engraver John Croker and his assistant Samuel Bull produced a portrait based on a painting of Anne by Sir Godfrey Kneller. After the Union of England and Scotland, the Scottish engraver James Clerk worked on the shilling and smaller denominations, but there is doubt about the exact attribution of some of the dies.

Provenance marks are: VIGO (below head) for silver obtained from Spanish galleons at Vigo Bay in 1702; plumes (in angles on reverse) for silver from Wales; roses and plumes (alternately in angles on reverse) for silver from the 'Company for smelting down lead with Pitcoale and Seacoale'. The mintmarks E and E* represent coins struck at Edinburgh. The shilling is the only denomination bearing the VIGO mark on coins struck in 1702, the same year as the capture of the silver bullion at Vigo Bay. All other VIGO coins are dated 1703.

By the Articles of the Union agreed on 22 July 1706 to take place on 1 May 1707, it was agreed that after the Union the coin should be of the same standard and value throughout the United Kingdom, and that a Mint should be continued in Scotland under the same rules as applied in England. In 1707, a quantity of Scottish silver coin valued at £411,117 10s 9d was brought into the Mint at Edinburgh to be recoined, and the resulting British coinage (much of it shillings of 1707 and 1708) bears the mintmark E (for Edinburgh) under the head on the obverse. However, a great deal of the silver was not recoined because of the 1707 invasion, and was re-issued, mainly as Scottish 40 shilling pieces. In 1708, this was again called in, and the resulting recoined British silver dated 1707 (sic), 1708 and 1709 was given the same mintmark, but with a six pointed mullet or star next to the E. Records show that the actual weight of the coins struck at Edinburgh was 103,346 pounds.

After the Union, two of the shields on the reverse were each divided into the arms of England and Scotland; previously the arms had been placed separately on two shields.

Collecting Hints

This series should be collected in at least very fine condition with the exception of the rarer varieties. The intricacies of the numerous varieties of 1707 and 1708 are such that one needs not only to have a good memory but also some expertise in identification unless one is prepared to carry an illustrated catalogue when buying. We trust that you will find the present catalogue an improvement on previous attempts to illustrate this series!

The 1711 is a coin which should always be examined carefully, since this date is shared by the common Head 5 and the rare Head 3. Luckily, the identification is easy, even with worn pieces. The rare Head 3 has what looks like an indentation or cut at the top, caused by the hair arrangement, whereas the common Head 5 is somewhat uneven but relatively smooth in comparison, rather as if the queen were wearing a hairnet.

The 1703, although much scarcer overall than, say, the 1711 Head 5, appears to have been preserved in quantities in higher grades, so that in very fine or extremely fine the 1703 is not all that much scarcer. It is, incidentally, more likely to be flecked or haymarked than the 1711. The 1707 plain variety is also frequently found in top condition.

Denomination	Metal	Weight (grams)	Diameter (mm)	Rev. alignment
Shilling	Silver	5.9–6.0	25–26	↓

Obverse 1 Head 1, left; two curls at top, relatively long tie; ANNA DEI GRATIA

Obverse 2 Head 2, left; curls different, tie shorter; same legend

Obverse 3 Head 3, left; curls flatter; same legend

Obverse 4 Head 4, so-called 'Edinburgh bust' (Edinburgh mint), left; very similar to Obverse 3 but the tie is noticeably shorter; same legend

Obverse 5 Head 5, left; deeply engraved 'hairnet' effect; same legend

Reverse 1 'Before Union reverse'; thin shields convex at top; English and Scottish arms on separate shields; MAG BR FRA ET HIB REG (date)

Reverse 2 'After Union reverse'; broader shields concave at top; English and Scottish arms impaled together on two identical divided shields;

MAG BRI FR ET HIB REG (date); London and Edinburgh Reverse 2 differ slightly

Edge milled (diagonally)

Obv. 1　　　Obv. 2　　　Obv. 3

Obv. 4　　　Obv. 5

Rev. 1　　　Rev. 2

Before Union of England and Scotland

No.	Date	Features	Obv.	Rev.	F	VF	EF
ANSH-005	1702	[1]	1	1	50	140	350
ANSH-010	1702	plumes on rev.	1	1	60	170	420
ANSH-015	1702	VIGO below head [1]	1	1	50	130	320
ANSH-020	1703	VIGO below head [1]	2	1	35	90	150
ANSH-025	1704		2	1	300	800	1800
ANSH-030	1704	plumes on rev.	2	1	70	180	450
ANSH-035	1705		2	1	70	180	450
ANSH-040	1705	plumes on rev.	2	1	50	140	350
ANSH-045	1705	roses and plumes on rev.	2	1	45	130	320
ANSH-050	1707	roses and plumes on rev.	2	1	50	140	350

1. Obverse punctuation varies.

After Union of England and Scotland

No.	Date	Features	mm	Obv.	Rev.	F	VF	EF
ANSH-055	1707		E	2	2	25	70	180
ANSH-060	1707	PROOF; edge plain [1]	E	2	2			2000
ANSH-065	1707	[2]	E*	2	2	50	150	400
ANSH-070	1707			3	2	20	55	140
ANSH-075	1707	plumes on rev.		3	2	30	80	220
ANSH-080	1707		E	3	2	22	60	160
ANSH-085	1707		E*	4	2	200		
ANSH-090	1708		E	2	2	50	140	380
ANSH-095	1708		E*	2	2	30	80	220
ANSH-100	1708	8 over 7	E*	2	2	80	180	500
ANSH-105	1708	roses and plumes on rev.		2	2	75	180	600
ANSH-110	1708			3	2	15	40	100
ANSH-115	1708	plumes on rev.		3	2	22	65	170
ANSH-120	1708	roses and plumes on rev.		3	2	25	70	180
ANSH-125	1708		E	3	2	35	95	280
ANSH-130	1708	8 over 7	E	3	2	45	120	380
ANSH-135	1708		E*	4	2	40	110	320
ANSH-140	1709			3	2	18	50	120

No.	Date	Features	mm	Obv.	Rev.	F	VF	EF
ANSH-145	1709	ANNA over DEI (obv.)		3	2	50	150	400
ANSH-150	1709	IIIB instead of HIB (rev.)		3	2	30	80	180
ANSH-155	1709	[3]	E*	4	2	60	180	500
ANSH-160	1709	rev. ↑ [3]	E*	4	2	65	200	550
ANSH-165	1710	roses and plumes on rev.		3	2	22	60	150
ANSH-170	1710	PROOF; edge plain		5	2			5000
ANSH-172	1710	PROOF on thick flan; edge plain [4]		5	2			8000
ANSH-175	1710	roses and plumes on rev.		5	2	35	100	350
ANSH-180	1710	PROOF; edge plain roses and plumes on rev.		5	2			3000
ANSH-185	1711	[5]		3	2	60	250	900
ANSH-190	1711			5	2	15	35	120
ANSH-195	1712	roses and plumes on rev.		5	2	18	50	140
ANSH-200	1713	3 over 2 roses and plumes on rev. [6]		5	2	22	70	180
ANSH-205	1714	roses and plumes on rev.		5	2	18	50	140
ANSH-210	1714	roses and plumes on rev. inverted 'L' instead of 'I' (both) in obv. legend		5	2	25	80	220
ANSH-215	1714	4 over 3		5	2	50	150	400

1. Reverse shields are slightly narrower than on usual Rev. 2.
2. Minor die differences exist.
3. Some have star filled in on die; some are underweight.
4. Weight 8.0 grams.
5. Virtually unknown above VF grade.
6. 3 not over 2 unknown.

The number of harp strings varies through this series. It is possible that the variation constituted a form of internal code denoting the die number.

George I (1714 – 1727)

The general design of cruciform shields continued with the accession of George Louis, Elector of Hanover, as George I, but one of the duplicated England/Scotland shields was replaced by one containing the arms of Brunswick-Lüneburg, with a central depiction of the crown of Charlemagne. The long German titles of the king also appear on both obverse and reverse in a greatly abbreviated form.

It is probable that John Croker was responsible for at least some of the work of the obverse design of this series, and there is evidence that a Swiss engraver, Johan Ochs, designed some of the reverse dies.

Provenance marks of this series are: roses and plumes (in reverse angles) for silver from the 'Company for smelting down lead with Pitcoale and Seacoale'; SS and C (in alternate angles on reverse) for silver from The South Sea Company; WCC (below head) for silver from the Welsh Copper Company, which coins also bear on the reverse as provenance marks two interlinked 'C's placed in the reverse angles alternately with a plume (i.e. totalling four 'C's and two plumes). It is an interesting possibility that this configuration may have been meant to denote Welsh Copper Company (i.e. plume, C and C). It is also worthy of note that the interlinked 'C's on the reverse are identical to those used on the coinage of Charles II, but, while those on the Charles coinage were an integral part of the design, being the initial of the king's name, in this case they are true provenance marks. For this reason

it is felt correct to place the WCC coinage under 'Reverse 1' rather than allocate a new reverse design.

Provenance marks in this and the following reign were now so prolific that their existence on a coin was the rule rather than the exception.

There are no pattern or proof shillings of George I, except for a piece ascribed to Norbert Roettier dated 1716, which may have been a pattern guinea or shilling. This was produced while Roettier was working in France, and has no official status.

Collecting Hints

This series should be collected in very fine or better condition except for the very rare pieces, but the WCC pieces do turn up in very fine or extremely fine from time to time. Possibly they were hoarded as curiosities.

The 1723 variety with arms of France at date is often missed through carelessness, but there is an easy way to check it, even with below-average eyesight, and this should always be done: with the date at the top, the rare type reads SS C across the date; the common one reads C SS. For 1723 coins, the difference between heads can be easily remembered; two loose ends to tie is Head 1; one loose end is Head 2.

The 1721 shilling with reversed roses and plumes is not a well-known coin, and therefore it is well worth checking any shilling of this date. The coin has even appeared, unnoticed and yet photographed, in the catalogue of a major London auctioneer! It should be remembered that, for a correctly orientated coin (i.e. the common variety), with the date at the top, the sequence is plume-rose from left to right across the obv. top of the coin.

Denomination	Metal	Weight (grams)	Diameter (mm)	Rev. alignment
Shilling	Silver	5.9–6.1	25–26	↓

Obverse 1 Head 1, right; two loose ends to tie; GEORGIVS D G M BR FR ET HIB REX F D

Obverse 2 Head 2, right; one loose end and one bow to tie; minor differences to portrait; same undivided legend

Reverse 1 Four crowned cruciform shields around central star; BRVN ET L DVX S R I A TH ET EL

Edge milled (diagonally)

Obv. 1	Obv. 2	Rev. 1

No.	Date	Features	Obv.	Rev.	F	VF	EF
G1SH-005	1715	roses and plumes on rev. [1]	1	1	20	70	200
G1SH-010	1716	roses and plumes on rev.	1	1	50	200	550
G1SH-015	1717	roses and plumes on rev.	1	1	20	70	200
G1SH-020	1718	roses and plumes on rev. [2]	1	1	20	55	150
G1SH-025	1719	roses and plumes on rev.	1	1	45	160	450
G1SH-030	1720	roses and plumes on rev.	1	1	20	70	200
G1SH-035	1720	roses and plumes on rev.; edge plain [3]	1	1	100	400	
G1SH-040	1720	(plain in angles) [4]	1	1	18	60	170
G1SH-045	1721	(plain in angles)	1	1	80	400	
G1SH-050	1721	roses and plumes on rev. [5]	1	1	30	100	300

No.	Date	Features	Obv.	Rev.	F	VF	EF
G1SH-055	1721	plumes and roses on rev. (i.e. reversed positions)	1	1	120	300	900
G1SH-058	1721	plumes and roses on rev. (i.e. reversed positions); 21 over 18	1	1	180	450	1200
G1SH-060	1721	latter 1 over 0; roses and plumes on rev. [6]	1	1	25	85	250
G1SH-065	1721	21 over 19 or 18 roses and plumes on rev.	1	1	35	120	350
G1SH-070	1722	roses and plumes on rev. [7]	1	1	25	85	260
G1SH-075	1723	roses and plumes on rev.	1	1	20	70	200
G1SH-080	1723	SS C in angles [8]	1	1	15	50	120
G1SH-085	1723	SS C in angles with one C over SS	1	1	30	90	200
G1SH-090	1723	SS C in angles arms of France at date [9]	1	1	75	300	
G1SH-095	1723	SS C in angles [10]	2	1	20	65	170
G1SH-100	1723	roses and plumes on rev.	2	1	22	75	240
G1SH-105	1723	WCC below head; plumes and interlinked 'C's on rev.	2	1	200	600	1300
G1SH-110	1724	roses and plumes on rev.	2	1	22	80	300
G1SH-115	1724	WCC below head; plumes and interlinked 'C's on rev.	2	1	200	600	1300
G1SH-120	1725	roses and plumes on rev.	2	1	22	80	300
G1SH-125	1725	roses and plumes on rev.; no stops on obv.	2	1	25	85	350
G1SH-130	1725	WCC below head; plumes and interlinked 'C's on rev.	2	1	200	600	1300
G1SH-135	1726	roses and plumes on rev.	2	1	450		
G1SH-140	1726	WCC below head; plumes and interlinked 'C's on rev.	2	1	200	600	1300
G1SH-145	1727	roses and plumes on rev.	2	1	350		
G1SH-150	1727	roses and plumes on rev.; no stops on obv.	2	1	350		

1. Stops varieties exist.
2. Often found in VF+ grade.
3. An error coin.
4. Date and letters vary in size.
5. Latter 1 not over 0.
6. Usually a remarkably clear overdate.
7. Obv stops vary.
8. Reads C SS across date (rev.); stops vary; a variety is reported with a slightly smaller obverse and reverse design.
9. Reads SS C across date (rev.).
10. Harp varies.

The number of harp strings varies through this series. It is possible that the variation constituted a form of internal code denoting the die number.

George II   (1727 – 1760)

Although Croker was responsible for designing most of the new coinage, the reverse of the first type of shilling has been attributed to J. R. Ochs, senior. The older portrait of the king, introduced in 1743, was largely the work of John Sigismund Tanner, who had become Chief Engraver in 1741. Croker had also worked on the dies before his death in March 1741 (1740 old style calendar).

Provenance marks are: plumes (silver from The Welsh Copper Company); roses (silver from mines in the West of England); roses and plumes (silver from the 'Company for smelting down lead with Pitcoale and Seacoale'), all of these in the reverse angles; LIMA below the head for coins struck in silver captured by Admiral Anson during his voyage around the world, possibly in the form of coinage with the LIMA mintmark.

Denomination	Metal	Weight (grams)	Diameter (mm)	Rev. alignment
Shilling	Silver	6.0	25–26	↓

Obverse 1   Head 1, left; GEORGIVS II (head) DEI GRATIA

Obverse 2   Head 2, left; GEORGIUS II (head) DEI GRATIA

Obverse 3   Head 2, left; GEORGIVS II (head) DEI GRATIA

Reverse 1   Four crowned cruciform shields; M B F ET H REX F D B ET L D S R I A T ET E (date)

Edge   milled (diagonally)

Obv. 1   Obv. 3   Rev. 1

No.	Date	Features	Obv.	Rev.	F	VF	EF
G2SH-005	1727	plumes on rev.	1	1	50	130	500
G2SH-010	1727	roses and plumes on rev.	1	1	30	80	250
G2SH-015	1728		1	1	40	100	350
G2SH-020	1728	roses and plumes on rev.	1	1	50	140	550
G2SH-025	1728	roses and plumes on rev.; E of GEOR over R (obv.)	1	1	60	160	650
G2SH-030	1729	roses and plumes on rev.	1	1	50	120	300
G2SH-035	1731	roses and plumes on rev.	1	1	30	80	200
G2SH-040	1731	plumes on rev.	1	1	70	200	500
G2SH-045	1732	roses and plumes on rev.	1	1	50	120	300
G2SH-050	1734	roses and plumes on rev. [1]	1	1	25	70	170
G2SH-055	1735	roses and plumes on rev.	1	1	25	70	170
G2SH-060	1736	roses and plumes on rev. [2]	1	1	25	70	170
G2SH-065	1736	6 over 5 roses and plumes on rev.	1	1	35	90	250
G2SH-070	1737	roses and plumes on rev.	1	1	25	70	170
G2SH-075	1739	roses on rev.	1	1	20	60	150
G2SH-080	1739	9 over 7; roses on rev.	1	1	40	95	200
G2SH-085	1739	unusually small Garter star (rev.); roses on rev.	1	1	150		
G2SH-090	1741	roses on rev.	1	1	20	60	150
G2SH-095	1743	roses on rev.	2	1	20	55	140
G2SH-100	1743	3 over 1 roses on rev.	2	1	35	80	170
G2SH-105	1745	roses on rev.	2	1	25	65	150
G2SH-110	1745	5 over 3 roses on rev.	2	1	30	80	170
G2SH-115	1745	LIMA below head	2	1	20	50	120
G2SH-118	1745	LIMA below head; A of LIMA unbarred	2	1	30	70	160
G2SH-120	1746	LIMA below head	3	1	50	150	600

No.	Date	Features	Obv.	Rev.	F	VF	EF
G2SH-125	1746	6 over 5 LIMA below head	3	1	50	150	600
G2SH-130	1746	PROOF [3]	3	1			700
G2SH-135	1747	roses on rev.	3	1	25	70	170
G2SH-140	1747	latter 7 over 6; roses on rev.	3	1	30	80	190
G2SH-145	1750	oval '0' in date	3	1	30	75	160
G2SH-150	1750	oval '0' over 6	3	1	35	85	180
G2SH-155	1750	5 over 4; round '0' in date	3	1	35	85	180
G2SH-160	1750	50 over 46; oval '0' in date	3	1	60	130	300
G2SH-165	1751		3	1	40	90	180
G2SH-170	1758	[4]	3	1	15	25	60

1. See comments below.
2. Reverse stops vary.
3. No LIMA; may have raised die flaw in reverse field; weight variations exist.
4. Possibly struck for some years.

The number of harp strings varies through this series. It is possible that the variation constituted a form of internal code denoting the die number.

Although there was a change to slightly larger lettering in 1734, this is not considered significant enough to assign new obverse and reverse numbers.

George III   (1760 – 1820)

The George III shilling series is, like the Curate's egg, an oddball, but it certainly contains some gems. Two classic rarities sandwich the ubiquitous 1787, which itself contains a multiplicity of interesting varieties. A long gap is then followed by the 'Great Recoinage' series of 1816 to 1820 with a smattering of proofs (including one in gold) to whet the appetite.

At the beginning of the reign, many of the shillings in circulation had been worn to complete blanks. Indeed, such blanks were produced in profusion by 'counterfeiters', if such a word can be used in this context. Much foreign coinage of similar size was imported and worn smooth to produce pieces similar to worn shillings.

The 'Northumberland' shilling of 1763 was distributed by the Earl of Northumberland on his appointment as Lord Lieutenant of Ireland, but the story that the issue was limited to £100 in face value is probably untrue. The portrait was designed by Richard Yeo (d. 1779), who also engraved the reverses based on the current standard design. These coins were undoubtedly hoarded, as they are probably more plentiful in very fine or extremely fine than in fair or fine condition.

The very large issue of 1787 may have been hoarded, possibly because the denomination had become so unusual that there was a reluctance to spend the coins, rather in the same way that crowns and £2 coins are hoarded today or used as gifts. The issue of 1787 is certainly as likely to be encountered in very fine or extremely fine condition as in fine. However, a curious comment is made by Stephen Martin Leake, writing in 1793, lamenting that 'we are at a loss to account for the reason of no coinage of shillings being issued, after so many dies had been engraved'. He further says that the coinage, 'made for the use of The Bank of England' is 'not in common currency'. Records show that a total value of £55,549 in silver coins was issued in 1787.

The series of 1787 includes a number of interesting and scarce varieties, as well as proofs and patterns. It is also divided into two main types, with and without the semee of hearts on the arms of Brunswick, although it is not generally realised that the issue without hearts was issued in error, corrected only after a large number had been minted.

The very rare issue of 1798 was struck from silver supplied by Mr. Magens Dorrien Magens (1761–1849) of the City of London. Apparently some £30,000 worth of coins were struck, but in May of that year a Privy Council Committee ruled that the issue was illegal and the coins were almost all melted down. They are so rare that even a photograph is missing from several reference works. Some years ago a club was in existence whose condition

of entry was ownership of one of these coins. They were the only silver coins struck in 1798.

After the Great Recoinage of 1816, the short series up to 1820 was made using the new machinery at Tower Hill. Initially, the design and engraving were carried out by Thomas Wyon, Junior, the obverse being based on a model by Benedetto Pistrucci. On the death of Wyon in 1817, Pistrucci himself took over the engraving of the dies. The quality of striking of this series was excellent, and again many pieces were hoarded; consequently, it is not too difficult to find specimens in the higher grades.

The shilling coinage of 1816 onwards remained legal tender until the end of 1990, when the size of the decimal 5 pence coin was reduced.

No provenance marks exist for the George III shilling coinage; the crowns in the angles of the 1787 coins resemble provenance marks but are an integral part of the design.

Collecting Hints

All of the shillings of George III should be collected in extremely fine condition, but the 1798 Dorrien Magens issue is so rare that one will be lucky if one even hears of it for sale in any condition.
The unusual GEOE error of 1817 and the plain edge 1816 and 1817 proofs are sometimes obtainable cheaply because not all dealers and auctioneers check their stock as thoroughly as they might.
The 1787 shilling should always be checked for the stop omissions, obverse and reverse. The very rare obverse without any stops at all is occasionally catalogued as the 'no stop over head' type (or even missed altogether!) because a dealer is unused to seeing the coin and does not trouble to check properly.
Shillings of the period 1816–20 sometimes occur with initials unofficially stamped on them, usually on the obverse.

Denomination	Metal	Weight (grams)	Diameter (mm)	Rev. alignment
Shilling 1763	Silver	6.0	26	↓
Shilling 1787 & 1798	Silver	6.0	25	↑
Shilling 1816–20	Silver	5.7	24	↑

Obverse 1   Head 1, right; GEORGIVS III DEI GRATIA

Obverse 2   Head 2, right; same legend

Obverse 3   Head 3, similar to 2, right; same legend, larger lettering; no stop over head

Obverse 4   Head 4, right; GEOR III D G BRITT REX F D (date)

Reverse 1   Cruciform shields around star, plain in angles; M B F ET H REX F D B ET L D S R I A T ET E 1763

Reverse 2   Cruciform pentagonal shields around star, with crowns in angles; no hearts behind lion in Hanoverian shield. M B F ET H REX F D B ET L D S R I A T ET E 1787

Reverse 3   As Reverse 2 but with hearts

Reverse 4   As Reverse 3 but with larger lettering and dated 1798

Reverse 5   Crowned shield within Garter; HONI SOIT Q(UI) MAL Y PENSE on Garter

Edge   milled

Obv. 1

Obv. 2

Obv. 3

Obv. 4

Rev. 1

Rev. 3

Rev. 4

Rev. 5

no hearts

hearts

No.	Date	Features	Obv.	Rev.	F	VF	EF	UNC
G3SH-005	1763	[1]	1	1	180	300	500	650
G3SH-010	1787		2	2	15	25	45	75
G3SH-015	1787	1 over reversed 1	2	2	60	90	150	250
G3SH-020	1787	PROOF on thick flan; edge plain [2]	2	2				700
G3SH-025	1787	no stop over head	2	2	14	20	45	75
G3SH-030	1787	no stop over head PROOF	2	2				400
G3SH-035	1787	no stop over head PROOF; edge plain	2	2				600
G3SH-040	1787	no stop over head PROOF on thick flan; edge plain	2	2				700
G3SH-045	1787	no stops on obv.	2	2	40	100	200	300
G3SH-050	1787	no stops on obv. PROOF; edge plain	2	2				800
G3SH-055	1787	no stops at date	2	2	18	30	45	75
G3SH-060	1787	latter 7 over 6; no stops at date	2	2	35	60	90	120
G3SH-065	1787		2	3	15	25	45	75
G3SH-070	1787	1 over reversed 1	2	3	60	90	150	250
G3SH-075	1787	PROOF	2	3				400
G3SH-080	1787	PROOF on thick flan; edge plain	2	3				700
G3SH-085	1798	[3]	3	4			5000	8000
G3SH-090	1816	[4]	4	5	7	12	30	55
G3SH-095	1816	PROOF	4	5				750
G3SH-100	1816	PROOF; edge plain	4	5				750
G3SH-105	1816	PROOF in gold	4	5				10000
G3SH-110	1817		4	5	7	12	30	55
G3SH-112	1817	I of HONI over S (rev.)	4	5	60	120	250	500
G3SH-113	1817	IIONI instead of HONI (rev.)	4	5	20	45	90	150
G3SH-115	1817	PROOF; edge plain	4	5			450	750
G3SH-120	1817	GEOE instead of GEOR (obv.)	4	5	50	150	400	
G3SH-122	1817	RRITT instead of BRITT (obv.)	4	5	70	200	600	
G3SH-125	1818	[5]	4	5	12	25	90	140
G3SH-130	1819	[6]	4	5	7	12	30	55
G3SH-135	1819	9 over 8 [7]	4	5	12	20	55	80

No.	Date	Features	Obv.	Rev.	F	VF	EF	UNC
G3SH-140	1820	[8]	4	5	8	14	35	55
G3SH-142	1820	reverse ↓ [8]	4	5	15	25	70	120
G3SH-145	1820	I of HONI over S (rev.) [8]	4	5	40	80	150	250
G3SH-150	1820	H of HONI over horizontal H [8]	4	5	30	75	150	250
G3SH-155	1820	PROOF	4	5				900

1. 'Northumberland' shilling.
2. Weight 7.6 grams.
3. 'Dorrien Magens' shilling.
4. Issued in 1817.
5. Recut date exists.
6. 9 varies in size.
7. Do not confuse overdate with double struck 8.
8. Continued to be minted after death of George III.

George IV (1820 – 1830)

The shillings initially used the Benedetto Pistrucci laureate head of the monarch, but this was changed during 1825 after the king's disapproval of the design, giving way to a more youthful portrait by William Wyon. The reverses, by Johann Baptiste Merlen, underwent two major changes in design, the second coinciding with the introduction of the new portrait in 1825. As with the half-crowns, the initials of William Wellesley Pole, Master of the Mint, are hidden in the centres of the shamrocks on the reverse.

Collecting Hints

The delicate design of the Pistrucci laureate head shillings and the relatively higher relief of the later bare head type make it advisable to collect the series in extremely fine or better condition if one wants to appreciate the craftsmanship put into their manufacture. Several dates, notably 1821, 1823 and 1827 are very difficult to find in mint state or near.

Denomination	Metal	Weight (grams)	Diameter (mm)	Rev. alignment
Shilling	Silver	5.7	24	↓

Obverse 1 Head 1, laureate, left; GEORGIUS IIII D G BRITANNIAR REX F D

Obverse 2 Head 2, 'bare head', left; GEORGIUS IV DEI GRATIA (date)

Reverse 1 Garnished shield with surmounting large crown; ANNO (date)

Reverse 2 Crowned shield within Garter; ANNO (date); HONI SOIT QUI MAL Y PENSE (on Garter)

Reverse 3 Lion on crown, ornament below; BRITANNIARUM REX FIDEI DEFENSOR

Edge milled

Obv. 1

Obv. 2

Rev. 1

Rev. 2

Rev. 3

No.	Date	Features	Obv.	Rev.	F	VF	EF	UNC
G4SH-005	1821		1	1	10	22	80	140
G4SH-010	1821	PROOF	1	1				600
G4SH-015	1823		1	2	25	70	200	300
G4SH-020	1823	PROOF	1	2				800
G4SH-025	1824		1	2	10	25	90	140
G4SH-030	1824	PROOF	1	2				800
G4SH-035	1825		1	2	10	25	90	140
G4SH-040	1825	5 over 3	1	2	15	35	130	200
G4SH-045	1825	PROOF	1	2				600
G4SH-050	1825		2	3	8	18	60	90
G4SH-055	1825	I instead of 1 in date	2	3	150	700		
G4SH-060	1825	PROOF	2	3				600
G4SH-065	1825	PROOF in Barton's metal; edge plain	2	3				1000
G4SH-070	1826		2	3	7	15	50	80
G4SH-075	1826	Roman I in date	2	3	20	50	150	250
G4SH-080	1826	PROOF [1]	2	3				350
G4SH-085	1826	6 over 2	2	3	12	25	70	110
G4SH-090	1827		2	3	12	45	130	190
G4SH-095	1829		2	3	10	35	110	170
G4SH-100	1829	PROOF	2	3				800

1. Issued in cased proof sets.

Barton's metal is a laminated product consisting of thin sheets of gold bonded to a copper base.

William IV (1830 – 1837)

The shillings of William IV were of one type only, using an obverse by William Wyon and a reverse by Johann Baptiste Merlen, which latter included the denomination 'ONE SHILLING' for the first time. William Wyon had by now shown himself to be an engraver of talent, while the antics of the temperamental Pistrucci had resulted in his being moved sideways to a new post of Chief Medallist.

Proofs exist for each of the five dates, with the unusual feature on three of them of a round-top '3' in the date.

Collecting Hints

This series is of a simple and elegant design which is best appreciated in very fine or extremely fine condition.

Denomination	Metal	Weight (grams)	Diameter (mm)	Rev. alignment
Shilling	Silver	5.7	24	↓

Obverse 1 Head 1, right; GULIELMUS IIII D G BRITANNIAR REX F D

Reverse 1 'ONE SHILLING' within wreath, crown above, date below

Edge milled

Obv. 1   Rev. 1

No.	Date	Features	Obv.	Rev.	F	VF	EF	UNC
W4SH-005	1831	PROOF; edge plain [1]	1	1				450
W4SH-010	1831	PROOF	1	1				800
W4SH-015	1834		1	1	10	25	85	140
W4SH-020	1834	PROOF	1	1				600
W4SH-025	1834	PROOF round-top '3' in date	1	1				1200
W4SH-030	1835		1	1	15	40	120	170
W4SH-035	1835	PROOF round-top '3' in date	1	1				1500

No.	Date	Features	Obv.	Rev.	F	VF	EF	UNC
W4SH-040	1836		1	1	10	25	85	140
W4SH-045	1836	PROOF round-top '3' in date	1	1				1500
W4SH-050	1836	PROOF in copper; edge plain	1	1				800
W4SH-055	1837		1	1	16	45	130	180
W4SH-060	1837	PROOF	1	1				800

1. Issued in cased proof sets.

All coins have flat-top 3 in date unless otherwise stated.

Victoria (1837 – 1901)

The Johann Baptiste Merlen 'ONE SHILLING' reverse was continued with the accession of Victoria, while the obverse used a portrait of the young queen by William Wyon, whose initials appear on the truncation for about the first year. Later coins up to 1887, while of similar design, exhibit progressively inferior workmanship and become somewhat more crude in style.

As with the florins, the placement on the reverse of die numbers between the years 1864 and 1879 add greatly to the numismatic interest of these pieces, as well as giving some indication of their respective scarcities.

The shilling was radically redesigned in 1887 for the Silver Jubilee, and again in 1893, when the unpopular Boehm Jubilee portrait was replaced by the veiled head design by Brock. The practice of including the words 'ONE SHILLING', discarded in 1887, was reintroduced in 1893.

Collecting Hints

The series should be collected in extremely fine or better condition unless the rarity of a piece prevents its acquisition in such a grade. Anyone brave enough to attempt the fascinating task of collecting by die number and date will probably be satisfied with any piece on which the die number is readable.
Care should be taken in distinguishing 1887 Jubilee issue early strikings from the proofs; the milling on the edge of the latter almost cuts the fingers, and is 'straight across' rather than displaying a concave/convex cross-section.

Denomination	Metal	Weight (grams)	Diameter (mm)	Rev. alignment
Shilling 1838–87 obvs 1–5	Silver	5.7	24	↓
Shilling 1887–1901 obvs 6–9	Silver	5.7	24	↑

Obverse 1 Head 1, left; W.W. in relief on truncation; VICTORIA DEI GRATIA BRITANNIAR REG F D

Obverse 2 Head 2, very slightly larger, left; W.W. in relief on truncation; same legend

Obverse 3 Head 2, left; no W.W. on truncation; same legend

Obverse 4 Head 3, left; lower relief, slightly different design; same legend

Obverse 5 Head 4, left; slightly older features; same legend

Obverse 6 Head 5, 'Jubilee' head, left; VICTORIA DEI GRATIA BRITT REGINA F D

Obverse 7 Head 6, similar but much larger, left; same legend

Obverse 8 Head 7, veiled and draped, left; VICTORIA DEI GRA BRITT REGINA FID DEF IND IMP

Obverse 9 Head 7, left; same legend but lettering slightly larger

Reverse 1 ONE SHILLING within wreath of olive and oak, crown above, date below, with or without die number above date (in listings, no die number unless stated)

Reverse 2 Similar but larger lettering. Slight alterations in design

Reverse 3 Crowned shield within Garter; HONI SOIT QUI MAL Y PENSE on Garter (date)

Reverse 4 Similar but slightly different design: row of jewels on crown on Reverse 3 replaced by lines; no loop inside QUI (on Garter) unlike on Reverse 3

Reverse 5 Three shields within Garter; HONI SOIT QUI MAL Y PENSE on Garter, partially hidden by shields ONE SHILLING (date)

Reverse 6 Similar but the rose is larger

Edge milled

Obv. 1 Obv. 3 Obv. 4

Obv. 5 Obv. 6 Obv. 7

Obv. 9 Rev. 1 Rev. 2

Rev. 3 Rev. 5

Young Head

No.	Date	Features	Obv.	Rev.	F	VF	EF	UNC
VYSH-005	1838		1	1	10	24	80	110
VYSH-010	1838	PROOF	1	1				850
VYSH-015	1839		1	1	12	28	90	120
VYSH-020	1839	PROOF; edge plain	1	1				800
VYSH-025	1839	PROOF; edge plain [1]	2	1				350
VYSH-030	1839		3	1	10	24	75	100
VYSH-035	1839	PROOF	3	1				1400
VYSH-040	1839	PROOF; edge plain	3	1				400
VYSH-045	1839	PROOF; edge plain; rev. ↑	3	1				400
VYSH-050	1840		3	1	12	30	100	130
VYSH-055	1840	PROOF	3	1				1200
VYSH-060	1841		3	1	14	45	130	160
VYSH-065	1842		3	1	12	30	90	120
VYSH-070	1842	PROOF	3	1				900
VYSH-075	1843		3	1	12	35	110	140
VYSH-080	1844		3	1	10	30	90	120
VYSH-085	1845		3	1	10	30	90	120
VYSH-090	1846		3	1	10	30	90	120
VYSH-095	1848	latter 8 over 6	3	1	30	90	300	500
VYSH-100	1849		3	1	10	30	90	120
VYSH-105	1850		3	1	120	400	1000	
VYSH-110	1850	50 over 46 or 49	3	1	140	450	1200	
VYSH-115	1851		3	1	30	80	400	800
VYSH-120	1851	PROOF	3	1				1500
VYSH-125	1852		3	1	10	30	90	120
VYSH-130	1853		3	1	10	30	90	120
VYSH-135	1853	PROOF [1]	3	1				500

No.	Date	Features	Obv.	Rev.	F	VF	EF	UNC
VYSH-140	1854		3	1	50	130	500	
VYSH-145	1854	4 over 1	3	1	80	200	800	
VYSH-150	1855		3	1	10	30	90	120
VYSH-155	1856		3	1	10	30	90	120
VYSH-160	1857	[2]	3	1	10	30	90	120
VYSH-165	1857	inverted G or broken D at end of obv. legend	3	1	25	90	200	
VYSH-170	1857	7 over 5	3	1	40	120	300	500
VYSH-175	1858		3	1	9	25	75	100
VYSH-178	1858	latter 8 over 6	3	1	15	40	110	180
VYSH-180	1858	PROOF	3	1				1500
VYSH-185	1859	[3]	3	1	9	25	75	100
VYSH-190	1860		3	1	12	30	90	120
VYSH-195	1861		3	1	12	30	90	120
VYSH-200	1862		3	1	20	45	120	170
VYSH-205	1863		3	1	24	50	130	180
VYSH-210	1863	3 over 1	3	1	30	70	160	220
VYSH-215	1863	3 over 2	3	1	28	65	150	210
VYSH-220	1864	die number above date [4]	3	1	10	30	90	120
VYSH-225	1865	die number above date	3	1	10	25	80	110
VYSH-230	1866	die number above date	3	1	10	25	80	110
VYSH-235	1866	die number above date BBITANNIAR instead of BRITANNIAR (obv.)	3	1	30	100		
VYSH-240	1867	die number above date	3	1	10	25	80	110
VYSH-245	1867	PROOF [5]	4	1				900
VYSH-250	1867	PROOF; edge plain [5]	4	1				1400
VYSH-255	1867	die number above date	4	1	60	200	1000	
VYSH-260	1868	die number above date	4	1	10	25	80	110
VYSH-265	1869	die number above date	4	1	12	30	90	120
VYSH-270	1870	die number above date	4	1	12	30	90	120
VYSH-275	1871	die number above date	4	1	9	20	60	80
VYSH-280	1871	PROOF die number above date [6]	4	1				900
VYSH-285	1871	PROOF; edge plain; rev. ↑ die number above date	4	1				1600
VYSH-290	1872	die number above date	4	1	8	18	50	70
VYSH-295	1873	die number above date	4	1	8	18	50	70
VYSH-300	1874	die number above date [4]	4	1	9	20	60	80
VYSH-305	1875	die number above date	4	1	9	20	60	80
VYSH-310	1876	die number above date	4	1	10	25	70	100
VYSH-315	1877	die number above date	4	1	9	20	60	80
VYSH-320	1878	die number above date	4	1	20	50	120	180
VYSH-322	1878	die number above date	5	1	9	20	60	80
VYSH-325	1878	PROOF; die number above date	4	1				1000
VYSH-330	1879	die number above date [7]	5	1	12	30	100	140
VYSH-335	1879	PROOF die number above date	5	1				700
VYSH-340	1879	[8]	5	1	9	20	60	80
VYSH-345	1879	PROOF; edge plain; rev. ↑ [9]	5	1				1500
VYSH-350	1880	[10]	5	2	9	16	45	65
VYSH-355	1880	PROOF	5	2				900
VYSH-360	1880	PROOF; edge plain	5	2				1200
VYSH-365	1881	[10]	5	2	9	16	45	65
VYSH-370	1881	PROOF	5	2				900
VYSH-375	1881	PROOF; edge plain	5	2				1500
VYSH-380	1882		5	2	12	25	80	110
VYSH-385	1883		5	2	9	16	45	65
VYSH-390	1884	[11]	5	2	9	16	45	65
VYSH-395	1884	PROOF	5	2				900

No.	Date	Features	Obv.	Rev.	F	VF	EF	UNC
VYSH-400	1885		5	2	8	14	35	50
VYSH-405	1885	PROOF	5	2				900
VYSH-410	1886		5	2	8	14	35	50
VYSH-415	1886	PROOF	5	2				900
VYSH-420	1887		5	2	8	14	35	50
VYSH-425	1887	PROOF	5	2				800

1. Issued in cased proof sets.
2. Date size varies.
3. Date often resembles 1839; minor obverse differences exist.
4. 4 of date varies.
5. No die number.
6. Some or all have die number 19.
7. Minor obverse/reverse differences exist.
8. No die number above date from now on.
9. Some may exist with obverse 1 (sic).
10. Lettering and length of line below SHILLING varies (rev.).
11. Length of line below SHILLING varies (rev.).

Jubilee Head

No.	Date	Features	Obv.	Rev.	F	VF	EF	UNC
VJSH-430	1887	[1]	6	3	5	7	10	20
VJSH-435	1887	PROOF [2]	6	3				80
VJSH-440	1888		6	3	6	8	22	35
VJSH-445	1888	last 8 over 7	6	3	6	8	22	35
VJSH-450	1889		6	3	15	80	300	600
VJSH-455	1889		6	4	18	90	350	700
VJSH-460	1889	[3]	7	4	6	9	24	40
VJSH-465	1889	PROOF	7	4				1000
VJSH-470	1890	[3]	7	4	7	10	26	45
VJSH-475	1891		7	4	7	10	26	45
VJSH-480	1891	PROOF	7	4				1400
VJSH-485	1892		7	4	7	10	28	50

1. Garter letters vary in size (rev.).
2. Issued in proof sets.
3. Minor obverse differences exist.

Old Head

No.	Date	Features	Obv.	Rev.	F	VF	EF	UNC
VOSH-490	1893		8	5	6	9	18	28
VOSH-495	1893		9	5	4	7	15	22
VOSH-500	1893	PROOF [1]	9	5				120
VOSH-505	1894		8	5	10	15	35	60
VOSH-510	1894		9	5	6	9	20	30
VOSH-515	1895		9	5	8	12	28	45
VOSH-520	1895		9	6	5	8	17	27
VOSH-525	1896		9	5	6	9	30	50
VOSH-530	1896		9	6	5	8	17	27
VOSH-535	1897		9	6	4	8	16	25
VOSH-540	1898		9	6	5	8	17	27
VOSH-545	1899		9	6	5	8	17	28
VOSH-550	1900		9	6	5	8	15	25
VOSH-555	1901		9	6	4	8	15	24

1. Issued in cased proof sets.

Edward VII (1901 – 1910)

As with the other denominations, the shilling was a one-type issue depicting the de Saulles portrait of Edward using a mechanical reduction process. The reverse of a lion on a crown was also by de Saulles and used the same motif as the reverse of the later type of George IV shilling.

After the death of de Saulles early in the reign, W.H.J. Blakemore became responsible for hand-finishing and re-engraving dies produced by the mechanical reducer.

Collecting Hints

In common with the halfcrown and florin, 1905 is the rarest date of the Edward VII shilling. However, most of the dates are difficult to find in top condition, although in fine or very fine they present less of a problem. Collectors should look

for at least extremely fine specimens, with the 1905 possibly in very fine.
The Edward VII shilling is often found somewhat weakly struck, and care should be taken in differentiating between wear and weak striking.

Denomination	Metal	Weight (grams)	Diameter (mm)	Rev. alignment
Shilling	Silver	5.7	24	↑

Obverse 1 Head 1, right; EDWARDVS VII DEI GRA BRITT OMN REX

Reverse 1 Lion on crown, with separated date, all within inner circle; FID DEF IND IMP ONE SHILLING

Edge milled

Obv. 1   Rev. 1

No.	Date	Features	Obv.	Rev.	F	VF	EF	UNC
E7SH-005	1902		1	1	5	9	20	40
E7SH-010	1902	matt PROOF [1]	1	1			20	40
E7SH-015	1903		1	1	7	12	50	90
E7SH-020	1904	[2]	1	1	7	11	45	75
E7SH-025	1905		1	1	30	95	400	900
E7SH-030	1906	[2]	1	1	6	10	25	50
E7SH-035	1907		1	1	6	12	30	55
E7SH-040	1908		1	1	7	14	60	110
E7SH-045	1909		1	1	7	14	60	110
E7SH-050	1910		1	1	5	10	24	45

1. Issued in cased proof sets.
2. Minor obverse differences exist.

George V (1910 – 1936)

The overall design of the shilling changed very little with the transition to a new monarch. The obverse used the portrait of the king by Sir Bertram Mackennal (1863–1931); the reverse retains the lion on crown design which was used on the Edward VII coinage and which originated on the George IV shilling.

As with the other silver denominations, the metal constituency underwent a number of changes during the reign. In 1920, the silver content was reduced to 50%, the remaining constituents being a nickel-containing copper-based alloy. This proved unsatisfactory in that it tarnished with yellow streaks. In 1922 a straight 1:1 silver-copper mix proved much more satisfactory. In 1923 and 1924, a few experimental pieces were struck in pure nickel. The silver-copper composition was changed again in 1927 to a silver-copper-nickel-zinc alloy when the new designs were introduced, and these later coins are considerably less prone to tarnishing.

From 1928 onwards small quantities of proofs were struck each year for record purposes. These were sent to museums, other mints, and occasionally presented to important visitors.

Unusually for a reign of this length, the shilling was struck for every year of the reign.

Collecting Hints

Collect in extremely fine condition or better, unless one is assembling merely a date sequence in the lower grades. Try to acquire at least one nice condition 'yellow streak

No.	Date	Features	Obv.	Rev.	VF	EF	UNC
G5SH-090	1925		1	1	10	60	90
G5SH-095	1926		1	1	6	15	30
G5SH-100	1926		2	1	6	15	25
G5SH-105	1927		2	1	6	18	32
G5SH-110	1927		2	2	5	15	25
G5SH-115	1927	PROOF [3]	2	2			25
G5SH-120	1927	PROOF from sandblasted dies [4]	2	2			350
G5SH-125	1928		2	2	4	8	12
G5SH-130	1928	PROOF	2	2			350
G5SH-135	1929		2	2	4	10	16
G5SH-140	1929	PROOF	2	2			350
G5SH-145	1930		2	2	10	30	50
G5SH-150	1930	PROOF	2	2			500
G5SH-155	1931		2	2	4	11	18
G5SH-160	1931	PROOF	2	2			350
G5SH-165	1932		2	2	4	14	25
G5SH-170	1932	PROOF	2	2			350
G5SH-175	1933		2	2	4	11	18
G5SH-180	1933	PROOF	2	2			350
G5SH-185	1934		2	2	5	16	25
G5SH-190	1934	PROOF	2	2			350
G5SH-195	1935		2	2	4	10	16
G5SH-200	1935	PROOF	2	2			350
G5SH-205	1936		2	2	3	7	10
G5SH-210	1936	PROOF	2	2			350

1. Minor obverse/reverse differences exist.
2. Nickel is slightly magnetic.
3. Issued in cased proof sets.
4. Struck to facilitate photography of coin.

Edward VIII   (1936)

The Edward VIII shilling is strictly speaking a pattern, as probable Royal approval was about to be granted at the time of the abdication. However, because its official status rests only on this technicality, and to provide continuity, it is included here.

The portrait of Edward VIII is by Thomas Humphrey Paget, and faces left at the insistence of the king, who considered this placement more flattering and wished to discontinue the tradition of opposite facings for successive monarchs. The reverse is by George Kruger Gray (1880–1943). The Scottish Crest was used on the shilling after protests from Scotland that the English Crest had been used on the shillings of Edward VII and George V. Although it was intended in addition to strike shillings with an English Crest, only Scottish type coins were in fact struck.

Denomination	Metal	Weight (grams)	Diameter (mm)	Rev. alignment
Shilling	Silver	5.6	24	↑

Obverse 1   Head 1, left; EDWARDVS VIII D G BR OMN REX

Reverse 1   Facing lion on crown dividing date (1937) and flanked by St Andrew's Cross and Thistle; FID DEF IND IMP ONE SHILLING

Edge   milled

Obv. 1

Rev. 1

No.	Date		Obv.	Rev.			UNC
E8SH-005	1937		1	1			15000

George VI   (1937 – 1952)

The George VI shilling saw the introduction of the unique concept of two different reverse designs for each year (apart from the very rare 1952). These were the 'English' and the 'Scottish' reverses. The design of the English reverses was influenced by the

---

tarnish' specimen of 1920–22 to demonstrate the problem with the metal constituency of the period.
Take care not to overgrade coins of the 1927–36 period, and always examine the high points of both sides carefully before grading.

Denomination	Metal	Weight (grams)	Diameter (mm)	Rev. alignment
Shilling 1911–19	0.925 Silver	5.7	24	↑
Shilling 1920–22	Silver 50%; copper 40%; nickel 10%	5.7	24	↑
Shilling 1922–27	Silver 50%; copper 50%	5.7	24	↑
Shilling 1927–36	Silver 50%; copper 40%; nickel 5%; zinc 5%	5.7	24	↑

Obverse 1   Head 1, left; B.M. on truncation; GEORGIVS V DEI GRA BRITT OMN REX

Obverse 2   Head 2, so-called 'modified effigy', left; BM (no stops) further to right; same legend. Beading recut

Reverse 1   Lion on crown with separated date, all within inner circle; FID DEF IND IMP ONE SHILLING

Reverse 2   Lion on crown, different design; no circle; FID DEF IND IMP ONE SHILLING (date)

Edge   milled

Obv. 1   Obv. 2

Rev. 1   Rev. 2

Sterling Silver Issue

No.	Date	Features	Obv.	Rev.	VF	EF	UNC
G5SH-005	1911	[1]	1	1	5	12	20
G5SH-010	1911	PROOF [2]	1	1		20	40
G5SH-015	1912	[3]	1	1	6	18	35
G5SH-020	1913		1	1	9	28	55
G5SH-025	1914		1	1	5	12	20
G5SH-030	1915		1	1	5	12	20
G5SH-035	1916		1	1	5	12	20
G5SH-040	1917		1	1	6	15	25
G5SH-045	1918		1	1	5	12	20
G5SH-050	1919		1	1	5	15	25

1. Obverse portrait varies.
2. Issued in cased proof sets.
3. Minor reverse differences exist.

50% Silver Issue

No.	Date	Features	Obv.	Rev.	VF	EF	UNC
G5SH-055	1920		1	1	5	20	35
G5SH-060	1921	[1]	1	1	5	25	45
G5SH-065	1922		1	1	5	20	35
G5SH-070	1923		1	1	5	18	30
G5SH-075	1923	struck in nickel [2]	1	1			700
G5SH-080	1924		1	1	6	25	50
G5SH-085	1924	struck in nickel [2]	1	1			700

lion on crown designs of earlier reigns; the Scottish reverse had a more symmetrically posed lion holding a sword and sceptre, and seated on a smaller crown, at the sides of which stand the St Andrew's Cross and the Scottish Thistle. Both reverses were designed by George Kruger Gray (1880–1943). The obverse uses the design of the monarch by Thomas Humphrey Paget (1893–1974). There is no difference in obverse design between the English and Scottish types.

As with the other silver coinage, there was a transition in 1947 to cupronickel.

Collecting Hints

An attempt should be made to collect this series in as near mint state as possible, and the existence of two types for each date renders the task doubly challenging. Some of the pieces are quite difficult to find in this grade.
The edges of 1950 and 1951 proofs should always be examined carefully for corrosion; the 1950 may also have ribbon stains on either side from the proof set case. This cannot be removed chemically.

Denomination	Metal	Weight (grams)	Diameter (mm)	Rev. alignment
Shilling 1937–46	Silver 50%; other 50%	5.7	24	↑
Shilling 1947–52	Copper 75%; nickel 25%	5.7	24	↑

Obverse 1   Head 1, left; GEORGIVS VI D G BR OMN REX

Reverse 1E   (English reverse): Lion on crown dividing date; (rose) FID DEF IND IMP (rose) ONE SHILLING

Reverse 1S   (Scottish reverse): Facing lion on crown dividing date and flanked by St Andrew's Cross and Thistle; same legend

Reverse 2E   Similar to 1E but IND IMP missing

Reverse 2S   Similar to 1S but IND IMP missing

Edge   milled. The milling is finer from 1947 onwards

Obv. 1   Rev. 1E   Rev. 1S

Rev. 2E   Rev. 2S

50% Silver Issue

No.	Date	Features	Obv.	Rev.	EF	UNC
G6SH-005	1937		1	1E	4	8
G6SH-010	1937	PROOF [1]	1	1E		12
G6SH-015	1937	PROOF from sandblasted dies [2]	1	1E		200
G6SH-020	1937	[3]	1	1S	4	8
G6SH-025	1937	PROOF [1][3]	1	1S		12
G6SH-030	1937	PROOF from sandblasted dies [2][3]	1	1S		200
G6SH-035	1938		1	1E	6	18
G6SH-040	1938	PROOF	1	1E		350
G6SH-045	1938		1	1S	6	18
G6SH-050	1938	PROOF	1	1S		350
G6SH-055	1939		1	1E	4	12

No.	Date	Features	Obv.	Rev.	EF	UNC
G6SH-060	1939	PROOF	1	1E		350
G6SH-065	1939		1	1S	4	12
G6SH-070	1939	PROOF	1	1S		350
G6SH-075	1940		1	1E	4	12
G6SH-080	1940	PROOF	1	1E		350
G6SH-085	1940		1	1S	4	12
G6SH-090	1940	PROOF	1	1S		350
G6SH-095	1941		1	1E	4	8
G6SH-100	1941	PROOF	1	1E		350
G6SH-105	1941		1	1S	4	8
G6SH-110	1941	PROOF	1	1S		350
G6SH-115	1942		1	1E	4	8
G6SH-120	1942		1	1S	4	8
G6SH-125	1943		1	1E	4	8
G6SH-128	1943	rev. ↓	1	1E	80	120
G6SH-130	1943		1	1S	4	8
G6SH-135	1944		1	1E	4	8
G6SH-140	1944	PROOF	1	1E		450
G6SH-145	1944		1	1S	4	8
G6SH-150	1944	PROOF	1	1S		450
G6SH-155	1945		1	1E	4	8
G6SH-160	1945	PROOF	1	1E		350
G6SH-165	1945		1	1S	4	8
G6SH-170	1945	PROOF	1	1S		350
G6SH-175	1946	[4]	1	1E	4	8
G6SH-180	1946	PROOF	1	1E		350
G6SH-185	1946	PROOF in cupronickel [5]	1	1E		800
G6SH-190	1946		1	1S	4	8
G6SH-195	1946	PROOF	1	1S		350

1. Issued in cased proof sets.
2. Struck to facilitate photography of coin.
3. Unusually, this has stop after date.
4. Minor reverse differences exist.
5. Trial piece for cupronickel coinage.

Cupronickel Issue

No.	Date	Features	Obv.	Rev.	EF	UNC
G6SH-200	1947		1	1E	3	7
G6SH-205	1947	struck in 0.5 silver	1	1E		750
G6SH-210	1947	PROOF	1	1E		400
G6SH-215	1947	[1]	1	1S	3	7
G6SH-220	1947	PROOF [1]	1	1S		400
G6SH-225	1948		1	1E	3	7
G6SH-230	1948	PROOF	1	1E		400
G6SH-235	1948		1	1S	3	7
G6SH-240	1948	PROOF	1	1S		400
G6SH-245	1949		1	2E	3	9
G6SH-250	1949	PROOF	1	2E		400
G6SH-255	1949		1	2S	3	9
G6SH-260	1949	PROOF	1	2S		400
G6SH-265	1950		1	2E	3	7
G6SH-270	1950	PROOF [2]	1	2E		12
G6SH-275	1950	PROOF from sandblasted dies [3]	1	2E		200
G6SH-280	1950		1	2S	3	12
G6SH-285	1950	PROOF [2]	1	2S		10
G6SH-290	1950	PROOF from sandblasted dies [3]	1	2S		200
G6SH-295	1951		1	2E	3	9
G6SH-300	1951	PROOF [2]	1	2E		12
G6SH-305	1951	PROOF from sandblasted dies [3]	1	2E		200
G6SH-310	1951		1	2S	3	7
G6SH-315	1951	PROOF [2]	1	2S		12
G6SH-320	1951	PROOF from sandblasted dies [3]	1	2S		200
G6SH-325	1952	PROOF	1	2E		8000
G6SH-330	1952	PROOF in nickel [4]	1	2E		5000

1. Unusually, this has stop after date.
2. Issued in cased proof sets.
3. Struck to facilitate photography of coin.
4. Weight 5.6 grams; nickel is slightly magnetic.

Elizabeth II   (1952 –)

The original design by Mary Gillick for the queen's portrait resulted in a weak striking lacking in detail, and the dies were soon recut to provide a sharper image. The first year (1953) is the only coin bearing the obverse 'BRITT OMN' (trans: of all the British possessions).

The reverses were designed by William Gardner.

No.	Date	Features	Obv.	Rev.	UNC
EZSH-180	1961		2	1E	3
EZSH-185	1961	PROOF	2	1E	300
EZSH-190	1961		2	1S	10
EZSH-195	1961	PROOF	2	1S	300
EZSH-200	1962		2	1E	3
EZSH-205	1962	PROOF	2	1E	300
EZSH-210	1962		2	1S	3
EZSH-215	1962	PROOF	2	1S	300
EZSH-220	1963		2	1E	3
EZSH-225	1963	PROOF	2	1E	300
EZSH-230	1963		2	1S	3
EZSH-235	1963	PROOF	2	1S	300
EZSH-240	1964		2	1E	3
EZSH-245	1964	PROOF	2	1E	300
EZSH-250	1964		2	1S	3
EZSH-255	1964	PROOF	2	1S	300
EZSH-260	1965		2	1E	3
EZSH-265	1965	PROOF	2	1E	300
EZSH-270	1965		2	1S	3
EZSH-275	1965	PROOF	2	1S	300
EZSH-280	1966		2	1E	3
EZSH-285	1966	PROOF	2	1E	300
EZSH-290	1966		2	1S	3
EZSH-295	1966	rev. ↓	2	1S	50
EZSH-300	1966	PROOF	2	1S	300
EZSH-305	1970	PROOF [6]	2	1E	4
EZSH-310	1970	PROOF [6]	2	1S	4

1. Minor obverse differences exist.
2. Can be dated from being obverse 1.
3. Issued in cased proof sets.
4. Struck to facilitate photography of coin.
5. Minor reverse differences exist.
6. Issued in sealed cased proof sets; no ordinary issue coins of this date.

<table>
<tr><td colspan="6" style="background:#888;">

Collecting Hints

Collect in mint state. Acquiring examples of the unofficially struck proofs is an interesting challenge.

</td></tr>
</table>

Denomination	Metal	Weight (grams)	Diameter (mm)	Rev. alignment
Shilling 1953–70	Copper 75%; nickel 25%	5.7	24	↑

Obverse 1　Head 1, right; ELIZABETH II DEI GRATIA BRITT OMN REGINA

Obverse 2　Head 1 (recut), right; ELIZABETH II DEI GRATIA REGINA

Reverse 1E　(English reverse): Three leopards within crowned shield; FID DEF ONE SHILLING (date)

Reverse 1S　(Scottish reverse): Rampant lion within crowned shield; same legend (date)

Edge　milled

Obv. 1

Obv. 2

Rev. 1E

Rev. 1S

No.	Date	Features	Obv.	Rev.	UNC
EZSH-005	1953	[1]	1	1E	3
EZSH-010	1953	'double headed' [2]	1	obv. 1	300
EZSH-015	1953	PROOF [3]	1	1E	8
EZSH-020	1953	PROOF from sandblasted dies [4]	1	1E	200
EZSH-025	1953		1	1S	3
EZSH-030	1953	PROOF [3]	1	1S	8
EZSH-035	1953	PROOF from sandblasted dies [4]	1	1S	200
EZSH-040	1954		2	1E	5
EZSH-045	1954	PROOF	2	1E	300
EZSH-050	1954		2	1S	5
EZSH-055	1954	PROOF	2	1S	300
EZSH-060	1955		2	1E	5
EZSH-065	1955	PROOF	2	1E	300
EZSH-070	1955	[5]	2	1S	5
EZSH-075	1955	PROOF	2	1S	300
EZSH-080	1956	[5]	2	1E	7
EZSH-085	1956	PROOF	2	1E	300
EZSH-090	1956		2	1S	7
EZSH-095	1956	PROOF	2	1S	300
EZSH-100	1957		2	1E	3
EZSH-105	1957	PROOF	2	1E	300
EZSH-110	1957		2	1S	20
EZSH-115	1957	PROOF	2	1S	300
EZSH-120	1958		2	1E	25
EZSH-125	1958	PROOF	2	1E	300
EZSH-130	1958		2	1S	3
EZSH-135	1958	PROOF	2	1S	300
EZSH-140	1959		2	1E	3
EZSH-145	1959	PROOF	2	1E	300
EZSH-150	1959		2	1S	30
EZSH-155	1959	PROOF	2	1S	300
EZSH-160	1960		2	1E	3
EZSH-165	1960	PROOF	2	1E	300
EZSH-170	1960		2	1S	4
EZSH-175	1960	PROOF	2	1S	300

Sorting out imperfect coins

Sixpence

Oliver Cromwell (Commonwealth 1649 – 1660)

Only a handful of Cromwell sixpences exist, possibly as few as four. All are dated 1658. The sixpence bears the same basic design as the other Cromwell coinage, being designed by Thomas Simon (also called Symonds) and portraying Cromwell as a Roman Emperor, draped and laureate.

Sixpences of Cromwell and Charles II are sometimes referred to as 'half shillings'.

Denomination	Metal	Weight (grams)	Diameter (mm)	Rev. alignment
Sixpence	Silver	3.0	21	↓

Obverse 1 Head 1, left; OLIVAR D G R P ANG SCO HIB &c PRO

Reverse 1 Crowned shield; PAX QVAERITVR BELLO 1658

Edge milled

Obv. 1

Rev. 1

No.	Date	Obv.	Rev.	F	VF
OC6D-005	1658	1	1	15000	25000

Charles II (1660 – 1685)

The milled sixpence, designed by John Roettier (1631–c.1703), was first struck in 1674. This was considerably later than the other silver denominations, and it was thus untouched by the problems of the Great Plague and Great Fire of London. As well as having a short span (only eleven years), it is also a much less complicated series, with only one basic design without provenance marks. Having a milled edge, it does not have the added complications of edge lettering varieties such as are encountered on the crowns and halfcrowns. As the first date of issue was 1674, there are no specimens displaying the 'straight across' milling which was used on the shilling and smaller gold coins until 1669.

Denomination	Metal	Weight (grams)	Diameter (mm)	Rev. alignment
Sixpence	Silver	2.9–3.0	21	↓

Obverse 1 Head 1, right; CAROLVS II DEI GRATIA

Reverse 1 Central star enclosed by four cruciform shields with surmounting crowns; interlinked 'C's in angles; MAG BR FRA ET HIB REX (date)

Edge milled (diagonally)

Obv. 1

Rev. 1

No.	Date	Features	Obv.	Rev.	F	VF	EF
C26DM-005	1674		1	1	40	120	350
C26DM-010	1675		1	1	40	120	350
C26DM-015	1675	5 over 4	1	1	50	130	400
C26DM-020	1676	latter 6 usually over 5 [1]	1	1	50	140	500
C26DM-025	1677		1	1	40	120	350
C26DM-030	1678	8 always over 7	1	1	45	130	400
C26DM-035	1679		1	1	45	130	400
C26DM-040	1680		1	1	60	180	600
C26DM-045	1681		1	1	40	120	350
C26DM-050	1682		1	1	55	160	550
C26DM-055	1682	2 over 1	1	1	50	140	450
C26DM-060	1683		1	1	40	110	320
C26DM-065	1684		1	1	45	130	400

1. 6 not over 5 may not exist.

James II (1685 – 1688)

John Roettier continued as designer and engraver during the reign of James II, and the overall appearance of the sixpence owes much to that of its predecessor. The practice of placing interlinked initials of the monarch in the reverse angles was discontinued, although it was reinstated during the following reign.

As with the Charles II sixpence, the series is simpler than that of the larger denominations, but there are two distinct reverses, distinguished by the shape of the shields. The date 1687 straddles both of these types. Again, there are no provenance marks, and there are no proofs or patterns.

Denomination	Metal	Weight (grams)	Diameter (mm)	Rev. alignment
Sixpence	Silver	2.8–3.0	21–22	↓

Obverse 1 Head 1, left; IACOBVS II DEI GRATIA

Reverse 1 Central star enclosed by four cruciform shields with surmounting crowns, the top of each shield being concave; plain in angles; MAG BR FRA ET HIB REX (date)

Reverse 2 Similar but top of each shield is convex

Reverse 3 Similar but each shield has superimposed convex/concave tops

Edge milled (diagonally)

Obv. 1   Rev. 1

Rev. 2   Rev. 3

No.	Date	Features	Obv.	Rev.	F	VF	EF
J26D-005	1686		1	1	60	160	500
J26D-010	1686	8 over 6	1	1	80	200	650
J26D-015	1687		1	1	65	170	550
J26D-020	1687	7 over 6	1	1	65	170	550
J26D-025	1687		1	2	60	160	500
J26D-030	1687		1	3	75	190	650
J26D-035	1687	7 over 6	1	3	70	180	600
J26D-040	1688		1	3	70	180	600

The number of harp strings varies through this series. It is possible that the variation constituted a form of internal code denoting the die number.

William & Mary (1688 – 1694)

The fact that the first sixpences were issued so late in the reign was probably responsible for the continuance of the cruciform shield reverse on this issue. It is interesting to note that the half-crowns and the gold, radically redesigned earlier in the reign, reverted to the cruciform shield design either later in the reign of William and Mary or during the period when William ruled alone. By 1693, when the first sixpence was issued, the halfcrown had already undergone this metamorphosis.

By the time the sixpences were issued, John Roettier, the Chief Engraver, had developed an affliction in his hands, and almost all of the work was carried out by his sons James (1663–98) and Norbert (b.1665), assisted by Henry Harris. There is some doubt as to the attribution of the sixpence. The style is similar to that of the later halfcrowns, which are probably by James Roettier, but are in the high relief style favoured by Norbert Roettier.

The brief series consists of only two dates, 1693 and 1694. It is worthy of note that the larger silver denominations were not struck in this final year.

There are again no provenance marks, patterns or proofs.

Collecting Hints

As there are only two dates, one should attempt to acquire both in about extremely fine condition. The William and Mary sixpence is a superbly crafted coin, and is much more attractive in this grade than in fine condition. It is frequently found with delightful toning in the higher grades. The 1694 coin is much more difficult to find than the 1693, and one may have to be satisfied with the best available.

Denomination	Metal	Weight (grams)	Diameter (mm)	Rev. alignment
Sixpence	Silver	2.9–3.0	21	↓

Obverse 1 Heads 1, right; GVLIELMVS ET MARIA DEI GRATIA

Reverse 1 Four crowned cruciform shields around lion of Orange-Nassau, with monogrammed 'WM' and one digit of date in each angle; MAG BR FR ET HI REX ET REGINA

Edge milled (diagonally)

Obv. 1   Rev. 1

No.	Date	Features	Obv.	Rev.	F	VF	EF
WM6D-005	1693		1	1	50	180	600
WM6D-010	1693	3 of date inverted (see note below)	1	1	150	500	1500
WM6D-015	1694		1	1	90	250	800

The date is read in two lines, left to right, with the English shield at the top of the coin.

William III (1695 – 1701)

The simplicity of the sixpence series of the previous three reigns disappeared with a vengeance on the death of Mary from small-pox in 1694. Not only are the listings of London and provincial coins complex, with many errors and varieties, but the majority of the examples exist with either large or small crowns surmounting the shields.

The early sixpences were probably the work of James Roettier, who died during the reign in 1698. Some later coins were produced by the German Johann Crocker, who took an Anglicised form for his name, John Croker. Attribution doubt exists in the intermediate period, and it is thought that some of the coins may have been the work of Henry Harris, who was Chief Engraver at the Mint during at least part of the reign.

As with the halfcrowns and shillings, the complexity of the work was due largely to the 'Great Recoinage', and the decision to withdraw the hammered coinage. The work done at the five provincial mints was often of doubtful quality. This was the result of using a new and inexperienced work-force, and the speed with which the work was expected to be done.

There exists a 1696 sixpence with what has usually been termed the 'second bust'. This provides a companion to the 1696 half-crown and shilling of this type. As stated elsewhere, the halfcrown and shilling are probably patterns and are therefore outside the scope of this book, and this may well be true of the sixpence also. However, in view of the fact that a number of these coins exist in well circulated state, and because of the use of this head in the 1697 circulating sixpence coinage, we have included it in the listings below for the sake of completion.

The very large number of varieties has again necessitated the use of expediency and selection in producing a listing of the various types existing. It is not to be taken, therefore, that the listing is exhaustive. However, it should be found to include all varieties of note which any collector should reasonably require. Some varieties are referred to in note form instead of being given a separate line.

Provenance marks are: plumes (either in angles on reverse or singly below head) for silver from Welsh mines; roses (in angles) for silver from West of England mines.

Collecting Hints

Because of the large number of varieties and errors issued during this reign, the safest course of action is to acquire the best example available bearing enough detail to identify the coin, rather than insisting upon a minimum grade such as fine.

Like the shilling, the sixpence is often found weakly struck. Some collectors do not object to this characteristic, while others prefer, say, a sharply struck very fine coin (i.e. bearing genuine wear) to a weak extremely fine specimen. Specimens of the 1700 sixpence occur in quantities in about mint condition because a sack of the coins was found around 1950 in a bank vault.

Denomination	Metal	Weight (grams)	Diameter (mm)	Rev. alignment
Sixpence	Silver	2.8–3.1	21	↓

Obverse 1   Head 1, right; GVLIELMVS III DEI GRA

Obverse 2   Head 2, right; hair more profuse and facial expression very different, with hooked nose. same legend

Obverse 3   Head 3, right; much more like Head 1, but tie longer and hair at back of head differently arranged

Reverse 1   four cruciform shields around lion of Nassau; MAG BR FRA ET HIB REX (date). Irish harp has top left corner higher than top right; shield are surmounted by crowns of similar width

Reverse 2   Similar but a different harp, with top left and right corners at roughly equal height

Reverse 3   Similar to Reverse 2 but the surmounting crowns are narrower than the shields

Edge   milled (diagonally)

Obv. 1   Obv. 2   Obv. 3

Rev. 1   Rev. 2   Rev. 3

No.	Date	Features	mm	Obv.	Rev.	F	VF	EF
W36D-005	1695			1	1	35	90	240
W36D-010	1696			1	1	15	45	85
W36D-015	1696	latter 6 over 5		1	1	30	80	180
W36D-020	1696	no stops on obv.		1	1	20	60	140
W36D-025	1696	shield of Scotland at date		1	1	250	1500	
W36D-030	1696	shield of France at date		1	1	500		
W36D-035	1696	struck on thick flan		1	1	300	1000	
W36D-040	1696		B	1	1	20	55	130
W36D-042	1696	GVLIFLMVS instead of GVLIELMVS	B over E	1	1	100	500	
W36D-045	1696		C	1	1	25	70	170
W36D-050	1696		E	1	1	30	80	200
W36D-055	1696		N	1	1	25	70	170
W36D-060	1696		y	1	1	20	50	120
W36D-065	1696		Y	1	1	30	80	200
W36D-070	1696	no stops on obv.	Y	1	1	40	110	250
W36D-075	1696			1	2	35	100	250
W36D-080	1696	no stops on rev.		1	2	45	120	280
W36D-085	1696			1	3	35	100	250

No.	Date	Features	mm	Obv.	Rev.	F	VF	EF
W36D-090	1696		B	1	2	35	110	280
W36D-095	1696	no stops on obv.	B	1	2	35	110	280
W36D-100	1696		B	1	3	35	110	280
W36D-105	1696	no stops on obv.	B	1	3	35	110	280
W36D-110	1696		C	1	3	60	180	500
W36D-115	1696		E	1	3	50	140	350
W36D-120	1696		N	1	3	45	120	300
W36D-125	1696			2	3	250	1000	
W36D-130	1696	GVLELMVS instead of GVLIELMVS [1] (obv.)		2	3	400	1500	
W36D-135	1696	[1]	Y	3	2	250	600	
W36D-140	1696	[1]	E	3	2	300	700	
W36D-145	1697			1	3	15	55	130
W36D-150	1697	Arms of France and Ireland transposed		1	3	400		
W36D-155	1697	GVLIELMⱯS instead of GVLIELMVS (obv.)		1	3	25	75	180
W36D-160	1697	struck on shilling blank		1	3	250		
W36D-165	1697		B	1	2	30	90	220
W36D-170	1697		B	1	3	20	70	160
W36D-172	1697	rev. ↑	B	1	3	40	130	300
W36D-175	1697	reads M.AG on rev.; extra stops after FRA & HIB	B	1	3	25	80	190
W36D-180	1697		C	1	2	35	100	240
W36D-185	1697		C	1	3	20	70	160
W36D-190	1697	shield of Ireland at date	C	1	3	400		
W36D-195	1697		E	1	2	25	80	190
W36D-200	1697		E	1	3	20	70	160
W36D-205	1697	E over B (mintmark)	E	1	3	50	150	400
W36D-208	1697	E over C (mintmark)	E	1	3	70	200	
W36D-210	1697		N	1	3	18	60	140
W36D-215	1697	rev. ↑	N	1	3	30	110	220
W36D-220	1697	GVLIEMVS instead of GVLIELMVS (obv.)	N	1	3	150	500	
W36D-225	1697		y	1	3	30	90	240
W36D-230	1697	tiny 7 in date [2]	y	1	3	60	250	800
W36D-235	1697	shield of Ireland at date [3]	y	1	3	400		
W36D-240	1697	[4]		2	3	60	400	
W36D-245	1697	GVLIEMVS instead of GVLIELMVS (obv.)		2	3	120	1200	
W36D-250	1697			3	2	15	45	110
W36D-255	1697	GVLIEIMVS instead of GVLIELMVS (obv.)		3	2	30	90	200
W36D-260	1697	GⱯLIELMVS instead of GVLIELMVS (obv.)		3	2	25	75	170
W36D-265	1697	[5]		3	3	22	60	130
W36D-270	1697		B	3	2	25	75	170
W36D-275	1697	IRA instead of FRA (obv.)	B	3	2	50	130	300
W36D-280	1697		C	3	2	45	120	270
W36D-285	1697		C	3	3	45	120	270
W36D-290	1697		E	3	2	50	140	320
W36D-295	1697		E	3	3	25	75	170
W36D-300	1697		Y	3	3	40	110	260
W36D-305	1698			3	2	20	55	120
W36D-310	1698	plumes on rev.		3	2	25	70	140
W36D-315	1699			3	2	60	150	400
W36D-320	1699	plumes on rev.		3	2	25	70	140
W36D-325	1699	roses on rev.		3	2	30	90	250

No.	Date	Features	mm	Obv.	Rev.	F	VF	EF
W36D-330	1699	roses on rev. GⱯLIELMVS instead of GVLIELMVS (obv.)		3	2	50	130	320
W36D-335	1700			3	2	20	50	80
W36D-340	1700	plume below head		3	2	1800	3000	5000
W36D-345	1701			3	2	25	70	140

1. A mule, possibly struck in 1697.
2. Punch for 7 same as for the unique 1697 fourpence.
3. The entire assembly of shields is rotated to the right by 90 degrees.
4. Various overstruck letters exist in obverse legend.
5. Some have no central bar in F of FRA (obv.).

Variations in the shape of the harp occur.

Anne (1702 – 1714)

John Croker produced a portrait based on a painting of Anne by Sir Godfrey Kneller, while his assistant Samuel Bull is thought to have worked on some of the reverses. A very considerable number of sixpences was struck, resulting in erosion of the dies, and the 'Edinburgh' bust on some of the 1708 coins was possibly the work of the Scottish engraver James Clerk or his assistant Cave.

The shields on the reverse of the sixpence underwent a number of changes. During 1705 they were redesigned, and, two years later, in common with those on the other denominations, they were altered to accommodate the combined Arms of England and Scotland following the union of the two countries.

Provenance marks denoting the origin of the silver were: VIGO (below head) for silver obtained from Spanish galleons at Vigo Bay in 1702; plumes (in reverse angles) for silver from Wales; roses and plumes (alternately in the reverse angles) for silver from the 'Company for smelting down lead with Pitcoale and Seacoale'. The mintmark E (with or without a star) below the head of Anne represents coins struck at Edinburgh.

Collecting Hints

The Anne sixpence was in general a well-circulated coin, and, with the exception of the 1703 and 1711 dates, can be difficult to find in extremely fine condition or near. Some of the dates and varieties are scarcer than is sometimes realised, and it is well worth making some study of how frequently one encounters the individual dates and varieties. It is all too easy to assume that a piece dated 1707 or 1708 is fairly common without realising that one is thinking back to the easy availability of, say, the crowns and half-crowns of those dates. Although few will make the error of assuming that the 1710 sixpence is common, it is perhaps not generally realised how difficult this coin is to obtain in very fine grade or above. In addition, this date is normally encountered weakly struck.

Denomination	Metal	Weight (grams)	Diameter (mm)	Rev. alignment
Sixpence	Silver	2.9–3.0	21	↓

Obverse 1   Head 1, left; ANNA DEI GRATIA

Obverse 2   Head 2, so-called 'Edinburgh Bust', left; less well defined, more pointed nose

Reverse 1   Four undivided cruciform shields (each having a concave top) with surmounting crowns; MAG BR FRA ET HIB REG (date); usually known as the 'Before Union' reverse

Reverse 2   Similar but each shield has a convex top

Reverse 3   Similar but top and bottom shields are each divided into the Arms of England and Scotland. Shields are again concave at the top; MAG BRI FR ET HIB REG (date); known as 'After Union' reverse

Reverse 4   Similar but MAG BR FRA ET HIB REG (date) (i.e. After Union type with legend as Revs 1/2)

Reverse 5   Similar to Reverse 3 but larger lis in Arms

Edge   milled (diagonally)

Obv. 1   Obv. 2   Rev. 1

Rev. 2   Rev. 3   Rev. 5

Before Union of England and Scotland

No.	Date	Features	Obv.	Rev.	F	VF	EF
AN6D-005	1703	VIGO below head	1	1	20	60	130
AN6D-010	1705		1	1	30	90	240
AN6D-015	1705	plumes on rev.	1	1	25	75	180
AN6D-020	1705	plumes on rev.	1	2	30	90	230
AN6D-025	1705	roses and plumes on rev.	1	2	25	80	210
AN6D-030	1707	roses and plumes on rev.	1	2	25	75	180

After Union of England and Scotland

No.	Date	Features	Obv.	Rev.	F	VF	EF
AN6D-035	1707		1	3	16	40	100
AN6D-040	1707		1	4	3000		
AN6D-045	1707	E below head	1	3	18	50	130
AN6D-050	1707	PROOF; edge plain E below head	1	3			2000
AN6D-055	1707	plumes on rev.	1	3	20	55	140
AN6D-060	1708		1	3	16	50	120
AN6D-065	1708	E below head	1	3	18	55	140
AN6D-070	1708	8 over 7; E below head	1	3	30	80	200
AN6D-075	1708	E* below head	1	3	18	55	140
AN6D-080	1708	8 over 7; E* below head	1	3	25	65	170
AN6D-085	1708	E* below head	2	3	20	65	200
AN6D-090	1708	plumes on rev.	1	3	20	55	140
AN6D-095	1710	roses and plumes on rev.	1	3	30	140	550
AN6D-100	1711		1	3	15	40	85
AN6D-105	1711		1	5	15	40	85

George I (1714 – 1727)

With the accession of George Louis, Elector of Hanover, as George I, one of the duplicated England/Scotland shields was replaced by one containing the Arms of Brunswick-Lüneburg surrounding the crown of Charlemagne. The design also incorporates the abbreviated titles of the king. The obverses were probably the work of John Croker, while the reverses were designed by Johan Ochs, senior (b.1673).

This series has the unusual feature that every coin bears a provenance mark denoting the origin of the silver. Roses and plumes (alternately in the reverse angles) were for silver from the 'Company for smelting down lead with Pitcoale and Seacoale'; SS and C (in alternate angles on the reverse) for silver from the South Sea Company.

Collecting Hints

When one considers that the sixpences of George I span only four dates, the provenance marks are surprisingly varied, culminating in 1726 with a sixpence bearing an unusually small roses and plumes. This coin is quite scarce and a choice specimen is a must for any collector if one turns up. The 1723 SSC sixpence is scarcer than its shilling stablemate and one must remember this when considering a purchase.

Overall, the George I sixpence series is a pleasing one. The coins are often found well struck, they seem to tone attractively and in such a way that the main features retain the crispness of their original appearance.

Denomination	Metal	Weight (grams)	Diameter (mm)	Rev. alignment
Sixpence	Silver	2.9–3.0	21	↓

Obverse 1   Head 1, right; GEORGIVS D G M BR ET HIB REX F D

Reverse 1   Four crowned cruciform shields around central star; BRVN ET L DVX S R I A TH ET EL (date)

Edge   milled (diagonally)

Obv. 1   Rev. 1

No.	Date	Features	Obv.	Rev.	F	VF	EF
G16D-005	1717	roses and plumes on rev.	1	1	50	130	400
G16D-010	1717	edge plain; roses and plumes on rev. [1]	1	1	200	500	1200
G16D-015	1720	20 always over 17 roses and plumes on rev.	1	1	50	130	400
G16D-020	1723	SSC in angles on rev. [2]	1	1	20	60	130
G16D-025	1726	roses and plumes on rev. [3]	1	1	55	140	420

1. Not proofs; some currency coins were not given a milled edge in error.
2. Lettering size may vary.
3. Roses and plumes smaller than on 1717 coin.

George II (1727 – 1760)

As with the larger silver denominations, the sixpence series incorporates the two very different portraits of the monarch. The young head was designed by John Croker, while the old head was probably produced by John Sigismund Tanner, who had joined the Mint as an apprentice around 1728. It is likely that this work on the old head was supervised by the aged Croker, in his last years of work before his death in 1741. The reverses were, as always, regarded as somewhat less important, and Tanner was possibly allowed to work on these with less supervision. It may be that this work was aided by Johan Ochs, junior (1704–88), who had by this time begun to work at the Mint.

Provenance marks are: plumes (silver from the Welsh Copper Company); roses (silver from mines in the West of England); roses and plumes (silver from the 'Company for smelting down lead with Pitcoale and Seacoale'), all of these in the reverse angles; LIMA below the head for coins struck in silver captured by Admiral Anson in Peru during his world voyage.

In 1742, Peter Vallavine observed that sixpences are 'the subject of daily complaint, many are reduced to about two-thirds of their just weight ... A good sixpence should weigh 46 and 56/124 grains, but not 1 in 50 weighs above 39 grains, and some 30 grains.'

Collecting Hints

The young head sixpences should be collected in at least very fine condition; much detail is missing on fine condition coins, especially on the hair and eye. The old head coins retain more detail in the lower grades, but if a type specimen is required, it is not difficult to find a choice example of 1757 or 1758.

Denomination	Metal	Weight (grams)	Diameter (mm)	Rev. alignment
Sixpence	Silver	3.0–3.2	21	↓

Obverse 1   Head 1, left; GEORGIVS II DEI GRATIA

Obverse 2   Head 2, left; same legend but GEORGIUS instead of GEORGIVS

Obverse 3   Head 2, left; same legend but GEORGIVS

Reverse 1   Four crowned cruciform shields; M B F ET H REX F D B ET L D S R I A T ET E (date)

Edge   milled (diagonally)

Obv. 1   Obv. 3   Rev. 1

No.	Date	Features	Obv.	Rev.	F	VF	EF
G26D-005	1728		1	1	50	120	400
G26D-010	1728	PROOF; edge plain	1	1			1500
G26D-015	1728	plumes on rev.	1	1	40	100	350
G26D-020	1728	roses and plumes on rev.	1	1	25	60	160
G26D-025	1731	roses and plumes on rev.	1	1	25	60	160
G26D-030	1732	roses and plumes on rev.	1	1	25	60	160
G26D-035	1734	roses and plumes on rev.	1	1	50	110	300
G26D-040	1735	roses and plumes on rev.	1	1	50	110	300
G26D-045	1735	5 over 4; roses and plumes on rev.	1	1	65	130	400
G26D-050	1736	roses and plumes on rev.	1	1	40	85	250
G26D-055	1739	roses on rev.	1	1	25	60	160
G26D-060	1739	0 in GEORGIVS over R (obv.)	1	1	40	90	240
G26D-065	1741	roses on rev.	1	1	20	50	130
G26D-070	1743	roses on rev.	2	1	20	50	130
G26D-075	1745	roses on rev.	2	1	25	65	170
G26D-080	1745	5 over 3 roses on rev.	2	1	35	85	220
G26D-085	1745	LIMA below head	2	1	18	45	110
G26D-090	1746	LIMA below head	3	1	15	35	85
G26D-095	1746	PROOF [1]	3	1			350
G26D-100	1750		3	1	40	90	250
G26D-105	1751		3	1	50	110	280
G26D-110	1757		3	1	10	18	30
G26D-115	1758		3	1	10	18	30
G26D-120	1758	8 over 7	3	1	14	25	45
G26D-125	1758	8 over 7; D of DEI over indeterminate letter (obv.)	3	1	20	40	70

1. No LIMA under head.

George III (1760 – 1820)

Compared with the complexities of the larger George III silver coins, the sixpence series is fairly simple. It is not, however, without interest. The popular 1787 coin provides a companion to the shilling, and is just as easily found in the higher grades. No doubt it was hoarded when first minted, being the first issue for 29 years.

Oman reports that in 1786 it was found that sixpences in circulation were almost worn flat, and on average 36% underweight. Like the 1787 shilling, the sixpence was initially struck in large quantities without the hearts on the arms of Brunswick, until the error was spotted. The theory that the coin was hoarded is lent credence by the report by Leake in 1793 that the 1787 sixpence was 'not in common currency', and by a Mint Report of 1798 that sixpences were by now on average 38% underweight.

The 1787 sixpence, like the shilling, was designed by Lewis Pingo, who had been appointed as Chief Engraver in 1780. A number of similarities in technique can be seen if one compares Pingo's design for the sixpence with the half guinea, another of his products.

With the Great Recoinage of 1816, the series was resumed, co-incidentally again after 29 years, and the new design was very similar to that of the shilling. The initial design for the obverse was by Benedetto Pistrucci and engraved by Thomas Wyon, junior (1792–1817). The reverse was both designed and engraved by Thomas Wyon, junior. After the latter's untimely death in 1817, engraving work was carried out by Pistrucci himself, but under the prevailing legislation foreigners were debarred from holding the position of Chief Engraver. The craftsmanship and quality of striking of this series was extremely good, and specimens in the higher grades frequently exhibit a prooflike appearance.

The sixpences of 1816 and later remained legal tender even after decimalization in 1971. The coin was later demonetized despite some degree of public opinion which wanted to retain a denomination of $2\frac{1}{2}$ (decimal) pence.

No provenance marks exist on these coins. The crowns in the angles of the 1787 sixpence, while being positioned similarly to other provenance marks, are instead an integral part of the design.

Collecting Hints

The sixpences of George III should be collected in extremely fine or better condition. In these grades the excellent quality of the workmanship will be best appreciated. There are a number of interesting varieties in the sixpences dated between 1817 and 1820. This is a series in which the coins are not always inspected thoroughly by dealers and auctioneers, all the more so because a good eyeglass and/or good eyesight is often needed on so small a coin. Also, these varieties are not as well known as they might be. Even the plain edge proof 1787 and 1817 sixpences can be found occasionally, sometimes in very fine!

Denomination	Metal	Weight (grams)	Diameter (mm)	Rev. alignment
Sixpence 1787	Silver	3.0	21	↑
Sixpence 1816–20	Silver	2.8	19	↑

Obverse 1   Head 1, right; GEORGIVS III DEI GRATIA

Obverse 2   Head 2, right; GEOR III D G BRITT REX F D (date)

Reverse 1   Cruciform pentagonal shields around star, with crowns in angles; no hearts behind lion in Hanoverian shield. M B F ET H REX F D B ET L D S R I A T ET E (date)

Reverse 2   As Reverse 1 but with hearts

Reverse 3   Crowned shield within Garter; HONI SOIT QUI MAL Y PENSE on Garter

Edge   milled (diagonally on 1787)

Obv. 1   Obv. 2   Rev. 1   Rev. 3

No.	Date	Features	Obv.	Rev.	F	VF	EF	UNC
G36D-005	1787	[1]	1	1	10	15	35	50
G36D-010	1787	PROOF; edge plain	1	1				350
G36D-015	1787	PROOF on thick flan; edge plain	1	1				600
G36D-020	1787	[1]	1	2	10	15	35	50
G36D-025	1816		2	3	8	16	30	45
G36D-030	1816	struck in gold [2]	2	3				7500
G36D-035	1817		2	3	8	16	30	45
G36D-040	1817	PROOF	2	3				750
G36D-045	1817	PROOF; edge plain	2	3		80	300	800
G36D-050	1818		2	3	12	22	45	60
G36D-055	1818	PROOF	2	3				800
G36D-060	1819		2	3	10	18	35	50
G36D-065	1819	8 in date very small	2	3	16	24	50	75
G36D-068	1819	9 over 8	2	3	16	24	50	75
G36D-070	1819	PROOF; 9 not over 8	2	3				750
G36D-075	1819	PROOF; 9 over 8	2	3				650
G36D-080	1820	[2]	2	3	12	22	45	70
G36D-085	1820	1 in date inverted; [3]	2	3	30	45	75	150
G36D-088	1820	I of HONI over S (rev.)	2	3	25	40	70	130
G36D-090	1820	PROOF	2	3				750

1. 7s in date occur with and without serifs.
2. Weight 4.0 grams.
3. This date continued to be minted after death of George III.

George IV   (1820 – 1830)

The first issue of George IV sixpences used the obverse by Benedetto Pistrucci, similar to that used on the larger denominations, the die being identical to that used for the half sovereigns. This depicted the laureate head of the king, an unflattering portrait much disapproved of by the monarch. In 1826 the laureate king's head was replaced by a bare head design by William Wyon, again with an identical half-sovereign die. The sixpence was thus the last of the main silver coins to have the laureate head discarded.

The reverses, by Johann Baptiste Merlen, were of three very different designs. These were similar to those used on the shillings, the last design introducing the lion on crown motif which was to be reintroduced on George V sixpences about a century later.

The 1821 sixpence with the BBITANNIAR error in the obverse legend came about when the word was originally engraved as BITANNIAR in error; the beginning of the word was then re-engraved as effectively as could be done. The first B is usually or always struck from a broken punch ans is open at the top.

Collecting Hints

This series should be collected in extremely fine or better condition to allow the fineness of the engraving of this small denomination to be appreciated. Some of the dates are quite difficult to obtain in this condition.
The 1821 sixpence should always be checked carefully for the BBITANNIAR error. This coin sometimes turns up in about fine condition in mixed auction lots.

Denomination	Metal	Weight (grams)	Diameter (mm)	Rev. alignment
Sixpence	Silver	2.8	19	↓

Obverse 1   Head 1, laureate, left; GEORGIUS IIII D G BRITANNIAR REX F D

Obverse 2   Head 2, 'bare head', left; GEORGIUS IV DEI GRATIA (date)

Reverse 1   Garnished shield with surmounting large crown; ANNO (date)

Reverse 2   Crowned shield within Garter; ANNO (date); HONI SOIT QUI MAL Y PENSE (on Garter)

Reverse 3   Lion on crown, ornament below; BRITANNIARUM REX FIDEI DEFENSOR

Edge   milled

Obv. 1

Obv. 2

Rev. 1

Rev. 2

Rev. 3

No.	Date	Features	Obv.	Rev.	F	VF	EF	UNC
G46D-005	1821		1	1	12	20	70	120
G46D-010	1821	BBITANNIAR instead of BRITANNIAR (obv.)	1	1	65	150	600	1200
G46D-015	1821	PROOF	1	1				250
G46D-020	1824		1	2	14	24	85	120
G46D-025	1824	PROOF	1	2				600
G46D-030	1825		1	2	12	22	75	110
G46D-035	1825	PROOF	1	2				700
G46D-040	1826		1	2	30	55	160	240
G46D-045	1826	rev. ↑	1	2	90	150	500	800
G46D-050	1826	PROOF	1	2				600
G46D-055	1826		2	3	10	18	55	80
G46D-060	1826	PROOF [1]	2	3				200
G46D-065	1826	PROOF in pewter; struck on thick flan	2	3				800
G46D-070	1827		2	3	20	40	120	180
G46D-075	1828		2	3	16	30	90	140
G46D-080	1829		2	3	14	22	75	110
G46D-085	1829	PROOF	2	3				800

1. Issued in cased proof sets.

William IV   (1830 – 1837)

The design of the William IV sixpence reflects that of the shilling. This is a one-type issue, with obverses by William Wyon and reverses by Johann Baptiste Merlen, and the words 'SIX PENCE' are used for the first time.

Collecting Hints

The series should be collected in at least very fine condition. It should be remembered that the 1836 sixpence is somewhat scarce, unlike the shilling of the same date.

Denomination	Metal	Weight (grams)	Diameter (mm)	Rev. alignment
Sixpence	Silver	2.8	19	↓

Obverse 1   Head 1, right; GULIELMUS IIII D G BRITANNIAR REX F D

Reverse 1   SIX PENCE within wreath, crown above, date below

Edge   milled

Obv. 1

Rev. 1

No.	Date	Features	Obv.	Rev.	F	VF	EF	UNC
W46D-005	1831		1	1	10	20	65	90
W46D-010	1831	PROOF	1	1				400
W46D-015	1831	PROOF on thin flan; edge plain [1]	1	1				1500
W46D-020	1831	PROOF; edge plain [2]	1	1				220
W46D-025	1831	PROOF in palladium [3]	1	1				2000
W46D-030	1834		1	1	11	22	70	100
W46D-035	1834	PROOF	1	1				700
W46D-040	1834	PROOF round-top 3 in date	1	1				900
W46D-045	1835		1	1	10	20	65	90
W46D-050	1835	PROOF round-top 3 in date	1	1				1000
W46D-055	1836		1	1	16	30	100	160
W46D-060	1836	PROOF round-top 3 in date	1	1				1200
W46D-065	1837		1	1	15	35	120	200
W46D-070	1837	PROOF	1	1				1000

1. Weight 1.9 grams.
2. Issued in cased proof sets.
3. Date size varies.

All coins have flat-top 3 in date unless otherwise stated.

Victoria   (1837 – 1901)

The first Victorian sixpences were struck in 1838. These retained the 'SIX PENCE' within wreath reverse by Johann Baptiste Merlen as used on the William IV coinage. The obverse portrait was by William Wyon as on the larger coins, but the engraver's initials on the truncation were absent. Presumably Wyon considered that the coin was too small to allow his initials to be read clearly, and he did not have the arrogance of his predecessor to allow him to spell his name in full, as Pistrucci did on the George III crown.

The sixpence was struck, usually with a mintage of a million or more in each year, but no pieces are confirmed dated 1847 or 1849, and the 1848 coin is quite rare. It is likely that this was connected with the interest in the possible advent of decimal currency around 1848. No doubt the future of a coin valued at one-fortieth of a pound was considered in some doubt.

As with the shilling, the reverse dies for the coins between 1864 and 1879 were generally marked with the die number, in order to determine the life of each die.

To mark the Golden Jubilee of Victoria's reign in 1887, the obverse and reverse of the sixpence were redesigned, incorporating a new portrait of Victoria by Sir Joseph Edgar Boehm (1834–90) and a shield reverse. The choice of design, however, proved unfortunate. Both sides of the coin resembled the half sovereign, which was of similar size, to such an extent that many pieces were gilded and passed off as the gold coin. The redesigned shilling did not lend itself to this trickery as the similarly sized sovereign bore a St George design on the reverse. The design of the reverse of the sixpence was therefore changed back during 1887 to the discarded 'SIX PENCE within wreath' type, while the shilling was allowed to retain its shield reverse. The July 1887 issue of *Numismatic Magazine* reported that, as it went to press, the issue of the sixpence had been temporarily stopped 'pending enquiries'. In 1893 the unpopular Boehm Jubilee portrait was replaced by a veiled head design by Sir Thomas Brock.

There exists a rare but distinct variety of 1887 shield sixpence hitherto unrecorded in almost all reference works. This has the engraver's initials J.E.B. on the obverse much higher, on the truncation instead of below it. In 1997, a specimen at a London auction was sold still wrapped in a segment of newspaper dated 2

July 1887, indicating that at least some of this variety were probably struck before this date.

Collecting Hints

At least some of the early Victorian sixpences should be collected in extremely fine condition. Only in this grade is it possible to appreciate fully the high standard of the work of William Wyon and the beauty of his Victoria portrait. The later coins are not so finely executed but are more plentiful and for this reason the extremely fine standard should be maintained.

To collect the 1864–79 series by die number is to enter virtually uncharted waters, and specimens in any grade will be acceptable.

1887 Jubilee issue early strikings exist with prooflike surfaces and are sometimes sold as proofs. The striking of the milled edges should be carefully examined. The edges of true proofs almost cut the fingers when handled.

Denomination	Metal	Weight (grams)	Diameter (mm)	Rev. alignment
Sixpence 1838–87 Obvs 1–3	Silver	2.8	19	↓
Sixpence 1887–1901 Obvs 4–6	Silver	2.8	19	↑

Obverse 1   Head 1, left; VICTORIA DEI GRATIA BRITANNIAR REG F D

Obverse 2   Head 2, in lower relief, left; same legend

Obverse 3   Head 3, slightly different design, left

Obverse 4   Head 4, 'Jubilee Head', left, initials JEB on truncation; VICTORIA DEI GRATIA BRITT REGINA F D

Obverse 5   Head 4, similar, left, initials JEB below truncation; same legend

Obverse 6   Head 5, veiled and draped, left; VICTORIA DEI GRA BRITT REGINA FID DEF IND IMP

Reverse 1   SIX PENCE within wreath, crown above, date below, with or without die number above date (in listings, no die number unless stated)

Reverse 2   Similar but SIX PENCE larger. No die number

Reverse 3   Crowned shield within Garter; HONI SOIT QUI MAL Y PENSE on Garter

Reverse 4   Similar to reverses 1,2 but redesigned; crown is very different (date)

Edge   milled

Obv. 1   Obv. 2   Obv. 3

Obv. 5   Obv. 6   Rev. 1

Rev. 2   Rev. 3   Rev. 4

Young Head

No.	Date	Features	Obv.	Rev.	F	VF	EF	UNC
VY6D-005	1838		1	1	7	18	60	85
VY6D-010	1838	PROOF	1	1				700
VY6D-015	1839		1	1	7	20	70	100
VY6D-020	1839	PROOF; edge plain [1]	1	1				180
VY6D-025	1839	PROOF; edge plain; rev. ↑	1	1				250
VY6D-030	1839	PROOF; rev. ↑ [2]	3	1				1500
VY6D-035	1840		1	1	8	24	80	110
VY6D-040	1841		1	1	8	25	85	120
VY6D-045	1842		1	1	8	24	80	110
VY6D-050	1842	each 'I' in VICTORIA is a numeral '1' (obv.)	1	1	30	90	200	
VY6D-055	1843		1	1	8	24	80	110
VY6D-060	1844		1	1	7	18	60	80
VY6D-065	1844	large 44 in date	1	1	8	22	75	95
VY6D-070	1845		1	1	8	24	80	110
VY6D-075	1846		1	1	7	18	60	80
VY6D-080	1848		1	1	40	120	400	650
VY6D-085	1848	8 over 6	1	1	40	120	400	650
VY6D-090	1848	8 over 7	1	1	40	120	400	650
VY6D-095	1850		1	1	8	22	80	100
VY6D-098	1850	5 over 3	1	1	12	35	120	180
VY6D-100	1851		1	1	8	22	80	100
VY6D-105	1852		1	1	8	22	80	100
VY6D-110	1853		1	1	7	18	60	80
VY6D-115	1853	PROOF [1]	1	1				500
VY6D-120	1854		1	1	75	300	900	1400
VY6D-125	1855		1	1	7	18	60	80
VY6D-130	1855	PROOF	1	1				700
VY6D-135	1856	[3]	1	1	8	20	75	95
VY6D-140	1857	[3]	1	1	8	20	80	100
VY6D-145	1858	[4]	1	1	8	22	90	120
VY6D-148	1858	latter 8 over 6	1	1	20	60	200	500
VY6D-150	1858	PROOF	1	1				750
VY6D-155	1859	[5]	1	1	7	17	55	75
VY6D-160	1859	9 over 8 [5]	1	1	8	24	95	130
VY6D-165	1860		1	1	9	18	60	80
VY6D-170	1860	6 over indeterminate figure, possibly 0	1	1	8	20	70	95
VY6D-175	1862		1	1	30	110	400	600
VY6D-180	1863		1	1	20	80	250	400
VY6D-185	1864	die number above date [6]	1	1	8	18	65	85
VY6D-190	1865	die number above date	1	1	9	20	75	100
VY6D-195	1866	die number above date	1	1	8	18	65	85
VY6D-200	1866		1	1	40	150	700	
VY6D-205	1867	die number above date	2	1	10	25	90	120
VY6D-210	1867	die number above date PROOF[7]	2	1				700
VY6D-215	1868	die number above date [4]	2	1	10	28	100	150
VY6D-220	1869	die number above date	2	1	10	30	110	170
VY6D-225	1869	die number above date PROOF	2	1				750
VY6D-230	1870	die number above date	2	1	10	32	115	180
VY6D-235	1870	die number above date PROOF; edge plain	2	1				900
VY6D-240	1871	die number above date	2	1	8	22	75	110
VY6D-245	1871		2	1	10	30	100	140
VY6D-250	1871	die number above date PROOF; rev. ↑	2	1				900
VY6D-255	1871	die number above date PROOF; edge plain	2	1				750
VY6D-260	1871	PROOF	2	1				700
VY6D-265	1872	die number above date	2	1	9	22	65	95
VY6D-270	1873	die number above date [8]	2	1	8	20	60	85
VY6D-275	1874	die number above date [4]	2	1	8	20	60	85
VY6D-280	1875	die number above date [4]	2	1	8	20	60	85
VY6D-285	1876	die number above date	2	1	10	26	80	120
VY6D-290	1877	die number above date	2	1	9	22	65	95

No.	Date	Features	Obv.	Rev.	F	VF	EF	UNC
VY6D-295	1877		2	1	10	26	80	120
VY6D-300	1878	die number above date	2	1	8	20	60	85
VY6D-305	1878	die number above date PROOF	2	1				700
VY6D-310	1878	8 over 7 die number above date	2	1	60	150	400	600
VY6D-315	1878	DRITANNIAR instead of BRITANNIAR (obv.) die number 6 above date [9]	2	1	40	100	300	500
VY6D-320	1879	die number above date	2	1	9	24	70	100
VY6D-325	1879		2	1	9	24	70	100
VY6D-330	1879	PROOF	2	1				700
VY6D-335	1879	PROOF; edge plain; rev. ↑ [10]	2	1				800
VY6D-340	1879	larger border beads [11]	2	1	10	26	75	110
VY6D-345	1880	larger border beads [11]	2	1	10	26	75	110
VY6D-350	1880		3	1	8	20	55	75
VY6D-355	1880	PROOF	3	1				600
VY6D-360	1881	[12]	3	1	8	20	55	75
VY6D-365	1881	PROOF	3	1				500
VY6D-370	1881	PROOF; edge plain	3	1				600
VY6D-375	1882		3	1	10	26	75	110
VY6D-380	1883		3	1	8	20	55	75
VY6D-385	1884		3	2	8	20	55	75
VY6D-390	1885		3	2	8	20	55	75
VY6D-395	1885	PROOF	3	2				500
VY6D-400	1886		3	2	7	18	45	65
VY6D-405	1886	PROOF	3	2				500
VY6D-410	1887		3	2	7	16	40	55
VY6D-415	1887	PROOF	3	2				400

1. Issued in cased proof sets.
2. An unexplained piece obviously struck at a much later date (cf. 1879 proofs).
3. Variety has longer line below PENCE.
4. Minor obverse differences exist.
5. A clear overdate is visible at the top of the digit; plain 9 coin resembles 9 over 8.
6. 4 in date varies.
7. Die number usually or always 2.
8. Minor reverse differences exist; well over 100 die numbers recorded.
9. Always die number 6; minted for use in Cyprus.
10. Some may have obverse 1 (sic).
11. 118 beads.
12. Date size may vary.

Jubilee Head

No.	Date	Features	Obv.	Rev.	F	VF	EF	UNC
VJ6D-420	1887		4	3	25	45	75	110
VJ6D-425	1887	[1]	5	3	4	7	11	15
VJ6D-430	1887	PROOF [2]	5	3				60
VJ6D-435	1887		5	4	4	8	14	20
VJ6D-440	1887	PROOF	5	4				300
VJ6D-445	1888	[3]	5	4	5	9	18	30
VJ6D-450	1888	PROOF	5	4				500
VJ6D-455	1889	[3]	5	4	5	10	20	32
VJ6D-460	1890	[3]	5	4	6	11	22	35
VJ6D-465	1890	PROOF	5	4				450
VJ6D-470	1891		5	4	6	11	22	35
VJ6D-475	1892		5	4	6	11	22	35
VJ6D-480	1893		5	4	150	500	1500	

1. R in VICTORIA may show traces of other letter such as b, i, v (obv.).
2. Issued in cased proof sets.
3. Minor reverse differences exist.

Old Head

No.	Date	Features	Obv.	Rev.	F	VF	EF	UNC
VO6D-485	1893	[1]	6	4	5	8	17	22
VO6D-490	1893	PROOF [2]	6	4				70
VO6D-495	1894		6	4	6	10	25	40
VO6D-500	1895		6	4	6	10	22	32
VO6D-505	1896		6	4	6	10	22	32
VO6D-510	1897		6	4	5	9	20	28
VO6D-515	1898	[3]	6	4	6	10	22	32
VO6D-520	1899		6	4	6	10	22	32
VO6D-525	1900		6	4	5	9	20	28
VO6D-530	1901		6	4	5	8	18	24

1. Minor obverse differences exist.

No.	Date	Features	Obv.	Rev.	F	VF	EF	UNC

2. Issued in cased proof sets.
3. Date slightly larger than usual.

Edward VII   (1901 – 1910)

The sixpence series of Edward VII is a one-type issue struck for each year of the reign. The obverse depicts the portrait of the king by George William de Saulles (1862–1903) which was engraved using a mechanical reducing machine. Unlike the halfcrown, florin and shilling, the reverse of the sixpence was not by de Saulles but continued the value in wreath design of the late Victorian pieces. This was itself a re-engraved version of the Merlen design first used on William IV sixpences.

After the death of de Saulles early in the reign, W.H.J. Blakemore became responsible for hand-finishing and re-engraving dies produced by the mechanical reducer.

Collecting Hints

This series should be collected in extremely fine or better condition. It must be remembered that the 1905 sixpence is not as rare as its larger companion coins.

Denomination	Metal	Weight (grams)	Diameter (mm)	Rev. alignment
Sixpence	Silver	2.8	19	↑

Obverse 1   Head 1, right; EDWARDVS VII DEI GRA BRITT OMN REX

Reverse 1   SIX PENCE within wreath, crown above, date below

Edge   milled

Obv. 1   Rev. 1

No.	Date	Features	Obv.	Rev.	F	VF	EF	UNC
E76D-005	1902		1	1	4	8	18	25
E76D-010	1902	matt PROOF [1]	1	1				28
E76D-015	1903		1	1	5	10	26	45
E76D-020	1904		1	1	6	12	35	65
E76D-025	1905		1	1	5	11	30	55
E76D-030	1906		1	1	5	10	26	40
E76D-035	1907		1	1	5	10	26	40
E76D-040	1908		1	1	6	12	35	55
E76D-045	1909		1	1	5	10	26	40
E76D-050	1910		1	1	4	9	20	30

1. Issued in cased proof sets.

George V   (1910 – 1936)

The obverse of the George V sixpence used the portrait of George V by Sir Bertram Mackennal (1863–1931) engraved using the mechanical reduction machine to the appropriate size. The reverse finally discarded the Merlen reverse first used in 1831. Ironically, however, the lion on crown design which replaced it was last used on sixpences in 1829! This modified version was almost identical to that designed by de Saulles for the Edward VII shilling, and carried forward to the George V shilling.

In line with the other silver denominations, the silver content of the metal was reduced to 50% in 1920, and further modified in 1922 after it was found that streaking occurred. Another modification to the metal content was made in 1927 when the new acorn reverse was introduced. This design, depicting six acorns (presumably indicating six pence) amongst oak leaves, was one of a number of new designs for coinage by George Kruger Gray (1880–1943) and was sometimes referred to somewhat unkindly as 'the garden of weeds'. The new designs were introduced to the public in 1927 by way of a proof set of six silver coins, and were all abandoned in 1937 on the advent of the George VI coinage.

Collecting Hints

This series should be collected in extremely fine to mint state, although some of the dates are quite difficult to obtain in this condition. The acorn reverse type sixpence of 1928–36 often turns up cleaned or polished, sometimes to such an extent that it appears lacquered. Care should be taken in grading this coin, with special attention being paid to the detail on the base of each of the six acorns.

Denomination	Metal	Weight (grams)	Diameter (mm)	Rev. alignment
Sixpence 1911–20	0.925 Silver	2.8	19	↑
Sixpence 1920–22	Silver 50%; copper 40%; nickel 10%	2.8	19	↑
Sixpence 1922–27	Silver 50%; copper 50%	2.8	19	↑
Sixpence 1927–36	Silver 50%; copper 40%; nickel 5%; zinc 5%	2.8	19	↑

Obverse 1   Head 1, left, B.M. on truncation; GEORGIVS V DEI GRA BRITT OMN REX

Obverse 2   Head 2, so-called 'modified effigy', left; BM (no stops) further to right; beading recut; GEORGIVS V D G BRITT OMN F D IND IMP

Reverse 1   Lion on crown with separated date, all within inner circle; FID DEF IND IMP SIXPENCE

Reverse 2   Oak sprigs with six acorns; SIXPENCE A (date) D

Edge   milled (finer milling 1931–36 than for previous years)

| Obv. 1 | Obv. 2 | Rev. 1 | Rev. 2 |

Sterling Silver Issue

No.	Date	Features	Obv.	Rev.	VF	EF	UNC
G56D-005	1911	[1]	1	1	4	12	18
G56D-010	1911	PROOF [2]	1	1			45
G56D-015	1912		1	1	5	18	28
G56D-020	1913		1	1	7	22	35
G56D-025	1914		1	1	4	12	18
G56D-030	1915		1	1	4	12	18
G56D-035	1916		1	1	4	12	18
G56D-040	1917		1	1	8	25	45
G56D-045	1918		1	1	4	12	18
G56D-050	1919		1	1	4	14	22
G56D-055	1920	silver content 0.925	1	1	4	14	24

1. Minor obverse/reverse differences exist.
2. Issued in cased proof sets.

50% Silver Issue

No.	Date	Features	Obv.	Rev.	VF	EF	UNC
G56D-060	1920	silver content 0.5	1	1	4	12	20
G56D-065	1921		1	1	4	12	20
G56D-070	1922	[1]	1	1	4	14	24
G56D-075	1923		1	1	5	18	35
G56D-080	1924		1	1	5	16	30

No.	Date	Features	Obv.	Rev.	VF	EF	UNC
G56D-085	1925	[2]	1	1	5	16	27
G56D-090	1926	[3]	1	1	5	16	27
G56D-095	1926		2	1	4	12	20
G56D-100	1927		2	1	4	14	24
G56D-105	1927	struck in nickel [4]	2	1			500
G56D-110	1927	PROOF [5]	2	2			28
G56D-115	1927	PROOF from sandblasted dies [6]	2	2			200
G56D-120	1928		2	2	3	8	14
G56D-125	1928	PROOF	2	2			300
G56D-130	1929		2	2	3	8	14
G56D-135	1929	PROOF	2	2			300
G56D-140	1930		2	2	3	8	14
G56D-145	1930	PROOF	2	2			400
G56D-150	1931		2	2	3	10	16
G56D-155	1931	PROOF	2	2			300
G56D-160	1932		2	2	4	18	35
G56D-165	1932	PROOF	2	2			400
G56D-170	1933		2	2	3	8	14
G56D-175	1933	PROOF	2	2			300
G56D-180	1934		2	2	3	10	18
G56D-185	1934	PROOF	2	2			400
G56D-190	1935		2	2	3	8	14
G56D-195	1935	PROOF	2	2			300
G56D-200	1936		2	2	3	7	12
G56D-205	1936	PROOF	2	2			250

1. Alloy occurs with and without nickel content; see table above.
2. Some have redesigned beads/rim on obverse.
3. Obverse beads/rim redesigned from 1924 issue.
4. Weight 2.9 grams; nickel is slightly magnetic.
5. Issued in cased proof sets.
6. Struck to facilitate photography of coin.

Edward VIII   (1936)

The Edward VIII sixpence is strictly speaking a pattern, as probable Royal approval was about to be granted at the time of the abdication. However, because its official status rests only on this technicality, and to provide continuity, it is included here.

The portrait of Edward VIII is by Thomas Humphrey Paget, and faces left at the insistence of the king, who considered this placement more flattering and wished to discontinue the tradition of opposite facings for successive monarchs. The reverse is by George Kruger Gray (1880–1943)

Denomination	Metal	Weight (grams)	Diameter (mm)	Rev. alignment
Sixpence	Silver	2.8	19	↑

Obverse 1   Head 1, left; EDWARDVS VIII D G BR OMN REX

Reverse 1   Six interlinked rings of St Edmund; FID DEF IND IMP 1937 SIXPENCE

Edge   milled

| Obv. 1 | Rev. 1 |

No.	Date	Obv.	Rev.	UNC
E86D-005	1937	1	1	12000

George VI   (1937 – 1952)

The obverse of the sixpence depicts the portrait of George VI designed by Thomas Humphrey Paget (1893–1974). The first reverse, by George Kruger Gray, depicts the crowned interlinked initials GRI (Georgius Rex Imperator = King George, Emperor). This was redesigned in 1949 to read GVIR (Georgius (6) Rex) after the title Emperor of India had been relinquished.

In 1947, the metal of the sixpence and other coins previously struck in silver was changed to cupronickel. At this time, Britain had to repay silver borrowed from the United States for the war effort.

Denomination	Metal	Weight (grams)	Diameter (mm)	Rev. alignment
Sixpence 1937–46	0.500 Silver	2.8	19	↑
Sixpence 1947–52	Copper 75%; nickel 25%	2.8	19	↑

Obverse 1   Head 1, left; GEORGIVS VI D G BR OMN REX

Reverse 1   Crowned 'GRI' with divided date; FID DEF IND IMP SIXPENCE

Reverse 2   Crowned 'GVIR' with divided date; FID DEF SIXPENCE

Edge   milled

Obv. 1   Rev. 1   Rev. 2

50% Silver Issue

No.	Date	Features	Obv.	Rev.	EF	UNC
G66D-005	1937		1	1	3	6
G66D-010	1937	PROOF [1]	1	1		10
G66D-015	1937	PROOF from sandblasted dies [2]	1	1		200
G66D-020	1938		1	1	4	9
G66D-025	1938	PROOF	1	1		250
G66D-030	1939		1	1	4	10
G66D-035	1939	PROOF	1	1		250
G66D-040	1940		1	1	3	9
G66D-045	1940	PROOF	1	1		300
G66D-050	1941		1	1	3	10
G66D-055	1941	PROOF	1	1		300
G66D-060	1942		1	1	3	6
G66D-065	1943		1	1	3	6
G66D-070	1943	PROOF	1	1		300
G66D-075	1944		1	1	3	6
G66D-080	1944	PROOF	1	1		300
G66D-085	1945		1	1	3	6
G66D-090	1945	PROOF	1	1		300
G66D-095	1946		1	1	3	6
G66D-100	1946	PROOF	1	1		300

1. Issued in cased proof sets.
2. Struck to facilitate photography of coin.

Cupronickel Issue

No.	Date	Features	Obv.	Rev.	VF	EF	UNC
G66D-105	1946	PROOF in cupronickel	1	1			600
G66D-110	1947		1	1		2	6
G66D-115	1947	PROOF	1	1			320
G66D-120	1948		1	1		2	6
G66D-125	1948	PROOF	1	1			320
G66D-130	1949		1	2		2	8
G66D-135	1949	PROOF	1	2			320
G66D-140	1950		1	2		2	6
G66D-145	1950	PROOF [1]	1	2			8
G66D-150	1950	PROOF from sandblasted dies [2]	1	2			200
G66D-155	1951		1	2		2	6
G66D-160	1951	PROOF [1]	1	2			9

No.	Date	Features	Obv.	Rev.	VF	EF	UNC
G66D-165	1951	PROOF from sandblasted dies [2]	1	2			200
G66D-170	1952		1	2	8	15	60
G66D-175	1952	PROOF [3]	1	2			1500

1. Issued in cased proof sets.
2. Struck to facilitate photography of coin.
3. Struck from polished dies.

Elizabeth II   (1952 –)

The original design by Mary Gillick for the queen's portrait resulted in a weak striking lacking in detail, and the dies were soon recut to provide a sharper image. The first year (1953) is the only coin bearing the obverse 'BRITT OMN' (trans.: of all the British possessions).

Denomination	Metal	Weight (grams)	Diameter (mm)	Rev. alignment
Sixpence 1953–70	Cupronickel	2.8	19	↑

Obverse 1   Head 1, right; ELIZABETH II DEI GRATIA BRITT OMN REGINA

Obverse 2   Head 1 (recut), right; ELIZABETH II DEI GRATIA REGINA

Obverse M   Head as designed by Cecil Thomas for Mauritius quarter rupee 1960–78

Reverse 1   Garland of rose, thistle, shamrock, leek; FID DEF SIX PENCE (date)

Edge   milled

Obv. 1   Obv. 2   Rev. 1

No.	Date	Features	Obv.	Rev.	UNC
EZ6D-005	1953	[1]	1	1	2
EZ6D-010	1953	PROOF [2]	1	1	7
EZ6D-015	1953	PROOF from sandblasted dies [3]	1	1	150
EZ6D-020	1954		2	1	9
EZ6D-025	1954	PROOF	2	1	220
EZ6D-030	1955	[4]	2	1	3
EZ6D-035	1955	PROOF	2	1	220
EZ6D-040	1956		2	1	3
EZ6D-045	1956	PROOF	2	1	220
EZ6D-050	1957		2	1	2
EZ6D-052	1957	rev. ↓	2	1	80
EZ6D-055	1957	PROOF	2	1	220
EZ6D-060	1958		2	1	9
EZ6D-065	1958	PROOF	2	1	220
EZ6D-070	1959		2	1	2
EZ6D-075	1959	PROOF	2	1	220
EZ6D-080	1960		2	1	9
EZ6D-085	1960	PROOF	2	1	220
EZ6D-090	1961		2	1	5
EZ6D-095	1961	PROOF	2	1	220
EZ6D-100	1962		2	1	2
EZ6D-105	1962	PROOF	2	1	220
EZ6D-110	1963		2	1	2
EZ6D-115	1963	PROOF	2	1	220
EZ6D-120	1964	[5]	2	1	2
EZ6D-125	1964	PROOF	2	1	220
EZ6D-130	1965	[5]	2	1	2

Sixpence — Elizabeth II   (1952 –)

No.	Date	Features	Obv.	Rev.	UNC
EZ6D-135	1965	PROOF	2	1	220
EZ6D-140	1966	[6]	2	1	2
EZ6D-145	1966	struck in bronze [7]	2	1	180
EZ6D-150	1966	PROOF	2	1	220
EZ6D-155	1966	Error obverse	M	1	300
EZ6D-160	1967	[8]	2	1	2
EZ6D-165	1967	PROOF [9]	2	1	220
EZ6D-170	1970	PROOF [10]	2	1	3

1. At least 2 minor varieties.
2. Issued in cased proof sets.
3. Struck to facilitate photography of coin.
4. Minor reverse differences exist.
5. Minor obverse differences exist.
6. Border teeth now become finer than on previous years.
7. Weight 3.1 grams.
8. Issued for some years.
9. At least one issued sealed in error in 1970 proof set.
10. Issued in sealed cased proof sets; no ordinary issue coins of this date.

Maundy Fourpence

Charles II (1660 – 1685)

The early silver fourpences were used exclusively as currency, even though they are now commonly referred to as Maundy coins. The first machine struck small silver coins are often termed the 'undated Maundy' despite the fact that for well over a century only the silver pennies (and occasionally the silver twopence) were distributed as Maundy Money. The dies for this undated coinage were probably prepared by Thomas Simon (1618–65) in 1664 or 1665. This was almost the only work he did following the appointment of John Roettier.

The first dated fourpence was struck in 1670, this first year of issue being shared with the threepence and the silver penny. The twopence had first been issued in 1668. The motif of interlinked 'C's (the king's initial) as used on the larger silver was here employed to represent the denomination, a cross formed from four 'C's representing four pence. This new dated small coinage was designed by John Roettier.

There are a relatively large number of overdates in this series, and on some dates an overdate is the more usually encountered variety. The date most usually seen is 1679.

Denomination	Metal	Weight (grams)	Diameter (mm)	Rev. alignment
Fourpence undated	Silver	2.0	19	varies
Fourpence 1670–84	Silver	2.0	19	↓

Obverse 1 Head 1, crowned, left; IIII behind head; CAROLVS II D G M B F & H REX

Obverse 2 Head 2, right; CAROLVS II DEI GRATIA

Reverse 1 Shield enclosing Arms of England, Scotland, Ireland, coinjoined England/France; CHRISTO AVSPICE REGNO

Reverse 2 Four crowned interlinked 'C's with rose, thistle, fleur-de-lis, harp; MAG BR FRA ET HIB REX (date)

Edge plain

Obv. 1   Obv. 2   Rev. 1   Rev. 2

No.	Date	Features	Obv.	Rev.	F	VF	EF
C24MM-005	none	[1]	1	1	18	35	70
C24MM-010	1670		2	2	22	40	85
C24MM-015	1671		2	2	16	28	60
C24MM-020	1672	2 over 1	2	2	16	28	60
C24MM-025	1673		2	2	16	28	60
C24MM-030	1674		2	2	16	28	60
C24MM-035	1674	7 over 6	2	2	18	35	70
C24MM-040	1674	4 over horizontal 4	2	2	30	70	120
C24MM-045	1675		2	2	16	28	60
C24MM-050	1675	5 over 4	2	2	30	70	120
C24MM-055	1676		2	2	18	35	70
C24MM-060	1676	7 over 6	2	2	18	35	70
C24MM-065	1676	latter 6 over 5	2	2	18	35	70
C24MM-070	1677	[2]	2	2	16	28	60
C24MM-075	1678		2	2	16	28	60
C24MM-080	1678	8 over 6	2	2	16	28	60
C24MM-085	1678	8 over 7	2	2	16	28	60
C24MM-090	1679	[3]	2	2	14	24	50
C24MM-095	1680		2	2	15	25	55
C24MM-100	1681		2	2	15	25	55
C24MM-105	1681	B of HIB over R (rev.)	2	2	20	35	80
C24MM-110	1681	1 over 0	2	2	16	28	60
C24MM-115	1682		2	2	16	28	60
C24MM-120	1682	2 over 1	2	2	16	28	60
C24MM-125	1683		2	2	16	28	60
C24MM-130	1684		2	2	18	35	70
C24MM-135	1684	4 over 3	2	2	16	28	60

1. Minor varieties exist.
2. Variety reads CAROLVS I.I.
3. Lettering and punctuation vary.

James II (1685 – 1688)

John Roettier redesigned the silver fourpence on the accession of James II. The obverse depicts the monarch with shorter hair than on the larger silver pieces, while on the reverse the denomination appears as IIII. What is often not realised is that this representation not only denotes '4' as a Roman numeral but also continues the tradition of signifying the fourfold initials of the monarch (IACOBUS).

Denomination	Metal	Weight (grams)	Diameter (mm)	Rev. alignment
Fourpence	Silver	2.0	19	↓

Obverse 1 Head 1, left; IACOBVS II DEI GRATIA

Reverse 1 Large IIII, crowned; MAG BR FRA ET HIB REX (date)

Edge plain

Obv. 1   Rev. 1

No.	Date	Features	Obv.	Rev.	F	VF	EF
J24M-005	1686		1	1	16	28	60
J24M-010	1686	date nearer top of crown	1	1	16	28	60
J24M-015	1687	7 over 6	1	1	16	28	60
J24M-020	1687	7 over 6; 8 over 7	1	1	16	28	60
J24M-025	1688	[1]	1	1	16	28	60
J24M-030	1688	1 over 8	1	1	25	50	120
J24M-035	1688	latter 8 over 7	1	1	16	28	60

1. A slightly different obverse lettering alignment introduced for this year.

William & Mary (1688 – 1694)

There is uncertainty about the identity of the designer of the small silver coins of William and Mary. The portraits of the king and queen are certainly very different from those on the larger coinage, and in some ways resemble caricatures. Although the designer has never been positively identified, if the medals of George Bower are studied, one often comes across very similar caricatured portraits. Bower was an engraver at the Royal Mint, a post he still held at his death on 1 March 1689 (old style calendar). He must remain a strong candidate for the designer of the early small silver. The striking of the obverse is usually sharp and in high relief, while the reverse is flatter. Whoever he was, this craftsman gave to the coinage a basic reverse design of a crowned '4' which lasted for over three hundred years.

The William and Mary obverse is unusual in that there are two distinct types, with and without a tie to the wreath on the portrait. In addition, there are a number of lettering and numeral varieties.

Small silver of William and Mary is fairly rare in extremely fine or better condition.

Denomination	Metal	Weight (grams)	Diameter (mm)	Rev. alignment
Fourpence	Silver	2.0	19	↓

Obverse 1 Heads 1, right; no tie at back of king's head; GVLIELMVS ET MARIA D G

Obverse 2 Heads 2, with tie, right; same legend

Reverse 1 Crowned '4'; MAG BR FR ET HIB REX ET REGINA

Edge plain

Obv. 1   Obv. 2   Rev. 1

No.	Date	Features	Obv.	Rev.	F	VF	EF
WM4M-005	1689	1	1	1	16	28	60
WM4M-010	1690	2	1	1	18	32	70
WM4M-015	1690	6 over 5	1	1	18	32	70
WM4M-020	1691	3	1	1	20	35	75
WM4M-025	1691	1 over 0	1	1	20	35	75
WM4M-030	1692	4	2	1	18	35	75
WM4M-035	1692	2 over 1	2	1	18	40	85
WM4M-040	1693		2	1	24	45	95
WM4M-045	1693	3 over 2	2	1	22	40	85
WM4M-050	1694	4	1	1	22	40	85
WM4M-055	1694		2	1	22	45	95

1. Many minor lettering, stop and head varieties exist.
2. Punctuation varieties exist.
3. Minor stop varieties exist.
4. Lettering size variations exist.

William III   (1695 – 1701)

After the death of Mary from smallpox in 1694, the obverse of the new fourpence was designed by Johann Crocker, aka John Croker (1670–1741). The reverse may have been the work of Croker or an assistant. The style of earlier reigns is continued and, being struck relatively late in the reign, none was struck at the provincial mints.

The 1702 coin is an oddity. William III died on 8th March 1701, and no coins of William III should thus bear the date 1702, even though under the old calendar 1702 began on 25th March. The fourpence is the only known English William III coin to bear this date, although Scottish 5 shillings of William were dated 1702. In Scotland, the year changeover had changed to 1st January in 1600.

Denomination	Metal	Weight (grams)	Diameter (mm)	Rev. alignment
Fourpence	Silver	2.0	19	↓

Obverse 1 Head 1, right; GVLIELMVS III DEI GRA

Reverse 1 Crowned '4'; MAG BR FRA ET HIB REX (date)

Edge plain

Obv. 1   Rev. 1

No.	Date	Features	Obv.	Rev.	F	VF	EF
W34M-005	1697	1	1	1			
W34M-010	1698		1	1	20	35	75
W34M-015	1699		1	1	20	35	75
W34M-020	1700	2	1	1	20	35	75
W34M-025	1701		1	1	20	50	100
W34M-030	1702	3	1	1	15	25	60

1. Only one known; see BNJ 1948, p.352 re exhibition by Albert Baldwin at BNJ.
2. Punctuation varies.
3. Dated posthumously.

Anne   (1702 – 1714)

The Anne fourpence was probably the work of John Croker and/ or his assistant Samuel Bull, although some doubt attaches to the identity of the engravers of the reverse. The coin appears at first glance to be of one type, but there are some major differences to the lettering and some minor varieties of the portrait and crown.

Denomination	Metal	Weight (grams)	Diameter (mm)	Rev. alignment
Fourpence	Silver	2.0	19	↓

Obverse 1 Head 1, left; ANNA DEI GRATIA

Obverse 2 Head 2, slightly different, left; same legend

Reverse 1 Crowned '4'; MAG BR FR ET HIB REG (date)

Reverse 2 Similar but MAG BR FRA ET HIB REG

Reverse 3 Similar but MAG BRI FR ET HIB REG

Reverse 4 As reverse 3 but crown is larger; serifs on '4' are larger

Edge plain

Obv. 1   Obv. 2   Rev. 1   Rev. 4

No.	Date	Features	Obv.	Rev.	F	VF	EF
AN4M-005	1703		1	1	20	45	90
AN4M-010	1704		1	1	15	30	60
AN4M-015	1705		2	1	20	45	90
AN4M-020	1706		2	2	15	30	60
AN4M-025	1708		2	3	15	30	60
AN4M-030	1709		2	3	15	30	60
AN4M-035	1710		2	4	10	20	45
AN4M-040	1713	1	2	4	15	30	60

1. Hair varies (obv.); variety exists with very close date.

George I   (1714 – 1727)

John Croker continued, with some assistance from Samuel Bull, to engrave the small silver coinage. The reverses may have been the work of Johann Rudolph Ochs, senior. Unlike the silver series from crown to sixpence, the small silver omitted the Hanoverian titles of the king. It was probably thought that the lengthy abbreviated titles would be too difficult to read on such a small scale. The series continues with the general overall design of earlier reigns.

Denomination	Metal	Weight (grams)	Diameter (mm)	Rev. alignment
Fourpence	Silver	2.0	19	↓

Obverse 1 Head 1, right; GEORGIVS DEI GRA

Reverse 1 Crowned '4'; MAG BRI FR ET HIB REX (date)

Edge plain

Obv. 1

Rev. 1

No.	Date	Obv.	Rev.	F	VF	EF
G14M-005	1717	1	1	20	35	75
G14M-010	1721	1	1	20	35	75
G14M-015	1723	1	1	25	45	90
G14M-020	1727	1	1	30	50	100

George II (1727 – 1760)

The elderly John Croker engraved the obverse dies for the silver fourpence. However, unlike on the larger silver coinage, there was no transition in 1743 to the older portrait by Tanner. The isolated issue of the coin in 1760, the year of the king's death, meant that the Croker young head design was still being issued two years after the last old head Tanner design was seen on the shilling and sixpence.

Denomination	Metal	Weight (grams)	Diameter (mm)	Rev. alignment
Fourpence	Silver	2.0	19	↓

Obverse 1 Head 1, left; GEORGIVS II DEI GRATIA

Obverse 2 Similar but a threepence obverse die (used in error)

Reverse 1 Crowned '4'; MAG BRI FR ET HIB REX (date)

Reverse 2 Similar but crown slightly different; '4' is larger; same legend

Edge plain

Obv. 1

Rev. 1

Rev. 2

No.	Date	Features	Obv.	Rev.	F	VF	EF
G24M-005	1729		1	1	15	25	45
G24M-010	1731		1	1	15	25	45
G24M-015	1732		1	2	15	25	45
G24M-020	1735		1	2	15	25	45
G24M-025	1737		1	2	18	30	50
G24M-030	1739		1	2	15	25	45
G24M-035	1740		2	2	15	25	45
G24M-040	1743		1	2	20	35	60
G24M-045	1743	3 over 0	1	2	30	60	120
G24M-050	1746		1	2	15	25	45
G24M-055	1760		1	2	18	30	50

George III (1760 – 1820)

The reign of George III probably saw the last of the 'crowned 4' silver fourpences struck for circulation. Late George III issues and those of subsequent reigns are usually encountered in higher grades, indicating that their source was probably a set of Maundy money.

The first fourpences bear a portrait very similar to that on the Northumberland shilling and the early guineas. Although uncertain, this possibly means that Richard Yeo was the designer. An intermediate type (1792–1800) depicts a very different head, the 1792 coin also incorporating a stylised reverse numeral which has caused this date of small coinage to become known as 'Wire Money'. The George III fourpences produced after the Great Recoinage incorporate the Benedetto Pistrucci head of the king. These are the only fourpences with the date on the obverse.

In 1784 the silver fourpence was redesigned with a much flatter '4' on the reverse; other minor changes were also made. The next issue, in 1786, also featured this new design, the silver penny having been similarly redesigned in lower relief in 1781. However, the twopence and threepence retained the high relief reverse. The 1784 and 1786 small silver coinage was the last struck before an even more radical redesign in 1792.

Fourpences apparently dated 1775 are dated 1776 with a broken '6'.

Denomination	Metal	Weight (grams)	Diameter (mm)	Rev. alignment
Fourpence 1762–86	Silver	2.0	19	↓
Fourpence 1792–1800	Silver	2.0	19	↑
Fourpence 1817–20	Silver	1.9	18	↑

Obverse 1 Head 1, right; GEORGIVS III DEI GRATIA

Obverse 2 Head 2, right; same legend

Obverse 3 Head 3, laureate, right; GEORGIUS III DEI GRATIA (date)

Reverse 1 Crowned '4' in high relief; MAG BRI FR ET HIB REX (date, across crown)

Reverse 2 Similar but in lower relief; the '4' is much flatter

Reverse 3 Completely redesigned; stylised '4' under small crown; date below '4'; same legend

Reverse 4 Redesigned; more similar to Reverse 2 but crown very different; same legend; date is below '4'

Reverse 5 Crowned '4'; BRITANNIARUM REX FID DEF (no date)

Edge plain

Obv. 1   Obv. 2   Obv. 3

Rev. 1   Rev. 3   Rev. 4   Rev. 5

No.	Date	Features	Obv.	Rev.	F	VF	EF
G34M-005	1763		1	1	5	10	25
G34M-010	1763	PROOF; rev. ↑	1	1			1200
G34M-015	1765		1	1	200	400	900
G34M-020	1765	E in GEORGIVS over R (obv.)	1	1	250	500	1000
G34M-025	1766		1	1	14	24	50
G34M-030	1770		1	1	14	24	50
G34M-035	1772		1	1	14	24	50
G34M-040	1772	2 over 0	1	1	14	24	50
G34M-045	1776	1	1	1	14	24	50
G34M-050	1780		1	1	14	24	50
G34M-055	1784		1	2	15	30	70
G34M-060	1786	2	1	2	15	26	50
G34M-065	1792	3	2	3	20	32	70
G34M-070	1795		2	4	14	24	50
G34M-075	1800		2	4	10	18	30
G34M-080	1817		3	5	12	16	30
G34M-085	1818		3	5	12	16	30
G34M-090	1820		3	5	12	16	30

1. Occurs with broken 6 in date resembling 5.
2. Larger lettering on obverse than previous dates.
3. 'Wire Money' issue.

George IV (1820 – 1830)

By the reign of George IV, the small silver coins bearing a crowned numeral reverse may be considered almost exclusively as

Maundy coinage. From 1822 this coinage has been minted with a similar design in each of the four denominations (1, 2, 3, 4 pence) for every year up to the present. Because of this, and the fact that few design varieties occur from now on, the individual pieces from 1822 will be tabulated in abbreviated form. Major varieties such as proofs will be noted. Few people collect, say, Maundy fourpences only, and so the expanded and detailed tables showing each year separately will appear under the heading of Maundy sets. Under this heading will also appear again full details of varieties of any individual pieces.

Denomination	Metal	Weight (grams)	Diameter (mm)	Rev. alignment
Maundy Fourpence	Silver	1.9	18	↓

Obverse 1   Head 1, left; GEORGIUS IIII D G BRITANNIAR REX F D

Reverse 1   Crowned '4' and divided date, all within wreath

Edge   plain

No.	Date	Features	Obv.	Rev.	VF	EF	FDC
G44M-005	1822–30 [1]		1	1	12	20	30

1. Proofs were struck in 1822, 1828.

William IV   (1830 – 1837)

Denomination	Metal	Weight (grams)	Diameter (mm)	Rev. alignment
Maundy Fourpence	Silver	1.9	18	↓

Obverse 1   Head 1, right; GULIELMUS IIII D G BRITANNIAR REX F D

Reverse 1   Crowned '4' and divided date, all within wreath

Edge   plain

No.	Date	Features	Obv.	Rev.	VF	EF	FDC
W44M-005	1831–37 [1]		1	1	15	25	35

1. Proofs in gold and silver were struck in 1831; proofs may exist for 1834.

Victoria   (1837 – 1901)

The Maundy fourpence of 1853 frequently turns up in about fine condition. Presumably it was used as currency in place of the groat, which had become scarce.

Denomination	Metal	Weight (grams)	Diameter (mm)	Rev. alignment
Maundy Fourpence 1838–87	Silver	1.9	18	↓
Maundy Fourpence 1888–1901	Silver	1.9	18	↑

Obverse 1   Head 1, left; VICTORIA D G BRITANNIAR REGINA F D

Obverse 2   Head 2, left; same legend

Obverse 3   Head 3, left; VICTORIA DEI GRA BRITT REGINA FID DEF IND IMP

Reverse 1   Crowned '4' and divided date, all within wreath

Reverse 2   Similar but crown very different

Edge   plain

No.	Date	Features	Obv.	Rev.	VF	EF	FDC
VY4M-005	1838–87 [1]		1	1	10	14	18
VJ4M-010	1888–92 [2]		2	2	12	15	18
VO4M-015	1893–1901		3	2	6	10	14

1. Proofs were struck in 1838 (silver and gold); 1839, 1853, 1867, 1871, 1878, 1881 (silver).
2. Proofs were struck in 1888.

For details of proofs see Maundy listings, p.624.

Edward VII   (1901 – 1910)

Denomination	Metal	Weight (grams)	Diameter (mm)	Rev. alignment
Maundy Fourpence	Silver	1.9	18	↑

Obverse 1   Head 1, right; EDWARDVS VII D G BRITT OMN REX F D IND IMP

Reverse 1   Crowned '4' and divided date, all within wreath

Edge   plain

No.	Date	Features	Obv.	Rev.	VF	EF	FDC
E74M-005	1902–1910 [1]		1	1	6	10	14

1. Matt proofs were struck in 1902.

George V   (1910 – 1936)

Denomination	Metal	Weight (grams)	Diameter (mm)	Rev. alignment
Maundy Fourpence 1911–20	0.925 Silver	1.9	18	↑
Maundy Fourpence 1921–36	0.500 Silver	1.9	18	↑

Obverse 1   Head 1, left; GEORGIVS V D G BRITT OMN REX F D IND IMP

Obverse 2   Head 2, so-called 'modified effigy', left; same legend

Obverse 3   Head 2, re-engraved, left; same legend

Reverse 1   Crowned '4' and divided date, all within wreath

Edge   plain

No.	Date	Features	Obv.	Rev.	VF	EF	FDC
G54M-005	1911–27 [1]		1	1	8	11	16
G54M-010	1928–29		2	1	8	11	16
G54M-015	1930–36		3	1	8	11	16

1. See comment on 1911 issue under Maundy sets, p. 625

George VI   (1937 – 1952)

Denomination	Metal	Weight (grams)	Diameter (mm)	Rev. alignment
Maundy Fourpence 1937–46	0.500 Silver	1.9	18	↑
Maundy Fourpence 1947–52	0.925 Silver	1.9	18	↑

Obverse 1   Head 1, left; GEORGIVS VI D G BR OMN REX F D IND IMP

Obverse 2   Head 1, left; GEORGIVS VI D G BR OMN REX FIDEI DEF

Reverse 1   Crowned '4' and divided date, all within wreath

Edge   plain

No.	Date	Features	Obv.	Rev.	VF	EF	FDC
G64M-005	1937–48 [1]		1	1	8	10	14
G64M-010	1949–52 [2]		2	1	8	11	15

1. See comment on 1937 issue under Maundy sets, p.626.
2. 1952 sets struck in copper also exist.

Elizabeth II   (1952 –)

Denomination	Metal	Weight (grams)	Diameter (mm)	Rev. alignment
Maundy Fourpence	0.925 Silver	1.9	18	↑

Obverse 1   Head 1, right; ELIZABETH II DEI GRA BRITT OMN REGINA F D

Obverse 2   Head 2, recut; ELIZABETH II DEI GRATIA REGINA F D

Reverse 1   Crowned '4' and divided date, all within wreath

Edge   plain

No.	Date	Features	Obv.	Rev.	VF	EF	FDC
EZ4M-005	1953	1	1	1	55	65	70
EZ4M-010	1954–97		2	1	14	17	20

1. Varieties: see under Maundy sets, p.626.

Groat

The Britannia groat is characteristically so different from its Maundy counterpart that it is here treated in a separate section. The Maundy-type small silver coinage had generally ceased to be used in circulation at the time of the inception of the Britannia groat. The latter was, therefore, together with the silver three-pence, the only silver coinage denominated below the sixpence; some pieces, however, notably the silver one and a half-pence series and the 1838 twopence, circulated in the colonies.

Because the William IV groat was struck for only two years, and the transition to Victoria involved no change of reverse, the listing covers the entire series across the change of monarch.

The groat appears to have been coined following a recommendation of the philanthropist Joseph Hume, M.P. It was thus the original coin to bear the nickname 'silver Joey', a term later used for the threepence. It was initially popular for the payment of London hackney (taxi) fares, being the exact fare for half a mile, but the popularity did not extend to the hackney driver, as prior to its inception the client had often paid for his fare using a six-pence, without asking for change!

The Britannia groat was introduced simultaneously into the currency of British Guiana as the equivalent of a quarter guilder. When, however, in 1845 the silver threepence became legal tender in Britain, confusion arose. It is not generally realised that the Britannia groat is exactly the same size as the threepence (although it is thicker and heavier). Despite the fact that the edges are different, the two could not live happily together, and no currency groats were struck after 1855 apart from the 1888 issue struck for British Guiana. Apparently the groat was more popular in Scotland, and circulated there for many years after its demise in England and Wales.

The dies for the Britannia groat were designed by William Wyon, although the obverse of the isolated 1888 issue uses the Boehm jubilee portrait of Victoria.

Collecting Hints

Although at first glance a series consisting of one basic design might appear uninteresting, this series is a fascinating one. Rare and spectacular overdates abound; several plain edge proofs exist, several of which turn up unnoticed in about very fine condition from time to time. Some of the dates are extremely difficult to locate.
One or two of the overdates are remarkably bold and appear to be 'underdates', i.e. the later figure appears to lie underneath the earlier one.
Victoria young head groat obverses were struck in high relief, and it is difficult to find specimens without a trace of wear on the portrait.

Denomination	Metal	Weight (grams)	Diameter (mm)	Rev. alignment
Groat	Silver	1.9	16	↑

Obverse 1 Head 1 (William IV), right; GULIELMUS IIII D G BRITANNIAR REX F D

Obverse 2 Head 2 (Victoria), left; VICTORIA D G BRITANNIAR REGINA F D

Obverse 3 Head 3 (Victoria), left; same legend

Reverse 1 Britannia, seated, with shield; FOUR PENCE; date in exergue

Edge milled

Obv. 1   Obv. 2   Obv. 3   Rev. 1

William IV

No.	Date	Features	Obv.	Rev.	F	VF	EF	UNC
W44D-005	1836	[1]	1	1	7	10	24	50
W44D-010	1836	PROOF	1	1				400
W44D-015	1836	PROOF; edge plain	1	1				400
W44D-020	1836	PROOF in gold	1	1				4000
W44D-025	1836	PROOF on thin flan [2]	1	1				800
W44D-030	1837	[3]	1	1	8	12	28	50
W44D-035	1837	PROOF	1	1				700
W44D-038	1837	PROOF; rev. ↓	1	1				700
W44D-040	1837	PROOF; edge plain	1	1				900

1. Occurs with either near or far colons after D G (obv.).
2. Weight 1.3 grams.
3. Minor differences occur to head (obv.).

Victoria

No.	Date	Features	Obv.	Rev.	F	VF	EF	UNC
VY4D-005	1837	PROOF or pattern; rev. ↓	2	1				1500
VY4D-010	1837	PROOF or pattern; edge plain [1]	2	1				1500
VY4D-015	1838		2	1	7	10	24	40
VY4D-020	1838	PROOF; edge plain	2	1				350
VY4D-025	1838	latter 8 over horizontal 8	2	1	15	22	50	100
VY4D-030	1839	[2]	2	1	7	11	26	42
VY4D-035	1839	PROOF; edge plain [3]	2	1				200
VY4D-040	1839	PROOF; edge plain; rev. ↓ [3]	2	1				220
VY4D-045	1840	[4]	2	1	7	10	24	45
VY4D-050	1841	latter 1 over inverted 1	2	1	8	12	28	55
VY4D-055	1842		2	1	7	11	26	50
VY4D-060	1842	PROOF; edge plain	2	1				600
VY4D-065	1842	2 over 1	2	1	9	15	35	60
VY4D-070	1843		2	1	9	15	35	60
VY4D-075	1843	4 over 5	2	1	15	25	50	110
VY4D-080	1844		2	1	10	16	38	65
VY4D-085	1845		2	1	9	15	35	60
VY4D-090	1846		2	1	9	15	35	60
VY4D-095	1847	7 over 6	2	1	30	100	300	
VY4D-100	1848		2	1	10	16	38	60
VY4D-102	1848	G of DG over sideways G (obv.)	2	1	35	75	200	350
VY4D-105	1848	latter 8 over 6	2	1	12	20	50	90
VY4D-110	1848	latter 8 over 7	2	1	15	25	60	120
VY4D-115	1849		2	1	10	16	38	60
VY4D-120	1849	9 over 8	2	1	12	20	50	85
VY4D-125	1851		2	1	25	90	300	
VY4D-130	1852	[5]	2	1	40	130	450	
VY4D-135	1853		2	1	50	160	500	
VY4D-140	1853	PROOF [6]	2	1				350
VY4D-145	1853	PROOF; edge plain	2	1				600
VY4D-150	1854		2	1	6	9	20	30
VY4D-155	1855		2	1	6	9	20	30
VY4D-160	1857	PROOF [7]	2	1				950
VY4D-165	1862	PROOF	2	1				900

No.	Date	Features	Obv.	Rev.	F	VF	EF	UNC
VY4D-170	1862	PROOF; edge plain [7]	2	1				900

1. Obverse differs slightly (from a threepence die).
2. 9 of date varies in size; can be larger or smaller than 3.
3. Some or all issued in cased proof sets.
4. 0 in date and size of date vary.
5. 2 in date is unusually large on some specimens.
6. Issued in cased proof sets; minor obverse differences exist.
7. Minor obverse differences exist (truncation).

No.	Date	Features	Obv.	Rev.	F	VF	EF	UNC
VJ4D-175	1888	[1]	3	1	8	14	35	65
VJ4D-180	1888	PROOF	3	1				850

1. Issued for Colonial use.

Silver Threepence

Charles II   (1660 – 1685)

Although the earlier threepence is often wrongly termed a Maundy coin, it is easier to appreciate it as a currency coin because it continued as such well into the 20th century. The so-called 'undated Maundy' coins were probably designed by Thomas Simon in 1664 or 1665, shortly before he died. The first dated issue, by John Roettier, appeared in 1670, together with most of the other small silver, although the twopence had first appeared in 1668. Like the other small silver, the dated threepence made use of a reverse motif of 'C's (the initial letter of Charles), the three 'C's indicating three pence. As with the fourpence and twopence, the date most usually encountered is 1679.

Denomination	Metal	Weight (grams)	Diameter (mm)	Rev. alignment
Threepence undated	Silver	1.5	17	varies
Threepence 1670–84	Silver	1.5	17	↓

Obverse 1   Head 1, crowned, left; III behind head; CAROLVS II D G M B F & H REX

Obverse 2   Head 2, right; CAROLVS II DEI GRATIA

Reverse 1   Shield enclosing arms of England, Scotland, Ireland, France; CHRISTO AVSPICE REGNO

Reverse 2   Three crowned interlinked 'C's; MAG BR FRA ET HIB REX (date)

Edge   plain

| Obv. 1 | Obv. 2 | Rev. 1 | Rev. 2 |

No.	Date	Features	Obv.	Rev.	F	VF	EF
C23MM-005	none		1	1	18	35	70
C23MM-010	1670		2	2	16	25	55
C23MM-015	1671		2	2	16	25	55
C23MM-020	1671	first A in GRATIA inverted	2	2	18	30	65
C23MM-025	1671	first A in GRATIA unbarred	2	2	18	30	65
C23MM-030	1672	2 over 1	2	2	16	25	55
C23MM-035	1673		2	2	16	25	55
C23MM-040	1674		2	2	18	30	65
C23MM-045	1675		2	2	18	30	65
C23MM-050	1676		2	2	16	25	55
C23MM-055	1676	latter 6 over 5	2	2	18	30	65
C23MM-060	1676	ERA instead of FRA (rev.)	2	2	18	30	65
C23MM-065	1677		2	2	18	30	65
C23MM-070	1678	[1]	2	2	16	25	55
C23MM-075	1679		2	2	15	22	45
C23MM-080	1679	O of CAROLVS over A (obv.)	2	2	18	30	65
C23MM-085	1680	[2]	2	2	16	25	55
C23MM-090	1681		2	2	16	25	55
C23MM-095	1681	latter 1 over 0	2	2	16	25	55
C23MM-100	1682		2	2	16	25	55
C23MM-105	1682	2 over 1	2	2	16	25	55
C23MM-110	1683		2	2	16	25	55
C23MM-115	1684		2	2	16	25	55
C23MM-120	1684	4 over 3	2	2	16	25	55

1. Lettering size varies.
2. Some are struck from a badly cracked die.

James II   (1685 – 1688)

John Roettier continued as designer, producing a threepence similar in style to the Charles II coin. The interlinked 'C's are replaced by the symbol III, continuing the motif of three regnal initials (IACOBUS) as well as denoting the denomination '3'.

The James threepence in particular suffers from metal transfer during striking, as a result of the somewhat high relief portrait to which metal was displaced during the process from the reverse. This resulted in the coin appearing to have a worn or weakly struck reverse in the centre. This phenomenon should be taken into account when grading this particular coin.

Denomination	Metal	Weight (grams)	Diameter (mm)	Rev. alignment
Threepence	Silver	1.5	17	↓

Obverse 1   Head 1, left; IACOBVS II DEI GRATIA

Reverse 1   Large III, crowned; MAG BR FRA ET HIB REX (date)

Edge   plain

| Obv. 1 | Rev. 1 |

No.	Date	Features	Obv.	Rev.	F	VF	EF
J23M-005	1685		1	1	16	25	50
J23M-010	1685	die axes at 90 degrees	1	1	50	80	150
J23M-015	1685	struck on fourpence flan	1	1	100	180	350
J23M-020	1686		1	1	16	25	50
J23M-022	1686	1I instead of II (obv)	1	1	25	40	80
J23M-025	1687		1	1	16	25	50
J23M-030	1687	7 over 6	1	1	16	25	50
J23M-035	1688		1	1	16	25	50
J23M-040	1688	latter 8 over 7	1	1	16	25	50

William & Mary   (1688 – 1694)

The unknown designer of the first type of William and Mary small silver coinage produced a somewhat caricatured portrait of the two monarchs. As postulated under the fourpence entry for this reign, the design may have been the work of George Bower. A rather more staid double portrait was introduced during 1691. The reverse, representing a crowned Arabic numeral has lasted, with modifications, up to the present day.

This series is fairly rare in extremely fine or better condition.

Denomination	Metal	Weight (grams)	Diameter (mm)	Rev. alignment
Threepence	Silver	1.5	17	↓

Obverse 1   Heads 1, right; little or no tie at back of king's head; GVLIELMVS ET MARIA D G

Obverse 2   Heads 2, with tie, right; same legend

Reverse 1   Crowned '3'; MAG BR FR ET HIB REX ET REGINA (date)

Edge   plain

| Obv. 1 | Obv. 2 | Rev. 1 |

No.	Date	Features	Obv.	Rev.	F	VF	EF
WM3M-005	1689	[1]	1	1	15	24	60
WM3M-010	1689	rev. stops are hyphens	1	1	15	24	60
WM3M-015	1689	GVLIE(LMV over MVS)S (obv.)	1	1	16	25	60
WM3M-020	1689	no stops on rev.	1	1	16	25	60
WM3M-025	1690		1	1	16	25	60
WM3M-030	1690	6 over 5	1	1	18	30	70
WM3M-035	1690	9 over 6 or inverted 9	1	1	18	30	70
WM3M-040	1690	9 over 6 or inverted 9; BR FR over BB FB (rev.)	1	1	24	38	85
WM3M-045	1691		1	1	25	45	110
WM3M-050	1691	[2]	2	1	18	30	70
WM3M-055	1692	[2]	2	1	18	30	70
WM3M-060	1693	[2]	2	1	18	30	70
WM3M-065	1693	3 over 2 [2]	2	1	18	30	70
WM3M-070	1694	[2]	2	1	18	30	70
WM3M-075	1694	MΛRIΛ instead of MARIA (obv.) [2]	2	1	18	30	70

1. Date and stop varieties exist.
2. Date and lettering positioning varies.

Variations in the shape of the crown occur on the reverse.

William III   (1695 – 1701)

The threepence obverse was the work of Johann Crocker (John Croker). The reverse may have been by him and/or an assistant. The design concept continues from that of William and Mary. As the coins were produced after the closure of the provincial mints, none bears a mintmark. Why no small silver was produced at the provincial mints or before 1698 (apart from the unique 1697 four-pence) is open to question. It has been conjectured that this was because the Maundy ceremony was always held in London, but in fact probably only silver pennies were used during the ceremony.

Denomination	Metal	Weight (grams)	Diameter (mm)	Rev. alignment
Threepence	Silver	1.5	17	↓

Obverse 1   Head 1, right; GVLIELMVS III DEI GRA

Reverse 1   Crowned '3'; MAG BR FRA ET HIB REX (date)

Edge   plain

| Obv. 1 | Rev. 1 |

No.	Date	Features	Obv.	Rev.	F	VF	EF
W33M-005	1698		1	1	18	30	70
W33M-010	1699		1	1	18	30	70
W33M-015	1700		1	1	18	30	70
W33M-020	1701	Z-type '1's in date	1	1	18	30	70
W33M-025	1701	Z-type '1's in date; GBA instead of GRA (obv.)	1	1	18	30	70
W33M-030	1701	J-type '1's in date [1]	1	1	18	30	70

1. Larger lettering than Z-type variety.

Anne   (1702 – 1714)

There is doubt about the attribution of the threepences of Anne, especially for the reverse. However, it appears that John Croker and/or his assistant Samuel Bull may have been responsible for the obverses.

Denomination	Metal	Weight (grams)	Diameter (mm)	Rev. alignment
Threepence	Silver	1.5	17	↓

Obverse 1   Head 1, left; ANNA DEI GRATIA

Obverse 2   Similar but head is larger; hair and brooch are different

Reverse 1   Crowned '3'; MAG BR FR ET HIB REG (date)

Reverse 2   Similar but MAG BR FRA ET HIB REG

Reverse 3   Similar but MAG BRI FR ET HIB REG

Edge   plain

| Obv. 1 | Obv. 2 | Rev. 3 |

No.	Date	Features	Obv.	Rev.	F	VF	EF
AN3M-005	1703	[1]	1	1	18	35	75
AN3M-010	1704		1	1	15	30	70
AN3M-015	1705		1	1	15	30	70
AN3M-020	1706		1	2	15	30	70
AN3M-025	1707		1	1	15	30	70
AN3M-030	1708		1	3	15	30	70
AN3M-035	1709		1	3	15	30	70
AN3M-040	1710		1	3	15	30	70
AN3M-045	1713		1	3	15	30	70
AN3M-050	1713		2	3	15	30	70

1. Position of date varies.

Minor head varieties may exist for some of these dates.

George I   (1714 – 1727)

The basic design of earlier reigns is continued through the reign of George I. Designed by John Croker, assisted by Samuel Bull, the obverse omits the lengthy German titles of the king which are included on the larger silver denominations. The reverse may have been the work of Johann Rudolf Ochs, senior.

Denomination	Metal	Weight (grams)	Diameter (mm)	Rev. alignment
Threepence	Silver	1.5	17	↓

Obverse 1   Head 1, right; GEORGIVS DEI GRA

Reverse 1   Crowned '3'; MAG BRI FR ET HIB REX (date)

Edge   plain

| Obv. 1 | Rev. 1 |

No.	Date	Obv.	Rev.	F	VF	EF
G13M-005	1717	1	1	20	35	80
G13M-010	1721	1	1	20	35	80
G13M-015	1723	1	1	20	40	90
G13M-020	1727	1	1	20	35	80

George II (1727 – 1760)

The young portrait of the king by John Croker was used throughout the series. This is remarkable, given that on the larger silver the portrait was superseded by an older portrait as early as 1743. The last striking of the threepence in 1760 occurred 19 years after Croker's death and two years after the issue of the last of the large silver. The reverses of this series may have been the work of the Assistant Engraver, Johann Sigismund Tanner.

Denomination	Metal	Weight (grams)	Diameter (mm)	Rev. alignment
Threepence	Silver	1.5	17	↓

Obverse 1   Head 1, left; GEORGIVS II DEI GRATIA

Reverse 1   Crowned '3'; MAG BRI FR ET HIB REX (date);

Reverse 2   Similar but a slightly different crown

Reverse 3   Similar but a different crown

Edge   plain

Obv. 1   Rev. 3

No.	Date	Features	Obv.	Rev.	F	VF	EF
G23M-005	1729		1	1	15	25	55
G23M-010	1731		1	2	18	30	65
G23M-015	1731	small obverse lettering	1	2	18	30	65
G23M-020	1732	no stop over head	1	3	18	30	65
G23M-025	1732	stop over head	1	3	18	30	65
G23M-030	1735		1	3	18	30	65
G23M-035	1737		1	3	15	25	55
G23M-040	1739	[1]	1	3	15	25	55
G23M-045	1740		1	3	15	25	55
G23M-050	1743	large obv. and rev. lettering	1	3	15	25	55
G23M-055	1743	small lettering no stop over head	1	3	15	25	55
G23M-060	1743	small lettering stop over head	1	3	15	25	55
G23M-065	1746	[2]	1	3	15	25	55
G23M-070	1746	6 over 3 or 5	1	3	15	25	55
G23M-075	1760		1	3	15	25	60

1. Several stops usually missing on reverse.
2. Exists without overdate?

George III (1760 – 1820)

Although the silver threepence was minted as a currency coin until well into the twentieth century, an alteration in the purpose of this coin undoubtedly occurred during the long reign of George III. The first two years of minting, 1762 and 1763, saw a prolific issue which was obviously intended for general circulation, as these coins normally turn up in fine or very fine condition. On the other hand, the threepences of the last type (1817–20) are usually found in very fine or extremely fine condition, indicating that their primary use was probably as a Maundy issue.

The first issue of 1762 and 1763 bears a portrait similar to that on the Northumberland shilling and the early guineas, which were the work of Richard Yeo. However, the obverse of this issue was designed and engraved by Ochs, junior. These dates, amongst the most easily found of all threepences, are followed by one of the rarest, 1765, and careful date checking is therefore essential!

The very different head of 1792 coincided with the new 'Wire Money' numerals on the reverse, thereafter abandoned. This issue was designed by Lewis Pingo. The obverse head was retained for the issue of 1795 and 1800, when the series was discontinued until after the 'Great Recoinage' in 1816.

Denomination	Metal	Weight (grams)	Diameter (mm)	Rev. alignment
Threepence 1762–86	Silver	1.5	17	↓
Threepence 1792–1800	Silver	1.5	17	↑
Threepence 1817–20	Silver	1.4	16	↑

Obverse 1   Head 1, right; GEORGIVS III DEI GRATIA

Obverse 2   Head 2, right; same legend

Obverse 3   Head 3, laureate, right; GEORGIUS III DEI GRATIA (date)

Reverse 1   Crowned '3' in high relief; MAG BRI FR ET HIB REX (date, across crown)

Reverse 2   Completely redesigned; stylised '3' under small crown; date below '3'; same legend

Reverse 3   Redesigned; more similar to Reverse 1 but crown very different; same legend; date is below '3'

Reverse 4   Crowned '3'; BRITANNIARUM REX FID DEF (no date)

Edge   plain

Obv. 1   Obv. 2   Obv. 3

Rev. 1   Rev. 2   Rev. 3   Rev. 4

No.	Date	Features	Obv.	Rev.	F	VF	EF
G33M-005	1762	[1]	1	1	8	15	35
G33M-010	1763	[2]	1	1	8	15	35
G33M-015	1763	PROOF; rev. ↑	1	1			1000
G33M-020	1765		1	1	150	350	800
G33M-022	1765	5 over 4	1	1	250	600	1500
G33M-025	1766		1	1	12	20	40
G33M-030	1770		1	1	12	20	40
G33M-035	1772	small lettering	1	1	12	20	40
G33M-040	1772	large lettering; large III	1	1	12	20	40
G33M-045	1772	large lettering; small III	1	1	12	20	40
G33M-050	1780		1	1	12	20	40
G33M-055	1784	[3]	1	1	14	22	45
G33M-060	1786		1	1	12	20	40
G33M-065	1792	[4]	2	2	20	32	80
G33M-070	1795		2	3	12	20	40
G33M-075	1800		2	3	10	18	40
G33M-080	1817		3	4	12	18	40
G33M-085	1818		3	4	12	18	40
G33M-090	1820		3	4	12	18	40

1. Minor design variations; possibly over 40 different dies.
2. Minor design variations.
3. Obverse legend larger than usual.
4. 'Wire Money' issue.

George IV (1820 – 1830)

By now the silver threepence was being struck primarily as a Maundy coin, although some were sent to the Colonies for use as currency. However, the George IV threepence is frequently found in well-circulated state, no doubt due to its being taken from Maundy sets and spent during the reign of Victoria when the circulation coin was reintroduced.

Because the Maundy coinage is dealt with separately, including details of varieties, Maundy issue threepences from George IV onwards appear in an abbreviated form.

It is worth mentioning, however, the odd case of the 1822 threepence. This bears an unusually small head, from a twopence punch. Hawkins (1887) states that the correct punch broke and the smaller one was substituted. The error was apparently rectified in time for coining the 1823 threepence.

Denomination	Metal	Weight (grams)	Diameter (mm)	Rev. alignment
Maundy Threepence	Silver	1.4	16	↓

Obverse 1   Head 1, left (small, from a twopence punch); GEORGIUS IIII D G BRITANNIAR REX F D

Obverse 2   Head 2, left (normal size); same legend

Reverse 1   Crowned '3' and divided date, all within wreath

Edge   plain

Obv. 2   Rev. 1

No.	Date	Feature	Obv.	Rev.	VF	EF	FDC
G43M-005	1822	1	1	1	20	35	50
G43M-010	1823–30	2	2	1	12	20	30

1. Proofs were struck.
2. Proofs were struck in 1828.

William IV   (1830 – 1837)

Denomination	Metal	Weight (grams)	Diameter (mm)	Rev. alignment
Maundy Threepence	Silver	1.4	16	↓

Obverse 1   Head 1, right; GULIELMUS IIII D G BRITANNIAR REX F D

Reverse 1   Crowned '3' and divided date, all within wreath

Edge   plain

No.	Date	Features	Obv.	Rev.	VF	EF	FDC
W43M-005	1831–37	1	1	1	20	35	50

1. Proofs in gold and silver were struck in 1831; proofs may exist for 1834.

Currency threepences of identical design were struck for Colonial use as below; these differ from the Maundy threepence in not having a prooflike surface.

Denomination	Metal	Weight (grams)	Diameter (mm)	Rev. alignment
Non-Maundy Threepence	Silver	1.4	16	↓

Obverse 1   Head 1, right; GULIELMUS IIII D G BRITANNIAR REX F D

Reverse 1   Crowned '3' and divided date, all within wreath

Edge   plain

Obv. 1   Rev. 1

No.	Date	Features	Obv.	Rev.	F	VF	EF	UNC
W43D-005	1834		1	1	5	20	55	90
W43D-010	1835		1	1	5	18	50	80
W43D-015	1836		1	1	5	20	55	90
W43D-020	1837		1	1	7	22	60	100

Victoria   (1837 – 1901)

Denomination	Metal	Weight (grams)	Diameter (mm)	Rev. alignment
Maundy Threepence 1838–87	Silver	1.4	16	↓
Maundy Threepence 1888–1901	Silver	1.4	16	↑

Obverse 1   Head 1, left; VICTORIA D G BRITANNIAR REGINA F D

Obverse 2   Head 2, left; same legend

Obverse 3   Head 3, left; VICTORIA DEI GRA BRITT REGINA FID DEF IND IMP

Reverse 1   Crowned '3' and divided date, all within wreath

Reverse 2   Similar but crown very different

Edge   plain

No.	Date	Features	Obv.	Rev.	EF	FDC
VY3M-005	1838–87	1	1	1	25	35
VJ3M-010	1888–92	2	2	2	25	35
VO3M-015	1893–1901		3	2	20	25

1. Proofs were struck in 1838 (silver and gold); 1839, 1853, 1867, 1871, 1878, 1881 (silver).
2. Proofs were struck in 1888.

For details of proofs see Maundy listings, p.624.

One of the oddities of the British series is the fact that the currency silver threepence from 1838 to 1926 was of identical design to that of the Maundy threepence, except for some of the 1887 and 1893 coins. In the higher grades, they can usually be distinguished from one another because the Maundy pieces are more sharply struck and usually have a more prooflike field. This difference is more apparent from 1888 onwards.

For the young head series of Victoria, the difference most usually cited, the prooflike field or lack of it, is by no means a certain indication as to whether a coin is a currency or Maundy issue. It is relatively easy to find mint state Maundy fourpences without any trace of a prooflike field, and presumably the same applies for the threepences. The better guideline is the sharpness of the strike, especially of the wreath on the reverse, and a trained eye will distinguish between the fineness of the detail on a Maundy piece as against a currency coin, especially on the reverse.

A curious legal anomaly has arisen because of the impossibility of distinguishing worn currency threepences from their Maundy counterparts. When decimalization was introduced in 1971, the Maundy coins maintained their legal tender status, and of course this had to be in new pence. Because of the indistinguishability of the two threepences, the currency and the Maundy threepences from 1870 were both decreed to be legal tender for 3 new pence, i.e. the old currency coins were revalued at 2.4 times their original value!

The first Victorian currency threepences used the young head portrait by William Wyon and a reverse by Johann Baptiste Merlen. They were initially struck for colonial use, but in 1845 entered general circulation in the British Isles. However, because of their close relationship to British coinage, all of the dates from 1838 are included in this book. No threepences are recorded as having been struck in 1847, 1848 and 1852 and the probable explanation for this is that at this time there was much interest in the possible advent of decimal currency; the threepence, at one-eighteenth of a pound, would not easily have fit into any decimal scheme. A. Milward, in a letter to the Chancellor of the Exchequer in 1853 advocating the issue of a decimal five-farthing piece, observed that 'shopkeepers do not offer threepenny and fourpenny pieces in change to the lower classes; their hands are hardened by manual labour and they dislike them.'

Collecting Hints

The Victorian silver threepence series is one of the most difficult to collect in top condition. A popular and much-used coin, it circulated extensively, and its small size did not at the time make it an obvious candidate for collecting. Now, however, it is recognised as a fascinating series and its rarity in higher grades increases its appeal. The rarity of some of the dates in extremely fine or better condition is probably much underrated. However, care must be taken that one does not buy a Maundy threepence sold as a currency piece.

Denomination	Metal	Weight (grams)	Diameter (mm)	Rev. alignment
Non-Maundy Threepence 1838–87 obv. 1	Silver	1.4	16	↓
Non-Maundy Threepence 1887–1901 obvs 2–3	Silver	1.4	16	↑

Obverse 1 Head 1, left; VICTORIA D G BRITANNIAR REGINA F D

Obverse 2 Head 2, left; same legend

Obverse 3 Head 3, left; VICTORIA DEI GRA BRITT REGINA FID DEF IND IMP

Reverse 1 Crowned '3' and divided date, all within wreath

Reverse 2 Similar but crown very different

Edge plain

Obv. 1 Obv. 2 Obv. 3 Rev. 1 Rev. 2

Young Head

No.	Date	Features	Obv.	Rev.	F	VF	EF	UNC
VY3D-005	1838	[1]	1	1	6	12	50	80
VY3D-010	1839	[2]	1	1	6	14	60	100
VY3D-015	1840		1	1	6	14	60	100
VY3D-020	1841		1	1	7	16	65	110
VY3D-025	1842		1	1	7	16	65	110
VY3D-030	1843		1	1	5	12	50	80
VY3D-035	1844		1	1	7	16	65	110
VY3D-040	1845	[3]	1	1	6	14	55	90
VY3D-045	1846		1	1	30	70	150	
VY3D-050	1849		1	1	8	20	80	130
VY3D-055	1850		1	1	5	12	50	80
VY3D-060	1851		1	1	5	12	50	80
VY3D-062	1851	8 under 5 (i.e. appears as 1551)	1	1	10	22	90	140
VY3D-065	1852		1	1	50	100	250	
VY3D-070	1853	[2]	1	1	30	70	150	
VY3D-075	1854		1	1	5	12	50	80
VY3D-080	1855		1	1	6	14	55	90
VY3D-085	1856		1	1	6	14	55	90
VY3D-090	1857		1	1	6	14	55	90
VY3D-095	1858		1	1	5	12	50	80
VY3D-098	1858	latter 8 over 6	1	1	8	18	75	110
VY3D-100	1858	BRITANNIAB instead of BRITANNIAR (obv.)	1	1	50	150		
VY3D-105	1859	[4]	1	1	5	10	40	65
VY3D-110	1860		1	1	7	16	65	110
VY3D-115	1861		1	1	5	10	40	65
VY3D-120	1862		1	1	5	12	50	80
VY3D-125	1863		1	1	5	12	50	80
VY3D-130	1864		1	1	5	10	40	65
VY3D-135	1865		1	1	5	12	50	80
VY3D-140	1866		1	1	5	10	40	65
VY3D-145	1867	[2]	1	1	5	10	40	65
VY3D-150	1868		1	1	5	9	35	60

No.	Date	Features	Obv.	Rev.	F	VF	EF	UNC
VY3D-155	1868	RRITANNIAR instead of BRITANNIAR (obv.)	1	1	30	100		
VY3D-160	1869		1	1	6	14	55	90
VY3D-165	1870		1	1	5	9	35	60
VY3D-170	1871	[2]	1	1	5	10	40	65
VY3D-175	1872		1	1	5	10	40	65
VY3D-180	1873		1	1	5	9	35	55
VY3D-185	1874		1	1	5	9	35	55
VY3D-190	1875		1	1	5	9	35	55
VY3D-195	1876		1	1	5	9	35	55
VY3D-200	1877		1	1	5	9	35	55
VY3D-205	1878	[2]	1	1	5	9	35	55
VY3D-208	1878	B of BRITANNIAR under R (obv.)	1	1	8	15	55	80
VY3D-210	1879		1	1	5	9	35	55
VY3D-215	1879	PROOF; rev. ↑	1	1				600
VY3D-220	1880		1	1	5	9	35	55
VY3D-225	1881	[2]	1	1	5	9	35	55
VY3D-230	1882		1	1	5	9	35	55
VY3D-235	1883		1	1	5	8	30	45
VY3D-240	1884		1	1	5	8	30	45
VY3D-245	1885		1	1	5	8	30	45
VY3D-250	1886		1	1	5	8	30	45
VY3D-255	1887		1	1	5	8	30	45
VY3D-260	1887	PROOF	1	1				200

1. Proofs in gold/silver included in Maundy set listings.
2. Proofs included in Maundy set listings.
3. Date numerals vary in size; coin introduced into British Isles this year.
4. Date numerals vary.

Jubilee Head

No.	Date	Features	Obv.	Rev.	F	VF	EF	UNC
VJ3D-265	1887	[1]	2	2	5	7	12	20
VJ3D-270	1887	PROOF [2]	2	2				50
VJ3D-275	1888	[3]	2	2	5	8	14	25
VJ3D-280	1889	[1]	2	2	5	8	12	30
VJ3D-285	1890		2	2	5	8	14	40
VJ3D-290	1891		2	2	5	8	15	42
VJ3D-295	1892		2	2	5	8	16	45
VJ3D-300	1893	[4]	2	2	7	25	130	350

1. Minor variations in crown occur (obv.).
2. Issued in cased proof sets.
3. Proofs included in Maundy set listings.
4. 3 in date varies.

Old Head

No.	Date	Features	Obv.	Rev.	F	VF	EF	UNC
VO3D-305	1893		3	2	4	7	10	18
VO3D-310	1893	PROOF [1]	3	2				70
VO3D-315	1894		3	2	5	8	14	25
VO3D-320	1895		3	2	5	8	14	25
VO3D-325	1896		3	2	4	7	10	20
VO3D-330	1897		3	2	4	7	10	20
VO3D-335	1898		3	2	4	7	10	20
VO3D-340	1899		3	2	4	7	10	20
VO3D-345	1900		3	2	4	7	10	20
VO3D-350	1901		3	2	4	7	10	20

1. Issued in cased proof sets.

Small progressive modifications are made to Head 1 from time to time.

Edward VII (1901 – 1910)

Denomination	Metal	Weight (grams)	Diameter (mm)	Rev. alignment
Maundy Threepence	Silver	1.4	16	↑

Obverse 1 Head 1, right; EDWARDVS VII D G BRITT OMN REX F D IND IMP

Reverse 1 Crowned '3' and divided date, all within wreath

Edge plain

No.	Date	Features	Obv.	Rev.	EF	FDC
E73M-005	1902–10 [1]		1	1	12	18

1. Matt proofs were struck in 1902.

The currency threepence, like the other denominations, was issued for each of the nine years of the reign. The obverse used the mechanically reduced portrait of Edward by de Saulles, while the reverse continued the design of earlier reigns.

Denomination	Metal	Weight (grams)	Diameter (mm)	Rev. alignment
Non-Maundy Threepence	Silver	1.4	16	↑

Obverse 1   Head 1, right; EDWARDVS VII D G BRITT OMN REX F D IND IMP

Reverse 1   Crowned '3' and divided date, all within wreath

Edge   plain

Obv. 1   Rev. 1

No.	Date	Features	Obv.	Rev.	F	VF	EF	UNC
E73D-005	1902	[1]	1	1	3	5	8	15
E73D-010	1903		1	1	4	7	14	20
E73D-015	1904		1	1	5	10	25	45
E73D-020	1905		1	1	5	10	25	40
E73D-025	1906		1	1	4	8	25	45
E73D-030	1907		1	1	4	7	14	20
E73D-035	1908		1	1	4	7	14	20
E73D-040	1909		1	1	4	7	14	20
E73D-045	1910		1	1	4	6	12	18

1. Matt proofs included in Maundy set listings.

George V   (1910 – 1936)

Denomination	Metal	Weight (grams)	Diameter (mm)	Rev. alignment
Maundy Threepence 1911–20	0.925 Silver	1.4	16	↑
Maundy Threepence 1921–36	0.500 Silver	1.4	16	↑

Obverse 1   Head 1, left; GEORGIVS V D G BRITT OMN REX F D IND IMP

Obverse 2   Head 2, so-called 'modified effigy', left; same legend

Obverse 3   Head 2, re-engraved, left; same legend

Reverse 1   Crowned '3' and divided date, all within wreath

Edge   plain

No.	Date	Features	Obv.	Rev.	EF	FDC
G53M-005	1911–27 [1]		1	1	14	20
G53M-010	1928–29		2	1	14	20
G53M-015	1930–36		3	1	14	20

1. See comment on 1911 issue under Maundy sets, p.625.

The currency threepence again used the same design as the Maundy threepence at the beginning of the reign, but underwent a radical change in 1927. The proof set of that year introduced the new acorn reverse, a smaller version of the new sixpence reverse. In 1927 the only threepences bearing the new acorn design were the ones struck for the proof set, and the currency coin bearing the new design entered circulation in 1928. Occasionally one comes across worn coins of 1927–36 bearing the earlier '3' reverse, but these are invariably refugees from a Maundy set which were spent at the time.

Anyone buying or selling currency threepences by weight should note that these coins wear considerably in circulation. A fine con-

dition coin weighs about 1.34 grams, about 5% less than when it was struck. The writer has weighed a counted quantity of 1300 average circulated (F–VF) threepences dated 1919/1920 at 1783 grams.

Denomination	Metal	Weight (grams)	Diameter (mm)	Rev. alignment
Non-Maundy Threepence 1911–20	0.925 Silver	1.4	16	↑
Non-Maundy Threepence 1920–22	Silver 50%; copper 40%; nickel 10%	1.4	16	↑
Non-Maundy Threepence 1922–27	Silver 50%; copper 50%	1.4	16	↑
Non-Maundy Threepence 1927–36	Silver 50%; copper 40%; nickel 5%; zinc 5%	1.4	16	↑

Obverse 1   Head 1, left; GEORGIVS V D G BRITT OMN REX F D IND IMP

Obverse 2   Head 2, so-called 'modified effigy', left; same legend

Reverse 1   Crowned '3' and divided date, all within wreath

Reverse 2   Three oak-sprigs with three acorns; G in centre; THREE PENCE (date)

Edge   plain

Obv. 1   Obv. 2   Rev. 1   Rev. 2

Sterling Silver Issue

No.	Date	Features	Obv.	Rev.	VF	EF	UNC
G53D-005	1911	[1]	1	1	2	5	10
G53D-010	1912		1	1	2	5	10
G53D-015	1913		1	1	2	5	10
G53D-020	1914		1	1	2	5	10
G53D-025	1915		1	1	2	5	10
G53D-030	1916		1	1	2	5	10
G53D-035	1917		1	1	2	5	10
G53D-040	1918	[2]	1	1	2	5	10
G53D-045	1919	[2]	1	1	2	5	10

1. Minor obverse variations occur.
2. Overdates possibly exist.

50% Silver Issue

No.	Date	Features	Obv.	Rev.	VF	EF	UNC
G53D-050	1920	[1]	1	1	2	5	8
G53D-055	1921	[2]	1	1	2	5	8
G53D-060	1922		1	1	2	6	10
G53D-065	1925		1	1	4	20	45
G53D-070	1926		1	1	2	12	25
G53D-075	1926		2	1	2	6	10
G53D-080	1927	PROOF [3]	2	2	20	35	50
G53D-085	1927	PROOF from sandblasted dies [4]	2	2			200
G53D-090	1928		2	2	4	12	30
G53D-095	1928	PROOF	2	2			300
G53D-100	1930		2	2	2	8	18
G53D-105	1930	PROOF	2	2			250
G53D-110	1931		2	2	2	4	6
G53D-115	1931	PROOF	2	2			250
G53D-120	1932		2	2	2	4	6
G53D-125	1932	PROOF	2	2			250
G53D-130	1933		2	2	2	4	6
G53D-135	1933	PROOF	2	2			250
G53D-140	1934		2	2	2	4	6
G53D-145	1934	PROOF	2	2			250
G53D-150	1935		2	2	2	4	6
G53D-155	1935	PROOF	2	2			250
G53D-160	1936		2	2	2	4	5
G53D-165	1936	PROOF	2	2			250

1. Struck in both 0.500 and 0.925 silver.
2. 2 of date varies in size.

Notes continued
3. Issued in cased proof sets.
4. Struck to facilitate photography of coin.

Edward VIII (1936)

The Edward VIII silver threepence is strictly speaking a pattern, as probable Royal approval was about to be granted at the time of the abdication. However, because its official status rests only on this technicality, and to provide continuity, it is included here.

The portrait of Edward VIII is by Thomas Humphrey Paget, and faces left at the insistence of the king, who considered this placement more flattering and wished to discontinue the tradition of opposite facings for successive monarchs. The reverse is by George Kruger Gray (1880–1943)

Denomination	Metal	Weight (grams)	Diameter (mm)	Rev. alignment
Non-Maundy Threepence	Silver	1.4	16	↑

Obverse 1 Head 1, left; EDWARDVS VIII D G BR OMN REX

Reverse 1 Three interlinked rings of St Edmund; FID DEF IND IMP 1937 THREE PENCE

Edge plain

Obv. 1   Rev. 1

No.	Date			Obv.	Rev.			Unc
E83D-005	1937			1	1			10000

George VI (1937 – 1952)

Denomination	Metal	Weight (grams)	Diameter (mm)	Rev. alignment
Maundy Threepence 1937–46	0.500 Silver (see below)	1.4	16	↑
Maundy Threepence 1947–52	0.925 Silver	1.4	16	↑

There is a very slight difference in the base metal constituency of the 1937 Maundy set given at the Maundy ceremony compared with that of the set included in the 1937 proof set.

Obverse 1 Head 1, left; GEORGIVS VI D G BR OMN REX F D IND IMP

Obverse 2 Head 1, left; GEORGIVS VI D G BR OMN REX FIDEI DEF

Reverse 1 Crowned '3' and divided date, all within wreath

Edge plain

No.	Date	Features	Obv.	Rev.	EF	FDC
G63M-005	1937–48	[1]	1	1	12	18
G63M-010	1949–52		2	1	14	20

1. See comment on 1937 issue under Maundy sets, p.626.

On the currency coin, the acorn reverse was abandoned in 1937 in favour of an elegant and simple shield and rose design by George Kruger Gray (1880–1943). This tiny coin was to last only a few more years. It did not survive long enough to suffer the indignity of the changeover to cupronickel, and in 1944/45 was superseded by its larger brother, the twelve-sided nickel-brass threepence; the two had coexisted since 1937.

Denomination	Metal	Weight (grams)	Diameter (mm)	Rev. alignment
Non-Maundy Threepence	0.500 Silver	1.4	16	↑

Obverse 1 Head 1, left; GEORGIVS VI D G BR OMN REX

Reverse 1 Shield of St George lying on Tudor rose with divided date; FID DEF IND IMP THREE PENCE

Edge plain

Obv. 1   Rev. 1

No.	Date	Features	Obv.	Rev.	VF	EF	UNC
G63D-005	1937		1	1	1	2	3
G63D-010	1937	PROOF [1]	1	1			10
G63D-015	1937	PROOF from sandblasted dies [2]	1	1			150
G63D-020	1938		1	1	1	3	7
G63D-025	1938	PROOF	1	1			200
G63D-030	1939		1	1	1	4	9
G63D-035	1939	PROOF	1	1			200
G63D-040	1940		1	1	1	3	6
G63D-045	1940	PROOF	1	1			200
G63D-050	1941		1	1	1	3	6
G63D-055	1941	PROOF	1	1			200
G63D-060	1942	[3]	1	1	2	10	20
G63D-065	1943	[3]	1	1	2	12	30
G63D-070	1944	[3]	1	1	3	20	35
G63D-075	1945	[4]	1	1	4000		

1. Issued in cased proof sets.
2. Struck to facilitate photography of coin.
3. Issued for circulation in the West Indies.
4. Almost all melted down.

Elizabeth II (1952 –)

Denomination	Metal	Weight (grams)	Diameter (mm)	Rev. alignment
Maundy Threepence	Silver	1.4	16	↑

Obverse 1 Head 1, right; ELIZABETH II DEI GRA BRITT OMN REGINA F D

Obverse 2 Head 2, recut, right; ELIZABETH II DEI GRATIA REGINA F D

Reverse 1 Crowned '3' and divided date, all within wreath

Edge plain

No.	Date	Features	Obv.	Rev.	VF	EF	FDC
EZ3M-005	1953	[1]	1	1	55	65	70
EZ3M-010	1954–1998		2	1	14	17	20

1. Varieties: see under Maundy sets, p.626.

Washing silver blanks in barrels which come out of shute into metal pans for drying

Brass Threepence

Edward VIII (1936)

The Edward VIII threepence is strictly speaking a pattern, as probable royal approval was about to be granted at the time of the abdication. However, because its official status rests only on this technicality, and also to provide continuity, it is included in the currency section of this catalogue.

The threepence with stylized reverse and divided date was produced for experimental purposes only, and can be found in the Patterns section.

The portrait of Edward VIII is by Thomas Humphrey Paget, and faces left at the insistence of the king, who considered this placement more flattering. He saw no reason to continue the tradition of opposite facings for successive monarchs. The reverse is by Percy Metcalfe, and was a modification of a proposed design by Frances Madge Kitchener.

Denomination	Metal	Weight (grams)	Diameter (mm)	Rev. alignment
Threepence	'Nickel-brass' (copper 79%; zinc 20%; nickel 1%)	6.6	12–sided figure: 21mm across sides; 22mm across corners	↑

Obverse 1   Head 1, left; EDWARDVS VIII D G BR OMN REX F D IND IMP

Reverse 1   Thrift plant; THREE PENCE 1937

Edge   plain, 12 sides

Obv. 1   Rev. 1

No.	Date		Obv.	Rev.		UNC
E83DB-005	1937		1	1		20000

George VI (1937 – 1952)

At the end of the reign of George V, the silver threepence had become somewhat unpopular in England, and especially in London, mainly on account of its small size. Inexplicably, the coin was popular in Scotland. The alternative, bronze pennies and halfpennies, were heavy and cumbersome in quantities of more than two or three. Because of this, it was decided to introduce a somewhat more substantial threepenny piece which had a more convenient weight/value ratio than the bronze coins. The silver threepence continued to be minted, however; it is possible that there was some doubt as to whether the new coin would prove successful. It is worthy of note that between 1937 and 1944 no fewer than three different types of threepence (including the Maundy coin) were being struck, and this excludes the Edward VIII coins dated 1937.

The new threepence was coined in a brass alloy (copper 80%, zinc 20%) to which 1% of nickel was substituted in lieu of an equal weight of copper, possibly to make the alloy more wear resistant. Initially, the coin was to have been thinner than the piece eventually produced, but during experimentation for production of the

Edward VIII coinage it was found that some sixpence and shilling slot machines could be worked using the trial pieces coined for testing purposes. Of special concern were the many electricity meters which at the time were fed using shillings and sixpences. The adopted coins were too thick to be inserted into the slots.

The resulting coin was distinctive in thickness and colour, and furthermore was given a unique shape for a coin of a regular 12–sided figure (a dodecagon). The obverse used the portrait of George VI by Thomas Humphrey Paget (1893–1974). The reverse design, a thrift plant, was a departure from the classical designs hitherto used on almost all base metal coinage in Britain, and continued the plant motif of the later sixpences and threepences of George V. It was a modification by Percy Metcalfe of the proposed design by Frances Madge Kitchener for the Edward VIII threepence. This had originally had the word 'THRIFT' under the plant, and Miss Kitchener possibly considered this appropriate for a coin extensively used for saving in money boxes.

Initially, the twelve-sided collar used in the striking had sharp corners, but it was found that metal fatigue occurred frequently because of the high stresses obtaining at these points. During 1941 the corners were rounded slightly, and the collars subsequently lasted longer at a time when the steel used in their manufacture was in short supply. After the war, when steel was more plentiful, some of the collars were again made with sharp corners.

Collecting Hints

The series should be collected in extremely fine or mint state with original lustre. The sharpness of the reverse is lost when the coin becomes worn below very fine condition.

Denomination	Metal	Weight (grams)	Diameter (mm)	Rev. alignment
Threepence	'Nickel-brass' (copper 79%; zinc 20%; nickel 1%)	6.8	12–sided figure: 21mm across sides; 22mm across corners	↑

Obverse 1   Head 1, left; GEORGIVS VI D G BR OMN REX F D IND IMP

Obverse 2   Head 1, left; GEORGIVS D G BR OMN REX FIDEI DEF

Reverse 1   Thrift plant; THREE PENCE (date)

Edge   plain, 12 sides; corners sharp unless stated

Obv. 1   Obv. 2   Rev. 1

No.	Date	Features	Obv.	Rev.	VF	EF	UNC
G63DB-005	1937		1	1	1	3	5
G63DB-010	1937	PROOF [1]	1	1		4	8
G63DB-015	1937	PROOF from sandblasted dies [2]	1	1			150
G63DB-020	1937	struck on round nickel blank for Hong Kong 10 cents [3]	1	1			300

No.	Date	Features	Obv.	Rev.	VF	EF	UNC
G63DB-025	1938		1	1	1	4	9
G63DB-030	1938	PROOF	1	1			200
G63DB-035	1939		1	1	1	5	20
G63DB-040	1939	PROOF	1	1			200
G63DB-045	1940		1	1	1	3	8
G63DB-050	1940	PROOF	1	1			200
G63DB-055	1941		1	1	1	3	5
G63DB-060	1941	rounded corners	1	1	1	3	5
G63DB-065	1941	PROOF	1	1			200
G63DB-070	1942	rounded corners	1	1	1	3	5
G63DB-075	1942	PROOF; rounded corners	1	1			200
G63DB-080	1943	rounded corners	1	1	1	3	5
G63DB-085	1943	PROOF; rounded corners	1	1			200
G63DB-090	1944	rounded corners	1	1	1	3	6
G63DB-095	1944	PROOF; rounded corners	1	1			200
G63DB-100	1945	rounded corners	1	1	1	4	8
G63DB-105	1945	PROOF; rounded corners	1	1			200
G63DB-110	1946	rounded corners	1	1	9	70	220
G63DB-115	1946	PROOF; rounded corners	1	1			300
G63DB-120	1948	rounded corners	1	1	1	5	16
G63DB-125	1948		1	1	1	5	16
G63DB-130	1948	PROOF	1	1			200
G63DB-135	1949	rounded corners	2	1	12	80	200
G63DB-140	1949	PROOF; rounded corners	2	1			600
G63DB-145	1950		2	1	4	20	60
G63DB-150	1950	PROOF [1]	2	1			20
G63DB-155	1950	PROOF from sandblasted dies [2]	2	1			200
G63DB-160	1951		2	1	4	22	65
G63DB-165	1951	PROOF [1]	2	1			22
G63DB-170	1951	PROOF from sandblasted dies [2]	2	1			200
G63DB-175	1952		2	1	1	4	8
G63DB-180	1952	PROOF	2	1			200

1. Issued in cased proof sets.
2. Struck to facilitate photography of coin.
3. Weight 4.5 grams; diameter 20mm.

Elizabeth II (1952 –)

The brass threepence for this reign used the obverse portrait of Elizabeth II by Mary Gillick and a Tudor portcullis design on the reverse by William Gardner.

The first threepences of this reign were issued in 1953 in the so-called 'plastic sets' of nine coins in a plastic envelope. These sets were sold at seven shillings and sixpence, not much more than the total face value of the coins. The threepence was not issued for general circulation until some months later, and the design was different in a few minute details. The proof set of that year contained a proof example of the second type.

In 1954, in common with other denominations, the low relief portrait was retouched because of striking difficulties with the 1953 coin. In addition, the legend was altered and the stops were made slightly more rounded in shape.

Collecting Hints

The series should be collected in mint state.

Denomination	Metal	Weight (grams)	Diameter (mm)	Rev. alignment
Threepence	'Nickel-brass' (copper 79%; zinc 20%; nickel 1%)	6.8	12–sided figure: 21mm across sides; 22mm across corners	↑

Obverse 1 Head 1, right; ELIZABETH II DEI GRA BRITT OMN REGINA F D. Stops are oval

Obverse 2 Head 2, recut, right; ELIZABETH II DEI GRATIA REGINA F D. Stops are rounder

Reverse 1 Tudor portcullis with chains; crown or coronet above. THREE PENCE (date)

Edge plain, 12 sides

Obv. 1

Obv. 2

Rev. 1

No.	Date	Features	Obv.	Rev.	EF	UNC
EZ3DB-005	1953	[1]	1	1	1	3
EZ3DB-010	1953	PROOF	1	1	4	8
EZ3DB-015	1953	PROOF from sandblasted dies [2]	1	1		150
EZ3DB-020	1954		2	1	2	8
EZ3DB-025	1954	PROOF	2	1		200
EZ3DB-030	1955		2	1	2	8
EZ3DB-035	1955	PROOF	2	1		200
EZ3DB-040	1956		2	1	2	8
EZ3DB-045	1956	PROOF	2	1		200
EZ3DB-050	1957		2	1	2	6
EZ3DB-055	1957	PROOF	2	1		200
EZ3DB-060	1958		2	1	2	12
EZ3DB-065	1958	struck in cupronickel	2	1	300	400
EZ3DB-070	1958	PROOF	2	1		200
EZ3DB-075	1959		2	1	2	6
EZ3DB-080	1959	PROOF	2	1		200
EZ3DB-085	1960		2	1	2	6
EZ3DB-090	1960	PROOF	2	1		200
EZ3DB-095	1961		2	1	1	2
EZ3DB-098	1961	struck on blank for Hong Kong 10 cents [3]	2	1		400
EZ3DB-100	1961	PROOF	2	1		200
EZ3DB-105	1962		2	1	1	2
EZ3DB-110	1962	PROOF	2	1		200
EZ3DB-115	1963		2	1	1	2
EZ3DB-120	1963	PROOF	2	1		200
EZ3DB-125	1964		2	1	1	2
EZ3DB-130	1964	PROOF	2	1		200
EZ3DB-135	1965		2	1	1	2
EZ3DB-140	1965	PROOF	2	1		200
EZ3DB-145	1966		2	1	1	2
EZ3DB-150	1966	struck in cupronickel [4]	2	1	300	400
EZ3DB-155	1966	PROOF	2	1		200
EZ3DB-160	1967		2	1	1	2
EZ3DB-165	1967	PROOF	2	1		200
EZ3DB-170	1970	PROOF [5]	2	1	1	3
EZ3DB-175		'double headed' error	2	obv. 2		350

1. Two almost identical types.
2. Struck to facilitate photography of coin.
3. Security edge; weight 4.4 grams.
4. Weight 5.9 grams.
5. Issued in sealed proof sets.

The brass threepence ceased to be legal tender after 31 August 1971.

Silver Twopence

Charles II (1660 – 1685)

The first machine-struck twopence belonged to the series of four coins usually referred to as the 'Undated Maundy'. The dies for these coins were probably the work of Thomas Simon. The first of the dated twopences was, exceptionally, struck in 1668, two years before the first dated fourpence, threepence and penny. Catalogues do not usually record die axes, and it is not generally realised that this one date is the only one struck 'en medaille', i.e. with obverse/reverse axis alignment top to top. All other silver coinage for the next century or so, apart from a few proofs, was struck 'top to bottom'. It has been conjectured that this single piece was a pattern by Roettier for his small silver coinage introduced in 1670. The fact that this coin is struck in this manner would lend some credence to this theory, as it has been the practice down the years of striking many pattern pieces 'en medaille'. It will be seen from this catalogue, however, that Charles II crowns, halfcrowns and shillings were all to a limited extent struck 'en medaille' in the first year of issue. Whether these are all worn patterns or proofs cannot be determined. Only the twopence appears to be exclusively struck thus during the first year.

The small silver coinage introduced a few years prior to the dated issue had been hoarded to an extent, and this fact was responsible for the issue of low denomination coinage in copper in 1672. The royal Proclamation of 16 August 1672 legalising this copper currency stated that 'we have found by experience...by having our small silver money bought in and hoarded up, so that there might be a scarcity thereof in common payments...'

Denomination	Metal	Weight (grams)	Diameter (mm)	Rev. alignment
Twopence undated	Silver	1.0	14	varies
Twopence 1668	Silver	1.0	14	↑
Twopence 1670–84	Silver	1.0	14	↓

Obverse 1 Head 1, crowned, left; II behind head; CAROLVS II D G M B F & H REX

Obverse 2 Head 2, right; CAROLVS II DEI GRATIA

Reverse 1 Shield enclosing arms of England, Scotland, Ireland, France; CHRISTO AVSPICE REGNO

Reverse 2 Two crowned interlinked 'C's; MAG BR FRA ET HIB REX (date)

Edge plain

Obv. 1	Obv. 2	Rev. 1	Rev. 2

No.	Date	Features	Obv.	Rev.	F	VF	EF
C22MM-005	none		1	1	16	30	60
C22MM-010	1668	unusual rev. ↑ as stated [1]	2	2	20	35	100
C22MM-015	1670		2	2	16	25	50
C22MM-020	1671		2	2	16	25	50
C22MM-025	1672	2 over 1 [2]	2	2	16	25	50
C22MM-030	1673		2	2	16	25	50
C22MM-035	1674		2	2	16	25	50
C22MM-040	1675		2	2	18	30	55
C22MM-045	1676		2	2	16	25	50
C22MM-050	1677		2	2	18	30	55
C22MM-055	1678		2	2	16	25	50
C22MM-060	1678	8 over 6	2	2	16	25	50
C22MM-065	1679		2	2	16	25	50
C22MM-070	1679	struck on large flan [3]	2	2	16	25	50
C22MM-075	1679	HIB over FRA (rev.)	2	2	20	30	70
C22MM-080	1680		2	2	16	25	50
C22MM-085	1680	80 over 79	2	2	18	28	60
C22MM-090	1681		2	2	16	25	50
C22MM-095	1682		2	2	16	25	50
C22MM-100	1682	2 over 1	2	2	16	25	50
C22MM-105	1682	2 over 1 ERA instead of FRA (rev.)	2	2	16	25	50
C22MM-110	1683		2	2	16	25	50
C22MM-115	1683	3 over 2	2	2	16	25	50
C22MM-120	1684	[4]	2	2	18	30	55

1. Possibly a pattern; see text above.
2. Coin without overdate may exist.
3. Diameter 15–16 mm; weight 1.2 grams.
4. Stop varieties exist.

James II (1685 – 1688)

The short series for James II was, as with the other small coinage, designed and engraved by John Roettier.

Denomination	Metal	Weight (grams)	Diameter (mm)	Rev. alignment
Twopence	Silver	1.0	14	↓

Obverse 1 Head 1, left; IACOBVS II DEI GRATIA

Reverse 1 Large II, crowned; MAG BR FRA ET HIB REX (date)

Edge plain

Obv. 1	Rev. 1

No.	Date	Features	Obv.	Rev.	F	VF	EF
J22M-005	1686	[1]	1	1	16	25	50
J22M-010	1686	IΛCOBVS instead of IACOBVS (obv.) [1]	1	1	16	25	50
J22M-015	1687		1	1	18	30	60
J22M-020	1687	ERA instead of FRA (rev.)	1	1	30	45	100
J22M-025	1688		1	1	16	25	50
J22M-030	1688	latter 8 over 7	1	1	16	25	50

1. O in IACOBVS sometimes smaller (obv.).

William & Mary (1688 – 1694)

Unlike the threepence and fourpence, the twopence has only a single obverse type. Like the other pieces, it bears a rather caricatured portrayal of the two monarchs by an unknown designer, possibly George Bower (see under 'fourpence', p. 553). The reverse introduces the crowned Arabic numeral which still exists on the modern Maundy coinage.

This issue is rare in extremely fine or better condition.

Denomination	Metal	Weight (grams)	Diameter (mm)	Rev. alignment
Twopence	Silver	1.0	14	↓

Obverse 1 Heads 1, right; GVLIELMVS ET MARIA D G

Reverse 1 Crowned '2'; MAG BR FR ET HIB REX ET REGINA (date)

Edge plain

Obv. 1

Rev. 1

No.	Date	Features	Obv.	Rev.	F	VF	EF
WM2M-005	1689		1	1	14	22	50
WM2M-010	1691		1	1	16	25	55
WM2M-015	1692		1	1	14	22	50
WM2M-020	1693	[1]	1	1	14	22	50
WM2M-025	1693	3 over 2	1	1	14	22	50
WM2M-030	1694	[2]	1	1	16	25	55
WM2M-035	1694	4 over 3	1	1	18	30	60
WM2M-040	1694	MARLA instead of MARIA (obv.)	1	1	16	25	55
WM2M-045	1694	HI instead of HIB (rev.)	1	1	16	25	55

1. Positioning of obverse lettering varies.
2. Positioning of obverse lettering and spacing varies.

William III   (1695 – 1701)

The William III twopence continues the general design concept of the previous reign, but unlike the other small silver the reverse appears to have undergone some modification. In particular the numeral is thinner and shorter. It is generally held that the obverses were by Johann Crocker (John Croker) and the reverses probably by him and/or an assistant.

There are no mintmarks on these coins as they were produced after the closure of the provincial mints.

Denomination	Metal	Weight (grams)	Diameter (mm)	Rev. alignment
Twopence	Silver	1.0	14	↓

Obverse 1   Head 1, right; GVLIELMVS III DEI GRA

Reverse 1   Crowned '2'; MAG BR FRA ET HIB REX (date)

Edge   plain

Obv. 1

Rev. 1

No.	Date	Obv.	Rev.	F	VF	EF
W32M-005	1698	1	1	20	32	55
W32M-010	1699	1	1	18	30	50
W32M-015	1700	1	1	18	30	50
W32M-020	1701	1	1	18	30	50

The denomination numeral '2' varies in style and thickness.

Anne   (1702 – 1714)

John Croker and/or Samuel Bull may have been responsible for the obverse of this series, but there is some doubt about the identity of the designers and engravers of the reverse. The '2' on the reverse reverted to a design much nearer that used during the reign of William and Mary. On some of the William III twopences the numeral had varied in style somewhat.

Denomination	Metal	Weight (grams)	Diameter (mm)	Rev. alignment
Twopence	Silver	1.0	14	↓

Obverse 1   Head 1, left; ANNA DEI GRATIA

Reverse 1   Crowned '2'; MAG BR FRA ET HIB REG (date)

Reverse 2   Similar but MAG BRI FR ET HIB REG; crown is larger

Edge   plain

Obv. 1

Rev. 1

No.	Date	Features	Obv.	Rev.	F	VF	EF
AN2M-005	1703		1	1	18	35	65
AN2M-010	1704	[1]	1	1	15	30	55
AN2M-015	1704	no obverse stops	1	1	15	30	55
AN2M-020	1705		1	1	15	30	55
AN2M-025	1706		1	1	15	30	55
AN2M-030	1707		1	1	15	30	55
AN2M-035	1708		1	2	16	32	60
AN2M-040	1709		1	2	16	32	60
AN2M-045	1710		1	2	15	30	55
AN2M-050	1713		1	2	15	30	55

1. Date position varies.

George I   (1714 – 1727)

The series continued with little alteration to the basic format. John Croker and Samuel Bull were responsible for the designs. The German titles of the king were omitted as they would not fit conveniently on such a small coin.

Denomination	Metal	Weight (grams)	Diameter (mm)	Rev. alignment
Twopence	Silver	1.0	14	↓

Obverse 1   Head 1, right; GEORGIVS DEI GRA

Reverse 1   Crowned '2'; MAG BRI FR ET HIB REX (date)

Edge   plain

Obv. 1

Rev. 1

No.	Date	Features	Obv.	Rev.	F	VF	EF
G12M-005	1717		1	1	15	25	50
G12M-010	1721		1	1	15	25	50
G12M-015	1723		1	1	20	32	65
G12M-020	1726		1	1	15	25	50
G12M-025	1727	[1]	1	1	16	28	55

1. O in GEORGIVS varies in size (obv.).

George II   (1727 – 1760)

As on the other small silver, the John Croker young portrait of the monarch was used throughout the series. It will be remembered that on the larger silver the young portrait was replaced in 1743. The reverse of the twopence was possibly executed by John Sigismund Tanner.

Denomination	Metal	Weight (grams)	Diameter (mm)	Rev. alignment
Twopence	Silver	1.0	14	↓

Obverse 1   Head 1, left; GEORGIVS II DEI GRATIA

Reverse 1   Crowned '2'; MAG BRI FR ET HIB REX (date)

Edge   plain

Obv. 1

Rev. 1

No.	Date	Features	Obv.	Rev.	F	VF	EF
G22M-005	1729		1	1	14	22	35
G22M-010	1731		1	1	14	22	35
G22M-015	1732		1	1	14	22	35
G22M-020	1735		1	1	14	22	35
G22M-025	1737		1	1	14	22	35
G22M-030	1739	[1]	1	1	14	22	35
G22M-035	1740		1	1	18	30	55
G22M-040	1743		1	1	14	22	35
G22M-045	1743	3 over 0	1	1	14	22	35
G22M-050	1746		1	1	14	22	35
G22M-055	1756		1	1	14	22	35
G22M-060	1756	large date	1	1	14	22	35
G22M-065	1759		1	1	14	22	35
G22M-070	1760		1	1	14	22	35

1. Some struck from cracked die.

George III   (1760 – 1820)

The first date of George III twopence, 1763, is not as common as sometimes thought. The error arises because of the large numbers of fourpences and threepences that were minted. In fact, apart from the very rare 1765 and the 1792, it is probably the scarcest date. As with the other small silver, the young head type was minted in isolated years until 1786, when after a gap the 'Wire Money' issue of 1792 was followed by the five different date issues up to 1820, the same years as the minting of the other three small silver coins. This period marks the beginning of the true Maundy 'set' of four coins, as opposed to a somewhat artificial assembling of the four small silver pieces in earlier years.

Denomination	Metal	Weight (grams)	Diameter (mm)	Rev. alignment
Twopence 1762–86	Silver	1.0	14	↓
Twopence 1792–1800	Silver	1.0	14	↑
Twopence 1817–20	Silver	0.9	13	↑

Obverse 1   Head 1, right; GEORGIVS III DEI GRATIA

Obverse 2   Head 2, right; same legend

Obverse 3   Head 3, laureate, right; GEORGIUS III DEI GRATIA (date)

Reverse 1   Crowned '2' in high relief; MAG BRI FR ET HIB REX (date, across crown)

Reverse 2   Completely redesigned; stylised '2' under small crown; date below '2'; same legend

Reverse 3   Redesigned; more similar to Reverse 1 but crown very different; same legend; date is below '2'

Reverse 4: Crowned '2'; BRITANNIARUM REX FID DEF (no date)

Edge   plain

Obv. 1   Obv. 2   Obv. 3

Rev. 1   Rev. 2   Rev. 3   Rev. 4

No.	Date	Features	Obv.	Rev.	F	VF	EF
G32M-005	1763		1	1	16	25	40
G32M-010	1763	PROOF; rev. ↑	1	1			600
G32M-015	1765		1	1	120	280	700
G32M-020	1766		1	1	12	18	26
G32M-025	1772		1	1	12	18	26
G32M-030	1772	second 7 over 6	1	1	12	18	26
G32M-035	1776		1	1	12	18	26
G32M-040	1780		1	1	12	18	26
G32M-045	1784		1	1	12	18	26
G32M-050	1786		1	1	12	18	26

No.	Date	Features	Obv.	Rev.	F	VF	EF
G32M-055	1792	[1]	2	2	20	35	70
G32M-060	1795		2	3	10	15	22
G32M-065	1800		2	3	8	14	20
G32M-070	1817		3	4	8	12	18
G32M-075	1818		3	4	8	12	18
G32M-080	1820		3	4	8	12	18

1. 'Wire Money' issue.

George IV   (1820 – 1830)

The twopence was by now primarily a Maundy coin. From 1822 onwards the coin was struck each year until the present day for Maundy purposes. Some may have been struck for circulation in the Colonies. Because of the change in use of this coin from about this time, the tables below from 1822 until the present day are abbreviated, but the detailed and expanded tables will be found under the heading of Maundy sets.

Denomination	Metal	Weight (grams)	Diameter (mm)	Rev. alignment
Maundy Twopence	Silver	0.9	13	↓

Obverse 1   Head 1, left; GEORGIUS IIII BRITANNIARUM REX F D

Reverse 1   Crowned '2' and divided date, all within wreath

Edge   plain

No.	Date	Features	Obv.	Rev.	VF	EF	FDC
G42M-005	1822–30	[1]	1	1	8	12	20

1. Proofs were struck in 1822, 1828.

William IV   (1830 – 1837)

Denomination	Metal	Weight (grams)	Diameter (mm)	Rev. alignment
Maundy Twopence	Silver	0.9	13	↓

Obverse 1   Head 1, right; GULIELMUS IIII D G BRITANNIAR REX F D

Reverse 1   Crowned '2' and divided date, all within wreath

Edge   plain

No.	Date	Features	Obv.	Rev.	VF	EF	FDC
W42M-005	1831–37	[1]	1	1	8	14	20

1. Proofs in gold and silver were struck in 1831.

Victoria   (1837 – 1901)

Denomination	Metal	Weight (grams)	Diameter (mm)	Rev. alignment
Maundy Twopence 1838–87	Silver	0.9	13	↓
Maundy Twopence 1888–1901	Silver	0.9	13	↑

Obverse 1   Head 1, left; VICTORIA D G BRITANNIAR REGINA F D

(this obverse is identical to that on the quarter farthing)

Obverse 2   Head 2, left; same legend

Obverse 3   Head 3, left; VICTORIA DEI GRA BRITT REGINA FID DEF IND IMP

Reverse 1   Crowned '2' and divided date, all within wreath

Reverse 2   Similar but crown and '2' very different

Edge   plain

No.	Date	Features	Obv.	Rev.	VF	EF	FDC
VY2M-005	1838–87	[1]	1	1	7	10	14
VJ2M-010	1888–92	[2]	2	2	8	12	16
VO2M-015	1893–1901		3	2	5	8	12

1. Proofs were struck in 1838, 1839, 1853, 1867, 1871, 1878, 1881.
2. Proofs were struck in 1888.

For details of proofs see Maundy listings, p.624.

Currency twopences of identical design but inferior strike were minted for colonial use (mainly for British Guiana) as below:

Denomination	Metal	Weight (grams)	Diameter (mm)	Rev. alignment
Twopence (currency issue)	Silver	0.9	13	↓

Obverse 1   Head 1, left; VICTORIA D G BRITANNIAR REGINA F D

Reverse 1   Crowned '2' and divided date, all within wreath

Edge   plain

No.	Date	Features	Obv.	Rev.	F	VF	EF	UNC
VY2M-020	1838	[1]	1	1	5	7	10	16
VY2M-025	1843		1	1	5	7	12	18
VY2M-030	1848		1	1	5	7	12	18

1. Latter '8' occurs in two very different styles.

Edward VII   (1901 – 1910)

Denomination	Metal	Weight (grams)	Diameter (mm)	Rev. alignment
Maundy Twopence	Silver	0.9	13	↑

Obverse 1   Head 1, right; EDWARDVS VII D G BRITT OMN REX F D IND IMP

Reverse 1   Crowned '2' and divided date, all within wreath

Edge   plain

No.	Date	Features	Obv.	Rev.	VF	EF	FDC
E72M-005	1902–10	[1]	1	1	6	10	14

1. Matt proofs were struck in 1902.

George V   (1910 – 1936)

Denomination	Metal	Weight (grams)	Diameter (mm)	Rev. alignment
Maundy Twopence 1911–20	0.925 Silver	0.9	13	↑
Maundy Twopence 1921–36	0.500 Silver	0.9	13	↑

Obverse 1   Head 1, left; GEORGIVS V D G BRITT OMN REX F D IND IMP

Obverse 2   Head 2, so-called 'modified effigy', left; same legend

Obverse 3   Head 2, re-engraved, left; same legend

Reverse 1   Crowned '2' and divided date, all within wreath

Edge   plain

No.	Date	Features	Obv.	Rev.	VF	EF	FDC
G52M-005	1911–27	[1]	1	1	8	11	16
G52M-010	1928–29		2	1	8	11	16
G52M-015	1930–36		3	1	8	11	16

1. See comment on 1911 issue under Maundy sets, p.625.

George VI   (1937 – 1952)

Denomination	Metal	Weight (grams)	Diameter (mm)	Rev. alignment
Maundy Twopence 1937–46	0.500 Silver	0.9	13	↑
Maundy Twopence 1947–52	0.925 Silver	0.9	13	↑

There is a very slight difference in the base metal constituency of the 1937 Maundy set given at the Maundy ceremony from that of the set included in the 1937 proof set.

Obverse 1   Head 1, left; GEORGIVS VI D G BR OMN REX F D IND IMP

Obverse 2   Head 1, left; GEORGIVS VI D G BR OMN REX FIDEI DEF

Reverse 1   Crowned '2' and divided date, all within wreath

Edge   plain

No.	Date	Obv.	Rev.	VF	EF	FDC
G62M-005	1937–48 [1]	1	1	8	10	14
G62M-010	1949–52	2	1	8	11	15

1. See comment on 1937 issue under Maundy sets, p.626.

Elizabeth II   (1952 –)

Denomination	Metal	Weight (grams)	Diameter (mm)	Rev. alignment
Maundy Twopence	0.925 Silver	0.9	13	↑

Obverse 1   Head 1, right; ELIZABETH II DEI GRA BRITT OMN REGINA F D

Obverse 2   Head 2, recut, right; ELIZABETH II DEI GRATIA REGINA F D

Reverse 1   Crowned '2' and divided date, all within wreath

Edge   plain

No.	Date	Features	Obv.	Rev.	VF	EF	FDC
EZ2M-005	1953	[1]	1	1	55	65	70
EZ2M-010	1954–97		2	1	14	17	20

1. Varieties, see under Maundy sets, p.626.

Copper Twopence

George III (1760 – 1820)

By the end of the 18th century the amount of counterfeit coinage had grown enormously. Indeed, it is difficult in modern times to imagine the state of affairs that existed. Stephen Martin Leake, writing in *An Historical Account of English Money* in 1793, noted that 'very few indeed of the shillings and sixpences now in use appear ever to have been legally coined'. The copper coinage appears to have been the subject of a mass industry in counterfeiting. Genuine coins were melted down and the metal refashioned into lightweight thin specimens of roughly correct diameter. Traders were offering goods priced at double value in counterfeit coinage which was then taken to Scotland and resold, where the best price could be obtained.

Into this maelstrom came one Matthew Boulton, a man with high ideals. His dream was to produce a coinage which was difficult to counterfeit, and in which the value of the coin and that of the intrinsic metal content were closely matched. Boulton opened a mint at Soho, near Birmingham, containing coining presses operated by steam, with many refinements in the preparation of blanks and dies.

For some years Boulton urged the Government to allow him to strike coinage, and finally secured a contract with them in 1797. In a Proclamation dated 26 July 1797, it was declared that 'certain pieces of copper should be coined, which should go and pass for one Penny and two Pennies, and that each of such pieces of one Penny should weigh one ounce Avoirdupois and that each such two Penny pieces should weigh two Ounces Avoirdupois; the intrinsic value of such pieces of 1 Penny and 2 Pennies, workmanship included, corresponding as nearly as possible with the nominal value of the same respectively.'

The new coinage was designed by Heinrich Küchler. The twopence is remarkable in a number of respects. It is the only pre-decimal base metal coin of this denomination, and it was struck bearing only one date. The coin had a most innovative design. It was inordinately large and thick, in order to fit Boulton's requirements as to intrinsic value. It was one of the heaviest regular British coins ever struck, heavier even than the five guinea piece. It has subsequently become known as the 'Cartwheel Twopence'. Because of its weight, it became very susceptible to edge damage, the pressure on the sharp rim when dropped on the floor being several tons per square inch. The incuse lettering around the broad rim on both sides was intended to foil the counterfeiters as well as being a means to reducing wear on the legend. Much of this coinage was melted down around 1800 when the price of copper increased. By 1805, the intrinsic value of the metal exceeded the face value by about 30%.

Denomination	Metal	Weight (grams)	Diameter (mm)	Rev. alignment
Twopence[1]	Copper	56.3–58.1	41	↓

1. Thickness 5 mm.

Obverse 1 Head 1, right; GEORGIUS III D G REX

Reverse 1 Britannia, seated, with shield, facing left, holding olive branch and trident; BRITANNIA 1797

Edge plain

Obv. 1   Rev. 1

No.	Date	Features	Obv.	Rev.	F	VF	EF	UNC
G32D-005	1797	[1]	1	1	25	60	200	450
G32D-010	1797	PROOF	1	1				600
G32D-015	1797	bronzed PROOF [2]	1	1				650
G32D-020	1797	gilt PROOF	1	1				750
G32D-025	1797	PROOF [3]	1	1				650
G32D-030	1797	PROOF on thin flan [3]	1	1				700
G32D-035	1797	bronzed PROOF [4]	1	1				650
G32D-040	1797	bronzed PROOF on thin flan [5]	1	1				600

No.	Date	Features	Obv.	Rev.	F	VF	EF	UNC
G32D-045	1797	gilt PROOF [4]	1	1				700
G32D-050	1797	gilt PROOF on thin flan [3]	1	1				1000
G32D-055	1797	PROOF in silver	1	1				8000
G32D-060	1797	PROOF in silver on thin flan [6]	1	1				6000
G32D-065	1797	PROOF in gold	1	1				15000

1. Many minor varieties; see below.
2. At least 2 different dies.
3. 'Late Soho' issue.
4. 'Late Soho' issue; at least 2 different dies.
5. 'Late Soho' issue; some or all have rev. ↑.
6. Thickness 3.5 mm.

The currency coin was struck from a number of different dies, and details on the ship on the reverse appear to have been frequently altered as a die identification mark. Dots on the drapery folds on the obverse may have been used similarly. Other minor variations can be found on the wreath berries, leaves and hair (obv.); waves, rock, drapery, sea position and stops (rev.).

Three Halfpence

William IV (1830 – 1837) & Victoria (1837 – 1901)

The silver three-halfpence (1½ pence) was issued for circulation in the colonies, mainly Ceylon and the West Indies, and not in Britain. However, it resembles the British coinage to such an extent that it has come to be regarded as a British denomination, and as such it merits inclusion in this catalogue.

The history of the coin parallels to some extent that of the Britannia groat, but was much more limited. As with the groat, the issue straddles only the reigns of William IV and Victoria, and, like the groat, there are no proofs struck in metals other than silver. For the sake of expediency, the issues of the two reigns are catalogued together rather than broken into two halves. The two issues share the same reverse, and all other characteristics are identical except for the change in monarch.

The portraits of William IV and Victoria are both by William Wyon, while Johann Baptiste Merlen designed the reverses.

Collecting Hints

While no doubt many of these coins became so worn that they were unusable, and others no doubt were lost through holes in pockets, it is surprising how many turn up in very fine or better condition. However, some of the dates are rare, and it is a considerable achievement to assemble a set in extremely fine or near mint state. The 1843 over 1834 overdate is possibly not as rare as some catalogues indicate.

Denomination	Metal	Weight (grams)	Diameter (mm)	Rev. alignment
1½ pence	Silver	0.7	12	↓

Obverse 1   Head 1 (William IV), right; GULIELMUS IIII D G BRITANNIAR REX F D

Obverse 2   Head 2 (Victoria), left; VICTORIA D G BRITANNIAR REGINA F D

Reverse 1   '1½', date below, crown above, all within wreath

Edge   plain

Obv. 1   Obv. 2   Rev. 1

William IV

No.	Date	Features	Obv.	Rev.	F	VF	EF	UNC
W43HD-005	1834		1	1	5	8	20	40
W43HD-010	1835		1	1	6	10	26	45
W43HD-015	1835	5 over 4	1	1	5	8	22	42
W43HD-020	1836		1	1	6	9	24	45
W43HD-025	1837		1	1	12	20	70	150

Victoria

No.	Date	Features	Obv.	Rev.	F	VF	EF	UNC
VY3HD-005	1838		2	1	4	7	20	40
VY3HD-010	1839		2	1	4	7	20	40
VY3HD-015	1840		2	1	8	15	50	100
VY3HD-020	1841		2	1	6	10	26	48
VY3HD-025	1842		2	1	6	11	30	50
VY3HD-030	1843		2	1	4	7	18	35
VY3HD-035	1843	PROOF	2	1				700
VY3HD-040	1843	43 over 34	2	1	8	16	50	80
VY3HD-045	1843	43 over 34; PROOF	2	1				1000
VY3HD-050	1860		2	1	10	18	50	80
VY3HD-055	1862		2	1	10	18	50	80
VY3HD-060	1862	PROOF	2	1				1000
VY3HD-065	1870	PROOF or PATTERN	2	1				2000

Silver Penny

Charles II   (1660 – 1685)

The silver penny is the only one of the small silver coins to have been regularly used for the Maundy ceremony in the 17th century. Although the 2–, 3– and 4–pence silver are often referred to as Maundy coinage, there is no doubt that their primary (or even their only) use was as currency coins. It was only during the reign of George III that the Maundy 'set' became an established feature. The silver penny was, of course, also used as currency, otherwise the recipients at the Maundy ceremony would have had no benefit from receiving it. All of the four small silver coins usually turn up in about fine condition; however, there is a tendency for the pennies to be found in the higher grades more often than the other three coins. This would be expected if one assumes that some of the Maundy coinage would have been kept as keepsakes. In addition, the currency small silver coinage was also hoarded, and it was this that was to some extent responsible for the issue of copper coinage in 1672. The hoarding of the silver coinage was mentioned in the royal Proclamation of 16 August 1672 declaring the copper coinage to be current (see p.571).

Apart from some of the later coinage in the hammered series, the first regular machine struck pennies, probably by Thomas Simon (1618–65) appeared around 1664 or 1665, and are undated. The issue of pennies by John Roettier, which began in 1670, established the basic design which was to continue for many years. The portrait of the monarch on the obverse was augmented by a crowned 'C' (for Charles) on the reverse.

Denomination	Metal	Weight (grams)	Diameter (mm)	Rev. alignment
Penny undated	Silver	0.5	12	varies
Penny 1670–84	Silver	0.5	12	↓

Obverse 1   Head 1, crowned, left; 'I' behind head; CAROLVS II D G M B F & H REX

Obverse 2   Head 2, right; CAROLVS II DEI GRATIA

Reverse 1   Shield enclosing Arms of England, Scotland, Ireland, France; CHRISTO AVSPICE REGNO

Reverse 2   Crowned 'C'; MAG BR FRA ET HIB REX (date)

Edge   plain

| Obv. 1 | Obv. 2 | Rev. 1 | Rev. 2 |

No.	Date	Features	Obv.	Rev.	F	VF	EF
C21MM-005	none	[1]	1	1	20	40	80
C21MM-010	1670	[2]	2	2	18	35	75
C21MM-015	1671		2	2	18	35	75
C21MM-020	1672	2 over 1	2	2	18	35	75
C21MM-025	1673		2	2	18	35	75
C21MM-030	1674		2	2	18	35	75
C21MM-035	1674	G of GRATIA inverted (obv.)	2	2	18	35	75
C21MM-040	1674	as last but GRACIA instead of GRATIA	2	2	18	35	75
C21MM-045	1675		2	2	20	40	85
C21MM-050	1676		2	2	22	45	90
C21MM-055	1676	G of GRATIA inverted (obv.)	2	2	22	45	90
C21MM-060	1677		2	2	18	35	75
C21MM-065	1677	G of GRATIA inverted (obv.)	2	2	18	35	75
C21MM-070	1678		2	2	22	45	90
C21MM-075	1678	G of GRATIA inverted (obv.)	2	2	22	45	90

No.	Date	Features	Obv.	Rev.	F	VF	EF
C21MM-080	1679		2	2	20	40	85
C21MM-085	1680		2	2	18	35	75
C21MM-090	1680	struck on larger thin flan [3]	2	2	100		
C21MM-095	1681		2	2	22	45	90
C21MM-100	1682		2	2	20	40	85
C21MM-105	1682	2 over 1	2	2	20	40	85
C21MM-110	1682	ERA instead of FRA (rev.)	2	2	22	45	90
C21MM-115	1683		2	2	18	35	75
C21MM-120	1684		2	2	20	40	85
C21MM-125	1684	4 over 3	2	2	20	40	85

1. Scarcer than 2–, 3– or 4–pence.
2. Date sometimes resembles 1679.
3. Lettering anomalies exist – coins genuine?

James II   (1685 – 1688)

John Roettier continued the basic design, replacing the 'C' on the reverse with 'I', which served not only as the initial of the monarch (IACOBVS), but also as a mark of denomination (1 penny).

Denomination	Metal	Weight (grams)	Diameter (mm)	Rev. alignment
Penny	Silver	0.5	12	↓

Obverse 1   Head 1, left; IACOBVS II DEI GRATIA

Reverse 1   Large I, crowned; MAG BR FRA ET HIB REX (date)

Edge   plain

| Obv. 1 | | Rev. 1 |

No.	Date	Features	Obv.	Rev.	F	VF	EF
J21M-005	1685		1	1	20	35	80
J21M-010	1686		1	1	22	40	90
J21M-015	1687		1	1	20	35	80
J21M-020	1687	7 over 6	1	1	20	35	80
J21M-022	1687	7 over 8	1	1	20	35	80
J21M-025	1688		1	1	20	35	80
J21M-030	1688	latter 8 over 7	1	1	20	35	80

William & Mary   (1688 – 1694)

The first issue of silver penny in this reign is a strange beast indeed. Not only does it have a different obverse from those of the remaining years, it is also very rare, and the date is unreadable! The writer has seen examples which appear to read 1681 and 1691, and on others the tiny distorted numerals are illegible. Luckily, the date can be identified by the fact that all silver pennies with the first obverse (continuous legend over the heads) are of 1689.

The identity of the designer of the small silver of William and Mary is uncertain. The heads of the monarchs are more stylized than on the other denominations, and are in relatively high relief. The portraits were possibly the work of George Bower (see p.553).

Although on the 2–, 3– and 4–pence coins the denomination on the reverse is changed to an Arabic numeral on the William and Mary series, on the penny the '1' was still engraved as a Roman

'I'. The general form of the reverse thus appears very similar to that of the James II penny.

As with the other small silver denominations, the penny is rare in Extremely Fine or better condition.

Denomination	Metal	Weight (grams)	Diameter (mm)	Rev. alignment
Penny	Silver	0.5	12	↓

Obverse 1   Heads 1, right; legend GVLIELMVS ET MARIA D G continuous over heads

Obverse 2   Similar but legend divided by heads

Reverse 1   Crowned 'I'; MAG BR FR ET HIB REX ET REGINA (date)

Edge   plain

Obv. 1   Obv. 2   Rev. 1

No.	Date	Features	Obv.	Rev.	F	VF	EF
WM1M-005	1689	[1]	1	1	120	300	500
WM1M-010	1689	GVIELMVS instead of GVLIELMVS (obv.) [2]	1	1	150	400	700
WM1M-015	1690		2	1	20	35	80
WM1M-020	1691	latter 1 over 0	2	1	20	35	80
WM1M-025	1692		2	1	40	60	120
WM1M-030	1692	2 over 1	2	1	40	60	120
WM1M-035	1693		2	1	25	40	90
WM1M-040	1694	stops on obv.	2	1	20	35	80
WM1M-045	1694	no stops on obv.	2	1	20	35	80
WM1M-050	1694	HI instead of HIB (rev.) [3]	2	1	20	35	80
WM1M-055	1694	9 over 6 or inverted 9; HI instead of HIB (rev.) [3]	2	1	20	35	80

1. Date can appear to read 1681, 1691 or be illegible. Minor stop and lettering varieties exist.
2. Date can be illegible. Minor stop and lettering varieties exist.
3. Occur with and without stops on obverse.

William III   (1695 – 1701)

Johann Crocker, aka John Croker (1670–1741) designed the new portrait for the silver penny after the death of Mary in 1694. This was a more conventional representation of William following the somewhat cartoon-style effigies on the William and Mary small coinage. The reverse, continuing the Roman I denomination, were designed by Croker and/or an assistant.

The small silver coinage was struck after the closure of the provincial mints and thus no mintmarks were placed on them.

Denomination	Metal	Weight (grams)	Diameter (mm)	Rev. alignment
Penny	Silver	0.5	12	↓

Obverse 1   Head 1, right; GVLIELMVS III DEI GRA

Reverse 1   Crowned 'I'; MAG BR FRA ET HIB REX (date)

Edge   plain

Obv. 1   Rev. 1

No.	Date	Features	Obv.	Rev.	F	VF	EF
W31M-005	1698	[1]	1	1	20	32	55
W31M-010	1698	IRA instead of FRA (rev.)	1	1	20	32	55
W31M-015	1698	HI.BREX instead of HIB.REX (rev.)	1	1	20	32	55
W31M-020	1699		1	1	25	40	75
W31M-025	1700		1	1	25	40	75
W31M-030	1701		1	1	20	32	55

1. Position of date varies.

Anne   (1702 – 1714)

The Anne penny was probably designed by John Croker and/or Samuel Bull, although the attribution of the reverse is in some doubt. The coin continues the general design of previous reigns.

Denomination	Metal	Weight (grams)	Diameter (mm)	Rev. alignment
Penny	Silver	0.5	12	↓

Obverse 1   Head 1, left; ANNA DEI GRATIA

Reverse 1   Crowned 'I'; MAG BR FRA ET HIB REG (date)

Reverse 2   Similar but MAG BR FR ET HIB REG

Reverse 3   Similar but MAG BRI FR ET HIB REG

Edge   plain

Obv. 1   Rev. 3

No.	Date	Features	Obv.	Rev.	F	VF	EF
AN1M-005	1703		1	1	20	40	70
AN1M-010	1705		1	2	22	45	80
AN1M-015	1706	[1]	1	2	20	40	70
AN1M-020	1708		1	3	35	70	120
AN1M-025	1709		1	3	20	40	70
AN1M-030	1710		1	3	30	60	110
AN1M-035	1713	3 over 0	1	3	20	40	70

1. Position of date varies.

George I   (1714 – 1727)

John Croker and Samuel Bull continued as designers and engravers of the small silver coinage. The design of this series is very similar to that of earlier reigns.

In the first year of minting of the silver penny, 1716, no other small silver coinage was struck. In 1717, the other three were struck without the penny; in 1718 and 1720, pennies only were struck, and in 1721 again the penny was the only piece not minted! One had to wait until 1723 before a full so-called 'Maundy set' was issued. Another anomaly which sets the penny apart in the period 1716–23 was that the reverse legend reads MAG BR, etc. whereas on the other three small silver coins the legend reads MAG BRI, etc.

Denomination	Metal	Weight (grams)	Diameter (mm)	Rev. alignment
Penny	Silver	0.5	12	↓

Obverse 1   Head 1, right; GEORGIVS DEI GRA

Reverse 1   Crowned 'I'; MAG BR FR ET HIB REX (date)

Reverse 2   Similar but BRI instead of BR

Edge   plain

Obv. 1   Rev. 2

No.	Date	Features	Obv.	Rev.	F	VF	EF
G11M-005	1716		1	1	15	25	45
G11M-010	1718		1	1	15	25	45
G11M-015	1720		1	1	15	25	45
G11M-020	1720	HIPEX or HIPREX instead of HIB REX (rev.)	1	1	15	25	45
G11M-025	1723		1	1	15	25	45
G11M-030	1725	[1]	1	1	15	25	45
G11M-035	1726		1	2	18	30	55

No.	Date	Features	Obv.	Rev.	F	VF	EF
G11M-040	1727	[2]	1	2	20	35	60

1. Lettering size varies; some or all read RR instead of BR (rev.).
2. Lettering smaller than on previous dates.

George II   (1727 – 1760)

While the sixpence and larger silver coins used an older portrait of the king by Tanner from 1743 onwards, the small silver coins used the young portrait by John Croker throughout until the king's death in 1760. Tanner, however, may have been responsible for the reverses of the small silver.

For seven of the years between 1750 and 1758 the silver penny was the only coin of the small silver series issued. This fact, coupled with the proliferation of these years in the higher grades, indicate that they were primarily issued for the Maundy ceremony. In some years, such as 1733 and 1744, the coin was not issued because Maundy Thursday fell before the date changeover on 25th March.

Denomination	Metal	Weight (grams)	Diameter (mm)	Rev. alignment
Penny	Silver	0.5	12	↓

Obverse 1   Head 1, left; GEORGIVS II DEI GRATIA

Reverse 1   Crowned 'I'; MAG BRI FR ET HIB REX (date)

Edge   plain

Obv. 1   Rev. 1

No.	Date	Features	Obv.	Rev.	F	VF	EF
G21M-005	1729		1	1	14	20	30
G21M-010	1731		1	1	14	20	30
G21M-015	1732	[1]	1	1	14	20	30
G21M-020	1735		1	1	15	22	35
G21M-025	1737		1	1	15	22	35
G21M-030	1739		1	1	14	20	30
G21M-035	1740		1	1	14	20	30
G21M-040	1743		1	1	14	20	30
G21M-045	1746		1	1	14	20	30
G21M-050	1746	6 over 3 (?)	1	1	15	22	35
G21M-055	1750		1	1	14	20	30
G21M-060	1752		1	1	14	20	30
G21M-065	1752	2 over 0	1	1	14	20	30
G21M-070	1753		1	1	14	20	30
G21M-075	1753	3 over 2	1	1	15	22	35
G21M-080	1754		1	1	14	20	30
G21M-085	1755		1	1	14	20	30
G21M-090	1756	[2]	1	1	14	20	30
G21M-095	1757	no colon after GRATIA (obv.) [2]	1	1	14	20	30
G21M-100	1757	colon after GRATIA (obv.) [2]	1	1	14	20	30
G21M-105	1758		1	1	14	20	30
G21M-110	1759		1	1	14	20	30
G21M-115	1760	[3]	1	1	14	20	30

1. Head design varies slightly.
2. Date size varies.
3. Obverse lettering size varies.

George III   (1760 – 1820)

The silver penny underwent a number of changes during the long reign of George III. Unlike the threepence and fourpence, the first date, 1763, is scarce, but not noticeably more so in the higher grades, since it was primarily used as a Maundy coin. By the end of the reign all of the four small silver coins were used mainly as Maundy pieces.

In 1781 the silver penny was redesigned with a much flatter '1' on the reverse; other minor changes were also made. The next

issues, in 1784 and 1786, also featured this new design, and the fourpence was similarly redesigned in lower relief. However, the twopence and threepence retained the high relief reverse. The 1784 and 1786 small silver coinage was the last struck before an even more radical redesign in 1792.

It is possible that the redesign of the '1' in 1781 was because of trouble with metal flowing from the obverse to fill the reverse die during striking. Some of the pennies prior to 1781 have a deep groove across the head of George III resembling a cut. If one examines the alignment of the axes carefully, however, it will be seen that this flaw follows exactly the line of the '1' on the reverse. The lower relief numeral used from 1781 onwards caused no trouble in this respect. Similar problems occurred with the early George V bronze pennies.

Denomination	Metal	Weight (grams)	Diameter (mm)	Rev. alignment
Penny 1763–86	Silver	0.5	12	↓
Penny 1792–1800	Silver	0.5	12	↑
Penny 1817–20	Silver	0.5	11	↑

Obverse 1   Head 1, right; GEORGIVS III DEI GRATIA

Obverse 2   Head 2, right; same legend

Obverse 3   Head 3, laureate, right; GEORGIUS III DEI GRATIA (date)

Reverse 1   Crowned '1' in high relief; MAG BRI FR ET HIB REX (date, across crown)

Reverse 2   Similar but in lower relief; the '1' is much flatter

Reverse 3   Completely redesigned; stylized '1' under small crown; date below '1'; same legend

Reverse 4   Redesigned; more similar to Reverse 1 but crown very different; same legend; date is below '1'

Reverse 5   Crowned '1'; BRITANNIARUM REX FID DEF (no date)

Edge   plain

Obv. 1   Obv. 2   Obv. 3

Rev. 1   Rev. 2   Rev. 3   Rev. 4   Rev. 5

No.	Date	Features	Obv.	Rev.	F	VF	EF
G31M-005	1763		1	1	16	22	32
G31M-010	1763	PROOF; rev. ↑	1	1			500
G31M-015	1766		1	1	12	18	24
G31M-020	1770		1	1	12	18	24
G31M-025	1772		1	1	12	18	24
G31M-030	1776		1	1	12	18	24
G31M-035	1779		1	1	12	18	24
G31M-040	1780		1	1	12	18	24
G31M-045	1781		1	2	12	18	24
G31M-050	1784		1	2	12	18	24
G31M-055	1786		1	2	12	18	24
G31M-060	1792	[1]	2	3	15	22	28
G31M-065	1795		2	4	10	15	20
G31M-070	1800		2	4	7	11	15
G31M-075	1817		3	5	8	12	18
G31M-080	1818		3	5	8	12	18
G31M-085	1820		3	5	8	12	18

1. 'Wire Money' issue.

George IV   (1820 – 1830)

By the reign of George IV, the role of the silver penny was simply that of the smallest of the four silver Maundy coins. From 1822, the four coins have been minted yearly up to the present day, and full details are listed under the heading of Maundy sets. For the sake of continuity, however, the listing of silver pence also continues below in an abbreviated form.

Denomination	Metal	Weight (grams)	Diameter (mm)	Rev. alignment
Maundy Penny	Silver	0.5	11	↓

Obverse 1   Head 1, left; GEORGIUS IIII BRITANNIAR REX F D

Reverse 1   Crowned '1' and divided date, all within wreath

Edge   plain

No.	Date	Features	Obv.	Rev.	VF	EF	FDC
G41M-005	1822–30	[1]	1	1	7	10	18

1. Proofs were struck in 1822, 1828.

William IV   (1830 – 1837)

Denomination	Metal	Weight (grams)	Diameter (mm)	Rev. alignment
Maundy Penny	Silver	0.5	11	↓

Obverse 1   Head 1, right; GULIELMUS IIII D G BRITANNIAR REX F D

Reverse 1   Crowned '1' and divided date, all within wreath

Edge   plain

No.	Date	Features	Obv.	Rev.	VF	EF	FDC
W41M-005	1831–37	[1]	1	1	8	14	20

1. Proofs in gold and silver were struck in 1831.

Victoria   (1837 – 1901)

Denomination	Metal	Weight (grams)	Diameter (mm)	Rev. alignment
Maundy Penny 1838–87	Silver	0.5	11	↓
Maundy Penny 1888–1901	Silver	0.5	11	↑

Obverse 1   Head 1, left; VICTORIA D G BRITANNIAR REGINA F D

Obverse 2   Head 2, left; same legend

Obverse 3   Head 3, left; VICTORIA DEI GRA BRITT REGINA FID DEF IND IMP

Reverse 1   Crowned '1' and divided date, all within wreath

Reverse 2   Similar but crown very different

Edge   plain

No.	Date	Features	Obv.	Rev.	VF	EF	FDC
VY1M-005	1838–87	[1]	1	1	6	9	12
VJ1M-010	1888–92	[2]	2	2	8	12	16
VO1M-015	1893–1901		3	2	5	8	12

1. Proofs were struck in 1838, 1839, 1853, 1867, 1871, 1878, 1881.
2. Proofs were struck in 1888.

For details of proofs see Maundy listings, p.624.

Edward VII   (1901 – 1910)

Denomination	Metal	Weight (grams)	Diameter (mm)	Rev. alignment
Maundy Penny	Silver	0.5	11	↑

Obverse 1   Head 1, right; EDWARDVS VII D G BRITT OMN REX F D IND IMP

Reverse 1   Crowned '1' and divided date, all within wreath

Edge   plain

No.	Date	Features	Obv.	Rev.	VF	EF	FDC
E71M-005	1902–10	[1]	1	1	6	10	14

1. Matt proofs were struck in 1902.

George V   (1910 – 1936)

Denomination	Metal	Weight (grams)	Diameter (mm)	Rev. alignment
Maundy Penny 1911–20	0.925 Silver	0.5	11	↑
Maundy Penny 1921–36	0.500 Silver	0.5	11	↑

Obverse 1   Head 1, left; GEORGIVS V D G BRITT OMN REX F D IND IMP

Obverse 2   Head 2, so-called 'modified effigy', left; same legend

Obverse 3   Head 2, re-engraved, left; same legend

Reverse 1   Crowned '1' and divided date, all within wreath

Edge   plain

No.	Date	Features	Obv.	Rev.	VF	EF	FDC
G51M-005	1911–27	[1]	1	1	9	12	18
G51M-010	1928–29		2	1	9	12	18
G51M-015	1930–36		3	1	9	12	18

1. See comment on 1911 issue under Maundy sets, p.625.

George VI   (1937 – 1952)

Denomination	Metal	Weight (grams)	Diameter (mm)	Rev. alignment
Maundy Penny 1937–46	0.500 Silver	0.5	11	↑
Maundy Penny 1947–52	0.925 Silver	0.5	11	↑

There is a very slight difference in the base metal constituency of the 1937 Maundy set given at the Maundy ceremony from that of the set included in the 1937 proof set

Obverse 1   Head 1, left; GEORGIVS VI D G BR OMN REX F D IND IMP

Obverse 2   Head 1, left; GEORGIVS VI D G BR OMN REX FIDEI DEF

Reverse 1   Crowned '1' and divided date, all within wreath

Edge   plain

No.	Date	Features	Obv.	Rev.	VF	EF	FDC
G61M-005	1937–48	[1]	1	1	10	12	16
G61M-010	1949–52		2	1	10	14	18

1. See comment on 1937 issue under Maundy sets, p.626.

Elizabeth II   (1952 –)

Denomination	Metal	Weight (grams)	Diameter (mm)	Rev. alignment
Maundy Penny	0.925 Silver	0.5	11	↑

Obverse 1   Head 1, right; ELIZABETH II DEI GRA BRITT OMN REGINA F D

Obverse 2   Head 2, recut, right; ELIZABETH II DEI GRATIA REGINA F D

Reverse 1   Crowned '1' and divided date, all within wreath

Edge   plain

No.	Date	Features	Obv.	Rev.	VF	EF	FDC
EZ1M-005	1953	[1]	1	1	60	70	80
EZ1M-010	1954–97		2	1	16	20	24

1. Varieties: see under Maundy sets, p.626.

Copper/Bronze Penny

Rev. 1   Rev. 2

Although Newton had considered minting a copper penny in 1702, the first were struck in 1797, coincidentally with the copper twopence, and the notes on the twopence apply generally also to the penny. Following Matthew Boulton's ideals about intrinsic value, the weight of the penny is exactly half that of the twopence.

As on the twopence, the details on the ship may have been used as an identification mark for a particular die. However, the penny has many more varieties of ship. Ernest Bramah, in *English Regal Copper Coins* (London, 1929) suggested that there may be as many as a hundred ship varieties on the penny against about eighteen for the twopence. This is probably because, unlike the twopence, the penny remained in circulation for some years. It appears to have been issued for a few years with the date unchanged from 1797.

The pennies of 1806 and 1807 were again struck at the Soho mint and designed by Küchler. The innovative format of the 1797 series was abandoned, and the coinage presents a more conventional appearance. A total of 150 tons of copper was used for the two years.

Collecting Hints

Because the 1797 penny remained in circulation longer than the twopence, the average condition as found is lower than that of the larger coin. However, it appears to be somewhat easier to locate in the top grades. In addition, the penny is less prone to have suffered edge knocks than the twopence. Unless one is intending to assemble a specialised collection of the minor varieties, a single specimen in extremely fine or mint state with original lustre should be the minimum standard to aim for.

The 1806 and 1807 coins are not difficult to find in the higher grades and these should be sought. These pieces exist in large quantities in fine condition.

No.	Date	Features	Obv.	Rev.	F	VF	EF	UNC
G31D-005	1797	[1]	1	1	15	28	100	200
G31D-010	1797	PROOF [2]	1	1				500
G31D-015	1797	bronzed PROOF [2]	1	1				250
G31D-020	1797	gilt PROOF [2]	1	1				200
G31D-025	1797	silvered PROOF [3]	1	1				800
G31D-030	1797	PROOF in tin [3]	1	1				800
G31D-035	1797	PROOF in silver [3]	1	1				1200
G31D-040	1797	PROOF in silver on thin flan [3]	1	1				1000
G31D-045	1797	PROOF in gold [4]	1	1				18000
G31D-050	1806		2	2	6	15	75	140
G31D-055	1806	gilt PROOF	2	2				400
G31D-058	1806	gilt PROOF; rev. ↑	2	2				400
G31D-060	1806	PROOF [2]	2	2				350
G31D-065	1806	PROOF on thin flan; edge plain [3]	2	2				500
G31D-070	1806	bronzed PROOF; rev. ↑	2	2				500
G31D-072	1806	bronzed PROOF [2]	2	2				300
G31D-075	1806	bronzed PROOF; edge plain [3]	2	2				400
G31D-080	1806	bronzed PROOF on thin flan; edge plain [3]	2	2				450
G31D-085	1806	gilt PROOF [5]	2	2				400
G31D-090	1806	gilt PROOF; edge plain [3]	2	2				500
G31D-095	1806	gilt PROOF on thin flan; edge plain [3]	2	2				500
G31D-100	1806	PROOF in silver; edge plain [3]	2	2				1500
G31D-105	1807		2	2	6	15	80	150
G31D-110	1807	bronzed PROOF	2	2				700
G31D-115	1807	gilt PROOF	2	2				1000
G31D-120	1808	[6]	2	2				35000

1. Many minor varieties; see below.
2. 'Late Soho' issue; several varieties.
3. 'Late Soho' issue.
4. 'Late Soho' issue; thickness varies; weight 27 to 39 grams.
5. 'Late Soho' issue; at least 2 varieties.
6. Unique. Probably a proof.

Denomination	Metal	Weight (grams)	Diameter (mm)	Rev. alignment
Penny 1797	Copper	28.3	36	↓
Penny 1806–08	Copper	18.9	34	↓

Obverse 1   Head 1, right; GEORGIUS III D G REX

Obverse 2   Head 2, right; GEORGIUS III D G REX (date)

Reverse 1   Britannia, seated, with shield, facing left, holding olive branch and trident; BRITANNIA 1797

Reverse 2   Britannia facing left, holding olive branch and trident; BRITANNIA

Edge   (1797): plain; (1806–08): grooved down the centre and milled with diagonal lines across the groove

The currency coin of 1797 was struck from a number of different dies, and details on the ship on the reverse appear to have been frequently altered as a die identification mark. Dots on the drapery folds on the obverse may have been used similarly. Other minor variations can be found on the wreath berries, leaves and hair (obverse); waves, rock, drapery, sea position and stops (reverse).

George IV   (1820 – 1830)

At the beginning of the 'Great Recoinage' in 1816, only silver coins were produced. The first copper coins were farthings of 1821–26 bearing the Pistrucci head of the king. By the time the first pennies were minted in 1825, Pistrucci had come into some disgrace at the Mint, not least because of his refusal to engrave a portrait of the monarch based on that of another artist, Chantrey. Pistrucci, an Italian with an inflated ego, considered that by

Obv. 1   Obv. 2

doing so his position as an artist would be compromised. The king did not like Pistrucci's representation of himself, especially as depicted on the crown piece. He presumably had no wish to see another coin of similar size issued with such an unflattering portrait. William Wyon was therefore commissioned to engrave the portrait for the penny, and comparison with the obverse of the first issue of farthings will show that the decision was a wise one.

The penny was issued for only three years, including 1826, when a proof example was included in the proof set of that year. The penny of 1827, the last year of issue, is particularly rare. The 1825 piece is scarce, since the order for the new coinage was not made until 14 November of that year.

Collecting Hints

Although the series spans only three years, a collection containing all of the varieties is difficult to achieve, as many of them are elusive. In particular, brilliant uncirculated specimens are very rare.

Denomination	Metal	Weight (grams)	Diameter (mm)	Rev. alignment
Penny	Copper	18.8	34	↑

Obverse 1   Head 1, left; GEORGIUS IV DEI GRATIA (date)

Reverse 1   Britannia, seated, with shield, facing right, holding trident; the arms of the saltire on the Union Flag on the shield has no central line; BRITANNIAR REX FID DEF

Reverse 2   Similar but thin line down arms of saltire

Reverse 3   Similar but thick line down arms of saltire

Edge   plain

Obv. 1

Rev. 1

Rev. 3

No.	Date	Features	Obv.	Rev.	F	VF	EF	UNC
G41D-005	1825		1	1	18	30	85	150
G41D-010	1825	PROOF	1	1				500
G41D-015	1826		1	1	10	20	60	120
G41D-020	1826	PROOF	1	1				350
G41D-025	1826	bronzed PROOF [1]	1	1				250
G41D-030	1826		1	2	12	24	75	150
G41D-035	1826	bronzed PROOF	1	2				250
G41D-040	1826		1	3	15	30	100	250
G41D-045	1826	PROOF	1	3				600
G41D-050	1826	bronzed PROOF	1	3				350
G41D-055	1827	[2]	1	1	70	250	1500	3000

1. Issued in cased proof sets.

No.	Date	Features	Obv.	Rev.	F	VF	EF	UNC
2. Struck for circulation in Australia.

William IV (1830 – 1837)

The obverse of the penny was engraved by William Wyon from a model by Sir Francis Chantrey. The layout of the obverse is similar to that of the George IV coin, while the reverse is identical.

Ernest Bramah (*English Regal Copper Coins*, 1929) reported that 'on very good authority' a penny of 1836 existed in Australia and that it had been sent to Britain for inspection. Montagu (*Copper, Tin and Bronze Coinage of England*, 1893) believed that its existence was doubtful. It is included in the tables below, therefore, with these provisos.

Collecting Hints

Specimens in extremely fine condition should be sought. Brilliant uncirculated specimens are very rare.

Denomination	Metal	Weight (grams)	Diameter (mm)	Rev. alignment
Penny	Copper	18.8	34	↑

Obverse 1   Head 1, right; .W.W incuse on truncation; GULIELMUS IIII DEI GRATIA (date)

Obverse 2   Similar but no initials on truncation

Reverse 1   Britannia, seated, with shield, facing right, holding trident; BRITANNIAR REX FID DEF (as Reverse 1 of George IV issue)

Edge   plain

Obv. 1   Rev. 1

No.	Date	Features	Obv.	Rev.	F	VF	EF	UNC
W41D-005	1831	[1]	1	1	14	55	160	400
W41D-010	1831		2	1	12	45	150	400
W41D-015	1831	bronzed PROOF	2	1				400
W41D-020	1831	bronzed PROOF; rev. ↓	2	1				300
W41D-025	1834		2	1	14	60	170	450
W41D-030	1836	[2]	2	1				
W41D-035	1837		2	1	40	100	250	650

1. Some exist without stop before first 'W' on truncation.
2. Existence doubtful; see above.

Victoria (1837 – 1901)

The Victorian penny is one of the most intricate and involved denominations of the British coinage. It comprises two broad divisions, the copper and the bronze series. Although the copper series possesses many varieties, mainly in colon position and type of trident, it is the bronze series from 1860 onwards which exhibits a remarkably wide range of varieties of all kinds. This is especially true up to the year 1883.

The Victorian penny has been the subject of much study, and a number of specialised books exist on the subject. Many of the varieties will be of interest only to a specialist collector of the series, and in a catalogue such as this some abbreviation is obviously necessary. For this reason, many of the minor varieties will be given in annotated form rather than allocating each variety a separate entry, and some may be omitted.

The copper penny was designed by William Wyon. He died in 1851, and the task of designing and engraving the bronze coinage fell to his elder son, Leonard Charles Wyon (1826–91). Unlike the silver coinage, there was no jubilee issue of bronze coins, and the veiled head design was not introduced on the bronze coinage until 1895. This was designed by Thomas Brock and engraved by G. W. de Saulles.

Some dates of Victoria young head pennies bear a small 'H' beneath the date. This signifies coins struck by Messrs. Ralph Heaton of Birmingham. This firm also assisted in the production during other years in which the mintmark was not used. In 1874, an individual wrote to 'The Times' newspaper to say that he had made a large number of forgeries on which he had placed the letter 'H'. Mr Heaton then wrote to the newspaper repudiating the story.

Denomination	Metal	Weight (grams)	Diameter (mm)	Rev. alignment
Penny 1839–60	Copper	18.8	34	↑
Penny 1860–1901	Bronze (copper 95%; tin 4%; zinc 1%)	9.4	31	↑

Obverse 1 Head 1, left, W.W. on truncation; VICTORIA DEI GRATIA (date)

Obverse 2 Similar but no W.W. on truncation

Obverse 3 Head 2, left; VICTORIA D G BRITT REG F D; 'L.C. Wyon' on bust near rim; beaded border

Obverse 4 Similar but toothed border

Obverse 5 Similar but 'L.C. Wyon' between bust and rim

Obverse 6 Similar but no 'L.C. Wyon'

Obverse 7 Head 3, left; slightly older features; same legend

Obverse 8 Head 4, left; VICTORIA DEI GRA BRITT REGINA FID DEF IND IMP

Reverse 1 Britannia, seated, with shield, holding trident, facing right; BRITANNIAR REG FID DEF (as reverse of William IV issue but trident head is ornamented except where described as plain, and REX becomes REG)

Reverse 2 Redesigned Britannia, seated with shield, holding trident, facing right; ONE PENNY; date in exergue below Britannia; 'L.C.W' on base line near shield; beaded border

Reverse 3 Similar but toothed border

Reverse 4 Similar but 'L.C.W.' below Britannia's foot at right

Reverse 5 Similar to Reverse 3 but 'L.C.W.' replaced by rock formation

Reverse 6 Similar but Britannia completely redesigned; 'P' of 'PENNY' is 2mm from trident head

Reverse 7 Similar but 'P' of 'PENNY' is 1mm from trident head. Sea level is higher

Reverse 8 Similar but sea level is even higher

Edge plain

It must be emphasised that on the young head bronze coinage (obverses 3 to 6; reverses 2 to 5) there exist a great many varieties. It would be impossible to cover these in detail or allocate different obverse/reverse numbers in a work of this nature. The major varieties are allocated different die types as above but the minor ones are referred to in annotated form in the tables, with details such as where on the die the varieties occur. Collectors requiring detailed information should refer to a specialised work such as by Peck, Gouby or Freeman.

Collecting Hints

The minimum grade of this series acceptable to a serious collector would be about very fine. Fine specimens, especially in the bronze series, do not show enough of the delicate workmanship of the design. In addition, if one is collecting the minor varieties, a fine condition specimen may not be detailed enough to provide identification.

The bronze penny provides an excellent subject for study by the serious numismatist, and is likely to appeal more to the intellectually inclined collector. However, because the collecting of bronze is not perhaps as popular as, say, the larger silver coins, there are excellent chances for the discovery of rarities. Many go unnoticed through ignorance. Indeed, one of the leading writers in this field once bought an unnoticed coronetted head pattern penny of Victoria from the tray of one of the top London dealers!

'Ghosting', caused by clashed dies, is prevalent throughout the Victorian series, and should not be a deterrent to the purchase of a specimen. What happens is that, prior to striking, the dies clash together when a blank is not in position and traces of design transfer between the dies on impact. The 1860 copper penny appears always to have ghosting markings under the chin of Victoria. These originate from the drapery of Britannia on the reverse, and provide a useful identification mark, as some forgeries exist where the date has been altered. A further check is that the genuine 1860 copper penny will not have W.W. on the truncation, although of course this does not preclude any forgeries made from pennies dated 1858 and 1859. Note also that the genuine 1860 penny itself has the date altered from 1859 on the die.

Proofs were never prepared from dies bearing clashing marks, and any prooflike specimen with ghosting may be assumed not to be a proof.

Original mint lustre is more important with copper and bronze than it is with silver. Not only does the retention of original lustre make the coin more pleasing, but it is also difficult or impossible to restore it artificially. One should become aware of the characteristics of various types of artificial lustre, and pay special attention to the amount of structural wear that the coin possesses. It is all too easy to see a lustrous coin, and fail to notice that much detail has worn off.

Collectors are often convinced they possess an 1860 (bronze) beaded border specimen, or even a mule beaded/toothed specimen, when they do not. This is because the border on some of the toothed issue is very prominent and the teeth are almost round. On a genuine beaded border specimen, the dots are circular and stand apart from the border in a way that leaves no room for doubt.

Obv. 1   Obv. 3

Obv. 5   Obv. 7

Obv. 8

Rev. 1

Rev. 1 ornamental trident

Rev. 1 plain trident

Rev. 2

Rev. 3

Rev. 6

Rev. 7

Copper Issue

No.	Date	Features	Obv.	Rev.	F	VF	EF	UNC
VY1D-005	1839	bronzed PROOF [1]	1	1		180	300	400
VY1D-010	1841	no colon after REG	1	1	5	10	45	80
VY1D-015	1841	colon after REG	1	1	10	25	100	200
VY1D-020	1841	colon after REG; PROOF	1	1				700
VY1D-025	1841	colon after REG; bronzed PROOF	1	1				600
VY1D-030	1841	colon after REG; PROOF in silver [2]	1	1				4000
VY1D-035	1843	no colon after REG	1	1	50	160	600	900
VY1D-040	1843	colon after REG	1	1	35	120	400	600
VY1D-045	1844		1	1	8	15	55	100
VY1D-050	1845		1	1	10	24	100	200
VY1D-055	1846		1	1	5	14	65	130
VY1D-060	1846	near colon (see below)	1	1	7	18	80	170
VY1D-065	1847		1	1	5	14	65	130
VY1D-070	1847	near colon	1	1	5	14	65	130
VY1D-075	1848		1	1	5	14	65	130
VY1D-080	1848	8 over 6	1	1	10	22	120	220
VY1D-085	1848	8 over 7	1	1	5	14	70	140
VY1D-090	1849		1	1	80	200	800	1400
VY1D-095	1851	[3]	1	1	8	18	65	130
VY1D-100	1851	near colon	1	1	8	18	75	150
VY1D-105	1853		1	1	4	9	32	55
VY1D-110	1853	PROOF	1	1			350	700

No.	Date	Features	Obv.	Rev.	F	VF	EF	UNC
VY1D-115	1853	bronzed PROOF rev. ↓ [4]	1	1			200	400
VY1D-120	1853	near colon; plain trident head	1	1	8	16	60	100
VY1D-125	1854		1	1	5	10	35	65
VY1D-130	1854	near colon; plain trident head	1	1	5	10	35	65
VY1D-135	1854	PROOF; near colon; plain trident head	1	1				250
VY1D-140	1854	near colon; plain trident head 4 over 3	1	1	20	50	150	250
VY1D-145	1855		1	1	5	10	40	70
VY1D-150	1855	near colon; plain trident head	1	1	5	10	40	70
VY1D-155	1856		1	1	18	50	250	400
VY1D-160	1856	near colon; plain trident head	1	1	10	30	150	280
VY1D-165	1856	near colon; plain trident head PROOF	1	1				700
VY1D-170	1857		1	1	6	12	48	90
VY1D-175	1857	near colon; plain trident head	1	1	5	10	40	70
VY1D-180	1857	near colon; plain trident head small date	1	1	5	10	40	70
VY1D-185	1858		1	1	4	8	30	65
VY1D-190	1858	small date	1	1	6	10	40	80
VY1D-192	1858	small date; latter 8 over 6	1	1	12	30	120	200
VY1D-195	1858	latter 8 over 7	1	1	4	8	30	65
VY1D-200	1858		2	1	4	8	30	65
VY1D-205	1859		2	1	5	10	40	70
VY1D-210	1859	small date	2	1	8	15	60	110
VY1D-215	1859	PROOF	2	1				500
VY1D-220	1860	60 altered from 59 [5]	2	1		500	900	1700
VY1D-225	1860	60 altered from 59 rev. ↓ [6]	2	1		700	1200	2200

1. Issued in cased proof sets; specimens with reverse ↓ not recorded (cf. halfpenny and farthing).
2. Slightly thicker than ordinary issue.
3. Issued also during 1852.
4. Issued in cased proof sets.
5. See 'Collecting Hints' above.
6. Unrecorded in Peck but a specimen (uncatalogued) sold at Glendining's March 1992.

Bronze Issue; Young Head

No.	Date	Features	Obv.	Rev.	F	VF	EF	UNC
VY1D-230	1860	[1]	3	2	15	35	70	120
VY1D-235	1860	rev. ↓	3	2	20	50	120	200
VY1D-240	1860	PROOF [2]	3	2				500
VY1D-245	1860	bronzed PROOF in copper	3	2				600
VY1D-250	1860	bronzed PROOF in copper on thick flan [3]	3	2			500	800
VY1D-255	1860	PROOF in silver on thick flan [4]	3	2				2500
VY1D-260	1860	PROOF in gold [5]	3	2				15000
VY1D-265	1860	[6]	3	3	150	220	450	800
VY1D-270	1860	[7]	4	2	200	300	700	1200
VY1D-275	1860	[8]	4	3	5	12	50	90
VY1D-280	1860	on thick flan [9]	4	3	250	450		
VY1D-285	1860	on very thick flan [10]	4	3	250	450		
VY1D-290	1860	PROOF	4	3				500
VY1D-295	1860		4	4	90	150	400	900
VY1D-300	1860	[11]	5	3	8	20	50	100
VY1D-305	1860	[12]	6	3	10	20	60	120
VY1D-310	1861	[13]	4	3	25	50	200	400
VY1D-315	1861	[14]	4	5	40	75	300	500
VY1D-320	1861		5	3	5	15	60	110
VY1D-325	1861	on thick flan [15]	5	3	200	500		
VY1D-330	1861	[14]	5	5	25	50	200	400
VY1D-335	1861	[16]	6	3	5	15	60	110
VY1D-340	1861	6 over 8	6	3	120	300		
VY1D-345	1861	PROOF	6	3				400
VY1D-350	1861	[17]	6	5	5	15	60	110
VY1D-355	1861	8 over 6	6	5	200	500		
VY1D-360	1861	PROOF	6	5				400
VY1D-365	1861	PROOF in gold; rev. ↓ [18]	6	5				8000
VY1D-370	1861	PROOF in silver on thin flan	6	5				1500

No.	Date	Features	Obv.	Rev.	F	VF	EF	UNC
VY1D-375	1861	PROOF in silver on thick flan [19]	6	5				2000
VY1D-380	1861	PROOF in copper [20]	6	5				500
VY1D-385	1862		4	5	150	300	1000	3000
VY1D-390	1862		6	5	4	10	40	70
VY1D-392	1862	B of BRITT over R (obv.)	6	5	80	180	350	600
VY1D-395	1862	8 over 6	6	5	100	200		
VY1D-400	1862	date numerals from halfpenny die	6	5	250	500		
VY1D-405	1862	PROOF	6	5				400
VY1D-410	1863	[21]	6	5	4	10	40	70
VY1D-415	1863	die number 2 below date	6	5	1000	4000		
VY1D-420	1863	die number 3 below date	6	5	1000	4000		
VY1D-425	1863	die number 4 below date	6	5	1000	4000		
VY1D-430	1863	PROOF	6	5				400
VY1D-435	1864	[22]	6	5	8	40	200	550
VY1D-440	1865		6	5	6	15	65	110
VY1D-445	1865	5 over 3	6	5	40	100	400	1000
VY1D-450	1866		6	5	6	15	55	95
VY1D-455	1867		6	5	6	15	65	170
VY1D-460	1867	PROOF	6	5				500
VY1D-465	1867	bronzed PROOF in copper	6	5				500
VY1D-470	1868		6	5	10	24	110	180
VY1D-475	1868	PROOF	6	5				500
VY1D-480	1868	PROOF in copper [23]	6	5				600
VY1D-485	1868	PROOF in cupronickel [24]	6	5			350	500
VY1D-490	1869		6	5	50	150	500	950
VY1D-495	1870		6	5	10	30	150	250
VY1D-500	1871		6	5	25	80	280	420
VY1D-505	1872		6	5	6	15	55	95
VY1D-510	1872	PROOF; rev. ↓	6	5				1000
VY1D-515	1873		6	5	6	15	55	95
VY1D-520	1874		6	5	7	18	65	110
VY1D-525	1874	narrow date [25]	6	5	15	50	150	300
VY1D-530	1874	H below date [26]	6	5	8	22	75	140
VY1D-535	1874	H below date narrow date	6	5	30	60	180	400
VY1D-540	1874	[27]	7	5	7	18	65	110
VY1D-545	1874	narrow date [28]	7	5	7	20	70	130
VY1D-550	1874	H below date [27]	7	5	8	22	75	140
VY1D-555	1874	H below date narrow date	7	5	8	22	75	140
VY1D-560	1874	H below date narrow date PROOF	7	5				400
VY1D-565	1875	[26]	7	5	4	10	35	65
VY1D-570	1875	narrow date [25]	7	5	5	15	40	80
VY1D-575	1875	narrow date PROOF	7	5				600
VY1D-580	1875	PROOF in cupronickel	7	5				1200
VY1D-585	1875	PROOF on thick flan [29]	7	5				1200
VY1D-590	1875	H below date	7	5	20	80	400	650
VY1D-595	1875	H below date PROOF	7	5				800
VY1D-600	1876	H below date	7	5	8	20	80	150
VY1D-605	1876	H below date narrow date	7	5	4	10	35	65
VY1D-610	1876	H below date narrow date PROOF	7	5				600
VY1D-615	1877	narrow date	7	5	500			
VY1D-620	1877	[25]	7	5	4	10	35	65
VY1D-625	1877	PROOF	7	5				500
VY1D-630	1877	PROOF in cupronickel [30]	7	5				1200
VY1D-635	1878		7	5	5	12	45	100
VY1D-640	1878	PROOF	7	5				400
VY1D-645	1879	[31]	7	5	3	8	30	70
VY1D-650	1879	PROOF	7	5				600
VY1D-655	1879	narrow date [25]	7	5	20	50	100	250
VY1D-660	1880	[32]	7	5	5	11	40	90
VY1D-665	1880	PROOF	7	5				600
VY1D-670	1881	[31]	7	5	6	15	50	120
VY1D-675	1881	PROOF [32]	7	5				800
VY1D-680	1881	H below date	7	5	4	10	35	80
VY1D-685	1881	H below date PROOF	7	5				600
VY1D-690	1882	[33]	7	5	400	700	1000	1500
VY1D-695	1882	H below date [34]	7	5	3	8	28	55
VY1D-700	1882	H below date 2 over 1 [35]	7	5	20	50	100	200

No.	Date	Features	Obv.	Rev.	F	VF	EF	UNC
VY1D-705	1882	H below date PROOF [36]	7	5				800
VY1D-710	1883	[37]	7	5	4	9	35	60
VY1D-715	1883	PROOF	7	5				400
VY1D-720	1884		7	5	3	7	25	50
VY1D-725	1884	PROOF	7	5				400
VY1D-730	1885		7	5	3	7	25	50
VY1D-735	1885	PROOF	7	5				400
VY1D-740	1886		7	5	3	7	25	50
VY1D-745	1886	PROOF	7	5				400
VY1D-750	1887		7	5	3	7	25	50
VY1D-755	1887	PROOF	7	5				400
VY1D-760	1888	[38]	7	5	3	7	25	50
VY1D-765	1888	both 'I's in VICTORIA have no top left serif [39]	7	5	5	11	40	80
VY1D-770	1889	[40]	7	5	3	6	22	40
VY1D-775	1889	PROOF [40]	7	5				400
VY1D-780	1890		7	5	3	6	22	40
VY1D-785	1890	PROOF	7	5				400
VY1D-790	1891		7	5	3	6	20	35
VY1D-795	1891	PROOF	7	5				400
VY1D-800	1892		7	5	3	6	20	35
VY1D-805	1892	PROOF	7	5				400
VY1D-810	1893		7	5	3	6	20	35
VY1D-815	1893	PROOF	7	5				400
VY1D-820	1894		7	5	4	8	30	65
VY1D-825	1894	PROOF	7	5				500

1. Slight variations in: portrait; shield; drapery; sea, etc.
2. Two slightly different obv. dies.
3. Weight 12.5–13.5 grams; thickness c.2.3mm.
4. Weight c.14.5 grams; thickness c.2.3mm.
5. Weight c.13.7 grams.
6. A 'mule' with beaded obverse and toothed reverse.
7. A 'mule' with toothed obverse and beaded reverse.
8. Slight variations (obv.) in: legend; portrait; position of 'L.C. Wyon'.
9. Possibly a proof; weight c.11.3 grams.
10. Weight 16.0–16.5 grams.
11. Some have the N in 'ONE' over a sideways N (rev.).
12. Some read 'ONF' instead of 'ONE' (rev.) (die flaw) slight variations (obv.) in: portrait; legend and portrait position.
13. Slight variations (obv.) in: position of 'L.C. Wyon'; legend size and alignment.
14. Slight variations (rev.) in: shield; legend size; sea; lighthouse; ship; trident, etc.
15. Weight c.11 grams.
16. Slight variations (obv.) in: portrait; legend and portrait position.
17. Many slight variations on obv. and rev.
18. Weight c.16 grams.
19. Weight c.18 grams.
20. Exists with or without bronzed finish.
21. Possibly occurs with narrow '3' in date.
22. Two different types of '4' in date; slight axis misalignments occur.
23. Rim is slightly wider.
24. See also halfpenny and farthing.
25. Minor reverse differences from coin above.
26. Minor reverse differences occur.
27. Minor portrait differences occur.
28. Minor portrait differences occur minor reverse differences from coin above.
29. Weight c.11.6 grams.
30. Weight c.9.0 grams.
31. Minor obverse differences occur.
32. Minor obverse/reverse differences occur.
33. No H below date; a major omission by Peck but noted by Freeman.
34. Minor reverse differences occur. Horizontal bar of H mintmark may be missing.
35. Overdate faint and fragmented.
36. Reverse is slightly modified and exists only on this coin. May be considered a pattern or proof.
37. Minor obverse differences occur, esp: hair; lettering.
38. Presumably proofs may have been struck.
39. Compare double florin of 1888/89.
40. Minor obverse differences occur, esp. wreath.

Old Head

No.	Date	Features	Obv.	Rev.	F	VF	EF	UNC
VO1D-830	1895		8	6	7	30	110	180
VO1D-835	1895	PROOF	8	6				1000
VO1D-840	1895		8	7	2	5	12	25
VO1D-845	1895	PROOF	8	7				400
VO1D-850	1896		8	7	2	5	10	18
VO1D-855	1896	PROOF	8	7				400
VO1D-860	1897		8	7	2	5	10	18
VO1D-865	1897		8	8	10	40	120	250
VO1D-870	1898		8	7	2	6	15	35
VO1D-875	1899		8	7	2	5	10	20
VO1D-880	1900		8	7	2	5	10	20
VO1D-885	1900	PROOF	8	7				350
VO1D-890	1901		8	7	2	4	6	12
VO1D-895	1901	PROOF	8	7				350

The term 'near colon' refers to copper pennies on which the colon after DEF (reverse) is decidedly nearer to DEF than midway between the F and Britannia's foot.

Edward VII   (1901 – 1910)

The obverse of the penny uses the portrait of Edward VII by George William de Saulles (1862–1903) as on the silver coinage. The reverse is very similar to that on the veiled head penny of Victoria. Both obverse and reverse exhibit minor alterations in design during this reign, of which by far the best known is the so-called 'Low Tide' penny of 1902. Other slight die variations exist in the series, and the 1908 penny actually exhibits at least four distinct varieties, not including the proof.

There is some variation in metal colour with the pennies of this reign, and specimens are sometimes found with a somewhat unpleasant yellow streaky appearance.

Collecting Hints

Unless one is collecting the die varieties, one specimen of each date in mint state with original lustre should be acquired. Most collectors will want to obtain a 1902 'Low Tide' specimen, and it is not too difficult to find this coin in extremely fine or better. This is because, being the first year of issue, many were put away as keepsakes.

Denomination	Metal	Weight (grams)	Diameter (mm)	Rev. alignment
Penny	Bronze (copper 95%; tin 4%; zinc 1%)	9.4	31	↑

Unofficial variations in metal composition occurred, resulting in some coins being lighter in colour than others

Obverse 1   Head 1, right; EDWARDVS VII DEI GRA BRITT OMN REX FID DEF IND IMP

Reverse 1   Britannia, seated, with shield and trident, facing right; ONE PENNY; date in exergue below Britannia

Reverse 2   Similar but sea is higher

Edge   plain

Obv. 1	Rev. 1
Rev. 1 (enl.)	Rev. 2 (enl.)

No.	Date	Features	Obv.	Rev.	VF	EF	UNC
E71D-005	1902	[1]	1	1	8	20	50
E71D-010	1902		1	2	4	7	12
E71D-015	1903	[2]	1	2	6	12	25
E71D-020	1904		1	2	7	15	35
E71D-025	1905	[3]	1	2	6	12	30

No.	Date	Features	Obv.	Rev.	VF	EF	UNC
E71D-030	1906		1	2	6	11	30
E71D-035	1907		1	2	6	11	30
E71D-040	1908	[4]	1	2	6	12	30
E71D-045	1908	matt PROOF on thick flan [5]	1	2			1000
E71D-050	1909	[6]	1	2	6	12	24
E71D-055	1910		1	2	5	10	20

1. Known as 'Low Tide' variety.
2. 3 in date varies in shape.
3. Orientation of 'E' in PENNY (rev.) varies.
4. Minor obverse/reverse differences occur.
5. Weight c.12.5 grams.
6. Minor reverse differences occur; colour of metal varies widely with composition variation.

George V   (1910 – 1936)

The portrait of George V used on the penny was by Sir Bertram Mackennal (1863–1931), while the reverse continued the same Britannia design used for the Edward VII series.

In the first years of production of the penny, problems were encountered with 'ghosting' (see p.575). The nature of this was different from that experienced on the Victorian coinage. While many Victorian coins had suffered faint but sharply defined 'ghost' images caused by clashed dies, the ghosting on the George V pennies was vague in outline and yet more widespread. It was caused by the dies, especially the obverse, being in too high relief. When the coin was struck, the amount of metal needed to fill the hollow of the portrait die was so much that it drew metal from the corresponding area on the reverse. This phenomenon can be seen on many specimens of penny, especially before 1920, where the field either side of Britannia exhibits a characteristic striation. The pennies of this period are also somewhat weakly struck, and this is particularly noticeable on the 'KN' specimens of 1918 and 1919 (see below).

A reduction in ghosting was achieved with the introduction of striking in lower relief in 1921 and 1926; finally the small head introduced in 1928 produced a sharply struck coin with little or no ghosting.

Some pennies of 1912, 1918 and 1919 were struck with a small 'H' to the left of the date, while some of 1918 and 1919 have the letters 'KN' in this position; these coins were struck at the Heaton works (later The Mint, Birmingham, Ltd.) and by the Kings Norton Metal Co Ltd (also at Birmingham) respectively.

Metal colouration of toned coins is a subject not normally touched on in catalogues, but which is worthy of some research. It is noticeable, for example, that while 'H' pennies normally tone to black, the 'KN' pieces and the 1928–36 series almost always achieve a dark reddish-brown finish, except for those of 1934 and some of 1935, which were issued artificially darkened.

Collecting Hints

Collect this series in extremely fine or mint state, with as much original lustre as possible. The 'H' and 'KN' varieties are difficult to find in this condition, but in considering specimens it must be remembered that these are invariably weakly struck.

The 1926 'modified effigy' penny is not at all easy to find in the higher grades, and some collectors have difficulty in distinguishing between the two heads of the 1926 coin. One distinguishing feature is that on the first obverse the lower dot of the colon between GRA and BRITT lies almost centrally between the A and the B. On the modified head obverse the dot is much nearer the A.

Only about seven specimens of the legendary 1933 penny exist, and it is unlikely that others will be found after this time. One should not therefore waste time and effort in checking dates of the 1928–36 type, the remainder of which are all fairly common. One is more likely to encounter one of the many forgeries with an altered date.

No.	Date	Features	Obv.	Rev.	VF	EF	UNC
G51D-005	1911	[1]	1	1	6	10	20
G51D-010	1912		1	1	6	10	20
G51D-015	1912	H to left of date	1	1	10	30	80
G51D-020	1913	[2]	1	1	6	11	22
G51D-025	1914		1	1	6	12	25
G51D-030	1915		1	1	6	12	28
G51D-035	1916		1	1	6	12	25
G51D-040	1917		1	1	6	10	18
G51D-045	1918		1	1	6	10	20
G51D-050	1918	H to left of date	1	1	15	80	180
G51D-055	1918	KN to left of date [3]	1	1	20	120	240
G51D-060	1919		1	1	6	10	20
G51D-065	1919	H to left of date	1	1	15	80	180
G51D-070	1919	KN to left of date	1	1	25	140	450
G51D-075	1920	[4]	1	1	6	10	20
G51D-080	1921	[4]	1	1	6	10	20
G51D-085	1922		1	1	10	30	60
G51D-090	1922	[5]	1	2	1500	4000	
G51D-095	1926		1	1	12	45	90
G51D-100	1926	PROOF	1	1			600
G51D-105	1926		2	1	30	250	900
G51D-110	1926	PROOF	2	1			1000
G51D-115	1927		2	2	4	7	12
G51D-120	1927	PROOF	2	2			400
G51D-125	1928		3	2	4	7	10
G51D-130	1928	PROOF	3	2			400
G51D-135	1929		3	2	4	8	11
G51D-140	1929	PROOF	3	2			400
G51D-145	1930		3	2	4	8	16
G51D-150	1930	PROOF	3	2			400
G51D-155	1931		3	2	4	9	16
G51D-160	1931	PROOF	3	2			450
G51D-165	1932		3	2	4	15	50
G51D-170	1932	PROOF	3	2			500
G51D-175	1933	artificially darkened at mint (?) [6]	3	2			30000
G51D-178	1933	PROOF; artificially darkened at mint (?)	3	2			35000
G51D-180	1934	artificially darkened at mint	3	2	4	14	28
G51D-185	1934	PROOF	3	2			500
G51D-190	1935	artificially darkened at mint	3	2	1	2	3
G51D-195	1935		3	2	1	2	3
G51D-200	1935	PROOF	3	2			400
G51D-205	1936		3	2	1	2	3
G51D-210	1936	PROOF	3	2			350

1. Minor obverse varieties exist.
2. Slightly different obverse/reverse dies introduced during this year.
3. Spacing of KN varies.
4. Slightly different obverse dies introduced during 1920/21.
5. Minor differences from the later Reverse 2; border teeth are longer.
6. Not issued for circulation.

It must be remembered that pennies of 1934 and some of 1935 were issued artificially darkened with sodium thio-sulphate, and particular attention must be paid to the structural wear when grading. As with all of this series, wear becomes apparent first on the hand gripping the trident, and on the arm which extends to the shield.

The 1922 penny with reverse 2 is not a well known coin but is very rare and worth looking for. An experienced collector will be able to distinguish reverse 2 at a glance, not by comparing characteristics but simply by the way this reverse is struck and the way it wears, quite differently from reverse 1. The reverse in fine condition resembles a halfpenny reverse of the later George V period on account of the larger border teeth.

Denomination	Metal	Weight (grams)	Diameter (mm)	Rev. alignment
Penny 1911–22	Bronze (copper 95%; tin 4%; zinc 1%)	9.4	31	↑
Penny 1926–36	Bronze (copper 95.5%; tin 3%; zinc 1.5%)	9.4	31	↑

Obverse 1 Head 1, left, B.M. on truncation; GEORGIVS V DEI GRA BRITT OMN REX FID DEF IND IMP

Obverse 2 Head 2, known as 'modified effigy', left; initials BM are without stops and further to right; same legend

Obverse 3 Head 3, smaller, more sharply struck, left; same legend

Reverse 1 Britannia, seated, with shield and trident, facing right; ONE PENNY; date in exergue below Britannia

Reverse 2 Similar but redesigned and more sharply struck

Edge plain

Obv. 1   Obv. 2

Obv. 3   Rev. 1 ('ghosting')

Rev. 2 early   Rev. 2 late

Edward VIII (1936)

The Edward VIII penny is strictly speaking a pattern, as probable Royal approval was about to be granted at the time of the abdication. However, because its official status rests only on this technicality, and to provide continuity, it is included here.

The portrait of Edward VIII is by Thomas Humphrey Paget, and faces left at the insistence of the king, who considered this placement more flattering and wished to discontinue the tradition of opposite facings for successive monarchs. The reverse was a revamped version of that used on previous reigns.

Denomination	Metal	Weight (grams)	Diameter (mm)	Rev. alignment
Penny	Bronze (copper 95.5%; tin 3%; zinc 1.5%)	9.4	31	↑

Obverse 1 Head 1, left; EDWARDVS VIII D G BR OMN REX F D IND IMP

Reverse 1 Britannia, seated, with shield and trident, facing right; ONE PENNY; date 1937 in exergue below Britannia

Edge plain

Obv. 1

Rev. 1

No.	Date		Obv.	Rev.	Unc
E81D-005	1937		1	1	25000

Denomination	Metal	Weight (grams)	Diameter (mm)	Rev. alignment
Penny 1937–40	Bronze (copper 95.5%; tin 3%; zinc 1.5%)	9.4	31	↑
Penny 1944–45	Bronze (copper 97%; tin 0.5%; zinc 2.5%)	9.4	31	↑
Penny 1945–51	Bronze (copper 95.5%; tin 3%; zinc 1.5%)	9.4	31	↑

Obverse 1   Head 1, left; GEORGIVS VI D G BR OMN REX F D IND IMP

Obverse 2   Head 1, left; GEORGIVS VI D G BR OMN REX FIDEI DEF

Reverse 1   Britannia, seated, with shield and trident, facing right; ONE PENNY; date in exergue below Britannia

Edge   plain

George VI   (1937 – 1952)

The pennies of George VI use a portrait of the king by Thomas Humphrey Paget, with a redesigned Britannia reverse. While pennies of the latter years of George V had been struck in proof in small quantities, a relatively large number of proofs of the 1937 penny needed to be struck to satisfy the issue of cased proof sets for the Coronation year. These proofs were struck to a higher standard than the George V proofs. Thereafter, proofs were again struck in small quantities for each year of the regular issue, but again in 1950 and 1951 the mintage was augmented by the issue of proof sets.

Although there were a number of minor changes to both obverse and reverse during this series, basically there were two main obverses and one reverse, the legend on the obverse being amended in 1949 when the title IND IMP (Emperor of India) was removed.

In 1940 it became apparent that a large amount of pennies were in circulation. Consequently, no pennies bearing the dates 1941 to 1943 were struck, and the few required for colonial issue were struck from dies with the 1940 date. When the issue was resumed in 1944, the world scarcity of tin had necessitated a reduction of the content of this metal in the bronze from 3% to 0.5%. It had been found that this reduced-tin bronze tarnished unattractively, and consequently the penny issue of 1944 to 1946 was treated with sodium thiosulphate, which gave it a darkened appearance. Subsequent coinage had the tin content increased to its original amount.

In 1950 and 1951 the issues of pennies in Great Britain was again discontinued, but unlike in 1941 those sent for colonial use bore the actual date of issue. In the early sixties, collecting by date became fashionable, and initially no denomination was more fashionable to collect than the bronze penny. The 1951 penny, in particular, acquired something of a cult status. At that time, someone in the coin business discovered that almost the entire issue had been sent to Bermuda. Considerable effort was made to buy as many of the 120,000 specimens as possible, and many wild claims were made about the investment potential of the coin.

Obv. 1

Obv. 2

Rev. 1

No.	Date	Features	Obv.	Rev.	VF	EF	UNC
G61D-005	1937	[1]	1	1	1	3	4
G61D-010	1937	PROOF [2]	1	1		4	10
G61D-015	1937	PROOF from sandblasted dies [3]	1	1			200
G61D-020	1938		1	1	1	3	5
G61D-025	1938	PROOF	1	1			250
G61D-030	1939		1	1	1	4	7
G61D-035	1939	PROOF	1	1			250
G61D-040	1940	[4]	1	1	1	4	10
G61D-045	1940	PROOF	1	1			250
G61D-050	1944	most artificially darkened at mint	1	1	1	4	8
G61D-055	1944	PROOF; artificially darkened at mint	1	1			300
G61D-060	1945	most artificially darkened at mint [5]	1	1	1	3	6
G61D-065	1945	PROOF; artificially darkened at mint	1	1			300
G61D-070	1946	most artificially darkened at mint	1	1	1	3	5
G61D-075	1946	PROOF; artificially darkened at mint	1	1			300
G61D-080	1947		1	1	1	3	5
G61D-085	1947	PROOF	1	1			300
G61D-090	1948		1	1	1	3	4
G61D-095	1948	PROOF	1	1			200
G61D-100	1949		2	1	1	3	4
G61D-105	1949	PROOF	2	1			200
G61D-110	1950	[6]	2	1	5	10	30
G61D-115	1950	PROOF [2]	2	1			15
G61D-120	1950	PROOF from sandblasted dies [3]	2	1			220
G61D-125	1951	[7]	2	1	10	18	30
G61D-130	1951	PROOF [2]	2	1			18
G61D-135	1951	PROOF from sandblasted dies [3]	2	1			250

Collecting Hints

This series should be collected in mint state with original lustre, or, in the case of the 1944–46 issue, with original patina. The 1951 penny overall is scarcer than the 1950, but in mint state the 1950 is considerably scarcer. The proofs of 1950 and 1951 are somewhat difficult to find with full lustre because the cases of the proof sets had a tendency to induce toning on the coins.

No.	Date	Features	Obv.	Rev.	VF	EF	UNC
G61D-140	1952	PROOF [8]	2	1			25000

1. Slight border teeth differences occur.
2. Issued in cased proof sets.
3. Struck to facilitate photography of coin.
4. Exergual line becomes double during this year.
5. 9 in date may be doubled.
6. Issued for colonial use.
7. Issued mainly for Bermuda.
8. Probably unique.

Elizabeth II   (1952 –)

The series continues the general overall design of the George VI penny, using a portrait of Elizabeth II by Mary Gillick. The toothed border of the George VI coinage was replaced by a border of fine circular dots, although at least one specimen of the 1953 penny exists with a toothed border on both sides. The reverse is a slightly redesigned Britannia.

Because of a surplus of pennies in circulation, no pennies dated 1953 were struck for circulation, but a large number of specimen sets of 1953 was issued, in which the coins were sealed in a plastic holder. Colloquially known as 'plastic sets', many of these were split open and the coinage spent, as they were issued for only a small premium over their face value. Later, in the mid-sixties, when date collecting of pennies became popular, many more were split open to obtain the penny.

The 1953 penny was also issued in proof condition in the cased proof sets marking the coronation of the queen. The penny of this date, as well as being scarce because it was not issued for circulation, is a popular piece also because it is a one-year type. On later coins the words 'BRITT OMN' were omitted from the obverse.

At least one specimen exists of a penny dated 1954, apparently struck for private internal purposes at the mint, but it was not until 1961 that demand again required the penny to be struck for circulation. The series was to last only another six years, during which a very large quantity of this coin was issued.

The amount of coinage struck between 1961 and 1967 necessitated a considerable amount of retouching to the waves and sealine on the reverse dies to maintain their sharpness, so much so that an expert in this field could no doubt date a coin from a close examination of the details on the sea.

Collecting Hints

The series should be collected in mint state. Apart from the 1953, the proofs are very difficult to find.

Denomination	Metal	Weight (grams)	Diameter (mm)	Rev. alignment
Penny 1953–54	Bronze (copper 95.5%; tin 3%; zinc 1.5%)	9.4	31	↑
Penny 1961–67	Bronze (copper 97%; tin 0.5%; zinc 2.5%)	9.4	31	↑

Obverse 1   Head 1, right; ELIZABETH II DEI GRA BRITT OMN REGINA F D. Border is toothed

Obverse 2   Similar but border is of fine circular or near-circular dots

Obverse 3   Similar but ELIZABETH II DEI GRATIA REGINA F D

Obverse J   Obverse intended for Jersey Elizabeth II penny: Head 2, crowned, right: QUEEN ELIZABETH THE SECOND

Reverse 1   Britannia, seated, with shield and trident, facing right; ONE PENNY; date in exergue below Britannia. Border is toothed

Reverse 2   Similar but border is of fine circular or near-circular dots

Edge   plain

Obv. 2

Obv. 3

Rev. 2

No.	Date	Features	Obv.	Rev.	EF	UNC
EZ1D-005	1953	[1]	1	1		750
EZ1D-010	1953	PROOF [1]	2	1		750
EZ1D-015	1953	[2]	2	2	4	6
EZ1D-020	1953	PROOF [3]	2	2	5	8
EZ1D-025	1953	PROOF from sandblasted dies [4]	2	2		200
EZ1D-030	1954	[5]	3	2		25000
EZ1D-035	1961	[6]	3	2		2
EZ1D-040	1961	PROOF	3	2		250
EZ1D-045	1962	[7]	3	2		1
EZ1D-048	1962	rev. →	3	2		80
EZ1D-050	1962	struck on heavy flan [8]	3	2		400
EZ1D-055	1962	PROOF	3	2		250
EZ1D-060	1963	[9]	3	2		1
EZ1D-065	1963	PROOF	3	2		250
EZ1D-070	1964	[10]	3	2		1
EZ1D-075	1964	struck without collar in cupronickel [11]	3	2		150
EZ1D-080	1964	PROOF	3	2		250
EZ1D-085	1965	[12]	3	2		1
EZ1D-090	1965	struck in gold [13]	3	2		2500
EZ1D-095	1965	struck in cupronickel [14]	3	2		300
EZ1D-100	1966	[12]	3	2		1
EZ1D-105	1966	struck in cupronickel [15]	3	2		300
EZ1D-110	1966	[16]	J	2		1200
EZ1D-115	1967	[17]	3	2		1
EZ1D-118	1967	struck on flan which does not 'ring'	3	2		25
EZ1D-120	1967	struck on thin flan [18]	3	2		200
EZ1D-125	1967	struck on heavy flan [19]	3	2		400
EZ1D-130	1967	struck in nickel-brass [20]	3	2	250	350
EZ1D-135	1970	PROOF [21]	3	2	2	4

1. Struck in 1952.
2. Issued in 'plastic sets'.
3. Issued in cased proof sets.
4. Struck to facilitate photography of coin.
5. Only 1 known but several struck; both sides slightly redesigned.
6. Both sides slightly redesigned.
7. Reverse slightly retouched.
8. Weight c.13 grams.
9. Reverse slightly redesigned.
10. Reverse slightly retouched (waves).
11. Weight 11.3 grams.
12. Reverse again retouched (waves); on 1965 minor helmet variations exist.
13. Weight c.18.3 grams.
14. Weight c.11.5 grams.
15. Weight c.11 grams.
16. Obverse is of Jersey Elizabeth II penny; weight 9.3 grams.
17. Reverse again retouched (waves and sealine; minor lighthouse varieties exist (rev.).
18. Weight c.7 grams.
19. Weight c.13 grams.
20. Weight 9.6 grams.
21. Issued in sealed cased proof sets.

The penny ceased to be legal tender after 31 August 1971.

Finished coin blanks ready for receiving the impression after drying

Halfpenny

Charles II   (1660 – 1685)

In the early part of the reign of Charles II there was a clear need for coins of low denomination to fund the day-to-day purchases of the common man. The silver penny and twopence issued in the first few years of the reign had been extensively hoarded, and it was the practice of tradesmen in many parts of the country to issue private tokens in base metal. Although, strictly speaking, the issue of such tokens was an offence, in practice any penalties exacted were minimal. This was no doubt because the authorities appreciated the need for such coinage which was not available legally.

A problem with the issuance of coinage is that if the face value is less than the cost of manufacture (including the metal), the exercise is conducted at a loss, and the coins may be subsequently clipped or melted down; if the face value is higher, counterfeit coins begin to appear.

It was not until 1672 that the mint was ready to produce coins in copper. By that time, the issue of 'Maundy-type' small silver was underway, and these were circulating widely. No copper pennies were therefore struck, but the Royal Proclamation in August decreed that halfpennies and farthings would be issued, and that these would have a face value equal to the value of the metal less the cost of producing them. The new coins were legal tender up to six pence, and depicted Britannia on the reverse, modelled by the Duchess of Richmond. They were issued from an office in Fenchurch Street, in the City of London, between the hours of 0900–1200 and 1400–1700.

It was soon found that the mint was incapable of producing the copper blanks necessary, and these eventually had to be imported from Sweden. To facilitate the process, the Customs Duty on import was waived. Further delays ensued, however, not least because of transportation problems. The first halfpennies did not appear until after Christmas (remembering that in those days the year ended on March 24, there were still three months until 1673 began).

The ideals of striking coinage with a value equal to its production costs were not maintained, and the coins were given a face value slightly higher. Inevitably, counterfeit coins began to appear within a few years.

A proclamation of 15 December 1674 threatened action against those who 'make and utter forgeries, halfpence or pieces of brass, or other base metals, with private stamps'. However, the high quality of the new coinage did much to limit the proliferation of counterfeits. Nevertheless, Chester and Norwich were specifically threatened with legal proceedings because of the problem.

The dies for the Charles II halfpenny were prepared by John Roettier, whose fee was a penny per pound weight of copper, and the reverse has been compared by some to a sestertius of Antoninus Pius. The reverse legend 'BRITANNIA' was presumably considered a wiser choice than 'QVATTVOR MARIA VINDICO' (I claim the four seas) seen on the pattern halfpenny of about 1665, especially following the naval defeat by the Dutch off Kent in 1667.

It is worthy of note that on the copper coinage the head of Charles II faces left, i.e. the opposite attitude to that on the silver and gold coins.

Collecting Hints

This issue is very rare in the higher grades, and scarce in any condition above fine. Even higher grade specimens are frequently found to be weakly struck and consequently grading is difficult. The 1672 and 1675 are of approximately equal rarity and the 1673 is somewhat less rare. The series should be collected in at least fine condition, with the CRAOLVS error coins in any readable grade.

Denomination	Metal	Weight (grams)	Diameter (mm)	Rev. alignment
Halfpenny	Copper	10.0–12.0	28–31	↓

Obverse 1   Head 1, left; CAROLVS A CAROLO

Reverse 1   Britannia, seated, with shield, facing left, holding spray and spear; BRITANNIA; (date) in exergue

Edge   plain

Obv. 1   Rev. 1

No.	Date	Features	Obv.	Rev.	VG	F	VF	EF
C2HDM-005	1672		1	1	50	100	400	1500
C2HDM-010	1672	CRAOLVS instead of CAROLVS (obv.)	1	1	150	250	1800	
C2HDM-015	1672	PROOF	1	1				1500
C2HDM-020	1672	PROOF in silver	1	1				2500
C2HDM-025	1673		1	1	20	40	150	650
C2HDM-030	1673	No stops on obverse	1	1	30	80	450	1400
C2HDM-035	1673	No stop on reverse	1	1	25	60	250	1000
C2HDM-040	1673	CRAOLVS instead of CAROLVS (obv.)	1	1	45	110	800	
C2HDM-045	1673	PROOF [1]	1	1				1500
C2HDM-050	1673	PROOF in silver [1]	1	1				1500
C2HDM-055	1675		1	1	25	50	200	800
C2HDM-060	1675	5 over 3	1	1	75	150	800	
C2HDM-065	1675	No stops on obverse	1	1	25	50	200	800

1. No stop on reverse.

Minor variations exist in: position of ribbon and lettering (obv.); position of B, N, N in legend (reverse).

James II   (1685 – 1688)

The halfpennies of this reign were struck in tin with a square plug of copper through the centre. A small quantity of farthings in copper-plugged tin had been struck at the end of the previous reign. By using tin, it was hoped that coinage could be produced at a profit while at the same time producing a coin which would be difficult to counterfeit. A further object was to assist the ailing tin industry.

The obverse for the halfpenny was by John Roettier, and the reverse used a Britannia from the same punch as for the Charles

II coin. The date, however, appeared not in the exergue but on the edge of the coin, a notable departure from common practice. In addition, as on the Charles II coins, the king's head faced the opposite way to the depiction on the silver and gold coins.

It is possible that the reason for the extensive corrosion of plugged coinage lies with the electrochemical difference in potential between copper and tin when in contact. Copper itself resists corrosion reasonably well, and tin is so resistant that it is used to plate steel to protect it from corrosion. This is a field requiring further research.

Collecting Hints

These coins are scarce in any condition, but especially so in the higher grades. Most specimens have corroded so badly that what is left is virtually unreadable. Unlike copper, where the oxidation of the metal forms a layer which is largely protective, the corrosion of tin is progressive and can continue until little is left. The coins should be collected in the best grade possible, and good condition specimens highly prized. Do not underestimate the value of such pieces.

Denomination	Metal	Weight (grams)	Diameter (mm)	Rev. alignment
Halfpenny	Tin with central copper plug	10.5–11.6	28–30	↓

Obverse 1 Head 1, right; IACOBVS SECVNDVS

Reverse 1 Britannia, seated, with shield, facing left, holding spray and spear; BRITANNIA. The exergue is blank

Edge NVMMORVM FAMVLVS (date)

Obv. 1   Rev. 1

No.	Date	Features	Edge date	Obv.	Rev.	VG	F	VF	EF
J2HD-005	1685	[1]	1685	1	1	60	120	450	1600
J2HD-010	1685	no star between NVMMORVM and FAMVLVS	1685	1	1	80	160	650	2300
J2HD-015	1686		1686	1	1	60	120	450	1600
J2HD-020	1687		1687	1	1	60	120	450	1600

1. Star varieties exist (edge).

William & Mary (1688 – 1694)

The production of tin halfpennies with a copper plug continued, with dies prepared by George Bower and James Roettier. However, the new tin coinage was becoming increasingly unpopular. By now, the corrosive tendencies of the coins were very apparent, and in addition the public did not feel that the coinage had any intrinsic value. Even worse, counterfeits in lead had begun to appear. The prevention of counterfeiting had been one of the principal reasons for introducing the tin coinage. The tin halfpenny survived until 1692, and in 1694, just before the queen's death from smallpox, a copper halfpenny was reintroduced. The obverse of this issue was designed by James or Norbert Roettier. The contract stipulated that the copper should be English and that the blanks should be struck at the Mint. Previously, blanks had been imported from Sweden for the Charles II copper coinage. It is noticeable that the Charles II issue tones to a dark red, while the William and Mary coins tone to black. This is presumably because of different trace elements in the copper. The English copper was difficult to strike, so in order to render it more malleable the blanks were made by casting the molten metal into moulds.

Collecting Hints

All of the tin series is as scarce as that of the previous reign, while the 1689 coin is considerably rarer. This should be acquired in any condition, almost irrespective of price. All of the other dates are desirable if in fine condition and attractive. The 1694 halfpenny is less scarce but is a useful one-year type. All of the dates, including 1694, are rare in extremely fine condition.

Denomination	Metal	Weight (grams)	Diameter (mm)	Rev. alignment
Halfpenny 1689–92	Tin with central copper plug	10.5–11.7	28–30	↓
Halfpenny 1694	Copper	9.1–11.7	28–31	↓

The weight range is narrower on the 1689 coin, averaging 10.8 grams.

Obverse 1 Heads 1, right; GVLIELMVS ET MARIA (heads divide GVLIELMVS... ET)

Obverse 2 Heads 2, more drapery, right; same legend (heads divide ET...MARIA)

Obverse 3 Heads 3, larger, with king wearing breastplate, right; same legend with lettering larger (heads divide GVLIELMVS...ET)

Obverse 4 Heads 4, right, the king with shorter hair; same legend (heads divide GVLIELMVS... ET)

Reverse 1 Britannia, seated, with shield, facing left, holding spray and spear; BRITANNIA. The exergue is blank

Reverse 2 Similar but the exergue contains the date

Edge (1689–92): (in relief) NVMMORVM FAMVLVS (date); (1694): plain

Obv. 1   Obv. 3   Obv. 4

Rev. 1   Rev. 2

No.	Date	Features	Edge date	Obv.	Rev.	VG	F	VF	EF
WMHD-005	1689		1689	1	1	350	700	1600	
WMHD-010	(1689)	PROOF, plain edge [1]		1	1				10000
WMHD-015	1689	[2]	1689	1	2				
WMHD-020	1689		1689	2	1	1500			
WMHD-025	1690	[3]	1690	3	1	60	100	280	1000
WMHD-030	1691	[3]	1691	3	2	60	100	280	1000
WMHD-035	1691	[4]	1692	3	2	60	100	280	1000
WMHD-040	1692		1692	3	2	60	100	280	1000
WMHD-045	1694			4	2	25	45	100	550

No.	Date	Features	Edge date	Obv.	Rev.	VG	F	VF	EF
WMHD-050	1694	GVLEELMVS instead of GVLIELMVS (obv.)		4	2	45	95	200	1200
WMHD-055	1694	GVLIEMVS instead of GVLIELMVS (obv.)		4	2	45	95	200	1200
WMHD-060	1694	MVRIA instead of MARIA (obv.)		4	2	35	75	150	1000
WMHD-065	1694	MΛRIΛ instead of MARIA (obv.)		4	2	30	55	120	750
WMHD-070	1694	BRITΛNNIΛ (last I over Λ) instead of BRITANNIA (rev.)		4	2	30	55	120	750
WMHD-072	1694	BRTΛNNIΛ instead of BRITANNIA (rev.)		4	2	30	55	120	750
WMHD-075	1694	no stop on rev.		4	2	30	55	120	750
WMHD-080	1694	PROOF [5]		4	2				900
WMHD-082	1694	PROOF; rev. ↑		4	2				900
WMHD-085	1694	PROOF, edge striated		4	2				900
WMHD-090	1694	PROOF on thin flan		4	2				900
WMHD-095	1694	PROOF in silver		4	2				1800
WMHD-100	1694	PROOF in silver on thin flan		4	2				1500
WMHD-105	1694	PROOF in gold on thin flan [6]		4	2				8000

1. Coin bears no date at all; possibly unique.
2. Reported by Snelling and Batty but doubted by Montagu.
3. Edge punctuation varies.
4. '1691' is the date on the reverse.
5. Minor varieties exist.
6. Possibly unique.

William III (1694 – 1701)

The production of halfpennies continued under the contract granted during the previous reign, but it was soon apparent that the terms of the contract were not always being kept. To save costs, not only were many of the blanks being cast rather than struck, but some of the coins themselves were being cast as a single operation. Claims were made about the convenience of casting and the quality of the product, but despite this there was no doubt that the manufacturers were in breach of contract.

There were other ways in which the contractors were saving on expenses. Cheap labour was used, including foreigners, and some could not spell the words they engraved on the dies, nor punctuate correctly. A somewhat similar situation existed in the provincial mints at around this time, when large quantities of silver coinage were being produced using an inefficient work-force.

Towards the end of the reign, both the workmanship and the design and production of dies for the copper coins had sunk to their lowest depths. It is curious that, at this time, the mint were producing the highest quality five-and two-guinea pieces made, the 'fine work' 1701 pieces.

By 1698 there was a glut of inferior copper coinage, and following representation from the public, an act was passed to stop the coining for one year. Stephen Martin Leake, writing in 1726, stated that the act 'seems to have had no effect', and that the proliferation continued. Further parliamentary efforts were later made to try to stop the glut of coinage.

James Roettier engraved the obverse dies for the halfpenny, including, according to Peck, those for the last type, which dated from 1699, after Roettier's death. The reverse initially continued the John Roettier Britannia from previous reigns until the last issue in 1699. Then a new and poorly executed Britannia reverse was introduced, possibly by Samuel Bull.

Because of the poor quality of many of the coins of this reign, it is not always possible to determine whether minor punctuation varieties are caused by such vagaries as die wear or poor striking. In addition, many of the variations are so minor and so widespread that they are of little interest except to a dedicated collector of varieties. Included in these are the substitution of an inverted 'V' for 'A' and vice versa, and the omission of one or more stops. Because of this, the tables below allocate a separate number only to major varieties, e.g. when a word is completely misspelt, although minor varieties are still included in the Remarks column. Because minor varieties are so commonplace in the William III series, they may be referred to only in annotated form where they would have received separate treatment if they had occurred, say, in the reign of William IV.

Collecting Hints

The whole of this series is rare in the highest grades, and the coins should be acquired in very fine condition or better, with the rarer varieties in fine condition or better. Ernest Bramah (English Regal Copper Coins, 1929) estimated the scarcity of the first issue as this distribution from 100 randomly acquired examples: 1695, 12; 1696, 38; 1697, 47; 1698, 3. He estimated the last issue as: 1699, 44; 1700, 38; 1701, 18.

Denomination	Metal	Weight (grams)	Diameter (mm)	Rev. alignment
Halfpenny	Copper	8.9–11.5	28–29	↓

Obverse 1 Head 1, right; GVLIELMVS TERTIVS

Obverse 2 Head 2, right; same legend

Reverse 1 Britannia, seated, with shield, facing left, holding spray and spear; BRITANNIA; date in exergue below

Reverse 2 Similar but legend reads BRITANNIA (date); exergue is blank

Reverse 3 Redesigned Britannia, seated, with shield, facing left, crude style; BRITANNIA; date in exergue below

Edge plain

Obv. 1 Obv. 2

Rev. 1 Rev. 2 Rev. 3

No.	Date	Features	Obv.	Rev.	F	VF	EF
W3HD-005	1695	[1]	1	1	18	75	350
W3HD-010	1695	struck on thick flan [2]	1	1	100		
W3HD-015	1696		1	1	15	65	300
W3HD-020	1696	GVLIEMVS instead of GVLIELMVS (obv.) [3]	1	1	100		
W3HD-025	1696	TERTVS instead of TERTIVS (obv.)	1	1	100		
W3HD-030	1696	PROOF in silver	1	1			1200

595

No.	Date	Features	Obv.	Rev.	F	VF	EF
W3HD-035	1696	PROOF in silver on thin flan [4]	1	1			1200
W3HD-040	1697	[5]	1	1	15	65	300
W3HD-045	1697	I of TERTIVS over E (obv.)	1	1	50	180	
W3HD-050	1697	GVLILMVS instead of GVLIELMVS (obv.) [3]	1	1	150		
W3HD-055	1697	gap instead of first N in BRITANNIA [6]	1	1	50	180	
W3HD-060	1698		1	1	20	90	450
W3HD-065	no date	[7]	1	obv. 1	150		
W3HD-070	1698	[8]	1	2	18	75	350
W3HD-075	1699	[9]	1	2	18	75	350
W3HD-080	1699	GVLIEMVS instead of GVLIELMVS (obv.)	1	2	100		
W3HD-085	1699	[1]	2	3	15	65	300
W3HD-090	1699	GVLIELMVS instead of GVLIELMVS (obv.)	2	3	100		
W3HD-095	1699	TERTVS instead of TERTIVS (obv.) [5]	2	3	100		
W3HD-100	1699	PROOF in silver	2	3			1500
W3HD-105	1700	[1]	2	3	15	65	300
W3HD-110	1700	GVLIELMS instead of GVLIELMVS (obv.)	2	3	70		
W3HD-115	1700	GVLIEEMVS instead of GVLIELMVS (obv.)	2	3	70		
W3HD-120	1700	I of TERTIVS over V (obv.)	2	3	50		
W3HD-125	1700	TER TIVS instead of TERTIVS (obv.)	2	3	40		
W3HD-130	1700	BRIVANNIA instead of BRITANNIA (obv.)	2	3	100		
W3HD-135	1701	[10]	2	3	18	75	350
W3HD-140	1701	PROOF in silver [11]	2	3			1800
W3HD-145	no date	[7]	2	obv. 2	150		

1. Inverted 'V' and stop varieties exist.
2. Weight c.14.4 grams.
3. No stop on reverse.
4. Diameter 31mm.
5. Stop varieties exist.
6. Gap is possibly die wear.
7. 'Double headed' coin.
8. Stop after date.
9. No stop after date; inverted 'V' varieties exist.
10. Inverted 'V', 'A' and stop varieties exist.
11. Edge striated.

Anne (1701 – 1714)

When Anne came to the throne, a very large quantity of copper coinage was in circulation. It was therefore decided to suspend striking until more was required. Consequently, no halfpennies of Anne were produced except for patterns.

George I (1714 – 1727)

No currency halfpennies had been struck during the reign of Anne, and by 1717 there was again a shortage of copper coinage. A new contract was signed and a Royal Warrant in 1717 proclaimed the issuance of a new halfpenny.

The first halfpennies struck had a somewhat unusual appearance. They were smaller, thicker, and somewhat lighter than those previously issued. Both obverse and reverse were boldly struck and in high relief, a marked difference from the poor strikings and cast specimens of William III. This first issue of George I has become known as the 'dump' issue. The dies were probably produced by Croker and/or Johann Rudolph Ochs, senior.

In 1719, a new issue of halfpennies began. These were nearer in proportions to those of earlier reigns. The diameter was greater than that of the 'dump' halfpenny, but the coin was thinner, thus retaining the same weight.

Unlike on most of the silver coinage, the Hanoverian titles of the king did not form part of the legend. The result was an uncluttered and simple design which resulted in one of the more attractive issues of copper halfpenny, despite the shortcomings of the king's appearance. Whether they were appreciated at the time is more doubtful; Leake, writing in 1726, described them as 'very clumsy pieces'.

Denomination	Metal	Weight (grams)	Diameter (mm)	Rev. alignment
Halfpenny 1717–18	Copper	9.4–10.3	25–27	↓
Halfpenny 1719–24	Copper	9.4–10.3	26–29	↓

Proofs are usually of diameter 27mm.

Obverse 1   Head 1, right; GEORGIVS REX

Obverse 2   Head 2, slightly different (tie, shoulder-strap) and rather larger, right; same legend

Obverse 3   Head 3, slightly different (shoulder-strap, hair, leaves), right; same legend

Reverse 1   Britannia, seated, with shield, facing left, holding spray and spear; BRITANNIA; date in exergue below

Edge   plain

Obv. 1   Obv. 2

Obv. 3   Rev. 1

No.	Date	Features	Obv.	Rev.	F	VF	EF
G1HD-005	1717		1	1	15	60	300
G1HD-010	1717	no stops on obv.	1	1	30	110	500
G1HD-015	1717	PROOF	1	1			500
G1HD-020	1717	PROOF in silver	1	1		250	400
G1HD-022	1717	PROOF in silver; rev. ↑	1	1		300	500
G1HD-025	1718		1	1	15	60	300
G1HD-028	1718	R in BRITANNIA over B	1	1	30	120	600
G1HD-030	1718	no stops on obv.	1	1	30	110	500
G1HD-035	1718	in silver [1]	1	1		300	500
G1HD-038	1718	struck on Irish Gun money piece dated 1689	1	1	100	300	
G1HD-040	1719	[2]	1	1	500		
G1HD-045	1719	diagonally grained edge	1	1	500		
G1HD-050	1719		2	1	10	60	300
G1HD-055	1719	diagonally grained edge	2	1	100		
G1HD-060	1719		3	1	15	90	450
G1HD-065	1719	diagonally grained edge	3	1	150		
G1HD-070	1720		3	1	10	60	300
G1HD-075	1721		3	1	10	60	300
G1HD-080	1721	latter 1 over 0	3	1	14	80	400
G1HD-085	1721	stop after date	3	1	12	70	350
G1HD-090	1721	struck on 3mm thick flan	3	1	150		

No.	Date	Features	Obv.	Rev.	F	VF	EF
G1HD-095	1722	3	3	1	10	60	300
G1HD-100	1722	GEORGI∀S instead of GEORGIVS	3	1	20	100	500
G1HD-105	1722	PROOF in brass; rev. ↑ 4	3	1			500
G1HD-110	1723		3	1	10	60	300
G1HD-115	1723	no stop on rev.	3	1	15	85	500
G1HD-120	1723	struck on thin flan	3	1	40	200	
G1HD-125	1724		3	1	12	80	400

1. Possibly a proof.
2. On larger flan from now on.
3. Orientation of head varies (obv.)
4. Weight c.10.8 grams.

George II   (1727 – 1760)

The halfpennies of George II were the most prolific issue yet produced, spanning a quarter of a century. To them was added a large number of counterfeits and curious pieces similar in appearance. Many of these sported legends markedly different from those on the genuine coin, in order to circumvent any accusation that the pieces were coined as imitations of coinage. Many genuine coins were melted down and underweight fabrications made from the molten metal. It is difficult in modern times to appreciate the extent to which counterfeiting had debased the currency, and for long periods forgeries outnumbered the genuine pieces.

The early head of George II used on the halfpennies of 1729 to 1739 was by Croker. The later head of the king from 1740 to 1754 was by Tanner. The reverses were possibly by Tanner and/or Johann Ochs, junior, although Peck considered that the early Britannia reverse was of such good workmanship that it was probably by Croker.

Collecting Hints

The series should be collected in at least very fine condition. Specimens in higher grades with original lustre are considerably more desirable. Although these are scarce, they are not as scarce as those of earlier reigns in top condition.

Denomination	Metal	Weight (grams)	Diameter (mm)	Rev. alignment
Halfpenny	Copper	9.7–10.3	28–30	↓

Obverse 1   Head 1, left; GEORGIVS II REX

Obverse 2   Head 2, older, left; GEORGIUS II REX

Obverse 3   Head 2, left; GEORGIVS II REX

Reverse 1   Britannia, seated, with shield, facing left, holding spray and spear; BRITANNIA; date in exergue below

Reverse 2   Redesigned Britannia, cruder style; other details similar

Edge   plain

Obv. 1

Obv. 2

Rev. 1

Rev. 2

No.	Date	Features	Obv.	Rev.	F	VF	EF
G2HD-005	1729	stop after legend (rev.)	1	1	8	35	140
G2HD-010	1729	no stop after legend (rev.)	1	1	12	50	200
G2HD-015	1729	PROOF 1	1	1			400
G2HD-020	1729	PROOF in silver 2	1	1			1200
G2HD-025	1729	PROOF in silver on thick flan; rev. ↑ 3	1	1			1800
G2HD-030	1730	4	1	1	10	40	160
G2HD-035	1730	GEOGIVS instead of GEORGIVS (obv.) 5	1	1	30	100	600
G2HD-040	1731	stop after legend (rev.)	1	1	8	35	140
G2HD-045	1731	no stop after legend (rev.)	1	1	10	45	180
G2HD-050	1732		1	1	10	40	160
G2HD-055	1732	no stop after legend (rev.)	1	1	14	55	220
G2HD-060	1732	on thick wide flan 6	1	1	50	150	600
G2HD-065	1733	4	1	1	8	35	140
G2HD-070	1734		1	1	8	35	140
G2HD-072	1734	R in GEORGIVS over O (obv.)	1	1	30	100	
G2HD-075	1734	4 over 3	1	1	15	60	220
G2HD-080	1734	no stops on obv.	1	1	12	45	170
G2HD-085	1735		1	1	8	35	140
G2HD-090	1736		1	1	10	40	160
G2HD-092	1736	6 over 0	1	1	40	100	400
G2HD-095	1737		1	1	10	40	160
G2HD-100	1738		1	1	8	35	140
G2HD-105	1738	V in GEORGIVS over S (obv.)	1	1	11	55	200
G2HD-110	1739		1	1	8	35	140
G2HD-115	1740		2	2	8	30	120
G2HD-120	1742		2	2	8	30	120
G2HD-125	1742	2 over 0	2	2	10	40	160
G2HD-130	1743		2	2	8	30	120
G2HD-135	1744		2	2	8	30	120
G2HD-140	1745		2	2	8	30	120
G2HD-145	1746		3	2	8	30	120
G2HD-150	1747		3	2	8	30	120
G2HD-155	1748		3	2	8	30	120
G2HD-160	1749		3	2	8	30	120
G2HD-165	1750		3	2	8	30	120
G2HD-170	1751		3	2	8	30	120
G2HD-175	1752		3	2	8	30	120
G2HD-180	1753		3	2	8	30	120
G2HD-185	1754		3	2	8	30	120

1. Occurs with and without stop after GEORGIVS.
2. No stop after GEORGIVS; weight c.10 grams.
3. No stop after GEORGIVS; thickness varies from 1.5mm to 2mm.
4. Stop varieties exist.
5. No stop on reverse.
6. Weight c.13.8 grams; diam. 33mm.

George III   (1760 – 1820)

The first issue of halfpennies was in 1770, ten years after the accession of George III. Counterfeiting was now rampant, and in 1771 the utterance of counterfeit copper coin became a felony. This, however, had little effect, and for the next twenty or so years most of the so-called coins in circulation were forgeries. In March 1782, a woman convicted of counterfeiting was hanged, then fixed to a stake and burnt before the debtor's door at Newgate prison.

On 14 April 1789, Boulton, in a letter to Lord Hawkesbury, wrote: 'In the course of my journeys, I observe that I receive upon an average two-thirds counterfeit halfpence for change at tollgates, etc., and I believe the evil is daily increasing, as the spurious money is carried into circulation by the lowest class of manufacturers, who pay with it the principal part of the wages of the poor people they employ.'

Boulton's contract in 1797 to produce the 'cartwheel' coinage thwarting the counterfeiters did not extend to the production of halfpennies, although Boulton clearly expected that it would, and had indeed prepared patterns of proportionate weight and size in accordance with his theories on intrinsic value. The reason given by the government for the omission of the halfpenny from the contract was that the large number of de facto halfpennies (including tokens and fakes!) would be driven out of circulation, and that Boulton would be unable to cope with the demand for his coinage that would ensue. Many tradesmen had at this time issued privately struck halfpenny tokens.

Public demand for legally struck halfpennies soon forced the Government to reconsider its position, and in 1798 a contract was effected with Boulton to strike at the Soho mint a quantity of halfpennies and farthings dated 1799. However, in the meantime the price of copper had risen, and in accordance with Boulton's theories the weight had to be reduced slightly. Moreover, the original cartwheel design had been discontinued in favour of a more conventional design, and the net result was that the new halfpennies were not popular at first. Perhaps if the weight reduction had been more, it might have been accepted, but it was less than 5%, and it was probably seen as some sort of deception.

In 1806, a further issue of halfpennies totalling 427.5 tons was struck by Boulton, but the price of copper had again risen, and the weight of these was even less than that of the 1799 issue. This time, there was no adverse reaction from the public. Perhaps the national obsession with 'intrinsic value' was over.

The first series of 1770–75 was possibly designed by Richard Yeo or Thomas Pingo. The coins of 1799 and 1806–07 produced by Boulton were designed by Conrad Heinrich Küchler (c.1740–c.1810).

Obv. 3   Obv. 4

Rev. 1   Rev. 2

Rev. 3

Collecting Hints

The halfpennies of George III are somewhat easier to find in top grades than are those of earlier reigns, and specimens with original lustre should be sought. Obviously, in the light of the discourse above, one must beware of counterfeits, but to a trained eye these are fairly easy to detect. The counterfeits are themselves historically interesting and worthy of acquisition.

Denomination	Metal	Weight (grams)	Diameter (mm)	Rev. alignment
Halfpenny 1770–75	Copper	9.2–10.8	29–30	↓
Halfpenny 1799	Copper	12.0–13.1	30–31	↓
Halfpenny 1806–07	Copper	9.2–9.8	29	↓

Obverse 1 Head 1, right; GEORGIVS III REX

Obverse 2 Head 2, with fuller face, right; same legend

Obverse 3 Head 3, right; GEORGIUS III DEI GRATIA REX

Obverse 4 Head 4, right; GEORGIUS III D G REX (date)

Reverse 1 Britannia, seated, with shield, facing left, holding spray and spear; BRITANNIA; date in exergue below

Reverse 2 Redesigned Britannia, smaller; BRITANNIA 1799

Reverse 3 Slightly different Britannia; BRITANNIA (no date)

Edge 1770–75: plain (1770 proofs slightly striated); 1799–1807: diagonally grained in groove

Obv. 1   Obv. 2

No.	Date	Features	Obv.	Rev.	F	VF	EF
G3HD-005	1770		1	1	8	24	100
G3HD-010	1770	no stop on rev.	1	1	12	35	140
G3HD-015	1770	PROOF	1	1			600
G3HD-018	1770	PROOF; rev. ↑	1	1			600
G3HD-020	1770	PROOF in silver	1	1			1200
G3HD-025	1771	[1]	1	1	7	20	90
G3HD-030	1771	no stop on rev.	1	1	10	30	120
G3HD-035	1772	[2]	1	1	7	20	90
G3HD-040	1772	GEORIVS instead of GEORGIVS (obv.)	1	1	20	55	180
G3HD-045	1772	no stop on rev.	1	1	10	30	120
G3HD-050	1773		1	1	7	20	90
G3HD-055	1773	no stop after REX (obv.)	1	1	9	25	110
G3HD-060	1773	no stop on rev.	1	1	10	30	120
G3HD-065	1774		2	1	8	22	95
G3HD-070	1775	[3]	2	1	8	22	95
G3HD-072	1775	rev. ↑	2	1	25	75	300
G3HD-075	1799	[3]	3	2	5	8	30
G3HD-080	1799	PROOF [4]	3	2			500
G3HD-082	1799	gilt PROOF	3	2			150
G3HD-085	1806	[5]	4	3	4	7	25
G3HD-090	1806	PROOF edge grained [5]	4	3			150
G3HD-095	1806	gilt PROOF edge grained [5]	4	3			150
G3HD-100	1807	[5]	4	3	5	8	30

1. Slight reverse differences exist.
2. Slight obverse and reverse differences exist.
3. Minor varieties exist.
4. Prooflike currency coins exist.
5. Varieties exist.

George IV   (1820 – 1830)

After the mint moved to Tower Hill, coinage in gold and silver took precedence. The production of copper coins did not resume until 1821, when farthings were produced, and the first halfpennies were not issued until after 14 November 1825. This was after the disagreements between the egocentric Pistrucci and the authorities, and the designing of the halfpenny fell to William Wyon. If one examines the farthing of 1821, one may be forgiven for considering that the halfpenny of George IV had a lucky escape.

The designs of William Wyon are generally considered to be amongst the most elegant of the British coinage.

In 1826, a proof set of British coins in a leather case was issued, and the proof halfpenny of that year was included in this set.

Wyon followed Pistrucci's and Küchler's practice of placing the date on the obverse under the head. Under the exergue on the reverse he depicted a rose, thistle and shamrock.

Collecting Hints

Counterfeits were no longer a problem during the minting of this series. The coins should be sought in extremely fine condition or better.

Denomination	Metal	Weight (grams)	Diameter (mm)	Rev. alignment
Halfpenny	Copper	9.1–9.5	28	↑

Obverse 1   Head 1, left; GEORGIUS IV DEI GRATIA (date)

Reverse 1   Britannia, seated, with shield, facing right, holding trident; two incuse lines down arms of saltire; BRITANNIAR REX FID DEF

Reverse 2   Similar but one raised line down arms of saltire; same legend

Edge   plain

Obv. 1   Rev. 1

No.	Date	Features	Obv.	Rev.	F	VF	EF	UNC
G4HD-005	1825		1	1	15	45	120	180
G4HD-010	1825	PROOF	1	1				400
G4HD-015	1826		1	1	6	12	40	65
G4HD-020	1826	PROOF	1	1				250
G4HD-025	1826	bronzed PROOF	1	1				180
G4HD-030	1826		1	2	12	35	100	150
G4HD-035	1826	PROOF	1	2				300
G4HD-040	1826	bronzed PROOF	1	2				250
G4HD-045	1827		1	1	7	16	60	90

William IV   (1830 – 1837)

The halfpenny series of William IV was a continuation of that of George IV, using a William Wyon obverse from a model by Sir Francis Chantrey. The reverse was virtually identical to that of the issue for the previous reign.

Collecting Hints

The series should be collected in extremely fine or mint state, with original lustre.

Denomination	Metal	Weight (grams)	Diameter (mm)	Rev. alignment
Halfpenny	Copper	9.2–9.5	28	↑

Obverse 1   Head 1, right; W.W. incuse on truncation; GULIELMUS IIII DEI GRATIA (date)

Reverse 1   Britannia, seated, with shield, facing right, holding trident; BRITANNIAR REX FID DEF (almost identical to Reverse 1 of George IV issue)

Edge   plain

Obv. 1   Rev. 1

No.	Date	Features	Obv.	Rev.	F	VF	EF	UNC
W4HD-005	1831		1	1	7	15	60	110
W4HD-010	1831	Bronzed PROOF	1	1				300
W4HD-015	1831	Bronzed PROOF; rev. ↓[1]	1	1				200
W4HD-020	1834		1	1	7	15	60	110
W4HD-025	1837		1	1	6	12	50	95

1. Issued in cased proof sets.

Victoria   (1837 – 1901)

The halfpenny of Victoria has, as a series, many of the characteristics of the Victorian penny, but on inspection many differences are revealed. Although the designers, William Wyon and his son Leonard Charles Wyon, later followed by Thomas Brock, are the same, the halfpenny series is not simply a scaled down version of the penny. Indeed, in some ways it is more interesting. It is probably also more challenging, as specimens in top condition are more difficult to find.

The copper halfpenny, struck from 1838 to 1860, is, like the penny, notable for a number of overdate varieties. 'Ghosting' caused by clashed dies is probably even more prevalent than on the penny. However, the copper series has fewer design variations than the penny. The trident on the reverse, for example, is always ornamented, and this reverse appears to be identical to that of the William IV halfpenny (apart from REX becoming REG). The head on the obverse has William Wyon's initials on the truncation on all dates, unlike the penny.

The bronze halfpenny, like the penny, has a large number of minor varieties and has been the subject of almost as much specialised study as the penny. In this work, many of these varieties will be referred to only in annotated form and not as a separate entry. A few may be omitted on the grounds that they are so minor as to be of little interest except to a specialised student.

Collecting Hints

The halfpenny suffered more wear generally than the penny. This is almost always the case with smaller coins, as the percentage of surface area making contact during circulation is greater with small coins. A minimum acceptable grade, unless the coin is very rare, is probably fine to very fine. Many of the minor varieties will not be identifiable on a fine condition coin. If possible, higher grade coins with original lustre should be sought.

Most dealers do not concern themselves with very minor varieties, and the serious collector or student with sufficient knowledge has an excellent chance of picking up rarities cheaply.

As mentioned, ghosting is prevalent on the halfpenny series. For collectors who do not object to the products of clashed dies, or even welcome them, superb crystal-sharp examples of this phenomenon can frequently be found.

Denomination	Metal	Weight (grams)	Diameter (mm)	Rev. alignment
Halfpenny 1838–60 Obv. 1, Rev. 1	Copper	9.1–9.5	28	↑
Halfpenny 1860–1901 Obvs 2–6, Revs 2–5	Bronze	5.5–5.8	25	↑

Obverse 1   Head 1, left; VICTORIA DEI GRATIA (date)

Obverse 2   Head 2, left; VICTORIA D G BRITT REG F D; beaded border

Obverse 3   Similar, but toothed border

Obverse 4   Head 3, left; slightly older features; same legend

Obverse 5   Head 3, left; drapery includes seven-pearled brooch (rose on previous obverses)

Obverse 6   Head 4, veiled, left; VICTORIA DEI GRA BRITT REGINA FID DEF IND IMP

Reverse 1   Britannia, seated, with shield and trident, facing right; BRITANNIAR REG FID DEF (as reverse of William IV issue but REX becomes REG)

Reverse 2   Redesigned Britannia, seated, with shield and trident, facing right; HALF PENNY; date in exergue below Britannia; beaded border.

Reverse 3   Similar but toothed border

Reverse 4   Similar but Britannia completely redesigned.

Reverse 5   Similar but waterline slightly higher

Edge   plain

Obv. 1   Obv. 2   Obv. 3

Obv. 4   Obv. 5   Obv. 6

Rev. 1   Rev. 2   Rev. 3

Rev. 4

Copper Issue

No.	Date	Features	Obv.	Rev.	F	VF	EF	UNC
VYHD-005	1838		1	1	5	9	35	60
VYHD-010	1839	PROOF	1	1				220
VYHD-015	1839	PROOF rev. ↓[1]	1	1				180
VYHD-020	1841		1	1	5	9	35	60
VYHD-025	1841	rev. ↓	1	1	25	50	150	250
VYHD-030	1841	Bronzed PROOF	1	1				350
VYHD-035	1841	PROOF in silver on thick flan [2]	1	1				2000
VYHD-040	1843		1	1	10	18	60	100
VYHD-045	1844		1	1	8	15	40	70
VYHD-050	1845		1	1	30	70	250	450
VYHD-055	1846		1	1	8	16	55	85
VYHD-060	1847		1	1	7	15	60	90
VYHD-065	1848	8 not over 7	1	1	30	60	150	300
VYHD-070	1848	8 over 7	1	1	6	11	40	70
VYHD-075	1851	[3]	1	1	8	15	40	70
VYHD-080	1852	[3]	1	1	6	12	45	75
VYHD-085	1853	[3]	1	1	5	8	25	45
VYHD-090	1853	3 over 2 [3]	1	1	10	20	60	120
VYHD-095	1853	PROOF [3]	1	1				250
VYHD-100	1853	Bronzed PROOF; rev. ↓[3]	1	1				300
VYHD-105	1854	[3]	1	1	5	8	25	45
VYHD-110	1855	[3]	1	1	5	8	25	45
VYHD-115	1856	[3]	1	1	8	14	60	90
VYHD-120	1857	[3]	1	1	6	11	40	70
VYHD-125	1858	[4]	1	1	5	8	30	55
VYHD-130	1858	latter 8 over 6	1	1	7	10	40	70
VYHD-135	1858	latter 8 over 7	1	1	5	8	30	55
VYHD-140	1859		1	1	12	18	65	120
VYHD-145	1859	9 over 8	1	1	10	16	55	95
VYHD-150	1860	[5]	1	1	1000	2000	3000	3800

1. Some (all?) issued in cased proof sets.
2. Thickness 2.8 mm.
3. Some examples of 1851, 1852, 1857, and all examples of 1853 to 1856, have seven incuse dots on and above the shield on the reverse.
4. Date size varies.
5. Some struck in bronze; some struck between 1860 and 1872; some or all proofs.

Bronze Issue; Young Head

No.	Date	Features	Obv.	Rev.	F	VF	EF	UNC
VYHD-155	1860	[1]	2	2	5	9	24	40
VYHD-160	1860	PROOF	2	2				600
VYHD-165	1860	Bronzed PROOF [1]	2	2				500
VYHD-170	1860	[2]	3	2	300	1200		
VYHD-175	1860	[3]	3	3	8	16	50	100
VYHD-180	1860	PROOF	3	3				600
VYHD-185	1860	Bronzed PROOF	3	3				600
VYHD-190	1861	[3]	3	3	5	9	24	40
VYHD-195	1861	HALP instead of HALF (rev.)	3	3	60	150		
VYHD-200	1861	6 over 8 [4]	3	3	100	250		
VYHD-205	1861	PROOF [5]	3	3				400
VYHD-210	1861	Bronzed PROOF	3	3				400
VYHD-215	1861	PROOF in brass	3	3				500
VYHD-220	1861	PROOF in cupronickel	3	3				700
VYHD-225	1861	PROOF in silver [5]	3	3				2000
VYHD-230	1861	PROOF in gold; rev. ↓[6]	3	3				5000
VYHD-235	1862		3	3	5	9	22	36
VYHD-240	1862	'A' to left of lighthouse (rev.) [7]	3	3	300	1200		
VYHD-245	1862	'B' to left of lighthouse (rev.) [8]	3	3	400	1500		
VYHD-250	1862	'C' to left of lighthouse (rev.) [8]	3	3	400	1500		
VYHD-255	1862	PROOF [9]	3	3				500
VYHD-260	1863	[10]	3	3	5	11	30	55
VYHD-265	1863	PROOF	3	3				500
VYHD-270	1864	[11]	3	3	6	14	45	80
VYHD-275	1864	PROOF	3	3				700
VYHD-280	1865		3	3	7	18	60	110
VYHD-285	1865	5 over 3	3	3	18	80	250	400
VYHD-290	1866		3	3	7	16	55	95
VYHD-295	1866	PROOF	3	3				600
VYHD-300	1867		3	3	8	18	65	120
VYHD-305	1867	PROOF; rev. ↓	3	3				700
VYHD-310	1867	PROOF in copper	3	3				700
VYHD-315	1868		3	3	7	16	55	95
VYHD-320	1868	PROOF	3	3				400
VYHD-325	1868	PROOF in copper	3	3				500
VYHD-330	1868	PROOF in cupronickel [12]	3	3			140	200

No.	Date	Features	Obv.	Rev.	F	VF	EF	UNC
VYHD-335	1869		3	3	12	35	130	200
VYHD-340	1870		3	3	7	16	55	90
VYHD-345	1871		3	3	20	60	200	350
VYHD-350	1872		3	3	7	15	50	85
VYHD-355	1872	PROOF in brass	3	3				600
VYHD-360	1873	[13]	3	3	7	16	55	90
VYHD-365	1874		3	3	20	50	130	220
VYHD-370	1874	narrow date [14]	3	3	20	50	130	220
VYHD-375	1874	[13]	3	3	20	50	130	220
VYHD-380	1874	narrow date	4	3	20	50	130	220
VYHD-385	1874	narrow date 'H' below date	4	3	5	9	25	45
VYHD-390	1874	narrow date 'H' below date struck on thick flan [15]	4	3	120	450		
VYHD-395	1874	narrow date 'H' below date PROOF [16]	4	3				500
VYHD-400	1875		4	3	5	9	25	45
VYHD-405	1875	'H' below date	4	3	10	18	50	95
VYHD-410	1875	'H' below date struck on thick flan	4	3	200	800		
VYHD-415	1875	'H' below date PROOF [17]	4	3				600
VYHD-420	1876	'H' below date [16]	4	3	4	8	25	45
VYHD-425	1876	'H' below date struck on thick flan	4	3	120	450		
VYHD-430	1876	'H' below date PROOF	4	3				500
VYHD-435	1877	[16]	4	3	4	8	25	45
VYHD-440	1877	PROOF	4	3				500
VYHD-445	1878	[16]	4	3	9	20	70	140
VYHD-450	1878	PROOF	4	3				500
VYHD-455	1879	[14]	4	3	4	8	25	45
VYHD-460	1880	[14]	4	3	5	10	30	50
VYHD-465	1880	PROOF	4	3				500
VYHD-470	1881	[16]	4	3	5	10	30	50
VYHD-475	1881	PROOF	4	3				500
VYHD-480	1881	'H' below date	4	3	4	8	25	40
VYHD-485	1881	PROOF	5	3				500
VYHD-490	1882	'H' below date	4	3	4	8	25	40
VYHD-495	1882	'H' below date PROOF [18]	4	3				600
VYHD-500	1883	[16]	4	3	10	20	55	95
VYHD-505	1883	PROOF	4	3				500
VYHD-510	1883		5	3	5	10	30	50
VYHD-515	1884		5	3	3	7	20	35
VYHD-520	1884	PROOF	5	3				400
VYHD-525	1885		5	3	3	7	20	35
VYHD-530	1885	PROOF	5	3				400
VYHD-535	1886		5	3	3	7	20	35
VYHD-540	1886	PROOF	5	3				400
VYHD-545	1887		5	3	3	6	18	30
VYHD-550	1887	PROOF	5	3				400
VYHD-555	1888		5	3	3	7	20	35
VYHD-560	1889		5	3	3	7	20	35
VYHD-565	1889	9 over 8	5	3	12	30	80	150
VYHD-570	1889	9 over 8 PROOF [19]	5	3				1000
VYHD-575	1890		5	3	3	6	18	28
VYHD-580	1890	PROOF	5	3				400
VYHD-585	1891		5	3	3	6	18	28
VYHD-590	1891	PROOF	5	3				350
VYHD-595	1892		5	3	4	8	24	36
VYHD-600	1892	PROOF	5	3				450
VYHD-605	1893		5	3	3	6	18	28
VYHD-610	1893	PROOF	5	3				400
VYHD-615	1894		5	3	4	8	24	36
VYHD-620	1894	PROOF	5	3				400

1. Minor portrait varieties exist.
2. Toothed/beaded 'mule'.
3. Many minor obverse/reverse varieties exist.
4. Some minor varieties exist.
5. At least two slightly different types.
6. One known; weight 8.3 grams.
7. Die identification letter; the 'A' is unbarred.
8. Die identification letter.
9. Minor differences from usual reverse.
10. '3' in date varies.
11. '4' has only one serif.
12. Weight c.5.5 grams.
13. Minor reverse varieties exist.
14. Minor obverse varieties exist.
15. Weight c.8.0 grams.
16. Minor obverse/reverse varieties exist.
17. Possibly early striking currency pieces; price if genuine proofs.
18. Possibly a pattern; reverse slightly different from any used on currency.
19. All overdate proofs are extremely rare.

Old Head

No.	Date	Features	Obv.	Rev.	F	VF	EF	UNC
VOHD-625	1895		6	4	2	6	12	18
VOHD-630	1895	PROOF	6	4				350
VOHD-635	1896	[1]	6	4	2	5	8	12
VOHD-640	1896	PROOF	6	4				350
VOHD-645	1897		6	4	4	10	18	28
VOHD-650	1897		6	5	2	5	9	14
VOHD-655	1898		6	4	2	5	9	14
VOHD-660	1899		6	4	2	5	9	14
VOHD-665	1900		6	4	2	4	6	10
VOHD-670	1900	PROOF	6	4				300
VOHD-675	1901		6	4	2	4	5	8
VOHD-680	1901	PROOF	6	4				300

1. Minor reverse varieties exist.

Edward VII (1901 – 1910)

The halfpenny is at first sight a scaled-down version of the penny, but on closer inspection it appears to be more straightforward. Although the 'low tide' variety of 1902 exists as on the penny, some of the minor varieties seen on the penny do not appear. Apart from the low tide variety, the only change in the series is the alteration of the date numerals.

The portrait of Edward is by George William de Saulles (1862–1903), with the reducing machine being used to effect the alteration of the portrait to the correct size. The reverse is virtually identical to that used for the veiled head halfpennies of Victoria.

The colour variation of toned pieces ranges from light to very dark brown, according to the composition of the alloy used.

Collecting Hints

The series should be collected in mint state or near. These coins usually occur sharply struck, and are very attractive when none or little of their original lustre has been lost. It should be noted that the 'low tide' halfpenny is rarer than this variety on the penny and commands a higher price.

Denomination	Metal	Weight (grams)	Diameter (mm)	Rev. alignment
Halfpenny	Bronze	5.7	25	↑

Obverse 1 Head 1, right; EDWARDVS VII DEI GRA BRITT OMN REX FID DEF IND IMP

Reverse 1 Britannia, seated, with shield and trident, facing right; HALF PENNY; date in exergue below Britannia

Reverse 2 Similar but sea is higher

Edge plain

Obv. 1   Rev. 2

No.	Date	Features	Obv.	Rev.	VF	EF	UNC
E7HD-005	1902	[1]	1	1	25	60	95
E7HD-010	1902		1	2	3	6	12
E7HD-015	1903		1	2	5	12	22
E7HD-020	1904		1	2	5	15	30
E7HD-025	1905		1	2	5	15	30
E7HD-030	1906		1	2	5	14	26
E7HD-035	1907		1	2	4	10	20
E7HD-040	1908		1	2	4	10	20

No.	Date	Features	Obv.	Rev.	VF	EF	UNC
E7HD-045	1909		1	2	5	15	30
E7HD-050	1910		1	2	4	12	20

1. Known as 'Low Tide' variety.

George V   (1910 – 1936)

The design for the halfpenny is again very similar to that of the penny, and uses a portrait of George V by Sir Bertram Mackennal (1863–1931). The reverse is more or less identical to that of the previous reign.

Ghosting was a problem in the earlier years. Attempts were made to reduce it in 1925, when a new obverse and reverse were introduced, but it was not until the introduction of the later obverse in 1928 that the problem was eradicated.

Unlike the pennies, no halfpennies were struck with provincial mintmarks.

Collecting Hints

The earlier dates of halfpenny were very prone to circulation wear on the reverse, owing to the fact that there was no significant raised rim on the obverse. Consequently, fine or very fine specimens before 1925 are somewhat scarcer than those after that date.

The series should be collected in mint state with original lustre. Some of the dates are significantly more difficult to find than is indicated in some catalogues. Unlike with the penny, it is possible to collect an unbroken series of dates throughout the reign, and no dates were issued artificially darkened at the mint.

Denomination	Metal	Weight (grams)	Diameter (mm)	Rev. alignment
Halfpenny	Bronze	5.7	25	↑

Obverse 1   Head 1, left; B.M. on truncation; GEORGIVS V DEI GRA BRITT OMN REX FID DEF IND IMP

Obverse 2   Head 2, left; known as 'modified effigy'; initials BM are without stops and further to right; same legend

Obverse 3   Head 3, smaller, more sharply struck, left; same legend

Reverse 1   Britannia, seated, with shield and trident, facing right; HALF PENNY; date in exergue below Britannia

Reverse 2   Similar but redesigned and more sharply struck

Edge   plain

Obv. 1   Obv. 2   Obv. 3

Rev. 1   Rev. 2

No.	Date	Features	Obv.	Rev.	VF	EF	UNC
G5HD-005	1911	1	1	1	3	7	12
G5HD-010	1912		1	1	3	7	12
G5HD-015	1913		1	1	3	8	14
G5HD-020	1914		1	1	3	7	12
G5HD-025	1915		1	1	3	7	12
G5HD-030	1916		1	1	3	7	12
G5HD-035	1917		1	1	3	7	12
G5HD-040	1918		1	1	3	7	12
G5HD-045	1919		1	1	3	7	12
G5HD-050	1920		1	1	3	7	12
G5HD-055	1921		1	1	3	7	12
G5HD-060	1922		1	1	4	9	16
G5HD-065	1923		1	1	3	8	14
G5HD-070	1924		1	1	3	8	14
G5HD-075	1925		1	1	3	8	14
G5HD-080	1925		2	2	4	9	20
G5HD-085	1926		2	2	4	9	16
G5HD-090	1926	PROOF	2	2			350
G5HD-095	1927		2	2	2	5	10
G5HD-100	1927	PROOF	2	2			300
G5HD-105	1928		3	2	2	4	8
G5HD-110	1928	PROOF	3	2			300
G5HD-115	1929		3	2	2	4	8
G5HD-120	1929	PROOF	3	2			300
G5HD-125	1930		3	2	2	4	8
G5HD-130	1930	PROOF	3	2			300
G5HD-135	1931		3	2	2	4	9
G5HD-140	1931	PROOF	3	2			300
G5HD-145	1932		3	2	2	4	10
G5HD-150	1932	PROOF	3	2			300
G5HD-155	1933		3	2	2	4	9
G5HD-160	1933	PROOF	3	2			300
G5HD-165	1934		3	2	2	5	12
G5HD-170	1934	PROOF	3	2			320
G5HD-175	1935		3	2	2	4	8
G5HD-180	1935	PROOF	3	2			300
G5HD-185	1936		3	2	2	3	5
G5HD-190	1936	PROOF	3	2			280

1. Minor obverse varieties exist.

Edward VIII   (1936)

The Edward VIII halfpenny is strictly speaking a pattern, as probable Royal approval was about to be granted at the time of the abdication. However, because its official status rests only on this technicality, and to provide continuity, it is included here.

The portrait of Edward VIII is by Thomas Humphrey Paget, and faces left at the insistence of the king, who considered this placement more flattering and wished to discontinue the tradition of opposite facings for successive monarchs. The reverse is by Thomas Humphrey Paget.

Denomination	Metal	Weight (grams)	Diameter (mm)	Rev. alignment
Halfpenny	Bronze	5.7	25	↑

Obverse 1   Head 1, left; EDWARDVS VIII D G BR OMN REX F D IND IMP

Reverse 1   Sailing ship; HALF PENNY 1937

Edge   plain

Obv. 1   Rev. 1

No.	Date		Obv.	Rev.			Unc
E8HD-005	1937		1	1			15000

No.	Date	Features	Obv.	Rev.	EF	UNC
G6HD-080	1944		1	1	2	4
G6HD-085	1944	PROOF	1	1		200
G6HD-090	1945		1	1	2	4
G6HD-095	1945	PROOF	1	1		200
G6HD-100	1946		1	1	3	12
G6HD-105	1946	PROOF	1	1		200
G6HD-110	1947		1	1	2	4
G6HD-115	1947	PROOF	1	1		200
G6HD-120	1948		1	1	2	4
G6HD-125	1948	PROOF	1	1		200
G6HD-130	1949		2	1	2	5
G6HD-135	1949	PROOF	2	1		200
G6HD-140	1950		2	1	2	4
G6HD-145	1950	PROOF [1]	2	1		8
G6HD-150	1950	PROOF from sandblasted dies [2]	2	1		180
G6HD-155	1951		2	1	2	5
G6HD-160	1951	PROOF [1]	2	1		9
G6HD-165	1951	PROOF from sandblasted dies [2]	2	1		180
G6HD-170	1952		2	1	2	4
G6HD-175	1952	PROOF	2	1		200

1. Issued in cased proof sets.
2. Struck to facilitate photography of coin.
3. Minor reverse differences exist.

Size of ship, orientation of legend against border teeth vary minutely within this series.

George VI   (1937 – 1952)

The omission of Britannia from the reverse of the George VI halfpenny was a bold innovation. Britannia had graced the coin from its inception in 1672, and continued to be depicted on the penny in a somewhat modernistic style.

The choice of symbol to replace Britannia was a three-masted sailing ship. This was not entirely the revolutionary idea it seemed at first glance; ships had occurred from time to time on British coinage, and the ship was to some extent as symbolic of Britain 'ruling the waves' as was Britannia. The vessel was said to represent the 'Golden Hind' of Sir Francis Drake. Both obverse and reverse were designed by Thomas Humphrey Paget.

As with the George V series, the halfpenny was struck for every year of the reign. It was not found necessary to curtail production in some years, as was done with the penny.

The size and orientation of the ship and the reverse legend vary very slightly from year to year and also, during 1940, within the year itself. Although Peck commented on these variations, he allocated only one reverse to the series, whereas Freeman allocated 16. These minute intricacies are not considered here to be of interest except to a specialist student of this series, and we therefore follow the Peck example.

Proofs were struck for the cased sets of 1937, 1950 and 1951, and in small quantities in all of the other years.

Collecting Hints

Mint state with full lustre is the order of the day for this series. There are no real rarities except for those proofs not issued for cased sets. Collecting a set of these presents a real challenge.

Denomination	Metal	Weight (grams)	Diameter (mm)	Rev. alignment
Halfpenny	Bronze	5.7	25	↑

Obverse 1   Head 1, left; HP on truncation; GEORGIVS VI D G BR OMN REX F D IND IMP

Obverse 2   Head 1, left; GEORGIVS VI D G BR OMN REX FIDEI DEF

Reverse 1   Sailing ship; HALF PENNY (date)

Edge   plain

Obv. 1   Obv. 2   Rev. 1

No.	Date	Features	Obv.	Rev.	EF	UNC
G6HD-005	1937		1	1	2	4
G6HD-010	1937	PROOF [1]	1	1		8
G6HD-015	1937	PROOF from sandblasted dies [2]	1	1		180
G6HD-020	1938		1	1	2	6
G6HD-025	1938	PROOF	1	1		200
G6HD-030	1939		1	1	2	5
G6HD-035	1939	PROOF	1	1		200
G6HD-040	1940	[3]	1	1	2	6
G6HD-045	1940	PROOF	1	1		200
G6HD-050	1941		1	1	2	5
G6HD-055	1941	PROOF	1	1		200
G6HD-060	1942		1	1	2	4
G6HD-065	1942	PROOF	1	1		200
G6HD-070	1943		1	1	2	4
G6HD-075	1943	PROOF	1	1		200

Elizabeth II   (1952 –)

The series uses the portrait of Elizabeth II by Mary Gillick. The halfpenny was struck for every year from 1953 to 1967 except 1961, unlike the penny. Small quantities of proofs were struck each year, and larger quantities for insertion in the proof sets of 1953 and 1970.

Collecting Hints

The series should be collected in mint state. Apart from the 1953 and 1970, the proofs are very difficult to find.

Denomination	Metal	Weight (grams)	Diameter (mm)	Rev. alignment
Halfpenny	Bronze	5.7	25	↑

Obverse 1   Head 1, right; ELIZABETH II DEI GRA BRITT OMN REGINA F D.

Obverse 2   Similar but ELIZABETH II DEI GRATIA REGINA F D

Reverse 1   Ship on sea with almost straight waves; HALF PENNY (date)

Reverse 2   Similar but waves are more irregular

Reverse NZ   Reverse of regular issue New Zealand halfpenny dated 1965

Edge   plain

Obv. 1   Obv. 2   Rev. 1

No.	Date	Features	Obv.	Rev.	UNC
EZHD-005	1953	[1]	1	1	5
EZHD-010	1953	PROOF [2]	1	1	7
EZHD-015	1953	PROOF from sandblasted dies [3]	1	1	150
EZHD-020	1954	[1]	2	1	6
EZHD-025	1954	PROOF	2	1	200
EZHD-030	1955		2	1	5

No.	Date	Features	Obv.	Rev.	UNC
EZHD-035	1955	PROOF	2	1	200
EZHD-040	1956	[1]	2	1	6
EZHD-045	1956	PROOF	2	1	200
EZHD-050	1957		2	1	10
EZHD-052	1957		2	2	2
EZHD-055	1957	PROOF	2	2	200
EZHD-060	1958	[1]	2	2	2
EZHD-065	1958	PROOF	2	2	200
EZHD-070	1959		2	2	2
EZHD-075	1959	PROOF	2	2	200
EZHD-080	1960		2	2	2
EZHD-085	1960	PROOF	2	2	200
EZHD-090	1962		2	2	2
EZHD-095	1962	PROOF	2	2	200
EZHD-100	1963		2	2	2
EZHD-105	1963	PROOF	2	2	200
EZHD-110	1964		2	2	2
EZHD-115	1964	PROOF	2	2	200
EZHD-120	1965		2	2	2
EZHD-125	1965	PROOF	2	2	200
EZHD-130	1965	struck in gold [4]	2	2	1500
EZHD-135	1965	[5]	2	NZ	500
EZHD-140	1966		2	2	2
EZHD-145	1966	PROOF	2	2	200
EZHD-150	1966	struck in aluminium [6]	2	2	300
EZHD-155	1966	struck in brass or nickel-brass [7]	2	2	400
EZHD-160	1967	[1]	2	2	2
EZHD-165	1967	PROOF	2	2	200
EZHD-170	1967	struck in cupronickel [8]	2	2	400
EZHD-175	1970	PROOF [9]	2	2	2

1. Minor design and orientation differences exist.
2. Issued in cased proof sets.
3. Struck to facilitate photography of coin.
4. Weight c.12.5 grams.
5. Error coin with New Zealand reverse; weight 5.8 grams; possibly unique.
6. Weight 2.3 grams.
7. Weight 6.8 grams.
8. Weight 5.6 grams.
9. Issued in sealed cased proof sets; not legal tender.

The halfpenny ceased to be legal tender after 31 July 1969.

Farthing

Charles II   (1660 – 1685)

In the first few years of this reign, there was a considerable shortage of coins of low denomination. It is always a sign that coins of a certain denomination are needed when tradesmen issue private tokens bearing that denomination, and the well-known farthing tokens of the 1660s are a clear indication of the need for this coin. An extensive series of pattern farthings was struck from the beginning of the reign, but it was not until 1672 that farthings were struck for circulation.

The royal Proclamation of 1672 authorised strikings of farthings and halfpennies with legal tender status up to a total of six pence, but the issue of halfpennies was delayed. The farthing thus became the first of the long series of base metal 'Britannia' coinage which was to last almost exactly 300 years.

The Proclamation decreed that there was to be a close correlation between the face value of the coins and their intrinsic metal content. Almost immediately, however, problems arose. The mint proved incapable of manufacturing the necessary blanks, and they had to be imported from Sweden. Eventually, the coins were struck with a face value slightly higher than the metal and production costs, and this resulted in counterfeits appearing shortly afterwards. In 1679 and 1680 there was some speculation about a possible new issue of farthings in tin, which had become very cheap. However, it was considered easy to counterfeit, and there were various disagreements with the tin miners. The project was postponed.

In 1684, five years after the last copper coinage of the reign had been struck, a quantity of tin farthings was issued, each coin having a plug of copper through its centre. With the price of tin at a very low level, it was hoped thus to produce coinage at a profit over production costs, while at the same time foiling the counterfeiters. An added bonus was that the ailing tin industry was bolstered by the new demand.

John Roettier prepared the dies for this series.

| Obv. 1 | Rev. 1 | Rev. 2 |

No.	Date	Features	Edge date	Obv.	Rev.	VG	F	VF	EF
C2FAM-005	1672	[1]		1	1	6	16	50	300
C2FAM-006	1672	A of CAROLVS over B (obv.)		1	1	15	45	150	750
C2FAM-007	1672	RO of CAROLO over OL (obv.)		1	1	20	60	200	1000
C2FAM-008	1672	rev. ↑		1	1	20	50	160	1000
C2FAM-010	1672	no stops on obv.		1	1	8	22	65	400
C2FAM-012	1672	no stop on rev.		1	1	15	45	120	700
C2FAM-015	1673			1	1	6	16	50	300
C2FAM-018	1673	R of CAROLVS over B (obv)		1	1	12	30	100	600
C2FAM-020	1673	CAROLA instead of CAROLO (obv.)		1	1	15	50	150	900
C2FAM-022	1673	last O of CAROLO over side-turned O		1	1	15	50	150	900
C2FAM-025	1673	BRITINNIA instead of BRITANNIA (rev.)		1	1	20	65	220	1200
C2FAM-030	1673	no stops on obv.		1	1	12	40	120	700
C2FAM-035	1673	no stop on rev.		1	1	8	22	65	400
C2FAM-040	1674			1	1	7	20	60	320
C2FAM-045	1675	[2]		1	1	7	20	60	300
C2FAM-048	1675	5 over 2 or 3		1	1	10	30	80	450
C2FAM-050	1675	no stop after CAROLVS (obv.)		1	1	10	30	75	420
C2FAM-055	1679			1	1	10	30	80	450
C2FAM-060	1679	no stop on rev.		1	1	8	22	65	400
C2FAM-065	1684	[3]	1684	1	2	45	100	300	1200
C2FAM-070	1685	[4]	1685	1	2	1200	1800		

1. Slight differences in drapery and spray exist (rev.).
2. Date spacing varies (rev.).
3. Edge punctuation varies.
4. Very few exist. Charles died on 6 February 1684 (old style calendar).

Denomination	Metal	Weight (grams)	Diameter (mm)	Rev. alignment
Farthing 1672–79	Copper	5.2–6.4	22–23	↓
Farthing 1684–85	Tin with central copper plug	5.4–6.0	23–24	↓

Obverse 1   Head 1, left; CAROLVS A CAROLO

Reverse 1   Britannia, seated, with shield, facing left, holding spray and spear; BRITANNIA; date in exergue below

Reverse 2   Similar but no date

Edge   (1672–1679) plain; (1684–1685) NVMMORVM FAMVLVS (date)

James II   (1685 – 1688)

The issue of farthings in copper plugged tin augmented the similar halfpenny of this reign, both attempting to foil counterfeiters and assist the ailing tin industry. The halfpenny was a new issue, but the farthing continued the general design of the previous reign, using a figure of Britannia from a punch used on the earlier coins. The patent for this issue was granted to Thomas Neale, Hoare and Duncombe, with 40 per cent of the profits accruing to the king.

The obverse portrait was by John Roettier. A later issue of farthing in 1687 used a somewhat different and draped bust, more like that on the halfpenny.

Collecting Hints

Because the series is highly prone to corrosion, specimens in the higher grades are very difficult to obtain. The corrosion tends to be progressive, and does not form a protective oxide coating such as is obtained with, for example, copper. Attractive specimens should be pursued without paying too much heed to catalogue prices.

Denomination	Metal	Weight (grams)	Diameter (mm)	Rev. alignment
Farthing	Tin with central copper plug	5.2–5.7	23–24	↓

Obverse 1 Head 1, right, with breastplate; IACOBVS SECVNDVS

Obverse 2 Head 2, right, draped; same legend

Reverse 1 Britannia, seated, with shield, facing left, holding spray and spear; BRITANNIA. The exergue is blank

Edge NVMMORVM FAMVLVS (date)

The coin has a square plug of copper through the centre.

Obv. 1   Obv. 2   Rev. 1

No.	Date	Features	Edge date	Obv.	Rev.	VG	F	VF	EF
J2FA-005	1684		1684	1	1	800			
J2FA-010	1685	¹	1685	1	1	40	70	300	1000
J2FA-015	1685	no copper plug	1685	1	1	300	800		
J2FA-020	1686	¹	1686	1	1	40	70	300	1000
J2FA-025	1687		1687	1	1				
J2FA-030	1687	¹	1687	2	1	100	180	700	3000

1. Punctuation varieties exist (edge).

William & Mary (1688 – 1694)

The farthing issue again followed that of the halfpenny, but there were some significant differences. The first issue, in tin, bears a caricatured portrait of William and Mary by George Bower somewhat similar to that on the halfpenny (and, incidentally, very like that on the small silver pieces which are by an unknown designer). However, the reverse of the farthing is also by Bower, whereas the halfpenny reverse is a continuation of the John Roettier Britannia. Papers referring to the 'Commission for Coyning Tynn Farthings' state that Bower was employed on this work from November 1689 to his death on the following 1st March.

The first issue of farthing was discontinued in 1690 in favour of a tin issue with a more conventional portrait of the monarchs by James Roettier. This resembles more closely the sixpence rather than the small silver. The reverse uses the figure of Britannia by James Roettier as on the coins of Charles II.

By 1692 it had become clear that the use of tin as a coinage metal left a great deal to be desired. The tendency to corrosion was now much in evidence; moreover, the coins were, after all, easy to counterfeit. In 1694, a petition by shopkeepers and the poor was presented to the House of Commons and on 17 April a committee reported that the present tin coins were 'an obstruction to trade and a great grievance' and that future coins should be made 'of English metal and of the intrinsic value'. In 1694 a new copper farthing was struck, together with a new halfpenny. Unlike the Charles II issue, the blanks were struck at the Mint rather than imported, and indeed this was one of the main conditions of the

contract. The portrait of the monarchs was by James or Norbert Roettier.

In addition to the above, a very few farthings dated 1693 exist as a result of a (subsequently revoked) contract granted to one Andrew Corbet. These bear a portrait similar to that on the last issue.

Collecting Hints

All farthings of this reign are very difficult to find in top condition. The first issue of tin farthings by Bower is very elusive in any grade, and should be acquired whenever the chance arises.

Denomination	Metal	Weight (grams)	Diameter (mm)	Rev. alignment
Farthing 1689–92	Tin with central copper plug	5.2–5.8	22–24	↓
Farthing 1693–94	Copper	4.7–6.2	22–25	↓

Obverse 1 Heads 1, right; GVLIELMVS ET MARIA (heads divide GVLIELMVS...ET)

Obverse 2 Heads 2, right, more drapery; same legend, which starts below busts. (heads divide ET...MARIA)

Obverse 3 Heads 3, right, with king wearing breastplate; same legend

Obverse 4 Heads 4, right; king's hair short; same legend

Reverse 1 Britannia, seated, with shield, facing left, crude style; date in exergue; BRITANNIA.

Reverse 2 Britannia, slightly different, same crude style; date in exergue; BRITANNIA

Reverse 3 Britannia, as on Charles II farthings; date in exergue; BRITANNIA

Edge (1689–1692): (in relief) NVMMORVM FAMVLVS (date); (1693–1694): plain

Obv. 1   Obv. 2   Obv. 3

Obv. 4

Rev. 1   Rev. 2   Rev. 3

No.	Date	Features	Edge date	Obv.	Rev.	VG	F	VF	EF
WMFA-005	1689		1689	1	1	300	700	2000	
WMFA-010	1689	PROOF in copper; edge plain		1	1				2000
WMFA-015	1689		1690	2	2	1000			
WMFA-020	1690		1689	3	3	1000			

No.	Date	Features	Edge date	Obv.	Rev.	VG	F	VF	EF
WMFA-025	1690	[1]	1690	3	3	40	90	250	900
WMFA-028	1690		1691	3	3	3000			
WMFA-030	1690	PROOF in copper; edge plain [2]		3	3				5000
WMFA-035	1691	[1]	1691	3	3	40	90	250	900
WMFA-040	1692		·1692	3	3	40	90	250	900
WMFA-045	1693	[3]		3	3	800	1200		
WMFA-050	1694	[4]		4	3	12	40	80	600
WMFA-055	1694	struck on thick wide flan [5]		4	3	150	350	800	
WMFA-060	1694	GVLIELMS instead of GVLIELMVS (obv.)		4	3	120	250	600	
WMFA-065	1694	PROOF		4	3				2000
WMFA-070	1694	PROOF in silver [6]		4	3		120	240	500

1. Edge punctuation varies.
2. Possibly unique.
3. 4 known.
4. Exergue line single or double; some 'A's may be unbarred; punctuation varies; often weakly struck.
5. Diameter 25–26 mm.
6. Some 'A's may be unbarred; punctuation varies.

William III (1694 – 1701)

The farthings of William III suffered from the same lack of control of production techniques as did the halfpenny. The production of the tin farthing (or 'white farthing' as it was sometimes known) did not resume, but the coin itself was still in circulation, corroding rapidly. These unpopular pieces were, theoretically at least, exchangeable for the new copper coinage. After the death of the queen, the farthings bearing the head of William ruling as king continued to be produced under the contract granted during the reign of William and Mary. However, sloppiness was the order of the day at the mint. Blanks, and indeed entire coins, were sometimes cast instead of being struck, and some of those benefiting financially from the savings thus produced were vociferous in exhorting the benefits of cast coinage.

Savings were made in addition by hiring cheap labour, often foreigners who were unable to spell even the king's name. Some of these craftsmen appear to have been selected to punch in the lettering on the dies.

In 1698, production of copper coinage was supposed to have been stopped following an Act of Parliament, but Stephen Martin Leake noted in 1726 that this had little effect. Nevertheless, the 1698 farthing of the first type is particularly rare, and some doubts have been raised about the authenticity of the known specimens.

The last farthings of the reign were struck in 1700. The coin did not follow the halfpenny into the degradation of the final 1699–1701 issue of much inferior workmanship and the new crude design of the reverse of the halfpenny.

The obverses of this series were engraved by James Roettier. The reverses continued to use the John Roettier punches of Britannia from the Charles II coins.

Collecting Hints

The series is rare in the top grades, and the serious collector will require specimens in very fine or better. As with the halfpenny, the scarcest date is 1698. As mentioned above, the 1698 first type farthing is particularly rare.

Denomination	Metal	Weight (grams)	Diameter (mm)	Rev. alignment
Farthing	Copper	4.5–6.2	22–23	↓

Obverse 1 Head 1, right; GVLIELMVS TERTIVS

Reverse 1 Britannia, seated, with shield, facing left, holding spray and spear; date in exergue below; BRITANNIA

Reverse 2 Similar but legend reads BRITANNIA (date); exergue is blank

Edge plain

Obv. 1	Rev. 1	Rev. 2

No.	Date	Features	Obv.	Rev.	F	VF	EF
W3FA-005	1695		1	1	20	70	350
W3FA-010	1695	struck on thick flan [1]	1	1	100	400	
W3FA-015	1695	GVLIELMV instead of GVLIELMVS (obv.)	1	1	80	300	
W3FA-020	1695	M in GVLIELMVS over V (obv.)	1	1	40	150	
W3FA-025	1695	PROOF in silver	1	1		700	1200
W3FA-030	1696	[2]	1	1	16	55	280
W3FA-035	1696	PROOF in silver	1	1		700	1200
W3FA-040	1697		1	1	16	55	280
W3FA-045	1697	GVLIELMS instead of GVLIELMVS (obv.)	1	1	80	300	
W3FA-050	1697	TERTIV instead of TERTIVS (obv.)	1	1	100	400	
W3FA-055	1697	PROOF in silver	1	1		700	1200
W3FA-060	1698		1	1	100	400	
W3FA-065	1698	B of BRITANNIA over G (rev.)	1	1	150	600	
W3FA-070	1698	[3]	1	2	40	130	550
W3FA-075	1698	PROOF in silver [3]	1	2	130	200	300
W3FA-080	1699		1	1	16	55	300
W3FA-085	1699	GVLILEMVS instead of GVLIELMVS (obv.)	1	1	80	300	
W3FA-088	1699	I in TERTIVS over V (obv.)	1	1	25	80	400
W3FA-090	1699	[4]	1	2	25	80	420
W3FA-095	1699	PROOF in silver [5]	1	2		700	1200
W3FA-100	1699	PROOF in silver on thick flan [6]	1	2		1000	1800
W3FA-105	1700	[7]	1	1	16	55	280
W3FA-110	1700	GVLILMVS instead of GVLIELMVS (obv.)	1	1	80	300	
W3FA-112	1700	BBITANNIA instead of BRITANNIA (rev.)	1	1	60	200	
W3FA-115	1700	RRITANNIA instead of BRITANNIA (rev.)	1	1	80	300	
W3FA-120	1700	R of BRITANNIA over B [8]	1	1	30	90	500
W3FA-125	1700	rev. ↑	1	1	30	90	500
W3FA-130	1700	PROOF in silver	1	1		450	750
W3FA-135	none	struck on wide flan [9]	1	obv. 1	200		

1. Weight c.7.2 grams.
2. Lettering size may vary.
3. Stop after date.
4. Stop varieties exist; one or both 'A's in BRITANNIA may be unbarred; obverse lettering spacing varies.
5. No stop after date.
6. No stop after date; weight 7.0 to 7.2 grams.
7. Stop varieties exist; 'A's in BRITANNIA may be unbarred; date size may vary.
8. First A of BRITANNIA may be unbarred.
9. 'Double headed' coin.

Anne (1701 – 1714)

The 1714 farthing of Anne is the only copper coin which is generally thought of as a regular coin. In fact, its status is in some doubt. The reign was characterised by a large number of patterns of varying designs and metals. If Anne had not died in 1714, no doubt the farthing would have entered circulation in quantity, but its actual legal status may well be that of a pattern. However, it is so widely accepted and catalogued as a coin that it is included here.

Copper coinage of Anne was not considered necessary because a very large quantity of copper had been struck during the previous reign, much of it of poor quality. Isaac Newton was the Master of the Mint at this time, and he had high ideals about the quality of the coinage. The Anne farthing is certainly greatly superior to the pieces of William III, not only in striking but also in design. The old Britannia figure used since the days of Charles II was discarded in favour of a sharper high relief design by John Croker, who also designed the obverse portrait of Anne. The bare leg on the figure of Britannia as on earlier coins is thought to have been covered on the 1714 coin on the orders of the queen. Representations by Dean Swift that the copper coinage should bear illustrations of historical events of the reign came to nothing.

The Anne farthing is somewhat smaller than its predecessors, and the total effect is that of a coin of quality and value. Unfortunately, circumstances dictated that the coin was never to enter circulation widely.

Around 1802, a curious rumour swept the country that the Anne farthing was worth a fortune, around £500, no less, and many advertisements appeared in newspapers offering specimens for sale. A specimen was sold by auction in London in March of that year for 750 guineas. The rumour persisted and *The Times* of 28 September 1826 reported that a poor man came to London from Bedfordshire with an Anne farthing, hoping to make his fortune.

Collecting Hints

As the Anne farthing did not enter circulation to any great extent, the coin is probably scarcer in fine condition than in extremely fine, although many low grade specimens do turn up. An extremely fine or better specimen is the obvious candidate for any collection.
Many cast and other forgeries exist, and one must be on guard. Electrotypes are deceptive, and the edge should be examined; these pieces are made in two halves and the seam is usually evident.

Denomination	Metal	Weight (grams)	Diameter (mm)	Rev. alignment
Farthing	Copper	4.8–5.8	21–22	↓

Obverse 1   Head 1, left; ANNA DEI GRATIA

Reverse 1   Britannia, seated, with shield, facing left, holding spray and spear; 1714 in exergue below; BRITANNIA

Edge   plain

Obv. 1   Rev. 1

No.	Date			Obv.	Rev.	F	VF	EF
ANFA-005	1714			1	1	250	450	1000

George I   (1714 – 1727)

The issue of the Anne farthing had been thwarted by the death of the queen, and when George I came to the throne there was again a need for copper coinage. However, the price of copper had risen. It was therefore decided to produce a somewhat lighter coin than previously. The first issue, known as the 'dump' issue, achieved this economy by means of a reduction in flan size, while the latter issue of 1719–1724 has a more conventional flan size but is thinner. Unfortunately, both issues suffer from metal and striking flaws. The dies, unlike those of the 17th century, were in bold relief, and difficulties were encountered in achieving the high pressure necessary to transfer all of the detail to the blanks.

Wisely, it was decided not to include the long abbreviated Hanoverian titles of the king, as had been done on most of the silver coinage. The result was a simple and elegant coin, despite the unattractiveness of the monarch. The dies were the work of John Croker, possibly assisted by Johann Rudolph Ochs, senior. The Britannia reverse is from the same punch as used on the Anne farthing.

Collecting Hints

As mentioned above, the series suffers from metal flaws and weak striking. However, the George I farthing is attractive and popular with collectors. The dump issue in particular has a chunky appearance and is much sought after in the higher grades. Collect in very fine condition or better. Remember that what appears as wear may in fact be weakness of strike.

Denomination	Metal	Weight (grams)	Diameter (mm)	Rev. alignment
Farthing 1717–18	Copper	4.5–5.3	20–21	↓
Farthing 1719–24	Copper	4.5–5.3	22–23	↓

Obverse 1   Head 1, right; GEORGIVS REX

Reverse 1   Britannia, seated, with shield, facing left, holding spray and spear; date in exergue below; BRITANNIA

Edge   plain

Obv. 1   Rev. 1

No.	Date	Features	Obv.	Rev.	F	VF	EF
G1FA-005	1717		1	1	100	250	600
G1FA-010	1717	PROOF	1	1			1000
G1FA-015	1717	PROOF on thick flan [1]	1	1			2000
G1FA-020	1717	PROOF in silver; rev. ↑	1	1		200	500
G1FA-025	1717	PROOF in silver on thin flan [2]	1	1		200	700
G1FA-030	1718	PROOF in silver on thin flan	1	1		300	800
G1FA-032	1718	PROOF in silver on thin flan; rev. ↑ [3]	1	1		300	800
G1FA-035	1719	[3]	1	1	8	50	200
G1FA-036	1719	no rev. linear circle; very small 9 in date	1	1	30	150	600
G1FA-037	1719	very small 9 in date[4]	1	1	20	100	400
G1FA-038	1719	very large 9 in date[4]	1	1	20	100	400
G1FA-039	1719	latter A in BRITANNIA over I	1	1	40	180	700
G1FA-040	1719	struck on 25mm diameter flan	1	1	20	100	400
G1FA-045	1719	obv. legend continues over head [5]	1	1	25	130	500
G1FA-050	1719	in silver [6]	1	1		300	800
G1FA-055	1720	[7]	1	1	8	50	200
G1FA-060	1720	edge vertically milled	1	1	20	120	600
G1FA-065	1720	edge vertically milled; struck on thin (0.7mm) flan	1	1	100	500	1200
G1FA-070	1721	[8]	1	1	8	50	200
G1FA-075	1721	latter 1 over 0	1	1	14	80	350
G1FA-080	1722	[7]	1	1	8	50	200
G1FA-085	1723		1	1	8	50	200
G1FA-090	1723	R of REX over horizontal R	1	1	16	100	400
G1FA-095	1724		1	1	8	50	200
G1FA-100	none	struck on 5 mm thick flan [9]	1	obv. 1	500		

1. Thickness 2.5 mm.
2. Weight 3.9 grams.
3. Weight 4.6 grams.

Notes continued
4. Obverse lettering size varies; stop varieties exist.
5. Small obverse lettering.
6. Possibly a proof.
7. Obverse lettering size varies.
8. Exists with and without stop after date.
9. 'Double headed'; possibly only one exists.

George II (1727 – 1760)

A large quantity of farthings was struck during this reign. Furthermore, counterfeits began to appear in very large numbers. The low denomination copper coinage did not have quite the same public image as it has in modern times, and was looked on separately from the silver coinage, rather like tokens which could be exchanged on demand. This public view of coins such as the farthing may have gone some way to explain the large proliferation of counterfeits, although greed was always the primary motive. Many of the counterfeits were produced from genuine coins which were melted down to produce lightweight copies.

The young head of George II used until 1739 was by John Croker, while the old head used from 1741 was by John Sigismund Tanner. The reverse continued to use the Britannia from the Anne farthing punch by John Croker.

According to Snelling, the 1754 farthing was minted at least as late as 1763, i.e. well into the reign of George III.

Collecting Hints

This series is more easily found in the high grades than are the farthings of earlier reigns. The minimum acceptable grade should be very fine.

Denomination	Metal	Weight (grams)	Diameter (mm)	Rev. alignment
Farthing	Copper	4.5–5.3	22–23	↓

Obverse 1 Head 1, left; GEORGIVS II REX

Obverse 2 Head 2, older, left; GEORGIUS II REX

Obverse 3 Head 2, left; GEORGIVS II REX

Reverse 1 Britannia, seated, with shield, facing left, holding spray and spear; BRITANNIA; date in exergue below

Edge plain

Obv. 1	Obv. 3	Rev. 1

No.	Date	Features	Obv.	Rev.	F	VF	EF
G2FA-005	1730		1	1	8	45	150
G2FA-010	1730	PROOF	1	1			700
G2FA-015	1730	PROOF in silver	1	1			750
G2FA-020	1730	PROOF in silver on thick flan; rev. ↑ [1]	1	1			900
G2FA-025	1731	[2]	1	1	8	55	200
G2FA-030	1732		1	1	8	45	150
G2FA-032	1732	2 over 1	1	1	20	100	400
G2FA-035	1733		1	1	8	45	150
G2FA-040	1734		1	1	8	45	150
G2FA-045	1734	no stops on obv.	1	1	15	80	250
G2FA-050	1735		1	1	7	40	130
G2FA-055	1735	3 double-struck	1	1	10	60	180
G2FA-060	1735	3 double-struck; struck on thick flan [3]	1	1	100		
G2FA-065	1736	[4]	1	1	7	40	130
G2FA-070	1737		1	1	7	40	130
G2FA-075	1737	large date	1	1	7	40	130
G2FA-080	1739		1	1	7	40	130

No.	Date	Features	Obv.	Rev.	F	VF	EF
G2FA-085	1739	9 over 5	1	1	18	100	300
G2FA-090	1741		2	1	8	50	170
G2FA-095	1744		2	1	8	50	170
G2FA-100	1746		3	1	7	40	130
G2FA-105	1746	V of GEORGIVS over U (obv.)	3	1	16	90	250
G2FA-110	1749		3	1	7	40	130
G2FA-115	1750		3	1	7	40	130
G2FA-120	1754	[5]	3	1	5	24	70
G2FA-125	1754	4 over 0	3	1	15	80	220

1. 2mm thick; weight c.7.8 grams.
2. Ribbons vary.
3. Weight c.7.1 grams.
4. Date spacing varies.
5. Struck for several years.

George III (1760 – 1820)

Apart from the 'posthumous' George II farthings dated 1754 mentioned earlier, the first farthings struck during this reign were those of 1771. In the same year, the production of counterfeit copper became a felony, but the new law did little to stop what had by now become an epidemic. For many years a situation existed in which the majority of copper pieces circulating were forgeries.

The Boulton anti-counterfeiting measures carried out at the Soho Mint to produce the 1797 'Cartwheel' coinage did not extend to the farthing, although several types of pattern cartwheel farthing were struck. Boulton was, however, granted a licence to produce farthings in 1799, but the weight of these was somewhat below those of the cartwheel patterns, owing to a rise in the price of copper. The wide-rimmed cartwheel design had by this time been abandoned, and the farthing of 1799 had a more conventional design, although two aspects of it were far from conventional. The reverse bore the legend '1 FARTHING', the first time that the name of a denomination had appeared on any English coin; the coin was also the first British coin to bear the date on the obverse. The issue of 1806–07 was even lighter in weight than the 1799 issue, owing to a further rise in the price of copper. A total of 22.5 tons of copper was used for the 1806–07 issue.

The portrait of George III used on the issue of 1771–75 was possibly by Richard Yeo or Thomas Pingo. The later coins were designed by Conrad Heinrich Küchler.

Collecting Hints

The series should be collected in extremely fine or better condition with original lustre. Counterfeits are easily detectable but are themselves an interesting field of study. The farthings of 1799–1807 did not wear as fast as those of the earlier series as the field on both sides was somewhat concave. The central design thus did not rub against other coins so readily when in circulation.

Denomination	Metal	Weight (grams)	Diameter (mm)	Rev. alignment
Farthing 1771–75	Copper	4.3–5.3	23–24	↓
Farthing 1799	Copper	5.8–6.6	23–24	↓
Farthing 1806–07	Copper	4.7–4.8	21–22	↓

Obverse 1 Head 1, right; GEORGIVS III REX

Obverse 2 Head 2, right; GEORGIUS III DEI GRATIA REX 1799

Obverse 3 Head 3, right; GEORGIUS III D G REX (date)

Reverse 1 Britannia, seated, with shield, facing left, holding spray and spear; BRITANNIA; date in exergue below

Reverse 2 Redesigned Britannia, smaller; BRITANNIA 1 FARTHING

Reverse 3 Slightly different Britannia; BRITANNIA

*Edge*1771–1775: plain

1799–1807: diagonally grained

609

Obv. 1   Obv. 2   Obv. 3

Rev. 1   Rev. 2   Rev. 3

No.	Date	Features	Obv.	Rev.	F	VF	EF
G3FA-005	1771		1	1	25	60	180
G3FA-008	1771	first 7 over 1	1	1	50	100	250
G3FA-010	1771	PROOF [1]	1	1			800
G3FA-015	1773	[2]	1	1	6	18	80
G3FA-020	1773	no stop on rev. [2]	1	1	8	22	110
G3FA-025	1773	no stop after REX (obv.)	1	1	10	25	140
G3FA-030	1774	[2]	1	1	8	24	130
G3FA-035	1775		1	1	10	26	150
G3FA-038	1775	V in GEORGIVS is ∀	1	1	15	40	250
G3FA-040	1799	[3]	2	2	4	10	40
G3FA-045	1799	PROOF [4]	2	2			200
G3FA-050	1799	PROOF; edge plain [5]	2	2			200
G3FA-055	1799	Bronzed PROOF [6]	2	2			150
G3FA-060	1799	Bronzed PROOF; edge plain [5]	2	2			150
G3FA-065	1799	gilt PROOF [6]	2	2			200
G3FA-070	1799	gilt PROOF; edge plain [5]	2	2			200
G3FA-075	1799	PROOF in silver; edge plain [5]	2	2			900
G3FA-080	1799	PROOF in gold; edge plain [5]	2	2			6000
G3FA-085	1806	[7]	3	3	4	9	35
G3FA-090	1806	PROOF [4]	3	3			150
G3FA-095	1806	Bronzed PROOF [4]	3	3			150
G3FA-100	1806	Bronzed PROOF; edge plain [6]	3	3			150
G3FA-105	1806	gilt PROOF	3	3			150
G3FA-110	1806	gilt PROOF; edge plain [5]	3	3			150
G3FA-115	1806	PROOF in silver; edge plain [5]	3	3			800
G3FA-120	1806	PROOF in gold; edge plain [5]	3	3			6000
G3FA-125	1807		3	3	6	12	60

1. No stop on reverse.
2. Breastplate varieties exist (obv.).
3. Wreath may have 3 or 4 berries.
4. Several varieties; some are 'Late Soho' issue.
5. 'Late Soho' issue.
6. Several varieties; 'Late Soho' issue.
7. Several minor varieties.

George IV (1820 – 1830)

The 'Great Recoinage' of 1816 ensured that the new mint at Tower Hill was working at full capacity. However, the production of gold and silver coinage was given priority, and the quantity of copper in circulation was sufficient for day-to-day needs. The first copper coins to be struck at the new mint were in 1821, when an issue of farthings was authorised. These were to be struck from copper at the mint which had already been obtained from melting down old coinage.

Pistrucci was still employed as a designer and engraver, and unfortunately for the farthing it fell to him to engrave the designs for the new coinage. He produced another of his ugly portraits of the king, with a bulging face and neck, and wiry hair. It was not difficult to see why his portraits caused the king so much displeasure. His treatment of Britannia was little better, cumbersome and pretentious, and facing the opposite way to the traditional position. This reversal of Britannia demonstrated Pis-

trucci's contempt for traditional design; on the silver coinage of George III he had already raised some eyebrows by placing the date on the obverse under the head.

Following Pistrucci's downgrading following his refusal to copy another artist's work, William Wyon was given the task of redesigning the coinage. This produced the so-called 'bare head' type farthing of 1826. The portrait of the king was more flattering, and the reverse Britannia was more elegant and uncluttered. It is interesting to note, however, that William Wyon continued Pistrucci's innovatory idea of placing the date under the head. The proof farthing of 1826 was included in the proof set issued in that year to inaugurate the new Wyon coinage.

Collecting Hints

The series should be collected in extremely fine condition or better. Counterfeits are no longer a problem.

Denomination	Metal	Weight (grams)	Diameter (mm)	Rev. alignment
Farthing 1821–26 Obv. 1; Rev. 1	Copper	4.5–4.8	22	↓
Farthing 1826–30 Obv. 2; Rev. 2	Copper	4.6–4.9	22	↑

Obverse 1   Head 1, left; GEORGIUS IIII DEI GRATIA

Obverse 2   Head 2, left; GEORGIUS IV DEI GRATIA (date)

Reverse 1   Britannia, seated, with shield, facing right, holding trident and spray; date in exergue below; BRITANNIAR REX FID DEF

Reverse 2   Redesigned Britannia, facing right, holding trident; same legend (no date)

Edge   plain

Obv. 1   Obv. 2

Rev. 1   Rev. 2

No.	Date	Features	Obv.	Rev.	F	VF	EF	UNC
G4FA-005	1821	[1]	1	1	4	8	25	40
G4FA-010	1821	PROOF [1]	1	1				500
G4FA-015	1822	[2]	1	1	4	8	25	40
G4FA-020	1822	PROOF; rev. ↑	1	1				500
G4FA-025	1823	1 in date is I [3]	1	1	10	20	60	95
G4FA-030	1823	1 in date is 1	1	1	4	8	25	50
G4FA-035	1825	[2]	1	1	4	8	25	40
G4FA-040	1825	D of DEI over U (obv.)	1	1	15	35	80	150
G4FA-045	1825	PROOF in gold	1	1				4000
G4FA-050	1826		1	1	6	11	35	55
G4FA-052	1826	R of GRATIA over E	1	1	20	40	100	200
G4FA-055	1826		2	2	4	7	24	35
G4FA-058	1826	Roman I in date	2	2	30	100	200	300
G4FA-060	1826	PROOF	2	2				150
G4FA-065	1826	Bronzed PROOF [4]	2	2				100
G4FA-070	1827		2	2	6	10	32	50
G4FA-075	1828		2	2	4	8	40	80
G4FA-080	1829		2	2	6	10	32	50
G4FA-085	1830		2	2	4	8	50	100

1. Stop after date (only on 1821).
2. Leaves vary (obv.).

Notes continued
3. Date 'l' is '1' over inverted '1'.
4. Issued in cased proof sets.

William IV   (1830 – 1837)

The farthing continued the William Wyon design of the previous reign, the head of the king being based by Wyon on a model by Sir Francis Chantrey. The reverse is identical to the George IV issue except that some of the dates have minor variations to the lines on the oval shield.

Collecting Hints

Collect in extremely fine or mint state with original lustre.

Denomination	Metal	Weight (grams)	Diameter (mm)	Rev. alignment
Farthing	Copper	4.6–4.8	22	↑

Obverse 1   Head 1, right; W.W. incuse on truncation; GULIELMUS IIII DEI GRATIA (date)

Reverse 1   Britannia, seated, with shield, facing right, holding trident; BRITANNIAR REX FID DEF (almost identical to Reverse 2 of George IV issue)

Edge   plain

Obv. 1   Rev. 1

No.	Date	Features	Obv.	Rev.	F	VF	EF	UNC
W4FA-005	1831		1	1	4	8	25	50
W4FA-010	1831	PROOF	1	1				250
W4FA-015	1831	Bronzed PROOF	1	1				180
W4FA-020	1831	Bronzed PROOF rev. ↓[1]	1	1				180
W4FA-025	1834	[2]	1	1	4	8	35	70
W4FA-030	1835	[2]	1	1	4	8	25	60
W4FA-035	1835	rev. ↓	1	1	25	50	200	400
W4FA-040	1836		1	1	5	10	45	75
W4FA-045	1837		1	1	8	16	60	100
W4FA-050	1837	7 over indeterminate digit	1	1	10	22	75	130

1. Issued in cased proof sets.
2. Minor shield variations (2 types).

Victoria   (1837 – 1901)

The long reign of Victoria produced in the farthing one of the longest series of copper and bronze coinage. The date sequence was broken only in 1870, 1871 and 1889. The curious 1877 proof was struck at a later date, but maintains the run of dates. It is possible that one reason contributing to the fact that the copper series has an unbroken run is that it appears that the same dies were used for the obverses of the sovereign and the farthing. Sovereigns were minted throughout the period, except for 1840. The use of the same dies may also explain the high prevalence of defects in the series. Presumably, it would have been considered that the gold coin was more important, and it is logical to assume that the new die was used to strike the sovereign first. By the time the die was used for the farthing, defects had appeared. It should be mentioned, however, that defects are also common on the reverses of farthings to a considerable degree. Bramah listed many of these as separate varieties, but it is not considered here that minor va-

rieties which are the result of die wear or die defect should merit special treatment. Some, however, have been included in annotated form.

In 1860, the farthing was redesigned for the introduction of the bronze coinage. The weight was also considerably reduced. This series produced a number of interesting varieties but these are not as extensive as on the penny and halfpenny. In 1895, the coin was again completely redesigned to incorporate the veiled head of Victoria. This design lasted until the death of the Queen in 1901.

The copper farthing was designed and engraved by William Wyon, using the same reverse as on the previous reign (except for the alteration of REX to REG); the bronze issue was the work of Leonard Charles Wyon, while the veiled head farthing was engraved by George William de Saulles (1862–1903), the obverse being designed by Thomas Brock, and the reverse owing much to the Wyon reverse.

Collecting Hints

Very fine is probably the minimum acceptable grade for this extensive series. Anyone seeking to acquire the minor varieties will probably look for them in fine condition or better. Ghosting is not quite as prevalent as on the larger copper and bronze coins.

Some of the rare varieties (such as the 1875-H narrow bust) are not at all well known, and can be picked up cheaply if they can be found. Others, such as the 1874 G over rotated G, are well known but are not always checked by dealers, sometimes because the coin is so small, and the variety may not be spotted. This latter variety is, however, very seldom found.

Warner points out that the copper series is notable for the imperfections of the reverse legends. The B is found with one or both serifs missing, and the bar of the A is often weak or missing.

The farthing is a fascinating series. It is perhaps more likely to appeal to the intellectual than, say, the five pound piece, and it is a coin worthy of considerable study.

Denomination	Metal	Weight (grams)	Diameter (mm)	Rev. alignment
Farthing 1838–60, 1864 Obvs 1–2, Rev. 1	Copper	4.5–4.9	22	↑
Farthing 1860–1901 Obvs 3–6, Revs 2–5	Bronze (copper 95%; tin 4%; zinc 1%)	2.8–3.0	20	↑

Obverse 1   Head 1, left, WW raised on truncation; VICTORIA DEI GRATIA (date)

Obverse 2   Head 1, left, WW incuse on truncation; same legend

Obverse 3   Head 2, left; VICTORIA D G BRITT REG F D; beaded border

Obverse 4   Similar but toothed border

Obverse 5   Head 3, left; slightly older features; same legend

Obverse 6   Head 4, veiled, left; VICTORIA DEI GRA BRITT REGINA FID DEF IND IMP

Reverse 1   Britannia, seated, with shield, facing right; BRITANNIAR REG FID DEF (as reverse of William IV issue but REX becomes REG)

Reverse 2   Redesigned Britannia, seated, with shield, facing right; FARTHING; date in exergue below Britannia; beaded border.

Reverse 3   Similar but toothed border

Reverse 4   Similar but Britannia completely redesigned.

Reverse 5   Similar but waterline slightly higher

Obv. 2   Obv. 3   Obv. 4

Obv. 5   Obv. 6   Rev. 1

Rev. 2   Rev. 3   Rev. 4

Copper Issue

No.	Date	Features	Obv.	Rev.	F	VF	EF	UNC
VYFA-005	1838	[1]	1	1	4	8	25	45
VYFA-010	1839		1	1	4	7	22	35
VYFA-015	1839	trident has only 2 prongs (rev.)	1	1	6	10	30	50
VYFA-018	1839	GRATIΛ instead of GRATIA (obv.)	1	1	8	15	50	90
VYFA-020	1839	PROOF	1	1				180
VYFA-025	1839	Bronzed PROOF	1	1				180
VYFA-030	1839	Bronzed PROOF; rev. ↓[2]	1	1				180
VYFA-035	1839	PROOF in silver	1	1				1500
VYFA-040	1840	[1]	1	1	4	7	22	35
VYFA-042	1840	trident has only 2 prongs (rev.)	1	1	70	200	400	800
VYFA-045	1841	[1]	1	1	4	7	22	40
VYFA-050	1841	PROOF [3]	1	1				1000
VYFA-055	1842		1	1	5	10	45	75
VYFA-060	1843	1 in date is I	1	1	100	300	700	
VYFA-065	1843	1 in date is 1	1	1	4	7	22	40
VYFA-068	1843	1 in date is 1; 3 over 2	1	1	40	80	200	
VYFA-070	1844	[1]	1	1	60	150	900	
VYFA-075	1845	[4]	1	1	4	8	24	45
VYFA-080	1846	[1]	1	1	5	10	40	70
VYFA-085	1847	[1]	1	1	4	8	24	40
VYFA-090	1848	[1]	1	1	4	8	24	45
VYFA-095	1849	[1]	1	1	12	50	150	300
VYFA-100	1850	[5]	1	1	4	8	24	45
VYFA-102	1850	5 over 7 [5]	1	1	10	20	60	120
VYFA-105	1851		1	1	6	20	70	110
VYFA-110	1851	D of DEI over horizontal D (obv.)	1	1	80	300	600	900
VYFA-115	1852		1	1	6	20	70	110
VYFA-120	1853	[1]	1	1	4	7	22	35
VYFA-122	1853	3 over 8(?)	1	1	8	15	50	90
VYFA-125	1853	PROOF	1	1				250
VYFA-130	1853	Bronzed PROOF rev. ↓[2]	1	1				250
VYFA-135	1853	[1]	2	1	6	15	45	70
VYFA-140	1853	PROOF	2	1				300
VYFA-145	1854		2	1	4	7	22	35
VYFA-150	1855		1	1	4	8	24	40
VYFA-155	1855		2	1	5	10	28	50
VYFA-160	1856	[1]	2	1	5	11	35	70
VYFA-165	1856	R of VICTORIA under E (obv.) [1]	2	1	7	14	50	85
VYFA-170	1857		2	1	4	8	24	40
VYFA-175	1858	[6]	2	1	4	8	24	40
VYFA-178	1858	small date [6]	2	1	25	50	120	400
VYFA-180	1859		2	1	8	16	50	90
VYFA-185	1860	[7]	2	1	1200	1800	3000	5000

1. Punctuation may vary.
2. Issued in cased proof sets.
3. Possibly struck after 1841.

Notes continued
4. Date size varies.
5. Head slightly redesigned; punctuation may vary.
6. 5 of date may resemble 3.
7. Possibly struck after 1860; proofs may exist.

Bronze Issue; Young Head

No.	Date	Features	Obv.	Rev.	F	VF	EF	UNC
VYFA-190	1860		3	2	5	9	20	35
VYFA-195	1860	PROOF	3	2				350
VYFA-200	1860	[1]	4	2	150	250	500	1500
VYFA-205	1860	[2]	4	3	3	5	12	20
VYFA-210	1860	PROOF	4	3				450
VYFA-215	1861	[2]	4	3	3	5	12	20
VYFA-220	1861	PROOF	4	3				400
VYFA-225	1861	PROOF in 0.97 silver	4	3				1200
VYFA-230	1861	PROOF in gold; rev. ↓ [3]	4	3				5000
VYFA-235	1862	[4]	4	3	3	5	12	25
VYFA-240	1862	PROOF	4	3				300
VYFA-245	1863	[5]	4	3	15	50	120	240
VYFA-250	1863	PROOF	4	3				1200
VYFA-255	1864	in copper; as copper issue [6]	2	1	6000	10000		
VYFA-260	1864	[4]	4	3	3	6	18	35
VYFA-265	1865	[4]	4	3	3	6	15	25
VYFA-270	1865	5 over 2	4	3	5	9	20	50
VYFA-275	1866		4	3	3	6	15	25
VYFA-280	1866	PROOF	4	3				400
VYFA-285	1867		4	3	4	7	16	28
VYFA-290	1867	PROOF	4	3				350
VYFA-295	1868		4	3	4	7	16	28
VYFA-300	1868	PROOF	4	3				250
VYFA-305	1868	PROOF in copper	4	3				400
VYFA-310	1868	PROOF in cupronickel	4	3				200
VYFA-315	1869		4	3	5	9	24	60
VYFA-320	1872		4	3	3	6	15	30
VYFA-325	1873		4	3	3	5	12	25
VYFA-330	1874	H below date [7]	5	3	3	5	12	25
VYFA-335	1874	H below date; 'G's on obv. both over horizontal 'G's [7]	5	3	100	200	800	
VYFA-340	1874	H below date; PROOF [7]	5	3				350
VYFA-345	1875	[8]	4	3	8	20	60	100
VYFA-350	1875	[7]	4	3	20	60	150	250
VYFA-355	1875	[7]	5	3	11	30	85	150
VYFA-360	1875	H below date [7]	4	3	40	80	250	450
VYFA-365	1875	H below date [7]	5	3	3	5	10	22
VYFA-370	1875	H below date; PROOF [7]	5	3				300
VYFA-375	1876	H below date [9]	5	3	10	24	60	120
VYFA-380	1877	PROOF	5	3				1500
VYFA-385	1878		5	3	3	5	10	20
VYFA-390	1878	PROOF	5	3				350
VYFA-395	1879	[10]	5	3	3	5	10	20
VYFA-400	1879	PROOF [16]	5	3				400
VYFA-405	1880	[11]	5	3	4	7	14	26
VYFA-410	1880	PROOF	5	3				300
VYFA-415	1881	[12]	5	3	3	5	12	22
VYFA-420	1881	PROOF	5	3				350
VYFA-425	1881	H below date [13]	5	3	4	7	14	24
VYFA-430	1882	H below date	5	3	4	7	14	30
VYFA-435	1882	H below date; PROOF	5	3				300
VYFA-440	1883		5	3	6	10	20	40
VYFA-445	1883	PROOF	5	3				350
VYFA-450	1884		5	3	3	5	8	16
VYFA-455	1884	PROOF	5	3				300
VYFA-460	1885		5	3	3	5	8	12
VYFA-465	1885	PROOF	5	3				300
VYFA-470	1886		5	3	3	5	8	12
VYFA-475	1886	PROOF	5	3				300
VYFA-480	1887		5	3	3	6	10	15
VYFA-485	1888		5	3	3	6	10	15
VYFA-490	1890		5	3	3	6	10	15
VYFA-495	1890	PROOF	5	3				300
VYFA-500	1891		5	3	3	6	10	15
VYFA-505	1891	PROOF	5	3				300
VYFA-510	1892		5	3	7	14	35	60
VYFA-515	1892	PROOF	5	3				400
VYFA-520	1893	[10]	5	3	3	6	10	15
VYFA-525	1894		5	3	3	6	11	17
VYFA-530	1894	PROOF	5	3				300
VYFA-535	1895		5	3	10	24	50	80

1. Toothed/beaded 'mule'.

No.	Date	Features	Obv.	Rev.	F	VF	EF	UNC

2. Minor obverse differences occur.
3. One known; weight 3.9 grams.
4. Date variations occur.
5. Date variations occur; all have square-top '3' (occurs only on this date).
6. Has I in relief on truncation before WW.
7. Date in small figures.
8. Date in large figures.
9. 6 in date varies; date is in small figures from now on.
10. 9 in date varies.
11. 2 slightly different obverses; hair often weakly struck.
12. 3 slightly different obverses.
13. Many have double 'H' mintmark (rev.).

Old Head

No.	Date	Features	Obv.	Rev.	F	VF	EF	UNC
VOFA-540	1895		6	4	2	4	8	15
VOFA-545	1895	PROOF	6	4				400
VOFA-550	1896		6	4	2	4	8	12
VOFA-555	1896	PROOF	6	4				400
VOFA-560	1897		6	4	4	8	14	20
VOFA-562	1897	issued artificially darkened	6	4	5	10	20	35
VOFA-565	1897	issued artificially darkened	6	5	2	4	10	20
VOFA-568	1897	issued with conventional bright finish	6	5			20	35
VOFA-570	1898	issued artificially darkened	6	4	2	4	10	30
VOFA-572	1898	issued with conventional bright finish	6	4			20	30
VOFA-575	1899	issued artificially darkened	6	4			20	30
VOFA-580	1900	issued artificially darkened	6	4	2	4	10	20
VOFA-585	1901	issued artificially darkened	6	4	2	4	10	20
VOFA-590	1901	issued with conventional bright finish	6	4				25

Edward VII (1901 – 1910)

The farthing continued to be issued in an artificially toned state to avoid confusion with the half sovereign. The only minor difference occurring to the design was in 1903, when the whole issue of that year had a 'low tide' reverse. This coin is not very well known amongst collectors. Presumably it would have achieved a greater fame if, like the halfpenny and penny, it had been a scarce variety of that year. The 'low tide' reverse is identical to that used on the Victorian veiled head farthing.

The portrait of Edward VII was by George William de Saulles (1862–1903), with the reducing machine being used to effect the correct size.

Collecting Hints

This issue is unusual and attractive in mint state, when the lustre of the original dark patina is untouched. A little care should be taken, however. Some years ago, the writer was told by a well-known dealer from the North of England that he always treated extremely fine or better farthings of this period with motor oil before selling them!

Denomination	Metal	Weight (grams)	Diameter (mm)	Rev. alignment
Farthing	Bronze (copper 95%; tin 4%; zinc 1%)	2.7–2.9	20	↑

Obverse 1 Head 1, right; EDWARDVS VII DEI GRA BRITT OMN REX FID DEF IND IMP

Reverse 1 Britannia, seated, with shield, holding trident, facing right; FARTHING; date in exergue below Britannia

Reverse 2 Similar but sea is lower

Edge plain

Obv. 1   Rev. 1

No.	Date	Obv.	Rev.	VF	EF	UNC
E7FA-005	1902	1	1	3	6	12
E7FA-010	1903	1	2	4	8	20
E7FA-015	1904	1	1	4	9	25
E7FA-020	1905	1	1	4	8	16
E7FA-025	1906	1	1	4	8	16
E7FA-030	1907	1	1	4	8	20
E7FA-035	1908	1	1	4	8	20
E7FA-040	1909	1	1	4	8	20
E7FA-045	1910	1	1	4	9	22

George V (1910 – 1936)

The head of George V used on the farthings was the Sir Bertram Mackennal design used on the larger coins. The reverse carried through from the Edward VII farthing. The principal difference from the halfpenny and penny was that the 'modified effigy' introduced in 1926 continued through to 1936 instead of being replaced by a smaller version in 1928. The new reverse, also introduced in 1926, was a reduced version of that used on the penny and halfpenny from 1927 and 1925 respectively.

Ghosting does not occur as frequently on the farthing as it does on the two larger bronze coins, and disappears with the new 1926 issue.

Artificial darkening continued from the inception of the series until 1917. Half sovereigns were by that time no longer being struck at the mint.

Collecting Hints

The first seven years of the series were issued artificially darkened, and the remarks made for the Edward VII farthing apply. The series as a whole should be collected in extremely fine or mint state.

Denomination	Metal	Weight (grams)	Diameter (mm)	Rev. alignment
Farthing 1911–22	Bronze (copper 95%; tin 4%; zinc 1%)	2.8–2.9	20	↑
Farthing 1923–36	Bronze (copper 95.5%; tin 3%; zinc 1.5%)	2.8–2.9	20	↑

Obverse 1 Head 1, left, B.M. on truncation; GEORGIVS V DEI GRA BRITT OMN REX FID DEF IND IMP

Obverse 2 Head 2, known as 'modified effigy', left; initials BM are without stops and further to right; same legend

Reverse 1 Britannia, seated, with shield and trident, facing right; FARTHING; date in exergue below Britannia

Reverse 2 Similar but redesigned and more sharply struck

| Obv. 1 | Obv. 2 | Rev. 1 | Rev. 2 |

No.	Date	Features	Obv.	Rev.	EF	UNC
G5FA-005	1911	issued artificially darkened [1]	1	1	4	8
G5FA-010	1912	issued artificially darkened	1	1	4	8
G5FA-015	1913	issued artificially darkened	1	1	4	8
G5FA-020	1914	issued artificially darkened [1]	1	1	4	8
G5FA-025	1915	issued artificially darkened [1]	1	1	5	10
G5FA-030	1916	issued artificially darkened	1	1	4	8
G5FA-035	1917	issued artificially darkened	1	1	4	8
G5FA-040	1918		1	1	4	8
G5FA-042	1918	issued artificially darkened	1	1	20	30
G5FA-045	1919		1	1	3	7
G5FA-050	1920		1	1	3	7
G5FA-055	1921		1	1	3	7
G5FA-060	1922		1	1	3	7
G5FA-065	1923		1	1	3	7
G5FA-070	1924		1	1	3	7
G5FA-075	1925		1	1	3	7
G5FA-080	1926		2	2	3	7
G5FA-085	1926	PROOF	2	2		200
G5FA-090	1927		2	2	3	6
G5FA-095	1927	PROOF	2	2		200
G5FA-100	1928		2	2	3	6
G5FA-105	1928	PROOF	2	2		200
G5FA-110	1929		2	2	3	6
G5FA-115	1929	PROOF	2	2		200
G5FA-120	1930		2	2	3	6
G5FA-125	1930	PROOF	2	2		200
G5FA-130	1931		2	2	3	6
G5FA-135	1931	PROOF	2	2		200
G5FA-140	1932		2	2	2	5
G5FA-145	1932	PROOF	2	2		200
G5FA-150	1933		2	2	2	5
G5FA-155	1933	PROOF	2	2		200
G5FA-160	1934		2	2	3	6
G5FA-165	1934	PROOF	2	2		200
G5FA-170	1935		2	2	4	8
G5FA-175	1935	PROOF	2	2		200
G5FA-180	1936		2	2	2	4
G5FA-185	1936	PROOF	2	2		200

1. Minor obverse differences occur.

Edward VIII (1936)

The Edward VIII farthing is strictly speaking a pattern, as probable Royal approval was about to be granted at the time of the abdication. However, because its official status rests only on this technicality, and to provide continuity, it is included here.

The use of the reducing machine to fit a design of considerable detail on to a farthing flan was now seen as unsatisfactory from an aesthetic viewpoint. Although the later pennies and halfpennies of George V were visually pleasing, it needed a magnifying glass to appreciate the farthing reverse. A simpler design was proposed for the reverse of the Edward VIII issue. The adopted wren design by H. Wilson Parker was a bold departure from previous reverses depicting Britannia. Moreover, other denominations had not previously departed from traditional British heraldic and similar representations.

The portrait of Edward VIII is by Thomas Humphrey Paget, and faces left at the insistence of the king, who considered this position more flattering and wished to discontinue the tradition of opposite facings for successive monarchs.

Denomination	Metal	Weight (grams)	Diameter (mm)	Rev. alignment
Farthing	Bronze	2.8	20	↑

Obverse 1 Head 1, left; EDWARDVS VIII D G BR OMN REX F D IND IMP

Reverse 1 Wren; 1937 FARTHING

Edge plain

| Obv. 1 | Rev. 1 |

No.	Date	Features	Obv.	Rev.	UNC
E8FA-005	1937		1	1	12000

George VI (1937 – 1952)

The wren design proposed for the reverse of the Edward VIII farthing was adopted for this series. The farthing was struck for every year of the reign but, unlike the halfpenny, it did not undergo minute differences of design from year to year.

Proofs were struck for the cased sets of 1937, 1950 and 1951, and in small quantities in all of the other years.

Collecting Hints

This series is easy to locate in mint state. However, the proofs of the years not issued for cased proof sets are very difficult to find. The edges of proofs of 1950 and 1951 should be examined for corrosion.

Denomination	Metal	Weight (grams)	Diameter (mm)	Rev. alignment
Farthing	Bronze	2.7–2.9	20	↑

Obverse 1 Head 1, left; HP on truncation; GEORGIVS VI D G BR OMN REX F D IND IMP

Obverse 2 Head 1, left; GEORGIVS VI D G BR OMN REX FIDEI DEF

Reverse 1 Wren; FARTHING (date)

| Obv. 1 | Obv. 2 | Rev. 1 |

No.	Date	Features	Obv.	Rev.	UNC
G6FA-005	1937		1	1	3
G6FA-010	1937	PROOF [1]	1	1	7
G6FA-015	1937	PROOF from sandblasted dies [2]	1	1	150
G6FA-020	1937	uniface rev. in silver [3]		1	500
G6FA-025	1938		1	1	5
G6FA-030	1938	PROOF	1	1	200
G6FA-035	1939		1	1	3
G6FA-040	1939	PROOF	1	1	200
G6FA-045	1940		1	1	3
G6FA-050	1940	PROOF	1	1	200
G6FA-055	1941		1	1	3
G6FA-060	1941	PROOF	1	1	200
G6FA-065	1942		1	1	2
G6FA-070	1942	PROOF	1	1	200

No.	Date	Features	Obv.	Rev.	UNC
G6FA-075	1943		1	1	2
G6FA-080	1943	PROOF	1	1	200
G6FA-085	1944		1	1	2
G6FA-090	1944	PROOF	1	1	200
G6FA-095	1945		1	1	2
G6FA-100	1945	PROOF	1	1	200
G6FA-105	1946		1	1	2
G6FA-110	1946	PROOF	1	1	200
G6FA-115	1947		1	1	2
G6FA-120	1947	PROOF	1	1	200
G6FA-125	1948		1	1	2
G6FA-130	1948	PROOF	1	1	200
G6FA-135	1949		2	1	2
G6FA-140	1949	PROOF	2	1	200
G6FA-145	1950		2	1	2
G6FA-150	1950	PROOF [1]	2	1	7
G6FA-155	1950	PROOF from sandblasted dies [2]	2	1	150
G6FA-160	1951		2	1	2
G6FA-165	1951	PROOF [1]	2	1	8
G6FA-170	1951	PROOF from sandblasted dies [2]	2	1	150
G6FA-175	1951	in cupronickel [4]	2	1	200
G6FA-180	1952		2	1	2
G6FA-185	1952	PROOF	2	1	200

1. Issued in cased proof sets.
2. Struck to facilitate photography of coin.
3. Weight 3.4 grams.
4. Weight c.2.8 grams.

Obv. 1   Obv. 2   Rev. 1

No.	Date	Features	Obv.	Rev.	UNC
EZFA-005	1953	[1]	1	1	2
EZFA-010	1953	PROOF [2]	1	1	5
EZFA-015	1953	PROOF from sandblasted dies [3]	1	1	150
EZFA-020	1954		2	1	2
EZFA-025	1954	PROOF	2	1	150
EZFA-030	1955		2	1	2
EZFA-035	1955	PROOF	2	1	150
EZFA-040	1956		2	1	4
EZFA-045	1956	PROOF	2	1	200

1. Minor obverse/reverse differences exist.
2. Minor reverse differences exist; issued in cased proof sets.
3. Struck to facilitate photography of coin.

The farthing ceased to be legal tender after 31 December 1960.

Elizabeth II (1952 –)

The farthing series of Elizabeth II consists of only four dates. The first date, 1953, is a one-year type, owing to the change to the legend in 1954. However, minor changes occurred to both obverse and reverse during 1953. In particular, the first coins did not strike up the portrait at all well, and it was recut in slightly higher relief. Later, when the 1954 obverse was introduced, the portrait was recut even more sharply.

The obverse head of Elizabeth II was by Mary Gillick. The series retained the wren design by H. Wilson Parker.

Proofs were again struck for the 1953 cased proof sets, and in small quantities in the other years. Some of the 1953 ordinary coins were issued in the 'plastic sets' of that year. The farthing of 1953 issued in that set is from a die pairing very slightly different from that used on the circulation issue.

In 1953, a correspondent wrote in 'The Times' newspaper that a bus conductor had refused to accept eight farthings in payment for a twopenny ticket, and that a newspaper vendor had become abusive when offered six farthings in payment. A subsequent letter in the newspaper pointed out that the farthing was still legal tender in amounts up to one shilling.

The ravages of inflation meant that by 1956 the farthing had outlived its usefulness as a circulation coin, and no farthings were minted after that date.

Collecting Hints

The four dates are easily found in mint state.

Denomination	Metal	Weight (grams)	Diameter (mm)	Rev. alignment
Farthing	Bronze	2.8–2.9	20	↑

Obverse 1   Head 1, right; ELIZABETH II DEI GRA BRITT OMN REGINA F D

Obverse 2   Head 1, recut, right; ELIZABETH II DEI GRATIA REGINA F D

Reverse 1   Wren; FARTHING (date)

Edge   plain

Ringing coins to detect dumb pieces

Half Farthing

George IV   (1820 – 1830)

The first issue of the half farthing was in 1828. Initially, it was issued for use only in Ceylon, and did not become a legal tender coin in Britain until 1842. The coin, however, bore no indication of the country of origin and, along with the third– and quarter farthing, is commonly regarded as a British coin.

The half farthing was the last denomination to be issued in this reign. Consequently, the controversies surrounding Pistrucci did not touch it, and by the time the coin was introduced William Wyon was safely established as the principal designer and engraver at the mint. Wyon's dies for obverse and reverse were similar to those used on the larger copper coins, but the obverse head does appear inordinately large compared with the size of the flan.

The coin was minted again during this reign only in 1830. The death of the king in June of that year may explain why the 1830 coin is markedly scarcer than the 1828.

Collecting Hints

The half farthing circulated widely in Ceylon where the corrosive salty air took its toll on the coinage. This series is difficult to locate in extremely fine or better condition.

Denomination	Metal	Weight (grams)	Diameter (mm)	Rev. alignment
Half farthing	Copper	2.4	18	↑

Obverse 1   Head 1, left; GEORGIUS IV DEI GRATIA (date)

Reverse 1   Britannia, seated, with shield, facing right, holding trident; BRITANNIAR REX FID DEF

Edge   plain

Obv. 1   Rev. 1

No.	Date	Features	Obv.	Rev.	F	VF	EF	UNC
G4HF-005	1828	1	1	1	12	30	120	220
G4HF-010	1828	PROOF	1	1				240
G4HF-015	1828	Bronzed PROOF rev. ↓	1	1				700
G4HF-020	1830	2	1	1	15	35	140	240
G4HF-025	1830	PROOF	1	1				500

1. Reverse legend/design orientation varies.
2. Reverse legend/design orientation varies; date numerals vary in size.

William IV   (1830 – 1837)

The half farthing was again minted in 1837 for circulation in Ceylon. The coin uses the William Wyon head of William IV as used on the larger coins. The reverse is virtually identical to that used on the George IV half farthing.

As with the half farthing of George IV, the minting and issue of the coin was interrupted by the death of the monarch, again in June. Consequently, the William IV half farthing became one of the most elusive of this denomination.

Collecting Hints

This coin is scarce in any grade, and particularly rare in extremely fine or better. The fact that it is a one-year type and much sought after makes it even more difficult to find.

Denomination	Metal	Weight (grams)	Diameter (mm)	Rev. alignment
Half farthing	Copper	2.3	18	↑

Obverse 1   Head 1, right; GULIELMUS IIII DEI GRATIA 1837

Reverse 1   Britannia, seated, with shield, facing right, holding trident; BRITANNIAR REX FID DEF

Edge   plain

Obv. 1   Rev. 1

No.	Date	Obv.	Rev.	F	VF	EF	UNC
W4HF-005	1837	1	1	35	75	300	500

Victoria   (1837 – 1901)

With the accession of Victoria to the throne, the half farthing was approaching its prime. Moreover, in 1842 it acquired legal tender status in Britain. Much cynicism was, however, displayed over this decision. It was widely commented that very little could be bought for a farthing, let alone half a farthing, and the inevitable letters to *The Times* appeared on the subject. Nevertheless, the coin did circulate widely both in Britain and in Ceylon.

The preparation of the dies again fell to William Wyon. The obverse portrayed the head of Victoria, and for the first time the obverse legend differed from that on the larger copper coins; this obverse is identical to that on the Maundy fourpence, both in design and size. The reverse was radically redesigned. At the beginning of the reign, silver groats were circulating in Ceylon, and these bore a Britannia reverse somewhat similar to that on the half farthings of the previous reign. In order to prevent the half farthings being silvered and passed off as groats, the new Victoria half farthing was given a reverse bearing the words HALF FARTHING, together with the date, sandwiched between a crown and a rose. It is often not realised, however, that the series bears two different reverses. When the coin acquired legal tender status on 13 June, 1842, the rose was replaced by a rose, thistle and shamrock. This was to make the design compatible with those of the farthing, halfpenny and penny. There is some doubt as to whether the coin entered circulation; Peter Seaby (*The Story of the English Coinage*) notes that street traders used to sell them at three-farthings each!

The 1868 proofs are curious anomalies to this series. Other coins in the bronze series were struck in cupronickel in 1868, possibly as trial strikings in connection with the forthcoming Jamaican issue in this metal. Although the legislation introducing the Jamaican coinage refers to this issue as being struck in nickel, both it and the 1868 British proofs are non-magnetic and must therefore be in cupronickel. It seems to have been decided to strike bronze proofs at the same time as these cupronickel proofs, but no circulation coins were struck dated 1868. The entire denomination was demonetised the following year.

Collecting Hints

The half farthing is a challenging series to collect. Several of the dates are so rare in top condition as to be almost unobtainable, and their rarity is probably underestimated in most catalogues. Rarely does one come across a series with such a profusion of coins concentrated on one date, in this case 1844. Bramah estimated that the 1844 coin is between 10 and 20 times more common than almost all of the other dates.

There are a considerable number of minor varieties in this series caused by die wear and flaws. Batty (*Copper Coinage of Great Britain*), a master of attention to detail, listed 142 different die flaws for the 1844 half farthing alone! It is not intended that this catalogue will provide this sort of service to its readers.

The series should be collected generally in extremely fine condition, but it will probably be difficult to find some of the dates in this grade. The 1844 should always be checked for the E over N variety as this is a popular coin. The 1856 coin appears to occur frequently with a rough surface, possibly because of die damage, although it has been speculated that some may have been cast.

Denomination	Metal	Weight (grams)	Diameter (mm)	Rev. alignment
Half farthing	Copper	2.4	18	↑

Obverse 1   Head 1, left; VICTORIA D G BRITANNIAR REGINA F D

Reverse 1   Crown above; rose with three leaves below; HALF FARTHING (date)

Reverse 2   Similar but rose replaced by rose, thistle and shamrock

Edge   plain

Obv. 1   Rev. 1   Rev. 2

No.	Date	Features	Obv.	Rev.	F	VF	EF	UNC
VYHF-005	1839	[1]	1	1	7	14	50	100
VYHF-010	1839	Bronzed PROOF [1]	1	1				200
VYHF-015	1842	[2]	1	2	5	10	35	70
VYHF-020	1843	[3]	1	2	4	7	15	30
VYHF-025	1844	[3]	1	2	3	5	12	25
VYHF-030	1844	E of REGINA over N (obv.)	1	2	20	35	75	150
VYHF-035	1847		1	2	5	10	30	60
VYHF-040	1851		1	2	7	14	50	100
VYHF-045	1851	first 1 over 5	1	2	10	20	80	140
VYHF-048	1851	5 over 0	1	2	15	30	120	200
VYHF-050	1852		1	2	10	20	40	85
VYHF-055	1853		1	2	8	20	80	150
VYHF-060	1853	PROOF	1	2				200
VYHF-065	1853	Bronzed PROOF rev. ↓ [4]	1	2				200
VYHF-070	1854		1	2	10	25	95	170
VYHF-075	1856	[5]	1	2	10	25	95	170
VYHF-080	1868	PROOF in bronze	1	2				250
VYHF-085	1868	PROOF in cupronickel [6]	1	2				350

1. Date numerals larger than on most years.
2. Becomes legal tender in Britain.
3. Many minor varieties exist.
4. Issued in cased proof sets.
5. Date numerals vary in size; many have rough surface.
6. Weight 2.3 grams.

The half farthing ceased to be legal tender after 31 December 1869.

Third Farthing

George IV   (1820 – 1830)

The third farthing was minted in 1827 exclusively for circulation in Malta. However, it is widely thought of as being included within the ambit of British coinage, and for this reason it is included in this catalogue. The coin bears no indication of the country of origin, and closely resembles a British coin. Furthermore, Malta, having become a British Possession in 1814, was considered more as a part of Britain at that time than during the twentieth century. The farthing was already in circulation there as a '3 grani' coin, and the third farthing was introduced as '1 grano'. A proclamation issued in Malta on 3 November 1827 legalised the new coins, referring to them as 'British Grains'. The cost of living in Malta was lower than in Britain, and the new coin was thought inappropriate for circulation in the home country.

As with the half farthing, minted for Ceylon in the following year, the dies were prepared by William Wyon. Pistrucci had already fallen into disfavour. The obverse was of smaller proportion relative to the flan than on the half farthing, and the striking was somewhat sharper.

Collecting Hints

The third farthing is easier to find in top condition than the half farthing, and should be collected in Extremely Fine or mint state. Beware of coins which have been bronzed to resemble proofs.

Denomination	Metal	Weight (grams)	Diameter (mm)	Rev. alignment
Third farthing	Copper	1.5–1.6	16	↑

Obverse 1   Head 1, left; GEORGIUS IV DEI GRATIA 1827

Reverse 1   Britannia, seated, with shield, facing right, holding trident; BRITANNIAR REX FID DEF

Edge   plain

Obv. 1   Rev. 1

No.	Date	Features	Obv.	Rev.	F	VF	EF	UNC
G4TF-005	1827		1	1	5	10	26	65
G4TF-010	1827	PROOF	1	1				450

William IV   (1830 – 1837)

The third farthing was again issued for Malta for only one of the years of this reign, in 1835. The obverse was by William Wyon as on the larger coinage, and once again the proportion of the head in relation to the flan was smaller than on the half farthing. The reverse was virtually identical to that of the third farthing of George IV.

Collecting Hints

The third farthing is far easier to locate than the half farthing, and should be sought in mint state.

Denomination	Metal	Weight (grams)	Diameter (mm)	Rev. alignment
Third farthing	Copper	1.5–1.6	16	↑

Obverse 1   Head 1, right; GULIELMUS IIII DEI GRATIA 1835

Reverse 1   Britannia, seated, with shield, right, holding trident; BRITANNIAR REX FID DEF

Edge   plain

Obv. 1   Rev. 1

No.	Date	Features	Obv.	Rev.	F	VF	EF	UNC
W4TF-005	1835		1	1	5	10	26	80
W4TF-010	1835	PROOF	1	1				350

Victoria   (1837 – 1901)

The relatively few coins required for circulation in Malta resulted in the minting of the copper issue of third farthings for one year only, in 1844. This issue used the young head of Victoria by William Wyon, with a Britannia reverse. This resembled to some extent a small version of the farthing, unlike the half farthing which had a different obverse legend and a redesigned reverse, to prevent its being silvered and passed off as a groat.

The bronze issue, again for circulation in Malta, was more prolific, being minted from 1866 to 1885. The head of Victoria, engraved by Leonard Charles Wyon, was very different. The Britannia reverse was discontinued in favour of a 'value in wreath' design.

Collecting Hints

The young head copper issue is difficult to find in the high grades. The reverse should be checked for the 'missing G' variety, but this is particularly rare. The bronze series is easier to find and should be collected in mint state.

Denomination	Metal	Weight (grams)	Diameter (mm)	Rev. alignment
Third farthing 1844	Copper	1.5–1.6	16	↑
Third farthing 1866–85	Bronze	0.9–1.0	15	↑

Obverse 1   Head 1, left; VICTORIA DEI GRATIA 1844

Obverse 2   Head 2, left; VICTORIA D G BRITT REG F D

Reverse 1   Britannia, seated, with shield, facing right, holding trident; BRITANNIAR REG FID DEF

Reverse 2   ONE THIRD FARTHING (date) within wreath, crown above

Edge   plain

| Obv. 1 | Obv. 2 | Rev. 1 | Rev. 2 |

No.	Date	Features	Obv.	Rev.	F	VF	EF	UNC
VYTF-005	1844		1	1	12	30	100	160
VYTF-010	1844	large G in REG (obv.)	1	1	18	45	140	220
VYTF-015	1844	RE instead of REG (obv.) [1]	1	1	120	250	800	1200
VYTF-020	1866		2	2	4	8	16	30
VYTF-025	1866	PROOF	2	2				300
VYTF-030	1868	[2]	2	2	4	8	16	30
VYTF-035	1868	PROOF	2	2				280
VYTF-040	1868	PROOF in cupronickel	2	2				400
VYTF-045	1868	PROOF in aluminium	2	2				600
VYTF-050	1876		2	2	4	8	16	30
VYTF-055	1878		2	2	4	8	16	30
VYTF-060	1881		2	2	4	8	16	30
VYTF-065	1881	PROOF	2	2				450
VYTF-070	1884	[2]	2	2	4	8	16	30
VYTF-075	1885		2	2	4	8	16	30

1. Flan thickness varies; all may be proofs struck at a later date.
2. Minor obverse differences exist.

On reverse 2, minor variations occur on the wreath, and the number of leaves and acorns may vary.

Edward VII   (1901 – 1910)

The third farthing continued to be struck for Malta. The face value of the mintage was £100 sterling, i.e. 288,000 pieces, and all were dated 1902. The general design was based on that for the last Victoria issue, using the head of Edward VII by George William de Saulles (1862–1903). The reverse was of identical layout, but the crown was the Imperial crown instead of the Royal crown used on the Victorian series.

As it was a coin minted for Malta, the third farthing was not included in the cased proof set for 1902.

Collecting Hints

The coin can be found in mint state without much difficulty.

Denomination	Metal	Weight (grams)	Diameter (mm)	Rev. alignment
Third farthing	Bronze	0.9–1.0	15	↑

Obverse 1   Head 1, right; EDWARDVS VII D G BRITT OMN REX F D IND IMP

Reverse 1   ONE THIRD FARTHING 1902 within wreath, crown above

Edge   plain

| Obv. 1 | Rev. 1 |

No.	Date	Obv.	Rev.	F	VF	EF	UNC
E7TF-005	1902	1	1	3	6	12	20

George V   (1910 – 1936)

A final issue of the third farthing for Malta was made in 1913, again to the total face value of £100 sterling. The head of the monarch was by Sir Bertram Mackennal (1863–1931), as used on the larger coinage. The reverse was identical to the 1902 issue, apart from the date.

Collecting Hints

The coin can be found in mint state without much difficulty.

Denomination	Metal	Weight (grams)	Diameter (mm)	Rev. alignment
Third farthing	Bronze	0.9–1.0	15	↑

Obverse 1   Head 1, left; GEORGIVS V D G BRITT OMN REX F D IND IMP

Reverse 1   ONE THIRD FARTHING 1913 within wreath, crown above

Edge   plain

| Obv. 1 | Rev. 1 |

No.	Date	Obv.	Rev.	F	VF	EF	UNC
G5TF-005	1913	1	1	3	6	12	20

Quarter Farthing

Victoria (1837 – 1901)

Like the half farthing, the quarter farthing was introduced for use in Ceylon, but it did not subsequently become legal tender in Britain as the half farthing did. The denomination was simply too small to have any purchasing power in the home country. In Ceylon, where the cost of living was lower, it was more useful.

Although the quarter farthing was never a British legal tender coin, it has become accepted as a British coin, as has the third farthing. It is consequently included in this catalogue.

The series is relatively short, consisting of only five dates, including the curious 1868 proofs. It is interesting to note that the British 1853 proof set (but not the 1839) included the quarter farthing, even though the coin had no legal tender status in Britain. This is possibly an indication of how much more closely the British colonies were regarded in the 19th century, almost as a part of the British Isles. The 1868 proofs may have been struck in connection with the proposed cupronickel issue of Jamaican coinage.

The obverse bears a head of Victoria by William Wyon, and is in fact taken from a die for the Maundy twopence. The reverse is very similar in design to the Victorian half farthing of 1839, i.e. before the rose was replaced by a larger emblem.

Before the coins were brought back to Britain for collectors, the series was regarded in numismatic circles as very rare. Batty (*Copper Coinage of Great Britain*, 1886) stated that he had only seen one specimen dated 1853.

Collecting Hints

This is a popular coin, and its limited mintage renders it scarcer than usual for a complete series. In addition, only a relatively small proportion of minted coins have survived in collectable condition. Some years ago a London dealer took space in newspapers in Ceylon to buy this coin in quantity, and received large numbers of tiny green corroded discs! The salty air of Ceylon had taken its toll on the coins in much the same way as the polluted air of London had destroyed the tin coinage two centuries earlier. Even otherwise fine or very fine coins are frequently encountered with pitting marks and edge corrosion. Consequently, mint state coins without damage are much sought after and are a worthy addition to any serious collection.

Denomination	Metal	Weight (grams)	Diameter (mm)	Rev. alignment
Quarter farthing 1839–53	Copper	1.2	13.5	↑
Quarter farthing 1868	Bronze	1.2	13.5	↑

A wide weight range exists for this denomination

Obverse 1 Head 1, left; VICTORIA D G BRITANNIAR REGINA F D

Reverse 1 Crown above; rose with three leaves below; QUARTER FARTHING (date)

Edge plain

Obv. 1

Rev. 1

No.	Date	Features	Obv.	Rev.	F	VF	EF	UNC
VYQF-005	1839		1	1	20	30	50	90
VYQF-010	1851		1	1	22	34	55	100
VYQF-015	1852		1	1	20	30	50	90
VYQF-020	1852	Bronzed PROOF [1]	1	1				1000
VYQF-025	1853	[2]	1	1	22	34	55	100
VYQF-030	1853	PROOF	1	1				300
VYQF-035	1853	Bronzed PROOF [3]	1	1				350
VYQF-040	1868	PROOF	1	1				500
VYQF-045	1868	PROOF in cupronickel [4]	1	1				700

1. Possibly unique.
2. Many minor varieties exist, esp. pearls on crown (rev.).
3. Issued in cased proof sets.
4. Weight c.1.1 grams.

Maundy Sets

The present-day Maundy ceremony is the product of the evolution of rituals through many centuries, and bears little similarity to the ancient rites to which it owes its origins.

A fundamental aspect of the early Maundy service was the washing of feet of the poor. This has its origins in the pedilavium, a ceremony in which senior clergy washed the feet of lower clergy. In other rituals, a person's feet would be washed by a person considered to be higher up in the hierarchical order. A clear parallel can be seen with the washing of the feet of the apostles by Jesus at the end of the Last Supper.

There appears to be evidence of a link between this ceremony and Maundy Thursday as early as the sixth century. The day was known in early times as Sheer, Shire (or similar) Thursday, the day before Good Friday.

Edward II (1307–27) appears to be the first monarch recorded as actively taking part in the washing of the feet of the poor, although John (1199–1216) is said to have taken part in a ceremony around 1210 donating small silver coins to the poor. Edward III (1327–77) washed feet and gave gifts, including money, to the poor. The practice continued regularly, with the participation of the monarch, until 1698.

Although the monarch did not take part personally, later ceremonies continued in which a selection of poor people were given Maundy money consisting of silver pennies totalling, in pence, the current age of the monarch, together with other allowances. The ceremony of 1736 was the last in which the foot washing ceremony occurred.

In 1838, because some recipients were found to be selling the gift allowances for money, an extra monetary allowance was made in lieu of the gifts. Clothing and other allowances, and the manner of their distribution, have been amended a number of times down the years.

In 1932, George V agreed to take part personally in the distribution of Maundy, and the participation of the monarch in now an accepted feature of the ceremony.

Although the Maundy 'set' of the four minor silver coins is usually thought of as the coinage of the Maundy ceremony, in the early years probably only the silver penny was used for this purpose. It was not until some time during the reign of George III that the set of four coins was distributed as Maundy.

During the period up to 1820, the small silver coinage was primarily used as circulation coinage. For this reason, the coins are listed in this catalogue as separate denominations, and their individual varieties will be found in these listings. From 1822 onwards, when the coins were minted mainly for the provision of sets of Maundy, the detailed listings are under the heading of Maundy sets. 1822 also marks the year from which sets were issued without a break up to the present day.

The Maundy ceremony currently takes place on Maundy Thursday (the day before Good Friday). The coins are given in a leather bag, the total number of pence equalling the age of the monarch. As one set totals 10 pence, the amount is made up by a number of complete sets plus, when appropriate, a part set.

George IV   (1820 – 1830)

As mentioned elsewhere, by the time George IV ascended the throne, the Maundy set of four coins was primarily used for the Maundy ceremony rather than for circulation. This is evident from the fact that these coins usually turn up in very fine or better condition.

The series used the laureate head of the king designed by Benedetto Pistrucci throughout the series. The William Wyon bare head used on the larger silver did not appear on the Maundy coinage, even though the king greatly disapproved of the Pistrucci portrayal of his image.

A curious incident produced an unusual obverse on the 1822 threepence. Before the coins were struck, the punch broke, and a die was hurriedly made with a punch of the twopence head. The portrait on this coin therefore appears unusually small.

Denomination	Metal	Weight (grams)	Diameter (mm)	Rev. alignment
Maundy Set	Silver	0.5; 0.9; 1.4; 1.9	11; 13; 16; 18	↓

Obverse 1   Head 1, left; GEORGIUS IIII D G BRITANNIAR REX F D

Reverse 1   Crowned numeral and divided date, all within wreath.

Edge   plain

No.	Date	Features	Obv.	Rev.	EF	FDC
G4MS-005	1822	[1]	1	1	130	220
G4MS-010	1822	PROOFS [1]	1	1		800
G4MS-015	1823		1	1	120	200
G4MS-020	1824		1	1	120	200
G4MS-025	1825	[2]	1	1	120	200
G4MS-030	1826		1	1	120	200
G4MS-035	1827		1	1	120	200
G4MS-040	1828		1	1	120	200
G4MS-045	1828	PROOFS	1	1		1000
G4MS-050	1829		1	1	120	200
G4MS-055	1830		1	1	120	200

1. Threepence has small king's head (obv.) from twopence punch.
2. A variety of the twopence reads TRITANNIAR (obv.).

William IV   (1830 – 1837)

The William Wyon portrait of the king was adopted for the Maundy coinage, the reverse continuing as on the previous series. The first date, 1831, boasts not only a proof Maundy set included in the proof set of that year, but also a small number of sets of the four pieces struck in gold.

Denomination	Metal	Weight (grams)	Diameter (mm)	Rev. alignment
Maundy Set	Silver	0.5; 0.9; 1.4; 1.9	11; 13; 16; 18	↓

Obverse 1   Head 1, right; GULIELMUS IIII D G BRITANNIAR REX F D

Reverse 1   Crowned numeral and divided date, all within wreath.

Edge   plain

No.	Date	Features	Obv.	Rev.	EF	FDC
W4MS-005	1831		1	1	130	240
W4MS-010	1831	PROOFS	1	1		500
W4MS-015	1831	PROOFS in gold	1	1		18000
W4MS-020	1832		1	1	140	250
W4MS-025	1833		1	1	130	240
W4MS-030	1834		1	1	130	240
W4MS-035	1835		1	1	130	240
W4MS-040	1836		1	1	150	280
W4MS-045	1837		1	1	150	280

Victoria   (1837 – 1901)

The Maundy sets of Victoria are amongst the most popular with collectors of this series. When one considers the longevity of the reign, and the fact that the denominations were minted for every year, one appreciates the uniqueness of this series. To assemble a complete set in perfect condition or near is a mammoth task.

The early Maundy sets bear the young head portrait of Victoria by William Wyon, and this was unchanged for fifty years! Unlike on the larger silver coins and the gold, the jubilee head portrait did not appear until 1888, as the Maundy ceremony in 1887 occurred before the jubilee.

Confusion sometimes occurs with Victorian young head Maundy sets over the status of the threepence. Many sets are encountered with fields which are not prooflike, and this sometimes leads to the description of sets bearing 'currency threepences' when in fact they do not. Experience is the only way to determine whether a threepence is a currency or Maundy strike. The distinguishing marks are often more to do with the quality of the strike rather than whether the field has a mirror finish. Particular attention should be paid to the fineness of the wreath on the reverse, and comparison with the other Maundy pieces of the set, if available, is helpful.

Maundy coins continued to be presented to recipients at the Maundy service in leather purses, but at some stage towards the end of the Victorian era those given to other recipients were in official presentation cases. Initially, these were rectangular and covered in black or dark red leather, and usually bore the date on the lid.

From 1888 to 1901 the obverses are similar to those of the larger coinage, with the jubilee head by Sir Joseph Edgar Boehm (engraved by L.C. Wyon) and the old head by Sir Thomas Brock (engraved by de Saulles).

Denomination	Metal	Weight (grams)	Diameter (mm)	Rev. alignment
Maundy set 1838–87	Silver	0.5; 0.9; 1.4; 1.9	11; 13; 16; 18	↓
Maundy set 1888–1901	Silver	0.5; 0.9; 1.4; 1.9	11; 13; 16; 18	↑

Obverse 1   Head 1, left; VICTORIA D G BRITANNIAR REGINA F D

Obverse 2   Head 2, left; same legend

Obverse 3   Head 3, left; VICTORIA DEI GRA BRITT REGINA FID DEF IND IMP

Reverse 1   Crowned numeral and divided date, all within wreath.

Reverse 2   Similar but crown very different; on the twopence the '2' is different

Edge   plain

Obv. 1   Obv. 2   Obv. 3

Rev. 1

Rev. 2

Young Head

No.	Date	Features	Obv.	Rev.	EF	FDC
VYMS-005	1838		1	1	85	130
VYMS-010	1838	PROOFS	1	1		600
VYMS-015	1838	PROOFS in gold; revs ↑	1	1		18000
VYMS-020	1839		1	1	80	120
VYMS-025	1839	PROOFS; revs ↑ [1]	1	1		450
VYMS-030	1840		1	1	85	130
VYMS-035	1841		1	1	90	140
VYMS-040	1842		1	1	90	140
VYMS-045	1843		1	1	80	120
VYMS-050	1844		1	1	85	130
VYMS-055	1845		1	1	80	120
VYMS-060	1846		1	1	90	140
VYMS-065	1847		1	1	80	120
VYMS-070	1848		1	1	80	120
VYMS-075	1849		1	1	90	140
VYMS-080	1850		1	1	60	100
VYMS-085	1851		1	1	60	100
VYMS-090	1852		1	1	60	100
VYMS-095	1853		1	1	80	120
VYMS-100	1853	PROOFS	1	1		400
VYMS-105	1854		1	1	60	100
VYMS-110	1855		1	1	60	100
VYMS-115	1856		1	1	60	100
VYMS-120	1857		1	1	60	100
VYMS-125	1857	2 pence reads BRITANNIAE EEGINA (obv.)	1	1	120	200
VYMS-130	1858		1	1	55	90
VYMS-135	1859		1	1	55	90
VYMS-140	1859	2 pence reads BEITANNIAR (obv.)	1	1	80	120
VYMS-145	1860		1	1	55	90
VYMS-150	1861	2 pence has 6 not over 1	1	1	100	130
VYMS-155	1861	2 pence has 6 over 1	1	1	55	90
VYMS-160	1862		1	1	55	90
VYMS-165	1863		1	1	55	90
VYMS-170	1864		1	1	55	90
VYMS-175	1865		1	1	55	90
VYMS-180	1866		1	1	55	90
VYMS-185	1867		1	1	55	90
VYMS-190	1867	PROOFS	1	1		500
VYMS-195	1868		1	1	55	90
VYMS-200	1869		1	1	55	90
VYMS-205	1870		1	1	55	90
VYMS-210	1871		1	1	55	90
VYMS-215	1871	PROOFS; revs ↑	1	1		800
VYMS-220	1872		1	1	55	90
VYMS-225	1873		1	1	55	90
VYMS-230	1874		1	1	55	90
VYMS-235	1875		1	1	55	90
VYMS-240	1876		1	1	55	90
VYMS-245	1877		1	1	55	90
VYMS-250	1878		1	1	55	90
VYMS-255	1878	PROOFS	1	1		500
VYMS-260	1879		1	1	55	90
VYMS-265	1879	PROOFS; revs ↑	1	1		1200
VYMS-270	1880		1	1	55	90
VYMS-275	1881		1	1	55	90

No.	Date	Features	Obv.	Rev.	EF	FDC
VYMS-280	1881	PROOFS	1	1		500
VYMS-285	1882		1	1	55	90
VYMS-290	1883		1	1	55	90
VYMS-295	1884		1	1	55	90
VYMS-300	1885		1	1	55	90
VYMS-305	1886		1	1	55	90
VYMS-310	1887		1	1	55	90

1. Issued in cased proof sets.

Jubilee Head

No.	Date	Features	Obv.	Rev.	EF	FDC
VJMS-315	1888		2	2	60	100
VJMS-320	1888	PROOFS	2	2		400
VJMS-325	1889		2	2	60	100
VJMS-330	1890		2	2	60	100
VJMS-335	1891		2	2	60	100
VJMS-340	1892		2	2	60	100

Old Head

No.	Date	Features	Obv.	Rev.	EF	FDC
VOMS-345	1893	1	3	2	45	80
VOMS-350	1894		3	2	45	80
VOMS-355	1895		3	2	45	80
VOMS-360	1896		3	2	45	80
VOMS-365	1897		3	2	45	80
VOMS-370	1898		3	2	45	80
VOMS-375	1899		3	2	45	80
VOMS-380	1900		3	2	45	80
VOMS-385	1901		3	2	45	80

1. Only the 4 pence has flat-top '3' in date.

Edward VII (1901 – 1910)

The Maundy set used the portrait of Edward VII by de Saulles which was adjusted to the size required using a mechanical reduction machine. The first year mintage included the matt proof set for the cased Royal Mint proof sets of that year. This set has a very distinctive appearance with wider rims. The unattractive streaky tarnish which is often found on the matt proof sets can be removed with chemical silver tarnish remover, as this does not affect the matt finish.

Until 1908 it was possible to obtain sets of Maundy money through banks and other outlets, but from 1909 the issue was restricted to Maundy ceremony recipients and a number of other specified persons. This is why the 1909 and 1910 sets are considerably scarcer than those of other years, and also why sets of later reigns are more difficult to find than those of Victoria and Edward VII.

Maundy cases continued to be similar to those issued in the late Victorian era.

Denomination	Metal	Weight (grams)	Diameter (mm)	Rev. alignment
Maundy set	Silver	0.5; 0.9; 1.4; 1.9	11; 13; 16; 18	↑

Obverse 1 Head 1, right; EDWARDVS VII D G BRITT OMN REX F D IND IMP

Reverse 1 Crowned numeral and divided date, all within wreath.

Edge plain

No.	Date	Features	Obv.	Rev.	EF	FDC
E7MS-005	1902		1	1	40	70
E7MS-010	1902	PROOFS 1	1	1	40	70
E7MS-015	1903	2	1	1	40	70
E7MS-020	1904	3	1	1	40	70
E7MS-025	1905		1	1	40	70
E7MS-030	1906		1	1	40	70
E7MS-035	1907		1	1	40	70
E7MS-040	1908		1	1	40	70
E7MS-045	1909	4	1	1	55	100
E7MS-050	1910	4	1	1	55	100

1. Matt surface; issued in cased proof sets.
2. Only the 4 pence has flat-top '3' in date.
3. Some issued in unusual oval case.
4. See comments above re distribution.

George V (1910 – 1936)

Sir Bertram Mackennal (1863–1931) executed the portrait of George V which replaced that of Edward VII on the new Maundy series. The reverse remained unchanged. Along with the other coinage, but a year later, a change was made to the metal content in 1921, the silver constituent of the alloy falling to 50%. In 1928, and again in 1930, minor alterations were made to the portrait.

One of the more common myths of British numismatics, repeated in most catalogues, is that of the 1911 proof Maundy set. Examination of a Royal Mint proof set of that year will reveal that, whilst all of the other coins have a prooflike field, the Maundy set is identical to the other Maundy sets of that year. Indeed, the field is less prooflike than many of the sets of previous or subsequent years! Nevertheless, there is a slight difference between the shape of the rim of the fourpence in the proof sets and that on the presentation Maundy set.

The set of 1932 was personally distributed by George V. Distribution of Maundy by the monarch had generally been discontinued in the 17th century. The set of 1936, although bearing the portrait of George V, was distributed by Edward VIII.

Maundy cases of this reign were usually rectangular, although some square and octagonal cases were issued. They were usually covered in red leather with embossed gold lettering, with or without a date.

Denomination	Metal	Weight (grams)	Diameter (mm)	Rev. alignment
Maundy Set 1911–20	0.925 Silver	0.5; 0.9; 1.4; 1.9	11; 13; 16; 18	↑
Maundy Set 1921–36	0.500 Silver	0.5; 0.9; 1.4; 1.9	11; 13; 16; 18	↑

Obverse 1 Head 1, left; GEORGIVS V D G BRITT OMN REX F D IND IMP

Obverse 2 Head 2, so-called 'modified effigy', left; same legend

Obverse 3 Head 2, re-engraved, left; same legend

Reverse 1 Crowned numeral and divided date, all within wreath

Edge plain

Obv. 1   Obv. 2

Rev. 1

Sterling Silver Issue

No.	Date	Features	Obv.	Rev.	EF	FDC
G5MS-005	1911	[1]	1	1	45	75
G5MS-010	1912		1	1	45	75
G5MS-015	1913		1	1	45	75
G5MS-020	1914		1	1	55	80
G5MS-025	1915		1	1	45	75
G5MS-030	1916		1	1	45	75
G5MS-035	1917		1	1	45	75
G5MS-040	1918		1	1	45	75
G5MS-045	1919		1	1	45	75
G5MS-050	1920		1	1	40	70

1. So-called 'proof' sets exist with a minor variation to the shape of the 4 pence rim.

50% Silver Issue

No.	Date	Features	Obv.	Rev.	EF	FDC
G5MS-055	1921		1	1	45	75
G5MS-060	1922		1	1	45	75
G5MS-065	1923		1	1	45	75
G5MS-070	1924		1	1	45	75
G5MS-075	1925		1	1	45	75
G5MS-080	1926		1	1	45	75
G5MS-085	1927		1	1	45	75
G5MS-090	1928		2	1	45	75
G5MS-095	1929		2	1	45	75
G5MS-100	1930		3	1	45	75
G5MS-105	1931		3	1	45	75
G5MS-110	1932	1	3	1	45	75
G5MS-115	1933		3	1	45	75
G5MS-120	1934		3	1	45	75
G5MS-125	1935		3	1	45	75
G5MS-130	1936	2	3	1	50	80

1. Distributed by George V; first distribution by reigning monarch since 17th century.
2. Distributed by Edward VIII.

George VI   (1937 – 1952)

The obverse portrait of George VI was designed by Thomas Humphrey Paget, the reverse continuing a slightly modified version of the previous reign. The Maundy set of the first year, 1937, was included in the Royal Mint proof set of that year, but there is no difference in the quality of the strike between the regular Maundy set and that included in the proof set. However, unlike the 1911 set, the 1937 set exhibit highly prooflike fields, as indeed do all of the George VI sets.

A somewhat curious decision was made when the changeover to cupronickel was made for silver coinage in 1947. It was considered inappropriate to strike Maundy money, to be distributed by the monarch, in such a debased material as cupronickel. However, rather than continuing to strike it in 0.500 silver, the silver content was once again upgraded to 0.925. This is one of the few times in which a regular denomination has had its precious metal content increased.

Maundy cases were usually square, undated, and covered in red leather.

Denomination	Metal	Weight (grams)	Diameter (mm)	Rev. alignment
Maundy set 1937–46	0.500 Silver	0.5; 0.9; 1.4; 1.9	11; 13; 16; 18	↑
Maundy set 1947–52	0.925 Silver	0.5; 0.9; 1.4; 1.9	11; 13; 16; 18	↑

Obverse 1   Head 1, left; GEORGIVS VI D G BR OMN REX F D IND IMP

Obverse 2   Head 1, left; GEORGIVS VI D G BR OMN REX FIDEI DEF

Reverse 1   Crowned numeral and divided date, all within wreath.

Edge   plain

Obv. 1   Obv. 2

Rev. 1

50% Silver Issue

No.	Date	Features	Obv.	Rev.	EF	FDC
G6MS-005	1937		1	1	40	60
G6MS-010	1937	PROOF from sandblasted dies [1]	1	1		250
G6MS-015	1938		1	1	45	70
G6MS-020	1939		1	1	45	70
G6MS-025	1940		1	1	45	70
G6MS-030	1941		1	1	45	70
G6MS-035	1942		1	1	45	70
G6MS-040	1943		1	1	45	70
G6MS-045	1944		1	1	45	70
G6MS-050	1945		1	1	45	70
G6MS-055	1946		1	1	45	70

1. Struck to facilitate photography of coin.

Sterling Silver Issue

No.	Date	Features	Obv.	Rev.	EF	FDC
G6MS-060	1947		1	1	50	80
G6MS-065	1948		1	1	50	80
G6MS-070	1949		2	1	50	80
G6MS-075	1950		2	1	50	80
G6MS-080	1951		2	1	50	80
G6MS-085	1951	PROOF from sandblasted dies [1]	2	1		250
G6MS-090	1952		2	1	50	80
G6MS-095	1952	struck in copper [2]	2	1		1200

1. Struck to facilitate photography of coin.
2. Weights 0.6; 0.9; 1.4; 1.6 grams.

Elizabeth II   (1952 –)

The Maundy coinage continued to be struck in sterling (0.925) silver, using the portrait of Elizabeth II by Mary Gillick. As with the other coinage, there were problems with weak striking, and the obverse dies were recut in time to strike the 1954 coinage. In addition, the obverse legend was revised in 1954, making the 1953 set a unique type which is much in demand by collectors. The fact that, unlike in 1911 and 1937, the Maundy set was not included in the Royal Mint proof set only served to increase its scarcity.

By 1953 the monarch or representative was distributing the Maundy personally each year, usually in London. Later, distributions were made at cathedrals in the Home Counties (e.g. St. Albans, Canterbury, Rochester). It was not until 1967 that the ceremony was held some considerable distance from London, at Durham. Thereafter, ceremonies were held in many parts of the country.

When the changeover to decimal currency occurred in 1971, there was no apparent change to the Maundy coinage. Certainly, no alterations were made to the design. However, Maundy coinage has always been legal tender, otherwise strictly speaking the recipients are receiving only trinkets (although they are usually exhorted to sell their sets by dealers!). Because the post–1971 sets could clearly not continue to be denominated in old pence, the entire series (including the older sets) was upgraded to legal tender status in New Pence. This is yet another unique aspect of this

No.	Date	Features	Obv.	Rev.	EF	FDC
EZMS-190	1988		2	1	70	90
EZMS-195	1989		2	1	70	90
EZMS-200	1990		2	1	75	95
EZMS-205	1991		2	1	80	100
EZMS-210	1992		2	1	85	110
EZMS-215	1993		2	1	85	110
EZMS-220	1994		2	1	90	120
EZMS-225	1995		2	1	90	120
EZMS-230	1996		2	1	95	130
EZMS-235	1997		2	1	95	130
EZMS-240	1998		2	1	100	140
EZMS-245	1999		2	1	100	140

1. Struck to facilitate photography of coins.
2. Weights 1.2 ; 1.8; 2.6; 2.9 grams.

remarkable coinage – an overnight revaluation by a factor of 2.4. Very few people nowadays spend Maundy sets as currency, but perhaps it is something to fall back on if ever coin collecting goes out of fashion! If the United Kingdom eventually adopts the Euro as the unit of currency, presumably the Maundy coinage will either become denominated in Euros, or will remain as pence. In the latter event, they will probably have to relinquish their legal tender status.

Maundy cases were square and covered in red leather, with the Royal Mint crest on the inside of the lid. From 1989, the coins were placed in a hard plastic insert inside the cases. Some 1953 sets were issued in blue and maroon cases.

Denomination	Metal	Weight (grams)	Diameter (mm)	Rev. alignment
Maundy set	0.925 Silver	0.5; 0.9; 1.4; 1.9	11; 13; 16; 18	↑

Obverse 1 Head 1, right; ELIZABETH II DEI GRA BRITT OMN REGINA F D

Obverse 2 Head 2, recut, right; ELIZABETH II DEI GRATIA REGINA F D

Reverse 1 Crowned numeral and divided date, all within wreath.

Edge plain

Obv. 1   Obv. 2

Rev. 1

No.	Date	Features	Obv.	Rev.	EF	FDC
EZMS-005	1953		1	1	240	350
EZMS-010	1953	PROOF from sandblasted dies [1]	1	1		800
EZMS-015	1953	struck in gold [2]	1	1		7000
EZMS-020	1954		2	1	60	80
EZMS-025	1955		2	1	60	80
EZMS-030	1956		2	1	60	80
EZMS-035	1957		2	1	60	80
EZMS-040	1958		2	1	60	80
EZMS-045	1959		2	1	60	80
EZMS-050	1960		2	1	60	80
EZMS-055	1961		2	1	60	80
EZMS-060	1962		2	1	60	80
EZMS-065	1963		2	1	60	80
EZMS-070	1964		2	1	60	80
EZMS-075	1965		2	1	60	80
EZMS-080	1966		2	1	60	80
EZMS-085	1967		2	1	60	80
EZMS-090	1968		2	1	60	80
EZMS-095	1969		2	1	60	80
EZMS-100	1970		2	1	60	80
EZMS-105	1971		2	1	60	80
EZMS-110	1972		2	1	60	80
EZMS-115	1973		2	1	60	80
EZMS-120	1974		2	1	60	80
EZMS-125	1975		2	1	60	80
EZMS-130	1976		2	1	60	80
EZMS-135	1977		2	1	60	80
EZMS-140	1978		2	1	60	80
EZMS-145	1979		2	1	60	80
EZMS-150	1980		2	1	60	80
EZMS-155	1981		2	1	60	80
EZMS-160	1982		2	1	60	80
EZMS-165	1983		2	1	60	80
EZMS-170	1984		2	1	60	80
EZMS-175	1985		2	1	60	80
EZMS-180	1986		2	1	60	80
EZMS-185	1987		2	1	70	90

Touchpieces

The touchpiece is an oddity on the numismatic scene, and hitherto collectors of these items have had little, if any, mention of their field of interest in standard catalogues. However, thanks to the researches of Helen Farquhar, Raymond Crawfurd, Marc Bloch, and, in particular, Noel Woolf, it is possible to put together these listings which may go some way to rectifying this omission.

For some centuries before the reign of Charles II there have been recorded instances of the ceremony of 'touching' by monarchs to attempt to cure scrofula, a disease afflicting a small but significant proportion of the population; this was an inflammation of the lymph nodes brought on by tuberculosis. It was common practice to give a token gift, usually one penny, to the sufferer at the same time. When the angel gold coin was introduced during the reign of Edward IV, this became adopted as the monetary gift, and its face value, six shillings and eight pence, was coincidentally the same as the recognised fee for a doctor. During the reign of Henry VII, it became the practice to pierce the coin, which was then used for crossing the sores of the sufferer prior to its being hung around the neck on a white silk ribbon personally by the king.

As can be imagined, the demand to be touched by the monarch was high, especially in view of the value of the gold received. A proclamation of 18th June 1626 decreed that intending recipients were required to bring with them a certificate that they had not been touched before. This gave rise to the issue of metal tokens of admission, although these are not covered in these listings. The scene was set for the issue of touchpieces struck specifically for the purpose of the touching ceremony.

Charles II

On 23rd June 1660, ten months before his coronation, Charles II held a touching ceremony in Whitehall, London, using gold coins from earlier reigns. The venue chosen by him was the Banqueting House, from the upper windows of which the unfortunate Charles I had stepped to his execution just over a decade earlier. Over 600 sufferers attended this ceremony, and, because of the large numbers, it was decided in July to limit the admission to 200. In September, Thomas Simon was ordered to prepare dies for a new Angel gold coin, but only one trial piece of the reverse was struck. During the winter months touching ceremonies were held around once a week, but in the heat of summer none took place because of the fear of spreading infection. Presumably, the King's mystical powers were insufficiently strong to prevent this.

The true touchpiece did not appear until some time later. A warrant of 25th February 1665 (1664 old style calendar) ordered specially made healing pieces to be coined from 22 carat gold, weighing about 3.5 grams each. The dies were probably the work of John Roettier, and the first striking accounted for about 6700 pieces. The design was clearly based on the Angel, with an obverse depicting a ship and a reverse of St. Michael as an angel fighting a dragon. The ship was 'The Sovereign of the Seas', later (1696) destroyed by fire, and the legends included a significant space where the piercing for the ribbon was to be made.

Between the years 1664 and 1684, 79,200 people had received gold touchpieces, and in August of that year it was decided to reduce the size considerably, with a weight reduction from 3.5 to about 2 grams. Records show payments for the new pieces of £176.10s on 13th August, £500 on 16th October, and £500 on 9th January 1685 (1684 old style calendar), a total of 4,700 pieces. Between 1st November and 4th February, when Charles was taken ill, a total of 2,800 were used. When the king died on 6th February, 1,905 pieces were left.

Denomination	Metal	Weight (grams)	Diameter (mm)	Rev. alignment
Touchpiece obvs. 1–3; revs. 1–2	0.916 gold	3.5	22–23	↑
Touchpiece obv. 4; rev. 3	0.916 gold	2.0–2.4	18–19	↑

Obv. 2   Rev. 1

Obverse 1   Ship with pillar next to main mast; CAR II D G M B (space) FR ET HI REX

Obverse 2   Similar but legend reads CAR II D G M B FR (space) ET HI REX

Obverse 3   Similar but no pillar. Legend as on obverse 2

Obverse 4   Similar to obverse 3 but on smaller flan

Reverse 1   St Michael as angel with spear, fighting dragon; SOLI DEO (space) GLORIA

Reverse 2   Similar but end of dragon's tail is much thinner; same legend

Reverse 3   Similar to reverse 1 but on smaller flan; dragon's tongue is different, and the bottom of the angel's wing (nearest SOLI) curves outwards; same legend

Edge   plain

No.	Features	Obv	Rev	F-VF
C2TP-005	1	1	1	400
C2TP-010		2	1	250
C2TP-015		3	1	200
C2TP-020		3	2	200
C2TP-025	2	4	3	200

1. Obverse 1 is identical to the reverse of the copper and silver pieces described by Peck as 'miscellaneous pieces' (Peck 493; 494) and by Montagu as pattern farthings.
2. Issued from August 1684 to February 1685 (1684 old style calendar).

Several minor differences occur on obverse and reverse (ship rigging, angel feathers, lettering size and shape, punctuation).

James II

James was a Catholic, and no doubt found it easy to accept the superstition surrounding the touching ceremony, the issuance of 14,364 touchpieces in the year 1687 giving some indication of his credulity. He first touched on 4th March 1685 (1684 old style calendar), less than a month after the death of Charles, using some of the pieces left over on Charles's demise.

The need now arose for a new issue of touchpieces, and these were again probably the work of John Roettier, using the old reverse. The first delivery of these was on 11th April 1685. James soon established a regular pattern on touching ceremonies on Fridays in London, except during hot weather. At first he used Anglican clergy, but these were soon replaced with Roman Catholic priests, using Latin, which James considered more appropriate.

James also undertook touching ceremonies in the provinces. The diary of Thomas Cartwright, Bishop of Chester, records that James touched 350 and 450 people on the 28th and 30th August 1687 respectively in Chester Cathedral.

Denomination	Metal	Weight (grams)	Diameter (mm)	Rev. alignment
Touchpiece	0.916 gold	1.7–2.0	19	↑

Obv. 1	Rev. 1

Obverse 1   Ship; IACO II D G M B FR (space) ET HI REX

Reverse 1   St. Michael as angel with spear, fighting dragon; SOLI DEO (space) GLORIA

Edge   plain

No.	Features	Obv	Rev	F-VF
J2TP-005		1	1	250

Several minor differences occur on obverse and reverse (ship rigging, lettering size and shape).

William and Mary
William III

William was not a believer in superstition and refused to undertake touching ceremonies.

Anne

Anne claimed no divine rights, but was advised by her ministers that it was the will of her people that she resume touching. This she did, using a simplified ceremony. Playing cards of the time depicted her on the nine of hearts, which was inscribed 'Her Majesty The Queen touching for scrofula'. On 6th October 1702 she touched 30 people in Bath, and an announcement in The London Gazette on 15th March 1703 (1702 old style calendar) stated: 'Mr. Charles Barnard, Her Majesty's Sergeant Surgeon ... will give his attendance there and deliver tickets every Friday at three in the afternoon during the time that Her Majesty shall please to touch for The Evil'. The ceremonies were held on Saturdays at St. James's in London at eleven in the morning.

The Hon. Daines Barrington, writing in 'Observations on our Ancient Statutes', mentions an old man who had said that when Queen Anne was at Oxford she touched him for evil when he was a child. When asked if he had been cured, he said with a smile that he had not been ill, but deserved to be touched as his parents were poor, and 'had no objection to the bit of gold'.

The touchpieces of Anne were of similar size to the earlier Charles II issue, but slightly thinner, weighing on average 47 grains. From February 1703 (1702 old style calendar) to May 1707, and from March 1711 to April 1714, 8,087 and 4,260 pieces were delivered respectively.

The last touching ceremony by a monarch was undertaken by Anne on 27th April 1714. Although touching is now accepted as a superstition, one of its beneficiaries may have had the last laugh. The parish register of Alrewas, Staffordshire for 1767 records that 'Edward Hall, who was touched and cured by His Majesty King Charles the Second for the King's Evil, was buried January 19th aged 110 years'.

Although touching died with Anne, the superstition lived on, especially in rural areas. Coinage of Charles I was handed down for healing purposes well into the 19th century in the Shetland Islands.

Denomination	Metal	Weight (grams)	Diameter (mm)	Rev. alignment
Touchpiece	0.916 gold	3.0–3.2	21	↑

Obv. 2	Rev. 1

Obverse 1   Ship; ANNA D G M BR (space) F ET H REG (each N in ANNA a standard N)

Obverse 2   Similar but left vertical of each N in ANNA is thin, slopes and tapers at foot with no serif

Reverse 1   St Michael as angel with spear, fighting dragon; SOLI DEO (space) GLORIA

Edge   plain

No.	Features	Obv	Rev	F-VF
ANTP-005		1	1	200
ANTP-010		2	1	200

Several punctuation differences occur on obverse and reverse.

Unofficial touchpieces of James II during his stay in France

James II arrived in France on 25th December 1688 following his unfortunate reign as King of England. The belief of Louis XIV in the divine right of kings led to the issue of a series of touchpieces in the name of the deposed king.

'The Prince' had been James's flagship during the battle of Sole Bay in 1672, and a depiction of this vessel appeared on the pieces, which were probably made in England by James and/or Norbert Roettier.

Maria Windfeda Francesca, the five year old daughter of Sir Nicholas Shireburn and his wife Catherine, was sent to the exiled Court at St. Germain-en-laye 'to be tutched for ye King's Evil by King James ye 2nd, 8th May 1698'.

Denomination	Metal	Weight (grams)	Diameter (mm)	Rev. alignment
Touchpiece Obv 1/Rev 1	Silver	1.5	20	↑
Touchpiece Obv 2/Rev 2	Silver	1.4	19	↑

The weights above are for unpierced pieces.

Obverse 1   Ship 'The Prince'; IAC II D G M B F (space) ET H REX (no stop after REX)

Obverse 2   Ship with several differences; same legend but smaller space between F and ET, and with a stop after REX

Reverse 1   St Michael as angel with spear, fighting dragon (dragon has tongue); SOLI DEO (space) GLORIA

Reverse 2   Similar but dragon has no tongue and angel's wing is slightly different; same legend but different spacing

Edge   plain

No.	Features	Obv	Rev	F-VF
J2FT-005		1	1	200
J2FT-010		2	2	200

Later touchpieces were made in France for 'James III', 'Charles III' and Henry IX. It is hoped to cover these in more details in future editions of this catalogue.

'Strangely visited people
All sworn and ulcerous,
Pitiful to the eye,
The mere despair of surgery he cures,
Hanging a golden stamp around their necks,
Put on with holy prayers.'

William Shakespeare (Macbeth)

Examining coins after receiving impressions for imperfect pieces etc.

Decimal Coinage Primarily Struck In Base Metals

A Committee of Enquiry appointed in 1961 to consider the adoption of decimal currency reported its findings in 1968. Despite the success of changeovers in Australia and New Zealand adopting a two-dollar pound, the Committee recommended that the pound be retained as the basic unit. The florin would become ten new pence (10p), the shilling five new pence (5p), and the sixpence a rather awkward 2½ new pence. New coinage of values 2, 1 and ½ pence would be introduced for use at the inception of decimal currency, together with a 50 pence coin which would replace the ten shilling note prior to the changeover date. The old halfcrown, threepence, penny and halfpenny would have no place in the new system.

Decimal day was fixed as 15th February 1971. The 50 pence coin was introduced in 1969, and the new bronze coinage was made available in 1968 as part of a specimen set in a wallet. The bronze coins in this set were dated 1971 and were not legal tender until decimal day in 1971. Despite some protests, the old sixpence was withdrawn in 1980 after it became obvious that a 2½ pence denomination was something of an anomaly. In 1982, a 20 pence coin was introduced, followed in 1983 by a nickel-brass pound coin. The new halfpenny was discontinued after 1984, and a few years later the 10 and 5 pence coins were reduced in size.

Base metal five pounds, two pounds and twenty-five pence coins were also issued from time to time but, although legal tender, they were not primarily intended for circulation. Some commemorative versions of the 50 pence coin were also struck.

In Coincraft's numbering system, decimal coins are denoted by a 'D', followed by the abbreviation for the denomination, a stroke and then the last two digits of the year they were issued. Because several different types are usually issued for each date of the decimal series, a suffix code is used to distinguish between them:

1: currency coin; 2: specimen (nonproof) issue; 3: proof issue in base metal; 4: proof in silver; 5: piedfort proof in silver; 6: proof in gold

On some coins, a further coding is incorporated into the suffix on an ad hoc basis where further classification of a variety is necessary.

Base Metal Five Pounds

Commemorative crowns of five shillings (later 25 new pence) in cupronickel were first issued in 1951 for the Festival of Britain. Subsequently they were struck on a number of occasions until the final issue in 1981 for the wedding of the Prince of Wales and Lady Diana. When in 1990 it was decided to strike a similar coin for the 90th Birthday of the Queen Mother, it was obvious that the cost of issuing the piece would be a substantial portion of the face value if the 25 pence value was retained. Moreover, a large coin weighing almost one ounce would sit distinctly oddly alongside the tiny 20 pence and the 50 pence coins. It was decided, therefore, that the denomination of the crown-size piece should be five pounds, no doubt also with one eye on the lucrative issue income which would ensue! The description of the coin as a 'crown' is unfortunate, as it debases a term used for well over 400 years to denote a coin of five shillings.

The striking of versions of these cupronickel commemoratives in gold is a source of some confusion alongside gold five pounds of the same years with a different design. In which listings should they be included? In this catalogue, these pieces are considered to be varieties of the base metal five pounds and are therefore listed in this section.

Denomination	Metal	Weight (grams)	Diameter (mm)	Rev. alignment
Five Pounds	Cupronickel	28.3	38.6	↑

Obverse 1   Head 1, right; ELIZABETH II DEI GRATIA REGINA F D FIVE POUNDS, all within beaded border

Obverse 2   Head 2, right, within eight mounted trumpeters separated by swords and sceptres; ELIZABETH II DEI GRATIA REGINA FID DEF FIVE POUNDS *(for the 40th anniversary of the Coronation)*

Obverse 3   As obverse 1 but without beaded border

Obverse 4   Conjoined portraits of Elizabeth and Philip; ELIZABETH II D G REG F D PHILIP PRINCEPS *(for the Queen's Golden Wedding anniversary)*

Obverse 5   Head 3, right; ELIZABETH II D G REG F D (date)

Reverse 1   Two intertwined 'E's, crown above, flanked by rose and thistle; QUEEN ELIZABETH THE QUEEN MOTHER 1900 1990

Reverse 2   St Edward's crown within 40 radiating trumpets; FAITH AND TRUTH I WILL BEAR UNTO YOU 1953–1993 *(for the 40th anniversary of the Coronation)*

Reverse 3   The Queen's personal flag, the Royal Standard, the Union Flag and two pennants bearing the dates 1926 and 1996, with background of Windsor Castle (*for the Queen's 70th Birthday*)

Reverse 4   Royal Arms and Arms of Prince Philip, crown above, anchor below; 1947 1997 20 NOVEMBER FIVE POUNDS

Reverse 5   Prince of Wales; FIFTIETH BIRTHDAY OF HRH THE PRINCE OF WALES 1948 FIVE POUNDS 1998; THE PRINCE'S TRUST HELPING YOUNG PEOPLE TO SUCCEED; CONFIDENCE, SUCCESS ... etc

Reverse 6   Head of Diana, facing right; 1961 1997 IN MEMORY OF DIANA PRINCESS OF WALES FIVE POUNDS

Reverse 7   Representation of clock face at 12 midnight, with centre of face positioned on map of British Isles at Greenwich; 1999 2000 FIVE POUNDS

Edge   (1996) (incuse) VIVAT REGINA ELIZABETHA
(1999) (incuse) WHAT'S PAST IS PROLOGUE
others: milled

Obv. 1   Obv. 2

Rev. 7

Obv. 4   Obv. 5

Rev. 1   Rev. 2

Rev. 3   Rev. 4

Rev. 5   Rev. 6

No.	Date	Features	Obv.	Rev.	UNC
D5P/90–1	1990		1	1	8
D5P/90–2	1990	SPECIMEN [1]	1	1	12
D5P/90–4	1990	PROOF in silver [2]	1	1	35
D5P/90–6	1990	PROOF in gold [3]	1	1	800
D5P/93–1	1993		2	2	8
D5P/93–2	1993	SPECIMEN [1]	2	2	12
D5P/93–3	1993	PROOF [4]	2	2	12
D5P/93–4	1993	PROOF in silver [2]	2	2	35
D5P/93–6	1993	PROOF in gold [3]	2	2	750
D5P/96–1	1996		3	3	8
D5P/96–2	1996	SPECIMEN [1]	3	3	14
D5P/96–3	1996	PROOF [4]	3	3	14
D5P/96–4	1996	PROOF in silver [2]	3	3	40
D5P/96–6	1996	PROOF in gold [3]	3	3	750
D5P/97–1	1997		4	4	8
D5P/97–2	1997	SPECIMEN [1]	4	4	14
D5P/97–3	1997	PROOF [4]	4	4	14
D5P/97–4	1997	PROOF in silver [2]	4	4	40
D5P/97–6	1997	PROOF in gold [3]	4	4	750
D5P/98–1	1998		5	5	8
D5P/98–2	1998	SPECIMEN [1]	5	5	14
D5P/98–3	1998	PROOF [4]	5	5	14
D5P/98–4	1998	PROOF in silver [2]	5	5	40
D5P/98–6	1998	PROOF in gold [3]	5	5	700
D5P/99–1	1999		5	6	8
D5P/99–2	1999	SPECIMEN [1]	5	6	14
D5P/98–3	1999	PROOF [4]	5	6	14
D5P/98–4	1999	PROOF in silver [2]	5	6	45
D5P/99–6	1999	PROOF in gold [3]	5	6	700
D5P/99A-1	1999		5	7	8

1. Issued in card holder.
2. Issued cased.
3. Issued cased; weight 39.9 grams.
4. Issued in cased proof sets.

Base Metal Two Pounds

Two pound coins were struck in nickel-brass to commemorate the Commonwealth Games in 1986; in 1989 for the 300th Anniversary of the Bill of Rights and (in Scotland) the Claim of Right (these were documents which sought to prevent a repetition of the dubious practices of James II); in 1994 for the 300th anniversary of the Bank of England, and in 1995 both for the 50th anniversary of the end of World War II and for the 50th anniversary of the United Nations. The commemorative series continued in 1996 with a two pounds struck for the Euro 96 Football Championship, while in 1997 and 1998 an unusual bi-metallic piece was issued to represent Man's technological progress. This last piece was the first two pounds coin in modern times genuinely intended for circulation; the designers were Raphael Maklouf (obverse); Bruce Rushin (reverse).

The two pounds of 1986 and some later dates have designs identical to those of the gold two pounds issued in the proof sets. This gives rise to something of a dilemma for cataloguers, as confusion arises as to which section the gold piece properly belongs. Normally, an identical gold version of a base metal coin would properly be incorporated in the base metal listings, but because of the inclusion of the gold coin in the proof sets it is considered here more appropriate to place the main listing in the gold section but to include a secondary listing in the base metal section but with the gold section reference number.

Denomination	Metal	Weight (grams)	Diameter (mm)	Rev. alignment
Two Pounds 1986–96	Nickel-brass	16.0	28.4	↑
Two Pounds 1997–99	Inner disc of cupro-nickel bonded to outer ring of nickel-brass	12.0	28.4	↑

Piedfort two pounds weigh twice the weight of the standard issue.

Obverse 1 Head 1, right; ELIZABETH II DEI GRATIA REGINA F D TWO POUNDS

Obverse 2 Similar but head larger; ELIZABETH II DEI GRA REG F D

Obverse 3 Similar head to that on Obverse 1 within beaded circle; ELIZABETH II DEI GRATIA REGINA F D

Obverse 4 Head 2, right; ELIZABETH II DEI GRA REG FID DEF

Reverse 1 Thistle on St Andrew's Cross; 1986 *(for the Commonwealth Games)*

Reverse 2 Cypher of William and Mary (intertwined W and M) threaded by mace, with crown above; TERCENTENARY OF THE BILL OF RIGHTS 1689 1989

Reverse 3 As above but with crown of Scotland; legend reads TERCENTENARY OF THE CLAIM OF RIGHT 1689 1989

Reverse 4 Bank of England's Corporate Seal ('Britannia looking on a Bank of money') with Crown and Cyphers of William and Mary; BANK OF ENGLAND 1694 1994

Reverse 5 Dove carrying olive branch *(for 50th anniversary of end of World War II)*

Reverse 6 Array of flags rising from UN 50 logo; NATIONS UNITED FOR PEACE 1945–1995 *(for 50th anniversary of United Nations)*

Reverse 7 Stylised football incorporating date 1996 and sixteen small circles representing teams in finals *(for the Euro 96 Championship)*

Reverse 8 Four concentric circles depicting Man's technological advancement from Iron Age to Internet; TWO POUNDS 1997

Reverse 9 Rugby ball and posts; 1999 TWO POUNDS

Edge 1 XIII COMMONWEALTH GAMES SCOTLAND 1986 incuse on milling

Edge 2 milled

Edge 3 (incuse on milling) SIC VOC NON VOBIS

Edge 4 (incuse on milling) 1945 IN PEACE GOODWILL 1995

Edge 5 (incuse on milling) TENTH EUROPEAN CHAMPIONSHIP

Edge 6 (incuse on milling) STANDING ON THE SHOULDERS OF GIANTS

Edge 7 (incuse on milling) RUGBY WORLD CUP 1999

Obv. 1   Obv. 2

Obv. 3   Obv. 4

Rev. 1   Rev. 2

Rev. 3   Rev. 4

Rev. 5   Rev. 6

Rev. 7   Rev. 8

Rev. 9

No.	Date	Features	Edge	Obv.	Rev.	UNC
D2P/86–1	1986		1	1	1	4
D2P/86–2	1986	SPECIMEN [1]	1	1	1	8
D2P/86–3	1986	PROOF [2]	1	1	1	7
D2P/86SP-4	1986	SPECIMEN in 0.500 silver [3]	1	1	1	20
D2P/86–4	1986	PROOF in silver [3]	1	1	1	30
EZ2P-030	1986	PROOF in gold [4]	2	1	1	220
D2P/89CB-1	1989		2	1	2	4
D2P/89CB-2	1989	SPECIMEN [1]	2	1	2	8
D2P/89CB-3	1989	PROOF [2]	2	1	2	7
D2P/89CB-4	1989	PROOF in silver [3]	2	1	2	25
D2P/89CB-5	1989	PIEDFORT PROOF in silver [3]	2	1	2	50
D2P/89CC-1	1989		2	1	3	8
D2P/89CC-2	1989	SPECIMEN [1]	2	1	3	12
D2P/89CC-3	1989	PROOF [2]	2	1	3	12
D2P/89CC-4	1989	PROOF in silver [3]	2	1	3	25
D2P/89CC-5	1989	PIEDFORT PROOF in silver [3]	2	1	3	50
D2P/94–1	1994		3	1	4	4
D2P/94–2	1994	SPECIMEN [1]	3	1	4	7
D2P/94–3	1994	PROOF [2]	3	1	4	6
D2P/94–4	1994	PROOF in silver [3]	3	1	4	25
D2P/94–5	1994	PIEDFORT PROOF in silver [3]	3	1	4	50
EZ2P-070	1994	PROOF in gold [4]	2	1	4	350
EZ2P-075	1994	PROOF in gold [5]	2	2	4	450
D2P/95C1–1	1995		4	1	5	4
D2P/95C1–2	1995	SPECIMEN [1]	4	1	5	7
D2P/95C1–3	1995	PROOF [2]	4	1	5	6
D2P/95C1–4	1995	PROOF in silver [3]	4	1	5	25
D2P/95C1–5	1995	PIEDFORT PROOF in silver [3]	4	1	5	50
EZ2P-080	1995	PROOF in gold [4]	4	1	5	350
D2P/95C2–1	1995		2	1	6	5
D2P/95C2–2	1995	SPECIMEN [1]	2	1	6	7
D2P/95C2–3	1995	PROOF [2]	2	1	6	6
D2P/95C2–4	1995	PROOF in silver [3]	2	1	6	25
D2P/95C2–5	1995	PIEDFORT PROOF in silver [3]	2	1	6	50
EZ2P-085	1995	PROOF in gold [4]	2	1	6	350
D2P/96–1	1996		5	1	7	5
D2P/96–2	1996	SPECIMEN [1]	5	1	7	7
D2P/96–3	1996	PROOF [2]	5	1	7	7
D2P/96–4	1996	PROOF in silver [3]	5	1	7	30
D2P/96–5	1996	PIEDFORT PROOF in silver [3]	5	1	7	50
D2P/96–6	1996	PROOF in gold [3]	5	1	7	350
D2P/97–1	1997		6	3	8	5
D2P/97–2	1997	SPECIMEN [1]	6	3	8	7
D2P/97–3	1997	PROOF [2]	6	3	8	7
D2P/97–4	1997	PROOF in silver [3]	6	3	8	30
D2P/97–5	1997	PIEDFORT PROOF in silver [3]	6	3	8	50

No.	Date	Features	Edge	Obv.	Rev.	UNC
EZ2P-095	1997	PROOF in gold [4]	2	3	8	350
D2P/98–1	1998		6	4	8	5
D2P/98–2	1998	SPECIMEN [1]	6	4	8	7
D2P/98–3	1998	PROOF [2]	6	4	8	7
D2P/98–4	1998	PROOF in silver [3]	6	4	8	30
D2P/98–5	1998	PIEDFORT PROOF in silver [3]	6	4	8	50
D2P/99–1	1999		7	4	9	5
D2P/99–2	1999	SPECIMEN [1]	7	4	9	7
D2P/99–3	1999	PROOF [2]	7	4	9	7
D2P/99–4	1999	PROOF in silver [3]	7	4	9	30
D2P/99–5	1999	PIEDFORT PROOF in silver [3]	7	4	9	50
EZ2P-105	1999	PROOF in gold [3]	2	4	9	350

1. Issued in card holder.
2. Issued in cased proof sets.
3. Issued cased.
4. Gold section reference number; issued cased and in cased proof sets.
5. Error obverse; gold section reference number; see p.431 for details; issued cased.

The 1997 silver issue has the outer concentric ring plated with fine gold.

The 1997 gold issue has the inner disc of gold 91.67%, silver 4.17%, copper 4.17% (yellow gold) and the outer ring of gold 91.67%, copper 8.33% (red gold).

Base Metal Pound

Inflationary pressures dictated that by 1983 it was considered more appropriate that the pound should be represented by a coin rather than a banknote. Although at first unpopular, the coin has now become widely accepted.

An unusual feature of the coin has been the annual change of reverse rotating through ten different designs. These feature aspects of different nations within the United Kingdom. The obverse at first used the Machin portrait of the queen, but from 1985 the Maklouf design was used. A number of collectors' versions were also struck each year, including cased silver proofs and, for some years, cased piedforts.

Denomination	Metal	Weight (grams)	Diameter (mm)	Rev. alignment
Pound	Nickel-brass	9.5	22.5	↑

Piedfort pounds weigh 19.0 grams.

Obverse 1 Head 1, right; ELIZABETH II D G REG F D (date)

Obverse 2 Head 2, right; same legend

Obverse 3 Head 3, right; same legend

Reverse 1 Royal Arms; ONE POUND

Reverse 2 Thistle sprig inside coronet (Scottish design); ONE POUND

Reverse 3 Leek inside coronet (Welsh design); ONE POUND

Reverse 4 Flax inside coronet (Northern Ireland design); ONE POUND

Reverse 5 Oak Tree inside coronet (English design); ONE POUND

Reverse 6 Arms within shield, crown above; ONE POUND

Reverse 7 Lion rampant within ornate border (Scottish design); ONE POUND

Reverse 8 Dragon of Wales; ONE POUND

Reverse 9 Celtic cross incorporating central pimpernel (Northern Ireland design); ONE POUND

Reverse 10 Three lions passant (English design); ONE POUND

All of the edge letterings below are superimposed on a milled edge:

Edge 1 DECUS ET TUTAMEN

Edge 2 NEMO ME IMPUNE LACESSIT

Edge 3 PLEIDIOL WYF I'M GWLAD

Obv. 1   Obv. 2   Obv. 3

Rev. 1   Rev. 2   Rev. 3

Rev. 4   Rev. 5   Rev. 6

Rev. 7   Rev. 8   Rev. 9

Rev. 10

No.	Date	Features	Edge	Obv.	Rev.	UNC
D1P/83–1	1983		1	1	1	4
D1P/83–2	1983	SPECIMEN [1]	1	1	1	10
D1P/83–3	1983	PROOF [2]	1	1	1	6
D1P/83–4	1983	PROOF in silver [3]	1	1	1	40
D1P/83–5	1983	PIEDFORT PROOF in silver [3]	1	1	1	150
D1P/84–1	1984		2	1	2	5
D1P/84–2	1984	SPECIMEN [1]	2	1	2	12
D1P/84–3	1984	PROOF [2]	2	1	2	6
D1P/84–4	1984	PROOF in silver [3]	2	1	2	30
D1P/84–5	1984	PIEDFORT PROOF in silver [3]	2	1	2	75
D1P/85–1	1985		3	2	3	5
D1P/85–2	1985	SPECIMEN [1]	3	2	3	10
D1P/85–3	1985	PROOF [2]	3	2	3	6
D1P/85–4	1985	PROOF in silver [3]	3	2	3	35
D1P/85–5	1985	PIEDFORT PROOF in silver [3]	3	2	3	60
D1P/86–1	1986		1	2	4	5
D1P/86–2	1986	SPECIMEN [1]	1	2	4	10
D1P/86–3	1986	PROOF [2]	1	2	4	6
D1P/86–4	1986	PROOF in silver [3]	1	2	4	35
D1P/86–5	1986	PIEDFORT PROOF in silver [3]	1	2	4	60
D1P/87–1	1987		1	2	5	5
D1P/87–2	1987	SPECIMEN [1]	1	2	5	10
D1P/87–3	1987	PROOF [2]	1	2	5	6
D1P/87–4	1987	PROOF in silver [3]	1	2	5	35
D1P/87–5	1987	PIEDFORT PROOF in silver [3]	1	2	5	60
D1P/88–1	1988		1	2	6	5
D1P/88–2	1988	SPECIMEN [1]	1	2	6	9
D1P/88–3	1988	PROOF [2]	1	2	6	7
D1P/88–4	1988	PROOF in silver [3]	1	2	6	40
D1P/88–5	1988	PIEDFORT PROOF in silver [3]	1	2	6	60
D1P/89–1	1989		2	2	2	4
D1P/89–2	1989	SPECIMEN [1]	2	2	2	9
D1P/89–3	1989	PROOF [2]	2	2	2	5
D1P/89–4	1989	PROOF in silver [3]	2	2	2	35
D1P/89–5	1989	PIEDFORT PROOF in silver [3]	2	2	2	80
D1P/90–1	1990		3	2	3	4
D1P/90–3	1990	PROOF [2]	3	2	3	5
D1P/90–4	1990	PROOF in silver [3]	3	2	3	35
D1P/91–1	1991		1	2	4	4
D1P/91–3	1991	PROOF [2]	1	2	4	6
D1P/91–4	1991	PROOF in silver [3]	1	2	4	35
D1P/92–1	1992		1	2	5	4
D1P/92–3	1992	PROOF [2]	1	2	5	6

No.	Date	Features	Edge	Obv.	Rev.	UNC
D1P/92–4	1992	PROOF in silver [3]	1	2	5	35
D1P/93–1	1993		1	2	1	4
D1P/93–3	1993	PROOF [2]	1	2	1	6
D1P/93–4	1993	PROOF in silver [3]	1	2	1	35
D1P/93–5	1993	PIEDFORT PROOF in silver [3]	1	2	1	75
D1P/94–1	1994		2	2	7	3
D1P/94–2	1994	SPECIMEN [1]	2	2	7	9
D1P/94–3	1994	PROOF [2]	2	2	7	5
D1P/94–4	1994	PROOF in silver [3]	2	2	7	35
D1P/94–5	1994	PIEDFORT PROOF in silver [3]	2	2	7	75
D1P/95–1	1995		3	2	8	3
D1P/95–2	1995	SPECIMEN [1]	2	2	8	9
D1P/95–3	1995	PROOF [2]	3	2	8	5
D1P/95–4	1995	PROOF in silver [3]	3	2	8	35
D1P/95–5	1995	PIEDFORT PROOF in silver [3]	3	2	8	75
D1P/96–1	1996		1	2	9	3
D1P/96–2	1996	SPECIMEN [1]	1	2	9	10
D1P/96–3	1996	PROOF [2]	1	2	9	6
D1P/96–4	1996	PROOF in silver [4]	1	2	9	35
D1P/96–5	1996	PIEDFORT PROOF in silver [3]	1	2	9	80
D1P/97–1	1997		1	2	10	3
D1P/97–2	1997	SPECIMEN [1]	1	2	10	10
D1P/97–3	1997	PROOF [2]	1	2	10	6
D1P/97–4	1997	PROOF in silver [3]	1	2	10	35
D1P/97–5	1997	PIEDFORT PROOF in silver [3]	1	2	10	80
D1P/98–1	1998		1	3	1	3
D1P/98–2	1998	SPECIMEN [1]	1	3	1	10
D1P/98–3	1998	PROOF [2]	1	3	1	6
D1P/98–4	1998	PROOF in silver [3]	1	3	1	35
D1P/98–5	1998	PIEDFORT PROOF in silver [3]	1	3	1	80
D1P/99–1	1999		2	3	7	3
D1P/99–2	1999	SPECIMEN [1]	2	3	7	10
D1P/99–3	1999	PROOF [2]	2	3	7	6
D1P/99–4	1999	PROOF in silver [3]	2	3	7	35
D1P/99–5	1999	PIEDFORT PROOF in silver [3]	2	3	7	80

1. Issued in card holder.
2. Issued in cased proof sets.
3. Issued cased.
4. Issued cased and in cased proof sets.

50 Pence

The 50 pence entered circulation on 14 October 1969, before the decimal changeover in 1971, and it circulated alongside the ten shilling note of equal value. The coin was of an unusual shape, with seven sides which were each slightly curved, so that the 'diameter' from one side to the other through the centre of the coin was always the same length (30mm) wherever it was measured. This enabled the coin to activate slot machines without any problem. The same principle applied to the 27mm diameter coin introduced in 1997.

Although widely encountered in circulation, several of the dates were struck only either as proofs or for incorporation in the yearly specimen sets in card wallets.

Denomination	Metal	Weight (grams)	Diameter (mm)	Rev. alignment
50 pence 1969–96	Cupronickel (copper 75%; nickel 25%)	13.5	30 [1]	↑
50 pence 1997–99	Cupronickel (copper 75%; nickel 25%)	8.1	27 [1]	↑

1. The coin is seven-sided but the diameter from any point on the edge across the centre of the face is constant.

Obverse 1 Head 1, right; ELIZABETH II D G REG F D (date)

Obverse 2 Head 1, right; ELIZABETH II D G REG F D

Obverse 3 Head 2, right; ELIZABETH II D G REG F D (date)

Obverse 4 Head 2, right; ELIZABETH II DEI GRA REG F D

Obverse 5 As Obverse 3 on smaller flan

Obverse 6 Head 3, right; ELIZABETH II D G REG F D (date)

Reverse 1 Britannia, seated, with shield, facing right; 50 in exergue; NEW PENCE

Reverse 2 Nine clasped hands forming circle; 1973 50 PENCE *(for Britain's entry into the EC)*

Reverse 3 As Reverse 1 but the trident is not so upright; legend reads FIFTY PENCE

Reverse 4 Plan of Conference table top and seats, with 12 stars; 1992 1993 50 PENCE *(for completion of the EC Single Market and Britain's Presidency)*

Reverse 5 Invasion Force of planes and ships; 50 PENCE *(for 50th anniversary of D-Day)*

Reverse 6 As Reverse 3 on smaller flan

Reverse 7 Twelve stars; 1973 EU 1998 50 PENCE *(for Britain's Presidency on the 25th anniversary of EU entry)*

Reverse 8 Light radiating from cupped hands; NHS NHS NHS NHS NHS FIFTIETH ANNIVERSARY 50 PENCE

Edge plain

Obv. 1

Obv. 2

Obv. 3   Obv. 4

Obv. 5   Obv. 6

Rev. 1   Rev. 2

Rev. 3   Rev. 4

Rev. 5   Rev. 6

Rev. 7   Rev. 8

30 mm diameter

No.	Date	Features	Obv.	Rev.	UNC
D50/69–1	1969		1	1	5
D50/69–1E	1969	[1]	1	obv. 1	200
D50/70–1	1970		1	1	10
D50/71–3	1971	PROOF [2]	1	1	8
D50/72–3	1972	PROOF [2]	1	1	7
D50/73–1	1973		2	2	4

No.	Date	Features	Obv.	Rev.	UNC
D50/73–3	1973	PROOF [3]	2	2	4
D50/73–5	1973	PIEDFORT PROOF in silver [4]	2	2	2500
D50/74–3	1974	PROOF [2]	1	1	8
D50/75–3	1975	PROOF [2]	1	1	8
D50/76–1	1976		1	1	9
D50/76–3	1976	PROOF [2]	1	1	7
D50/77–1	1977		1	1	4
D50/77–3	1977	PROOF [2]	1	1	8
D50/78–1	1978		1	1	4
D50/78–3	1978	PROOF [2]	1	1	7
D50/79–1	1979		1	1	4
D50/79–3	1979	PROOF [2]	1	1	7
D50/80–1	1980		1	1	4
D50/80–3	1980	PROOF [2]	1	1	6
D50/81–1	1981		1	1	4
D50/81–3	1981	PROOF [2]	1	1	6
D50/RR–1E		[5]	rev. 1	1	200
D50/82–1	1982		1	3	4
D50/82–3	1982	PROOF [2]	1	3	6
D50/83–1	1983		1	3	4
D50/83–3	1983	PROOF [2]	1	3	6
D50/84–1	1984	[6]	1	3	6
D50/84–3	1984	PROOF [2]	1	3	7
D50/85–1	1985		3	3	8
D50/85–3	1985	PROOF [2]	3	3	6
D50/86–1	1986	[6]	3	3	7
D50/86–3	1986	PROOF [2]	3	3	9
D50/87–1	1987	[6]	3	3	8
D50/87–3	1987	PROOF [2]	3	3	10
D50/88–1	1988	[6]	3	3	8
D50/88–3	1988	PROOF [2]	3	3	10
D50/89–1	1989	[6]	3	3	8
D50/89–3	1989	PROOF [3]	3	3	10
D50/90–1	1990	[6]	3	3	7
D50/90–3	1990	PROOF [2]	3	3	9
D50/91–1	1991	[6]	3	3	10
D50/91–3	1991	PROOF [2]	3	3	12
D50/92–1	1992	[6]	3	3	6
D50/92–3	1992	PROOF [2]	3	3	7
D50/93–1	1993	[6]	3	3	6
D50/93–3	1993	PROOF [2]	3	3	7
D50/92C–1	1992/93		4	4	4
D50/92C–3	1992/93	PROOF [2]	4	4	7
D50/92C–4	1992/93	PROOF in silver [7]	4	4	50
D50/92C–5	1992/93	PIEDFORT PROOF in silver [8]	4	4	95
D50/92C–6	1992/93	PROOF in gold [9]	4	4	500
D50/94C–1	1994	[6]	3	5	5
D50/94C–2	1994	SPECIMEN [10]	3	5	8
D50/94C–3	1994	PROOF [2]	3	5	8
D50/94C–4	1994	PROOF in silver [7]	3	5	50
D50/94C–5	1994	PIEDFORT PROOF in silver [8]	3	5	95
D50/94C–6	1994	PROOF in gold [9]	3	5	500
D50/95–1	1995	[6]	3	3	5
D50/95–3	1995	PROOF [2]	3	3	8
D50/96–1	1996	[6]	3	3	5
D50/96–3	1996	PROOF [2]	3	3	8
D50/96–4	1996	PROOF in silver [2]	3	3	20
D50/97–3L	1997	PROOF [2]	3	3	8
D50/97–4L	1997	PROOF in silver [2]	3	3	25

1. 'Double headed' coin.
2. Issued in cased proof sets.
3. Issued cased and in cased proof sets.
4. About 20 struck.
5. 'Double tailed' coin; bears no date.
6. All issued in uncirculated sets in holders.
7. Issued cased.
8. Weight 27.0 grams; issued cased.
9. Weight 26.3 grams; issued cased.
10. Issued in card holder.

27 mm diameter

No.	Date	Features	Obv.	Rev.	UNC
D50/97–1	1997		5	6	2
D50/97–3S	1997	PROOF [1]	5	6	6
D50/97–4S	1997	PROOF in silver [2]	5	6	20
D50/97–5S	1997	PIEDFORT PROOF in silver [2]	5	6	80
D50/98–1	1998		6	6	2
D50/98–3	1998	PROOF [1]	6	6	6
D50/98–4	1998	PROOF in silver [2]	6	6	20
D50/98C–1	1998		6	7	3
D50/98C–3	1998	PROOF [1]	6	7	7
D50/98C–4	1998	PROOF in silver [2]	6	7	20

No.	Date	Features	Obv.	Rev.	UNC
D50/98C-6	1998	PROOF in gold [2]	6	7	500
D50/98N-1	1998		6	8	3
D50/98N-4	1998	PROOF in silver [2]	6	8	20
D50/98N-6	1998	PROOF in gold [2]	6	8	300
D50/99-1	1999		6	6	3
D50/99-3	1999	PROOF [1]	6	6	7

1. Issued in cased proof sets.
2. Issued cased.

25 Pence

During the reign of Elizabeth II, crowns of five shillings had been issued on three occasions, but these were not intended as circulation pieces. The year after decimalization, a crown denominated at 25 pence was struck for the Royal Silver Wedding, although no mark of denomination appears on this, or on any subsequent 25 pence coin. Three further commemorative crowns were struck as listed, and proof versions in silver were also issued. The 1977 coin is unusual in having no legend or digits whatsoever on the reverse.

In 1990 a cupronickel crown-size coin of five pounds was issued, and it appears unlikely that any future crowns of 25 pence will be issued.

Denomination	Metal	Weight (grams)	Diameter (mm)	Rev. alignment
25 Pence	Cupronickel (copper 75%; nickel 25%)	28.3	38.6	↑

Obverse 1   Head 1, right; ELIZABETH II D G REG F D

Obverse 2   Queen on horseback; ELIZABETH II D G REG F D 1977 *(for the 25th anniversary of the Queen's accession)*

Reverse 1   EP on floral motif, crown above; ELIZABETH AND PHILIP 20 NOVEMBER 1947–1972

Reverse 2   Coronation regalia with floral border, crown above

Reverse 3   Head of Queen Mother, left, within decoration; QUEEN ELIZABETH THE QUEEN MOTHER AUGUST 4TH 1980 *(for the Queen Mother's 80th Birthday)*

Reverse 4   Conjoined heads of Charles and Diana, left; HRH THE PRINCE OF WALES AND LADY DIANA SPENCER 1981 *(for the Wedding of Prince of Wales and Lady Diana)*

Edge   milled

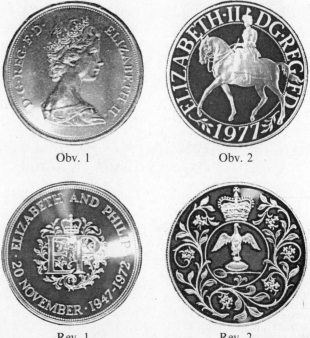

Obv. 1   Obv. 2

Rev. 1   Rev. 2

Rev. 3	Rev. 4

No.	Date	Features	Obv.	Rev.	UNC
D25/72–1	1972		1	1	3
D25/72–3	1972	PROOF [1]	1	1	12
D25/72–4	1972	PROOF in silver [2]	1	1	30
D25/77–1	1977	[3]	2	2	3
D25/77–2	1977	SPECIMEN [4]	2	2	8
D25/77–3	1977	PROOF [1]	2	2	12
D25/77–4	1977	PROOF in silver [2]	2	2	25
D25/80–1	1980		1	3	3
D25/80–2	1980	SPECIMEN [4]	1	3	8
D25/80–4	1980	PROOF in silver [2]	1	3	30
D25/81–1	1981		1	4	3
D25/81–2	1981	SPECIMEN [4]	1	4	10
D25/81–4	1981	PROOF in silver [2]	1	4	35

1. Issued in cased proof sets.
2. Issued cased.
3. Has no words or figures on reverse.
4. Issued in card holder.

For later crown-size pieces see under base metal five pounds, p.633.

20 Pence

Although crowns denominated at 25 pence had been issued from time to time, these were not primarily intended for circulation, and in any event were too large for practical use. After decimal currency had been circulating for some time it became obvious that it would be convenient to have a new coin to bridge the gap between the 50 pence and 10 pence coins. The 20 pence was first issued in 1982, with a reverse by William Gardner, and soon became a popular addition to the decimal range, with its distinctive seven-sided shape, a smaller version of the 50 pence coin. It is interesting to contrast the success of the 20 pence with the unpopularity of the double florin (equivalent face value) in 1887. The latter coin failed to survive beyond 1890 in competition with the crown piece. Ironically, the proclamation of 1971 included the double florin in the list of coins which continued to have legal tender status after decimal day.

The first 20 pence was issued in the same year that the term 'new pence' was abandoned in favour of 'pence', and so no specimens with the old wording were struck. The coins were issued also in proof each year for the proof set, and in 1986 no ordinary coins were struck except for those issued in official card wallets.

The cupronickel used for the 20 pence has a copper content of 84%, compared with the 75% in the cupronickel used for the 50, 10 and 5 pence coins.

Denomination	Metal	Weight (grams)	Diameter (mm)	Rev. alignment
20 Pence	Cupronickel (copper 84%; nickel 16%)	5.0	21.4	↑

The coin is seven-sided but the diameter from any point on the edge across the centre of the face is constant.

Obverse 1   Head 1, right; ELIZABETH II D G REG F D

Obverse 2   Head 2, right; same legend

Obverse 3   Head 2, right; 1mm longer than on obverse 2; same legend

Obverse 4   Head 3, right; same legend

Reverse 1   Crowned double rose; TWENTY PENCE (date), '20' below

Edge   plain

Obv. 1	Obv. 2	Obv. 4

Rev. 1

No.	Date	Features	Obv.	Rev.	UNC
D20/82–1	1982		1	1	2
D20/82–3	1982	PROOF [1]	1	1	5
D20/82–5	1982	PIEDFORT PROOF in silver [2]	1	1	50
D20/83–1	1983		1	1	2
D20/83–3	1983	PROOF [1]	1	1	5
D20/84–1	1984		1	1	2
D20/84–3	1984	PROOF [1]	1	1	5
D20/85–1	1985		2	1	2
D20/85–3	1985	PROOF [1]	2	1	5
D20/86–1	1986	[3]	2	1	3
D20/86–3	1986	PROOF [1]	2	1	6
D20/87–1	1987		2	1	2
D20/87–3	1987	PROOF [1]	2	1	5

No.	Date	Features	Obv.	Rev.	UNC
D20/88–1	1988		2	1	2
D20/88–3	1988	PROOF [1]	2	1	5
D20/89–1	1989		2	1	2
D20/89–3	1989	PROOF [1]	2	1	5
D20/90–1	1990		2	1	2
D20/90–3	1990	PROOF [1]	2	1	5
D20/91–1	1991		2	1	2
D20/91–3	1991	PROOF [1]	2	1	5
D20/92–1	1992		3	1	2
D20/92–3	1992	PROOF [1]	3	1	5
D20/93–1	1993		3	1	2
D20/93–3	1993	PROOF [1]	3	1	5
D20/94–1	1994		3	1	2
D20/94–3	1994	PROOF [1]	3	1	5
D20/95–1	1995		3	1	2
D20/95–3	1995	PROOF [1]	3	1	5
D20/96–1	1996		3	1	2
D20/96–3	1996	PROOF [1]	3	1	5
D20/96–4	1996	PROOF in silver [1]	3	1	15
D20/97–1	1997		3	1	2
D20/97–3	1997	PROOF [1]	3	1	5
D20/98–1	1998		4	1	2
D20/98–3	1998	PROOF [1]	4	1	5
D20/99–1	1999		4	1	2
D20/99–3	1999	PROOF [1]	4	1	5

1. Issued in cased proof sets.
2. Weight 10.0 grams; issued cased.
3. All issued in uncirculated sets in holders.

10 Pence

The 10 new pence coin was one of the two denominations intended to circulate alongside a pre-decimal coin of the same size, weight and value (the florin). There was therefore no bar to its being introduced prior to decimalization in order to familiarise the public, and consequently in 1968, 1969 and 1970 a large quantity was struck and issued. In 1968 the 10 pence was also issued as part of an official decimal set in a blue wallet. This set also contained three bronze coins dated 1971.

In 1992, a smaller size 10 pence was issued, and the larger coins were progressively withdrawn.

Denomination	Metal	Weight (grams)	Diameter (mm)	Rev. alignment
10 Pence 1968–92	Cupronickel (copper 75%; nickel 25%)	11.3	28.5	↑
10 Pence 1992–99	Cupronickel (copper 75%; nickel 25%)	6.5	24.5	↑

Obverse 1 Head 1, right; ELIZABETH II D G REG F D (date)
Obverse 2 Head 2, right; same legend
Obverse 3 As Obverse 2 on smaller flan
Obverse 4 Head 3, right; same legend
Reverse 1 Lion Passant, '10' below; NEW PENCE
Reverse 2 Similar but legend reads TEN PENCE
Reverse 3 As Reverse 2 on smaller flan
Edge milled

Obv. 1   Obv. 2   Obv. 3

Obv. 4

Rev. 1   Rev. 2   Rev. 3

28.5 mm diameter

No.	Date	Features	Obv.	Rev.	UNC
D10/68–1	1968	[1]	1	1	2
D10/68–1A	1968	some border beads on rev. double struck	1	1	25
D10/69–1E	1969	rev. ↓	1	1	80
D10/69–1	1969		1	1	3
D10/69–1A	1969	die axis about 90 degrees from vertical	1	1	40
D10/70–1	1970		1	1	4
D10/71–1	1971		1	1	4

No.	Date	Features	Obv.	Rev.	UNC
D10/71–3	1971	PROOF [2]	1	1	5
D10/72–3	1972	PROOF [2]	1	1	6
D10/73–1	1973		1	1	3
D10/73–3	1973	PROOF [2]	1	1	5
D10/74–1	1974		1	1	3
D10/74–1E	1974	struck on thin flan [3]	1	1	50
D10/74–3	1974	PROOF [2]	1	1	5
D10/75–1	1975		1	1	4
D10/75–3	1975	PROOF [2]	1	1	5
D10/76–1	1976		1	1	4
D10/76–3	1976	PROOF [2]	1	1	5
D10/77–1	1977		1	1	3
D10/77–3	1977	PROOF [2]	1	1	4
D10/78–3	1978	PROOF [2]	1	1	8
D10/79–1	1979		1	1	4
D10/79–3	1979	PROOF [2]	1	1	5
D10/80–1	1980		1	1	3
D10/80–3	1980	PROOF [2]	1	1	5
D10/81–1	1981		1	1	10
D10/81–3	1981	PROOF [2]	1	1	11
D10/82–1	1982	[4]	1	2	7
D10/82–3	1982	PROOF [2]	1	2	8
D10/83–1	1983	[4]	1	2	8
D10/83–3	1983	PROOF [2]	1	2	9
D10/84–1	1984	[4]	1	2	4
D10/84–3	1984	PROOF [2]	1	2	4
D10/85–1	1985	[4]	2	2	4
D10/85–3	1985	PROOF [2]	2	2	4
D10/86–1	1986	[4]	2	2	4
D10/86–3	1986	PROOF [2]	2	2	4
D10/87–1	1987	[4]	2	2	4
D10/87–3	1987	PROOF [2]	2	2	5
D10/88–1	1988	[4]	2	2	5
D10/88–3	1988	PROOF [2]	2	2	6
D10/89–1	1989	[4]	2	2	5
D10/89–3	1989	PROOF [2]	2	2	6
D10/90–1	1990	[4]	2	2	5
D10/90–3	1990	PROOF [2]	2	2	6
D10/91–1	1991	[4]	2	2	5
D10/91–3	1991	PROOF [2]	2	2	6
D10/92–1L	1992	[4]	2	2	8
D10/92–3L	1992	PROOF [2]	2	2	10
D10/92–4L	1992	PROOF in silver [5]	2	2	20

1. Some issued in 1968 in decimal set wallets.
2. Issued in cased proof sets.
3. Weight 8.1 grams.
4. All issued in uncirculated sets in holders.
5. Issued cased.

24.5 mm diameter

No.	Date	Features	Obv.	Rev.	UNC
D10/92–1S	1992	[1]	3	3	2
D10/92–3S	1992	PROOF [2]	3	3	4
D10/92–4S	1992	PROOF in silver [3]	3	3	10
D10/92–5S	1992	PIEDFORT PROOF in silver [4]	3	3	50
D10/93–1	1993	[5]	3	3	6
D10/93–3	1993	PROOF [2]	3	3	4
D10/94–1	1994	[5]	3	3	5
D10/94–3	1994	PROOF [2]	3	3	4
D10/95–1	1995		3	3	2
D10/95–3	1995	PROOF [2]	3	3	4
D10/96–1	1996		3	3	2
D10/96–3	1996	PROOF [2]	3	3	4
D10/96–4	1996	PROOF in silver [2]	3	3	15
D10/97–1	1997		3	3	2
D10/97–3	1997	PROOF [2]	3	3	4
D10/98–1	1998		4	3	2
D10/98–3	1998	PROOF [2]	4	3	4
D10/99–1	1999		4	3	2
D10/99–3	1999	PROOF [2]	4	3	4

1. Milling varies.
2. Issued in cased proof sets.
3. Issued cased.
4. Weight 13.0 grams; issued cased.
5. All issued in uncirculated sets in holders.

5 Pence

As with the 10 pence, the 5 pence coin was first issued in 1968, and took its place alongside the old shilling, having the same size and value. So many were issued prior to decimalization that no more were needed to be struck between 1972 and 1974 apart from proofs. When the coinage of circulation pieces was resumed, some of the dies were chromium-plated to protect them against wear. Coins from these dies have a somewhat glossy surface.

In 1990, the coin was succeeded by a 5 pence of similar design but reduced size, resulting in arguably the most unpopular coin since the double florin. Indeed, it is very difficult to find anyone who approves of the coin.

Denomination	Metal	Weight (grams)	Diameter (mm)	Rev. alignment
5 Pence 1968–90	Cupronickel (copper 75%; nickel 25%)	5.65	24.0	↑
5 Pence 1990–99	Cupronickel (copper 75%; nickel 25%)	3.25	18.0	↑

Obverse 1 Head 1, right; ELIZABETH II D G REG F D (date)

Obverse 2 Head 2, right; same legend

Obverse 3 As Obverse 2 on smaller flan

Obverse 4 Head 3, right; same legend

Reverse 1 Crowned thistle, '5' below; NEW PENCE

Reverse 2 Similar but legend reads FIVE PENCE

Reverse 3 As Reverse 2 on smaller flan

Edge milled

Obv. 1

Obv. 2

Obv. 3

Obv.4

Rev. 1

Rev. 2

Rev. 3

24 mm diameter

No.	Date	Features	Obv.	Rev.	UNC
D05/68–1	1968	[1]	1	1	1
D05/69–1	1969		1	1	2
D05/70–1	1970		1	1	2
D05/71–1	1971		1	1	2
D05/71–3	1971	PROOF [2]	1	1	5
D05/72–3	1972	PROOF [2]	1	1	7
D05/73–3	1973	PROOF [2]	1	1	7
D05/74–3	1974	PROOF [2]	1	1	8
D05/75–1	1975		1	1	2
D05/75–3	1975	PROOF [2]	1	1	4
D05/76–3	1976	PROOF [2]	1	1	8
D05/77–1	1977		1	1	1

No.	Date	Features	Obv.	Rev.	UNC
D05/77-3	1977	PROOF [2]	1	1	4
D05/78-1	1978		1	1	2
D05/78-3	1978	PROOF [2]	1	1	10
D05/79-1	1979		1	1	2
D05/79-3	1979	PROOF [2]	1	1	4
D05/80-1	1980		1	1	2
D05/80-3	1980	PROOF [2]	1	1	4
D05/81-3	1981	PROOF [2]	1	1	7
D05/82-1	1982	[3]	1	2	7
D05/82-3	1982	PROOF [2]	1	2	7
D05/83-1	1983	[3]	1	2	7
D05/83-3	1983	PROOF [2]	1	2	7
D05/84-1	1984	[3]	1	2	5
D05/84-3	1984	PROOF [2]	1	2	6
D05/85-1	1985	[3]	2	2	4
D05/85-3	1985	PROOF [2]	2	2	5
D05/86-1	1986	[3]	2	2	3
D05/86-3	1986	PROOF [2]	2	2	4
D05/87-1	1987		2	2	3
D05/87-3	1987	PROOF [2]	2	2	4
D05/88-1	1988		2	2	3
D05/88-3	1988	PROOF [2]	2	2	4
D05/89-1	1989		2	2	3
D05/89-3	1989	PROOF [2]	2	2	4
D05/90-1L	1990	[3]	2	2	8
D05/90-3L	1990	PROOF [2]	2	2	8
D05/90-4L	1990	PROOF in silver [4]	2	2	20

1. Some issued in 1968 in decimal set wallets.
2. Issued in cased proof sets.
3. All issued in uncirculated sets in holders.
4. Issued cased.

18 mm diameter

No.	Date	Features	Obv.	Rev.	UNC
D05/90-1S	1990		3	3	1
D05/90-3S	1990	PROOF [1]	3	3	5
D05/90-4S	1990	PROOF in silver [2]	3	3	10
D05/90-5S	1990	PIEDFORT PROOF in silver [3]	3	3	40
D05/91-1	1991		3	3	1
D05/91-3	1991	PROOF [1]	3	3	5
D05/92-1	1992		3	3	1
D05/92-3	1992	PROOF [1]	3	3	6
D05/93-1	1993	[4]	3	3	3
D05/93-3	1993	PROOF [1]	3	3	7
D05/94-1	1994		3	3	3
D05/94-3	1994	PROOF [1]	3	3	4
D05/95-1	1995		3	3	1
D05/95-3	1995	PROOF [1]	3	3	4
D05/96-1	1996		3	3	1
D05/96-3	1996	PROOF [1]	3	3	4
D05/96-4	1996	PROOF in silver [1]	3	3	15
D05/97-1	1997		3	3	1
D05/97-3	1997	PROOF [1]	3	3	4
D05/98-1	1998		4	3	1
D05/98-3	1998	PROOF [1]	4	3	4
D05/99-1	1999		4	3	1
D05/99-3	1999	PROOF [1]	4	3	4

1. Issued in cased proof sets.
2. Issued cased.
3. Weight 6.5 grams; issued cased.
4. All issued in uncirculated sets in holders.

Minor changes in the milled edge were brought in during 1990 and 1991; coins of these two dates can be found with differing types of edge.

2 Pence

Although the bronze 2 pence coin had no legal tender status until decimal day in 1971, it was first issued to the public in 1968 in the official decimal sets in blue wallets. All of the bronze coins in this set were dated 1971.

In 1982, the words NEW PENCE on the reverse were replaced by TWO PENCE, but a few coins dated 1983 have been found with the earlier NEW PENCE legend; all were from specimen sets.

From 1992 the 2 pence was struck in steel which was subsequently plated with copper. These coins have a bright pink hue, and are slightly magnetic.

Denomination	Metal	Weight (grams)	Diameter (mm)	Rev. alignment
2 Pence 1971–92	Bronze	7.1	25.9	↑
2 Pence 1992–99	Copper-plated steel	7.1	25.9	↑

Obverse 1 Head 1, right; ELIZABETH II D G REG F D (date)

Obverse 2 Head 2, right; same legend

Obverse 3 Head 3, right; same legend

Reverse 1 Plumes within coronet (Badge of the Prince of Wales), '2' below; ICH DIEN (on ribbon); NEW PENCE

Reverse 2 Similar but TWO PENCE instead of NEW PENCE

Edge plain

Obv. 1   Obv. 2   Obv. 3

Rev. 1   Rev. 2

Bronze Issue

No.	Date	Features	Obv.	Rev.	UNC
D02/71-1	1971	[1]	1	1	1
D02/71-3	1971	PROOF [2]	1	1	4
D02/72-3	1972	PROOF [2]	1	1	6
D02/73-3	1973	PROOF [2]	1	1	7
D02/74-3	1974	PROOF [2]	1	1	7
D02/75-1	1975		1	1	2
D02/75-3	1975	PROOF [2]	1	1	4
D02/76-1	1976		1	1	2
D02/76-3	1976	PROOF [2]	1	1	4
D02/77-1	1977		1	1	1
D02/77-3	1977	PROOF [2]	1	1	3
D02/78-1	1978		1	1	4
D02/78-3	1978	PROOF [2]	1	1	5
D02/79-1	1979		1	1	1
D02/79-3	1979	PROOF [2]	1	1	3
D02/80-1	1980		1	1	1
D02/80-3	1980	PROOF [2]	1	1	3
D02/81-1	1981		1	1	1
D02/81-3	1981	PROOF [2]	1	1	3
D02/RR-1		[3]	rev. 1	1	150
D02/82-1	1982	[4]	1	2	7
D02/82-3	1982	PROOF [2]	1	2	4
D02/83-1E	1983	[5]	1	1	800
D02/83-1	1983	[4]	1	2	7
D02/83-3	1983	PROOF [2]	1	2	4

No.	Date	Features	Obv.	Rev.	UNC
D02/84–1	1984	[4]	1	2	3
D02/84–3	1984	PROOF [2]	1	2	5
D02/85–1	1985		2	2	1
D02/85–3	1985	PROOF [2]	2	2	4
D02/86–1	1986		2	2	1
D02/86–3	1986	PROOF [2]	2	2	4
D02/87–1	1987		2	2	1
D02/87–3	1987	PROOF [2]	2	2	4
D02/88–1	1988		2	2	1
D02/88–3	1988	PROOF [2]	2	2	4
D02/89–1	1989		2	2	1
D02/89–3	1989	PROOF [2]	2	2	4
D02/90–1	1990		2	2	1
D02/90–3	1990	PROOF [2]	2	2	4
D02/91–1	1991		2	2	1
D02/91–3	1991	PROOF [2]	2	2	4
D02/92–1BR	1992	[4]	2	2	6
D02/92–3	1992	PROOF [2]	2	2	6

1. Some issued in 1968 in decimal set wallets.
2. Issued in cased proof sets.
3. 'Double tailed' coin.
4. All issued in uncirculated sets in holders.
5. Error reverse; probably all issued in uncirculated sets in holders.

Copper Plated Steel Issue

No.	Date	Features	Obv.	Rev.	UNC
D02/92–1ST	1992		2	2	1
D02/93–1	1993		2	2	1
D02/93–3	1993	PROOF [1]	2	2	5
D02/94–1	1994		2	2	1
D02/94–3	1994	PROOF [1]	2	2	5
D02/95–1	1995		2	2	1
D02/95–3	1995	PROOF [1]	2	2	4
D02/96–1	1996		2	2	1
D02/96–3	1996	PROOF [1]	2	2	4
D02/96–4	1996	PROOF in silver [1]	2	2	12
D02/97–1	1997		2	2	1
D02/97–3	1997	PROOF [1]	2	2	4
D02/98–1	1998		3	2	1
D02/98–3	1998	PROOF [1]	3	2	4
D02/99–1	1999		3	2	1
D02/99–3	1999	PROOF [1]	3	2	4

1. Issued in cased proof sets.

Penny

As with the 2 pence and half penny coins, the decimal penny was issued in 1968 in decimal set wallets, but at that time had no legal tender status and the issue was all dated 1971.

From 1992 the penny was struck in steel which was subsequently plated with copper. These coins have a bright pink hue, and are slightly magnetic.

Since decimalization, many people seem to refer to this coin as 'one pence'. The correct term is still 'one penny'.

Denomination	Metal	Weight (grams)	Diameter (mm)	Rev. alignment
Penny 1971–92	Bronze	3.6	20.3	↑
Penny 1992–99	Copper-plated steel	3.6	20.3	↑

Obverse 1 Head 1, right; ELIZABETH II D G REG F D (date)

Obverse 2 Head 2, right; same legend

Obverse 3 Head 3, right; same legend

Reverse 1 Crowned portcullis, '1' below; NEW PENNY

Reverse 2 Similar but ONE PENNY instead of NEW PENNY

Edge plain

Obv. 1   Obv. 2   Obv. 3

Rev. 1   Rev. 2

Bronze Issue

No.	Date	Features	Obv.	Rev.	UNC
D01/71–1	1971	[1]	1	1	1
D01/71–3	1971	PROOF [2]	1	1	4
D01/72–3	1972	PROOF [2]	1	1	7
D01/73–1	1973		1	1	2
D01/73–3	1973	PROOF [2]	1	1	4
D01/74–1	1974		1	1	2
D01/74–3	1974	PROOF [2]	1	1	4
D01/75–1	1975		1	1	2
D01/75–3	1975	PROOF [2]	1	1	4
D01/76–1	1976		1	1	2
D01/76–3	1976	PROOF [2]	1	1	4
D01/77–1	1977		1	1	1
D01/77–3	1977	PROOF [2]	1	1	3
D01/78–1	1978		1	1	5
D01/78–3	1978	PROOF [2]	1	1	4
D01/79–1	1979		1	1	1
D01/79–3	1979	PROOF [2]	1	1	4
D01/80–1	1980		1	1	1
D01/80–3	1980	PROOF [2]	1	1	4
D01/81–1	1981		1	1	3
D01/81–3	1981	PROOF [2]	1	1	4
D01/82–1	1982		1	2	1
D01/82–3	1982	PROOF [2]	1	2	4
D01/83–1	1983		1	2	3
D01/83–3	1983	PROOF [2]	1	2	4
D01/84–1	1984		1	2	1
D01/84–3	1984	PROOF [2]	1	2	5
D01/85–1	1985		2	2	1
D01/85–3	1985	PROOF [2]	2	2	4
D01/86–1	1986		2	2	1
D01/86–3	1986	PROOF [2]	2	2	4
D01/87–1	1987		2	2	1
D01/87–3	1987	PROOF [2]	2	2	4
D01/88–1	1988		2	2	1

No.	Date	Features	Obv.	Rev.	UNC
D01/88–3	1988	PROOF [2]	2	2	4
D01/89–1	1989		2	2	1
D01/89–3	1989	PROOF [2]	2	2	4
D01/90–1	1990		2	2	1
D01/90–3	1990	PROOF [2]	2	2	4
D01/91–1	1991		2	2	1
D01/91–3	1991	PROOF [2]	2	2	4
D01/92–1BR	1992	[3]	2	2	6
D01/92–3	1992	PROOF [2]	2	2	6

1. Some issued in 1968 in decimal set wallets.
2. Issued in cased proof sets.
3. All issued in uncirculated sets in holders.

Copper Plated Steel Issue

No.	Date	Features	Obv.	Rev.	UNC
D01/92–1ST	1992		2	2	1
D01/93–1	1993		2	2	1
D01/93–3	1993	PROOF [1]	2	2	4
D01/94–1	1994		2	2	1
D01/94–3	1994	PROOF [1]	2	2	4
D01/95–1	1995		2	2	1
D01/95–3	1995	PROOF [1]	2	2	4
D01/96–1	1996		2	2	1
D01/96–3	1996	PROOF [1]	2	2	4
D01/96–4	1996	PROOF in silver [1]	2	2	12
D01/97–1	1997		2	2	1
D01/97–3	1997	PROOF [1]	2	2	4
D01/98–1	1998		3	2	1
D01/98–3	1998	PROOF [1]	3	2	4
D01/99–1	1999		3	2	1
D01/99–3	1999	PROOF [1]	3	2	4

1. Issued in cased proof sets.

Half Penny

As with the 2 pence and penny coins, the decimal halfpenny was issued in 1968 in decimal set wallets, but at that time had no legal tender status and the issue was all dated 1971.

The coin was not popular, being very small and also causing problems with electronic accounting systems, which began in the early 1970s. High inflation of the period soon made the halfpenny too trivial a coin to serve any useful function, and it was demonetised in 1984. No circulation pieces were issued that year, but some were struck for inclusion in official decimal sets.

Denomination	Metal	Weight (grams)	Diameter (mm)	Rev. alignment
Half Penny	Bronze	1.8	17	↑

Obverse 1 Head 1, right; ELIZABETH II D G REG F D (date)

Reverse 1 Crown, '1/2' below; NEW PENNY

Reverse 2 Similar but HALF PENNY instead of NEW PENNY

Edge plain

Obv. 1	Rev. 1	Rev. 2

No.	Date	Features	Obv.	Rev.	UNC
DHP/71–1	1971	[1]	1	1	1
DHP/71–1E	1971	[2]	1	obv. 1	200
DHP/71–3	1971	PROOF [3]	1	1	4
DHP/72–3	1972	PROOF [3]	1	1	7
DHP/73–1	1973		1	1	1
DHP/73–3	1973	PROOF [3]	1	1	5
DHP/74–1	1974		1	1	1
DHP/74–3	1974	PROOF [3]	1	1	4
DHP/75–1	1975		1	1	1
DHP/75–3	1975	PROOF [3]	1	1	4
DHP/76–1	1976		1	1	1
DHP/76–3	1976	PROOF [3]	1	1	4
DHP/77–1	1977		1	1	1
DHP/77–3	1977	PROOF [3]	1	1	3
DHP/78–1	1978		1	1	2
DHP/78–3	1978	PROOF [3]	1	1	5
DHP/79–1	1979		1	1	1
DHP/79–3	1979	PROOF [3]	1	1	4
DHP/80–1	1980		1	1	1
DHP/80–3	1980	PROOF [3]	1	1	4
DHP/81–1	1981		1	1	2
DHP/81–3	1981	PROOF [3]	1	1	4
DHP/82–1	1982		1	2	1
DHP/82–3	1982	PROOF [3]	1	2	4
DHP/83–1	1983		1	2	2
DHP/83–3	1983	PROOF [3]	1	2	4
DHP/84–1	1984	[4]	1	2	5
DHP/84–3	1984	PROOF	1	2	6

1. Some issued in 1968 in decimal set wallets.
2. 'Double headed' coin.
3. Issued in cased proof sets.
4. All issued in uncirculated sets in holders.

The decimal halfpenny was demonetised in December 1984.

Britannia Coinage

From 1987 a series of bullion gold issues was struck annually. The coins were denominated at 100, 50, 25 and 10 pounds, and contained respectively fine gold contents of 1, 1/2, 1/4 and 1/10th ounces. This closely followed the South African Krugerrand and fractional Krugerrand gold specifications, and, like the South African issues, the coins were struck in 22 carat gold, the actual weight of the coins being about 9.1% above the stated fine gold content.

The reverse of the Britannia series depicted an elegant portrayal of a standing Britannia, strongly reminiscent of the de Saulles engraving for the reverse of the Edward VII florin. Proofs of the coins were also struck annually, these generally being issued cased.

From 1997, a similar series of Britannia silver coinage was issued.

100 Pounds

Denomination	Metal	Weight (grams)	Diameter (mm)	Rev. alignment
100 Pounds	Gold	34.0	33	↑

Obverse 1 Head 1, right; ELIZABETH II DEI GRATIA REGINA FID DEF 100 POUNDS

Obverse 2 Head 2, right; ELIZABETH II D G REG FID DEF 100 POUNDS

Reverse 1 Britannia, standing, with trident and shield; ONE OUNCE FINE GOLD BRITANNIA (date)

Reverse 2 Britannia, standing, with trident, driving two horses and chariot; same legend.

Edge milled

Obv. 1   Rev. 1

No.	Date	Features	Obv.	Rev.	Unc
BR100–005	1987		1	1	BV
BR100–010	1987	PROOF	1	1	350
BR100–015	1988		1	1	BV
BR100–020	1988	PROOF	1	1	350
BR100–025	1989		1	1	BV
BR100–030	1989	PROOF	1	1	350
BR100–035	1990		1	1	BV
BR100–040	1990	PROOF	1	1	350
BR100–045	1991		1	1	BV
BR100–050	1991	PROOF	1	1	380
BR100–055	1992		1	1	BV
BR100–060	1992	PROOF	1	1	400
BR100–065	1993		1	1	BV
BR100–070	1993	PROOF	1	1	420
BR100–075	1994		1	1	BV
BR100–080	1994	PROOF	1	1	420
BR100–085	1995		1	1	BV
BR100–090	1995	PROOF	1	1	440
BR100–095	1996		1	1	BV
BR100–100	1996	PROOF	1	1	440
BR100–105	1997		1	2	BV
BR100–110	1997	PROOF	1	2	440
BR100–115	1998		2	1	BV
BR100–120	1998	PROOF	2	1	440

50 Pounds

Denomination	Metal	Weight (grams)	Diameter (mm)	Rev. alignment
50 Pounds	Gold	17.0	27	↑

Obverse 1 Head 1, right; ELIZABETH II DEI GRATIA REGINA FID DEF 50 POUNDS

Obverse 2 Head 2, right; ELIZABETH II D G REG FID DEF 50 POUNDS

Reverse 1 Britannia, standing, with trident and shield; 1/2 OUNCE FINE GOLD BRITANNIA (date)

Reverse 2 Britannia, standing, with trident, driving two horses and chariot; HALF OUNCE FINE GOLD BRITANNIA (date)

Edge milled

Obv. 1   Rev. 1

No.	Date	Features	Obv.	Rev.	Unc
BR50–005	1987		1	1	BV
BR50–010	1987	PROOF	1	1	180
BR50–015	1988		1	1	BV
BR50–020	1988	PROOF	1	1	180
BR50–025	1989		1	1	BV
BR50–030	1989	PROOF	1	1	190
BR50–035	1990		1	1	BV
BR50–040	1990	PROOF	1	1	200
BR50–045	1991		1	1	BV
BR50–050	1991	PROOF	1	1	200
BR50–055	1992		1	1	BV
BR50–060	1992	PROOF	1	1	220
BR50–065	1993		1	1	BV
BR50–070	1993	PROOF	1	1	240
BR50–075	1994		1	1	BV
BR50–080	1994	PROOF	1	1	240
BR50–085	1995		1	1	BV
BR50–090	1995	PROOF	1	1	250
BR50–095	1996		1	1	BV
BR50–100	1996	PROOF	1	1	250
BR50–105	1997		1	2	BV
BR50–110	1997	PROOF	1	2	250
BR50–115	1998		2	1	BV
BR50–120	1998	PROOF	2	1	250

25 Pounds

Denomination	Metal	Weight (grams)	Diameter (mm)	Rev. alignment
25 Pounds	Gold	8.5	22	↑

Obverse 1 Head 1, right; ELIZABETH II DEI GRATIA REGINA FID DEF 25 POUNDS

Obverse 2 Head 2, right; ELIZABETH II D G REG FID DEF 25 POUNDS

Reverse 1 Britannia, standing, with trident and shield; 1/4 OUNCE FINE GOLD BRITANNIA (date)

Reverse 2 Britannia, standing, with trident, driving two horses and chariot; QUARTER OUNCE FINE GOLD BRITANNIA (date)

Edge milled

Obv. 1   Rev. 1

No.	Date	Features	Obv.	Rev.	Unc
BR25–005	1987		1	1	BV
BR25–010	1987	PROOF	1	1	100
BR25–015	1988		1	1	BV
BR25–020	1988	PROOF	1	1	100
BR25–025	1989		1	1	BV
BR25–030	1989	PROOF	1	1	110.
BR25–035	1990		1	1	BV
BR25–040	1990	PROOF	1	1	120
BR25–045	1991		1	1	BV
BR25–050	1991	PROOF	1	1	120
BR25–055	1992		1	1	BV
BR25–060	1992	PROOF	1	1	130
BR25–065	1993		1	1	BV
BR25–070	1993	PROOF	1	1	130
BR25–075	1994		1	1	BV
BR25–080	1994	PROOF	1	1	130
BR25–085	1995		1	1	BV
BR25–090	1995	PROOF	1	1	130
BR25–095	1996		1	1	BV
BR25–100	1996	PROOF	1	1	130
BR25–105	1997		1	2	BV
BR25–110	1997	PROOF	1	2	130
BR25–115	1998		2	1	BV
BR25–120	1998	PROOF	2	1	130

10 Pounds

Denomination	Metal	Weight (grams)	Diameter (mm)	Rev. alignment
10 Pounds	Gold	3.4	16.5	↑

Obverse 1 Head 1, right; ELIZABETH II DEI GRATIA REGINA FID DEF 10 POUNDS

Obverse 2 Head 2, right; ELIZABETH II D G REG FID DEF 10 POUNDS

Reverse 1 Britannia, standing, with trident and shield; 1/10 OUNCE FINE GOLD BRITANNIA (date)

Reverse 2 Britannia, standing, with trident, driving two horses and chariot; TENTH OUNCE FINE GOLD BRITANNIA (date)

Edge milled

Obv. 1   Rev. 1

No.	Date	Features	Obv.	Rev.	Unc
BR10–005	1987		1	1	BV
BR10–010	1987	PROOF	1	1	55
BR10–015	1988		1	1	BV
BR10–020	1988	PROOF	1	1	55
BR10–025	1989		1	1	BV
BR10–030	1989	PROOF	1	1	60
BR10–035	1990		1	1	BV
BR10–040	1990	PROOF	1	1	60
BR10–045	1991		1	1	BV
BR10–050	1991	PROOF	1	1	65
BR10–055	1992		1	1	BV
BR10–060	1992	PROOF	1	1	65
BR10–065	1993		1	1	BV
BR10–070	1993	PROOF	1	1	65
BR10–075	1994		1	1	BV
BR10–080	1994	PROOF	1	1	70
BR10–085	1995		1	1	BV
BR10–090	1995	PROOF	1	1	70
BR10–095	1996		1	1	BV
BR10–100	1996	PROOF	1	1	70
BR10–105	1997		1	2	BV
BR10–110	1997	PROOF	1	2	70
BR10–115	1998		2	1	BV
BR10–120	1998	PROOF	2	1	70

2 Pounds

Denomination	Metal	Weight (grams)	Diameter (mm)	Rev. alignment
2 Pounds	0.958 Silver	32.4	40	↑

Obverse 1 Head 1, right; ELIZABETH II DEI GRATIA REGINA F D 2 POUNDS

Obverse 2 Head 2, right; ELIZABETH II D G REG FID DEF 2 POUNDS

Reverse 1 Britannia, standing, with trident, driving two horses and chariot; ONE OUNCE FINE SILVER BRITANNIA (date)

Reverse 2 Britannia, standing, with trident and shield; same legend

Edge milled

Obv. 1   Rev. 1

No.	Date	Features	Obv.	Rev.	Unc
BR02–005	1997		1	1	15
BR02–010	1997	PROOF	1	1	30
BR02–015	1998		2	2	15
BR02–020	1998	PROOF	2	2	30
BR02–025	1999		2	1	15
BR02–030	1999	PROOF	2	1	30

Pound

Denomination	Metal	Weight (grams)	Diameter (mm)	Rev. alignment
Pound	0.958 Silver	16.2	27	↑

Obverse 1 Head 1, right; ELIZABETH II DEI GRATIA REGINA F D ONE POUND

Obverse 2 Head 2, right; ELIZABETH II D G REG FID DEF ONE POUND

Reverse 1 Britannia, standing, with trident, driving two horses and chariot; HALF OUNCE FINE SILVER BRITANNIA (date)

Reverse 2 Britannia, standing, with trident and shield; 1/2 OUNCE FINE SILVER BRITANNIA (date)

Edge milled

Obv. 1   Rev. 1

No.	Date	Features	Obv.	Rev.	Unc
BR01–005	1997		1	1	10
BR01–010	1997	PROOF	1	1	20
BR01–015	1998		2	2	10
BR01–020	1998	PROOF	2	2	20
BR01–025	1999		2	1	10
BR01–030	1999	PROOF	2	1	20

50 Pence

Denomination	Metal	Weight (grams)	Diameter (mm)	Rev. alignment
50 Pence	0.958 Silver	8.1	22	↑

Obverse 1 Head 1, right; ELIZABETH II DEI GRATIA REGINA F D 50 PENCE

Obverse 2 Head 2, right; ELIZABETH II D G REG FID DEF 50 PENCE

Reverse 1 Britannia, standing, with trident, driving two horses and chariot; QUARTER OUNCE FINE SILVER BRITANNIA (date)

Reverse 2 Britannia, standing, with trident and shield; 1/4 OUNCE FINE SILVER BRITANNIA (date)

Edge milled

Obv. 1   Rev. 1

No.	Date	Features	Obv.	Rev.	Unc
BR50P-005	1997		1	1	8
BR50P-010	1997	PROOF	1	1	15
BR50P-015	1998		2	2	8
BR50P-020	1998	PROOF	2	2	15
BR50P-025	1999		2	1	8
BR50P-030	1999	PROOF	2	1	15

20 Pence

Denomination	Metal	Weight (grams)	Diameter (mm)	Rev. alignment
20 Pence	0.958 Silver	3.2	16.5	↑

Obverse 1 Head 1, right; ELIZABETH II DEI GRATIA REGINA F D 20 PENCE

Obverse 2 Head 2, right; ELIZABETH II D G REG FID DEF 20 PENCE

Reverse 1 Britannia, standing, with trident, driving two horses and chariot; TENTH OUNCE FINE SILVER BRITANNIA (date)

Reverse 2 Britannia, standing, with trident and shield; 1/10 OUNCE FINE SILVER BRITANNIA (date)

Edge milled

Obv. 1   Rev. 1

No.	Date	Features	Obv.	Rev.	Unc
BR20P-005	1997		1	1	6
BR20P-010	1997	PROOF	1	1	12
BR20P-015	1998		2	2	6
BR20P-020	1998	PROOF	2	2	12
BR20P-025	1999		2	1	6
BR20P-030	1999	PROOF	2	1	12

Proof Sets

From time to time over the last 200 years or so coins have been issued as sets in cases rather than individually for circulation. In recent times several such sets have been issued by the Royal Mint each year as a commercial exercise, but in the early years the sets were issued by the Mint or by the engravers, usually at the time of a change of monarch or when the design of the coinage underwent a radical revision. These earlier sets were invariably specially struck proofs, but in recent times the issues have been supplemented by sets of specimen or ordinary coinage, usually in card holders.

The listings below include the conventional issues but omit some of the isolated rare proofs such as the 1877 three-coin bronze set or the 1879 silver set. Also omitted are the somewhat contrived 'sets' spanning several years issued by the Royal Mint.

The numbering system for cased sets consists of a prefix PS or (for decimal) DPS for proof sets and MS or DMS for mint sets; a suffix of the last two digits of the date or, in the case of sets before 1902, the four digits of the date; an optional suffix allocated on an ad hoc basis to distinguish different types of set of the same date.

George II   (1727 – 1760)

1746

No.	Date	Striking Standard	No. of Coins	Price
PS-1746	1746	Proof [1]	4	10000

1. Issued in wedge shaped case.

Denomination	Metal
Crown	Silver
Halfcrown	Silver
Shilling	Silver
Sixpence	Silver

George IV   (1820 – 1830)

1826

No.	Date	Striking Standard	No. of Coins	Price
PS-1826	1826	Proof [1]	11	22000

1. Issued in oval case; probably about 150 struck.

Denomination	Metal
5 Pounds	Gold
2 Pounds	Gold
Sovereign	Gold
Half Sovereign	Gold
Crown	Silver
Halfcrown	Silver
Shilling	Silver
Sixpence	Silver
Penny	Copper
Halfpenny	Copper
Farthing	Copper

William IV   (1830 – 1837)

1831

No.	Date	Striking Standard	No. of Coins	Price
PS-1831	1831	Proof [1]	14	22000

1. Issued in round case.

Denomination	Metal
2 Pounds	Gold
Sovereign	Gold
Half Sovereign	Gold
Crown	Silver
Halfcrown	Silver
Shilling	Silver
Sixpence	Silver
Maundy set	Silver
Penny	Copper
Halfpenny	Copper
Farthing	Copper

Victoria   (1837 – 1901)

1839

No.	Date	Striking Standard	No. of Coins	Price
PS-1839	1839	Proof [1]	15	30000

1. Issued in spade-shaped case.

Denomination	Metal
5 Pounds	Gold
Sovereign	Gold
Half Sovereign	Gold
Crown	Silver
Halfcrown	Silver
Shilling	Silver
Sixpence	Silver
Groat	Silver
Maundy set	Silver
Penny	Copper
Halfpenny	Copper
Farthing	Copper

1853

No.	Date	Striking Standard	No. of Coins	Price
PS-1853	1853	Proof [1]	16	25000

1. A small number of sets exist with additional proof penny, halfpenny and farthing of 1862 (total 19 coins).

Denomination	Metal
Sovereign	Gold
Half Sovereign	Gold
Crown	Silver
Halfcrown	Silver
Florin	Silver
Shilling	Silver
Sixpence	Silver
Groat	Silver
Maundy set	Silver
Penny	Copper
Halfpenny	Copper
Farthing	Copper
Half Farthing	Copper

1877

No.	Date	Striking Standard	No. of Coins	Price
PS-1877	1877	Proof	3	2500

Denomination	Metal
Penny	Bronze
Halfpenny	Bronze
Farthing	Bronze

1887

No.	Date	Striking Standard	No. of Coins	Price
PS-1887L	1887	Proof	11	6500

Denomination	Metal
5 Pounds	Gold
2 Pounds	Gold
Sovereign	Gold
Half Sovereign	Gold
Crown	Silver
Double Florin	Silver

Denomination	Metal
Halfcrown	Silver
Florin	Silver
Shilling	Silver
Sixpence	Silver
Threepence	Silver

No.	Date	Striking Standard	No. of Coins	Price
PS-1887S	1887	Proof	7	1300

Denomination	Metal
Crown	Silver
Double Florin	Silver
Halfcrown	Silver
Florin	Silver
Shilling	Silver
Sixpence	Silver
Threepence	Silver

1893

No.	Date	Striking Standard	No. of Coins	Price
PS-1893L	1893	Proof	10	7000

Denomination	Metal
5 Pounds	Gold
2 Pounds	Gold
Sovereign	Gold
Half Sovereign	Gold
Crown	Silver
Halfcrown	Silver
Florin	Silver
Shilling	Silver
Sixpence	Silver
Threepence	Silver

No.	Date	Striking Standard	No. of Coins	Price
PS-1893S	1893	Proof	6	1400

Denomination	Metal
Crown	Silver
Halfcrown	Silver
Florin	Silver
Shilling	Silver
Sixpence	Silver
Threepence	Silver

Edward VII   (1901 – 1910)

1902

No.	Date	Striking Standard	No. of Coins	Price
PS-02L	1902	Matt Proof [1]	13	1800

1. 8066 issued in red leatherette case.

Denomination	Metal
5 Pounds	Gold
2 Pounds	Gold
Sovereign	Gold
Half Sovereign	Gold
Crown	Silver
Halfcrown	Silver
Florin	Silver
Shilling	Silver
Sixpence	Silver
Maundy set	Silver

No.	Date	Striking Standard	No. of Coins	Price
PS-02S	1902	Matt Proof [1]	11	600

1. 7057 issued in red leatherette case.

Denomination	Metal
Sovereign	Gold
Half Sovereign	Gold
Crown	Silver
Halfcrown	Silver
Florin	Silver
Shilling	Silver
Sixpence	Silver
Maundy set	Silver

George V   (1910 – 1936)

1911

No.	Date	Striking Standard	No. of Coins	Price
PS-11L	1911	Proof [1]	12	3000

1. Maundy set does not have proof surface but rim of 4d slightly different from that on standard Maundy set; 2812 issued in red leatherette case.

Denomination	Metal
5 Pounds	Gold
2 Pounds	Gold
Sovereign	Gold
Half Sovereign	Gold
Halfcrown	Silver
Florin	Silver
Shilling	Silver
Sixpence	Silver
Maundy set	Silver

No.	Date	Striking Standard	No. of Coins	Price
PS-11SH	1911	Proof [1]	10	900

1. Maundy set does not have proof surface but rim of 4d slightly different from that on standard Maundy set; 952 issued in red leatherette case.

Denomination	Metal
Sovereign	Gold
Half Sovereign	Gold
Halfcrown	Silver
Florin	Silver
Shilling	Silver
Sixpence	Silver
Maundy set	Silver

No.	Date	Striking Standard	No. of Coins	Price
PS-11SV	1911	Proof [1]	8	450

1. Maundy set does not have proof surface but rim of 4d slightly different from that on standard Maundy set; 2241 issued in red leatherette case (a few in a card box).

Denomination	Metal
Halfcrown	Silver
Florin	Silver
Shilling	Silver
Sixpence	Silver
Maundy set	Silver

1927

No.	Date	Striking Standard	No. of Coins	Price
PS-27	1927	Proof or Prooflike [1]	6	250
PS-27SB	1927	as above; struck from sandblasted dies [2]	6	1500

1. 5 of the 6 coins are proof only issues; 15030 issued in red leatherette case or card box.
2. As above; struck to facilitate photography of coin.

Denomination	Metal
Crown	0.500 Silver
Halfcrown	0.500 Silver
Florin	0.500 Silver
Shilling	0.500 Silver
Sixpence	0.500 Silver
Threepence	0.500 Silver

George VI   (1937 – 1952)

1937

No.	Date	Striking Standard	No. of Coins	Price
PS-37G	1937	Proof [1]	4	1800

1. 5501 issued in red leatherette case.

Denomination	Metal
5 Pounds	Gold
2 Pounds	Gold
Sovereign	Gold
Half Sovereign	Gold

No.	Date	Striking Standard	No. of Coins	Price
PS-37S	1937	Proof [1]	15	200
PS-37SSB	1937	Proof struck from sandblasted dies [2]	15	1500

1. 26402 issued in red leatherette case or card box.
2. As above; struck to facilitate photography of coin.

Denomination	Metal
Crown	0.500 Silver
Halfcrown	0.500 Silver
Florin	0.500 Silver
Scottish Shilling	0.500 Silver
English Shilling	0.500 Silver
Sixpence	0.500 Silver
Maundy set	0.500 Silver
Threepence	0.500 Silver
Threepence	Nickel-brass
Penny	Bronze
Halfpenny	Bronze
Farthing	Bronze

No.	Date	Striking Standard	No. of Coins	Price
PS-37B	1937	Proof [1]	4	500

1. Issued in octagonal red leatherette case.

Denomination	Metal
Threepence	Nickel-brass
Penny	Bronze
Halfpenny	Bronze
Farthing	Bronze

1950

No.	Date	Striking Standard	No. of Coins	Price
PS-50	1950	Proof [1]	9	75
PS-50SB	1950	Proof struck from sandblasted dies [2]	9	1500

1. 17513 issued in red box.
2. As above; struck to facilitate photography of coin.

Denomination	Metal
Halfcrown	Cupronickel
Florin	Cupronickel
Scottish Shilling	Cupronickel
English Shilling	Cupronickel
Sixpence	Cupronickel
Threepence	Nickel-brass
Penny	Bronze
Halfpenny	Bronze
Farthing	Bronze

1951

No.	Date	Striking Standard	No. of Coins	Price
PS-51	1951	Proof [1]	10	100
PS-51SB	1951	Proof struck from sandblasted dies [2]	10	1500

1. 20000 issued in maroon, green or blue card box.
2. As above; struck to facilitate photography of coin.

Denomination	Metal
Crown	Cupronickel
Halfcrown	Cupronickel
Florin	Cupronickel
Scottish Shilling	Cupronickel
English Shilling	Cupronickel
Sixpence	Cupronickel
Threepence	Nickel-brass
Penny	Bronze
Halfpenny	Bronze
Farthing	Bronze

Elizabeth II   (1952 –)

1953

No.	Date	Striking Standard	No. of Coins	Price
PS-53	1953	Proof [1]	10	70
PS-53SB	1953	Proof struck from sandblasted dies [2]	10	1500

1. 40000 issued in maroon leatherette case. A very small number are in a dark blue case.
2. As above; struck to facilitate photography of coin.

Denomination	Metal
Crown	Cupronickel
Halfcrown	Cupronickel
Florin	Cupronickel
Scottish Shilling	Cupronickel
English Shilling	Cupronickel
Sixpence	Cupronickel
Threepence	Nickel-brass
Penny	Bronze
Halfpenny	Bronze
Farthing	Bronze

1970

No.	Date	Striking Standard	No. of Coins	Price
PS-70	1970	Proof [1]	8	18

1. Issued in hard plastic holder with outer maroon card cover.

Denomination	Metal
Halfcrown	Cupronickel
Florin	Cupronickel
Scottish Shilling	Cupronickel
English Shilling	Cupronickel
Sixpence	Cupronickel
Threepence	Nickel-brass
Penny	Bronze
Halfpenny	Bronze

1971

No.	Date	Striking Standard	No. of Coins	Price
DPS-71	1971	Proof [1]	6	15

1. Issued in hard plastic holder with outer black card cover.

Denomination	Metal
50 Pence	Cupronickel
10 Pence	Cupronickel
5 Pence	Cupronickel
2 Pence	Bronze
1 Penny	Bronze
Halfpenny	Bronze

1972

No.	Date	Striking Standard	No. of Coins	Price
DPS-72	1972	Proof [1]	7	18

1. Issued in hard plastic holder with outer dark blue card cover.

Denomination	Metal
50 Pence	Cupronickel
25 Pence	Cupronickel
10 Pence	Cupronickel
5 Pence	Cupronickel
2 Pence	Bronze
1 Penny	Bronze
Halfpenny	Bronze

1973

No.	Date	Striking Standard	No. of Coins	Price
DPS-73	1973	Proof [1]	6	15

1. Issued in hard plastic holder with outer red card cover.

Denomination	Metal
50 Pence	Cupronickel
10 Pence	Cupronickel
5 Pence	Cupronickel
2 Pence	Bronze
1 Penny	Bronze
Halfpenny	Bronze

1974

No.	Date	Striking Standard	No. of Coins	Price
DPS-74	1974	Proof [1]	6	15

1. Issued in hard plastic holder with outer brown card cover.

Denomination	Metal
50 Pence	Cupronickel
10 Pence	Cupronickel
5 Pence	Cupronickel
2 Pence	Bronze
1 Penny	Bronze
Halfpenny	Bronze

1975

No.	Date	Striking Standard	No. of Coins	Price
DPS-75	1975	Proof [1]	6	15

1. Issued in hard plastic holder with outer green card cover.

Denomination	Metal
50 Pence	Cupronickel
10 Pence	Cupronickel
5 Pence	Cupronickel
2 Pence	Bronze
1 Penny	Bronze
Halfpenny	Bronze

1976

No.	Date	Striking Standard	No. of Coins	Price
DPS-76	1976	Proof [1]	6	15

1. Issued in hard plastic holder with outer grey card cover.

Denomination	Metal
50 Pence	Cupronickel
10 Pence	Cupronickel
5 Pence	Cupronickel
2 Pence	Bronze
1 Penny	Bronze
Halfpenny	Bronze

1977

No.	Date	Striking Standard	No. of Coins	Price
DPS-77	1977	Proof [1]	7	18

1. Issued in hard plastic holder with outer blue card cover.

Denomination	Metal
50 Pence	Cupronickel
25 Pence	Cupronickel
10 Pence	Cupronickel
5 Pence	Cupronickel
2 Pence	Bronze
1 Penny	Bronze
Halfpenny	Bronze

1978

No.	Date	Striking Standard	No. of Coins	Price
DPS-78	1978	Proof [1]	6	20

1. Issued in hard plastic holder with outer brown card cover.

Denomination	Metal
50 Pence	Cupronickel
10 Pence	Cupronickel
5 Pence	Cupronickel
2 Pence	Bronze
1 Penny	Bronze
Halfpenny	Bronze

1979

No.	Date	Striking Standard	No. of Coins	Price
DPS-79	1979	Proof [1]	6	15

1. Issued in hard plastic holder with outer slate blue card cover.

Denomination	Metal
50 Pence	Cupronickel
10 Pence	Cupronickel
5 Pence	Cupronickel
2 Pence	Bronze
1 Penny	Bronze
Halfpenny	Bronze

1980

No.	Date	Striking Standard	No. of Coins	Price
DPS-80GL	1980	Proof [1]	4	1000

1. Issued in green leatherette case.

Denomination	Metal
5 Pounds	Gold
2 Pounds	Gold
Sovereign	Gold
Half Sovereign	Gold

No.	Date	Striking Standard	No. of Coins	Price
DPS-80	1980	Proof [1]	6	16

1. Issued in hard plastic holder with outer purple card cover.

Denomination	Metal
50 Pence	Cupronickel
10 Pence	Cupronickel
5 Pence	Cupronickel
2 Pence	Bronze
1 Penny	Bronze
Halfpenny	Bronze

1981

No.	Date	Striking Standard	No. of Coins	Price
DPS-81G	1981	Proof [1]	9	700

1. Issued in red leatherette case.

Denomination	Metal
5 Pounds	Gold
Sovereign	Gold
50 Pence	Cupronickel
25 Pence	Cupronickel
10 Pence	Cupronickel
5 Pence	Cupronickel
2 Pence	Bronze
1 Penny	Bronze
Halfpenny	Bronze

No.	Date	Striking Standard	No. of Coins	Price
DPS-81	1981	Proof [1]	6	16

1. Issued in hard plastic holder with outer black card cover.

Denomination	Metal
50 Pence	Cupronickel
10 Pence	Cupronickel
5 Pence	Cupronickel
2 Pence	Bronze
1 Penny	Bronze
Halfpenny	Bronze

1982

No.	Date	Striking Standard	No. of Coins	Price
DPS-82G	1982	Proof [1]	4	1000

1. Issued in dark blue leatherette case.

Denomination	Metal
5 Pounds	Gold
2 Pounds	Gold
Sovereign	Gold
Half Sovereign	Gold

No.	Date	Striking Standard	No. of Coins	Price
DPS-82	1982	Proof [1]	7	16

1. Issued in hard plastic holder with outer blue card cover.

Denomination	Metal
50 Pence	Cupronickel
20 Pence	Cupronickel
10 Pence	Cupronickel
5 Pence	Cupronickel
2 Pence	Bronze
1 Penny	Bronze
Halfpenny	Bronze

1983

No.	Date	Striking Standard	No. of Coins	Price
DPS-83G	1983	Proof [1]	3	450

1. Issued in brown leatherette case.

Denomination	Metal
2 Pounds	Gold
Sovereign	Gold
Half Sovereign	Gold

No.	Date	Striking Standard	No. of Coins	Price
DPS-83	1983	Proof [1]	8	30

1. Issued in hard plastic and dark blue leatherette case.

Denomination	Metal
1 Pound	Nickel-brass
50 Pence	Cupronickel
20 Pence	Cupronickel
10 Pence	Cupronickel
5 Pence	Cupronickel

2 Pence	Bronze			
1 Penny	Bronze			
Halfpenny	Bronze			

1984

No.	Date	Striking Standard	No. of Coins	Price
DPS-84G	1984	Proof [1]	3	750

1. Issued in leatherette case.

Denomination	Metal
5 Pounds	Gold
Sovereign	Gold
Half Sovereign	Gold

No.	Date	Striking Standard	No. of Coins	Price
DPS-84	1984	Proof [1]	8	30

1. Issued in hard plastic and dark blue leatherette case.

Denomination	Metal
1 Pound	Nickel-brass
50 Pence	Cupronickel
20 Pence	Cupronickel
10 Pence	Cupronickel
5 Pence	Cupronickel
2 Pence	Bronze
1 Penny	Bronze
Halfpenny	Bronze

1985

No.	Date	Striking Standard	No. of Coins	Price
DPS-85G	1985	Proof [1]	4	1000

1. Issued in leatherette case.

Denomination	Metal
5 Pounds	Gold
2 Pounds	Gold
Sovereign	Gold
Half Sovereign	Gold

No.	Date	Striking Standard	No. of Coins	Price
DPS-85DL	1985	Proof [1]	7	28
DPS-85	1985	Proof [2]	7	24

1. Issued in hard plastic and red leatherette case.
2. Issued in hard plastic and dark blue leatherette case.

Denomination	Metal
1 Pound	Nickel-brass
50 Pence	Cupronickel
20 Pence	Cupronickel
10 Pence	Cupronickel
5 Pence	Cupronickel
2 Pence	Bronze
1 Penny	Bronze

1986

No.	Date	Striking Standard	No. of Coins	Price
DPS-86G	1986	Proof [1]	3	450

1. Issued in red leatherette case.

Denomination	Metal
2 Pounds	Gold
Sovereign	Gold
Half Sovereign	Gold

No.	Date	Striking Standard	No. of Coins	Price
DPS-86DL	1986	Proof [1]	8	30
DPS-86	1986	Proof [2]	8	26

1. Issued in hard plastic and red leatherette case.
2. Issued in hard plastic and dark blue leatherette case.

Denomination	Metal
2 Pounds	Nickel-brass
1 Pound	Nickel-brass
50 Pence	Cupronickel
20 Pence	Cupronickel
10 Pence	Cupronickel
5 Pence	Cupronickel
2 Pence	Bronze
1 Penny	Bronze

1987

No.	Date	Striking Standard	No. of Coins	Price
DPS-87BRL	1987	Proof [1]	4	800

1. Issued in black leatherette case.

Denomination	Metal
100 Pounds	Gold
50 Pounds	Gold
25 Pounds	Gold
10 Pounds	Gold

No.	Date	Striking Standard	No. of Coins	Price
DPS-87BRS	1987	Proof [1]	2	200

1. Issued in brown leatherette case.

Denomination	Metal
25 Pounds	Gold
10 Pounds	Gold

No.	Date	Striking Standard	No. of Coins	Price
DPS-87G	1987	Proof [1]	3	450

1. Issued in red leatherette case.

Denomination	Metal
2 Pounds	Gold
Sovereign	Gold
Half Sovereign	Gold

No.	Date	Striking Standard	No. of Coins	Price
DPS-87DL	1987	Proof [1]	7	32
DPS-87	1987	Proof [2]	7	28

1. Issued in hard plastic and red leatherette case.
2. Issued in hard plastic and dark blue leatherette case.

Denomination	Metal
1 Pound	Nickel-brass
50 Pence	Cupronickel
20 Pence	Cupronickel
10 Pence	Cupronickel
5 Pence	Cupronickel
2 Pence	Bronze
1 Penny	Bronze

1984–1987

No.	Date	Striking Standard	No. of Coins	Price
DPS-84PFP	1984–87	Piedfort Proof [1]	4	240

1. Issued in black leatherette case.

Denomination	Metal
Pound 1984	Silver
Pound 1985	Silver
Pound 1986	Silver
Pound 1987	Silver

No.	Date	Striking Standard	No. of Coins	Price
DPS-84PP	1984–87	Proof [1]	4	120

1. Issued in red leatherette case.

Denomination	Metal
Pound 1984	Silver
Pound 1985	Silver
Pound 1986	Silver
Pound 1987	Silver

1988

No.	Date	Striking Standard	No. of Coins	Price
DPS-88BRL	1988	Proof [1]	4	800

1. Issued in leatherette case.

Denomination	Metal
100 Pounds	Gold
50 Pounds	Gold
25 Pounds	Gold
10 Pounds	Gold

No.	Date	Striking Standard	No. of Coins	Price
DPS-88BRS	1988	Proof [1]	2	200

1. Issued in leatherette case.

Denomination	Metal
25 Pounds	Gold
10 Pounds	Gold

No.	Date	Striking Standard	No. of Coins	Price
DPS-88G	1988	Proof [1]	3	450

1. Issued in blue leatherette case.

Denomination	Metal
2 Pounds	Gold
Sovereign	Gold
Half Sovereign	Gold

No.	Date	Striking Standard	No. of Coins	Price
DPS-88DL	1988	Proof [1]	7	32
DPS-88	1988	Proof [2]	7	28

1. Issued in hard plastic and red leatherette case.
2. Issued in hard plastic and dark blue leatherette case.

Denomination	Metal
1 Pound	Nickel-brass
50 Pence	Cupronickel

Denomination	Metal
20 Pence	Cupronickel
10 Pence	Cupronickel
5 Pence	Cupronickel
2 Pence	Bronze
1 Penny	Bronze

1989

No.	Date	Striking Standard	No. of Coins	Price
DPS-89BRL	1989	Proof [1]	4	900

1. Issued in leatherette case.

Denomination	Metal
100 Pounds	Gold
50 Pounds	Gold
25 Pounds	Gold
10 Pounds	Gold

No.	Date	Striking Standard	No. of Coins	Price
DPS-89BRS	1989	Proof [1]	2	240

1. Issued in leatherette case.

Denomination	Metal
25 Pounds	Gold
10 Pounds	Gold

No.	Date	Striking Standard	No. of Coins	Price
DPS-89GL	1989	Proof [1]	4	1100

1. For the 500th anniversary of the gold sovereign; issued in black leatherette case.

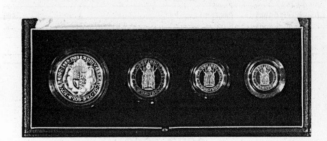

Denomination	Metal
5 Pounds	Gold
Double Sovereign	Gold
Sovereign	Gold
Half Sovereign	Gold

No.	Date	Striking Standard	No. of Coins	Price
DPS-89GS	1989	Proof [1]	3	550

1. For the 500th anniversary of the gold sovereign; issued in leatherette case.

Denomination	Metal
Double Sovereign	Gold
Sovereign	Gold
Half Sovereign	Gold

No.	Date	Striking Standard	No. of Coins	Price
DPS-89DL	1989	Proof [1]	9	40
DPS-89	1989	Proof [2]	9	35

1. Issued in hard plastic and red leatherette case.
2. Issued in hard plastic and dark blue leatherette case.

Denomination	Metal
2 Pounds (Bill of Rights)	Nickel-brass
2 Pounds (Claim of Right)	Nickel-brass
1 Pound	Nickel-brass
50 Pence	Cupronickel
20 Pence	Cupronickel
10 Pence	Cupronickel
5 Pence	Cupronickel
2 Pence	Bronze
1 Penny	Bronze

No.	Date	Striking Standard	No. of Coins	Price
DPS-89PF2P	1989	Piedfort Proof [1]	2	100
DPS-89P2P	1989	Proof [2]	2	50

1. 10000 issued in brown leatherette case.
2. 25000 issued in blue leatherette case.

Denomination	Metal
2 Pound	Silver
2 Pound	Silver

1983–1989

No.	Date	Striking Standard	No. of Coins	Price
DPS-83PFP	1983–89	Piedfort Proof [1]	7	600

1. 500 sets issued in black leatherette case.

Denomination	Metal
Pound 1983	Silver
Pound 1984	Silver
Pound 1985	Silver
Pound 1986	Silver
Pound 1987	Silver
Pound 1988	Silver
Pound 1989	Silver

1990

No.	Date	Striking Standard	No. of Coins	Price
DPS-90BR	1990	Proof [1]	4	900

1. Issued in leatherette case.

Denomination	Metal
100 Pounds	Gold
50 Pounds	Gold
25 Pounds	Gold
10 Pounds	Gold

No.	Date	Striking Standard	No. of Coins	Price
DPS-90GL	1990	Proof [1]	4	1000

1. Issued in red leatherette case.

Denomination	Metal
5 Pounds	Gold
2 Pounds	Gold
Sovereign	Gold
Half Sovereign	Gold

No.	Date	Striking Standard	No. of Coins	Price
DPS-90GS	1990	Proof [1]	3	520

1. Issued in red leatherette case.

Denomination	Metal
2 Pounds	Gold
Sovereign	Gold
Half Sovereign	Gold

No.	Date	Striking Standard	No. of Coins	Price
DPS-90DL	1990	Proof [1]	8	40
DPS-90	1990	Proof [2]	8	35

1. Issued in hard plastic and red leatherette case.
2. Issued in hard plastic and dark blue leatherette case.

Denomination	Metal
1 Pound	Nickel-brass
50 Pence	Cupronickel
20 Pence	Cupronickel
10 Pence	Cupronickel
5 Pence (on 24mm flan)	Cupronickel
5 Pence (on 18mm flan)	Cupronickel
2 Pence	Bronze
1 Penny	Bronze

No.	Date	Striking Standard	No. of Coins	Price
DPS-90–05	1990	Proof [1]	2	30

1. 35000 issued in red case.

Denomination	Metal
5 Pence	Silver
5 Pence	Silver

1991

No.	Date	Striking Standard	No. of Coins	Price
DPS-91BR	1991	Proof [1]	4	900

1. Issued in leatherette case.

Denomination	Metal
100 Pounds	Gold
50 Pounds	Gold
25 Pounds	Gold
10 Pounds	Gold

No.	Date	Striking Standard	No. of Coins	Price
DPS-91GL	1991	Proof [1]	4	1000

1. Issued in red leatherette case.

Denomination	Metal
5 Pounds	Gold
2 Pounds	Gold
Sovereign	Gold
Half Sovereign	Gold

No.	Date	Striking Standard	No. of Coins	Price
DPS-91GS	1991	Proof [1]	3	550

1. Issued in leatherette case.

Denomination	Metal
2 Pounds	Gold
Sovereign	Gold
Half Sovereign	Gold

No.	Date	Striking Standard	No. of Coins	Price
DPS-91DL	1991	Proof [1]	7	40
DPS-91	1991	Proof [2]	7	35

1. Issued in hard plastic and red leatherette case.
2. Issued in hard plastic and dark blue leatherette case.

Denomination	Metal
1 Pound	Nickel-brass
50 Pence	Cupronickel
20 Pence	Cupronickel
10 Pence	Cupronickel
5 Pence	Cupronickel
2 Pence	Bronze
1 Penny	Bronze

1992

No.	Date	Striking Standard	No. of Coins	Price
DPS-92BR	1992	Proof [1]	4	1000

1. Issued in leatherette case.

Denomination	Metal
100 Pounds	Gold
50 Pounds	Gold
25 Pounds	Gold
10 Pounds	Gold

No.	Date	Striking Standard	No. of Coins	Price
DPS-92GL	1992	Proof [1]	4	1000

1. Issued in red leatherette case.

Denomination	Metal
5 Pounds	Gold
2 Pounds	Gold
Sovereign	Gold
Half Sovereign	Gold

No.	Date	Striking Standard	No. of Coins	Price
DPS-92GS	1992	Proof [1]	3	580

1. Issued in leatherette case.

Denomination	Metal
2 Pounds	Gold
Sovereign	Gold
Half Sovereign	Gold

No.	Date	Striking Standard	No. of Coins	Price
DPS-92DL	1992	Proof [1]	9	38
DPS-92	1992	Proof [2]	9	32

1. Issued in hard plastic and red leatherette case.
2. Issued in hard plastic and dark blue leatherette case; at least one set contains two regular issue (non-EEC) Proof 50 pence coins in error.

Denomination	Metal
1 Pound	Nickel-brass
50 Pence (regular issue)	Cupronickel
50 Pence (EEC issue)	Cupronickel
20 Pence	Cupronickel
10 Pence (on 28.5 mm flan)	Cupronickel
10 Pence (on 24.5mm flan)	Cupronickel
5 Pence	Cupronickel
2 Pence	Bronze
1 Penny	Bronze

No.	Date	Striking Standard	No. of Coins	Price
DPS-92-10	1992	Proof [1]	2	30

1. 35000 issued in blue case.

Denomination	Metal
10 Pence	Silver
10 Pence	Silver

1992 1993

No.	Date	Striking Standard	No. of Coins	Price
DPS-92-50	1992–93 double dated coin	Proof & Piedfort Proof [1]	2	200

1. Issued in red case.

Denomination	Metal
Piedfort proof 50 pence (Single Market issue)	Silver
Proof 50 pence (Single Market issue)	Silver

No.	Date	Striking Standard	No. of Coins	Price
DPS-92A	1992–93	Proof [1]	3	100

1. 1000 issued in blue case.

Denomination	Metal
5 Pounds 1993	Silver
Pound 1993	Silver
50 Pence 1992–93	Silver

1993

No.	Date	Striking Standard	No. of Coins	Price
DPS-93BR	1993	Proof [1]	4	1000

1. Issued in leatherette case.

Denomination	Metal
100 Pounds	Gold
50 Pounds	Gold
25 Pounds	Gold
10 Pounds	Gold

No.	Date	Striking Standard	No. of Coins	Price
DPS-93GL	1993	Proof [1]	4	1000

1. 1250 issued in purple leatherette case.

Denomination	Metal
5 Pounds	Gold
2 Pounds	Gold
Sovereign	Gold
Half Sovereign	Gold

No.	Date	Striking Standard	No. of Coins	Price
DPS-93GS	1993	Proof [1]	3	550

1. 1250 issued in red leatherette case.

Denomination	Metal
2 Pounds	Gold
Sovereign	Gold
Half Sovereign	Gold

No.	Date	Striking Standard	No. of Coins	Price
DPS-93DL	1993	Proof [1]	8	60
DPS-93	1993	Proof [2]	8	50

1. Issued in hard plastic and red leatherette case.
2. Issued in hard plastic and dark blue leatherette case.

Denomination	Metal
5 Pounds	Cupronickel
1 Pound	Nickel-brass
50 Pence	Cupronickel
20 Pence	Cupronickel
10 Pence	Cupronickel
5 Pence	Cupronickel
2 Pence	Copper-plated steel
1 Penny	Copper-plated steel

No.	Date	Striking Standard	No. of Coins	Price
DPS-93A	1993	Proof [1]	2	200

1. 500 issued in green case.

Denomination	Metal
Sovereign	Gold
1 Pound	Silver

1994

No.	Date	Striking Standard	No. of Coins	Price
DPS-94BR	1994	Proof [1]	4	1150

1. Issued in leatherette case.

Denomination	Metal
100 Pounds	Gold
50 Pounds	Gold
25 Pounds	Gold
10 Pounds	Gold

No.	Date	Striking Standard	No. of Coins	Price
DPS-94GL	1994	Proof [1]	4	1300

1. Issued in red leatherette case.

Denomination	Metal
5 Pounds	Gold
2 Pounds (Bank of England)	Gold
Sovereign	Gold
Half Sovereign	Gold

No.	Date	Striking Standard	No. of Coins	Price
DPS-94GS	1994	Proof [1]	3	620

1. Issued in leatherette case.

Denomination	Metal
2 Pounds	Gold
Sovereign	Gold
Half Sovereign	Gold

No.	Date	Striking Standard	No. of Coins	Price
DPS-94DL	1994	Proof [1]	8	35
DPS-94	1994	Proof [2]	8	30

1. Issued in hard plastic and red leatherette case.
2. Issued in hard plastic and dark blue leatherette case.

Denomination	Metal
2 Pounds	Nickel-brass
1 Pound	Nickel-brass
50 Pence	Cupronickel
20 Pence	Cupronickel
10 Pence	Cupronickel
5 Pence	Cupronickel
2 Pence	Copper-plated steel
1 Penny	Copper-plated steel

1995

No.	Date	Striking Standard	No. of Coins	Price
DPS-95BR	1995	Proof [1]	4	1200

1. Issued in leatherette case.

Denomination	Metal
100 Pounds	Gold
50 Pounds	Gold
25 Pounds	Gold
10 Pounds	Gold

No.	Date	Striking Standard	No. of Coins	Price
DPS-95GL	1995	Proof [1]	4	1000

1. 1250 issued in red leatherette case.

Denomination	Metal
5 Pounds	Gold
2 Pounds (World War II)	Gold
Sovereign	Gold
Half Sovereign	Gold

No.	Date	Striking Standard	No. of Coins	Price
DPS-95GS	1995	Proof [1]	3	600

1. 1250 issued in leatherette case.

Denomination	Metal
2 Pounds(World War II)	Gold
Sovereign	Gold
Half Sovereign	Gold

No.	Date	Striking Standard	No. of Coins	Price
DPS-95DL	1995	Proof [1]	8	.35
DPS-95	1995	Proof [2]	8	28

1. Issued in hard plastic and red leatherette case.
2. Issued in hard plastic and dark blue leatherette case.

Denomination	Metal
2 Pounds (World War II)	Nickel-brass
1 Pound	Nickel-brass
50 Pence	Cupronickel
20 Pence	Cupronickel
10 Pence	Cupronickel
5 Pence	Cupronickel
2 Pence	Copper-plated steel
1 Penny	Copper-plated steel

No.	Date	Striking Standard	No. of Coins	Price
DPS-95A	1995	Proof [1]	2	160

1. 250 issued in black case.

Denomination	Metal
Half Sovereign	Gold
10 Pounds	Gold

No.	Date	Striking Standard	No. of Coins	Price
DPS-95B	1995	Proof [1]	3	80

1. 1000 issued in blue case.

Denomination	Metal
2 Pounds (World War II)	Silver
2 Pounds (United Nations)	Silver
1 Pound	Silver

No.	Date	Striking Standard	No. of Coins	Price
DPS-95C	1995	Proof [1]	2	200

1. 250 issued in maroon case.

Denomination	Metal
Sovereign	Gold
1 Pound	Silver

No.	Date	Striking Standard	No. of Coins	Price
DPS-95D	1995	Proof [1]	2	60

1. 1500 issued in green case.

Denomination	Metal
2 Pounds (World War II)	Silver
2 Pounds (United Nations)	Silver

1996

No.	Date	Striking Standard	No. of Coins	Price
DPS-96BR	1996	Proof [1]	4	1200

1. Issued in leatherette case.

Denomination	Metal
100 Pounds	Gold
50 Pounds	Gold
25 Pounds	Gold
10 Pounds	Gold

No.	Date	Striking Standard	No. of Coins	Price
DPS-96GL	1996	Proof [1]	4	1000

1. Issued in leatherette case.

Denomination	Metal
5 Pounds	Gold
2 Pounds	Gold
Sovereign	Gold
Half Sovereign	Gold

No.	Date	Striking Standard	No. of Coins	Price
DPS-96GS	1996	Proof [1]	3	500

1. Issued in leatherette case.

Denomination	Metal
2 Pounds	Gold
Sovereign	Gold
Half Sovereign	Gold

No.	Date	Striking Standard	No. of Coins	Price
DPS-96DL	1996	Proof [1]	9	35
DPS-96	1996	Proof [2]	9	28

1. Issued in hard plastic and red leatherette case.
2. Issued in hard plastic and dark blue leatherette case.

Denomination	Metal
5 Pounds (Queen's Birthday)	Cupronickel
2 Pounds (Football)	Nickel-brass
1 Pound	Nickel-brass
50 Pence	Cupronickel
20 Pence	Cupronickel
10 Pence	Cupronickel
5 Pence	Cupronickel
2 Pence	Copper-plated steel
1 Penny	Copper-plated steel

No.	Date	Striking Standard	No. of Coins	Price
DPS-96S	1996	Proof [1]	7	150

1. Up to 15,000 issued in hard plastic and maroon velvet case.

Denomination	Metal
1 Pound	Silver
50 Pence	Silver
20 Pence	Silver
10 Pence	Silver
5 Pence	Silver
2 Pence	Silver
1 Penny	Silver

1997

No.	Date	Striking Standard	No. of Coins	Price
DPS-97BR	1997	Proof [1]	4	1200

1. Issued in red leatherette case.

Denomination	Metal
100 Pounds	Gold
50 Pounds	Gold
25 Pounds	Gold
10 Pounds	Gold

No.	Date	Striking Standard	No. of Coins	Price
DPS-97BRS	1997	Proof [1]	4	80

1. Issued in green leatherette case.

Denomination	Metal
2 Pounds	Silver
1 Pound	Silver
50 Pence	Silver
20 Pence	Silver

No.	Date	Striking Standard	No. of Coins	Price
DPS-97GL	1997	Proof [1]	4	1000

1. Issued in leatherette case.

Denomination	Metal
5 Pounds	Gold
2 Pounds	Gold
Sovereign	Gold
Half Sovereign	Gold

No.	Date	Striking Standard	No. of Coins	Price
DPS-97GS	1997	Proof [1]	3	500

1. Issued in leatherette case.

Denomination	Metal
2 Pounds	Gold
Sovereign	Gold
Half Sovereign	Gold

No.	Date	Striking Standard	No. of Coins	Price
DPS-97DL	1997	Proof [1]	10	60
DPS-97	1997	Proof [2]	10	50

1. Issued in hard plastic and red leatherette case.
2. Issued in hard plastic and dark blue leatherette case.

Denomination	Metal
5 Pounds (Golden Wedding)	Cupronickel
2 Pounds	Cupronickel and nickel-brass
1 Pound	Nickel-brass
50 Pence (30 mm)	Cupronickel
50 Pence (27 mm)	Cupronickel
20 Pence	Cupronickel
10 Pence	Cupronickel
5 Pence	Cupronickel
2 Pence	Copper-plated steel
1 Penny	Copper-plated steel

No.	Date	Striking Standard	No. of Coins	Price
DPS-97A	1997	Proof [1]	2	50

1. Issued in green case.

Denomination	Metal
50 Pence (30 mm)	Silver
50 Pence (27 mm)	Silver

No.	Date	Striking Standard	No. of Coins	Price
DPS-97B	1997	Proof [1]	2	50

1. Issued in red case.

Denomination	Metal
2 Pounds	Silver
2 Pounds	Silver

1998

No.	Date	Striking Standard	No. of Coins	Price
DPS-98BR	1998	Proof [1]	4	1200

1. Issued in leatherette case.

Denomination	Metal
100 Pounds	Gold
50 Pounds	Gold
25 Pounds	Gold
10 Pounds	Gold

No.	Date	Striking Standard	No. of Coins	Price
DPS-98BRS	1998	Proof [1]	4	80

1. Issued in green leatherette case.

Denomination Metal

2 Pounds	Silver
1 Pound	Silver
50 Pence	Silver
20 Pence	Silver

No.	Date	Striking Standard	No. of Coins	Price
DPS-98GL	1998	Proof [1]	4	1000

1. Issued in red leatherette case.

Denomination Metal

5 Pounds	Gold
2 Pounds	Gold
Sovereign	Gold
Half Sovereign	Gold

No.	Date	Striking Standard	No. of Coins	Price
DPS-98GS	1998	Proof [1]	3	500

1. Issued in leatherette case.

Denomination Metal

2 Pounds	Gold
Sovereign	Gold
Half Sovereign	Gold

No.	Date	Striking Standard	No. of Coins	Price
DPS-98DL	1998	Proof [1]	10	60
DPS-98	1998	Proof [2]	10	50

1. Issued in hard plastic and red leatherette case.
2. Issued in hard plastic and dark blue leatherette case.

Denomination Metal

5 Pounds (Prince of Wales)	Cupronickel
2 Pounds	Cupronickel and nickel-brass
1 Pound	Nickel-brass
50 Pence	Cupronickel
50 Pence (European Union)	Cupronickel
20 Pence	Cupronickel
10 Pence	Cupronickel

5 Pence	Cupronickel
2 Pence	Copper-plated steel
1 Penny	Copper-plated steel

No.	Date	Striking Standard	No. of Coins	Price
DPS-98A	1998	Proof [1]	2	40

1. Issued in green case.

Denomination Metal

50 Pence (European Union)	Silver
50 Pence (NHS)	Silver

1999

No.	Date	Striking Standard	No. of Coins	Price
DPS-99GL	1999	Proof [1]	4	1000

1. Issued in red case.

Denomination Metal

5 Pounds	Gold
2 Pounds (Rugby)	Gold
Sovereign	Gold
Half Sovereign	Gold

No.	Date	Striking Standard	No. of Coins	Price
DPS-99GS	1999	Proof [1]	3	500

1. Issued in red case.

Denomination Metal

2 Pounds (Rugby)	Gold
Sovereign	Gold
Half Sovereign	Gold

No.	Date	Striking Standard	No. of Coins	Price
DPS-99DL	1999	Proof [1]	9	40
DPS-99	1999	Proof [2]	9	30

1. Issued in hard plastic and red leatherette case.
2. Issued in hard plastic and dark blue leatherette case.

Denomination	Metal
5 Pounds (Diana)	Cupronickel
2 Pounds (Rugby)	Cupronickel and nickel-brass
1 Pound	Nickel-brass
50 Pence	Cupronickel
20 Pence	Cupronickel
10 Pence	Cupronickel
5 Pence	Cupronickel
2 Pence	Copper-plated steel
1 Penny	Copper-plated steel

Specimen Sets

1953

No.	Date	Striking Standard	No. of Coins	Price
MS-53	1953	Currency [1]	9	15

1. Issued in clear plastic holder.

Denomination	Metal
Halfcrown	Cupronickel
Florin	Cupronickel
Scottish Shilling	Cupronickel
English Shilling	Cupronickel
Sixpence	Cupronickel
Threepence	Nickel-brass
Penny	Bronze
Halfpenny	Bronze
Farthing	Bronze

1968/1971

No.	Date	Striking Standard	No. of Coins	Price
DMS-68	1968/1971	Currency [1]	5	3

1. Issued in 1968 in blue wallet.

Denomination	Metal
10 pence 1968	Cupronickel
5 pence 1968	Cupronickel
2 pence 1971	Bronze
1 penny 1971	Bronze
Halfpenny 1971	Bronze

1982

No.	Date	Striking Standard	No. of Coins	Price
DMS-82	1982	Specimen [1]	7	10

1. Issued in card holder.

Denomination	Metal
50 pence	Cupronickel
20 pence	Cupronickel
10 pence	Cupronickel
5 pence	Cupronickel
2 pence	Bronze
1 penny	Bronze
Halfpenny	Bronze

1983

No.	Date	Striking Standard	No. of Coins	Price
DMS-83	1983	Specimen [1]	8	20
DMS-83E	1983	Specimen [2]	8	1000

1. Issued in card holder.
2. Issued in card holder; contains error twopence D02/83–1E.

Denomination	Metal
1 pound	Nickel-brass
50 pence	Cupronickel
20 pence	Cupronickel
10 pence	Cupronickel
5 pence	Cupronickel
2 pence	Bronze
1 penny	Bronze
Halfpenny	Bronze

1984

No.	Date	Striking Standard	No. of Coins	Price
DMS-84	1984	Specimen [1]	8	15

1. Issued in card holder.

Denomination	Metal
1 pound	Nickel-brass
50 pence	Cupronickel
20 pence	Cupronickel
10 pence	Cupronickel
5 pence	Cupronickel
2 pence	Bronze
1 penny	Bronze
Halfpenny	Bronze

1985

No.	Date	Striking Standard	No. of Coins	Price
DMS-85	1985	Specimen [1]	7	10

1. Issued in card holder.

Denomination	Metal
1 pound	Nickel-brass
50 pence	Cupronickel
20 pence	Cupronickel
10 pence	Cupronickel
5 pence	Cupronickel
2 pence	Bronze
1 penny	Bronze

1986

No.	Date	Striking Standard	No. of Coins	Price
DMS-86	1986	Specimen [1]	8	18

1. Issued in card holder.

Denomination	Metal
2 pounds	Nickel-brass
1 pound	Nickel-brass
50 pence	Cupronickel
20 pence	Cupronickel
10 pence	Cupronickel
5 pence	Cupronickel
2 pence	Bronze
1 penny	Bronze

1987

No.	Date	Striking Standard	No. of Coins	Price
DMS-87	1987	Specimen [1]	7	10

1. Issued in card holder.

Denomination	Metal
1 pound	Nickel-brass
50 pence	Cupronickel
20 pence	Cupronickel
10 pence	Cupronickel
5 pence	Cupronickel
2 pence	Bronze
1 penny	Bronze

1988

No.	Date	Striking Standard	No. of Coins	Price
DMS-88	1988	Specimen [1]	7	12

1. Issued in card holder.

Denomination	Metal
1 pound	Nickel-brass
50 pence	Cupronickel
20 pence	Cupronickel
10 pence	Cupronickel
5 pence	Cupronickel
2 pence	Bronze
1 penny	Bronze

1989

No.	Date	Striking Standard	No. of Coins	Price
DMS-89	1989	Specimen [1]	7	20

1. Issued in card holder.

Denomination	Metal
1 pound	Nickel-brass
50 pence	Cupronickel
20 pence	Cupronickel
10 pence	Cupronickel
5 pence	Cupronickel
2 pence	Bronze
1 penny	Bronze

No.	Date	Striking Standard	No. of Coins	Price
DMS-89–2P	1989	Specimen [1]	2	20

1. Issued in card holder. Also issued in two separate card holders.

Denomination	Metal
2 pounds (Bill of Rights)	Nickel-brass
2 pounds (Claim of Right)	Nickel-brass

1990

No.	Date	Striking Standard	No. of Coins	Price
DMS-90	1990	Specimen [1]	8	20

1. Issued in card holder.

Denomination	Metal
1 pound	Nickel-brass
50 pence	Cupronickel
20 pence	Cupronickel
10 pence	Cupronickel
5 pence (on 24mm flan)	Cupronickel
5 pence (on 18mm flan)	Cupronickel
2 pence	Bronze
1 penny	Bronze

1991

No.	Date	Striking Standard	No. of Coins	Price
DMS-91	1991	Specimen [1]	7	18

1. Issued in card holder.

Denomination	Metal
1 pound	Nickel-brass
50 pence	Cupronickel
20 pence	Cupronickel
10 pence	Cupronickel
5 pence	Cupronickel
2 pence	Bronze
1 penny	Bronze

1992

No.	Date	Striking Standard	No. of Coins	Price
DMS-92	1992	Specimen [1]	9	15

1. Issued in card holder.

Denomination	Metal
1 pound	Nickel-brass
50 pence (regular issue)	Cupronickel
50 pence (EEC issue)	Cupronickel
20 pence	Cupronickel
10 pence (on 28.5 mm flan)	Cupronickel
10 pence (on 24.5mm flan)	Cupronickel
5 pence	Cupronickel
2 pence	Bronze
1 penny	Bronze

1992/93

No.	Date	Striking Standard	No. of Coins	Price
DMS-92A	1992/93	Specimen [1]	2	10

1. Issued in card holder.

Denomination	Metal
50 pence (EEC issue)	Cupronickel
50 pence (EEC issue)	Cupronickel

1993

No.	Date	Striking Standard	No. of Coins	Price
DMS-93	1993	Specimen [1]	8	12

1. Issued in card holder.

Denomination	Metal
1 pound	Nickel-brass
50 pence (regular issue)	Cupronickel
50 pence (Single Market)	Cupronickel
20 pence	Cupronickel
10 pence	Cupronickel
5 pence	Cupronickel
2 pence	Copper-plated steel
1 penny	Copper-plated steel

1994

No.	Date	Striking Standard	No. of Coins	Price
DMS-94	1994	Specimen [1]	8	12

1. Issued in card holder.

Denomination	Metal
2 pounds	Nickel-brass
1 pound	Nickel-brass
50 pence	Cupronickel
20 pence	Cupronickel
10 pence	Cupronickel
5 pence	Cupronickel
2 pence	Copper-plated steel
1 penny	Copper-plated steel

1995

No.	Date	Striking Standard	No. of Coins	Price
DMS-95	1995	Specimen [1]	8	10

1. Issued in card holder.

Denomination	Metal
2 pounds (World War II)	Nickel-brass
1 pound	Nickel-brass

50 pence Cupronickel
20 pence Cupronickel
10 pence Cupronickel
5 pence Cupronickel
2 pence Copper-plated steel
1 penny Copper-plated steel

1996

No.	Date	Striking Standard	No. of Coins	Price
DMS-96	1996	Specimen [1]	8	9

1. Issued in card holder.

Denomination Metal
2 pounds (Football) Nickel-brass
1 pound Nickel-brass
50 pence Cupronickel
20 pence Cupronickel
10 pence Cupronickel
5 pence Cupronickel
2 pence Copper-plated steel
1 penny Copper-plated steel

1997

No.	Date	Striking Standard	No. of Coins	Price
DMS-97	1997	Specimen [1]	9	15

1. Issued in card holder.

Denomination Metal
2 pounds Cupronickel and nickel-brass
1 pound Nickel-brass
50 pence (30 mm) Cupronickel
50 pence (27 mm) Cupronickel
20 pence Cupronickel
10 pence Cupronickel
5 pence Cupronickel
2 pence Copper-plated steel
1 penny Copper-plated steel

1998

No.	Date	Striking Standard	No. of Coins	Price
DMS-98	1998	Specimen [1]	9	15

1. Issued in card holder.

Denomination Metal
2 pounds Cupronickel and nickel-brass
1 pound Nickel-brass
50 pence Cupronickel
50 pence (European Union) Cupronickel
20 pence Cupronickel
10 pence Cupronickel
5 pence Cupronickel
2 pence Copper-plated steel
1 penny Copper-plated steel

No.	Date	Striking Standard	No. of Coins	Price
DMS-98A	1998	Specimen [1]	2	8

1. Issued in card holder.

Denomination Metal
50 pence Cupronickel
50 pence (European Union) Cupronickel

1999

No.	Date	Striking Standard	No. of Coins	Price
DMS-99	1999	Specimen [1]	8	12

1. Issued in card holder.

Denomination Metal
2 pounds (Rugby) Cupronickel and nickel-brass
1 pound Nickel-brass
50 pence Cupronickel
20 pence Cupronickel
10 pence Cupronickel
5 pence Cupronickel
2 pence Copper-plated steel
1 penny Copper-plated steel

£26,000 worth of silver coins ready to enter the Mint safe

Mintage Figures

In response to many requests, we are listing below official issue ('mintage') figures as far as is practicable between 1816 and the changeover to decimal currency in 1971, together with Maundy mintage figures after that date. Dates for which no coins were minted, or for which information is unavailable, are omitted.

Mintage figures are notoriously unreliable as a guide to rarity, as the figures are for coins issued, not minted, in that year. They can sometimes include coins bearing previous, or even subsequent, dates to the year of issue.

Decimal coins from 1971 are not included in these listings. The situation is greatly complicated by the existence of issue limits, where coins can be struck because of public demand well after the original issue.

Gold Five Pounds

Date	Remarks	Mintage
1887	non-proof issue	53,844
1887	proof issue	797
1893	non-proof issue	20,405
1893	proof issue	773
1902	non-proof issue	34,911
1902	proof issue	8,066
1911	proof only	2,812
1937	proof-only issue	5,501

Gold Two Pounds

Date	Remarks	Mintage
1831	proof-only issue	225
1887	non-proof issue	91,345
1887	proof issue	797
1893	non-proof issue	52,212
1893	proof issue	773
1902	non-proof issue	45,807
1902	proof issue	8,066
1911	proof-only issue	2,812
1937	proof-only issue	5,501

Guinea

The Gazetteer and London Daily Advertiser of 23 January 1755 contained the following table of numbers of guineas minted out of gold imported by the Royal African Company. These coins usually carry the elephant or elephant and castle symbol:

Date	Mintage
1675	12,271
1676	15,278
1677	83,871
1678	5,005
1679	25,277
1680	17,147
1681	24,852
1682	23,235
1683	25,589
1684	20,684
1685	46,066
1686	23,434
1687	32,440
1688	39,371
1689	25,493
1690	1,562
1691	26,700
1692	19,036
1693	7,506
1694	15,801
1695	21,504
1696	2,410
1697	11,443
1698	17,828
1699	2,214
1700	0
1701	4,984
1702	0
1703	397
1704	1,836
1705	1,358
1706	0
1707	5,568
1708	2,918
1709	11,155
1710	10,382
1711	0
1712	2,925
1713	146
1714	0
1715	591
1716	0
1717	0
1718	0
1719	0
1720	0
1721	2,962
1722	12,284
1723	5,427
1724	14,388
1725	4,916
Total:	578,754

All gold coins (1760–1813) (value in pounds sterling)

Date	Sterling value £
1760	111,299
1761	550,888
1762	553,691
1763	513,041
1764	883,102
1765	538,272
1766	820,725
1767	1,271,808
1768	844,554
1769	626,582
1770	623,779
1771	637,796
1772	843,853
1773	1,317,645
1774	4,685,624
1775	4,901,219
1776	5,006,350
1777	3,680,995
1778	350,438
1779	1,696,117

1780	0
1781	876,795
1782	698,074
1783	227,084
1784	822,126
1785	2,488,106
1786	1,107,382
1787	2,849,057
1788	3,664,174
1789	1,530,711
1790	2,660,522
1791	2,456,567
1792	1,171,863
1793	2,747,430
1794	2,558,895
1795	493,416
1796	464,680
1797	2,000,297
1798	2,967,505
1799	449,962
1800	189,937
1801	450,240
1802	437,019
1803	596,445
1804	718,397
1805	54,616
1806	405,106
1807	0
1808	371,744
1809	298,946
1810	316,935
1811	312,263
1812	0
1813	519,722

Sovereign

London mint

Date	Remarks	Mintage
1817		3,235,239
1818		2,347,230
1819	probably almost all dated 1818	3,574
1820		931,994
1821		9,405,114
1822		5,356,787
1823		616,770
1824		3,767,904
1825		4,200,343
1826		5,724,046
1827		2,266,629
1828	most probably dated 1827	386,182
1829		2,444,652
1830		2,387,881
1831		598,547
1832		3,737,065
1833		1,225,269
1835		723,441
1836		1,714,349
1837		1,172,984
1838		2,718,694
1839		503,695
1841		124,054
1842		4,865,375
1843		5,981,968
1844		3,000,445
1845		3,800,845
1846		3,802,947
1847		4,667,126
1848		2,246,701
1849		1,755,399
1850		1,402,039

Date	Remarks	Mintage
1851		4,013,624
1852		8,053,435
1853		10,597,993
1854		3,589,611
1855		8,448,482
1856		4,806,160
1857		4,495,748
1858		803,234
1859		1,547,603
1860		2,555,958
1861		7,624,736
1862		7,836,413
1863		5,921,669
1864		8,656,352
1865		1,450,238
1866		4,047,288
1868		1,653,384
1869		6,441,322
1870		2,189,960
1871		8,767,250
1872		13,486,708
1873		2,368,215
1874		520,713
1876		3,318,866
1878		1,091,275
1879		20,013
1880		3,650,080
1884		1,769,635
1885		717,723
1887	non-proof issue	1,111,280
1887	proof issue	797
1888		2,277,424
1889		7,257,455
1890		6,529,887
1891		6,329,476
1892		7,104,720
1893	non-proof issue	6,898,260
1893	proof issue	773
1894		3,782,611
1895		2,285,317
1896		3,334,065
1898		4,361,347
1899		7,515,978
1900		10,846,741
1901		1,578,948
1902	non-proof issue	4,737,796
1902	proof issue	15,123
1903		8,888,627
1904		10,041,369
1905		5,910,403
1906		10,466,981
1907		18,458,663
1908		11,729,006
1909		12,157,099
1910		22,379,624
1911	non-proof issue	30,044,105
1911	proof issue	3,764
1912		30,317,921
1913		24,539,672
1914		11,501,117
1915		20,295,280
1916	many not issued	1,554,120
1917	many not issued	1,014,714
1925	see entries 1949–52	3,520,431
1937	proof-only issue	5,501
1949	all dated 1925	138,000
1951	all dated 1925	318,000
1952	all dated 1925	430,000
1957		2,072,000
1958		8,700,140
1959	140 were dated 1958	1,385,368
1962		3,000,000

1963	7,400,000
1965	3,800,000
1966	7,050,000
1967	5,000,000
1968	4,203,000
1974	5,002,566
1976	4,150,000
1978	6,550,000
1979	9,100,000
1980	5,100,000
1981	5,000,000
1982	2,950,000

Figures since 1962 exclude proof and specimen strikings and may not be exact.

Australia: Melbourne mint

Date	Remarks	Mintage
1872		748,000
1873		752,000
1874		1373,000
1875		1,888,000
1876		2,124,000
1877		1,487,000
1878		2,171,000
1879		2,740,000
1880		3,052,800
1881		2,324,800
1882		371,400
1883		427,000
1884		2,942,000
1885		2,966,500
1886		2,901,500
1887	young head issue	1,916,424
1887	jubilee head issue	940,000
1888		2,830,000
1889		2,732,000
1890		2,473,000
1891		2,749,000
1892		3,488,000
1893	jubilee head issue	1,649,352
1893	old head issue	1,914,400
1894		4,166,000
1895		4,165,000
1896		4,456,000
1897		5,129,500
1898		5,508,000
1899		5,578,000
1900		4,305,000
1901		3,986,000
1902		4,265,000
1903		3,520,000
1904		3,742,000
1905		3,632,000
1906		3,656,000
1907		3,331,000
1908		3,078,500
1909		3,028,000
1910		3,053,000
1911		2,850,000
1912		2,468,000
1913		2,322,000
1914		2,011,000
1915		1,637,000
1916		1,272,000
1917		934,000
1918		4,907,000
1919		514,000
1920		530,000
1921		240,000
1922		608,000
1923		510,870

1924	278,000
1925	3,310,000
1926	211,000
1927	310,000
1928	413,000
1929	436,719
1930	77,547
1931	57,779

Australia: Perth mint

Date	Mintage
1899	690,992
1900	1,886,089
1901	2,889,333
1902	4,289,122
1903	4,674,783
1904	4,506,756
1905	4,876,193
1906	4,829,817
1907	4,972,289
1908	4,875,617
1909	4,524,241
1910	4,690,625
1911	4,373,165
1912	4,278,144
1913	4,635,287
1914	4,815,996
1915	4,373,596
1916	4,096,771
1917	4,110,286
1918	3,812,884
1919	2,995,216
1920	2,421,196
1921	2,314,360
1922	2,298,884
1923	2,124,154
1924	1,464,416
1925	1,837,901
1926	1,313,578
1927	1,383,578
1928	1,333,417
1929	1,606,625
1930	1,915,352
1931	1,173,568

Australia: Sydney mint

Date	Remarks	Mintage
1871		2,814,000
1872		1,815,000
1873		1,478,000
1874		1,899,000
1875		2,122,000
1876		1,613,000
1877		1,590,000
1878		1,259,000
1879		1,366,000
1880		1,459,000
1881		1,360,000
1882		1,298,000
1883		1,108,000
1884		1,595,000
1885		1,486,000
1886		1,667,000
1887	young head issue	1,000,000
1887	jubilee head issue	1,002,000
1888		2,187,000
1889		3,262,000
1890		2,808,000
1891		2,596,000
1892		2,837,000

Date	Remarks	Mintage
1893	jubilee head issue	1,498,000
1893	old head issue	1,346,000
1894		3,067,000
1895		2,758,000
1896		2,544,000
1897		2,532,000
1898		2,548,000
1899		3,259,000
1900		3,586,000
1901		3,012,000
1902		2,813,000
1903		2,806,000
1904		2,986,000
1905		2,778,000
1906		2,792,000
1907		2,539,000
1908		2,017,000
1909		2,057,000
1910		2,135,000
1911		2,519,000
1912		2,227,000
1913		2,249,000
1914		1,774,000
1915		1,346,000
1916		1,242,000
1917		1,666,000
1918		3,716,000
1919		1,835,000
1920		360,000
1921		839,000
1922		578,000
1923		416,000
1924		394,000
1925		5,632,000
1926		1,031,050

Canada: Ottawa mint

Date	Mintage
1908	636
1909	16,273
1910	28,012
1911	256,946
1913	3,715
1914	14,891
1916	6,111
1917	58,845
1918	106,516
1919	135,889

India: Bombay mint

Date	Mintage
1918	1,295,372

South Africa: Pretoria mint

Date	Mintage
1923	719
1924	3,184
1925	6,086,264
1926	11,107,611
1927	16,379,704
1928	18,235,057
1929	12,024,107
1930	10,027,756
1931	8,511,792
1932	1,066,680

Half sovereign

(London mint only)

Date	Remarks	Mintage
1817		2,080,197
1818		1,030,286
1820		35,043
1821		231,288
1823		224,280
1824		591,530
1825		761,150
1826		344,830
1827		492,014
1828	some struck in 1829	1,244,754
1834		133,899
1835		772,554
1836		146,865
1837		160,207
1838		273,341
1839		1,230
1841		508,835
1842		2,223,352
1843		1,251,762
1844		1,127,007
1845		887,526
1846		1,063,928
1847		982,326
1848		410,595
1849		845,112
1850		175,595
1851		173,573
1852		1,377,671
1853		2,708,796
1854		1,125,144
1855		1,120,362
1856		2,391,909
1857		728,223
1858		855,578
1859		2,203,813
1860		1,131,500
1861		1,130,867
1863		1,371,574
1864		1,758,490
1865		1,834,750
1866		2,058,776
1867		992,795
1869		1,861,764
1870		1,159,544
1871		2,062,970
1872		3,248,627
1873		1,927,050
1874		1,884,432
1875		516,240
1876		2,785,187
1877		2,197,482
1878		2,081,941
1879		35,201
1880		1,009,049
1883		2,870,457
1884		1,133,756
1885		4,468,871
1887	non-proof issue	871,770
1887	proof issue	797
1890		2,266,023
1891		1,079,286
1892		13,680,486
1893	non-proof issue	4,426,625
1893	proof issue	773
1894		3,794,591
1895		2,869,183
1896		2,946,605

1897		3,568,156
1898		2,878,527
1899		3,361,881
1900		4,307,372
1901		2,037,664
1902	non-proof issue	4,244,457
1902	proof issue	15,123
1903		2,522,057
1904		1,717,440
1905		3,023,993
1906		4,245,437
1907		4,233,421
1908		3,996,992
1909		4,010,715
1910		5,023,881
1911	non-proof issue	6,104,106
1911	proof issue	3,764
1912		6,224,316
1913		6,094,290
1914		7,251,124
1915		2,042,747
1937	proof-only issue	5,501
1982	non-proof issue	2,500,000

Crown

Date	Remarks	Mintage
1818		155,232
1819		683,496
1820		448,272
1821		437,976
1822		124,929
1844		94,248
1845		159,192
1847	young head issue	140,976
1847	Gothic issue	8,000
1853		460
1887	non-proof issue	273,581
1887	proof issue	1,084
1888		131,899
1889		1,807,223
1890		997,862
1891		566,394
1892		451,334
1893	non-proof issue	497,845
1893	proof issue	1,312
1894		144,906
1895		252,862
1896		317,599
1897		262,118
1898		161,450
1899		166,300
1900		353,356
1902	non-proof issue	256,020
1902	proof issue	15,123
1927	proof-only issue	15,030
1928		9,034
1929		4,994
1930		4,847
1931		4,056
1932		2,395
1933		7,132
1934		932
1935	non-proof issue	714,769
1935	proof issue -not gold	2,500
1935	proof issue -gold	25
1936		2,473
1937	non-proof issue	418,699
1937	proof issue	26,402
1951	proof-only issue	1,183,540
1953	non-proof issue	5,962,621

1953	proof issue	40,000
1960	non-proof issue	1,024,038
1960	proof and prooflike issue	70,000
1965		12,080,000
1966	all dated 1965	7,560,000

Double Florin

Date	Remarks	Mintage
1887	non-proof issue	483,347
1887	proof issue	1,084
1888		243,340
1889		1,185,111
1890		782,146

Halfcrown

Date	Remarks	Mintage
1817	includes 1816 dated coins	8,092,656
1818		2,905,056
1819		4,790,016
1820		2,396,592
1821		1,435,104
1823		2,003,760
1824		465,696
1825		2,258,784
1826		2,189,088
1828		49,890
1829		508,464
1834		993,168
1835		281,952
1836		1,588,752
1837		150,526
1840		386,496
1841		42,768
1842		486,288
1843		454,608
1844		1,999,008
1845		2,231,856
1846		1,907,136
1848		91,872
1849		261,360
1850		483,120
1874		2,188,599
1875		1,113,483
1876		633,221
1877		447,059
1878		1,466,323
1879		901,356
1880		1,346,350
1881		2,301,495
1882		808,227
1883		2,982,779
1884		1,569,175
1885		1,628,438
1886		891,767
1887	non-proof issue	1,438,046
1887	proof issue	1,084
1888		1,428,787
1889		4,811,954
1890		3,228,111
1891		2,284,632
1892		1,710,946
1893	non-proof issue	1,792,600
1893	proof issue	1,312
1894		1,524,960
1895		1,772,662
1896		2,148,505
1897		1,678,643
1898		1,870,055

Date	Remarks	Mintage
1899		2,863,872
1900		4,479,128
1901		1,516,570
1902	non-proof issue	1,316,008
1902	proof issue	15,123
1903		274,840
1904		709,652
1905		166,008
1906		2,886,206
1907		3,693,930
1908		1,758,889
1909		3,051,592
1910		2,557,685
1911	non-proof issue	2,914,573
1911	proof issue	6,007
1912		4,700,789
1913		4,090,169
1914		18,333,003
1915		32,433,066
1916		29,530,020
1917		11,172,052
1918		29,079,592
1919		10,266,737
1920		17,982,077
1921		23,677,889
1922		16,396,724
1923		26,308,526
1924		5,866,294
1925		1,413,461
1926		4,473,516
1927	non-proof issue	6,852,872
1927	proof issue	15,000
1928		18,762,727
1929		17,632,636
1930		809,051
1931		11,264,468
1932		4,793,643
1933		10,311,494
1934		2,422,399
1935		7,022,216
1936		7,039,423
1937	non-proof issue	9,106,440
1937	proof issue	26,402
1938		6,426,478
1939		15,478,635
1940		17,948,439
1941		15,773,984
1942		31,220,090
1943		15,462,875
1944		15,255,165
1945		19,849,242
1946		22,724,873
1947		21,911,484
1948		71,164,703
1949		28,272,512
1950	non-proof issue	28,335,500
1950	proof issue	17,513
1951	non-proof issue	9,003,520
1951	proof issue	20,000
1953	non-proof issue	3,883,214
1953	proof issue	40,000
1954		11,614,953
1955		23,628,726
1956		33,934,909
1957		34,200,563
1958		15,745,668
1959		9,028,844
1960		19,929,191
1961		25,887,897
1962		23,998,112
1963	includes 15,200 dated 1962	17,572,800
1964	includes 77,600 dated 1963	4,576,800
1965	includes 1,474,400 dated 1964	8,124,800
1966	includes 3,228,000 dated 1965	14,811,200
1967		18,895,200
1968	all dated 1967	14,163,200
1970	proof only	750,476

Florin

Date	Remarks	Mintage
1849		413,820
1851		1,540
1852		1,014,552
1853		3,919,950
1854	rarer than these figures suggest	550,413
1855		831,017
1856		2,201,760
1857		1,671,120
1858		2,239,380
1859		2,568,060
1860		1,475,100
1862		594,000
1863		938,520
1864		1,861,200
1865		1,580,040
1866		914,760
1867		423,720
1868		896,940
1869		297,000
1870		1,080,648
1871		3,425,605
1872		7,199,690
1873		5,921,839
1874		1,642,630
1875		1,117,030
1876		580,034
1877		682,292
1878		1,786,680
1879		1,512,247
1880		2,167,170
1881		2,570,337
1883		3,555,667
1884		1,447,379
1885		1,758,210
1886		591,773
1887	non-proof issue	1,776,903
1887	proof issue	1,084
1888		1,547,540
1889		2,973,561
1890		1,684,737
1891		836,438
1892		283,401
1893	non-proof issue	1,666,103
1893	proof issue	1,312
1894		1,952,842
1895		2,182,968
1896		2,944,416
1897		1,699,921
1898		3,061,343
1899		3,966,953
1900		5,528,630
1901		2,648,870
1902	non-proof issue	2,189,575
1902	proof issue	15,123
1903		1,995,298
1904		2,769,932
1905		1,187,596
1906		6,910,128
1907		5,947,895
1908		3,280,010
1909		3,482,829
1910		5,650,713

1911	non-proof issue	5,951,284
1911	proof issue	6,007
1912		8,571,731
1913		4,545,278
1914		21,252,701
1915		12,367,939
1916		21,064,337
1917		11,181,617
1918		29,211,792
1919		9,469,292
1920		15,387,833
1921		34,863,895
1922		23,861,044
1923		21,546,533
1924		4,582,372
1925		1,404,136
1926		5,125,410
1927	1927 florin was proof-only issue; mintage figure as reported	116,497
1927	proof issue	15,000
1928		11,087,186
1929		16,397,279
1930		5,753,568
1931		6,556,331
1932		717,041
1933		8,685,303
1935		7,540,546
1936		9,897,448
1937	non-proof issue	13,006,781
1937	proof issue	26,402
1938		7,909,388
1939		20,850,607
1940		18,700,338
1941		24,451,079
1942		39,895,243
1943		26,711,987
1944		27,560,005
1945		25,858,049
1946		22,300,254
1947		22,910,085
1948		67,553,636
1949		28,614,939
1950	non-proof issue	24,357,490
1950	proof issue	17,513
1951	non-proof issue	27,411,747
1951	proof issue	20,000
1953	non-proof issue	11,958,710
1953	proof issue	40,000
1954		13,085,422
1955		25,887,253
1956		47,824,500
1957		33,071,282
1958		9,564,580
1959		14,080,319
1960		13,831,782
1961		37,735,315
1962		35,129,903
1963	includes 18,000 dated 1962	25,580,000
1964	includes 909,000 dated 1963	16,313,000
1965	includes 1,135,000 dated 1964	48,723,000
1966	includes 575,000 dated 1965	84,574,000
1967		22,152,000
1968	all dated 1967	17,566,000
1970	proof only	750,476

1820		7,975,440
1821		2,463,120
1823		693,000
1824		4,158,000
1825		2,459,160
1826		6,351,840
1827		574,200
1829		879,120
1834		3,223,440
1835		1,449,360
1836		3,567,960
1837		479,160
1838		1,956,240
1839		5,666,760
1840		1,639,440
1841		875,160
1842		2,094,840
1843		1,465,200
1844		4,466,880
1845		4,082,760
1846		4,031,280
1847	no coins dated 1847 known	847,440
1848		194,040
1849		645,480
1850		685,080
1851		470,071
1852		1,306,574
1853		4,256,188
1854		552,414
1855		1,368,499
1856		3,168,000
1857		2,562,120
1858		3,108,600
1859		4,561,920
1860		1,671,120
1861		1,382,040
1862		954,360
1863		859,320
1864		4,518,360
1865		5,619,240
1866		4,989,600
1867		2,166,120
1868		3,330,360
1869		736,560
1870		1,467,471
1871		4,910,010
1872		8,897,781
1873		6,489,598
1874		5,503,747
1875		4,353,983
1876		1,057,487
1877		2,980,703
1878		3,127,131
1879		3,611,507
1880		4,842,786
1881		5,255,332
1882		1,611,786
1883		7,281,450
1884		3,923,993
1885		3,336,527
1886		2,086,819
1887	non-proof issue	4,034,133
1887	proof issue	1,084
1888		4,526,856
1889		7,039,628
1890		8,794,042

1896		9,264,551
1897		6,270,364
1898		9,768,703
1899		10,965,382
1900		10,937,590
1901		3,426,294
1902	non-proof issue	7,809,481
1902	proof issue	15,123
1903		2,061,823
1904		2,040,161
1905		488,390
1906		10,791,025
1907		14,083,418
1908		3,806,969
1909		5,664,982
1910		26,547,236
1911	non-proof issue	20,065,901
1911	proof issue	6,007
1912		15,594,009
1913		9,011,509
1914		23,415,843
1915		39,279,024
1916		35,862,015
1917		22,202,608
1918		34,915,934
1919		10,823,824
1920		22,825,142
1921		22,648,763
1922		27,215,738
1923		14,575,243
1924		9,250,095
1925		5,418,764
1926		22,516,453
1927	non-proof issue	9,262,344
1927	proof issue	15,000
1928		18,136,778
1929		19,343,006
1930		3,137,092
1931		6,993,926
1932		12,168,101
1933		11,511,624
1934		6,138,463
1935		9,183,462
1936		11,910,613
1937E	non-proof issue;[1]	8,359,122
1937E	proof issue	26,402
1937S	non-proof issue;[2]	6,748,875
1937S	proof issue	26,402
1938E		4,833,436
1938S		4,797,852
1939E		11,052,677
1939S		10,263,892
1940E		11,099,126
1940S		9,913,089
1941E		11,391,883
1941S		8,086,030
1942E		17,453,643
1942S		13,676,759
1943E		11,404,213
1943S		9,824,214
1944E		11,586,751
1944S		10,990,167
1945E		15,143,404
1945S		15,106,270
1946E		18,663,797
1946S		16,381,501

1950E	non-proof issue	19,243,872
1950E	proof issue	17,513
1950S	non-proof issue	14,299,601
1950S	proof issue	17,513
1951E	non-proof issue	9,956,930
1951E	proof issue	20,000
1951S	non-proof issue	10,961,174
1951S	proof issue	20,000
1953E	non-proof issue	41,942,894
1953E	proof issue	40,000
1953S	non-proof issue	20,663,528
1953S	proof issue	40,000
1954E		30,262,032
1954S		26,771,735
1955E		45,259,908
1955S		27,950,906
1956E		44,970,008
1956S		42,853,639
1957E		42,774,217
1957S		17,959,988
1958E		14,392,305
1958S		40,822,557
1959E		19,442,778
1959S		1,012,988
1960E		27,027,914
1960S		14,376,932
1961E		39,816,907
1961S		2,762,558
1962E		36,395,179
1962S		17,470,510
1963E	includes 9,200 dated 1962E	44,723,200
1963S	includes 1,496,800 dated 1962S	33,796,800
1964E	includes 5,029,440 dated 1963E	13,617,440
1964S	includes 8,560 dated 1963S	5,246,560
1965E	includes 2,900 dated 1964E	9,218,900
1965S	includes 1,100 dated 1964S	2,017,100
1966E		15,002,000
1966S	includes 758,000 dated 1965S	16,362,000
1970E	proof only	750,476
1970S	proof only	750,476

1. 'E' after date signifies 'English' type shilling.
2. 'S' after date signifies 'Scottish' type shilling.

Sixpence

Date	Remarks	Mintage
1817	includes coins dated 1816	10,921,680
1818		4,284,720
1819		4,712,400
1820		1,488,960
1821		863,280
1824		633,600
1825		483,120
1826		689,040
1827		166,320
1828		15,840
1829		403,920
1831		1,340,195
1834		5,892,480
1835		1,552,320
1836		1,987,920
1837		506,880
1838		1,607,760
1839		3,310,560

1847	all dated 1848	586,080
1849	none known dated 1849	205,920
1850		498,960
1851		2,288,107
1852		904,587
1853		3,837,930
1854		840,116
1855		1,129,084
1856		2,779,920
1857		2,233,440
1858		1,932,480
1859		4,688,640
1860		1,100,880
1861	none known dated 1861	601,920
1862		990,000
1863		491,040
1864		4,253,040
1865		1,631,520
1866		5,140,080
1867		1,362,240
1868		1,069,200
1869		388,080
1870		479,613
1871		3,662,684
1872		3,382,048
1873		4,594,733
1874		4,225,726
1875		3,256,545
1876		841,435
1877		4,066,486
1878		2,624,525
1879		3,326,313
1880		3,892,501
1881		6,239,447
1882		759,809
1883		4,986,558
1884		3,422,565
1885		4,652,771
1886		2,728,249
1887	non-proof issue	3,675,607
1887	proof issue	1,084
1888		4,197,698
1889		8,738,928
1890		9,386,955
1891		7,022,734
1892		6,245,746
1893	non-proof issue	7,350,619
1893	proof issue	1,312
1894		3,467,704
1895		7,024,631
1896		6,651,699
1897		5,031,498
1898		5,914,100
1899		7,996,804
1900		8,984,354
1901		5,108,757
1902	non-proof issue	6,367,378
1902	proof issue	15,123
1903		5,410,096
1904		4,487,098
1905		4,235,556
1906		7,641,146
1907		8,733,673
1908		6,739,491
1909		6,584,017
1910		12,490,724
1911	non-proof issue	9,155,310
1911	proof issue	6,007
1912		10,984,129
1913		7,499,833
1914		22,714,602
1915		15,694,597

1916		2,207,178
1917		7,725,475
1918		27,558,743
1919		13,375,447
1920		14,136,287
1921		30,339,741
1922		16,878,890
1923		6,382,793
1924		17,444,218
1925		12,720,558
1926		21,809,621
1927	non-proof issue	8,939,873
1927	proof issue	15,000
1928		23,123,384
1929		28,319,326
1930		16,990,289
1931		16,873,268
1932		9,406,117
1933		22,185,083
1934		9,304,009
1935		13,995,621
1936		24,380,171
1937	non-proof issue	22,302,524
1937	proof issue	26,402
1938		13,402,701
1939		28,670,304
1940		20,875,196
1941		23,086,616
1942		44,942,785
1943		46,927,111
1944		37,952,600
1945		39,939,259
1946		43,466,407
1947		29,993,263
1948		88,323,540
1949		41,355,515
1950	non-proof issue	32,741,955
1950	proof issue	17,513
1951	non-proof issue	40,399,491
1951	proof issue	20,000
1952		1,013,477
1953	non-proof issue	70,323,876
1953	proof issue	40,000
1954		105,241,150
1955		109,929,554
1956		109,841,555
1957		105,654,290
1958		123,518,527
1959		93,089,441
1960		103,288,346
1961		111,284,384
1962	includes 3,767,633 dated 1961	158,355,270
1963	includes 11,896,000 dated 1962	124,860,000
1964	includes 7,092,000 dated 1963	137,352,000
1965	includes 22,076,000 dated 1964	149,948,000
1966		171,636,000
1967		240,788,000
1970	proof only	750,476

Groat

Date	Remarks	Mintage
1836		4,253,040
1837		962,280
1838		2,150,280
1839		1,461,240
1840		1,496,880
1841		344,520
1842		724,680
1843		1,817,640
1844		855,360

1845	914,760
1846	1,366,200
1847	225,720
1848	712,800
1849	380,160
1850 ....none dated 1850 known	594,000
1851	31,300
1853	11,880
1854	1,096,613
1855	646,041
1856 ....probably all dated 1855	95,040

Silver Threepence

(not including Maundy issues)

Date	Remarks	Mintage
1845		1,314,720
1846		47,520
1849		126,720
1850		950,400
1851		479,065
1853		31,680
1854		1,467,246
1855		383,350
1856		1,013,760
1857		1,758,240
1858		1,441,440
1859		3,579,840
1860		3,405,600
1861		3,294,720
1862		1,156,320
1863		950,400
1864		1,330,560
1865		1,742,400
1866		1,900,800
1867		712,800
1868		1,457,280
1870		1,283,218
1871		999,633
1872		1,293,271
1873		4,055,550
1874		4,427,031
1875		3,306,500
1876		1,834,389
1877		2,622,393
1878		2,419,975
1879		3,140,265
1880		1,610,069
1881		3,248,265
1882		472,965
1883		4,369,971
1884		3,322,424
1885		5,183,653
1886		6,152,669
1887	non-proof issue	2,780,761
1887	proof issue	1,084
1888		518,199
1889		4,587,010
1890		4,465,834
1891		6,323,027
1892		2,578,226
1893	non-proof issue	3,067,293
1893	proof issue	1,312
1894		1,608,603
1895		4,788,609
1896		4,598,442
1897		4,541,294
1898		4,597,177
1899		6,246,281
1900		10,644,480
1901		6,098,400

Date	Remarks	Mintage
1902		8,268,480
1903		5,227,200
1904		3,627,360
1905		3,548,160
1906		3,152,160
1907		4,831,200
1908		8,157,600
1909		4,055,040
1910		4,563,380
1911		5,841,084
1912		8,932,825
1913		7,143,242
1914		6,733,584
1915		5,450,617
1916		18,555,201
1917		21,662,490
1918		20,630,909
1919		16,845,687
1920		16,703,597
1921		8,749,301
1922		7,979,998
1925		3,731,859
1926		4,107,910
1927	proof only	15,022
1928		1,302,106
1930		1,319,412
1931		6,251,936
1932		5,887,325
1933		5,578,541
1934		7,405,954
1935		7,027,654
1936		3,238,670
1937	non-proof issue	8,148,156
1937	proof issue	26,402
1938		6,402,473
1939		1,355,860
1940		7,914,401
1941		7,979,411
1942		4,144,051
1943		1,379,220
1944		2,005,553
1945	almost all melted down	371,600

Brass Threepence

Date	Remarks	Mintage
1937	non-proof issue	45,707,957
1937	proof issue	26,402
1938		14,532,332
1939		5,603,021
1940		12,636,018
1941		60,239,489
1942		103,214,400
1943		101,702,400
1944		69,760,000
1945		33,942,466
1946		620,734
1948		4,230,400
1949		464,000
1950	non-proof issue	1,600,000
1950	proof issue	17,513
1951	non-proof issue	1,184,000
1951	proof issue	20,000
1952		25,494,400
1953	non-proof issue	30,618,000
1953	proof issue	40,000
1954		41,720,000
1955		41,075,200
1956		36,801,600
1957		24,294,400
1958		20,504,000

Date		Mintage
1959		28,499,200
1960		83,078,400
1961		41,102,400
1962		51,545,600
1963		35,280,000
1964		44,867,200
1965		27,160,000
1966		53,760,000
1967		151,780,800
1970	proof only	750,476

Copper Twopence

Date	Mintage
1797	722,160

Copper Penny

Date	Mintage
1825	1,075,200
1826	5,913,000
1827	1,451,520
1831	806,400
1834	322,560
1837	174,720
1841	913,920
1843	483,830
1844	215,040
1845	322,560
1846	483,840
1847	430,080
1848	161,280
1849	268,800
1851	432,224
1853	1,021,440
1854	6,720,000
1855	5,273,866
1856	1,212,288
1857	752,640
1858	1,559,040
1859	1,075,200
1860	32,256

Bronze Penny

Date	Remarks	Mintage
1860		5,053,440
1861		36,449,280
1862		50,534,400
1863		28,062,720
1864		3,440,646
1865		8,601,600
1866		9,999,360
1867		5,483,520
1868		1,182,720
1869		2,580,480
1870		5,695,022
1871		1,290,318
1872		8,494,572
1873		8,494,200
1874	London mint	5,621,865
1874	Heaton mint, Birmingham	6,666,240
1875	London mint	10,691,040
1875	Heaton mint, Birmingham	752,640
1876	Heaton mint, Birmingham	11,074,560
1877		9,624,747
1878		2,764,470
1879		7,666,476
1880		3,000,831

Date	Remarks	Mintage
1881	London mint	2,302,261
1881	Heaton mint, Birmingham	3,763,200
1882	Heaton mint, Birmingham	7,526,400
1883		6,237,438
1884		11,702,802
1885		7,145,862
1886		6,087,759
1887		5,315,085
1888		7,145,862
1889		12,559,737
1890		15,330,840
1891		17,885,961
1892		10,501,671
1893		8,161,737
1894		3,883,452
1895		5,395,830
1896		24,147,156
1897		20,756,620
1898		14,296,836
1899		26,441,069
1900		31,778,109
1901		22,205,568
1902		26,976,768
1903		21,415,296
1904		12,913,152
1905		17,783,808
1906		37,989,504
1907		47,322,240
1908		31,506,048
1909		19,617,024
1910		29,549,184
1911		23,079,168
1912	London mint	48,306,048
1912	Heaton mint, Birmingham	16,800,000
1913		65,497,872
1914		50820,997
1915		47,310,807
1916		86,411,165
1917		107,905,436
1918	London mint	84,227,372
1918	Heaton and Kings Norton mints, Birmingham	3,660,800
1919		113,761,090
1919	Heaton and Kings Norton mints, Birmingham	5,209,600
1920		124,693,485
1921		129,717,693
1922		16,346,711
1926		4,498,519
1927		60,989,561
1928		50,178,000
1929		49,132,800
1930		29,097,600
1931		19,843,200
1932		8,277,600
1933		7
1934		13,965,600
1935		56,070,000
1936		134,160,000
1937	non-proof issue	109,032,000
1937	proof issue	26,402
1938		121,560,000
1939		55,560,000
1940		42,284,400
1944		42,600,000
1945		79,531,200
1946		66,855,600
1947		52,220,400
1948		63,961,200
1949		14,324,400
1950	non-proof issue	240,000
1950	proof issue	17,513

1951	non-proof issue	120,000
1951	proof issue	20,000
1953	non-proof issue	1,308,400
1953	proof issue	40,000
1954		1
1961		48,313,400
1962		157,588,600
1963		119,733,600
1964		153,294,000
1965		121,310,400
1966		165,739,200
1967		155,280,000
1968	all dated 1967	170,400,000
1969	all dated 1967	219,360,000
1970	non-proof issue; all dated 1967	109,524,000
1970	proof issue	750,424

Copper Halfpenny

Date	Remarks	Mintage
1825		215,040
1826		9,031,630
1827		5,376,000
1831		806,400
1834		537,600
1837		349,400
1838		456,960
1839	proof issue; about 400 issued in sets	268,800
1841		1,075,200
1843		967,680
1844		1,075,200
1845		1,075,200
1846		860,160
1847		752,640
1848		322,560
1851		215,040
1852		637,056
1853		1,559,040
1854		12,354,048
1855		1,455,837
1856		1,942,080
1857		1,182,720
1858		2,472,960
1859		1,290,340

Bronze Halfpenny

Date	Remarks	Mintage
1860		6,630,400
1861		54,118,400
1862		61,107,200
1863		15,948,800
1864		537,600
1865		8,064,000
1866		2,508,800
1867		2,508,800
1868		3,046,400
1869		3,225,600
1870		4,350,739
1871		1,075,280
1872		4,659,410
1873		3,404,880
1874	London mint	1,347,665
1874	Heaton mint, Birmingham	5,017,600
1875	London mint	5,430,815
1875	Heaton mint, Birmingham	1,254,400
1876	Heaton mint, Birmingham	6,809,600
1877		5,209,505
1878		1,425,535

1879		3,582,545
1880		2,423,465
1881	London mint	2,007,515
1881	Heaton mint, Birmingham	1,792,000
1882	Heaton mint, Birmingham	4,480,000
1883		3,000,725
1884		6,989,580
1885		8,600,574
1886		8,586,155
1887		10,701,305
1888		6,814,070
1889		7,748,234
1890		11,254,235
1891		13,192,260
1892		2,478,335
1893		7,229,344
1894		1,767,635
1895		3,032,154
1896		9,142,500
1897		8,690,315
1898		8,595,180
1899		12,108,001
1900		13,805,190
1901		11,127,360
1902		13,672,960
1903		11,450,880
1904		8,131,200
1905		10,124,800
1906		11,101,440
1907		16,849,280
1908		16,620,800
1909		8,279,040
1910		10,769,920
1911		12,570,880
1912		21,185,920
1913		17,476,480
1914		20,289,111
1915		21,563,040
1916		39,386,143
1917		38,245,436
1918		22,321,072
1919		28,104,001
1920		35,146,793
1921		28,027,293
1922		10,734,964
1923		12,266,282
1924		13,971,038
1925		12,216,123
1926		6,712,306
1927		15,589,622
1928		20,935,200
1929		25,680,000
1930		12,532,800
1931		16,137,600
1932		14,448,000
1933		10,560,000
1934		7,704,000
1935		12,180,000
1936		19,807,200
1937	non-proof issue	27,705,600
1937	proof issue	26,402
1938		40,320,000
1939		28,924,800
1940		32,162,400
1941		45,120,000
1942		71,908,800
1943		76,200,000
1944		81,840,000
1945		57,000,000
1946		22,725,600
1947		21,266,400
1948		26,947,200

1949		24,744,000
1950	non-proof issue	24,153,600
1950	proof issue	17,513
1951	non-proof issue	14,868,000
1951	proof issue	20,000
1952		33,278,400
1953	non-proof issue	8,910,000
1953	proof issue	40,000
1954		19,375,200
1955		18,465,600
1956		21,799,200
1957		39,672,000
1958		66,283,200
1959		79,224,000
1960		41,340,000
1962		41,779,200
1963		42,720,000
1964		78,583,200
1965		98,083,200
1966		95,289,600
1967		100,264,000
1968	all dated 1967	46,226,400
1970	proof only	750,424

Copper Farthing

Date	Mintage
1821	2,688,000
1822	5,924,352
1823	2,365,440
1825	4,300,800
1826	6,666,240
1827	2,365,440
1828	2,365,440
1829	1,505,280
1830	2,365,440
1831	2,688,000
1834	1,935,360
1835	1,720,320
1836	1,290,240
1837	3,010,560
1838	591,360
1839	4,300,800
1840	3,010,560
1841	1,720,320
1842	1,290,240
1843	4,085,760
1844	430,080
1845	3,225,600
1846	2,580,480
1847	3,879,720
1848	1,290,240
1849	645,120
1850	430,080
1851	1,935,360
1852	822,528
1853	1,028,628
1854	6,504,960
1855	3,440,640
1856	1,771,392
1857	1,075,200
1858	1,720,320
1859	1,290,240

Bronze Farthing

Date	Remarks	Mintage
1860		2,867,200
1861		8,601,600
1862		14,336,000
1863		1,433,600
1864		2,508,800
1865		4,659,200
1866		3,584,000
1867		5,017,600
1868		4,851,208
1869		3,225,600
1872		2,150,400
1873		3,225,620
1874	Heaton mint, Birmingham	3,584,000
1875		712,760
1875	Heaton mint, Birmingham	6,092,800
1876	Heaton mint, Birmingham	1,175,200
1878		4,008,540
1879		3,977,180
1880		1,842,710
1881	London mint	3,494,670
1881	Heaton mint, Birmingham	1,792,000
1882	Heaton mint, Birmingham	1,792,000
1883		1,128,680
1884		5,782,000
1885		5,442,308
1886		7,767,790
1887		1,340,800
1888		1,887,250
1890		2,133,070
1891		4,959,690
1892		887,240
1893		3,904,320
1894		2,396,770
1895		2,852,852
1896		3,668,610
1897		4,579,800
1898		4,010,080
1899		3,864,616
1900		5,969,317
1901		8,016,459
1902		5,125,120
1903		5,331,200
1904		3,628,800
1905		4,076,800
1906		5,340,160
1907		4,399,360
1908		4,264,960
1909		8,852,480
1910		2,598,400
1911		5,196,800
1912		7,669,760
1913		4,184,320
1914		6,126,988
1915		7,129,254
1916		10,993,325
1917		21,434,844
1918		19,362,818
1919		15,089,425
1920		11,480,536
1921		9,469,097
1922		9,956,983
1923		8,034,457
1924		8,733,414
1925		12,634,697
1926		9,792,397
1927		7,868,355
1928		11,625,600
1929		8,419,200
1930		4,195,200
1931		6,595,200
1932		9,292,800
1933		4,560,000
1934		3,052,800
1935		2,227,200
1936		9,734,400

1937	non-proof issue	8,131,200
1937	proof issue	26,402
1938		7,449,600
1939		31,440,000
1940		18,360,000
1941		27,312,000
1942		28,857,600
1943		33,345,600
1944		25,137,600
1945		23,736,000
1946		24,364,800
1947		14,745,600
1948		16,622,400
1949		8,424,000
1950	non-proof issue	10,324,800
1950	proof issue	17,513
1951	non-proof issue	14,016,000
1951	proof issue	20,000
1952		5,251,200
1953	non-proof issue	6,109,200
1953	proof issue	40,000
1954		6,566,400
1955		5,779,200
1956		1,996,800

Half Farthing

Date	Mintage
1828	7,680,000
1830	8,776,320
1837	1,935,360
1839	2,042,880
1843	3,440,640
1844	6,451,000
1847	3,010,560
1852	989,184
1853	955,224
1854	677,376
1856	913,920

Third Farthing

Date	Mintage
1844	1,301,040
1866	576,000
1868	144,000
1876	162,000
1878	288,000
1881	144,000
1884	144,000
1885	288,000
1902	288,000
1913	288,000

Quarter Farthing

Date	Mintage
1839	3,840,000
1852	2,215,000

Mintage Figures – Decimal Coinage

Base Metal Five Pounds

Date	Remarks	Mintage
1990	non-proof issue	2,754,631
1993	non-proof issue	1,776,201

Base Metal Two Pounds

Date	Remarks	Mintage
1986	non-proof issue	8,212,184
1989	non-proof issue	4,777,891

Base Metal Pound

Date	Remarks	Mintage
1983	non-proof issue	443,053,510
1984	non-proof issue	146,256,501
1985	non-proof issue	228,430,749
1986	non-proof issue	10,409,501
1987	non-proof issue	39,298,502
1988	non-proof issue	7,118,825
1989	non-proof issue	70,580,501
1990	non-proof issue	97,269,302
1991	non-proof issue	38,443,575
1992	non-proof issue	36,320,487
1993	non-proof issue	44,392,000

50 Pence

Date	Remarks	Mintage
1969	non-proof issue	188,400,000
1970	non-proof issue	19,461,500
1973	non-proof issue	89,775,000
1976	non-proof issue	43,746,500
1977	non-proof issue	49,536,000
1978	non-proof issue	72,005,500
1979	non-proof issue	58,680,000
1980	non-proof issue	89,086,000
1981	non-proof issue	74,002,000
1982	non-proof issue	51,312,000
1983	non-proof issue	62,824,904
1985	non-proof issue	682,103
1992	non-proof issue	109,000

25 Pence

Date	Remarks	Mintage
1972	non-proof issue	7,452,100
1977	non-proof issue	37,061,160
1980	non-proof issue	9,306,000
1981	non-proof issue	26,773,600

20 Pence

Date	Remarks	Mintage
1982	non-proof issue	740,815,000
1983	non-proof issue	158,463,000
1984	non-proof issue	65,350,965

1985	non-proof issue	74,273,699
1987	non-proof issue	137,450,000
1988	non-proof issue	38,038,344
1989	non-proof issue	132,013,890
1990	non-proof issue	88,097,500
1991	non-proof issue	35,901,250
1992	non-proof issue	31,205,000
1993	non-proof issue	50,330,000

10 Pence

Date	Remarks	Mintage
1968	non-proof issue	336,143,250
1969	non-proof issue	314,008,000
1970	non-proof issue	133,571,000
1971	non-proof issue	63,205,000
1973	non-proof issue	152,174,000
1974	non-proof issue	92,741,000
1975	non-proof issue	181,559,000
1976	non-proof issue	228,220,000
1977	non-proof issue	59,323,000
1979	non-proof issue	115,457,000
1980	non-proof issue	88,650,000
1981	non-proof issue	3,487,000
1992	non-proof issue	1,291,743,170

5 Pence

Date	Remarks	Mintage
1968	non-proof issue	98,868,250
1969	non-proof issue	120,270,000
1970	non-proof issue	225,948,525
1971	non-proof issue	81,783,475
1975	non-proof issue	141,539,000
1977	non-proof issue	24,308,000
1978	non-proof issue	61,094,000
1979	non-proof issue	155,456,000
1980	non-proof issue	220,566,000
1987	non-proof issue	48,220,000
1988	non-proof issue	120,744,610
1989	non-proof issue	101,406,000
1990	non-proof issue	1,634,976,005
1991	non-proof issue	724,979,000
1992	non-proof issue	247,611,500

2 Pence

Date	Remarks	Mintage
1971	non-proof issue	1,454,856,250
1975	non-proof issue	145,545,000
1976	non-proof issue	181,379,000
1977	non-proof issue	109,281,000
1978	non-proof issue	189,658,000
1979	non-proof issue	260,200,000
1980	non-proof issue	408,527,000
1981	non-proof issue	353,191,000
1985	non-proof issue	107,113,000
1986	non-proof issue	168,967,500
1987	non-proof issue	218,100,750
1988	non-proof issue	419,889,000
1989	non-proof issue	359,226,000
1990	non-proof issue	204,499,700

Date	Remarks	Mintage
1991	non-proof issue	86,625,250
1992	non-proof issue	102,247,000
1993	non-proof issue	109,985,000

Penny

Date	Remarks	Mintage
1971	non-proof issue	1,521,666,250
1973	non-proof issue	280,196,000
1974	non-proof issue	330,892,000
1975	non-proof issue	221,604,000
1976	non-proof issue	300,160,000
1977	non-proof issue	285,430,000
1978	non-proof issue	292,770,000
1979	non-proof issue	459,000,000
1980	non-proof issue	416,304,000
1981	non-proof issue	301,800,000
1982	non-proof issue	100,292,000
1983	non-proof issue	243,002,000
1984	non-proof issue	154,759,625
1985	non-proof issue	200,605,245
1986	non-proof issue	369,989,130
1987	non-proof issue	499,946,000
1988	non-proof issue	793,492,000
1989	non-proof issue	658,142,000
1990	non-proof issue	529,047,500
1991	non-proof issue	206,457,600
1992	non-proof issue	253,867,000
1993	non-proof issue	356,274,000

Half Penny

Date	Remarks	Mintage
1971	non-proof issue	1,394,188,250
1973	non-proof issue	365,680,000
1974	non-proof issue	365,448,000
1975	non-proof issue	197,600,000
1976	non-proof issue	412,172,000
1977	non-proof issue	66,368,000
1978	non-proof issue	59,532,000
1979	non-proof issue	219,132,000
1980	non-proof issue	202,788,000
1981	non-proof issue	46,748,000
1982	non-proof issue	190,752,000
1983	non-proof issue	7,600,000

Maundy Money

(not including sets in cased proof sets)

Date	4d	3d	2d	1d
1816	1,584	1,584	2,376	4,752
1817	1,386	1,584	2,376	10,296
1818	1,188	1,584	2,376	9,504
1819	792	1,320	1,980	6,336
1820	990	1,320	1,584	7,920
1821	990	1,320	1,980	3,960
1822	2,970	3,960	5,940	11,880
1823	1,980	2,640	3,960	12,672
1824	1,584	2,112	3,168	9,504
1825	2,376	3,432	3,960	8,712
1826		3,432		8,712
1827	2,772	3,168	3,960	7,920
1828	2,772	3,168	3,960	7,920
1829	2,772	3,168	3,960	7,920
1830	2,772	3,168	3,960	7,920
1831	3,564	3,960	4,752	10,296
1832	2,574	2,904	3,564	8,712
1833	2,574	2,904	3,564	8,712
1834	2,574	2,904	3,564	8,712
1835	2,574	2,904	3,564	8,712
1836	2,544	2,904	3,564	8,712
1837	2,574	2,904	3,564	8,712
1838	4,158	4,312	4,488	8,976
1839	4,125	4,356	4,488	8,976
1840	4,125	4,356	4,488	8,976
1841	2,574	2,904	3,960	7,920
1842	4,125	4,356	4,488	8,976
1843	4,158	4,488	4,752	7,920
1844	4,158	4,488	4,752	7,920
1845	4,158	4,488	4,752	7,920
1846	4,158	4,488	4,752	7,920
1847	4,158	4,488	4,752	7,920
1848	4,158	4,488	4,752	7,920
1849	4,158	4,488	4,752	7,920
1850	4,158	4,488	4,752	7,920
1851	4,158	4,488	4,752	7,920
1852	4,158	4,488	4,752	7,920
1853	4,158	4,488	4,752	7,920
1854	4,158	4,488	4,752	7,920
1855	4,158	4,488	4,752	7,920
1856	4,158	4,488	4,752	7,920
1857	4,158	4,488	4,752	7,920
1858	4,158	4,488	4,752	7,920
1859	4,158	4,488	4,752	7,920
1860	4,158	4,488	4,752	7,920
1861	4,158	4,488	4,752	7,920
1862	4,158	4,488	4,752	7,920
1863	4,158	4,488	4,752	7,920
1864	4,158	4,488	4,752	7,920
1865	4,158	4,488	4,752	7,920
1866	4,158	4,488	4,752	7,920
1867	4,158	4,488	4,752	7,920
1868	4,158	4,488	4,752	7,920
1869	4,158	4,488	4,752	7,920
1870	4,569	4,488	5,347	9,002
1871	4,627	4,488	4,753	9,286
1872	4,328	4,488	4,719	8,956
1873	4,162	4,488	4,756	7,932
1874	5,937	4,488	5,578	8,741
1875	4,154	4,488	5,745	8,459
1876	4,862	4,488	6,655	10,426
1877	4,850	4,488	7,189	8,936
1878	5,735	4,488	6,709	9,903
1879	5,202	4,488	6,925	10,626
1880	5,199	4,488	6,247	11,088
1881	6,203	4,488	6,001	9,017
1882	4,146	4,488	7,264	10,607
1883	5,096	4,488	7,232	11,673
1884	5,353	4,488	6,042	14,109
1885	5,791	4,488	5,958	12,302
1886	6,785	4,488	9,167	15,952
1887	5,292	4,488	8,296	17,506
1888	9,583	4,488	9,528	14,480
1889	6,088	4,488	6,727	14,028
1890	9,087	4,488	8,613	13,115
1891	11,303	4,488	10,000	21,743
1892	8,524	4,488	11,583	15,525
1893	10,832	8,976	14,182	21,593
1894	9,385	8,976	12,099	18,391
1895	8,877	8,976	10,766	17,408
1896	8,476	8,976	10,795	17,380
1897	9,388	8,976	11,000	16,477
1898	9,147	8,976	11,945	16,634
1899	13,561	8,976	14,514	17,402
1900	9,571	8,976	10,987	17,299
1901	11,928	8,976	13,539	17,644
1902	10,117	8,976	14,079	21,278
1903	9,729	8,976	13,386	17,209
1904	11,568	8,976	13,827	18,524

1905	10,998	–	8,976	–	11,139	–	17,504
1906	11,065	–	8,800	–	11,325	–	17,850
1907	11,132	–	8,760	–	13,238	–	18,388
1908	9,929	–	8,760	–	14,815	–	18,150
1909	2,428	–	1,983	–	2,695	–	2,948
1910	2,755	–	1,440	–	2,998	–	3,392
1911	1,768	–	1,991	–	1,635	–	1,913
1912	1,700	–	1,246	–	1,678	–	1,616
1913	1,798	–	1,228	–	1,880	–	1,590
1914	1,651	–	982	–	1,659	–	1,818
1915	1,441	–	1,293	–	1,465	–	2,072
1916	1,499	–	1,128	–	1,509	–	1,647
1917	1,478	–	1,237	–	1,506	–	1,820
1918	1,479	–	1,375	–	1,547	–	1,911
1919	1,524	–	1,258	–	1,567	–	1,699
1920	1,460	–	1,399	–	1,630	–	1,715
1921	1,542	–	1,386	–	1,794	–	1,847
1922	1,609	–	1,373	–	3,074	–	1,758
1923	1,635	–	1,430	–	1,527	–	1,840
1924	1,665	–	1,515	–	1,602	–	1,619
1925	1,786	–	1,438	–	1,670	–	1,890
1926	1,762	–	1,504	–	1,902	–	2,180
1927	1,681	–	1,690	–	1,766	–	1,647
1928	1,642	–	1,835	–	1,706	–	1,846
1929	1,969	–	1,761	–	1,862	–	1,837
1930	1,744	–	1,948	–	1,901	–	1,724
1931	1,915	–	1,818	–	1,897	–	1,759
1932	1,937	–	2,042	–	1,960	–	1,835
1933	1,931	–	1,920	–	2,066	–	1,872
1934	1,893	–	1,887	–	1,927	–	1,872
1935	1,995	–	2,007	–	1,928	–	1,975
1936	1,323	–	1,307	–	1,365	–	1,329
1937	1,325	–	1,351	–	1,472	–	1,329
1938	1,424	–	1,350	–	1,374	–	1,275
1939	1,332	–	1,234	–	1,436	–	1,253
1940	1,367	–	1,290	–	1,277	–	1,375
1941	1,345	–	1,253	–	1,345	–	1,255
1942	1,325	–	1,325	–	1,231	–	1,243
1943	1,335	–	1,335	–	1,239	–	1,347
1944	1,345	–	1,345	–	1,345	–	1,259
1945	1,355	–	1,355	–	1,355	–	1,367
1946	1,365	–	1,365	–	1,365	–	1,479
1947	1,375	–	1,375	–	1,479	–	1,387
1948	1,385	–	1,491	–	1,385	–	1,397
1949	1,503	–	1,395	–	1,395	–	1,407
1950	1,515	–	1,405	–	1,405	–	1,527
1951	1,580	–	1,468	–	1,580	–	1,480
1952	1,064	–	1,012	–	1,064	–	1,024
1953	1,078	–	1,078	–	1,025	–	1,050
1954	1,076	–	1,076	–	1,020	–	1,088
1955	1,082	–	1,082	–	1,082	–	1,036
1956	1,088	–	1,088	–	1,088	–	1,100
1957	1,094	–	1,094	–	1,094	–	1,168
1958	1,100	–	1,100	–	1,164	–	1,112
1959	1,106	–	1,172	–	1,106	–	1,118
1960	1,180	–	1,112	–	1,112	–	1,124
1961	1,118	–	1,118	–	1,118	–	1,200
1962	1,197	–	1,125	–	1,197	–	1,127
1963	1,205	–	1,205	–	1,131	–	1,133
1964	1,213	–	1,213	–	1,137	–	1,215
1965	1,221	–	1,221	–	1,221	–	1,143
1966	1,206	–	1,206	–	1,206	–	1,206
1967	986	–	986	–	986	–	1,068
1968	964	–	964	–	1,048	–	964
1969	1,002	–	1,088	–	1,002	–	1,002
1970	1,068	–	980	–	980	–	980
1971	1,108	–	1,018	–	1,018	–	1,108
1972	1,118	–	1,026	–	1,118	–	1,026
1973	1,098	–	1,098	–	1,004	–	1,004
1974	1,138	–	1,138	–	1,042	–	1,138
1975	1,148	–	1,148	–	1,148	–	1,050
1976	1,158	–	1,158	–	1,158	–	1,158

1977	1,138	–	1,138	–	1,138	–	1,240
1978	1,178	–	1,178	–	1,282	–	1,178
1979	1,188	–	1,294	–	1,188	–	1,188
1980	1,306	–	1,198	–	1,198	–	1,198
1981	1,288	–	1,178	–	1,178	–	1,288
1982	1,330	–	1,218	–	1,330	–	1,218
1983	1,342	–	1,342	–	1,228	–	1,228
1984	1,354	–	1,354	–	1,238	–	1,354
1985	1,366	–	1,366	–	1,366	–	1,248
1986	1,378	–	1,378	–	1,378	–	1,378
1987	1,390	–	1,390	–	1,390	–	1,512
1988	1,402	–	1,528	–	1,526	–	1,402
1989	1,353	–	1,353	–	1,353	–	1,353
1990	1,523	–	1,523	–	1,523	–	1,523
1991	1,514	–	1,384	–	1,384	–	1,514
1992	1,556	–	1,424	–	1,424	–	1,556
1993	1,440	–	1,440	–	1,440	–	1,440
1994	1,433	–	1,433	–	1,433	–	1,433
1995	1,466	–	1,466	–	1,466	–	1,466

Maundy Sets

The following table indicates the number of complete sets struck annually since 1902, together with averages for the last two types of Victorian set. These figures do not include sets issued in cased proof sets.

Date	Mintage of complete sets
Victoria jubilee head	4488
Victoria old head	8909
1902	8976
1903	8976
1904	8976
1905	8976
1906	8800
1907	8760
1908	8760
1909	1983
1910	1440
1911	1635
1912	1246
1913	1228
1914	982
1915	1293
1916	1128
1917	1237
1918	1375
1919	1258
1920	1399
1921	1386
1922	1373
1923	1430
1924	1515
1925	1438
1926	1504
1927	1647
1928	1642
1929	1761
1930	1724
1931	1759
1932	1835
1933	1872
1934	1872
1935	1928
1936	1307
1937	1325
1938	1275
1939	1234
1940	1277
1941	1253
1942	1231
1943	1239

1944	1259
1945	1355
1946	1365
1947	1375
1948	1385
1949	1395
1950	1405
1951	1468
1952	1012
1953	1025
1954	1020
1955	1036
1956	1088
1957	1094
1958	1100
1959	1106
1960	1112
1961	1118
1962	1125
1963	1131
1964	1137
1965	1143
1966	1206
1967	986
1968	964
1969	1002
1970	980
1971	1018
1972	1026
1973	1004
1974	1042
1975	1050
1976	1158
1977	1138
1978	1178
1979	1188
1980	1198
1981	1178
1982	1218
1983	1228
1984	1238
1985	1248
1986	1378
1987	1390
1988	1402
1989	1353
1990	1523
1991	1384
1992	1424
1993	1440
1994	1433
1995	1466

Patterns

Patterns of the Hammered Coinage

A pattern is a proposed design for a new coin which was never officially released into circulation. During the 17th century in particular, various engravers struck patterns in the hope that their design would be accepted by the mint and produced for circulation. It should be noted however that during medieval and early Tudor times, several issues were struck on flans of double or even triple thickness; known as piedforts. Such issues are not patterns, but presentation or trial pieces and were perhaps gifts to royalty or foreign officials. Medallions and medalets, as well as jettons, were also produced during the 16th and 17th centuries. These issues are not coins or patterns, but there is uncertainty whether certain pieces are patterns or medallions/medalets, whose size or weight are similar to an issued coin, and such cases have been discussed in the relevant sections of this catalogue. Medallions and medalets (which are just small medallions) were produced to commemorate an event or anniversary. A jetton is similar to a medalet but was produced either as a gaming counter or as an aid in mathematical calculations.

Collecting Hints

By their very nature, nearly all patterns are extremely rare and many can only be found in museum collections, so we have only listed 'Collecting Hints' for issues that are fairly available to collectors. If however an issue is extremely rare or very rare, it is unlikely that collectors will be able to obtain an example.

Henry III   (1216 – 1272)

Double Penny

This issue should not be confused with the smaller penny issue.

Obverse Legend   HENRICUS REX III — King Henry III

Reverse Legend   WILLEM ON CANT — Willem of Canterbury

Obverse   Crowned bust of the king front-facing and holding a sceptre, as the class 5G penny (see p.331).

Reverse   Long cross, three pellets in each quarter.

H3PT-005   probably unique

Henry VII   (1485 – 1509)

Silver Groat (?)

Obverse Legend   None

Reverse Legend   POSUI DEUM ADIUTOR MEU — I have made God my helper

Obverse   King enthroned with 'LONDON' below.

Reverse   Royal shield over long cross.

H7PT-005   ex. rare

Henry VIII   (1509 – 1547)

No patterns were made during Henry VIII's reign, although several modern sources list a pattern silver crown. This issue, which has a half-length bust of the king on the obverse and the arms of England and France with a lion and dragon on the reverse, is in fact a medallion. The original issue is of the highest rarity but later copies exist.

Edward VI   (1547 – 1553)

Gold Six Angel Piece

Obverse Legend   EDWARD VI D.G. REX ANGL FRAN HIBER — Edward VI by the grace of God King of England France Ireland

Reverse Legend   PER CRUCEM TUAM SALUA NOS XPE RED — By the cross save us O Christ our Redeemer

Obverse   Archangel Michael spearing the Devil.

Reverse   A ship.

E6PT-005   ex. rare

Gold Half Sovereign

Obverse Legend   SCUTUM FIDEI PROTEGET EUM — The shield of faith shall protect him

Reverse Legend   EDWARD VI D.G. REX AGL FRA HI — Edward VI by the grace of God King of England France Ireland (varieties of legend layout exist)

Obverse   Uncrowned right-facing bust of the king; mintmark rose.

Reverse   Crowned rose dividing 'E.R.'.

E6PT-010   ex. rare

Gold Noble

It is possible that this issue is in fact a medallion.

Obverse Legend   EDWARD VI REX ANG FRANC HIBER Z — Edward VI King of England France and Ireland

Reverse Legend   INSIGNIA POTENTISSI MI REGIS ANGLIE 1547 — ?

Obverse   Crowned rose dividing 'E.R.'.

Reverse   Legend in five lines.

E6PT-015   ex. rare

Gold Crown

Obverse Legend   EDWARD VI D.G. REX AGL FRA HI — Edward VI by the grace of God King of England France and Ireland

Reverse Legend   SCUTUM FIDEI PROTEGET EUM — The shield of faith shall protect him

Obverse   Uncrowned right-facing bust of the king.

Reverse   Crowned rose dividing 'E.R.'.

E6PT-020   ex. rare

E6PT-040   ex. rare

Gold Halfcrown

Obverse Legend   SCUTUM FIDEI PROTEGET EUM — The shield of faith shall protect him

Reverse Legend   EDWARD VI D.G. REX AGL FRA HI — Edward VI by the grace of God King of England France and Ireland

Obverse   Uncrowned right-facing bust of the king; mintmark cross.

Reverse   Crowned rose dividing 'E.R.'.

E6PT-025   ex. rare

Silver Shilling

This issue (E6PT-030) has a variety of weights.

Obverse Legend   EDWARD VI D.G. AGL FRA Z HIB REX — Edward VI by the grace of God King of England France and Ireland

Reverse Legend   TIMOR DOMINI FONS VITE MDXLVII — The fear of the Lord is the fountain of life 1547

Obverse   Crowned right-facing bust of the king.

Reverse   Oval shield dividing 'E.R.'; mintmark rose.

E6PT-030   ex. rare

Obverse Legend   TIMOR DOMIN FONS VITAE MDLV7 — The fear of the Lord is the fountain of life 1547

Reverse Legend   POSUI DEUM ADIUTORE MEU — I have made the Lord my helper

Obverse   Crowned right-facing bust of the king; mintmark rose.

Reverse   Long cross over royal shield; mintmark arrow.

E6PT-035   ex. rare

Obverse Legend   EDWARD VI D.G. AGLIE FRAN Z HIB REX — Edward VI by the grace of God King of England France and Ireland

Reverse Legend   TIMOR DOMINI FONS VITE MDLI — The fear of the Lord is the fountain of life 1551

Obverse   King on horseback; mintmark ostrich head.

Reverse   Crowned arms dividing 'E.R.'; mintmark ostrich head.

Philip and Mary   (1554 – 1558)

Silver Halfcrown

Obverse Legend   PHILIPUS D.G.R. ANG FR NEAP PR HISP — Philip by the grace of God King of England France and Naples Prince of Spain

Reverse Legend   MARIA D.G.R. ANG FR NEAP PR HISP -Mary by the grace of God Queen of England France and Naples Princess of Spain

Obverse   Right-facing bust of Philip, a crown above.

Reverse   Left-facing bust of Mary, a crown above and the date 1554 below.

PMPT-005   ex. rare

Elizabeth I   (1558 – 1603)

Gold Pound (1565 issue)

Obverse Legend   ELIZABETH D.G. ANG FRA ET HIB REGINA — Elizabeth by the grace of God Queen of England France and Ireland

Reverse Legend   IHS AUTEM TRANSIENS PER MEDUIM ILLORUM IBAT — But Jesus passing through their midst went His way

Obverse   Crowned left-facing bust of the queen wearing a plain dress; mintmark rose.

Reverse   Crowned square shield dividing 'E.R.'; mintmark rose.

ELPT-005   ex. rare

Gold Halfpound

Obverse Legend   ELIZABETH D.G. ANG FRA ET HI REGINA — Elizabeth by the grace of God Queen of England France and Ireland

Reverse Legend   SCUTUM FIDEI PROTEGET EAM — The shield of the faith shall protect her

Obverse   Crowned left-facing bust of the queen in plain dress, no inner circle; mintmark tun.

Reverse   Crowned shield dividing 'E.R.', no inner circle; mintmark tun.

ELPT-010   ex. rare

Several publications from the last century list the milled gold crown as a pattern, but we consider it a regular issue (ELCR-020, p.159).

Milled Silver Halfcrown

This issue is a piedfort of ELSH-020 or ELSH-025 (see p.230), except that the obverse legend reads REGI instead of REGINA. Sometimes listed as a pattern halfcrown, it could also be a presentation piece due to its weight. The queen's bust is in high relief.

ELPT-015   ex. rare

Milled Silver Shilling

Obverse Legend   ELIZABETH D.G. ANG FRA ET HIB REGINA — Elizabeth by the grace of God Queen of England France and Ireland

Reverse Legend   POSUI DEU ADUITOREM MEU — I have made God my helper

Obverse   Crowned left-facing bust of the queen, no inner circles; mintmark martlet.

Reverse   Royal shield over long cross; mintmark martlet.

ELPT-020   ex. rare

The following two patterns (ELPT-025 and -030) should not be confused with the regular currency issue ELSH-040, p.231.

Obverse Legend   ELIZAB D.G. ANG FR ET HIB REGI — Elizabeth by the grace of God Queen of England France and Ireland

Reverse Legend   POSUI DEU ADITOREM MEU — I have made the Lord my helper

Obverse   Left-facing bust of the queen in very ornate dress; mintmark key.

Reverse   Royal shield over long cross; mintmark key.

ELPT-025   ex. rare

Obverse Legend   As previous, but REGINA instead of REGI.
Reverse Legend   As previous.
Obverse   As previous.
Reverse   Ornate shield over long cross; mintmark key.

ELPT-030   ex. rare

Milled Sixpence

Obverse Legend   ELIZABETH D.G. ANG FRA ET HIB REGINA — Elizabeth by the grace of God Queen of England France and Ireland

Reverse Legend   POSUI DEUM ADUITOREM MEUM — I have made God my helper

Obverse   Crowned bust with rose behind; mintmark pierced mullet.

Reverse   Cross over royal shield, dated 1570 above the shield; mintmark pierced mullet.

ELPT-035   ex. rare

Sixpence

Obverse Legend   ELIZABETH DE GR ANG FR & HIB REGINA — Elizabeth by the grace of God Queen of England France and Ireland (irregular sized lettering)

Reverse Legend   POSUI DEUM ADIUTOREM MEUM — I have made God my helper (irregular sized lettering)

Obverse   Very elaborate bust of the queen with a rose behind, the queen's crown touches the top of the coin; mintmark mullet.

Reverse   Shield over cross dated 1574 or 1575 above shield; mintmark mullet.

ELPT-040   ex. rare

Threepence

As previous, but dated 1575 only.

ELPT-045   ex. rare

Halfgroat

Obverse Legend   E.D.G. ROSA SINE SPINA — Elizabeth by the grace of God a rose without a thorn

Reverse Legend   CIVITAS LONDON — City of London

Obverse   Left-facing crowned bust of the queen, a lis behind her head; mintmark bell.

Reverse   Shield over long cross; mintmark bell.

ELPT-050   ex. rare

Obverse Legend   ELIZABETH D.G. ANG FRA ET HIB REGINA — Elizabeth by the grace of God Queen of England France and Ireland

Reverse Legend   POSUI DEU ADIVTOREM MEU — I have made God my helper

Obverse   Crowned bust of the queen facing left, no inner circle; mintmark cross crosslet.

Reverse   Shield over long cross, no inner circle; mintmark cross crosslet.

ELPT-055   ex. rare

Penny

Type 1

This issue, which was struck in gold, silver, copper or tin, could be a pattern or a medalet. Victorian copies exist.

Obverse Legend   UNUM A DEO DUOBUS SUSTINEO — ?

Reverse Legend   AFFLICTORUM CONSERVATRIX — ?

Obverse   Front-facing crowned bust of the queen.

Reverse   Crowned monogram of the word 'Elizabeth', 1601.

Gold

ELPT-060   ex. rare

Silver

ELPT-065   VG £100   F £300   VF v. rare

Copper

ELPT-070   v. rare

Tin

ELPT-075   v. rare

Type 2

This pattern was struck in silver and copper. Some low denomination patterns had legends in English as they were intended for the poor who it was thought could not read Latin, although it is equally unlikely that they could read English.

Obverse Legend   THE PLEDGE OF

Reverse Legend   A PENNY 1601

Obverse   Front-facing crowned bust of the queen.

Reverse   Crowned monogram of Elizabeth.

Silver

ELPT-080   v. rare

Copper

ELPT-085   v. rare

Type 3

This pattern was struck in silver, copper and tin.

Obverse Legend   ROSA SINE SPINA — A rose without a thorn

Reverse Legend   PRO LEGE REGE ET GREGE — ?

Obverse   Crowned rose.

Reverse   Shield of St George.

Silver

ELPT-090   v. rare

Copper

ELPT-095   v. rare

Tin

ELPT-100   v. rare

Halfpenny

Type 1

This pattern was struck in silver and copper.

Obverse Legend   THE PLEDGE OF

Reverse Legend   A HALFPENNY 1601

Obverse   Front-facing crowned bust of the queen.

Reverse   Crowned monogram of 'Elizabeth'.

Silver

ELPT-105   v. rare

Copper

ELPT-110   v. rare

Type 2

This pattern was struck in silver and copper.

Obverse Legend   THE PLEDGE OF

Reverse Legend   A HALFPENNY

Obverse   Crowned monogram of 'Elizabeth'.

Reverse   Crowned rose.

Silver

ELPT-115   v. rare

Copper

ELPT-120   v. rare

Type 3

This pattern was struck in silver, copper and tin.

Obverse Legend   ROSA SINE SPINA — A rose without a thorn

Reverse Legend   PRO LEGE REGE ET GREGE — ?

Obverse   Crowned rose.

Reverse   Shield of St George.

Silver

ELPT-125   v. rare

Copper

ELPT-130   v. rare

Tin

ELPT-135   v. rare

Type 4

This issue was struck in silver and is sometimes considered to be a pattern twopence.

Obverse Legend   E.D.G. ROSA SINE SPINA — Elizabeth by the grace of God a rose without a thorn

Reverse Legend   TURRIS LONDINENSIS — Tower of London

Obverse   Crowned rose dividing 'E.R.'.

Reverse   Shield of St George.

ELPT-140   ex. rare

Type 5

This pattern was struck in billon silver.

Obverse Legend   ELIZAB D.G. AN FR ET H REG — Elizabeth by the grace of God Queen of England France and Ireland

Reverse Legend   A HALFPENNY PECE

Obverse   Crowned bust of the queen facing right.

Reverse   Crowned shield.

ELPT-145   ex. rare

Farthing

Type 1

This pattern was struck in silver.

Obverse Legend   None.

Reverse Legend   None.

Obverse   Crowned monogram of Elizabeth.

Reverse   Portcullis with '1601' above.

ELPT-150   ex. rare

Type 2

This pattern was struck in copper and it is possible that this issue was struck at a later date.

Obverse Legend   ROSA SINE SPINA — A rose without a thorn

Reverse Legend   PRO LEGE REGE ET GREGE — ?

Obverse   A crowned rose.

Reverse   Shield of St George.

ELPT-155   ex. rare

Type 3

This pattern was struck in silver.

Obverse Legend   None.

Reverse Legend   None.

Obverse   Crowned 'E.R.' with bell below.

Reverse   A rose.

ELPT-160   ex. rare

James I   (1603 – 1625)

Gold Unite

This pattern was struck on a small thick flan.

Obverse Legend   IACOBUS D.G. MAG BRIT FRA ET HIB REX — James by the grace of God King of Great Britain, France and Ireland

Reverse Legend   None.

Obverse   Laureate bust of the king facing left.

Reverse   Royal arms in square shield over a cross.

J1PT-005   ex. rare

Gold Quarter Angel

Obverse Legend   None.

Reverse Legend   TUEATUR UNITA DEUS -May God guard these united kingdoms

Obverse   St Michael slaying the dragon.

Reverse   Square royal shield.

J1PT-010   ex. rare

Copper Halfpenny

Obverse Legend   BEATI PACIFIC — Blessed peace

Reverse Legend   HOC OPUS DEI — This work of God

Obverse   Crown with a small tun below.

Reverse   A thistle and rose.

J1PT-015   ex. rare

Silver Farthing

This issue in Victorian times was considered a halfpenny.

Obverse Legend   None.

Reverse Legend   None.

Obverse   'I.R.' with crown above, a rose to the left and a thistle-head to the right.

Reverse   Crowned portcullis.

J1PT-020   v. rare

Charles I   (1625 – 1649)

Charles I's coinage was very complex in terms of both the number and the variety of coins issued, and the pattern coinage is no exception, with several issues being considered possible medallions and medalets, while others saw circulation as currency. We have noted this at the appropriate instances. Several patterns are fairly common, making it possible for the collector to obtain an example.

Gold Five Unite

This pattern is unique and was presented by King Charles on the scaffold to Bishop Juxon. Sometimes referred to as the Juxon medal, it was probably struck by Abraham Vanderdoort.

Obverse Legend   CAROLUS D.G. MAG BRIT FRAN ET HIBERNIAE REX — Charles by the grace of God King of Great Britain France and Ireland

Reverse Legend FLORENT CONCORDIA REGNA — Through concord kingdoms flourish

Obverse Uncrowned left-facing bust of the king with a pointed beard.

Reverse Crowned and garnished shield dividing crowned 'C.R.'.

C1PT-005 unique

Triple Unite

Obverse Legend As previous.

Reverse Legend As previous.

Obverse Crowned bust facing left and wearing armour.

Reverse Crowned oval garnished shield dividing 'C.R.'.

C1PT-010 ex. rare

Oxford Mint

Obverse Legend CAROLUS D.G. MAG BRIT FRAN ET HI REX — Charles by the grace of God King of Great Britain France and Ireland

Outer Reverse Legend EXURGAT DEUS DISSIPENTUR INIMICI — Let God arise and His enemies be scattered

Inner Reverse Legend RELIG PROT LEG AND LIBER PAR — The religion of the Protestants the laws of England the liberty of Parliament

Obverse Half-length bust of the king holding a sword, a plume behind the bust; mintmark small lis.

Reverse Declaration in continuous scroll with date 1643 below (as C1TU-015, p. 103).

C1PT-015 ex. rare

Unite

Abraham Vanderdoort Issues

These issues were struck in high relief in gold, silver, tin and pewter, and some could be medallions.

Obverse Legend CAROLUS D.G. MAG BRIT FR ET HI REX — Charles by the grace of God King of Great Britain France and Ireland

Reverse Legend FLORERT CONCORDIA REGNA — Through concord kingdoms flourish

Obverse Uncrowned left-facing bust of the king; mintmark lis at the start of the legend.

Reverse Crowned oval garnished shield, dividing crowned 'C.R.'; mintmark lis at the end of the legend.

C1PT-020 v. rare

As previous, but with 'XX' behind the king's head; mintmark plume.

C1PT-025 v. rare

As previous, but the 'C.R.' on the reverse is uncrowned.

C1PT-030 v. rare

As previous, but the king's bust reaches the edge of the coin, dated 1630 on the reverse; mintmark heart.

C1PT-035 ex. rare

Briot Unite or Shilling

Struck in gold and silver, it is uncertain whether these issues were for the unite, the shilling or both. It is possible that they were considered medallions and some of the silver issues appear to have seen circulation as currency.

Obverse Legend CAROLUS D.G. MAGN BRITANN FRANC ET HIB REX — Charles by the grace of God King of Great Britain France and Ireland

Reverse Legend AUSPICIIS REX MAGNE TUIS — Under the auspices Great King

Obverse Uncrowned bust of the king with long hair and beard; mintmark flower at the start of the legend.

Reverse Crown over garnished royal shield dividing crowned 'C.R.', dated 1630, small 'B' for Briot at the end of the legend, small St George and dragon at the start of the legend.

C1PT-040 ex. rare

Obverse Legend As previous (minor varieties).

Reverse Legend As previous.

Obverse Crowned bust of the king, small 'B' at the start of the legend.

Reverse As previous.

C1PT-045 v. rare

Obverse Legend   As previous, but the king's name is spelt CAR instead of CAROLUS.

Reverse Legend   As previous.

Obverse   Uncrowned bust of the king with the bust reaching the bottom of the coin, 'B' at the start of the of the legend.

Reverse   As previous.

> **C1PT-050   ex. rare**

As previous, but the obverse bears a crowned bust of the king reaching the bottom of the coin and a 'B' at the end of the legend which has the king's name spelt 'C.A.R.'.

> **C1PT-055   ex. rare**

Briot Silver Unite

Obverse Legend   CAROLUS D.G. MAGN BRIT FRANC ET HIB REX — Charles by the grace of God King of Great Britain France and Ireland

Reverse Legend   ARCHETYPUS MONETAE AURAE ANGLIAE — The original money of England is gold

Obverse   Crowned left-facing bust of the king.

Reverse   Crowned square shield dividing crowned 'C.R.' and dated 1635, 'B' in the legend.

> **C1PT-060   ex. rare**

Briot Silver Unite or Shilling

Obverse Legend   CAR D.G. MAG BRIT FR ET HIB REX — Charles by the grace of God King of Great Britain France and Ireland

Reverse Legend   FIDEI DEFENSOR — Defender of the faith

Obverse   Crowned right-facing bust reaching the bottom of the coin, a 'B' at the bottom of the coin.

Reverse   Crowned shield with garter.

> **C1PT-065   ex. rare**

Tower Gold Issue Unite

Obverse Legend   CAROLUS D.G. MAG BRIT FR ET HIB REX — Charles by the grace of God King of Great Britain France and Ireland

Reverse Legend   FLORENT CONCORDIA REGNA — Through concord kingdoms flourish

Obverse   Crowned bust of the king as C1UN-035 (p.113), with value behind the king's head; mintmark sideways heart.

Reverse   Crown over shield dividing 'C.R.; mintmark heart.

> **C1PT-070   ex. rare**

Obverse Legend   As previous.

Reverse Legend   As previous.

Obverse   Crowned bust of the king as C1UN-040 (p.113, with value behind the head; mintmark plume.

Reverse   As previous, but mintmark plume.

> **C1PT-075   ex. rare**

Briot Gold Angel

Obverse Legend   CAROLUS D.G. MAGN BRITTAN FRAN ET HIB REX — Charles by the grace of God King of Great Britain France and Ireland

Reverse Legend   AMOR POPULI PRAESIDIUM REGIS — The love of the people is the king's protection

Obverse   St Michael killing the dragon, value 'X' (ten shillings) in the field.

Reverse   Ship in full sail, a small 'B' for Briot at the end of the legend.

> **C1PT-080   ex. rare**

Gold Double Crown

Obverse Legend   CAROLUS D.G. MAG BRIT FRA ET HIB REX — Charles by the grace of God King of Great Britain France and Ireland

Reverse Legend   CULTORES SUI DEUS PROTEGIT — God protects His worshippers

Obverse   Bust of the king wearing a large ruff with value 'X' behind his head, as C1DC-005 (p.128), but mintmark trefoil.

Reverse   Crown over square-topped shield, as C1DC-005; mintmark trefoil.

> **C1PT-085   ex. rare**

Obverse Legend   As previous.

Reverse Legend   As previous.

Obverse   Crowned bust of the king with pointed beard as C1DC-020 (p.128), but large mintmark rose only on obverse.

Reverse   Crown over oval shield dividing 'C.R.', as C1DC-020.

> **C1PT-090   ex. rare**

Briot Silver Crowns

Obverse Legend   CAROLUS D.G. MAG BRITANNIAE FRAN ET HIB REX FIDEI DEFENSOR — Charles by the grace of God King of Great Britain France and Ireland Defender of the faith

Reverse Legend   HAND VLLI VETERUM VIRTUTE SECUNDUS — By no means second to any predecessors in virtue

Obverse   Uncrowned bust of the king; mintmark flower.

Reverse   King on horseback.

C1PT-095   ex. rare

As previous, but crowned bust of the king.

C1PT-100   ex. rare

Obverse Legend   CAROLUS D.G. MAG BRIT FRAN ET HIB REX FIDEI DE — Charles by the grace of God King of Great Britain France and Ireland Defender of the faith

Reverse Legend   As previous.

Obverse   Shields of England, France, Scotland and Ireland in cruciform pattern with a crown above.

Reverse   King on horseback, a 'B' in wreath in exergue.

C1PT-105   ex. rare

Halfcrown

Briot Silver Issue

Obverse Legend   O REX DA FACILEM CURSUM — Grant our King a prosperous course

Reverse Legend   ATQUE AUDACIBUS ANNUE COEPTIS — And favour bold undertakings

Obverse   King on horseback with Briot's name below the groundline.

Reverse   Crown over oval royal shield dividing 1628.

C1PT-110   ex. rare

Tower Mint Issue

Obverse Legend   CAROLUS D.G. MAG BRI FRA ET HI REX — Charles by the grace of God King of Great Britain France and Ireland

Reverse Legend   CHRISTO AUSPICE REGNO — I reign under the auspices of Christ

Obverse   King on horseback, as C1HC-065 (p.194); mintmark portcullis.

Reverse   Oval shield; mintmark portcullis with rose stops and scrolls in legend.

C1PT-115   ex. rare

Shilling

Briot Gold or Silver Issue

This issue could be a jetton or medalet.

Obverse Legend   CAROLUS D.G. MAG BRIT FR ET HIB REX — Charles by the grace of God King of Great Britain France and Ireland

Reverse Legend   REGIT UNUS UNTROQUE — One rules with both

Obverse   Right-facing bust of the king wearing a radiate crown.

Reverse   Sceptre and trident dividing crowned 'C.R.', a rose below.

Gold

C1PT-120   ex. rare

Silver

C1PT-125   v. rare

Briot Silver Issue

Obverse Legend   CAROLUS D.G. MAGN BRITANN FRANC ET HIBER REX — Charles by the grace of God King of Great Britain France and Ireland

Reverse Legend   ARCHETYPUS MONETAE ARGENTAE ANGLIE — The original money in silver of England

Obverse   Crowned left-facing bust of the king.

Reverse   Crowned square shield dividing crowned 'C.R.', 1635 above crown; mintmark 'B' at the end of the legend.

C1PT-130   ex. rare

Silver Issue

This issue is probably a jetton or medalet.

Obverse Legend   CAROLUS D.G. ANG SCO FRAN ET HIB REX FIDEI DEF — Charles by the grace of God King of England Scotland France and Ireland defender of the faith

Reverse Legend   REGIT VNUS VTROQUE — One rules with both

Obverse   Crowned royal shield within garter.

Reverse   Sceptre and trident, dated 1628 in exergue.

C1PT-135   v. rare

Tower Silver Issue

Obverse Legend CAROLUS D.G. MAG BR FR ET HIB REX -Charles by the grace of God King of Great Britain France and Ireland

Reverse Legend CHRISTO AUSPICE REGNO — I reign under the auspices of Christ

Obverse Crowned bust of the king with value behind, as C1SH-050 (p.234) but without inner circles; mintmark rose.

Reverse Garnished royal shield dividing 'C.R.'.

C1PT-140 ex. rare

Obverse Legend As previous.

Reverse Legend As previous.

Obverse Crowned bust of the king with value behind his head, as C1SH-060 (p.234); mintmark portcullis.

Reverse Round oval shield, rose stops in legend; mintmark portcullis.

C1PT-145 ex. rare

Oxford Silver Issues

Obverse Legend CAROLUS D.G. MAG BR F ET HI REX — Charles by the grace of God King of Great Britain France and Ireland

Outer Reverse Legend EXURGAT DEUS DISSIPENTUR INIMICI — Let God arise and His enemies be scattered

Inner Reverse Legend RELIG PRO LEG ANG LIB PAR — The religion of the Protestants the laws of England the liberty of Parliament

Obverse Left-facing crowned bust wearing armour with a lion's head on shoulders and small plain collar with value 'XII' (twelve pence) behind the bust; mintmark Shrewsbury plume between two lozenges.

Reverse Declaration within three lines between two scrolls with Shrewsbury plume between two Oxford plumes, date 1644 and 'OX' below declaration; mintmark four lozenges.

C1PT-150 ex. rare

Obverse Legend As previous.

Reverse Legends As previous.

Obverse Crowned bust facing right in armour with plain collar and scarf, value 'IIX' behind bust; mintmark Shrewsbury plume with lozenge to the left.

Reverse Declaration in three lines between two straight lines, three Oxford plumes above declaration and date (1644) and 'OX' below.

C1PT-155 ex. rare

Obverse Legend As previous.

Reverse Legends As previous.

Obverse As previous, but the bust reaches to the bottom of the coin.

Reverse Declaration within three lines within a cartouche, a large Shrewsbury plume above, dated 1644 below; no inner circle or mintmark.

C1PT-160 ex. rare

Groat
Briot Silver Issue

Obverse Legend CAROLUS D.G. MA B F ET H REX — Charles by the grace of God King of Great Britain France and Ireland

Reverse Legend CHRISTO AUSPICE REGNO — I reign under the auspices of Christ

Obverse Crowned bust of the king with value 'IIIId' behind the head.

Reverse Square shield dated 1634 above.

C1PT-165 ex. rare

Tower Silver Issue

Obverse Legend CAROLUS D.G. MA B F ET H REX — Charles by the grace of God King of Great Britain France and Ireland

Reverse Legend As previous.

Obverse Crowned bust of the king; mintmark bell (no mark of value).

Reverse Round shield; mintmark bell.

C1PT-170 ex. rare

Silver Threepence
Briot Issue

Obverse Legend CAROLUS D.G. MA BR FR ET H REX — Charles by the grace of God King of Great Britain France and Ireland

Reverse Legend SALUS REIPUBLICAE SUPREMA LEX — The safety of the people is the supreme law

Obverse Crowned bust of the king with rose behind the bust; mintmark bell.

Reverse Oval shield; mintmark bell.

C1PT-175 v. rare

As previous, but a rose and 'III' (mark of value) behind the king's bust.

C1PT-180 v. rare

Obverse Legend CAR D.G. MAG BRIT FR ET H.R. — Charles by the grace of God King of Great Britain France Ireland

Reverse Legend As previous.

Obverse Left-facing crowned bust reaching the bottom of the coin, a rose and 'IIId' behind the king's bust.

Reverse Square royal shield over cross with 1634 above.

C1PT-185 v. rare

Silver Halfgroat

Obverse Legend CAROLUS D.G. MAG B F ET H REX — Charles by the grace of God King of Great Britain France and Ireland

Reverse Legend IUSTITIA THRONUM FIRMAT — Justice strengthens the throne

Obverse Bust of the king with value behind; mintmark heart.

Reverse Square shield; mintmark heart.

C1PT-190 ex. rare

Obverse Legend CAR D.G. MAG BRIT FR ET H R — Charles by the grace of God King of Great Britain France and Ireland

Reverse Legend IUSTITIA THRONUM FIRMAT — Justice strengthens the throne

Obverse Crowned bust with a rose and 'II' behind it.

Reverse Square shield over a cross.

C1PT-195   ex. rare

Briot Issue

The following two pattern halfgroats (C1PTR-200 and -205) sometimes saw unofficial circulation.

Obverse Legend CAR D.G. ANG SCO FR ET HIB REX — Charles by the grace of God King of England Scotland France and Ireland

Reverse Legend REGIT UNUS UTCOQUE — One rules with both

Obverse Uncrowned bust facing right and wearing a ruff.

Reverse Sceptre and trident in saltire.

C1PT-200   VG —   F £150   VF £350

As previous, but crowned 'C's on the reverse. A variety of revere legends exists.

C1PT-205   VG —   F £150   VF £350

The following issue was struck in silver and gold.

Obverse Legend As previous.

Reverse Legend FLOREBIT IN AEVUM — He will flourish in his lifetime

Obverse As previous.

Reverse Large radiate rose; mintmark small rose.

Silver

C1PT-210   v. rare

Gold

C1PT-215   ex. rare

The following issue was struck in silver and copper by N. Briot and saw circulation.

Obverse Legend CAR D.G. MAG BRIT FRAN ET HI R(EX) — Charles by the grace of God King of Great Britain France and Ireland

Reverse Legend FIDEL DEFENSOR — Defender of the faith

Obverse As previous.

Reverse Two 'C's interlocked with crown above, sometimes with a small 'B' below the 'C's.

Silver

C1PT-220   VG £50   F £100   VF £200

Copper

C1PT-225   v. rare

The following issue was struck in silver and copper by Nicholas Briot.

Obverse Legend None.

Reverse Legend None.

Obverse Rose with large crown above and 'B' below dividing crowned 'C.R.'.

Reverse Rose or thistle with large crown above and 1640 below, dividing crowned 'C.R.'.

Silver

C1PT-230   v. rare

Copper

C1PT-235   v. rare

The following issue is a silver pattern for an uncertain provincial mint and it is also uncertain who produced the dies.

Obverse Legend None.

Reverse Legend CHRISTO AUSPICE REGNO — I reign under the auspices of Christ

Obverse Large plume dividing 'C.R.' and mark of value 'II' below.

Reverse Oval royal shield.

C1PT-240   ex. rare

Silver Six Farthings

Obverse Legend CAR D.G. MAG BRIT FR ET H R — Charles by the grace of God King of Great Britain France and Ireland

Reverse Legend CHRIS AUSPICE REGN — I reign under the auspices of Christ

Obverse Crowned bust facing left reaching the bottom of the coin.

Reverse Rose with 'VI F' below.

C1PT-245   ex. rare

Silver Five Farthings

Obverse Legend As previous.

Reverse Legend As previous.

Obverse As previous.

Reverse Rose with 'V F' below.

C1PT-250   ex. rare

Silver Penny

Obverse Legend CAROLUS D.G. MA B F ET HI REX — Charles by the grace of God King of Great Britain France and Ireland

Reverse Legend IUSTITIA THRONUM FIRMAT — Justice strengthens the throne

Obverse Crowned left-facing bust wearing a lace collar, value 'I' behind the king's bust as C11D-050 (p.372); mintmark rose.

Reverse Oval shield dividing 'C.R.'; mintmark rose.

C1PT-255   ex. rare

Obverse Legend CAR D.G. MAG BRIT FR ET H R — Charles by the grace of God King of Great Britain France and Ireland

Reverse Legend IUSTITIA THRONUM FIRMAT — Justice strengthens the throne

Obverse Left-facing crowned bust reaching the bottom of the coin, a rose and 'I' behind the bust.

Reverse Square shield over cross.

C1PT-260   v. rare

Obverse Legend CAR D.G. MAG BRIT FR ET H REX — Charles by the grace of God King of Great Britain France and Ireland

Reverse Legend FLOREBIT IN AEVUM — He will flourish in his lifetime

Obverse A crowned 'C'.

Reverse A large rose.

> **C1PT-265 v. rare**

Silver Halfpenny

Obverse Legend CAROLUS REX — King Charles

Reverse Legend A HALF PENI

Obverse Crowned rose with crown dividing 'C.R.'.

Reverse As obverse.

> **C1PT-270 v. rare**

Obverse Legend None.

Reverse Legend None.

Obverse Crowned 'C.R.'.

Reverse Rose.

> **C1PT-275 v. rare**

Obverse Legend CAROLUS D.G. MAG BRIT — Charles by the grace of God (of) Great Britain

Reverse Legend FRAN ET HIBER REX — France and Ireland King

Obverse Radiate draped left-facing bust of the king.

Reverse Crown with 'C½DR' below.

> **C1PT-280 v. rare**

Copper Farthing

These issues are sometimes considered tokens and they did circulate as such, mostly in London.

Obverse Legend FARTHING TOAKENS

Reverse Legend TYPUS MONETAE ANGL AERIS — The original money of England Copper

Obverse Crossed sceptres crowned with a rose with three lis around.

Reverse Crowned cross sceptres with three lions around.

> **C1PT-285 v. rare**

Obverse Legend CITTIE OF LONDON

Reverse Legend As previous.

Obverse Crowned rose and 1644 between two swords.

Reverse As previous.

> **C1PT-290 v. rare**

Obverse Legend CAROLUS D.G. M. B REX — Charles by the grace of God King of Great Britain

Reverse Legend A FARTHING PLEDGE

Obverse Crowned rose dividing 'C.R.'.

Reverse As obverse.

> **C1PT-295 v. rare**

Obverse Legend CAROLUS D.G. MAG BRIT — Charles by the grace of God of Great Britain

Reverse Legend FRA ET HIBER REX — France and Ireland King

Obverse Helmeted bust of the king that reaches to the edge of the coin.

Reverse Oval garnished shield.

> **C1PT-300 v. rare**

Obverse Legend None.

Reverse Legend EXURGAT DEUS DISSIPENTUR INIMICI — Let God arise and His enemies be scattered

Obverse Square shield.

Reverse Crowned portcullis.

> **C1PT-305 v. rare**

Obverse Legend TAM COMMUNI QUAM — So much shared

Reverse Legend BONO PAUPERUM — Good for the poor

Obverse A crown.

Reverse A rose.

> **C1PT-310 ex. rare**

Commonwealth (1649 – 1660)

The silver patterns of the Commonwealth were mainly struck to show new minting techniques rather than new designs. Although Eloye Mestrelle and Nicholas Briot had already tried to introduce milled and machine-made coins under Elizabeth I and Charles I, they had faced the opposition of the Tower Mint workers who favoured the continuation of hammered coin production and opposed the proposed innovations, fearing that the new machinery would make their own skills (and jobs) obsolete. Nevertheless the authorities, impressed by reports of milled coins in Europe, in 1651 invited Peter Blondeau from Paris to strike some patterns on his new machinery at the London mint. This resulted in the production of the first English issues to bear an inscription on the coin edge. It also prompted the mint workers to commission a series of machine-made patterns by the Englishman David Ramage to show that the work of Blondeau, whose presence in London they resented, was not required.

The halfcrown, silver and sixpence was struck in silver unless stated.

Halfcrown

Peter Blondeau Issues

Obverse Legend THE COMMONWEALTH OF ENGLAND

Reverse Legend GOD WITH US 1651

Edge Legend IN THE THIRD YEARE OF FREEDOME BY GODS BLESSING RESTORED 1651

Obverse Arms of St George within wreath; mintmark sun.

Reverse Arms of St George and Ireland with value 'II VI' above.

> **CWPT-005 ex. rare**

Obverse Legend   As previous.

Reverse Legend   As previous.

Edge Legend   TRUTH AND PEACE 1651 PETRUS BLONDAEUS INVENTOR FECIT

Obverse   As previous.

Reverse   As previous.

CWPT-010   ex. rare

As previous, but plain edge struck in copper on a thin flan.

CWPT-015   ex. rare

Issue by Uncertain Engraver

Obverse Legend   THE COMMONWEALTH OF ENGLAND

Reverse Legend   GOD WITH US 1651

Edge   Plain.

Obverse   Arms of St George within wreath, the palm of the wreath has leaves on the inside the stem.

Reverse   Arms of St George and Ireland within circle of hairline, with beaded border, value above shield.

CWPT-020   ex. rare

David Ramage Issues

The next two issues were struck on thick or thin flans.

Obverse Legend   THE COMMOWEALTH OF ENGLAND

Reverse Legend   GAURDED WITH ANGELES 1651

Edge   TRUTH AND PEACE 1651

Obverse   Arms of St George within wreath.

Reverse   Arms of St George and Ireland being held by an angel.

CWPT-025   ex. rare

As previous, but a plain edge.

CWPT-030   ex. rare

This issue is probably also by David Ramage.

Obverse Legend   THE COMMONWEALTH OF ENGLAND

Reverse Legend   GOD WITH US. 1651

Edge   Plain.

Obverse   Small shield of St George within wreath.

Reverse   Small shields of St George and Ireland.

CWPT-035   ex. rare

Shilling

This machine-made issue was produced by Peter Blondeau.

Obverse Legend   THE COMMONWEALTH OF ENGLAND

Reverse Legend   GOD WITH US 1651

Edge   Milled or plain.

Obverse   Arms of St George within wreath; mintmark sun.

Reverse   Arms of St George and Ireland with value 'XII' above.

CWPT-040   ex. rare

Sixpence
Peter Blondeau Milled Issue

Obverse Legend   THE COMMONWEALTH OF ENGLAND

Reverse Legend   GOD WITH US 1651

Edge   Milled.

Obverse   Arms of St George within wreath.

Reverse   Arms of St George and Ireland with value 'VI' above.

CWPT-045   ex. rare

As previous, but struck on a thin flan with a plain edge.

CWPT-050   ex. rare

David Ramage Issues

Obverse Legend   TRUTH AND PEACE

Reverse Legend   TRUTH AND PEACE

Edge   TRUTH AND PEACE 1651

Obverse   Arms of St George.

Reverse   Arms of Ireland.

CWPT-055   ex. rare

As previous, but struck in gold.

CWPT-060   ex. rare

As previous, but struck in copper with a plain edge.

CWPT-065   ex. rare

As previous, but silver plated with edge of a series of stars.

CWPT-070   ex. rare

As previous, but struck in copper.

CWPT-075   ex. rare

Farthing

Pattern farthings in a variety of base metals were struck with numerous designs during the Commonwealth period. Often referred to as tokens, there is no doubt that some of these issues saw circulation along with contemporary unofficial Tradesman's tokens. Despite the large number of patterns, no farthings were officially struck for circulation during the Commonwealth. All issues are machine-made and have a plain edge.

Copper (1649)

Obverse Legend   FARTHING TOKENS OF ENGLAND

Reverse Legend   FOR NECESSITY OF CHANGE 1649

Obverse   Shield of St George.

Reverse   Shield of Ireland.

CWPT-080   v. rare

Copper or Brass (c.1650)

Obverse Legend   THE FARTHING TOKENS FOR

Reverse Legend   THE RELEFE OF THE PORE

Obverse   As previous.

Reverse   As previous.

CWPT-085   v. rare

Copper (1851)

Obverse Legend   GOD IS OUR SUN AND SHIELD

Outer Reverse Legend   OUR FOUNDATION IS A ROCKE

Inner Reverse Legend A TOKENE 1651

Obverse   A sun within a shield.

Reverse   Some rocks.

CWPT-090   v. rare

Copper (date uncertain)

Obverse Legend   THUS UNITED INVINCIBLE

Reverse Legend   AND GOD DIRECT OUR COURSE (varieties exist)

Obverse   Three pillars.

Reverse   Ship.

CWPT-095   v. rare

Copper (1652)

Obverse Legend   THE COMMONS PETICON

Reverse Legend   THE POORES RELEFE

Obverse   Shields of St George and Ireland.

Reverse   Shields of St George and Ireland with 'E.R.' below. It is thought that E.R. are the initials of an unidentified engraver.

CWPT-100   ex. rare

Silver, Brass or Copper (1652)

Obverse Legend   PITTY THE POORE 1652

Reverse Legend   SUCH GOD LOVES

Obverse   Shields of St George and Ireland.

Reverse   Shields of St George and Ireland with 'E.R.' below.

CWPT-105   ex. rare

Copper (1654)

Obverse Legend   ENGLANDS FARDIN (varieties exist)

Reverse Legend   FOR NECESSARY CHANGE (varieties exist)

Obverse   Shield of St George within wreath.

Reverse   Shield of Ireland with wreath above.

CWPT-110   v. rare

Pewter (1654)

Obverse Legend   ¼ OUNCE OF FINE PEWTER

Reverse Legend   FOR NECESSARY CHANGE

Obverse   Shield of St George with 'T.K.' within wreath above. It thought 'T.K.' are the initials of the engraver.

Reverse   Shield of Ireland with wreath above.

CWPT-115   v. rare

Tin (c.1650s)

Obverse Legend   THE FARTHING TOKEN OF THE

Reverse Legend   COMMONWEALTH OF ENGLAND

Obverse   Shield of Ireland.

Reverse   Shield of St George.

CWPT-120   ex. rare

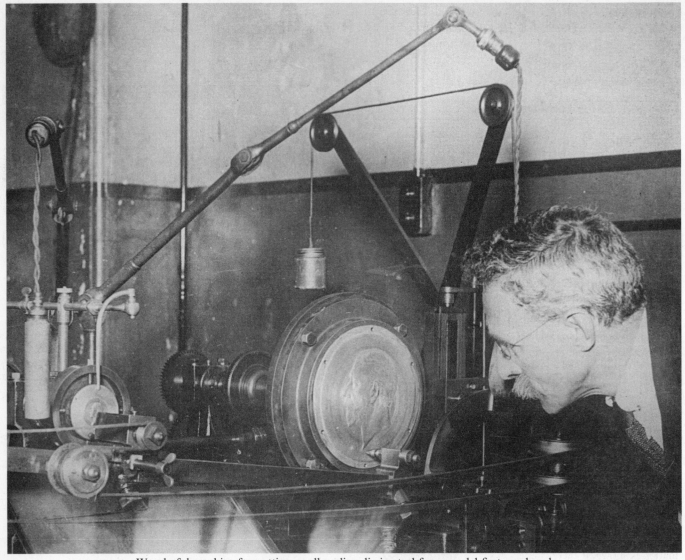

Wonderful machine for cutting small replica die in steel from model first produced

Patterns of the Milled Coinage

Most collectors and dealers probably believe that they could provide a satisfactory definition of a proof and of a pattern. However, the distinction between the two is not so obviously clear-cut, and neither is it always easy to say into which category a particular piece falls. For example, a pattern struck from dies which are later adopted for the striking of currency pieces is, strictly speaking, a pattern; however, it would probably be universally regarded as a proof. A coin such as a modern decimal proof taken from a cased proof set could by no stretch of the imagination be called a pattern. Some coins, such as the 1831 crown, were issued only for inclusion in sets and were never intended to circulate; such pieces may be considered to be either proofs or patterns.

The occasions on which there is very little doubt as to the status of a piece as a pattern is when it is struck from dies which were not those subsequently used to strike the series. The pieces in the listings that follow will mostly fall within such a definition. **Those struck from adopted dies will usually be included in the main coinage listings**.

The listings that follow are necessarily only a representative sample of the patterns known to exist in the milled coinage series. In later editions it is hoped to expand the pattern section and to provide more information on individual pieces. The quoted values are retail prices of specimens in perfect state. In assessing condition, it should be borne in mind that plain edge patterns frequently exhibit what appear to be random scratches around the edge. However, these marks identically match up coin to coin, and are caused by a metallic band used during manufacture.

To list patterns by denomination would not be a practical option; some of the denominations are unclear, and in any event patterns are not official coinage but quasi-medallic pieces struck to show how the designs would appear on a coin. For this reason, the pieces are listed in chronological order, but the intended denomination is shown, if there is one.

Some of the information tables display blanks where information is not to hand at the time of going to press.

Cromwell (Commonwealth 1649 – 1660)

Half Broad 1656

This piece was struck by J. S. Tanner in 1738. About 8 are known.

No.	Date	Denomination	Metal	Weight (grams)	Diameter (mm)	Rev. align.	Current Value
OCPT-005	1656	Half broad	Gold		25		12000

Obverse Head, left; OLIVAR D G R P ANG SCO HIB &c PRO

Reverse Crowned shield; PAX QVAERITVR BELLO 1656

Edge plain

Crown 1658

These pieces, known as the 'Dutch Copy' crowns, were struck from false dies prepared in the Low Countries around 1680–1700 using genuine puncheons acquired after Simon's death. The gilt silver specimens are thought to have been struck after those in silver.

Obverse Head, left; OLIVAR D G R P ANG SCO HIB &c PRO

Reverse Crowned shield: PAX QVAERITVR BELLO 1658

Edge HAS NISI PERITVRVS MIHI ADIMAT NEMO

Characteristics The facial features are slightly different from those on the current coin; top leaf in laurel points to N of ANG; this letter is inverted, i.e. the top left of the character has no serif (obv.). On the reverse, the harp strings slope to the perpendicular much more than on the current coin.

Crown 1658

These pieces were struck after the Cromwell era from dies prepared by J.S. Tanner using original puncheons.

No.	Date	Denomination	Metal	Weight (grams)	Diameter (mm)	Rev. align.	Current Value
OCPT-030	1658	Crown	Silver	31.7	40–41	↑	3000

Obverse Head, left; OLIVAR D G R P ANG SCO HIB &c PRO

Reverse Crowned shield: PAX QVAERITVR BELLO 1658

Edge HAS NISI PERITVRVS MIHI ADIMAT NEMO

Characteristics The facial features are slightly different from those on the current coin; top leaf in laurel points to space between A and N of ANG (obv.); wider border beading than on current coin; each P in legends is flawed near the downstroke (obv/rev).

Farthing

The designer was D. Ramage.

No.	Date	Denomination	Metal	Weight (grams)	Diameter (mm)	Rev. align.	Current Value
OCPT-040	None	Farthing	Copper	4.4–4.7	22	↓	4000

Obverse Laureate head, left; OLIVAR PRO ENG SC IRL

Reverse Crowned Arms; CHARITIE AND CHANGE

Edge plain

No.	Date	Denomination	Metal	Weight (grams)	Diameter (mm)	Rev. align.	Current Value
C2PTM-010	1660	Broad	Gold	8.4–8.8	29	↓	15000

Obverse Laureate head, right, star above; CAROLVS II REX

Reverse Four crowned cruciform shields of England, Scotland, France, Ireland with interlinked 'C's over 'II's in angles; MAGNALIA DEI 1660

Edge milled

Crown 1662

This is the piece prepared by John Roettier which was preferred to Simon's 'petition' crown.

No.	Date	Denomination	Metal	Weight (grams)	Diameter (mm)	Rev. align.	Current Value
C2PTM-020	1662	Crown	Silver	29–31	40	↓	10000
C2PTM-030	1662	Crown	Gold	51–52	40	↓	40000

Obverse Head, right; CAROLVS II DEI GRATIA

Reverse Four cruciform shields, top and bottom two quartered (England/France), interlinked pair of 'C's in angles; MAG BR FRA ET HIB REX 1662

Edge (in relief) DECVS ET TVTAMEN

Characteristics Truncation of (undraped) head is pointed unlike on current coin, but somewhat similar to head on guinea; no rose below head.

Crown 1662

No.	Date	Denomination	Metal	Weight (grams)	Diameter (mm)	Rev. align.	Current Value
C2PTM-040	1662	Crown	Gold	58.5	40		40000

Obverse Head, right; CAROLVS II DEI GRATIA

Reverse Four cruciform shields, top and bottom two quartered (England/France), interlinked pair of 'C's in angles; MAG BR FRA ET HIB REX 1662

Edge plain

Characteristics Truncation of (undraped) head is pointed unlike on current coin, but somewhat similar to head on guinea; no rose below head.

Crown 1663

In 1662, a competition was held between Thomas Simon and John Roettier to produce a crown piece for the restored monarch. This is the Simon pattern which was rejected in favour of that by

Obverse Head, right; CAROLVS II DEI GRA

Reverse Four ornate cruciform shields of England, Ireland, France, Scotland, interlinked pairs of 'C's in angles; MAG BRI FR ET HIB REX 1663

Edge (in two lines; penultimate word with original spelling) THOMAS SIMON MOST HVMBLY PRAYS YOUR MAJESTY TO COMPARE THIS HIS TRYALL PIECE WITH THE DVTCH AND IF MORE TRVLY DRAWN & EMBOSS'D MORE GRACE FVLLY ORDER'D AND MORE ACCVRATELY ENGRAVEN TO RELEIVE HIM

Characteristics Head much larger than on current coin. Legend on rev. includes BRI FR unlike BR FRA on all current pieces.

Crown 1663

See Petition crown C2PTM-050. The edge inscription on this piece, including POST with a depiction of the sun and clouds, is evocative of the Latin POST NUBILA PHOEBUS (After the storm the sun shines), i.e. the monarchy is restored.

No.	Date	Denomination	Metal	Weight (grams)	Diameter (mm)	Rev. align.	Current Value
C2PTM-060	1663	Crown	Silver	29.8–32.9	40	↑	12000
C2PTM-070	1663	Crown	Pewter	19.6–21.6	40	↑	5000

Obverse Head, right; CAROLVS II DEI GRA

Reverse Four ornate cruciform shields of England, Ireland, France, Scotland, interlinked pairs of 'C's in angles; MAG BRI FR ET HIB REX 1663

Edge REDDITE QVAE CAESARIS CAESARI &CT POST (followed by sun with clouds)

Characteristics Head much larger than on current coin. Legend on rev. includes BRI FR unlike BR FRA on all current pieces.

Shilling 1663

No.	Date	Denomination	Metal	Weight (grams)	Diameter (mm)	Rev. align.	Current Value
C2PTM-075	1663	Shilling	Silver		25–26	↓	1500

Obverse   Head, right; CAROLVS II DEI GRATIA

Reverse   Crowned rose, thistle, lis, harp in cruciform with four interlinked 'C's at centre; MAG BR FRA ET HI REX 1663

Edge

Characteristics   The obverse is identical to that of the currency issue

Farthing 1665

The designer was John Roettier, and this piece is only one example of a lengthy series of official patterns of the period. The reverse is based on a sestertius of Antoninus Pius, and the Duchess of Richmond modelled for the figure of Britannia. The Count de Grammont mentions in his memoirs that the King was a noted admirer of her legs.

No.	Date	Denomination	Metal	Weight (grams)	Diameter (mm)	Rev. align.	Current Value
C2PTM-080	1665	Farthing	Copper		22–26		120
C2PTM-090	1665	Farthing	Silver		22–26		600
C2PTM-100	1665	Farthing	Gold	12.5	22–26		5000

Obverse   Head, left; CAROLVS A CAROLO 1665

Reverse   Britannia seated on globe with shield, spear and spray; QVATVOR MARIA VINDICO; BRITANNIA in exergue

Edge   milled

Halfpenny

No.	Date	Denomination	Metal	Weight (grams)	Diameter (mm)	Rev. align.	Current Value
C2PTM-200	none	Halfpenny	Copper		29–30	↑	500

Obverse   Head, left; CAROLVS A CAROLO

Reverse   Britannia seated on globe, facing left; QVATVOR MARIA VINDICO; BRITANNIA in exergue

Edge   plain

Characteristics   Minor reverse lettering orientation differences occur

Obverse   Heads, right; GVLIELMVS ET MARIA

Reverse   Britannia seated on chair with shield, spear and spray; BRITANNIA 1694

Edge   plain

Halfpenny 1694

No.	Date	Denomination	Metal	Weight (grams)	Diameter (mm)	Rev. align.	Current Value
WMPT-030	1694	Halfpenny	Copper		35		600
WMPT-040	1694	Halfpenny	Copper		30		800

Obverse   Heads, right; GVLIELMVS ET MARIA

Reverse   Britannia seated on globe with shield, spear and spray; BRITANNIA 1694

Edge   plain

Farthing 1694

No.	Date	Denomination	Metal	Weight (grams)	Diameter (mm)	Rev. align.	Current Value
WMPT-050	1694	Farthing	Copper		26		

Obverse   Heads, right; GVLIELMVS ET MARIA

Reverse   Britannia seated on globe with shield, spear and spray; BRITANNIA 1694

Edge   plain

William III (1694 – 1701)

Crown 1696

Anne   (1702 – 1714)

Guinea 1702

The designer was John Croker. Anne considered the portrait somewhat immodest.

No.	Date	Denomination	Metal	Weight (grams)	Diameter (mm)	Rev. align.	Current Value
ANPT-010	1702	Guinea	Gold	8.2	25	↓	10000

Obverse   Head, left; ANNA DEI GRATIA

Reverse   Four crowned cruciform shields with sceptres in angles and monogrammed AR in centre; MAG BR FRA ET HIB REG 1702

Edge   plain

Characteristics   The portrait has a pronounced lock of hair on the left shoulder, unlike that on the adopted coin.

Guinea 1702

No.	Date	Denomination	Metal	Weight (grams)	Diameter (mm)	Rev. align.	Current Value
ANPT-012	1702	Guinea	Gold	8.2	25	↓	

Obverse   Head, left; ANNA DEI GRATIA

Reverse   Four crowned cruciform shields with sceptres in angles and rose in centre; MAG BR FRA ET HIB REG 1702

Edge   plain

Characteristics   The portrait is identical to that of ANPT-010

Halfpenny

The designer was John Croker. Minor varieties exist.

No.	Date	Denomination	Metal	Weight (grams)	Diameter (mm)	Rev. align.	Current Value
ANPT-020	None	Halfpenny	Copper	11.7	28	↓	200

Obverse   Draped head, left; ANNA D G MAG BR FR ET HIB REG

Reverse   Britannia seated on a globe, facing left, holding rose and thistle, crown above

Edge   plain

Halfpenny 1713

Obverse   Draped head, left; ANNA DEI GRATIA

Reverse   As obverse, but legend slightly displaced

Edge   inscribed DECVS ET TVTAME ANNO REGNI DVODE (or a somewhat similar blundered legend)

Farthing 1713

The designer was John Croker. This piece is only one of several types of Anne pattern farthing.

No.	Date	Denomination	Metal	Weight (grams)	Diameter (mm)	Rev. align.	Current Value
ANPT-040	1713	Farthing	Copper	5.7–6.0	21–25	↓	400

Obverse   Head, left; ANNA DEI GRATIA

Reverse   Britannia seated on globe with shield, spear and spray; BRITANNIA 1713

Edge   plain

George I   (1714 – 1727)

Halfcrown 1715

See currency listings.

Guinea 1727

The designer was possibly John Croker.

No.	Date	Denomination	Metal	Weight (grams)	Diameter (mm)	Rev. align.	Current Value
G1PT-010	1727	Guinea	Gold	8.3–8.4	25–26	↓	5000

Obverse   Head, right; GEORGIVS D G M BR FR ET HIB REX F D

Reverse   Four crowned cruciform shields with sceptres in angles, with central Star of the Garter; BRVN ET L DVX S R I A TH ET EL 1727

No.	Date	Denomination	Metal	Weight (grams)	Diameter (mm)	Rev. align.	Current Value
G2PT-030	1733	Two guineas	Gold	16.3–16.5	31–32	↓	10000

Obverse   Head, left; GEORGIVS II DEI GRATIA

Reverse   ·Crowned garnished shield; M B F ET H REX F D B ET L D S R I A T ET E 1733

Edge   plain

George III   (1760 – 1820)

Guinea 1761

The designer was John Tanner.

No.	Date	Denomination	Metal	Weight (grams)	Diameter (mm)	Rev. align.	Current Value
G3PT-010	1761	Guinea	Gold	7.6–8.4	24–25	↑	4000

Obverse   Head, left; GEORGIVS III DEI GRATIA

Reverse   Crowned garnished shield; M B F ET H REX F D B ET L D S R I A T ET E 1761

Edge   plain

Characteristics   The bust has a rounded truncation, unlike the adopted coin for 1761; there are other differences, especially the facial features; the adopted coin was designed by Richard Yeo.

Half Guinea 1762

The designer was Richard Yeo.

No.	Date	Denomination	Metal	Weight (grams)	Diameter (mm)	Rev. align.	Current Value
G3PT-020	1762	Half guinea	Gold	4.0–4.2	20	↑	4000

Obverse   Head, right; GEORGIVS III DEI GRATIA

Reverse   Crowned garnished shield; M B F ET H REX F D B ET L D S R I A T ET E 1762

Edge   plain

Half Guinea 1763

The designer was Richard Yeo. Mint records show that for the year ending 7 January 1764, Reuben Fletcher, the Mint smith, charged ten shillings for 'a pair of shouldered half guinea dies for pattern pieces.'

No.	Date	Denomination	Metal	Weight (grams)	Diameter (mm)	Rev. align.	Current Value
G3PT-030	1763	Half guinea	Gold	4.2	20	↑	5000

Obverse   Head, right; GEORGIVS III DEI GRATIA

Reverse   Crowned garnished shield; M B F ET H REX F D B ET L D S R I A T ET E 1762

Edge   plain

Characteristics   The hair is shorter than on the 1762 pattern half guinea.

Quarter Guinea 1764

The designer was probably Richard Yeo. Tanner's eyesight had deteriorated and by this time he may have been employed merely in an advisory capacity. Die cracks may be visible on both sides.

No.	Date	Denomination	Metal	Weight (grams)	Diameter (mm)	Rev. align.	Current Value
G3PT-040	1764	Quarter guinea	Gold	2.1–2.2	16	↑	2000

Obverse   Head, right; GEORGIVS III DEI GRATIA

Reverse   Crowned shield; M B F ET H REX F D B ET L D S R I A T ET E 1764

Edge   plain

Characteristics   Identical to adopted coin except for edge.

Shilling 1764

The designer was Richard Yeo.

No.	Date	Denomination	Metal	Weight (grams)	Diameter (mm)	Rev. align.	Current Value
G3PT-050	1764	Shilling	Silver	6.0	26	↑	2000

Obverse   Head, right; GEORGIVS III DEI GRATIA

Reverse   Four crowned cruciform shields around star, plain in angles; M B F ET H REX F D B ET L D S R I A T ET E 1764

Edge   plain

Characteristics   Similar to adopted 'Northumberland' coin of 1763 but portrait slightly different.

Guinea 1765

The designer was Thomas Pingo, and the head of the King is very similar to that on Pingo's design for the guineas of 1774 to 1786. Two specimens are known.

No.	Date	Denomination	Metal	Weight (grams)	Diameter (mm)	Rev. align.	Current Value
G3PT-060	1765	Guinea	Gold	8.4	24	↑	5000

Obverse   Head, right; GEORGIVS III DEI GRATIA

Reverse   Crowned garnished shield; M B F ET H REX F D B ET L D S R I A T ET E 1765

Edge   plain, one specimen with rim struck up and the other with bevelled edge

Two Guineas 1768, 1773

The designer was John Tanner. No two guinea pieces were struck for circulation after 1753.

No.	Date	Denomination	Metal	Weight (grams)	Diameter (mm)	Rev. align.	Current Value
G3PT-070	1768	Two guineas	Gold	15.9–16.6	31–32	↑	25000
G3PT-080	1773	Two guineas	Gold	16.6–18.3	31–33	↑	20000

Obverse Laureate head, right; GEORGIVS III DEI GRATIA

Reverse Crowned garnished shield; M B F ET H REX F D B ET L D S R I A T ET E (date)

Edge plain

Five Guineas 1770, 1773

The designer was John Tanner. No five guinea pieces were struck for circulation after 1753.

No.	Date	Denomination	Metal	Weight (grams)	Diameter (mm)	Rev. align.	Current Value
G3PT-090	1770	Five guineas	Gold	40.0–42.0	37	↑	55000
G3PT-100	1773	Five guineas	Gold	38.3–42.9	37	↑	40000

Obverse Laureate head, right; GEORGIVS III DEI GRATIA

Reverse Crowned garnished shield; M B F ET H REX F D B ET L D S R I A T ET E (date)

Edge plain

Characteristics The 1773 piece usually has a die flaw above the 73 of the date.

Guinea 1773

No.	Date	Denomination	Metal	Weight (grams)	Diameter (mm)	Rev. align.	Current Value
G3PT-105	1773	Guinea	Gold	8.4	24	↑	

Obverse Head, right; GEORGIVS III DEI GRATIA

Reverse Crowned shield; M B F ET H REX F D B ET L D S R I A T ET E 1733

Edge plain

Characteristics The piece is identical to the issue of 1774–1786 except for the date

Third Guinea 1775

The designer was Richard Yeo. 9 were struck. See note for third guinea 1776.

No.	Date	Denomination	Metal	Weight (grams)	Diameter (mm)	Rev. align.	Current Value
G3PT-107	1775	Third guinea	Gold	2.8	19	↓	1200

Obverse Head, right; GEORGIVS III DEI GRATIA

Reverse Lion on crown; MAG BRI FR ET HIB REX 1775

Edge milled (diagonally)

Shilling 1775

The designer was Richard Yeo.

No.	Date	Denomination	Metal	Weight (grams)	Diameter (mm)	Rev. align.	Current Value
G3PT-110	1775	Shilling	Silver	6.0	25–26	↑	3000

Obverse Head, right; GEORGIVS III DEI GRATIA

Reverse Four crowned cruciform shields around star, plain in angles; M B F ET H REX F D B ET L D S R I A T ET E 1775

Edge plain

Characteristics Similar to adopted 'Northumberland' coin but portrait slightly different.

Third Guinea 1776

The designer was Richard Yeo. No third guineas were struck for circulation until 1797, but in 1770 an indenture had been made between the King and the Master of the Mint, C. S. Cadogan, to coin this denomination with the proviso that the Master should not be obliged to do so until ordered expressly by the King or the Lord High Treasurer or the Commissioners of the Treasury.

No.	Date	Denomination	Metal	Weight (grams)	Diameter (mm)	Rev. align.	Current Value
G3PT-120	1776	Third guinea	Gold	2.8–2.9	19	↑	800

Obverse Head, right; GEORGIVS III DEI GRATIA

Reverse Lion on crown; MAG BRI FR ET HIB REX 1776

Edge plain

Characteristics Some pieces may exhibit traces of double striking.

Five Guineas 1777

The designer of the obverse was Richard Yeo, the reverse being as on the Tanner pattern. No five guinea pieces were struck for circulation after 1753.

No.	Date	Denomination	Metal	Weight (grams)	Diameter (mm)	Rev. align.	Current Value
G3PT-130	1777	Five guineas	Gold	39.8–44.1	37	↑	35000
G3PT-132	1777	Five guineas	White metal	20.5	37	↑	

Obverse   Laureate head, right; GEORGIVS III DEI GRATIA

Reverse   Crowned garnished shield; M B F ET H REX F D B ET L D S R I A T ET E 1777

Edge   plain

Two Guineas 1777

The designer of the obverse was Richard Yeo, the reverse being as on the Tanner pattern. No two guinea pieces were struck for circulation after 1753.

No.	Date	Denomination	Metal	Weight (grams)	Diameter (mm)	Rev. align.	Current Value
G3PT-140	1777	Two guineas	Gold	16.8	31–32	↑	25000

Obverse   Laureate head, right; GEORGIVS III DEI GRATIA

Reverse   Crowned garnished shield; M B F ET H REX F D B ET L D S R I A T ET E 1777

Edge   plain

Shilling 1778

No.	Date	Denomination	Metal	Weight (grams)	Diameter (mm)	Rev. align.	Current Value
G3PT-142	1778	Shilling	Silver	6.8	27	↓	

Obverse   Head, right; GEORGIVS III DEI GRATIA

Reverse   Four crowned cruciform shields; M B F ET H REX F D B ET L D S R I A T ET E 1778

Edge   plain

Characteristics   relatively thin flan

Guinea 1782

The designer was Earl Stanhope, and the engraver Lewis Pingo.

No.	Date	Denomination	Metal	Weight (grams)	Diameter (mm)	Rev. align.	Current Value
G3PT-143	1782	Guinea	Gold	7.1–8.2	23	↓	3000
G3PT-145	1782	Guinea	Copper	4.5–5.9	23	↓	180

Obverse   Head, right; GEORGIVS III DEI GRATIA

Reverse   Crowned garnished shield of Arms; M B F ET H REX F D B ET L D S R I A T ET E 1782

Edge   plain

Shilling 1786

The designer was Lewis Pingo.

No.	Date	Denomination	Metal	Weight (grams)	Diameter (mm)	Rev. align.	Current Value
G3PT-150	1786	Shilling	Silver	6.0	25	↑	3000

Obverse   Head, right; GEORGIVS III DEI GRATIA

Reverse   Four cruciform pentagonal shields around star; M B F ET H REX F D B ET L D S R I A T ET E 1786

Edge   milled (diagonally)

Characteristics   Identical to adopted coin variety of 1787 without hearts, with no stop over head or at date.

Sixpence 1786

No.	Date	Denomination	Metal	Weight (grams)	Diameter (mm)	Rev. align.	Current Value
G3PT-155	1786	Sixpence	Silver	3.1	21	↑	2500

Obverse   Head, right; GEORGIVS III DEI GRATIA

Reverse   Four cruciform pentagonal shields around star; M B F ET H REX F D B ET L D S R I A T ET E 1786

Edge   milled

Characteristics   Similar to adopted variety of 1787 without hearts. No stops at date.

Shilling 1787

The designer was Lewis Pingo.

No.	Date	Denomination	Metal	Weight (grams)	Diameter (mm)	Rev. align.	Current Value
G3PT-160	1787	Shilling	Silver	6.7	26–27	↑	400

Obverse   Head, right within border of dots; GEORGIVS III DEI GRATIA

Reverse   Four cruciform pentagonal shields around star, all within border of dots; M B F ET H REX F D B ET L D S R I A T ET E 1787

Edge   plain

Characteristics   Similar to 'with hearts' adopted coin except for dotted border.

Sixpence 1787

The designer was Lewis Pingo.

No.	Date	Denomination	Metal	Weight (grams)	Diameter (mm)	Rev. align.	Current Value
G3PT-170	1787	Sixpence	Silver	3.1–3.4	22–23	↑	200

Obverse   Head, right within border of dots; GEORGIVS III DEI GRATIA

Reverse   Four cruciform pentagonal shields around star, all within border of dots; hearts in Hanoverian shield; M B F ET H REX F D B ET L D S R I A T ET E 1787

Edge   plain

Characteristics   Similar to 'with hearts' adopted coin except for dotted border.

Sixpence 1788

The designer was J. P. Droz.

No.	Date	Denomination	Metal	Weight (grams)	Diameter (mm)	Rev. align.	Current Value
G3PT-180	1788	Sixpence	Silver	2.6–3.0	21	↑	180
G3PT-182	1788	Sixpence	Silver	2.6–3.0	21	↓	180
G3PT-185	1788	Sixpence	Copper		21	↑	300
G3PT-188	1788	Sixpence	Copper		21	↓	400
G3PT-190	1788	Sixpence	Gold	3.6	21	↑	3000

Obverse   Crowned monogram GR within branches

Reverse   Britannia seated; BRITANNIA; 1788 in exergue

Edge   milled

Halfpenny 1788

The designer was Lewis Pingo.

No.	Date	Denomination	Metal	Weight (grams)	Diameter (mm)	Rev. align.	Current Value
G3PT-200	1788	Halfpenny	Copper	17.6–17.7	35	↓	750

Obverse   Small laureate head, right; GEORGIVS III REX

Reverse   Britannia facing, holding spear and laurel branch; BRITANNIA 1788

Edge   milled (diagonally)

Sixpence 1790

The designer was J. P. Droz.

No.	Date	Denomination	Metal	Weight (grams)	Diameter (mm)	Rev. align.	Current Value
G3PT-210	1790	Sixpence	Silver	2.8	19–20	↑	200

Obverse   Crowned monogram GR within branches

Reverse   Britannia seated; BRITANNIA 1790

Edge   milled

Sixpence 1790

The designer was J. P. Droz.

No.	Date	Denomination	Metal	Weight (grams)	Diameter (mm)	Rev. align.	Current Value
G3PT-220	1790	Sixpence	Silver	2.8	19–20	↑	200

Obverse   Crowned monogram GR within branches

Reverse   Britannia seated; BRITANNIA 1790

Edge   plain

Guinea 1791

The designer was C. H. Küchler.

No.	Date	Denomination	Metal	Weight (grams)	Diameter (mm)	Rev. align.	Current Value
G3PT-230	1791	Guinea	Gilt copper	4.4	24	↑	400

Obverse   Small laureate head, right, within wide raised border bearing ornament and incuse legend GEORGIVS III DEI GRATIA

Reverse   Crowned spade-shaped shield within wide raised border bearing incuse legend M B F ET H REX F D B ET L D S R I A T ET E 1791

Edge   plain

Characteristics   The items depicted on the shield are reversed (i.e they are mirror images) but they are in their customary positions.

Sixpence 1791

The designer was J. P. Droz.

No.	Date	Denomination	Metal	Weight (grams)	Diameter (mm)	Rev. align.	Current Value
G3PT-240	1791	Sixpence	Silver	2.8	19–20	↑	120
G3PT-245	1791	Sixpence	Copper	3.4	19–20	↑	150
G3PT-250	1791	Sixpence	Gold	4.0	19–20	↑	4000

Obverse   Crowned monogram GR within branches

Reverse   Britannia seated; BRITANNIA; 1791 in exergue

Edge   plain

Very large numbers of copper patterns were struck around the period 1790–98. It is hoped to include many of these in the next edition of this catalogue.

Guinea 1798

The designer was Lewis Pingo, the piece being struck from half guinea dies very similar to those used for the currency issue.

No.	Date	Denomination	Metal	Weight (grams)	Diameter (mm)	Rev. align.	Current Value
G3PT-520	1798	Guinea	Gold	8.4	24	↑	5000

Obverse   Head, right; GEORGIVS III DEI GRATIA, all within plain outer border

Reverse   Crowned spade-shaped shield; M B F ET H REX F D B ET L D S R I A T ET E 1798, all within plain outer border

Edge   slightly curved 'straight across' milling

Guinea 1798

The designer was C. H. Küchler.

No.	Date	Denomination	Metal	Weight (grams)	Diameter (mm)	Rev. align.	Current Value
G3PT-540	1798	Guinea	Gold	8.0–8.3	24	↓	3000
G3PT-550	1798	Guinea	Silver	5.2	24	↑	400
G3PT-555	1798	Guinea	Silver	5.2	24	↓	400
G3PT-560	1798	Guinea	Copper	6.1	24	↑	200
G3PT-570	1798	Guinea	Copper	6.1	24	↓	200

Obverse   Head, right, within wide raised border bearing incuse legend GEORGIVS III DEI GRATIA

Reverse   Crowned spade-shaped shield within wide raised border bearing incuse legend M B F ET H REX F D B ET L D S R I A T ET E 1798

Edge   plain

Bank of England Dollar 1798

No.	Date	Denomination	Metal	Weight (grams)	Diameter (mm)	Rev. align.	Current Value
G3PT-600	1798	Bank dollar	Silver	26–32	41	↓	2000

Obverse   Head, right; GEORGIVS III DEI GRATIA REX

Reverse   Crowned shield bearing Royal Arms; M B F ET H REX F D B ET L D S R I A T ET E 1798

Edge   plain

Characteristics   Obverse is similar to adopted coin.

Shilling 1798

The designer was John Milton

No.	Date	Denomination	Metal	Weight (grams)	Diameter (mm)	Rev. align.	Current Value
G3PT-610	1798	Shilling	Silver	8.5	25	↑	1200
G3PT-612	1798	Shilling	Gilt silver	8.3	25	↑	2000
G3PT-615	1798	Shilling	Copper on thick flan	8.9	25	↑	500
G3PT-616	1798	Shilling	Copper on thick flan	10.1	25	↑	1000

Obverse   Large laureate head, right; GEORGIVS III DEI GRATIA REX 1798

Reverse   Large crowned shield; M B F ET H F D B ET L D S R I A T ET E

Edge   plain

Bank of England Dollar 1804

These coins are usually struck over Spanish American dollars.

No.	Date	Denomination	Metal	Weight (grams)	Diameter (mm)	Rev. align.	Current Value
G3PT-620	1804	Bank dollar	Silver	26–27	41	↑	1200
G3PT-625	1804	Bank dollar	Silver	26–27	41	↓	1200

Obverse   Head, right; GEORGIUS III DEI GRATIA REX

Reverse   Shield bearing Royal Arms, this within Garter, all surmounted by crown dividing date 1804; BRITANNIARUM REX FIDEI DEFENSOR; DOLLAR (last beneath Garter)

Edge   plain, but may show traces of the 'host' coin

Characteristics   Obverse is similar to adopted coin.

Twopence 1805

The designer, W. J. Taylor, acquired a number of old Soho Mint punches and dies in 1848 when the mint closed down. Amongst the contrived pieces made by him using these items were these twopences. The obverse is struck from a die prepared using the Küchler portrait from the 1804 bank dollar. An attempt has been made to remove the initials CHK from the original design, but the K is still discernible. Taylor has designed the reverse using modified punches from other pieces.

No.	Date	Denomination	Metal	Weight (grams)	Diameter (mm)	Rev. align.	Current Value
G3PT-640	1805	Twopence	Copper		41		800
G3PT-645	1805	Twopence	Bronzed copper on 5mm flan		41		350
G3PT-650	1805	Twopence	Bronzed copper on 2.5mm flan		41		800
G3PT-655	1805	Twopence	White metal		41		800
G3PT-660	1805	Twopence	Silver		41		
G3PT-665	1805	Twopence	Gold		41		

Obverse   Head, right; GEORGIUS III D G REX

Reverse   Britannia seated on rock, with shield, trident, spray; BRITANNIARUM 1805

Edge   plain

Farthing 1806

No.	Date	Denomination	Metal	Weight (grams)	Diameter (mm)	Rev. align.	Current Value
G3PT-675	1806	Farthing	Copper	4.7–4.8	21–22		

Obverse Head, right; GEORGIUS III D G REX

Reverse Britannia seated on rock, with shield, trident, spray; BRITANNIA

Edge milled

Characteristics The piece is similar but not identical to the adopted coin. The portrait is more similar to that on the Irish currency farthing of 1806.

Bank of England 5s 6d Token 1811

The designer was John Phillp.

No.	Date	Denomination	Metal	Weight (grams)	Diameter (mm)	Rev. align.	Current Value
G3PT-680	1811	5 shillings and 6 pence	Silver	26–27	41	↑	3000
G3PT-682	1811	5 shillings and 6 pence	Copper	26–27	41	↓	1000

Obverse Head, left; GEORGIUS III DEI GRATIA REX (minor differences exist)

Reverse Britannia, seated facing left on rock; BANK OF ENGLAND TOKEN FIVE SHILLINGS & SIXPENCE 1811

Edge plain

Bank of England 5s 6d Token 1811

No.	Date	Denomination	Metal	Weight (grams)	Diameter (mm)	Rev. align.	Current Value
G3PT-685	1811	5 shillings and 6 pence	Silver	26–27	41		2000

Obverse Head, right; GEORGIUS III DEI GRATIA REX (minor varieties exist)

Reverse Oak wreath enclosing legend BANK TOKEN 5S 6D 1811 (minor varieties exist)

Edge plain

Characteristics Obverse is similar to adopted Bank of England dollar.

Bank of England 5s 6d Token 1811

No.	Date	Denomination	Metal	Weight (grams)	Diameter (mm)	Rev. align.	Current Value
G3PT-690	1811	5 shillings and 6 pence	Silver	26–27	41	↑	2500
G3PT-692	1811	5 shillings and 6 pence	Copper	22–23	41	↑	400

Obverse Head, left; GEORGIUS III DEI GRATIA REX

Reverse Oak wreath enclosing legend BANK TOKEN 5S 6D 1811

Edge plain

Ninepence 1812

The designer was T. Wyon, junior.

No.	Date	Denomination	Metal	Weight (grams)	Diameter (mm)	Rev. align.	Current Value
G3PT-695	1812	Ninepence	Silver		22	↑	300
G3PT-700	1812	Ninepence	Copper		22		200

Obverse Laureate head, right; GEORGIUS III DEI GRATIA REX

Reverse Wreath of oak and olive enclosing BANK TOKEN 9D 1812

Edge plain

Characteristics Coin is similar in appearance to last issue of 1s6d bank tokens

Guinea 1813

The designer was Lewis Pingo.

No.	Date	Denomination	Metal	Weight (grams)	Diameter (mm)	Rev. align.	Current Value
G3PT-710	1813	Guinea	Gold	7.7–9.6	24–25	↑	5000

Obverse Head, right; GEORGIVS III DEI GRATIA

Reverse Royal Standard; BRITANNIARUM REX FIDEI DEFENSOR 1813

Edge plain

Characteristics Obverse is identical to that on adopted coin.

Guinea 1813

The designer was Lewis Pingo.

No.	Date	Denomination	Metal	Weight (grams)	Diameter (mm)	Rev. align.	Current Value
G3PT-720	1813	Guinea	Gold	9.6–10.2	24–25	↑	5000

Obverse Head, right; GEORGIVS III DEI GRATIA

Reverse Royal Standard; BRITANNIARUM REX FIDEI DEFENSOR 1813

Edge   milled

Characteristics   Obverse is identical to that on adopted coin; the piece is unusually heavy.

Guinea 1813

The designer was Thomas Wyon.

No.	Date	Denomination	Metal	Weight (grams)	Diameter (mm)	Rev. align.	Current Value
G3PT-730	1813	Guinea	Gold	8.1	24	↑	5000

Obverse   Head, right; GEORGIVS III DEI GRATIA

Reverse   Crowned shield of Arms dividing date 1813; BRITANNIARVM REX FIDEI DEFENSOR

Edge   milled (straight or diagonally)

Characteristics   Obverse is similar but not identical to that on adopted coin.

Guinea 1813

The designer was Thomas Wyon.

No.	Date	Denomination	Metal	Weight (grams)	Diameter (mm)	Rev. align.	Current Value
G3PT-732	1813	Guinea	Gold	9.5	24	↓	

Obverse   Head, right; GEORGIVS III DEI GRATIA

Reverse   Crowned shield of Arms dividing date 1813; BRITANNIARVM REX FIDEI DEFENSOR

Edge   milled

Guinea 1813

The designer was Thomas Wyon.

No.	Date	Denomination	Metal	Weight (grams)	Diameter (mm)	Rev. align.	Current Value
G3PT-735	1813	Guinea	Gold	8.4	24	↑	6000
G3PT-736	1813	Guinea	Gold	10.0	24	↓	

Obverse   Head, right; GEORGIVS III DEI GRATIA

Reverse   Crowned shield of Arms dividing date 1813 flanked by sprays of rose, thistle, shamrock; BRITANNIARVM REX FIDEI DEFENSOR

Edge   plain

Guinea 1813

The designer was Thomas Wyon.

No.	Date	Denomination	Metal	Weight (grams)	Diameter (mm)	Rev align.	Current Value
G3PT-737	1813	Guinea	Gold	8.2–8.7	24	↑	
G3PT-738	1813	Guinea	Bronzed copper		24	↑	600

Obverse   Head, right; GEORGIVS III DEI GRATIA

Reverse   Crowned shield of Arms dividing date 1813 flanked by sprays of rose, thistle, shamrock; BRITANNIARVM REX FIDEI DEFENSOR

Edge   milled (diagonally or vertically)

Sovereign 1816

The designer was Thomas Wyon.

No.	Date	Denomination	Metal	Weight (grams)	Diameter (mm)	Rev. align.	Current Value
G3PT-740	1816	Sovereign	Gold	9.5–10.4	22–23	↑	5000

Obverse   Very large laureate head, right; GEORGIUS III D G BRITT REX F D

Reverse   Crowned shield; BRITANNIARUM REX FID DEF 1816

Edge   plain

Characteristics   The coin is unusually heavy; the obverse is usually or always slightly off-centre.

Sovereign 1816

The designer was Thomas Wyon, after a model by Benedetto Pistrucci.

No.	Date	Denomination	Metal	Weight (grams)	Diameter (mm)	Rev. align.	Current Value
G3PT-745	1816	Sovereign	Gold	9.7	23	↓	6000

Obverse   Laureate head, right; GEORGIUS III DEI GRATIA

Reverse   Crowned shield; BRITANNIARUM REX FID DEF 1816

Edge   plain

Half Sovereign or Sixpence 1816

The designer was Thomas Wyon, possibly retouched by Pistrucci. Mint workers are reported to have had difficulty in striking the high relief coin. The Murdoch sale of 1904 included a piece with a milled edge.

No.	Date	Denomination	Metal	Weight (grams)	Diameter (mm)	Rev. align.	Current Value
G3PT-750	1816	Half sovereign or sixpence	Gold	3.6–4.0	19	↑	3000
G3PT-752	1816	Half sovereign or sixpence	Gold	3.6–4.0	19	↓	3500

Obverse   Large head, right; GEORGIUS III DEI GRATIA

Reverse   Crowned Royal Arms within Garter, crown dividing date 1816; HONI SOIT QUI MAL Y PENSE on Garter; BRITT REX FID DEF

Edge   plain

Shilling c.1816

The designer was William Wyon.

No.	Date	Denomination	Metal	Weight (grams)	Diameter (mm)	Rev. align.	Current Value
G3PT-760	c.1816	Shilling	Silver	5.7	24		800

Obverse   Head, right; GEORGIUS III DEI GRATIA

Reverse   Crowned and garnished square shield; BRITANNIARUM REX FIDEI DEFENSOR

Edge   milled

Characteristics   The head is similar to that on the adopted coin but is smaller; the piece is undated.

Crown c.1817–1820

The designers were Thomas Webb (obv.) and George Mills (rev.). The piece was commissioned by James Mudie.

No.	Date	Denomination	Metal	Weight (grams)	Diameter (mm)	Rev. align.	Current Value
G3PT-770	c.1817 -1820	Crown	Silver	28.0–28.1	39	↑	700
G3PT-775	c.1817 -1820	Crown	Lead		39		

Obverse   Head, right; GEORGIVS III DEI GRATIA

Reverse   Four cruciform shields with rose, thistle, shamrock, horse in angles, with central Garter; MILLS FECIT at edge; HONI SOIT QUIT MAL Y PENSE on Garter

Edge   plain

Crown 1817

No.	Date	Denomination	Metal	Weight (grams)	Diameter (mm)	Rev. align.	Current Value
G3PT-780	1817	Crown	Silver		39	↓	8000

Obverse   Head, right; GEORGIUS III DEI GRATIA BRITANNIARUM REX F D 1817

Reverse   St George and Dragon within Garter bearing legend HONI SOIT QUI MAL Y PENSE

Edge   plain

Crown 1817

The designer was William Wyon. The Three Graces in classical dress represent England, Scotland and Ireland. The Rev. Rogers Ruding wrote at the time: 'Britain is drawn with considerable dignity and character, and appears to be the eldest sister of the three; the other two look towards her with affection and respect. Of all the three figures, Scotia has the most originality and grace; but should she not, as the elder sister of Hibernia, so far at least as union goes, have been placed on the right hand of Britannia?'

No.	Date	Denomination	Metal	Weight (grams)	Diameter (mm)	Rev. align.	Current Value
G3PT-785	1817	Crown	Silver	25.2–27.2	39	↑	3000
G3PT-790	1817	Crown	Gold	45–53	39		60000
G3PT-795	1817	Crown	Lead on thick (5.2mm) flan	62.0	39	↑	1000
G3PT-800	1817	Crown	Copper		39		2500
G3PT-805	1817	Crown	Tin on thick flan		39		3000

Obverse   Head, right; GEORGIUS III D G BRITANNIARUM REX F D 1817

Reverse   'The Three Graces', with harp, thistle, palm branch, quiver; FOEDUS INVIOLABILE

Edge   plain

Crown 1817

The designer was William Wyon, but the reverse is clearly based on the reverse of the Cromwell crown by Simon. About 7 specimens of the gold variety exist, and the silver piece was first exhibited in Cork (Ireland) in 1817.

No.	Date	Denomination	Metal	Weight (grams)	Diameter (mm)	Rev. align.	Current Value
G3PT-810	1817	Crown	Silver	28.7–28.9	39	↑	5000
G3PT-815	1817	Crown	Gold	45.2–48.6	39	↑	65000

Obverse   Head, right; GEORGIUS III D G BRITANNIARUM REX 1817

Reverse   Crowned shield; INCORRUPTA FIDES VERITASQUE

Edge   plain

Crown 1818

The designer was Benedetto Pistrucci.

No.	Date	Denomination	Metal	Weight (grams)	Diameter (mm)	Rev. align.	Current Value
G3PT-825	1818	Crown	Silver	28.0–28.1	39	↑	6000
G3PT-828	1818	Crown	Silver	28.0	39	↓	7000
G3PT-830	1818	Crown	White metal		39		2000
G3PT-832	1818	Crown	Lead		39		1500
G3PT-835	1818	Crown	Gold	c.45	39		60000

Obverse   Head, right; GEORGIUS III D G BRITANNIARUM REX F D 1818

Reverse St George and dragon within Garter; HONI SOIT QUI MAL Y PENSE

Edge plain

Characteristics The head is very large; the reverse is very similar to that on adopted coin.

Crown 1818

No.	Date	Denomination	Metal	Weight (grams)	Diameter (mm)	Rev. align.	Current Value
G3PT-838	1818	Crown	Silver	27.9–28.4	39	↓	7000

Obverse Head, right; GEORGIUS III D G BRITANNIARUM REX F D 1818

Reverse St George and Dragon within Garter bearing legend HONI SOIT QUI MAL Y PENSE

Edge (incuse) DECUS ET TUTAMEN ANNO REGNI LVIII

Crown 1818

No.	Date	Denomination	Metal	Weight (grams)	Diameter (mm)	Rev. align.	Current Value
G3PT-840	1818	Crown	Silver	28.4	39	↓	

Obverse Head, right; GEORGIUS III D G BRITANNIARUM REX F D 1818

Reverse St George and Dragon within Garter bearing legend HONI SOIT QUI MAL Y PENSE

Edge (in relief) DECUS ET TUTAMEN ANNO REGNI LVIII

Five Pounds 1820

The designer was Benedetto Pistrucci. A fascinating episode of numismatic history lies hidden within the pages of a single copy of Crowther's 'English Pattern Coins' (publ: Upcott Gill, 1887) bearing the dedication 'With the Publisher's Compliments' (to whom?). In faint pencil in the margin of page 37 is written: 'It is said that the dies for this piece were completed by Pistrucci a few days before the death of George III. On the day of the death of the King, Pistrucci on his way home heard the bell of St Paul's tolling. He then immediately returned to the Mint and ordered that a few specimens (25?) should be struck the first thing the next morning. This account was told to me by the late Lord Dillon who knew Pistrucci–H.G.'

No.	Date	Denomination	Metal	Weight (grams)	Diameter (mm)	Rev. align.	Current Value
G3PT-845	1820	Five pounds	Gold	39.9–40.3	38	↓	60000
G3PT-850	1820	Five pounds	Silver	c.25	38		10000

Obverse Laureate head, right, PISTRUCCI in tiny letters below; GEORGIUS III D G BRITANNIAR REX F D 1820

Reverse St George and dragon; PISTRUCCI in tiny letters in exergue

Edge (in relief) DECUS ET TUTAMEN ANNO REGNI LX

Five Pounds 1820

The designer was Benedetto Pistrucci. The pattern is identical to G3PT-845 (notes q.v.) except for the edge. Two are known.

No.	Date	Denomination	Metal	Weight (grams)	Diameter (mm)	Rev. align.	Current Value
G3PT-854	1820	Five pounds	Gold	39.8	38		70000

Obverse Laureate head, right, PISTRUCCI in tiny letters below; GEORGIUS III D G BRITANNIAR REX F D 1820

Reverse St George and Dragon; PISTRUCCI in tiny letters in exergue

Edge plain

Two Pounds (Double Sovereign) 1820

The designer was Benedetto Pistrucci. 60 pieces are reported to have been struck.

No.	Date	Denomination	Metal	Weight (grams)	Diameter (mm)	Rev. align.	Current Value
G3PT-860	1820	Two pounds	Gold	15.8–16.0	28	↓	8000

Obverse Laureate head, right, GEORGIUS III D G BRITANNIARUM REX F D 1820

Reverse St George and dragon; BP in exergue

Edge (in relief) DECUS ET TUTAMEN ANNO REGNI LX

Two Pounds 1820

This piece is identical to G3PT-860 except for the edge and the en medaille striking. Probably unique.

No.	Date	Denomination	Metal	Weight (grams)	Diameter (mm)	Rev. align.	Current Value
G3PT-862	1820	Two pounds	Gold	16.0	28	↑	20000

Obverse Laureate head, right; GEORGIUS III D G BRITANNIAR REX F D 1820

Reverse St George and Dragon; BP in exergue

Edge plain

Half Sovereign 1820

The designer was Benedetto Pistrucci, engraved by Thomas Wyon (obv.); the reverse was probably by Thomas Wyon.

No.	Date	Denomination	Metal	Weight (grams)	Diameter (mm)	Rev. align.	Current Value
G3PT-870	1820	Half sovereign	Gold	3.9	19	↑	5000
G3PT-872	1820	Half sovereign	Gold	3.9	19	↓	5000
G3PT-875	1820	Half sovereign	Silver	2.8	19	↑	1500

Obverse Laureate head, right; GEOR III D G BRITT REX F D 1820

Reverse Crowned rose, shamrock, thistle on single stem; BRITANNIARUM REX FID DEF

Edge plain

Characteristics Obverse is identical to that on adopted sixpence 1816–1820.

Crown 1820

The designer was Jean-Pierre Droz, after Monneron's 1792 pattern by Augustin Dupre.

No.	Date	Denomination	Metal	Weight (grams)	Diameter (mm)	Rev. align.	Current Value
G3PT-900	1820	Crown	Silver	26.0–26.8	39	↑	4000
G3PT-905	1820	Crown	Bronzed copper	28.2	39	↑	700
G3PT-910	1820	Crown	Gilt copper		39		1500
G3PT-920	1820	Crown	Copper		39	↓	700

Obverse Hercules seated on lion skin breaking sticks across his knee; background of sea, ships and trees; VIS VNITATE FORTIOR 1820

Reverse Shield of Arms, crown above; DECVS ET TVTAMEN

Edge plain

Guinea

The designer was William Wyon. The piece is possibly unique.

No.	Date	Denomination	Metal	Weight (grams)	Diameter (mm)	Rev. align.	Current Value
G3PT-950	none	Guinea	Gold	10.1	24	not applicable	4000

Obverse Head, right; GEORGIUS III DEI GRATIA

Reverse blank, with beaded border

Edge plain

George IV (1820 – 1830)

Half Sovereign 1820

The designer was Benedetto Pistrucci. The coin is possibly unique.

No.	Date	Denomination	Metal	Weight (grams)	Diameter (mm)	Rev. align.	Current Value
G4PT-010	1820	Half sovereign	Gold	4.0	19	↓	8000

Obverse Laureate head, left; GEORGIUS IIII D G BRITANNIAR REX F D

Reverse Crowned shield garnished with rose, shamrock, thistle; ANNO 1820

Edge milled

Characteristics Identical to adopted coin 1821 except for the date.

Crown 1820

The designer was T. Mills and the piece issued by R, Whiteaves.

No.	Date	Denomination	Metal	Weight (grams)	Diameter (mm)	Rev. align.	Current Value
G4PT-020	1820	Crown	Silver	35.5–36.1	39–41	↑	6000
G4PT-030	1820	Crown	Gold	c.50	39–41		50000

Obverse Large head, left; GEORGIUS IV DEI GRATIA MDCCCXX

Reverse Royal Arms on shield within Garter supported by lion and unicorn with embellishments; BRITANNIARUM ET HAN REX FIDEI DEFENSOR; PUB BY R WHITEAVES (last in small lettering beneath design)

Edge plain

Crown 1820

No.	Date	Denomination	Metal	Weight (grams)	Diameter (mm)	Rev. align.	Current Value
G4PT-035	1820	Crown	Silver	36.2	38	↑	

Obverse Large head, left, wearing collar and tie; GEORGIUS IV DEI GRATIA MDCCCXX

Reverse Royal Arms on shield within Garter supported by lion and unicorn with embellishments; BRITANNIARUM ET HAN REX FIDEI DEFENSOR; PUB BY R WHITEAVES (last in small lettering beneath design)

Edge plain

Crown 1820

The designer was Benedetto Pistrucci.

No.	Date	Denomination	Metal	Weight (grams)	Diameter (mm)	Rev. align.	Current Value
G4PT-037	1820	Crown	Silver	28.2	39	↓	

Obverse Laureate head, left; GEORGIUS IIII D G BRITANNIAR REX F D

Reverse St George and Dragon, 1820 in exergue below

Edge plain

Characteristics The piece is similar to the currency coin 1821–22 except for the date and the edge; there are other minor differences

Shilling 1820

No.	Date	Denomination	Metal	Weight (grams)	Diameter (mm)	Rev. align.	Current Value
G4PT-038	1820	Shilling	Silver		24		

Obverse Laureate head, left; GEORGIUS IIII D G BRITANNIAR REX F D

Reverse Garnished shield with surmounting large crown; ANNO 1820

Edge milled

Characteristics Identical to currency issue 1821 except for the date and the lack of initials JBM in obverse border

Half Sovereign 1821

The designer was Benedetto Pistrucci.

No.	Date	Denomination	Metal	Weight (grams)	Diameter (mm)	Rev. align.	Current Value
G4PT-040	1821	Half sovereign	Gold	4.0	19		2500

Obverse Laureate head, left; GEORGIUS IIII D G BRITANNIAR REX F D

Reverse Crowned flat-topped shield, rose, shamrock, thistle below; ANNO 1821

Edge milled

Characteristics Identical to adopted coin 1823–1825 except for the date.

Halfcrown 1822

No.	Date	Denomination	Metal	Weight (grams)	Diameter (mm)	Rev. align.	Current Value
G4PT-045	1822	Halfcrown	Silver		32		

Obverse Laureate head, left; GEORGIUS IIII D G BRITANNIAR REX F D

Reverse Crowned shield within Garter and collar; ANNO 1822; on Garter HONI SOIT QUI MAL Y PENSE

Edge milled

Characteristics As adopted coin 1823–24 but with minor reverse differences

Two Pounds c.1823

The designer was Benedetto Pistrucci. The coin is possibly unique.

No.	Date	Denomination	Metal	Weight (grams)	Diameter (mm)	Rev. align.	Current Value
G4PT-050	None	Two pounds	Silver	13.6	27–28	↑	2000

Obverse St George and Dragon (no date in exergue)

Reverse As obverse

Edge plain

Characteristics Both sides are as the gold two pounds of 1823 without the date, The piece is struck on a thick (2.9mm) flan.

Two Pounds 1824

The designers were William Wyon (obv.); J. B. Merlen (rev.).

No.	Date	Denomination	Metal	Weight (grams)	Diameter (mm)	Rev. align.	Current Value
G4PT-052	1824	Two pounds	Copper	8.6	28	↓	500

Obverse Head, left; GEORGIUS IV DEI GRATIA 1824

Reverse Shield within mantle, crown above; BRITANNIARUM REX FID DEF

Edge plain

Characteristics The piece is identical to the adopted 1826 coin apart from the date, metal and edge.

Halfcrown 1824

No.	Date	Denomination	Metal	Weight (grams)	Diameter (mm)	Rev. align.	Current Value
G4PT-052A	1824	Halfcrown	Silver	13.9	32	↓	
G4PT-052B	1824	Halfcrown	Copper	12.9	32	↓	
G4PT-052C	1824	Halfcrown	Gold	24.1	32	↓	

Obverse Bare head, left; GEORGIUS IV DEI GRATIA 1824

Reverse Garnished flat-top shield with surmounting helmet and small crown; BRITANNIARUM REX FID DEF; on scroll DIEU ET MON DROIT

Edge plain

Characteristics The piece is identical to the currency issue 1825–29 except for the date and the edge

Half Sovereign 1825

No.	Date	Denomination	Metal	Weight (grams)	Diameter (mm)	Rev. align.	Current Value
G4PT-053	1825	Half sovereign	Gold	4.0	19	↓	

Obverse Head, left; GEORGIUS IV DEI GRATIA 1825

Reverse Crowned shield; BRITANNIARUM REX FID DEF

Edge plain

Characteristics The piece is identical to the currency issue 1826–28 except for the date and the edge

Shilling 1825

No.	Date	Denomination	Metal	Weight (grams)	Diameter (mm)	Rev. align.	Current Value
G4PT-054	1825	Shilling	Silver		24	↓	800
G4PT-054A	1825	Shilling	Barton's Metal [1]		24	↓	1200

1. Barton's Metal is a laminated product consisting of thin sheets of gold bonded to a copper base

Obverse Head, left; GEORGIUS IV DEI GRATIA 1825

Reverse Lion on crown, ornament below; BRITANNIARUM REX FID DEF

Edge milled

Characteristics The obverse is identical to that of the adopted coin. The reverse is very similar but there are several differences, including the legend.

Crown 1825

See currency listings.

Ninepence/Farthing 1825

This curious piece in platinum uses the obverse of the 1812 pattern ninepence and the reverse of the currency 1825 farthing. The use of a die for the wrong monarch suggests that the choice of dies was arbitrary, possibly merely to test the use of platinum as a striking medium.

No.	Date	Denomination	Metal	Weight (grams)	Diameter (mm)	Rev. align.	Current Value
G4PT-055	1825	Farthing (?)	Platinum		22		

Obverse Head of George III, right; GEORGIUS III DEI GRATIA REX

Reverse Britannia seated, with shield, trident; BRITANNIA REX FID DEF 1825

Edge plain

Five Pounds 1826 (weight 46.5 grams)

The designer was William Wyon (obv.) and J. B. Merlen (rev.). The coin is possibly unique. See currency listings for this piece (Five pounds: proof on thick flan).

Two Pounds 1826 (weight 21.5 grams)

The designer was William Wyon (obv.) and J. B. Merlen (rev.). The coin is possibly unique. See currency listings for this piece. (Two pounds: proof on thick flan).

Crown 1828

The designers were William Wyon (obv.); J. B. Merlen (rev.). The piece was officially defaced at the Mint.

No.	Date	Denomination	Metal	Weight (grams)	Diameter (mm)	Rev. align.	Current Value
G4PT-057	1828	Crown	Silver		39	↓	

Obverse Head, left; GEORGIUS IV DEI GRATIA 1828

Reverse Crowned garnished shield; BRITANNIARUM REX FID DEF; scroll below inscribed DIEU ET MON DROIT

Edge DECUS ET TUTAMEN ANNO REGNI NONO

Crown 1828

The designers were William Wyon (obv.); J. B. Merlen (rev.).

No.	Date	Denomination	Metal	Weight (grams)	Diameter (mm)	Rev. align.	Current Value
G4PT-058	1828	Crown	Copper		39		1800

Obverse Head, left; GEORGIUS IV D G BRITANNIAR REX F D 1828

Reverse Crowned garnished shield; BRITANNIARUM REX FID DEF; scroll below inscribed DIEU ET MON DROIT

Edge DECUS ET TUTAMEN ANNO REGNI OCTAVO

Crown 1829

The designer was William Wyon (obv.) and J. B. Merlen (rev.). The piece was engraved with a view to adapting the dies to the new coining press imported from the Prussian Mint.

No.	Date	Denomination	Metal	Weight (grams)	Diameter (mm)	Rev. align.	Current Value
G4PT-060	1829	Crown	Silver	26.5–28.0	39	↓	10000
G4PT-065	1829	Crown	Silver	28.3	39	↑	

Obverse Head, left; GEORGIUS IV DEI GRATIA 1829

Reverse Shield bearing Royal Arms, crowned and encircled by Collar of the Garter; BRITANNARUM REX FID DEF

Edge plain

Characteristics Obverse similar to that of 1826 proof crown but initials on truncation are in relief, and the bust is larger

Crown 1829

The designers were William Wyon (obv.) and J. B. Merlen (rev.).

No.	Date	Denomination	Metal	Weight (grams)	Diameter (mm)	Rev. align.	Current Value
G4PT-066	1829	Crown	Silver	28.0	39	↓	
G4PT-067	1829	Crown	Copper		39		

Obverse Head, left; GEORGIUS IV DEI GRATIA 1829

Reverse Shield bearing Royal Arms, crowned and encircled by Collar of the Garter

Edge (in relief): DECUS ET TUTAMEN ANNO REGNI NONO

Characteristics   Similar to G4PT-060 except for the edge

Crown c.1829

The designers were Benedetto Pistrucci (obv.); J. B. Merlen (rev.).

No.	Date	Denomination	Metal	Weight (grams)	Diameter (mm)	Rev. align.	Current Value
G4PT-075	none	Crown	Copper		39		

Obverse   Laureate head, left; GEORGIUS IIII D G BRITANNIAR REX F D

Reverse   Shield within mantle, crown above; BRITANNIARUM REX F D

Edge   DECVS ET TVTAMEN ANNO REGNI NONO

Characteristics   The obverse is identical to that of the crowns 1821, 1822

Crown c.1829

No.	Date	Denomination	Metal	Weight (grams)	Diameter (mm)	Rev. align.	Current Value
G4PT-100	none	Crown	White metal	17.0	35	↑	

Obverse   Laureate head, left; GEORGIUS IIII D G BRITANNIAR REX F D

Reverse   Royal Arms supported, Garter and gothic 'M' below

Edge   plain

William IV   (1830 – 1837)

Sovereign 1830

No.	Date	Denomination	Metal	Weight (grams)	Diameter (mm)	Rev. align.	Current Value
W4PT-010	1830	Sovereign	Gold	7.7	22	↓	4000

Obverse   Head, right; GULIELMUS IIII D G BRITANNIAR REX F D

Reverse   Crowned shield on mantle; ANNO 1830

Edge   plain

Characteristics   This piece is identical to adopted coin except for the date and the edge.

Crown 1834

This pattern is in the British Museum and is officially sheared at the Mint.

No.	Date	Denomination	Metal	Weight (grams)	Diameter (mm)	Rev. align.	Current Value
W4PT-015	1834	Crown	Silver	28.3	39	↓	

Obverse   Head, right; GULIELMUS IIII D G BRITANNIAR REX F D; W.W. incuse on truncation

Reverse   Crowned shield on mantle; ANNO 1834

Edge   DECUS ET TUTAMEN ANNO REGNI QUINQUAGESIMO SEPTIMO incuse on milling

Groat 1836

The designer was William Wyon.

No.	Date	Denomination	Metal	Weight (grams)	Diameter (mm)	Rev. align.	Current Value
W4PT-020	1836	Groat	Silver	1.9	16	↑	600

Obverse   Head, right; GULIELMUS IIII D G BRITANNIAR REX F D

Reverse   Britannia seated, with shield; FOUR PENCE; 1836 in exergue

Edge   milled

Characteristics   Obverse is identical to that on adopted coin; reverse is similar but FOUR PENCE is continuous and not broken by Britannia as on adopted coin.

Groat 1836

The designer was William Wyon.

No.	Date	Denomination	Metal	Weight (grams)	Diameter (mm)	Rev. align.	Current Value
W4PT-030	1836	Groat	Silver	1.9	16	↑	600

Obverse   Head, right; GULIELMUS IIII D G BRITANNIAR REX F D

Reverse   Britannia seated, with shield; FOUR PENCE; 1836 in exergue

Edge   plain

Characteristics   Obverse is identical to that on adopted coin; reverse is similar but FOUR PENCE is continuous and not broken by Britannia as on adopted coin.

Groat 1836

The designer was William Wyon.

No.	Date	Denomination	Metal	Weight (grams)	Diameter (mm)	Rev. align.	Current Value
W4PT-040	1836	Groat	Silver	1.9	16	↑	400

Obverse   Head, right; GULIELMUS IIII D G BRITANNIAR REX F D

Reverse   Britannia seated, with shield; 4 P in field broken by Britannia; 1836 in exergue

Edge   milled

Characteristics   Obverse is identical to that on adopted coin.

Groat 1836

The designer was William Wyon.

No.	Date	Denomination	Metal	Weight (grams)	Diameter (mm)	Rev. align.	Current Value
W4PT-050	1836	Groat	Silver	1.9	16	↑	400
W4PT-060	1836	Groat	Gold		16		

Obverse   Head, right; GULIELMUS IIII D G BRITANNIAR REX F D

Reverse   Britannia seated, with shield; 4 P in field broken by Britannia; 1836 in exergue

Edge   plain

Characteristics   Obverse is identical to that on adopted coin.

Victoria   (1837 – 1901)

Sovereign 1837

The designer was William Wyon (obv.); J. B. Merlen (rev.).

No.	Date	Denomination	Metal	Weight (grams)	Diameter (mm)	Rev. align.	Current Value
VPT-010	1837	Sovereign	Gold	7.8	22	↓	3500

Obverse   Small head, left, flanked by two tiny roses; VICTORIA DEI GRATIA 1837

Reverse   Crowned shield within wreath; BRITANNIARUM REGINA FID DEF

Edge   plain

Characteristics   Reverse is identical to that on adopted coin.

Crown 1837

The so-called pattern crowns by Joseph Bonomi were concoctions in various metals issued in 1893 (not 1887 as usually stated) by J. Rochelle Thomas from Bonomi's original 1837 designs. They were engraved by Theophilus Pinches, and the design strongly reflects Bonomi's reputation as an admirer of ancient Egyptian culture.

No.	Date	Denomination	Metal	Weight (grams)	Diameter (mm)	Rev. align.	Current Value
VPT-020	1837 (issued 1893)	Crown	Silver	31–35	38	↑	1500
VPT-025	1837 (issued 1893)	Crown	Copper	26–27	38	↑	900
VPT-030	1837 (issued 1893)	Crown	Lead	39–40	38	↑	500
VPT-035	1837 (issued 1893)	Crown	White metal	19–20	38	↑	500

Obverse   Head, left; VICTORIA REG DEI GRA 1837 (all incuse), within ornate beaded border

Reverse   Britannia, depicted as Minerva, standing with trident, shield, and Victory; BRITT MINERVA VICTRIX FID DEF (all incuse) within ornate beaded border

Edge   plain except for T plus (number = 1 to 150)

Crown or Five Pounds 1839

The designer was William Wyon. This is one of a number of different strikings similar to the 'Una' five pounds. For the gold pieces, see the currency listings.

No.	Date	Denomination	Metal	Weight (grams)	Diameter (mm)	Rev. align.	Current Value
VPT-045	1839	Crown or Five pounds	White metal	20.8	39	↑	4000

Obverse   Head, left; VICTORIA D G BRITANNIARUM REGINA F D

Reverse   Victoria as Una, standing, leading a lion left; DIRIGE DEUS GRESSUS MEOS; MDCCCXXXIX (=1839) in exergue

Edge   DECUS ET TUTAMEN ANNO REGNI TERTIO

Characteristics   The piece is more or less identical to one of the varieties of Una and the Lion five pounds except that it is struck in white metal and is on a thicker and wider flan.

Crown 1839

The designer was William Wyon.

No.	Date	Denomination	Metal	Weight (grams)	Diameter (mm)	Rev. align.	Current Value
VPT-048	1839	Crown	Silver		39		

Obverse   Head, left; VICTORIA DEI GRATIA 1839

Reverse   Crowned shield within branches; BRITANNIARUM REGINA FID DEF

Edge   plain

Characteristics   The reverse is identical to that of the proof crown of 1839 and the currency pieces of 1844, 1845, 1847

Crown 1839

The designer was William Wyon.

No.	Date	Denomination	Metal	Weight (grams)	Diameter (mm)	Rev. align.	Current Value
VPT-050	1839	Crown	Silver		39		

Obverse Small head with plain fillets, left; VICTORIA DEI GRATIA 1839

Reverse Crowned shield within branches; BRITANNIARUM REGINA FID DEF

Edge plain

Characteristics The reverse is identical to that of the proof crown of 1839 and the currency pieces of 1844, 1845, 1847

Crown 1844

The designer was William Wyon.

No.	Date	Denomination	Metal	Weight (grams)	Diameter (mm)	Rev. align.	Current Value
VPT-052	1844	Crown	Silver		38		

Obverse Head, left; VICTORIA DEI GRATIA 1844

Reverse Crowned shield within branches; BRITANNIARUM REGINA FID DEF

Edge plain

Characteristics The reverse is similar to that of the proof crown of 1839 and the currency pieces of 1844, 1845, 1847, but the legend is in smaller lettering

'Gothic' Crown 1846

No.	Date	Denomination	Metal	Weight (grams)	Diameter (mm)	Rev. align.	Current Value
VPT-055	1846	Crown	Silver	28.2	39	↑	8000

Obverse Head left; VICTORIA DEI GRATIA BRITANNIAR REG F D in Gothic script

Reverse Cruciform shields; TUEATUR UNITA DEUS ANNO DOM MDCCCXLVI (=1846) in Gothic script

Edge plain

Characteristics Very similar to adopted Gothic crown except for date and that the Queen's robe is plain.

Florin 1848

The designer was William Wyon. About 2 of the gold variety are known.

No.	Date	Denomination	Metal	Weight (grams)	Diameter (mm)	Rev. align.	Current Value
VPT-065	1848	Florin	Silver	11.3	28	↑	600
VPT-070	1848	Florin	Silver	11.3	28	↓	600
VPT-075	1848	Florin	Gold	21.7 and 22.7	28	↑	14000

Obverse Head, left; VICTORIA REGINA 1848

Reverse Four crowned cruciform shields with rose at centre; rose, thistle, rose, shamrock in angles; ONE FLORIN ONE TENTH OF A POUND

Edge plain

Characteristics As adopted coin but with plain edge.

Florin 1848

The designer was William Wyon.

No.	Date	Denomination	Metal	Weight (grams)	Diameter (mm)	Rev. align.	Current Value
VPT-085	1848	Florin	Silver	11.0–11.4	28	↓	1400

Obverse Head, left; VICTORIA REGINA 1848

Reverse Four crowned cruciform shields with rose at centre; rose, thistle, rose, shamrock in angles; ONE FLORIN ONE TENTH OF A POUND

Edge milled

Characteristics As adopted coin.

Dime (Florin) 1848

The designer was William Wyon.

No.	Date	Denomination	Metal	Weight (grams)	Diameter (mm)	Rev. align.	Current Value
VPT-095	1848	Dime or florin	Silver	11.0–11.4	28	↑	600

Obverse Head, left; VICTORIA REGINA 1848

Reverse Four crowned cruciform shields with rose at centre; rose, thistle, rose, shamrock in angles; ONE DIME ONE TENTH OF A POUND

Edge milled

Characteristics As adopted coin except for reverse legend.

Florin 1848

The designer was William Wyon.

No.	Date	Denomination	Metal	Weight (grams)	Diameter (mm)	Rev. align.	Current Value
VPT-100	1848	Florin	Silver	11.0–11.4	28	↑	1000

Obverse Large unlaureate head, left; VICTORIA REGINA 1848

Reverse VR with ornamentation within quatrefoil; ONE FLORIN ONE TENTH OF A POUND

Edge milled

Florin 1848

The designer was William Wyon.

No.	Date	Denomination	Metal	Weight (grams)	Diameter (mm)	Rev. align.	Current Value
VPT-110	1848	Florin	Silver	11.0–11.4	28	↑	800

Obverse Large unlaureate head, left; VICTORIA REGINA 1848

Reverse Oak wreath and trident; ONE FLORIN ONE TENTH OF A POUND

Edge milled

Florin 1848

The designer was William Wyon.

No.	Date	Denomination	Metal	Weight (grams)	Diameter (mm)	Rev. align.	Current Value
VPT-115	1848	Florin	Silver	11.0–11.4	28	↑	800

Obverse Large unlaureate head, left; VICTORIA REGINA 1848

Reverse Oak wreath and trident; ONE CENTUM 100 MILLES ONE TENTH OF A POUND

Edge plain

Decade (Florin) 1848

The designer was William Wyon.

No.	Date	Denomination	Metal	Weight (grams)	Diameter (mm)	Rev. align.	Current Value
VPT-117	1848	Decade or Florin	Silver	11.0–11.4	28	↑	800

Obverse Large unlaureate head, left; VICTORIA REGINA 1848

Reverse Oak wreath and trident; ONE DECADE 100 MILLES ONE TENTH OF A POUND

Edge plain

Decade (Florin) 1848

The designer was William Wyon.

No.	Date	Denomination	Metal	Weight (grams)	Diameter (mm)	Rev. align.	Current Value
VPT-118	1848	Decade or Florin	Silver	11.0–11.4	28	↑	800

Obverse Large laureate head, left; VICTORIA REGINA 1848

Reverse Oak wreath and trident; ONE DECADE 100 MILLES ONE TENTH OF A POUND

Edge plain

Quarter Sovereign (Five Shillings) 1853

The designer was W. Wyon.

No.	Date	Denomination	Metal	Weight (grams)	Diameter (mm)	Rev. align.	Current Value
VPT-120	1853	Quarter sovereign	Gold	1.9	13	↑	1500

Obverse Head, left; VICTORIA D G BRITANNIAR REGINA F D

Reverse FIVE SHILLINGS 1853; crown above; rose, shamrock, thistle below

Edge plain

Characteristics The obverse is struck from the die for the Maundy twopence and quarter farthing.

Quarter Sovereign (Five Shillings) 1853

The designers were W. Wyon (obv.); L. C. Wyon (rev.).

No.	Date	Denomination	Metal	Weight (grams)	Diameter (mm)	Rev. align.	Current Value
VPT-130	1853	Quarter sovereign	Gold	1.9	13	↑	1500

Obverse Head, left; VICTORIA D G BRITANNIAR REGINA F D

Reverse Crowned flat-topped shield dividing date 18 53; QUARTER SOVEREIGN

Edge plain

Characteristics   The obverse is struck from the die for the Maundy twopence and quarter farthing.

Sixpence 1856

The designers were William Wyon and L. C. Wyon.

No.	Date	Denomination	Metal	Weight (grams)	Diameter (mm)	Rev. align.	Current Value
VPT-140	1856	Sixpence	Silver	2.8	19	↑	1000

Obverse   Head left; VICTORIA DEI GRATIA BRITANNIAR REG F D

Reverse   Crowned wreath enclosing HALF SHILLING; 1856 below

Edge   plain

Characteristics   Obverse is identical to that on adopted coin.

Five Farthings (10 Centimes) 1857

The designers were L. C. Wyon (obv.); J. Wyon (rev.).

No.	Date	Denomination	Metal	Weight (grams)	Diameter (mm)	Rev. align.	Current Value
VPT-145	1857	Five farthings (10 centimes)	Bronze	11.5	33.5	↑	

Obverse   Head, left, within beaded circle; VICTORIA D G BRITANNIAR REGINA F D

Reverse   Britannia seated, facing right, with shield and trident within inner beaded circle; FIVE FARTHINGS 10 CENTIMES

Edge   plain

Decimal Penny 1857, 1859

The designers were L. C. Wyon (obv.); J. Wyon (rev.).

No.	Date	Denomination	Metal	Weight (grams)	Diameter (mm)	Rev. align.	Current Value
VPT-150	1857	Decimal penny	Bronze	11.2	32.5	↑	300
VPT-160	1859	Decimal penny	Bronze	11.2	32.5	↑	400

Obverse   Head, left, within beaded circle; VICTORIA D G BRITANNIAR REGINA F D (date)

Reverse   Britannia seated, facing right, with shield and trident within inner beaded circle; DECIMAL PENNY ONE TENTH OF A SHILLING

Edge   plain

10 Cents 1857

The designers were L. C. Wyon (obv.); J. Wyon (rev.).

No.	Date	Denomination	Metal	Weight (grams)	Diameter (mm)	Rev. align.	Current Value
VPT-165	1857	10 cents [1]	Bronze	11.2	32.5	↑	400
VPT-170	1857	10 cents [2]	Bronze	16.0	32.5	↑	1000

1. Thickness 1.75 mm.
2. Thickness 2.5mm.

Obverse   Head, left, within beaded circle; VICTORIA D G BRITANNIAR REGINA F D 1857

Reverse   Britannia seated, facing right, with shield and trident within inner beaded circle; TEN CENTS ONE TENTH OF A SHILLING

Edge   plain

Penny(?) 1859

The designer was William Wyon. The piece is probably unique, but a similar piece exists on a 31.4 mm diameter flan.

No.	Date	Denomination	Metal	Weight (grams)	Diameter (mm)	Rev. align.	Current Value
VPT-200	1859	Penny(?)	Cupronickel(?)	6.3	30	↑	800

Obverse   Head, left; VICTORIA DEI GRATIA

Reverse   Britannia, seated, with shield, facing right; BRITANNIAR REG FID DEF

Edge   plain

Characteristics   As currency halfpenny but struck on a broader flan

Penny 1860

No.	Date	Denomination	Metal	Weight (grams)	Diameter (mm)	Rev. align.	Current Value
VPT-250	1860	Penny	Bronze		31		

Obverse   Head, left; VICTORIA D G BRITANNIARUM REGINA

Reverse   Britannia seated facing right, with shield, trident, spray; ONE PENNY 1860

Edge plain

Characteristics The reverse is somewhat similar to that of the currency round beads variety but the date numerals are markedly different and the exergue is larger. There is an obverse die flaw around the top of the beaded circle

Penny 1860

No.	Date	Denomination	Metal	Weight (grams)	Diameter (mm)	Rev. align.	Current Value
VPT-255	1860	Penny	Bronze		31		

Obverse Head, left; VICTORIA D G BRITANNIAR REG F D

Reverse Britannia seated facing right, with shield, trident, spray; ONE PENNY 1860

Edge plain

Characteristics The reverse is somewhat similar to that of the currency round beads variety but the date numerals are markedly different and the exergue is larger.

Penny 1862, 1865, 1870

This piece is similar in appearance to the currency coin except for the coronetted head of Victoria designed by T. J. Minton from a model by W. Theed. The reverse was designed by L. C. Wyon.

No.	Date	Denomination	Metal	Weight (grams)	Diameter (mm)	Rev. align.	Current Value
VPT-300	1862	Penny	Bronze	9.3	31	↑	
VPT-305	1862	Penny	Cupronickel	c.9.0	31	↑	
VPT-310	1865	Penny	Bronze	9.3	31	↑	
VPT-315	1870	Penny	Bronze	9.3	31	↑	
VPT-320	1870	Penny	Nickel-bronze	9.3	31	↑	

Obverse Coronetted head, left; VICTORIA D G BRITT REG F D

Reverse Britannia seated facing right, with shield, trident, spray; ONE PENNY (date)

Edge plain

Sovereign 1863

The designer of the obverse was C. W. Wiener. The Montagu sale catalogue of 1890 notes that 'this portrait was rejected by the Queen at once'. One specimen is known.

No.	Date	Denomination	Metal	Weight (grams)	Diameter (mm)	Rev. align.	Current Value
VPT-325	1863	Sovereign	Copper	4.15	22		1200

Obverse Head, left, wearing wreath of roses, shamrocks and thistles; VICTORIA REGINA

Reverse Crowned shield within wreath; BRITANNIARUM REGINA FID DEF

Edge plain

Shilling 1863

The designers were C. W. Wiener and Wyon. The piece was possibly struck on the death of Prince Albert.

No.	Date	Denomination	Metal	Weight (grams)	Diameter (mm)	Rev. align.	Current Value
VPT-330	1863	Shilling	Silver	6.3	24	↓	700
VPT-332	1863	Shilling	Silver	6.3	24	↑	700

Obverse Head, left, wearing wreath of roses, shamrocks and thistles; two tie ends; VICTORIA DEI GRATIA BRITANNIAR REG F D

Reverse ONE SHILLING within wreath, crown above, 1863 below

Edge plain

Characteristics The reverse is identical to that on adopted coin.

Shilling 1863

The designers were C. W. Wiener and Wyon. The piece was possibly struck on the death of Prince Albert.

No.	Date	Denomination	Metal	Weight (grams)	Diameter (mm)	Rev. align.	Current Value
VPT-340	1863	Shilling	Silver	6.3	24	↑	700

Obverse Head, left, wearing wreath of roses, shamrocks and thistles; no tie ends; CHW in relief on neck; VICTORIA DEI GRATIA BRITANNIAR REG F D

Reverse ONE SHILLING within wreath, crown above, 1863 below

Edge plain

Characteristics The reverse is identical to that on adopted coin.

Shilling 1863

The designers were C. W. Wiener and Wyon.

No.	Date	Denomination	Metal	Weight (grams)	Diameter (mm)	Rev. align.	Current Value
VPT-350	1863	Shilling	Silver	6.3	24	↓	700

Obverse Coronetted head, left, hair decorated with pearls; CHW incuse on neck; VICTORIA DEI GRATIA BRITANNIAR REG F D

Reverse ONE SHILLING within wreath, crown above, 1863 below

Edge plain

Characteristics The reverse is identical to that on adopted coin.

Half Florin (Shilling) 1863

The designers were C. W. Wiener and W. J. Taylor.

No.	Date	Denomination	Metal	Weight (grams)	Diameter (mm)	Rev. align.	Current Value
VPT-360	1863	Shilling	Silver	6.3	24	↑	450
VPT-362	1863	Shilling	Copper	5.3	24	↑	400

Obverse Coronetted head left; VICTORIA DEI GRATIA 1863

Reverse Crowned flat-topped shield with circle and cross; HALF FLORIN 1863

Edge plain

Half Florin (Shilling) 1863

The designers were C. W. Wiener and W. J. Taylor.

No.	Date	Denomination	Metal	Weight (grams)	Diameter (mm)	Rev. align.	Current Value
VPT-370	1863	Shilling	Silver	6.3	24		450
VPT-375	1863	Shilling	Copper	5.3	24	↑	400

Obverse Coronetted head left; VICTORIA REGINA

Reverse Crowned flat-topped shield with circle and cross; HALF FLORIN 1863

Edge plain

Half Florin (Shilling) 1863

The designers were C. W. Wiener and W. J. Taylor.

No.	Date	Denomination	Metal	Weight (grams)	Diameter (mm)	Rev. align.	Current Value
VPT-385	1863	Shilling	Silver	6.3	24		700
VPT-390	1863	Shilling	Copper	5.3	24	↑	500

Obverse Coronetted head left; VICTORIA REGINA

Reverse Crowned flat-topped shield with circle and cross; HALF FLORIN 1863

Edge milled

Half Florin (Shilling) 1865

The designers were C. W. Wiener and W. J. Taylor.

No.	Date	Denomination	Metal	Weight (grams)	Diameter (mm)	Rev. align.	Current Value
VPT-400	1865	Shilling	Silver	6.3	24	↑	450
VPT-405	1865	Shilling	Copper	5.3	24		400

Obverse Coronetted head left; VICTORIA REGINA

Reverse Crowned flat-topped shield with circle and cross; HALF FLORIN MDCCCLXV (= 1865)

Edge plain

Half Florin (Shilling) 1865

The designers were C. W. Wiener and W. J. Taylor.

No.	Date	Denomination	Metal	Weight (grams)	Diameter (mm)	Rev. align.	Current Value
VPT-415	1865	Shilling	Silver	6.3	24	↑	450
VPT-420	1865	Shilling	Copper	5.3	24	↑	400

Obverse Coronetted head left; VICTORIA DEI GRATIA

Reverse Crowned flat-topped shield with circle and cross; HALF FLORIN MDCCCLXV (= 1865)

Edge plain

Half Florin (Shilling) 1865

The designers were C. W. Wiener and W. J. Taylor.

No.	Date	Denomination	Metal	Weight (grams)	Diameter (mm)	Rev. align.	Current Value
VPT-425	1865	Half florin or shilling	Silver	5.6–5.7	24		

Obverse Head, left, wearing wreath of roses, shamrocks, thistles; VICTORIA DEI GRATIA

Reverse Crowned flat-topped shield with circle and cross; HALF FLORIN MDCCCLXV (= 1865)

Edge plain

Franc (Tenpence) 1867

The designer was L. C. Wyon.

No.	Date	Denomination	Metal	Weight (grams)	Diameter (mm)	Rev. align.	Current Value
VPT-430	1867	Tenpence	Silver	4.2	23	↑	600

Obverse Coronetted head left; VICTORIA D G BRITANNIAR REG F D 1867

Reverse Crowned flat-top shield within wreath; ONE FRANC TEN PENCE

Edge plain

Ducat (100 Pence) 1867

No.	Date	Denomination	Metal	Weight (grams)	Diameter (mm)	Rev. align.	Current Value
VPT-435	1867	Ducat (100 pence)	Gold				2500

Obverse   Head, left; VICTORIA D G BRITANNIAR REG F D

Reverse   ONE DUCAT within wreath; ONE HUNDRED PENCE 1867

Edge   plain

Double Florin 1868

The designer was L. C. Wyon.

No.	Date	Denomination	Metal	Weight (grams)	Diameter (mm)	Rev. align.	Current Value
VPT-440	1868	Double florin	Gold	1.6	16	↑	1000

Obverse   Coronetted head, left; VICTORIA D G BRITANNIAR REG F D

Reverse   Oak wreath enclosing DOUBLE FLORIN 1868; around wreath 5 FRANCS INTERNATIONAL

Edge   plain

Double Florin 1868

The designer was L. C. Wyon.

No.	Date	Denomination	Metal	Weight (grams)	Diameter (mm)	Rev. align.	Current Value
VPT-445	1868	Double florin	Gold	1.6	16	↑	1200

Obverse   Coronetted head, left; VICTORIA D G BRITANNIAR REG F D

Reverse   Oak wreath enclosing DOUBLE FLORIN 1868; around wreath 5 FRANCS INTERNATIONAL

Edge   milled

Threepence 1868

The designer was L. C. Wyon.

No.	Date	Denomination	Metal	Weight (grams)	Diameter (mm)	Rev. align.	Current Value
VPT-450	1868	Threepence	Silver	1.4	16	↑	1500

Obverse   Laureate head left; VICTORIA D G BRITT REG F D

Reverse   Crowned 3 and divided date 18 68, all within wreath

Edge   plain

Characteristics   Reverse is identical to that on adopted coin; obverse is identical to that on third farthing issue of 1866–1885 but coin is marginally wider.

Half Sovereign 1869

This piece, struck by Thomas Graham, is usually stated to have been struck in the somewhat exotically termed yet non-existent metal 'palladium hydrogenium' referred to on the reverse. However, this alludes merely to the fact that the metal palladium (in which the piece is struck) is capable of physically absorbing hydrogen gas to a remarkable degree, a process known as occlusion. This non-chemical process is reversible, and the structure of the palladium is not affected in any way.

The obverse portrait was designed by William Wyon.

No.	Date	Denomination	Metal	Weight (grams)	Diameter (mm)	Rev. align.	Current Value
VPT-455	1869	Half sovereign	Palladium	2.3	19	↑	1000

Obverse   Head, left

Reverse   PALLADIUM-HYDROGENIUM GRAHAM 1869

Edge   plain

Sovereign 1870

The designer was William Wyon (obv.) and B. Pistrucci (rev.). The coin is probably unique. Pattern sovereigns in copper exist, but some differ from this piece in design.

No.	Date	Denomination	Metal	Weight (grams)	Diameter (mm)	Rev. align.	Current Value
VPT-460	1870	Sovereign	Gold	8.0	22		15000

Obverse   Head, left; VICTORIA DEI GRATIA 1870

Reverse   St George and Dragon; HONI SOIT QUI MAL Y PENSE on Garter

Edge   milled

Characteristics   The obverse is identical to that of a Victorian shield sovereign; the reverse is identical to that of a George III sovereign.

Halfcrown 1875

No.	Date	Denomination	Metal	Weight (grams)	Diameter (mm)	Rev. align.	Current Value
VPT-463	1875	Halfcrown	Silver		32		2500

Obverse   Head, left; VICTORIA DEI GRATIA BRITANNIAR REG F D

Reverse   St George and Dragon; 1875 in exergue

Edge   plain

Florin 1875

No.	Date	Denomination	Metal	Weight (grams)	Diameter (mm)	Rev. align.	Current Value
VPT-465	1875	Florin	Silver		29		1800

Obverse Head, left; VICTORIA DEI GRATIA BRITANNIAR REG F D

Reverse St George and Dragon; 1875 in exergue

Edge plain

Shilling 1875

No.	Date	Denomination	Metal	Weight (grams)	Diameter (mm)	Rev. align.	Current Value
VPT-467	1875	Shilling	Silver		24		1500

Obverse Head, left; VICTORIA DEI GRATIA BRITANNIAR REG F D

Reverse St George and Dragon; 1875 in exergue

Edge plain

Shilling 1875

The designer was William Wyon (obv.), the reverse using the St George and dragon design by Pistrucci.

No.	Date	Denomination	Metal	Weight (grams)	Diameter (mm)	Rev. align.	Current Value
VPT-470	1875	Shilling	Silver	5.4–5.7	24		1200

Obverse Head left; VICTORIA DEI GRATIA BRITANNIAR REG F D

Reverse St George and dragon with beaded border; 1875 in exergue

Edge plain

Characteristics Obverse is identical to that on adopted coin; reverse similar to that on sovereign except for beaded border.

Shilling 1875

The designer was William Wyon (obv.), the reverse using the St George and dragon design by Pistrucci.

No.	Date	Denomination	Metal	Weight (grams)	Diameter (mm)	Rev. align.	Current Value
VPT-480	1875	Shilling	Silver	5.4	24	↑	1800

Obverse Head left; VICTORIA DEI GRATIA BRITANNIAR REG F D

Reverse St George and dragon with beaded border; 1875 in exergue

Edge milled

Characteristics Obverse is identical to that on adopted coin; reverse similar to that on sovereign except for beaded border.

Shilling c.1875

The designer was William Wyon (obv.), the reverse using the St George and dragon design by Pistrucci.

No.	Date	Denomination	Metal	Weight (grams)	Diameter (mm)	Rev. align.	Current Value
VPT-490	c.1875	Shilling	Silver	5.4–5.7	24		1000
VPT-495	c.1875	Shilling	Aluminium	1.5	24		500

Obverse Head left; VICTORIA DEI GRATIA BRITANNIAR REG F D

Reverse St George and dragon; no date in exergue

Edge milled

Characteristics Obverse is identical to that on adopted coin; reverse similar to that on sovereign.

Halfcrown 1876

The designer was L. C. Wyon.

No.	Date	Denomination	Metal	Weight (grams)	Diameter (mm)	Rev. align.	Current Value
VPT-500	1876	Halfcrown	Silver	14.0–14.2	32	↑	2500

Obverse Coronetted head, left; VICTORIA D G BRITANNIAR REG F D 1876

Reverse Stylized St George and Dragon

Edge plain

Half Sovereign 1880

The designer of the obverse was J. E. Boehm, using the Pistrucci reverse.

No.	Date	Denomination	Metal	Weight (grams)	Diameter (mm)	Rev. align.	Current Value
VPT-505	1880	Half sovereign	Silver	2.7	19	↑	2000

Obverse Jubilee type head, with large crown, left; VICTORIA D G BRITT REG F D

Reverse St George and Dragon; 1880 in exergue

Edge plain

Shilling 1880

No.	Date	Denomination	Metal	Weight (grams)	Diameter (mm)	Rev. align.	Current Value
VPT-508	1880	Shilling	Silver		24		

Obverse   Head, left; VICTORIA DEI GRATIA BRITANNIAR REG F D 1880

Reverse   Crowned shield within Garter bearing legend HONI SOIT QUI MAL Y PENSE

Edge   plain

Characteristics   The obverse is identical to that on the currency shilling (obv. 5) with the addition of the date.

Half Sovereign 1884

The designer was probably L. C. Wyon. The coin is possibly unique.

No.	Date	Denomination	Metal	Weight (grams)	Diameter (mm)	Rev. align.	Current Value
VPT-510	1884	Half sovereign	Gold	4.0	19		8000

Obverse   Head with large crown and veil, left; VICTORIA DEI GRA 1884

Reverse   Four crowned cruciform shields with sceptres in angles and central Star of Garter; BRITT REGINA FIDEI DEFENSOR

Edge   milled

Sixpence 1884

The designer was probably L. C. Wyon. The coin is possibly unique.

No.	Date	Denomination	Metal	Weight (grams)	Diameter (mm)	Rev. align.	Current Value
VPT-520	1884	Sixpence	Silver	2.9	19	↑	2000

Obverse   Head with large crown and veil, left; VICTORIA DEI GRA 1884

Reverse   Four crowned cruciform shields with rose, thistle, rose, shamrock in angles and central Star of Garter; BRITT REGINA FIDEI DEFENSOR

Edge   milled

Sovereign 1885

The designer of the obverse was J. E. Boehm, using the Pistrucci reverse. The piece is possibly unique.

No.	Date	Denomination	Metal	Weight (grams)	Diameter (mm)	Rev. align.	Current Value
VPT-525	1885	Sovereign	Silver	3.85	22	↑	4000

Obverse   Jubilee type head, left; VICTORIA D G BRITT REG F D

Reverse   St George and Dragon; 1885 in exergue

Edge   plain

Crown 1887

The designer was J. Rochelle Thomas from a commission by Spink and Son. The pieces were struck by Lauer. A number of minor varieties exist, occasioned by the presence or absence of initials or name of the designer and commissioner.

No.	Date	Denomination	Metal	Weight (grams)	Diameter (mm)	Rev. align.	Current Value
VPT-530	1887	Crown	Silver	28.0–28.3	39	↑	1400

Obverse   Head, left, with tiny crown, all within ornate borders; VICTORIA BY THE GRACE OF GOD QUEEN OF GREAT BRITAIN EMP OF INDIA

Reverse   Royal Arms on oval shield with supporters, spray below, all within ornate border; FIVE SHILLINGS MDCCCLXXXVII (= 1887)

Edge   plain, with or without MADE IN BAVARIA (incuse)

Shilling 1887

The designers were J. E. Boehm (obv.); L. C. Wyon (rev.).

No.	Date	Denomination	Metal	Weight (grams)	Diameter (mm)	Rev. align.	Current Value
VPT-540	1887	Shilling	Silver	5.7	24	↑	1800

Obverse   Jubilee type head, left; VICTORIA DEI GRATIA BRITT REGINA F D

Reverse   Crowned shield within Garter, 1887 above; ONE SHILLING below

Edge   milled

Characteristics   Obverse is identical to that on adopted coin.

Sixpence 1887

The designers were J. E. Boehm (obv.); L. C. Wyon (rev.).

No.	Date	Denomination	Metal	Weight (grams)	Diameter (mm)	Rev. align.	Current Value
VPT-550	1887	Sixpence	Silver	2.8	19	↑	1000

Obverse   Jubilee type head, left; VICTORIA DEI GRATIA BRITT REGINA F D

Reverse   Crowned shield within Garter, 1887 above; SIX PENCE below

Edge   milled

Characteristics   Obverse is identical to that on adopted coin.

Sixpence 1887

The designer was J. Rochelle Thomas for Spink and Son.

No.	Date	Denomination	Metal	Weight (grams)	Diameter (mm)	Rev. align.	Current Value
VPT-560	1887	Sixpence	Silver		19		300
VPT-565	1887	Sixpence	Aluminium		19	↓	400
VPT-570	1887	Sixpence	Tin		19		700
VPT-575	1887	Sixpence	Copper		19		800
VPT-580	1887	Sixpence	Gold		19		1000

Obverse · Head, left, with tiny crown; VICTORIA BY THE GRACE OF GOD QUEEN OF GREAT BRITAIN EMP OF INDIA

Reverse Royal Arms on oval shield with supporters, spray below; SIX PENCE MDCCCLXXXVII (= 1887) with or without SPINK & SON

Edge plain, with or without MADE IN BAVARIA (incuse)

Sixpence 1887

The designer was J. Rochelle Thomas for Spink and Son.

No.	Date	Denomination	Metal	Weight (grams)	Diameter (mm)	Rev. align.	Current Value
VPT-590	1887	Sixpence	Silver		19		300
VPT-595	1887	Sixpence	Brass		19	↑	250
VPT-600	1887	Sixpence	Copper		19		600
VPT-605	1887	Sixpence	Gold		19	↓	1000

Obverse Head, left, with tiny crown; VICTORIA BY THE GRACE OF GOD QUEEN OF GREAT BRITAIN EMP OF INDIA

Reverse Royal Arms on oval shield with supporters, spray below; SIX PENCE MDCCCLXXXVII (= 1887)

Edge milled

Crown 1888

The designers were L. C. Wyon (obv.); Benedetto Pistrucci (rev.).

No.	Date	Denomination	Metal	Weight (grams)	Diameter (mm)	Rev. align.	Current Value
VPT-620	1888	Crown	Silver		39		

Obverse Veiled head, left (LCW on truncation); VICTORIA D G BRITT REG F D

Reverse St George and Dragon; 1888 in exergue below

Edge milled

Crown 1888

The designers were L. C. Wyon (obv.); Benedetto Pistrucci (rev.).

No.	Date	Denomination	Metal	Weight (grams)	Diameter (mm)	Rev. align.	Current Value
VPT-621	1888	Crown	Silver		39		

Obverse Veiled head, left (no initials on truncation); VICTORIA D G BRITT REG F D

Reverse St George and Dragon; 1888 in exergue below

Edge milled

Crown 1892

The designers were Thomas Brock (obv.); Benedetto Pistrucci (rev.).

No.	Date	Denomination	Metal	Weight (grams)	Diameter (mm)	Rev. align.	Current Value
VPT-640	1892	Crown	Silver		39		

Obverse Head, left; VICTORIA DEI GRA BRITT REG FID DEF IND IMP

Reverse St George and Dragon; 1892 in exergue below

Edge DECVS ET TVTAMEN ANNO REGNI LVI

Characteristics The obverse is similar to that of the currency crown 1893–1900 but the legend reads REG instead of REGINA, and there are other minor differences. The reverse is identical to that of the crowns 1887–1900

Penny 1894

No.	Date	Denomination	Metal	Weight (grams)	Diameter (mm)	Rev. align.	Current Value
VPT-645	1894	Penny	Bronze		31		

Obverse Veiled head, left; VICTORIA DEI GRA BRITT REGINA FID DEF IND IMP

Reverse Britannia, seated, with shield, holding trident, facing right, with sailing ship at Britannia's feet; ONE PENNY 1894

Edge plain

Characteristics The obverse identical to that of the currency issue of 1895 to 1901. The reverse is similar to that of this issue except for the ship and some extra drapery from Britannia's arm

Farthing 1894

No.	Date	Denomination	Metal	Weight (grams)	Diameter (mm)	Rev. align.	Current Value
VPT-650	1894	Farthing	Bronze		20		

Obverse Veiled head, left; VICTORIA DEI GRA BRITT REGINA FID DEF IND IMP

Reverse   Britannia, seated, with shield, holding trident, facing right, with sailing ship at Britannia's feet; FARTHING 1894

Edge   plain

Farthing 1896

No.	Date	Denomination	Metal	Weight (grams)	Diameter (mm)	Rev. align.	Current Value
VPT-660	1896	Farthing	Bronze		20		

Obverse   Small veiled head, left; VICTORIA DEI GRA BRITT REGINA FID DEF IND IMP

Reverse   Britannia, seated, with shield, holding trident, facing right; FARTHING 1896

Edge   plain

Characteristics   The reverse is identical to that of the currency farthing

Farthing 1896

No.	Date	Denomination	Metal	Weight (grams)	Diameter (mm)	Rev. align.	Current Value
VPT-662	1896	Farthing	Bronze		20		

Obverse   Small veiled head, left, within raised circle; VICTORIA DEI GRA BRITT REGINA FID DEF IND IMP

Reverse   Britannia, seated, with shield, holding trident, facing right; FARTHING 1896

Edge   plain

Characteristics   The reverse is identical to that of the currency farthing

Double Florin 1900

This piece was struck for Reginald Huth by Pinches to commemorate Victoria's visit to Ireland.

No.	Date	Denomination	Metal	Weight (grams)	Diameter (mm)	Rev. align.	Current Value
VPT-670	1900	Double florin	Silver		34	↑	600

Obverse   Veiled head, left; VICTORIA DEI GRA HIBERNIAE &c REGINA

Reverse   Four crowned cruciform shields; CEAD MILE FAILTE (in Irish script) 1900

Edge   milled

Edward VII (1901 – 1910)

Crown 1902

This piece, based on the Charles I Tower Mint crown, was struck by Spink and Son.

No.	Date	Denomination	Metal	Weight (grams)	Diameter (mm)	Rev. align.	Current Value
E7PT-010	1902	Crown	Silver		47		2000

Obverse   King in coronation robes with sword upright on horseback, facing left, monogram of London behind; EDWARD VII D G BRITT ET TERRAR TRANSMARIN 1902

Reverse   Oval garnished shield within border; Q 1 D S BRITANNICA REX FID DEF IND IMP

Edge   plain

George V   (1910 – 1936)

Crown 1910

The designer was A. G. Wyon.

No.	Date	Denomination	Metal	Weight (grams)	Diameter (mm)	Rev. align.	Current Value
G5PT-010	1910	Crown	Silver	27–28	39	↑	7000
G5PT-012	1910	Crown	Copper		39		3000
G5PT-014	1910	Crown	Gold		39		30000

Obverse   Head, left; GEORGIUS V D G BRITT OMN REX MDCDX
(= 1910)

Reverse   Stylized St George and dragon without exergue

Edge   plain

Crown 1910

The designer was A. G. Wyon. 10 were struck.

No.	Date	Denomination	Metal	Weight (grams)	Diameter (mm)	Rev. align.	Current Value
G5PT-020	1910	Crown	Silver	27–33.5	39	↑	6000
G5PT-022	1910	Crown	Copper		39		3000
G5PT-024	1910	Crown	Gold	56.0	39		30000

Obverse   Head, left; GEORGIVS V D G BRITANNIARVM OMNIVM REX

Reverse   Stylized St George and dragon; 1910 in exergue

Edge   plain

Crown 1910

The designer was A. G. Wyon. 2 known.

No.	Date	Denomination	Metal	Weight (grams)	Diameter (mm)	Rev. align.	Current Value
G5PT-028	1910	Crown	Silver	27–33	39	↑	6000
G5PT-030	1910	Crown	Gold	56.0	39	↑	30000

Obverse   Head, left; GEORGIVS V D G BRITANNIARVM OMNIVM REX

Reverse   Stylized St George and dragon; 1910 in exergue

Edge   milled

Double Florin 1911

These pieces were struck by Messrs. John Pinches for Reginald Huth; the designer was possibly A. G. Wyon.

No.	Date	Denomination	Metal	Weight (grams)	Diameter (mm)	Rev. align.	Current Value
G5PT-040	1911	Double florin	Silver	22.7	36	↑	400

Obverse   Head, left, in high relief; GEORGIVS V DEI GRATIA

Reverse   Four crowned cruciform shields with emblems in angles and Legs of Man (triune) in centre; BRITANIARVM (sic) REX 1911

Edge   plain

Eightpence 1913

These pieces were struck by Messrs. John Pinches for Reginald Huth; the designer was possibly A. G. Wyon.

No.	Date	Denomination	Metal	Weight (grams)	Diameter (mm)	Rev. align.	Current Value
G5PT-050	1913	Eightpence	Silver	3.8	22	↑	600
G5PT-055	1913	Eightpence	Copper		22		200
G5PT-060	1913	Eightpence	Nickel		22		300

Obverse   Head left; GEORGIVS V DEI GRATIA

Reverse   Four crowned cruciform shields with ornaments in angles; BRI REX EIGHT PENCE 1913

Edge   milled

Octorino 1913

No.	Date	Denomination	Metal	Weight (grams)	Diameter (mm)	Rev. align.	Current Value
G5PT-063	1913	Octorino	Silver	3.8	22	↑	600
G5PT-065	1913	Octorino	Copper		22		200
G5PT-067	1913	Octorino	Nickel		22		300

Obverse   Head, left; GEORGIVS V DEI GRATIA

Reverse   Four crowned cruciform shields with Isle of Man triune in centre and ornaments in angles; BRI REX OCTORINO 1913

Edge   milled

Double Florin (12 Groats) 1914

These pieces were struck by Messrs. John Pinches for Reginald Huth; the designer was possibly A. G. Wyon.

No.	Date	Denomination	Metal	Weight (grams)	Diameter (mm)	Rev. align.	Current Value
G5PT-070	1914	Double florin	Silver	22.6	36	↑	450

Obverse Head, left, in high relief; GEORGIVS V DEI GRATIA

Reverse Four crowned cruciform shields with emblems in angles and Legs of Man (triune) in centre; BRI 1914 REX TWELVE GROATS

Edge milled

Shilling 1925

The designers were Bertram Mackennal (obv.); George Kruger Gray (rev.). Around 1923, it was decided that the reverses of the silver coinage were not satisfactory for striking purposes. These 1925 pieces are probably amongst those considered for the replacement of the existing coinage.

No.	Date	Denomination	Metal	Weight (grams)	Diameter (mm)	Rev. align.	Current Value
G5PT-080	1925	Shilling	Nickel	5.6–5.7	24	↑	800

Obverse Head left; GEORGIVS V DEI GRA BRITT OMN REX

Reverse Lion on crown; FID DEF IND IMP ONE SHILLING

Edge milled

Characteristics Similar to adopted shilling 1927 onwards but lion's tail different.

Sixpence 1925

The designers were Bertram Mackennal (obv.); George Kruger Gray (rev.). See notes for G5PT-080.

No.	Date	Denomination	Metal	Weight (grams)	Diameter (mm)	Rev. align.	Current Value
G5PT-090	1925	Sixpence	Nickel	2.8	19	↑	500

Obverse Head left; GEORGIVS V D G BRITT OMN REX F D IND IMP

Reverse Oak sprigs with six acorns; SIXPENCE A 1925 D

Edge milled

Characteristics Similar to adopted coin of 1927.

Threepence 1925

The designers were Bertram Mackennal (obv.); George Kruger Gray (rev.). See notes for G5PT-080.

No.	Date	Denomination	Metal	Weight (grams)	Diameter (mm)	Rev. align.	Current Value
G5PT-100	1925	Threepence	Nickel	1.6	16	↑	600

Obverse Head left; GEORGIVS V D G BRITT OMN REX F D IND IMP

Reverse Three oak sprigs with three acorns; THREE PENCE 1925

Edge plain

Characteristics Similar to adopted coin of 1927.

Penny 1933

No.	Date	Denomination	Metal	Weight (grams)	Diameter (mm)	Rev. align.	Current Value
G5PT-105	1933	Penny	Bronze		31		

Obverse Head, left; GEORGIVS V DEI GRA BRITT OMN REX FID DEF IND IMP

Reverse Britannia seated, with shield and trident, facing right; ONE PENNY 1933

Edge plain

Crown 1935

The designers were Bertram Mackennal (obv.) and George Kruger Gray (rev.).

No.	Date	Denomination	Metal	Weight (grams)	Diameter (mm)	Rev. align.	Current Value
G5PT-110	1935	Crown	Silver	28.0	39	↑	8000

Obverse Head, left; GEORGIVS V DG BRITT OMN REX FD IND IMP

Reverse Stylized St George and dragon; 1935 CROWN

Edge (in relief) DECUS ET TUTAMEN ANNO REGNI XXV

Characteristics Obverse is identical to that of adopted coin.

Edward VIII   (1936)

Crown 1936

These fantasy pieces were part of a series struck for Geoffrey Hearn by Pinches.

No.	Date	Denomination	Metal	Weight (grams)	Diameter (mm)	Rev. align.	Current Value
E8PT-010	1936	Crown	Silver	28.0	39	↑	25
E8PT-020	1936	Crown	Gold	35.8	39	↑	500

Obverse Head, left; EDWARD VIII KING & EMPEROR

Reverse Stylized St George and dragon; 1936

Edge plain

Threepence 1937

The designers were T. H. Paget (obv.); Madge Kitchener (rev.). The rumour that Kitchener wove her initials into the stems of the plant is unfounded.

No.	Date	Denomination	Metal	Weight (grams)	Diameter (mm)	Rev. align.	Current Value
E8PT-100	1937	Threepence	Nickel-brass 2.5 mm thick	6.8	12 sided figure; 21mm across sides; 22mm across corners	↑	25000
E8PT-105	1937	Threepence	Nickel-brass 2.0 mm thick	5.2	12 sided figure; 21mm across sides; 22mm across corners	↑	25000
E8PT-110	1937	Threepence	Nickel-brass 1.75 mm thick	4.5	12 sided figure; 21mm across sides; 22mm across corners	↑	

Obverse   Head, left; EDWARDVS VIII D G BR OMN REX F D IND IMP

Reverse   Thrift plant within circle, all dividing date 19 37; THREE PENCE

Edge   plain

George VI   (1937 – 1952)

Crown or Double Florin 1950

The designer was T. Paget (obv.); Benedetto Pistrucci (rev.).

No.	Date	Denomination	Metal	Weight (grams)	Diameter (mm)	Rev. align.	Current Value
G6PT-020	1950	Crown or double florin	Cupronickel	22.7	36	↑	3000

Obverse   Head, left; GEORGIVS VI D G BR OMN REX FID DEF 1950

Reverse   St George and dragon within Garter; HONI SOIT QUI MAL Y PENSE

Edge   milled

Characteristics   The obverse head is identical to that on the adopted 1951 crown; the reverse is very similar to that on the adopted 1818 crown but the design is smaller within a prominent toothed border.

Double Florin 1950

The designer was T. Paget (obv.); Benedetto Pistrucci (rev.).

No.	Date	Denomination	Metal	Weight (grams)	Diameter (mm)	Rev. align.	Current Value
G6PT-030	1950	Double florin	Cupronickel (?)	22.7	36	↑	6000

Obverse   Head, left; GEORGIVS VI D G BR OMN REX FID DEF 1950

Reverse   St George and dragon within Garter; HONI SOIT QUI MAL Y PENSE

Edge   milled with incuse FOUR SHILLINGS

Characteristics   The obverse head is identical to that on the adopted 1951 crown; the reverse is very similar to that on the adopted 1818 crown but the design is smaller within a prominent toothed border.

Elizabeth II   (1952 –)

Crown 1953

No.	Date	Denomination	Metal	Weight (grams)	Diameter (mm)	Rev. align.	Current Value
EZPT-010	1953	Crown	Cupronickel	28.3	39	↑	10000

Obverse   Queen on horseback; ELIZABETH II DEI GRATIA BRITT OMN REGINA FIDEI DEFENSOR FIVE SHILLINGS

Reverse   Cruciform shields and emblems around crown superimposed on cross; 1953

Edge   (incuse) FAITH AND TRUTH I WILL BEAR UNTO YOU

Characteristics   Similar to adopted coin but in higher relief, and reverse is slightly different design; the adopted coin does not have the superimposed cross.

Two Cents 1961

No.	Date	Denomination	Metal	Weight (grams)	Diameter (mm)	Rev. align.	Current Value
EZPT-050	1961	2 cents	Bronze	89.5	25	↑	

Obverse   Head, right; ELIZABETH II DEI GRATIA REGINA F D

Reverse   Ornamented trident head, crown above; 2 CENTS 2 CENTS 1961

Edge   plain

Characteristics   The obverse is identical to that of the current halfpenny.

Cent 1961

No.	Date	Denomination	Metal	Weight (grams)	Diameter (mm)	Rev. align.	Current Value
EZPT-060	1961	Cent	Bronze	45	20	↑	

Obverse   Head, right; ELIZABETH II DEI GRATIA REGINA F D
Reverse   Monogrammed EIIR; 1 CENT ONE DECIMAL PENNY 1961
Edge   plain
Characteristics   The obverse is identical to that of the farthing 1954–56.

Bibliography

Bibliography

Batty, D. T., *Descriptive Catalogue of Copper Coinage*, Manchester, 1886.

Besley, E., *Coins and Medals of the Civil War*, Batsfords, 1950.

Boon, George C., *Cardiganshire Silver and the Aberystwyth Mint in Peace and War*, National Museum of Wales, 1981.

Bramah, E., *Varieties of English Regal Copper Coins*, Methuen, 1929.

Bressett, K., *Guide Book of English Coins*, Western Publishing, USA, 1982.

Brooke, G., *English Coins*, Methuen, 1942.

Challis, C. E. (ed.), *A New History of the Royal Mint*, Cambridge University Press, 1992.

Cleveland Museum, *English Gold Coins*, Cleveland, 1968.

Cope, G. and A. Rayner, *English Milled Coinage 1662–1972*, Spink, 1972.

Craig, J., *The Mint*, Cambridge University Press, 1953.

Crowther, Rev. G.F., *A Guide to English Pattern Coins in Gold, Silver, Copper and Pewter*, L. Upcolt Gill, 1887.

Cullimore Allen, J., *Sovereigns of the British Empire*, Spink, 1965.

Davies, Peter J., *British silver coins since 1816*, 1982.

Dickinson, M., *Victorian Godless and Gothic Florins*, SCMB, 1978/80.

Doty, Richard C., *Encyclopaedic Dictionary of Numismatics*, Robert Hale, 1972.

Duveen, G. and H.G. Stride, *A History of the Gold Sovereign*, 1962.

Dyer, G., *The proposed Coinage of King Edward VIII*, HMSO, 1973.

Dyer, G., ed., *Royal Sovereign, 1489–1989*, Royal Mint, 1989.

Farquhar, H., *Portraiture of our Stuart Monarchs on their Coins and Medals*, Harrison, 1914.

Farquhar, H., *Royal Charities*, Harrison, 1929.

Freeman, M., *Bronze Coinage of Great Britain*, Barrie and Jenkins, 1985.

Garside, H., *British Imperial Copper and Bronze Coinage 1838–1920*, Spink, 1920, suppl. 1925.

Grueber, H., *Handbook of Coins of Great Britain in the British Musuem*, 1899.

Hawkins, E., *The Silver Coins of England*, Quaritch, 1887.

Henfrey, H. W., *A Guide to the Study of English Coins*, Bell, 1885.

Jackson Kent, E., *The Silver Coinage of William III*, Spink, 1961.

Jewitt, L., *Handbook of English Coins*, 1810.

Junge, E. Ward, *The Seaby Coin Encyclopaedia*, Seaby, 1992.

Kenyon, R., *Gold Coins of England*, Quaritch, 1884.

Kinnaird, George, *Royal Mint treatement of brittle gold*, 1871.

Krause, Mishler and Bruce II, *Standard Catalogue of World Coins and Talers, 1601 to Date*, Krause, 1994.

Krause, Mishler and Bruce II, *Standard Catalogue of World Coins, 1701–1801*, Krause, 1993.

Lawrence, L.A., *The Coinage of Edward III from 1351*.

Leake, S. Martin, *Historical account of English Money*, London, 1793.

Li, Ming-Hsun, *The Great Recoinage of 1696–9*, Weidenfeld and Nicolson, 1963.

Linecar, H. and Stone, A., *English Proof and Pattern Crown-size Pieces 1658–1960*, Spink, 1968.

Linecar, H., *British Coin Designs and Designers*, Bell, 1977.

Linecar, H., *Crown Pieces of Great Britain*, Benn, 1969.

Linecar, H., ed., *The Milled Coinage of England 1662–1946*, Spink, 1950.

Marles, J., *Collectors' Coins*, Rotographic Publications.

Marsh, M., *The Gold Half Sovereign*, Cambridge Coins.

Marsh, M., *The Gold Sovereign*, Cambridge Coins.

Marshall, George, *View of the Silver Coin and Coinage*, 1838.

Mayhew, N.J., *Sterling Imitations of Edwardian type (Pennies)*, Royal Numismatic Society, 1983.

Mays, James O'Donald, *The Splendid Shilling*, New Forest Leaves, 1982.

McDonald, G., *Australian Coin and Banknote Guide*, Rigby, Australia, 1983.

Milward, A., *Decimal Coinage*, 1853.

Montagu, H., *The Copper, Tin, and Bronze Coinage of England*, Rollin and Feuardent, 1885.

Morrieson, H.W., *A Review of the Coinage of Charles II*, 1921.

Nicholson, Alan J., *Thomas Simon, his life and works, 1618–1665*, Seaby, 1975.

North, J.J. and P.J. Preston, *The John Brooker Collection, Coins of Charles I*, Spink, 1984.

North, J.J., *Edwardian English Silver Coins, 1279–1351*, Spink.

North, J.J., *English Hammered Coinage*, Spink, Vol. 1: 1994, Vol. 2: 1992 (revised editions).

Oman, C., *The Coinage of England*, Clarendon, 1931.

Peck, C.W., *English Copper, Tin and Bronze Coins in the British Museum 1558–1958*, British Museum, 1964.

Purvey, Frank, *Collecting Coins*, Seaby, 1985.

Rayner, P. Alan, *Designers and Engravers of English milled coinage*, 1954.

Rayner, P. Alan, *English Silver Coinage since 1649*, Seaby, 1992.

Robinson, B., *Silver Pennies & Linen Towels, The Story of the Royal Maundy*, Spink, 1992.

Robinson, B., *The Royal Maundy*, Kaye and Ward, 1977.

Royal Almonry, *The Royal Maundy*, Royal Almonry, 1952.

Royal Mint, *Statutes relating to Coinage*, HMSO, 1915.

Ruding, R., *Annals of the Coinage of Great Britain*, 1840.

Sainthill, Richard, *Numismatic crumbs*, 1855.

Salzman, M., *Modern British Coins and their varieties 1797–1970*, Salzman, 1982.

Seaby, Mitchell and Reeds, *Standard Catalogue, Coins of England and the United Kingdom*, 30th edition, Seaby, 1995.

Seaby, P., *The Story of the English Coinage*, Seaby, 1952.

Snelling, T., *A view of the Coins at this time current throughout Europe*, London, 1766.

Stainer, C.L., *Oxford Silver Pennies*, 1904.

Sutherland, C.H.V., *English Coins*, Oxford, 1973.

Thorburn, S., *Guide to the Coins of Great Britain and Ireland*, Upcott Gill, 1884.

Vallavine, Peter, *Observations on present coindition of current coin*, 1742.

Woolf, N., *The Sovereign Remedy; Touch-pieces and the King's Evil*, 1990.

Wren, C.R., *The English Long Cross Pennies, 1279–1489*, Plantagenet Books, 1995.

Wren, C.R., *The Short Cross Coinage, 1180–1247*, Plantagenet Books, 1992.

Wren, C.R., *The Voided Cross Coinage, 1247–1279*, Plantagenet Books, 1993.

Index of Engravers
and Designers

Index
of designers and engravers of milled coins

W.H.J. Blakemore
E76D, *549*
E7SH, *536*

Joseph Edgar **Boehm** (1834–1890)
V2P, *440*
V4D, *559*
V6D, *547*
VCR, *488*
VDFL, *495*
VFL, *517*
VHC, *509*
VHS, *468*
VMS, *624*
VSH, *534*
VSV, *454*

George **Bower** (?–1689)
WM1M, *579*
WM2M, *571*
WM3M, *561*
WM4M, *553*
WMFA, *606*
WMHD, *594*
WMHG, *462*

Thomas **Brock** (1847–1922)
V1D, *584*
V2P, *440*
V5P, *427*
V6D, *547*
VCR, *488*
VFA, *611*
VFL, *517*
VHC, *509*
VHD, *599*
VHS, *468*
VMS, *624*
VSH, *534*
VSV, *454*

Samuel **Bull** (?–c.1720)
A1M, *580*
A2G, *437*
A2M, *572*
A3M, *562*
A4M, *554*
A5G, *424*
A6D, *544*
ACR, *481*
AGN, *448*

AHC, *504*
AHG, *462*
ASH, *528*
G11M, *580*
G12M, *572*
G13M, *562*
G14M, *554*
G1GN, *448*
W3HD, *595*

Joseph **Cave** (?–c.1760)
A6D, *544*

Francis Legatt **Chantrey** (1781–1842)
G42P, *439*
G45P, *427*
G4CR, *487*
W41D, *584*
W42P, *439*
W4FA, *611*
W4HD, *599*
W4HS, *467*
W4SV, *454*

James **Clerk**
A6D, *544*
ASH, *528*

John **Croker** (1670–1741) (1740 old style calendar)
A1M, *580*
A2G, *437*
A2M, *572*
A3M, *562*
A4M, *554*
A5G, *424*
A6D, *544*
ACR, *481*
AFA, *607*
AGN, *448*
AHC, *504*
AHG, *462*
ASH, *528*
G11M, *580*
G12G, *437*
G12M, *572*
G13M, *562*
G14M, *554*
G15G, *425*
G16D, *544*
G1CR, *482*
G1FA, *608*

G1GN,   448
G1HC,   505
G1HD,   596
G1HG,   463
G1QG,   475
G1SH,   530
G22G,   437
G22M,   572
G23M,   563
G24M,   555
G25G,   425
G25G,   425
G26D,   545
G2CR,   483
G2FA,   609
G2GN,   449
G2HC,   506
G2HD,   597
G2HG,   463
G2SH,   531
W31M,   580
W32G,   436
W32M,   572
W33M,   562
W34M,   554
W35G,   423
W36D,   542
W3CR,   480
W3GN,   447
W3HG,   462
W3SH,   527

George William **de Saulles** (1862–1903)
E71D,   588
E72P,   440
E73D,   565
E75P,   428
E76D,   549
E7CR,   490
E7FA,   613
E7FL,   519
E7HC,   511
E7HD,   601
E7HS,   470
E7MS,   625
E7SH,   536
E7SV,   457
E7TF,   620
V1D,   584
VFA,   611
VMS,   624

William **Dyce** (1806–1864)
VCR,   488
VFL,   517

William **Gardner** (1914–)
EL23DB,   570
EL2SH,   538

Mary **Gillick** (1881–1965)
EL21D,   591
EL22P,   441
EL23DB,   570
EL25P,   430
EL26D,   551
EL2FA,   615
EL2FL,   522
EL2HC,   514
EL2HD,   603
EL2HS,   471
EL2MS,   626
EL2SH,   538
EL2SV,   459

George **Gray**, see **Kruger Gray**

Henry **Harris** (?–1704)
W36D,   542
WM6D,   542
WMHC,   501

Frances Madge **Kitchener**
E83DB,   569
G63DB,   569

Godfrey **Kneller** (1646–1723)
A2G,   437
A5G,   424
A6D,   544
ACR,   481
AGN,   448
AHC,   504
AHG,   462
ASH,   528

George **Kruger Gray** (1880–1943)
E83M,   567
E86D,   550
E8CR,   491
E8FL,   521
E8HC,   513
E8SH,   537
G56D,   549
G5CR,   490
G5FL,   520
G5HC,   512
G63M,   566
G66D,   550
G6CR,   492
G6FL,   521
G6HC,   513
G6SH,   537

Conrad Heinrich **Küchler** (c.1740–1810)
G31D,   583

G32D, *575*
G3FA, *609*
G3HD, *597*

Arnold **Machin** (1911–1999)
D1P, *637*
EL22P, *441*
EL25P, *430*
EL2HS, *471*
EL2SV, *459*

Bertram **Mackennal** (1863–1931)
G51D, *588*
G52P, *440*
G55P, *429*
G56D, *549*
G5CR, *490*
G5FA, *613*
G5FL, *520*
G5HC, *512*
G5HD, *602*
G5HS, *470*
G5MS, *625*
G5SH, *536*
G5SV, *458*
G5TF, *620*

Raphael David **Maklouf** (1937–)
D1P, *637*
EL22P, *441*
EL25P, *430*
EL2HS, *471*
EL2SV, *459*

Nathaniel **Marchant** (1739–1816)
G318D, *523*
G33S, *497*
G3GN, *451*
G3HG, *464*
G3TG, *473*

Johann Baptiste **Merlen** (1769–c.1850)
G42P, *439*
G45P, *427*
G46D, *546*
G4HC, *508*
G4HS, *467*
G4SV, *453*
V3HD, *577*
V3M, *564*
V6D, *547*
VCR, *488*
VHS, *468*
VSH, *534*
VSV, *454*
W42P, *439*
W43HD, *577*
W46D, *547*
W4CR, *487*

W4HC, *509*
W4HS, *467*
W4SH, *534*
W4SV, *454*

Percy **Metcalfe** (1895–1970)
E83DB, *569*
G5CR, *490*
G63DB, *569*

Johann Rudolf **Ochs, junior** (1704–1788)
G22G, *437*
G26D, *545*
G2GN, *449*
G2HD, *597*
G2HG, *463*
G33M, *563*

Johann Rudolf **Ochs, senior** (1673–c.1748)
G12G, *437*
G13M, *562*
G14M, *554*
G15G, *425*
G16D, *544*
G1CR, *482*
G1FA, *608*
G1GN, *448*
G1HC, *505*
G1HD, *596*
G1HG, *463*
G1QG, *475*
G1SH, *530*
G2GN, *449*
G2SH, *531*

Thomas Humphrey **Paget** (1893–1974)
E81D, *589*
E82P, *441*
E83DB, *569*
E83M, *567*
E85P, *429*
E86D, *550*
E8CR, *491*
E8FA, *614*
E8FL, *521*
E8HC, *513*
E8HD, *602*
E8SH, *537*
E8SV, *459*
G61D, *590*
G62P, *441*
G63DB, *569*
G65P, *429*
G66D, *550*
G6CR, *492*
G6FL, *521*
G6HC, *513*
G6HD, *603*

G6HS, *471*
G6MS, *626*
G6SH, *537*
G6SV, *459*

H. Wilson **Parker** (1896–1980)
EL2FA, *615*

Lewis **Pingo** (1743–1830)
G318D, *523*
G33M, *563*
G33S, *497*
G36D, *545*
G3GN, *451*
G3HG, *464*
G3TG, *473*
G3GN, *451*
G3HG, *464*

Thomas **Pingo** (?–1776)
G3HG, *464*
G3HD, *597*
G3FA, *609*

Benedetto **Pistrucci** (1784–1855)
E72P, *440*
E75P, *428*
E7SV, *457*
E82P, *441*
E85P, *429*
E8SV, *459*
EL22P, *441*
EL25P, *430*
EL2SV, *459*
G34M, *555*
G36D, *545*
G3CR, *484*
G3HC, *507*
G3HS, *467*
G3SH, *532*
G3SV, *453*
G41D, *583*
G42P, *439*
G46D, *546*
G4CR, *487*
G4FA, *610*
G4HC, *508*
G4HS, *467*
G4MS, *623*
G4SH, *533*
G4SV, *453*
G52P, *440*
G55P, *429*
G5SV, *458*
G62P, *441*
G65P, *429*
G6SV, *459*
V2P, *440*

V5P, *427*
VSV, *454*

Edward **Poynter** (1836–1919)
VFL, *517*

James **Roettier** (1663–1698)
W32G, *436*
W35G, *423*
W36D, *542*
W3CR, *480*
W3FA, *607*
W3HD, *595*
W3HG, *462*
W3SH, *527*
WM2G, *436*
WM5G, *423*
WM6D, *542*
WMCR, *480*
WMFA, *606*
WMGN, *446*
WMHC, *501*
WMHD, *594*
WMHG, *462*
WMSH, *526*

John **Roettier** (1631–1700)
C21MM, *579*
C22G, *435*
C22M, *571*
C23M, *561*
C24M, *553*
C25G, *421*
C26D, *541*
C2CR, *477*
C2FAM, *605*
C2GN, *445*
C2HC, *499*
C2HDM, *593*
C2HG, *461*
C2SH, *245*
J21M, *579*
J22G, *435*
J22M, *571*
J23M, *561*
J24M, *553*
J25G, *422*
J26D, *541*
J2CR, *479*
J2FA, *605*
J2GN, *446*
J2HC, *501*
J2HD, *593*
J2HG, *461*
J2SH, *526*
VDFL, *495*
WM6D, *542*

WMSH, *526*

Norbert **Roettier** (1665–?)
G1SH, *530*
WM2G, *436*
WM5G, *423*
WM6D, *542*
WMCR, *480*
WMFA, *606*
WMGN, *446*
WMHC, *501*
WMHD, *594*
WMHG, *462*
WMSH, *526*

Thomas **Simon** (1618–1665)
C21MM, *579*
C22MM, *571*
C23MM, *561*
C24MM, *553*
OC50S, *433*
OC6D, *541*
OCBR, *443*
OCCR, *477*
OCHC, *499*
OCSH, *525*

Johann Sigismund **Tanner** (c.1706–1775)
G21M, *581*
G22G, *437*
G22M, *572*
G23M, *563*
G25G, *425*
G26D, *545*
G2CR, *483*
G2FA, *609*
G2GN, *449*
G2HC, *506*
G2HD, *597*
G2HG, *463*
G2SH, *531*
G3GN, *451*

Leonard Charles **Wyon** (1826–1891)
V1D, *584*
VDFL, *495*
VFA, *611*
VFL, *517*
VHD, *599*
VMS, *624*
VSV, *454*
VTF, *619*

Thomas **Wyon** (1792–1817)
G318D, *523*
G36D, *545*
G3HC, *507*
G3SH, *532*
G4HS, *467*

W42P, *439*
W4FA, *611*

William **Wyon** (1795–1851)
G3HS, *467*
G41D, *583*
G42P, *439*
G45P, *427*
G46D, *546*
G4CR, *487*
G4FA, *610*
G4HC, *508*
G4HD, *598*
G4HF, *617*
G4SH, *533*
G4SV, *453*
G4TF, *619*
V1D, *584*
V3HD, *577*
V3M, *564*
V4D, *559*
V5P, *427*
V6D, *547*
VCR, *488*
VFA, *611*
VFL, *517*
VHD, *599*
VHF, *617*
VHS, *468*
VMS, *624*
VQF, *621*
VSH, *534*
VSV, *454*
VTF, *619*
W41D, *584*
W43HD, *577*
W44D, *559*
W46D, *547*
W4CR, *487*
W4HC, *509*
W4HD, *599*
W4HF, *617*
W4HS, *467*
W4MS, *623*
W4SH, *534*
W4SV, *454*
W4TF, *619*

Richard **Yeo** (?–1779)
G33M, *563*
G34M, *555*
G3FA, *609*
G3GN, *451*
G3HD, *597*
G3HG, *464*
G3QG, *475*
G3SH, *532*

Index

Index

Page numbers in **bold** type refer to the Hammered section, those in *italic* type refer to the Milled section.

adjustment marks, *479*

Africa Company, *445*

Albert Memorial, halfcrown struck for 1864opening, *511*

angel, **145**

Anne
  crown, *481*
  farthing, *607*
  five guineas, *424*
  fourpence, *554*
  guinea, *448*
  half guinea, *462*
  halfcrown, *504*
  patterns, *708*
  penny, *580*
  shilling, *528*
  sixpence, *544*
  threepence, *562*
  two guineas, *437*
  twopence, *572*

Ansell sovereign, *454*

Assize of the Moneyers, **81, 317**

Australian mints, *456*

Bank of England dollars, *484*

Barton's metal, *487*

bibliography, *739*

blanks, imported from Sweden, *593*

Boulton, Matthew, *575*

Briot's coinage
  crown, **163**
  half sovereign, **129**
  halfcrown, **195**
  halfgroat, **308**
  penny, **373**
  shilling, **236**
  sixpence, **253**
  sovereign, **114**

Britain crown, **160**

Britannia coinage, *647*
  100 Pounds, *647*
  50 Pounds, *647*
  25 Pounds, *648*

10 Pounds, *458*
2 Pounds, *649*

Britannia groat, *559*

broad, *443*

Canadian mint, *457*

Cartwheel twopence, *575*

Charles I
  angel **151**
  crown, **162**
  double crown, **128**
  farthing, **402**
  groat, **279**
  half unite, **130**
  halfcrown, **192**
  halfgroat, **307**
  halfpenny, **394**
  halfpound, **130**
  ninepence, **409**
  patterns, **695**
  penny, **371**
  pound, **116**
  rose farthing, **404**
  Scarborough siege issues, **409**
  shilling, **232**
  siege issues, **409**
  sixpence, **251**
  three shillings, **409**
  threepence, **284**
  touch pieces, **152**
  triple unite, **103**
  two shillings, **409**
  unite, **111**

Charles II
  crown, hammered, **169**
  crown, milled, *477*
  double crown, **132**
  farthing, *605*
  five guineas, *421*
  fourpence, *553*
  groat, **282**
  guinea, *445*
  half guinea, *461*
  halfcrown, hammered, **211**
  halfcrown, milled, *499*
  halfgroat, **311**
  halfpenny, *593*

patterns milled, *705*
penny, hammered, **375**
penny, milled, *579*
shilling, hammered, **245**
shilling, milled, *525*
sixpence, hammered, **257**
sixpence, milled *541*
threepence, hammered, **283**
threepence, milled, *561*
two guineas, *435*
twopence, *571*
unite, **119**

clashed dies
halfpenny, *599*
penny, *585*

clipping
hammered coins, **81**
milled coins, *446*

coin weights, **412**

Colonies
half farthing issued for, *617*
quarter farthing issued for, *621*
third farthing issued for, *619*
three-halfpence issued for, *564*
threepence issued for, *563*

commemorative crown
1937 and 1951, *492*
1953, 1960 and 1965, *492*
1972, 1977, 1980 and 1981, *640*

commemorative five pounds, *633*

commemorative sovereign, Australian, permission to
mint refused, *458*

commemorative twenty five pence, *640*

commemorative two pounds, *635*

Commonwealth
crown, **168**
double crown, **132**
halfcrown, **210**
halfgroat, **310**
halfpenny, **394**
patterns, **701**
penny, **375**
shilling, **245**
sixpence, **256**
unite, **119**

Corbet farthing, *606*

countermarked coins
eight reales, *484*
Elizabeth I, **407**
four reales, *507*

Cromwell, depicted as Roman Emperor, *477*
Cromwell-Commonwealth
broad, *443*
crown, *477*
fifty shillings, *433*
halfcrown, *499*
patterns, *705*
shilling, *525*
sixpence, *541*

crown of the double rose, **155**

crown of the rose, **171**

crown
decimal, *633, 635, 640*
hammered, **155**
milled, *477*

decimal crown, *633, 635, 640*

decimal currency, *633*
fifty pence, *638*
five pence, *643*
five pounds, *633*
halfpenny, *646*
penny, *645*
pound, *637*
ten pence, *642*
twenty pence, *641*
twenty-five pence, *640*
two pounds, *635*
twopence, *644*

decimalization
1847 proposals, *517*
1961 proposals, *633*

Decus et Tutamen, origin of, *421*

denomination in legend
first use of Crown, *491*
first use of Halfcrown, *509*
first use of One Shilling, *534*
first use of Six Pence, *547*
first use, list, *419*

designers of milled coins, see index of, *743*

Dorrien Magens shilling, *532*

double florin, *495*

double leopard, **153**

dump coinage
farthing, *608*
halfpence, *596*

ecus, French, Charles II crown, possibly struck
from, *477*

edge date, see *regnal date, 477*

edge lettering
manufacture, *421*

used by French after use in England, *477*

Edinburgh mintmark, *504*

Edward I and Edward II pennies, distinguishing
  between, **334**

Edward I
  farthing, **395**
  groat, **259**
  halfpenny, **379**
  long cross coinage, **333**
  penny, **333**
  Recoinage of 1279, **334**

Edward II
  farthing, **397**
  halfpenny, **381**
  penny, **341**

Edward III
  double leopard, **153**
  farthing, **397**
  florin, **153**
  florin coinage farthing, **397**
  florin coinage halfpenny, **382**
  florin coinage penny, **344**
  fourth coinage, **345**
  groat, **260**
  half florin, **185**
  half noble, **173**
  halfgroat, **289**
  halfpenny, **381**
  helm, **223**
  leopard, **185**
  noble, **135**
  penny, **343**
  quarter florin, **223**
  quarter noble, **215**

Edward IV or V
  angel, **146**
  groat, **271**
  half angel, **180**
  halfpenny, **389**
  penny, **361**

Edward IV
  angel (first reign), **145**
  angel (second reign), **145**
  farthing, **400**
  groat (first reign), **267**
  groat (second reign), **270**
  half angel, **179**
  half noble, **177**
  halfgroat (first reign), **295**
  halfgroat (second reign), **298**
  halfpenny (first reign), **387**
  halfpenny (second reign), **388**
  noble, **142**

  penny (first reign), **356**
  penny (second reign), **359**
  quarter noble, **219**
  quarter ryal, **219**
  rose noble or ryal, **142**

Edward V
  angel, **146**
  groat, **271**
  half angel, **180**
  halfgroat, **298**
  penny, **362**

Edward VI
  angel, **149**
  crown, **157**
  crown, gold, **157**
  crown, silver, **157**
  farthing, **401**
  groat, **277**
  half angel, **181**
  half sovereign, **124**
  halfcrown, **188**
  halfcrown, fine silver, **189**
  halfcrown, gold, **188**
  halfgroat, **304**
  halfpenny, **393**
  patterns, **691**
  penny, **368**
  penny, fine silver, **369**
  shilling, **226**
  shilling, base silver, **226**
  shilling, fine silver, **228**
  sixpence, **247**
  sovereign, **108**
  sovereign, fine, **108**
  threepence, **283**

Edward VII
  crown, *490*
  farthing, *613*
  five pounds, *428*
  florin, *519*
  fourpence, Maundy *556*
  half sovereign, *470*
  halfcrown, *511*
  halfpenny, *601*
  Maundy set, *625*
  penny, copper/bronze, *588*
  penny, Maundy, *582*
  shilling, *536*
  sixpence, *549*
  sovereign, *457*
  third farthing, *620*
  threepence, Maundy, *565*
  threepence, silver, *566*
  two pounds, *440*

twopence, Maundy, *574*

Edward VIII
  crown, *491*
  farthing, *614*
  five pounds, *429*
  florin *521*
  halfcrown, *513*
  halfpenny, *602*
  patterns, *734*
  penny, bronze, *589*
  shilling, *537*
  sixpence, *550*
  sovereign, *459*
  threepence, brass, *569*
  threepence, silver, *567*
  two pounds, *441*

eighteen pence bank token, *523*

electrotypes, *488*

Elizabeth I
  angel **150**
  countermarked coins, **407**
  crown, **158**
  crown, milled, **159**
  crown, silver, **159**
  groat, **278**
  half angel, **182**
  halfcrown, **189**
  halfcrown, milled, **190**
  halfcrown, silver, **190**
  halfgroat, **305**
  halfpenny, **393**
  halfpound, **125**
  patterns, **692**
  penny, **370**
  portcullis coinage, **408**
  pound, gold **109**
  quarter angel, **221**
  ryal, **121**
  shilling, **229**
  shilling, milled, **230**
  sixpence, **248**
  sixpence, milled, **249**
  sovereign, **108**
  sovereign, fine, **109**
  three-farthings, **377**
  three-halfpence, **313**
  threepence, **283**
  threepence, milled, **284**

Elizabeth II
  Britannia gold coinage *647*
  Britannia silver coinage *649*
  crown, *492*
  decimal coinage, *633*
  farthing, *615*

five pounds, *430*
florin *522*
fourpence, Maundy, *556*
half sovereign, *471*
halfcrown, *514*
halfpenny, *603*
Maundy set, *626*
pattterns, *735*
penny, bronze, *591*
penny, Maundy, *582*
shilling, *538*
sixpence, *551*
sovereign, *459*
threepence, brass, *570*
threepence, Maundy, *567*
two pounds, *441*
twopence, Maundy, *574*

engravers of milled coins, see index of, 743

Falkland Islands, Victoria crown used in, *488*

farthing
  hammered, **395**
  milled, *605*
  struck from sovereign die, *454*

Festival of Britain, 1951, *633*

Fidei Defensor, *483*

fifty pence, decimal, *638*

fifty shillings, *433*

fine sovereign
  Edward VI, **108**
  Elizabeth I, **109**
  Mary, **108**

fine work coinage, William III, *423, 436*

five guineas, *421*

five pence, decimal, *643*

five pounds, *427*
  decimal, in base metal, *633*

flecking, see *haymarking*, *502, 526*

florin coinage, Edward III
  farthing, **397**
  halfpenny, **382**
  penny, **344**

florin
  hammered, **153**
  milled, *517*

foreign coins, circulating unofficially, **411**

forgeries
  crown, Gothic, *489*
  detection, *454, 451, 489, 502*

farthing, hammered **405**
five pounds, *427*
guinea, *450*
guinea, 1798 *451*
halfcrown, Edward VII 1905, *511*
halfcrown, Victoria, *510*
halfcrown, William and Mary, *502*
halfpenny, George III, *597*
milling, *454*
sovereign, *454*
two guineas, George II, *438*
two pounds, *440, 440, 441*

George I
  crown, *482*
  farthing, *608*
  five guineas, *425*
  fourpence, *554*
  guinea, *448*
  half guinea, *463*
  halfcrown, *505*
  halfpenny, *596*
  patterns, *708*
  penny, *580*
  quarter guinea, *475*
  shilling, *530*
  sixpence, *544*
  threepence, *562*
  two guineas, *437*
  twopence, *572*

George II
  crown, *483*
  farthing, *609*
  five guineas, *425*
  fourpence, *555*
  guinea, *449*
  half guinea, *463*
  halfcrown, *506*
  halfpenny, *597*
  patterns, *708*
  penny, *581*
  shilling, *531*
  sixpence, *545*
  threepence, *563*
  two guineas, *437*
  twopence, *572*

George III
  crown, *484*
  eighteen pence bank token, *523*
  farthing, *609*
  fourpence, *555*
  guinea, *451*
  guinea, military, *451*
  guinea, spade, *451*
  half guinea, *464*

half sovereign, *467*
halfcrown, *507*
halfpenny, *597*
patterns, *709*
penny, copper, *583*
penny, silver, *581*
quarter guinea, *475*
shilling, *532*
sixpence, *545*
sovereign, *453*
third guinea, *473*
three shillings bank token, *497*
threepence, *563*
twopence, copper, *575*
twopence, silver, *573*

George IV
  crown, *487*
  farthing, *610*
  five pounds, *427*
  fourpence, Maundy, *555*
  half farthing, *617*
  half sovereign, *467*
  halfcrown, *508*
  halfpenny, *598*
  Maundy set, *623*
  patterns, *718*
  penny, copper, *583*
  penny, Maundy, *581*
  shilling, *533*
  sixpence, *546*
  sovereign, *453*
  third farthing, *619*
  threepence, Maundy, *563*
  two pounds, *439*
  twopence, Maundy, *573*

George noble, **149**

George V
  crown, *490*
  farthing, *613*
  five pounds, *429*
  florin, *520*
  fourpence, Maundy, *556*
  half sovereign, *470*
  halfcrown, *512*
  halfpenny, *602*
  Maundy set, *625*
  patterns, *732*
  penny, bronze, *588*
  penny, Maundy, *582*
  shilling, *536*
  sixpence, *549*
  sovereign, *593*
  third farthing, *620*
  threepence, Maundy, *566*

threepence, silver, *566*
two pounds, *440*
twopence, Maundy, *574*

George VI
  crown, *492*
  farthing, *614*
  five pounds, *429*
  florin, *521*
  fourpence, Maundy *556*
  half sovereign, *471*
  halfcrown, *513*
  halfpenny, *603*
  Maundy set, *626*
  patterns, *735*
  penny, bronze, *590*
  penny, Maundy, *582*
  shilling, *537*
  sixpence, *550*
  sovereign, *459*
  threepence, brass, *569*
  threepence, Maundy, *567*
  threepence, silver, *567*
  two pounds, *441*
  twopence, Maundy, *574*

ghosting
  halfpenny, *599*
  penny, *585*
  see also *metal transfer, 561*

Glossary, 55

Godless florin, *517*

gold bullion, sovereign used as, *454*

Gothic crown, *488*

Gothic florin, *517*

grading, 22

Great Exhibition, 1851, crown commemorating
 centenary of, *492*

Great Fire, 1666, possible loss of dies in, *245*

Great plague, 1665, effect on coin production, *499*

Great Recoinage, 1816 *484*

groat
  hammered, **259**
  milled, *559*

guinea, *445*
  fluctuation in value, *447, 449*
  melting for re-use, *451*
  military, *451*
  misplaced sceptres variety, *447*
  origin of name, *445*
  Prince Elector, *448*
  spade, *451*

half angel, **179**

half farthing, *617*

half florin, **185**

half guinea, *461*

half laurel, **127**

half noble, **173**

half sovereign
  hammered, **123**
  milled, *467*

half unite, **130**

halfcrown
  hammered, **187**
  milled, *499*

halfgroat, **289**

halfpenny
  decimal, *646*
  hammered, **379**
  milled, *593*

halfpound
  Charles I, **130**
  Elizabeth I, **125**

hammered coinage, introduction to, **81**

Harrington farthing, **402**

haymarking
  halfcrown, *502*
  shilling, *526*

heaviest regular coin, *575*

helm, **223**

Henry I
  halfpenny, **379**
  penny, **317**

Henry II
  penny, **322**
  short cross coinage, **323**
  Tealby issue, **322**

Henry III
  farthing, **395**
  halfpenny, **379**
  long cross coinage, **329**
  pattern, **691**
  penny, **328**
  short cross coinage, **328**
  twenty pence, **213**

Henry IV
  farthing, **398**
  groat, **262**
  half noble, **175**

halfgroat, **291**
halfpenny, **384**
noble, **138**
penny, **350**
quarter noble, **217**

Henry V
farthing, **399**
groat, **263**
half noble, **176**
halfgroat, **292**
halfpenny, **384**
noble, **139**
penny, **351**
quarter noble, **217**

Henry VI
angel, **145**
farthing, **399**
groat (first reign), **264**
groat (restored), **270**
half angel, **179**
half noble, **176**
halfgroat (first reign), **293**
halfgroat (restored), **297**
halfpenny (first reign), **385**
halfpenny (restored), **388**
noble, **140**
penny (first reign), **353**
penny (restored), **359**
quarter noble, **218**

Henry VII
angel, **147**
farthing, **400**
groat, **272**
half angel, **180**
halfgroat, **299**
halfpenny, **390**
patterns, **691**
penny, **362**
profile issue groat, 273
profile issue halfgroat, **300**
profile issue testoon, **225**
ryal, **121**
sovereign, **105**
sovereign coinage penny, **363**
testoon, **225**

Henry VIII
angel, **148**
crown, **155**
crown of the rose, **171**
farthing, **401**
George noble, **149**
groat, **274**
half angel, **181**
half sovereign, **123**

halfcrown, **187**
halfgroat, **300**
halfpenny, **391**
penny, **365**
penny, debased, **366**
posthumous coinage crown, **156**
posthumous coinage groat, **277**
posthumous coinage half sovereign, **123**
posthumous coinage halfcrown, **188**
posthumous coinage halfgroat, **303**
posthumous coinage halfpenny, **392**
posthumous coinage penny, **367**
posthumous coinage sovereign, **107**
posthumous coinage testoon, **226**
quarter angel, **221**
sovereign, **106**
testoon, **225**

Hume, Joseph, *559*

James I
angel, **151**
crown, **159**
crown, gold, **160**
crown, silver, **161**
double crown, **127**
farthing, **401**
half angel, **183**
half laurel, **127**
half sovereign, **127**
halfcrown, **190**
halfcrown, gold, **190**
halfcrown, silver, **191**
halfgroat, **306**
halfpenny, **393**
laurel, **110**
patterns, **695**
penny, **371**
rose ryal, **121**
ryal, **121**
shilling, **231**
sixpence, **250**
sovereign, **109**
touch pieces, **151**
unite, **110**

James II
crown, *479*
farthing, *605*
five guineas, *422*
fourpence, *553*
guinea, *446*
half guinea, *461*
halfcrown, *501*
halfpenny, *593*
penny, *579*
shilling, *526*

sixpence, *541*
threepence, *561*
two guineas, *435*
twopence, *571*

jetons, **411**

John
penny, **326**

laurel, **110**

legends, translation of foreign, milled section, *416*

leopard, **185**

Lima, provenance mark, *425, 449, 483, 506, 531, 545*

Mary
angel **149**
groat, **278**
half angel, **182**
halfgroat, **304**
penny, **369**
penny, base issue, **369**
ryal, **121**
sovereign, **108**

Matilda
penny, **321**

Maundy coinage, *579*

Maundy fourpence, *553*

Maundy set, *623*

Maundy threepence, how to distinguish, *564*

Merlen, J. B., initials hidden in design, *508*

metal transfer, *561*
see *ghosting, halfpenny, 599*
see *ghosting, penny, 585*

military guinea, *451*

milled coinage, introduction to using the tables, *415*

milling, chevron type, *438*
chevron type, not used on half guinea *464*

mintage figures, *671*

mintmark E, *504*

mintmarks, on hammered coins, **89**

ninepence, **409**

noble, **135**

Northumberland shilling, *532*

Numbering System, 6

patterns, hammered
Charles I, **695**

Commonwealth, **701**
Edward VI, **691**
Elizabeth I, **692**
Henry VII, **691**
James I, **695**
Philip and Mary, **692**

patterns, milled
Anne, *708*
Charles II milled, *705*
Cromwell, *705*
Edward VIII, *734*
Elizabeth II, *735*
George I, *708*
George II, *708*
George III, *709*
George IV, *718*
George V, *732*
George VI, *735*
Victoria, *722*
William and Mary, *707*
William IV, *721*

Pax issue
Henry I, **318**
William I, **316**

penny
decimal, *645*
hammered, **315**
milled, copper/bronze, *583*
milled, silver, *579*
short cross classes by reign, **323**

Pepys's Diary, coin manufacture described in, *421*

Philip and Mary
angel, **150**
groat, **278**
half angel, **182**
halfgroat, **305**
patterns, **692**
penny, **369**
shilling, **228**
sixpence, **247**

Pistrucci, BenedettoGeorge IV dislike of portrait, *487*
egotism, *484*

plastic set, *591*

plugged coinage, corrosion of, *594*

Pole, William Wellesley, initials hidden in design, *467*

popularity
of groat, in Scotland, *559*
of silver threepence, in Scotland, *569*

portcullis coinage, **408**

pound
decimal, *637*
gold, Elizabeth I, **109**
silver, Charles I, **116**

Prince Elector guinea, *448*

proof sets, *651*

provenance mark
common on early Georgian silver, *530*
EIC, *425*
elephant and castle, *421*
elephant, *435*
Lima, *483*
plume, *526*
plumes, *481*
roses and plumes, *481*
roses, *477*
SSC, *483*
Vigo, *481*
WCC, *530*

Quakers' money, *482*

quarter angel, **221**

quarter farthing, *621*

quarter florin, **223**

quarter guinea, *475*

quarter noble, **215**

quarter ryal, **219**

Quick-Index-Charts, 8

regnal date, *477*

Richard I
penny, **325**

Richard II
farthing, **398**
groat, **262**
half noble, **174**
halfgroat, **291**
halfpenny, **383**
noble, **137**
penny, **349**
quarter noble, **216**

Richard III
angel, **146**
groat, **272**
half angel, **180**
halfgroat, **298**
halfpenny, **389**
penny, **362**

Roettier, James, dismissal for smuggling, *480*

rose farthing, **404**

rose noble, **142**

rose ryal, **121**

ryal, **121**

sceptres, transposed, *422*

sets, proof and specimen
Edward VII, *652*
Elizabeth II, *654*
George II, *651*
George IV, *651*
George V, *653*
George VI, *653*
Victoria, *651*
William IV, *651*

seven shilling piece, known as *third guinea*, *473*

shilling
George VI, English and Scottish types introduced, *537*
hammered, **225**
milled, *525*

silver dip, *512*
inadvisable for cupronickel, *513*

silver Joey, *559*

silver
high price prevents coinage use, *451*
shortage prevents use in coinage, *484*

sixpence
hammered, **247**
milled, *541*

size
of Charles II halfcrown inconvenient, *499*
of groat the same as threepence, *559*
of hammered farthing, **395**
of quarter guinea too small, *475*
of three-halfpence too small, *577*

Soho mint, *575*
late Soho strikings, *575*

South Sea Company, *483*

sovereign
Ansell type, *454*
die used for farthing, *454*
hammered, **105**
milled, *453*
used as gold bullion, *454*

spade guinea, *451*

specimen sets, *651*

spur ryal, **122**

Stephen
penny, **320**

Tealby issue penny, Henry II, **322**

ten pence, decimal, *642*

third farthing, *619*

third guinea, *473*

Thistle crown, **160**

three shillings token, *497*

three shillings, **409**

three-farthings, **377**

three-halfpence
hammered, **313**
milled, *577*

threepence
brass, *569*
hammered,
silver, *561*

tin, used in coinage, *593*

token, bank
eighteen pence, *523*
three shillings, *497*

tokens
ecclesiastical, **412**
struck to replace coinage, *605, 598*
trade, **412**

touch pieces
Charles I, **152**
James I, **151**

transposed sceptres
meaning of, *422*
on five guineas, *422*
on guinea, *447*

triple unite, **103**

twenty pence
decimal, *641*
Henry III, **213**

twenty-five pence, decimal, *640*

two guineas, *435*

two pounds, *439*
decimal, *635*

twopence
copper, *575*

decimal, *644*
hammered, see *halfgroat*, **289**
silver, *571*

two shillings, **409**

Una and the Lion, five pound piece, *427*

unite
Charles I, **111**
Charles II, **119**
Commonwealth, **119**
James I, **110**

unpopularity
of decimal five pence, *643*
of double florin, *495*
of half farthing, *617*

Vallavine, P.
and James II guinea, *446*
and George II guinea, *450*
and George II sixpence *545*

Victoria
crown, *488*
crown, gothic, *488*
double florin, *495*
farthing, *611*
five pounds, *427*
florin, *517*
florin, Godless, *517*
florin, gothic, *517*
fourpence, Maundy, *556*
groat, *559*
half farthing, *617*
half sovereign, *468*
halfcrown, *509*
halfpenny, *599*
Maundy set, *624*
patterns, *722*
penny, copper & bronze, *584*
penny, Maundy, *582*
quarter farthing, *621*
shilling, *534*
sixpence, *547*
sovereign, *454*
sovereign, Ansell, *454*
third farthing, *619*
three-halfpence, *577*
threepence, Maundy, *564*
threepence, silver, *564*
two pounds, *440*
twopence, Maundy, *573*

Vigo provenance mark, *424*

weight of coins
and intrinsic value, *182*
heaviest, *182*

Welsh Copper Company, *530*

William and Mary
  crown, *480*
  farthing, *606*
  five guineas, *423*
  fourpence, silver, *553*
  guinea, *446*
  half guinea, *462*
  halfcrown, *501*
  halfpenny, *594*
  patterns, *707*
  penny, silver, *579*
  shilling, *526*
  sixpence, *542*
  threepence, silver, *561*
  two guineas, *436*
  twopence, silver, *571*

William I
  mints, **316**
  penny, **315**

William II
  mints, **316**
  penny, **317**

William III
  crown, *480*
  farthing, *607*
  fine work coinage, *423, 436*
  five guineas, *423*
  fourpence, silver, *554*
  groat, posthumous issue, *554*
  guinea, *447*
  half guinea, *462*
  halfcrown, *502*
  halfpenny, *595*
  penny, silver, *580*
  shilling, *527*
  sixpence, *542*
  threepence, silver, *562*
  two guineas, *436*
  twopence, silver, *572*

William IV
  crown, *487*
  farthing, *611*
  fourpence, Maundy, *556*
  groat, *559*
  half farthing, *617*
  half sovereign, *467*
  halfcrown, *509*
  halfpenny, *599*
  Maundy set, *623*
  patterns, *721*
  penny, copper, *584*
  penny, silver, *582*
  shilling, *534*

sixpence, *547*
sovereign, *454*
third farthing, *619*
three-halfpence, *577*
threepence, Maundy, *564*
threepence, silver, *564*
two pounds, *439*
twopence, Maundy, *573*

wire money
  fourpence, *555*
  threepence, *563*
  twopence, *573*

wreath crown, *490*